175 YEARS OF DICTIONARY PUBLISHING

Collins

Collins

175 YEARS OF DICTIONARY PUBLISHING

Thesaurus

Collins

HarperCollins Publishers
Westerhill Road
Bishopbriggs
Glasgow
G64 2QT
Great Britain

Fourth Edition 2008

Reprint 10 9 8 7 6 5 4 3 2

© HarperCollins Publishers 1992,
2000, 2004, 2005, 2008

ISBN 978-0-00-726137-6

www.collinslanguage.com

A catalogue record for this book is
available from the British Library.

Typeset by Wordcraft, Glasgow

Printed in Italy by
Rotolito Lombarda S.p.A.

Acknowledgements
We would like to thank those authors
and publishers who kindly gave
permission for copyright material to
be used in the Collins Word Web. We
would also like to thank Times
Newspapers Ltd for providing
valuable data.

CONTENTS

ABBREVIATIONS USED IN THIS THESAURUS

AD	anno Domini	*meteorol*	meteorology
adj	adjective	*mil*	military
adv	adverb	*n*	noun
anat	anatomy	*N*	North
archit	architecture	*naut*	nautical
astrol	astrology	*NZ*	New Zealand
Aust	Australia(n)	*obs*	obsolete
BC	before Christ	*offens*	offensive
biol	biology	*orig*	originally
Brit	British	*photog*	photography
chem	chemistry	*pl*	plural
C of E	Church of England	*prep*	preposition
conj	conjunction	*pron*	pronoun
E	East	*psychol*	psychology
eg	for example	®	trademark
esp	especially	*RC*	Roman Catholic
etc	et cetera	*S*	South
fem	feminine	*S Afr*	South Africa(n)
foll	followed	*Scot*	Scottish
geom	geometry	*sing*	singular
hist	history	*US*	United States
interj	interjection	*usu*	usually
lit	literary	*v*	verb
masc	masculine	*W*	West
med	medicine	*zool*	zoology

Main Entry Words

Main entry words are printed in blue bold type:

altogether

Parts of Speech

Parts of speech are shown in small capitals. Where a word has several senses for one part of speech, the senses are numbered:

altogether ADVERB 1

Alternatives

The key synonym for each sense is given in bold, with other alternatives given in roman:

> **altogether** ADVERB 1 **absolutely**, quite, completely, totally, perfectly, fully, thoroughly, wholly 2 **completely**, fully, entirely, thoroughly, wholly, in every respect

Opposites

Opposites are indented, with an inequation sign:

≠ partially

Related words

Related words are introduced by rightfacing arrows:

▷ **RELATED WORD** circle

Word Power

Word Power notes are shown in indented panels:

- The use of actress is now very
- much in decline, and women
- who work in the profession
- invariably prefer to be
- referred to as actors

Aa

abandon VERB 1 = **leave**, strand, ditch, forsake, run out on, desert, dump 2 = **stop**, give up, halt, pack in (*Brit. informal*), discontinue, leave off ≠ continue 3 = **give up**, yield, surrender, relinquish ≠ keep
▷ NOUN = **recklessness**, wildness ≠ restraint

abandonment NOUN = **desertion**, leaving, forsaking

abbey NOUN = **monastery**, convent, priory, nunnery, friary

abduct VERB = **kidnap**, seize, carry off, snatch (*slang*)

abide VERB = **tolerate**, suffer, accept, bear, endure, put up with, take, stand ▷ PHRASE: **abide by something** = **obey**, follow, agree to, carry out, observe, fulfil, act on, comply with

abiding ADJECTIVE = **enduring**, lasting, continuing, permanent, persistent, everlasting ≠ brief

ability NOUN 1 = **capability**, potential, competence, proficiency ≠ inability 2 = **skill**, talent, expertise, competence, aptitude, proficiency, cleverness

able ADJECTIVE = **capable**, qualified, efficient, accomplished, competent, skilful, proficient ≠ incapable

abnormal ADJECTIVE = **unusual**, different, odd, strange, extraordinary, remarkable, exceptional, peculiar, daggy (*Austral. & N.Z. informal*) ≠ normal

abnormality NOUN 1 = **strangeness**, peculiarity, irregularity, singularity 2 = **anomaly**, oddity, exception, peculiarity, deformity, irregularity

abolish VERB = **do away with**, end, destroy, eliminate, cancel, get rid of, ditch (*slang*), throw out ≠ establish

abolition NOUN = **eradication**, ending, end, destruction, wiping out, elimination, cancellation, termination

abort VERB 1 = **terminate** (*a pregnancy*), miscarry 2 = **stop**, end, finish, check, arrest, halt, cease, axe (*informal*)

abortion NOUN = **termination**, miscarriage, deliberate miscarriage

abound VERB = **be plentiful**, thrive, flourish, be numerous, proliferate, be abundant, be thick on the ground

about PREPOSITION 1 = **regarding**, on, concerning, dealing with, referring to, relating to, as regards 2 = **near**, around, close to, nearby, beside, adjacent to, in the neighbourhood of
▷ ADVERB = **approximately**, around, almost, nearly, approaching, close to, roughly, just about

above PREPOSITION 1 = **over**,

upon, beyond, on top of, exceeding, higher than ≠ under **2** = **senior to**, over, ahead of, in charge of, higher than, superior to, more powerful than

abroad ADVERB = **overseas**, out of the country, in foreign lands

abrupt ADJECTIVE **1** = **sudden**, unexpected, rapid, surprising, quick, rash, precipitate ≠ slow **2** = **curt**, brief, short, rude, impatient, terse, gruff, succinct ≠ polite

absence NOUN **1** = **time off**, leave, break, vacation, recess, truancy, absenteeism, nonattendance **2** = **lack**, deficiency, omission, scarcity, want, need, shortage, dearth

absent ADJECTIVE **1** = **away**, missing, gone, elsewhere, unavailable, nonexistent ≠ present **2** = **absent-minded**, blank, vague, distracted, vacant, preoccupied, oblivious, inattentive ≠ alert ▷ PHRASE: **absent yourself** = **stay away**, withdraw, keep away, play truant

absolute ADJECTIVE **1** = **complete**, total, perfect, pure, sheer, utter, outright, thorough **2** = **supreme**, sovereign, unlimited, ultimate, full, unconditional, unrestricted, pre-eminent **3** = **autocratic**, supreme, all-powerful, imperious, domineering, tyrannical

absolutely ADVERB = **completely**, totally, perfectly, fully, entirely, altogether, wholly, utterly ≠ somewhat

absorb VERB **1** = **soak up**, suck up, receive, digest, imbibe **2** = **engross**, involve, engage, fascinate, rivet, captivate

absorbed ADJECTIVE = **engrossed**, lost, involved, gripped, fascinated, caught up, wrapped up, preoccupied

absorbing ADJECTIVE = **fascinating**, interesting, engaging, gripping, compelling, intriguing, enticing, riveting ≠ boring

absorption NOUN **1** = **soaking up**, consumption, digestion, sucking up **2** = **immersion**, involvement, concentration, fascination, preoccupation, intentness

abstract ADJECTIVE = **theoretical**, general, academic, speculative, indefinite, hypothetical, notional, abstruse ≠ actual ▷ NOUN = **summary**, résumé, outline, digest, epitome, rundown, synopsis, précis ≠ expansion ▷ VERB = **extract**, draw, pull, remove, separate, withdraw, isolate, pull out ≠ add

absurd ADJECTIVE = **ridiculous**, crazy (*informal*), silly, foolish, ludicrous, unreasonable, irrational, senseless ≠ sensible

abundance NOUN = **plenty**, bounty, exuberance, profusion, plethora, affluence, fullness, fruitfulness ≠ shortage

abundant ADJECTIVE = **plentiful**, full, rich, liberal, generous, ample, exuberant, teeming ≠ scarce

abuse NOUN 1 = **maltreatment**, damage, injury, hurt, harm, exploitation, manhandling, ill-treatment 2 = **insults**, blame, slights, put-downs, censure, reproach, scolding, defamation 3 = **misuse**, misapplication
▷ VERB 1 = **ill-treat**, damage, hurt, injure, harm, molest, maltreat, knock about or around ≠ care for 2 = **insult**, offend, curse, put down, malign, scold, disparage, castigate ≠ praise

abusive ADJECTIVE 1 = **violent**, rough, cruel, savage, brutal, vicious, destructive, harmful ≠ kind 2 = **insulting**, offensive, rude, degrading, scathing, contemptuous, disparaging, scurrilous ≠ complimentary

academic ADJECTIVE
1 = **scholastic**, educational
2 = **scholarly**, learned, intellectual, literary, erudite, highbrow, studious
3 = **theoretical**, abstract, speculative, hypothetical, impractical, notional, conjectural
▷ NOUN = **scholar**, intellectual, don, master, professor, fellow, lecturer, tutor, acca (Austral. slang)

accelerate VERB 1 = **increase**, grow, advance, extend, expand, raise, swell, enlarge ≠ fall
2 = **expedite**, further, speed up, hasten ≠ delay 3 = **speed up**, advance, quicken, gather momentum ≠ slow down

acceleration NOUN = **hastening**, hurrying, stepping up (informal), speeding up, quickening

accent NOUN = **pronunciation**, tone, articulation, inflection, brogue, intonation, diction, modulation
▷ VERB = **emphasize**, stress, highlight, underline, underscore, accentuate

accept VERB 1 = **receive**, take, gain, pick up, secure, collect, get, obtain 2 = **acknowledge**, believe, allow, admit, approve, recognize, yield, concede

acceptable ADJECTIVE
= **satisfactory**, fair, all right, suitable, sufficient, good enough, adequate, tolerable ≠ unsatisfactory

acceptance NOUN 1 = **accepting**, taking, receiving, obtaining, acquiring, reception, receipt
2 = **acknowledgement**, agreement, approval, recognition, admission, consent, adoption, assent

accepted ADJECTIVE = **agreed**, common, established, traditional, approved, acknowledged, recognized, customary ≠ unconventional

access NOUN 1 = **admission**, entry, passage 2 = **entrance**, road, approach, entry, path, gate, opening, passage

accessible ADJECTIVE = **handy**, near, nearby, at hand, within reach, at your fingertips, reachable, achievable ≠ inaccessible

accessory NOUN 1 = **extra**, addition, supplement, attachment, adjunct, appendage 2 = **accomplice**, partner, ally, associate, assistant, helper, colleague, collaborator

accident NOUN 1 = **crash**, smash, wreck, collision 2 = **misfortune**, disaster, tragedy, setback, calamity, mishap, misadventure 3 = **chance**, fortune, luck, fate, hazard, coincidence, fluke, fortuity

accidental ADJECTIVE 1 = **unintentional**, unexpected, incidental, unforeseen, unplanned ≠ deliberate 2 = **chance**, random, casual, unplanned, fortuitous, inadvertent

accidentally ADVERB = **unintentionally**, incidentally, by accident, by chance, inadvertently, unwittingly, randomly, haphazardly ≠ deliberately

acclaim VERB = **praise**, celebrate, honour, cheer, admire, hail, applaud, compliment ▷ NOUN = **praise**, honour, celebration, approval, tribute, applause, kudos, commendation ≠ criticism

accommodate VERB 1 = **house**, put up, take in, lodge, shelter, entertain, cater for 2 = **help**, support, aid, assist, cooperate with, abet, lend a hand to 3 = **adapt**, fit, settle, alter, adjust, modify, comply, reconcile

accommodating ADJECTIVE = **obliging**, willing, kind, friendly, helpful, polite, cooperative, agreeable ≠ unhelpful

accommodation NOUN = **housing**, homes, houses, board, quarters, digs (*Brit. informal*), shelter, lodging(s)

accompaniment NOUN 1 = **backing music**, backing, support, obbligato 2 = **supplement**, extra, addition, companion, accessory, complement, decoration, adjunct

accompany VERB 1 = **go with**, lead, partner, guide, attend, conduct, escort, shepherd 2 = **occur with**, belong to, come with, supplement, go together with, follow

accompanying ADJECTIVE = **additional**, extra, related, associated, attached, attendant, complementary, supplementary

accomplish VERB = **realize**, produce, effect, finish, complete, manage, achieve, perform ≠ fail

accomplished ADJECTIVE = **skilled**, able, professional, expert, masterly, talented, gifted, polished ≠ unskilled

accomplishment NOUN 1 = **achievement**, feat, act, stroke, triumph, coup, exploit, deed 2 = **accomplishing**, finishing, carrying out, conclusion, bringing about, execution, completion, fulfilment

accord NOUN 1 = **treaty**, contract, agreement, arrangement, settlement, pact, deal (*informal*)

2 = **sympathy**, agreement, harmony, unison, rapport, conformity ≠ conflict ▷ **PHRASE**: **accord with something** = **agree with**, match, coincide with, fit with, correspond with, conform with, tally with, harmonize with

accordingly ADVERB
1 = **consequently**, so, thus, therefore, hence, subsequently, in consequence, ergo 2 = **appropriately**, correspondingly, properly, suitably, fitly

account NOUN 1 = **description**, report, story, statement, version, tale, explanation, narrative
2 = **importance**, standing, concern, value, note, worth, weight, honour 3 (*commerce*) = **ledger**, charge, bill, statement, balance, tally, invoice
▷ **VERB** = **consider**, rate, value, judge, estimate, think, count, reckon

accountability NOUN
= **responsibility**, liability, culpability, answerability, chargeability

accountable ADJECTIVE
= **answerable**, subject, responsible, obliged, liable, amenable, obligated, chargeable

accountant NOUN = **auditor**, book-keeper, bean counter (*informal*)

accumulate VERB = **build up**, increase, be stored, collect, gather, pile up, amass, hoard ≠ disperse

accumulation NOUN
1 = **collection**, increase, stock, store, mass, build-up, pile, stack
2 = **growth**, collection, gathering, build-up

accuracy NOUN = **exactness**, precision, fidelity, authenticity, correctness, closeness, veracity, truthfulness ≠ inaccuracy

accurate ADJECTIVE 1 = **precise**, close, correct, careful, strict, exact, faithful, explicit ≠ inaccurate 2 = **correct**, true, exact, spot-on (*Brit. informal*)

accurately ADVERB 1 = **precisely**, correctly, closely, truly, strictly, exactly, faithfully, to the letter
2 = **exactly**, closely, correctly, precisely, strictly, faithfully, explicitly, scrupulously

accusation NOUN = **charge**, complaint, allegation, indictment, recrimination, denunciation, incrimination

accuse VERB 1 = **point a** *or* **the finger at**, blame for, denounce, hold responsible for, impute blame to ≠ exonerate 2 = **charge with**, indict for, impeach for, censure with, incriminate for ≠ absolve

accustom VERB = **familiarize**, train, discipline, adapt, instruct, school, acquaint, acclimatize

accustomed ADJECTIVE 1 = **used**, trained, familiar, given to, adapted, acquainted, in the habit of, familiarized ≠ unaccustomed
2 = **usual**, established, expected, common, standard, traditional,

normal, regular ≠ unusual

ace NOUN 1 (*cards*, *dice*) = **one**, single point 2 (*informal*) = **expert**, star, champion, authority, professional, master, specialist, guru

▷ ADJECTIVE (*informal*) = **great**, brilliant, fine, wonderful, excellent, outstanding, superb, fantastic (*informal*), booshit (*Austral. slang*), exo (*Austral. slang*), sik (*Austral. slang*), ka pai (*N.Z.*), rad (*informal*), phat (*slang*), schmick (*Austral. informal*)

ache VERB = **hurt**, suffer, burn, pain, smart, sting, pound, throb

▷ NOUN = **pain**, discomfort, suffering, hurt, throbbing, irritation, tenderness, pounding

achieve VERB = **accomplish**, fulfil, complete, gain, perform, do, get, carry out

achievement NOUN = **accomplishment**, effort, feat, deed, stroke, triumph, coup, exploit

acid ADJECTIVE 1 = **sour**, tart, pungent, acerbic, acrid, vinegary ≠ sweet 2 = **sharp**, cutting, biting, bitter, harsh, barbed, caustic, vitriolic ≠ kindly

acknowledge VERB 1 = **admit**, own up, allow, accept, reveal, grant, declare, recognize ≠ deny 2 = **greet**, address, notice, recognize, salute, accost ≠ snub 3 = **reply to**, answer, notice, recognize, respond to, react to, retort to ≠ ignore

acquaintance NOUN

1 = **associate**, contact, ally, colleague, comrade ≠ intimate 2 = **relationship**, connection, fellowship, familiarity ≠ unfamiliarity

acquire VERB = **get**, win, buy, receive, gain, earn, secure, collect ≠ lose

acquisition NOUN 1 = **acquiring**, gaining, procurement, attainment 2 = **purchase**, buy, investment, property, gain, prize, asset, possession

acquit VERB = **clear**, free, release, excuse, discharge, liberate, vindicate ≠ find guilty ▷ PHRASE: **acquit yourself** = **behave**, bear yourself, conduct yourself, comport yourself

act VERB 1 = **do something**, perform, function 2 = **perform**, mimic

▷ NOUN 1 = **deed**, action, performance, achievement, undertaking, exploit, feat, accomplishment 2 = **pretence**, show, front, performance, display, attitude, pose, posture 3 = **law**, bill, measure, resolution, decree, statute, ordinance, enactment 4 = **performance**, show, turn, production, routine, presentation, gig (*informal*), sketch

acting NOUN = **performance**, playing, performing, theatre, portrayal, impersonation, characterization, stagecraft

▷ ADJECTIVE = **temporary**, substitute, interim, provisional, surrogate, stopgap, pro tem

action NOUN **1** = **deed**, act, performance, achievement, exploit, feat, accomplishment **2** = **measure**, act, manoeuvre **3** = **lawsuit**, case, trial, suit, proceeding, dispute, prosecution, litigation **4** = **energy**, activity, spirit, force, vitality, vigour, liveliness, vim **5** = **effect**, working, process, operation, activity, movement, functioning, motion **6** = **battle**, fight, conflict, clash, contest, encounter, combat, engagement

activate VERB = **start**, move, initiate, rouse, mobilize, set in motion, galvanize ≠ stop

active ADJECTIVE **1** = **busy**, involved, occupied, lively, energetic, bustling, on the move, strenuous ≠ sluggish **2** = **energetic**, quick, alert, dynamic, lively, vigorous, animated, forceful ≠ inactive **3** = **in operation**, working, acting, at work, in action, operative, in force, effectual

activist NOUN = **militant**, partisan

activity NOUN **1** = **action**, labour, movement, energy, exercise, spirit, motion, bustle ≠ inaction **2** = **pursuit**, project, scheme, pleasure, interest, hobby, pastime

actor or **actress** NOUN = **performer**, player, Thespian, luvvie (*informal*)

● **WORD POWER**
● The use of *actress* is now very
● much on the decline, and
● women who work in the
● profession invariably prefer to
● be referred to as *actors*.

actual ADJECTIVE = **real**, substantial, concrete, definite, tangible

● **WORD POWER**
● The words *actual* and *actually*
● are often used when speaking,
● but should only be used
● in writing where they add
● something to the meaning
● of a sentence. For example,
● in the sentence *he actually*
● *rather enjoyed the film*, the word
● *actually* is only needed if there
● was originally some doubt as to
● whether he would enjoy it.

actually ADVERB = **really**, in fact, indeed, truly, literally, genuinely, in reality, in truth

acute ADJECTIVE **1** = **serious**, important, dangerous, critical, crucial, severe, grave, urgent **2** = **sharp**, shooting, powerful, violent, severe, intense, fierce, piercing **3** = **perceptive**, sharp, keen, smart, sensitive, clever, astute, insightful ≠ slow

adamant ADJECTIVE = **determined**, firm, fixed, stubborn, uncompromising, resolute, unbending, obdurate ≠ flexible

adapt VERB **1** = **adjust**, change, alter, modify, accommodate, conform, acclimatize **2** = **convert**, change, transform, alter, modify, tailor, remodel

adaptation NOUN
1 = **acclimatization**, naturalization, familiarization
2 = **conversion**, change, variation, adjustment, transformation, modification, alteration

add VERB 1 = **count up**, total, reckon, compute, add up, tot up ≠ take away 2 = **include**, attach, supplement, adjoin, augment, affix, append

addict NOUN 1 = **junkie** (informal), freak (informal), fiend (informal)
2 = **fan**, lover, nut (slang), follower, enthusiast, admirer, buff (informal), junkie (informal)

addicted ADJECTIVE = **hooked**, dependent

addiction NOUN = **dependence**, habit, obsession, craving, enslavement with **to** = **love of**, passion for, attachment to

addition NOUN 1 = **extra**, supplement, increase, gain, bonus, extension, accessory, additive 2 = **inclusion**, adding, increasing, extension, attachment, insertion, incorporation, augmentation ≠ removal 3 = **counting up**, totalling, adding up, computation, totting up ≠ subtraction ▷ PHRASE: **in addition to** = **as well as**, along with, on top of, besides, to boot, additionally, over and above, to say nothing of

additional ADJECTIVE = **extra**, new, other, added, further, fresh, spare, supplementary

address NOUN 1 = **location**, home, place, house, point, position, situation, site
2 = **speech**, talk, lecture, discourse, sermon, dissertation, homily, oration
▷ VERB = **speak to**, talk to, greet, hail, approach, converse with, korero (N.Z.)

adept ADJECTIVE = **skilful**, able, skilled, expert, practised, accomplished, versed, proficient ≠ unskilled
▷ NOUN = **expert**, master, genius, hotshot (informal), dab hand (Brit. informal)

adequate ADJECTIVE
1 = **passable**, acceptable, average, fair, satisfactory, competent, mediocre, so-so (informal) ≠ inadequate 2 = **sufficient**, enough ≠ insufficient

adhere to VERB = **stick to**, attach to, cling to, glue to, fix to, fasten to, hold fast to, paste to

adjacent ADJECTIVE = **adjoining**, neighbouring, nearby ≠ far away

adjoin VERB = **connect with** or **to**, join, link with, touch on, border on

adjoining ADJECTIVE = **connecting**, touching, bordering, neighbouring, next door, adjacent, abutting

adjourn VERB = **postpone**, delay, suspend, interrupt, put off, defer, discontinue ≠ continue

adjust VERB 1 = **adapt**, change, alter, accustom, conform

2 = **change**, reform, alter, adapt, revise, modify, amend, make conform **3** = **modify**, alter, adapt

adjustable ADJECTIVE = **alterable**, flexible, adaptable, malleable, movable, modifiable

adjustment NOUN
1 = **alteration**, change, tuning, repair, conversion, modifying, adaptation, modification
2 = **acclimatization**, orientation, change, regulation, amendment, adaptation, revision, modification

administer VERB **1** = **manage**, run, control, direct, handle, conduct, command, govern
2 = **dispense**, give, share, provide, apply, assign, allocate, allot
3 = **execute**, give, provide, apply, perform, carry out, impose, implement

administration NOUN
1 = **management**, government, running, control, handling, direction, conduct, application
2 = **directors**, board, executive(s), employers **3** = **government**, leadership, regime

administrative ADJECTIVE = **managerial**, executive, directing, regulatory, governmental, organizational, supervisory, directorial

administrator NOUN = **manager**, head, official, director, executive, boss (*informal*), governor, supervisor, baas (*S. African*)

admirable ADJECTIVE = **praiseworthy**, good, great, fine, wonderful, excellent, brilliant, outstanding, booshit (*Austral. slang*), exo (*Austral. slang*), sik (*Austral. slang*), ka pai (*N.Z.*), rad (*informal*), phat (*slang*), schmick (*Austral. informal*) ≠ deplorable

admiration NOUN = **regard**, wonder, respect, praise, approval, recognition, esteem, appreciation

admire VERB **1** = **respect**, value, prize, honour, praise, appreciate, esteem, approve of ≠ despise
2 = **adore**, like, love, take to, fancy (*Brit. informal*), treasure, cherish, glorify **3** = **marvel at**, look at, appreciate, delight in, wonder at, be amazed by, take pleasure in, gape at

admirer NOUN **1** = **fan**, supporter, follower, enthusiast, partisan, disciple, devotee **2** = **suitor**, lover, boyfriend, sweetheart, beau, wooer

admission NOUN
1 = **admittance**, access, entry, introduction, entrance, acceptance, initiation, entrée
2 = **confession**, declaration, revelation, allowance, disclosure, acknowledgement, unburdening, divulgence

admit VERB **1** = **confess**, confide, own up, come clean (*informal*)
2 = **allow**, agree, accept, reveal, grant, declare, acknowledge, recognize ≠ deny **3** = **let in**, allow, receive, accept, introduce, take in, initiate, give access to ≠ keep out

adolescence NOUN = **teens**, youth, minority, boyhood, girlhood

adolescent ADJECTIVE 1 = **young**, junior, teenage, juvenile, youthful, childish, immature, boyish 2 = **teenage**, young, teen (*informal*)
▷ NOUN = **teenager**, girl, boy, kid (*informal*), youth, lad, minor, young man

adopt VERB 1 = **take on**, follow, choose, maintain, assume, take up, engage in, become involved in 2 = **take in**, raise, nurse, mother, rear, foster, bring up, take care of ≠ abandon

adoption NOUN 1 = **fostering**, adopting, taking in 2 = **embracing**, choice, taking up, selection, assumption, endorsement, appropriation, espousal

adore VERB = **love**, honour, admire, worship, esteem, cherish, revere, dote on ≠ hate

adoring ADJECTIVE = **admiring**, loving, devoted, fond, affectionate, doting ≠ hating

adorn VERB = **decorate**, array, embellish, festoon

adrift ADJECTIVE 1 = **drifting**, afloat, unmoored, unanchored 2 = **aimless**, goalless, directionless, purposeless
▷ ADVERB = **wrong**, astray, off course, amiss, off target, wide of the mark

adult NOUN = **grown-up**, mature person, person of mature age, grown or grown-up person, man or woman
▷ ADJECTIVE 1 = **fully grown**, mature, grown-up, of age, ripe, fully fledged, fully developed, full grown 2 = **pornographic**, blue, dirty, obscene, filthy, indecent, lewd, salacious

advance VERB 1 = **progress**, proceed, come forward, make inroads, make headway ≠ retreat 2 = **accelerate**, speed, promote, hasten, bring forward, crack on (*informal*) 3 = **improve**, rise, develop, pick up, progress, upgrade, prosper, make strides 4 = **suggest**, offer, present, propose, advocate, submit, prescribe, put forward ≠ withhold 5 = **lend**, loan, supply on credit ≠ withhold payment
▷ NOUN 1 = **down payment**, credit, fee, deposit, retainer, prepayment 2 = **attack**, charge, strike, assault, raid, invasion, offensive, onslaught 3 = **improvement**, development, gain, growth, breakthrough, step, headway, inroads
▷ MODIFIER = **prior**, early, beforehand ▷ PHRASE: **in advance** = **beforehand**, earlier, ahead, previously

advanced ADJECTIVE = **sophisticated**, foremost, modern, revolutionary, up-to-date, higher, leading, recent ≠ backward

advancement NOUN = **promotion**, rise, gain, progress,

improvement, betterment, preferment

advantage NOUN 1 = **benefit**, help, profit, favour ≠ disadvantage 2 = **lead**, sway, dominance, precedence 3 = **superiority**, good

adventure NOUN = **venture**, experience, incident, enterprise, undertaking, exploit, occurrence, caper

adventurous ADJECTIVE = **daring**, enterprising, bold, reckless, intrepid, daredevil ≠ cautious

adversary NOUN = **opponent**, rival, enemy, competitor, foe, contestant, antagonist ≠ ally

adverse ADJECTIVE 1 = **harmful**, damaging, negative, destructive, detrimental, hurtful, injurious, inopportune ≠ beneficial 2 = **unfavourable**, hostile, unlucky 3 = **negative**, opposing, hostile, contrary, dissenting, unsympathetic, ill-disposed

advert NOUN (Brit. informal) = **advertisement**, notice, commercial, ad (informal), announcement, poster, plug (informal), blurb

advertise VERB = **publicize**, promote, plug (informal), announce, inform, hype, notify, tout

advertisement NOUN = **advert** (Brit. informal), notice, commercial, ad (informal), announcement, poster, plug (informal), blurb

advice NOUN = **guidance**, help, opinion, direction, suggestion, instruction, counsel, counselling

advise VERB 1 = **recommend**, suggest, urge, counsel, advocate, caution, prescribe, commend 2 = **notify**, tell, report, announce, warn, declare, inform, acquaint

adviser NOUN = **counsellor**, guide, consultant, aide, guru, mentor, helper, confidant

advisory ADJECTIVE = **advising**, helping, recommending, counselling, consultative

advocate VERB = **recommend**, support, champion, encourage, propose, promote, advise, endorse ≠ oppose ▷ NOUN 1 = **supporter**, spokesman, champion, defender, campaigner, promoter, counsellor, proponent 2 (law) = **lawyer**, attorney, solicitor, counsel, barrister

affair NOUN 1 = **matter**, business, happening, event, activity, incident, episode, topic 2 = **relationship**, romance, intrigue, fling, liaison, flirtation, amour, dalliance

affect¹ VERB 1 = **influence**, concern, alter, change, manipulate, act on, bear upon, impinge upon 2 = **emotionally move**, touch, upset, overcome, stir, disturb, perturb

affect² VERB = **put on**, assume, adopt, pretend, imitate, simulate, contrive, aspire to

affected³ ADJECTIVE = **pretended**,

artificial, contrived, put-on, mannered, unnatural, feigned, insincere ≠ genuine

affection NOUN = **fondness**, liking, feeling, love, care, warmth, attachment, goodwill, aroha (*N.Z.*)

affectionate ADJECTIVE = **fond**, loving, kind, caring, friendly, attached, devoted, tender ≠ cool

affiliate VERB = **associate**, unite, join, link, ally, combine, incorporate, amalgamate

affinity NOUN 1 = **attraction**, liking, leaning, sympathy, inclination, rapport, fondness, partiality, aroha (*N.Z.*) ≠ hostility 2 = **similarity**, relationship, connection, correspondence, analogy, resemblance, closeness, likeness ≠ difference

affirm VERB 1 = **declare**, state, maintain, swear, assert, testify, pronounce, certify ≠ deny 2 = **confirm**, prove, endorse, ratify, verify, validate, bear out, substantiate ≠ refute

affirmative ADJECTIVE = **agreeing**, confirming, positive, approving, consenting, favourable, concurring, assenting ≠ negative

afflict VERB = **torment**, trouble, pain, hurt, distress, plague, grieve, harass

affluent ADJECTIVE = **wealthy**, rich, prosperous, loaded (*slang*), well-off, opulent, well-heeled (*informal*), well-to-do, minted (*Brit. slang*) ≠ poor

afford VERB 1 = **have the money for**, manage, bear, pay for, spare, stand, stretch to 2 = **bear**, stand, sustain, allow yourself 3 = **give**, offer, provide, produce, supply, yield, render

affordable ADJECTIVE = **inexpensive**, cheap, reasonable, moderate, modest, low-cost, economical ≠ expensive

afraid ADJECTIVE 1 = **scared**, frightened, nervous, terrified, shaken, startled, fearful, cowardly ≠ unafraid 2 = **reluctant**, frightened, scared, unwilling, hesitant, loath, disinclined, unenthusiastic 3 = **sorry**, apologetic, regretful, sad, distressed, unhappy ≠ pleased

after PREPOSITION = **at the end of**, following, subsequent to ≠ before
▷ ADVERB = **following**, later, next, succeeding, afterwards, subsequently, thereafter
▷ RELATED WORD: *prefix* post-

aftermath NOUN = **effects**, results, wake, consequences, outcome, sequel, end result, upshot

again ADVERB 1 = **once more**, another time, anew, afresh 2 = **also**, in addition, moreover, besides, furthermore

against PREPOSITION 1 = **beside**, on, up against, in contact with, abutting 2 = **opposed to**, anti (*informal*), hostile to, in opposition to, averse to, opposite to 3 = **in opposition to**, resisting, versus, counter to, in the opposite direction of **4** = **in preparation for**, in case of, in anticipation of, in expectation of, in provision for

▷ RELATED WORDS: *prefixes* anti-, contra-, counter-

age NOUN **1** = **years**, days, generation, lifetime, length of existence **2** = **old age**, experience, maturity, seniority, majority, senility, decline, advancing years ≠ youth **3** = **time**, day(s), period, generation, era, epoch

▷ VERB **1** = **grow old**, decline, weather, fade, deteriorate, wither **2** = **mature**, season, condition, soften, mellow, ripen

aged ADJECTIVE = **old**, getting on, grey, ancient, antique, elderly, antiquated ≠ young

agency NOUN **1** = **business**, company, office, firm, department, organization, enterprise, establishment **2** (*old-fashioned*) = **medium**, means, activity, vehicle, instrument, mechanism

agenda NOUN = **programme**, list, plan, schedule, diary, calendar, timetable

agent NOUN **1** = **representative**, rep (*informal*), negotiator, envoy, surrogate, go-between **2** = **author**, worker, vehicle, instrument, operator, performer, catalyst, doer **3** = **force**, means, power, cause, instrument

aggravate VERB **1** = **make worse**, exaggerate, intensify, worsen, exacerbate, magnify, inflame,

increase ≠ improve **2** (*informal*) = **annoy**, bother, provoke, irritate, nettle, get on your nerves (*informal*) ≠ please

aggregate NOUN = **total**, body, whole, amount, collection, mass, sum, combination

▷ ADJECTIVE = **collective**, mixed, combined, collected, accumulated, composite, cumulative

▷ VERB = **combine**, mix, collect, assemble, heap, accumulate, pile, amass

aggression NOUN **1** = **hostility**, malice, antagonism, antipathy, ill will, belligerence, destructiveness, pugnacity **2** = **attack**, campaign, injury, assault, raid, invasion, offensive, onslaught

aggressive ADJECTIVE **1** = **hostile**, offensive, destructive, belligerent, unfriendly, contrary, antagonistic, pugnacious, aggers (*Austral. slang*), biffo (*Austral. slang*) ≠ friendly **2** = **forceful**, powerful, convincing, effective, enterprising, dynamic, bold, militant ≠ submissive

agitate VERB **1** = **stir**, beat, shake, disturb, toss, rouse **2** = **upset**, worry, trouble, excite, distract, unnerve, disconcert, fluster ≠ calm

agony NOUN = **suffering**, pain, distress, misery, torture, discomfort, torment, hardship

agree VERB **1** = **concur**, be as one, sympathize, assent, see eye

to eye, be of the same opinion
≠ disagree **2 = correspond**,
match, coincide, tally, conform
▷ **PHRASE: agree with someone**
= **suit**, get on, befit

agreement NOUN **1 = treaty**,
contract, arrangement,
alliance, deal (*informal*),
understanding, settlement,
bargain **2 = concurrence**,
harmony, compliance, union,
agreeing, consent, unison,
assent ≠ disagreement
3 = correspondence, similarity,
consistency, correlation,
conformity, compatibility,
congruity ≠ difference

agricultural ADJECTIVE
= **farming**, country, rural, rustic,
agrarian

agriculture NOUN = **farming**,
culture, cultivation, husbandry,
tillage

ahead ADVERB **1 = in front**, in
advance, towards the front,
frontwards **2 = at an advantage**,
in advance, in the lead **3 = in the
lead**, winning, leading, at the
head, to the fore, at an advantage
4 = in front, before, in advance, in
the lead

aid NOUN = **help**, backing, support,
benefit, favour, relief, promotion,
assistance ≠ hindrance
▷ VERB **1 = help**, support, serve,
sustain, assist, avail, subsidize,
be of service to ≠ hinder
2 = promote, help, further,
forward, encourage, favour,
facilitate, pave the way for

aide NOUN = **assistant**, supporter,
attendant, helper, right-hand
man, second

ailing ADJECTIVE **1 = weak**,
failing, poor, flawed, unstable,
unsatisfactory, deficient **2 = ill**,
poorly, sick, weak, crook (*Austral.
& N.Z. informal*), unwell, infirm,
under the weather (*informal*),
indisposed

ailment NOUN = **illness**, disease,
complaint, disorder, sickness,
affliction, malady, infirmity

aim VERB **1 = try for**, seek, work
for, plan for, strive, set your sights
on **2 = point**
▷ NOUN = **intention**, point, plan,
goal, design, target, purpose,
desire

air NOUN **1 = wind**, breeze,
draught, gust, zephyr
2 = atmosphere, sky, heavens,
aerosphere **3 = tune**, song,
theme, melody, strain, lay, aria
4 = manner, appearance, look,
aspect, atmosphere, mood,
impression, aura
▷ VERB **1 = publicize**, reveal,
exhibit, voice, express,
display, circulate, make public
2 = ventilate, expose, freshen,
aerate ▷ **RELATED WORD**: *adjective*
aerial

airborne ADJECTIVE = **flying**,
floating, in the air, hovering,
gliding, in flight, on the wing

airing NOUN **1 = ventilation**,
drying, freshening, aeration
2 = exposure, display, expression,
publicity, vent, utterance,

dissemination

airplane (*U.S. & Canad.*) NOUN
= **plane**, aircraft, jet, aeroplane, airliner

airs PLURAL NOUN = **affectation**, arrogance, pretensions, pomposity, swank (*informal*), hauteur, haughtiness, superciliousness

aisle NOUN = **passageway**, path, lane, passage, corridor, alley, gangway

alarm NOUN 1 = **fear**, panic, anxiety, fright, apprehension, nervousness, consternation, trepidation ≠ calmness
2 = **danger signal**, warning, bell, alert, siren, alarm bell, hooter, distress signal
▷ VERB = **frighten**, scare, panic, distress, startle, dismay, daunt, unnerve ≠ calm

alarming ADJECTIVE
= **frightening**, shocking, scaring, disturbing, distressing, startling, horrifying, menacing

alcoholic NOUN = **drunkard**, drinker, drunk, toper, lush (*slang*), tippler, wino (*informal*), inebriate, alko *or* alco (*Austral. slang*)
▷ ADJECTIVE = **intoxicating**, hard, strong, stiff, brewed, fermented, distilled

alert ADJECTIVE 1 = **attentive**, awake, vigilant, watchful, on the lookout, circumspect, observant, on guard ≠ careless 2 = **quick-witted**, bright, sharp
▷ NOUN = **warning**, signal, alarm, siren ≠ all clear

▷ VERB = **warn**, signal, inform, alarm, notify, tip off, forewarn ≠ lull

alien NOUN = **foreigner**, incomer, immigrant, stranger, outsider, newcomer, asylum seeker ≠ citizen
▷ ADJECTIVE 1 = **foreign**, strange, imported, unknown, exotic, unfamiliar 2 = **strange**, new, foreign, novel, unknown, exotic, unfamiliar, untried ≠ similar

alienate VERB = **antagonize**, anger, annoy, offend, irritate, hassle (*informal*), estrange, hack off (*informal*)

alienation NOUN
= **estrangement**, setting against, separation, turning away, disaffection, remoteness

alight¹ VERB 1 = **get off**, descend, get down, disembark, dismount
2 = **land**, light, settle, come down, descend, perch, touch down, come to rest ≠ take off

alight² ADJECTIVE = **lit up**, bright, brilliant, shining, illuminated, fiery

align VERB 1 = **ally**, side, join, associate, affiliate, cooperate, sympathize 2 = **line up**, order, range, regulate, straighten, even up

alike ADJECTIVE = **similar**, close, the same, parallel, resembling, identical, corresponding, akin ≠ different
▷ ADVERB = **similarly**, identically, equally, uniformly, correspondingly, analogously

≠ differently

alive ADJECTIVE 1 = **living**, breathing, animate, subsisting, existing, functioning, in the land of the living (*informal*) ≠ dead 2 = **in existence**, existing, functioning, active, operative, in force, on-going, prevalent ≠ inoperative 3 = **lively**, active, vital, alert, energetic, animated, agile, perky ≠ dull

all DETERMINER 1 = **the whole amount**, everything, the total, the aggregate, the totality, the sum total, the entirety, the entire amount 2 = **every**, each, every single, every one of, each and every ▷ ADJECTIVE = **complete**, greatest, full, total, perfect, entire, utter ▷ ADVERB = **completely**, totally, fully, entirely, absolutely, altogether, wholly, utterly

allegation NOUN = **claim**, charge, statement, declaration, accusation, assertion, affirmation

allege VERB = **claim**, charge, challenge, state, maintain, declare, assert, uphold ≠ deny

alleged ADJECTIVE = **claimed**, supposed, declared, assumed, so-called, apparent, stated, described

allegiance NOUN = **loyalty**, devotion, fidelity, obedience, constancy, faithfulness ≠ disloyalty

allergic ADJECTIVE = **sensitive**, affected, susceptible, hypersensitive

allergy NOUN = **sensitivity**, reaction, susceptibility, antipathy, hypersensitivity, sensitiveness

alleviate VERB = **ease**, reduce, relieve, moderate, soothe, lessen, lighten, allay

alley NOUN = **passage**, walk, lane, pathway, alleyway, passageway, backstreet

alliance NOUN = **union**, league, association, agreement, marriage, connection, combination, coalition ≠ division

allied ADJECTIVE 1 = **united**, linked, related, combined, integrated, affiliated, cooperating, in league 2 = **connected**, linked, associated

allocate VERB = **assign**, grant, distribute, designate, set aside, earmark, give out, consign

allocation NOUN 1 = **allowance**, share, portion, quota, lot, ration 2 = **assignment**, allowance, allotment

allow VERB 1 = **permit**, approve, enable, sanction, endure, license, tolerate, authorize ≠ prohibit 2 = **let**, permit, sanction, authorize, license, tolerate, consent to, assent to ≠ forbid 3 = **give**, provide, grant, spare, devote, assign, allocate, set aside 4 = **acknowledge**, accept, admit, grant, recognize, yield, concede, confess ▷ PHRASE: **allow for something** = **take into account**, consider, plan for, accommodate, provide for, make provision for, make allowances for, make concessions for

allowance NOUN 1 = **portion**, lot, share, amount, grant, quota, allocation, stint 2 = **pocket money**, grant, fee, payment, ration, handout, remittance 3 = **concession**, discount, reduction, repayment, deduction, rebate

all right ADJECTIVE
1 = **satisfactory**, O.K. or okay (informal), average, fair, sufficient, standard, acceptable, good enough ≠ unsatisfactory
2 = **well**, O.K. or okay (informal), whole, sound, fit, safe, healthy, unharmed ≠ ill

ally NOUN = **partner**, friend, colleague, associate, mate, comrade, helper, collaborator, cobber (Austral. & N.Z. old-fashioned, informal), E hoa (N.Z.) ≠ opponent
▷ VERB = **unite with**, associate with, unify, collaborate with, join forces with, band together with

almost ADVERB = **nearly**, about, close to, virtually, practically, roughly, just about, not quite

alone ADJECTIVE 1 = **solitary**, isolated, separate, apart, by yourself, unaccompanied, on your tod (slang) ≠ accompanied
2 = **lonely**, abandoned, isolated, solitary, desolate, forsaken, forlorn, destitute
▷ ADVERB 1 = **solely**, only, individually, singly, exclusively, uniquely 2 = **by yourself**, independently, unaccompanied, without help, on your own,

without assistance ≠ with help

aloud ADVERB = **out loud**, clearly, plainly, distinctly, audibly, intelligibly

already ADVERB = **before now**, before, previously, at present, by now, by then, even now, just now

also ADVERB = **and**, too, further, in addition, as well, moreover, besides, furthermore

alter VERB 1 = **modify**, change, reform, vary, transform, adjust, adapt, revise 2 = **change**, turn, vary, transform, adjust, adapt

alternate VERB 1 = **interchange**, change, fluctuate, take turns, oscillate, chop and change
2 = **intersperse**, interchange, exchange, swap, stagger, rotate
▷ ADJECTIVE = **alternating**, interchanging, every other, rotating, every second, sequential

alternative NOUN = **substitute**, choice, other, option, preference, recourse
▷ ADJECTIVE = **different**, other, substitute, alternate

alternatively ADVERB = **or**, instead, otherwise, on the other hand, if not, then again, as an alternative, as another option

although CONJUNCTION = **though**, while, even if, even though, whilst, albeit, despite the fact that, notwithstanding

altogether ADVERB
1 = **absolutely**, quite, completely, totally, perfectly, fully, thoroughly, wholly 2 = **completely**, fully, entirely, thoroughly, wholly, in

every respect ≠ partially **3** = **on the whole**, generally, mostly, in general, collectively, all things considered, on average, for the most part **4** = **in total**, in all, all told, taken together, in sum, everything included

● **WORD POWER**
● The single-word form
● *altogether* should not be used
● as an alternative to *all together*
● because the meanings are very
● distinct. *Altogether* is an adverb
● meaning 'absolutely' or, in a
● different sense, ' in total'. *All*
● *together*, however, means 'all
● at the same time' or 'all in the
● same place'. The distinction
● can be seen in the following
● example: *altogether there were six*
● *or seven families sharing the flat's*
● *facilities* means ' in total', while
● *there were six or seven families all*
● *together in one flat*, means 'all
● crowded in together'.

always ADVERB **1** = **habitually**, regularly, every time, consistently, invariably, perpetually, without exception, customarily ≠ seldom **2** = **forever**, for keeps, eternally, for all time, evermore, till the cows come home (*informal*), till Doomsday **3** = **continually**, constantly, all the time, forever, repeatedly, persistently, perpetually, incessantly

amass VERB = **collect**, gather, assemble, compile, accumulate, pile up, hoard

amateur NOUN

= **nonprofessional**, outsider, layman, dilettante, layperson, non-specialist, dabbler

amaze VERB = **astonish**, surprise, shock, stun, alarm, stagger, startle, bewilder

amazement NOUN
= **astonishment**, surprise, wonder, shock, confusion, admiration, awe, bewilderment

amazing ADJECTIVE
= **astonishing**, surprising, brilliant, stunning, overwhelming, staggering, sensational (*informal*), bewildering

ambassador NOUN
= **representative**, minister, agent, deputy, diplomat, envoy, consul, attaché

ambiguity NOUN = **vagueness**, doubt, uncertainty, obscurity, equivocation, dubiousness

ambiguous ADJECTIVE
= **unclear**, obscure, vague, dubious, enigmatic, indefinite, inconclusive, indeterminate ≠ clear

ambition NOUN **1** = **goal**, hope, dream, target, aim, wish, purpose, desire **2** = **enterprise**, longing, drive, spirit, desire, passion, enthusiasm, striving

ambitious ADJECTIVE
= **enterprising**, spirited, daring, eager, intent, enthusiastic, hopeful, striving ≠ unambitious

ambush VERB = **trap**, attack, surprise, deceive, dupe, ensnare, waylay, bushwhack (*U.S.*)

▷ NOUN = **trap**, snare, lure, waylaying

amend VERB = **change**, improve, reform, fix, correct, repair, edit, alter

amendment NOUN 1 = **addition**, change, adjustment, attachment, adaptation, revision, modification, alteration 2 = **change**, improvement, repair, edit, remedy, correction, revision, modification

amends PLURAL NOUN = **compensation**, redress, reparation, restitution, atonement, recompense

amenity NOUN = **facility**, service, advantage, comfort, convenience

amid or **amidst** PREPOSITION 1 = **during**, among, at a time of, in an atmosphere of 2 = **in the middle of**, among, surrounded by, amongst, in the midst of, in the thick of

ammunition NOUN = **munitions**, rounds, shot, shells, powder, explosives, armaments

amnesty NOUN = **general pardon**, mercy, pardoning, immunity, forgiveness, reprieve, remission, clemency

among or **amongst** PREPOSITION 1 = **in the midst of**, with, together with, in the middle of, amid, surrounded by, amidst, in the thick of 2 = **in the group of**, one of, part of, included in, in the company of, in the class of, in the number of 3 = **between**, to

amount NOUN = **quantity**, measure, size, supply, mass, volume, capacity, extent

▷ PHRASE: **amount to something** 1 = **add up to**, mean, total, equal, constitute, comprise, be equivalent to 2 = **come to**, become, develop into, advance to, progress to, mature into

● WORD POWER
● Although it is common to use a
● plural noun after *amount of*, for
● example in *the amount of people*
● and *the amount of goods*, this
● should be avoided. Preferred
● alternatives would be to use
● *quantity*, as in *the quantity of*
● *people*, or *number*, as in *the*
● *number of goods*.

ample ADJECTIVE 1 = **plenty of**, generous, lavish, abundant, plentiful, expansive, copious, profuse ≠ insufficient 2 = **large**, full, extensive, generous, abundant, bountiful

amply ADVERB = **fully**, completely, richly, generously, abundantly, profusely, copiously ≠ insufficiently

amuse VERB 1 = **entertain**, please, delight, charm, cheer, tickle ≠ bore 2 = **occupy**, interest, involve, engage, entertain, absorb, engross

amusement NOUN 1 = **enjoyment**, entertainment, cheer, mirth, merriment ≠ boredom 2 = **diversion**, fun, pleasure, entertainment 3 = **pastime**, game, sport, joke, entertainment, hobby, recreation,

a

diversion

amusing ADJECTIVE = **funny**, humorous, comical, droll, interesting, entertaining, comic, enjoyable ≠ boring

anaesthetic NOUN = **painkiller**, narcotic, sedative, opiate, anodyne, analgesic, soporific
▷ ADJECTIVE = **pain-killing**, dulling, numbing, sedative, deadening, anodyne, analgesic, soporific

analogy NOUN = **similarity**, relation, comparison, parallel, correspondence, resemblance, correlation, likeness

analyse VERB 1 = **examine**, test, study, research, survey, investigate, evaluate, inspect
2 = **break down**, separate, divide, resolve, dissect, think through

analysis NOUN = **examination**, test, inquiry, investigation, interpretation, breakdown, scanning, evaluation

analytic or **analytical** ADJECTIVE = **rational**, organized, exact, precise, logical, systematic, inquiring, investigative

anarchy NOUN = **lawlessness**, revolution, riot, disorder, confusion, chaos, disorganization ≠ order

anatomy NOUN 1 = **structure**, build, make-up, frame, framework, composition
2 = **examination**, study, division, inquiry, investigation, analysis, dissection

ancestor NOUN = **forefather**, predecessor, precursor, forerunner, forebear, antecedent, tupuna or tipuna (N.Z.) ≠ descendant

ancient ADJECTIVE 1 = **classical**, old, former, past, bygone, primordial, primeval, olden
2 = **very old**, aged, antique, archaic, timeworn **3** = **old-fashioned**, dated, outdated, obsolete, out of date, unfashionable, outmoded, passé ≠ up-to-date

and CONJUNCTION 1 = **also**, including, along with, together

● **AMPHIBIANS**
● axolotl
● brown-striped frog (*Austral.*)
● bullfrog
● caecilian
● cane toad (*Austral.*)
● congo eel or snake
● frog or (*Caribbean*) crapaud
● Goliath frog
● hairy frog
● hyla
● midwife toad
● natterjack
● newt or (*dialect* or *archaic*) eft
● olm
● Queensland cane toad
● salamander
● siren
● toad or (*Caribbean*) crapaud
● tree frog

with, in addition to, as well as

2 = **moreover**, plus, furthermore

● **WORD POWER**
● The forms *try and do something*
● and *wait and do something*
● should only be used in informal
● or spoken English. In more
● formal writing, use *try to* and
● *wait to*, for example: *we must try*
● *to prevent this happening* (not *try*
● *and prevent*).

anecdote NOUN = **story**, tale, sketch, short story, yarn, reminiscence, urban myth, urban legend

angel NOUN **1** = **divine messenger**, cherub, archangel, seraph **2** (*informal*) = **dear**, beauty, saint, treasure, darling, jewel, gem, paragon

anger NOUN = **rage**, outrage, temper, fury, resentment, wrath, annoyance, ire ≠ calmness
▷ **VERB** = **enrage**, outrage, annoy, infuriate, incense, gall, madden, exasperate ≠ soothe

angle NOUN **1** = **gradient**, bank, slope, incline, inclination
2 = **intersection**, point, edge, corner, bend, elbow, crook, nook
3 = **point of view**, position, approach, direction, aspect, perspective, outlook, viewpoint

angry ADJECTIVE = **furious**, cross, mad (*informal*), outraged, annoyed, infuriated, incensed, enraged, tooshie (*Austral. slang*), off the air (*Austral. slang*) ≠ calm
● **WORD POWER**
● Some people feel it is more

● correct to talk about being
● *angry with* someone than
● being *angry at* them. In British
● English, *angry with* is still more
● common than *angry at*, but
● *angry at* is used more commonly
● in American English.

angst NOUN = **anxiety**, worry, unease, apprehension ≠ peace of mind

anguish NOUN = **suffering**, pain, distress, grief, misery, agony, torment, sorrow

animal NOUN **1** = **creature**, beast, brute **2** = **brute**, devil, monster, savage, beast, bastard (*informal* or *offensive*), villain, barbarian
▷ **ADJECTIVE** = **physical**, gross, bodily, sensual, carnal, brutish, bestial
▷ *see* **amphibians, animals, birds, dinosaurs, fish, insects, invertebrates, mammals, reptiles**

animate ADJECTIVE = **living**, live, moving, alive, breathing, alive and kicking
▷ **VERB** = **enliven**, excite, inspire, move, fire, stimulate, energize, kindle ≠ inhibit

animated ADJECTIVE = **lively**, spirited, excited, enthusiastic, passionate, energetic, ebullient, vivacious ≠ listless

animation NOUN = **liveliness**, energy, spirit, passion, enthusiasm, excitement, verve, zest

announce VERB = **make known**, tell, report, reveal, declare, advertise, broadcast, disclose ≠ keep secret

announcement NOUN
 1 = **statement**, communication,
 broadcast, declaration,
 advertisement, bulletin,
 communiqué, proclamation
 2 = **declaration**, report, reporting,
 revelation, proclamation
annoy VERB = **irritate**, trouble,
 anger, bother, disturb, plague,
 hassle (informal), madden, hack
 you off (informal) ≠ soothe
annoying ADJECTIVE = **irritating**,
 disturbing, troublesome,
 maddening, exasperating
 ≠ delightful

annual ADJECTIVE 1 = **once a year**,
 yearly 2 = **yearlong**, yearly
annually ADVERB 1 = **once a year**,
 yearly, every year, per year, by the
 year, every twelve months, per
 annum 2 = **per year**, yearly, every
 year, by the year, per annum
anomaly NOUN = **irregularity**,
 exception, abnormality,
 inconsistency, eccentricity,
 oddity, peculiarity,
 incongruity
anonymous ADJECTIVE
 1 = **unnamed**, unknown,
 unidentified, nameless,

● ANIMALS			
● animal	collective noun	● animal	collective noun
● antelopes	herd	● crows	murder
● apes	shrewdness	● cubs	litter
● asses	pace or herd	● curlews	herd
● badgers	cete	● curs	cowardice
● bears	sloth	● deer	herd
● bees	swarm or grist	● dolphins	school
● birds	flock, congregation, flight, or volery	● doves	flight or dule
		● ducks	paddling or team
		● dunlins	flight
● bitterns	sedge or siege	● elk	gang
● boars	sounder	● fish	shoal, draught, haul, run, or catch
● bucks	brace or lease		
● buffaloes	herd	● flies	swarm or grist
● capercailzies	tok	● foxes	skulk
● cats	clowder	● geese	gaggle or skein
● cattle	drove or herd	● giraffes	herd
● choughs	chattering	● gnats	swarm or cloud
● colts	rag	● goats	herd or tribe
● coots	covert	● goldfinches	charm
● cranes	herd, sedge, or siege	● grouse	brood, covey, or pack

animal	collective noun
gulls	colony
hares	down or husk
hawks	cast
hens	brood
herons	sedge or siege
herrings	shoal or glean
hounds	pack, mute, or cry
insects	swarm
kangaroos	troop
kittens	kindle
lapwings	desert
larks	exaltation
leopards	leap
lions	pride or troop
mallards	sord or sute
mares	stud
martens	richesse
moles	labour
monkeys	troop
mules	barren
nightingales	watch
owls	parliament
oxen	yoke, drove, team, or herd
partridges	covey
peacocks	muster
pheasants	nye or nide
pigeons	flock or flight
pigs	litter
plovers	stand or wing
pochards	flight, rush, bunch, or knob
ponies	herd

animal	collective noun
porpoises	school or gam
poultry	run
pups	litter
quails	bevy
rabbits	nest
racehorses	field or string
ravens	unkindness
roes	bevy
rooks	building or clamour
ruffs	hill
seals	herd or pod
sheep	flock
sheldrakes	dopping
snipe	walk or wisp
sparrows	host
starlings	murmuration
swallows	flight
swans	herd or bevy
swifts	flock
swine	herd, sounder, or dryft
teal	bunch, knob, or spring
whales	school, gam, or run
whelps	litter
whiting	pod
wigeon	bunch, company, knob, or flight
wildfowl	plump, sord, or sute
wolves	pack, rout, or herd
woodcocks	fall

unacknowledged, incognito ≠ identified **2** = **unsigned**, uncredited, unattributed ≠ signed

answer VERB = **reply**, explain, respond, resolve, react, return, retort ≠ ask

▷ NOUN **1** = **reply**, response, reaction, explanation, comeback, retort, return, defence ≠ question

a

● **ANTS, BEES, AND WASPS**
● Amazon ant
● ant *or* (*archaic or dialect*) emmet
● army ant *or* legionary ant
● bee
● blue ant (*Austral.*)
● bulldog ant, bull ant, *or* (*Austral.*) bull Joe
● bumblebee *or* humblebee
● carpenter bee
● cicada hunter (*Austral.*)
● cuckoo bee
● digger wasp
● driver ant
● flower wasp (*Austral.*)
● gall wasp
● honeypot ant *or* honey ant (*Austral.*)
● honeybee *or* hive bee
● horntail *or* wood wasp
● ichneumon fly *or* ichneumon wasp
● killer bee
● kootchar (*Austral.*)
● leafcutter ant
● leafcutter bee
● mason bee
● mason wasp
● minga (*Austral.*)
● mining bee
● mud dauber
● native bee *or* sugarbag fly (*Austral.*)
● Pharaoh ant
● policeman fly (*Austral.*)
● ruby-tail wasp
● sand wasp
● Sirex wasp (*Austral.*)
● slave ant
● spider-hunting wasp
● termite *or* white ant
● velvet ant
● wasp
● wood ant
● yellow jacket (*U.S. & Canad.*)

2 = **solution**, resolution, explanation **3** = **remedy**, solution

anthem NOUN = **song of praise**, carol, chant, hymn, psalm, paean, chorale, canticle

anthology NOUN = **collection**, selection, treasury, compilation, compendium, miscellany

anticipate VERB **1** = **expect**, predict, prepare for, hope for, envisage, foresee, bank on, foretell **2** = **await**, look forward to, count the hours until

● **WORD POWER**
● The Bank of English reveals
● that the use of *anticipate*
● and *expect* as synonyms is
● well established. However,
● although both words relate
● to a person's knowledge of
● something that will happen
● in the future, there are subtle
● differences in meaning that
● should be understood when
● choosing which word to use.
● *Anticipate* means that someone
● foresees an event and has
● prepared for it, while expect
● means 'to regard something
● as probable', but does not
● necessarily suggest the state
● of being prepared. Similarly,

● using *foresee* as a synonym
● of *anticipate*, as in *they failed*
● *to foresee the vast explosion*
● *in commercial revenue which*
● *would follow*, is not entirely
● appropriate.

anticipation NOUN
= **expectancy**, expectation,
foresight, premonition,
prescience, forethought

antics PLURAL NOUN = **clowning**,
tricks, mischief, pranks,
escapades, playfulness, horseplay,
tomfoolery

antique NOUN = **period piece**,
relic, bygone, heirloom, collector's
item, museum piece
▷ ADJECTIVE = **vintage**, classic,
antiquarian, olden

anxiety NOUN = **uneasiness**,
concern, worry, doubt, tension,
angst, apprehension, misgiving
≠ confidence

anxious ADJECTIVE 1 = **eager**,
keen, intent, yearning, impatient,
itching, desirous ≠ reluctant
2 = **uneasy**, concerned,
worried, troubled, nervous,
uncomfortable, tense, fearful
≠ confident

apart ADVERB 1 = **to pieces**, to
bits, asunder 2 = **away from
each other**, distant from each
other 3 = **aside**, away, alone,
isolated, to one side, by yourself
▷ PHRASE: **apart from** = **except
for**, excepting, other than,
excluding, besides, not including,
aside from, but

apartment NOUN 1 (*U.S.*) = **flat**,
room, suite, penthouse, duplex
(*U.S. & Canad.*), crib, bachelor
apartment (*Canad.*) 2 = **rooms**,
quarters, accommodation, living
quarters

apathy NOUN = **lack of interest**,
indifference, inertia, coolness,
passivity, nonchalance, torpor,
unconcern ≠ interest

apiece ADVERB = **each**,
individually, separately, for each,
to each, respectively, from each
≠ all together

apologize VERB = **say sorry**,
express regret, ask forgiveness,
make an apology, beg pardon

apology NOUN = **regret**,
explanation, excuse,
confession ▷ PHRASE: apology
for something *or* someone
= **mockery of**, excuse for,
imitation of, caricature of,
travesty of, poor substitute for

appal VERB = **horrify**, shock,
alarm, frighten, outrage, disgust,
dishearten, revolt

appalling ADJECTIVE
1 = **horrifying**, shocking,
alarming, awful, terrifying,
horrible, dreadful, fearful
≠ reassuring 2 = **awful**, dreadful,
horrendous

apparatus NOUN
1 = **organization**, system,
network, structure, bureaucracy,
hierarchy, setup (*informal*), chain
of command 2 = **equipment**,
tackle, gear, device, tools,
mechanism, machinery,
appliance

apparent ADJECTIVE 1 = **seeming**, outward, superficial, ostensible ≠ actual 2 = **obvious**, marked, visible, evident, distinct, manifest, noticeable, unmistakable ≠ unclear

apparently ADVERB = **seemingly**, outwardly, ostensibly

appeal VERB = **plead**, ask, request, pray, beg, entreat ≠ refuse ▷ NOUN 1 = **plea**, call, application, request, prayer, petition, overture, entreaty ≠ refusal 2 = **attraction**, charm, fascination, beauty, allure ≠ repulsiveness ▷ PHRASE: **appeal to someone** ▷ **attract**, interest, draw, please, charm, fascinate, tempt, lure

appealing ADJECTIVE = **attractive**, engaging, charming, desirable, alluring, winsome ≠ repellent

appear VERB 1 = **look (like or as if)**, seem, occur, look to be, come across as, strike you as 2 = **come into view**, emerge, occur, surface, come out, turn up, be present, show up (informal) ≠ disappear

appearance NOUN 1 = **look**, form, figure, looks, manner, expression, demeanour, mien (literary) 2 = **arrival**, presence, introduction, emergence 3 = **impression**, air, front, image, illusion, guise, façade, pretence

appease VERB 1 = **pacify**, satisfy, calm, soothe, quiet, placate, mollify, conciliate ≠ anger 2 = **ease**, calm, relieve, soothe, alleviate, allay

appendix NOUN = **supplement**, postscript, adjunct, appendage, addendum, addition

appetite NOUN 1 = **hunger** 2 = **desire**, liking, longing, demand, taste, passion, stomach, hunger ≠ distaste

applaud VERB 1 = **clap**, encourage, praise, cheer, acclaim ≠ boo 2 = **praise**, celebrate, approve, acclaim, compliment, salute, commend, extol ≠ criticize

applause NOUN = **ovation**, praise, cheers, approval, clapping, accolade, big hand

appliance NOUN = **device**, machine, tool, instrument, implement, mechanism, apparatus, gadget

applicable ADJECTIVE = **appropriate**, fitting, useful, suitable, relevant, apt, pertinent ≠ inappropriate

applicant NOUN = **candidate**, claimant, inquirer

application NOUN 1 = **request**, claim, appeal, inquiry, petition, requisition 2 = **effort**, work, industry, trouble, struggle, pains, commitment, hard work

apply VERB 1 = **request**, appeal, put in, petition, inquire, claim, requisition 2 = **be relevant**, relate, refer, be fitting, be appropriate, fit, pertain, be applicable 3 = **use**, exercise, carry out, employ, implement, practise, exert, enact 4 = **put on**,

work in, cover with, lay on, paint on, spread on, rub in, smear on
▷ **PHRASE: apply yourself** = **work hard**, concentrate, try, commit yourself, buckle down (*informal*), devote yourself, be diligent, dedicate yourself

appoint VERB 1 = **assign**, name, choose, commission, select, elect, delegate, nominate ≠ fire 2 = **decide**, set, choose, establish, fix, arrange, assign, designate ≠ cancel

appointed ADJECTIVE 1 = **decided**, set, chosen, established, fixed, arranged, assigned, designated 2 = **assigned**, named, chosen, selected, elected, delegated, nominated 3 = **equipped**, provided, supplied, furnished, fitted out

appointment NOUN 1 = **selection**, naming, election, choice, nomination, assignment 2 = **job**, office, position, post, situation, place, employment, assignment 3 = **meeting**, interview, date, arrangement, engagement, fixture, rendezvous, assignation

appraisal NOUN = **assessment**, opinion, estimate, judgment, evaluation, estimation

appreciate VERB 1 = **enjoy**, like, value, respect, prize, admire, treasure, rate highly ≠ scorn 2 = **be aware of**, understand, realize, recognize, perceive, take account of, be sensitive to, sympathize with ≠ be unaware of

3 = **be grateful for**, be obliged for, be thankful for, give thanks for, be indebted for, be in debt for, be appreciative of ≠ be ungrateful for 4 = **increase**, rise, grow, gain, improve, enhance, soar ≠ fall

appreciation NOUN 1 = **admiration**, enjoyment 2 = **gratitude**, thanks, recognition, obligation, acknowledgment, indebtedness, thankfulness, gratefulness ≠ ingratitude 3 = **awareness**, understanding, recognition, perception, sympathy, consciousness, sensitivity, realization ≠ ignorance 4 = **increase**, rise, gain, growth, improvement, escalation, enhancement ≠ fall

apprehension NOUN 1 = **anxiety**, concern, fear, worry, alarm, suspicion, dread, trepidation ≠ confidence 2 = **arrest**, catching, capture, taking, seizure ≠ release 3 = **awareness**, understanding, perception, grasp, comprehension ≠ incomprehension

apprentice NOUN = **trainee**, student, pupil, novice, beginner, learner, probationer ≠ master

approach VERB 1 = **move towards**, reach, near, come close, come near, draw near 2 = **make a proposal to**, speak to, apply to, appeal to, proposition, solicit, sound out, make overtures to 3 = **set about**, tackle, undertake, embark on, get down to, launch into, begin work on, commence on ▷ **NOUN 1 = advance**, coming, nearing, appearance, arrival, drawing near **2 = access**, way, drive, road, passage, entrance, avenue, passageway **3** *often plural* **= proposal**, offer, appeal, advance, application, invitation, proposition, overture **4 = way**, means, style, method, technique, manner

appropriate

ADJECTIVE **= suitable**, fitting, relevant, to the point, apt, pertinent, befitting, well-suited ≠ unsuitable
▷ **VERB 1 = seize**, claim, acquire, confiscate, usurp, impound, commandeer, take possession of ≠ relinquish **2 = allocate**, allow, budget, devote, assign, designate, set aside, earmark ≠ withhold **3 = steal**, take, nick (*slang, chiefly Brit.*), pocket, pinch (*informal*), lift (*informal*), embezzle, pilfer

approval NOUN **1 = consent**, agreement, sanction, blessing, permission, recommendation, endorsement, assent **2 = favour**, respect, praise, esteem, appreciation, admiration, applause ≠ disapproval

approve VERB **= agree to**, allow, pass, recommend, permit, sanction, endorse, authorize ≠ veto ▷ **PHRASE: approve of something** *or* **someone = favour**, like, respect, praise, admire, commend, have a good opinion of, regard highly

apt ADJECTIVE **1 = appropriate**, fitting, suitable, relevant, to the point, pertinent ≠ inappropriate **2 = inclined**, likely, ready, disposed, prone, liable, given, predisposed **3 = gifted**, skilled, quick, talented, sharp, capable, smart, clever ≠ slow

● **WORD POWER**
● Arabic has contributed many
● words to English over the
● ages, particularly in the areas
● of mathematics and science.
● These were adopted into
● English via Latin and French
● with their sounds and spellings
● adapted for the Romance
● languages. For example, *alcohol*
● derives from the Arabic *al-kuhl*
● but these two elements were
● fused together in Medieval
● Latin, entering English in the
● 16th century. The cosmetic
● powder *kohl*, used to darken
● the eyelids, is from the same
● derivation, without *al*, the
● Arabic word for 'the'. Other
● borrowings from Arabic
● describe aspects of Islamic
● religion, such as *muezzin*, *imam*,
● *madrasah*, and *hajj*; food eaten
● in the Middle East, such as
● *kebabs*, *falafel*, *hummus*, and
● *tabbouleh*; and clothes worn in
● Muslim countries, such as the
● *hijab* and *jellaba*. The adoption
● of loan words from other
● languages takes place when
● there is contact between two

- cultures. For this reason, many
- servicemen have introduced
- loan words into English.
- Sometimes, military slang
- remains restricted to army-
- speak, but at other times it
- passes into mainstream usage.
- An example of this is **shufti** (also
- **shufty**) from Arabic *sufti* 'have
- you seen?' We talk about **having**
- **a shufti at something** when we
- want to have a quick look at it.
- It is still chiefly a British slang
- expression, and is now quite
- dated. It is thought to have
- first been used by the RAF in
- the 1920s and was in common
- currency in the British army
- in the Middle East during the
- Second World War.

arbitrary ADJECTIVE = **random**,
chance, subjective, inconsistent,
erratic, personal, whimsical,
capricious ≠ logical

arbitration NOUN = **decision**,
settlement, judgment,
determination, adjudication

arc NOUN = **curve**, bend, bow, arch,
crescent, half-moon

arcade NOUN = **gallery**, cloister,
portico, colonnade

arch¹ NOUN 1 = **archway**, curve,
dome, span, vault 2 = **curve**,
bend, bow, crook, arc, hunch,
sweep, hump
  ▷ VERB = **curve**, bridge, bend,
  bow, span, arc

arch² ADJECTIVE = **playful**, sly,
mischievous, saucy, pert, roguish,
frolicsome, waggish

archetypal ADJECTIVE = **typical**,
standard, model, original, classic,
ideal, prototypic or prototypical

architect NOUN = **designer**,
planner, draughtsman, master
builder

architecture NOUN 1 = **design**,
planning, building, construction
2 = **construction**, design,
style 3 = **structure**, design,
shape, make-up, construction,
framework, layout, anatomy

archive NOUN = **record office**,
museum, registry, repository
  ▷ PLURAL NOUN = **records**, papers,
  accounts, rolls, documents, files,
  deeds, chronicles

arctic ADJECTIVE (*informal*)
= **freezing**, cold, frozen, icy, chilly,
glacial, frigid

Arctic ADJECTIVE = **polar**, far-
northern, hyperborean

ardent ADJECTIVE
1 = **enthusiastic**, keen, eager,
avid, zealous ≠ indifferent
2 = **passionate**, intense,
impassioned, lusty, amorous, hot-
blooded ≠ cold

area NOUN 1 = **region**, quarter,
district, zone, neighbourhood,
locality 2 = **part**, section,
sector, portion 3 = **realm**, part,
department, field, province,
sphere, domain

arena NOUN 1 = **ring**, ground,
field, theatre, bowl, pitch,
stadium, enclosure 2 = **scene**,
world, area, stage, field, sector,
territory, province

argue VERB 1 = **quarrel**, fight,

row, clash, dispute, disagree,
squabble, bicker **2** = **discuss**,
debate, dispute **3** = **claim**, reason,
challenge, insist, maintain, allege,
assert, uphold

argument NOUN **1** = **reason**,
case, reasoning, ground(s),
defence, logic, polemic, dialectic
2 = **debate**, questioning, claim,
discussion, dispute, controversy,
plea, assertion **3** = **quarrel**, fight,
row, clash, dispute, controversy,
disagreement, feud ≠ agreement

arise VERB **1** = **happen**, start,
begin, follow, result, develop,
emerge, occur **2** (old-fashioned)
= **get to your feet**, get up, rise,
stand up, spring up, leap up
3 = **get up**, wake up, awaken, get
out of bed

aristocrat NOUN = **noble**, lord,
lady, peer, patrician, grandee,
aristo (informal), peeress

aristocratic ADJECTIVE = **upper-
class**, lordly, titled, elite,
gentlemanly, noble, patrician,
blue-blooded ≠ common

arm¹ NOUN = **upper limb**, limb,
appendage

arm² VERB = **equip**, provide,
supply, array, furnish, issue with,
deck out, accoutre
▷ PLURAL NOUN = **weapons**, guns,
firearms, weaponry, armaments,
ordnance, munitions,
instruments of war

● **WORD POWER**
● The core meaning of **arm** is a
● limb of the human body from
● the shoulder to the hand. By
● extension, arm can mean any
● offshoot from a larger area,
● particularly when applied to
● bodies of water, e.g. *an arm*
● *of the North Sea*. This term is
● also used in organisations
● where arm refers to a specific
● branch or division of a larger
● whole, as in *the manufacturing*
● *arm of the company*. Arm has
● also come to mean 'power' or
● 'command', especially in the
● phrase *the (long) arm of the law*.
● It is thought that this phrase
● may derive from a proverb
● found from 16th century
● English: *Kings have long arms,*
● *hands, many ears, and many eyes*
● meaning that royal authority
● was far-reaching. Arms are seen
● as valuable commodities in the
● expressions *(cost) an arm and a*
● *leg* and (would) *give one's right*
● *arm for something*.

armed ADJECTIVE = **carrying
weapons**, protected, equipped,
primed, fitted out

armour NOUN = **protection**,
covering, shield, sheathing,
armour plate, chain mail,
protective covering

armoured ADJECTIVE
= **protected**, mailed, reinforced,
toughened, bulletproof, armour-
plated, steel-plated, ironclad

army NOUN **1** = **soldiers**, military,
troops, armed force, legions,
infantry, military force, land force
2 = **vast number**, host, gang,
mob, flock, array, legion, swarm

aroma NOUN = **scent**, smell, perfume, fragrance, bouquet, savour, odour, redolence

around PREPOSITION
1 = **approximately**, about, nearly, close to, roughly, just about, in the region of, circa (*of a date*) 2 = **surrounding**, about, enclosing, encompassing, framing, encircling, on all sides of, on every side of
▷ ADVERB 1 = **everywhere**, about, throughout, all over, here and there, on all sides, in all directions, to and fro 2 = **near**, close, nearby, at hand, close at hand

● **WORD POWER**
● In American English, *around* is
● used more often than *round* as
● an adverbial and preposition,
● except in a few fixed phrases
● such as *all year round*. In
● British English, *round* is more
● commonly used as an adverb
● than *around*.

arouse VERB 1 = **stimulate**, encourage, inspire, prompt, spur, provoke, rouse, stir up ≠ quell 2 = **inflame**, move, excite, spur, provoke, stir up, agitate 3 = **awaken**, wake up, rouse, waken

arrange VERB 1 = **plan**, agree, prepare, determine, organize, construct, devise, contrive, jack up (*N.Z. informal*) 2 = **put in order**, group, order, sort, position, line up, organize, classify, jack up (*N.Z. informal*) ≠ disorganize 3 = **adapt**, score, orchestrate,

harmonize, instrument

arrangement NOUN 1 *often plural* = **plan**, planning, provision, preparation 2 = **agreement**, contract, settlement, appointment, compromise, deal (*informal*), pact, compact 3 = **display**, system, structure, organization, exhibition, presentation, classification, alignment 4 = **adaptation**, score, version, interpretation, instrumentation, orchestration, harmonization

array NOUN 1 = **arrangement**, show, supply, display, collection, exhibition, line-up, mixture 2 (*poetic*) = **clothing**, dress, clothes, garments, apparel, attire, finery, regalia
▷ VERB 1 = **arrange**, show, group, present, range, display, parade, exhibit 2 = **dress**, clothe, deck, decorate, adorn, festoon, attire

arrest VERB 1 = **capture**, catch, nick (*slang, chiefly Brit.*), seize, detain, apprehend, take prisoner ≠ release 2 = **stop**, end, limit, block, slow, delay, interrupt, suppress ≠ speed up 3 = **fascinate**, hold, occupy, engage, grip, absorb, entrance, intrigue
▷ NOUN 1 = **capture**, bust (*informal*), detention, seizure ≠ release 2 = **stoppage**, suppression, obstruction, blockage, hindrance ≠ acceleration

arresting ADJECTIVE = **striking**,

surprising, engaging, stunning, impressive, outstanding, remarkable, noticeable ≠ unremarkable

arrival NOUN 1 = **appearance**, coming, arriving, entrance, advent, materialization 2 = **coming**, happening, taking place, emergence, occurrence, materialization 3 = **newcomer**, incomer, visitor, caller, entrant

arrive VERB 1 = **come**, appear, turn up, show up (*informal*), draw near ≠ depart 2 = **occur**, happen, take place 3 (*informal*) = **succeed**, make it (*informal*), triumph, do well, thrive, flourish, be successful, make good

arrogance NOUN = **conceit**, pride, swagger, insolence, high-handedness, haughtiness, superciliousness, disdainfulness ≠ modesty

arrogant ADJECTIVE = **conceited**, proud, cocky, overbearing, haughty, scornful, egotistical, disdainful ≠ modest

arrow NOUN 1 = **dart**, flight, bolt, shaft (*archaic*), quarrel 2 = **pointer**, indicator, marker

arsenal NOUN 1 = **store**, supply, stockpile 2 = **armoury**, storehouse, ammunition dump, arms depot, ordnance depot

art NOUN 1 = **artwork**, style of art, fine art, creativity 2 = **skill**, craft, expertise, competence, mastery, ingenuity, virtuosity, cleverness

article NOUN 1 = **feature**, story, paper, piece, item, creation, essay,

composition 2 = **thing**, piece, unit, item, object, device, tool, implement 3 = **clause**, point, part, section, item, passage, portion, paragraph

articulate
ADJECTIVE = **expressive**, clear, coherent, fluent, eloquent, lucid ≠ incoherent
▷ VERB 1 = **express**, say, state, word, declare, phrase, communicate, utter
2 = **pronounce**, say, talk, speak, voice, utter, enunciate

artificial ADJECTIVE 1 = **synthetic**, manufactured, plastic, man-made, non-natural 2 = **insincere**, forced, affected, phoney *or* phony (*informal*), false, contrived, unnatural, feigned ≠ genuine
3 = **fake**, mock, imitation, bogus, simulated, sham, counterfeit ≠ authentic

artillery NOUN = **big guns**, battery, cannon, ordnance, gunnery

artistic ADJECTIVE 1 = **creative**, cultured, original, sophisticated, refined, aesthetic, discerning, eloquent ≠ untalented
2 = **beautiful**, creative, elegant, stylish, aesthetic, tasteful ≠ unattractive

as CONJUNCTION 1 = **when**, while, just as, at the time that 2 = **in the way that**, like, in the manner that 3 = **since**, because, seeing that, considering that, on account of the fact that
▷ PREPOSITION = **in the role of**,

being, under the name of, in the character of

ashamed ADJECTIVE
1 = **embarrassed**, sorry, guilty, distressed, humiliated, self-conscious, red-faced, mortified ≠ proud 2 = **reluctant**, embarrassed

ashore ADVERB = **on land**, on the beach, on the shore, aground, to the shore, on dry land, shorewards, landwards

aside ADVERB = **to one side**, separately, apart, beside, out of the way, on one side, to the side
▷ NOUN = **interpolation**, parenthesis

ask VERB 1 = **inquire**, question, quiz, query, interrogate ≠ answer 2 = **request**, appeal to, plead with, demand, beg 3 = **invite**, bid, summon

asleep ADJECTIVE = **sleeping**, napping, dormant, dozing, slumbering, snoozing (informal), fast asleep, sound asleep

aspect NOUN 1 = **feature**, side, factor, angle, characteristic, facet 2 = **position**, view, situation, scene, prospect, point of view, outlook 3 = **appearance**, look, air, condition, quality, bearing, attitude, cast

aspiration NOUN = **aim**, plan, hope, goal, dream, wish, desire, objective

aspire to VERB = **aim for**, desire, hope for, long for, seek out, wish for, dream about, set your heart on

ass NOUN 1 = **donkey**, moke (slang) 2 = **fool**, idiot, twit (informal, chiefly Brit.), oaf, jackass, blockhead, halfwit, numbskull or numskull, dorba or dorb (Austral. slang), bogan (Austral. slang)

assassin NOUN = **murderer**, killer, slayer, liquidator, executioner, hit man (slang), hatchet man (slang)

assassinate VERB = **murder**, kill, eliminate (slang), take out (slang), terminate, hit (slang), slay, liquidate

assault NOUN = **attack**, raid, invasion, charge, offensive, onslaught, foray ≠ defence
▷ VERB = **strike**, attack, beat, knock, bang, slap, smack, thump

assemble VERB 1 = **gather**, meet, collect, rally, come together, muster, congregate ≠ scatter 2 = **bring together**, collect, gather, rally, come together, muster, amass, congregate 3 = **put together**, join, set up, build up, connect, construct, piece together, fabricate ≠ take apart

assembly NOUN 1 = **gathering**, group, meeting, council, conference, crowd, congress, collection, hui (N.Z.), runanga (N.Z.) 2 = **putting together**, setting up, construction, building up, connecting, piecing together

assert VERB 1 = **state**, argue, maintain, declare, swear, pronounce, affirm, profess ≠ deny 2 = **insist upon**, stress, defend, uphold, put forward, press, stand up for ≠ retract ▷ **PHRASE: assert yourself** = **be forceful**, put your foot down (*informal*), put yourself forward, make your presence felt, exert your influence

assertion NOUN 1 = **statement**, claim, declaration, pronouncement 2 = **insistence**, stressing, maintenance

assertive ADJECTIVE = **confident**, positive, aggressive, forceful, emphatic, insistent, feisty (*informal, chiefly U.S. & Canad.*), pushy (*informal*) ≠ meek

assess VERB 1 = **judge**, estimate, analyse, evaluate, rate, value, check out, weigh up 2 = **evaluate**, rate, tax, value, estimate, fix, impose, levy

assessment NOUN 1 = **judgment**, analysis, evaluation, valuation, appraisal, rating, opinion, estimate 2 = **evaluation**, rating, charge, fee, toll, levy, valuation

asset NOUN = **benefit**, help, service, aid, advantage, strength, resource, attraction ≠ disadvantage

assign VERB 1 = **give**, set, grant, allocate, give out, consign, allot, apportion 2 = **select for**, post, commission, elect, appoint, delegate, nominate, name 3 = **attribute**, credit, put down, set down, ascribe, accredit

assignment NOUN = **task**, job, position, post, commission, exercise, responsibility, duty

assist VERB 1 = **help**, support, aid, cooperate with, abet, lend a helping hand to 2 = **facilitate**, help, further, serve, aid, forward, promote, speed up ≠ hinder

assistance NOUN = **help**, backing, support, aid, cooperation, helping hand ≠ hindrance

assistant NOUN = **helper**, ally, colleague, supporter, aide, second, attendant, accomplice

associate VERB 1 = **connect**, link, ally, identify, join, combine, attach, fasten ≠ separate 2 = **socialize**, mix, accompany, mingle, consort, hobnob ≠ avoid ▷ NOUN = **partner**, friend, ally, colleague, mate (*informal*), companion, comrade, affiliate, cobber (*Austral. & N.Z. old-fashioned, informal*), E hoa (*N.Z.*)

association NOUN 1 = **group**, club, society, league, band, set, pack, collection 2 = **connection**, union, joining, pairing, combination, mixture, blend, juxtaposition

assorted ADJECTIVE = **various**, different, mixed, varied, diverse, miscellaneous, sundry, motley ≠ similar

assume VERB 1 = **presume**, think, believe, expect, suppose, imagine, fancy, take for granted ≠ know 2 = **take on**, accept, shoulder, take over, put on, enter upon 3 = **simulate**, affect, adopt, put on, imitate, mimic, feign, impersonate 4 = **take over**, take, appropriate, seize, commandeer ≠ give up

assumed ADJECTIVE = **false**,

made-up, fake, bogus,
counterfeit, fictitious, make-
believe ≠ real

assumption NOUN
1 = **presumption**, belief, guess,
hypothesis, inference, conjecture,
surmise, supposition **2** = **taking
on**, managing, handling,
shouldering, putting on, taking
up, takeover, acquisition
3 = **seizure**, taking, takeover,
acquisition, appropriation,
wresting, confiscation,
commandeering

assurance NOUN **1** = **promise**,
statement, guarantee,
commitment, pledge, vow,
declaration, assertion ≠ lie
2 = **confidence**, conviction,
certainty, self-confidence, poise,
faith, nerve, aplomb ≠ self-doubt

assure VERB **1** = **convince**,
encourage, persuade, satisfy,
comfort, reassure, hearten,
embolden **2** = **make certain**,
ensure, confirm, guarantee,
secure, make sure, complete, seal
3 = **promise to**, pledge to, vow to,
guarantee to, swear to, confirm
to, certify to, give your word to

assured ADJECTIVE **1** = **confident**,
certain, positive, poised, fearless,
self-confident, self-assured,
dauntless ≠ self-conscious
2 = **certain**, sure, ensured,
confirmed, settled, guaranteed,
fixed, secure, nailed-on (slang)
≠ doubtful

astonish VERB = **amaze**, surprise,
stun, stagger, bewilder, astound,

daze, confound

astounding ADJECTIVE
= **amazing**, surprising, brilliant,
impressive, astonishing,
staggering, sensational (informal),
bewildering

astute ADJECTIVE = **intelligent**,
sharp, clever, subtle, shrewd,
cunning, canny, perceptive
≠ stupid

asylum NOUN **1** (old-fashioned)
= **mental hospital**, hospital,
institution, psychiatric hospital,
madhouse (informal) **2** = **refuge**,
haven, safety, protection,
preserve, shelter, retreat, harbour

athlete NOUN = **sportsperson**,
player, runner, competitor,
sportsman, contestant, gymnast,
sportswoman

athletic ADJECTIVE = **fit**, strong,
powerful, healthy, active, trim,
strapping, energetic ≠ feeble

athletics PLURAL NOUN = **sports**,
games, races, exercises, contests,
sporting events, gymnastics,
track and field events

atmosphere NOUN **1** = **air**, sky,
heavens, aerosphere **2** = **feeling**,
character, environment, spirit,
surroundings, tone, mood,
climate

atom NOUN = **particle**, bit, spot,
trace, molecule, dot, speck

atrocity NOUN **1** = **act of cruelty**,
crime, horror, evil, outrage,
abomination **2** = **cruelty**, horror,
brutality, savagery, wickedness,
barbarity, viciousness,
fiendishness

attach VERB 1 = **affix**, stick, secure, add, join, couple, link, tie ≠ detach 2 = **ascribe**, connect, attribute, assign, associate

attached ADJECTIVE = **spoken for**, married, partnered, engaged, accompanied ▷ PHRASE: **attached to** = **fond of**, devoted to, affectionate towards, full of regard for

attachment NOUN 1 = **fondness**, liking, feeling, relationship, regard, attraction, affection, affinity, aroha (N.Z.) ≠ aversion 2 = **accessory**, fitting, extra, component, extension, supplement, fixture, accoutrement

attack VERB 1 = **assault**, strike (at), mug, ambush, tear into, set upon, lay into (informal) ≠ defend 2 = **invade**, occupy, raid, infringe, storm, encroach 3 = **criticize**, blame, abuse, condemn, knock (informal), put down, slate (informal), have a go (at) (informal) ▷ NOUN 1 = **assault**, charge, campaign, strike, raid, invasion, offensive, blitz ≠ defence 2 = **criticism**, censure, disapproval, abuse, bad press, vilification, denigration, disparagement 3 = **bout**, fit, stroke, seizure, spasm, convulsion, paroxysm

attacker NOUN = **assailant**, assaulter, raider, intruder, invader, aggressor, mugger

attain VERB 1 = **obtain**, get, reach, complete, gain, achieve, acquire, fulfil 2 = **reach**, achieve, acquire, accomplish

attempt VERB = **try**, seek, aim, struggle, venture, undertake, strive, endeavour ▷ NOUN 1 = **try**, go (informal), shot (informal), effort, trial, bid, crack (informal), stab (informal) 2 = **attack**

attend VERB 1 = **be present**, go to, visit, frequent, haunt, appear at, turn up at, patronize ≠ be absent 2 = **pay attention**, listen, hear, mark, note, observe, heed, pay heed ≠ ignore ▷ PHRASE: **attend to something** = **apply yourself to**, concentrate on, look after, take care of, see to, get to work on, devote yourself to, occupy yourself with

attendance NOUN 1 = **presence**, being there, attending, appearance 2 = **turnout**, audience, gate, congregation, house, crowd, throng, number present

attendant NOUN = **assistant**, guard, servant, companion, aide, escort, follower, helper ▷ ADJECTIVE = **accompanying**, related, associated, accessory, consequent, resultant, concomitant

attention NOUN 1 = **thinking**, thought, mind, consideration, scrutiny, heed, deliberation, intentness 2 = **care**, support, concern, treatment, looking after, succour, ministration 3 = **awareness**, regard, notice, recognition, consideration, observation, consciousness ≠ inattention

attic NOUN = **loft**, garret, roof space

attitude NOUN 1 = **opinion**, view, position, approach, mood, perspective, point of view, stance 2 = **position**, bearing, pose, stance, carriage, posture

attract VERB 1 = **allure**, draw, persuade, charm, appeal to, win over, tempt, lure (*informal*) ≠ repel 2 = **pull**, draw, magnetize

attraction NOUN 1 = **appeal**, pull (*informal*), charm, lure, temptation, fascination, allure, magnetism 2 = **pull**, magnetism

attractive ADJECTIVE 1 = **seductive**, charming, tempting, pretty, fair, inviting, lovely, pleasant, hot (*informal*), fit (*Brit. informal*) ≠ unattractive 2 = **appealing**, pleasing, inviting, tempting, irresistible ≠ unappealing

attribute VERB = **ascribe**, credit, refer, trace, assign, charge, allocate, put down ▷ NOUN = **quality**, feature, property, character, element, aspect, characteristic, distinction

audience NOUN 1 = **spectators**, company, crowd, gathering, gallery, assembly, viewers, listeners 2 = **interview**, meeting, hearing, exchange, reception, consultation

aura NOUN = **air**, feeling, quality, atmosphere, tone, mood, ambience

austerity NOUN 1 = **plainness**, simplicity, starkness 2 = **asceticism**, self-discipline, sobriety, puritanism, self-denial

authentic ADJECTIVE 1 = **real**, pure, genuine, valid, undisputed, lawful, bona fide, dinkum (*Austral. & N.Z. informal*), true-to-life ≠ fake 2 = **accurate**, legitimate, authoritative

authenticity NOUN 1 = **genuineness**, purity 2 = **accuracy**, certainty, validity, legitimacy, faithfulness, truthfulness

author NOUN 1 = **writer**, composer, novelist, hack, creator, scribbler, scribe, wordsmith 2 = **creator**, father, producer, designer, founder, architect, inventor, originator

authoritarian ADJECTIVE = **strict**, severe, autocratic, dictatorial, dogmatic, tyrannical, doctrinaire ≠ lenient ▷ NOUN = **disciplinarian**, dictator, tyrant, despot, autocrat, absolutist

authoritative ADJECTIVE 1 = **commanding**, masterly, imposing, assertive, imperious, self-assured ≠ timid 2 = **reliable**, accurate, valid, authentic, definitive, dependable, trustworthy ≠ unreliable

authority NOUN 1 *usually plural* = **powers that be**, government, police, officials, the state, management, administration, the system **2** = **prerogative**, influence, power, control, weight, direction, command, licence, mana (*N.Z.*) **3** = **expert**, specialist, professional, master, guru, virtuoso, connoisseur, fundi (*S. African*) **4** = **command**, power, control, rule, management, direction, mastery

authorize VERB **1** = **empower**, commission, enable, entitle, mandate, accredit, give authority to **2** = **permit**, allow, grant, approve, sanction, license, warrant, consent to ≠ forbid

automatic ADJECTIVE
1 = **mechanical**, automated, mechanized, push-button, self-propelling ≠ done by hand **2** = **involuntary**, natural, unconscious, mechanical, spontaneous, reflex, instinctive, unwilled ≠ conscious

autonomous ADJECTIVE = **self-ruling**, free, independent, sovereign, self-sufficient, self-governing, self-determining

autonomy NOUN
= **independence**, freedom, sovereignty, self-determination, self-government, self-rule, self-sufficiency, home rule, rangatiratanga (*N.Z.*) ≠ dependency

availability NOUN
= **accessibility**, readiness, handiness, attainability

available ADJECTIVE = **accessible**, ready, to hand, handy, at hand, free, to be had, achievable ≠ in use

avalanche NOUN **1** = **snow-slide**, landslide, landslip **2** = **large amount**, barrage, torrent, deluge, inundation

avant-garde ADJECTIVE
= **progressive**, pioneering, experimental, innovative, unconventional, ground-breaking ≠ conservative

avenue NOUN = **street**, way, course, drive, road, approach, route, path

average NOUN = **standard**, normal, usual, par, mode, mean, medium, norm
▷ ADJECTIVE **1** = **usual**, standard, general, normal, regular, ordinary, typical, commonplace ≠ unusual **2** = **mean**, middle, medium, intermediate, median ≠ minimum
▷ VERB = **make on average**, be on average, even out to, do on average, balance out to ▷ PHRASE: **on average** = **usually**, generally, normally, typically, for the most part, as a rule

avert VERB **1** = **ward off**, avoid, prevent, frustrate, fend off, preclude, stave off, forestall **2** = **turn away**, turn aside

avoid VERB **1** = **prevent**, stop, frustrate, hamper, foil, inhibit, avert, thwart **2** = **refrain from**, bypass, dodge, eschew, escape, duck (out of) (*informal*), fight shy of, shirk from **3** = **keep away from**, dodge, shun, evade, steer clear of, bypass

await VERB 1 = **wait for**, expect, look for, look forward to, anticipate, stay for 2 = **be in store for**, wait for, be ready for, lie in wait for, be in readiness for

awake VERB 1 = **wake up**, come to, wake, stir, awaken, rouse 2 = **alert**, stimulate, provoke, revive, arouse, stir up, kindle 3 = **stimulate**, provoke, alert, stir up, kindle ▷ ADJECTIVE 1 = **not sleeping**, sleepless, wide-awake, aware, conscious, aroused, awakened, restless ≠ asleep

award VERB 1 = **present with**, give, grant, hand out, confer, endow, bestow 2 = **grant**, give, confer ▷ NOUN = **prize**, gift, trophy, decoration, grant, bonsela (*S. African*), koha (*N.Z.*)

aware ADJECTIVE = **informed**, enlightened, knowledgeable, learned, expert, versed, up to date, in the picture ≠ ignorant

awareness NOUN ▷ PHRASE: **awareness of** = **knowledge of**, understanding of, recognition of, perception of, consciousness of, realization of, familiarity with

away ADJECTIVE = **absent**, out, gone, elsewhere, abroad, not here, not present, on vacation ▷ ADVERB 1 = **off**, elsewhere, abroad, hence, from here 2 = **aside**, out of the way, to one side 3 = **at a distance**, far, apart, remote, isolated 4 = **continuously**, repeatedly, relentlessly, incessantly, interminably, unremittingly, uninterruptedly

awe NOUN = **wonder**, fear, respect, reverence, horror, terror, dread, admiration ≠ contempt ▷ VERB = **impress**, amaze, stun, frighten, terrify, astonish, horrify, intimidate

awesome ADJECTIVE = **awe-inspiring**, amazing, stunning, impressive, astonishing, formidable, intimidating, breathtaking

awful ADJECTIVE 1 = **disgusting**, offensive, gross, foul, dreadful, revolting, sickening, frightful, festy (*Austral. slang*), yucko (*Austral. slang*) 2 = **bad**, poor, terrible, appalling, foul, rubbish (*slang*), dreadful, horrendous ≠ wonderful ka pai (*N.Z.*) 3 = **shocking**, dreadful 4 = **unwell**, poorly (*informal*), ill, terrible, sick, crook (*Austral. & N.Z. informal*), unhealthy, off-colour, under the weather (*informal*)

awfully ADVERB 1 (*informal*) = **very**, extremely, terribly, exceptionally, greatly, immensely, exceedingly, dreadfully 2 = **badly**, woefully, dreadfully, disgracefully, wretchedly, unforgivably, reprehensibly

awkward ADJECTIVE 1 = **embarrassing**, difficult, sensitive, delicate, uncomfortable, humiliating, disconcerting, inconvenient, barro (*Austral. slang*)

≠ comfortable **2** = **inconvenient**,
difficult, troublesome,
cumbersome, unwieldy,
unmanageable, clunky (*informal*)
≠ convenient **3** = **clumsy**,
lumbering, bumbling, unwieldy,
ponderous, ungainly, gauche,
gawky, unco (*Austral. slang*)
≠ graceful

axe NOUN = **hatchet**, chopper,
tomahawk, cleaver, adze
▷ VERB **1** (*informal*) = **abandon**,
end, eliminate, cancel, scrap, cut
back, terminate, dispense with
2 (*informal*) = **dismiss**, fire
(*informal*), sack (*informal*), remove,
get rid of, kennet (*Austral. slang*),
jeff (*Austral. slang*) ▷ PHRASE:
the axe (*informal*) = **the sack**
(*informal*), dismissal, the boot
(*slang*), termination, the chop
(*slang*)

axis NOUN = **pivot**, shaft, axle,
spindle, centre line

Bb

baas (*S. African*) NOUN = **master**, chief, ruler, commander, head, overlord, overseer

baby NOUN = **child**, infant, babe, bairn (*Scot. & Northern English*), newborn child, babe in arms, ankle biter (*Austral. slang*), tacker (*Austral. slang*)
▷ ADJECTIVE = **small**, little, minute, tiny, mini, wee, miniature, petite

back NOUN 1 = **spine**, backbone, vertebrae, spinal column, vertebral column 2 = **rear** ≠ front
3 = **reverse**, rear, other side, wrong side, underside, flip side
▷ ADJECTIVE 1 = **rear** ≠ front
2 = **rearmost**, hind, hindmost
3 = **previous**, earlier, former, past, elapsed ≠ future 4 = **tail**, end, rear, posterior
▷ VERB 1 = **support**, help, aid, champion, defend, promote, assist, advocate ≠ oppose
2 = **subsidize**, help, support, sponsor, assist

● WORD POWER
● The *back* is the posterior part
● of the human body, extending
● from the neck to the pelvis. It
● is conceived as the part of any
● object opposite the front or to
● the rear, in examples like *the*
● *back of a car*. It can also mean
● the tail end, e.g. *the back of a*
● *queue*. The reverse side of an
● object can equally be denoted
● by back, e.g. *the back of a packet*.
● We describe the past and the
● future in terms of backwards
● and forwards. As an adjective,
● back means 'previous' in the
● expression *back catalogue*,
● and, as an adverb, back means
● 'previously' in the expression *a*
● *few years back*. The back plays an
● important role in supporting
● the human body, therefore
● *backing* is another word for
● support and assistance. We
● cannot see what is going on
● *behind our backs*, therefore this
● expression denotes secrecy and
● even wrongdoing.

backbone NOUN 1 = **spinal column**, spine, vertebrae, vertebral column 2 = **strength of character**, character, resolution, nerve, daring, courage, determination, pluck

backer NOUN 1 = **supporter**, second, angel (*informal*), patron, promoter, subscriber, helper, benefactor 2 = **advocate**, supporter, patron, sponsor, promoter

backfire VERB = **fail**, founder, flop (*informal*), rebound, boomerang, miscarry, misfire

background NOUN
1 = **upbringing**, history, culture, environment,

tradition, circumstances
2 = **experience**, grounding,
education 3 = **circumstances**,
history, conditions, situation,
atmosphere, environment,
framework, ambience

backing NOUN 1 = **support**,
encouragement, endorsement,
moral support 2 = **assistance**,
support, help, aid, sponsorship,
patronage

backlash NOUN = **reaction**,
response, resistance, retaliation,
repercussion, counterblast,
counteraction

backward ADJECTIVE
1 = **underdeveloped**,
undeveloped 2 = **slow**, behind,
retarded, subnormal, half-witted,
slow-witted, intellectually
handicapped (*Austral.*)

backwards or **backward**
ADVERB = **towards the rear**,
behind you, in reverse, rearwards

bacteria PLURAL NOUN
= **microorganisms**, viruses,
bugs (*slang*), germs, microbes,
pathogens, bacilli

● **WORD POWER**
● *Bacteria* is a plural noun. It is
● therefore incorrect to talk
● about *a bacteria*, even though
● this is quite commonly heard,
● especially in the media. The
● correct singular is *a bacterium*.

bad ADJECTIVE 1 = **harmful**,
damaging, dangerous,
destructive, unhealthy,
detrimental, hurtful, ruinous

≠ beneficial 2 = **unfavourable**,
distressing, unfortunate, grim,
unpleasant, gloomy, adverse
3 = **inferior**, poor, inadequate,
faulty, unsatisfactory, defective,
imperfect, substandard,
bush-league (*Austral.* & *N.Z.
informal*), half-pie (*N.Z. informal*),
bodger or bodgie (*Austral. slang*)
≠ satisfactory 4 = **incompetent**,
poor, useless, incapable, unfit,
inexpert 5 = **grim**, severe, hard,
tough 6 = **wicked**, criminal, evil,
corrupt, immoral, sinful, depraved
≠ virtuous 7 = **naughty**, defiant,
wayward, mischievous, wicked,
unruly, impish, undisciplined
≠ well-behaved 8 = **rotten**, off,
rank, sour, rancid, mouldy, putrid,
festy (*Austral. slang*)

badge NOUN 1 = **image**, brand,
stamp, identification, crest,
emblem, insignia 2 = **mark**, sign,
token

badger VERB = **pester**, harry,
bother, bug (*informal*), bully,
plague, hound, harass

badly ADVERB 1 = **poorly**,
incorrectly, carelessly,
inadequately, imperfectly, ineptly
≠ well 2 = **severely**, greatly,
deeply, seriously, desperately,
intensely, exceedingly
3 = **unfavourably**, unsuccessfully

baffle VERB = **puzzle**, confuse,
stump, bewilder, confound,
perplex, mystify, flummox
≠ explain

bag NOUN = **sack**, container, sac,
receptacle

▷ **VERB 1** = **get**, land, score (*slang*), capture, acquire, procure **2** = **catch**, kill, shoot, capture, acquire, trap

baggage NOUN = **luggage**, things, cases, bags, equipment, gear, suitcases, belongings

baggy ADJECTIVE = **loose**, slack, bulging, sagging, sloppy, floppy, roomy, ill-fitting ≠ tight

bail NOUN (*law*) = **security**, bond, guarantee, pledge, warranty, surety ▷ PHRASES: **bail out** = **escape**, withdraw, get away, retreat, make your getaway, break free *or* out; **bail something** *or* **someone out** (*informal*) = **save**, help, release, aid, deliver, recover, rescue, get out

bait NOUN = **lure**, attraction, incentive, carrot (*informal*), temptation, snare, inducement, decoy
▷ **VERB** = **tease**, annoy, irritate, bother, mock, wind up (*Brit. slang*), hound, torment

baked ADJECTIVE = **dry**, desert, seared, scorched, barren, sterile, arid, torrid

bakkie NOUN (*S. African*) = **truck**, pick-up, van, lorry, pick-up truck

balance VERB **1** = **stabilize**, level, steady ≠ overbalance **2** = **weigh**, consider, compare, estimate, contrast, assess, evaluate, set against **3** (*accounting*) = **calculate**, total, determine, estimate, settle, count, square, reckon
▷ **NOUN 1** = **equilibrium**,

stability, steadiness, evenness ≠ instability **2** = **stability**, equanimity, steadiness **3** = **parity**, equity, fairness, impartiality, equality, correspondence, equivalence **4** = **remainder**, rest, difference, surplus, residue **5** = **composure**, stability, restraint, self-control, poise, self-discipline, equanimity, self-restraint

balcony NOUN **1** = **terrace**, veranda **2** = **upper circle**, gods, gallery

bald ADJECTIVE **1** = **hairless**, depilated, baldheaded **2** = **plain**, direct, frank, straightforward, blunt, rude, forthright, unadorned

ball NOUN = **sphere**, drop, globe, pellet, orb, globule, spheroid

balloon VERB = **expand**, rise, increase, swell, blow up, inflate, bulge, billow

ballot NOUN = **vote**, election, voting, poll, polling, referendum, show of hands

ban VERB **1** = **prohibit**, bar, block, veto, forbid, boycott, outlaw, banish ≠ permit **2** = **bar**, prohibit, exclude, forbid, disqualify, preclude, debar, declare ineligible
▷ **NOUN** = **prohibition**, restriction, veto, boycott, embargo, injunction, taboo, disqualification, rahui (*N.Z.*), restraining order (*U.S. law*) ≠ permission

band[1] NOUN **1** = **ensemble**, group, orchestra, combo **2** = **gang**, company, group, party, team, body, crowd, pack

band² NOUN = **headband**, strip, ribbon

bandage NOUN = **dressing**, plaster, compress, gauze
▷ **VERB** = **dress**, cover, bind, swathe

bandit NOUN = **robber**, outlaw, raider, plunderer, mugger (*informal*), looter, highwayman, desperado

bang NOUN 1 = **explosion**, pop, clash, crack, blast, slam, discharge, thump **2** = **blow**, knock, stroke, punch, bump, sock (*slang*), smack, thump
▷ **VERB 1** = **resound**, boom, explode, thunder, thump, clang **2** = **bump**, knock, elbow, jostle **3** *often with* **on** = **hit**, strike, knock, belt (*informal*), slam, thump, clatter, beat *or* knock seven bells out of (*informal*)
▷ **ADVERB** = **exactly**, straight, square, squarely, precisely, slap, smack, plumb (*informal*)

banish VERB 1 = **exclude**, ban, dismiss, expel, throw out, eject, evict **2** = **expel**, exile, outlaw, deport ≠ admit **3** = **get rid of**, remove

bank¹ NOUN 1 = **financial institution**, repository, depository **2** = **store**, fund, stock, source, supply, reserve, pool, reservoir
▷ **VERB** = **deposit**, keep, save

bank² NOUN 1 = **side**, edge, margin, shore, brink **2** = **mound**, banking, rise, hill, mass, pile, heap, ridge, kopje *or* koppie (*S. African*)
▷ **VERB** = **tilt**, tip, pitch, heel, slope, incline, slant, cant

bank³ NOUN = **row**, group, line, range, series, file, rank, sequence

bankrupt ADJECTIVE = **insolvent**, broke (*informal*), ruined, wiped out (*informal*), impoverished, in the red, destitute, gone bust (*informal*) ≠ solvent

bankruptcy NOUN = **insolvency**, failure, disaster, ruin, liquidation

banner NOUN 1 = **flag**, standard, colours, pennant, ensign, streamer **2** = **placard**

banquet NOUN = **feast**, spread (*informal*), dinner, meal, revel, repast, hakari (*N.Z.*)

bar NOUN 1 = **public house**, pub (*informal, chiefly Brit.*), counter, inn, saloon, tavern, canteen, watering hole (*facetious or slang*), beer parlour (*Canad.*) **2** = **rod**, staff, stick, stake, rail, pole, paling, shaft **3** = **obstacle**, block, barrier, hurdle, hitch, barricade, snag, deterrent ≠ aid
▷ **VERB 1** = **lock**, block, secure, attach, bolt, blockade, barricade, fortify **2** = **block**, restrict, restrain, hamper, thwart, hinder, obstruct, impede **3** = **exclude**, ban, forbid, prohibit, keep out of, disallow, shut out of, blackball ≠ admit

barbarian NOUN 1 = **savage**, monster, beast, brute, yahoo, swine, sadist **2** = **lout**, yahoo, bigot, philistine, hoon (*Austral.*

& N.Z.), cougan (Austral. slang), scozza (Austral. slang), bogan (Austral. slang), boor, vulgarian

bare ADJECTIVE 1 = **naked**, nude, stripped, uncovered, undressed, unclothed, unclad, without a stitch on (informal) ≠ dressed 2 = **simple**, spare, stark, austere, spartan, unadorned, unembellished, unornamented, bare-bones ≠ adorned 3 = **plain**, simple, basic, obvious, sheer, patent, evident, stark

barely ADVERB = **only just**, just, hardly, scarcely, at a push ≠ completely

bargain NOUN 1 = **good buy**, discount purchase, good deal, steal (informal), snip (informal), giveaway, cheap purchase 2 = **agreement**, deal (informal), promise, contract, arrangement, settlement, pledge, pact ▷ VERB = **negotiate**, deal, contract, mediate, covenant, stipulate, transact, cut a deal

barge NOUN = **canal boat**, lighter, narrow boat, flatboat

bark¹ VERB = **yap**, bay, howl, snarl, growl, yelp, woof ▷ NOUN = **yap**, bay, howl, snarl, growl, yelp, woof

bark² NOUN = **covering**, casing, cover, skin, layer, crust, cortex (anatomy, botany), rind

barracks PLURAL NOUN = **camp**, quarters, garrison, encampment, billet

barrage NOUN 1 = **bombardment**, attack, bombing, assault, shelling, battery, volley, blitz 2 = **torrent**, mass, burst, stream, hail, spate, onslaught, deluge

barren ADJECTIVE 1 = **desolate**, empty, desert, waste ≠ fertile 2 (old-fashioned) = **infertile**, sterile, childless, unproductive

barricade NOUN = **barrier**, wall, fence, blockade, obstruction, rampart, bulwark, palisade ▷ VERB = **bar**, block, defend, secure, lock, bolt, blockade, fortify

barrier NOUN = **barricade**, wall, bar, fence, boundary, obstacle, blockade, obstruction

base¹ NOUN 1 = **bottom**, floor, lowest part ≠ top 2 = **support**, stand, foot, rest, bed, bottom, foundation, pedestal 3 = **foundation**, institution, organization, establishment, starting point 4 = **centre**, post, station, camp, settlement, headquarters 5 = **home**, house, pad (slang), residence 6 = **essence**, source, basis, root, core ▷ VERB 1 = **ground**, found, build, establish, depend, construct, derive, hinge 2 = **place**, set, post, station, establish, locate, install

base² ADJECTIVE = **dishonourable**, evil, disgraceful, shameful, immoral, wicked, sordid, despicable, scungy (Austral. & N.Z.) ≠ honourable

bash VERB = **hit**, beat, strike, knock, smash, belt (informal), slap, sock (slang)

basic ADJECTIVE 1 = **fundamental**,

● BATS
● flying fox
● fruit bat
● hammerhead
● horseshoe bat
● kalong
● noctule
● pipistrelle
● serotine
● vampire bat

main, essential, primary, vital, principal, cardinal, elementary **2** = **vital**, needed, important, key, necessary, essential, primary, crucial **3** = **essential**, key, vital, fundamental ≠ secondary **4** = **main**, key, essential, primary **5** = **plain**, simple, classic, unfussy, unembellished, bare-bones ▷ PLURAL NOUN = **essentials**, principles, fundamentals, nuts and bolts (*informal*), nitty-gritty (*informal*), rudiments, brass tacks (*informal*)

basically ADVERB = **essentially**, mainly, mostly, principally, fundamentally, primarily, at heart, inherently

basis NOUN **1** = **arrangement**, way, system, footing, agreement **2** = **foundation**, support, base, ground, footing, bottom, groundwork

bask VERB = **lie**, relax, lounge, sprawl, loaf, lie about, swim in, sunbathe, outspan (*S. African*)

bass ADJECTIVE = **deep**, low, resonant, sonorous, low-pitched, deep-toned

batch NOUN = **group**, set, lot, crowd, pack, collection, quantity, bunch

bath NOUN = **wash**, cleaning, shower, soak, cleansing, scrub,

scrubbing, douche ▷ VERB = **clean**, wash, shower, soak, cleanse, scrub, bathe, rinse

bathe VERB **1** = **swim 2** = **wash**, clean, bath, shower, soak, cleanse, scrub, rinse **3** = **cleanse**, clean, wash, soak, rinse **4** = **cover**, flood, steep, engulf, immerse, overrun, suffuse, wash over

baton NOUN = **stick**, club, staff, pole, rod, crook, cane, mace, mere (*N.Z.*), patu (*N.Z.*)

batter VERB = **beat**, hit, strike, knock, bang, thrash, pound, buffet

battery NOUN = **artillery**, ordnance, gunnery, gun emplacement, cannonry

battle NOUN **1** = **fight**, attack, action, struggle, conflict, clash, encounter, combat, biffo (*Austral. slang*), boilover (*Austral.*) ≠ peace **2** = **conflict**, campaign, struggle, dispute, contest, crusade **3** = **campaign**, drive, movement, push, struggle ▷ VERB **1** = **wrestle**, war, fight, argue, dispute, grapple, clamour, lock horns **2** = **struggle**, work, labour, strain, strive, toil, go all out (*informal*), give it your best shot (*informal*)

battlefield NOUN = **battleground**, front, field,

● **FAMOUS BATTLES**

● Aboukir or Abukir Bay	1798	● Manassas	1861; 1862
● Actium	31 BC	● Marathon	490 BC
● Agincourt	1415	● Marengo	1800
● Alamo	1836	● Marston Moor	1644
● Arnhem	1944	● Missionary Ridge	1863
● Austerlitz	1805	● Navarino	425 BC
● Balaklava or Balaclava	1854	● Omdurman	1898
● Bannockburn	1314	● Passchendaele	1917
● Barnet	1471	● Philippi	42 BC
● Bautzen	1813	● Plains of Abraham	1759
● Belleau Wood	1918	● Plassey	1757
● Blenheim	1704	● Plataea	479 BC
● Borodino	1812	● Poltava	1709
● Bosworth Field	1485	● Prestonpans	1745
● Boyne	1690	● Pydna	168 BC
● Cannae	216 BC	● Quatre Bras	1815
● Crécy	1346	● Ramillies	1706
● Culloden	1746	● Roncesvalles	778
● Dien Bien Phu	1954	● Sadowa or Sadová	1866
● Edgehill	1642	● Saint-Mihiel	1918
● El Alamein	1942	● Salamis	480 BC
● Falkirk	1298; 1746	● Sedgemoor	1685
● Flodden	1513	● Sempach	1386
● Gettysburg	1863	● Shipka Pass	1877–78
● Guadalcanal	1942-3	● Somme	1916; 1918
● Hastings	1066	● Stamford Bridge	1066
● Imphal	1944	● Tannenberg	1410; 1914
● Inkerman	1854	● Tewkesbury	1471
● Issus	333 BC	● Thermopylae	480 BC
● Jemappes	1792	● Tobruk	1941; 1942
● Jena	1806	● Trafalgar	1805
● Killiecrankie	1689	● Trenton	1776
● Kursk	1943	● Verdun	1916
● Ladysmith	1899–1900	● Vitoria	1813
● Leipzig	1813	● Wagram	1809
● Lepanto	1571	● Waterloo	1815
● Leyte Gulf	1944	● Ypres	1914; 1915; 1917; 1918
● Little Bighorn	1876		
● Lützen	1632	● Zama	202 BC

combat zone, field of battle

batty ADJECTIVE = **crazy**, odd, mad, eccentric, peculiar, daft (*informal*), touched, potty (*Brit. informal*), off the air (*Austral. slang*), porangi (*N.Z.*), daggy (*Austral. & N.Z. informal*)

bay¹ NOUN = **inlet**, sound, gulf, creek, cove, fjord, bight, natural harbour

bay² NOUN = **recess**, opening, corner, niche, compartment, nook, alcove

bay³ VERB = **howl**, cry, roar (*of a hound*), bark, wail, growl, bellow, clamour
  ▷ NOUN = **cry**, roar (*of a hound*), bark, howl, wail, growl, bellow, clamour

bazaar NOUN 1 = **market**, exchange, fair, marketplace
  2 = **fair**, fête, gala, bring-and-buy

be VERB = **be alive**, live, exist, survive, breathe, be present, endure

beach NOUN = **shore**, coast, sands, seaside, water's edge, seashore

beached ADJECTIVE = **stranded**, grounded, abandoned, deserted, wrecked, ashore, marooned, aground

beacon NOUN 1 = **signal**, sign, beam, flare, bonfire
  2 = **lighthouse**, watchtower

bead NOUN = **drop**, tear, bubble, pearl, dot, drip, blob, droplet

beam VERB 1 = **smile**, grin
  2 = **transmit**, show, air, broadcast, cable, send out, relay, televise 3 = **radiate**, flash, shine, glow, glitter, glare, gleam
  ▷ NOUN 1 = **ray**, flash, stream, glow, streak, shaft, gleam, glint
  2 = **rafter**, support, timber, spar, plank, girder, joist 3 = **smile**, grin

bear VERB 1 = **carry**, take, move, bring, transfer, conduct, transport, haul ≠ put down
  2 = **support**, shoulder, sustain, endure, uphold, withstand ≠ give up 3 = **display**, have, show, hold, carry, possess
  4 = **suffer**, experience, go through, sustain, stomach, endure, brook, abide 5 = **bring yourself to**, allow, accept, permit, endure, tolerate 6 = **produce**, generate, yield, bring forth
  7 = **give birth to**, produce, deliver, breed, bring forth, beget
  8 = **exhibit**, hold, maintain
  9 = **conduct**, carry, move, deport
  ▷ PHRASE: **bear something out** = **support**, prove, confirm, justify, endorse, uphold, substantiate, corroborate

bearer NOUN 1 = **agent**, carrier, courier, herald, envoy, messenger, conveyor, emissary 2 = **carrier**, runner, servant, porter

bearing NOUN 1 *usually with* **on** *or* **upon** = **relevance**, relation, application, connection, import, reference, significance, pertinence ≠ irrelevance

2 = **manner**, attitude, conduct, aspect, behaviour, posture, demeanour, deportment
▷ PLURAL NOUN = **way**, course, position, situation, track, aim, direction, location

beast NOUN 1 = **animal**, creature, brute 2 = **brute**, monster, savage, barbarian, fiend, swine, ogre, sadist

beastly ADJECTIVE (*informal*) = **unpleasant**, mean, awful, nasty, rotten, horrid, disagreeable ≠ pleasant

beat VERB 1 = **batter**, hit, strike, knock, pound, smack, thrash, thump 2 = **pound**, strike, hammer, batter, thrash 3 = **throb**, thump, pound, quake, vibrate, pulsate, palpitate 4 = **hit**, strike, bang 5 = **flap**, thrash, flutter, wag 6 = **defeat**, outdo, trounce, overcome, crush, overwhelm, conquer, surpass
▷ NOUN 1 = **throb**, pounding, pulse, thumping, vibration, pulsating, palpitation, pulsation 2 = **route**, way, course, rounds, path, circuit ▷ PHRASE: **beat someone up** (*informal*) = **assault**, attack, batter, thrash, set about, set upon, lay into (*informal*), beat the living daylights out of (*informal*)

beaten ADJECTIVE 1 = **stirred**, mixed, whipped, blended, whisked, frothy, foamy 2 = **defeated**, overcome, overwhelmed, cowed, thwarted, vanquished

beautiful ADJECTIVE = **attractive**, pretty, lovely, charming, tempting, pleasant, handsome, fetching, hot (*informal*), fit (*Brit. informal*) ≠ ugly

beauty NOUN 1 = **attractiveness**, charm, grace, glamour, elegance, loveliness, handsomeness, comeliness ≠ ugliness 2 = **good-looker**, lovely (*slang*), belle, stunner (*informal*), beaut (*Austral. & N.Z. slang*)

because CONJUNCTION = **since**, as, in that ▷ PHRASE: **because of** = **as a result of**, on account of, by reason of, thanks to, owing to

● WORD POWER
● The phrase *on account of* can
● provide a useful alternative
● to *because of* in writing. It
● occurs relatively infrequently
● in spoken language, where it
● is sometimes followed by a
● clause, as in *on account of I don't*
● *do drugs*. However, this use is
● considered nonstandard.

beckon VERB = **gesture**, sign, wave, indicate, signal, nod, motion, summon

become VERB 1 = **come to be**, develop into, be transformed into, grow into, change into, alter to, mature into, ripen into 2 = **suit**, fit, enhance, flatter, embellish, set off

becoming ADJECTIVE
1 = **flattering**, pretty, attractive, enhancing, neat, graceful, tasteful, well-chosen ≠ unflattering 2 = **appropriate**,

seemly, fitting, suitable, proper, worthy, in keeping, compatible ≠ inappropriate

bed NOUN 1 = **bedstead**, couch, berth, cot, divan 2 = **plot**, area, row, strip, patch, ground, land, garden 3 = **bottom**, ground, floor 4 = **base**, footing, basis, bottom, foundation, underpinning, groundwork, bedrock

bee NOUN
  ▷ *see* **ants, bees and wasps**

beer parlour NOUN (*Canad.*) = **tavern**, inn, bar, pub (*informal, chiefly Brit.*), public house, beverage room (*Canad.*), hostelry, alehouse (*archaic*)

before PREPOSITION 1 = **earlier than**, ahead of, prior to, in advance of ≠ after 2 = **in front of**, ahead of, in advance of 3 = **in the presence of**, in front of 4 = **ahead of**, in front of, in advance of
  ▷ ADVERB 1 = **previously**, earlier,

● **BEETLES**
● ambrosia beetle
● Asiatic beetle
● bacon beetle
● bark beetle
● bee beetle
● black beetle *or* (N.Z.) kekerengu *or* Māori bug
● blister beetle
● bloody-nosed beetle
● boll weevil
● bombardier beetle
● burying beetle *or* sexton
● cabinet beetle
● cardinal beetle
● carpet beetle *or* (U.S.) carpet bug
● chafer
● Christmas beetle *or* king beetle
● click beetle, snapping beetle, *or* skipjack
● cockchafer, May beetle, *or* May bug
● Colorado beetle *or* potato beetle
● deathwatch beetle
● diving beetle
● dung beetle *or* chafer

● firefly
● flea beetle
● furniture beetle
● glow-worm
● gold beetle *or* goldbug
● goldsmith beetle
● ground beetle
● Japanese beetle
● June bug, June beetle, May bug, *or* May beetle
● ladybird *or* (U.S. & Canad.) ladybug
● leaf beetle
● leather beetle
● May beetle, cockchafer, *or* June bug
● scarab
● scavenger beetle
● snapping beetle
● water beetle
● weevil *or* snout beetle
● weevil, pea weevil, *or* bean weevil

sooner, in advance, formerly ≠ after **2 = in the past**, earlier, once, previously, formerly, hitherto, beforehand ▷ **RELATED WORDS**: prefixes ante-, fore-, pre-

beforehand ADVERB = **in advance**, before, earlier, already, sooner, ahead, previously, in anticipation

beg VERB **1 = implore**, plead with, beseech, request, petition, solicit, entreat **2 = scrounge**, bum (informal), touch (someone) for (slang), cadge, sponge on (someone) for, freeload (slang), seek charity, solicit charity ≠ give

beggar NOUN = **tramp**, bum (informal), derelict, drifter, down-and-out, pauper, vagrant, bag lady (chiefly U.S.), derro (Austral. slang)

begin VERB **1 = start**, commence, proceed ≠ stop **2 = commence**, start, initiate, embark on, set about, instigate, institute, make a beginning **3 = start talking**, start, initiate, commence **4 = come into existence**, start, appear, emerge, arise, originate, come into being **5 = emerge**, start, spring, stem, derive, originate ≠ end

beginner NOUN = **novice**, pupil, amateur, newcomer, starter, trainee, apprentice, learner ≠ expert

beginning NOUN **1 = start**, opening, birth, origin, outset, onset, initiation, inauguration ≠ end **2 = outset**, start, opening, birth, onset, commencement

3 = origins

behave VERB **1 = act 2** often reflexive = **be well-behaved**, mind your manners, keep your nose clean, act correctly, conduct yourself properly ≠ misbehave

behaviour NOUN **1 = conduct**, ways, actions, bearing, attitude, manner, manners, demeanour **2 = action**, performance, operation, functioning

behind PREPOSITION **1 = at the rear of**, at the back of, at the heels of **2 = after**, following **3 = supporting**, for, backing, on the side of, in agreement with **4 = causing**, responsible for, initiating, at the bottom of, instigating **5 = later than**, after ▷ ADVERB **1 = after**, next, following, afterwards, subsequently, in the wake (of) ≠ in advance of **2 = behind schedule**, delayed, running late, behind time ≠ ahead **3 = overdue**, in debt, in arrears, behindhand ▷ NOUN (informal) = **bottom**, butt (U.S. & Canad. informal), buttocks, posterior

being NOUN **1 = individual**, creature, human being, living thing **2 = life**, reality ≠ nonexistence **3 = soul**, spirit, substance, creature, essence, organism, entity

beleaguered ADJECTIVE **1 = harassed**, troubled, plagued, hassled (informal), badgered, persecuted, pestered, vexed

b

2 = **besieged**, surrounded, blockaded, beset, encircled, assailed, hemmed in

belief NOUN **1** = **trust**, confidence, conviction ≠ disbelief **2** = **faith**, principles, doctrine, ideology, creed, dogma, tenet, credo **3** = **opinion**, feeling, idea, impression, assessment, notion, judgment, point of view

believe VERB **1** = **think**, judge, suppose, estimate, imagine, assume, gather, reckon **2** = **accept**, trust, credit, depend on, rely on, have faith in, swear by, be certain of ≠ disbelieve

believer NOUN = **follower**, supporter, convert, disciple, devotee, apostle, adherent, zealot ≠ sceptic

bellow VERB = **shout**, cry (out), scream, roar, yell, howl, shriek, bawl
▷ NOUN = **shout**, cry, scream, roar, yell, howl, shriek, bawl

belly NOUN = **stomach**, insides (*informal*), gut, abdomen, tummy, paunch, potbelly, corporation (*informal*), puku (*N.Z.*)

belong VERB = **go with**, fit into, be part of, relate to, be connected with, pertain to

belonging NOUN = **fellowship**, relationship, association, loyalty, acceptance, attachment, inclusion, affinity

belongings PLURAL NOUN = **possessions**, goods, things, effects, property, stuff, gear, paraphernalia

beloved ADJECTIVE = **dear**, loved, valued, prized, admired, treasured, precious, darling

below PREPOSITION **1** = **under**, underneath, lower than **2** = **less than**, lower than **3** = **subordinate to**, subject to, inferior to, lesser than
▷ ADVERB **1** = **lower**, down, under, beneath, underneath **2** = **beneath**, following, at the end, underneath, at the bottom, further on

belt NOUN **1** = **waistband**, band, sash, girdle, girth, cummerbund **2** = **conveyor belt**, band, loop, fan belt, drive belt **3** (*geography*) = **zone**, area, region, section, district, stretch, strip, layer

bemused ADJECTIVE = **puzzled**, confused, baffled, at sea, bewildered, muddled, perplexed, mystified

bench NOUN **1** = **seat**, stall, pew **2** = **worktable**, stand, table, counter, trestle table, workbench
▷ PHRASE: **the bench** = **court**, judges, magistrates, tribunal, judiciary, courtroom

benchmark NOUN = **reference point**, gauge, yardstick, measure, level, standard, model, par

bend VERB = **twist**, turn, wind, lean, hook, bow, curve, arch
▷ NOUN = **curve**, turn, corner, twist, angle, bow, loop, arc

beneath PREPOSITION **1** = **under**, below, underneath, lower than ≠ over **2** = **inferior to**, below **3** = **unworthy of**, unfitting for, unsuitable for, inappropriate for, unbefitting

▷ **ADVERB** = **underneath**, below, in a lower place ▷ **RELATED WORD**: *prefix* **sub-**

beneficial ADJECTIVE
= **favourable**, useful, valuable, helpful, profitable, benign, wholesome, advantageous ≠ harmful

beneficiary NOUN 1 = **recipient**, receiver, payee **2** = **heir**, inheritor

benefit NOUN 1 = **good**, help, profit, favour ≠ harm
2 = **advantage**, aid, favour, assistance
▷ **VERB 1** = **profit from**, make the most of, gain from, do well out of, reap benefits from, turn to your advantage **2** = **help**, aid, profit, improve, enhance, assist, avail ≠ harm

benign ADJECTIVE 1 = **benevolent**, kind, kindly, warm, friendly, obliging, sympathetic, compassionate ≠ unkind
2 (*medical*) = **harmless**, innocent, innocuous, curable, inoffensive, remediable ≠ malignant

bent ADJECTIVE 1 = **misshapen**, twisted, angled, bowed, curved, arched, crooked, distorted ≠ straight **2** = **stooped**, bowed, arched, hunched
▷ **NOUN** = **inclination**, ability, leaning, tendency, preference, penchant, propensity, aptitude
▷ **PHRASE**: **bent on** = **intent on**, set on, fixed on, predisposed to, resolved on, insistent on

bequeath VERB 1 = **leave**, will, give, grant, hand down, endow, bestow, entrust **2** = **give**, accord, grant, afford, yield, lend, pass on, confer

berth NOUN 1 = **bunk**, bed, hammock, billet **2** (*nautical*) = **anchorage**, haven, port, harbour, dock, pier, wharf, quay
▷ **VERB** (*nautical*) = **anchor**, land, dock, moor, tie up, drop anchor

beside PREPOSITION = **next to**, near, close to, neighbouring, alongside, adjacent to, at the side of, abreast of ▷ **PHRASE**:
beside yourself = **distraught**, desperate, distressed, frantic, frenzied, demented, unhinged, overwrought

● **WORD POWER**
● People occasionally confuse
● *beside* and *besides*. *Besides* is used
● for mentioning something that
● adds to what you have already
● said, for example: *I didn't feel like*
● *going and besides, I had nothing*
● *to wear.* *Beside* usually means
● *next to or at the side of something*
● *or someone*, for example: *he was*
● *standing beside me* (not *besides*
● *me*).

besides PREPOSITION = **apart from**, barring, excepting, other than, excluding, as well (as), in addition to, over and above
▷ **ADVERB** = **also**, too, further, otherwise, in addition, as well, moreover, furthermore

besiege VERB 1 = **harass**, harry, plague, hound, hassle (*informal*), badger, pester **2** = **surround**, enclose, blockade, encircle, hem in, shut in, lay siege to

best ADJECTIVE = **finest**, leading, supreme, principal, foremost, pre-eminent, unsurpassed, most accomplished
▷ ADVERB = **most highly**, most fully, most deeply ▷ PHRASE: **the best** = **the finest**, the pick, the flower, the cream, the elite, the rème de la crème (*French*)

bestow VERB = **present**, give, award, grant, commit, hand out, lavish, impart ≠ obtain

bet VERB = **gamble**, chance, stake, venture, hazard, speculate, wager, risk money
▷ NOUN = **gamble**, risk, stake, venture, speculation, flutter (*informal*), punt, wager

betray VERB **1** = **be disloyal to**, dob in (*Austral. slang*), double-cross (*informal*), stab in the back, be unfaithful to, inform on *or* against **2** = **give away**, reveal, expose, disclose, uncover, divulge, unmask, let slip

betrayal NOUN = **disloyalty**, sell-out (*informal*), deception, treason, treachery, trickery, double-cross (*informal*), breach of trust ≠ loyalty

better ADVERB **1** = **to a greater degree**, more completely, more thoroughly **2** = **in a more excellent manner**, more effectively, more attractively, more advantageously, more competently, in a superior way

≠ worse
▷ ADJECTIVE **1** = **well**, stronger, recovering, cured, fully recovered, on the mend (*informal*) ≠ worse **2** = **superior**, finer, higher-quality, surpassing, preferable, more desirable ≠ inferior

between PREPOSITION = **amidst**, among, mid, in the middle of, betwixt ▷ RELATED WORD: *prefix* **inter-**

● **WORD POWER**
● After *distribute* and words with
● a similar meaning, *among*
● should be used rather than
● *between*: *share out the sweets*
● *among the children* (not *between*
● *the children*, unless there are
● only two children).

beverage NOUN = **drink**, liquid, liquor, refreshment

beverage room NOUN (*Canad.*) = **tavern**, inn, bar, pub (*informal, chiefly Brit.*), public house, beer parlour (*Canad.*), hostelry, alehouse (*archaic*)

beware VERB **1** = **be careful**, look out, watch out, be wary, be cautious, take heed, guard against something **2** = **avoid**, mind

bewilder VERB = **confound**, confuse, puzzle, baffle, perplex, mystify, flummox, bemuse

bewildered ADJECTIVE = **confused**, puzzled, baffled, at sea, muddled, perplexed, at a loss, mystified

beyond PREPOSITION **1** = **on the other side of 2** = **after**, over, past, above **3** = **past 4** = **except for**, but, save, apart from, other than, excluding, besides, aside from **5** = **exceeding**, surpassing, superior to, out of reach of **6** = **outside**, over, above

bias NOUN = **prejudice**, leaning, tendency, inclination, favouritism, partiality
≠ impartiality
▷ VERB = **influence**, colour, weight, prejudice, distort, sway, warp, slant

biased ADJECTIVE = **prejudiced**, weighted, one-sided, partial, distorted, slanted

bid NOUN **1** = **attempt**, try, effort, go (*informal*), shot (*informal*), stab (*informal*), crack (*informal*)
2 = **offer**, price, amount, advance, proposal, sum, tender
▷ VERB **1** = **make an offer**, offer, propose, submit, tender, proffer
2 = **wish**, say, call, tell, greet
3 = **tell**, ask, order, require, direct, command, instruct

bidding NOUN = **order**, request, command, instruction, summons, beck and call

big ADJECTIVE **1** = **large**, great, huge, massive, vast, enormous, substantial, extensive, supersize
≠ small **2** = **important**, significant, urgent, far-reaching
≠ unimportant **3** = **powerful**, important, prominent, dominant, influential, eminent, skookum (*Canad.*) **4** = **grown-up**, adult, grown, mature, elder, full-grown ≠ young **5** = **generous**,

good, noble, gracious, benevolent, altruistic, unselfish, magnanimous

bill¹ NOUN **1** = **charges**, rate, costs, score, account, statement, reckoning, expense **2** = **act of parliament**, measure, proposal, piece of legislation, projected law **3** = **list**, listing, programme, card, schedule, agenda, catalogue, inventory **4** = **advertisement**, notice, poster, leaflet, bulletin, circular, handout, placard
▷ VERB **1** = **charge**, debit, invoice, send a statement to, send an invoice to **2** = **advertise**, post, announce, promote, plug (*informal*), tout, publicize, give advance notice of

bill² NOUN = **beak**, nib, neb (*archaic or dialect*), mandible

bind VERB **1** = **oblige**, make, force, require, engage, compel, constrain, necessitate **2** = **tie**, join, stick, secure, wrap, knot, strap, lash ≠ untie
▷ NOUN (*informal*) = **nuisance**, inconvenience, hassle (*informal*), drag (*informal*), spot (*informal*), difficulty, bore, dilemma, uphill (*S. African*)

binding ADJECTIVE = **compulsory**, necessary, mandatory, obligatory, irrevocable, unalterable, indissoluble ≠ optional

binge NOUN (*informal*) = **bout**, spell, fling, feast, stint, spree, orgy, bender (*informal*)

biography NOUN = **life story**, life, record, account, profile, memoir,

CV, curriculum vitae

bird NOUN = **feathered friend**, fowl, songbird ▷ **RELATED WORDS**: *adjective* **avian**, *male* **cock**, *female* **hen**, *young* **chick**, **fledgeling** *or* **fledgling**, **nestling**, *collective nouns* **flock**, **flight**, *habitation* **nest**
▷ *see* **birds of prey**, **seabirds**, **types of fowl**

bird of prey NOUN
▷ *see* **birds of prey**

birth NOUN 1 = **childbirth**,

● **BIRDS**
● accentor
● amokura (N.Z.)
● apostle bird *or* happy family bird (Austral.)
● avocet
● axebird (Austral.)
● banded dotterel (N.Z.)
● banded rail (N.Z.)
● bee-eater
● bellbird *or* (N.Z.) koromako *or* makomako
● bittern
● blackbird
● blackcap
● black-fronted tern *or* tara (N.Z.)
● black robin (N.Z.)
● blue duck, mountain duck, whio *or* whistling duck (N.Z.)
● boobook (Austral.)
● brain-fever bird *or* (Austral.) pallid cuckoo
● brambling
● brolga, Australian crane, *or* (Austral.) native companion
● brown creeper *or* pipipi (N.Z.)
● brown duck (N.Z.)
● brown kiwi (N.Z.)
● budgerigar *or* (Austral.) zebra parrot
● bunting
● bush wren (N.Z.)
● bustard *or* (Austral.) plain turkey, plains turkey, *or* wild turkey
● button quail *or* (Austral.) bustard quail
● Californian quail (N.Z.)
● canary
● capercaillie *or* capercailzie
● chaffinch
● chicken *or* (Austral. informal) chook
● chiffchaff
● chough
● chukar
● crane
● crossbill
● crow *or* (Scot.) corbie
● cuckoo
● curlew
● dipper *or* water ouzel
● diver
● dove *or* (archaic *or* poetic) culver
● dunlin *or* red-backed sandpiper
● egret
● fernbird (N.Z.)
● fieldfare
● finch
● firecrest
● flamingo
● flycatcher
● galah *or* (Austral.) galar *or* gillar
● godwit

- goldcrest
- grebe
- greenshank
- grey-crowned babbler, happy family bird, Happy Jack, or parson bird (*Austral.*)
- grey warbler or riroriro (*N.Z.*)
- grouse
- hen harrier or (*U.S. & Canad.*) marsh harrier
- heron
- hoopoe
- jabiru or (*Austral.*) policeman bird
- jackdaw
- jaeger (*U.S. & Canad.*)
- jay
- kaka (*N.Z.*)
- kakapo (*N.Z.*)
- kakariki (*N.Z.*)
- karoro or blackbacked gull (*N.Z.*)
- kea (*N.Z.*)
- kingfisher or (*N.Z.*) kotare
- kiwi or apteryx
- knot
- koel or (*Austral.*) black cuckoo or cooee bird
- kokako or blue-wattled crow (*N.Z.*)
- kookaburra, laughing jackass, or (*Austral.*) bushman's clock, settler's clock, goburra, or great brown kingfisher
- kotuku or white heron (*N.Z.*)
- lapwing or green plover
- lark
- linnet
- lorikeet
- lyrebird or (*Austral.*) buln-buln
- magpie or (*Austral.*) piping shrike or piping crow-shrike

- magpie lark or (*Austral.*) mudlark, Murray magpie, mulga, or peewit
- Major Mitchell or Leadbeater's cockatoo
- makomako (*Austral.*)
- martin
- metallic starling or shining starling (*Austral.*)
- miromiro (*N.Z.*)
- mistletoe bird (*Austral.*)
- mohua or bush canary (*N.Z.*)
- New Zealand pigeon or kereru (*N.Z.*)
- nightingale
- nightjar, (*U.S. & Canad.*) goatsucker, or (*Austral.*) nighthawk
- noisy miner or (*Austral.*) micky or soldier bird
- nutcracker
- nuthatch
- ouzel or ousel
- paradise duck or putangitangi (*N.Z.*)
- pardalote (*Austral.*)
- partridge
- pheasant
- pigeon
- pipit or (*N.Z.*) pihoihoi
- pipiwharauroa or bronze-winged cuckoo (*N.Z.*)
- pitta (*Austral.*)
- plover
- ptarmigan
- puffin
- quail
- rainbow lorikeet
- raven
- redpoll

b

- redshank
- redstart
- redwing
- ringneck parrot, Port Lincoln parrot, or buln-buln (*Austral.*)
- robin or robin redbreast
- roller
- rook
- ruff
- saddlebill or jabiru
- sanderling
- sandpiper
- serin
- shrike or butcherbird
- silver-eye (*Austral.*)
- siskin or (*formerly*) aberdevine
- skylark
- snipe
- sparrow
- spoonbill
- spotted crake or (*Austral.*) water crake
- starling
- stint
- stonechat
- stork
- sulphur-crested cockatoo or white cockatoo

- superb blue wren (*Austral.*)
- superb lyrebird (*Austral.*)
- swallow
- swift
- thrush or (*poetic*) throstle
- tit
- topknot pigeon (*Austral.*)
- tree creeper
- tui or parson bird (*N.Z.*)
- twite
- wagtail
- warbler
- waxwing
- weka, weka rail, Māori hen, or wood hen (*N.Z.*)
- whinchat
- white-eye or (*N.Z.*) blighty, silvereye, tauhou or waxeye
- white-fronted tern or kahawai bird (*N.Z.*)
- whitethroat
- woodcock
- woodlark
- woodpecker
- wren
- yellowhammer
- yellowtail or yellowtail kingfisher (*Austral.*)

delivery, nativity, parturition ≠ death **2** = **ancestry**, stock, blood, background, breeding, pedigree, lineage, parentage
▷ **RELATED WORD**: *adjective* **natal**
bit¹ NOUN **1** = **slice**, fragment, crumb, morsel **2** = **piece**, scrap **3** = **jot**, iota **4** = **part**
bit² NOUN = **curb**, check, brake, restraint, snaffle
bite VERB = **nip**, cut, tear, wound,

snap, pierce, pinch, chew
▷ NOUN **1** = **snack**, food, piece, taste, refreshment, mouthful, morsel, titbit **2** = **wound**, sting, pinch, nip, prick
biting ADJECTIVE **1** = **piercing**, cutting, sharp, frozen, harsh, penetrating, arctic, icy
2 = **sarcastic**, cutting, stinging, scathing, acrimonious, incisive, virulent, caustic

bitter ADJECTIVE 1 = **resentful**, angry, offended, sour, sore, acrimonious, sullen, miffed (*informal*) ≠ happy 2 = **freezing**, biting, severe, intense, raw, fierce, chill, stinging ≠ mild 3 = **sour**, sharp, acid, harsh, tart, astringent, acrid, unsweetened ≠ sweet

bitterness NOUN
1 = **resentment**, hostility, indignation, animosity, acrimony, rancour, ill feeling, bad blood
2 = **sourness**, acidity, sharpness, tartness, acerbity

bizarre ADJECTIVE = **strange**, unusual, extraordinary, fantastic, weird, peculiar, eccentric, ludicrous, daggy (*Austral. & N.Z. informal*) ≠ normal

black ADJECTIVE 1 = **dark**, raven, ebony, sable, jet, dusky, pitch-black, swarthy ≠ light 2 = **gloomy**, sad, depressing, grim, bleak, hopeless, dismal, ominous ≠ happy 3 = **terrible**, bad, devastating, tragic, fatal, catastrophic, ruinous, calamitous 4 = **wicked**, bad, evil, corrupt, vicious, immoral, depraved, villainous ≠ good 5 = **angry**, cross, furious, hostile, sour, menacing, moody, resentful ≠ happy

● WORD POWER
● When referring to people with
● dark skin, the adjective black or
● Black is widely used. For people
● of the U.S. whose origins lie
● in Africa, the preferred term
● is African-American. To use 'a
● Black' or 'Blacks' as a noun is
● considered offensive, and it
● is better to talk about a Black
● person and Black people.

● WORD POWER
● *Black* is a colour which has
● nearly no hue due to its
● absorption of light. It has long
● been associated with night-
● time and darkness in Western
● cultures. It is also symbolic
● of death, with the bereaved
● expected to wear black clothes
● to signify mourning in many
● cultures. Some of the senses
● of black include: gloomy as in
● *black despair*; dirty as in *black*
● *with dirt*; terrible as in *Black*
● *Tuesday*; wicked as in *blackest*
● *act*; macabre as in *black comedy*;
● and angry as in *black look*. A
● *black sheep* is a person who is
● a disgrace or an outcast in a
● group, from the proverb 'there
● is a black sheep in every flock'.
● Another phrase involving black
● is *in the black* which means to
● be in credit financially, from
● the practice of marking credit
● items in black ink in a balance
● book. Black is sometimes used
● as a term relating to ethnic
● origin.

blackmail NOUN = **threat**, intimidation, ransom, extortion, hush money (*slang*)
▷ VERB = **threaten**, squeeze, compel, intimidate, coerce, dragoon, extort, hold to ransom

blame VERB 1 = **hold responsible**, accuse, denounce, indict, impeach, incriminate, impute ≠ absolve 2 = **attribute to**, credit to, assign to, put down to, impute to 3 *used in negative constructions* = **criticize**, condemn, censure, reproach, chide, find fault with ≠ praise
  ▷ NOUN = **responsibility**, liability, accountability, onus, culpability, answerability ≠ praise

bland ADJECTIVE 1 = **dull**, boring, plain, flat, dreary, run-of-the-mill, uninspiring, humdrum ≠ exciting 2 = **tasteless**, insipid, flavourless, thin

blank ADJECTIVE 1 = **unmarked**, white, clear, clean, empty, plain, bare, void ≠ marked 2 = **expressionless**, empty, vague, vacant, deadpan, impassive, poker-faced (*informal*) ≠ expressive
  ▷ NOUN 1 = **empty space**, space, gap 2 = **void**, vacuum, vacancy, emptiness, nothingness

blanket NOUN 1 = **cover**, rug, coverlet 2 = **covering**, sheet, coat, layer, carpet, cloak, mantle, thickness
  ▷ VERB = **coat**, cover, hide, mask, conceal, obscure, cloak

blast NOUN 1 = **explosion**, crash, burst, discharge, eruption, detonation 2 = **gust**, rush, storm, breeze, puff, gale, tempest, squall 3 = **blare**, blow, scream, trumpet, wail, resound, clamour, toot
  ▷ VERB = **blow up**, bomb, destroy, burst, ruin, break up, explode, shatter

blatant ADJECTIVE = **obvious**, clear, plain, evident, glaring, manifest, noticeable, conspicuous ≠ subtle

blaze VERB 1 = **burn**, glow, flare, be on fire, go up in flames, be ablaze, fire, flame 2 = **shine**, flash, beam, glow, flare, glare, gleam, radiate
  ▷ NOUN 1 = **inferno**, fire, flames, bonfire, combustion, conflagration 2 = **flash**, glow, glitter, flare, glare, gleam, brilliance, radiance

bleach VERB = **lighten**, wash out, blanch, whiten

bleak ADJECTIVE 1 = **dismal**, dark, depressing, grim, discouraging, gloomy, hopeless, dreary ≠ cheerful 2 = **exposed**, empty, bare, barren, desolate, windswept, weather-beaten, unsheltered ≠ sheltered 3 = **stormy**, severe, rough, harsh, tempestuous, intemperate

bleed VERB 1 = **lose blood**, flow, gush, spurt, shed blood 2 = **blend**, run, meet, unite, mix, combine, flow, fuse 3 (*informal*) = **extort**, milk, squeeze, drain, exhaust, fleece

blend VERB 1 = **mix**, join, combine, compound, merge, unite, mingle, amalgamate 2 = **go well**, match, fit, suit, go with, correspond, complement, coordinate 3 = **combine**, mix, link, integrate, merge, unite, amalgamate
  ▷ NOUN = **mixture**, mix,

combination, compound, brew, union, synthesis, alloy

bless VERB 1 = **sanctify**, dedicate, ordain, exalt, anoint, consecrate, hallow ≠ curse 2 = **endow**, give to, provide for, grant for, favour, grace, bestow to ≠ afflict

blessed ADJECTIVE = **holy**, sacred, divine, adored, revered, hallowed, sanctified, beatified

blessing NOUN 1 = **benefit**, help, service, favour, gift, windfall, kindness, good fortune ≠ disadvantage
2 = **approval**, backing, support, agreement, favour, sanction, permission, leave ≠ disapproval
3 = **benediction**, grace, dedication, thanksgiving, invocation, commendation, consecration, benison ≠ curse

blight NOUN 1 = **curse**, suffering, evil, corruption, pollution, plague, hardship, woe ≠ blessing
2 = **disease**, pest, fungus, mildew, infestation, pestilence, canker
▷ VERB = **frustrate**, destroy, ruin, crush, mar, dash, wreck, spoil, crool or cruel (*Austral. slang*)

blind ADJECTIVE 1 = **sightless**, unsighted, unseeing, eyeless, visionless ≠ sighted 2 *usually followed by* **to** = **unaware of**, unconscious of, ignorant of, indifferent to, insensitive to, oblivious of, unconcerned about, inconsiderate of ≠ aware
3 = **unquestioning**, prejudiced, wholesale, indiscriminate, uncritical, unreasoning,

undiscriminating

blindly ADVERB 1 = **thoughtlessly**, carelessly, recklessly, indiscriminately, senselessly, heedlessly 2 = **wildly**, aimlessly

blink VERB 1 = **flutter**, wink, bat 2 = **flash**, flicker, wink, shimmer, twinkle, glimmer ▷ PHRASE: **on the blink** (*slang*) = **not working (properly)**, faulty, defective, playing up, out of action, malfunctioning, out of order

bliss NOUN 1 = **joy**, ecstasy, euphoria, rapture, nirvana, felicity, gladness, blissfulness ≠ misery 2 = **beatitude**, blessedness

blister NOUN = **sore**, boil, swelling, cyst, pimple, carbuncle, pustule

blitz NOUN = **attack**, strike, assault, raid, offensive, onslaught, bombardment, bombing campaign

bloc NOUN = **group**, union, league, alliance, coalition, axis

block NOUN 1 = **piece**, bar, mass, brick, lump, chunk, hunk, ingot
2 = **obstruction**, bar, barrier, obstacle, impediment, hindrance
▷ VERB 1 = **obstruct**, close, stop, plug, choke, clog, stop up, bung up (*informal*) ≠ clear 2 = **obscure**, bar, obstruct 3 = **shut off**, stop, bar, hamper, obstruct

blockade NOUN = **stoppage**, block, barrier, restriction, obstacle, barricade, obstruction, impediment

bloke NOUN (*informal*) = **man**, person, individual, character

b

(*informal*), guy (*informal*), fellow, chap

blonde *or* **blond** ADJECTIVE
1 = **fair**, light, flaxen 2 = **fair-haired**, golden-haired, tow-headed

blood NOUN 1 = **lifeblood**, gore, vital fluid 2 = **family**, relations, birth, descent, extraction, ancestry, lineage, kinship

● **WORD POWER**
● The literal meaning of
● *blood* is that of the red fluid
● circulating in the veins and
● arteries of human beings and
● some animals. Its essential
● role in transporting oxygen
● around the body has led blood
● to represent vitality and
● rejuvenation in phrases such
● as *the lifeblood of the economy*.
● We also associate blood
● with feelings and emotions,
● particularly those of passion
● and temper, when we talk
● about *hot-blooded* people,
● acts being performed *in cold*
● *blood*, or *bad blood* stirred
● up between people. These
● expressions demonstrate
● that different temperatures
● represent different feelings,
● with anger and passion as
● heat, and indifference and
● cruelty as cold. Blood has
● long been symbolic of family,
● lineage, and race, from the
● expression *flesh and blood* to
● the proverb *blood is thicker than*
● *water*, meaning that family

● ties take precedence. Blood
● also signifies loss of life from
● *blood-letting* as a therapeutic
● surgical procedure in the past,
● to *bloodshed* which indicates
● murder and death.

bloodshed NOUN = **killing**, murder, massacre, slaughter, slaying, carnage, butchery, blood-letting

bloody ADJECTIVE 1 = **cruel**, fierce, savage, brutal, vicious, ferocious, cut-throat, warlike 2 = **bloodstained**, raw, bleeding, blood-soaked, blood-spattered

bloom NOUN 1 = **flower**, bud, blossom 2 = **prime**, flower, beauty, height, peak, flourishing, heyday, zenith 3 = **glow**, freshness, lustre, radiance ≠ pallor
▷ VERB 1 = **flower**, blossom, open, bud ≠ wither 2 = **grow**, develop, wax 3 = **succeed**, flourish, thrive, prosper, fare well ≠ fail

blossom NOUN 1 = **flower**, bloom, bud, efflorescence, floret
▷ VERB 1 = **bloom**, grow, develop, mature 2 = **succeed**, progress, thrive, flourish, prosper 3 = **flower**, bloom, bud

blow¹ VERB 1 = **move**, carry, drive, sweep, fling, buffet, waft 2 = **be carried**, flutter 3 = **exhale**, breathe, pant, puff 4 = **play**, sound, pipe, trumpet, blare, toot ▷ PHRASES: **blow something up 1** = **explode**, bomb, blast, detonate, blow sky-high **2** = **inflate**, pump up, fill,

b

expand, swell, enlarge, puff up, distend **3** = **magnify**, increase, extend, expand, widen, broaden, amplify; **blow up 1** = **explode**, burst, shatter, erupt, detonate **2** (*informal*) = **lose your temper**, rage, erupt, see red (*informal*), become angry, hit the roof (*informal*), fly off the handle (*informal*), go crook (*Austral. & N.Z. slang*), blow your top

blow² NOUN **1** = **knock**, stroke, punch, bang, sock (*slang*), smack, thump, clout (*informal*) **2** = **setback**, shock, disaster, reverse, disappointment, catastrophe, misfortune, bombshell

bludge VERB (*Austral. & N.Z. informal*) = **slack**, skive (*Brit. informal*), idle, shirk

blue ADJECTIVE **1** = **depressed**, low, sad, unhappy, melancholy, dejected, despondent, downcast ≠ happy **2** = **smutty**, obscene, indecent, lewd, risqué, X-rated (*informal*) ≠ respectable ▷ PLURAL NOUN = **depression**, gloom, melancholy, unhappiness, low spirits, the dumps (*informal*), doldrums

● WORD POWER
● *Blue* has developed many
● figurative meanings in English.
● The colour of the sky in nature,
● blue has come to symbolize
● constancy and lack of change,
● leading to the phrase *true-blue*,
● meaning staunch, as applied
● to members of the Scottish
● Whig party in the 17th century
● and now applied to British
● Conservatives. In Australia,
● *true blue* means genuine. Blue
● denotes right-wing in Britain,
● from the choice of this colour
● to represent the Conservative
● party. It refers to the aristocracy
● in the phrase *blue-blood*, but
● to manual workers in the
● phrase *blue-collar*. Blue-collar
● stems from the dress codes
● of these industries, where
● traditionally shirts had to be
● made of a durable material and
● non-staining colour. Against
● appearances, in Australia *bluey*
● is a slang term for someone
● with red hair. Though its
● origins are not certain, blue

● SHADES OF BLUE

aqua	navy blue	sky blue
aquamarine	Oxford blue	steel blue
azure	peacock blue	teal
Cambridge blue	perse	turquoise
clear blue	royal blue	ultramarine
cobalt blue	sapphire	
indigo	saxe blue	

- has become associated with
- pornography, as in the phrase
- *blue movies*. This may derive
- from so-called 'blue laws'
- which promoted morality in
- the 18th century United States
- by restricting activities such
- as drinking and gaming. Blue
- is also related to depression
- and low spirits, especially
- appearing in the plural form *the*
- *blues*. This is also the name of a
- style of melancholy music.

blue-collar ADJECTIVE = **manual**, industrial, physical, manufacturing, labouring

blueprint NOUN 1 = **scheme**, plan, design, system, programme, proposal, strategy, pattern **2** = **plan**, scheme, pattern, draft, outline, sketch

bluff¹ NOUN = **deception**, fraud, sham, pretence, deceit, bravado, bluster, humbug
▷ VERB = **deceive**, trick, fool, pretend, cheat, con, fake, mislead

bluff² NOUN = **precipice**, bank, peak, cliff, ridge, crag, escarpment, promontory
▷ ADJECTIVE = **hearty**, open, blunt, outspoken, genial, ebullient, jovial, plain-spoken ≠ tactful

blunder NOUN = **mistake**, slip, fault, error, oversight, gaffe, slip-up (*informal*), indiscretion, barry or Barry Crocker (*Austral. slang*) ≠ correctness
▷ VERB 1 = **make a mistake**, blow it (*slang*), err, slip up (*informal*), foul up, put your foot in it (*informal*) ≠ be correct **2** = **stumble**, fall, reel, stagger, lurch

blunt ADJECTIVE 1 = **frank**, forthright, straightforward, rude, outspoken, bluff, brusque, plain-spoken ≠ tactful **2** = **dull**, rounded, dulled, edgeless, unsharpened ≠ sharp
▷ VERB = **dull**, weaken, soften, numb, dampen, water down, deaden, take the edge off ≠ stimulate

blur NOUN = **haze**, confusion, fog, obscurity, indistinctness
▷ VERB 1 = **become indistinct**, become vague, become hazy, become fuzzy **2** = **obscure**, make indistinct, mask, obfuscate, make vague, make hazy

blush VERB = **turn red**, colour, glow, flush, redden, go red (as a beetroot), turn scarlet ≠ turn pale
▷ NOUN = **reddening**, colour, glow, flush, pink tinge, rosiness, ruddiness, rosy tint

board NOUN 1 = **plank**, panel, timber, slat, piece of timber **2** = **council**, directors, committee, congress, advisers, panel, assembly, trustees **3** = **meals**, provisions, victuals, daily meals
▷ VERB = **get on**, enter, mount, embark ≠ get off

boast VERB 1 = **brag**, crow, vaunt, talk big (*slang*), blow your own trumpet, show off, be proud of, congratulate yourself on, skite (*Austral. & N.Z. informal*) ≠ cover up **2** = **possess**, exhibit

▷ NOUN = **bragging** ≠ disclaimer

bob VERB = **bounce**, duck, hop, oscillate

bodily ADJECTIVE = **physical**, material, actual, substantial, tangible, corporal, carnal, corporeal

body NOUN 1 = **physique**, build, form, figure, shape, frame, constitution 2 = **torso**, trunk 3 = **corpse**, dead body, remains, stiff (*slang*), carcass, cadaver 4 = **organization**, company, group, society, association, band, congress, institution 5 = **main part**, matter, material, mass, substance, bulk, essence 6 = **expanse**, mass ▷ RELATED WORDS: *adjectives* **corporal, physical**

bog NOUN = **marsh**, swamp, slough, wetlands, fen, mire, quagmire, morass, pakihi (*N.Z.*), muskeg (*Canad.*)

bogey NOUN = **bugbear**, bête noire, horror, nightmare, bugaboo

bogus ADJECTIVE = **fake**, false, artificial, forged, imitation, sham, fraudulent, counterfeit ≠ genuine

Bohemian ADJECTIVE *often not cap.* = **unconventional**, alternative, artistic, unorthodox, arty (*informal*), offbeat, left bank, nonconformist ≠ conventional ▷ NOUN *often not cap.* = **nonconformist**, rebel, radical, eccentric, maverick, hippy, dropout, individualist

boil¹ VERB = **simmer**, bubble, foam, seethe, fizz, froth, effervesce

boil² NOUN = **pustule**, gathering, swelling, blister, carbuncle

bold ADJECTIVE 1 = **fearless**, enterprising, brave, daring, heroic, adventurous, courageous, audacious ≠ timid 2 = **impudent**, forward, confident, rude, cheeky, feisty (*informal*), chiefly U.S. & Canad.), brazen, shameless, insolent ≠ shy

bolster VERB = **support**, help, boost, strengthen, reinforce, shore up, augment

bolt NOUN 1 = **pin**, rod, peg, rivet 2 = **bar**, catch, lock, latch, fastener, sliding bar ▷ VERB 1 = **lock**, close, bar, secure, fasten, latch 2 = **dash**, fly 3 = **gobble**, stuff, wolf, cram, gorge, devour, gulp, guzzle

bomb NOUN = **explosive**, mine, shell, missile, device, rocket, grenade, torpedo ▷ VERB = **blow up**, attack, destroy, assault, shell, blitz, bombard, torpedo

bombard VERB 1 = **attack**, assault, besiege, beset, assail 2 = **bomb**, shell, blitz, open fire, strafe, fire upon

bombardment NOUN = **bombing**, attack, assault, shelling, blitz, barrage, fusillade

bond NOUN 1 = **tie**, union, coupling, link, association, relation, connection, alliance 2 = **fastening**, tie, chain, cord, shackle, fetter, manacle 3 = **agreement**, word, promise,

contract, guarantee, pledge, obligation, covenant
▷ VERB 1 = **form friendships**, connect 2 = **fix**, hold, bind, connect, glue, stick, paste, fasten, fit (*Brit. informal*)

bonus NOUN 1 = **extra**, prize, gift, reward, premium, dividend 2 = **advantage**, benefit, gain, extra, plus, asset, icing on the cake

book NOUN 1 = **work**, title, volume, publication, tract, tome 2 = **notebook**, album, journal, diary, pad, notepad, exercise book, jotter
▷ VERB = **reserve**, schedule, engage, organize, charter, arrange for, make reservations ▷ PHRASE: **book in** = **register**, enter

booklet NOUN = **brochure**, leaflet, hand-out, pamphlet, folder, mailshot, handbill

boom NOUN 1 = **expansion**, increase, development, growth, jump, boost, improvement, upsurge ≠ decline 2 = **bang**, crash, clash, blast, burst, explosion, roar, thunder
▷ VERB 1 = **increase**, flourish, grow, boost, expand, strengthen, swell, thrive ≠ fall 2 = **bang**, roll, crash, blast, explode, roar, thunder, rumble

boon NOUN 1 = **benefit**, blessing, godsend, gift 2 (*archaic*) = **gift**, favour

boost VERB = **increase**, develop, raise, boost, expand, add to, heighten, enlarge, amplify ≠ decrease

▷ NOUN 1 = **rise**, increase, jump, addition, improvement, expansion, upsurge, upturn ≠ fall 2 = **encouragement**, help

boot VERB = **kick**, punt, put the boot in(to) (*slang*), drop-kick

border NOUN 1 = **frontier**, line, limit, bounds, boundary, perimeter, borderline 2 = **edge**, margin, verge, rim
▷ VERB = **edge**, bound, decorate, trim, fringe, rim, hem

bore¹ VERB = **drill**, mine, sink, tunnel, pierce, penetrate, burrow, puncture

bore² VERB = **tire**, fatigue, weary, wear out, jade, be tedious, pall on, send to sleep ≠ excite
▷ NOUN = **nuisance**, pain (*informal*), yawn (*informal*), anorak (*informal*)

bored ADJECTIVE = **fed up**, tired, wearied, uninterested, sick and tired (*informal*), listless, brassed off (*Brit. slang*), hoha (*N.Z.*)

boredom NOUN = **tedium**, apathy, weariness, monotony, sameness, ennui, flatness, world-weariness ≠ excitement

boring ADJECTIVE = **uninteresting**, dull, tedious, tiresome, monotonous, flat, humdrum, mind-numbing

borrow VERB 1 = **take on loan**, touch (someone) for (*slang*), scrounge (*informal*), cadge, use temporarily ≠ lend 2 = **steal**, take, copy, adopt, pinch (*informal*)

boss NOUN = **manager**, head, leader, director, chief, master, employer, supervisor, baas (S. African), sherang (Austral. & N.Z.) ▷ PHRASE: **boss someone around** (informal) = **order around**, dominate, bully, oppress, push around (slang)

bother VERB 1 = **trouble**, concern, worry, alarm, disturb, disconcert, perturb 2 = **pester**, plague, harass, hassle (informal), inconvenience ≠ help
▷ NOUN = **trouble**, problem, worry, difficulty, fuss, irritation, hassle (informal), nuisance, uphill (S. African) ≠ help

bottle shop NOUN (Austral. & N.Z.) = **off-licence** (Brit.), liquor store (U.S. & Canad.), bottle store (S. African), package store (U.S. & Canad.), offie or offy (Brit. informal)

bottle store NOUN (S. African) = **off-licence** (Brit.), liquor store (U.S. & Canad.), bottle shop (Austral. & N.Z.), package store (U.S. & Canad.), offie or offy (Brit. informal)

bottom NOUN 1 = **lowest part**, base, foot, bed, floor, foundation, depths ≠ top 2 = **underside**, sole, underneath, lower side 3 (informal) = **buttocks**, behind (informal), rear, backside, rump, seat, posterior
▷ ADJECTIVE = **lowest**, last ≠ higher

bounce VERB 1 = **rebound**, recoil, ricochet 2 = **bound**, spring, jump, leap, skip, gambol
▷ NOUN 1 = **springiness**, give, spring, resilience, elasticity, recoil

2 (informal) = **life**, go (informal), energy, zip (informal), vigour, exuberance, dynamism, vivacity

bound[1] ADJECTIVE 1 = **compelled**, obliged, forced, committed, pledged, constrained, beholden, duty-bound 2 = **tied**, fixed, secured, attached, tied up, fastened, pinioned 3 = **certain**, sure, fated, doomed, destined

bound[2] VERB = **leap**, bob, spring, jump, bounce, skip, vault
▷ NOUN = **leap**, bob, spring, jump, bounce, hurdle, skip, vault

bound[3] VERB 1 = **surround**, confine, enclose, encircle, hem in, demarcate 2 = **limit**, restrict, confine, restrain, circumscribe

boundary NOUN 1 = **frontier**, edge, border, barrier, margin, brink 2 = **edges**, limits, fringes, extremities 3 = **dividing line**, borderline

bounds PLURAL NOUN = **boundary**, limit, edge, border, confine, verge, rim, perimeter

bouquet NOUN 1 = **bunch of flowers**, spray, garland, wreath, posy, buttonhole, corsage, nosegay 2 = **aroma**, smell, scent, perfume, fragrance, savour, odour, redolence

bourgeois ADJECTIVE = **middle-class**, traditional, conventional, materialistic, hidebound

bout NOUN 1 = **period**, term, fit, spell, turn, interval 2 = **round**, series, session, cycle, sequence, stint 3 = **fight**, match, competition, struggle, contest, set-to, encounter, engagement

bow¹ VERB = **bend**, bob, nod, stoop, droop, genuflect
▷ NOUN = **bending**, bob, nod, obeisance, kowtow, genuflection

bow² NOUN (*nautical*) = **prow**, head, stem, fore, beak

bowels PLURAL NOUN 1 = **guts**, insides (*informal*), intestines, innards (*informal*), entrails, viscera, vitals 2 = **depths**, hold, inside, deep, interior, core, belly

bowl¹ NOUN = **basin**, plate, dish, vessel

bowl² VERB = **throw**, hurl, launch, cast, pitch, toss, fling, chuck (*informal*)

box¹ NOUN = **container**, case, chest, trunk, pack, package, carton, casket
▷ VERB = **pack**, package, wrap, encase, bundle up

box² VERB = **fight**, spar, exchange blows

boxer NOUN = **fighter**, pugilist, prizefighter

boy NOUN = **lad**, kid (*informal*), youth, fellow, youngster, schoolboy, junior, stripling

boycott VERB = **embargo**, reject, snub, black ≠ support

boyfriend NOUN = **sweetheart**, man, lover, beloved, admirer, suitor, beau, date

brace VERB 1 = **steady**, support, secure, stabilize 2 = **support**, strengthen, steady, reinforce, bolster, fortify, buttress
▷ NOUN = **support**, stay, prop, bolster, bracket, reinforcement, strut, truss

bracing ADJECTIVE = **refreshing**, fresh, stimulating, crisp, brisk, exhilarating, invigorating ≠ tiring

brain PLURAL NOUN = **intelligence**, understanding, sense, intellect

● **WORD POWER**
● The *brain* controls the nervous
● system and is the seat of
● thought in the human body.
● A brain is a person who is
● intelligent and has great
● intellectual ability; this is
● also expressed in the recent
● coinage *brainiac*. In the plural,
● *brains* refers to intelligence,
● e.g. *He hasn't the brains to do it*.
● If someone is *the brains behind*
● *something*, it has implications
● of masterminding an idea
● or operation. We talk about
● *brainwaves* when an idea comes
● into the brain, and *brainwashing*
● when thought is deliberately
● censored. Both of these words
● show that the physical brain
● is strongly equated with the
● processes of thought in the
● mind.

brake NOUN = **control**, check, curb, restraint, constraint, rein
▷ VERB = **slow**, decelerate, reduce speed

branch NOUN 1 = **bough**, shoot, arm, spray, limb, sprig, offshoot 2 = **office**, department, unit, wing, chapter, bureau
3 = **division**, part, section, subdivision, subsection

4 = **discipline**, section, subdivision

brand NOUN 1 = **trademark** 2 = **label**, mark, sign, stamp, symbol, logo, trademark, marker ▷ VERB 1 = **stigmatize**, mark, expose, denounce, disgrace, discredit, censure 2 = **mark**, burn, label, stamp, scar

brash ADJECTIVE = **bold**, rude, cocky, pushy (*informal*), brazen, impertinent, insolent, impudent ≠ timid

brave ADJECTIVE = **courageous**, daring, bold, heroic, adventurous, fearless, resolute, audacious ≠ timid ▷ VERB = **confront**, face, suffer, tackle, endure, defy, withstand, stand up to ≠ give in to

bravery NOUN = **courage**, nerve, daring, pluck, spirit, fortitude, heroism, mettle ≠ cowardice

brawl NOUN = **fight**, clash, fray, skirmish, scuffle, punch-up (*Brit. informal*), fracas, altercation, biffo (*Austral. slang*) ▷ VERB = **fight**, scrap (*informal*), wrestle, tussle, scuffle

breach NOUN 1 = **nonobservance**, abuse, violation, infringement, trespass, transgression, contravention, infraction ≠ compliance 2 = **opening**, crack, split, gap, rift, rupture, cleft, fissure

bread NOUN 1 = **food**, fare, kai (*N.Z. informal*), nourishment, sustenance 2 (*slang*) = **money**, cash, dough (*slang*)

breadth NOUN 1 = **width**, spread, span, latitude, broadness, wideness 2 = **extent**, range, scale, scope, compass, expanse

break VERB 1 = **shatter**, separate, destroy, crack, snap, smash, crush, fragment ≠ repair 2 = **fracture**, crack, smash 3 = **burst**, tear, split 4 = **disobey**, breach, defy, violate, disregard, flout, infringe, contravene ≠ obey 5 = **stop**, cut, suspend, interrupt, cut short, discontinue 6 = **disturb**, interrupt 7 = **end**, stop, cut, drop, give up, abandon, suspend, interrupt 8 = **weaken**, undermine, tame, subdue, demoralize, dispirit 9 = **be revealed**, be published, be announced, be made public, be proclaimed, be let out 10 = **reveal**, tell, announce, declare, disclose, proclaim, make known 11 = **beat**, top, better, exceed, go beyond, excel, surpass, outstrip ▷ NOUN 1 = **fracture**, opening, tear, hole, split, crack, gap, fissure 2 = **interval**, pause, interlude, intermission 3 = **holiday**, leave, vacation, time off, recess, awayday, schoolie (*Austral.*), acumulated day off or ADO (*Austral.*) 4 (*informal*) = **stroke of luck**, chance, opportunity, advantage, fortune, opening ▷ PHRASES: **break off** = **stop talking**, pause; **break out** = **begin**, start, happen, occur, arise, set in, commence, spring

b

up; **break something off**
= **detach**, separate, divide, cut
off, pull off, sever, part, remove;
break something up = **stop**, end,
suspend, dismantle, terminate,
disband, diffuse; **break up**
1 = **finish**, be suspended, adjourn
2 = **split up**, separate, part,
divorce

breakdown NOUN = **collapse**

break-in NOUN = **burglary**,
robbery, breaking and entering,
home invasion (*Austral. & N.Z.*)

breakthrough NOUN
= **development**, advance,
progress, discovery, find,
invention, step forward, leap
forwards

breast NOUN = **bosom**

breath NOUN = **inhalation**,
breathing, pant, gasp, gulp,
wheeze, exhalation, respiration

breathe VERB 1 = **inhale and
exhale**, pant, gasp, puff, gulp,
wheeze, respire, draw in breath
2 = **whisper**, sigh, murmur

breathless ADJECTIVE 1 = **out
of breath**, panting, gasping,
gulping, wheezing, short-winded
2 = **excited**, curious, eager,
enthusiastic, impatient, on
tenterhooks, in suspense

breathtaking ADJECTIVE
= **amazing**, exciting, stunning
(*informal*), impressive, thrilling,
magnificent, astonishing,
sensational

breed NOUN 1 = **variety**, race,
stock, type, species, strain,
pedigree 2 = **kind**, sort, type,
variety, brand, stamp
▷ VERB 1 = **rear**, tend, keep, raise,
maintain, farm, look after, care
for 2 = **reproduce**, multiply,
propagate, procreate, produce
offspring, bear young, bring forth
young 3 = **produce**, cause, create,
generate, bring about, arouse,
give rise to, stir up

breeding NOUN = **refinement**,
culture, taste, manners, polish,
courtesy, sophistication,
cultivation

breeze NOUN = **light wind**, air,
draught, gust, waft, zephyr,
breath of wind, current of air
▷ VERB = **sweep**, move briskly,
pass, sail, hurry, glide, flit

brew VERB 1 = **boil**, make, soak,
steep, stew, infuse (*tea*) 2 = **make**,
ferment 3 = **start**, develop,
gather, foment 4 = **develop**,
form, gather, foment
▷ NOUN = **drink**, preparation,
mixture, blend, liquor, beverage,
infusion, concoction

bribe NOUN = **inducement**, payoff (*informal*), sweetener (*slang*),
kickback (*U.S.*), backhander
(*slang*), enticement, allurement
▷ VERB = **buy off**, reward, pay off
(*informal*), corrupt, suborn, grease
the palm or hand of (*slang*)

bribery NOUN = **corruption**,
inducement, buying off, payola
(*informal*), palm-greasing (*slang*)

bridge NOUN = **arch**, span,
viaduct, flyover, overpass
▷ VERB 1 = **span**, cross
2 = **reconcile**, resolve

brief ADJECTIVE 1 = **short**, quick, fleeting, swift, short-lived, momentary, ephemeral, transitory ≠ long
▷ VERB = **inform**, prime, prepare, advise, fill in (*informal*), instruct, put in the picture (*informal*), keep (someone) posted
▷ NOUN = **summary**, résumé, outline, sketch, abstract, digest, epitome, rundown

briefing NOUN 1 = **conference**, priming 2 = **instructions**, information, priming, directions, preparation, guidance, rundown

briefly ADVERB 1 = **quickly**, shortly, hastily, momentarily, hurriedly 2 = **in outline**, in brief, in a nutshell, concisely

brigade NOUN 1 = **corps**, company, force, unit, division, troop, squad, team 2 = **group**, band, squad, organization

bright ADJECTIVE 1 = **vivid**, rich, brilliant, glowing, colourful 2 = **shining**, glowing, dazzling, gleaming, shimmering, radiant, luminous, lustrous 3 (*informal*) = **intelligent**, smart, clever, aware, sharp, enlightened, astute, wide-awake ≠ stupid 4 (*informal*) = **clever**, smart, ingenious 5 = **sunny**, clear, fair, pleasant, lucid, cloudless, unclouded ≠ cloudy

brighten VERB 1 = **light up**, shine, glow, gleam, lighten ≠ dim 2 = **enliven**, animate, make brighter, vitalize 3 = **become brighter**, light up, glow, gleam

brilliance *or* **brilliancy** NOUN 1 = **cleverness**, talent, wisdom, distinction, genius, excellence, greatness, inventiveness ≠ stupidity 2 = **brightness**, intensity, sparkle, dazzle, lustre, radiance, luminosity, vividness ≠ darkness 3 = **splendour**, glamour, grandeur, magnificence, éclat, illustriousness

brilliant ADJECTIVE 1 = **intelligent**, sharp, intellectual, clever, profound, penetrating, inventive, perspicacious ≠ stupid 2 = **expert**, masterly, talented, gifted, accomplished ≠ untalented 3 = **splendid**, famous, celebrated, outstanding, superb, magnificent, glorious, notable 4 = **bright**, shining, intense, sparkling, glittering, dazzling, vivid, radiant ≠ dark

brim NOUN = **rim**, edge, border, lip, margin, verge, brink
▷ VERB 1 = **be full**, spill, well over, run over 2 = **fill**, well over, fill up, overflow

bring VERB 1 = **fetch**, take, carry, bear, transfer, deliver, transport, convey 2 = **take**, guide, conduct, escort 3 = **cause**, produce, create, effect, occasion, result in, contribute to, inflict ▷ PHRASES: **bring someone up** = **rear**, raise, support, train, develop, teach, breed, foster; **bring something about** = **cause**, produce, create, effect, achieve, generate, accomplish, give rise to; **bring something off** = **accomplish**, achieve, perform, succeed, execute, pull off, carry off; **bring something up** = **mention**, raise, introduce, point out, refer to, allude to, broach

brink NOUN = **edge**, limit, border, lip, margin, boundary, skirt, frontier

brisk ADJECTIVE 1 = **quick**, lively, energetic, active, vigorous, bustling, sprightly, spry ≠ slow 2 = **short**, brief, blunt, abrupt, terse, gruff, brusque, monosyllabic

briskly ADVERB = **quickly**, smartly, promptly, rapidly, readily, actively, efficiently, energetically

bristle NOUN = **hair**, spine, thorn, whisker, barb, stubble, prickle ▷ VERB 1 = **stand up**, rise, stand on end 2 = **be angry**, rage, seethe, flare up, bridle, see red

brittle ADJECTIVE = **fragile**, delicate, crisp, crumbling, frail, crumbly, breakable, friable ≠ tough

broad ADJECTIVE 1 = **wide**, large, ample, generous, expansive 2 = **large**, huge, vast, extensive, ample, spacious, expansive, roomy ≠ narrow 3 = **full**, general, comprehensive, complete, wide, sweeping, wide-ranging, thorough 4 = **universal**, general, common, wide, sweeping, worldwide, widespread, wide-ranging 5 = **general**, loose, vague, approximate, indefinite, ill-defined, inexact, unspecific

broadcast NOUN = **transmission**, show, programme, telecast, podcast ▷ VERB 1 = **transmit**, show, air, radio, cable, beam, send out, relay, podcast 2 = **make public**, report, announce, publish, spread, advertise, proclaim, circulate

broaden VERB = **expand**, increase, develop, spread, extend, stretch, swell, supplement ≠ restrict

brochure NOUN = **booklet**, advertisement, leaflet, hand-out, circular, pamphlet, folder, mailshot

broekies PLURAL NOUN (S. African informal) = **underpants**, pants, briefs, drawers, knickers, panties, boxer shorts, Y-fronts (trademark), underdaks (Austral. slang)

broke ADJECTIVE (informal) = **penniless**, short, ruined, bust (informal), bankrupt, impoverished, in the red, insolvent ≠ rich

broken ADJECTIVE 1 = **interrupted**, incomplete, erratic, intermittent, fragmentary, spasmodic, discontinuous 2 = **imperfect**, halting, hesitating, stammering, disjointed 3 = **smashed**, burst, shattered, fragmented, fractured, severed, ruptured, separated 4 = **defective**, not working, imperfect, out of order, on the blink (slang), kaput (informal)

broker NOUN = **dealer**, agent, trader, supplier, merchant, negotiator, mediator, intermediary

bronze ADJECTIVE = **reddish-**

brown, copper, tan, rust, chestnut, brownish
▷ *see* **shades of brown**
brood NOUN 1 = **offspring**, issue, clutch, litter, progeny
2 = **children**, family, nearest and dearest, flesh and blood, ainga (*N.Z.*)
▷ VERB = **think**, obsess, muse, ponder, agonize, mull over, mope, ruminate
brook NOUN = **stream**, burn (*Scot. & Northern English*), rivulet, beck, watercourse, rill
brother NOUN 1 = **male sibling**
2 = **monk**, cleric, friar, religious
▷ RELATED WORD: *adjective* **fraternal**
brotherly ADJECTIVE = **fraternal**, friendly, neighbourly, sympathetic, affectionate, benevolent, kind, amicable
brown ADJECTIVE 1 = **brunette**,

bay, coffee, chocolate, chestnut, hazel, dun, auburn 2 = **tanned**, bronze, tan, sunburnt
▷ VERB = **fry**, cook, grill, sear, sauté
browse VERB 1 = **skim**, scan, glance at, survey, look through, look round, dip into, leaf through
2 = **graze**, eat, feed, nibble
bruise NOUN = **discoloration**, mark, injury, blemish, contusion
▷ VERB 1 = **hurt**, injure, mark
2 = **damage**, mark, mar, discolour
brush¹ NOUN 1 = **broom**, sweeper, besom 2 = **conflict**, clash, confrontation, skirmish, tussle 3 = **encounter**, meeting, confrontation, rendezvous
▷ VERB 1 = **clean**, wash, polish, buff 2 = **touch**, sweep, kiss, stroke, glance, flick, scrape, graze
▷ PHRASES: **brush someone off** (*slang*) = **ignore**, reject, dismiss,

---

● **SHADES OF BROWN**

● amber	● cinnamon	● oxblood
● auburn	● cocoa	● russet
● bay	● coffee	● rust
● beige	● copper	● sable
● biscuit	● dun	● sepia
● bisque	● fawn	● sienna
● bronze	● ginger	● tan
● buff	● hazel	● taupe
● burnt sienna	● henna	● tawny
● burnt umber	● khaki	● terracotta
● café au lait	● liver	● tortoiseshell
● camel	● mahogany	● walnut
● chestnut	● mocha	
● chocolate	● nutbrown	

snub, disregard, scorn, disdain, spurn; **brush something up** or **brush up on something** = **revise**, study, go over, cram, polish up, read up on, relearn, bone up on (*informal*)

brush² NOUN = **shrubs**, bushes, scrub, undergrowth, thicket, copse, brushwood

brutal ADJECTIVE 1 = **cruel**, savage, vicious, ruthless, callous, sadistic, heartless, inhuman ≠ kind
2 = **harsh**, tough, severe, rough, rude, indifferent, insensitive, callous ≠ sensitive

brutality NOUN = **cruelty**, atrocity, ferocity, savagery, ruthlessness, barbarism, inhumanity, viciousness

bubble NOUN = **air ball**, drop, bead, blister, blob, droplet, globule
▷ VERB 1 = **boil**, seethe 2 = **foam**, fizz, froth, percolate, effervesce
3 = **gurgle**, splash, murmur, trickle, ripple, babble, burble, lap

bubbly ADJECTIVE 1 = **lively**, happy, excited, animated, merry, bouncy, elated, sparky 2 = **frothy**, sparkling, fizzy, effervescent, carbonated, foamy

buckle NOUN = **fastener**, catch, clip, clasp, hasp
▷ VERB 1 = **fasten**, close, secure, hook, clasp 2 = **distort**, bend, warp, crumple, contort
3 = **collapse**, bend, twist, fold, give way, subside, cave in, crumple

bud NOUN = **shoot**, branch, sprout,

sprig, offshoot
▷ VERB = **develop**, grow, shoot, sprout, burgeon, burst forth

budding ADJECTIVE = **developing**, beginning, growing, promising, potential, burgeoning, fledgling, embryonic

budge VERB 1 = **move**, stir
2 = **dislodge**, move, push, transfer, shift, stir

budget NOUN = **allowance**, means, funds, income, finances, resources, allocation
▷ VERB = **plan**, estimate, allocate, cost, ration, apportion

buff¹ ADJECTIVE = **fawn**, tan, beige, yellowish, straw-coloured, sand-coloured, yellowish-brown
▷ VERB = **polish**, smooth, brush, shine, rub, wax, brighten, burnish
▷ see **shades of brown, shades of yellow**

buff² NOUN (*informal*) = **expert**, fan, addict, enthusiast, admirer, devotee, connoisseur, aficionado, fundi (*S. African*)

buffer NOUN = **safeguard**, screen, shield, cushion, intermediary, bulwark

buffet NOUN 1 = **smorgasbord**
2 = **snack bar**, café, cafeteria, brasserie, refreshment counter

bug NOUN 1 (*informal*) = **illness**, disease, virus, infection, disorder, sickness, ailment, affliction
2 = **fault**, error, defect, flaw, glitch, gremlin
▷ VERB 1 = **tap**, eavesdrop, listen in on 2 (*informal*) = **annoy**, bother, disturb, irritate, hassle

(informal), pester, vex, get on your nerves *(informal)*

build VERB = **construct**, make, raise, put up, assemble, erect, fabricate, form ≠ demolish
▷ NOUN = **physique**, form, body, figure, shape, structure, frame

building NOUN = **structure**, house, construction, dwelling, erection, edifice, domicile

build-up NOUN = **increase**, development, growth, expansion, accumulation, enlargement, escalation

bulge VERB 1 = **swell out**, project, expand, stick out, protrude, puff out, distend 2 = **stick out**, stand out, protrude
▷ NOUN = **lump**, swelling, bump, projection, hump, protuberance, protrusion ≠ hollow 2 = **increase**, rise, boost, surge, intensification

bulk NOUN 1 = **size**, volume, dimensions, magnitude, substance, immensity, largeness 2 = **weight**, size, mass, heaviness, poundage 3 = **majority**, mass, most, body, best part, lion's share, better part, preponderance

● WORD POWER
● The use of a plural noun after
● *bulk*, when it has the meaning
● 'majority', although common,
● is considered by some to
● be incorrect and should be
● avoided. This usage is most
● commonly encountered,
● according to the Bank of
● English, when referring to

● funds and profits: *the bulk of our*
● *profits stem from the sale of beer*.
● The synonyms *majority* and
● *most* would work better in this
● context.

bullet NOUN = **projectile**, ball, shot, missile, slug, pellet

bulletin NOUN = **report**, account, statement, message, communication, announcement, dispatch, communiqué

bully NOUN = **persecutor**, tough, oppressor, tormentor, bully boy, browbeater, coercer, ruffian
▷ VERB 1 = **persecute**, intimidate, torment, oppress, pick on, victimize, terrorize, push around *(slang)* 2 = **force**, coerce, browbeat, hector, domineer

bump VERB 1 = **knock**, hit, strike, crash, smash, slam, bang 2 = **jerk**, shake, bounce, rattle, jog, lurch, jolt
▷ NOUN 1 = **knock**, blow, impact, collision, thump 2 = **thud**, crash, knock, bang, smack, thump 3 = **lump**, swelling, bulge, hump, nodule, protuberance, contusion

bumper ADJECTIVE = **exceptional**, excellent, exo *(Austral. slang)*, massive, jumbo *(informal)*, abundant, whopping *(informal)*, bountiful

bunch NOUN 1 *(informal)* = **group**, band, crowd, party, team, gathering, gang, flock 2 = **bouquet**, sheaf 3 = **cluster**, clump ▷ PHRASE: **bunch together** or **up** = **group**, mass, collect, assemble, cluster, huddle

bundle NOUN = **bunch**, group, collection, mass, pile, stack, heap, batch
▷ VERB = **push**, thrust, shove, throw, rush, hurry, jostle, hustle
▷ PHRASE: **bundle someone up** = **wrap up**, swathe

bungle VERB = **mess up**, blow (*slang*), ruin, spoil, blunder, botch, make a mess of, muff, crool *or* cruel (*Austral. slang*) ≠ accomplish

bungling ADJECTIVE = **incompetent**, blundering, clumsy, inept, cack-handed (*informal*), maladroit, ham-fisted (*informal*), unco (*Austral. slang*)

bunk *or* **bunkum** NOUN (*informal*) = **nonsense**, rubbish, garbage (*informal*), hot air (*informal*), twaddle, moonshine, malarkey, baloney (*informal*), hogwash, bizzo (*Austral. slang*), bull's wool (*Austral. & N.Z. slang*), kak (*S. African taboo*)

buoy NOUN = **float**, guide, signal, marker, beacon

buoyant ADJECTIVE = **cheerful**, happy, upbeat (*informal*), carefree, jaunty, chirpy (*informal*), light-hearted ≠ gloomy = **floating**, light

burden NOUN 1 = **trouble**, worry, weight, responsibility, strain, affliction, onus, millstone 2 = **load**, weight, cargo, freight, consignment, encumbrance
▷ VERB = **weigh down**, worry, load, tax, bother, handicap, oppress, inconvenience

bureau NOUN 1 = **agency** 2 = **office**, department, section, branch, station, unit, division, subdivision 3 = **desk**, writing desk

bureaucracy NOUN 1 = **government**, officials, authorities, administration, the system, civil service, corridors of power 2 = **red tape**, regulations, officialdom

bureaucrat NOUN = **official**, officer, administrator, civil servant, public servant, functionary, mandarin

burglar NOUN = **housebreaker**, thief, robber, pilferer, filcher, cat burglar, sneak thief

burglary NOUN = **breaking and entering**, housebreaking, break-in, home invasion (*Austral. & N.Z.*)

burial NOUN = **funeral**, interment, obsequies, entombment, exequies

burn VERB 1 = **be on fire**, blaze, be ablaze, smoke, flame, glow, flare, go up in flames 2 = **set on fire**, light, ignite, kindle, incinerate 3 = **scorch**, toast, sear, char, singe 4 = **be passionate**, be aroused, be inflamed 5 = **seethe**, fume, be angry, simmer, smoulder

burning ADJECTIVE 1 = **intense**, passionate, eager, ardent, fervent, impassioned, vehement ≠ mild 2 = **crucial**, important, pressing, significant, essential, vital, critical, acute

burrow NOUN = **hole**, shelter, tunnel, den, lair, retreat
▷ VERB 1 = **dig**, tunnel, excavate 2 = **delve**, search, probe, ferret, rummage, forage, fossick (*Austral. & N.Z.*)

burst VERB 1 = **explode**, blow up, break, split, crack, shatter, puncture, rupture 2 = **rush**, run, break, break out, erupt, spout, gush forth 3 = **barge**, charge, rush, shove
▷ NOUN 1 = **rush**, surge, outbreak, outburst, spate, gush, torrent, spurt 2 = **explosion**, crack, blast, bang, discharge

bury VERB 1 = **inter**, lay to rest, entomb, consign to the grave, inhume ≠ dig up 2 = **hide**, cover, conceal, stash (*informal*), secrete, stow away ≠ uncover 3 = **sink**, embed, immerse, enfold 4 = **forget**

bush NOUN = **shrub**, plant, hedge, thicket, shrubbery ▷ PHRASE: **the bush** = **the wilds**, brush, scrub, woodland, backwoods, scrubland

business NOUN 1 = **trade**, selling, industry, manufacturing, commerce, dealings 2 = **establishment**, company, firm, concern, organization, corporation, venture, enterprise 3 = **profession**, work, job, line, trade, career, function, employment 4 = **matter**, issue, subject, point, problem, responsibility, task, duty 5 = **concern**, affair

businessman NOUN = **executive**, director, manager, merchant, capitalist, administrator, entrepreneur, tycoon

bust[1] NOUN = **bosom**, breasts, chest, front

bust[2] (*informal*) VERB 1 = **break**, smash, split, burst, shatter, fracture, rupture 2 = **arrest**, catch, raid ▷ PHRASE: **go bust** = **go bankrupt**, fail, be ruined, become insolvent

bustle VERB = **hurry**, rush, fuss, hasten, scuttle, scurry, scamper ≠ idle
▷ NOUN = **activity**, to-do, stir, excitement, fuss, flurry, commotion, ado ≠ inactivity

bustling ADJECTIVE = **busy**, full, crowded, active, lively, buzzing, humming, swarming

busy ADJECTIVE 1 = **active**, industrious, rushed off your feet ≠ idle 2 = **occupied with**, working, engaged in, on duty, employed in, hard at work ≠ unoccupied 3 = **hectic**, full, exacting, energetic ▷ PHRASE: **busy yourself** = **occupy yourself**, be engrossed, immerse yourself, involve yourself, absorb yourself, employ yourself, engage yourself

but CONJUNCTION = **however**, still, yet, nevertheless
▷ PREPOSITION = **except (for)**, save, bar, barring, excepting, excluding, with the exception of
▷ ADVERB = **only**, just, simply, merely

butcher NOUN = **murderer**, killer, slaughterer, slayer, destroyer, executioner, cut-throat, exterminator
▷ VERB 1 = **slaughter**, prepare, carve, cut up, dress, cut, clean, joint 2 = **kill**, slaughter, massacre, destroy, cut down, assassinate,

slay, liquidate

butt¹ NOUN 1 = **end**, handle, shaft, stock, shank, hilt, haft 2 = **stub**, tip, leftover, fag end (*informal*)

butt² NOUN = **target**, victim, dupe, laughing stock, Aunt Sally

butt³ VERB = **knock**, push, bump, thrust, ram, shove, poke, prod
▷ PHRASE: **butt in** 1 = **interfere**, meddle, intrude, heckle, barge in (*informal*), stick your nose in, put your oar in 2 = **interrupt**, cut in, break in, chip in (*informal*)

butt⁴ NOUN = **cask**, barrel

butterfly NOUN ▷ RELATED WORDS: *young* **caterpillar, chrysalis** *or* **chrysalid**, *enthusiast* **lepidopterist**

buy VERB = **purchase**, get, pay for, obtain, acquire, invest in, shop for, procure ≠ sell
▷ NOUN = **purchase**, deal, bargain, acquisition, steal (*informal*), snip (*informal*), giveaway

by PREPOSITION 1 = **through**, through the agency of 2 = **via**, over, by way of 3 = **near**, past, along, close to, closest to,

---

● **BUTTERFLIES AND MOTHS**

- argus
- bag moth (*N.Z.*)
- brown-tail moth
- cabbage white
- cactoblastis
- cardinal
- carpet moth
- clearwing *or* clearwing moth
- death's-head moth
- ermine moth *or* ermine
- ghost moth
- gipsy moth
- grayling
- hairstreak
- herald moth
- hawk moth, sphinx moth, *or* hummingbird moth

- house moth
- lackey moth
- large white *or* cabbage white
- leopard moth
- magpie moth
- marbled white
- monarch
- orange-tip
- painted lady
- peacock butterfly
- peppered moth
- privet hawk
- processionary moth
- purple emperor
- puss moth
- red admiral
- red underwing
- ringlet
- silver-Y
- skipper

- small white
- snout
- speckled wood
- swallowtail
- swift
- tapestry moth
- tiger (moth)
- umber (moth)
- wax moth, honeycomb moth, *or* bee moth
- white
- white admiral
- winter moth
- yellow underwing

neighbouring, next to, beside
▷ ADVERB = **nearby**, close, handy,
at hand, within reach
bypass VERB 1 = **get round**, avoid
2 = **go round**, circumvent, depart
from, deviate from, pass round,
detour round ≠ cross

Cc

c

cab NOUN = **taxi**, minicab, taxicab, hackney carriage

cabin NOUN 1 = **room**, berth, quarters, compartment 2 = **hut**, shed, cottage, lodge, shack, chalet, shanty, whare (*N.Z.*)

cabinet NOUN = **cupboard**, case, locker, dresser, closet, press, chiffonier

Cabinet NOUN = **council**, committee, administration, ministry, assembly, board

cad NOUN (*old-fashioned or informal*) = **scoundrel** (*slang*), rat (*informal*), bounder (*Brit. old-fashioned or slang*), rotter (*slang, chiefly Brit.*), heel, wrong 'un (*Austral. slang*)

café NOUN = **snack bar**, restaurant, cafeteria, coffee shop, brasserie, coffee bar, tearoom, lunchroom

cage NOUN = **enclosure**, pen, coop, hutch, pound

cake NOUN = **block**, bar, slab, lump, cube, loaf, mass

calculated ADJECTIVE = **deliberate**, planned, considered, intended, intentional, designed, aimed, purposeful ≠ unplanned

calculating ADJECTIVE = **scheming**, sharp, shrewd, cunning, sly, devious, manipulative, crafty ≠ direct

calculation NOUN 1 = **computation**, working out, reckoning, estimate, forecast, judgment, result, answer 2 = **planning**, intention, deliberation, foresight, contrivance, forethought, premeditation

calibre *or* (*U.S.*) **caliber** NOUN 1 = **worth**, quality, ability, talent, capacity, merit, distinction, stature 2 = **diameter**, bore, gauge, measure

call VERB 1 = **name**, entitle, dub, designate, term, style, label, describe as 2 = **cry**, shout, scream, yell, whoop ≠ whisper 3 = **phone**, telephone, ring (up) (*informal, chiefly Brit.*) 4 = **hail**, summon 5 = **summon**, gather, rally, assemble, muster, convene ≠ dismiss 6 = **waken**, arouse, rouse

▷ NOUN 1 = **visit** 2 = **request**, order, demand, appeal, notice, command, invitation, plea 3 *used in negative constructions* = **need**, cause, reason, grounds, occasion, excuse, justification 4 = **attraction**, pull (*informal*), appeal, lure, allure, magnetism 5 = **cry**, shout, scream, yell, whoop ≠ whisper ▷ PHRASES: **call for someone** = **fetch**, pick up, collect; **call for something** 1 = **demand**, order, request, insist on, cry out for 2 = **require**, need, involve, demand, occasion, entail, necessitate

calling NOUN = **profession**, trade, career, mission, vocation, life's work

calm ADJECTIVE 1 = **cool**, relaxed, composed, sedate, collected, dispassionate, unemotional, self-possessed, chilled (*informal*) ≠ excited 2 = **still**, quiet, smooth, mild, serene, tranquil, balmy, windless ≠ rough
▷ NOUN 1 = **peacefulness**, peace, serenity 2 = **stillness**, peace, quiet, hush, serenity, tranquillity, repose, peacefulness 3 = **peace**, calmness ≠ disturbance
▷ VERB 1 = **soothe**, quiet, relax, appease, still, allay, assuage, quieten ≠ excite 2 = **placate**, hush, pacify, mollify ≠ aggravate

camouflage NOUN
1 = **protective colouring**
2 = **disguise**, cover, screen, blind, mask, cloak, masquerade, subterfuge
▷ VERB = **disguise**, cover, screen, hide, mask, conceal, obscure, veil ≠ reveal

camp[1] NOUN 1 = **camp site**, tents, encampment, camping ground 2 = **bivouac**, cantonment (*military*)

camp[2] (*informal*) ADJECTIVE
1 = **effeminate** 2 = **affected**, mannered, artificial, posturing, ostentatious

campaign NOUN 1 = **drive**, appeal, movement, push (*informal*), offensive, crusade
2 = **operation**, drive, attack, movement, push, offensive, expedition, crusade

canal NOUN = **waterway**, channel, passage, conduit, duct, watercourse

cancel VERB 1 = **call off**, drop, forget about 2 = **annul**, abolish, repeal, abort, do away with, revoke, eliminate ▷ PHRASE: **cancel something out** = **counterbalance**, offset, make up for, compensate for, neutralize, nullify, balance out

cancellation NOUN
1 = **abandonment**
2 = **annulment**, abolition, repeal, elimination, revocation

cancer NOUN 1 = **growth**, tumour, malignancy 2 = **evil**, corruption, sickness, pestilence

candidate NOUN = **contender**, competitor, applicant, nominee, entrant, claimant, contestant, runner

cannabis NOUN = **marijuana**, pot (*slang*), dope (*slang*), grass (*slang*), hemp, dagga (*S. African*)

cannon NOUN = **gun**, big gun, field gun, mortar

canon NOUN 1 = **rule**, standard, principle, regulation, formula, criterion, dictate, statute 2 = **list**, index, catalogue, roll

canopy NOUN = **awning**, covering, shade, sunshade

cap VERB 1 (*informal*) = **beat**, top, better, exceed, eclipse, surpass, transcend, outstrip 2 = **top**, crown

capability NOUN = **ability**, means, power, potential, capacity, qualification(s), competence, proficiency ≠ inability

capable ADJECTIVE 1 = **able** ≠ incapable 2 = **accomplished**, qualified, talented, gifted, efficient, competent, proficient ≠ incompetent

capacity NOUN 1 = **ability**, facility, gift, genius, capability, aptitude, aptness, competence or competency 2 = **size**, room, range, space, volume, extent, dimensions, scope 3 = **function**, position, role, post, office

cape NOUN = **headland**, point, head, peninsula, promontory

capital NOUN = **money**, funds, investment(s), cash, finances, resources, assets, wealth
▷ ADJECTIVE (old-fashioned) = **first-rate**, fine, excellent, superb

capitalism NOUN = **private enterprise**, free enterprise, private ownership, laissez faire or laisser faire

capsule NOUN 1 = **pill**, tablet, lozenge 2 (botany) = **pod**, case, shell, vessel, sheath, receptacle, seed case

captain NOUN 1 = **leader**, boss, master, skipper, head, chief 2 = **commander**, skipper

captivate VERB = **charm**, attract, fascinate, entrance, enchant, enthral, beguile, allure ≠ repel

captive ADJECTIVE = **confined**, caged, imprisoned, locked up, enslaved, incarcerated, ensnared, subjugated
▷ NOUN = **prisoner**, hostage, convict, prisoner of war, detainee, internee

captivity NOUN = **confinement**, custody, detention, imprisonment, incarceration, internment

capture VERB = **catch**, arrest, take, bag, secure, seize, collar (informal), apprehend ≠ release
▷ NOUN = **arrest**, catching, trapping, imprisonment, seizure, apprehension, taking, taking captive

car NOUN 1 = **vehicle**, motor, wheels (informal), auto (U.S.), automobile, jalopy (informal), motorcar, machine 2 (U.S. & Canad.) = **(railway) carriage**, coach, cable car, dining car, sleeping car, buffet car, van

cardinal ADJECTIVE = **principal**, first, leading, chief, main, central, key, essential ≠ secondary

care VERB = **be concerned**, mind, bother, be interested, be bothered, give a damn, concern yourself
▷ NOUN 1 = **custody**, keeping, control, charge, management, protection, supervision, guardianship 2 = **caution**, attention, pains, consideration, heed, prudence, vigilance, forethought ≠ carelessness 3 = **worry**, concern, pressure, trouble, responsibility, stress, anxiety, disquiet ≠ pleasure
▷ PHRASES: **care for someone** 1 = **look after**, mind, tend, attend, nurse, minister to, watch over

2 = **love**, desire, be fond of, want, prize; **care for something** or **someone** = **like**, enjoy, take to, relish, be fond of, be keen on, be partial to **1** = **look after**, mind, watch, protect, tend, nurse, care for, provide for **2** = **deal with**, manage, cope with, see to, handle

career NOUN = **occupation**, calling, employment, pursuit, vocation, livelihood, life's work
▷ VERB = **rush**, race, speed, tear, dash, barrel (along) (*informal, chiefly U.S. & Canad.*), bolt, hurtle

careful ADJECTIVE **1** = **cautious**, scrupulous, circumspect, chary, thoughtful, discreet ≠ careless **2** = **thorough**, full, particular, precise, intensive, in-depth, meticulous, conscientious ≠ casual **3** = **prudent**, sparing, economical, canny, provident, frugal, thrifty

careless ADJECTIVE **1** = **slapdash**, irresponsible, sloppy (*informal*), cavalier, offhand, neglectful, slipshod, lackadaisical ≠ careful **2** = **negligent**, hasty, thoughtless, unthinking, forgetful, absent-minded, remiss ≠ careful **3** = **nonchalant**, casual, offhand, artless, unstudied ≠ careful

caretaker NOUN = **warden**, keeper, porter, superintendent, curator, custodian, watchman, janitor

cargo NOUN = **load**, goods, contents, shipment, freight, merchandise, baggage, consignment

caricature NOUN = **parody**, cartoon, distortion, satire, send-up (*Brit. informal*), travesty, takeoff (*informal*), lampoon
▷ VERB = **parody**, take off (*informal*), mock, distort, ridicule, mimic, send up (*Brit. informal*), lampoon

carnage NOUN = **slaughter**, murder, massacre, holocaust, havoc, bloodshed, shambles, mass murder

carnival NOUN = **festival**, fair, fête, celebration, gala, jubilee, jamboree, revelry

carol NOUN = **song**, hymn, Christmas song

carp VERB = **find fault**, complain, criticize, reproach, quibble, cavil, pick holes, nit-pick (*informal*) ≠ praise

carpenter NOUN = **joiner**, cabinet-maker, woodworker

carriage NOUN **1** = **vehicle**, coach, trap, gig, cab, wagon, hackney, conveyance **2** = **bearing**, posture, gait, deportment, air

carry VERB **1** = **convey**, take, move, bring, bear, transfer, conduct, transport **2** = **transport**, take, transfer **3** = **transmit**, transfer, spread, pass on **4** = **win**, gain, secure, capture, accomplish ▷ PHRASES: **carry on 1** = **continue**, last, endure, persist, keep going, persevere, crack on (*informal*) **2** (*informal*) = **make a fuss**, misbehave, create (*slang*),

CARNIVORES

- aardwolf
- arctic fox
- badger
- bear
- binturong
- black bear
- bobcat
- brown bear
- caracal or desert lynx
- cat
- catamount, catamountain, or cat-o'-mountain
- cheetah or chetah
- cinnamon bear
- civet
- coyote or prairie wolf
- dhole
- dingo or (Austral.) native dog or warrigal
- dog
- ermine
- fennec
- ferret
- fox
- genet or genette
- giant panda
- grey fox (U.S.)
- grey wolf or timber wolf
- grizzly bear or grizzly
- hyena or hyaena
- ichneumon
- jackal
- jaguar
- jaguarondi, jaguarundi, or (Austral.) eyra
- kinkajou, honey bear, or potto
- Kodiak bear
- laughing hyena or spotted hyena
- leopard or panther
- linsang
- lion
- lynx
- margay
- marten
- meerkat
- mink
- mongoose
- mountain lion
- ocelot
- otter
- otter shrew
- palm civet
- panda
- panther
- pine marten or sweet marten
- polar bear or (N. Canad.) nanook
- polecat
- prairie dog
- puma or cougar
- raccoon, racoon, or coon
- raccoon dog
- ratel
- red fox
- sable
- sea otter
- serval
- silver fox
- skunk
- sloth bear
- snow leopard or ounce
- stoat
- strandwolf
- sun bear
- swift fox or kit fox
- tayra
- teledu
- tiger
- tiger cat
- timber wolf
- weasel
- wolf
- wolverine, glutton, or carcajou

raise Cain; **carry something on** = **engage in**, conduct, carry out, undertake, embark on, enter into; **carry something out** = **perform**, effect, achieve, realize, implement, fulfil, accomplish, execute

carry-on NOUN (*informal, chiefly Brit.*) = **fuss**, disturbance, racket, commotion

carton NOUN = **box**, case, pack, package, container

cartoon NOUN 1 = **drawing**, parody, satire, caricature, comic strip, takeoff (*informal*), lampoon, sketch 2 = **animation**, animated film, animated cartoon

carve VERB 1 = **sculpt**, cut, chip, whittle, chisel, hew, fashion 2 = **etch**, engrave

cascade NOUN = **waterfall**, falls, torrent, flood, shower, fountain, avalanche, deluge
▷ VERB = **flow**, fall, flood, pour, plunge, surge, spill, tumble

case¹ NOUN 1 = **situation**, event, circumstance(s), state, position, condition, context, contingency 2 = **instance**, example, occasion, specimen, occurrence 3 (*law*) = **lawsuit**, trial, suit, proceedings, dispute, action

case² NOUN 1 = **cabinet**, box, chest, holder 2 = **container**, carton, canister, casket, receptacle 3 = **suitcase**, bag, grip, holdall, portmanteau, valise 4 = **crate**, box 5 = **covering**, casing, shell, jacket, envelope, capsule, sheath, wrapper

cash NOUN = **money**, funds, notes, currency, silver, brass (*Northern English dialect*), dough (*slang*), coinage

cast NOUN 1 = **actors**, company, players, characters, troupe, dramatis personae 2 = **type**, sort, kind, style, stamp
▷ VERB 1 = **choose**, name, pick, select, appoint, assign, allot

2 = **bestow**, give, level, direct 3 = **give out**, spread, deposit, shed, distribute, scatter, emit, radiate 4 = **throw**, launch, pitch, toss, thrust, hurl, fling, sling 5 = **mould**, set, found, form, model, shape

caste NOUN = **class**, order, rank, status, stratum, social order

castle NOUN = **fortress**, keep, palace, tower, chateau, stronghold, citadel

casual ADJECTIVE 1 = **careless**, relaxed, unconcerned, blasé, offhand, nonchalant, lackadaisical ≠ serious 2 = **chance**, unexpected, random, accidental, incidental ≠ planned 3 = **informal**, leisure, sporty, non-dressy ≠ formal

casualty NOUN 1 = **fatality**, death, loss, wounded 2 = **victim**, sufferer

cat NOUN = **feline**, pussy (*informal*), moggy (*slang*), puss (*informal*), ballarat (*Austral. informal*), tabby
▷ RELATED WORDS: *adjective* **feline**, *male* **tom**, *female* **queen**, *young* **kitten**

catalogue *or* (*U.S.*) **catalog** NOUN = **list**, record, schedule, index, register, directory, inventory, gazetteer
▷ VERB = **list**, file, index, register, classify, inventory, tabulate, alphabetize

catastrophe NOUN = **disaster**, tragedy, calamity, cataclysm, trouble, adversity, fiasco

catch VERB 1 = **capture**, arrest,

trap, seize, snare, apprehend, ensnare, entrap ≠ free **2** = **trap**, capture, snare, ensnare, entrap **3** = **seize**, get, grab, snatch **4** = **grab**, take, grip, seize, grasp, clutch, lay hold of ≠ release **5** = **discover**, surprise, find out, expose, detect, catch in the act, take unawares **6** = **contract**, get, develop, suffer from, incur, succumb to, go down with ≠ escape
▷ NOUN **1** = **fastener**, clip, bolt, latch, clasp **2** (*informal*) = **drawback**, trick, trap, disadvantage, hitch, snag, stumbling block, fly in the ointment ≠ advantage
▷ PHRASE: **catch on 1** (*informal*) = **understand**, see, find out, grasp, see through, comprehend, twig (*Brit. informal*), get the picture **2** = **become popular**, take off, become trendy, come into fashion

catchcry NOUN (*Austral.*) = **catchphrase**, slogan, saying, quotation, motto

catching ADJECTIVE = **infectious**, contagious, transferable, communicable, transmittable ≠ non-infectious

category NOUN = **class**, grouping, heading, sort, department, type, division, section

cater VERB ▷ PHRASE: **cater for something** *or* **someone** **1** = **provide for**, supply, purvey **2** = **take into account**, consider, bear in mind, make allowance for, have regard for

cattle PLURAL NOUN = **cows**, stock, beasts, livestock, bovines
▷ RELATED WORDS: *adjective* **bovine**, *collective nouns* **drove, herd**

cause NOUN **1** = **origin**, source, spring, agent, maker, producer, root, beginning ≠ result **2** = **reason**, call, need, grounds, basis, incentive, motive, motivation **3** = **aim**, movement, principle, ideal, enterprise
▷ VERB = **produce**, create, lead to, result in, generate, induce, bring about, give rise to ≠ prevent

caution NOUN **1** = **care**, discretion, heed, prudence, vigilance, alertness, forethought, circumspection ≠ carelessness **2** = **reprimand**, warning, injunction, admonition
▷ VERB **1** = **warn**, urge, advise, alert, tip off, forewarn **2** = **reprimand**, warn, admonish, give an injunction to

cautious ADJECTIVE = **careful**, guarded, wary, tentative, prudent, judicious, circumspect, cagey (*informal*) ≠ careless

cavalry NOUN = **horsemen**, horse, mounted troops ≠ infantrymen

cave NOUN = **hollow**, cavern, grotto, den, cavity

cavity NOUN = **hollow**, hole, gap, pit, dent, crater

cease VERB **1** = **stop**, end, finish, come to an end ≠ start **2** = **discontinue**, end, stop, finish, conclude, halt, terminate, break off ≠ begin

celebrate VERB 1 = **rejoice**,
party, enjoy yourself, carouse,
live it up (*informal*), make merry,
put the flags out, kill the fatted
calf 2 = **commemorate**, honour,
observe, toast, drink to, keep
3 = **perform**, observe, preside
over, officiate at, solemnize

celebrated ADJECTIVE
= **renowned**, popular, famous,
distinguished, well-known,
prominent, acclaimed, notable
≠ unknown

celebration NOUN 1 = **party**,
festival, gala, jubilee,
festivity, revelry, red-
letter day, merrymaking
2 = **commemoration**, honouring,
remembrance 3 = **performance**,
observance, solemnization

celebrity NOUN 1 = **personality**,
star, superstar, big name,
dignitary, luminary, big shot
(*informal*), V.I.P. ≠ nobody
2 = **fame**, reputation, distinction,
prestige, prominence, stardom,
renown, repute ≠ obscurity

cell NOUN 1 = **room**, chamber, lockup, compartment, cavity, cubicle,
dungeon, stall 2 = **unit**, group,
section, core, nucleus, caucus,
coterie

cement NOUN 1 = **mortar**, plaster,
paste 2 = **sealant**, glue, gum,
adhesive
▷ VERB = **stick**, join, bond, attach,
seal, glue, plaster, weld

cemetery NOUN = **graveyard**,
churchyard, burial ground,
necropolis, God's acre

censor VERB = **expurgate**, cut,
blue-pencil, bowdlerize

censure VERB = **criticize**, blame,
condemn, denounce, rebuke,
reprimand, reproach, scold
≠ applaud
▷ NOUN = **disapproval**, criticism,
blame, condemnation, rebuke,
reprimand, reproach, stick (*slang*)
≠ approval

central ADJECTIVE 1 = **inner**,
middle, mid, interior ≠ outer
2 = **main**, chief, key, essential,
primary, principal, fundamental,
focal ≠ minor

centre NOUN = **middle**, heart,
focus, core, nucleus, hub, pivot,
kernel ≠ edge ▷ PHRASE: **centre
on something** *or* **someone**
= **focus**, concentrate, cluster,
revolve, converge

ceremonial ADJECTIVE = **formal**,
public, official, ritual, stately,
solemn, liturgical, courtly
≠ informal
▷ NOUN = **ritual**, ceremony, rite,
formality, solemnity

ceremony NOUN 1 = **ritual**,
service, rite, observance,
commemoration, solemnities
2 = **formality**, ceremonial,
propriety, decorum

certain ADJECTIVE 1 = **sure**,
convinced, positive, confident,
satisfied, assured ≠ unsure
2 = **bound**, sure, fated, destined
≠ unlikely 3 = **inevitable**,
unavoidable, inescapable
4 = **known**, true, positive,
conclusive, unequivocal,

undeniable, irrefutable,
unquestionable, nailed-on (*slang*)
≠ doubtful **5 = fixed**, decided,
established, settled, definite
≠ indefinite

certainly ADVERB = **definitely**,
surely, truly, undoubtedly,
without doubt, undeniably,
indisputably, assuredly

certainty NOUN **1 = confidence**,
trust, faith, conviction, assurance,
sureness, positiveness ≠ doubt
2 = inevitability ≠ uncertainty
3 = fact, truth, reality, sure thing
(*informal*), banker

certificate NOUN = **document**,
licence, warrant, voucher,
diploma, testimonial,
authorization, credential(s)

certify VERB = **confirm**, declare,
guarantee, assure, testify, verify,
validate, attest

chain NOUN **1 = tether**, coupling,
link, bond, shackle, fetter,
manacle **2 = series**, set, train,
string, sequence, succession,
progression
▷ VERB = **bind**, confine, restrain,
handcuff, shackle, tether, fetter,
manacle

chairman *or* **chairwoman**
NOUN **1 = director**, president,
chief, executive, chairperson
2 = master of ceremonies,
spokesman, chair, speaker, MC,
chairperson

● **WORD POWER**
● The general trend of nonsexist
● language is to find a term
● which can apply to both sexes

● equally, as in the use of *actor*
● to refer to both men and
● women. *Chairman* can seem
● inappropriate when applied
● to a woman, while *chairwoman*
● specifies gender, and so, as
● the entry above illustrates, the
● terms *chair* and *chairperson* are
● often preferred as alternatives.

challenge NOUN **1 = dare**,
provocation, wero (*N.Z.*) **2 = test**,
trial, opposition, confrontation,
ultimatum
▷ VERB **1 = dispute**, question,
tackle, confront, defy, object to,
disagree with, take issue with
2 = dare, invite, defy, throw
down the gauntlet **3 = test**
4 = question, interrogate

chamber NOUN **1 = hall**, room
2 = council, assembly, legislature,
legislative body **3 = room**,
bedroom, apartment, enclosure,
cubicle **4 = compartment**

champion NOUN **1 = winner**,
hero, victor, conqueror, title
holder **2 = defender**, guardian,
patron, backer, protector,
upholder
▷ VERB = **support**, back, defend,
promote, advocate, fight for,
uphold, espouse

chance NOUN **1 = probability**,
odds, possibility, prospect,
likelihood ≠ certainty
2 = opportunity, opening,
occasion, time **3 = accident**,
fortune, luck, fate, destiny,
coincidence, providence ≠ design
4 = risk, speculation, gamble,

hazard
▷ VERB = **risk**, try, stake, venture, gamble, hazard, wager

change NOUN 1 = **alteration**, innovation, transformation, modification, mutation, metamorphosis, difference, revolution 2 = **variety**, break (*informal*), departure, variation, novelty, diversion ≠ monotony 3 = **exchange**, trade, conversion, swap, substitution, interchange
▷ VERB 1 = **alter**, reform, transform, adjust, revise, modify, reorganize, restyle ≠ keep 2 = **shift**, vary, transform, alter, modify, mutate ≠ stay 3 = **exchange**, trade, replace, substitute, swap, interchange

channel NOUN 1 = **means**, way, course, approach, medium, route, path, avenue 2 = **strait**, sound, route, passage, canal, waterway 3 = **duct**, artery, groove, gutter, furrow, conduit
▷ VERB = **direct**, guide, conduct, transmit, convey

chant NOUN = **song**, carol, chorus, melody, psalm
▷ VERB = **sing**, chorus, recite, intone, carol

chaos NOUN = **disorder**, confusion, mayhem, anarchy, lawlessness, pandemonium, bedlam, tumult ≠ orderliness

chaotic ADJECTIVE = **disordered**, confused, uncontrolled, anarchic, tumultuous, lawless, riotous, topsy-turvy

chap NOUN (*informal*) = **fellow**, man, person, individual, character, guy (*informal*), bloke (*Brit. informal*)

chapter NOUN 1 = **section**, part, stage, division, episode, topic, segment, instalment 2 = **period**, time, stage, phase

character NOUN 1 = **personality**, nature, attributes, temperament, complexion, disposition 2 = **nature**, kind, quality, calibre 3 = **reputation**, honour, integrity, good name, rectitude 4 = **role**, part, persona 5 = **eccentric**, card (*informal*), original, oddball (*informal*) 6 = **symbol**, mark, sign, letter, figure, device, rune, hieroglyph

characteristic NOUN = **feature**, mark, quality, property, attribute, faculty, trait, quirk
▷ ADJECTIVE = **typical**, special, individual, representative, distinguishing, distinctive, peculiar, singular ≠ rare

characterize VERB = **distinguish**, mark, identify, brand, stamp, typify

charge VERB 1 = **accuse**, indict, impeach, incriminate, arraign ≠ acquit 2 = **attack**, assault, assail ≠ retreat 3 = **rush**, storm, stampede 4 = **fill**, load
▷ NOUN 1 = **price**, rate, cost, amount, payment, expense, toll, expenditure 2 = **accusation**, allegation, indictment, imputation ≠ acquittal 3 = **care**, trust, responsibility, custody, safekeeping 4 = **duty**, office,

responsibility, remit **5** = **ward**,
pupil, protégé, dependant
6 = **attack**, rush, assault, onset,
onslaught, stampede, sortie
≠ retreat

charisma NOUN = **charm**,
appeal, personality, attraction,
lure, allure, magnetism, force of
personality

charismatic ADJECTIVE
= **charming**, appealing, attractive,
influential, magnetic, enticing,
alluring

charitable ADJECTIVE
1 = **benevolent**, liberal, generous,
lavish, philanthropic, bountiful,
beneficent ≠ mean **2** = **kind**,
understanding, forgiving,
sympathetic, favourable, tolerant,
indulgent, lenient ≠ unkind

charity NOUN **1** = **charitable
organization**, fund,
movement, trust, endowment
2 = **donations**, help, relief,
gift, contributions, assistance,
hand-out, philanthropy, koha
(*N.Z.*) ≠ meanness **3** = **kindness**,
humanity, goodwill, compassion,
generosity, indulgence, altruism,
benevolence, aroha (*N.Z.*) ≠ ill
will

charm NOUN **1** = **attraction**,
appeal, fascination, allure,
magnetism ≠ repulsiveness
2 = **trinket 3** = **talisman**,
amulet, fetish **4** = **spell**, magic,
enchantment, sorcery, makutu
(*N.Z.*)
▷ VERB **1** = **attract**, delight,
fascinate, entrance, win over,

enchant, captivate, beguile
≠ repel **2** = **persuade**, seduce,
coax, beguile, sweet-talk (*informal*)

charming ADJECTIVE = **attractive**,
pleasing, appealing, fetching,
delightful, cute, seductive,
captivating ≠ unpleasant

chart NOUN = **table**, diagram,
blueprint, graph, plan, map
▷ VERB **1** = **plot**, map out,
delineate, sketch, draft, tabulate
2 = **monitor**, follow, record, note,
document, register, trace, outline

charter NOUN **1** = **document**,
contract, permit, licence, deed,
prerogative **2** = **constitution**,
laws, rules, code
▷ VERB **1** = **hire**, commission,
employ, rent, lease **2** = **authorize**,
permit, sanction, entitle, license,
empower, give authority

chase VERB **1** = **pursue**, follow,
track, hunt, run after, course
2 = **drive away**, drive, expel,
hound, send away, send packing,
put to flight **3** (*informal*) = **rush**,
run, race, shoot, fly, speed, dash,
bolt
▷ NOUN = **pursuit**, race, hunt,
hunting

chat VERB = **talk**, gossip, jaw
(*slang*), natter, blather, blether
(*Scot.*)
▷ NOUN = **talk**, tête-à-tête,
conversation, gossip, heart-to-
heart, natter, blather, blether
(*Scot.*), korero (*N.Z.*)

chatter VERB = **prattle**, chat,
rabbit on (*Brit. informal*), babble,
gab (*informal*), natter, blather,

schmooze (slang)
▷ NOUN = **prattle**, chat, gossip, babble, gab (informal), natter, blather, blether (Scot.)

cheap ADJECTIVE 1 = **inexpensive**, reduced, keen, reasonable, bargain, low-priced, low-cost, cut-price ≠ expensive 2 = **inferior**, poor, worthless, second-rate, shoddy, tawdry, tatty, trashy, bodger or bodgie (Austral. slang) ≠ good 3 (informal) = **despicable**, mean, contemptible, scungy (Austral. & N.Z.) ≠ decent

cheat VERB = **deceive**, trick, fool, con (informal), mislead, rip off (slang), fleece, defraud, scam (slang)
▷ NOUN = **deceiver**, sharper, shark, charlatan, trickster, con man (informal), double-crosser (informal), swindler, rorter (Austral. slang), rogue trader

check VERB 1 often with **out** = **examine**, test, study, look at, research, investigate, monitor, vet ≠ overlook 2 = **stop**, limit, delay, halt, restrain, inhibit, hinder, obstruct ≠ further
▷ NOUN 1 = **examination**, test, research, investigation, inspection, scrutiny, once-over (informal) 2 = **control**, limitation, restraint, constraint, obstacle, curb, obstruction, stoppage

cheek NOUN (informal) = **impudence**, nerve, disrespect, audacity, lip (slang), temerity, chutzpah (U.S. & Canad. informal), insolence

cheeky ADJECTIVE = **impudent**, rude, forward, insulting, saucy, audacious, pert, disrespectful ≠ respectful

cheer VERB 1 = **applaud**, hail, acclaim, clap ≠ boo 2 = **hearten**, encourage, comfort, uplift, brighten, cheer up, buoy up, gladden ≠ dishearten
▷ NOUN = **applause**, ovation
▷ PHRASES: **cheer someone up** = **comfort**, encourage, hearten, enliven, gladden, gee up, jolly along (informal); **cheer up** = **take heart**, rally, perk up, buck up (informal)

cheerful ADJECTIVE 1 = **happy**, optimistic, enthusiastic, jolly, merry, upbeat (informal), buoyant, cheery ≠ sad 2 = **pleasant** ≠ gloomy

chemical NOUN = **compound**, drug, substance, synthetic substance, potion

chemist NOUN = **pharmacist**, apothecary (obsolete), dispenser

cherish VERB 1 = **cling to**, prize, treasure, hold dear, cleave to ≠ despise 2 = **care for**, love, support, comfort, look after, shelter, nurture, hold dear ≠ neglect 3 = **harbour**, nurse, sustain, foster, entertain

chest NOUN 1 = **breast**, front 2 = **box**, case, trunk, crate, coffer, casket, strongbox ▷ RELATED WORD: adjective **pectoral**

chew VERB = **munch**, bite, grind, champ, crunch, gnaw, chomp, masticate

chic ADJECTIVE = **stylish**, smart, elegant, fashionable, trendy (*Brit. informal*), schmick (*Austral. informal*) ≠ unfashionable

chief NOUN = **head**, leader, director, manager, boss (*informal*), captain, master, governor, baas (*S. African*), ariki (*N.Z.*), sherang (*Austral. & N.Z.*) ≠ subordinate
▷ ADJECTIVE = **primary**, highest, leading, main, prime, key, premier, supreme ≠ minor

chiefly ADVERB 1 = **especially**, essentially, principally, primarily, above all 2 = **mainly**, largely, usually, mostly, in general, on the whole, predominantly, in the main

child NOUN 1 = **youngster**, baby, kid (*informal*), infant, babe, juvenile, toddler, tot, littlie (*Austral. informal*), ankle-biter (*Austral. slang*), tacker (*Austral. slang*) 2 = **offspring** ▷ RELATED WORDS: *adjective* filial, *prefix* paedo-

childbirth NOUN = **child-bearing**, labour, delivery, lying-in, confinement, parturition

childhood NOUN = **youth**, minority, infancy, schooldays, immaturity, boyhood *or* girlhood

childish ADJECTIVE 1 = **youthful**, young, boyish *or* girlish 2 = **immature**, juvenile, foolish, infantile, puerile ≠ mature

chill VERB 1 = **cool**, refrigerate, freeze 2 = **dishearten**, depress, discourage, dismay, dampen,

deject
▷ NOUN 1 = **coldness**, bite, nip, sharpness, coolness, rawness, crispness, frigidity 2 = **shiver**, frisson
▷ ADJECTIVE = **chilly**, biting, sharp, freezing, raw, bleak, chilly, wintry

chilly ADJECTIVE 1 = **cool**, fresh, sharp, crisp, penetrating, brisk, draughty, nippy ≠ warm 2 = **unfriendly**, hostile, unsympathetic, frigid, unresponsive, unwelcoming ≠ friendly

china¹ NOUN = **pottery**, ceramics, ware, porcelain, crockery, tableware, service

china² NOUN (*Brit. & S. African informal*) = **friend**, pal, mate (*informal*), buddy (*informal*), companion, best friend, intimate, comrade, cobber (*Austral. & N.Z. old-fashioned, informal*), E hoa (*N.Z.*)

● **WORD POWER**
● Some words borrowed into
● English from Chinese have
● further developed in meaning.
● For example, *gung-ho*, which
● literally means 'work together',
● was appropriated as a slogan
● by the U.S. Marines in the
● Second World War. From this
● sense of military co-operation
● arose the idea of militant
● zeal, and nowadays the term
● gung-ho is still used to describe
● those who are all too keen to
● participate in combat. It is also
● used in non-military contexts
● to mean proactive, upbeat,

enthusiastic, and eager,
particularly as an attitude or
approach. It sometimes has the
implication of inflexibility and
aggression, perhaps as a nod
to its military origins. Another
Chinese word which was
originally very specific in its
application is *kowtow*. Literally
'knock the head', it refers to
the former Chinese custom of
touching the forehead to the
ground as an act of deference.
In its extended sense, it means
to behave in an obsequious way
towards someone. Its meaning
has worsened from an act of
submission and deference into
one of servility. It is often found
in statements such as *wouldn't
kowtow to*, *refusal to kowtow*,
too willing to kowtow, showing
the negative associations now
attached to this word.

chip NOUN 1 = **fragment**, shaving,
wafer, sliver, shard 2 = **scratch**,
nick, notch 3 = **counter**, disc,
token
▷ VERB 1 = **nick**, damage, gash
2 = **chisel**, whittle

choice NOUN 1 = **range**,
variety, selection, assortment
2 = **selection**, preference, pick
3 = **option**, say, alternative
▷ ADJECTIVE = **best**, prime, select,
excellent, exclusive, elite, booshit
(*Austral. slang*), exo (*Austral. slang*),
sik (*Austral. slang*), rad (*informal*),
phat (*slang*), schmick (*Austral.
informal*)

choke VERB 1 = **suffocate**, stifle,
smother, overpower, asphyxiate
2 = **strangle**, throttle, asphyxiate
3 = **block**, clog, obstruct, bung,
constrict, congest, stop, bar

choose VERB 1 = **pick**, prefer,
select, elect, adopt, opt for,
designate, settle upon ≠ reject
2 = **wish**, want

chop VERB = **cut**, fell, hack, sever,
cleave, hew, lop

chore NOUN = **task**, job, duty,
burden, hassle (*informal*), errand

chorus NOUN 1 = **refrain**,
response, strain, burden
2 = **choir**, singers, ensemble,
vocalists, choristers ▷ PHRASE:
in chorus = **in unison**, as one, all
together, in concert, in harmony,
in accord, with one voice

christen VERB 1 = **baptize**, name
2 = **name**, call, term, style, title,
dub, designate

Christmas NOUN = **the festive
season**, Noël, Xmas (*informal*),
Yule (*archaic*), Yuletide (*archaic*)

chronicle VERB = **record**, tell,
report, enter, relate, register,
recount, set down
▷ NOUN = **record**, story, history,
account, register, journal, diary,
narrative, blog (*informal*)

chuck VERB 1 (*informal*) = **throw**,
cast, pitch, toss, hurl, fling, sling,
heave 2 *often with* **away** *or* **out**
(*informal*) = **throw out**, dump
(*informal*), scrap, get rid of, ditch
(*slang*), dispose of, dispense with,
jettison 3 (*informal*) = **give up**
or **over**, leave, abandon, cease,

resign from, pack in **4** (*slang*)
= **vomit**, throw up (*informal*), spew,
heave (*slang*), puke (*slang*), barf
(*U.S. slang*), chunder (*slang, chiefly
Austral.*)

chuckle VERB = **laugh**, giggle,
snigger, chortle, titter
▷ NOUN = **laugh**, giggle, snigger,
chortle, titter

chum NOUN (*informal*) = **friend**,
mate (*informal*), pal (*informal*),
companion, comrade, crony,
cobber (*Austral. & N.Z. old-
fashioned*) (*informal*), E hoa (*N.Z.*)

chunk NOUN = **piece**, block, mass,
portion, lump, slab, hunk, nugget

churn VERB **1** = **stir up**, beat,
disturb, swirl, agitate **2** = **swirl**,
toss

cinema NOUN **1** = **pictures**,
movies, picture-house, flicks
(*slang*) **2** = **films**, pictures, movies,
the big screen (*informal*), motion
pictures, the silver screen

circle NOUN **1** = **ring**, disc, hoop,
halo **2** = **group**, company, set,
club, society, clique, coterie
▷ VERB **1** = **go round**, ring,
surround, enclose, envelop,
encircle, circumscribe,
circumnavigate **2** = **wheel**, spiral

circuit NOUN **1** = **course**,
tour, track, route, journey
2 = **racetrack**, course, track,
racecourse **3** = **lap**, tour,
revolution, orbit

circular ADJECTIVE **1** = **round**,
ring-shaped **2** = **circuitous**,
cyclical, orbital
▷ NOUN = **advertisement**, notice,

ad (*informal*), announcement,
advert (*Brit. informal*), press release

circulate VERB **1** = **spread**, issue,
publish, broadcast, distribute,
publicize, disseminate,
promulgate **2** = **flow**, revolve,
rotate, radiate

circulation NOUN
1 = **distribution**, currency,
readership **2** = **bloodstream**,
blood flow **3** = **flow**, circling,
motion, rotation **4** = **spread**,
distribution, transmission,
dissemination

circumstance NOUN **1** *usually
plural* = **situation**, condition,
contingency, state of affairs, lie of
the land **2** *usually plural* = **detail**,
event, particular, respect **3**
usually plural = **situation**, state,
means, position, station, status
4 = **chance**, the times, accident,
fortune, luck, fate, destiny,
providence

cite VERB = **quote**, name, advance,
mention, extract, specify, allude
to, enumerate

citizen NOUN = **inhabitant**,
resident, dweller, denizen,
subject, townsman ▷ RELATED
WORD: *adjective* civil

city NOUN = **town**, metropolis,
municipality, conurbation
▷ RELATED WORD: *adjective* civic
▷ *see* **capital cities**

civic ADJECTIVE = **public**,
municipal, communal, local

civil ADJECTIVE **1** = **civic**, political,
domestic, municipal ≠ state
2 = **polite**, obliging, courteous,

considerate, affable, well-mannered ≠ rude

civilization NOUN 1 = **society**, people, community, nation, polity 2 = **culture**, development, education, progress, enlightenment, sophistication, advancement, cultivation

civilize VERB = **cultivate**, educate, refine, tame, enlighten, sophisticate

civilized ADJECTIVE 1 = **cultured**, educated, sophisticated, enlightened, humane ≠ primitive 2 = **polite**, mannerly, tolerant, gracious, courteous, well-behaved, well-mannered

claim VERB 1 = **assert**, insist, maintain, allege, uphold, profess 2 = **demand**, call for, ask for, insist on
▷ NOUN 1 = **assertion**, statement, allegation, declaration, pretension, affirmation, protestation 2 = **demand**, application, request, petition, call 3 = **right**, title, entitlement

clamour NOUN = **noise**, shouting, racket, outcry, din, uproar, commotion, hubbub

clamp NOUN = **vice**, press, grip, bracket, fastener
▷ VERB = **fasten**, fix, secure, brace, make fast

clan NOUN 1 = **family**, group, society, tribe, fraternity, brotherhood, ainga (N.Z.), ngai or ngati (N.Z.) 2 = **group**, set, circle, gang, faction, coterie, cabal

clap VERB = **applaud**, cheer, acclaim ≠ boo

clarify VERB = **explain**, interpret, illuminate, clear up, simplify, make plain, elucidate, throw or shed light on

clarity NOUN 1 = **clearness**, precision, simplicity, transparency, lucidity, straightforwardness ≠ obscurity 2 = **transparency**, clearness ≠ cloudiness

clash VERB 1 = **conflict**, grapple, wrangle, lock horns, cross swords, war, feud, quarrel 2 = **disagree**, conflict, vary, counter, differ, contradict, diverge, run counter to 3 = **not go**, jar, not match 4 = **crash**, bang, rattle, jar, clatter, jangle, clang, clank
▷ NOUN 1 = **conflict**, fight, brush, confrontation, collision, showdown (*informal*), boilover (*Austral.*) 2 = **disagreement**, difference, argument, dispute, dissent, difference of opinion

clasp VERB = **grasp**, hold, press, grip, seize, squeeze, embrace, clutch
▷ NOUN 1 = **grasp**, hold, grip, embrace, hug 2 = **fastening**, catch, grip, hook, pin, clip, buckle, brooch

class NOUN 1 = **group**, set, division, rank 2 = **type**, set, sort, kind, category, genre
▷ VERB = **classify**, group, rate, rank, brand, label, grade, designate

classic ADJECTIVE 1 = **typical**, standard, model, regular, usual,

ideal, characteristic, definitive,
dinki-di (*Austral. informal*)
2 = **masterly**, best, finest,
world-class, consummate, first-
rate ≠ second-rate **3** = **lasting**,
enduring, abiding, immortal,
undying, ageless, deathless
▷ NOUN = **standard**, masterpiece,
prototype, paradigm, exemplar,
model

classification NOUN
1 = **categorization**, grading,
taxonomy, sorting, analysis,
arrangement **2** = **class**, grouping,
heading, sort, department, type,
division, section

classify VERB = **categorize**, sort,
rank, arrange, grade, catalogue,
pigeonhole, tabulate

classy ADJECTIVE (*informal*) = **high-
class**, exclusive, superior, elegant,
stylish, posh (*informal, chiefly Brit.*),
up-market, top-drawer, schmick
(*Austral. informal*)

clause NOUN = **section**, condition,
article, chapter, passage, part,
paragraph

claw NOUN **1** = **nail**, talon
2 = **pincer**
▷ VERB = **scratch**, tear, dig, rip,
scrape, maul, mangulate (*Austral.
slang*), lacerate

clean ADJECTIVE **1** = **hygienic**,
fresh, sterile, pure,
purified, antiseptic,
sterilized, uncontaminated
≠ contaminated **2** = **spotless**,
fresh, immaculate, impeccable,
flawless, unblemished, unsullied
≠ dirty **3** = **moral**, good, pure,

decent, innocent, respectable,
upright, honourable ≠ immoral
4 = **complete**, final, whole, total,
perfect, entire, decisive, thorough
▷ VERB = **cleanse**, wash, scrub,
rinse, launder, scour, purify,
disinfect ≠ dirty

cleanse VERB **1** = **purify**, clear,
purge **2** = **absolve**, clear, purge,
purify **3** = **clean**, wash, scrub,
rinse, scour

clear ADJECTIVE
1 = **comprehensible**, explicit,
understandable ≠ confused
2 = **distinct** ≠ indistinct
3 = **obvious**, plain, apparent,
evident, distinct, pronounced,
manifest, blatant ≠ ambiguous
4 = **certain**, sure, convinced,
positive, satisfied, resolved,
definite, decided ≠ confused
5 = **transparent**, see-through,
translucent, crystalline, glassy,
limpid, pellucid ≠ opaque
6 = **unobstructed**, open, free,
empty, unhindered, unimpeded
≠ blocked **7** = **bright**, fine,
fair, shining, sunny, luminous,
cloudless, light ≠ cloudy
8 = **untroubled**, clean, pure,
innocent, immaculate,
unblemished, untarnished
▷ VERB **1** = **unblock**, free, loosen,
extricate, open, disentangle
2 = **remove**, clean, wipe,
cleanse, tidy (up), sweep away
3 = **brighten**, break up, lighten
4 = **pass over**, jump, leap,
vault, miss **5** = **absolve**, acquit,
vindicate, exonerate ≠ blame

clear-cut ADJECTIVE
= **straightforward**, specific, plain,
precise, black-and-white, explicit,
definite, unequivocal

clearly ADVERB 1 = **obviously**,
undoubtedly, evidently, distinctly,
markedly, overtly, undeniably,
beyond doubt 2 = **legibly**,
distinctly 3 = **audibly**, distinctly,
intelligibly, comprehensibly

clergy NOUN = **priesthood**,
ministry, clerics, clergymen,
churchmen, the cloth, holy orders

clever ADJECTIVE 1 = **intelligent**,
bright, talented, gifted, smart,
knowledgeable, quick-witted
≠ stupid 2 = **shrewd**, bright,
ingenious, resourceful, canny
≠ unimaginative 3 = **skilful**,
talented, gifted ≠ inept

cliché NOUN = **platitude**,
stereotype, commonplace,
banality, truism, hackneyed
phrase

client NOUN = **customer**,
consumer, buyer, patron, shopper,
patient

cliff NOUN = **rock face**, overhang,
crag, precipice, escarpment, scar,
bluff

climate NOUN = **weather**,
temperature

climax NOUN = **culmination**, top,
summit, height, highlight, peak,
high point, zenith

climb VERB 1 = **ascend**, scale,
mount, go up, clamber, shin up
2 = **clamber**, descend, scramble,
dismount 3 = **rise**, go up, soar,
ascend, fly up ▷ PHRASE: **climb**

down = **back down**, withdraw,
yield, concede, retreat, surrender,
give in, cave in (informal)

clinch VERB 1 = **secure**, close,
confirm, conclude, seal, sew
up (informal), set the seal on
2 = **settle**, decide, determine

cling VERB 1 = **clutch**, grip,
embrace, grasp, hug, hold on to,
clasp 2 = **stick to**, adhere to

clinical ADJECTIVE = **unemotional**,
cold, scientific, objective,
detached, analytic, impersonal,
dispassionate

clip¹ VERB 1 = **trim**, cut, crop,
prune, shorten, shear, snip, pare 2
(informal) = **smack**, strike, knock,
punch, thump, clout (informal),
cuff, whack
▷ NOUN (informal) = **smack**,
strike, knock, punch, thump, clout
(informal), cuff, whack

clip² VERB = **attach**, fix, secure,
connect, pin, staple, fasten, hold

cloak NOUN 1 = **cape**, coat, wrap,
mantle 2 = **covering**, layer,
blanket, shroud
▷ VERB 1 = **cover**, coat, wrap,
blanket, shroud, envelop 2 = **hide**,
cover, screen, mask, disguise,
conceal, obscure, veil

clog VERB = **obstruct**, block, jam,
hinder, impede, congest

close¹ VERB 1 = **shut**, lock, fasten,
secure ≠ open 2 = **shut down**,
finish, cease 3 = **wind up**, finish,
shut down, terminate 4 = **block
up**, bar, seal ≠ open 5 = **end**,
finish, complete, conclude, wind
up, terminate ≠ begin 6 = **clinch**,

confirm, secure, conclude, seal, sew up (*informal*), set the seal on **7 = come together**, join, connect ≠ separate

▷ NOUN = **end**, ending, finish, conclusion, completion, finale, culmination, denouement

close² ADJECTIVE **1 = near**, neighbouring, nearby, handy, adjacent, adjoining, cheek by jowl ≠ far **2 = intimate**, loving, familiar, thick (*informal*), attached, devoted, confidential, inseparable ≠ distant **3 = noticeable**, marked, strong, distinct, pronounced **4 = careful**, detailed, intense, minute, thorough, rigorous, painstaking **5 = even**, level, neck and neck, fifty-fifty (*informal*), evenly matched **6 = imminent**, near, impending, at hand, nigh ≠ far away **7 = stifling**, oppressive, suffocating, stuffy, humid, sweltering, airless, muggy ≠ airy

closed ADJECTIVE **1 = shut**, locked, sealed, fastened ≠ open **2 = shut down**, out of service **3 = exclusive**, select, restricted **4 = finished**, over, ended, decided, settled, concluded, resolved, terminated

cloth NOUN = **fabric**, material, textiles

clothe VERB = **dress**, array, robe, drape, swathe, attire, fit out, garb ≠ undress

clothes PLURAL NOUN = **clothing**, wear, dress, gear (*informal*), outfit, costume, wardrobe, garments

clothing NOUN = **clothes**, wear, dress, gear (*informal*), outfit, costume, wardrobe, garments

cloud NOUN = **mist**, haze, vapour, murk, gloom

▷ VERB **1 = confuse**, distort, impair, muddle, disorient **2 = darken**, dim, be overshadowed

clout (*informal*) VERB = **hit**, strike, punch, slap, sock (*slang*), smack, thump, clobber (*slang*)

▷ NOUN **1 = thump**, blow, punch, slap, sock (*slang*), wallop (*informal*) **2 = influence**, power, authority, pull, weight, prestige, mana (*N.Z.*)

clown NOUN **1 = comedian**, fool, harlequin, jester, buffoon **2 = joker**, comic, prankster **3 = fool**, idiot, twit (*informal, chiefly Brit.*), imbecile (*informal*), ignoramus, dolt, blockhead, dorba *or* dorb (*Austral. slang*), bogan (*Austral. slang*)

▷ VERB *usually with* **around** = **play the fool**, mess about, jest, act the fool

club NOUN **1 = association**, company, group, union, society, lodge, guild, fraternity **2 = stick**, bat, bludgeon, truncheon, cosh (*Brit.*), cudgel

▷ VERB = **beat**, strike, hammer, batter, bash, bludgeon, pummel, cosh (*Brit.*)

clue NOUN = **indication**, lead, sign, evidence, suggestion, trace, hint, suspicion

clump NOUN = **cluster**, group, bunch, bundle

▷ VERB = **stomp**, thump, lumber, tramp, plod, thud

clumsy ADJECTIVE = **awkward**, lumbering, bumbling, ponderous, ungainly, gauche, gawky, uncoordinated, unco (*Austral. slang*) ≠ skilful

cluster NOUN = **gathering**, group, collection, bunch, knot, clump, assemblage
▷ VERB = **gather**, group, collect, bunch, assemble, flock, huddle

clutch VERB 1 = **hold**, grip, embrace, grasp, cling to, clasp 2 = **seize**, catch, grab, grasp, snatch
▷ PLURAL NOUN = **power**, hands, control, grip, possession, grasp, custody, sway

clutter NOUN = **untidiness**, mess, disorder, confusion, litter, muddle, disarray, jumble ≠ order
▷ VERB = **litter**, scatter, strew, mess up ≠ tidy

coach NOUN 1 = **instructor**, teacher, trainer, tutor, handler 2 = **bus**, charabanc
▷ VERB = **instruct**, train, prepare, exercise, drill, tutor

coalition NOUN = **alliance**, union, association, combination, merger, conjunction, bloc, confederation

coarse ADJECTIVE 1 = **rough**, crude, unfinished, homespun, impure, unrefined, unprocessed, unpolished ≠ smooth 2 = **vulgar**, rude, indecent, improper, earthy, smutty, ribald, indelicate

coast NOUN = **shore**, border, beach, seaside, coastline, seaboard
▷ VERB = **cruise**, sail, drift, taxi, glide, freewheel

coat NOUN 1 = **fur**, hair, skin, hide, wool, fleece, pelt 2 = **layer**, covering, coating, overlay
▷ VERB = **cover**, spread, plaster, smear

coax VERB = **persuade**, cajole, talk into, wheedle, sweet-talk (*informal*), prevail upon, entice, allure ≠ bully

cobber NOUN (*Austral. & N.Z. old-fashioned, informal*) = **friend**, pal, mate (*informal*), buddy (*informal*), china (*Brit. & S. African informal*), best friend, intimate, comrade, E hoa (*N.Z.*)

cocktail NOUN = **mixture**, combination, compound, blend, mix

cocky or **cockie** NOUN (*Austral. & N.Z. informal*) = **farmer**, smallholder, crofter (*Scot.*), grazier, agriculturalist, rancher

code NOUN 1 = **principles**, rules, manners, custom, convention, ethics, maxim, etiquette, kawa (*N.Z.*), tikanga (*N.Z.*) 2 = **cipher**, cryptograph

coherent ADJECTIVE 1 = **consistent**, reasoned, organized, rational, logical, meaningful, systematic, orderly ≠ inconsistent 2 = **articulate**, lucid, comprehensible, intelligible ≠ unintelligible

coil VERB 1 = **wind**, twist, curl, loop, spiral, twine 2 = **curl**, wind, twist, snake, loop, twine, wreathe

coin NOUN = **money**, change, cash, silver, copper, specie, kembla (*Austral. slang*)
▷ VERB = **invent**, create, make up, forge, originate, fabricate

coincide VERB 1 = **occur simultaneously**, coexist, synchronize, be concurrent 2 = **agree**, match, accord, square, correspond, tally, concur, harmonize ≠ disagree

coincidence NOUN = **chance**, accident, luck, fluke, stroke of luck, happy accident

cold ADJECTIVE 1 = **chilly**, freezing, bleak, arctic, icy, frosty, wintry, frigid ≠ hot 2 = **distant**, reserved, indifferent, aloof, frigid, undemonstrative, standoffish ≠ emotional 3 = **unfriendly**, indifferent, frigid ≠ friendly
▷ NOUN = **coldness**, chill, frigidity, frostiness, iciness

collaborate VERB 1 = **work together**, team up, join forces, cooperate, play ball (*informal*), participate 2 = **conspire**, cooperate, collude, fraternize

collaboration NOUN
1 = **teamwork**, partnership, cooperation, association, alliance 2 = **conspiring**, cooperation, collusion, fraternization

collaborator NOUN 1 = **co-worker**, partner, colleague, associate, team-mate, confederate 2 = **traitor**, turncoat, quisling, fraternizer

collapse VERB 1 = **fall down**,

fall, give way, subside, cave in, crumple, fall apart at the seams 2 = **fail**, fold, founder, break down, fall through, come to nothing, go belly-up (*informal*)
▷ NOUN 1 = **falling down**, ruin, falling apart, cave-in, disintegration, subsidence 2 = **failure**, slump, breakdown, flop, downfall 3 = **faint**, breakdown, blackout, prostration

collar VERB (*informal*) = **seize**, catch, arrest, grab, capture, nail (*informal*), nab (*informal*), apprehend

colleague NOUN = **fellow worker**, partner, ally, associate, assistant, team-mate, comrade, helper

collect VERB 1 = **gather**, save, assemble, heap, accumulate, amass, stockpile, hoard ≠ scatter 2 = **assemble**, meet, rally, cluster, come together, convene, converge, congregate ≠ disperse

collected ADJECTIVE = **calm**, cool, composed, poised, serene, unperturbed, unruffled, self-possessed, chilled (*informal*) ≠ nervous

collection NOUN
1 = **accumulation**, set, store, mass, pile, heap, stockpile, hoard 2 = **compilation**, accumulation, anthology 3 = **group**, company, crowd, assembly, cluster, assortment 4 = **gathering** 5 = **contribution**, donation, alms 6 = **offering**, offertory

collective ADJECTIVE 1 = **joint**, united, shared, combined,

corporate, unified ≠ individual
2 = combined, aggregate, composite, cumulative ≠ separate

collide VERB **1 = crash**, clash, meet head-on, come into collision **2 = conflict**, clash, be incompatible, be at variance

collision NOUN **1 = crash**, impact, accident, smash, bump, pile-up (*informal*), prang (*informal*) **2 = conflict**, opposition, clash, encounter, disagreement, incompatibility

colony NOUN **= settlement**, territory, province, possession, dependency, outpost, dominion, satellite state

colour or (*U.S.*) **color** NOUN **1 = hue**, tone, shade, tint, colourway **2 = paint**, stain, dye, tint, pigment, colorant
▷ VERB **= blush**, flush, redden
▷ *see* **shades from black to white, shades of blue, shades of brown, shades of green, shades of orange, shades of purple, shades of red, shades of yellow**

colourful ADJECTIVE **1 = bright**, brilliant, psychedelic, variegated, multicoloured ≠ drab **2 = interesting**, rich, graphic, lively, distinctive, vivid, picturesque ≠ boring

column NOUN **1 = pillar**, support, post, shaft, upright, obelisk **2 = line**, row, file, rank, procession, cavalcade

coma NOUN **= unconsciousness**, trance, oblivion, stupor

comb VERB **1 = untangle**, arrange, groom, dress **2 = search**, hunt through, rake, sift, scour, rummage, ransack, forage, fossick (*Austral. & N.Z.*)

combat NOUN **= fight**, war, action, battle, conflict, engagement, warfare, skirmish ≠ peace
▷ VERB **= fight**, oppose, resist, defy, withstand, do battle with ≠ support

combination NOUN **1 = mixture**, mix, blend, composite, amalgamation, coalescence **2 = association**, union, alliance, coalition, federation, consortium, syndicate, confederation

combine VERB **1 = amalgamate**, mix, blend, integrate, merge ≠ separate **2 = join together**, link, connect, integrate, merge, amalgamate **3 = unite**, associate, team up, get together, collaborate, join forces, join together, pool resources ≠ split up

come VERB **1 = approach**, near, advance, move towards, draw near **2 = arrive**, turn up (*informal*), show up (*informal*) **3 = reach**, extend **4 = happen**, fall, occur, take place, come about, come to pass **5 = be available**, be made, be offered, be produced, be on offer **6 = seem**, look, seem to be, appear to be, give the impression of being ▷ PHRASES: **come across someone = meet**, encounter, run into, bump into (*informal*); **come across something = find**, discover, notice, unearth, stumble upon, chance upon **VERB** = **be obtained**, be from, issue, emerge, flow, arise, originate, emanate

comeback NOUN **1** (*informal*) = **return**, revival, rebound, resurgence, rally, recovery, triumph **2** = **response**, reply, retort, retaliation, riposte, rejoinder

comedian NOUN = **comic**, wit, clown, funny man, humorist, wag, joker, jester, dag (*N.Z. informal*)

comedy NOUN **1** = **light entertainment**, soap opera (*slang*), soapie *or* soapy (*Austral.*) ≠ tragedy **2** = **humour**, fun, joking, farce, jesting, hilarity ≠ seriousness

comfort NOUN **1** = **ease**, luxury, wellbeing, opulence **2** = **consolation**, succour, help, support, relief, compensation ≠ annoyance
  ▷ **VERB** = **console**, reassure, soothe, hearten, commiserate with ≠ distress

comfortable ADJECTIVE **1** = **pleasant**, homely, relaxing, cosy, agreeable, restful ≠ unpleasant **2** = **at ease**, happy, at home, contented, relaxed, serene ≠ uncomfortable **3** (*informal*) = **well-off**, prosperous, affluent, well-to-do, comfortably-off, in clover (*informal*)

comforting ADJECTIVE = **consoling**, encouraging, cheering, reassuring, soothing, heart-warming ≠ upsetting

comic ADJECTIVE = **funny**, amusing, witty, humorous, farcical, comical, droll, jocular ≠ sad
  ▷ NOUN = **comedian**, funny man, humorist, wit, clown, wag, jester, dag (*N.Z. informal*), buffoon

coming ADJECTIVE = **approaching**, near, forthcoming, imminent, in store, impending, at hand, nigh
  ▷ NOUN = **arrival**, approach, advent

command VERB **1** = **order**, tell, charge, demand, require, direct, bid, compel ≠ beg **2** = **have authority over**, lead, head, control, rule, manage, handle, dominate ≠ be subordinate to
  ▷ NOUN **1** = **order**, demand, instruction, requirement, decree, directive, ultimatum, commandment **2** = **domination**, control, rule, mastery, power, government **3** = **management**, power, control, charge, authority, supervision

commander NOUN = **leader**, chief, officer, boss, head, captain, bass (*S. African*), ruler, sherang (*Austral. & N.Z.*)

commanding ADJECTIVE = **dominant**, controlling, dominating, superior, decisive, advantageous

commemorate VERB = **celebrate**, remember, honour, recognize, salute, pay tribute to, immortalize ≠ ignore

commence VERB **1** = **embark on**, start, open, begin, initiate,

originate, instigate, enter upon
≠ stop 2 = **start**, open, begin, go
ahead ≠ end

commend VERB 1 = **praise**,
acclaim, applaud, compliment,
extol, approve, speak highly
of ≠ criticize 2 = **recommend**,
suggest, approve, advocate,
endorse

comment VERB 1 = **remark**, say,
note, mention, point out, observe,
utter 2 *usually with* **on** = **remark
on**, explain, talk about, discuss,
speak about, say something
about, allude to, elucidate
▷ NOUN 1 = **remark**, statement,
observation 2 = **note**,
explanation, illustration,
commentary, exposition,
annotation, elucidation

commentary NOUN
1 = **narration**, report, review,
explanation, description, voice-
over 2 = **analysis**, notes, review,
critique, treatise

commentator NOUN
1 = **reporter**, special
correspondent, sportscaster
2 = **critic**, interpreter, annotator

commercial ADJECTIVE
1 = **mercantile**, trading
2 = **materialistic**, mercenary,
profit-making

commission VERB = **appoint**,
order, contract, select, engage,
delegate, nominate, authorize
▷ NOUN 1 = **duty**, task, mission,
mandate, errand 2 = **fee**, cut,
percentage, royalties, rake-off
(*slang*) 3 = **committee**, board,

representatives, commissioners,
delegation, deputation

commit VERB 1 = **do**, perform,
carry out, execute, enact,
perpetrate 2 = **put in custody**,
confine, imprison ≠ release

commitment NOUN
1 = **dedication**, loyalty,
devotion ≠ indecisiveness
2 = **responsibility**, tie, duty,
obligation, liability, engagement

common ADJECTIVE 1 = **usual**,
standard, regular, ordinary,
familiar, conventional, routine,
frequent ≠ rare 2 = **popular**,
general, accepted, standard,
routine, widespread, universal,
prevailing 3 = **shared**, collective
4 = **ordinary**, average, typical,
dinki-di (*Austral. informal*)
≠ important 5 = **vulgar**, inferior,
coarse, plebeian ≠ refined
6 = **collective**, public, community,
social, communal ≠ personal

commonplace
ADJECTIVE = **everyday**, common,
ordinary, widespread, mundane,
banal, run-of-the-mill, humdrum
≠ rare
▷ NOUN = **cliché**, platitude,
banality, truism

common sense NOUN = **good
sense**, sound judgment, level-
headedness, prudence, gumption
(*Brit. informal*), horse sense, native
intelligence, wit

communal ADJECTIVE = **public**,
shared, general, joint, collective
≠ private

commune NOUN = **community**,

collective, cooperative, kibbutz

communicate VERB 1 = **contact**, talk, speak, make contact, get in contact, e-mail, text 2 = **make known**, declare, disclose, pass on, proclaim, transmit, convey, impart ≠ keep secret 3 = **pass on**, transfer, spread, transmit

communication NOUN
1 = **contact**, conversation, correspondence, link, relations
2 = **passing on**, circulation, transmission, disclosure, imparting, dissemination, conveyance 3 = **message**, news, report, word, information, statement, announcement, disclosure, e-mail, text

communism NOUN *usually cap.* = **socialism**, Marxism, collectivism, Bolshevism, state socialism

communist NOUN *often cap.* = **socialist**, Red (*informal*), Marxist, Bolshevik, collectivist

community NOUN = **society**, people, public, residents, commonwealth, general public, populace, state

commuter NOUN = **daily traveller**, passenger, suburbanite

compact¹ ADJECTIVE 1 = **closely packed**, solid, thick, dense, compressed, condensed, pressed together ≠ loose 2 = **concise**, brief, to the point, succinct, terse ≠ lengthy
▷ VERB = **pack closely**, stuff, cram, compress, condense, tamp ≠ loosen

compact² NOUN = **agreement**, deal, understanding, contract, bond, arrangement, treaty, bargain

companion NOUN 1 = **friend**, partner, ally, colleague, associate, mate (*informal*), comrade, accomplice, cobber (*Austral. & N.Z. old-fashioned, informal*)
2 = **assistant**, aide, escort, attendant

company NOUN 1 = **business**, firm, association, corporation, partnership, establishment, syndicate, house 2 = **group**, set, community, band, crowd, collection, gathering, assembly
3 = **troop**, unit, squad, team
4 = **companionship**, society, presence, fellowship 5 = **guests**, party, visitors, callers

comparable ADJECTIVE 1 = **equal**, equivalent, on a par, tantamount, a match, proportionate, commensurate, as good ≠ unequal 2 = **similar**, related, alike, corresponding, akin, analogous, of a piece, cognate

comparative ADJECTIVE = **relative**, qualified, by comparison

compare VERB = **contrast**, balance, weigh, set against, juxtapose ▷ PHRASES: **compare to something** = **liken to**, parallel, identify with, equate to, correlate to, mention in the same breath as; **compare with something** = **be as good as**, match, approach, equal, compete with, be on a

par with, be the equal of, hold a
candle to

comparison NOUN 1 = **contrast**,
distinction, differentiation,
juxtaposition 2 = **similarity**,
analogy, resemblance,
correlation, likeness,
comparability

compartment NOUN
1 = **section**, carriage, berth
2 = **bay**, booth, locker, niche,
cubicle, alcove, pigeonhole,
cubbyhole

compass NOUN = **range**, field,
area, reach, scope, limit, extent,
boundary

compassion NOUN = **sympathy**,
understanding, pity, humanity,
mercy, sorrow, kindness,
tenderness, aroha (*N.Z.*)
≠ indifference

compassionate ADJECTIVE
= **sympathetic**, understanding,
pitying, humanitarian, charitable,
humane, benevolent, merciful
≠ uncaring

compatible ADJECTIVE
1 = **consistent**, in keeping,
congruous ≠ inappropriate
2 = **like-minded**, harmonious, in
harmony ≠ incompatible

compel VERB = **force**, make,
railroad (*informal*), oblige,
constrain, coerce, impel, dragoon

compelling ADJECTIVE
1 = **convincing**, telling,
powerful, forceful, conclusive,
weighty, cogent, irrefutable
2 = **fascinating**, gripping,
irresistible, enchanting,

enthralling, hypnotic,
spellbinding, mesmeric ≠ boring

compensate VERB
1 = **recompense**, repay, refund,
reimburse, remunerate, make
good 2 = **make amends for**,
make up for, atone for, pay for,
do penance for, cancel out, make
reparation for 3 = **balance**, cancel
(out), offset, make up for, redress,
counteract, counterbalance

compensation NOUN
1 = **reparation**, damages,
recompense, remuneration,
restitution, reimbursement
2 = **recompense**, amends,
reparation, restitution,
atonement

compete VERB 1 = **contend**,
fight, vie, challenge, struggle,
contest, strive 2 = **take part**,
participate, be in the running,
be a competitor, be a contestant,
play

competence NOUN 1 = **ability**,
skill, talent, capacity, expertise,
proficiency, capability
≠ incompetence 2 = **fitness**,
suitability, adequacy,
appropriateness ≠ inadequacy

competent ADJECTIVE 1 = **able**,
skilled, capable, proficient
≠ incompetent 2 = **fit**, qualified,
suitable, adequate ≠ unqualified

competition NOUN 1 = **rivalry**,
opposition, struggle, strife
2 = **opposition**, field, rivals,
challengers 3 = **contest**, event,
championship, tournament,
head-to-head

competitive ADJECTIVE 1 = **cut-throat**, aggressive, fierce, ruthless, relentless, antagonistic, dog-eat-dog 2 = **ambitious**, pushing, opposing, aggressive, vying, contentious, combative

competitor NOUN 1 = **rival**, adversary, antagonist 2 = **contestant**, participant, contender, challenger, entrant, player, opponent

compilation NOUN = **collection**, treasury, accumulation, anthology, assortment, assemblage

compile VERB = **put together**, collect, gather, organize, accumulate, marshal, garner, amass

complacency NOUN = **smugness**, satisfaction, contentment, self-congratulation, self-satisfaction

complacent ADJECTIVE = **smug**, self-satisfied, pleased with yourself, resting on your laurels, contented, satisfied, serene, unconcerned ≠ insecure

complain VERB = **find fault**, moan, grumble, whinge (informal), carp, groan, lament, whine, nit-pick (informal)

complaint NOUN 1 = **protest**, objection, grievance, charge 2 = **grumble**, criticism, moan, lament, grievance, grouse, gripe (informal) 3 = **disorder**, problem, disease, upset, illness, sickness, ailment, affliction

complement VERB = **enhance**, complete, improve, boost, crown, add to, set off, heighten ▷ NOUN 1 = **accompaniment**, companion, accessory, completion, finishing touch, rounding-off, adjunct, supplement 2 = **total**, capacity, quota, aggregate, contingent, entirety

● **WORD POWER**
● This is sometimes confused
● with *compliment* but the two
● words have very different
● meanings. As the synonyms
● show, the verb form of
● *complement* means 'to enhance'
● and 'to complete' something. In
● contrast, common synonyms of
● *compliment* as a verb are *praise*,
● *commend*, and *flatter*.

complementary ADJECTIVE = **matching**, companion, corresponding, compatible, reciprocal, interrelating, interdependent, harmonizing ≠ incompatible

complete ADJECTIVE 1 = **total**, perfect, absolute, utter, outright, thorough, consummate, out-and-out 2 = **whole**, full, entire ≠ partial 3 = **entire**, full, whole, intact, unbroken, faultless ≠ incomplete 4 = **unabridged**, full, entire 5 = **finished**, done, ended, achieved, concluded, fulfilled, accomplished ≠ unfinished ▷ VERB 1 = **perfect**, finish off, round off, crown ≠ spoil 2 = **finish**, conclude, end, close,

settle, wrap up (*informal*), finalize
≠ start

completely ADVERB = **totally**,
entirely, wholly, utterly, perfectly,
fully, absolutely, altogether

completion NOUN = **finishing**,
end, close, conclusion, fulfilment,
culmination, fruition

complex ADJECTIVE
1 = **compound**, multiple,
composite, manifold,
heterogeneous, multifarious
2 = **complicated**, difficult,
involved, elaborate, tangled,
intricate, tortuous, convoluted
≠ simple
▷ NOUN 1 = **structure**, system,
scheme, network, organization,
aggregate, composite 2 (*informal*)
= **obsession**, preoccupation,
phobia, fixation, fixed idea, idée
fixe (*French*)
● **WORD POWER**
● Although *complex* and
● *complicated* are close in
● meaning, care should be taken
● when using one as a synonym
● of the other. *Complex* should
● be used to say that something
● consists of several parts rather
● than that it is difficult to
● understand, analyse, or deal
● with, which is what *complicated*
● inherently means. In the
● following real example a clear
● distinction is made between
● the two words: *the British*
● *benefits system is phenomenally*
● *complex and is administered by a*
● *complicated range of agencies.*

complexion NOUN 1 = **skin**,
colour, colouring, hue, skin
tone, pigmentation 2 = **nature**,
character, make-up

complexity NOUN
= **complication**, involvement,
intricacy, entanglement

complicate VERB = **make
difficult**, confuse, muddle,
entangle, involve ≠ simplify

complicated ADJECTIVE
1 = **involved**, difficult, puzzling,
troublesome, problematic,
perplexing ≠ simple
2 = **complex**, involved, elaborate,
intricate ≠ understandable 3
(*of an attitude*) = **convoluted**,
labyrinthine

complication NOUN
1 = **problem**, difficulty, obstacle,
drawback, snag, uphill (*S. African*)
2 = **complexity**, web, confusion,
intricacy, entanglement

compliment NOUN = **praise**,
honour, tribute, bouquet, flattery,
eulogy ≠ criticism
▷ PLURAL NOUN 1 = **greetings**,
regards, respects, good
wishes, salutation ≠ insult
2 = **congratulations**, praise,
commendation
▷ VERB = **praise**, flatter, salute,
congratulate, pay tribute to,
commend, extol, wax lyrical about
≠ criticize
● **WORD POWER**
● *Compliment* is sometimes
● confused with *complement*.

complimentary ADJECTIVE
1 = **flattering**, approving,

appreciative, congratulatory, commendatory ≠ critical
2 = **free**, donated, courtesy, honorary, on the house, gratuitous, gratis

comply VERB = **obey**, follow, observe, submit to, conform to, adhere to, abide by, acquiesce with ≠ defy

component NOUN = **part**, piece, unit, item, element, ingredient, constituent
▷ ADJECTIVE = **constituent**, inherent, intrinsic

compose VERB 1 = **put together**, make up, constitute, comprise, make, build, form, fashion ≠ destroy 2 = **create**, write, produce, invent, devise, contrive 3 = **arrange**, make up, construct, put together, order, organize
▷ PHRASE: compose yourself = **calm yourself**, control yourself, collect yourself, pull yourself together

composed ADJECTIVE = **calm**, cool, collected, relaxed, poised, at ease, serene, sedate, chilled (*informal*), grounded ≠ agitated

composition NOUN 1 = **design**, structure, make-up, organization, arrangement, formation, layout, configuration 2 = **creation**, work, piece, production, opus, masterpiece 3 = **essay**, exercise, treatise, literary work 4 = **production**, creation, making, fashioning, formation, putting together, compilation, formulation

compound NOUN = **combination**, mixture, blend, composite, fusion, synthesis, alloy, medley ≠ element
▷ ADJECTIVE = **complex**, multiple, composite, intricate ≠ simple
▷ VERB 1 = **intensify**, add to, complicate, worsen, heighten, exacerbate, aggravate, magnify ≠ lessen 2 = **combine**, unite, mix, blend, synthesize, amalgamate, intermingle ≠ divide

comprehend VERB = **understand**, see, take in, perceive, grasp, conceive, make out, fathom ≠ misunderstand

comprehension NOUN = **understanding**, grasp, conception, realization, intelligence, perception, discernment ≠ incomprehension

comprehensive ADJECTIVE = **broad**, full, complete, blanket, thorough, inclusive, exhaustive, all-inclusive ≠ limited

compress VERB 1 = **squeeze**, crush, squash, press 2 = **condense**, contract, concentrate, shorten, abbreviate

comprise VERB 1 = **be composed of**, include, contain, consist of, take in, embrace, encompass 2 = **make up**, form, constitute, compose
● **WORD POWER**
● The use of *of* after *comprise*
● should be avoided: *the library*
● *comprises* (not *comprises*
● *of*) 6,500,000 books and
● manuscripts. *Consist*, however,

- should be followed by *of* when
- used in this way: *Her crew*
- *consisted of children from Devon*
- *and Cornwall.*

compromise NOUN = **give-and-take**, agreement, settlement, accommodation, concession, adjustment, trade-off ≠ disagreement
▷ VERB 1 = **meet halfway**, concede, make concessions, give and take, strike a balance, strike a happy medium, go fifty-fifty (*informal*) ≠ disagree
2 = **undermine**, expose, embarrass, weaken, prejudice, discredit, jeopardize, dishonour ≠ support

compulsive ADJECTIVE
1 = **obsessive**, confirmed, chronic, persistent, addictive, uncontrollable, incurable, inveterate 2 = **fascinating**, gripping, absorbing, compelling, captivating, enthralling, hypnotic, engrossing
3 = **irresistible**, overwhelming, compelling, urgent, neurotic, uncontrollable, driving

compulsory ADJECTIVE
= **obligatory**, forced, required, binding, mandatory, imperative, requisite, de rigueur (*French*) ≠ voluntary

compute VERB = **calculate**, total, count, reckon, figure out, add up, tally, enumerate

comrade NOUN = **companion**, friend, partner, ally, colleague, associate, fellow, co-worker, cobber (*Austral. & N.Z. old-fashioned, informal*)

con (*informal*) VERB = **swindle**, trick, cheat, rip off (*slang*), deceive, defraud, dupe, hoodwink, scam (*slang*)
▷ NOUN = **swindle**, trick, fraud, deception, scam (*slang*), sting (*informal*), fastie (*Austral. slang*)

conceal VERB 1 = **hide**, bury, cover, screen, disguise, obscure, camouflage ≠ reveal 2 = **keep secret**, hide, disguise, mask, suppress, veil ≠ show

concede VERB 1 = **admit**, allow, accept, acknowledge, own, grant, confess ≠ deny 2 = **give up**, yield, hand over, surrender, relinquish, cede ≠ conquer

conceive VERB 1 = **imagine**, envisage, comprehend, visualize, think, believe, suppose, fancy
2 = **think up**, create, design, devise, formulate, contrive
3 = **become pregnant**, get pregnant, become impregnated

concentrate VERB 1 = **focus your attention**, focus, pay attention, be engrossed, apply yourself ≠ pay no attention
2 = **focus**, centre, converge, bring to bear 3 = **gather**, collect, cluster, accumulate, congregate ≠ scatter

concentrated ADJECTIVE
1 = **condensed**, rich, undiluted, reduced, evaporated, thickened, boiled down 2 = **intense**, hard, deep, intensive, all-out (*informal*)

concentration NOUN

1 = **attention**, application, absorption, single-mindedness, intentness ≠ inattention 2 = **focusing**, centring, consolidation, convergence, bringing to bear, intensification, centralization 3 = **convergence**, collection, mass, cluster, accumulation, aggregation ≠ scattering

concept NOUN = **idea**, view, image, theory, notion, conception, hypothesis, abstraction

conception NOUN 1 = **idea**, plan, design, image, concept, notion 2 = **impregnation**, insemination, fertilization, germination

concern NOUN 1 = **anxiety**, fear, worry, distress, unease, apprehension, misgiving, disquiet 2 = **worry**, care, anxiety 3 = **affair**, issue, matter, consideration 4 = **care**, interest, attentiveness 5 = **business**, job, affair, responsibility, task 6 = **company**, business, firm, organization, corporation, enterprise, establishment 7 = **importance**, interest, bearing, relevance
▷ VERB 1 = **worry**, trouble, bother, disturb, distress, disquiet, perturb, make anxious 2 = **be about**, cover, deal with, go into, relate to, have to do with 3 = **be relevant to**, involve, affect, regard, apply to, bear on, have something to do with, pertain to

concerned ADJECTIVE

1 = **involved**, interested, active, mixed up, implicated, privy to 2 = **worried**, troubled, upset, bothered, disturbed, anxious, distressed, uneasy ≠ indifferent

concerning PREPOSITION = **regarding**, about, re, touching, respecting, relating to, on the subject of, with reference to

concession NOUN

1 = **compromise**, agreement, settlement, accommodation, adjustment, trade-off, give-and-take 2 = **privilege**, right, permit, licence, entitlement, indulgence, prerogative 3 = **reduction**, saving, grant, discount, allowance 4 = **surrender**, yielding, conceding, renunciation, relinquishment

conclude VERB 1 = **decide**, judge, assume, gather, work out, infer, deduce, surmise 2 = **come to an end**, end, close, finish, wind up ≠ begin 3 = **bring to an end**, end, close, finish, complete, wind up, terminate, round off ≠ begin 4 = **accomplish**, effect, bring about, carry out, pull off

conclusion NOUN 1 = **decision**, opinion, conviction, verdict, judgment, deduction, inference 2 = **end**, ending, close, finish, completion, finale, termination, bitter end 3 = **outcome**, result, upshot, consequence, culmination, end result

concrete ADJECTIVE 1 = **specific**, precise, explicit, definite, clear-cut, unequivocal ≠ vague

2 = **real**, material, actual, substantial, sensible, tangible, factual ≠ abstract

condemn VERB **1** = **denounce**, damn, criticize, disapprove, censure, reprove, upbraid, blame ≠ approve **2** = **sentence**, convict, damn, doom, pass sentence on ≠ acquit

condemnation NOUN = **denunciation**, blame, censure, disapproval, reproach, stricture, reproof

condition NOUN = **state**, order, shape, nick (*Brit. informal*), trim **2** = **situation**, state, position, status, circumstances **3** = **requirement**, terms, rider, restriction, qualification, limitation, prerequisite, proviso **4** = **health**, shape, fitness, trim, form, kilter, state of health, fettle **5** = **ailment**, problem, complaint, weakness, malady, infirmity ▷ PLURAL NOUN = **circumstances**, situation, environment, surroundings, way of life, milieu ▷ VERB = **train**, teach, adapt, accustom

conditional ADJECTIVE = **dependent**, limited, qualified, contingent, provisional, with reservations ≠ unconditional

condone VERB = **overlook**, excuse, forgive, pardon, turn a blind eye to, look the other way, make allowance for, let pass ≠ condemn

conduct VERB **1** = **carry out**, run, control, manage, direct, handle, organize, administer **2** = **accompany**, lead, escort, guide, steer, convey, usher ▷ NOUN **1** = **management**, running, control, handling, administration, direction, organization, guidance **2** = **behaviour**, ways, bearing, attitude, manners, demeanour, deportment ▷ PHRASE: **conduct yourself** = **behave yourself**, act, carry yourself, acquit yourself, deport yourself, comport yourself

confer VERB **1** = **discuss**, talk, consult, deliberate, discourse, converse **2** = **grant**, give, present, accord, award, hand out, bestow

conference NOUN = **meeting**, congress, discussion, convention, forum, consultation, seminar, symposium, hui (*N.Z.*)

confess VERB **1** = **admit**, acknowledge, disclose, confide, own up, come clean (*informal*), divulge ≠ cover up **2** = **declare**, allow, reveal, confirm, concede, assert, affirm, profess

confession NOUN = **admission**, revelation, disclosure, acknowledgment, exposure, unbosoming

confidant *or* **confidante** NOUN = **close friend**, familiar, intimate, crony, alter ego, bosom friend

confide VERB = **tell**, admit, reveal, confess, whisper, disclose, impart, divulge

confidence NOUN **1** = **trust**, belief, faith, dependence, reliance, credence ≠ distrust

2 = **self-assurance**, courage, assurance, aplomb, boldness, self-possession, nerve ≠ shyness 3 = **secret** ▷ PHRASE: **in confidence** = **in secrecy**, privately, confidentially, between you and me (and the gatepost), (just) between ourselves

confident ADJECTIVE 1 = **certain**, sure, convinced, positive, secure, satisfied, counting on ≠ unsure 2 = **self-assured**, positive, assured, bold, self-confident, self-reliant, sure of yourself ≠ insecure

confidential ADJECTIVE 1 = **secret**, private, intimate, classified, privy, off the record, hush-hush (*informal*) 2 = **secretive**, low, soft, hushed

confine VERB 1 = **imprison**, enclose, shut up, intern, incarcerate, hem in, keep, cage 2 = **restrict**, limit ▷ PLURAL NOUN = **limits**, bounds, boundaries, compass, precincts, circumference, edge

confirm VERB 1 = **prove**, support, establish, back up, verify, validate, bear out, substantiate 2 = **ratify**, establish, sanction, endorse, authorize 3 = **strengthen**, establish, fix, secure, reinforce, fortify

confirmation NOUN 1 = **proof**, evidence, testimony, verification, ratification, validation, corroboration, authentication ≠ repudiation 2 = **affirmation**, approval, acceptance, endorsement, ratification, assent, agreement ≠ disapproval

confirmed ADJECTIVE = **long-established**, seasoned, chronic, hardened, habitual, ingrained, inveterate, dyed-in-the-wool

confiscate VERB = **seize**, appropriate, impound, commandeer, sequester ≠ give back

conflict NOUN 1 = **dispute**, difference, opposition, hostility, disagreement, friction, strife, fighting ≠ agreement 2 = **struggle**, battle, clash, strife 3 = **battle**, war, fight, clash, contest, encounter, combat, strife, boilover (*Austral.*) ≠ peace ▷ VERB = **be incompatible**, clash, differ, disagree, collide, be at variance ≠ agree

conflicting ADJECTIVE = **incompatible**, opposing, clashing, contrary, contradictory, inconsistent, paradoxical, discordant ≠ agreeing

conform VERB 1 = **fit in**, follow, adjust, adapt, comply, obey, fall in, toe the line 2 *with* **with** = **fulfil**, meet, match, suit, satisfy, agree with, obey, abide by

confound VERB = **bewilder**, baffle, confuse, astound, perplex, mystify, flummox, dumbfound

confront VERB 1 = **tackle**, deal with, cope with, meet head-on 2 = **trouble**, face, perturb, bedevil 3 = **challenge**, face, oppose, tackle, encounter, defy, stand up to, accost ≠ evade

confrontation NOUN = **conflict**, fight, contest, set-to (*informal*), encounter, showdown (*informal*), head-to-head, boilover (*Austral.*)

confuse VERB 1 = **mix up with**, take for, muddle with 2 = **bewilder**, puzzle, baffle, perplex, mystify, fluster, faze, flummox 3 = **obscure**, cloud, make more difficult

confused ADJECTIVE 1 = **bewildered**, puzzled, baffled, at sea, muddled, perplexed, taken aback, disorientated ≠ enlightened 2 = **disorderly**, disordered, chaotic, mixed up, jumbled, untidy, in disarray, topsy-turvy ≠ tidy

confusing ADJECTIVE = **bewildering**, puzzling, misleading, unclear, baffling, contradictory, perplexing ≠ clear

confusion NOUN 1 = **bewilderment**, doubt, uncertainty ≠ enlightenment 2 = **disorder**, chaos, turmoil, upheaval, muddle, shambles, commotion ≠ order

congestion NOUN = **overcrowding**, crowding, jam, clogging, bottleneck

congratulate VERB = **compliment**, pat on the back, wish joy to

congratulations PLURAL NOUN = **good wishes**, greetings, compliments, best wishes, felicitations
 ▷ INTERJECTION = **good wishes**, greetings, compliments, best wishes, felicitations

congregation NOUN = **parishioners**, brethren, crowd, assembly, flock, fellowship, multitude, throng, flock

congress NOUN 1 = **meeting**, council, conference, assembly, convention, conclave, hui (*N.Z.*), runanga (*N.Z.*) 2 = **legislature**, council, parliament, House of Representatives (*N.Z.*)

conjure VERB = **produce**, generate, bring about, give rise to, make, create, effect, produce as if by magic ▷ PHRASE: **conjure something up** = **bring to mind**, recall, evoke, recreate, recollect, produce as if by magic

connect VERB 1 = **link**, join, couple, attach, fasten, affix, unite ≠ separate 2 = **associate**, join, link, identify, lump together

connected ADJECTIVE = **linked**, united, joined, coupled, related, allied, associated, combined

connection NOUN 1 = **association**, relationship, link, bond, relevance, tie-in 2 = **communication**, alliance, attachment, liaison, affinity, union 3 = **link**, coupling, junction, fastening, tie 4 = **contact**, friend, ally, associate, acquaintance

conquer VERB 1 = **seize**, obtain, acquire, occupy, overrun, annex, win 2 = **defeat**, overcome, overthrow, beat, master, crush, overpower, quell ≠ lose to 3 = **overcome**, beat, defeat, master, overpower

conquest NOUN 1 = **takeover**, coup, invasion, occupation, annexation, subjugation 2 = **defeat**, victory, triumph, overthrow, rout, mastery

conscience NOUN 1 = **principles**, scruples, moral sense, sense of right and wrong, still small voice 2 = **guilt**, shame, regret, remorse, contrition, self-reproach

conscious ADJECTIVE 1 *often with* **of** = **aware of**, alert to, responsive to, sensible of ≠ unaware 2 = **deliberate**, knowing, studied, calculated, self-conscious, intentional, wilful, premeditated ≠ unintentional 3 = **awake**, wide-awake, sentient, alive ≠ asleep

consciousness NOUN = **awareness**, understanding, knowledge, recognition, sensibility, realization, apprehension

consecutive ADJECTIVE = **successive**, running, succeeding, in turn, uninterrupted, sequential, in sequence

consensus NOUN = **agreement**, general agreement, unanimity, common consent, unity, harmony, assent, concord, kotahitanga (*N.Z.*)

● **WORD POWER**
● The original meaning of the
● word *consensus* is *a collective*
● *opinion*. Because the concept of
● 'opinion' is contained within
● this word, a few people argue
● that the phrase *a consensus*
● *of opinion* is incorrect and
● should be avoided. However,
● this common use of the word
● is unlikely to jar with the
● majority of speakers.

consent NOUN = **agreement**, sanction, approval, go-ahead (*informal*), permission, compliance, assent, acquiescence ≠ refusal
▷ VERB = **agree**, approve, permit, concur, assent, acquiesce ≠ refuse

consequence NOUN 1 = **result**, effect, outcome, repercussion, issue, sequel, end result, upshot 2 = **importance**, concern, moment, value, account, weight, import, significance

consequently ADVERB = **as a result**, thus, therefore, hence, subsequently, accordingly, for that reason, thence

conservation NOUN 1 = **preservation**, saving, protection, maintenance, safeguarding, upkeep, guardianship, safekeeping 2 = **economy**, saving, thrift, husbandry

conservative
ADJECTIVE = **traditional**, conventional, cautious, sober, reactionary, die-hard, hidebound ≠ radical
▷ NOUN = **traditionalist**, reactionary, die-hard, stick-in-the-mud (*informal*) ≠ radical

Conservative ADJECTIVE = **Tory**,

Republican (U.S.), right-wing

▷ NOUN = **Tory**, Republican (U.S.), right-winger

conserve VERB 1 = **save**, husband, take care of, hoard, store up, use sparingly ≠ waste 2 = **protect**, keep, save, preserve

consider VERB 1 = **think**, see, believe, rate, judge, suppose, deem, view as 2 = **think about**, reflect on, weigh, contemplate, deliberate, ponder, meditate, ruminate 3 = **bear in mind**, remember, respect, think about, take into account, reckon with, take into consideration, make allowance for

considerable ADJECTIVE = **large**, goodly, great, marked, substantial, noticeable, plentiful, appreciable ≠ small

considerably ADVERB = **greatly**, very much, significantly, remarkably, substantially, markedly, noticeably, appreciably

consideration NOUN 1 = **thought**, review, analysis, examination, reflection, scrutiny, deliberation 2 = **thoughtfulness**, concern, respect, kindness, tact, considerateness 3 = **factor**, point, issue, concern, element, aspect 4 = **payment**, fee, reward, remuneration, recompense, tip

considering PREPOSITION = **taking into account**, in the light of, bearing in mind, in view of, keeping in mind, taking into consideration

consist VERB ▷ PHRASES: consist **in something** = **lie in**, involve, reside in, be expressed by, subsist in, be found or contained in; **consist of something** = **be made up of**, include, contain, incorporate, amount to, comprise, be composed of

consistency NOUN 1 = **agreement**, regularity, uniformity, constancy, steadiness, steadfastness, evenness 2 = **texture**, density, thickness, firmness, viscosity, compactness

consistent ADJECTIVE 1 = **steady**, even, regular, stable, constant, persistent, dependable, unchanging ≠ erratic 2 = **compatible**, agreeing, in keeping, harmonious, in harmony, consonant, in accord, congruous ≠ incompatible 3 = **coherent**, logical, compatible, harmonious, consonant ≠ contradictory

consolation NOUN = **comfort**, help, support, relief, cheer, encouragement, solace, succour

console VERB = **comfort**, cheer, soothe, support, encourage, calm, succour, express sympathy for ≠ distress

consolidate VERB 1 = **strengthen**, secure, reinforce, fortify, stabilize 2 = **combine**, unite, join, merge, unify, amalgamate, federate

conspicuous ADJECTIVE = **obvious**, clear, patent, evident, noticeable, blatant, salient ≠ inconspicuous

conspiracy NOUN = **plot**, scheme, intrigue, collusion, machination

conspire VERB 1 = **plot**, scheme, intrigue, manoeuvre, contrive, machinate, plan 2 = **work together**, combine, contribute, cooperate, concur, tend

constant ADJECTIVE
1 = **continuous**, sustained, perpetual, interminable, unrelenting, incessant, ceaseless, nonstop ≠ occasional
2 = **unchanging**, even, fixed, permanent, stable, steady, uniform, invariable ≠ changing
3 = **faithful**, true, devoted, loyal, stalwart, staunch, trustworthy, trusty ≠ undependable

constantly ADVERB
= **continuously**, always, all the time, invariably, continually, endlessly, perpetually, incessantly ≠ occasionally

constituent NOUN 1 = **voter**, elector, member of the electorate 2 = **component**, element, ingredient, part, unit, factor
▷ ADJECTIVE = **component**, basic, essential, integral, elemental

constitute VERB 1 = **represent**, be, consist of, embody, exemplify, be equivalent to 2 = **make up**, form, compose, comprise

constitution NOUN 1 = **state of health**, build, body, frame, physique, physical condition
2 = **structure**, form, nature, make-up, composition, character, disposition

constitutional ADJECTIVE

= **legitimate**, official, legal, chartered, statutory, vested

constrain VERB 1 = **restrict**, confine, curb, restrain, constrict, straiten, check 2 = **force**, bind, compel, oblige, necessitate, coerce, impel, pressurize

constraint NOUN 1 = **restriction**, limitation, curb, rein, deterrent, hindrance, check 2 = **force**, pressure, necessity, restraint, compulsion, coercion

construct VERB 1 = **build**, make, form, create, fashion, shape, manufacture, assemble ≠ demolish 2 = **create**, make, form, compose, put together

construction NOUN 1 = **building**, creation, composition 2 (*formal*) = **interpretation**, reading, explanation, rendering, inference

constructive ADJECTIVE
= **helpful**, positive, useful, practical, valuable, productive ≠ unproductive

consult VERB 1 = **ask**, refer to, turn to, take counsel, pick (someone's) brains, question 2 = **confer**, talk, compare notes 3 = **refer to**, check in, look in

consultant NOUN = **specialist**, adviser, counsellor, authority

consultation NOUN
1 = **discussion**, talk, council, conference, dialogue
2 = **meeting**, interview, session, appointment, examination, deliberation, hearing

consume VERB 1 = **eat**, swallow, devour, put away, gobble (up), eat up **2** = **use up**, spend, waste, absorb, exhaust, squander, dissipate, expend **3** = **destroy**, devastate, demolish, ravage, annihilate, lay waste **4** *often passive* = **obsess**, dominate, absorb, preoccupy, eat up, monopolize, engross

consumer NOUN = **buyer**, customer, user, shopper, purchaser

consumption NOUN **1** = **using up**, use, loss, waste, expenditure, exhaustion, depletion, dissipation
2 (*old-fashioned*) = **tuberculosis**, T.B.

contact NOUN
1 = **communication**, link, association, connection, correspondence **2** = **touch**, contiguity **3** = **connection**, colleague, associate, liaison, acquaintance, confederate
▷ VERB = **get** *or* **be in touch with**, call, reach, approach, write to, speak to, communicate with, e-mail, text

contain VERB **1** = **hold**, incorporate, accommodate, enclose, have capacity for
2 = **include**, consist of, embrace, comprise, embody, comprehend
3 = **restrain**, control, hold in, curb, suppress, hold back, stifle, repress

container NOUN = **holder**, vessel, repository, receptacle

contaminate VERB = **pollute**, infect, stain, corrupt, taint, defile, adulterate, befoul ≠ purify

contamination NOUN
= **pollution**, infection, corruption, poisoning, taint, impurity, contagion, defilement

contemplate VERB **1** = **consider**, plan, think of, intend, envisage, foresee **2** = **think about**, consider, ponder, reflect upon, ruminate (upon), muse over, deliberate over
3 = **look at**, examine, inspect, gaze at, eye up, view, study, regard

contemporary ADJECTIVE
1 = **modern**, recent, current, up-to-date, present-day, à la mode, newfangled, present
≠ old-fashioned **2** = **coexisting**, concurrent, contemporaneous
▷ NOUN = **peer**, fellow, equal
● **WORD POWER**
● Since *contemporary* can mean
● either 'of the same period'
● or 'of the present period',
● it is best to avoid it where
● ambiguity might arise, as
● in *a production of Othello in*
● *contemporary dress*. A synonym
● such as *modern* or *present-day*
● would clarify if the sense 'of
● the present period' were being
● used, while a specific term,
● such as *Elizabethan*, would be
● appropriate if the sense 'of the
● same period' were being used.

contempt NOUN = **scorn**, disdain, mockery, derision, disrespect, disregard ≠ respect

contend VERB **1** = **argue**, hold, maintain, allege, assert, affirm
2 = **compete**, fight, struggle, clash, contest, strive, vie, jostle

content¹ NOUN 1 = **subject matter**, material, theme, substance, essence, gist 2 = **amount**, measure, size, load, volume, capacity
▷ PLURAL NOUN = **constituents**, elements, load, ingredients

content² ADJECTIVE = **satisfied**, happy, pleased, contented, comfortable, fulfilled, at ease, gratified
▷ NOUN = **satisfaction**, ease, pleasure, comfort, peace of mind, gratification, contentment
▷ PHRASE: content yourself with something = **satisfy yourself with**, be happy with, be satisfied with, be content with

contented ADJECTIVE = **satisfied**, happy, pleased, content, comfortable, glad, thankful, gratified ≠ discontented

contentious ADJECTIVE = **argumentative**, wrangling, bickering, quarrelsome, querulous, cavilling, disputatious, captious

contest NOUN 1 = **competition**, game, match, trial, tournament 2 = **struggle**, fight, battle, conflict, dispute, controversy, combat
▷ VERB 1 = **compete in**, take part in, fight in, go in for, contend for, vie in 2 = **oppose**, question, challenge, argue, debate, dispute, object to, call in or into question

contestant NOUN = **competitor**, candidate, participant, contender, entrant, player

context NOUN 1 = **circumstances**, conditions, situation, ambience 2 = **frame of reference**, background, framework, relation, connection

contingency NOUN = **possibility**, happening, chance, event, incident, accident, emergency, eventuality

continual ADJECTIVE 1 = **constant**, interminable, incessant, unremitting ≠ erratic 2 = **frequent**, regular, repeated, recurrent ≠ occasional

continually ADVERB 1 = **constantly**, always, all the time, forever, incessantly, nonstop, interminably 2 = **repeatedly**, often, frequently, many times, over and over, persistently

continuation NOUN 1 = **continuing**, lasting, carrying on, keeping up, endurance, perpetuation, prolongation 2 = **addition**, extension, supplement, sequel, resumption, postscript

continue VERB 1 = **keep on**, go on, maintain, sustain, carry on, persist in, persevere, stick at ≠ stop 2 = **go on**, progress, proceed, carry on, keep going, crack on (informal) 3 = **resume**, return to, take up again, proceed, carry on, recommence, pick up where you left off ≠ stop 4 = **remain**, last, stay, survive, carry on, live on, endure, persist ≠ quit

continuing ADJECTIVE = **lasting**, sustained, enduring, ongoing, in progress

continuity NOUN = **cohesion**, flow, connection, sequence, succession, progression

continuous ADJECTIVE = **constant**, extended, prolonged, unbroken, uninterrupted, unceasing ≠ occasional

contract NOUN = **agreement**, commitment, arrangement, settlement, bargain, pact, covenant
▷ VERB 1 = **agree**, negotiate, pledge, bargain, undertake, come to terms, covenant, make a deal ≠ refuse 2 = **constrict**, confine, tighten, shorten, compress, condense, shrivel 3 = **tighten**, narrow, shorten ≠ stretch 4 = **lessen**, reduce, shrink, diminish, decrease, dwindle ≠ increase 5 = **catch**, get, develop, acquire, incur, be infected with, go down with, be afflicted with ≠ avoid

contraction NOUN
1 = **tightening**, narrowing, shortening, constricting, shrinkage 2 = **abbreviation**, reduction, shortening, compression

contradict VERB 1 = **dispute**, deny, challenge, belie, fly in the face of, be at variance with 2 = **negate**, deny, rebut, controvert ≠ confirm

contradiction NOUN 1 = **conflict**, inconsistency, contravention, incongruity 2 = **negation**, opposite, denial

contradictory ADJECTIVE = **inconsistent**, conflicting, opposed, opposite, contrary, incompatible, paradoxical

contrary ADJECTIVE 1 = **opposite**, different, opposed, clashing, counter, reverse, adverse, contradictory ≠ in agreement 2 = **perverse**, difficult, awkward, intractable, obstinate, stroppy (*Brit. slang*), cantankerous, disobliging ≠ cooperative
▷ NOUN = **opposite**, reverse, converse, antithesis

contrast NOUN = **difference**, opposition, comparison, distinction, foil, disparity, divergence, dissimilarity
▷ VERB 1 = **differentiate**, compare, oppose, distinguish, set in opposition 2 = **differ**, be contrary, be at variance, be dissimilar

contribute VERB = **give**, provide, supply, donate, subscribe, chip in (*informal*), bestow ▷ PHRASE: **contribute to something** = **be partly responsible for**, lead to, be instrumental in, be conducive to, help

contribution NOUN = **gift**, offering, grant, donation, input, subscription, koha (*N.Z.*)

contributor NOUN = **donor**, supporter, patron, subscriber, giver

contrive VERB 1 = **devise**, plan, fabricate, create, design, scheme, manufacture, plot **2** = **manage**, succeed, arrange, manoeuvre

contrived ADJECTIVE = **forced**, planned, laboured, strained, artificial, elaborate, unnatural, overdone ≠ natural

control NOUN **1** = **power**, authority, management, command, guidance, supervision, supremacy, charge **2** = **restraint**, check, regulation, brake, limitation, curb **3** = **self-discipline**, self-restraint, restraint, self-command **4** = **switch**, instrument, button, dial, lever, knob

▷ PLURAL NOUN = **instruments**, dash, dials, console, dashboard, control panel

▷ VERB **1** = **have power over**, manage, direct, handle, command, govern, administer, supervise **2** = **limit**, restrict, curb **3** = **restrain**, limit, check, contain, curb, hold back, subdue, repress

controversial ADJECTIVE = **disputed**, contentious, at issue, debatable, under discussion, open to question, disputable

controversy NOUN = **argument**, debate, row, dispute, quarrel, squabble, wrangling, altercation

convene VERB **1** = **call**, gather, assemble, summon, bring together, convoke **2** = **meet**, gather, assemble, come together, congregate

convenience NOUN **1** = **benefit**, good, advantage **2** = **suitability**, fitness, appropriateness

3 = **usefulness**, utility ≠ uselessness **4** = **accessibility**, availability, nearness **5** = **appliance**, facility, comfort, amenity, labour-saving device, help

convenient ADJECTIVE **1** = **suitable**, fit, handy, satisfactory **2** = **useful**, practical, handy, serviceable, labour-saving ≠ useless **3** = **nearby**, available, accessible, handy, at hand, within reach, close at hand, just round the corner ≠ inaccessible **4** = **appropriate**, timely, suitable, helpful

convention NOUN **1** = **custom**, practice, tradition, code, usage, protocol, etiquette, propriety, kawa (*N.Z.*), tikanga (*N.Z.*) **2** = **agreement**, contract, treaty, bargain, pact, protocol **3** = **assembly**, meeting, council, conference, congress, convocation, hui (*N.Z.*), runanga (*N.Z.*)

conventional ADJECTIVE **1** = **proper**, conservative, respectable, genteel, conformist **2** = **ordinary**, standard, normal, regular, usual **3** = **traditional**, accepted, orthodox, customary **4** = **unoriginal**, routine, stereotyped, banal, prosaic, run-of-the-mill, hackneyed ≠ unconventional

converge VERB = **come together**, meet, join, combine, gather, merge, coincide, intersect

▷ PHRASE: **converge on**

something = **close in on**, arrive
at, move towards, home in on,
come together at

conversation NOUN = **talk**,
discussion, dialogue, tête-à-
tête, conference, chat, gossip,
discourse, korero (N.Z.) ▷ **RELATED
WORD**: *adjective* colloquial

conversion NOUN 1 = **change**,
transformation, metamorphosis
2 = **adaptation**, reconstruction,
modification, alteration,
remodelling, reorganization

convert VERB 1 = **change**, turn,
transform, alter, transpose
2 = **adapt**, modify, remodel,
reorganize, customize, restyle
3 = **reform**, convince, proselytize
▷ NOUN = **neophyte**, disciple,
proselyte

convey VERB 1 = **communicate**,
impart, reveal, relate, disclose,
make known, tell 2 = **carry**,
transport, move, bring, bear,
conduct, fetch

convict VERB 1 = **find guilty**,
sentence, condemn, imprison,
pronounce guilty
▷ NOUN = **prisoner**, criminal, lag
(*slang*), felon, jailbird

conviction NOUN 1 = **belief**,
view, opinion, principle, faith,
persuasion, creed, tenet,
kaupapa (N.Z.) 2 = **certainty**,
confidence, assurance, firmness,
certitude

convince VERB 1 = **assure**,
persuade, satisfy, reassure
2 = **persuade**, induce, coax, talk
into, prevail upon, bring round to

the idea of
● **WORD POWER**
● The use of *convince* to talk
● about persuading someone to
● do something is considered
● by many British speakers to
● be wrong or unacceptable. It
● would be preferable to use an
● alternative such as *persuade* or
● *talk into*.

convincing ADJECTIVE
= **persuasive**, credible, conclusive,
telling, powerful, impressive,
plausible, cogent ≠ unconvincing

cool ADJECTIVE 1 = **cold**, chilled,
refreshing, chilly, nippy ≠ warm
2 = **calm**, collected, relaxed,
composed, sedate, self-controlled,
unruffled, unemotional,
chilled (*informal*) ≠ agitated
3 = **unfriendly**, distant,
indifferent, aloof, lukewarm,
offhand, unenthusiastic,
unwelcoming ≠ friendly
4 = **unenthusiastic**, indifferent,
lukewarm, unwelcoming
▷ VERB 1 = **lose heat**, cool off
≠ warm (up) 2 = **make cool**,
freeze, chill, refrigerate, cool off
≠ warm (up)
▷ NOUN 1 = **coldness**, chill,
coolness 2 (*slang*) = **calmness**,
control, temper, composure,
self-control, poise, self-discipline,
self-possession

cooperate VERB = **work
together**, collaborate,
coordinate, join forces, conspire,
pull together, pool resources,
combine your efforts ≠ conflict

cooperation NOUN = **teamwork**, unity, collaboration, give-and-take, combined effort, esprit de corps, kotahitanga (N.Z.) ≠ opposition

cooperative ADJECTIVE
1 = **shared**, joint, combined, collective, collaborative
2 = **helpful**, obliging, accommodating, supportive, responsive, onside (informal)

cope VERB = **manage**, get by (informal), struggle through, survive, carry on, make the grade, hold your own ▷ PHRASE: **cope with something** = **deal with**, handle, struggle with, grapple with, wrestle with, contend with, weather

copy NOUN = **reproduction**, duplicate, replica, imitation, forgery, counterfeit, likeness, facsimile ≠ original
▷ VERB 1 = **reproduce**, replicate, duplicate, transcribe, counterfeit ≠ create 2 = **imitate**, act like, emulate, behave like, follow, repeat, mirror, ape

cord NOUN = **rope**, line, string, twine

cordon NOUN = **chain**, line, ring, barrier, picket line
▷ PHRASE: **cordon something off** = **surround**, isolate, close off, fence off, separate, enclose, picket, encircle

core NOUN 1 = **centre** 2 = **heart**, essence, nucleus, kernel, crux, gist, nub, pith

corner NOUN 1 = **angle**, joint, crook 2 = **bend**, curve 3 = **space**, hideaway, nook, hide-out
▷ VERB 1 = **trap**, catch, run to earth 2 (a market) = **monopolize**, take over, dominate, control, hog (slang), engross

corporation NOUN 1 = **business**, company, concern, firm, society, association, organization, enterprise 2 = **town council**, council, municipal authorities, civic authorities

corps NOUN = **team**, unit, regiment, detachment, company, band, division, troop

corpse NOUN = **body**, remains, carcass, cadaver, stiff (slang)

correct ADJECTIVE 1 = **accurate**, right, true, exact, precise, flawless, faultless, O.K. or okay (informal) ≠ inaccurate
2 = **right**, standard, appropriate, acceptable, proper, precise
3 = **proper**, seemly, standard, fitting, kosher (informal) ≠ inappropriate
▷ VERB 1 = **rectify**, remedy, redress, right, reform, cure, adjust, amend ≠ spoil
2 = **rebuke**, discipline, reprimand, chide, admonish, chastise, chasten, reprove ≠ praise

correction NOUN
1 = **rectification**, improvement, amendment, adjustment, modification, alteration, emendation 2 = **punishment**, discipline, reformation, admonition, chastisement, reproof, castigation

correctly ADVERB = **rightly**, right, perfectly, properly, precisely, accurately

correctness NOUN 1 = **truth**, accuracy, precision, exactitude, exactness, faultlessness
2 = **decorum**, propriety, good manners, civility, good breeding

correspond VERB 1 = **be consistent**, match, agree, accord, fit, square, tally, conform ≠ differ
2 = **communicate**, write, keep in touch, exchange letters, e-mail, text

correspondence NOUN
1 = **communication**, writing, contact 2 = **letters**, post, mail 3 = **relation**, match, agreement, comparison, harmony, coincidence, similarity, correlation

correspondent NOUN
1 = **reporter**, journalist, contributor, hack 2 = **letter writer**, pen friend or pen pal

corresponding ADJECTIVE
= **equivalent**, matching, similar, related, complementary, reciprocal, analogous

corridor NOUN = **passage**, alley, aisle, hallway, passageway

corrupt ADJECTIVE 1 = **dishonest**, bent (slang), crooked (informal), fraudulent, unscrupulous, venal, unprincipled ≠ honest
2 = **depraved**, vicious, degenerate, debased, profligate, dissolute 3 = **distorted**, doctored, altered, falsified
▷ VERB 1 = **bribe**, fix (informal), buy

off, suborn, grease (someone's) palm (slang) 2 = **deprave**, pervert, subvert, debauch ≠ reform
3 = **distort**, doctor, tamper with

corruption NOUN
1 = **dishonesty**, fraud, bribery, extortion, venality, shady dealings (informal) 2 = **depravity**, vice, evil, perversion, decadence, wickedness, immorality
3 = **distortion**, doctoring, falsification

cosmetic ADJECTIVE = **superficial**, surface, nonessential

cosmic ADJECTIVE
1 = **extraterrestrial**, stellar
2 = **universal**, general, overarching

cosmopolitan ADJECTIVE
= **sophisticated**, cultured, refined, cultivated, urbane, well-travelled, worldly-wise ≠ unsophisticated

cost NOUN 1 = **price**, worth, expense, charge, damage (informal), amount, payment, outlay 2 = **loss**, suffering, damage, injury, penalty, hurt, expense, harm
▷ PLURAL NOUN = **expenses**, spending, expenditure, overheads, outgoings, outlay, budget
▷ VERB 1 = **sell at**, come to, set (someone) back (informal), be priced at, command a price of
2 = **lose**, deprive of, cheat of

costly ADJECTIVE 1 = **expensive**, dear, stiff, steep (informal), highly-priced, exorbitant, extortionate ≠ inexpensive 2 = **damaging**, disastrous, harmful, catastrophic, loss-making, ruinous, deleterious

costume NOUN = **outfit**, dress, clothing, uniform, ensemble, livery, apparel, attire

cosy ADJECTIVE 1 = **comfortable**, homely, warm, intimate, snug, comfy (*informal*), sheltered
2 = **snug**, warm, comfortable, sheltered, comfy (*informal*), tucked up 3 = **intimate**, friendly, informal

cottage NOUN = **cabin**, lodge, hut, shack, chalet, whare (*N.Z.*)

cough VERB = **clear your throat**, bark, hack
▷ NOUN = **frog** *or* **tickle in your throat**, bark, hack

council NOUN 1 = **committee**, governing body, board
2 = **governing body**, parliament, congress, cabinet, panel, assembly, convention, conference, runanga (*N.Z.*)

counsel NOUN 1 = **advice**, information, warning, direction, suggestion, recommendation, guidance 2 = **legal adviser**, lawyer, attorney, solicitor, advocate, barrister
▷ VERB = **advise**, recommend, advocate, warn, urge, instruct, exhort

count VERB 1 *often with* **up** = **add (up)**, total, reckon (up), tot up, calculate, compute, tally, number
2 = **matter**, be important, carry weight, tell, rate, weigh, signify
3 = **consider**, judge, regard, deem, think of, rate, look upon

4 = **include**, number among, take into account *or* consideration
▷ NOUN = **calculation**, poll, reckoning, sum, tally, numbering, computation, enumeration
▷ PHRASE: **count on** *or* **upon something** *or* **someone**
= **depend on**, trust, rely on, bank on, take for granted, lean on, reckon on, take on trust

counter VERB 1 = **oppose**, meet, block, resist, parry, deflect, repel, rebuff 2 = **retaliate**, answer, reply, respond, retort, hit back, rejoin, strike back ≠ yield
▷ ADVERB = **opposite to**, against, versus, conversely, in defiance of, at variance with, contrariwise ≠ in accordance with

counterpart NOUN = **opposite number**, equal, twin, equivalent, match, fellow, mate

countless ADJECTIVE
= **innumerable**, legion, infinite, myriad, untold, limitless, incalculable, immeasurable ≠ limited

country NOUN 1 = **nation**, state, land, commonwealth, kingdom, realm, people 2 = **people**, community, nation, society, citizens, inhabitants, populace, public 3 = **countryside**, provinces, sticks (*informal*), farmland, outback (*Austral. & N.Z.*), green belt, backwoods, bush (*N.Z. & S. African*) ≠ town

countryside NOUN = **country**, rural areas, outback (*Austral. & N.Z.*), green belt, sticks (*informal*)

county NOUN = **province**, district, shire

coup NOUN = **masterstroke**, feat, stunt, action, exploit, manoeuvre, deed, accomplishment

couple NOUN = **pair**, two, brace, duo, twosome ▷ PHRASE: **couple something to something** = **link to**, connect to, pair with, unite with, join to, hitch to, yoke to

coupon NOUN = **slip**, ticket, certificate, token, voucher, card

courage NOUN = **bravery**, nerve, resolution, daring, pluck, heroism, mettle, gallantry ≠ cowardice

courageous ADJECTIVE = **brave**, daring, bold, gritty, fearless, gallant, intrepid, valiant ≠ cowardly

courier NOUN 1 = **messenger**, runner, carrier, bearer, envoy 2 = **guide**, representative, escort, conductor

course NOUN 1 = **route**, way, line, road, track, direction, path, passage 2 = **procedure**, plan, policy, programme, method, conduct, behaviour, manner 3 = **progression**, order, unfolding, development, movement, progress, flow, sequence 4 = **classes**, programme, schedule, lectures, curriculum 5 = **racecourse**, circuit 6 = **period**, time, duration, term, passing ▷ VERB 1 = **run**, flow, stream, gush, race, speed, surge 2 = **hunt**, follow, chase, pursue ▷ PHRASE:

of course = **naturally**, certainly, obviously, definitely, undoubtedly, needless to say, without a doubt, indubitably

court NOUN 1 = **law court**, bar, bench, tribunal 2 = **palace**, hall, castle, manor 3 = **royal household**, train, suite, attendants, entourage, retinue, cortege ▷ VERB 1 = **cultivate**, seek, flatter, solicit, pander to, curry favour with, fawn upon 2 = **invite**, seek, attract, prompt, provoke, bring about, incite 3 = **woo**, go (out) with, date, take out, run after, walk out with, set your cap at, step out with (*informal*)

courtesy NOUN 1 = **politeness**, good manners, civility, gallantry, graciousness, affability, urbanity 2 = **favour**, kindness, indulgence

courtyard NOUN = **yard**, square, piazza, quadrangle, plaza, enclosure, cloister, quad (*informal*)

cove NOUN = **bay**, sound, inlet, anchorage

covenant NOUN = **promise**, contract, agreement, commitment, arrangement, pledge, pact

cover VERB 1 = **conceal**, hide, mask, disguise, obscure, veil, cloak, shroud ≠ reveal 2 = **clothe**, dress, wrap, envelop ≠ uncover 3 = **overlay**, blanket 4 = **coat**, cake, plaster, smear, envelop, spread, encase, daub 5 = **submerge**, flood, engulf, overrun, wash over 6 = **travel**

over, cross, traverse, pass through *or* over **7** = **protect**, guard, defend, shield **8** = **consider**, deal with, investigate, describe, tell of **9** = **report on**, write about, commentate on, relate, tell of, narrate, write up **10** = **pay for**, fund, provide for, offset, be enough for

▷ NOUN **1** = **protection**, shelter, shield, defence, guard, camouflage, concealment **2** = **insurance**, protection, compensation, indemnity, reimbursement **3** = **covering**, case, top, coating, envelope, lid, canopy, wrapper **4** = **bedclothes**, bedding, sheet, blanket, quilt, duvet, eiderdown **5** = **jacket**, case, wrapper **6** = **disguise**, front, screen, mask, veil, façade, pretext, smoke screen

covering NOUN = **cover**, coating, casing, wrapping, layer, blanket
▷ ADJECTIVE = **explanatory**, accompanying, introductory, descriptive

covet VERB = **long for**, desire, envy, crave, aspire to, yearn for, lust after, set your heart on

coward NOUN = **wimp**, chicken (*slang*), scaredy-cat (*informal*), yellow-belly (*slang*)

cowardly ADJECTIVE = **faint-hearted**, scared, spineless, soft, yellow (*informal*), weak, chicken (*slang*), fearful, sookie (*N.Z.*)
≠ brave

cowboy NOUN = **cowhand**, drover, rancher, stockman, cattleman, herdsman, gaucho

crack VERB **1** = **break**, split, burst, snap, fracture, splinter **2** = **snap**, ring, crash, burst, explode, pop, detonate **3** (*informal*) = **hit**, clip (*informal*), slap, smack, clout (*informal*), cuff, whack **4** = **break**, cleave **5** = **solve**, work out, resolve, clear up, fathom, decipher, suss (out) (*slang*), get to the bottom of **6** = **break down**, collapse, yield, give in, give way, succumb, lose control, be overcome

▷ NOUN **1** = **break**, chink, gap, fracture, rift, cleft, crevice, fissure **2** = **split**, break, fracture **3** = **snap**, pop, crash, burst, explosion, clap, report **4** (*informal*) = **blow**, slap, smack, clout (*informal*), cuff, whack, clip (*informal*) **5** (*informal*) = **joke**, dig, gag (*informal*), quip, jibe, wisecrack, witticism, funny remark

▷ ADJECTIVE (*slang*) = **first-class**, choice, excellent, ace, elite, superior, world-class, first-rate

crackdown NOUN = **clampdown**, crushing, repression, suppression

cracked ADJECTIVE = **broken**, damaged, split, chipped, flawed, faulty, defective, imperfect

cradle NOUN **1** = **crib**, cot, Moses basket, bassinet **2** = **birthplace**, beginning, source, spring, origin, fount, fountainhead, wellspring
▷ VERB = **hold**, support, rock, nurse, nestle

craft NOUN **1** = **vessel**, boat, ship, plane, aircraft, spacecraft

2 = **occupation**, work, business, trade, employment, pursuit, vocation, handicraft **3** = **skill**, art, ability, technique, know-how (*informal*), expertise, aptitude, artistry

craftsman NOUN = **skilled worker**, artisan, master, maker, wright, technician, smith

cram VERB **1** = **stuff**, force, jam, shove, compress **2** = **pack**, fill, stuff **3** = **squeeze**, press, pack in **4** = **study**, revise, swot, bone up (*informal*), mug up (*slang*)

cramp¹ NOUN = **spasm**, pain, ache, contraction, pang, stitch, convulsion, twinge

cramp² VERB = **restrict**, hamper, inhibit, hinder, handicap, constrain, obstruct, impede

cramped ADJECTIVE = **restricted**, confined, overcrowded, crowded, packed, uncomfortable, closed in, congested ≠ spacious

crash NOUN **1** = **collision**, accident, smash, wreck, prang (*informal*), bump, pile-up (*informal*) **2** = **smash**, clash, boom, bang, thunder, racket, din, clatter **3** = **collapse**, failure, depression, ruin, downfall ▷ VERB **1** = **fall**, plunge, topple, lurch, hurtle, overbalance, fall headlong **2** = **plunge**, hurtle **3** = **collapse**, fail, go under, be ruined, go bust (*informal*), fold up, go to the wall, go belly up (*informal*) ▷ PHRASE: **crash into** = **collide with**, hit, bump into, drive into, plough into

crate NOUN = **container**, case, box, packing case, tea chest

crater NOUN = **hollow**, hole, depression, dip, cavity

crave VERB **1** = **long for**, yearn for, hanker after, want, desire, hope for, lust after **2** (*informal*) = **beg**, ask for, seek, petition, pray for, plead for, solicit, implore

craving NOUN = **longing**, hope, desire, yen (*informal*), hunger, appetite, yearning, thirst

crawl VERB **1** = **creep**, slither, inch, wriggle, writhe, worm your way, advance slowly ≠ run **2** = **grovel**, creep, humble yourself ▷ PHRASE: **crawl to someone** = **fawn on**, toady to

craze NOUN = **fad**, fashion, trend, rage, enthusiasm, vogue, mania, infatuation

crazed ADJECTIVE = **mad**, crazy, raving, insane, lunatic, berko (*Austral. slang*), off the air (*Austral. slang*), porangi (*N.Z.*)

crazy ADJECTIVE **1** (*informal*) = **ridiculous**, absurd, foolish, ludicrous, senseless, preposterous, idiotic, nonsensical, porangi (*N.Z.*) ≠ sensible **2** = **insane**, mad, unbalanced, deranged, nuts (*slang*), crazed, demented, off the air (*Austral. slang*), out of your mind, porangi (*N.Z.*) ≠ sane **3** = **fanatical**, wild (*informal*), mad, devoted, enthusiastic, passionate, infatuated ≠ uninterested

cream NOUN **1** = **lotion**, ointment,

oil, essence, cosmetic, paste, emulsion, salve **2** = **best**, elite, prime, pick, flower, crème de la crème (*French*)

▷ ADJECTIVE = **off-white**, ivory, yellowish-white

▷ *see* **shades from black to white**

creamy ADJECTIVE **1** = **milky**, buttery **2** = **smooth**, soft, velvety, rich

crease NOUN **1** = **fold**, line, ridge, groove, corrugation **2** = **wrinkle**, line, crow's-foot

▷ VERB **1** = **crumple**, rumple, fold, double up, corrugate **2** = **wrinkle**, crumple, screw up

create VERB **1** = **cause**, lead to, occasion, bring about **2** = **make**, produce, invent, compose, devise, originate, formulate, spawn ≠ destroy **3** = **appoint**, make, establish, set up, invest, install, constitute

creation NOUN **1** = **universe**, world, nature, cosmos **2** = **invention**, production, achievement, brainchild (*informal*), concoction, handiwork, pièce de résistance (*French*), magnum opus **3** = **making**, generation, formation, conception, genesis **4** = **setting up**, development, production, institution, foundation, establishment, formation, inception

creative ADJECTIVE = **imaginative**, gifted, artistic, inventive, original, inspired, clever, ingenious

creativity NOUN = **imagination**, inspiration, ingenuity, originality, inventiveness, cleverness

creator NOUN **1** = **maker**, father, author, designer, architect, inventor, originator **2** *usually with cap.* = **God**, Maker

creature NOUN **1** = **living thing**, being, animal, beast, brute **2** = **person**, man, woman, individual, soul, human being, mortal

credentials PLURAL NOUN **1** = **qualifications**, ability, skill, fitness, attribute, capability, eligibility, aptitude **2** = **certification**, document, reference(s), papers, licence, passport, testimonial, authorization

credibility NOUN = **believability**, reliability, plausibility, trustworthiness

credible ADJECTIVE **1** = **believable**, possible, likely, reasonable, probable, plausible, conceivable, imaginable ≠ unbelievable **2** = **reliable**, honest, dependable, trustworthy, sincere, trusty ≠ unreliable

credit NOUN **1** = **praise**, honour, recognition, approval, tribute, acclaim, acknowledgment, kudos **2** = **source of satisfaction** *or* **pride**, asset, honour, feather in your cap **3** = **prestige**, reputation, standing, position, influence, regard, status, esteem **4** = **belief**, trust, confidence, faith, reliance, credence

▷ **VERB** = **believe**, rely on, have faith in, trust, accept ▷ **PHRASE**: **credit someone with something** = **attribute to**, assign to, ascribe to, impute to

creed NOUN = **belief**, principles, doctrine, dogma, credo, catechism, articles of faith

creek NOUN **1** = **inlet**, bay, cove, bight, firth or frith (Scot.) **2** (U.S., Canad., Austral. & N.Z.) = **stream**, brook, tributary, bayou, rivulet, watercourse, runnel

creep VERB = **sneak**, steal, tiptoe, slink, skulk, approach unnoticed ▷ NOUN (slang) = **bootlicker** (informal), sneak, sycophant, crawler (slang), toady (informal) ▷ VERB = **disgust**, frighten, scare, repel, repulse, make your hair stand on end, make you squirm

crescent NOUN = **meniscus**, sickle, new moon

crest NOUN **1** = **top**, summit, peak, ridge, highest point, pinnacle, apex, crown **2** = **tuft**, crown, comb, plume, mane **3** = **emblem**, badge, symbol, insignia, bearings, device

crew NOUN **1** = **(ship's) company**, hands, (ship's) complement **2** = **team**, squad, gang, corps, posse **3** (informal) = **crowd**, set, bunch (informal), band, pack, gang, mob, horde

crime NOUN **1** = **offence**, violation, trespass, felony, misdemeanour, misdeed, transgression, unlawful act **2** = **lawbreaking**, corruption, illegality, vice, misconduct, wrongdoing

criminal NOUN = **lawbreaker**, convict, offender, crook (informal), villain, culprit, sinner, felon, rorter (Austral. slang), skelm (S. African), rogue trader, perp (U.S. & Canad. informal) ▷ ADJECTIVE **1** = **unlawful**, illicit, lawless, wrong, illegal, corrupt, crooked (informal), immoral ≠ lawful **2** (informal) = **disgraceful**, ridiculous, foolish, senseless, scandalous, preposterous, deplorable

cripple VERB **1** = **disable**, paralyse, lame, maim, incapacitate, weaken, hamstring **2** = **damage**, destroy, ruin, spoil, impair, put paid to, put out of action ≠ help

crippled ADJECTIVE = **disabled**, handicapped, challenged, paralysed, lame, incapacitated

crisis NOUN **1** = **emergency**, plight, predicament, trouble, deep water, meltdown (informal), dire straits **2** = **critical point**, climax, height, crunch (informal), turning point, culmination, crux, moment of truth, tipping point

crisp ADJECTIVE **1** = **firm**, crunchy, crispy, crumbly, fresh, brittle, unwilted ≠ soft **2** = **bracing**, fresh, refreshing, brisk, invigorating ≠ warm **3** = **clean**, smart, trim, neat, tidy, spruce, well-groomed, well-pressed

criterion NOUN = **standard**, test, rule, measure, principle, gauge, yardstick, touchstone

● **WORD POWER**
● The word criteria is the plural

- of *criterion* and it is incorrect to
- use it as an alternative singular
- form; *these criteria are not valid*
- is correct, and so is *this criterion*
- *is not valid*, but not *this criteria is*
- *not valid*.

critic NOUN 1 = **judge**, authority, expert, analyst, commentator, pundit, reviewer, connoisseur 2 = **fault-finder**, attacker, detractor, knocker (*informal*)

critical ADJECTIVE 1 = **crucial**, decisive, pressing, serious, vital, urgent, all-important, pivotal ≠ unimportant 2 = **grave**, serious, acute, precarious ≠ safe 3 = **disparaging**, disapproving, scathing, derogatory, nit-picking (*informal*), censorious, fault-finding, captious, nit-picky (*informal*) ≠ complimentary 4 = **analytical**, penetrating, discriminating, discerning, perceptive, judicious ≠ undiscriminating

criticism NOUN 1 = **fault-finding**, censure, disapproval, disparagement, stick (*slang*), flak (*informal*), bad press, character assassination 2 = **analysis**, assessment, judgment, commentary, evaluation, appreciation, appraisal, critique

criticize VERB 1 = **find fault with**, censure, disapprove of, knock (*informal*), condemn, carp, put down, slate (*informal*), nit-pick (*informal*) ≠ praise

crook NOUN (*informal*) = **criminal**, rogue, cheat, thief, shark, villain,

robber, racketeer, skelm (*S. African*) ▷ ADJECTIVE (*Austral. & N.Z. informal*) = **ill**, sick, poorly (*informal*), unhealthy, seedy (*informal*), unwell, queasy, out of sorts (*informal*) ▷ PHRASE: **go (off) crook** (*Austral. & N.Z. informal*) = **lose your temper**, be furious, rage, go mad, lose it (*informal*), crack up (*informal*), see red (*informal*), blow your top

crooked ADJECTIVE 1 = **bent**, twisted, curved, irregular, warped, out of shape, misshapen ≠ straight 2 = **deformed**, distorted 3 = **at an angle**, uneven, slanting, squint, awry, lopsided, askew, off-centre 4 (*informal*) = **dishonest**, criminal, illegal, corrupt, unlawful, shady (*informal*), fraudulent, bent (*slang*) ≠ honest

crop NOUN = **yield**, produce, gathering, fruits, harvest, vintage, reaping ▷ VERB 1 = **graze**, eat, browse, feed on, nibble 2 = **cut**, trim, clip, prune, shear, snip, pare, lop ▷ PHRASE: **crop up** (*informal*) = **happen**, appear, emerge, occur, arise, turn up, spring up

cross VERB 1 = **go across**, pass over, traverse, cut across, move across, travel across 2 = **span**, bridge, go across, extend over 3 = **intersect**, intertwine, crisscross 4 = **oppose**, interfere with, obstruct, block, resist, impede 5 = **interbreed**, mix, blend, cross-pollinate, crossbreed, hybridize, cross-fertilize, intercross

▷ NOUN 1 = **crucifix** 2 = **trouble**, worry, trial, load, burden, grief, woe, misfortune 3 = **mixture**, combination, blend, amalgam, amalgamation

▷ ADJECTIVE = **angry**, annoyed, put out, grumpy, short, ill-tempered, irascible, tooshie (*Austral. slang*), in a bad mood, hoha (*N.Z.*) ≠ good-humoured

▷ PHRASE: **cross something out** *or* **off** = **strike off** *or* **out**, eliminate, cancel, delete, blue-pencil, score off *or* out

crouch VERB = **bend down**, kneel, squat, stoop, bow, duck, hunch

crow VERB = **gloat**, triumph, boast, swagger, brag, exult, blow your own trumpet

crowd NOUN 1 = **multitude**, mass, throng, army, host, pack, mob, swarm 2 = **group**, set, lot, circle, gang, bunch (*informal*), clique 3 = **audience**, spectators, house, gate, attendance

▷ VERB 1 = **flock**, mass, collect, gather, stream, surge, swarm, throng 2 = **squeeze**, pack, pile, bundle, cram 3 = **congest**, pack, cram

crowded ADJECTIVE = **packed**, full, busy, cramped, swarming, teeming, congested, jam-packed

crown NOUN 1 = **coronet**, tiara, diadem, circlet 2 = **laurel wreath**, trophy, prize, honour, garland, laurels, wreath 3 = **high point**, top, tip, summit, crest, pinnacle, apex

▷ VERB 1 = **install**, honour, dignify, ordain, inaugurate 2 = **top**, cap, be on top of, surmount 3 = **cap**, finish, complete, perfect, round off, put the finishing touch to, be the climax *or* culmination of 4 (*slang*) = **strike**, belt (*informal*), bash, hit over the head, box, punch, cuff, biff (*slang*) ▷ PHRASE: **the Crown** 1 = **monarch**, ruler, sovereign, emperor *or* empress, king *or* queen 2 = **monarchy**, sovereignty, royalty

crucial ADJECTIVE 1 (*informal*) = **vital**, important, pressing, essential, urgent, momentous, high-priority 2 = **critical**, central, key, psychological, decisive, pivotal

crude ADJECTIVE 1 = **rough**, basic, makeshift 2 = **simple**, rudimentary, basic, primitive, coarse, clumsy, rough-and-ready 3 = **vulgar**, dirty, rude, obscene, coarse, indecent, tasteless, smutty ≠ tasteful 4 = **unrefined**, natural, raw, unprocessed ≠ processed

crudely ADVERB 1 = **roughly**, basically 2 = **simply**, roughly, basically, coarsely 3 = **vulgarly**, rudely, coarsely, crassly, obscenely, lewdly, impolitely, tastelessly

cruel ADJECTIVE 1 = **brutal**, ruthless, callous, sadistic, inhumane, vicious, monstrous, unkind ≠ kind 2 = **bitter**, ruthless, traumatic, grievous, unrelenting, merciless, pitiless

cruelly ADVERB 1 = **brutally**, severely, mercilessly, in cold blood, callously, monstrously, sadistically, pitilessly 2 = **bitterly**, deeply, severely, ruthlessly, mercilessly, grievously, pitilessly, traumatically

cruelty NOUN = **brutality**, ruthlessness, depravity, inhumanity, barbarity, callousness, spitefulness, mercilessness

cruise NOUN = **sail**, voyage, boat trip, sea trip
▷ VERB 1 = **sail**, coast, voyage 2 = **travel along**, coast, drift, keep a steady pace

crumb NOUN 1 = **bit**, grain, fragment, shred, morsel 2 = **morsel**, scrap, shred, snippet, soupçon (*French*)

crumble VERB 1 = **disintegrate**, collapse, deteriorate, decay, fall apart, degenerate, tumble down, go to pieces 2 = **crush**, fragment, pulverize, pound, grind, powder, granulate 3 = **collapse**, deteriorate, decay, fall apart, degenerate, go to pieces, go to wrack and ruin

crumple VERB 1 = **crush**, squash, screw up, scrumple 2 = **crease**, wrinkle, rumple, ruffle, pucker 3 = **collapse**, sink, go down, fall 4 = **break down**, fall, collapse, give way, cave in, go to pieces 5 = **screw up**

crunch VERB = **chomp**, champ, munch, chew noisily, grind
▷ PHRASE: **the crunch** (*informal*) = **critical point**, test, crisis, emergency, crux, moment of truth

crusade NOUN 1 = **campaign**, drive, movement, cause, push 2 = **holy war**
▷ VERB = **campaign**, fight, push, struggle, lobby, agitate, work

crush VERB 1 = **squash**, break, squeeze, compress, press, pulverize 2 = **crease**, wrinkle, crumple 3 = **overcome**, overwhelm, put down, subdue, overpower, quash, quell, stamp out 4 = **demoralize**, depress, devastate, discourage, humble, put down (*slang*), humiliate, squash
▷ NOUN = **crowd**, mob, horde, throng, pack, mass, jam, huddle

crust NOUN = **layer**, covering, coating, skin, surface, shell

cry VERB 1 = **weep**, sob, shed tears, blubber, snivel ≠ laugh 2 = **shout**, scream, roar, yell, howl, call out, exclaim, shriek ≠ whisper
▷ NOUN 1 = **weep**, sob, bawl, blubber 2 = **shout**, call, scream, roar, yell, howl, shriek, bellow 3 = **weeping**, sobbing, blubbering, snivelling ▷ PHRASE: **cry off** (*informal*) = **back out**, withdraw, quit, excuse yourself

cuddle VERB 1 = **hug**, embrace, fondle, cosset 2 = **pet**, hug, bill and coo ▷ PHRASE: **cuddle up** = **snuggle**

cue NOUN = **signal**, sign, hint, prompt, reminder, suggestion

● CRUSTACEANS
- barnacle
- crab
- crayfish, crawfish, (U.S.) or (Austral. & N.Z. informal) craw
- freshwater shrimp
- hermit crab
- horseshoe crab or king crab
- king prawn
- koura (N.Z.)
- krill
- land crab
- langoustine
- lobster
- oyster crab
- prawn
- robber crab
- sand shrimp
- scorpion
- sea spider
- shrimp
- soft-shell crab
- spider crab
- spiny lobster, rock lobster, crawfish, or langouste

culminate VERB = **end up**, close, finish, conclude, wind up, climax, come to a head, come to a climax

culprit NOUN = **offender**, criminal, felon, guilty party, wrongdoer, miscreant, evildoer, transgressor, perp (U.S. & Canad. informal)

cult NOUN 1 = **sect**, faction, school, religion, clique, hauhau (N.Z.)
2 = **craze**, fashion, trend, fad
3 = **obsession**, worship, devotion, idolization

cultivate VERB 1 = **farm**, work, plant, tend, till, plough
2 = **develop**, establish, foster
3 = **court**, seek out, run after, dance attendance upon
4 = **improve**, refine

cultural ADJECTIVE 1 = **ethnic**, national, native, folk, racial
2 = **artistic**, educational, aesthetic, enriching, enlightening, civilizing, edifying

culture NOUN 1 = **the arts**
2 = **civilization**, society, customs, way of life 3 = **lifestyle**, habit, way of life, mores
4 = **refinement**, education, enlightenment, sophistication,

good taste, urbanity

cultured ADJECTIVE = **refined**, intellectual, educated, sophisticated, enlightened, well-informed, urbane, highbrow ≠ uneducated

cunning ADJECTIVE 1 = **crafty**, sly, devious, artful, sharp, wily, Machiavellian, shifty ≠ frank
2 = **ingenious**, imaginative, sly, devious, artful, Machiavellian
3 = **skilful**, clever ≠ clumsy
▷ NOUN 1 = **craftiness**, guile, trickery, deviousness, artfulness, slyness ≠ candour 2 = **skill**, subtlety, ingenuity, artifice, cleverness ≠ clumsiness

cup NOUN 1 = **mug**, goblet, chalice, teacup, beaker, bowl 2 = **trophy**

cupboard NOUN = **cabinet**, press

curb VERB = **restrain**, control, check, restrict, suppress, inhibit, hinder, retard
▷ NOUN = **restraint**, control, check, brake, limitation, rein, deterrent, bridle

cure VERB 1 = **make better**, correct, heal, relieve, remedy, mend, ease 2 = **restore to health**,

restore, heal **3** = **preserve**,
smoke, dry, salt, pickle
▷ NOUN = **remedy**, treatment,
antidote, panacea, nostrum

curiosity NOUN
1 = **inquisitiveness**, interest,
prying, snooping (*informal*),
nosiness (*informal*) **2** = **oddity**,
wonder, sight, phenomenon,
spectacle, freak, novelty, rarity

curious ADJECTIVE **1** = **inquisitive**,
interested, questioning,
searching, inquiring, meddling,
prying, nosy (*informal*)
≠ uninterested **2** = **strange**,
unusual, bizarre, odd, novel,
rare, extraordinary, unexpected
≠ ordinary

curl NOUN **1** = **ringlet**, lock
2 = **twist**, spiral, coil, kink, whorl
▷ VERB **1** = **crimp**, wave, perm
2 = **twirl**, turn, bend, twist, curve,
loop, spiral, coil **3** = **wind**

curly ADJECTIVE = **wavy**, curled,
curling, fuzzy, frizzy

currency NOUN **1** = **money**,
coinage, legal tender, notes,
coins **2** = **acceptance**, popularity,
circulation, vogue, prevalence

current NOUN **1** = **flow**, course,
undertow, jet, stream, tide,
progression, river **2** = **draught**,
flow, breeze, puff **3** = **mood**,
feeling, spirit, atmosphere, trend,
tendency, undercurrent
▷ ADJECTIVE **1** = **present**,
fashionable, up-to-date,
contemporary, trendy (*Brit.
informal*), topical, present-
day, in fashion ≠ out-of-date
2 = **prevalent**, common,
accepted, popular, widespread,
customary, in circulation

curse VERB **1** = **swear**, cuss
(*informal*), blaspheme, take the
Lord's name in vain **2** = **abuse**,
damn, scold, vilify
▷ NOUN **1** = **oath**, obscenity,
blasphemy, expletive, profanity,
imprecation, swearword
2 = **malediction**, jinx,
anathema, hoodoo (*informal*),
excommunication **3** = **affliction**,
plague, scourge, trouble, torment,
hardship, bane

cursed ADJECTIVE = **under a**

● **CRUSTACEANS**
● barnacle
● crab
● crayfish, crawfish,
  (*U.S.*) or (*Austral. &
  N.Z. informal*) craw
● freshwater shrimp
● hermit crab
● horseshoe crab *or*
  king crab

● king prawn
● koura (*N.Z.*)
● krill
● land crab
● langoustine
● lobster
● oyster crab
● prawn
● robber crab

● sand shrimp
● scorpion
● sea spider
● shrimp
● soft-shell crab
● spider crab
● spiny lobster, rock
  lobster, crawfish, *or*
  langouste

curse, damned, doomed, jinxed, bedevilled, accursed, ill-fated

curtail VERB = **reduce**, diminish, decrease, dock, cut back, shorten, lessen, cut short

curtain NOUN = **hanging**, drape (*chiefly U.S.*), portière

curve NOUN = **bend**, turn, loop, arc, curvature
▷ VERB = **bend**, turn, wind, twist, arch, snake, arc, coil

curved ADJECTIVE = **bent**, rounded, twisted, bowed, arched, serpentine, sinuous

cushion NOUN = **pillow**, pad, bolster, headrest, beanbag, hassock
▷ VERB 1 = **protect** 2 = **soften**, dampen, muffle, mitigate, deaden, suppress, stifle

custody NOUN 1 = **care**, charge, protection, supervision, safekeeping, keeping
2 = **imprisonment**, detention, confinement, incarceration

custom NOUN 1 = **tradition**, practice, convention, ritual, policy, rule, usage, kaupapa (*N.Z.*) 2 = **habit**, way, practice, procedure, routine, wont
3 = **customers**, business, trade, patronage

customary ADJECTIVE 1 = **usual**, common, accepted, established, traditional, normal, ordinary, conventional ≠ unusual
2 = **accustomed**, regular, usual

customer NOUN = **client**, consumer, regular (*informal*), buyer, patron, shopper, purchaser

customs PLURAL NOUN = **import charges**, tax, duty, toll, tariff

cut VERB 1 = **slit**, score, slice, slash, pierce, penetrate 2 = **chop**, split, slice, dissect 3 = **carve**, slice
4 = **sever**, cut in two 5 = **shape**, carve, engrave, chisel, form, score, fashion, whittle 6 = **slash**, wound
7 = **clip**, mow, trim, prune, snip, pare, lop 8 = **trim**, shave, snip
9 = **reduce**, lower, slim (down), diminish, slash, decrease, cut back, kennet (*Austral. slang*), jeff (*Austral. slang*) ≠ increase
10 = **abridge**, edit, shorten, curtail, condense, abbreviate
≠ extend 11 = **delete**, take out, expurgate 12 = **hurt**, wound, upset, sting, hurt someone's feelings 13 (*informal*) = **ignore**, avoid, slight, blank (*slang*), snub, spurn, cold-shoulder, turn your back on ≠ greet 14 = **cross**, bisect
▷ NOUN 1 = **incision**, nick, stroke, slash, slit 2 = **gash**, nick, wound, slash, laceration 3 = **reduction**, fall, lowering, slash, decrease, cutback 4 (*informal*) = **share**, piece, slice, percentage, portion
5 = **style**, look, fashion, shape

cutback NOUN = **reduction**, cut, retrenchment, economy, decrease, lessening

cute ADJECTIVE = **appealing**, sweet, attractive, engaging, charming, delightful, lovable, winsome

cutting ADJECTIVE = **hurtful**, wounding, bitter, malicious, scathing, acrimonious, barbed, sarcastic ≠ kind

cycle NOUN = **series of events**,
circle, revolution, rotation

cynic NOUN = **sceptic**, doubter,
pessimist, misanthrope,
misanthropist, scoffer

cynical ADJECTIVE 1 = **sceptical**,
mocking, pessimistic, scoffing,
contemptuous, scornful,
distrustful, derisive ≠ trusting
2 = **unbelieving**, sceptical,
disillusioned, pessimistic,
disbelieving, mistrustful
≠ optimistic

cynicism NOUN 1 = **scepticism**,
pessimism, misanthropy
2 = **disbelief**, doubt, scepticism,
mistrust

Dd

dab VERB 1 = **pat**, touch, tap
2 = **apply**, daub, stipple
▷ NOUN 1 = **spot**, bit, drop, pat, smudge, speck 2 = **touch**, stroke, flick

daft (*chiefly Brit.*) ADJECTIVE
1 = **stupid**, crazy, silly, absurd, foolish, idiotic, witless, crackpot (*informal*), off the air (*Austral. slang*)
2 (*slang*) = **crazy**, mad, touched, nuts (*slang*), crackers (*Brit. slang*), insane, demented, deranged, off the air (*Austral. slang*), porangi (*N.Z.*)

dag NOUN (*N.Z. informal*) = **joker**, comic, wag, wit, comedian, clown, humorist, prankster
▷ PHRASE: **rattle your dags** (*N.Z. informal*) = **hurry up**, get a move on, step on it (*informal*), get your skates on (*informal*), make haste

dagga NOUN (*S. African*)
= **cannabis**, marijuana, pot (*slang*), dope (*slang*), hash (*slang*), grass (*slang*), weed (*slang*), hemp

daggy (*Austral. & N.Z. informal*)
ADJECTIVE 1 = **untidy**, unkempt, dishevelled, tousled, disordered, messy, ruffled, scruffy, rumpled, bedraggled, ratty (*informal*), straggly, windblown, disarranged, mussed up (*informal*)
2 = **eccentric**, odd, strange, bizarre, weird, peculiar, abnormal, queer (*informal*), irregular, uncommon, quirky, singular, unconventional, idiosyncratic, off-the-wall (*slang*), outlandish, whimsical, rum (*Brit. slang*), capricious, anomalous, freakish, aberrant, wacko (*slang*), outré

daily ADJECTIVE = **everyday**, diurnal, quotidian
▷ ADVERB = **every day**, day by day, once a day

dam NOUN = **barrier**, wall, barrage, obstruction, embankment
▷ VERB = **block up**, restrict, hold back, barricade, obstruct

damage NOUN 1 = **destruction**, harm, loss, injury, suffering, hurt, ruin, devastation ≠ improvement
2 (*informal*) = **cost**, price, charge, bill, amount, payment, expense, outlay
▷ VERB = **spoil**, hurt, injure, harm, ruin, crush, devastate, wreck ≠ fix
▷ PLURAL NOUN (*law*)
= **compensation**, fine, satisfaction, amends, reparation, restitution, reimbursement, atonement

damaging ADJECTIVE = **harmful**, detrimental, hurtful, ruinous, deleterious, injurious, disadvantageous ≠ helpful

dame NOUN *with cap.* = **lady**, baroness, dowager, grande dame (*French*), noblewoman, peeress

damn VERB = **criticize**, condemn, blast, denounce, put down, censure ≠ praise

damned ADJECTIVE (*slang*)
= **infernal**, detestable,
confounded, hateful, loathsome

damp ADJECTIVE = **moist**, wet,
soggy, humid, dank, sopping,
clammy, dewy ≠ dry
▷ NOUN = **moisture**, liquid,
drizzle, dampness, wetness,
dankness ≠ dryness
▷ VERB = **moisten**, wet, soak,
dampen, moisturize ▷ PHRASE:
damp something down = **curb**,
reduce, check, diminish, inhibit,
stifle, allay, pour cold water on

dampen VERB 1 = **reduce**, check,
moderate, dull, restrain, stifle,
lessen 2 = **moisten**, wet, spray,
make damp

dance VERB 1 = **prance**, trip,
hop, skip, sway, whirl, caper,
jig 2 = **caper**, trip, spring, jump,
bound, skip, frolic, cavort
▷ NOUN = **ball**, social, hop
(*informal*), disco, knees-up (*Brit.
informal*), discotheque, B and S
(*Austral. informal*)

dancer NOUN = **ballerina**,
Terpsichorean

danger NOUN 1 = **jeopardy**,
vulnerability 2 = **hazard**, risk,
threat, menace, peril, pitfall

dangerous ADJECTIVE = **perilous**,
risky, hazardous, vulnerable,
insecure, unsafe, precarious,
breakneck ≠ safe

dangerously ADVERB
= **perilously**, alarmingly,
precariously, recklessly, riskily,
hazardously, unsafely

dangle VERB 1 = **hang**, swing,
trail, sway, flap, hang down
2 = **offer**, flourish, brandish,
flaunt

dare VERB 1 = **risk doing**, venture,
presume, make bold (*archaic*),
hazard doing 2 = **challenge**,
provoke, defy, taunt, goad, throw
down the gauntlet

daring ADJECTIVE = **brave**, bold,
adventurous, reckless, fearless,
audacious, intrepid, daredevil
≠ timid
▷ NOUN = **bravery**, nerve
(*informal*), courage, spirit, bottle
(*Brit. slang*), pluck, audacity,
boldness ≠ timidity

dark ADJECTIVE 1 = **dim**, murky,
shady, shadowy, grey, dingy, unlit,
poorly lit 2 = **black**, brunette,
ebony, dark-skinned, sable, dusky,
swarthy ≠ fair 3 = **evil**, foul,
sinister, vile, wicked, infernal
4 = **secret**, hidden, mysterious,
concealed 5 = **gloomy**, sad,
grim, miserable, bleak, dismal,
pessimistic, melancholy
≠ cheerful
▷ NOUN 1 = **darkness**, shadows,
gloom, dusk, obscurity, murk,
dimness, semi-darkness
2 = **night**, twilight, evening, evo
(*Austral. slang*), dusk, night-time,
nightfall

darken VERB 1 = **cloud**, obscure,
dim, overshadow, blacken
≠ brighten 2 = **make dark**,
blacken

darkness NOUN = **dark**, shadows,
shade, gloom, blackness, murk,
duskiness

darling NOUN = **beloved**, love, dear, dearest, angel, treasure, precious, sweetheart
▷ ADJECTIVE = **beloved**, dear, treasured, precious, adored, cherished

dart VERB = **dash**, run, race, shoot, fly, speed, spring, tear

dash VERB 1 = **rush**, run, race, shoot, fly, career, speed, tear ≠ dawdle 2 = **throw**, cast, pitch, slam, toss, hurl, fling, chuck (*informal*) 3 = **crash**, break, smash, shatter, splinter
▷ NOUN 1 = **rush**, run, race, sprint, dart, spurt, sortie 2 = **drop**, little, bit, shot (*informal*), touch, spot, trace, hint ≠ lot 3 = **style**, spirit, flair, flourish, verve, panache, élan, brio

dashing ADJECTIVE (*old-fashioned*) = **stylish**, smart, elegant, flamboyant, sporty, jaunty, showy

data NOUN 1 = **details**, facts, figures, intelligence, statistics (*computing*) 2 = **information**

date NOUN 1 = **time**, stage, period 2 = **appointment**, meeting, arrangement, commitment, engagement, rendezvous, tryst, assignation 3 = **partner**, escort, friend
▷ VERB 1 = **put a date on**, assign a date to, fix the period of 2 = **become dated**, become old-fashioned ▷ PHRASE: **date from** *or* **date back to** (*a time or date*) = **come from**, belong to, originate in, exist from, bear a date of

dated ADJECTIVE = **old-fashioned**, outdated, out of date, obsolete, unfashionable, outmoded, passé, old hat ≠ modern

daunting ADJECTIVE = **intimidating**, alarming, frightening, discouraging, unnerving, disconcerting, demoralizing, off-putting (*Brit. informal*) ≠ reassuring

dawn NOUN 1 = **daybreak**, morning, sunrise, daylight, aurora (*poetic*), crack of dawn, sunup, cockcrow 2 (*literary*) = **beginning**, start, birth, rise, origin, emergence, advent, genesis
▷ VERB 1 = **begin**, start, rise, develop, emerge, unfold, originate 2 = **grow light**, break, brighten, lighten ▷ PHRASE: **dawn on** *or* **upon someone** = **hit**, strike, occur to, register (*informal*), become apparent, come to mind, come into your head

day NOUN 1 = **twenty-four hours** 2 = **daytime**, daylight 3 = **date** 4 = **time**, age, era, period, epoch

daylight NOUN = **sunlight**, sunshine, light of day

daze VERB = **stun**, shock, paralyse, numb, stupefy, benumb
▷ NOUN = **shock**, confusion, distraction, trance, bewilderment, stupor, trancelike state

dazzle VERB 1 = **impress**, amaze, overwhelm, astonish, overpower, bowl over (*informal*), take your breath away 2 = **blind**, confuse, daze, bedazzle

d

▷ NOUN = **splendour**, sparkle, glitter, brilliance, magnificence, razzmatazz (*slang*)

dazzling ADJECTIVE = **splendid**, brilliant, stunning, glorious, sparkling, glittering, sensational (*informal*), virtuoso ≠ ordinary

dead ADJECTIVE 1 = **deceased**, departed, late, perished, extinct, defunct, passed away ≠ alive 2 = **boring**, dull, dreary, flat, plain, humdrum, uninteresting 3 = **not working**, useless, inactive, inoperative ≠ working 4 = **numb**, frozen, paralysed, insensitive, inert, deadened, immobilized, unfeeling 5 (*of a centre, silence, or a stop*) = **total**, complete, absolute, utter, outright, thorough, unqualified 6 (*informal*) = **exhausted**, tired, worn out, spent, done in (*informal*), all in (*slang*), drained, knackered (*slang*)

▷ NOUN = **middle**, heart, depth, midst

▷ ADVERB = **exactly**, completely, totally, directly, fully, entirely, absolutely, thoroughly

deadline NOUN = **time limit**, cutoff point, target date *or* time, limit

deadlock NOUN 1 = **impasse**, stalemate, standstill, gridlock, standoff 2 = **tie**, draw, stalemate, impasse, standstill, gridlock, standoff, dead heat

deadly ADJECTIVE 1 = **lethal**, fatal, deathly, dangerous, devastating, mortal, murderous, malignant

2 (*informal*) = **boring**, dull, tedious, flat, monotonous, uninteresting, mind-numbing, wearisome

deaf ADJECTIVE 1 = **hard of hearing**, without hearing, stone deaf 2 = **oblivious**, indifferent, unmoved, unconcerned, unsympathetic, impervious, unhearing

▷ *see* **disabled**

deal NOUN 1 (*informal*) = **agreement**, understanding, contract, arrangement, bargain, transaction, pact 2 = **amount**, quantity, measure, degree, mass, volume, share, portion

▷ PHRASES: **deal in something** = **sell**, trade in, stock, traffic in, buy and sell; **deal something out** = **distribute**, give, share, assign, allocate, dispense, allot, mete out; **deal with something** = **be concerned with**, involve, concern, touch, regard, apply to, bear on, pertain to; **deal with something** *or* **someone** = **handle**, manage, treat, cope with, take care of, see to, attend to, get to grips with

dealer NOUN = **trader**, merchant, supplier, wholesaler, purveyor, tradesman

dear ADJECTIVE 1 = **beloved**, close, valued, favourite, prized, treasured, precious, intimate ≠ hated 2 = **expensive**, costly, high-priced, pricey (*informal*), at a premium, overpriced, exorbitant ≠ cheap

▷ NOUN = **darling**, love, dearest, angel, treasure, precious, beloved, loved one

dearly ADVERB 1 = **very much**, greatly, extremely, profoundly 2 = **at great cost**, at a high price

death NOUN 1 = **dying**, demise, end, passing, departure ≠ birth 2 = **destruction**, finish, ruin, undoing, extinction, downfall ≠ beginning ▷ RELATED WORDS: *adjectives* fatal, lethal, mortal

deathly ADJECTIVE = **deathlike**, white, pale, ghastly, wan, pallid, ashen

debacle *or* **débâcle** NOUN = **disaster**, catastrophe, fiasco

debate NOUN = **discussion**, talk, argument, dispute, analysis, conversation, controversy, dialogue ▷ VERB 1 = **discuss**, question, talk about, argue about, dispute, examine, deliberate 2 = **consider**, reflect, think about, weigh, contemplate, deliberate, ponder, ruminate

debris NOUN = **remains**, bits, waste, ruins, fragments, rubble, wreckage, detritus

debt NOUN = **debit**, commitment, obligation, liability ▷ PHRASE: **in debt** = **owing**, liable, in the red (*informal*), in arrears

debtor NOUN = **borrower**, mortgagor

debut NOUN 1 = **entrance**, beginning, launch, introduction, first appearance 2 = **presentation**, coming out, introduction, first appearance, initiation

decay VERB 1 = **rot**, spoil, crumble, deteriorate, perish, decompose, moulder, go bad 2 = **decline**, diminish, crumble, deteriorate, fall off, dwindle, lessen, wane ≠ grow ▷ NOUN 1 = **rot**, corruption, mould, blight, decomposition, gangrene, canker, caries 2 = **decline**, collapse, deterioration, failing, fading, degeneration ≠ growth

deceased ADJECTIVE = **dead**, late, departed, expired, defunct, lifeless

deceive VERB = **take in**, trick, fool (*informal*), cheat, con (*informal*), mislead, dupe, swindle, scam (*slang*)

decency NOUN 1 = **propriety**, correctness, decorum, respectability, etiquette 2 = **courtesy**, politeness, civility, graciousness, urbanity, courteousness

decent ADJECTIVE 1 = **satisfactory**, fair, all right, reasonable, sufficient, good enough, adequate, ample ≠ unsatisfactory 2 = **proper**, becoming, seemly, fitting, appropriate, suitable, respectable, befitting ≠ improper 3 (*informal*) = **good**, kind, friendly, neighbourly, generous, helpful, obliging, accommodating 4 = **respectable**, pure, proper, modest, chaste, decorous

deception NOUN 1 = **trickery**,

d

fraud, deceit, cunning, treachery, guile, legerdemain ≠ honesty **2 = trick**, lie, bluff, hoax, decoy, ruse, subterfuge, fastie (*Austral. slang*)

decide VERB **1 = make a decision**, make up your mind, reach or come to a decision, choose, determine, conclude ≠ hesitate **2 = resolve**, answer, determine, conclude, clear up, ordain, adjudicate, adjudge **3 = settle**, determine, resolve

decidedly ADVERB **= definitely**, clearly, positively, distinctly, downright, unequivocally, unmistakably

decision NOUN **1 = judgment**, finding, ruling, sentence, resolution, conclusion, verdict, decree **2 = decisiveness**, purpose, resolution, resolve, determination, firmness, forcefulness, strength of mind or will

decisive ADJECTIVE **1 = crucial**, significant, critical, influential, momentous, conclusive, fateful ≠ uncertain **2 = resolute**, decided, firm, determined, forceful, incisive, trenchant, strong-minded ≠ indecisive

deck VERB **= decorate**, dress, clothe, array, adorn, embellish, festoon, beautify

declaration NOUN
1 = announcement, proclamation, decree, notice, notification, edict, pronouncement **2 = affirmation**, profession, assertion, revelation, disclosure, acknowledgment, protestation, avowal
3 = statement, testimony

declare VERB **1 = state**, claim, announce, voice, express, maintain, assert, proclaim
2 = testify, state, swear, assert, affirm, bear witness, vouch
3 = make known, reveal, show, broadcast, confess, communicate, disclose

decline VERB **1 = fall**, drop, lower, sink, fade, shrink, diminish, decrease ≠ rise **2 = deteriorate**, weaken, pine, decay, worsen, languish, degenerate, droop ≠ improve **3 = refuse**, reject, turn down, avoid, spurn, abstain, say 'no' ≠ accept
▷ NOUN **1 = depression**, recession, slump, falling off, downturn, dwindling, lessening ≠ rise **2 = deterioration**, failing, weakening, decay, worsening, degeneration ≠ improvement

decor or **décor** NOUN
= decoration, colour scheme, ornamentation, furnishing style

decorate VERB **1 = adorn**, trim, embroider, ornament, embellish, festoon, beautify, grace **2 = do up**, paper, paint, wallpaper, renovate (*informal*), furbish **3 = pin a medal on**, cite, confer an honour on or upon

decoration NOUN
1 = adornment, trimming, enhancement, elaboration, embellishment, ornamentation,

beautification **2** = **ornament**, trimmings, garnish, frill, bauble **3** = **medal**, award, star, ribbon, badge

decorative ADJECTIVE
= **ornamental**, fancy, pretty, attractive, for show, embellishing, showy, beautifying

decrease VERB **1** = **drop**, decline, lessen, lower, shrink, diminish, dwindle, subside **2** = **reduce**, cut, lower, moderate, weaken, diminish, cut down, shorten ≠ increase
▷ NOUN = **lessening**, decline, reduction, loss, falling off, dwindling, contraction, cutback ≠ growth

decree NOUN **1** = **law**, order, ruling, act, command, statute, proclamation, edict **2** = **judgment**, finding, ruling, decision, verdict, arbitration
▷ VERB = **order**, rule, command, demand, proclaim, prescribe, pronounce, ordain

dedicate VERB **1** = **devote**, give, apply, commit, pledge, surrender, give over to **2** = **offer**, address, inscribe

dedicated ADJECTIVE
= **committed**, devoted, enthusiastic, single-minded, zealous, purposeful, wholehearted ≠ indifferent

dedication NOUN
1 = **commitment**, loyalty, devotion, allegiance, adherence, single-mindedness, faithfulness, wholeheartedness ≠ indifference

2 = **inscription**, message, address

deduct VERB = **subtract**, remove, take off, take away, reduce by, knock off (*informal*), decrease by ≠ add

deduction NOUN **1** = **conclusion**, finding, verdict, judgment, assumption, inference **2** = **reasoning**, thinking, thought, analysis, logic **3** = **discount**, reduction, cut, concession, decrease, rebate, diminution **4** = **subtraction**, reduction, concession

deed NOUN **1** = **action**, act, performance, achievement, exploit, feat **2** (*law*) = **document**, title, contract

deep ADJECTIVE **1** = **big**, wide, broad, profound, yawning, bottomless, unfathomable ≠ shallow **2** = **intense**, great, serious (*informal*), acute, extreme, grave, profound, heartfelt ≠ superficial = **sound**, profound, unbroken, undisturbed, untroubled **3** with **in** = **absorbed in**, lost in, gripped by, preoccupied with, immersed in, engrossed in, rapt by **4** = **dark**, strong, rich, intense, vivid ≠ light **5** = **low**, booming, bass, resonant, sonorous, low-pitched ≠ high **6** = **secret**, hidden, mysterious, obscure, abstract, esoteric, mystifying, arcane
▷ NOUN = **middle**, heart, midst, dead
▷ ADVERB = **far**, a long way, a good way, miles, a great distance

d

▷ **PHRASE**: **the deep** (*poetic*) = **the ocean**, the sea, the waves, the main, the high seas, the briny (*informal*)

deepen VERB 1 = **intensify**, increase, grow, strengthen, reinforce, escalate, magnify 2 = **dig out**, excavate, scoop out, hollow out

deeply ADVERB = **thoroughly**, completely, seriously, sadly, severely, gravely, profoundly, intensely

de facto ADVERB = **in fact**, really, actually, in effect, in reality ▷ **ADJECTIVE** = **actual**, real, existing

default NOUN 1 = **failure**, neglect, deficiency, lapse, omission, dereliction 2 = **nonpayment**, evasion ▷ **VERB** = **fail to pay**, dodge, evade, neglect

defeat VERB 1 = **beat**, crush, overwhelm, conquer, master, rout, trounce, vanquish ≠ surrender 2 = **frustrate**, foil, thwart, ruin, baffle, confound, balk, get the better of ▷ **NOUN** 1 = **conquest**, beating, overthrow, rout ≠ victory 2 = **frustration**, failure, reverse, setback, thwarting

defect NOUN = **deficiency**, failing, fault, error, flaw, imperfection ▷ **VERB** = **desert**, rebel, quit, revolt, change sides

defence or (*U.S.*) **defense** NOUN 1 = **protection**, cover, security, guard, shelter, safeguard,

immunity 2 = **armaments**, weapons 3 = **argument**, explanation, excuse, plea, justification, vindication, rationalization 4 = **plea** (*law*), testimony, denial, alibi, rebuttal ▷ **PLURAL NOUN** = **shield**, barricade, fortification, buttress, rampart, bulwark, fortified pa (*N.Z.*)

defend VERB 1 = **protect**, cover, guard, screen, preserve, look after, shelter, shield 2 = **support**, champion, justify, endorse, uphold, vindicate, stand up for, speak up for

defendant NOUN = **accused**, respondent, prisoner at the bar

defender NOUN 1 = **supporter**, champion, advocate, sponsor, follower 2 = **protector**, guard, guardian, escort, bodyguard

defensive ADJECTIVE 1 = **protective**, watchful, on the defensive, on guard 2 = **oversensitive**, uptight (*informal*)

defer VERB = **postpone**, delay, put off, suspend, shelve, hold over, procrastinate, put on ice (*informal*)

defiance NOUN = **resistance**, opposition, confrontation, contempt, disregard, disobedience, insolence, insubordination ≠ obedience

defiant ADJECTIVE = **resisting**, rebellious, daring, bold, provocative, audacious, antagonistic, insolent ≠ obedient

deficiency NOUN 1 = **lack**, want, deficit, absence, shortage, scarcity, dearth ≠ sufficiency 2 = **failing**, fault, weakness, defect, flaw, drawback, shortcoming, imperfection

deficit NOUN = **shortfall**, shortage, deficiency, loss, arrears

define VERB 1 = **mark out**, outline, limit, bound, delineate, circumscribe, demarcate 2 = **describe**, interpret, characterize, explain, spell out, expound 3 = **establish**, specify, designate

definite ADJECTIVE 1 = **specific**, exact, precise, clear, particular, fixed, black-and-white, cut-and-dried (*informal*) ≠ vague 2 = **clear**, black-and-white, unequivocal, unambiguous, guaranteed, cut-and-dried (*informal*) 3 = **noticeable**, marked, clear, decided, striking, particular, distinct, conspicuous 4 = **certain**, decided, sure, settled, convinced, positive, confident, assured ≠ uncertain

definitely ADVERB = **certainly**, clearly, surely, absolutely, positively, without doubt, unquestionably, undeniably

definition NOUN 1 = **description**, interpretation, explanation, clarification, exposition, elucidation, statement of meaning 2 = **sharpness**, focus, clarity, contrast, precision, distinctness

definitive ADJECTIVE 1 = **final**, convincing, absolute, clinching, decisive, definite, conclusive, irrefutable 2 = **authoritative**, greatest, ultimate, reliable, exhaustive, superlative

deflect VERB = **turn aside**, bend

defy VERB = **resist**, oppose, confront, brave, disregard, stand up to, spurn, flout

degenerate VERB = **decline**, slip, sink, decrease, deteriorate, worsen, decay, lapse
▷ ADJECTIVE = **depraved**, corrupt, low, perverted, immoral, decadent, debauched, dissolute

degrade VERB = **demean**, disgrace, humiliate, shame, humble, discredit, debase, dishonour ≠ ennoble

degree NOUN = **amount**, stage, grade

delay VERB 1 = **put off**, suspend, postpone, shelve, defer, hold over 2 = **hold up**, detain, hold back, hinder, obstruct, impede, bog down, set back ≠ speed (up)
▷ NOUN = **hold-up**, wait, setback, interruption, stoppage, impediment, hindrance

delegate NOUN = **representative**, agent, deputy, ambassador, commissioner, envoy, proxy, legate
▷ VERB 1 = **entrust**, transfer, hand over, give, pass on, assign, consign, devolve 2 = **appoint**, commission, select, contract, engage, nominate, designate, mandate

delegation NOUN

1 = **deputation**, envoys, contingent, commission, embassy, legation

2 = **commissioning**, assignment, devolution, committal

delete VERB = **remove**, cancel, erase, strike out, obliterate, efface, cross out, expunge

deliberate ADJECTIVE

1 = **intentional**, meant, planned, intended, conscious, calculated, wilful, purposeful ≠ accidental

2 = **careful**, measured, slow, cautious, thoughtful, circumspect, methodical, unhurried ≠ hurried

▷ VERB = **consider**, think, ponder, discuss, debate, reflect, consult, weigh

deliberately ADVERB

= **intentionally**, on purpose, consciously, knowingly, wilfully, by design, in cold blood, wittingly

deliberation NOUN

1 = **consideration**, thought, reflection, calculation, meditation, forethought, circumspection

2 *usually plural* = **discussion**, talk, conference, debate, analysis, conversation, dialogue, consultation

delicacy NOUN 1 = **fragility**, flimsiness 2 = **daintiness**, charm, grace, elegance, neatness, prettiness, slenderness, exquisiteness 3 = **difficulty** 4 = **sensitivity**, understanding, consideration, diplomacy, discretion, tact, thoughtfulness,

sensitiveness 5 = **treat**, luxury, savoury, dainty, morsel, titbit

6 = **lightness**, accuracy, precision, elegance, sensibility, purity, subtlety, refinement

delicate ADJECTIVE 1 = **fine**, elegant, exquisite, graceful

2 = **subtle**, fine, delicious, faint, refined, understated, dainty ≠ bright 3 = **fragile**, weak, frail, brittle, tender, flimsy, dainty, breakable 4 = **skilled**, precise, deft 5 = **diplomatic**, sensitive, thoughtful, discreet, considerate, tactful ≠ insensitive

delicious ADJECTIVE = **delectable**, tasty, choice, savoury, dainty, mouthwatering, scrumptious (*informal*), appetizing, lekker (*S. African slang*), yummo (*Austral. slang*) ≠ unpleasant

delight VERB = **please**, satisfy, thrill, charm, cheer, amuse, enchant, gratify ≠ displease

▷ PHRASE: **delight in** or **take a delight in something** or **someone** = **like**, love, enjoy, appreciate, relish, savour, revel in, take pleasure in NOUN = **pleasure**, joy, satisfaction, happiness, ecstasy, enjoyment, bliss, glee ≠ displeasure

delightful ADJECTIVE = **pleasant**, charming, thrilling, enjoyable, enchanting, agreeable, pleasurable, rapturous ≠ unpleasant

deliver VERB 1 = **bring**, carry, bear, transport, distribute, convey, cart **2** *sometimes with* **over** *or* **up** = **hand over**, commit, give up, yield, surrender, turn over, relinquish, make over **3** = **give**, read, present, announce, declare, utter **4** = **strike**, give, deal, launch, direct, aim, administer, inflict **5** = **release**, free, save, rescue, loose, liberate, ransom, emancipate

delivery NOUN **1** = **handing over**, transfer, distribution, transmission, dispatch, consignment, conveyance **2** = **consignment**, goods, shipment, batch **3** = **speech**, utterance, articulation, intonation, elocution, enunciation **4** = **childbirth**, labour, confinement, parturition

delusion NOUN = **misconception**, mistaken idea, misapprehension, fancy, illusion, hallucination, fallacy, false impression

demand VERB **1** = **request**, ask (for), order, expect, claim, seek, insist on, exact **2** = **challenge**, ask, question, inquire **3** = **require**, want, need, involve, call for, entail, necessitate, cry out for ≠ provide
▷ NOUN **1** = **request**, order **2** = **need**, want, call, market, claim, requirement

demanding ADJECTIVE = **difficult**, trying, hard, taxing, wearing, challenging, tough, exacting ≠ easy

demise NOUN **1** = **failure**, end, fall, defeat, collapse, ruin, breakdown,

overthrow **2** (*euphemistic*) = **death**, end, dying, passing, departure, decease

democracy NOUN = **self-government**, republic, commonwealth

Democrat NOUN = **left-winger**

democratic ADJECTIVE = **self-governing**, popular, representative, autonomous, populist, egalitarian

demolish VERB **1** = **knock down**, level, destroy, dismantle, flatten, tear down, bulldoze, raze ≠ build **2** = **destroy**, wreck, overturn, overthrow, undo

demolition NOUN = **knocking down**, levelling, destruction, explosion, wrecking, tearing down, bulldozing, razing

demon NOUN **1** = **evil spirit**, devil, fiend, goblin, ghoul, malignant spirit, atua (*N.Z.*), wairua (*N.Z.*) **2** = **wizard**, master, ace (*informal*), fiend

demonstrate VERB **1** = **prove**, show, indicate, make clear, manifest, testify to, flag up **2** = **show**, express, display, indicate, exhibit, manifest, flag up **3** = **march**, protest, rally, object, parade, picket, remonstrate, express disapproval, hikoi (*N.Z.*) **4** = **describe**, show, explain, teach, illustrate

demonstration NOUN **1** = **march**, protest, rally, sit-in, parade, picket, mass lobby, hikoi (*N.Z.*) **2** = **display**, show, performance, explanation,

d

description, presentation, exposition **3 = indication**, proof, testimony, confirmation, substantiation **4 = exhibition**, display, expression, illustration

den NOUN **1 = lair**, hole, shelter, cave, haunt, cavern, hide-out **2** (*chiefly U.S.*) **= study**, retreat, sanctuary, hideaway, sanctum, cubbyhole

denial NOUN **1 = negation**, contradiction, dissent, retraction, repudiation ≠ admission **2 = refusal**, veto, rejection, prohibition, rebuff, repulse

denomination NOUN **1 = religious group**, belief, sect, persuasion, creed, school, hauhau (*N.Z.*) **2 = unit**, value, size, grade

denounce VERB **1 = condemn**, attack, censure, revile, vilify, stigmatize **2 = report**, dob in (*Austral. slang*)

dense ADJECTIVE **1 = thick**, heavy, solid, compact, condensed, impenetrable, close-knit ≠ thin **2 = heavy**, thick, opaque, impenetrable **3 = stupid** (*informal*), thick, dull, dumb (*informal*), dozy (*Brit. informal*), stolid, dopey (*informal*), moronic ≠ bright

density NOUN **1 = tightness**, thickness, compactness, impenetrability, denseness **2 = mass**, bulk, consistency, solidity

dent NOUN **= hollow**, chip, indentation, depression, impression, pit, dip, crater, ding (*Austral. & N.Z. dated, informal*) ▷ VERB **= make a dent in**, press in, gouge, hollow, push in

deny VERB **1 = contradict**, disagree with, rebuff, negate, rebut, refute ≠ admit **2 = renounce**, reject, retract, repudiate, disown, recant, disclaim **3 = refuse**, forbid, reject, rule out, turn down, prohibit, withhold, preclude ≠ permit

depart VERB **1 = leave**, go, withdraw, retire, disappear, quit, retreat, exit, rack off (*Austral. & N.Z. slang*) ≠ arrive **2 = deviate**, vary, differ, stray, veer, swerve, diverge, digress

department NOUN **= section**, office, unit, station, division, branch, bureau, subdivision

departure NOUN **1 = leaving**, going, retirement, withdrawal, exit, going away, removal, exodus ≠ arrival **2 = retirement**, going, withdrawal, exit, going away, removal **3 = shift**, change, difference, variation, innovation, novelty, deviation, divergence

dependent or (*U.S.sometimes*) **dependant** ADJECTIVE **1 = reliant**, vulnerable, helpless, powerless, weak, defenceless ≠ independent **2 = determined by**, depending on, subject to, influenced by, conditional on, contingent on ▷ PHRASE: **dependent on** or **upon = reliant on**, relying on

depend on VERB **1 = be determined by**, be based on,

be subject to, hang on, rest on, revolve around, hinge on, be subordinate to **2 = count on**, turn to, trust in, bank on, lean on, rely upon, reckon on

depict VERB **1 = illustrate**, portray, picture, paint, outline, draw, sketch, delineate **2 = describe**, present, represent, outline, characterize

deplete VERB **= use up**, reduce, drain, exhaust, consume, empty, lessen, impoverish ≠ increase

deplore VERB **= disapprove of**, condemn, object to, denounce, censure, abhor, take a dim view of

deploy VERB (*troops or military resources*) **= use**, station, position, arrange, set out, utilize

deployment NOUN (*of troops or military resources*) **= use**, stationing, spread; organization, arrangement, positioning, utilization

deport VERB **= expel**, exile, throw out, oust, banish, expatriate, extradite, evict

depose VERB **= oust**, dismiss, displace, demote, dethrone, remove from office

deposit VERB **1 = put**, place, lay, drop **2 = store**, keep, put, bank, lodge, entrust, consign
▷ NOUN **1 = down payment**, security, stake, pledge, instalment, retainer, part payment **2 = accumulation**, mass, build-up, layer **3 = sediment**, grounds, residue, lees, precipitate, silt, dregs

depot NOUN **1 = arsenal**, warehouse, storehouse, repository, depository **2** (*U.S. & Canad.*) **= bus station**, station, garage, terminus

depreciation NOUN **= devaluation**, fall, drop, depression, slump, deflation

depress VERB **1 = sadden**, upset, distress, discourage, grieve, oppress, weigh down, make sad ≠ cheer **2 = lower**, cut, reduce, diminish, decrease, lessen ≠ raise **3 = devalue**, depreciate, cheapen **4 = press down**, push, squeeze, lower, flatten, compress, push down

depressed ADJECTIVE **1 = sad**, blue, unhappy, discouraged, fed up, mournful, dejected, despondent **2 = poverty-stricken**, poor, deprived, disadvantaged, rundown, impoverished, needy **3 = lowered**, devalued, weakened, depreciated, cheapened **4 = sunken**, hollow, recessed, indented, concave

depressing ADJECTIVE **= bleak**, sad, discouraging, gloomy, dismal, harrowing, saddening, dispiriting

depression NOUN **1 = despair**, misery, sadness, dumps (*informal*), the blues, melancholy, unhappiness, despondency **2 = recession**, slump, economic decline, stagnation, inactivity, hard *or* bad times **3 = hollow**, pit, dip, bowl, valley, dent, cavity, indentation

deprivation NOUN 1 = **lack**, denial, withdrawal, removal, expropriation, dispossession 2 = **want**, need, hardship, suffering, distress, privation, destitution

deprive VERB = **dispossess**, rob, strip, despoil, bereave

deprived ADJECTIVE = **poor**, disadvantaged, needy, in need, lacking, bereft, destitute, down at heel ≠ prosperous

depth NOUN 1 = **deepness**, drop, measure, extent 2 = **insight**, wisdom, penetration, profundity, discernment, sagacity, astuteness, profoundness ≠ superficiality 3 = **breadth**

deputy NOUN = **substitute**, representative, delegate, lieutenant, proxy, surrogate, second-in-command, legate

derelict ADJECTIVE = **abandoned**, deserted, ruined, neglected, discarded, forsaken, dilapidated ▷ NOUN = **tramp**, outcast, drifter, down-and-out, vagrant, bag lady, derro (*Austral. slang*)

descend VERB 1 = **fall**, drop, sink, go down, plunge, dive, tumble, plummet ≠ rise = **get off** 2 = **go down**, come down, walk down, move down, climb down 3 = **slope**, dip, incline, slant ▷ PHRASE: **be descended from** = **originate from**, derive from, spring from, proceed from, issue from

descent NOUN 1 = **fall**, drop, plunge, coming down, swoop 2 = **slope**, drop, dip, incline, slant, declivity 3 = **decline**, deterioration, degeneration 4 = **origin**, extraction, ancestry, lineage, family tree, parentage, genealogy, derivation

describe VERB 1 = **relate**, tell, report, explain, express, recount, recite, narrate 2 = **portray**, depict 3 = **trace**, draw, outline, mark out, delineate

description NOUN 1 = **account**, report, explanation, representation, sketch, narrative, portrayal, depiction 2 = **calling**, naming, branding, labelling, dubbing, designation 3 = **kind**, sort, type, order, class, variety, brand, category

desert¹ NOUN = **wilderness**, waste, wilds, wasteland

desert² VERB 1 = **abandon**, leave, quit (*informal*), forsake 2 = **leave**, abandon, strand, maroon, walk out on (*informal*), forsake, jilt, leave stranded ≠ take care of 3 = **abscond**

deserted ADJECTIVE 1 = **empty**, abandoned, desolate, neglected, vacant, derelict, unoccupied 2 = **abandoned**, neglected, forsaken

deserve VERB = **merit**, warrant, be entitled to, have a right to, rate, earn, justify, be worthy of

deserved ADJECTIVE = **well-earned**, fitting, due, earned, justified, merited, proper, warranted

deserving ADJECTIVE = **worthy**,

righteous, commendable, laudable, praiseworthy, meritorious, estimable
≠ undeserving

design VERB 1 = **plan**, draw, draft, trace, outline, devise, sketch, formulate 2 = **create**, plan, fashion, propose, invent, conceive, originate, fabricate 3 = **intend**, mean, plan, aim, purpose
▷ NOUN 1 = **pattern**, form, style, shape, organization, arrangement, construction 2 = **plan**, drawing, model, scheme, draft, outline, sketch, blueprint 3 = **intention**, end, aim, goal, target, purpose, object, objective

designate VERB 1 = **name**, call, term, style, label, entitle, dub 2 = **choose**, reserve, select, label, flag, assign, allocate, set aside 3 = **appoint**, name, choose, commission, select, elect, delegate, nominate

designer NOUN 1 = **couturier** 2 = **producer**, architect, deviser, creator, planner, inventor, originator

desirable ADJECTIVE
1 = **advantageous**, useful, valuable, helpful, profitable, of service, convenient, worthwhile
≠ disadvantageous = **popular**
≠ unpopular 2 = **attractive**, appealing, pretty, fair, inviting, lovely, charming, sexy (*informal*)
≠ unattractive

desire VERB = **want**, long for, crave, hope for, ache for, wish for, yearn for, thirst for
▷ NOUN 1 = **wish**, want, longing, hope, urge, aspiration, craving, thirst 2 = **lust**, passion, libido, appetite, lasciviousness, lonesome (*chiefly U.S. & Canad.*)

despair VERB = **lose hope**, give up, lose heart
▷ NOUN = **despondency**, depression, misery, gloom, desperation, anguish, hopelessness, dejection

despatch ▷ *see* dispatch

desperate ADJECTIVE 1 = **grave**, pressing, serious, severe, extreme, urgent, drastic 2 = **last-ditch**, daring, furious, risky, frantic, audacious

desperately ADVERB = **gravely**, badly, seriously, severely, dangerously, perilously

desperation NOUN 1 = **misery**, worry, trouble, despair, agony, anguish, unhappiness, hopelessness 2 = **recklessness**, madness, frenzy, impetuosity, rashness, foolhardiness

despise VERB = **look down on**, loathe, scorn, detest, revile, abhor
≠ admire

despite PREPOSITION = **in spite of**, in the face of, regardless of, even with, notwithstanding, in the teeth of, undeterred by

destination NOUN = **stop**, station, haven, resting-place, terminus, journey's end

destined ADJECTIVE = **fated**, meant, intended, certain, bound, doomed, predestined

d

destiny NOUN 1 = **fate**, fortune, lot, portion, doom, nemesis 2 *usually cap.* = **fortune**, chance, karma, providence, kismet, predestination, divine will

destroy VERB 1 = **ruin**, crush, devastate, wreck, shatter, wipe out, demolish, eradicate 2 = **slaughter**, kill

destruction NOUN 1 = **ruin**, havoc, wreckage, demolition, devastation, annihilation 2 slaughter, extermination, eradication

destructive ADJECTIVE = **devastating**, fatal, deadly, lethal, harmful, damaging, catastrophic, ruinous

detach VERB 1 = **separate**, remove, divide, cut off, sever, disconnect, tear off, disengage ≠ attach 2 = **free**, remove, separate, isolate, cut off, disengage

detached ADJECTIVE 1 = **objective**, neutral, impartial, reserved, impersonal, disinterested, unbiased, dispassionate ≠ subjective 2 = **separate**, disconnected, discrete, unconnected, undivided

detachment NOUN 1 = **indifference**, fairness, neutrality, objectivity, impartiality, coolness, remoteness, nonchalance 2 (*military*) = **unit**, party, force, body, squad, patrol, task force

detail NOUN 1 = **point**, fact, feature, particular, respect, factor, element, aspect 2 = **fine point**, particular, nicety, triviality 3 (*military*) = **party**, force, body, duty, squad, assignment, fatigue, detachment
▷ VERB = **list**, relate, catalogue, recount, rehearse, recite, enumerate, itemize

detailed ADJECTIVE = **comprehensive**, full, complete, minute, particular, thorough, exhaustive, all-embracing ≠ brief

detain VERB 1 = **hold**, arrest, confine, restrain, imprison, intern, take prisoner, hold in custody 2 = **delay**, hold up, hamper, hinder, retard, impede, keep back, slow up *or* down

detect VERB 1 = **discover**, find, uncover, track down, unmask 2 = **notice**, see, spot, note, identify, observe, recognize, perceive

detective NOUN = **investigator**, cop (*slang*), private eye, sleuth (*informal*), private investigator, gumshoe (*U.S. slang*)

detention NOUN = **imprisonment**, custody, quarantine, confinement, incarceration ≠ release

deter VERB 1 = **discourage**, inhibit, put off, frighten, intimidate, dissuade, talk out of 2 = **prevent**, stop

deteriorate VERB = **decline**, worsen, degenerate, slump, go downhill ≠ improve

determination NOUN = **resolution**, purpose, resolve,

dedication, fortitude, persistence, tenacity, perseverance
≠ indecision

determine VERB 1 = **affect**, decide, regulate, ordain
2 = **settle**, learn, establish, discover, find out, work out, detect, verify **3** = **decide on**, choose, elect, resolve **4** = **decide**, conclude, resolve, make up your mind

determined ADJECTIVE
= **resolute**, firm, dogged, intent, persistent, persevering, single-minded, tenacious

deterrent NOUN
= **discouragement**, obstacle, curb, restraint, impediment, check, hindrance, disincentive
≠ incentive

devastate VERB = **destroy**, ruin, sack, wreck, demolish, level, ravage, raze

devastation NOUN
= **destruction**, ruin, havoc, demolition, desolation

develop VERB 1 = **grow**, advance, progress, mature, evolve, flourish, ripen **2** = **establish**, set up, promote, generate, undertake, initiate, embark on, cultivate
3 = **form**, establish, breed, generate, originate **4** = **expand**, extend, work out, elaborate, unfold, enlarge, broaden, amplify

development NOUN 1 = **growth**, increase, advance, progress, spread, expansion, evolution, enlargement **2** = **establishment**, forming, generation, institution, invention, initiation, inauguration, instigation
3 = **event**, happening, result, incident, improvement, evolution, unfolding, occurrence

deviant ADJECTIVE = **perverted**, sick (*informal*), twisted, warped, kinky (*slang*) ≠ normal
▷ NOUN = **pervert**, freak, misfit

device NOUN 1 = **gadget**, machine, tool, instrument, implement, appliance, apparatus, contraption **2** = **ploy**, scheme, plan, trick, manoeuvre, gambit, stratagem, wile

devil NOUN 1 = **evil spirit**, demon, fiend, atua (*N.Z.*), wairua (*N.Z.*)
2 = **brute**, monster, beast, barbarian, fiend, terror, swine, ogre **3** = **person**, individual, soul, creature, thing, beggar
4 = **scamp**, rogue, rascal, scoundrel, scallywag (*informal*), nointer (*Austral. slang*) ▷ PHRASE: **the Devil** = **Satan**, Lucifer, Prince of Darkness, Mephistopheles, Evil One, Beelzebub, Old Nick (*informal*)

devise VERB = **work out**, design, construct, invent, conceive, formulate, contrive, dream up

devoid ADJECTIVE *with* **of**
= **lacking in**, without, free from, wanting in, bereft of, empty of, deficient in

devote VERB = **dedicate**, give, commit, apply, reserve, pledge, surrender, assign

devoted ADJECTIVE = **dedicated**, committed, true, constant,

loyal, faithful, ardent, staunch
≠ disloyal

devotee NOUN = **enthusiast**, fan,
supporter, follower, admirer, buff
(*informal*), fanatic, adherent

devotion NOUN 1 = **love**,
passion, affection, attachment,
fondness 2 = **dedication**,
commitment, loyalty,
allegiance, fidelity, adherence,
constancy, faithfulness
≠ indifference 3 = **worship**,
reverence, spirituality, holiness,
piety, godliness, devoutness
≠ irreverence

▷ PLURAL NOUN = **prayers**,
religious observance, church
service, divine office

devour VERB 1 = **eat**, consume,
swallow, wolf, gulp, gobble,
guzzle, polish off (*informal*)
2 = **enjoy**, take in, read
compulsively *or* voraciously

devout ADJECTIVE = **religious**,
godly, pious, pure, holy, orthodox,
saintly, reverent ≠ irreverent

diagnose VERB = **identify**,
determine, recognize,
distinguish, interpret, pronounce,
pinpoint

diagnosis NOUN = **identification**,
discovery, recognition, detection

diagram NOUN = **plan**, figure,
drawing, chart, representation,
sketch, graph

dialogue NOUN 1 = **discussion**,
conference, exchange, debate
2 = **conversation**, discussion,
communication, discourse

diary NOUN 1 = **journal**, chronicle,

blog (*informal*) 2 = **engagement
book**, Filofax (*trademark*),
appointment book

dictate VERB = **speak**, say, utter,
read out
▷ NOUN 1 = **command**, order,
decree, demand, direction,
injunction, fiat, edict
2 = **principle**, law, rule, standard,
code, criterion, maxim ▷ PHRASE:
dictate to someone = **order
(about)**, direct, lay down the law,
pronounce to

dictator NOUN = **absolute
ruler**, tyrant, despot, oppressor,
autocrat, absolutist, martinet

dictatorship NOUN = **absolute
rule**, tyranny, totalitarianism,
authoritarianism, despotism,
autocracy, absolutism

dictionary NOUN = **wordbook**,
vocabulary, glossary, lexicon

die VERB 1 = **pass away**, expire,
perish, croak (*slang*), give up
the ghost, snuff it (*slang*), peg
out (*informal*), kick the bucket
(*slang*), cark it (*Austral. & N.Z.
slang*) ≠ live 2 = **stop**, fail, halt,
break down, run down, stop
working, peter out, fizzle out
3 = **dwindle**, decline, sink, fade,
diminish, decrease, decay, wither
≠ increase ▷ PHRASE: **be dying
for something** = **long for**, want,
desire, crave, yearn for, hunger for,
pine for, hanker after

diet¹ NOUN 1 = **food**, provisions,
fare, rations, kai (*N.Z. informal*),
nourishment, sustenance,
victuals 2 = **fast**, regime,

abstinence, regimen
▷ VERB = **slim**, fast, lose
weight, abstain, eat sparingly
≠ overindulge

diet² NOUN *often cap.* = **council**,
meeting, parliament, congress,
chamber, convention, legislature

differ VERB 1 = **be dissimilar**,
contradict, contrast with, vary,
belie, depart from, diverge,
negate ≠ accord 2 = **disagree**,
clash, dispute, dissent ≠ agree

difference NOUN
1 = **dissimilarity**, contrast,
variation, change, variety,
diversity, alteration, discrepancy
≠ similarity 2 = **remainder**,
rest, balance, remains, excess
3 = **disagreement**, conflict,
argument, clash, dispute, quarrel,
contretemps ≠ agreement

different ADJECTIVE
1 = **dissimilar**, opposed,
contrasting, changed, unlike,
altered, inconsistent, disparate
2 = **various**, varied, diverse,
assorted, miscellaneous, sundry
3 = **unusual**, special, strange,
extraordinary, distinctive,
peculiar, uncommon, singular

● **WORD POWER**
● On the whole, *different from* is
● preferable to *different to* and
● *different than*, both of which
● are considered unacceptable
● by some people. *Different to* is
● often heard in British English,
● but is thought by some people
● to be incorrect; and *different*
● *than*, though acceptable in

● American English, is often
● regarded as unacceptable in
● British English. This makes
● *different from* the safest option:
● *this result is only slightly different*
● *from that obtained in the U.S.* – or
● you can rephrase the sentence:
● *this result differs only slightly from*
● *that obtained in the U.S.*.

differentiate VERB
1 = **distinguish**, separate,
discriminate, contrast, mark
off, make a distinction, tell
apart, set off *or* apart 2 = **make**
different, separate, distinguish,
characterize, single out,
segregate, individualize, mark off
3 = **become different**, change,
convert, transform, alter, adapt,
modify

difficult ADJECTIVE 1 = **hard**,
tough, taxing, demanding,
challenging, exacting, formidable,
uphill ≠ easy 2 = **problematical**,
involved, complex, complicated,
obscure, baffling, intricate, knotty
≠ simple 3 = **troublesome**,
demanding, perverse, fussy,
fastidious, hard to please,
refractory, unaccommodating
≠ cooperative

difficulty NOUN 1 = **problem**,
trouble, obstacle, hurdle,
dilemma, complication, snag,
uphill (*S. African*) 2 = **hardship**,
strain, awkwardness,
strenuousness, arduousness,
laboriousness

dig VERB 1 = **hollow out**, mine,
quarry, excavate, scoop out

2 = **delve**, tunnel, burrow 3 = **turn over** 4 = **search**, hunt, root, delve, forage, dig down, fossick (*Austral. & N.Z.*) 5 = **poke**, drive, push, stick, punch, stab, thrust, shove

▷ NOUN 1 = **cutting remark**, crack (*slang*), insult, taunt, sneer, jeer, barb, wisecrack (*informal*) 2 = **poke**, thrust, nudge, prod, jab, punch

digest VERB 1 = **ingest**, absorb, incorporate, dissolve, assimilate 2 = **take in**, absorb, grasp, soak up

▷ NOUN = **summary**, résumé, abstract, epitome, synopsis, précis, abridgment

dignity NOUN 1 = **decorum**, gravity, majesty, grandeur, respectability, nobility, solemnity, courtliness 2 = **self-importance**, pride, self-esteem, self-respect

dilemma NOUN = **predicament**, problem, difficulty, spot (*informal*), mess, puzzle, plight, quandary

● WORD POWER
● The use of *dilemma* to refer to a
● problem that seems incapable
● of solution is considered by
● some people to be incorrect. To
● avoid this misuse of the word,
● an appropriate alternative such
● as *predicament* could be used.

dilute VERB 1 = **water down**, thin (out), weaken, adulterate, make thinner, cut (*informal*) ≠ condense 2 = **reduce**, weaken, diminish, temper, decrease, lessen, diffuse, mitigate ≠ intensify

dim ADJECTIVE 1 = **poorly lit**, dark,

gloomy, murky, shady, shadowy, dusky, tenebrous 2 = **cloudy**, grey, gloomy, dismal, overcast, leaden ≠ bright 3 = **unclear**, obscured, faint, blurred, fuzzy, shadowy, hazy, bleary ≠ distinct 4 = **stupid** (*informal*), thick, dull, dense, dumb (*informal*), daft (*informal*), dozy (*Brit. informal*), obtuse ≠ bright

▷ VERB 1 = **turn down**, fade, dull 2 = **grow** *or* **become faint**, fade, dull, grow *or* become dim 3 = **darken**, dull, cloud over

dimension NOUN 1 = **aspect**, side, feature, angle, facet 2 = **extent**, size

diminish VERB 1 = **decrease**, decline, lessen, shrink, dwindle, wane, recede, subside ≠ grow 2 = **reduce**, cut, decrease, lessen, lower, curtail ≠ increase

din NOUN = **noise**, row, racket, crash, clamour, clatter, uproar, commotion ≠ silence

dine VERB = **eat**, lunch, feast, sup

dinkum ADJECTIVE (*Austral. & N.Z. informal*) = **genuine**, honest, natural, frank, sincere, candid, upfront (*informal*), artless

dinner NOUN 1 = **meal**, main meal, spread (*informal*), repast 2 = **banquet**, feast, repast, hakari (*N.Z.*)

dip VERB 1 = **plunge**, immerse, bathe, duck, douse, dunk 2 = **drop (down)**, fall, lower, sink, descend, subside 3 = **slope**, drop (down), descend, fall, decline, sink, incline, drop away

▷ NOUN 1 = **plunge**, ducking,

soaking, drenching, immersion, douche **2** = **nod**, drop, lowering, slump, sag **3** = **hollow**, hole, depression, pit, basin, trough, concavity ▷ **PHRASE**: **dip into something** = **sample**, skim, glance at, browse, peruse, surf (*computing*)

diplomacy NOUN

1 = **statesmanship**, statecraft, international negotiation

2 = **tact**, skill, sensitivity, craft, discretion, subtlety, delicacy, finesse ≠ tactlessness

diplomat NOUN = **official**, ambassador, envoy, statesman, consul, attaché, emissary, chargé d'affaires

diplomatic ADJECTIVE

1 = **consular**, official, foreign-office, ambassadorial, foreign-

politic **2** = **tactful**, politic, sensitive, subtle, delicate, polite, discreet, prudent ≠ tactless

dire ADJECTIVE = **desperate**, pressing, critical, terrible, crucial, extreme, awful, urgent

direct VERB **1** = **aim**, point, level, train, focus **2** = **guide**, show, lead, point the way, point in the direction of **3** = **control**, run, manage, lead, guide, handle, conduct, oversee **4** = **order**, command, instruct, charge, demand, require, bid **5** = **address**, send, mail, route, label ▷ ADJECTIVE **1** = **quickest**, shortest **2** = **straight**, through ≠ circuitous **3** = **first-hand**, personal, immediate ≠ indirect **4** = **clear**, specific, plain, absolute, definite, explicit, downright,

d

DINOSAURS

- allosaur(us)
- ankylosaur(us)
- apatosaur(us)
- atlantosaur(us)
- brachiosaur(us)
- brontosaur(us)
- ceratosaur(us)
- compsognathus
- dimetrodon
- diplodocus
- dolichosaur(us)
- dromiosaur(us)
- elasmosaur(us)
- hadrosaur(us)
- ichthyosaur(us)
- iguanodon or iguanodont
- megalosaur(us)
- mosasaur(us)
- oviraptor
- plesiosaur(us)
- pteranodon
- pterodactyl or pterosaur
- protoceratops
- stegodon or stegodont
- stegosaur(us)
- theropod
- titanosaur(us)
- trachodon
- triceratops
- tyrannosaur(us)
- velociraptor

point-blank ≠ ambiguous
5 = **straightforward**, open,
straight, frank, blunt, honest,
candid, forthright ≠ indirect
6 = **verbatim**, exact, word-for-
word, strict, accurate, faithful,
letter-for-letter
▷ ADVERB = **non-stop**, straight

direction NOUN **1** = **way**, course,
line, road, track, bearing,
route, path **2** = **management**,
control, charge, administration,
leadership, command, guidance,
supervision

directions PLURAL
NOUN = **instructions**, rules,
information, plan, briefing,
regulations, recommendations,
guidelines

directive NOUN = **order**,
ruling, regulation, command,
instruction, decree, mandate,
injunction

directly ADVERB **1** = **straight**,
unswervingly, without deviation,
by the shortest route, in a beeline
2 = **immediately**, promptly, right
away, straightaway **3** = **at once**,
as soon as possible, straightaway,
forthwith **4** = **honestly**, openly,
frankly, plainly, point-blank,
unequivocally, truthfully,
unreservedly

director NOUN = **controller**, head,
leader, manager, chief, executive,
governor, administrator, baas
(S. African), sherang (Austral. &
N.Z.)

dirt NOUN **1** = **filth**, muck, grime,
dust, mud, impurity, kak (S. African

taboo or slang) **2** = **soil**, ground,
earth, clay, turf, loam

dirty ADJECTIVE **1** = **filthy**, soiled,
grubby, foul, muddy, polluted,
messy, grimy, festy (Austral.
slang) ≠ clean **2** = **dishonest**,
illegal, unfair, cheating, crooked,
fraudulent, treacherous,
unscrupulous ≠ honest
3 = **obscene**, indecent, blue,
offensive, filthy, pornographic,
sleazy, lewd ≠ decent
▷ VERB = **soil**, foul, stain, spoil,
muddy, pollute, blacken, defile
≠ clean

disability NOUN = **handicap**,
affliction, disorder, defect,
impairment, infirmity

disable VERB = **handicap**, cripple,
damage, paralyse, impair,
incapacitate, immobilize,
enfeeble

disabled ADJECTIVE = **differently
abled**, physically challenged,
handicapped, challenged,
weakened, crippled, paralysed,
lame, incapacitated ≠ able-
bodied

● **WORD POWER**
● Referring to people with
● disabilities as the disabled can
● cause offence and should be
● avoided. Instead, refer to them
● as people with disabilities or
● who are physically challenged,
● or, possibly, disabled people
● or differently abled people.
● In general, the terms used
● for disabilities or medical
● conditions should be avoided

● as collective nouns for people
● who have them – so, for
● example, instead of *the blind*,
● it is preferable to refer to
● *sightless people*, *vision-impaired*
● *people*, or *partially-sighted people*,
● depending on the degree of
● their condition.

disadvantage NOUN
1 = **drawback**, trouble, handicap, nuisance, snag, inconvenience, downside ≠ advantage
2 = **harm**, loss, damage, injury, hurt, prejudice, detriment, disservice ≠ benefit

disagree VERB 1 = **differ (in opinion)**, argue, clash, dispute, dissent, quarrel, take issue with, cross swords ≠ agree 2 = **make ill**, upset, sicken, trouble, hurt, bother, distress, discomfort

disagreement NOUN
= **argument**, row, conflict, clash, dispute, dissent, quarrel, squabble ≠ agreement

disappear VERB 1 = **vanish**, recede, evanesce ≠ appear
2 = **pass**, fade away 3 = **cease**, dissolve, evaporate, perish, die out, pass away, melt away, leave no trace

disappearance NOUN
1 = **vanishing**, going, passing, melting, eclipse, evaporation, evanescence 2 = **flight**, departure
3 = **loss**, losing, mislaying

disappoint VERB = **let down**, dismay, fail, disillusion, dishearten, disenchant, dissatisfy, disgruntle

disappointment NOUN
1 = **regret**, discontent, dissatisfaction, disillusionment, chagrin, disenchantment, dejection, despondency
2 = **letdown**, blow, setback, misfortune, calamity, choker (*informal*) 3 = **frustration**

disapproval NOUN
= **displeasure**, criticism, objection, condemnation, dissatisfaction, censure, reproach, denunciation

disapprove VERB = **condemn**, object to, dislike, deplore, frown on, take exception to, take a dim view of, find unacceptable ≠ approve

disarm VERB 1 = **demilitarize**, disband, demobilize, deactivate
2 = **win over**, persuade

disarmament NOUN = **arms reduction**, demobilization, arms limitation, demilitarization, de-escalation

disarming ADJECTIVE = **charming**, winning, irresistible, persuasive, likable *or* likeable

disarray NOUN 1 = **confusion**, disorder, indiscipline, disunity, disorganization, unruliness ≠ order 2 = **untidiness**, mess, chaos, muddle, clutter, shambles, jumble, hotchpotch ≠ tidiness

disaster NOUN 1 = **catastrophe**, trouble, tragedy, ruin, misfortune, adversity, calamity, cataclysm
2 = **failure**, mess, flop (*informal*), catastrophe, debacle, cock-up (*Brit. slang*), washout (*informal*)

disastrous ADJECTIVE
1 = **terrible**, devastating, tragic, fatal, catastrophic, ruinous, calamitous, cataclysmic
2 = **unsuccessful**

disbelief NOUN = **scepticism**, doubt, distrust, mistrust, incredulity, unbelief, dubiety ≠ belief

discard VERB = **get rid of**, drop, throw away or out, reject, abandon, dump (informal), dispose of, dispense with ≠ keep

discharge VERB 1 = **release**, free, clear, liberate, pardon, allow to go, set free 2 = **dismiss**, sack (informal), fire (informal), remove, expel, discard, oust, cashier, kennet (Austral. slang), jeff (Austral. slang) 3 = **carry out**, perform, fulfil, accomplish, do, effect, realize, observe 4 = **pay**, meet, clear, settle, square (up), honour, satisfy, relieve 5 = **pour forth**, release, leak, emit, dispense, ooze, exude, give off 6 = **fire**, shoot, set off, explode, let off, detonate, let loose (informal)
▷ NOUN 1 = **release**, liberation, clearance, pardon, acquittal
2 = **dismissal**, notice, removal, the boot (slang), expulsion, the push (slang), marching orders (informal), ejection 3 = **emission**, ooze, secretion, excretion, pus, seepage, suppuration 4 = **firing**, report, shot, blast, burst, explosion, volley, salvo

disciple NOUN 1 = **apostle**
2 = **follower**, student, supporter, pupil, devotee, apostle, adherent ≠ teacher

discipline NOUN 1 = **control**, authority, regulation, supervision, orderliness, strictness 2 = **self-control**, control, restraint, self-discipline, willpower, self-restraint, orderliness 3 = **training**, practice, exercise, method, regulation, drill, regimen 4 = **field of study**, area, subject, theme, topic, course, curriculum, speciality
▷ VERB 1 = **punish**, correct, reprimand, castigate, chastise, chasten, penalize, bring to book
2 = **train**, educate

disclose VERB 1 = **make known**, reveal, publish, relate, broadcast, confess, communicate, divulge ≠ keep secret 2 = **show**, reveal, expose, unveil, uncover, lay bare, bring to light ≠ hide

disclosure NOUN 1 = **revelation**, announcement, publication, leak, admission, declaration, confession, acknowledgment
2 = **uncovering**, publication, revelation, divulgence

discomfort NOUN 1 = **pain**, hurt, ache, throbbing, irritation, tenderness, pang, malaise ≠ comfort 2 = **uneasiness**, worry, anxiety, doubt, distress, misgiving, qualms, trepidation ≠ reassurance
3 = **inconvenience**, trouble, difficulty, bother, hardship, irritation, nuisance, uphill (S. African)

discontent NOUN
= **dissatisfaction**, unhappiness, displeasure, regret, envy, restlessness, uneasiness

discontented ADJECTIVE
= **dissatisfied**, unhappy, fed up, disgruntled, disaffected, vexed, displeased ≠ satisfied

discount VERB 1 = **mark down**, reduce, lower 2 = **disregard**, reject, ignore, overlook, discard, set aside, dispel, pass over
▷ NOUN = **deduction**, cut, reduction, concession, rebate

discourage VERB 1 = **dishearten**, depress, intimidate, overawe, demoralize, put a damper on, dispirit, deject ≠ hearten 2 = **put off**, deter, prevent, dissuade, talk out of ≠ encourage

discourse NOUN
1 = **conversation**, talk, discussion, speech, communication, chat, dialogue
2 = **speech**, essay, lecture, sermon, treatise, dissertation, homily, oration, whaikorero (N.Z.)

discover VERB 1 = **find out**, learn, notice, realize, recognize, perceive, detect, uncover 2 = **find**, come across, uncover, unearth, turn up, dig up, come upon

discovery NOUN 1 = **finding out**, news, revelation, disclosure, realization 2 = **invention**, launch, institution, pioneering, innovation, inauguration
3 = **breakthrough**, find, development, advance, leap, invention, step forward, quantum

leap 4 = **finding**, revelation, uncovering, disclosure, detection

discredit VERB 1 = **disgrace**, shame, smear, humiliate, taint, disparage, vilify, slander ≠ honour 2 = **dispute**, question, challenge, deny, reject, discount, distrust, mistrust
▷ NOUN = **disgrace**, scandal, shame, disrepute, stigma, ignominy, dishonour, ill-repute ≠ honour

discreet ADJECTIVE = **tactful**, diplomatic, guarded, careful, cautious, wary, prudent, considerate ≠ tactless

discrepancy NOUN
= **disagreement**, difference, variation, conflict, contradiction, inconsistency, disparity, divergence

discretion NOUN 1 = **tact**, consideration, caution, diplomacy, prudence, wariness, carefulness, judiciousness ≠ tactlessness 2 = **choice**, will, pleasure, preference, inclination, volition

discriminate VERB
= **differentiate**, distinguish, separate, tell the difference, draw a distinction ▷ PHRASE:
discriminate against someone
= **treat differently**, single out, victimize, treat as inferior, show bias against, show prejudice against

discriminating ADJECTIVE
= **discerning**, particular, refined, cultivated, selective, tasteful,

fastidious ≠ undiscriminating

discrimination NOUN
1 = **prejudice**, bias, injustice, intolerance, bigotry, favouritism, unfairness 2 = **discernment**, taste, judgment, perception, subtlety, refinement

discuss VERB = **talk about**, consider, debate, examine, argue about, deliberate about, converse about, confer about

discussion NOUN 1 = **talk**, debate, argument, conference, conversation, dialogue, consultation, discourse, korero (*N.Z.*) 2 = **examination**, investigation, analysis, scrutiny, dissection

disdain NOUN = **contempt**, scorn, arrogance, derision, haughtiness, superciliousness
▷ VERB = **scorn**, reject, slight, disregard, spurn, deride, look down on, sneer at

disease NOUN = **illness**, condition, complaint, infection, disorder, sickness, ailment, affliction

diseased ADJECTIVE = **unhealthy**, sick, infected, rotten, ailing, sickly, unwell, crook (*Austral. & N.Z. informal*), unsound

disgrace NOUN 1 = **shame**, degradation, disrepute, ignominy, dishonour, infamy, opprobrium, odium ≠ honour 2 = **scandal**, stain, stigma, blot, blemish
▷ VERB = **shame**, humiliate, discredit, degrade, taint, sully, dishonour, bring shame upon ≠ honour

disgraceful ADJECTIVE = **shameful**, shocking, scandalous, unworthy, ignominious, disreputable, contemptible, dishonourable

disgruntled ADJECTIVE = **discontented**, dissatisfied, annoyed, irritated, put out, grumpy, vexed, displeased, hoha (*N.Z.*)

disguise VERB = **hide**, cover, conceal, screen, mask, suppress, withhold, veil
▷ NOUN = **costume**, mask, camouflage

disguised ADJECTIVE 1 = **in disguise**, masked, camouflaged, undercover, incognito 2 = **false**, artificial, forged, fake, mock, imitation, sham, counterfeit

disgust VERB 1 = **sicken**, offend, revolt, put off, repel, nauseate ≠ delight 2 = **outrage**, shock, anger, hurt, fury, resentment, wrath, indignation

disgusting ADJECTIVE 1 = **sickening**, foul, revolting, gross, repellent, nauseating, repugnant, loathsome, festy (*Austral. slang*), yucko (*Austral. slang*) 2 = **appalling**, shocking, awful, offensive, dreadful, horrifying

dish NOUN 1 = **bowl**, plate, platter, salver 2 = **food**, fare, recipe

dishonest ADJECTIVE = **deceitful**, corrupt, crooked (*informal*), lying, bent (*slang*), false, cheating, treacherous ≠ honest

disintegrate VERB = **break up**,

crumble, fall apart, separate, shatter, splinter, break apart, go to pieces

dislike VERB = **hate**, object to, loathe, despise, disapprove of, detest, recoil from, take a dim view of ≠ like
  ▷ NOUN = **hatred**, hostility, disapproval, distaste, animosity, aversion, displeasure, antipathy ≠ liking

dismal ADJECTIVE 1 = **bad**, awful, dreadful, rotten (*informal*), terrible, poor, dire, abysmal 2 = **sad**, gloomy, dark, depressing, discouraging, bleak, dreary, sombre ≠ happy 3 = **gloomy**, depressing, dull, dreary ≠ cheerful

dismantle VERB = **take apart**, strip, demolish, disassemble, take to pieces *or* bits

dismay VERB 1 = **alarm**, frighten, scare, panic, distress, terrify, appal, startle 2 = **disappoint**, upset, discourage, daunt, disillusion, let down, dishearten, dispirit
  ▷ NOUN 1 = **alarm**, fear, horror, anxiety, dread, apprehension, nervousness, consternation 2 = **disappointment**, frustration, dissatisfaction, disillusionment, chagrin, disenchantment, discouragement

dismiss VERB 1 = **reject**, disregard 2 = **banish**, dispel, discard, set aside, cast out, lay aside, put out of your mind 3 = **sack**, fire (*informal*), remove (*informal*),

axe (*informal*), discharge, lay off, cashier, give notice to, kennet (*Austral. slang*), jeff (*Austral. slang*) 4 = **let go**, free, release, discharge, dissolve, liberate, disperse, send away

dismissal NOUN = **the sack**, removal, notice, the boot (*slang*), expulsion (*informal*), the push (*slang*), marching orders (*informal*)

disobey VERB 1 = **defy**, ignore, rebel, disregard, refuse to obey 2 = **infringe**, defy, refuse to obey, flout, violate, contravene, overstep, transgress

disorder NOUN 1 = **illness**, disease, complaint, condition, sickness, ailment, affliction, malady 2 = **untidiness**, mess, confusion, chaos, muddle, clutter, shambles, disarray 3 = **disturbance**, riot, turmoil, unrest, uproar, commotion, unruliness, biffo (*Austral. slang*)

disorderly ADJECTIVE 1 = **untidy**, confused, chaotic, messy, jumbled, shambolic (*informal*), disorganized, higgledy-piggledy (*informal*) ≠ tidy 2 = **unruly**, disruptive, rowdy, turbulent, tumultuous, lawless, riotous, ungovernable

dispatch *or* **despatch** VERB 1 = **send**, consign 2 = **kill**, murder, destroy, execute, slaughter, assassinate, slay, liquidate 3 = **carry out**, perform, fulfil, effect, finish, achieve, settle, dismiss
  ▷ NOUN = **message**, news, report,

story, account, communication, bulletin, communiqué

dispel VERB = **drive away**, dismiss, eliminate, expel, disperse, banish, chase away

dispense VERB 1 = **distribute**, assign, allocate, allot, dole out, share out, apportion, deal out 2 = **prepare**, measure, supply, mix 3 = **administer**, operate, carry out, implement, enforce, execute, apply, discharge ▷ PHRASE: **dispense with something** or **someone** 1 = **do away with**, give up, cancel, abolish, brush aside, forgo 2 = **do without**, get rid of, dispose of, relinquish

disperse VERB 1 = **scatter**, spread, distribute, strew, diffuse, disseminate, throw about 2 = **break up**, separate, scatter, dissolve, disband ≠ gather 3 = **dissolve**, break up

displace VERB 1 = **replace**, succeed, supersede, oust, usurp, supplant, take the place of 2 = **move**, shift, disturb, budge, misplace

display VERB 1 = **show**, present, exhibit, put on view ≠ conceal 2 = **expose**, show, reveal, exhibit, uncover 3 = **demonstrate**, show, reveal, register, expose, disclose, manifest 4 = **show off**, parade, exhibit, sport (*informal*), flash (*informal*), flourish, brandish, flaunt ▷ NOUN 1 = **proof**, exhibition, demonstration, evidence, expression, illustration,

revelation, testimony 2 = **exhibition**, show, demonstration, presentation, array 3 = **ostentation**, show, flourish, fanfare, pomp 4 = **show**, exhibition, parade, spectacle, pageant

disposable ADJECTIVE 1 = **throwaway**, nonreturnable 2 = **available**, expendable, consumable

disposal NOUN = **throwing away**, dumping (*informal*), scrapping, removal, discarding, jettisoning, ejection, riddance ▷ PHRASE: **at your disposal** = **available**, ready, to hand, accessible, handy, at hand, on tap, expendable

dispose VERB = **arrange**, put, place, group, order, distribute, array ▷ PHRASES: **dispose of someone** = **kill**, murder, destroy, execute, slaughter, assassinate, slay, liquidate; **dispose of something** 1 = **get rid of**, destroy, dump (*informal*), scrap, discard, unload, jettison, throw out or away 2 = **deal with**, manage, treat, handle, settle, cope with, take care of, see to

disposition NOUN 1 = **character**, nature, spirit, make-up, constitution, temper, temperament 2 = **tendency**, inclination, propensity, habit, leaning, bent, bias, proclivity 3 (*archaic*) = **arrangement**, grouping, ordering, organization, distribution, placement

dispute VERB 1 = **contest**,

question, challenge, deny, doubt, oppose, object to, contradict
2 = argue, fight, clash, disagree, fall out (*informal*), quarrel, squabble, bicker
▷ NOUN **1 = disagreement**, conflict, argument, dissent, altercation **2 = argument**, row, clash, controversy, contention, feud, quarrel, squabble
disqualify VERB **= ban**, rule out, prohibit, preclude, debar, declare ineligible
disregard VERB **= ignore**, discount, overlook, neglect, pass over, turn a blind eye to, make light of, pay no heed to ≠ pay attention to
▷ NOUN **= ignoring**, neglect, contempt, indifference, negligence, disdain, disrespect
disrupt VERB **1 = interrupt**, stop, upset, hold up, interfere with, unsettle, obstruct, cut short
2 = disturb, upset, confuse, disorder, spoil, disorganize, disarrange
disruption NOUN **= disturbance**, interference, interruption, stoppage
disruptive ADJECTIVE **= disturbing**, upsetting, disorderly, unsettling, troublesome, unruly ≠ well-behaved
dissatisfaction NOUN **= discontent**, frustration, resentment, disappointment, irritation, unhappiness, annoyance, displeasure

dissatisfied ADJECTIVE **= discontented**, frustrated, unhappy, disappointed, fed up, disgruntled, displeased, unsatisfied ≠ satisfied
dissent NOUN **= disagreement**, opposition, protest, resistance, refusal, objection, discord, demur ≠ assent
dissident ADJECTIVE **= dissenting**, disagreeing, nonconformist, heterodox
▷ NOUN **= protester**, rebel, dissenter, demonstrator, agitator
dissolve VERB **1 = melt**, soften, thaw, liquefy, deliquesce
2 = end, suspend, break up, wind up, terminate, discontinue, dismantle, disband
distance NOUN **1 = space**, length, extent, range, stretch, gap, interval, span **2 = aloofness**, reserve, detachment, restraint, stiffness, coolness, coldness, standoffishness
distant ADJECTIVE **1 = far-off**, far, remote, abroad, out-of-the-way, far-flung, faraway, outlying ≠ close **2 = remote 3 = reserved**, withdrawn, cool, remote, detached, aloof, unfriendly, reticent ≠ friendly **4 = faraway**, blank, vague, distracted, vacant, preoccupied, oblivious, absent-minded
distinct ADJECTIVE **1 = different**, individual, separate, discrete, unconnected ≠ similar
2 = striking, dramatic, outstanding, noticeable, well-

defined **3 = definite**, marked,
clear, decided, obvious, evident,
noticeable, conspicuous ≠ vague

distinction NOUN **1 = difference**,
contrast, variation, differential,
discrepancy, disparity,
dissimilarity **2 = excellence**,
importance, fame, merit,
prominence, greatness,
eminence, repute **3 = feature**,
quality, characteristic, mark,
individuality, peculiarity,
distinctiveness, particularity
4 = merit, honour, integrity,
excellence, rectitude

distinctive ADJECTIVE
= characteristic, special,
individual, unique, typical,
peculiar, singular, idiosyncratic
≠ ordinary

distinctly ADVERB **1 = definitely**,
clearly, obviously, plainly,
patently, decidedly, markedly,
noticeably **2 = clearly**, plainly

distinguish VERB
1 = differentiate, determine,
separate, discriminate, decide,
judge, ascertain, tell the
difference **2 = characterize**,
mark, separate, single out, set
apart **3 = make out**, recognize,
perceive, know, see, tell, pick out,
discern

distinguished ADJECTIVE
= eminent, noted, famous,
celebrated, well-known,
prominent, esteemed, acclaimed
≠ unknown

distort VERB **1 = misrepresent**,
twist, bias, disguise, pervert,

slant, colour, misinterpret
2 = deform, bend, twist, warp,
buckle, mangle, mangulate
(*Austral. slang*), disfigure, contort

distortion NOUN
1 = misrepresentation, bias,
slant, perversion, falsification
2 = deformity, bend, twist, warp,
buckle, contortion, malformation,
crookedness

distract VERB **1 = divert**,
sidetrack, draw away, turn
aside, lead astray, draw or lead
away from **2 = amuse**, occupy,
entertain, beguile, engross

distracted ADJECTIVE **= agitated**,
troubled, puzzled, at sea,
perplexed, flustered, in a flap
(*informal*)

distraction NOUN
1 = disturbance, interference,
diversion, interruption
2 = entertainment, recreation,
amusement, diversion, pastime

distraught ADJECTIVE **= frantic**,
desperate, distressed,
distracted, worked-up, agitated,
overwrought, out of your mind

distress VERB **= upset**, worry,
trouble, disturb, grieve, torment,
harass, agitate
▷ NOUN **1 = suffering**, pain,
worry, grief, misery, torment,
sorrow, heartache **2 = need**,
trouble, difficulties, poverty, hard
times, hardship, misfortune,
adversity

distressed ADJECTIVE **1 = upset**,
worried, troubled, distracted,
tormented, distraught, agitated,

wretched 2 = **poverty-stricken**, poor, impoverished, needy, destitute, indigent, down at heel, straitened

distressing ADJECTIVE = **upsetting**, worrying, disturbing, painful, sad, harrowing, heart-breaking

distribute VERB 1 = **hand out**, pass round 2 = **circulate**, deliver, convey 3 = **share**, deal, allocate, dispense, allot, dole out, apportion

distribution NOUN 1 = **delivery**, mailing, transportation, handling 2 (*economics*) = **sharing**, division, assignment, rationing, allocation, allotment, apportionment 3 = **spread**, organization, arrangement, placement

district NOUN = **area**, region, sector, quarter, parish, neighbourhood, vicinity, locality

distrust VERB = **suspect**, doubt, be wary of, mistrust, disbelieve, be suspicious of ≠ trust ▷ NOUN = **suspicion**, question, doubt, disbelief, scepticism, mistrust, misgiving, wariness ≠ trust

disturb VERB 1 = **interrupt**, trouble, bother, plague, disrupt, interfere with, hassle, inconvenience 2 = **upset**, concern, worry, trouble, alarm, distress, unsettle, unnerve ≠ calm 3 = **muddle**, disorder, mix up, mess up, jumble up, disarrange, muss (*U.S. & Canad.*)

disturbance NOUN 1 = **disorder**, fray, brawl, fracas, commotion, rumpus 2 = **upset**, bother, distraction, intrusion, interruption, annoyance

disturbed ADJECTIVE 1 (*psychiatry*) = **unbalanced**, troubled, disordered, unstable, neurotic, upset, deranged, maladjusted ≠ balanced 2 = **worried**, concerned, troubled, upset, bothered, nervous, anxious, uneasy ≠ calm

disturbing ADJECTIVE = **worrying**, upsetting, alarming, frightening, distressing, startling, unsettling, harrowing

ditch NOUN = **channel**, drain, trench, dyke, furrow, gully, moat, watercourse ▷ VERB 1 (*slang*) = **get rid of**, dump (*informal*), scrap, discard, dispose of, dispense with, jettison, throw out *or* overboard 2 (*slang*) = **leave**, drop, abandon, dump (*informal*), get rid of, forsake

dive VERB 1 = **plunge**, drop, duck, dip, descend, plummet 2 = **go underwater** 3 = **nose-dive**, plunge, crash, swoop, plummet ▷ NOUN = **plunge**, spring, jump, leap, lunge, nose dive

diverse ADJECTIVE 1 = **various**, mixed, varied, assorted, miscellaneous, several, sundry, motley 2 = **different**, unlike, varying, separate, distinct, disparate, discrete, dissimilar

diversify VERB = **vary**, change, expand, spread out, branch out

diversion NOUN 1 = **distraction**,

deviation, digression
2 = **pastime**, game, sport,
entertainment, hobby, relaxation,
recreation, distraction
3 (*chiefly Brit.*) = **detour**,
roundabout way, indirect course
4 (*chiefly Brit.*) = **deviation**,
departure, straying, divergence,
digression

diversity NOUN **1** = **difference**,
multiplicity, heterogeneity,
diverseness **2** = **range**, variety,
scope, sphere

divert VERB **1** = **redirect**, switch,
avert, deflect, deviate, turn aside
2 = **distract**, sidetrack, lead
astray, draw or lead away from
3 = **entertain**, delight, amuse,
please, charm, gratify, beguile,
regale

divide VERB **1** = **separate**,
split, segregate, bisect ≠ join
2 = **share**, distribute, allocate,
dispense, allot, mete, deal out
3 = **split**, break up, come between,
estrange, cause to disagree

dividend NOUN = **bonus**, share,
cut (*informal*), gain, extra, plus,
portion, divvy (*informal*)

divine ADJECTIVE **1** = **heavenly**,
spiritual, holy, immortal,
supernatural, celestial, angelic,
superhuman **2** = **sacred**,
religious, holy, spiritual, blessed,
revered, hallowed, consecrated **3**
(*informal*) = **wonderful**, perfect,
beautiful, excellent, lovely,
glorious, marvellous, splendid
▷ VERB = **guess**, suppose,
perceive, discern, infer, deduce,

apprehend, surmise

division NOUN **1** = **separation**,
dividing, splitting up, partition,
cutting up **2** = **sharing**, sharing,
distribution, assignment,
rationing, allocation,
allotment, apportionment
3 = **disagreement**, split, rift,
rupture, abyss, chasm, variance,
discord ≠ unity **4** = **department**,
group, branch **5** = **part**, bit, piece,
section, class, category, fraction

divorce NOUN = **separation**, split,
break-up, parting, split-up, rift,
dissolution, annulment
▷ VERB = **separate**, split up, part
company, dissolve your marriage

dizzy ADJECTIVE **1** = **giddy**, faint,
light-headed, swimming, reeling,
shaky, wobbly, off balance
2 = **confused**, dazzled, at sea,
bewildered, muddled, bemused,
dazed, disorientated

do VERB **1** = **perform**, achieve,
carry out, complete, accomplish,
execute, pull off **2** = **make**,
prepare, fix, arrange, look after,
see to, get ready **3** = **solve**, work
out, resolve, figure out, decode,
decipher, puzzle out **4** = **be**
adequate, be sufficient, satisfy,
suffice, pass muster, cut the
mustard, meet requirements
5 = **produce**, make, create,
develop, manufacture, construct,
invent, fabricate
▷ NOUN (*informal, chiefly Brit.*
& *N.Z.*) = **party**, gathering,
function, event, affair, occasion,
celebration, reception ▷ PHRASES:

do away with something
= **get rid of**, remove, eliminate, abolish, discard, put an end to, dispense with, discontinue;
do without something or someone = **manage without**, give up, dispense with, forgo, kick (*informal*), abstain from, get along without

dock¹ NOUN = **port**, haven, harbour, pier, wharf, quay, waterfront, anchorage
▷ VERB 1 = **moor**, land, anchor, put in, tie up, berth, drop anchor 2 (*of a spacecraft*) = **link up**, unite, join, couple, rendezvous, hook up

dock² VERB 1 = **cut**, reduce, decrease, diminish, lessen ≠ increase 2 = **deduct**, subtract 3 = **cut off**, crop, clip, shorten, curtail, cut short

doctor NOUN = **physician**, medic (*informal*), general practitioner, medical practitioner, G.P.
▷ VERB 1 = **change**, alter, interfere with, disguise, pervert, tamper with, tinker with, misrepresent 2 = **add to**, spike, cut, mix something with something, dilute, water down, adulterate

doctrine NOUN = **teaching**, principle, belief, opinion, conviction, creed, dogma, tenet, kaupapa (*N.Z.*)

document NOUN = **paper**, form, certificate, report, record, testimonial, authorization
▷ VERB = **support**, certify, verify, detail, validate, substantiate, corroborate, authenticate

dodge VERB 1 = **duck**, dart, swerve, sidestep, shoot, turn aside 2 = **evade**, avoid, escape, get away from, elude 3 = **avoid**, evade, shirk
▷ NOUN = **trick**, scheme, ploy, trap, device, fraud, manoeuvre, deception, fastie (*Austral. slang*)

dodgy ADJECTIVE 1 (*Brit., Austral. & N.Z. informal*) = **nasty**, offensive, unpleasant, revolting, distasteful, repellent, obnoxious, repulsive, shonky (*Austral. & N.Z. informal*) 2 (*Brit., Austral. & N.Z. informal*) = **risky**, difficult, tricky, dangerous, delicate, uncertain, dicey (*informal, chiefly Brit.*), chancy (*informal*), shonky (*Austral. & N.Z. informal*)

dog NOUN = **hound**, canine, pooch (*slang*), cur, man's best friend, kuri *or* goorie (*N.Z.*), brak (*S. African*)
▷ VERB 1 = **plague**, follow, trouble, haunt, hound, torment 2 = **pursue**, follow, track, chase, trail, hound, stalk ▷ RELATED WORDS: *adjective* canine, *female* bitch, *young* pup, puppy

dogged ADJECTIVE = **determined**, persistent, stubborn, resolute, tenacious, steadfast, obstinate, indefatigable ≠ irresolute

dole NOUN = **share**, grant, gift, allowance, handout, koha (*N.Z.*)
▷ PHRASE: **dole something out** = **give out**, distribute, assign, allocate, hand out, dispense, allot, apportion

dolphin NOUN ▷ RELATED WORD: *collective noun* school

▷ *see* **whales and dolphins**

domestic ADJECTIVE 1 = **home**, internal, native, indigenous 2 = **household**, home, family, private 3 = **home-loving**, homely, housewifely, stay-at-home, domesticated 4 = **domesticated**, trained, tame, pet, house-trained ▷ NOUN = **servant**, help, maid, daily, char (*informal*), charwoman

dominant ADJECTIVE 1 = **main**, chief, primary, principal, prominent, predominant, pre-eminent ≠ minor 2 = **controlling**, ruling, commanding, supreme, governing, superior, authoritative

dominate VERB 1 = **control**, rule, direct, govern, monopolize, tyrannize, have the whip hand over 2 = **tower above**, overlook, survey, stand over, loom over, stand head and shoulders above

domination NOUN = **control**, power, rule, authority, influence, command, supremacy, ascendancy

don VERB = **put on**, get into, dress in, pull on, change into, get dressed in, clothe yourself in, slip on *or* into

donate VERB = **give**, present, contribute, grant, subscribe, endow, entrust, impart

donation NOUN = **contribution**, gift, subscription, offering, present, grant, hand-out, koha (*N.Z.*)

donor NOUN = **giver**, contributor, benefactor, philanthropist, donator ≠ recipient

doom NOUN = **destruction**, ruin, catastrophe, downfall ▷ VERB = **condemn**, sentence, consign, destine

doomed ADJECTIVE = **hopeless**, condemned, ill-fated, fated, unhappy, unfortunate, cursed, unlucky

door NOUN = **opening**, entry, entrance, exit, doorway

dope NOUN 1 (*slang*) = **drugs**, narcotics, opiates, dadah (*Austral. slang*) 2 (*informal*) = **idiot**, fool, twit (*informal, chiefly Brit.*), dunce, simpleton, dimwit (*informal*), nitwit (*informal*), dumb-ass (*slang*), dorba *or* dorb (*Austral. slang*), bogan (*Austral. slang*) ▷ VERB = **drug**, knock out, sedate, stupefy, anaesthetize, narcotize

dorp NOUN (*S. African*) = **town**, village, settlement, municipality, kainga *or* kaika (*N.Z.*)

dose NOUN 1 (*medical*) = **measure**, amount, allowance, portion, prescription, ration, draught, dosage 2 = **quantity**, measure, supply, portion

dot NOUN = **spot**, point, mark, fleck, jot, speck, speckle ▷ PHRASE: **on the dot** = **on time**, promptly, precisely, exactly (*informal*), to the minute, on the button (*informal*), punctually VERB = **spot**, stud, fleck, speckle

double ADJECTIVE 1 = **matching**, coupled, paired, twin, duplicate, in pairs 2 = **dual**, enigmatic, twofold

▷ **NOUN** = **twin**, lookalike, spitting image, clone, replica, dead ringer (*slang*), Doppelgänger, duplicate
▷ **PHRASE**: **at** *or* **on the double** = **at once**, now, immediately, directly, quickly, promptly, straight away, right away **VERB** 1 = **multiply by two**, duplicate, increase twofold, enlarge, magnify 2 = **fold up** *or* **over** 3 *with* **as** = **function as**, serve as

doubt NOUN 1 = **uncertainty**, confusion, hesitation, suspense, indecision, hesitancy, lack of conviction, irresolution ≠ certainty 2 = **suspicion**, scepticism, distrust, apprehension, mistrust, misgivings, qualms ≠ belief
▷ **VERB** 1 = **be uncertain**, be sceptical, be dubious 2 = **waver**, hesitate, vacillate, fluctuate 3 = **disbelieve**, question, suspect, query, distrust, mistrust, lack confidence in ≠ believe

doubtful ADJECTIVE 1 = **unlikely**, unclear, dubious, questionable, improbable, debatable, equivocal ≠ certain 2 = **unsure**, uncertain, hesitant, suspicious, hesitating, sceptical, tentative, wavering ≠ certain

doubtless ADVERB = **probably**, presumably, most likely

down ADJECTIVE = **depressed**, low, sad, unhappy, discouraged, miserable, fed up, dejected
▷ **VERB** (*informal*) = **swallow**, drink (down), drain, gulp (down), put away (*informal*), toss off

downfall NOUN = **ruin**, fall, destruction, collapse, disgrace, overthrow, undoing, comeuppance (*slang*)

downgrade VERB = **demote**, degrade, take down a peg (*informal*), lower *or* reduce in rank ≠ promote

downright ADJECTIVE = **complete**, absolute, utter, total, plain, outright, unqualified, out-and-out

down-to-earth ADJECTIVE = **sensible**, practical, realistic, matter-of-fact, sane, no-nonsense, unsentimental, plain-spoken, grounded

downward ADJECTIVE = **descending**, declining, heading down, earthward

draft NOUN 1 = **outline**, plan, sketch, version, rough, abstract 2 = **money order**, bill (of exchange), cheque, postal order
▷ **VERB** = **outline**, write, plan, produce, create, design, draw, compose

drag VERB = **pull**, draw, haul, trail, tow, tug, jerk, lug
▷ **NOUN** (*informal*) = **nuisance**, bore, bother, pest, hassle (*informal*), inconvenience, annoyance

drain NOUN 1 = **sewer**, channel, pipe, sink, ditch, trench, conduit, duct 2 = **reduction**, strain, drag, exhaustion, sapping, depletion
▷ **VERB** 1 = **remove**, draw, empty, withdraw, tap, pump, bleed 2 = **empty** 3 = **flow out**, leak,

trickle, ooze, seep, exude, well out, effuse **4** = **drink up**, swallow, finish, put away (*informal*), quaff, gulp down **5** = **exhaust**, wear out, strain, weaken, fatigue, debilitate, tire out, enfeeble **6** = **consume**, exhaust, empty, use up, sap, dissipate

drama NOUN **1** = **play**, show, stage show, dramatization **2** = **theatre**, acting, stagecraft, dramaturgy **3** = **excitement**, crisis, spectacle, turmoil, histrionics
▷ *see* **dramatists**

dramatic ADJECTIVE **1** = **exciting**, thrilling, tense, sensational, breathtaking, electrifying, melodramatic, climactic **2** = **theatrical**, Thespian, dramaturgical **3** = **expressive** **4** = **powerful**, striking, impressive, vivid, jaw-dropping ≠ ordinary

drape VERB = **cover**, wrap, fold, swathe

drastic ADJECTIVE = **extreme**, strong, radical, desperate, severe, harsh

draught *or* (U.S.) **draft** NOUN **1** = **breeze**, current, movement, flow, puff, gust, current of air **2** = **drink**

draw VERB **1** = **sketch**, design, outline, trace, portray, paint, depict, mark out **2** = **pull**, drag, haul, tow, tug **3** = **extract**, take, remove **4** = **deduce**, make, take, derive, infer **5** = **attract** **6** = **entice**
▷ NOUN **1** = **tie**, deadlock,

stalemate, impasse, dead heat **2** (*informal*) = **appeal**, pull (*informal*), charm, attraction, lure, temptation, fascination, allure ▷ PHRASE: **draw on** *or* **upon something** = **make use of**, use, employ, rely on, exploit, extract, take from, fall back on

drawback NOUN = **disadvantage**, difficulty, handicap, deficiency, flaw, hitch, snag, downside ≠ advantage

drawing NOUN = **picture**, illustration, representation, cartoon, sketch, portrayal, depiction, study

drawn ADJECTIVE = **tense**, worn, stressed, tired, pinched, haggard

dread VERB = **fear**, shrink from, cringe at the thought of, quail from, shudder to think about, have cold feet about (*informal*), tremble to think about
▷ NOUN = **fear**, alarm, horror, terror, dismay, fright, apprehension, trepidation

dreadful ADJECTIVE **1** = **terrible**, shocking, awful, appalling, horrible, fearful, hideous, atrocious **2** = **serious**, terrible, awful, horrendous, monstrous, abysmal **3** = **awful**, terrible, horrendous, frightful

dream NOUN **1** = **vision**, illusion, delusion, hallucination **2** = **ambition**, wish, fantasy, desire, pipe dream **3** = **daydream** **4** = **delight**, pleasure, joy, beauty, treasure, gem, marvel, pearler (*Austral. slang*), beaut (*Austral. &*

N.Z. slang)

▷ **VERB 1** = **have dreams**, hallucinate **2** = **daydream**, stargaze, build castles in the air *or* in Spain ▷ **PHRASE**: **dream of something** *or* **someone** = **daydream about**, fantasize about

dreamer NOUN = **idealist**, visionary, daydreamer, utopian, escapist, Walter Mitty, fantasist

dreary ADJECTIVE = **dull**, boring, tedious, drab, tiresome, monotonous, humdrum, uneventful ≠ exciting

drench VERB = **soak**, flood, wet, drown, steep, swamp, saturate, inundate

dress NOUN **1** = **frock**, gown, robe **2** = **clothing**, clothes, costume, garments, apparel, attire, garb, togs

▷ **VERB 1** = **put on clothes**, don clothes, slip on *or* into something ≠ undress **2** = **clothe 3** = **bandage**, treat, plaster, bind up **4** = **arrange**, prepare, get ready

dribble VERB **1** = **run**, drip, trickle, drop, leak, ooze, seep, fall in drops **2** = **drool**, drivel, slaver, slobber

drift VERB **1** = **float**, go (aimlessly), bob, coast, slip, sail, slide, glide **2** = **wander**, stroll, stray, roam, meander, rove, range **3** = **stray**, wander, digress, get off the point **4** = **pile up**, gather, accumulate, amass, bank up

▷ **NOUN 1** = **pile**, bank, mass, heap, mound, accumulation

2 = **meaning**, point, gist, direction, import, intention, tendency, significance

drill¹ NOUN **1** = **bit**, borer, gimlet, boring tool **2** = **training**, exercise, discipline, instruction, preparation, repetition **3** (*informal*) = **practice**

▷ **VERB 1** = **bore**, pierce, penetrate, sink in, puncture, perforate **2** = **train**, coach, teach, exercise, discipline, practise, instruct, rehearse

drink VERB **1** = **swallow**, sip, suck, gulp, sup, guzzle, imbibe, quaff **2** = **booze** (*informal*), tipple, tope, hit the bottle (*informal*)

▷ **NOUN 1** = **glass**, cup, draught **2** = **beverage**, refreshment, potion, liquid **3** = **alcohol**, booze (*informal*), liquor, spirits, the bottle (*informal*), hooch *or* hootch (*informal, chiefly U.S. & Canad.*)

drip VERB = **drop**, splash, sprinkle, trickle, dribble, exude, plop

▷ **NOUN 1** = **drop**, bead, trickle, dribble, droplet, globule, pearl **2** (*informal*) = **weakling**, wet (*Brit. informal*), weed (*informal*), softie (*informal*), mummy's boy (*informal*), namby-pamby

drive VERB **1** = **go (by car)**, ride (by car), motor, travel by car **2** = **operate**, manage, direct, guide, handle, steer **3** = **push**, propel **4** = **thrust**, push, hammer, ram **5** = **herd**, urge, impel **6** = **force**, press, prompt, spur, prod, constrain, coerce, goad

▷ **NOUN 1** = **run**, ride, trip,

journey, spin (*informal*), outing, excursion, jaunt **2** = **initiative**, energy, enterprise, ambition, motivation, zip (*informal*), vigour, get-up-and-go (*informal*) **3** = **campaign**, push (*informal*), crusade, action, effort, appeal

drop VERB **1** = **fall**, decline, diminish **2** *often with* **away** = **decline**, fall, sink **3** = **plunge**, fall, tumble, descend, plummet **4** = **drip**, trickle, dribble, fall in drops **5** = **sink**, fall, descend **6** = **quit**, give up, axe (*informal*), kick (*informal*), relinquish, discontinue
▷ NOUN **1** = **decrease**, fall, cut, lowering, decline, reduction, slump, fall-off **2** = **droplet**, bead, globule, bubble, pearl, drip **3** = **dash**, shot (*informal*), spot, trace, sip, tot, trickle, mouthful **4** = **fall**, plunge, descent ▷ PHRASES: **drop off 1** = **fall asleep**, nod (off), doze (off), snooze (*informal*), have forty winks (*informal*) **2** = **decrease**, lower, decline, shrink, diminish, dwindle, lessen, subside; **drop out** = **leave**, stop, give up, withdraw, quit, pull out, fall by the wayside; **drop out of something** = **discontinue**, give up, quit

dross = **nonsense**, garbage (*chiefly U.S.*), twaddle, rot, trash, hot air (*informal*), tripe (*informal*), claptrap (*informal*), bizzo (*Austral. slang*), bull's wool (*Austral. & N.Z. slang*)

drought NOUN = **water shortage**, dryness, dry spell, aridity ≠ flood

drove NOUN *often plural* = **herd**, company, crowds, collection, mob, flocks, swarm, horde

drown VERB **1** = **go down**, go under **2** = **drench**, flood, soak, steep, swamp, saturate, engulf, submerge **3** *often with* **out** = **overwhelm**, overcome, wipe out, overpower, obliterate, swallow up

drug NOUN **1** = **medication**, medicine, remedy, physic, medicament **2** = **dope** (*slang*), narcotic (*slang*), stimulant, opiate, dadah (*Austral. slang*)
▷ VERB = **knock out**, dope (*slang*), numb, deaden, stupefy, anaesthetize

drum VERB = **pound**, beat, tap, rap, thrash, tattoo, throb, pulsate
▷ PHRASE: **drum something into someone** = **drive**, hammer, instil, din, harp on about

drunk ADJECTIVE = **intoxicated**, plastered (*slang*), drunken, merry (*Brit. informal*), under the influence (*informal*), tipsy, legless (*informal*), inebriated, out to it (*Austral. & N.Z. slang*), babalas (*S. African*)
▷ NOUN = **drunkard**, alcoholic, lush (*slang*), boozer (*informal*), wino (*informal*), inebriate, alko or alco (*Austral. slang*)

dry ADJECTIVE **1** = **dehydrated**, dried-up, arid, parched, desiccated ≠ wet **2** = **thirsty**, parched **3** = **sarcastic**, cynical, low-key, sly, sardonic, deadpan, droll, ironical **4** = **dull**, boring, tedious, dreary, tiresome,

monotonous, run-of-the-mill, humdrum ≠ interesting **5** = **plain**, simple, bare, basic, stark, unembellished
▷ VERB **1** = **drain**, make dry **2** *often with* **out** = **dehydrate**, make dry, desiccate, sear, parch, dehumidify ≠ wet ▷ PHRASE: **dry out** *or* **up** = **become dry**, harden, wither, shrivel up, wizen

dual ADJECTIVE = **twofold**, double, twin, matched, paired, duplicate, binary, duplex

dubious ADJECTIVE **1** = **suspect**, suspicious, crooked, dodgy (*Brit., Austral. & N.Z. informal*), questionable, unreliable, fishy (*informal*), disreputable ≠ trustworthy **2** = **unsure**, uncertain, suspicious, hesitating, doubtful, sceptical, tentative, wavering ≠ sure

duck VERB **1** = **bob**, drop, lower, bend, bow, dodge, crouch, stoop **2** (*informal*) = **dodge**, avoid, escape, evade, elude, sidestep, shirk **3** = **dunk**, wet, plunge, dip, submerge, immerse, douse, souse

due ADJECTIVE **1** = **expected**, scheduled **2** = **fitting**, deserved, appropriate, justified, suitable, merited, proper, rightful **3** = **payable**, outstanding, owed, owing, unpaid, in arrears
▷ NOUN = **right(s)**, privilege, deserts, merits, comeuppance (*informal*)
▷ ADVERB = **directly**, dead, straight, exactly, undeviatingly

duel NOUN **1** = **single combat**, affair of honour **2** = **contest**, fight, competition, clash, encounter, engagement, rivalry
▷ VERB = **fight**, struggle, clash, compete, contest, contend, vie with, lock horns

dues PLURAL NOUN = **membership fee**, charges, fee, contribution, levy

duff ADJECTIVE (*Brit., Austral. & N.Z. informal*) = **bad**, poor, useless, inferior, unsatisfactory, defective, imperfect, substandard, bodger *or* bodgie (*Austral. slang*)

dull ADJECTIVE **1** = **boring**, tedious, dreary, flat, plain, monotonous, run-of-the-mill, humdrum ≠ exciting **2** = **lifeless**, indifferent, apathetic, listless, unresponsive, passionless ≠ lively **3** = **cloudy**, dim, gloomy, dismal, overcast, leaden ≠ bright **4** = **blunt**, blunted, unsharpened ≠ sharp
▷ VERB = **relieve**, blunt, lessen, moderate, soften, alleviate, allay, take the edge off

duly ADVERB **1** = **properly**, fittingly, correctly, appropriately, accordingly, suitably, deservedly, rightfully **2** = **on time**, promptly, punctually, at the proper time

dumb ADJECTIVE **1** = **unable to speak**, mute ≠ articulate **2** = **silent**, mute, speechless, tongue-tied, wordless, voiceless, soundless, mum **3** (*informal*) = **stupid**, thick, dull, foolish, dense, unintelligent, asinine, dim-witted (*informal*) ≠ clever

d

dummy NOUN 1 = **model**, figure, mannequin, form, manikin 2 = **imitation**, copy, duplicate, sham, counterfeit, replica 3 (slang) = **fool**, idiot, dunce, oaf, simpleton, nitwit (informal), blockhead, dumb-ass (slang), dorba or dorb (Austral. slang), bogan (Austral. slang)
▷ MODIFIER = **imitation**, false, fake, artificial, mock, bogus, simulated, sham

dump VERB 1 = **drop**, deposit, throw down, let fall, fling down 2 = **get rid of**, tip, dispose of, unload, jettison, empty out, throw away or out 3 = **scrap**, get rid of, abolish, put an end to, discontinue, jettison, put paid to
▷ NOUN 1 = **rubbish tip**, tip, junkyard, rubbish heap, refuse heap 2 (informal) = **pigsty**, hole (informal), slum, hovel

dunny NOUN (Austral. & N.Z. old-fashioned, informal) = **toilet**, lavatory, bathroom, loo (Brit. informal), W.C., bog (slang), Gents or Ladies, can (U.S. & Canad. slang), bogger (Austral. slang), brasco (Austral. slang)

duplicate ADJECTIVE = **identical**, matched, matching, twin, corresponding, twofold
▷ NOUN 1 = **copy**, facsimile 2 = **photocopy**, copy, reproduction, replica, carbon copy
▷ VERB 1 = **repeat**, reproduce, copy, clone, replicate 2 = **copy**

durable ADJECTIVE 1 = **hard-wearing**, strong, tough, reliable, resistant, sturdy, long-lasting ≠ fragile 2 = **enduring**, continuing, dependable, unwavering, unfaltering

duration NOUN = **length**, time, period, term, stretch, extent, spell, span, time frame, timeline

dusk NOUN = **twilight**, evening, evo (Austral. slang), nightfall, sunset, dark, sundown, eventide, gloaming (Scot. poetic) ≠ dawn

dust NOUN 1 = **grime**, grit, powder 2 = **particles**
▷ VERB = **sprinkle**, cover, powder, spread, spray, scatter, sift, dredge

dusty ADJECTIVE = **dirty**, grubby, unclean, unswept

- **WORD POWER**
- Dutch is a member of the
- western branch of the
- Germanic family of languages,
- as is English. Several compound
- words, whose combination
- of parts contributes a new
- meaning, have been borrowed
- from Dutch into English. The
- word *poppycock*, which came
- into English in the 19th century,
- literally means 'soft excrement',
- which evolved into its modern
- meaning of 'nonsense'. The
- association between words
- for faeces and words meaning
- rubbish has also given us
- stronger terms 'crap', 'cack',
- and 'bullshit'. Poppycock has
- nothing to do with either
- poppies or cocks, but the
- perception that this was an odd
- mixture may have contributed

to the meaning of nonsense.
It is an informal term, often
used on its own as a mild
expletive, or in combination
with *a bunch /load of*. Another
compound word which has an
interesting juxtaposition of
parts is *maelstrom*. From the
obsolete Dutch 17th century
maelstroom meaning 'whirl-
stream', it originally denoted an
authentic strong tidal current
off the west coast of Norway,
responsible for shipwrecks.
This specialized sense, which
is often capitalized, has been
superseded by the much more
common figurative sense
of maelstrom, meaning a
turbulent confusion, e.g. *a
maelstrom of emotions*. It is
quite a literary word, much
less common in speech than
in writing. The second part
'strom' evokes 'storm' which
has reinforced the meaning of
tumult.

duty NOUN **1** = **responsibility**,
job, task, work, role, function,
obligation, assignment **2** = **tax**,
toll, levy, tariff, excise ▷ PHRASE:
on duty = **at work**, busy,
engaged, on active service

dwarf NOUN = **gnome**, midget,
Lilliputian, Tom Thumb, pygmy
or pigmy

▷ MODIFIER = **miniature**, small,
baby, tiny, diminutive, bonsai,
undersized

▷ VERB **1** = **tower above** *or*
over, dominate, overlook, stand
over, loom over, stand head and
shoulders above **2** = **eclipse**,
tower above *or* over, put in the
shade, diminish

dwell VERB (*formal* or *literary*)
= **live**, reside, lodge, abide

dwelling NOUN (*formal* or *literary*)
= **home**, house, residence, abode,
quarters, lodging, habitation,
domicile, whare (*N.Z.*)

dwindle VERB = **lessen**, decline,
fade, shrink, diminish, decrease,
wane, subside ≠ increase

dye NOUN = **colouring**, colour,
pigment, stain, tint, tinge,
colorant

▷ VERB = **colour**, stain, tint, tinge,
pigment

dying ADJECTIVE **1** = **near death**,
moribund, in extremis (*Latin*),
at death's door, not long for this
world **2** = **final**, last, parting,
departing **3** = **failing**, declining,
foundering, diminishing,
decreasing, dwindling, subsiding

dynamic ADJECTIVE = **energetic**,
powerful, vital, go-ahead, lively,
animated, high-powered, forceful
≠ apathetic

dynasty NOUN = **empire**, house,
rule, regime, sovereignty

Ee

each ADJECTIVE = **every**, every single

▷ PRONOUN = **every one**, all, each one, each and every one, one and all

▷ ADVERB = **apiece**, individually, for each, to each, respectively, per person, per head, per capita

● WORD POWER
● *Each* is a singular pronoun and
● should be used with a singular
● verb – for example, *each of*
● *the candidates was interviewed*
● *separately* (not *were interviewed*
● *separately*).

eager ADJECTIVE 1 *often with to* *or* **for** = **anxious**, keen, hungry, impatient, itching, thirsty ≠ unenthusiastic 2 = **keen**, interested, intense, enthusiastic, passionate, avid (*informal*), fervent ≠ uninterested

ear NOUN = **sensitivity**, taste, discrimination, appreciation

▷ RELATED WORD: *adjectives* **aural**

● WORD POWER
● The *ear* is the organ of hearing
● and balance in humans. In
● the phrase *walls have ears*,
● walls are given the human
● characteristic of a sense of
● hearing. This expression was
● used as a slogan of national
● security in the Second World
● War to discourage indiscreet
● talk along the general
● population. The ability to
● discriminate sounds has led
● to ear meaning sensitivity,
● especially *an ear for music* and
● *an ear for language*. Hearing and
● listening are activities which
● can be selective, therefore ear
● also means paying attention:
● closely in *all ears*; as a conscious
● decision in *lend an ear*; and not
● at all in *turn a deaf ear*. Although
● it might be expected that *ears*
● *of corn* are related to the human
● ear in their resemblance, these
● are actually two different
● words which look the same.

early ADVERB 1 = **in good time**, beforehand, ahead of schedule, in advance, with time to spare ≠ late 2 = **too soon**, before the usual time, prematurely, ahead of time ≠ late

▷ ADJECTIVE 1 = **first**, opening, initial, introductory 2 = **premature**, forward, advanced, untimely, unseasonable ≠ belated 3 = **primitive**, first, earliest, young, original, undeveloped, primordial, primeval ≠ developed

earmark VERB 1 = **set aside**, reserve, label, flag, allocate, designate, mark out 2 = **mark out**, identify, designate

earn VERB 1 = **be paid**, make, get, receive, gain, net, collect, bring in 2 = **deserve**, win, gain, attain, justify, merit, warrant, be entitled to

earnest ADJECTIVE 1 = **serious**, grave, intense, dedicated, sincere, thoughtful, solemn, ardent ≠ frivolous 2 = **determined**, dogged, intent, persistent, persevering, resolute, wholehearted ≠ half-hearted

earnings PLURAL NOUN = **income**, pay, wages, revenue, proceeds, salary, receipts, remuneration

earth NOUN 1 = **world**, planet, globe, sphere, orb, earthly sphere 2 = **ground**, land, dry land, terra firma 3 = **soil**, ground, land, dust, clay, dirt, turf, silt

earthly ADJECTIVE 1 = **worldly**, material, secular, mortal, temporal, human ≠ spiritual 2 = **sensual**, worldly, physical, fleshly, bodily, carnal 3 (*informal*) = **possible**, likely, practical, feasible, conceivable, imaginable

ease NOUN 1 = **straightforwardness**, simplicity, readiness 2 = **comfort**, luxury, leisure, relaxation, prosperity, affluence, rest, repose ≠ hardship 3 = **peace of mind**, peace, content, quiet, comfort, happiness, serenity, tranquillity ≠ agitation ▷ VERB 1 = **relieve**, calm, soothe, lessen, alleviate, lighten, lower, relax ≠ aggravate 2 *often with* **off** *or* **up** = **reduce**, diminish, lessen, slacken 3 = **move carefully**, edge, slip, inch, slide, creep, manoeuvre

easily ADVERB = **without difficulty**, smoothly, readily, comfortably, effortlessly, with ease, straightforwardly

easy ADJECTIVE 1 = **simple**, straightforward, no trouble, not difficult, effortless, painless, uncomplicated, child's play (*informal*) ≠ hard 2 = **untroubled**, relaxed, peaceful, serene, tranquil, quiet 3 = **carefree**, comfortable, leisurely, trouble-free, untroubled, cushy (*informal*) ≠ difficult 4 = **tolerant**, soft, mild, laid-back (*informal*), indulgent, easy-going, lenient, permissive ≠ strict

eat VERB 1 = **consume**, swallow, chew, scoff (*slang*), devour, munch, tuck into (*informal*), put away 2 = **have a meal**, lunch, breakfast, dine, snack, feed, graze (*informal*), have lunch

ebb VERB 1 = **flow back**, go out, withdraw, retreat, wane, recede 2 = **decline**, flag, diminish, decrease, dwindle, lessen, subside, fall away ▷ NOUN = **flowing back**, going out, withdrawal, retreat, wane, low water, low tide, outgoing tide

eccentric ADJECTIVE = **odd**, strange, peculiar, irregular, quirky, unconventional, idiosyncratic, outlandish, daggy (*Austral. & N.Z. informal*) ≠ normal ▷ NOUN = **crank** (*informal*), character (*informal*), oddball (*informal*), nonconformist, weirdo *or* weirdie (*informal*)

echo NOUN 1 = **reverberation**,

ringing, repetition, answer, resonance, resounding **2** = **copy**, reflection, clone, reproduction, imitation, duplicate, double, reiteration

▷ VERB **1** = **reverberate**, repeat, resound, ring, resonate **2** = **recall**, reflect, copy, mirror, resemble, imitate, ape

eclipse NOUN = **obscuring**, covering, blocking, shading, dimming, extinction, darkening, blotting out

▷ VERB = **surpass**, exceed, overshadow, excel, transcend, outdo, outclass, outshine

economic ADJECTIVE
1 = **financial**, industrial, commercial **2** (*Brit.*) = **profitable**, successful, commercial, rewarding, productive, lucrative, worthwhile, viable **3** (*informal*) = **economical**, cheap, reasonable, modest, low-priced, inexpensive

economical ADJECTIVE
1 = **thrifty**, sparing, careful, prudent, provident, frugal, parsimonious, scrimping ≠ extravagant **2** = **efficient**, sparing, cost-effective, money-saving, time-saving ≠ wasteful

economy NOUN **1** = **financial system**, financial state **2** = **thrift**, restraint, prudence, husbandry, frugality, parsimony

ecstasy NOUN = **rapture**, delight, joy, bliss, euphoria, fervour, elation ≠ agony

ecstatic ADJECTIVE = **rapturous**, entranced, joyous, elated,

overjoyed, blissful, euphoric, enraptured, stoked (*Austral. & N.Z. informal*)

edge NOUN **1** = **border**, side, limit, outline, boundary, fringe, verge, brink **2** = **verge**, point, brink, threshold **3** = **advantage**, lead, dominance, superiority, upper hand, head start, ascendancy, whip hand **4** = **power**, force, bite, effectiveness, incisiveness, powerful quality **5** = **sharpness**, point, bitterness, keenness

▷ VERB **1** = **inch**, ease, creep, slink, steal, sidle, move slowly **2** = **border**, fringe, hem, pipe

▷ PHRASE: **on edge** = **tense**, nervous, impatient, irritable, apprehensive, edgy, ill at ease, on tenterhooks, adrenalized

edit VERB = **revise**, improve, correct, polish, adapt, rewrite, condense, redraft

edition NOUN **1** = **printing**, publication **2** = **copy**, impression **3** = **version**, volume, issue **4** = **programme** (*tv, radio*)

educate VERB = **teach**, school, train, develop, improve, inform, discipline, tutor

educated ADJECTIVE **1** = **cultured**, intellectual, learned, sophisticated, refined, cultivated, enlightened, knowledgeable ≠ uncultured **2** = **taught**, schooled, coached, informed, tutored, instructed, nurtured, well-informed ≠ uneducated

education NOUN **1** = **teaching**, schooling, training, development, discipline, instruction, nurture, tuition **2 = learning**, schooling, cultivation, refinement

educational ADJECTIVE
1 = academic, school, learning, teaching, scholastic, pedagogical, pedagogic **2 = instructive**, useful, cultural, illuminating, enlightening, informative, instructional, edifying

eerie ADJECTIVE **= uncanny**, strange, frightening, ghostly, weird, mysterious, scary (*informal*), sinister

effect NOUN **1 = result**, consequence, conclusion, outcome, event, end result, upshot **2 = impression**, feeling, impact, influence **3 = purpose**, impression, sense, intent, essence, thread, tenor
▷ VERB **= bring about**, produce, complete, achieve, perform, fulfil, accomplish, execute

● WORD POWER
● It is quite common for the
● verb *effect* to be mistakenly
● used where *affect* is intended.
● *Effect* is relatively uncommon
● and rather formal, and is a
● synonym of 'bring about'.
● Conversely, the noun *effect* is
● quite often mistakenly written
● with an initial *a*. The following
● are correct: *the group is still*
● *recovering from the effects of the*
● *recession; they really are powerless*
● *to effect any change.* The next
● two examples are incorrect: *the*
● *full affects of the shutdown won't*

● *be felt for several more days; men*
● *whose lack of hair doesn't effect*
● *their self-esteem.*

effective ADJECTIVE **1 = efficient**, successful, useful, active, capable, valuable, helpful, adequate ≠ ineffective **2 = powerful**, strong, convincing, persuasive, telling, impressive, compelling, forceful ≠ weak **3 = virtual**, essential, practical, implied, implicit, tacit, unacknowledged **4 = in operation**, official, current, legal, active, in effect, valid, operative ≠ inoperative

effects PLURAL NOUN **= belongings**, goods, things, property, stuff, gear, possessions, paraphernalia

efficiency NOUN
1 = effectiveness, power, economy, productivity, organization, cost-effectiveness, orderliness **2 = competence**, expertise, capability, professionalism, proficiency, adeptness

efficient ADJECTIVE **1 = effective**, successful, structured, productive, systematic, streamlined, cost-effective, methodical ≠ inefficient **2 = competent**, professional, capable, organized, productive, proficient, businesslike, well-organized ≠ incompetent

effort NOUN **1 = attempt**, try, endeavour, shot (*informal*), bid, essay, go (*informal*), stab (*informal*) **2 = exertion**, work, trouble, energy, struggle, application, graft, toil

egg¹ NOUN = **ovum**, gamete, germ cell ▷ PHRASE: **egg someone on** = **incite**, push, encourage, urge, prompt, spur, provoke, prod

eject VERB 1 = **throw out**, remove, turn out, expel (*slang*), oust, banish, drive out, evict 2 = **bail out**, escape, get out

elaborate ADJECTIVE
1 = **complicated**, detailed, studied, complex, precise, thorough, intricate, painstaking
2 = **ornate**, involved, complex, fancy, complicated, intricate, baroque, ornamented ≠ plain
▷ VERB 1 = **develop**, flesh out
2 *usually with* **on** *or* **upon**
= **expand upon**, extend upon, enlarge on, amplify upon, embellish, flesh out, add detail to ≠ simplify

elastic ADJECTIVE 1 = **flexible**, supple, rubbery, pliable, plastic, springy, pliant, tensile ≠ rigid
2 = **adaptable**, yielding, variable, flexible, accommodating, tolerant, adjustable, supple ≠ inflexible

elbow NOUN = **joint**, angle, curve

elder ADJECTIVE = **older**, first, senior, first-born
▷ NOUN = **older person**, senior

elect VERB 1 = **vote for**, choose, pick, determine, select, appoint, opt for, settle on 2 = **choose**, decide, prefer, select, opt

election NOUN 1 = **vote**, poll, ballot, referendum, franchise, plebiscite, show of hands
2 = **appointment**, picking, choice, selection

electric ADJECTIVE 1 = **electric-powered**, powered, cordless, battery-operated, electrically-charged, mains-operated
2 = **charged**, exciting, stirring, thrilling, stimulating, dynamic, tense, rousing, adrenalized

elegance NOUN = **style**, taste, grace, dignity, sophistication, grandeur, refinement, gracefulness

elegant ADJECTIVE = **stylish**, fine, sophisticated, delicate, handsome, refined, chic, exquisite, schmick (*Austral. informal*) ≠ inelegant

element NOUN 1 = **component**, part, unit, section, factor, principle, aspect, foundation
2 = **group**, faction, clique, set, party, circle 3 = **trace**, suggestion, hint, dash, suspicion, tinge, smattering, soupçon
▷ PLURAL NOUN = **weather conditions**, climate, the weather, wind and rain, atmospheric conditions, powers of nature
▷ PHRASE: **in your element** = **in a situation you enjoy**, in your natural environment, in familiar surroundings

elementary ADJECTIVE = **simple**, clear, easy, plain, straightforward, rudimentary, uncomplicated, undemanding ≠ complicated

elevate VERB 1 = **promote**, raise, advance, upgrade,

exalt, kick upstairs (*informal*),
aggrandize, give advancement to
2 = **increase**, lift, raise, step up,
intensify, move up, hoist, raise
high **3** = **raise**, lift, heighten,
uplift, hoist, lift up, raise up, hike
up

elevated ADJECTIVE **1** = **exalted**,
important, august, grand,
superior, noble, dignified, high-
ranking **2** = **high-minded**, fine,
grand, noble, inflated, dignified,
sublime, lofty ≠ humble
3 = **raised**, high, lifted up,
upraised

elicit VERB **1** = **bring about**, cause,
derive, bring out, evoke, give
rise to, draw out, bring forth
2 = **obtain**, extract, exact, evoke,
wrest, draw out, extort

eligible ADJECTIVE **1** = **entitled**, fit,
qualified, suitable ≠ ineligible
2 = **available**, free, single,
unmarried, unattached

eliminate VERB = **remove**, end,
stop, withdraw, get rid of, abolish,
cut out, dispose of

elite NOUN = **aristocracy**, best,
pick, cream, upper class, nobility,
crème de la crème (*French*), flower
≠ rabble

eloquent ADJECTIVE
1 = **silver-tongued**, moving,
powerful, effective, stirring,
articulate, persuasive, forceful
≠ inarticulate **2** = **expressive**,
telling, pointed, significant,
vivid, meaningful, indicative,
suggestive

elsewhere ADVERB = **in** *or* **to**

another place, away, abroad,
hence (*archaic*), somewhere else,
not here, in other places, in *or* to a
different place

elude VERB **1** = **evade**, escape,
lose, avoid, flee, duck (*informal*),
dodge, get away from **2** = **escape**,
baffle, frustrate, puzzle, stump,
foil, be beyond (someone), thwart

● WORD POWER
● *Elude* is sometimes wrongly
● used where *allude* is meant: *he*
● *was alluding* (not *eluding*) *to his*
● *previous visit to the city.*

elusive ADJECTIVE **1** = **difficult**
to catch, tricky, slippery,
difficult to find, evasive, shifty
2 = **indefinable**, fleeting, subtle,
indefinite, transient, intangible,
indescribable, transitory

● WORD POWER
● The spelling of *elusive*, as in *a*
● *shy, elusive character*, should be
● noted. This adjective derives
● from the verb *elude*, and should
● not be confused with the rare
● word *illusive* meaning 'not real'
● or 'based on illusion'.

emanate VERB *often with* **from**
= **flow**, emerge, spring, proceed,
arise, stem, derive, originate

embargo NOUN = **ban**, bar,
restriction, boycott, restraint,
prohibition, moratorium,
stoppage, rahui (*N.Z.*)
▷ VERB = **block**, stop, bar, ban,
restrict, boycott, prohibit,
blacklist

embark VERB = **go aboard**, climb
aboard, board ship, step aboard,

go on board, take ship ≠ get off

▷ PHRASE: **embark on something** = **begin**, start, launch, enter, take up, set out, set about, plunge into

embarrass VERB = **shame**, distress, show up (*informal*), humiliate, disconcert, fluster, mortify, discomfit

embarrassed ADJECTIVE = **ashamed**, shamed, uncomfortable, awkward, abashed, humiliated, uneasy, unsettled

embarrassing ADJECTIVE = **humiliating**, upsetting, compromising, delicate, uncomfortable, awkward, sensitive, troublesome, barro (*Austral. slang*)

embarrassment NOUN **1** = **shame**, distress, showing up (*informal*), humiliation, discomfort, unease, self-consciousness, awkwardness **2** = **problem**, difficulty, nuisance, source of trouble, thorn in your flesh **3** = **predicament**, problem, difficulty (*informal*), mess, jam (*informal*), plight, scrape (*informal*), pickle (*informal*)

embody VERB **1** = **personify**, represent, stand for, manifest, exemplify, symbolize, typify, actualize **2** *often with* **in** = **incorporate**, include, contain, combine, collect, take in, encompass

embrace VERB **1** = **hug**, hold, cuddle, seize, squeeze, clasp, envelop, canoodle (*slang*)

2 = **accept**, support, welcome, adopt, take up, seize, espouse, take on board **3** = **include**, involve, cover, contain, take in, incorporate, comprise, encompass

▷ NOUN = **hug**, hold, cuddle, squeeze, clinch (*slang*), clasp

embroil VERB = **involve**, mix up, implicate, entangle, mire, ensnare, enmesh

embryo NOUN **1** = **fetus**, unborn child, fertilized egg **2** = **germ**, beginning, source, root, seed, nucleus, rudiment

emerge VERB **1** = **come out**, appear, surface, rise, arise, turn up, spring up, emanate ≠ withdraw **2** = **become apparent**, come out, become known, come to light, crop up, transpire, become evident, come out in the wash

emergence NOUN **1** = **coming**, development, arrival, surfacing, rise, appearance, arising, turning up **2** = **disclosure**, publishing, broadcasting, broadcast, publication, declaration, revelation, becoming known

emergency NOUN = **crisis**, danger, difficulty, accident, disaster, necessity, plight, scrape (*informal*)

▷ ADJECTIVE **1** = **urgent**, crisis, immediate **2** = **alternative**, extra, additional, substitute, replacement, temporary, makeshift, stopgap

emigrate VERB = **move abroad**,

move, relocate, migrate, resettle, leave your country

eminent ADJECTIVE = **prominent**, noted, respected, famous, celebrated, distinguished, well-known, esteemed ≠ unknown

emission NOUN = **giving off** *or* **out**, release, shedding, leak, radiation, discharge, transmission, ejaculation

emit VERB 1 = **give off**, release, leak, transmit, discharge, send out, radiate, eject ≠ absorb
2 = **utter**, produce, voice, give out, let out

emotion NOUN 1 = **feeling**, spirit, soul, passion, excitement, sensation, sentiment, fervour
2 = **instinct**, sentiment, sensibility, intuition, tenderness, gut feeling, soft-heartedness

emotional ADJECTIVE
1 = **psychological**, private, personal, hidden, spiritual, inner 2 = **moving**, touching, affecting, stirring, sentimental, poignant, emotive, heart-rending 3 = **emotive**, sensitive, controversial, delicate, contentious, heated, inflammatory, touchy
4 = **passionate**, sentimental, temperamental, excitable, demonstrative, hot-blooded

emphasis NOUN 1 = **importance**, attention, weight, significance, stress, priority, prominence
2 = **stress**, accent, force, weight

emphasize VERB 1 = **highlight**, stress, underline, draw attention

to, dwell on, play up, make a point of, give priority to ≠ minimize
2 = **stress**, accentuate, lay stress on

emphatic ADJECTIVE 1 = **forceful**, positive, definite, vigorous, unmistakable, insistent, unequivocal, vehement
≠ hesitant 2 = **significant**, pronounced, decisive, resounding, conclusive

empire NOUN 1 = **kingdom**, territory, province, federation, commonwealth, realm, domain
2 = **organization**, company, business, firm, concern, corporation, consortium, syndicate ▷ **RELATED WORD**: *adjective* imperial

empirical ADJECTIVE = **first-hand**, direct, observed, practical, actual, experimental, pragmatic, factual ≠ hypothetical

employ VERB 1 = **hire**, commission, appoint, take on, retain, engage, recruit, sign up
2 = **use**, apply, exercise, exert, make use of, utilize, ply, bring to bear 3 = **spend**, fill, occupy, involve, engage, take up, make use of, use up

employed ADJECTIVE
1 = **working**, in work, having a job, in employment, in a job, earning your living ≠ out of work 2 = **busy**, active, occupied, engaged, hard at work, in harness, rushed off your feet ≠ idle

employee *or* (U.S.) **employe** NOUN = **worker**, labourer, workman, staff member, member of staff, hand, wage-earner, white-collar worker

employer NOUN 1 = **boss** (*informal*), manager, head, leader, director, chief, owner, master, baas (*S. African*), sherang (*Austral. & N.Z.*) 2 = **company**, business, firm, organization, establishment, outfit (*informal*)

employment NOUN 1 = **job**, work, position, trade, post, situation, profession, occupation 2 = **taking on**, commissioning, appointing, hire, hiring, retaining, engaging, appointment 3 = **use**, application, exertion, exercise, utilization

empower VERB 1 = **authorize**, allow, commission, qualify, permit, sanction, entitle, delegate 2 = **enable**, equip, emancipate, give means to, enfranchise

empty ADJECTIVE 1 = **bare**, clear, abandoned, deserted, vacant, free, void, desolate ≠ full 2 = **meaningless**, cheap, hollow, vain, idle, futile, insincere 3 = **worthless**, meaningless, hollow, pointless, futile, senseless, fruitless, inane ≠ meaningful
▷ VERB 1 = **clear**, drain, void, unload, pour out, unpack, remove the contents of ≠ fill 2 = **exhaust**, consume the contents of, void, deplete, use up ≠ replenish 3 = **evacuate**, clear, vacate

emulate VERB = **imitate**, follow,

copy, mirror, echo, mimic, model yourself on

enable VERB 1 = **allow**, permit, empower, give someone the opportunity, give someone the means ≠ prevent 2 = **authorize**, allow, permit, qualify, sanction, entitle, license, warrant ≠ stop

enact VERB 1 = **establish**, order, command, approve, sanction, proclaim, decree, authorize 2 = **perform**, play, present, stage, represent, put on, portray, depict

enchant VERB = **fascinate**, delight, charm, entrance, dazzle, captivate, enthral, beguile

enclose or **inclose** VERB 1 = **surround**, circle, bound, fence, confine, close in, wall in, encircle 2 = **send with**, include, put in, insert

encompass VERB 1 = **include**, hold, cover, admit, deal with, contain, take in, embrace 2 = **surround**, circle, enclose, close in, envelop, encircle, fence in, ring

encounter VERB 1 = **experience**, meet, face, suffer, have, go through, sustain, endure 2 = **meet**, confront, come across, bump into (*informal*), run across, come upon, chance upon, meet by chance
▷ NOUN 1 = **meeting**, brush, confrontation, rendezvous, chance meeting 2 = **battle**, conflict, clash, contest, run-in (*informal*), confrontation, head-to-head

encourage VERB 1 = **inspire**,

comfort, cheer, reassure,
console, hearten, cheer up,
embolden ≠ discourage **2** = **urge**,
persuade, prompt, spur, coax,
egg on ≠ dissuade **3** = **promote**,
back, support, increase, foster,
advocate, stimulate, endorse
≠ prevent

encouragement NOUN
1 = **inspiration**, support, comfort,
comforting, cheer, cheering,
reassurance, morale boosting
2 = **urging**, prompting, stimulus,
persuasion, coaxing, egging
on, incitement **3** = **promotion**,
backing, support, endorsement,
stimulation, furtherance

end NOUN **1** = **close**, ending, finish,
expiry, expiration ≠ beginning
2 = **conclusion**, ending, climax,
completion, finale, culmination,
denouement, consummation
≠ start **3** = **finish**, close, stop,
resolution, conclusion, closure,
completion, termination
4 = **extremity**, limit, edge,
border, extent, extreme, margin,
boundary **5** = **tip**, point, head,
peak, extremity **6** = **purpose**,
point, reason, goal, target, aim,
object, mission **7** = **outcome**,
resolution, conclusion **8** = **death**,
dying, ruin, destruction, passing
on, doom, demise, extinction
9 = **remnant**, butt, stub, scrap,
fragment, stump, remainder,
leftover
▷ VERB **1** = **stop**, finish, halt,
cease, wind up, terminate,
call off, discontinue ≠ start

2 = **finish**, close, conclude, wind
up, culminate, terminate, come
to an end, draw to a close ≠ begin
▷ RELATED WORDS: *adjectives* **final,
terminal, ultimate**

endanger VERB = **put at risk**,
risk, threaten, compromise,
jeopardize, imperil, put in danger,
expose to danger ≠ save

endearing ADJECTIVE
= **attractive**, winning, pleasing,
appealing, sweet, engaging,
charming, pleasant

endeavour (*formal*) VERB = **try**,
labour, attempt, aim, struggle,
venture, strive, aspire
▷ NOUN = **attempt**, try, effort,
trial, bid, venture, enterprise,
undertaking

ending NOUN = **finish**, end,
close, conclusion, summing up,
completion, finale, culmination
≠ start

endless ADJECTIVE = **eternal**,
infinite, continual, unlimited,
interminable, incessant,
boundless, everlasting
≠ temporary

endorse VERB **1** = **approve**, back,
support, champion, promote,
recommend, advocate, uphold
2 = **sign**, initial, countersign, sign
on the back of

endorsement NOUN = **approval**,
backing, support, favour,
recommendation, acceptance,
agreement, upholding

endow VERB **1** = **finance**, fund,
pay for, award, confer, bestow,
bequeath, donate money to

2 = **imbue**

endowed ADJECTIVE *usually with* **with** = **provided**, favoured, graced, blessed, supplied, furnished

endowment NOUN = **provision**, funding, award, grant, gift, contribution, subsidy, donation, koha (*N.Z.*)

endurance NOUN **1** = **staying power**, strength, resolution, determination, patience, stamina, fortitude, persistence **2** = **permanence**, stability, continuity, duration, longevity, durability, continuance

endure VERB **1** = **experience**, suffer, bear, meet, encounter, cope with, sustain, undergo **2** = **last**, continue, remain, stay, stand, go on, survive, live on

enemy NOUN = **foe**, rival, opponent, the opposition, competitor, the other side, adversary, antagonist ≠ friend

energetic ADJECTIVE **1** = **forceful**, determined, active, aggressive, dynamic, vigorous, hard-hitting, strenuous **2** = **lively**, active, dynamic, vigorous, animated, tireless, bouncy, indefatigable ≠ lethargic **3** = **strenuous**, hard, taxing, demanding, tough, exhausting, vigorous, arduous

energy NOUN **1** = **strength**, might, stamina, forcefulness **2** = **liveliness**, drive, determination, pep, vitality, vigour, verve, resilience **3** = **power**

enforce VERB **1** = **carry out**, apply, implement, fulfil, execute, administer, put into effect, put into action **2** = **impose**, force, insist on

engage VERB **1** = **participate in**, join in, take part in, undertake, embark on, enter into, become involved in, set about **2** = **captivate**, catch, arrest, fix, capture **3** = **occupy**, involve, draw, grip, absorb, preoccupy, immerse, engross **4** = **employ**, appoint, take on, hire, retain, recruit, enlist, enrol ≠ dismiss **5** = **set going**, apply, trigger, activate, switch on, energize, bring into operation **6** (*military*) = **begin battle with**, attack, take on, encounter, fall on, battle with, meet, assail

engaged ADJECTIVE **1** = **occupied**, working, employed, busy, tied up **2** = **betrothed**, promised, pledged, affianced, promised in marriage ≠ unattached **3** = **in use**, busy, tied up, unavailable ≠ free

engagement NOUN **1** = **appointment**, meeting, interview, date, commitment, arrangement, rendezvous **2** = **betrothal**, marriage contract, troth (*archaic*), agreement to marry **3** = **battle**, fight, conflict, action, struggle, clash, encounter, combat **4** = **participation**, joining, taking part, involvement

engaging ADJECTIVE = **charming**, interesting, pleasing, attractive,

lovely, entertaining, winning,
fetching (*informal*) ≠ unpleasant

engine NOUN = **machine**, motor,
mechanism, generator, dynamo

engineer NOUN 1 = **designer**,
producer, architect, developer,
deviser, creator, planner, inventor
2 = **worker**, specialist, operator,
practitioner, operative, driver,
conductor, technician
▷ VERB 1 = **design**, plan, create,
construct, devise 2 = **bring
about**, plan, effect, set up
(*informal*), scheme, arrange, plot,
mastermind

engraving NOUN = **print**, carving,
etching, inscription, plate,
woodcut, dry point

engulf VERB 1 = **immerse**,
swamp, submerge, overrun,
inundate, envelop, swallow up
2 = **overwhelm**, overcome, crush,
swamp

enhance VERB = **improve**, better,
increase, lift, boost, add to,
strengthen, reinforce ≠ reduce

enjoy VERB 1 = **take pleasure in**
or **from**, like, love, appreciate,
relish, delight in, be pleased with,
be fond of ≠ hate 2 = **have**, use,
own, experience, possess, have
the benefit of, reap the benefits of,
be blessed *or* favoured with

enjoyable ADJECTIVE
= **pleasurable**, good, great,
fine, nice, satisfying, lovely,
entertaining ≠ unpleasant

enjoyment NOUN 1 = **pleasure**,
liking, fun, delight,
entertainment, joy, happiness,

relish 2 = **benefit**, use, advantage,
favour, possession, blessing

enlarge VERB 1 = **expand**,
increase, extend, add to, build
up, widen, intensify, broaden
≠ reduce 2 = **grow**, increase,
extend, expand, swell, become
bigger, puff up, grow larger
▷ PHRASE: **enlarge on something**
= **expand on**, develop, add to,
fill out, elaborate on, flesh out,
expatiate on, give further details
about

enlighten VERB = **inform**, tell,
teach, advise, counsel, educate,
instruct, illuminate

enlightened ADJECTIVE
= **informed**, aware, reasonable,
educated, sophisticated,
cultivated, open-minded,
knowledgeable ≠ ignorant

enlightenment NOUN
= **understanding**, learning,
education, knowledge,
instruction, awareness, wisdom,
insight

enlist VERB 1 = **join up**, join, enter
(into), register, volunteer, sign
up, enrol 2 = **obtain**, get, gain,
secure, engage, procure

enormous ADJECTIVE = **huge**,
massive, vast, extensive,
tremendous, gross, immense,
gigantic, supersize ≠ tiny

enough ADJECTIVE = **sufficient**,
adequate, ample, abundant, as
much as you need, as much as is
necessary
▷ PRONOUN = **sufficiency**, plenty,
sufficient, abundance, adequacy,

right amount, ample supply
▷ ADVERB = **sufficiently**,
amply, reasonably, adequately,
satisfactorily, abundantly,
tolerably

enquire ▷ see **inquire**

enquiry ▷ see **inquiry**

enrage VERB = **anger**, infuriate,
incense, madden, inflame,
exasperate, antagonize, make you
angry ≠ calm

enrich VERB 1 = **enhance**, develop,
improve, boost, supplement,
refine, heighten, augment
2 = **make rich**, make wealthy,
make affluent, make prosperous,
make well-off

enrol or (U.S.) **enroll** VERB
1 = **enlist**, register, be accepted,
be admitted, join up, put your
name down for, sign up or on
2 = **recruit**, take on, enlist

en route ADVERB = **on** or **along
the way**, travelling, on the road,
in transit, on the journey

ensemble NOUN 1 = **group**,
company, band, troupe, cast,
orchestra, chorus 2 = **collection**,
set, body, whole, total, sum,
combination, entity 3 = **outfit**,
suit, get-up (informal), costume

ensue VERB = **follow**, result,
develop, proceed, arise, stem,
derive, issue ≠ come first

ensure VERB 1 = **make certain**,
guarantee, secure, make sure,
confirm, warrant, certify
2 = **protect**, defend, secure,
safeguard, guard, make safe

entail VERB = **involve**, require,

produce, demand, call for,
occasion, need, bring about

enter VERB 1 = **come** or **go
in** or **into**, arrive, set foot in
somewhere, cross the threshold
of somewhere, make an entrance
≠ exit 2 = **penetrate**, get in,
pierce, pass into, perforate
3 = **join**, start work at, begin
work at, enrol in, enlist in ≠ leave
4 = **participate in**, join (in), be
involved in, get involved in, play
a part in, partake in, associate
yourself with, start to be in
5 = **begin**, start, take up, move
into, commence, set out on,
embark upon 6 = **compete in**,
contest, join in, fight, sign up for,
go in for 7 = **record**, note, register,
log, list, write down, take down,
inscribe

enterprise NOUN 1 = **firm**,
company, business, concern,
operation, organization,
establishment, commercial
undertaking 2 = **venture**,
operation, project, adventure,
undertaking, programme,
pursuit, endeavour 3 = **initiative**,
energy, daring, enthusiasm,
imagination, drive, ingenuity,
originality

enterprising ADJECTIVE
= **resourceful**, original, spirited,
daring, bold, enthusiastic,
imaginative, energetic

entertain VERB 1 = **amuse**,
interest, please, delight,
charm, enthral, cheer, regale
2 = **show hospitality to**, receive,

accommodate, treat, put up, lodge, be host to, have company of **3** = **consider**, imagine, think about, contemplate, conceive of, bear in mind, keep in mind, give thought to

entertainment NOUN
1 = **enjoyment**, fun, pleasure, leisure, relaxation, recreation, enjoyment, amusement
2 = **pastime**, show, sport, performance, treat, presentation, leisure activity

enthusiasm NOUN = **keenness**, interest, passion, motivation, relish, zeal, zest, fervour

enthusiast NOUN = **fan**, supporter, lover, follower, addict, buff (*informal*), fanatic, devotee

enthusiastic ADJECTIVE = **keen**, committed, eager, passionate, vigorous, avid, fervent, zealous ≠ apathetic

entice VERB = **lure**, attract, invite, persuade, tempt, induce, seduce, lead on

entire ADJECTIVE = **whole**, full, complete, total

entirely ADVERB = **completely**, totally, absolutely, fully, altogether, thoroughly, wholly, utterly ≠ partly

entitle VERB **1** = **give the right to**, allow, enable, permit, sanction, license, authorize, empower
2 = **call**, name, title, term, label, dub, christen, give the title of

entity NOUN = **thing**, being, individual, object, substance, creature, organism

entrance¹ NOUN **1** = **way in**, opening, door, approach, access, entry, gate, passage ≠ exit
2 = **appearance**, coming in, entry, arrival, introduction ≠ exit
3 = **admission**, access, entry, entrée, admittance, permission to enter, right of entry

entrance² VERB **1** = **enchant**, delight, charm, fascinate, dazzle, captivate, enthral, beguile ≠ bore **2** = **mesmerize**, bewitch, hypnotize, put a spell on, cast a spell on, put in a trance

entrant NOUN = **competitor**, player, candidate, entry, participant, applicant, contender, contestant

entrenched *or* **intrenched** ADJECTIVE = **fixed**, set, rooted, well-established, ingrained, deep-seated, deep-rooted, unshakeable *or* unshakable

entrepreneur NOUN = **businessman** *or* **businesswoman**, tycoon, executive, industrialist, speculator, magnate, impresario, business executive

entrust *or* **intrust** VERB **1** = **give custody of**, deliver, commit, delegate, hand over, turn over, confide **2** *usually with* **with** = **assign**

entry NOUN **1** = **admission**, access, entrance, admittance, entrée, permission to enter, right of entry **2** = **coming in**, entering, appearance, arrival, entrance ≠ exit **3** = **introduction**,

presentation, initiation,
inauguration, induction, debut,
investiture **4** = **record**, listing,
account, note, statement,
item **5** = **way in**, opening, door,
approach, access, gate, passage,
entrance

envelope NOUN = **wrapping**,
casing, case, covering, cover,
jacket, sleeve, wrapper

environment NOUN
1 = **surroundings**, setting,
conditions, situation, medium,
circumstances, background,
atmosphere **2** (*ecology*) = **habitat**,
home, surroundings, territory,
terrain, locality, natural home

environmental ADJECTIVE
= **ecological**, green

environmentalist NOUN
= **conservationist**, ecologist,
green

envisage VERB **1** = **imagine**,
contemplate, conceive (of),
visualize, picture, fancy, think
up, conceptualize **2** = **foresee**,
see, expect, predict, anticipate,
envision

envoy NOUN **1** = **ambassador**,
diplomat, emissary
2 = **messenger**, agent,
representative, delegate, courier,
intermediary, emissary

envy NOUN = **covetousness**,
resentment, jealousy, bitterness,
resentfulness, enviousness
(*informal*)
▷ VERB **1** = **be jealous (of)**,
resent, begrudge, be envious (of)
2 = **covet**, desire, crave, aspire to,

yearn for, hanker after

epidemic NOUN **1** = **outbreak**,
plague, growth, spread, scourge,
contagion **2** = **spate**, plague,
outbreak, wave, rash, eruption,
upsurge

episode NOUN **1** = **event**,
experience, happening, matter,
affair, incident, adventure,
occurrence **2** = **instalment**,
part, act, scene, section, chapter,
passage

equal ADJECTIVE *often with* **to**
or with = **identical**, the same,
matching, equivalent, uniform,
alike, corresponding ≠ unequal
2 = **fair**, just, impartial,
egalitarian, unbiased, even-
handed ≠ unfair **3** = **even**,
balanced, fifty-fifty (*informal*),
evenly matched ≠ uneven
▷ NOUN = **match**, equivalent,
twin, counterpart
▷ VERB **1** = **amount to**, make,
come to, total, level, parallel,
tie with, equate ≠ be unequal
to **2** = **be equal to**, match,
reach **3** = **be as good as**, match,
compare with, equate with,
measure up to, be as great as

equality NOUN **1** = **fairness**,
equal opportunity, equal
treatment, egalitarianism, fair
treatment, justness ≠ inequality
2 = **sameness**, balance, identity,
similarity, correspondence, parity,
likeness, uniformity ≠ disparity

equate VERB **1** = **identify**,
associate, connect, compare,
relate, mention in the same

breath, think of in connection with **2** = **make equal**, match, even up

equation NOUN = **equating**, comparison, parallel, correspondence

equilibrium NOUN = **stability**, balance, symmetry, steadiness, evenness, equipoise

equip VERB **1** = **supply**, provide, stock, arm, array, furnish, fit out, kit out **2** = **prepare**, qualify, educate, get ready

equipment NOUN = **apparatus**, stock, supplies, stuff, tackle, gear, tools, provisions

equitable ADJECTIVE = **even-handed**, just, fair, reasonable, proper, honest, impartial, unbiased

equivalent ADJECTIVE = **equal**, same, comparable, parallel, identical, alike, corresponding, tantamount ≠ different
▷ NOUN = **equal**, counterpart, twin, parallel, match, opposite number

era NOUN = **age**, time, period, date, generation, epoch, day or days

eradicate VERB = **wipe out**, eliminate, remove, destroy, get rid of, erase, extinguish, obliterate

erase VERB **1** = **delete**, cancel out, wipe out, remove, eradicate, obliterate, blot out, expunge **2** = **rub out**, remove, wipe out, delete

erect ADJECTIVE = **upright**, straight, stiff, vertical, elevated, perpendicular, pricked-up ≠ bent

▷ VERB **1** = **build**, raise, set up, construct, put up, assemble, put together ≠ demolish **2** = **found**, establish, form, create, set up, institute, organize, put up

erode VERB **1** = **disintegrate**, crumble, deteriorate, corrode, break up, grind down, waste away, wear down or away **2** = **destroy**, consume, crumble, eat away, corrode, break up, grind down, abrade **3** = **weaken**, destroy, undermine, diminish, impair, lessen, wear away

erosion NOUN **1** = **disintegration**, deterioration, wearing down or away, grinding down **2** = **deterioration**, undermining, destruction, weakening, attrition, eating away, abrasion, grinding down

erotic ADJECTIVE = **sexual**, sexy (*informal*), crude, explicit, sensual, seductive, vulgar, voluptuous

erratic ADJECTIVE = **unpredictable**, variable, unstable, irregular, inconsistent, uneven, unreliable, wayward ≠ regular

error NOUN = **mistake**, slip, blunder, oversight, howler (*informal*), bloomer (*Brit. informal*), miscalculation, solecism, barry or Barry Crocker (*Austral. slang*)

erupt VERB **1** = **explode**, blow up, emit lava **2** = **gush**, burst out, pour forth, belch forth, spew forth or out **3** = **start**, break out, began, explode, flare up, burst out, boil over **4** (*medical*) = **break out**, appear, flare up

escalate VERB 1 = **grow**, increase, extend, intensify, expand, surge, mount, heighten ≠ decrease 2 = **increase**, develop, extend, intensify, expand, build up, heighten ≠ lessen

escape VERB 1 = **get away**, flee, take off, fly, bolt, slip away, abscond, make a break for it, do a Skase (*Austral. informal*) 2 = **avoid**, miss, evade, dodge, shun, elude, duck, steer clear of 3 *usually with* **from** = **leak out**, flow out, gush out, emanate, seep out, exude, spill out, pour forth
▷ NOUN 1 = **getaway**, break, flight, break-out 2 = **avoidance**, evasion, circumvention 3 = **relaxation**, recreation, distraction, diversion, pastime 4 = **leak**, emission, outpouring, seepage, issue, emanation

escort NOUN 1 = **guard**, bodyguard, train, convoy, entourage, retinue, cortege 2 = **companion**, partner, attendant, guide, beau, chaperon
▷ VERB = **accompany**, lead, partner, conduct, guide, shepherd, usher, chaperon

especially ADVERB 1 = **notably**, mostly, strikingly, conspicuously, outstandingly 2 = **very**, specially, extremely, remarkably, unusually, exceptionally, markedly, uncommonly

espionage NOUN = **spying**, intelligence, surveillance, counter-intelligence, undercover work

essay NOUN = **composition**, study, paper, article, piece, assignment, discourse, tract
▷ VERB (*formal*) = **attempt**, try, undertake, endeavour

essence NOUN 1 = **fundamental nature**, nature, being, heart, spirit, soul, core, substance 2 = **concentrate**, spirits, extract, tincture, distillate

essential ADJECTIVE 1 = **vital**, important, needed, necessary, critical, crucial, key, indispensable ≠ unimportant 2 = **fundamental**, main, basic, principal, cardinal, elementary, innate, intrinsic ≠ secondary
▷ NOUN = **prerequisite**, fundamental, necessity, must, basic, sine qua non (*Latin*), rudiment, must-have

establish VERB 1 = **set up**, found, create, institute, constitute, inaugurate 2 = **prove**, confirm, demonstrate, certify, verify, substantiate, corroborate, authenticate 3 = **secure**, form, ground, settle

establishment NOUN 1 = **creation**, founding, setting up, foundation, institution, organization, formation, installation 2 = **organization**, company, business, firm, concern, operation, institution, corporation

Establishment NOUN ▷ PHRASE: **the Establishment** = **the authorities**, the system, the powers that be, the ruling class

estate NOUN 1 = **lands**, property, area, grounds, domain, manor, holdings, homestead (*U.S. & Canad.*) 2 (*chiefly Brit.*) = **area**, centre, park, development, site, zone, plot 3 (*law*) = **property**, capital, assets, fortune, goods, effects, wealth, possessions

esteem VERB = **respect**, admire, think highly of, love, value, prize, treasure, revere
▷ NOUN = **respect**, regard, honour, admiration, reverence, estimation, veneration

estimate VERB 1 = **calculate roughly**, value, guess, judge, reckon, assess, evaluate, gauge 2 = **think**, believe, consider, rate, judge, hold, rank, reckon
▷ NOUN 1 = **approximate calculation**, guess, assessment, judgment, valuation, guesstimate (*informal*), rough calculation, ballpark figure (*informal*)
2 = **assessment**, opinion, belief, appraisal, evaluation, judgment, estimation

estuary NOUN = **inlet**, mouth, creek, firth, fjord

etch VERB 1 = **engrave**, cut, impress, stamp, carve, imprint, inscribe 2 = **corrode**, eat into, burn into

etching NOUN = **print**, carving, engraving, imprint, inscription

eternal ADJECTIVE 1 = **everlasting**, lasting, permanent, enduring, endless, perpetual, timeless, unending ≠ transitory

2 = **interminable**, endless, infinite, continual, immortal, never-ending, everlasting ≠ occasional

eternity NOUN 1 = **the afterlife**, heaven, paradise, the next world, the hereafter 2 = **perpetuity**, immortality, infinity, timelessness, endlessness
3 = **ages**

ethical ADJECTIVE 1 = **moral**, behavioural 2 = **right**, morally acceptable, good, just, fair, responsible, principled ≠ unethical

ethics PLURAL NOUN = **moral code**, standards, principles, morals, conscience, morality, moral values, moral principles, tikanga (*N.Z.*)

ethnic *or* **ethnical** ADJECTIVE = **cultural**, national, traditional, native, folk, racial, genetic, indigenous

euphoria NOUN = **elation**, joy, ecstasy, rapture, exhilaration, jubilation ≠ despondency

evacuate VERB 1 = **remove**, clear, withdraw, expel, move out, send to a safe place 2 = **abandon**, leave, clear, desert, quit, withdraw from, pull out of, move out of

evade VERB 1 = **avoid**, escape, dodge, get away from, elude, steer clear of, sidestep, duck ≠ face
2 = **avoid answering**, parry, fend off, fudge, hedge, equivocate

evaluate VERB = **assess**, rate, judge, estimate, reckon, weigh, calculate, gauge

evaporate VERB 1 = **disappear**,
vaporize, dematerialize, vanish,
dissolve, dry up, fade away, melt
away 2 = **dry up**, dry, dehydrate,
vaporize, desiccate 3 = **fade
away**, disappear, vanish, dissolve,
melt away

eve NOUN 1 = **night before**, day
before, vigil 2 = **brink**, point,
edge, verge, threshold

even ADJECTIVE 1 = **regular**,
stable, constant, steady, smooth,
uniform, unbroken, uninterrupted
≠ variable 2 = **level**, straight,
flat, smooth, true, steady,
uniform, parallel ≠ uneven
3 = **equal**, like, matching, similar,
identical, comparable ≠ unequal
4 = **equally matched**, level, tied,
on a par, neck and neck, fifty-fifty
(*informal*), all square ≠ ill-
matched 5 = **square**, quits, on the
same level, on an equal footing
6 = **calm**, composed, cool,
well-balanced, placid, unruffled,
imperturbable, even-tempered
≠ excitable

evening NOUN = **dusk** (*archaic*),
night, sunset, twilight, sundown,
gloaming (*Scot. poetic*), close of
day, evo (*Austral. slang*)

event NOUN 1 = **incident**,
happening, experience, affair,
occasion, proceeding, business,
circumstance 2 = **competition**,
game, tournament, contest, bout

eventual ADJECTIVE = **final**,
overall, concluding, ultimate

eventually ADVERB = **in the end**,
finally, one day, after all, some
time, ultimately, at the end of the
day, when all is said and done

ever ADVERB 1 = **at any time**, at
all, in any case, at any point, by
any chance, on any occasion,
at any period 2 = **always**, for
ever, at all times, evermore
3 = **constantly**, continually,
perpetually

every ADJECTIVE = **each**, each and
every, every single

everybody PRONOUN
= **everyone**, each one, the whole
world, each person, every person,
all and sundry, one and all
▷ *see* **everyone**

everyday ADJECTIVE = **ordinary**,
common, usual, routine, stock,
customary, mundane, run-of-the-
mill ≠ unusual

everyone PRONOUN
= **everybody**, each one, the whole
world, each person, every person,
all and sundry, one and all

● **WORD POWER**
● *Everyone* and *everybody* are
● interchangeable, and can be
● used as synonyms of each other
● in any context. Care should be
● taken, however, to distinguish
● between *everyone* as a single
● word and *every one* as two
● words, the latter form correctly
● being used to refer to each
● individual person or thing in
● a particular group: *every one of*
● *them is wrong.*

everything PRONOUN = **all**, the
lot, the whole lot, each thing

everywhere ADVERB 1 = **all over**, all around, the world over, high and low, in every nook and cranny, far and wide or near, to or in every place 2 = **all around**, all over, in every nook and cranny, ubiquitously, far and wide or near, to or in every place

evidence NOUN 1 = **proof**, grounds, demonstration, confirmation, verification, corroboration, authentication, substantiation 2 = **sign(s)**, suggestion, trace, indication 3 (*law*) = **testimony**, statement, submission, avowal
▷ VERB = **show**, prove, reveal, display, indicate, witness, demonstrate, exhibit

evident ADJECTIVE = **obvious**, clear, plain, apparent, visible, manifest, noticeable, unmistakable ≠ hidden

evidently ADVERB 1 = **obviously**, clearly, plainly, undoubtedly, manifestly, without question, unmistakably 2 = **apparently**, seemingly, outwardly, ostensibly, so it seems, to all appearances

evil ADJECTIVE 1 = **wicked**, bad, malicious, immoral, sinful, malevolent, depraved, villainous 2 = **harmful**, disastrous, destructive, dire, catastrophic, pernicious, ruinous 3 = **demonic**, satanic, diabolical, hellish, devilish, infernal, fiendish 4 = **offensive**, nasty, foul, unpleasant, vile, noxious, disagreeable, pestilential

5 = **unfortunate**, unfavourable, ruinous, calamitous
▷ NOUN 1 = **wickedness**, bad, vice, sin, wrongdoing, depravity, badness, villainy 2 = **harm**, suffering, hurt, woe 3 = **act of cruelty**, crime, ill, horror, outrage, misfortune, mischief, affliction

evoke VERB = **arouse**, cause, induce, awaken, give rise to, stir up, rekindle, summon up ≠ suppress

evolution NOUN 1 (*biology*) = **rise**, development, adaptation, natural selection, Darwinism, survival of the fittest 2 = **development**, growth, advance, progress, working out, expansion, extension, unfolding

evolve VERB 1 = **develop**, metamorphose, adapt yourself 2 = **grow**, develop, advance, progress, mature 3 = **work out**, develop, progress, expand, unfold

exact ADJECTIVE = **accurate**, correct, true, right, specific, precise, definite, faultless ≠ approximate
▷ VERB 1 = **demand**, claim, force, command, extract, compel, extort 2 = **inflict**, apply, administer, mete out, deal out

exacting ADJECTIVE 1 = **demanding**, hard, taxing, difficult, tough ≠ easy 2 = **strict**, severe, harsh, rigorous, stringent

exactly ADVERB 1 = **accurately**, correctly, precisely, faithfully, explicitly, scrupulously, truthfully, unerringly 2 = **precisely**, specifically, bang on (*informal*), to the letter

exaggerate VERB = **overstate**, enlarge, embroider, amplify, embellish, overestimate, overemphasize, pile it on about (*informal*)

examination NOUN 1 (*medical*) = **checkup**, analysis, going-over (*informal*), exploration, health check, check 2 = **exam**, test, research, paper, investigation, practical, assessment, quiz

examine VERB 1 = **inspect**, study, survey, investigate, explore, analyse, scrutinize, peruse 2 (*medical*) = **check**, analyse, check over

3 (*education*) = **test**, question, assess, quiz, evaluate, appraise 4 (*law*) = **question**, quiz, interrogate, cross-examine, grill (*informal*), give the third degree to (*informal*)

example NOUN 1 = **instance**, specimen, case, sample, illustration, particular case, particular instance, typical case 2 = **illustration**, model, ideal, standard, prototype, paradigm, archetype, paragon 3 = **warning**, lesson, caution, deterrent

exceed VERB 1 = **surpass**, better, pass, eclipse, beat, cap (*informal*), top, be over 2 = **go over the limit of**, go beyond, overstep

excel VERB = **be superior**, eclipse, beat, surpass, transcend, outdo, outshine ▷ PHRASE: **excel in** or **at something** = **be good at**, shine

at, be proficient in, show talent in, be skilful at, be talented at

excellence NOUN = **high quality**, merit, distinction, goodness, superiority, greatness, supremacy, eminence

excellent ADJECTIVE = **outstanding**, good, great, fine, cool (*informal*), brilliant, very good, superb, booshit (*Austral. slang*), exo (*Austral. slang*), sik (*Austral. slang*), rad (*informal*), phat (*slang*), schmick (*Austral. informal*) ≠ terrible

except PREPOSITION *often with* **for** = **apart from**, but for, saving, barring, excepting, other than, excluding, omitting
▷ VERB = **exclude**, leave out, omit, disregard, pass over

exception NOUN = **special case**, freak, anomaly, inconsistency, deviation, oddity, peculiarity, irregularity

exceptional ADJECTIVE 1 = **remarkable**, special, excellent, extraordinary, outstanding, superior, first-class, marvellous ≠ average 2 = **unusual**, special, odd, strange, extraordinary, unprecedented, peculiar, abnormal ≠ ordinary

excerpt NOUN = **extract**, part, piece, section, selection, passage, fragment, quotation

excess NOUN 1 = **surfeit**, surplus, overload, glut, superabundance, superfluity ≠ shortage 2 = **overindulgence**, extravagance, profligacy,

debauchery, dissipation,
intemperance, indulgence,
prodigality ≠ moderation

excessive ADJECTIVE

1 = **immoderate**, too much,
extreme, exaggerated,
unreasonable, disproportionate,
undue, uncontrolled
2 = **inordinate**, unfair,
unreasonable, disproportionate,
undue, unwarranted, exorbitant,
extortionate

exchange VERB = **interchange**,
change, trade, switch, swap,
barter, give to each other, give to
one another
▷ NOUN 1 = **conversation**,
talk, word, discussion, chat,
dialogue, natter, powwow
2 = **interchange**, trade, switch,
swap, trafficking, swapping,
substitution, barter

excite VERB 1 = **thrill**, inspire,
stir, provoke, animate, rouse,
exhilarate, inflame 2 = **arouse**,
provoke, rouse, stir up
3 = **titillate**, thrill, stimulate,
turn on (slang), arouse, get going
(informal), electrify

excitement NOUN
= **exhilaration**, action, activity,
passion, thrill, animation, furore,
agitation

exciting ADJECTIVE
1 = **stimulating**, dramatic,
gripping, stirring, thrilling,
sensational, rousing, exhilarating
≠ boring 2 = **titillating**,
stimulating, arousing, erotic

exclaim VERB = **cry out**, declare,

shout, proclaim, yell, utter, call
out

exclude VERB 1 = **keep out**, bar,
ban, refuse, forbid, boycott,
prohibit, disallow ≠ let in
2 = **omit**, reject, eliminate, rule
out, miss out, leave out ≠ include
3 = **eliminate**, reject, ignore, rule
out, leave out, set aside, omit,
pass over

exclusion NOUN 1 = **ban**,
bar, veto, boycott, embargo,
prohibition, disqualification
2 = **elimination**, missing out,
rejection, leaving out, omission

exclusive ADJECTIVE 1 = **select**,
fashionable, stylish, restricted,
posh (informal, chiefly Brit.),
chic, high-class, up-market
≠ unrestricted 2 = **sole**, full,
whole, complete, total, entire,
absolute, undivided ≠ shared
3 = **entire**, full, whole, complete,
total, absolute, undivided
4 = **limited**, unique, restricted,
confined, peculiar

excursion NOUN = **trip**, tour,
journey, outing, expedition,
ramble, day trip, jaunt

excuse VERB 1 = **justify**, explain,
defend, vindicate, mitigate,
apologize for, make excuses for
≠ blame 2 = **forgive**, pardon,
overlook, tolerate, acquit, turn
a blind eye to, exonerate, make
allowances for 3 = **free**, relieve,
exempt, release, spare, discharge,
let off, absolve ≠ convict
▷ NOUN = **justification**, reason,
explanation, defence, grounds,

e

plea, apology, vindication ≠ accusation

execute VERB 1 = **put to death**, kill, shoot, hang, behead, decapitate, guillotine, electrocute 2 = **carry out**, effect, implement, accomplish, discharge, administer, prosecute, enact 3 = **perform**, carry out, accomplish

execution NOUN 1 = **killing**, hanging, the death penalty, the rope, capital punishment, beheading, the electric chair, the guillotine 2 = **carrying out**, performance, operation, administration, prosecution, enforcement, implementation, accomplishment

executive NOUN
1 = **administrator**, official, director, manager, chairman, managing director, controller, chief executive officer
2 = **administration**, government, directors, management, leadership, hierarchy, directorate
▷ ADJECTIVE = **administrative**, controlling, directing, governing, regulating, decision-making, managerial

exemplify VERB = **show**, represent, display, demonstrate, illustrate, exhibit, embody, serve as an example of

exempt VERB = **grant immunity**, free, excuse, release, spare, relieve, discharge, let off
▷ ADJECTIVE = **immune**, free, excepted, excused, released, spared, not liable to ≠ liable

exemption NOUN = **immunity**, freedom, relief, exception, discharge, release, dispensation, absolution

exercise VERB 1 = **put to use**, use, apply, employ, exert, utilize, bring to bear, avail yourself of 2 = **train**, work out, practise, keep fit, do exercises
▷ NOUN 1 = **use**, practice, application, operation, discharge, implementation, fulfilment, utilization 2 = **exertion**, training, activity, work, labour, effort, movement, toil 3 (*military*) = **manoeuvre**, campaign, operation, movement, deployment 4 = **task**, problem, lesson, assignment, practice

exert VERB = **apply**, use, exercise, employ, wield, make use of, utilize, bring to bear ▷ PHRASE: **exert yourself** = **make an effort**, work, labour, struggle, strain, strive, endeavour, toil

exhaust VERB 1 = **tire out**, fatigue, drain, weaken, weary, sap, wear out, debilitate 2 = **use up**, spend, consume, waste, go through, run through, deplete, squander

exhausted ADJECTIVE 1 = **worn out**, tired out, drained, spent, bushed (*informal*), done in (*informal*), all in (*slang*), fatigued ≠ invigorated 2 = **used up**, consumed, spent, finished, depleted, dissipated, expended ≠ replenished

exhaustion NOUN 1 = **tiredness**, fatigue, weariness, debilitation 2 = **depletion**, emptying, consumption, using up

exhibit VERB 1 = **show**, reveal, display, demonstrate, express, indicate, manifest 2 **display**, show, set out, parade, unveil, put on view

exhibition NOUN 1 = **show**, display, representation, presentation, spectacle, showcase, exposition 2 = **display**, show, performance, demonstration, revelation

exile NOUN 1 = **banishment**, expulsion, deportation, eviction, expatriation 2 = **expatriate**, refugee, outcast, émigré, deportee ▷ VERB = **banish**, expel, throw out, deport, drive out, eject, expatriate, cast out

exist VERB 1 = **live**, be present, survive, endure, be in existence, be, have breath 2 = **occur**, be present 3 = **survive**, stay alive, make ends meet, subsist, eke out a living, scrape by, scrimp and save, support yourself

existence NOUN 1 = **reality**, being, life, subsistence, actuality 2 = **life**, situation, way of life, life style

existent ADJECTIVE = **in existence**, living, existing, surviving, standing, present, alive, extant

exit NOUN 1 = **way out**, door, gate, outlet, doorway, gateway, escape route ≠ entry 2 = **departure**, withdrawal, retreat, farewell, going, goodbye, exodus, decamping ▷ VERB = **depart**, leave, go out, withdraw, retire, quit, retreat, go away ≠ enter

exodus NOUN = **departure**, withdrawal, retreat, leaving, flight, exit, migration, evacuation

exotic ADJECTIVE 1 = **unusual**, striking, strange, fascinating, mysterious, colourful, glamorous, unfamiliar ≠ ordinary 2 = **foreign**, alien, tropical, external, naturalized

expand VERB 1 = **get bigger**, increase, grow, extend, swell, widen, enlarge, become bigger ≠ contract 2 = **make bigger**, increase, develop, extend, widen, enlarge, broaden, magnify ≠ reduce 3 = **spread (out)**, stretch (out), unfold, unravel, diffuse, unfurl, unroll ▷ PHRASE: **expand on something** = **go into detail about**, embellish, elaborate on, develop, flesh out, expound on, enlarge on, expatiate on

expansion NOUN 1 = **increase**, development, growth, spread, magnification, amplification 2 = **enlargement**, increase, growth, opening out

expatriate ADJECTIVE = **exiled**, refugee, banished, emigrant, émigré, expat ▷ NOUN = **exile**, refugee, emigrant, émigré

e

expect VERB 1 = **think**, believe, suppose, assume, trust, imagine, reckon, presume 2 = **anticipate**, look forward to, predict, envisage, await, hope for, contemplate 3 = **require**, demand, want, call for, ask for, hope for, insist on

expectation NOUN 1 usually plural = **projection**, supposition, assumption, belief, forecast, likelihood, probability, presumption 2 = **anticipation**, hope, promise, excitement, expectancy, apprehension, suspense

expedition NOUN = **journey**, mission, voyage, tour, quest, trek

expel VERB 1 = **throw out**, exclude, ban, dismiss, kick out (informal), ask to leave, turf out (informal), debar ≠ let in 2 = **banish**, exile, deport, evict, force to leave ≠ take in 3 = **drive out**, discharge, force out, let out, eject, issue, spew, belch

expenditure NOUN 1 = **spending**, payment, expense, outgoings, cost, outlay 2 = **consumption**, using, output

expense NOUN = **cost**, charge, expenditure, payment, spending, outlay

expensive ADJECTIVE = **costly**, high-priced, lavish, extravagant, dear, stiff, steep (informal), pricey ≠ cheap

experience NOUN 1 = **knowledge**, practice, skill, contact, expertise, involvement, exposure, participation

2 = **event**, affair, incident, happening, encounter, episode, adventure, occurrence
▷ VERB = **undergo**, feel, face, taste, go through, sample, encounter, endure

experienced ADJECTIVE = **knowledgeable**, skilled, tried, tested, seasoned, expert, veteran, practised ≠ inexperienced

experiment NOUN 1 = **test**, trial, investigation, examination, procedure, demonstration, observation, try-out
2 = **research**, investigation, analysis, observation, research and development, experimentation
▷ VERB = **test**, investigate, trial, research, try, examine, pilot, sample

experimental ADJECTIVE 1 = **test**, trial, pilot, preliminary, provisional, tentative, speculative, exploratory
2 = **innovative**, new, original, radical, creative, ingenious, avant-garde, inventive

expert NOUN = **specialist**, authority, professional, master, genius, guru, pundit, maestro, fundi (S. African) ≠ amateur
▷ ADJECTIVE = **skilful**, experienced, professional, masterly, qualified, talented, outstanding, practised ≠ unskilled

expertise NOUN = **skill**, knowledge, know-how (informal), facility, judgment, mastery, proficiency, adroitness

expire VERB 1 = **become invalid**, end, finish, conclude, close, stop, run out, cease 2 = **die**, depart, perish, kick the bucket (*informal*), depart this life, meet your maker, cark it (*Austral. & N.Z. slang*), pass away or on

explain VERB 1 = **make clear** or **plain**, describe, teach, define, resolve, clarify, clear up, simplify 2 = **account for**, excuse, justify, give a reason for

explanation NOUN 1 = **reason**, answer, account, excuse, motive, justification, vindication 2 = **description**, report, definition, teaching, interpretation, illustration, clarification, simplification

explicit ADJECTIVE 1 = **clear**, obvious, specific, direct, precise, straightforward, definite, overt ≠ vague 2 = **frank**, specific, graphic, unambiguous, unrestricted, unrestrained, uncensored ≠ indirect

explode VERB 1 = **blow up**, erupt, burst, go off, shatter 2 = **detonate**, set off, discharge, let off 3 = **lose your temper**, rage, erupt, become angry, hit the roof (*informal*), go crook (*Austral. & N.Z. slang*) 4 = **increase**, grow, develop, extend, advance, shoot up, soar, boost 5 = **disprove**, discredit, refute, demolish, repudiate, put paid to, invalidate, debunk

exploit NOUN 1 = **feat**, act, achievement, enterprise, adventure, stunt, deed, accomplishment
▷ VERB 1 = **take advantage of**, abuse, use, manipulate, milk, misuse, ill-treat, play on or upon 2 = **make the best use of**, use, make use of, utilize, cash in on (*informal*), capitalize on, use to good advantage, profit by or from

exploitation NOUN = **misuse**, abuse, manipulation, using, ill-treatment

exploration NOUN 1 = **expedition**, tour, trip, survey, travel, journey, reconnaissance 2 = **investigation**, research, survey, search, inquiry, analysis, examination, inspection

explore VERB 1 = **travel around**, tour, survey, scout, reconnoitre 2 = **investigate**, consider, research, survey, search, examine, probe, look into

explosion NOUN 1 = **blast**, crack, burst, bang, discharge, report, blowing up, clap 2 = **increase**, rise, development, growth, boost, expansion, enlargement, escalation 3 = **outburst**, fit, storm, attack, surge, flare-up, eruption 4 = **outbreak**, flare-up, eruption, upsurge

explosive ADJECTIVE 1 = **unstable**, dangerous, volatile, hazardous, unsafe, perilous, combustible, inflammable 2 = **fiery**, violent, volatile, stormy, touchy, vehement
▷ NOUN = **bomb**, mine, shell, missile, rocket, grenade, charge,

torpedo

expose VERB 1 = **uncover**, show, reveal, display, exhibit, present, unveil, lay bare ≠ hide 2 = **make vulnerable**, subject, leave open, lay open

exposure NOUN
1 = **hypothermia**, frostbite, extreme cold, intense cold
2 = **uncovering**, showing, display, exhibition, revelation, presentation, unveiling

express VERB 1 = **state**, communicate, convey, articulate, say, word, voice, declare
2 = **show**, indicate, exhibit, demonstrate, reveal, intimate, convey, signify
▷ ADJECTIVE 1 = **explicit**, clear, plain, distinct, definite, unambiguous, categorical
2 = **specific**, exclusive, particular, sole, special, singular, clear-cut, especial 3 = **fast**, direct, rapid, priority, prompt, swift, high-speed, speedy

expression NOUN 1 = **statement**, declaration, announcement, communication, utterance, articulation 2 = **indication**, demonstration, exhibition, display, showing, show, sign, symbol 3 = **look**, countenance, face, air, appearance, aspect
4 = **phrase**, saying, word, term, remark, maxim, idiom, adage

expressive ADJECTIVE = **vivid**, striking, telling, moving, poignant, eloquent ≠ impassive

expulsion NOUN 1 = **ejection**, exclusion, dismissal, removal, eviction, banishment
2 = **discharge**, emission, spewing, secretion, excretion, ejection, seepage, suppuration

exquisite ADJECTIVE
1 = **beautiful**, elegant, graceful, pleasing, attractive, lovely, charming, comely ≠ unattractive
2 = **fine**, beautiful, lovely, elegant, precious, delicate, dainty
3 = **intense**, acute, severe, sharp, keen, extreme

extend VERB 1 = **spread out**, reach, stretch 2 = **stretch**, stretch out, spread out, straighten out
3 = **last**, continue, go on, stretch, carry on 4 = **protrude**, project, stand out, bulge, stick out, hang, overhang, jut out 5 = **widen**, increase, expand, add to, enhance, supplement, enlarge, broaden ≠ reduce 6 = **make longer**, prolong, lengthen, draw out, spin out, drag out ≠ shorten 7 = **offer**, present, confer, stick out, impart, proffer ≠ withdraw

extension NOUN 1 = **annexe**, addition, supplement, appendix, appendage 2 = **lengthening**, extra time, continuation, additional period of time
3 = **development**, expansion, widening, increase, broadening, enlargement, diversification

extensive ADJECTIVE 1 = **large**, considerable, substantial, spacious, wide, broad, expansive ≠ confined 2 = **comprehensive**, complete, wide, pervasive

≠ restricted **3** = **great**, vast,
widespread, large-scale, far-
reaching, far-flung, voluminous
≠ limited

extent NOUN **1** = **magnitude**,
amount, scale, level, stretch,
expanse **2** = **size**, area, length,
width, breadth

exterior NOUN = **outside**, face,
surface, covering, skin, shell,
coating, façade
▷ ADJECTIVE = **outer**, outside,
external, surface, outward,
outermost ≠ inner

external ADJECTIVE **1** = **outer**,
outside, surface, outward,
exterior, outermost ≠ internal
2 = **foreign**, international, alien,
extrinsic ≠ domestic **3** = **outside**,
visiting ≠ inside

extinct ADJECTIVE = **dead**, lost,
gone, vanished, defunct ≠ living

extinction NOUN = **dying out**,
destruction, abolition, oblivion,
extermination, annihilation,
eradication, obliteration

extra ADJECTIVE **1** = **additional**,
more, added, further,
supplementary, auxiliary,
ancillary ≠ vital **2** = **surplus**,
excess, spare, redundant, unused,
leftover, superfluous
▷ NOUN = **addition**, bonus,
supplement, accessory
≠ necessity
▷ ADVERB **1** = **in addition**,
additionally, over and above
2 = **exceptionally**, very, specially,
especially, particularly, extremely,
remarkably, unusually

extract VERB **1** = **take out**, draw,
pull, remove, withdraw, pull out,
bring out **2** = **pull out**, remove,
take out, draw, uproot, pluck out
3 = **elicit**, obtain, force, draw,
derive, glean, coerce
▷ NOUN **1** = **passage**, selection,
excerpt, cutting, clipping,
quotation, citation **2** = **essence**,
solution, concentrate, juice,
distillation

● **WORD POWER**
● People sometimes use *extract*
● where *extricate* would be
● better. Although both words
● can refer to a physical act of
● removal from a place, *extract*
● has a more general sense than
● *extricate*. *Extricate* has additional
● overtones of 'difficulty', and
● is most commonly used with
● reference to getting a person
● – particularly *yourself* – out of a
● situation. So, for example, you
● might say *he will find it difficult*
● *to extricate himself* (not *extract*
● *himself*) from this situation.

extraordinary ADJECTIVE
1 = **remarkable**, outstanding,
amazing, fantastic, astonishing,
exceptional, phenomenal,
extremely good ≠ unremarkable
2 = **unusual**, strange, remarkable,
uncommon ≠ ordinary

extravagant ADJECTIVE
1 = **wasteful**, lavish, prodigal,
profligate, spendthrift
≠ economical **2** = **excessive**,
outrageous, over the top (*slang*),
unreasonable, preposterous

≠ moderate

extreme ADJECTIVE 1 = **great**, highest, supreme, acute, severe, maximum, intense, ultimate ≠ mild 2 = **severe**, radical, strict, harsh, rigid, drastic, uncompromising 3 = **radical**, excessive, fanatical, immoderate ≠ moderate 4 = **farthest**, furthest, far, remotest, far-off, outermost, most distant ≠ nearest
▷ NOUN = **limit**, end, edge, opposite, pole, boundary, antithesis, extremity

extremely ADVERB = **very**, particularly, severely, terribly, unusually, exceptionally, extraordinarily, tremendously

extremist NOUN = **radical**, activist, militant, fanatic, die-hard, bigot, zealot
▷ ADJECTIVE = **extreme**, wild, passionate, frenzied, obsessive, fanatical, fervent, zealous *often with* **over**

eye NOUN 1 = **eyeball**, optic (*informal*), organ of vision, organ of sight 2 *often plural* = **eyesight**, sight, vision, perception, ability to see, power of seeing 3 = **appreciation**, taste, recognition, judgment, discrimination, perception, discernment 4 = **observance**, observation, surveillance, vigil, watch, lookout 5 = **centre**, heart, middle, mid, core, nucleus
▷ VERB = **look at**, view, study, watch, survey, observe, contemplate, check out (*informal*)
▷ **RELATED WORDS**: *adjectives* **ocular, ophthalmic, optic**

● **WORD POWER**
● The primary meaning of **eye**
● is that of the organ of sight in
● humans and other animals.
● Sight is perhaps the most
● fundamental sense in humans.
● Eyes are associated with vision
● in descriptions like **prying eyes**
● and **sharp eyes**, and observation
● in **all eyes**, **a watchful eye**, and
● **keeping an eye on someone**.
● When we are attracted to
● someone, eye develops the
● sense 'ogle' in **eye someone up**.
● The ability to discriminate
● with the eyes has led to the
● meaning of appreciation and
● taste, particularly in the visual
● sphere, e.g. **an eye for colour**,
● **design**, **detail**, **quality**, and
● **style**. The physical location
● and shape of the eyes has
● inspired the meaning of
● central in the phrase **the eye
● of the storm**, which is applied
● both literally and figuratively.
● Although we understand the
● biblical phrase **eye for an eye**
● to mean retribution, it was
● originally intended as an
● appeal to restrict the degree of
● punishment to fit that of the
● crime. Conversely, when we see
● **eye to eye**, it means agreement,
● and **in the eyes of (the law**,
● **others**, **the world)** it means
● opinion.

Ff

fable NOUN 1 = **legend**, myth, parable, allegory, story, tale 2 = **fiction**, fantasy, myth, invention, yarn (*informal*), fabrication, urban myth, tall story (*informal*) ≠ fact

fabric NOUN 1 = **cloth**, material, stuff, textile, web 2 = **framework**, structure, make-up, organization, frame, foundations, construction, constitution 3 = **structure**, foundations, construction, framework

fabulous ADJECTIVE 1 (*informal*) = **wonderful**, excellent, brilliant, superb, spectacular, fantastic (*informal*), marvellous, sensational (*informal*) ≠ ordinary 2 = **astounding**, amazing, extraordinary, remarkable, incredible, astonishing, unbelievable, breathtaking 3 = **legendary**, imaginary, mythical, fictitious, made-up, fantastic, invented, unreal

façade NOUN 1 = **front**, face, exterior 2 = **show**, front, appearance, mask, exterior, guise, pretence, semblance

face NOUN 1 = **countenance**, features, profile, mug (*slang*), visage 2 = **expression**, look, air, appearance, aspect, countenance

3 = **side**, front, outside, surface, exterior, elevation, vertical surface ▷ VERB 1 *often with* **to**, **towards**, *or* **on** = **look onto**, overlook, be opposite, look out on, front onto 2 = **confront**, meet, encounter, deal with, oppose, tackle, experience, brave

● **WORD POWER**
● The core sense of *face* is that
● of the front of the head. In
● humans, face can mean facial
● expression, particularly that
● of negative emotion in the
● phrase *make* or *pull a face*. When
● applied to inanimate objects,
● face refers to the functional
● side of an object or the side
● facing front, e.g. *clock face*
● and *cliff face*. There is some
● semantic overlap between the
● terms *façade* and *face*. Both
● can refer to the frontage of a
● building, and equally can refer
● to the outer appearance of a
● person or situation, especially
● the presentation of a deceptive
● image, e.g. *a façade of unity*
● and *on the face of it*. The idea
● of self-image is also present in
● the phrases *lose face* and *save*
● *face*, where face is self-respect.
● The verbal sense of face is
● associated with movement
● forwards or towards the
● front, having the meaning
● of opposite in location in
● *facing south*, and opposing in
● argument in *facing down*.

f

face up to VERB = **accept**, deal with, tackle, acknowledge, cope with, confront, come to terms with, meet head-on

facilitate VERB = **further**, help, forward, promote, speed up, pave the way for, make easy, expedite ≠ hinder

facility NOUN 1 *often plural* = **amenity**, means, aid, opportunity, advantage, resource, equipment, provision 2 = **opportunity**, possibility, convenience 3 = **ability**, skill, efficiency, fluency, proficiency, dexterity, adroitness 4 = **ease**, fluency, effortlessness ≠ difficulty

fact NOUN 1 = **truth**, reality, certainty, verity ≠ fiction 2 = **event**, happening, act, performance, incident, deed, occurrence, fait accompli (*French*)

faction¹ NOUN 1 = **group**, set, party, gang, bloc, contingent, clique, coterie, public-interest group (*U.S. & Canad.*) 2 = **dissension**, division, conflict, rebellion, disagreement, variance, discord, infighting ≠ agreement

factor NOUN = **element**, part, cause, influence, item, aspect, characteristic, consideration

● **WORD POWER**
● In strict usage, *factor* should
● only be used to refer to
● something which contributes
● to a result. It should not be used
● to refer to a part of something,
● such as a plan or arrangement;
● more appropriate alternatives

● to *factor* in this sense are words
● such as *component* or *element*.

factory NOUN = **works**, plant, mill, workshop, assembly line, shop floor

factual ADJECTIVE = **true**, authentic, real, correct, genuine, exact, precise, dinkum (*Austral. & N.Z. informal*), true-to-life ≠ fictitious

faculty NOUN 1 = **ability**, power, skill, facility, capacity, propensity, aptitude ≠ failing 2 = **department**, school 3 = **teaching staff**, staff, teachers, professors, lecturers (*chiefly U.S.*) 4 = **power**, reason, sense, intelligence, mental ability, physical ability

fad NOUN = **craze**, fashion, trend, rage, vogue, whim, mania

fade VERB 1 = **become pale**, bleach, wash out, discolour, lose colour, decolour 2 = **make pale**, dim, bleach, wash out, blanch, discolour, decolour 3 = **grow dim**, fade away, become less loud 4 *usually with* **away** *or* **out** = **dwindle**, disappear, vanish, melt away, decline, dissolve, wane, die away

fail VERB 1 = **be unsuccessful**, founder, fall, break down, flop (*informal*), fizzle out (*informal*), come unstuck, miscarry ≠ succeed 2 = **disappoint**, abandon, desert, neglect, omit, let down, forsake, be disloyal to 3 = **stop working**, stop, die, break down, stall, cut out, malfunction,

conk out (*informal*) **4** = **wither**, perish, sag, waste away, shrivel up **5** = **go bankrupt**, collapse, fold (*informal*), close down, go under, go bust (*informal*), go out of business, be wound up **6** = **decline**, deteriorate, degenerate **7** = **give out**, dim, peter out, die away, grow dim
▷ PHRASE: **without fail** = **without exception**, regularly, constantly, invariably, religiously, unfailingly, conscientiously, like clockwork

failing NOUN = **shortcoming**, fault, weakness, defect, deficiency, flaw, drawback, blemish ≠ strength
▷ PREPOSITION = **in the absence of**, lacking, in default of

failure NOUN **1** = **lack of success**, defeat, collapse, breakdown, overthrow, miscarriage, fiasco, downfall ≠ success **2** = **loser**, disappointment, flop (*informal*), write-off, no-hoper (*chiefly Austral.*), dud (*informal*), black sheep, washout (*informal*), dead duck (*slang*) **3** = **bankruptcy**, crash, collapse, ruin, closure, winding up, downfall, going under ≠ prosperity

faint ADJECTIVE **1** = **dim**, low, soft, faded, distant, vague, unclear, muted ≠ clear **2** = **slight**, weak, feeble, unenthusiastic, remote, slim, vague, slender **3** = **dizzy**, giddy, light-headed, weak, exhausted, wobbly, muzzy, woozy (*informal*) ≠ energetic
▷ VERB = **pass out**, black out, lose consciousness, keel over (*informal*), go out, collapse, swoon (*literary*), flake out (*informal*)
▷ NOUN = **blackout**, collapse, coma, swoon (*literary*), unconsciousness

faintly ADVERB **1** = **slightly**, rather, a little, somewhat, dimly **2** = **softly**, weakly, feebly, in a whisper, indistinctly, unclearly

fair¹ ADJECTIVE **1** = **unbiased**, impartial, even-handed, unprejudiced, just, reasonable, proper, legitimate ≠ unfair **2** = **respectable**, average, reasonable, decent, acceptable, moderate, adequate, satisfactory **3** = **light**, golden, blonde, blond, yellowish, fair-haired, light-coloured, flaxen-haired **4** = **fine**, clear, dry, bright, pleasant, sunny, cloudless, unclouded **5** = **beautiful**, pretty, attractive, lovely, handsome, good-looking, bonny, comely, fit (*Brit. informal*) ≠ ugly

fair² NOUN **1** = **carnival**, fête, gala, bazaar **2** = **exhibition**, show, festival, mart

fairly ADVERB **1** = **equitably**, objectively, legitimately, honestly, justly, lawfully, without prejudice, dispassionately **2** = **moderately**, rather, quite, somewhat, reasonably, adequately, pretty well, tolerably **3** = **positively**, really, simply, absolutely **4** = **deservedly**, objectively, honestly, justifiably, justly, impartially, equitably, without fear or favour

fairness NOUN = **impartiality**, justice, equity, legitimacy, decency, disinterestedness, rightfulness, equitableness

fairy NOUN = **sprite**, elf, brownie, pixie, puck, imp, leprechaun, peri

fairy tale or **fairy story** NOUN
1 = **folk tale**, romance, traditional story 2 = **lie**, fiction, invention, fabrication, untruth, urban myth, tall story, urban legend

faith NOUN 1 = **confidence**, trust, credit, conviction, assurance, dependence, reliance, credence ≠ distrust 2 = **religion**, church, belief, persuasion, creed, communion, denomination, dogma ≠ agnosticism

faithful ADJECTIVE 1 = **loyal**, true, committed, constant, devoted, dedicated, reliable, staunch ≠ disloyal 2 = **accurate**, close, true, strict, exact, precise

fake VERB 1 = **forge**, copy, reproduce, fabricate, counterfeit, falsify 2 = **sham**, put on, pretend, simulate, feign, go through the motions of
▷ NOUN 1 = **forgery**, copy, fraud, reproduction, dummy, imitation, hoax, counterfeit 2 = **charlatan**, deceiver, sham, quack
▷ ADJECTIVE = **artificial**, false, forged, counterfeit, put-on, pretend (*informal*), mock, imitation ≠ genuine

fall VERB 1 = **drop**, plunge, tumble, plummet, collapse, sink, go down, come down ≠ rise 2 = **decrease**,

drop, decline, go down, slump, diminish, dwindle, lessen ≠ increase 3 = **be overthrown**, surrender, succumb, submit, capitulate, be conquered, pass into enemy hands ≠ triumph 4 = **be killed**, die, perish, meet your end ≠ survive 5 = **occur**, happen, come about, chance, take place, befall, come to pass
▷ NOUN 1 = **drop**, slip, plunge, dive, tumble, descent, plummet, nose dive 2 = **decrease**, drop, lowering, decline, reduction, slump, dip, lessening 3 = **collapse**, defeat, downfall, ruin, destruction, overthrow, submission, capitulation

false ADJECTIVE 1 = **incorrect**, wrong, mistaken, misleading, faulty, inaccurate, invalid, erroneous ≠ correct 2 = **untrue**, fraudulent, trumped up, fallacious, untruthful ≠ true 3 = **artificial**, forged, fake, reproduction, replica, imitation, bogus, simulated ≠ real

falter VERB 1 = **hesitate**, delay, waver, vacillate ≠ persevere 2 = **tumble**, totter 3 = **stutter**, pause, stumble, hesitate, stammer

fame NOUN = **prominence**, glory, celebrity, stardom, reputation, honour, prestige, stature ≠ obscurity

familiar ADJECTIVE 1 = **well-known**, recognized, common, ordinary, routine, frequent, accustomed, customary

≠ unfamiliar **2** = **friendly**, close, dear, intimate, amicable ≠ formal **3** = **relaxed**, easy, friendly, comfortable, intimate, casual, amicable **4** = **disrespectful**, forward, bold, intrusive, presumptuous, impudent, overfamiliar

familiarity NOUN
1 = **acquaintance**, experience, understanding, knowledge, awareness, grasp ≠ unfamiliarity **2** = **friendliness**, intimacy, ease, openness, informality, sociability ≠ formality **3** = **disrespect**, forwardness, overfamiliarity, cheek, presumption, boldness ≠ respect

family NOUN **1** = **relations**, relatives, household, folk (*informal*), kin, nuclear family, next of kin, kith and kin, ainga (*N.Z.*), rellies (*Austral. slang*) **2** = **children**, kids (*informal*), offspring, little ones, littlies (*Austral. informal*) **3** = **ancestors**, house, race, tribe, clan, dynasty, line of descent **4** = **species**, group, class, system, order, network, genre, subdivision

● WORD POWER
● Some careful writers insist
● that a singular verb should
● always be used with collective
● nouns such as *government*,
● *team*, *family*, *committee*, and
● *class*, for example: *the class is*
● *doing a project on Vikings*; *the*
● *company is mounting a big sales*
● *campaign*. In British usage,
● however, a plural verb is often
● used with a collective noun,
● especially where the emphasis
● is on a collection of individual
● objects or people rather than
● a group regarded as a unit:
● *the family are all on holiday*.
● The most important thing to
● remember is never to treat
● the same collective noun as
● both singular and plural in the
● same sentence: *the family is well*
● *and sends its best wishes* or *the*
● *family are well and send their best*
● *wishes*, but not *the family is well*
● *and send their best wishes*.

famine NOUN = **hunger**, want, starvation, deprivation, scarcity, dearth

famous ADJECTIVE = **well-known**, celebrated, acclaimed, noted, distinguished, prominent, legendary, renowned ≠ unknown

fan¹ NOUN = **blower**, ventilator, air conditioner
▷ VERB = **blow**, cool, refresh, air-condition, ventilate

fan² NOUN **1** = **supporter**, lover, follower, enthusiast, admirer **2** = **devotee**, buff (*informal*), aficionado

fanatic NOUN = **extremist**, activist, militant, bigot, zealot

fancy ADJECTIVE = **elaborate**, decorative, extravagant, intricate, baroque, ornamental, ornate, embellished ≠ plain
▷ NOUN **1** = **whim**, thought, idea, desire, urge, notion, humour, impulse **2** = **delusion**, dream, vision, fantasy, daydream,

chimera
▷ VERB 1 (*informal*) = **wish for**, want, desire, hope for, long for, crave, yearn for, thirst for 2 (*Brit. informal*) = **be attracted to**, find attractive, lust after, like, take to, be captivated by, have a thing about (*informal*), have eyes for 3 = **suppose**, think, believe, imagine, reckon, conjecture, think likely

fantastic ADJECTIVE 1 (*informal*) = **wonderful**, great, excellent, very good, smashing (*informal*), superb, tremendous (*informal*), magnificent, booshit (*Austral. slang*), exo (*Austral. slang*), sik (*Austral. slang*), rad (*informal*), phat (*slang*), schmick (*Austral. informal*) ≠ ordinary 2 = **strange**, bizarre, grotesque, fanciful, outlandish 3 = **implausible**, unlikely, incredible, absurd, preposterous, cock-and-bull (*informal*)

fantasy *or* **phantasy** NOUN 1 = **daydream**, dream, wish, reverie, flight of fancy, pipe dream 2 = **imagination**, fancy, invention, creativity, originality

far ADVERB 1 = **a long way**, miles, deep, a good way, afar, a great distance 2 = **much**, greatly, very much, extremely, significantly, considerably, decidedly, markedly
▷ ADJECTIVE *often with* **off** = **remote**, distant, far-flung, faraway, out-of-the-way, far-off, outlying, off the beaten track ≠ near

farce NOUN 1 = **comedy**, satire, slapstick, burlesque, buffoonery 2 = **mockery**, joke, nonsense, parody, shambles, sham, travesty

fare NOUN 1 = **charge**, price, ticket price, ticket money 2 = **food**, provisions, board, rations, kai (*N.Z. informal*), nourishment, sustenance, victuals, nutriment
▷ VERB = **get on**, do, manage, make out, prosper, get along

farewell
INTERJECTION = **goodbye**, bye (*informal*), so long, see you, take care, good morning, bye-bye (*informal*), good day, haere ra (*N.Z.*)
▷ NOUN = **goodbye**, parting, departure, leave-taking, adieu, valediction, sendoff (*informal*)

farm NOUN = **smallholding**, ranch (*chiefly U.S. & Canad.*), farmstead, station (*Austral. & N.Z.*), vineyard, plantation, croft (*Scot.*), grange, homestead
▷ VERB = **cultivate**, work, plant, grow crops on, keep animals on

fascinate VERB = **entrance**, absorb, intrigue, rivet, captivate, enthral, beguile, transfix ≠ bore

fascinating ADJECTIVE = **captivating**, engaging, gripping, compelling, intriguing, very interesting, irresistible, enticing ≠ boring

fascination NOUN = **attraction**, pull, magic, charm, lure, allure, magnetism, enchantment

fashion NOUN 1 = **style**, look, trend, rage, custom, mode, vogue, craze 2 = **method**, way, style, manner, mode

▷ VERB = **make**, shape, cast, construct, form, create, manufacture, forge

fashionable ADJECTIVE = **popular**, in fashion, trendy (*Brit. informal*), in (*informal*), modern, with it (*informal*), stylish, chic, schmick (*Austral. informal*), funky ≠ unfashionable

fast[1] ADJECTIVE 1 = **quick**, flying, rapid, fleet, swift, speedy, brisk, hasty ≠ slow 2 = **fixed**, firm, sound, stuck, secure, tight, jammed, fastened ≠ unstable 3 = **dissipated**, wild, exciting, loose, extravagant, reckless, self-indulgent, wanton 4 = **close**, firm, devoted, faithful, steadfast
▷ ADVERB 1 = **quickly**, rapidly, swiftly, hastily, hurriedly, speedily, in haste, at full speed ≠ slowly 2 = **securely**, firmly, tightly, fixedly 3 = **fixedly**, firmly, soundly, deeply, securely, tightly

fast[2] VERB = **go hungry**, abstain, go without food, deny yourself
▷ NOUN = **fasting**, diet, abstinence

fasten VERB 1 = **secure**, close, do up 2 = **tie**, bind, tie up 3 = **fix**, join, link, connect, attach, affix

fat NOUN = **fatness**, flesh, bulk, obesity, flab, blubber, paunch, fatty tissue
▷ ADJECTIVE 1 = **overweight**, large, heavy, plump, stout, obese, tubby, portly ≠ thin 2 = **fatty**, greasy, adipose, oleaginous, oily ≠ lean

fatal ADJECTIVE 1 = **disastrous**, devastating, crippling, catastrophic, ruinous, calamitous, baleful, baneful ≠ minor 2 = **lethal**, deadly, mortal, causing death, final, killing, terminal, malignant ≠ harmless

fate NOUN 1 = **destiny**, chance, fortune, luck, the stars, providence, nemesis, kismet 2 = **fortune**, destiny, lot, portion, cup, horoscope

fated ADJECTIVE = **destined**, doomed, predestined, preordained, foreordained

father NOUN 1 = **daddy** (*informal*), dad (*informal*), male parent, pop (*U.S. informal*), old man (*Brit. informal*), pa (*informal*), papa (*old-fashioned* or *informal*), pater 2 = **founder**, author, maker, architect, creator, inventor, originator, prime mover 3 *often plural* = **forefather**, predecessor, ancestor, forebear, progenitor, tupuna *or* tipuna (*N.Z.*)
▷ VERB = **sire**, parent, conceive, bring to life, beget, procreate, bring into being, give life to ▷ RELATED WORD: *adjective* paternal

Father NOUN = **priest**, minister, vicar, parson, pastor, cleric, churchman, padre (*informal*)

fatherly ADJECTIVE = **paternal**, kindly, protective, supportive, benign, affectionate, patriarchal, benevolent

fatigue NOUN = **tiredness**, lethargy, weariness, heaviness, languor, listlessness ≠ freshness

▷ VERB = **tire**, exhaust, weaken, weary, drain, wear out, take it out of (*informal*), tire out ≠ refresh

fatty ADJECTIVE = **greasy**, fat, creamy, oily, adipose, oleaginous, suety, rich

faucet NOUN (*U.S. & Canad.*) = **tap**, spout, spigot, stopcock, valve

fault NOUN 1 = **responsibility**, liability, guilt, accountability, culpability 2 = **mistake**, slip, error, blunder, lapse, oversight, indiscretion, howler (*informal*), barry *or* Barry Crocker (*Austral. slang*) 3 = **failing**, weakness, defect, deficiency, flaw, shortcoming, blemish, imperfection ≠ strength

▷ VERB = **criticize**, blame, complain, condemn, moan about, censure, hold (someone) responsible, find fault with

▷ PHRASES: **find fault with something** *or* **someone** = **criticize**, complain about, whinge about (*informal*), whine about (*informal*), quibble, carp at, take to task, pick holes in, nit-pick (*informal*); **to a fault** = **excessively**, unduly, in the extreme, overmuch, immoderately

faulty ADJECTIVE 1 = **defective**, damaged, malfunctioning, broken, flawed, impaired, imperfect, out of order 2 = **incorrect**, flawed, unsound

favour *or* (*U.S.*) **favor** NOUN 1 = **approval**, goodwill, commendation, approbation ≠ disapproval 2 = **favouritism**, preferential treatment 3 = **support**, backing, aid, assistance, patronage, good opinion 4 = **good turn**, service, benefit, courtesy, kindness, indulgence, boon, good deed ≠ wrong

▷ VERB 1 = **prefer**, opt for, like better, incline towards, choose, pick, desire, go for ≠ object to 2 = **indulge**, reward, side with, smile upon 3 = **support**, champion, encourage, approve, advocate, subscribe to, commend, stand up for ≠ oppose 4 = **help**, benefit

favourable *or* (*U.S.*) **favorable** ADJECTIVE 1 = **positive**, encouraging, approving, praising, reassuring, enthusiastic, sympathetic, commending ≠ disapproving 2 = **affirmative**, agreeing, confirming, positive, assenting, corroborative 3 = **advantageous**, promising, encouraging, suitable, helpful, beneficial, auspicious, opportune ≠ disadvantageous

favourite *or* (*U.S.*) **favorite** ADJECTIVE = **preferred**, favoured, best-loved, most-liked, special, choice, dearest, pet

▷ NOUN = **darling**, pet, blue-eyed boy (*informal*), beloved, idol, fave (*informal*), teacher's pet, the apple of your eye

fear NOUN 1 = **dread**, horror, panic, terror, fright, alarm, trepidation,

fearfulness **2** = **bugbear**, bête noire, horror, nightmare, anxiety, terror, dread, spectre
▷ **VERB 1** = **be afraid of**, dread, shudder at, be fearful of, tremble at, be terrified by, take fright at, shake in your shoes about **2** = **regret**, feel, suspect, have a feeling, have a hunch, have a sneaking suspicion, have a funny feeling ▷ **PHRASE**: **fear for something** or **someone** = **worry about**, be anxious about, feel concern for

fearful ADJECTIVE **1** = **scared**, afraid, alarmed, frightened, nervous, terrified, petrified ≠ unafraid **2** = **timid**, afraid, frightened, scared, alarmed, nervous, uneasy, jumpy ≠ brave **3** (*informal*) = **frightful**, terrible, awful, dreadful, horrific, dire, horrendous, gruesome

feasible ADJECTIVE = **practicable**, possible, reasonable, viable, workable, achievable, attainable, likely ≠ impracticable

feast NOUN **1** = **banquet**, repast, spread (*informal*), dinner, treat, hakari (*N.Z.*) **2** = **festival**, holiday, fête, celebration, holy day, red-letter day, religious festival, saint's day
▷ **VERB** = **eat your fill**, wine and dine, overindulge, consume, indulge, gorge, devour, pig out (*slang*)

feat NOUN = **accomplishment**, act, performance, achievement, enterprise, undertaking, exploit, deed

feather NOUN = **plume**

feature NOUN **1** = **aspect**, quality, characteristic, property, factor, trait, hallmark, facet **2** = **article**, report, story, piece, item, column **3** = **highlight**, attraction, speciality, main item **4** = **face**, countenance, physiognomy, lineament
▷ **VERB 1** = **spotlight**, present, emphasize, play up, foreground, give prominence to **2** = **star**, appear, participate, play a part

federation NOUN = **union**, league, association, alliance, combination, coalition, partnership, consortium

fed up ADJECTIVE = **cheesed off**, depressed, bored, tired, discontented, dissatisfied, glum, sick and tired (*informal*), hoha (*N.Z.*)

fee NOUN = **charge**, price, cost, bill, payment, wage, salary, toll

feeble ADJECTIVE **1** = **weak**, frail, debilitated, sickly, puny, weedy (*informal*), infirm, effete ≠ strong **2** = **inadequate**, pathetic, insufficient, lame **3** = **unconvincing**, poor, thin, tame, pathetic, lame, flimsy, paltry ≠ effective

feed VERB **1** = **cater for**, provide for, nourish, provide with food, supply, sustain, cook for, wine and dine **2** = **graze**, eat, browse, pasture **3** = **eat**, drink milk
▷ **NOUN 1** = **food**, fodder, provender, pasturage **2** (*informal*)

= **meal**, spread (*informal*), dinner, lunch, tea, breakfast, feast, supper

feel VERB 1 = **experience**, bear 2 = **touch**, handle, manipulate, finger, stroke, paw, caress, fondle 3 = **be aware of** 4 = **perceive**, detect, discern, experience, notice, observe 5 = **sense**, be aware, be convinced, have a feeling, intuit 6 = **believe**, consider, judge, deem, think, hold ▷ NOUN 1 = **texture**, finish, touch, surface, surface quality 2 = **impression**, feeling, air, sense, quality, atmosphere, mood, aura

feeling NOUN 1 = **emotion**, sentiment 2 = **opinion**, view, attitude, belief, point of view, instinct, inclination 3 = **passion**, emotion, intensity, warmth 4 = **ardour**, love, care, warmth, tenderness, fervour 5 = **sympathy**, understanding, concern, pity, sensitivity, compassion, sorrow, sensibility 6 = **sensation**, sense, impression, awareness 7 = **sense of touch**, perception, sensation 8 = **impression**, idea, sense, notion, suspicion, hunch, inkling, presentiment 9 = **atmosphere**, mood, aura, ambience, feel, air, quality

feisty ADJECTIVE (*informal*) = **fiery**, spirited, bold, plucky, vivacious, (as) game as Ned Kelly (*Austral. slang*)

fell VERB 1 = **cut down**, cut, level, demolish, knock down, hew 2 = **knock down**

fellow NOUN 1 (*old-fashioned*) = **man**, person, individual, character, guy (*informal*), bloke (*Brit. informal*), chap (*informal*) 2 = **associate**, colleague, peer, partner, companion, comrade, crony

fellowship NOUN 1 = **society**, club, league, association, organization, guild, fraternity, brotherhood 2 = **camaraderie**, brotherhood, companionship, sociability

feminine ADJECTIVE = **womanly**, pretty, soft, gentle, tender, delicate, ladylike ≠ masculine

fence NOUN = **barrier**, wall, defence, railings, hedge, barricade, hedgerow, rampart ▷ VERB with **in** or **off** = **enclose**, surround, bound, protect, pen, confine, encircle

ferocious ADJECTIVE 1 = **fierce**, violent, savage, ravening, predatory, rapacious, wild ≠ gentle 2 = **cruel**, bitter, brutal, vicious, ruthless, bloodthirsty

ferry NOUN = **ferry boat**, boat, ship, passenger boat, packet boat, packet ▷ VERB = **transport**, bring, carry, ship, take, run, shuttle, convey

fertile ADJECTIVE = **productive**, rich, lush, prolific, abundant, plentiful, fruitful, teeming ≠ barren

fertility NOUN = **fruitfulness**, abundance, richness, fecundity, luxuriance, productiveness

fertilizer or **fertiliser** NOUN

= **compost**, muck, manure, dung, bone meal, dressing

festival NOUN 1 = **celebration**, fair, carnival, gala, fête, entertainment, jubilee, fiesta 2 = **holy day**, holiday, feast, commemoration, feast day, red-letter day, saint's day, fiesta

festive ADJECTIVE = **celebratory**, happy, merry, jubilant, cheery, joyous, joyful, jovial ≠ mournful

fetch VERB 1 = **bring**, pick up, collect, go and get, get, carry, deliver, transport 2 = **sell for**, make, raise, earn, realize, go for, yield, bring in

fetching ADJECTIVE (*informal*) = **attractive**, charming, cute, enticing, captivating, alluring, winsome

feud NOUN = **hostility**, row, conflict, argument, disagreement, rivalry, quarrel, vendetta ▷ VERB = **quarrel**, row, clash, dispute, fall out, contend, war, squabble

fever NOUN = **excitement**, frenzy, ferment, agitation, fervour, restlessness, delirium

few ADJECTIVE = **not many**, one or two, scarcely any, rare, meagre, negligible, sporadic, sparse

fiasco NOUN = **flop**, failure, disaster, mess (*informal*), catastrophe, debacle, cock-up (*Brit. slang*), washout (*informal*)

fibre or (U.S.) **fiber** NOUN = **thread**, strand, filament, tendril, pile, texture, wisp

fiction NOUN 1 = **tale**, story, novel, legend, myth, romance, narration, creative writing 2 = **lie**, invention, fabrication, falsehood, untruth, urban myth, tall story, urban legend

fictional ADJECTIVE = **imaginary**, made-up, invented, legendary, unreal, nonexistent

fiddle NOUN 1 (*Brit. informal*) = **fraud**, racket, scam (*slang*), fix, swindle 2 (*informal*) = **violin** ▷ VERB 1 (*informal*) *often with* **with** = **fidget**, play, finger, tamper, mess about *or* around 2 (*informal*) *often with* **with** = **tinker**, adjust, interfere, mess about *or* around 3 (*informal*) = **cheat**, cook (*informal*), fix, diddle (*informal*), wangle (*informal*)

fiddling ADJECTIVE = **trivial**, small, petty, trifling, insignificant, unimportant, pettifogging, futile

fidelity NOUN 1 = **loyalty**, devotion, allegiance, constancy, faithfulness, dependability, trustworthiness, staunchness ≠ disloyalty 2 = **accuracy**, precision, correspondence, closeness, faithfulness, exactness, scrupulousness ≠ inaccuracy

field NOUN 1 = **meadow**, land, green, lea (*poetic*), pasture 2 = **speciality**, line, area, department, territory, discipline, province, sphere 3 = **line**, reach, sweep 4 = **competitors**, competition, candidates, runners, applicants, entrants, contestants ▷ VERB 1 (*informal*) = **deal with**,

f

answer, handle, respond to, reply
to, deflect, turn aside **2** (*sport*)
= **retrieve**, return, stop, catch,
pick up

fierce ADJECTIVE **1** = **ferocious**,
wild, dangerous, cruel, savage,
brutal, aggressive, menacing,
aggers (*Austral. slang*), biffo
(*Austral. slang*) ≠ gentle
2 = **intense**, strong, keen,
relentless, cut-throat **3** = **stormy**,
strong, powerful, violent,
intense, raging, furious, howling
≠ tranquil

fiercely ADVERB = **ferociously**,
savagely, passionately, furiously,
viciously, tooth and nail,
tigerishly, with no holds barred

fiery ADJECTIVE **1** = **burning**,
flaming, blazing, on fire, ablaze,
aflame, afire **2** = **excitable**, fierce,
passionate, irritable, impetuous,
irascible, hot-headed

fight VERB **1** = **oppose**, campaign
against, dispute, contest,
resist, defy, contend, withstand
2 = **battle**, combat, do battle
3 = **engage in**, conduct, wage,
pursue, carry on
▷ NOUN **1** = **battle**, campaign,
movement, struggle **2** = **conflict**,
clash, contest, encounter
3 = **brawl**, scrap (*informal*),
confrontation, rumble (*U.S. & N.Z.
slang*), duel, skirmish, tussle, biffo
(*Austral. slang*), boilover (*Austral.*)
4 = **row**, argument, dispute,
quarrel, squabble **5** = **resistance**,
spirit, pluck, militancy,
belligerence, pluckiness

fighter NOUN **1** = **boxer**, wrestler,
pugilist, prize fighter **2** = **soldier**,
warrior, fighting man, man-at-
arms

figure NOUN **1** = **digit**,
character, symbol, number,
numeral **2** = **shape**, build,
body, frame, proportions,
physique **3** = **personage**, person,
individual, character, personality,
celebrity, big name, dignitary
4 = **diagram**, drawing, picture,
illustration, representation,
sketch **5** = **design**, shape, pattern
6 = **price**, cost, value, amount,
total, sum
▷ VERB **1** *usually with* **in** = **feature**,
act, appear, contribute to, play a
part, be featured **2** = **calculate**,
work out, compute, tot up, total,
count, reckon, tally ▷ PHRASE:
figure something *or* **someone
out** = **understand**, make out,
fathom, see, solve, comprehend,
make sense of, decipher

figurehead NOUN = **nominal
head**, titular head, front man,
puppet, mouthpiece

file¹ NOUN **1** = **folder**, case,
portfolio, binder **2** = **dossier**,
record, information, data,
documents, case history, report,
case **3** = **line**, row, chain, column,
queue, procession
▷ VERB **1** = **arrange**, order,
classify, put in place, categorize,
pigeonhole, put in order
2 = **register**, record, enter, log,
put on record **3** = **march**, troop,
parade, walk in line, walk behind

one another

file² VERB = **smooth**, shape, polish, rub, scrape, rasp, abrade

fill VERB 1 = **top up**, fill up, make full, become full, brim over 2 = **swell**, expand, become bloated, extend, balloon, fatten 3 = **pack**, crowd, squeeze, cram, throng 4 = **stock**, supply, pack, load 5 = **plug**, close, stop, seal, cork, bung, block up, stop up 6 = **saturate**, charge, pervade, permeate, imbue, impregnate, suffuse 7 = **fulfil**, hold, perform, carry out, occupy, execute, discharge 8 *often with* **up** = **satisfy**, stuff, glut

filling NOUN = **stuffing**, padding, filler, wadding, inside, insides, contents
 ▷ ADJECTIVE = **satisfying**, heavy, square, substantial, ample

film NOUN 1 = **movie**, picture, flick (*slang*), motion picture 2 = **cinema**, the movies 3 = **layer**, covering, cover, skin, coating, dusting, tissue, membrane
 ▷ VERB 1 = **photograph**, record, shoot, video, videotape, take 2 = **adapt for the screen**, make into a film

filter NOUN = **sieve**, mesh, gauze, strainer, membrane, riddle, sifter
 ▷ VERB 1 = **trickle**, seep, percolate, escape, leak, penetrate, ooze, dribble 2 *with* **through** = **purify**, treat, strain, refine, riddle, sift, sieve, winnow

filthy ADJECTIVE 1 = **dirty**, foul, polluted, squalid, slimy, unclean, putrid, festy (*Austral. slang*) 2 = **grimy**, muddy, blackened, grubby, begrimed, festy (*Austral. slang*) 3 = **obscene**, corrupt, indecent, pornographic, lewd, depraved, impure, smutty

final ADJECTIVE 1 = **last**, latest, closing, finishing, concluding, ultimate, terminal ≠ first 2 = **irrevocable**, absolute, definitive, decided, settled, definite, conclusive, irrefutable

finale NOUN = **climax**, ending, close, conclusion, culmination, denouement, last part, epilogue ≠ opening

finally ADVERB 1 = **eventually**, at last, in the end, ultimately, at length, at long last, after a long time 2 = **lastly**, in the end, ultimately 3 = **in conclusion**, lastly, in closing, to conclude, to sum up, in summary

finance NOUN = **economics**, business, money, banking, accounts, investment, commerce
 ▷ PLURAL NOUN = **resources**, money, funds, capital, cash, affairs, budgeting, assets
 ▷ VERB = **fund**, back, support, pay for, guarantee, invest in, underwrite, endow

financial ADJECTIVE = **economic**, business, commercial, monetary, fiscal, pecuniary

find VERB 1 = **discover**, uncover, spot, locate, detect, come across, hit upon, put your finger on ≠ lose 2 = **encounter**, meet, recognize 3 = **observe**, learn, note, discover, notice, realize, come up with, perceive

▷ **NOUN** = **discovery**, catch, asset, bargain, acquisition, good buy

▷ **PHRASE**: **find something out** = **learn**, discover, realize, observe, perceive, detect, become aware, come to know

fine¹ ADJECTIVE **1** = **excellent**, good, striking, masterly, very good, impressive, outstanding, magnificent ≠ poor **2** = **satisfactory**, good, all right, suitable, acceptable, convenient, fair, O.K. or okay (informal) **3** = **thin**, light, narrow, wispy **4** = **delicate**, light, thin, sheer, flimsy, wispy, gossamer, diaphanous ≠ coarse **5** = **stylish**, expensive, elegant, refined, tasteful, quality, schmick (Austral. informal) **6** = **exquisite**, delicate, fragile, dainty **7** = **minute**, exact, precise, nice **8** = **keen**, minute, nice, sharp, acute, subtle, precise, hairsplitting **9** = **brilliant**, quick, keen, alert, clever, penetrating, astute **10** = **sunny**, clear, fair, dry, bright, pleasant, clement, balmy ≠ cloudy

fine² NOUN = **penalty**, damages, punishment, forfeit, financial penalty

▷ **VERB** = **penalize**, charge, punish

finger VERB = **touch**, feel, handle, play with, manipulate, paw (informal), maul, toy with

● **WORD POWER**
● The **fingers** are any of the
● digits of the hand, excluding
● the thumb. Their shape and
● function are referred to in many
● of the extended meanings of
● finger. The long and thin shape
● of a finger has come to mean
● a strip or sliver, in *a finger of*
● *land* and *finger sandwich*. Our
● sense of touch is experienced
● through the fingers, which
● are employed to manipulate
● objects. As a verb, *finger* can
● simply mean to touch, often in
● a restless way, e.g. *He fingered*
● *the coins in his pocket*. Fingers
● are also used for pointing,
● selection, and identification,
● particularly as a means of
● assigning blame, in the phrase
● *point the finger at* or *finger*
● *someone to the police*. We pin
● physical objects down with our
● fingers, but can also pin down
● thoughts and memories in our
● minds, e.g. *I couldn't put my*
● *finger on it*.

finish VERB **1** = **stop**, close, complete, conclude, cease, wrap up (informal), terminate, round off ≠ start **2** = **get done**, complete, conclude **3** = **end**, stop, conclude, wind up, terminate **4** = **consume**, dispose of, devour, polish off, eat, get through **5** = **use up**, empty, exhaust **6** = **coat**, polish, stain, texture, wax, varnish, gild, veneer **7** often with **off** = **destroy**, defeat, overcome, bring down, ruin, dispose of, rout, put an end to **8** often with **off** = **kill**, murder, destroy, massacre, butcher,

slaughter, slay, exterminate
▷ NOUN 1 = **end**, close,
conclusion, run-in, completion,
finale, culmination, cessation
≠ beginning 2 = **surface**, polish,
shine, texture, glaze, veneer,
lacquer, lustre

finished ADJECTIVE 1 = **over**, done,
through, ended, closed, complete,
executed, finalized ≠ begun
2 = **ruined**, done for (*informal*),
doomed, through, lost, defeated,
wiped out, undone

fire NOUN 1 = **flames**, blaze,
combustion, inferno,
conflagration, holocaust
2 = **passion**, energy, spirit,
enthusiasm, excitement,
intensity, sparkle, vitality
3 = **bombardment**, shooting,
firing, shelling, hail, volley,
barrage, gunfire
▷ VERB 1 = **let off**, shoot, shell,
set off, discharge, detonate
2 = **shoot**, explode, discharge,
detonate, pull the trigger
3 (*informal*) = **dismiss**, sack
(*informal*), get rid of, discharge, lay
off, make redundant, cashier, give
notice, kennet (*Austral. slang*), jeff
(*Austral. slang*) 4 = **inspire**, excite,
stir, stimulate, motivate, awaken,
animate, rouse

fireworks PLURAL NOUN
1 = **pyrotechnics**, illuminations,
feux d'artifice 2 (*informal*)
= **trouble**, row, storm, rage,
uproar, hysterics

firm¹ ADJECTIVE 1 = **hard**, solid,
dense, set, stiff, compacted, rigid,
inflexible ≠ soft 2 = **secure**,
fixed, rooted, stable, steady,
fast, embedded, immovable
≠ unstable 3 = **strong**, close,
tight, steady 4 = **strict**,
unshakeable, resolute, inflexible,
unyielding, unbending
5 = **determined**, resolved,
definite, set on, adamant,
resolute, inflexible, unyielding
≠ wavering 6 = **definite**, hard,
clear, confirmed, settled, fixed,
hard-and-fast, cut-and-dried
(*informal*)

firm² NOUN = **company**,
business, concern, association,
organization, corporation,
venture, enterprise

firmly ADVERB 1 = **securely**,
safely, tightly 2 = **immovably**,
securely, steadily, like a rock,
unflinchingly, unshakeably
3 = **steadily**, securely, tightly,
unflinchingly 4 = **resolutely**,
staunchly, steadfastly, definitely,
unwaveringly, unchangeably

first ADJECTIVE = **earliest**,
initial, opening, introductory,
original, maiden, primordial
2 = **top**, best, winning, premier
3 = **elementary**, key, basic,
primary, fundamental, cardinal,
rudimentary, elemental
4 = **foremost**, highest, greatest,
leading, head, ruling, chief, prime
▷ NOUN = **novelty**, innovation,
originality, new experience
▷ ADVERB = **to begin with**, firstly,
initially, at the beginning, in the
first place, beforehand, to start

with, at the outset ▷ **PHRASE:
from the first** = **start**, beginning,
outset, the very beginning,
introduction, starting point,
inception, commencement

fish VERB = **angle**, net, cast, trawl
▷ *see* **sharks**

fit¹ VERB 1 = **adapt**, shape, arrange,
alter, adjust, modify, tweak
(*informal*), customize 2 = **place**,
insert 3 = **suit**, meet, match,
belong to, conform to, correspond
to, accord with, be appropriate to
4 = **equip**, provide, arm, prepare,
fit out, kit out
▷ ADJECTIVE 1 = **appropriate**,
suitable, right, becoming,
seemly, fitting, skilled, correct
≠ inappropriate 2 = **healthy**,
strong, robust, sturdy, well, trim,
strapping, hale ≠ unfit

fit² NOUN 1 (*pathology*) = **seizure**,
attack, bout, spasm, convulsion,
paroxysm 2 = **bout**, burst,
outbreak, outburst, spell

fitness NOUN
1 = **appropriateness**,
competence, readiness, eligibility,
suitability, propriety, aptness
2 = **health**, strength, good health,
vigour, good condition, wellness,
robustness

fitting ADJECTIVE = **appropriate**,
suitable, proper, apt, right,
becoming, seemly, correct
≠ unsuitable
▷ NOUN = **accessory**, part, piece,
unit, component, attachment

fix VERB 1 = **place**, join, stick,
attach, set, position, plant, link

2 *often with* **up** = **decide**, set,
choose, establish, determine,
settle, arrange, arrive at 3 *often
with* **up** = **arrange**, organize, sort
out, see to, make arrangements
for 4 = **repair**, mend, service,
correct, restore, see to, overhaul,
patch up 5 = **focus**, direct at,
fasten on 6 (*informal*) = **rig**, set up
(*informal*), influence, manipulate,
fiddle (*informal*)
▷ NOUN (*informal*) = **mess**,
corner, difficulty, dilemma,
embarrassment, plight, pickle
(*informal*), uphill (*S. African*)
▷ PHRASES: **fix someone up** *often
with* **with** = **provide**, supply, bring
about, lay on, arrange for; **fix
something up** = **arrange**, plan,
settle, fix, organize, sort out,
agree on, make arrangements for

fixed ADJECTIVE 1 = **inflexible**,
set, steady, resolute, unwavering
≠ wavering 2 = **immovable**,
set, established, secure, rooted,
permanent, rigid ≠ mobile
3 = **agreed**, set, planned, decided,
established, settled, arranged,
resolved

fizz VERB 1 = **bubble**, froth, fizzle,
effervesce, produce bubbles
2 = **sputter**, buzz, sparkle, hiss,
crackle *often with* **out**

flag¹ NOUN = **banner**, standard,
colours, pennant, ensign,
streamer, pennon
▷ VERB 1 = **mark**, identify,
indicate, label, pick out, note
2 *often with* **down** = **hail**, stop,
signal, wave down

● **FISH**

● ahuru (N.Z.)
● alewife
● albacore
● alfonsino
● amberjack
● anabas
● anchovy
● angelfish
● archerfish
● argentine
● aua (N.Z.)
● Australian salmon, native salmon, salmon trout, bay trout or kahawai (N.Z. & Austral.)
● barbel
● barracouta or (Austral.) hake
● barracuda
● barramundi or (Austral.) barra or giant perch
● bass
● beluga
● bib, pout, or whiting pout
● black cod or Māori chief (N.Z.)
● blackfish or (Austral.) nigger
● bleak
● blenny
● blowfish or (Austral.) toado
● blue cod, rock cod, or (N.Z.) rawaru, pakirikiri, or patutuki

● bluefin tuna
● bluefish or snapper
● blue nose (N.Z.)
● bonito or (Austral.) horse mackerel
● bony bream (Austral.)
● bowfin or dogfish
● bream or (Austral.) brim
● brill
● brook trout or speckled trout
● brown trout
● bullhead
● bully or (N.Z.) pakoko, titarakura, or toitoi
● burbot, eelpout, or ling
● butterfish, greenbone, or (N.Z.) koaea or marari
● capelin or caplin
● carp
● catfish
● Chinook salmon, quinnat salmon, or king salmon
● chub
● cisco or lake herring
● clingfish
● coalfish or (Brit.) saithe or coley
● cockabully
● cod or codfish
● coelacanth
● coho or silver salmon

● coley
● conger
● coral trout
● dab
● dace
● dart (Austral.)
● darter
● dory
● dragonet
● eel or (N.Z.) tuna
● eelpout
● electric eel
● fighting fish or betta
● filefish
● flatfish or (N.Z.) flattie
● flathead
● flounder or (N.Z.) patiki
● flying fish
● flying gurnard
● garpike, garfish, gar, or (Austral.) ballahoo
● geelbek
● gemfish or (Austral.) hake
● goby
● golden perch, freshwater bream, Murray perch, or yellow-belly (Austral.)
● goldfish
● gourami
● grayling or (Austral.) yarra herring
● grenadier or rat-tail

f

- groper or grouper
- grunion
- grunt
- gudgeon
- gunnel
- guppy
- gurnard or gurnet
- haddock
- hagfish, hag or blind eel
- hake
- halfbeak
- halibut
- hapuku (*Austral. & N.Z.*)
- herring
- hogfish
- hoki (*N.Z.*)
- horse mackerel
- jewelfish
- jewfish or (*Austral. informal*) jewie
- John Dory
- kelpfish or (*Austral. informal*) kelpie
- killifish
- kingfish
- kingklip (*S. African*)
- kokanee
- kokopu (*N.Z.*)
- lamprey or lamper eel
- leatherjacket
- lemon sole
- ling or (*Austral.*) beardie
- loach
- luderick or (*N.Z.*) parore
- lumpfish or

- lumpsucker
- lungfish
- mackerel or (*colloquial*) shiner
- mangrove Jack (*Austral.*)
- manta, manta ray, devilfish, or devil ray
- maomao (*N.Z.*)
- marlin or spearfish
- menhaden
- miller's thumb
- minnow or (*Scot.*) baggie minnow
- mirror carp
- moki or blue moki (*N.Z.*)
- molly
- monkfish or (*U.S.*) goosefish
- moray
- morwong, black perch, or (*N.Z.*) porae
- mudfish
- mudskipper
- opah, moonfish, or kingfish
- orange roughy (*Austral.*)
- orfe
- ouananiche
- ox-eye herring (*Austral.*)
- parore, blackfish, black rockfish or mangrove fish (*N.Z.*)
- parrotfish

- pearl perch (*Austral.*)
- perch or (*Austral.*) redfin
- pickerel
- pike, luce, or jackfish
- pikeperch
- pilchard or (*Austral. informal*) pillie
- pilot fish
- pipefish or needlefish
- piranha or piraña
- plaice
- pollack or pollock
- pollan
- pompano
- porae (*N.Z.*)
- porcupine fish or globefish
- porgy or pogy
- pout
- powan or lake herring
- puffer or globefish
- rainbow trout
- ray
- redfin
- redfish
- red mullet or (*U.S.*) goatfish
- red salmon
- red snapper
- remora
- ribbonfish
- roach
- rock bass
- rockfish or (*formerly*) rock salmon

f

- rockling
- rudd
- ruffe, ruff, or pope
- salmon
- sand eel, sand lance, or launce
- sardine
- sauger
- saury or skipper
- sawfish
- scad
- scaldfish
- scorpion fish
- scup or northern porgy
- sea bass
- sea bream
- sea horse
- sea scorpion
- sea snail or snailfish
- sea trout
- Sergeant Baker
- shad
- shanny
- shiner
- Siamese fighting fish
- sild
- silver belly (N.Z.)
- silverfish
- silverside or silversides
- skate
- skipjack or skipjack tuna

- smelt
- smooth hound
- snapper, red bream, or (Austral.) wollomai or wollamai
- snipefish or bellows fish
- snoek
- snook
- sockeye or red salmon
- sole
- Spanish mackerel or Queensland kingfish
- sprat
- steelhead
- stickleback
- stingray
- stonefish
- sturgeon
- sucker
- sunfish
- surgeonfish
- swordfish
- swordtail
- tailor
- tarakihi or terakihi (N.Z.)
- tarpon
- tarwhine
- tautog or blackfish
- tench
- toadfish

- tommy rough or tommy ruff (Austral.)
- trevalla (Austral.)
- trevally, araara or samson fish (Austral. & N.Z.)
- triggerfish
- trout
- trunkfish, boxfish, or cowfish
- tuna or tunny
- turbot
- vendace
- wahoo
- walleye, walleyed pike, or dory
- warehou (N.Z.)
- weever
- whitebait
- whitefish
- whiting
- witch
- wobbegong, wobbygong, or wobegong
- wolffish or catfish
- wrasse
- yellowfin (N.Z.)
- yellow jack

f

flag² VERB =**weaken**, fade, weary, falter, wilt, wane, sag, languish

flagging ADJECTIVE =**weakening**, declining, waning, fading, deteriorating, wearying, faltering, wilting

flair NOUN 1 =**ability**, feel, talent, gift, genius, faculty, mastery, knack **2** (*informal*) = **style**, taste, dash, chic, elegance, panache, discernment, stylishness

flake NOUN = **chip**, scale, layer, peeling, shaving, wafer, sliver
▷ VERB = **chip**, peel (off), blister

flamboyant ADJECTIVE **1** = **camp** (*informal*), dashing, theatrical, swashbuckling **2** = **showy**, elaborate, extravagant, ornate, ostentatious **3** = **colourful**, striking, brilliant, glamorous, stylish, dazzling, glitzy (*slang*), showy, bling (*slang*)

flame NOUN **1** = **fire**, light, spark, glow, blaze, brightness, inferno **2** (*informal*) = **sweetheart**, partner, lover, girlfriend, boyfriend, heart-throb (*Brit.*), beau
▷ VERB = **burn**, flash, shine, glow, blaze, flare, glare

flank NOUN **1** = **side**, hip, thigh, loin **2** = **wing**, side, sector, aspect

flap VERB **1** = **flutter**, wave, flail **2** = **beat**, wave, thrash, flutter, wag, vibrate, shake
▷ NOUN **1** = **flutter**, beating, waving, shaking, swinging, swish **2** (*informal*) = **panic**, state (*informal*), agitation, commotion, sweat (*informal*), dither (*chiefly Brit.*), fluster, tizzy (*informal*)

flare VERB **1** = **blaze**, flame, glare, flicker, burn up **2** = **widen**, spread, broaden, spread out, dilate, splay
▷ NOUN = **flame**, burst, flash, blaze, glare, flicker

flash NOUN = **blaze**, burst, spark, beam, streak, flare, dazzle, glare
▷ VERB **1** = **blaze**, shine, beam, sparkle, flare, glare, gleam, light up **2** = **speed**, race, shoot, fly, tear, dash, whistle, streak **3** (*informal*) = **show quickly**, display, expose, exhibit, flourish, show off, flaunt
▷ ADJECTIVE (*informal*) = **ostentatious**, smart, trendy, showy, bling (*slang*)

flat¹ ADJECTIVE **1** = **even**, level, levelled, smooth, horizontal ≠ uneven **2** = **punctured**, collapsed, burst, blown out, deflated, empty **3** = **used up**, finished, empty, drained, expired **4** = **absolute**, firm, positive, explicit, definite, outright, downright, unequivocal **5** = **dull**, dead, empty, boring, depressing, tedious, lacklustre, tiresome ≠ exciting **6** = **without energy**, empty, weak, tired, depressed, drained, weary, worn out **7** = **monotonous**, boring, dull, tedious, tiresome, unchanging
▷ ADVERB = **completely**, directly, absolutely, categorically, precisely, exactly, utterly, outright
▷ PHRASE: **flat out** (*informal*) = **at full speed**, all out, to the full, hell for leather (*informal*), as hard as possible, at full tilt, for all you are worth

flat² NOUN = **apartment**, rooms, quarters, digs, suite, penthouse, living quarters, duplex (*U.S. & Canad.*), bachelor apartment (*Canad.*)

flatly ADVERB = **absolutely**, completely, positively,

categorically, unequivocally, unhesitatingly

flatten VERB **1** *sometimes with* **out** = **level**, squash, compress, trample, iron out, even out, smooth off
2 *sometimes with* **out** = **destroy**, level, ruin, demolish, knock down, pull down, raze, kennet (*Austral. slang*), jeff (*Austral. slang*)

flatter VERB **1** = **praise**, compliment, pander to, sweet-talk (*informal*), wheedle, soft-soap (*informal*), butter up
2 = **suit**, become, enhance, set off, embellish, do something for, show to advantage

flattering ADJECTIVE
1 = **becoming**, kind, effective, enhancing, well-chosen ≠ unflattering **2** = **ingratiating**, complimentary, fawning, fulsome, laudatory, adulatory ≠ uncomplimentary

flavour (*U.S.*) *or* **flavor** NOUN
1 = **taste**, seasoning, flavouring, savour, relish, smack, aroma, zest ≠ blandness **2** = **quality**, feeling, feel, style, character, tone, essence, tinge
▷ VERB = **season**, spice, add flavour to, enrich, infuse, imbue, pep up, leaven

flaw NOUN = **weakness**, failing, defect, weak spot, fault, blemish, imperfection, chink in your armour

flawed ADJECTIVE **1** = **damaged**, defective, imperfect, blemished, faulty **2** = **erroneous**, incorrect, invalid, wrong, mistaken, false, faulty, unsound

flee VERB = **run away**, escape, bolt, fly, take off (*informal*), depart, run off, take flight

fleet NOUN = **navy**, task force, flotilla, armada

fleeting ADJECTIVE = **momentary**, passing, brief, temporary, short-lived, transient, ephemeral, transitory ≠ lasting

flesh NOUN **1** = **fat**, muscle, tissue, brawn **2** (*informal*) = **fatness**, fat, adipose tissue, corpulence, weight **3** = **meat** **4** = **physical nature**, carnality, human nature, flesh and blood, sinful nature
▷ PHRASE: **your own flesh and blood** = **family**, blood, relations, relatives, kin, kith and kin, blood relations, kinsfolk, ainga (*N.Z.*), rellies (*Austral. slang*)

flexibility NOUN **1** = **elasticity**, pliability, springiness, pliancy, give (*informal*) **2** = **adaptability**, openness, versatility, adjustability **3** = **complaisance**, accommodation, give and take, amenability

flexible ADJECTIVE **1** = **pliable**, plastic, elastic, supple, lithe, springy, pliant, stretchy ≠ rigid
2 = **adaptable**, open, variable, adjustable, discretionary ≠ inflexible

flick VERB **1** = **jerk**, pull, tug, lurch, jolt **2** = **strike**, tap, remove quickly, hit, touch, stroke, flip, whisk ▷ PHRASE: **flick through something** = **browse**, glance at, skim, leaf through, flip through, thumb through, skip through

flicker VERB 1 = **twinkle**, flash, sparkle, flare, shimmer, gutter, glimmer 2 = **flutter**, waver, quiver, vibrate

▷ NOUN 1 = **glimmer**, flash, spark, flare, gleam 2 = **trace**, breath, spark, glimmer, iota

flight¹ NOUN 1 = **journey**, trip, voyage 2 = **aviation**, flying, aeronautics 3 = **flock**, group, unit, cloud, formation, squadron, swarm, flying group

flight² NOUN = **escape**, fleeing, departure, retreat, exit, running away, exodus, getaway

fling VERB = **throw**, toss, hurl, launch, cast, propel, sling, catapult

▷ NOUN = **binge**, good time, bash, party, spree, night on the town, rave-up (*Brit. slang*)

flip VERB 1 = **flick**, switch, snap, slick 2 = **spin**, turn, overturn, turn over, roll over 3 = **toss**, throw, flick, fling, sling

▷ NOUN = **toss**, throw, spin, snap, flick

flirt VERB 1 = **chat up**, lead on (*informal*), make advances at, make eyes at, philander, make sheep's eyes at 2 *usually with* **with** = **toy with**, consider, entertain, play with, dabble in, trifle with, give a thought to, expose yourself to

▷ NOUN = **tease**, philanderer, coquette, heart-breaker

float VERB 1 = **glide**, sail, drift,

move gently, bob, coast, slide, be carried 2 = **be buoyant**, hang, hover ≠ sink 3 = **launch**, offer, sell, set up, promote, get going ≠ dissolve

floating ADJECTIVE

1 = **uncommitted**, wavering, undecided, indecisive, vacillating, sitting on the fence (*informal*), unaffiliated, independent

2 = **free**, wandering, variable, fluctuating, unattached, movable

flock NOUN 1 = **herd**, group, flight, drove, colony, gaggle, skein

2 = **crowd**, company, group, host, collection, mass, gathering, herd

▷ VERB 1 = **stream**, crowd, mass, swarm, throng 2 = **gather**, crowd, mass, collect, assemble, herd, huddle, converge

flog VERB = **beat**, whip, lash, thrash, whack, scourge, hit hard, trounce

flood NOUN 1 = **deluge**, downpour, inundation, tide, overflow, torrent, spate 2 = **torrent**, flow, rush, stream, tide, abundance, glut, profusion 3 = **series**, stream, avalanche, barrage, spate, torrent 4 = **outpouring**, rush, stream, surge, torrent

▷ VERB 1 = **immerse**, swamp, submerge, inundate, drown, cover with water 2 = **pour over**, swamp, run over, overflow, inundate 3 = **engulf**, sweep into, overwhelm, surge into, swarm into, pour into 4 = **saturate**, fill, choke, swamp, glut, oversupply, overfill 5 = **stream**, flow, rush, pour, surge

floor NOUN 1 = **ground** 2 = **storey**, level, stage, tier
▷ VERB 1 (*informal*) = **disconcert**, stump, baffle, confound, throw (*informal*), defeat, puzzle, bewilder 2 = **knock down**, fell, knock over, prostrate, deck (*slang*)

flop VERB 1 = **slump**, fall, drop, collapse, sink 2 = **hang down**, hang, dangle, sag, droop 3 (*informal*) = **fail**, fold (*informal*), founder, fall flat, come unstuck, misfire, go belly-up (*slang*) ≠ succeed
▷ NOUN (*informal*) = **failure**, disaster, fiasco, debacle, washout (*informal*), nonstarter ≠ success

floppy ADJECTIVE = **droopy**, soft, loose, limp, sagging, baggy, flaccid, pendulous

floral ADJECTIVE = **flowery**, flower-patterned

flounder VERB 1 = **falter**, struggle, stall, slow down, run into trouble, come unstuck (*informal*), be in difficulties, hit a bad patch 2 = **dither**, struggle, blunder, be confused, falter, be in the dark, be out of your depth 3 = **struggle**, struggle, toss, thrash, stumble, fumble, grope

● **WORD POWER**
● *Flounder* is sometimes wrongly
● used where *founder* is meant:
● *the project foundered* (not
● *floundered*) *because of lack of*
● *funds*.

flourish VERB 1 = **thrive**, increase, advance, progress, boom,
bloom, blossom, prosper ≠ fail 2 = **succeed**, move ahead, go places (*informal*) 3 = **grow**, thrive, flower, succeed, bloom, blossom, prosper 4 = **wave**, brandish, display, shake, wield, flaunt
▷ NOUN 1 = **wave**, sweep, brandish, swish, swing, twirl 2 = **show**, display, parade, fanfare 3 = **curlicue**, sweep, decoration, swirl, plume, embellishment, ornamentation

flourishing ADJECTIVE = **thriving**, successful, blooming, prospering, rampant, going places, in the pink

flow VERB 1 = **run**, course, rush, sweep, move, pass, roll, flood 2 = **pour**, move, sweep, flood, stream 3 = **issue**, follow, result, emerge, spring, proceed, arise, derive
▷ NOUN = **stream**, current, movement, motion, course, flood, drift, tide

flower NOUN 1 = **bloom**, blossom, efflorescence 2 = **elite**, best, prime, finest, pick, choice, cream, crème de la crème (*French*) 3 = **height**, prime, peak
▷ VERB 1 = **bloom**, open, mature, flourish, unfold, blossom 2 = **blossom**, grow, develop, progress, mature, thrive, flourish, bloom ▷ RELATED WORD: *adjective* **floral**

fluctuate VERB 1 = **change**, swing, vary, alternate, waver, veer, seesaw 2 = **shift**, oscillate

fluent ADJECTIVE = **effortless**, natural, articulate, well-versed, voluble

fluid NOUN = **liquid**, solution, juice, liquor, sap
▷ ADJECTIVE = **liquid**, flowing, watery, molten, melted, runny, liquefied ≠ solid

flurry NOUN 1 = **commotion**, stir, bustle, flutter, excitement, fuss, disturbance, ado 2 = **gust**, shower, gale, swirl, squall, storm

flush¹ VERB 1 = **blush**, colour, glow, redden, turn red, go red 2 = **cleanse**, wash out, rinse out, flood, swill, hose down 3 = **expel**, drive, dislodge
▷ NOUN = **blush**, colour, glow, reddening, redness, rosiness

flush² ADJECTIVE 1 = **level**, even, true, flat, square 2 (*informal*) = **wealthy**, rich, well-off, in the money (*informal*), well-heeled (*informal*), replete, moneyed, minted (*Brit. slang*)

flutter VERB 1 = **beat**, flap, tremble, ripple, waver, quiver, vibrate, palpitate 2 = **flit**
▷ NOUN 1 = **tremor**, tremble, shiver, shudder, palpitation 2 = **vibration**, twitching, quiver 3 = **agitation**, state (*informal*), confusion, excitement, flap (*informal*), dither (*chiefly Brit.*), commotion, fluster

fly VERB 1 = **take wing**, soar, glide, wing, sail, hover, flutter, flit 2 = **pilot**, control, operate, steer, manoeuvre, navigate 3 = **airlift**, send by plane, take by plane, take in an aircraft 4 = **flutter**, wave, float, flap 5 = **display**, show,
flourish, brandish 6 = **rush**, race, shoot, career, speed, tear, dash, hurry 7 = **pass swiftly**, pass, glide, slip away, roll on, flit, elapse, run its course 8 = **leave**, get away, escape, flee, run for it, skedaddle (*informal*), take to your heels

flying ADJECTIVE = **hurried**, brief, rushed, fleeting, short-lived, hasty, transitory

foam NOUN = **froth**, spray, bubbles, lather, suds, spume, head
▷ VERB = **bubble**, boil, fizz, froth, lather, effervesce

focus NOUN 1 = **centre**, focal point, central point 2 = **focal point**, heart, target, hub
▷ VERB 1 *often with on* = **concentrate**, centre, spotlight, direct, aim, pinpoint, zoom in 2 = **fix**, train, direct, aim

foe NOUN (*formal or literary*) = **enemy**, rival, opponent, adversary, antagonist ≠ friend

fog NOUN = **mist**, gloom, haze, smog, murk, miasma, peasouper (*informal*)

foil¹ VERB = **thwart**, stop, defeat, disappoint, counter, frustrate, hamper, balk

foil² NOUN = **complement**, relief, contrast, antithesis

fold VERB 1 = **bend**, crease, double over 2 *often with* **up** (*informal*) = **go bankrupt**, fail, crash, collapse, founder, shut down, go under, go bust (*informal*)
▷ NOUN = **crease**, gather, bend, overlap, wrinkle, pleat, ruffle, furrow

folk NOUN 1 = **people**, persons, individuals, men and women, humanity, inhabitants, mankind, mortals 2 *usually plural* (*informal*) = **family**, parents, relations, relatives, tribe, clan, kin, kindred, ainga (*N.Z.*), rellies (*Austral. slang*)

follow VERB 1 = **accompany**, attend, escort, go behind, tag along behind, come behind 2 = **pursue**, track, dog, hunt, chase, shadow, trail, hound ≠ avoid 3 = **come after**, go after, come next ≠ precede 4 = **result**, issue, develop, spring, flow, proceed, arise, ensue 5 = **obey**, observe, adhere to, stick to, heed, conform to, keep to, pay attention to ≠ ignore 6 = **succeed**, replace, come after, take over from, come next, supersede, supplant, take the place of 7 = **understand**, realize, appreciate, take in, grasp, catch on (*informal*), comprehend, fathom 8 = **keep up with**, support, be interested in, cultivate, be a fan of, keep abreast of

follower NOUN = **supporter**, fan, disciple, devotee, apostle, pupil, adherent, groupie (*slang*) ≠ leader

following ADJECTIVE 1 = **next**, subsequent, successive, ensuing, later, succeeding, consequent 2 = **coming**, about to be mentioned ▷ NOUN = **supporters**, backing, train, fans, suite, clientele, entourage, coterie

folly NOUN = **foolishness**, nonsense, madness, stupidity, indiscretion, lunacy, imprudence, rashness ≠ wisdom

fond ADJECTIVE 1 = **loving**,

● **FLIES**
● aphid *or* plant louse
● aphis
● blackfly *or* bean aphid
● blowfly, bluebottle, *or* (*Austral. informal*) blowie
● botfly
● bushfly
● crane fly *or* (*Brit.*) daddy-longlegs
● damselfly
● dragonfly *or* (*colloquial*) devil's darning-needle
● drosophila, fruit fly, *or* vinegar fly
● fly
● fruit fly
● gadfly

● gallfly
● gnat
● green blowfly *or* (*Austral. informal*) blue-arsed fly
● greenfly
● horsefly *or* cleg
● housefly
● hover fly
● lacewing
● mayfly *or* dayfly
● sandfly
● stonefly
● tsetse fly *or* tzetze fly
● warble fly
● whitefly

caring, warm, devoted, tender, adoring, affectionate, indulgent ≠ indifferent **2** = **unrealistic**, empty, naive, vain, foolish, deluded, overoptimistic, delusive ≠ sensible ▷ **PHRASE: fond of 1** = **attached to**, in love with, keen on, attracted to, having a soft spot for, enamoured of **2** = **keen on**, into (*informal*), hooked on, partial to, having a soft spot for, addicted to

fondly ADVERB **1** = **lovingly**, tenderly, affectionately, amorously, dearly, possessively, with affection, indulgently **2** = **unrealistically**, stupidly, vainly, foolishly, naively, credulously

food NOUN = **nourishment**, fare, diet, tucker (*Austral. & N.Z. informal*), rations, nutrition, cuisine, refreshment, nibbles, kai (*N.Z. informal*)

fool NOUN **1** = **simpleton**, idiot, mug (*Brit. slang*), dummy (*slang*), git (*Brit. slang*), twit (*informal, chiefly Brit.*), dunce, imbecile (*informal*), dorba or dorb (*Austral. slang*), bogan (*Austral. slang*) ≠ genius **2** = **dupe**, mug (*Brit. slang*), sucker (*slang*), stooge (*slang*), laughing stock, pushover (*informal*), fall guy (*informal*) **3** = **jester**, clown, harlequin, buffoon, court jester ▷ VERB = **deceive**, mislead, delude, trick, take in, con (*informal*), dupe, beguile, scam (*slang*)

foolish ADJECTIVE = **unwise**, silly, absurd, rash, senseless, foolhardy, ill-judged, imprudent ≠ sensible

● **WORD POWER**
● The literal meaning of *foot*
● is the part of the leg below
● the ankle in humans and
● some animals. The function,
● location, and shape of the foot
● have inspired many extended
● meanings. A foot is a unit of
● length in the imperial system,
● originally equal to the length
● of a man's foot. Foot can also
● mean the bottom or base of
● something, from its position at
● the lowest part of the body, e.g.
● *the foot of the hill*, *page*, or *bed*.
● Many phrases with foot involve
● movement, not just the literal
● act of walking *on foot*, but many
● figurative senses to do with
● initiating and deferring your
● actions, as in *drag your feet*.
● The idea of having a physically
● stable and strong position in
● *foothold* or *footing* is also used
● to mean a basis or foundation
● in fact or reality, e.g. *a firm*
● *foothold* and *a solid footing*.

footing NOUN **1** = **basis**, foundation, base position, groundwork **2** = **relationship**, position, basis, standing, rank, status, grade

footpath NOUN (*Austral. & N.Z.*) = **pavement**, sidewalk (*U.S. & Canad.*)

footstep NOUN = **step**, tread, footfall

foray NOUN = **raid**, sally, incursion, inroad, attack, assault, invasion, swoop

forbid VERB = **prohibit**, ban, disallow, exclude, rule out, veto, outlaw, preclude ≠ permit

● WORD POWER
● Traditionally, it has been
● considered more correct to
● talk about *forbidding someone*
● *to do something*, rather than
● *forbidding someone from doing*
● *something*. Recently, however,
● the *from* option has become
● generally more acceptable, so
● that *he was forbidden to come in*
● and *he was forbidden from coming*
● *in* may both now be considered
● correct.

forbidden ADJECTIVE = **prohibited**, banned, vetoed, outlawed, taboo, out of bounds, proscribed

forbidding ADJECTIVE = **threatening**, severe, frightening, hostile, menacing, sinister, daunting, ominous ≠ inviting

force NOUN 1 = **compulsion**, pressure, violence, constraint, oppression, coercion, duress, arm-twisting (*informal*) 2 = **power**, might, pressure, energy, strength, momentum, impulse, vigour ≠ weakness 3 = **intensity**, vigour, vehemence, fierceness, emphasis 4 = **army**, unit, company, host, troop, squad, patrol, regiment ▷ VERB 1 = **compel**, make, drive, press, oblige, constrain, coerce,

impel 2 = **push**, thrust, propel 3 = **break open**, blast, wrench, prise, wrest ▷ PHRASE: **in force** 1 = **valid**, working, current, effective, binding, operative, operational, in operation 2 = **in great numbers**, all together, in full strength

forced ADJECTIVE 1 = **compulsory**, enforced, mandatory, obligatory, involuntary, conscripted ≠ voluntary 2 = **false**, affected, strained, wooden, stiff, artificial, contrived, unnatural ≠ natural

forceful ADJECTIVE 1 = **dynamic**, powerful, assertive ≠ weak 2 = **powerful**, strong, convincing, effective, compelling, persuasive, cogent

forecast VERB = **predict**, anticipate, foresee, foretell, divine, prophesy, augur, forewarn ▷ NOUN = **prediction**, prognosis, guess, prophecy, conjecture, forewarning

forefront NOUN = **lead**, centre, front, fore, spearhead, prominence, vanguard, foreground

foreign ADJECTIVE = **alien**, exotic, unknown, strange, imported, remote, external, unfamiliar ≠ native

foreigner NOUN = **alien**, incomer, immigrant, non-native, stranger, settler

foremost ADJECTIVE = **leading**, best, highest, chief, prime, primary, supreme, most important

foresee VERB = **predict**, forecast, anticipate, envisage, prophesy, foretell

forever or **for ever** ADVERB **1** = **evermore**, always, ever, for good, for keeps, for all time, in perpetuity, till the cows come home (*informal*) **2** = **constantly**, always, all the time, continually, endlessly, persistently, eternally, perpetually

● WORD POWER
● *Forever* and *for ever* can both be
● used to say that something
● is without end. For all other
● meanings, *forever* is the
● preferred form.

forfeit NOUN = **penalty**, fine, damages, forfeiture, loss, mulct
▷ VERB = **relinquish**, lose, give up, surrender, renounce, be deprived of, say goodbye to, be stripped of

forge VERB **1** = **form**, build, create, establish, set up, fashion, shape, frame **2** = **fake**, copy, reproduce, imitate, counterfeit, feign, falsify **3** = **create**, make, work, found, form, model, fashion, shape

forget VERB **1** = **neglect**, overlook, omit, not remember, be remiss, fail to remember **2** = **leave behind**, lose, lose sight of, mislay

forgive VERB = **excuse**, pardon, not hold something against, understand, acquit, condone, let off (*informal*), turn a blind eye to ≠ blame

forgiveness NOUN = **pardon**, mercy, absolution, exoneration, amnesty, acquittal, remission

fork VERB = **branch**, part, separate, split, divide, diverge, subdivide, bifurcate

forked ADJECTIVE = **branching**, split, branched, divided, angled, pronged, zigzag, Y-shaped

form NOUN **1** = **type**, sort, kind, variety, class, style **2** = **shape**, formation, configuration, structure, pattern, appearance **3** = **condition**, health, shape, nick (*informal*), fitness, trim, fettle **4** = **document**, paper, sheet, questionnaire, application **5** = **procedure**, etiquette, use, custom, convention, usage, protocol, wont, kawa (*N.Z.*), tikanga (*N.Z.*) **6** (*education, chiefly Brit.*) = **class**, year, set, rank, grade, stream
▷ VERB **1** = **arrange**, combine, line up, organize, assemble, draw up **2** = **make**, produce, fashion, build, create, shape, construct, forge **3** = **constitute**, make up, compose, comprise **4** = **establish**, start, launch **5** = **take shape**, grow, develop, materialize, rise, appear, come into being, crystallize **6** = **draw up**, devise, formulate, organize **7** = **develop**, pick up, acquire, cultivate, contract

formal ADJECTIVE **1** = **serious**, stiff, detached, official, correct, conventional, remote, precise ≠ informal **2** = **official**, authorized, endorsed, certified, solemn **3** = **ceremonial**, traditional, solemn, ritualistic,

dressy **4** = **conventional**,
established, traditional

formality NOUN **1** = **correctness**,
seriousness, decorum, protocol,
etiquette **2** = **convention**,
procedure, custom, ritual, rite

format NOUN = **arrangement**,
form, style, make-up, look, plan,
design, type

formation NOUN
1 = **establishment**, founding,
forming, setting up, starting,
production, generation,
manufacture **2** = **development**,
shaping, constitution, moulding,
genesis **3** = **arrangement**,
grouping, design, structure,
pattern, organization, array,
configuration

former ADJECTIVE = **previous**,
one-time, erstwhile, earlier, prior,
sometime, foregoing ≠ current

formerly ADVERB = **previously**,
earlier, in the past, at one time,
before, lately, once

formidable ADJECTIVE
1 = **impressive**, great,
powerful, tremendous, mighty,
terrific, awesome, invincible
2 = **intimidating**, threatening,
terrifying, menacing, dismaying,
fearful, daunting, frightful
≠ encouraging

formula NOUN = **method**, plan,
policy, rule, principle, procedure,
recipe, blueprint

formulate VERB **1** = **devise**,
plan, develop, prepare, work
out, invent, forge, draw up
2 = **express**, detail, frame, define,

specify, articulate, set down, put
into words

fort NOUN = **fortress**, keep,
camp, tower, castle, garrison,
stronghold, citadel, fortified pa
(*N.Z.*) ▷ PHRASE: **hold the fort**
(*informal*) = **take responsibility**,
cover, stand in, carry on, take over
the reins, deputize, keep things
on an even keel

forte NOUN = **speciality**, strength,
talent, strong point, métier, long
suit (*informal*), gift ≠ weak point

forth ADVERB **1** (*formal or old-
fashioned*) = **forward**, out, away,
ahead, onward, outward **2** = **out**

forthcoming ADJECTIVE
1 = **approaching**, coming,
expected, future, imminent,
prospective, impending,
upcoming **2** = **available**, ready,
accessible, at hand, in evidence,
obtainable, on tap (*informal*)
3 = **communicative**, open, free,
informative, expansive, sociable,
chatty, talkative

fortify VERB **1** = **protect**, defend,
strengthen, reinforce, support,
shore up, augment, buttress
2 = **strengthen**, add alcohol to
≠ dishearten

fortitude NOUN = **courage**,
strength, resolution, grit, bravery,
backbone, perseverance, valour

fortress NOUN = **castle**, fort,
stronghold, citadel, redoubt,
fastness, fortified pa (*N.Z.*)

fortunate ADJECTIVE **1** = **lucky**,
favoured, jammy (*Brit. slang*),
in luck ≠ unfortunate

2 = **providential**, fortuitous, felicitous, timely, helpful, convenient, favourable, advantageous

fortunately ADVERB = **luckily**, happily, as luck would have it, providentially, by good luck, by a happy chance

fortune NOUN **1** = **wealth**, means, property, riches, resources, assets, possessions, treasure ≠ poverty **2** = **luck**, fluke (*informal*), stroke of luck, serendipity, twist of fate, run of luck **3** = **chance**, fate, destiny, providence, the stars, Lady Luck, kismet **4** *often plural* = **destiny**, lot, experiences, history, condition, success, means, adventures

▷ ADJECTIVE **1** = **leading**, first, head, front, advance, foremost **2** = **future**, advanced, premature, prospective **3** = **presumptuous**, familiar, bold, cheeky, brash, pushy (*informal*), brazen, shameless ≠ shy

▷ VERB **1** = **further**, advance, promote, assist, hurry, hasten, expedite **2** = **send on**, send, post, pass on, dispatch, redirect

forwards ADVERB **1** = **forth**, on, ahead, onwards ≠ backward(s) **2** = **on**, onward, onwards

fossick VERB (*Austral. & N.Z.*) = **search**, hunt, explore, ferret, check, forage, rummage

foster VERB **1** = **bring up**, mother, raise, nurse, look after, rear, care for, take care of **2** = **develop**, support, further, encourage,

feed, promote, stimulate, uphold ≠ suppress

foul ADJECTIVE **1** = **dirty**, unpleasant, stinking, filthy, grubby, repellent, squalid, repulsive, festy (*Austral. slang*), yucko (*Austral. slang*) ≠ clean **2** = **obscene**, crude, indecent, blue, abusive, coarse, vulgar, lewd **3** = **unfair**, illegal, crooked, shady (*informal*), fraudulent, dishonest, unscrupulous, underhand **4** = **offensive**, bad, wrong, evil, corrupt, disgraceful, shameful, immoral ≠ admirable

▷ VERB = **dirty**, stain, contaminate, pollute, taint, sully, defile, besmirch ≠ clean

found VERB = **establish**, start, set up, begin, create, institute, organize, constitute

foundation NOUN **1** = **basis** **2** *often plural* = **substructure**, underpinning, groundwork, bedrock, base, footing, bottom **3** = **setting up**, institution, instituting, organization, settlement, establishment, initiating, originating

founder¹ NOUN = **initiator**, father, author, architect, creator, beginner, inventor, originator

founder² VERB **1** = **fail**, collapse, break down, fall through, be unsuccessful, come unstuck, miscarry, misfire **2** = **sink**, go down, be lost, submerge, capsize, go to the bottom

● **WORD POWER**
● *Founder* is sometimes wrongly

used where *flounder* is meant:
*this unexpected turn of events left
him floundering* (not *foundering*).

fountain NOUN 1 = **font**, spring,
reservoir, spout, fount, water
feature, well 2 = **jet**, stream,
spray, gush 3 = **source**, fount,
wellspring, cause, origin,
derivation, fountainhead

fowl NOUN = **poultry**

foyer NOUN = **entrance hall**,
lobby, reception area, vestibule,
anteroom, antechamber

fraction NOUN = **percentage**,
share, section, slice, portion

fracture NOUN 1 = **break**, split,
crack 2 = **cleft**, opening, split,
crack, rift, rupture, crevice, fissure
▷ VERB 1 = **break**, crack 2 = **split**,
separate, divide, rend, fragment,
splinter, rupture

fragile ADJECTIVE 1 = **unstable**,
weak, vulnerable, delicate,
uncertain, insecure, precarious,
flimsy 2 = **fine**, weak, delicate,
frail, brittle, flimsy, dainty, easily
broken ≠ durable 3 = **unwell**,
poorly, weak, delicate, crook
(*Austral. & N.Z. informal*), shaky,
frail, feeble, sickly

fragment NOUN = **piece**, bit,
scrap, particle, portion, shred,
speck, sliver
▷ VERB 1 = **break**, shatter,
crumble, disintegrate, splinter,
come apart, break into pieces,
come to pieces ≠ fuse 2 = **break
up**, split up

fragrance *or* **fragrancy** NOUN
1 = **scent**, smell, perfume,

bouquet, aroma, sweet smell,
sweet odour, redolence ≠ stink
2 = **perfume**, scent, cologne, eau
de toilette, eau de Cologne, toilet
water, Cologne water

fragrant ADJECTIVE = **aromatic**,
perfumed, balmy, redolent, sweet-
smelling, sweet-scented, odorous
≠ stinking

frail ADJECTIVE 1 = **feeble**, weak,
puny, infirm ≠ strong 2 = **flimsy**,
weak, vulnerable, delicate, fragile,
insubstantial

frame NOUN 1 = **casing**,
framework, structure, shell,
construction, skeleton, chassis
2 = **physique**, build, form, body,
figure, anatomy, carcass
▷ VERB 1 = **mount**, case, enclose
2 = **surround**, ring, enclose,
encompass, envelop, encircle,
hem in 3 = **devise**, draft,
compose, sketch, put together,
draw up, formulate, map out
▷ PHRASE: **frame of mind** = **mood**,
state, attitude, humour, temper,
outlook, disposition, mind-set

framework NOUN 1 = **system**,
plan, order, scheme, arrangement,
the bare bones 2 = **structure**,
body, frame, foundation, shell,
skeleton

frank ADJECTIVE = **candid**, open,
direct, straightforward, blunt,
sincere, outspoken, honest
≠ secretive

frankly ADVERB 1 = **honestly**,
sincerely, in truth, candidly, to tell
you the truth, to be frank, to be
frank with someone, to be honest

f

- **TYPES OF FOWL**
- barnacle goose
- brush turkey *or* scrub turkey
- bufflehead
- Canada goose
- canvasback
- chicken *or (Austral. slang)* chook
- cock *or* cockerel
- duck
- eider *or* eider duck
- gadwall
- goldeneye
- goosander
- goose
- greylag *or* greylag goose
- hen
- mallard
- mallee fowl *or (Austral.)* gnow
- mandarin duck
- megapode
- merganser *or* sawbill
- moorhen
- Muscovy duck *or* musk duck
- mute swan
- paradise duck
- pintail
- pochard
- redhead
- Rhode Island Red chicken
- scaup *or* scaup duck
- screamer
- shelduck
- shoveler
- smew
- snow goose
- sultan
- swan
- teal
- trumpeter swan
- turkey
- whooper *or* whooper swan
- wigeon *or* widgeon

2 = **openly**, freely, directly, plainly, bluntly, candidly, without reserve

frantic ADJECTIVE **1** = **frenzied**, wild, furious, distracted, distraught, berserk, at the end of your tether, beside yourself, berko *(Austral. slang)* ≠ calm **2** = **hectic**, desperate, frenzied, fraught *(informal)*, frenetic

fraternity NOUN
   1 = **companionship**, fellowship, brotherhood, kinship, camaraderie **2** = **circle**, company, guild **3** *(U.S. & Canad.)* = **brotherhood**, club, union, society, league, association

fraud NOUN **1** = **deception**, deceit, treachery, swindling, trickery, duplicity, double-dealing, chicanery ≠ honesty **2** = **scam**,

deception *(slang)* **3** = **hoax**, trick, con *(informal)*, deception, sham, spoof *(informal)*, prank, swindle, fastie *(Austral. slang)* **4** *(informal)* = **impostor**, fake, hoaxer, pretender, charlatan, fraudster, swindler, phoney *or* phony *(informal)*

fraudulent ADJECTIVE = **deceitful**, crooked *(informal)*, untrue, sham, treacherous, dishonest, swindling, double-dealing ≠ genuine

fray VERB = **wear thin**, wear, rub, wear out, chafe

freak MODIFIER = **abnormal**, chance, unusual, exceptional, unparalleled
   ▷ NOUN **1** *(informal)* = **enthusiast**, fan, nut *(slang)*, addict, buff

(informal), fanatic, devotee, fiend (informal) **2** = **aberration**, eccentric, anomaly, oddity, monstrosity, malformation **3** (informal) = **weirdo** or **weirdie** (informal), eccentric, character (informal), oddball (informal), nonconformist

free ADJECTIVE

1 = **complimentary**, for free (informal), for nothing, unpaid, for love, free of charge, on the house, without charge **2** = **allowed**, permitted, unrestricted, unimpeded, clear, able **3** = **at liberty**, loose, liberated, at large, on the loose ≠ confined **4** = **independent**, unfettered, footloose **5** = **available**, empty, spare, vacant, unused, unoccupied, untaken **6** often with **of** or **with** = **generous**, liberal, lavish, unstinting, unsparing ≠ mean
▷ VERB **1** often with **of** or **from** = **clear**, disengage, cut loose, release, rescue, extricate **2** = **release**, liberate, let out, set free, deliver, loose, untie, unchain ≠ confine **3** = **disentangle**, extricate, disengage, loose, unravel, disconnect, untangle

freedom NOUN

1 = **independence**, democracy, sovereignty, self-determination, emancipation, autarchy, rangatiratanga (N.Z.) **2** = **liberty**, release, discharge, emancipation, deliverance ≠ captivity **3** = **licence**, latitude, free

rein, opportunity, discretion, carte blanche, blank cheque ≠ restriction

freely ADVERB **1** = **abundantly**, liberally, lavishly, extravagantly, copiously, unstintingly, amply **2** = **openly**, frankly, plainly, candidly, unreservedly, straightforwardly, without reserve **3** = **willingly**, readily, voluntarily, spontaneously, without prompting, of your own free will, of your own accord

freeway NOUN (U.S. & Austral.) = **motorway** (Brit.), autobahn (German), autoroute (French), autostrada (Italian)

freeze VERB **1** = **ice over** or **up**, harden, stiffen, solidify, become solid **2** = **chill 3** = **fix**, hold, limit, hold up **4** = **suspend**, stop, shelve, curb, cut short, discontinue

freezing (informal) ADJECTIVE
1 = **icy**, biting, bitter, raw, chill, arctic, frosty, glacial **2** = **frozen**, very cold

freight NOUN **1** = **transportation**, traffic, delivery, carriage, shipment, haulage, conveyance, transport **2** = **cargo**, goods, load, delivery, burden, shipment, merchandise, consignment

French ADJECTIVE = **Gallic**
● **WORD POWER**
● The number of words which
● English has borrowed from
● French is considerable. In the
● following passage, French
● loan words are highlighted
● in bold: *Close* to half the

- *general* vocabulary of *modern*
- English *derives* from either
- French or Latin and, of this, a
- *remarkable amount* is *directly*
- *descended* from French. Words
- from French *tend* to be longer,
- with more *syllables*, and of
- a higher *register* than their
- English *counterparts*. They also
- *tend* to be *nouns*, *adjectives*,
- *verbs*, and *adverbs* rather than
- *grammatical* words. There
- were *several historical periods*
- *during* which the *majority* of
- borrowing took *place*. After
- the Norman *Conquest*, the
- *ruling class* spoke Anglo-
- Norman, a *dialect* of French,
- for nearly 300 hundred years.
- French was the *language* of
- *government*, law, *administration*,
- and *literature*, but words were
- also *adopted* into the fields of
- *medicine*, *art*, *and fashion*. A later
- *period* of *influx* was *during* the
- *Renaissance* when *developments*
- in *science* and technology,
- and a focus on education and
- learning, led to a deliberate
- *attempt* to *enrich* the English
- *language* with *foreign* words.
- Equally, the French *language*
- has borrowed words from
- English and the *close* contact
- between the two *cultures* has
- even *inspired* a *corrupt version* of
- French called *Franglais*.

frenzied ADJECTIVE
= **uncontrolled**, wild, crazy,
furious, frantic, frenetic, feverish,
rabid

frenzy NOUN = **fury**, passion,
rage, seizure, hysteria, paroxysm,
derangement ≠ calm

frequent ADJECTIVE = **common**,
repeated, usual, familiar,
everyday, persistent, customary,
recurrent ≠ infrequent
▷ VERB = **visit**, attend, haunt,
be found at, patronize, hang out
at (*informal*), visit often, go to
regularly ≠ keep away

frequently ADVERB = **often**,
commonly, repeatedly,
many times, habitually,
not infrequently, much
≠ infrequently

fresh ADJECTIVE 1 = **additional**,
more, new, other, added, further,
extra, supplementary 2 = **natural**,
unprocessed, unpreserved
≠ preserved 3 = **new**, original,
novel, different, recent, modern,
up-to-date, unorthodox ≠ old
4 = **invigorating**, clean, pure,
crisp, bracing, refreshing, brisk,
unpolluted ≠ stale 5 = **cool**, cold,
refreshing, brisk, chilly, nippy
6 = **lively**, keen, alert, refreshed,
vigorous, energetic, sprightly,
spry ≠ weary 7 (*informal*)
= **cheeky** (*informal*), impertinent,
forward, familiar, audacious,
disrespectful, presumptuous,
insolent ≠ well-mannered

fret VERB = **worry**, brood, agonize,
obsess, lose sleep, upset yourself,
distress yourself

friction NOUN 1 = **conflict**,
hostility, resentment,

disagreement, animosity, discord, bad blood, dissension **2** = **resistance**, rubbing, scraping, grating, rasping, chafing, abrasion **3** = **rubbing**, scraping, grating, rasping, chafing, abrasion

friend NOUN **1** = **companion**, pal, mate (*informal*), buddy (*informal*), best friend, close friend, comrade, chum (*informal*), cobber (*Austral. & N.Z.*), E hoa (*N.Z. old-fashioned or informal*) ≠ foe **2** = **supporter**, ally, associate, sponsor, patron, well-wisher

friendly ADJECTIVE **1** = **amiable**, welcoming, warm, neighbourly, pally (*informal*), helpful, sympathetic, affectionate **2** = **amicable**, warm, familiar, pleasant, intimate, informal, cordial, congenial ≠ unfriendly

friendship NOUN
1 = **attachment**, relationship, bond, link, association, tie **2** = **friendliness**, affection, harmony, goodwill, intimacy, familiarity, rapport, companionship ≠ unfriendliness

fright NOUN **1** = **fear**, shock, alarm, horror, panic, dread, consternation, trepidation ≠ courage **2** = **scare**, start, turn, surprise, shock, jolt, the creeps (*informal*), the willies (*slang*)

frighten VERB = **scare**, shock, alarm, terrify, startle, intimidate, unnerve, petrify ≠ reassure

frightened ADJECTIVE = **afraid**, alarmed, scared, terrified,

shocked, startled, petrified, flustered

frightening ADJECTIVE
= **terrifying**, shocking, alarming, startling, horrifying, menacing, scary (*informal*), fearful

fringe NOUN **1** = **border**, edging, edge, trimming, hem, frill, flounce **2** = **edge**, limits, border, margin, outskirts, perimeter, periphery, borderline
▷ MODIFIER = **unofficial**, alternative, radical, innovative, avant-garde, unconventional, unorthodox

frog NOUN
▷ *see* **amphibians**

front NOUN **1** = **head**, start, lead, forefront **2** = **exterior**, face, façade, frontage **3** = **foreground**, fore, forefront, nearest part **4** (*military*) = **front line**, trenches, vanguard, firing line **5** (*informal*) = **disguise**, cover, blind, mask, cover-up, cloak, façade, pretext
▷ ADJECTIVE **1** = **foremost**, at the front ≠ back **2** = **leading**, first, lead, head, foremost, topmost
▷ VERB *often with* **on** *or* **onto** = **face onto**, overlook, look out on, have a view of, look over *or* onto

frontier NOUN = **border**, limit, edge, boundary, verge, perimeter, borderline, dividing line

frost NOUN = **hoarfrost**, freeze, rime

frown VERB = **glare**, scowl, glower, make a face, look daggers, knit your brows, lour *or* lower
▷ NOUN = **scowl**, glare, glower,

dirty look

frozen ADJECTIVE **1** = **icy**, hard, solid, frosted, arctic, ice-covered, icebound **2** = **chilled**, cold, iced, refrigerated, ice-cold **3** = **ice-cold**, freezing, numb, very cold, frigid, frozen stiff

fruit NOUN **1** (*botany*) = **produce**, crop, yield, harvest **2** *often plural* = **result**, reward, outcome, end result, return, effect, benefit, profit

frustrate VERB = **thwart**, stop, check, block, defeat, disappoint, counter, spoil, crool *or* cruel (*Austral. slang*) ≠ further

frustrated ADJECTIVE = **disappointed**, discouraged, infuriated, exasperated, resentful, embittered, disheartened

frustration NOUN **1** = **annoyance**, disappointment, resentment, irritation, grievance, dissatisfaction, exasperation, vexation **2** = **obstruction**, blocking, foiling, spoiling, thwarting, circumvention

fudge VERB = **misrepresent**, hedge, stall, flannel (*Brit. informal*), equivocate

fuel NOUN = **incitement**, ammunition, provocation, incentive

fugitive NOUN = **runaway**, refugee, deserter, escapee

fulfil *or* (*U.S.*) **fullfil** VERB **1** = **carry out**, perform, complete, achieve, accomplish ≠ neglect **2** = **achieve**, realize, satisfy, attain, consummate, bring to

fruition **3** = **satisfy**, please, content, cheer, refresh, gratify, make happy **4** = **comply with**, meet, fill, satisfy, observe, obey, conform to, answer

fulfilment *or* (*U.S.*) **fullfilment** NOUN = **achievement**, implementation, completion, accomplishment, realization, attainment, consummation

full ADJECTIVE **1** = **filled**, stocked, brimming, replete, complete, loaded, saturated ≠ empty **2** = **satiated**, having had enough, replete **3** = **extensive**, complete, generous, adequate, ample, abundant, plentiful ≠ incomplete **4** = **comprehensive**, complete, exhaustive, all-embracing **5** = **rounded**, strong, rich, powerful, intense, pungent **6** = **plump**, rounded, voluptuous, shapely, well-rounded, buxom, curvaceous **7** = **voluminous**, large, loose, baggy, billowing, puffy, capacious, loose-fitting ≠ tight **8** (*music*) = **rich**, strong, deep, loud, distinct, resonant, sonorous, clear ≠ thin

full-scale ADJECTIVE = **major**, wide-ranging, all-out, sweeping, comprehensive, thorough, in-depth, exhaustive

fully ADVERB **1** = **completely**, totally, perfectly, entirely, altogether, thoroughly, wholly, utterly **2** = **in all respects**, completely, totally, entirely, altogether, thoroughly, wholly

fumble VERB *often with* **for** *or* **with**

= **grope**, flounder, scrabble, feel around

fume VERB = **rage**, seethe, see red (*informal*), storm, rant, smoulder, get hot under the collar (*informal*)
▷ NOUN *often plural* = **smoke**, gas, exhaust, pollution, vapour, smog

fun NOUN 1 = **amusement**, sport, pleasure, entertainment, recreation, enjoyment, merriment, jollity
2 = **enjoyment**, pleasure, mirth ≠ gloom
▷ MODIFIER = **enjoyable**, entertaining, pleasant, amusing, lively, diverting, witty, convivial ▷ PHRASE: **make fun of something** *or* **someone** = **mock**, tease, ridicule, poke fun at, laugh at, mimic, parody, send up (*Brit. informal*)

function NOUN 1 = **purpose**, business, job, use, role, responsibility, task, duty
2 = **reception**, party, affair, gathering, bash (*informal*), social occasion, soiree, do (*informal*)
▷ VERB 1 = **work**, run, operate, perform, go 2 *with* **as** = **act**, operate, perform, behave, do duty, have the role of

functional ADJECTIVE
1 = **practical**, utilitarian, serviceable, hard-wearing, useful 2 = **working**, operative, operational, going, prepared, ready, viable, up and running

fund NOUN = **reserve**, stock, supply, store, collection, pool
▷ VERB = **finance**, back, support, pay for, subsidize, provide money for, put up the money for

fundamental ADJECTIVE
1 = **central**, key, basic, essential, primary, principal, cardinal ≠ incidental 2 = **basic**, essential, underlying, profound, elementary, rudimentary

fundamentally ADVERB
1 = **basically**, at heart, at bottom
2 = **essentially**, radically, basically, primarily, profoundly, intrinsically

fundi NOUN (*S. African*) = **expert**

funds PLURAL NOUN = **money**, capital, cash, finance, means, savings, resources, assets

funeral NOUN = **burial**, committal, laying to rest, cremation, interment, obsequies, entombment

funny ADJECTIVE 1 = **humorous**, amusing, comical, entertaining, comic, witty, hilarious, riotous ≠ unfunny 2 = **comic**, comical 3 = **peculiar**, odd, strange, unusual, bizarre, curious, weird, mysterious
4 (*informal*) = **ill**, poorly (*informal*), sick, odd, crook (*Austral. & N.Z. informal*), ailing, unhealthy, unwell, off-colour (*informal*)

furious ADJECTIVE 1 = **angry**, raging, fuming, infuriated, incensed, enraged, inflamed, very angry, tooshie (*Austral. slang*) ≠ pleased 2 = **violent**, intense, fierce, savage, turbulent, vehement, unrestrained

furnish VERB 1 = **decorate**, fit

out, stock, equip **2** = **supply**, give,
offer, provide, present, grant,
hand out

furniture NOUN = **household
goods**, furnishings, fittings,
house fittings, goods, things
(*informal*), possessions, appliances

furore or (U.S.) **furor** NOUN
= **commotion**, to-do, stir,
disturbance, outcry, uproar,
hullabaloo

further ADVERB = **in addition**,
moreover, besides, furthermore,
also, to boot, additionally, into
the bargain
  ▷ ADJECTIVE = **additional**,
  more, new, other, extra, fresh,
  supplementary
  ▷ VERB = **promote**, help, develop,
  forward, encourage, advance,
  work for, assist ≠ hinder

furthermore ADVERB
= **moreover**, further, in addition,
besides, too, as well, to boot,
additionally

furthest ADJECTIVE = **most
distant**, extreme, ultimate,
remotest, furthermost, outmost

fury NOUN **1** = **anger**, passion,
rage, madness, frenzy, wrath,
impetuosity ≠ calmness
  2 = **violence**, force, intensity,
  severity, ferocity, savagery,
  vehemence, fierceness ≠ peace

fuss NOUN **1** = **commotion**, to-do,
bother, stir, excitement, ado,
hue and cry, palaver **2** = **bother**,
trouble, struggle, hassle (*informal*),
nuisance, inconvenience,
hindrance **3** = **complaint**, row,

protest, objection, trouble,
argument, squabble, furore
  ▷ VERB = **worry**, flap (*informal*),
  fret, fidget, take pains, be
  agitated, get worked up

futile ADJECTIVE = **useless**,
vain, unsuccessful, pointless,
worthless, fruitless, ineffectual,
unprofitable ≠ useful

future NOUN **1** = **time to come**,
hereafter, what lies ahead
  2 = **prospect**, expectation,
  outlook
  ▷ ADJECTIVE = **forthcoming**,
  coming, later, approaching,
  to come, succeeding, fated,
  subsequent ≠ past

fuzzy ADJECTIVE **1** = **frizzy**, fluffy,
woolly, downy **2** = **indistinct**,
blurred, vague, distorted, unclear,
bleary, out of focus, ill-defined
≠ distinct

Gg

gadget NOUN = **device**, thing, appliance, machine, tool, implement, invention, instrument

- **WORD POWER**
- Gaelic is a member of the Celtic
- family of languages whose
- varieties can still be found in
- parts of Scotland (Scottish
- Gaelic), Ireland (Irish Gaelic),
- and the Isle of Man (Manx
- Gaelic). Although Gaelic has
- influenced Scottish and Irish
- English through colourful loan
- words, only a few Gaelic words
- have become assimilated into
- today's Standard English. The
- Irish Gaelic loan word *brogue*,
- referring to a broad gentle-
- sounding dialectal accent, was
- borrowed in the 18th century
- into English. It is not known
- whether it is related to the
- walking shoe of that name. It
- refers first and foremost to the
- accent with which the Irish
- speak English, known as *the
- brogue*, but has been applied
- more widely to other British
- regional accents, particularly
- those of Celtic origin. Another
- Irish Gaelic word is *galore*,
- meaning 'to sufficiency' or 'in

- abundance' which came into
- English in the 17th century. It
- is one of a very small group
- of words which are only ever
- used after the noun they
- describe, and this structure is
- typical of some words English
- has borrowed, e.g. There had
- been *opportunities galore* in
- the 1980s. It can be compared
- to the adjective *aplenty*, both
- in its meaning and in its
- grammatical behaviour. Unlike
- 'abundance' which describes
- a surplus which can be good,
- bad, or neutral, 'galore' tends to
- have positive connotations and
- is often used in advertising, e.g.
- *bargains galore*.

gag¹ NOUN = **muzzle**, tie, restraint ▷ VERB 1 = **suppress**, silence, muffle, curb, stifle, muzzle, quieten 2 = **retch**, heave

gag² NOUN (*informal*) = **joke**, crack (*slang*), funny (*informal*), quip, pun, jest, wisecrack (*informal*), witticism

gain VERB 1 = **acquire**, get, receive, pick up, secure, collect, gather, obtain 2 = **profit**, get, land, secure, collect, gather, capture, acquire ≠ lose 3 = **put on**, increase in, gather, build up 4 = **attain**, get, reach, get to, secure, obtain, acquire, arrive at ▷ NOUN 1 = **rise**, increase, growth, advance, improvement, upsurge, upturn, upswing 2 = **profit**, return, benefit, advantage, yield, dividend ≠ loss

▷ PLURAL NOUN = **profits**, earnings, revenue, proceeds, winnings, takings ▷ PHRASE: **gain on something** or **someone** = **get nearer to**, close in on, approach, catch up with, narrow the gap on

gala NOUN = **festival**, fête, celebration, carnival, festivity, pageant, jamboree

gale NOUN 1 = **storm**, hurricane, tornado, cyclone, blast, typhoon, tempest, squall 2 (*informal*) = **outburst**, scream, roar, fit, storm, shout, burst, explosion

gall VERB = **annoy**, provoke, irritate, trouble, disturb, madden, exasperate, vex

gallop VERB 1 = **run**, race, career, speed, bolt 2 = **dash**, run, race, career, speed, rush, sprint

gamble NOUN 1 = **risk**, chance, venture, lottery, speculation, uncertainty, leap in the dark ≠ certainty 2 = **bet**, flutter (*informal*), punt (*chiefly Brit.*), wager
▷ VERB 1 *often with* **on** = **take a chance**, speculate, stick your neck out (*informal*) 2 = **risk**, chance, hazard, wager 3 = **bet**, play, game, speculate, punt, wager, have a flutter (*informal*)

game NOUN 1 = **pastime**, sport, activity, entertainment, recreation, distraction, amusement, diversion ≠ job 2 = **match**, meeting, event, competition, tournament, clash, contest, head-to-head 3 = **amusement**, joke, entertainment, diversion 4 = **wild animals** or **birds**, prey, quarry 5 = **scheme**, plan, design, trick, plot, tactic, manoeuvre, ploy, fastie (*Austral. slang*)
▷ ADJECTIVE 1 = **willing**, prepared, ready, keen, eager, interested, desirous 2 = **brave**, courageous, spirited, daring, persistent, gritty, feisty (*informal, chiefly U.S. & Canad.*), intrepid, plucky, (as) game as Ned Kelly (*Austral. slang*) ≠ cowardly

gang NOUN = **group**, crowd, pack, company, band, bunch, mob

gangster NOUN = **hoodlum** (*chiefly U.S.*), crook (*informal*), bandit, hood (*U.S. slang*), robber, mobster (*U.S. slang*), racketeer, ruffian, tsotsi (*S. African*)

gap NOUN 1 = **opening**, space, hole, break, crack, slot, aperture, cleft 2 = **interval**, pause, interruption, respite, lull, interlude, breathing space, hiatus 3 = **difference**, gulf, contrast, disagreement, discrepancy, inconsistency, disparity, divergence

gape VERB 1 = **stare**, wonder, goggle, gawp (*Brit. slang*), gawk 2 = **open**, split, crack, yawn

gaping ADJECTIVE = **wide**, great, open, broad, vast, yawning, wide open, cavernous

garland NOUN = **wreath**, band, bays, crown, honours, laurels, festoon, chaplet
▷ VERB = **adorn**, crown, deck, festoon, wreathe

garment NOUN *often plural*
= **clothes**, dress, clothing, gear
(*slang*), uniform, outfit, costume,
apparel

garnish NOUN = **decoration**,
embellishment, adornment,
ornamentation, trimming
▷ VERB = **decorate**, adorn,
ornament, embellish, trim ≠ strip

garrison NOUN 1 = **troops**, group,
unit, section, command, armed
force, detachment 2 = **fort**,
fortress, camp, base, post,
station, stronghold, fortification,
fortified pa (*N.Z.*)
▷ VERB = **station**, position, post,
install, assign, put on duty

gas NOUN 1 = **fumes**, vapour 2
(*U.S., Canad. & N.Z.*) = **petrol**,
gasoline

gasp VERB = **pant**, blow, puff,
choke, gulp, catch your breath
▷ NOUN = **pant**, puff, gulp, sharp
intake of breath

gate NOUN = **barrier**, opening,
door, entrance, exit, gateway,
portal

gather VERB 1 = **congregate**,
assemble, collect, meet, mass,
come together, muster, converge
≠ scatter 2 = **assemble**, collect,
bring together, muster, call
together ≠ disperse 3 = **collect**,
assemble, accumulate, mass,
muster, garner, amass, stockpile
4 = **pick**, harvest, pluck, reap,
garner, glean 5 = **build up**,
rise, increase, grow, expand,
swell, intensify, heighten
6 = **understand**, believe, hear,

learn, assume, conclude, presume,
infer 7 = **fold**, tuck, pleat

gathering NOUN = **assembly**,
group, crowd, meeting,
conference, company, congress,
mass, hui (*N.Z.*), runanga (*N.Z.*)

gauge VERB 1 = **measure**,
calculate, evaluate, value,
determine, count, weigh,
compute 2 = **judge**, estimate,
guess, assess, evaluate, rate,
appraise, reckon
▷ NOUN = **meter**, dial, measuring
instrument

gay ADJECTIVE 1 = **homosexual**,
lesbian, queer (*informal* or
derogatory), moffie (*S. African slang*)
2 = **cheerful**, lively, sparkling,
merry, upbeat (*informal*),
buoyant, cheery, carefree ≠ sad
3 = **colourful**, rich, bright,
brilliant, vivid, flamboyant, flashy,
showy ≠ drab
▷ NOUN = **homosexual**, lesbian,
auntie *or* aunty (*Austral. slang*), lily
(*Austral. slang*) ≠ heterosexual
● **WORD POWER**
● By far the most common and
● up-to-date use of the word
● *gay* is in reference to being
● homosexual. Other senses
● of the word have become
● uncommon and dated.

gaze VERB = **stare**, look, view,
watch, regard, gape
▷ NOUN = **stare**, look, fixed look

gazette NOUN = **newspaper**,
paper, journal, periodical, news-
sheet

g'day *or* **gidday** INTERJECTION

(*Austral. & N.Z.*) = **hello**, hi
(*informal*), greetings, how do you
do?, good morning, good evening,
good afternoon, welcome, kia ora
(*N.Z.*)

gear NOUN 1 = **mechanism**,
works, machinery, cogs,
cogwheels, gearwheels
2 = **equipment**, supplies, tackle,
tools, instruments, apparatus,
paraphernalia, accoutrements
3 = **clothing**, wear, dress, clothes,
outfit, costume, garments, togs
▷ VERB *with* **to** *or* **towards**
= **equip**, fit, adjust, adapt

gem NOUN 1 = **precious stone**,
jewel, stone **2** = **treasure**,
prize, jewel, pearl, masterpiece,
humdinger (*slang*), taonga (*N.Z.*)

general ADJECTIVE
1 = **widespread**, accepted,
popular, public, common, broad,
extensive, universal ≠ individual
2 = **overall**, complete, total,
global, comprehensive, blanket,
inclusive, all-embracing
≠ restricted **3** = **universal**,
overall, widespread, collective,
across-the-board ≠ exceptional
4 = **vague**, loose, blanket,
sweeping, unclear, approximate,
woolly, indefinite ≠ specific

generally ADVERB 1 = **usually**,
commonly, typically, normally, on
the whole, by and large, ordinarily,
as a rule ≠ occasionally
2 = **commonly**, widely, publicly,
universally, extensively, popularly,
conventionally, customarily
≠ individually

generate VERB = **produce**,
create, make, cause, give rise to,
engender ≠ end

generation NOUN 1 = **age group**,
peer group **2** = **age**, period, era,
time, lifetime, span, epoch

generic ADJECTIVE = **collective**,
general, common, wide,
comprehensive, universal,
blanket, inclusive ≠ specific

generosity NOUN 1 = **liberality**,
charity, bounty, munificence,
beneficence, largesse *or* largess
2 = **magnanimity**, goodness,
kindness, selflessness, charity,
unselfishness, high-mindedness,
nobleness

generous ADJECTIVE 1 = **liberal**,
lavish, charitable, hospitable,
bountiful, open-handed,
unstinting, beneficent ≠ mean
2 = **magnanimous**, kind, noble,
good, high-minded, unselfish,
big-hearted **3** = **plentiful**, lavish,
ample, abundant, full, rich, liberal,
copious ≠ meagre

genesis NOUN = **beginning**,
origin, start, birth, creation,
formation, inception ≠ end

genius NOUN 1 = **brilliance**,
ability, talent, capacity, gift, bent,
excellence, flair **2** = **master**,
expert, mastermind, maestro,
virtuoso, whiz (*informal*), hotshot
(*informal*), brainbox, fundi
(*S. African*) ≠ dunce

genre NOUN = **type**, group, order,
sort, kind, class, style, species

gentle ADJECTIVE 1 = **kind**,
kindly, tender, mild, humane,

compassionate, meek, placid
≠ unkind **2 = slow**, easy, slight,
moderate, gradual, imperceptible
3 = moderate, light, soft, slight,
mild, soothing ≠ violent

gentlemanly ADJECTIVE
= **chivalrous**, refined, polite, civil,
courteous, gallant, genteel, well-
mannered

genuine ADJECTIVE **1 = authentic**,
real, actual, true, valid,
legitimate, veritable, bona fide,
dinkum (*Austral. & N.Z. informal*)
≠ counterfeit **2 = heartfelt**,
sincere, honest, earnest, real,
true, frank, unaffected ≠ affected
3 = sincere, honest, frank, candid,
dinkum (*Austral. & N.Z. informal*),
guileless ≠ hypocritical

germ NOUN **1 = microbe**, virus,
bug (*informal*), bacterium, bacillus,
microorganism **2 = beginning**,
root, seed, origin, spark, embryo,
rudiment

● **WORD POWER**
● German has provided English
● with some very evocative
● words which have distinct
● meanings from their English
● synonyms. *Schadenfreude*,
● borrowed in the 19th century,
● literally means of 'harm-joy'
● and describes a feeling of
● enjoyment at the misfortunes
● of others. Schadenfreude
● conveys a feeling of
● satisfaction that another
● has got their comeuppance,
● usually without the agency of
● the person experiencing it. It

● is often experienced as a guilty
● pleasure, rather than an open
● gloat and contains elements
● of voyeurism, titillation, and
● shame. It has retained its core
● meaning through the ages,
● precisely because there is no
● other word in English for this
● phenomenon. It is used solidly
● as a noun or noun-modifier,
● and is never used as a verb,
● because of its unwieldly and
● foreign sound. It can be found
● both with a capital (common
● to all nouns in German) or
● without. Another word which
● has no direct equivalent in
● English is *Zeitgeist* which
● entered the language in the
● 19th century. Literally it means
● 'time-spirit' and is loosely
● translated as 'the spirit of the
● times'. It conveys a sense of
● shared outlook in a culture
● at a particular point in time,
● especially when it is reflected
● in the arts or philosophy, and
● can be contrasted with its
● synonyms mood, attitude,
● trend, spirit and outlook.
● Zeitgeists are conceptualized
● in English as transitory and
● even elusive; they are captured
● or caught and pinned down, or
● else, like a wave, you can ride
● or surf them. The tautologous
● 'zeitgeist of our times' shows
● that the original German is
● not always known, though its
● meaning obviously is. The more

recent *zeitgeisty* shows that the concept is now being used as an adjective.

gesture NOUN = **sign**, action, signal, motion, indication, gesticulation
▷ VERB = **signal**, sign, wave, indicate, motion, beckon, gesticulate

get VERB 1 = **become**, grow, turn, come to be 2 = **persuade**, convince, induce, influence, entice, incite, impel, prevail upon 3 (*informal*) = **annoy**, upset, anger, disturb, trouble, bug (*informal*), irritate, gall 4 = **obtain**, receive, gain, acquire, win, land, net, pick up 5 = **fetch**, bring, collect 6 = **understand**, follow, catch, see, realize, take in, perceive, grasp 7 = **catch**, develop, contract, succumb to, fall victim to, go down with, come down with 8 = **arrest**, catch, grab, capture, seize, take, nab (*informal*), apprehend ▷ PHRASES: **get at someone** = **criticize**, attack, blame, put down, knock (*informal*), nag, pick on, disparage; **get at something 1** = **reach**, touch, grasp, get (a) hold of, stretch to VERB 2 = **find out**, learn, reach, reveal, discover, acquire, detect, uncover 3 = **imply**, mean, suggest, hint, intimate, lead up to, insinuate; **get by** = **manage**, survive, cope, fare, exist, get along, make do, muddle through; **get something across** = **communicate**, pass on,

transmit, convey, impart, bring home, make known, put over

ghastly ADJECTIVE = **horrible**, shocking, terrible, awful, dreadful, horrendous, hideous, frightful ≠ lovely

ghost NOUN 1 = **spirit**, soul, phantom, spectre, spook (*informal*), apparition, wraith, atua (*N.Z.*), kehua (*N.Z.*), wairua (*N.Z.*) 2 = **trace**, shadow, suggestion, hint, suspicion, glimmer, semblance ▷ RELATED WORD: adjective spectral

ghostly ADJECTIVE = **unearthly**, phantom, eerie, supernatural, spooky (*informal*), spectral

giant ADJECTIVE = **huge**, vast, enormous, tremendous, immense, titanic, gigantic, monumental, supersize ≠ tiny ▷ NOUN = **ogre**, monster, titan, colossus

gift NOUN 1 = **donation**, offering, present, contribution, grant, legacy, hand-out, endowment, bonsela (*S. African*), koha (*N.Z.*) 2 = **talent**, ability, capacity, genius, power, capability, flair, knack

gifted ADJECTIVE = **talented**, able, skilled, expert, masterly, brilliant, capable, clever ≠ talentless

gigantic ADJECTIVE = **huge**, large, giant, massive, enormous, tremendous, immense, titanic, supersize ≠ tiny

giggle VERB = **laugh**, chuckle, snigger, chortle, titter, twitter ▷ NOUN = **laugh**, chuckle, snigger, chortle, titter, twitter

girl NOUN = **female child**, lass, lassie (*informal*), miss, maiden (*archaic*), maid (*archaic*)

give VERB 1 = **perform**, do, carry out, execute 2 = **communicate**, announce, transmit, pronounce, utter, issue 3 = **produce**, make, cause, occasion, engender 4 = **present**, contribute, donate, provide, supply, award, grant, deliver ≠ take 5 = **concede**, allow, grant 6 = **surrender**, yield, devote, hand over, relinquish, part with ▷ PHRASES: **give in** = **admit defeat**, yield, concede, collapse, quit, submit, surrender, succumb; **give something away** = **reveal**, expose, leak, disclose, betray, uncover, let out, divulge; **give something off** *or* **out** = **emit**, produce, release, discharge, send out, throw out, exude; **give something up** = **abandon**, stop, quit, cease, renounce, leave off, desist

glad ADJECTIVE 1 = **happy**, pleased, delighted, contented, gratified, joyful, overjoyed ≠ unhappy 2 (*archaic*) = **pleasing**, happy, cheering, pleasant, cheerful, gratifying

gladly ADVERB 1 = **happily**, cheerfully, gleefully 2 = **willingly**, freely, happily, readily, cheerfully, with pleasure ≠ reluctantly

glamorous ADJECTIVE 1 = **attractive**, elegant, dazzling ≠ unglamorous 2 = **exciting**, glittering, prestigious, glossy, bling (*slang*) ≠ unglamorous

glamour NOUN 1 = **charm**, appeal, beauty, attraction, fascination, allure, enchantment 2 = **excitement**, magic, thrill, romance, prestige, glitz (*slang*)

glance VERB = **peek**, look, view, glimpse, peep ≠ scrutinize ▷ NOUN = **peek**, look, glimpse, peep, dekko (*slang*) ≠ good look

● **WORD POWER**
● Care should be taken not to
● confuse *glance* and *glimpse*: *he*
● *caught a glimpse* (not *glance*) *of*
● *her making her way through the*
● *crowd; he gave a quick glance* (not
● *glimpse*) *at his watch. A glance*
● is a deliberate action, while a
● *glimpse* seems opportunistic.

glare VERB 1 = **scowl**, frown, glower, look daggers, lour *or* lower 2 = **dazzle**, blaze, flare, flame ▷ NOUN 1 = **scowl**, frown, glower, dirty look, black look, lour *or* lower 2 = **dazzle**, glow, blaze, flame, brilliance

glaring ADJECTIVE = **obvious**, gross, outrageous, manifest, blatant, conspicuous, flagrant, unconcealed ≠ inconspicuous

glaze NOUN = **coat**, finish, polish, shine, gloss, varnish, enamel, lacquer ▷ VERB = **coat**, polish, gloss, varnish, enamel, lacquer

gleam VERB = **shine**, flash, glow, sparkle, glitter, shimmer, glint, glimmer ▷ NOUN 1 = **glimmer**, flash, beam, glow, sparkle 2 = **trace**, suggestion, hint, flicker, glimmer, inkling

glide VERB = **slip**, sail, slide

glimpse NOUN = **look**, sighting, sight, glance, peep, peek
▷ VERB = **catch sight of**, spot, sight, view, spy, espy

glitter VERB = **shine**, flash, sparkle, glare, gleam, shimmer, twinkle, glint
▷ NOUN 1 = **glamour**, show, display, splendour, tinsel, pageantry, gaudiness, showiness
2 = **sparkle**, flash, shine, glare, gleam, sheen, shimmer, brightness

global ADJECTIVE 1 = **worldwide**, world, international, universal
2 = **comprehensive**, general, total, unlimited, exhaustive, all-inclusive ≠ limited

globe NOUN = **planet**, world, earth, sphere, orb

gloom NOUN 1 = **darkness**, dark, shadow, shade, twilight, dusk, obscurity, blackness ≠ light
2 = **depression**, sorrow, woe, melancholy, unhappiness, despondency, dejection, low spirits ≠ happiness

gloomy ADJECTIVE 1 = **dark**, dull, dim, dismal, black, grey, murky, dreary ≠ light 2 = **miserable**, sad, pessimistic, melancholy, glum, dejected, dispirited, downcast
≠ happy 3 = **depressing**, bad, dreary, sombre, dispiriting, disheartening, cheerless

glorious ADJECTIVE 1 = **splendid**, beautiful, brilliant, shining, superb, gorgeous, dazzling
≠ dull 2 = **delightful**, fine, wonderful, excellent, marvellous, gorgeous 3 = **illustrious**, famous, celebrated, distinguished, honoured, magnificent, renowned, eminent ≠ ordinary

glory NOUN 1 = **honour**, praise, fame, distinction, acclaim, prestige, eminence, renown
≠ shame 2 = **splendour**, majesty, greatness, grandeur, nobility, pomp, magnificence, pageantry
▷ VERB = **triumph**, boast, relish, revel, exult, take delight, pride yourself

gloss¹ NOUN = **shine**, gleam, sheen, polish, brightness, veneer, lustre, patina

gloss² NOUN = **interpretation**, comment, note, explanation, commentary, translation, footnote, elucidation
▷ VERB = **interpret**, explain, comment, translate, annotate, elucidate

glossy ADJECTIVE = **shiny**, polished, shining, glazed, bright, silky, glassy, lustrous ≠ dull

glow NOUN = **light**, gleam, splendour, glimmer, brilliance, brightness, radiance, luminosity
≠ dullness
▷ VERB 1 = **shine**, burn, gleam, brighten, glimmer, smoulder
2 = **be pink**

glowing ADJECTIVE
= **complimentary**, enthusiastic, rave (*informal*), ecstatic, rhapsodic, laudatory, adulatory ≠ scathing

glue NOUN = **adhesive**, cement, gum, paste

▷ VERB = **stick**, fix, seal, cement, gum, paste, affix

go VERB 1 = **move**, travel, advance, journey, proceed, pass, set off ≠ stay 2 = **leave**, withdraw, depart, move out, slope off, make tracks 3 = **elapse**, pass, flow, fly by, expire, lapse, slip away 4 = **be given**, be spent, be awarded, be allotted 5 = **function**, work, run, move, operate, perform ≠ fail 6 = **match**, blend, correspond, fit, suit, chime, harmonize 7 = **serve**, help, tend

▷ NOUN 1 = **attempt**, try, effort, bid, shot (*informal*), crack (*informal*) 2 = **turn**, shot (*informal*), stint 3 (*informal*) = **energy**, life, drive, spirit, vitality, vigour, verve, force

▷ PHRASES: **go off** 1 = **depart**, leave, quit, go away, move out, decamp, slope off, rack off (*Austral.*

& *N.Z. slang*) 2 = **explode**, fire, blow up, detonate, come about 3 (*informal*) = **go bad**, turn, spoil, rot, go stale; **go out** 1 = **see someone**, court, date (*informal, chiefly U.S.*), woo, go steady (*informal*), be romantically involved with, step out with (*informal*) 2 = **be extinguished**, die out, fade out; **go through something** 1 = **suffer**, experience, bear, endure, brave, undergo, tolerate, withstand 2 = **search**, look through, rummage through, rifle through, hunt through, fossick through (*Austral. & N.Z.*), ferret about in 3 = **examine**, check, search, explore, look through

goal NOUN = **aim**, end, target, purpose, object, intention, objective, ambition

god NOUN = **deity**, immortal, divinity, divine being, supreme being, atua (*N.Z.*)

● GODS AND GODDESSES

● **Greek**

● Aeolus	winds
● Aphrodite	love and beauty
● Apollo	light, youth, and music
● Ares	war
● Artemis	hunting and the moon
● Asclepius	healing
● Athene *or* Pallas Athene	wisdom
● Bacchus	wine
● Boreas	north wind
● Cronos	fertility of the earth
● Demeter	agriculture
● Dionysus	wine
● Eos	dawn
● Eros	love
● Fates	destiny
● Gaea *or* Gaia	the earth
● Graces	charm and beauty
● Hades	underworld
● Hebe	youth and spring
● Hecate	underworld
● Helios	sun
● Hephaestus	fire and metalworking

Hera	queen of the gods	Cupid	love
Hermes	messenger of the gods	Cybele	nature
		Diana	hunting and the moon
Horae *or* the Hours	seasons		
		Faunus	forests
Hymen	marriage	Flora	flowers
Hyperion	sun	Janus	doors and beginnings
Hypnos	sleep		
Iris	rainbow	Juno	queen of the gods
Momus	blame and mockery	Jupiter *or* Jove	king of the gods
Morpheus	sleep and dreams		
Nemesis	vengeance	Lares	household
Nike	victory	Luna	moon
Pan	woods and shepherds	Mars	war
		Mercury	messenger of the gods
Poseidon	sea and earthquakes		
		Minerva	wisdom
Rhea	fertility	Neptune	sea
Selene	moon	Penates	storeroom
Uranus	sky	Phoebus	sun
Zephyrus	west wind	Pluto	underworld
Zeus	king of the gods	Quirinus	war
		Saturn	agriculture and vegetation
Roman			
Aesculapius	medicine	Sol	sun
Apollo	light, youth, and music	Somnus	sleep
		Trivia	crossroads
Aurora	dawn	Venus	love
Bacchus	wine	Victoria	victory
Bellona	war	Vulcan	fire and metalworking
Bona Dea	fertility		
Ceres	agriculture		

godly ADJECTIVE = **devout**, religious, holy, righteous, pious, good, saintly, god-fearing

gogga NOUN (*S. African*) = **insect**, bug, creepy-crawly (*Brit. informal*)

golden ADJECTIVE 1 = **yellow**, blonde, blond, flaxen ≠ dark 2 = **successful**, glorious, prosperous, rich, flourishing, halcyon ≠ worst 3 = **promising**, excellent, favourable, opportune ≠ unfavourable

▷ *see* **shades of orange, shades of yellow**

● **WORD POWER**
● Gold is a precious metal
● used as a monetary standard
● and in jewellery; in many
● societies it signifies wealth,
● status, and luxury. The
● colour adjective **golden**
● has taken on some of the
● positive connotations of the
● substance. The value of gold
● has resulted in the meaning
● 'successful' or 'prosperous'
● in phrases like a ***golden age***,
● denoting a thriving period
● in history in a particular
● field. Closely related to
● this, a ***golden opportunity***
● is one which is promising
● and advantageous. Gold
● symbolizes winning first
● place in a race, as in a ***gold***
● ***medal***, which has led people
● to be described as ***golden boys***
● or ***golden girls*** when they are
● prized and popular.

gone ADJECTIVE **1** = **missing**, lost, away, vanished, absent, astray **2** = **past**, over, ended, finished, elapsed

good ADJECTIVE **1** = **excellent**, great, fine, pleasing, acceptable, first-class, splendid, satisfactory, booshit (*Austral. slang*), exo (*Austral. slang*), sik (*Austral. slang*), rad (*informal*), phat (*slang*), schmick (*Austral. informal*) ≠ bad **2** = **proficient**, able, skilled, expert, talented, clever, accomplished, first-class ≠ bad **3** = **beneficial**, useful, helpful, favourable, wholesome, advantageous ≠ harmful **4** = **honourable**, moral, worthy, ethical, upright, admirable, honest, righteous ≠ bad **5** = **well-behaved**, polite, orderly, obedient, dutiful, well-mannered ≠ naughty **6** = **kind**, kindly, friendly, obliging, charitable, humane, benevolent, merciful ≠ unkind **7** = **true**, real, genuine, proper, dinkum (*Austral. & N.Z. informal*) **8** = **full**, complete, extensive ≠ scant **9** = **considerable**, large, substantial, sufficient, adequate, ample **10** = **valid**, convincing, compelling, legitimate, authentic, persuasive, bona fide ≠ invalid **11** = **convenient**, timely, fitting, appropriate, suitable ≠ inconvenient ▷ NOUN **1** = **benefit**, interest, gain, advantage, use, profit, welfare, usefulness ≠ disadvantage **2** = **virtue**, goodness, righteousness, worth, merit, excellence, morality, rectitude ≠ evil ▷ PHRASE: **for good** = **permanently**, finally, for ever, once and for all, irrevocably

goodbye NOUN = **farewell**, parting, leave-taking ▷ INTERJECTION = **farewell**, see you, see you later, ciao (*Italian*), cheerio, adieu, ta-ta, au revoir (*French*), haere ra (*N.Z.*)

goodness NOUN **1** = **virtue**,

honour, merit, integrity, morality,
honesty, righteousness, probity
≠ badness **2** = **excellence**, value,
quality, worth, merit, superiority
3 = **nutrition**, benefit, advantage,
wholesomeness, salubriousness
4 = **kindness**, charity, humanity,
goodwill, mercy, compassion,
generosity, friendliness

goods PLURAL NOUN
1 = **merchandise**, stock, products,
stuff, commodities, wares
2 = **property**, things, effects,
gear, possessions, belongings,
trappings, paraphernalia

goodwill NOUN = **friendliness**,
friendship, benevolence, amity,
kindliness

gore¹ NOUN = **blood**, slaughter,
bloodshed, carnage, butchery

gore² VERB = **pierce**, wound,
transfix, impale

gorge NOUN = **ravine**, canyon,
pass, chasm, cleft, fissure, defile,
gulch (*U.S. & Canad.*)
▷ VERB **1** = **overeat**, devour,
gobble, wolf, gulp, guzzle **2**
usually reflexive = **stuff**, feed, cram,
glut

gorgeous ADJECTIVE
1 = **magnificent**, beautiful,
superb, spectacular, splendid,
dazzling, sumptuous ≠ shabby
2 (*informal*) = **beautiful**, lovely,
stunning (*informal*), elegant,
handsome, exquisite, ravishing,
hot (*informal*) ≠ dull

gospel NOUN **1** = **doctrine**, news,
teachings, message, revelation,
creed, credo, tidings **2** = **truth**,

fact, certainty, the last word

gossip NOUN **1** = **idle talk**,
scandal, hearsay, tittle-tattle,
goss (*informal*), small talk,
chitchat, blether, chinwag
(*Brit. informal*) **2** = **busybody**,
chatterbox (*informal*), chatterer,
scandalmonger, gossipmonger,
tattletale (*chiefly U.S. & Canad.*)
▷ VERB = **chat**, chatter, jaw
(*slang*), blether

gourmet NOUN = **connoisseur**,
foodie (*informal*), bon vivant
(*French*), epicure, gastronome

govern VERB **1** = **rule**, lead,
control, command, manage,
direct, guide, handle **2** = **restrain**,
control, check, master, discipline,
regulate, curb, tame

government NOUN
1 = **administration**, executive,
ministry, regime, powers-
that-be **2** = **rule**, authority,
administration, sovereignty,
governance, statecraft

governor NOUN = **leader**,
administrator, ruler, head,
director, manager, chief,
executive, baas (*S. African*)

gown NOUN = **dress**, costume,
garment, robe, frock, garb, habit

grab VERB = **snatch**, catch, seize,
capture, grip, grasp, clutch, snap
up

grace NOUN **1** = **elegance**,
poise, ease, polish, refinement,
fluency, suppleness, gracefulness
≠ ungainliness **2** = **manners**,
decency, etiquette, consideration,
propriety, tact, decorum ≠ bad

manners 3 = **indulgence**, mercy, pardon, reprieve
4 = **benevolence**, favour, goodness, goodwill, generosity, kindness, kindliness ≠ ill will
5 = **prayer**, thanks, blessing, thanksgiving, benediction
6 = **favour**, regard, respect, approval, approbation, good opinion ≠ disfavour
▷ VERB 1 = **adorn**, enhance, decorate, enrich, set off, ornament, embellish 2 = **honour**, favour, dignify ≠ insult

graceful ADJECTIVE = **elegant**, easy, pleasing, beautiful ≠ inelegant

gracious ADJECTIVE = **courteous**, polite, civil, accommodating, kind, friendly, cordial, well-mannered ≠ ungracious

grade VERB = **classify**, rate, order, class, group, sort, range, rank
▷ NOUN 1 = **class** 2 degree
3 = **level**, rank, group, class, stage, category, echelon

gradual ADJECTIVE = **steady**, slow, regular, gentle, progressive, piecemeal, unhurried ≠ sudden

gradually ADVERB = **steadily**, slowly, progressively, gently, step by step, little by little, by degrees, unhurriedly

graduate VERB 1 = **mark off**, grade, proportion, regulate, gauge, calibrate, measure out
2 = **classify**, rank, grade, group, order, sort, arrange

graft NOUN = **shoot**, bud, implant, sprout, splice, scion

▷ VERB = **join**, insert, transplant, implant, splice, affix

graft NOUN (*informal*) = **labour**, work, effort, struggle, sweat, toil, slog, exertion
▷ VERB = **work**, labour, struggle, sweat (*informal*), slave, strive, toil

grain NOUN 1 = **seed**, kernel, grist
2 = **cereal**, corn 3 = **bit**, piece, trace, scrap, particle, fragment, speck, morsel 4 = **texture**, pattern, surface, fibre, weave, nap

grand ADJECTIVE 1 = **impressive**, great, large, magnificent, imposing, splendid, regal, stately ≠ unimposing 2 = **ambitious**, great, grandiose 3 = **superior**, great, dignified, stately
4 = **excellent**, great (*informal*), fine, wonderful, outstanding, smashing (*informal*), first-class, splendid ≠ bad

grandeur NOUN = **splendour**, glory, majesty, nobility, pomp, magnificence, sumptuousness, sublimity

grant NOUN = **award**, allowance, donation, endowment, gift, subsidy, hand-out
▷ VERB 1 = **give**, allow, present, award, permit, assign, allocate, hand out 2 = **accept**, allow, admit, acknowledge, concede

graphic ADJECTIVE 1 = **vivid**, clear, detailed, striking, explicit, expressive ≠ vague 2 = **pictorial**, visual, diagrammatic ≠ impressionistic

grapple VERB 1 = **deal**, tackle, struggle, take on, confront, get to grips, address yourself to **2** = **struggle**, fight, combat, wrestle, battle, clash, tussle, scuffle

grasp VERB **1** = **grip**, hold, catch, grab, seize, snatch, clutch, clinch **2** = **understand**, realize, take in, get, see, catch on, comprehend, catch *or* get the drift of
▷ NOUN **1** = **grip**, hold, possession, embrace, clutches, clasp **2** = **understanding**, knowledge, grip, awareness, mastery, comprehension **3** = **reach**, power, control, scope

grasping ADJECTIVE = **greedy**, acquisitive, rapacious, avaricious, covetous, snoep (*S. African informal*) ≠ generous

grate VERB **1** = **shred**, mince, pulverize **2** = **scrape**, grind, rub, scratch, creak, rasp

grateful ADJECTIVE = **thankful**, obliged, in (someone's) debt, indebted, appreciative, beholden

grating¹ NOUN = **grille**, grid, grate, lattice, trellis, gridiron

grating² ADJECTIVE = **irritating**, harsh, annoying, jarring, unpleasant, raucous, strident, discordant ≠ pleasing

gratitude NOUN = **thankfulness**, thanks, recognition, obligation, appreciation, indebtedness, gratefulness ≠ ingratitude

grave¹ NOUN = **tomb**, vault, crypt, mausoleum, sepulchre, pit, burying place

grave² ADJECTIVE **1** = **serious**, important, critical, pressing, threatening, dangerous, acute, severe ≠ trifling **2** = **solemn**, sober, sombre, dour, unsmiling ≠ carefree

graveyard NOUN = **cemetery**, churchyard, burial ground, charnel house, necropolis

gravity NOUN **1** = **seriousness**, importance, significance, urgency, severity, acuteness, weightiness, momentousness ≠ triviality **2** = **solemnity**, seriousness, gravitas ≠ frivolity

graze¹ VERB = **feed**, crop, browse, pasture

graze² VERB **1** = **scratch**, skin, scrape, chafe, abrade **2** = **touch**, brush, rub, scrape, shave, skim, glance off
▷ NOUN = **scratch**, scrape, abrasion

greasy ADJECTIVE = **fatty**, slippery, oily, slimy, oleaginous

great ADJECTIVE **1** = **large**, big, huge, vast, enormous, immense, gigantic, prodigious, supersize ≠ small **2** = **important**, serious, significant, critical, crucial, momentous ≠ unimportant **3** = **famous**, outstanding, remarkable, prominent, renowned, eminent, illustrious, noteworthy **4** (*informal*) = **excellent**, fine, wonderful, superb, fantastic (*informal*), tremendous (*informal*), marvellous (*informal*), terrific (*informal*), booshit (*Austral. slang*), exo (*Austral. slang*), sik (*Austral. slang*), rad (*informal*), phat (*slang*), schmick (*Austral. informal*) ≠ poor

5 = **very**, really, extremely, exceedingly

greatly ADVERB = **very much**, hugely, vastly, considerably, remarkably, enormously, immensely, tremendously

greatness NOUN **1** = **grandeur**, glory, majesty, splendour, pomp, magnificence **2** = **fame**, glory, celebrity, distinction, eminence, note, renown, illustriousness

greed or **greediness** NOUN
1 = **gluttony**, voracity
2 = **avarice**, longing, desire, hunger, craving, selfishness, acquisitiveness, covetousness
≠ generosity

greedy ADJECTIVE **1** = **gluttonous**, insatiable, voracious, ravenous, piggish **2** = **avaricious**, grasping, selfish, insatiable, acquisitive, rapacious, materialistic, desirous
≠ generous

● **WORD POWER**
● The period of greatest
● borrowing from Greek
● into English was during
● the Renaissance when the
● classical languages were
● plundered for terms to
● describe new developments
● in science, technology,
● and medicine. Concepts
● from Greek philosophy and
● mythology were brought to
● the English public for the first
● time through translations of
● classical texts. *Nemesis*, a word
● adopted into English in the
● 16th century, was the goddess
● of retribution in classical
● mythology. Both people and
● situations can embody the
● concept of nemesis in today's
● English. A nemesis is an agent
● of retribution, a person who
● avenges a wrongdoing, or
● more loosely, an arch-enemy
● or rival. The coinage *arch-
● nemesis* reiterates the latter
● meaning. Nemesis can also
● refer to a situation which is
● inevitable or unavoidable,
● and overlaps semantically
● with the notion of downfall,
● e.g. Spyware may now be
● the nemesis of PCs. Another
● Greek word which came
● into English during the 16th
● century is *nous*. Philosophers
● used *nous* in different senses
● to refer to the mind, the
● intellect, intelligence, or
● reason. Nowadays it means
● common sense, acumen, and
● applied intelligence, and is
● particularly found in British
● English. It is among several
● other slang words for common
● sense, including smarts and
● savvy, and is commonly used in
● collocations like *economic nous*
● and *political nous*.

green ADJECTIVE **1** = **verdant**, leafy, grassy **2** = **ecological**, conservationist, environment-friendly, ozone-friendly, non-polluting **3** = **inexperienced**, new, raw, naive, immature, gullible, untrained, wet behind the ears (*informal*) **4** =**jealous**, grudging, resentful, envious, covetous

▷ NOUN = **lawn**, common, turf, sward

● **WORD POWER**
● *Green* is the colour of plants
● and vegetation and many of
● its extended meanings derive
● from this. If an area is described
● as having green spaces, it
● has parkland, gardens, fields
● and the like. Similarly, *green*
● *belt* is a zone of open country
● surrounding a city which
● is protected from urban
● development. *Green politics* are
● those which concentrate on
● preserving the environment
● and natural resources. Green
● is also the colour of unripe
● fruit and plants, which has
● led to the meanings of youth,
● lack of maturity, and lack of
● experience. When applied to
● human physiology, green is
● the colour of biliousness and
● sickness as in the phrase *green*
● *around the gills*. Jealousy was
● formerly linked with the colour
● yellow, but now is expressed
● in various phrases with green,
● such as Shakespeare's *green-*
● *eyed monster* (jealousy) and
● *green with envy*. One modern
● metaphorical meaning of
● green is in traffic signalling,
● where a *green light* means go.
● The verb *greenlight*, meaning to
● authorize or permit something
● to proceed, shows a recent
● extension of this sense.

greet VERB **1** = **salute**, hail, say hello to, address, accost **2** = **welcome**, meet, receive, karanga (*N.Z.*), mihi (*N.Z.*) **3** = **receive**, take, respond to, react to

greeting NOUN = **welcome**, reception, salute, address, salutation, hongi (*N.Z.*), kia ora (*N.Z.*)

grey ADJECTIVE **1** = **dull**, dark, dim, gloomy, drab **2** = **boring**, dull, anonymous, faceless, colourless, nondescript, characterless **3** = **pale**, wan, pallid, ashen **4** = **ambiguous**, uncertain, neutral, unclear, debatable

▷ *see* **shades from black to white**

● **WORD POWER**
● *Grey* is a neutral tone which
● is intermediate between
● black and white. Because it

● **SHADES OF GREEN**

● apple green	● lime green	● pistachio
● aquamarine	● Lincoln green	● sea green
● avocado	● Nile green	● teal
● emerald green	● olive	● turquoise
● jade	● pea green	

● only reflects a little light, it is
● perceived as a dull colour. By
● extension, it has been used to
● describe many things which
● are dull in colour, such as
● weather conditions, as in a *grey*
● *day*. If human personalities
● are described as grey, it means
● they are boring or colourless.
● The hair of humans and some
● animals turns grey with age –
● this has lead to applications of
● grey meaning older, such as the
● *grey vote*. Grey can also mean
● pale in an unhealthy way when
● used of a person's skin-tone. As
● grey is neither entirely black
● nor white but a combination
● of both, it has developed the
● meaning 'ambiguous', as in the
● phrase *grey area*. Colloquially,
● the brain is referred to as *grey*
● *matter* or as *grey cells* because
● of the greyish colour of the
● physical brain.

grief NOUN = **sadness**, suffering,
regret, distress, misery, sorrow,
woe, anguish ≠ joy

grievance NOUN = **complaint**,
gripe (*informal*), axe to grind

grieve VERB 1 = **mourn**, suffer,
weep, lament 2 = **sadden**, hurt,
injure, distress, wound, pain,
afflict, upset ≠ gladden

grim ADJECTIVE = **terrible**, severe,
harsh, forbidding, formidable,
sinister

grind VERB 1 = **crush**, mill, powder,
grate, pulverize, pound, abrade,
granulate 2 = **press**, push, crush,

jam, mash, force down 3 = **grate**,
scrape, gnash 4 = **sharpen**,
polish, sand, smooth, whet
▷ NOUN 1 = **hard work** (*informal*),
labour, sweat (*informal*), chore,
toil, drudgery

grip VERB 1 = **grasp**, hold, catch,
seize, clutch, clasp, take hold of
2 = **engross**, fascinate, absorb,
entrance, hold, compel, rivet,
enthral
▷ NOUN 1 = **clasp**, hold, grasp
2 = **control**, rule, influence,
command, power, possession,
domination, mastery 3 = **hold**,
purchase, friction, traction
4 = **understanding**, sense,
command, awareness, grasp,
appreciation, mastery,
comprehension

gripping ADJECTIVE = **fascinating**,
exciting, thrilling, entrancing,
compelling, riveting, enthralling,
engrossing

grit NOUN 1 = **gravel**, sand, dust,
pebbles 2 = **courage**, spirit,
resolution, determination, guts
(*informal*), backbone, fortitude,
tenacity
▷ VERB = **clench**, grind, grate,
gnash

gritty ADJECTIVE 1 = **rough**, sandy,
dusty, rasping, gravelly, granular
2 = **courageous**, dogged,
determined, spirited, brave, feisty
(*informal, chiefly U.S. & Canad.*),
resolute, tenacious, plucky, (as)
game as Ned Kelly (*Austral. slang*)

groan VERB 1 = **moan**, cry, sigh
2 (*informal*) = **complain**, object,

moan, grumble, gripe (*informal*), carp, lament, whine

▷ NOUN 1 = **moan**, cry, sigh, whine 2 (*informal*) **complaint**, protest, objection, grumble, grouse, gripe (*informal*)

groom NOUN 1 = **stableman**, stableboy, hostler *or* ostler (*archaic*) 2 = **newly-wed**, husband, bridegroom, marriage partner

▷ VERB 1 = **brush**, clean, tend, rub down, curry 2 = **smarten up**, clean, tidy, preen, spruce up, primp 3 = **train**, prime, prepare, coach, ready, educate, drill, nurture

groove NOUN = **indentation**, cut, hollow, channel, trench, flute, trough, furrow

grope VERB = **feel**, search, fumble, flounder, fish, scrabble, cast about, fossick (*Austral. & N.Z.*)

gross ADJECTIVE 1 = **flagrant**, blatant, rank, sheer, utter, grievous, heinous, unmitigated ≠ qualified 2 = **vulgar**, offensive, crude, obscene, coarse, indelicate ≠ decent 3 = **fat**, obese, overweight, hulking, corpulent ≠ slim 4 = **total**, whole, entire, aggregate, before tax, before deductions ≠ net

▷ VERB = **earn**, make, take, bring in, rake in (*informal*)

grotesque ADJECTIVE 1 = **unnatural**, bizarre, strange, fantastic, distorted, deformed, outlandish, freakish ≠ natural 2 = **absurd**, preposterous ≠ natural

ground NOUN 1 = **earth**, land, dry land, terra firma 2 = **arena**, pitch, stadium, park (*informal*), field, enclosure

▷ PLURAL NOUN 1 = **estate**, land, fields, gardens, territory 2 = **reason**, cause, basis, occasion, foundation, excuse, motive, justification 3 = **dregs**, lees, deposit, sediment

▷ VERB 1 = **base**, found, establish, set, settle, fix 2 = **instruct**, train, teach, initiate, tutor, acquaint with, familiarize with

group NOUN = **crowd**, party, band, pack, gang, bunch

▷ VERB = **arrange**, order, sort, class, classify, marshal, bracket

grove NOUN = **wood**, plantation, covert, thicket, copse, coppice, spinney

grow VERB 1 = **develop**, get bigger ≠ shrink 2 = **get bigger**, spread, swell, stretch, expand, enlarge, multiply 3 = **cultivate**, produce, raise, farm, breed, nurture, propagate 4 = **become**, get, turn, come to be 5 = **originate**, spring, arise, stem, issue 6 = **improve**, advance, progress, succeed, thrive, flourish, prosper

grown-up NOUN = **adult**, man, woman

▷ ADJECTIVE = **mature**, adult, of age, fully-grown

growth NOUN 1 = **increase**, development, expansion, proliferation, enlargement, multiplication ≠ decline 2 = **progress**, success,

improvement, expansion,
advance, prosperity ≠ failure
3 (*medical*) = **tumour**, cancer,
swelling, lump, carcinoma
(*pathology*), sarcoma (*medical*)

grudge NOUN = **resentment**,
bitterness, grievance, dislike,
animosity, antipathy, enmity,
rancour ≠ goodwill
▷ VERB = **resent**, mind, envy,
covet, begrudge ≠ welcome

gruelling ADJECTIVE
= **exhausting**, demanding,
tiring, taxing, severe, punishing,
strenuous, arduous ≠ easy

gruesome ADJECTIVE = **horrific**,
shocking, terrible, horrible,
grim, ghastly, grisly, macabre
≠ pleasant

grumble VERB **1** = **complain**,
moan, gripe (*informal*), whinge
(*informal*), carp, whine, grouse,
bleat **2** = **rumble**, growl, gurgle
▷ NOUN **1** = **complaint**, protest,
objection, moan, grievance,
grouse, gripe (*informal*), grouch
(*informal*) **2** = **rumble**, growl,
gurgle

guarantee VERB **1** = **ensure**,
secure, assure, warrant, make
certain **2** = **promise**, pledge,
undertake
▷ NOUN **1** = **promise**, pledge,
assurance, certainty, word of
honour **2** = **warranty**, contract,
bond

guard VERB = **protect**, defend,
secure, mind, preserve, shield,
safeguard, watch over
▷ NOUN **1** = **sentry**, warder,

warden, custodian, watch,
lookout, watchman, sentinel
2 = **shield**, security, defence,
screen, protection, safeguard,
buffer

guarded ADJECTIVE = **cautious**,
reserved, careful, suspicious,
wary, prudent, reticent,
circumspect

guardian NOUN = **keeper**,
champion, defender, guard,
warden, curator, protector,
custodian

guerrilla NOUN = **freedom
fighter**, partisan, underground
fighter

guess VERB **1** = **estimate**, predict,
work out, speculate, conjecture,
postulate, hypothesize ≠ know
2 = **suppose**, think, believe,
suspect, judge, imagine, reckon,
fancy
▷ NOUN **1** = **estimate**,
speculation, judgment,
hypothesis, conjecture,
shot in the dark ≠ certainty
2 = **supposition**, idea, theory,
hypothesis

guest NOUN = **visitor**, company,
caller, manu(w)hiri (*N.Z.*)

guidance NOUN = **advice**,
direction, leadership, instruction,
help, management, teaching,
counselling

guide NOUN **1** = **handbook**,
manual, guidebook, instructions,
catalogue **2** = **directory**, street
map **3** = **escort**, leader, usher
4 = **pointer**, sign, landmark,
marker, beacon, signpost,

guiding light, lodestar **5** = **model**, example, standard, ideal, inspiration, paradigm
▷ VERB **1** = **lead**, direct, escort, conduct, accompany, shepherd, usher, show the way **2** = **steer**, control, manage, direct, handle, command, manoeuvre **3** = **supervise**, train, teach, influence, advise, counsel, instruct, oversee

guild NOUN = **society**, union, league, association, company, club, order, organization

guilt NOUN **1** = **shame**, regret, remorse, contrition, guilty conscience, self-reproach ≠ pride **2** = **culpability**, blame, responsibility, misconduct, wickedness, sinfulness, guiltiness ≠ innocence

guilty ADJECTIVE **1** = **ashamed**, sorry, rueful, sheepish, contrite, remorseful, regretful, shamefaced ≠ proud **2** = **culpable**, responsible, to blame, offending, erring, at fault, reprehensible, blameworthy ≠ innocent

guise NOUN **1** = **form**, appearance, shape, aspect, mode, semblance **2** = **pretence**, disguise, aspect, semblance

gulch NOUN (*U.S. & Canad.*) = **ravine**, canyon, defile, gorge, gully, pass

gulf NOUN **1** = **bay**, bight, sea inlet **2** = **chasm**, opening, split, gap, separation, void, rift, abyss

gum NOUN = **glue**, adhesive, resin, cement, paste
▷ VERB = **stick**, glue, affix, cement, paste

gun NOUN = **firearm**, shooter (*slang*), piece (*slang*), handgun

gunman NOUN = **armed man**, gunslinger (*U.S. slang*)

guru NOUN **1** = **authority**, expert, leader, master, pundit, Svengali, fundi (*S. African*) **2** = **teacher**, mentor, sage, master, tutor

gush VERB **1** = **flow**, run, rush, flood, pour, stream, cascade, spurt **2** = **enthuse**, rave, spout, overstate, effuse
▷ NOUN = **stream**, flow, rush, flood, jet, cascade, torrent, spurt

gut NOUN = **paunch** (*informal*), belly, spare tyre (*Brit. slang*), potbelly, puku (*N.Z.*)
▷ VERB **1** = **disembowel**, clean **2** = **ravage**, empty, clean out, despoil
▷ ADJECTIVE = **instinctive**, natural, basic, spontaneous, intuitive, involuntary, heartfelt, unthinking

guts PLURAL NOUN **1** = **intestines**, insides (*informal*), stomach, belly, bowels, innards (*informal*), entrails **2** (*informal*) = **courage**, spirit, nerve, daring, pluck, backbone, bottle (*slang*), audacity

gutter NOUN = **drain**, channel, ditch, trench, trough, conduit, sluice

guy NOUN (*informal*) = **man**, person, fellow, lad, bloke (*Brit. informal*), chap

Gypsy or **Gipsy** NOUN = **traveller**, roamer, wanderer, Bohemian, rover, rambler, nomad, Romany

Hh

habit NOUN 1 = **mannerism**, custom, way, practice, characteristic, tendency, quirk, propensity 2 = **addiction**, dependence, compulsion

hack¹ VERB = **cut**, chop, slash, mutilate, mangle, mangulate (*Austral. slang*), hew, lacerate

hack² NOUN = **reporter**, writer, correspondent, journalist, scribbler, contributor, literary hack

hail³ NOUN 1 = **hailstones**, sleet, hailstorm, frozen rain 2 = **shower**, rain, storm, battery, volley, barrage, bombardment, downpour
▷ VERB 1 = **rain**, shower, pelt 2 = **batter**, rain, bombard, pelt, rain down on, beat down upon

hail⁴ VERB 1 = **acclaim**, honour, acknowledge, cheer, applaud ≠ condemn 2 = **salute**, greet, address, welcome, say hello to, halloo ≠ snub 3 = **flag down**, summon, signal to, wave down
▷ PHRASE: **hail from somewhere** = **come from**, be born in, originate in, be a native of, have your roots in

hair NOUN = **locks**, mane, tresses, shock, mop, head of hair

● **WORD POWER**
● *Hair* has long been a focus of
● care and attention for humans,
● even seen as our 'crowning
● glory'. The extended meanings
● and idioms involving hair tend
● to refer either to the physical
● appearance of hair or the
● emotions. A hair describes a
● very small amount or distance
● in the expression *by a hair ('s*
● *breadth)*, meaning 'very close',
● which is also like the phrase
● *by a whisker*. Physical fineness
● of hair is also referenced in
● the expression *split hairs*
● whereby petty distinctions
● are made. Other expressions
● with hair allude to emotional
● states, such as *get in your hair*
● meaning 'annoy'. The idea that
● emotions can affect the hair
● has its foundation in fact in
● that cold, fear, and shock cause
● body hair to erect, literally
● *hair-raising* or *making your hair*
● *stand on end*. In olden times,
● the elaborate hairdressing of
● ladies and gentlemen in public
● meant that they would only
● *let their hair down* in private,
● thus the meaning of relaxing,
● or becoming confidential,
● developed.

hairdresser NOUN = **stylist**, barber, coiffeur *or* coiffeuse

hairy ADJECTIVE 1 = **shaggy**, woolly, furry, stubbly, bushy, unshaven, hirsute 2 (*slang*) = **dangerous**, risky, unpredictable, hazardous, perilous

hale ADJECTIVE (*old-fashioned*)
= **healthy**, well, strong, sound, fit, flourishing, robust, vigorous

half NOUN = **fifty per cent**, equal part
▷ ADJECTIVE = **partial**, limited, moderate, halved
▷ ADVERB = **partially**, partly, in part ▷ RELATED WORDS: *prefixes* **bi-, hemi-, demi-, semi-**

halfway ADVERB = **midway**, to *or* in the middle
▷ ADJECTIVE = **midway**, middle, mid, central, intermediate, equidistant

hall NOUN 1 = **passage**, lobby, corridor, hallway, foyer, entry, passageway, entrance hall
2 = **meeting place**, chamber, auditorium, concert hall, assembly room

hallmark NOUN 1 = **trademark**, sure sign, telltale sign 2 (*Brit.*) = **mark**, sign, device, stamp, seal, symbol

halt VERB 1 = **stop**, break off, stand still, wait, rest ≠ continue
2 = **come to an end**, stop, cease
3 = **hold back**, end, check, block, curb, terminate, cut short, bring to an end ≠ aid
▷ NOUN = **stop**, end, close, pause, standstill, stoppage ≠ continuation

halting ADJECTIVE = **faltering**, stumbling, awkward, hesitant, laboured, stammering, stuttering

halve VERB 1 = **cut in half**, reduce by fifty per cent, decrease by fifty per cent, lessen by fifty per cent

2 = **split in two**, cut in half, bisect, divide in two, share equally, divide equally

hammer VERB 1 = **hit**, drive, knock, beat, strike, tap, bang
2 (*informal*) = **defeat**, beat, thrash, trounce, run rings around (*informal*), wipe the floor with (*informal*), drub

hamper VERB = **hinder**, handicap, prevent, restrict, frustrate, hamstring, interfere with, obstruct ≠ help

hand NOUN 1 = **palm**, fist, paw (*informal*), mitt (*slang*)
2 = **worker**, employee, labourer, workman, operative, craftsman, artisan, hired man 3 = **round of applause**, clap, ovation, big hand
4 = **writing**, script, handwriting, calligraphy
▷ VERB = **give**, pass, hand over, present to, deliver

● WORD POWER
● The primary meaning of *hand* is
● the part of the body at the end
● of the arm. Other meanings
● of hand make reference to its
● shape, position, and function,
● especially its use in touching
● and moving objects in the
● physical world. The size of
● a hand is still used as a unit
● of measurement in horses.
● The appearance of a hand is
● reflected in a *hand of bananas*
● and pointing *clock hands*.
● The use of a hand for holding
● objects can be seen in a *hand of*
● *cards* and its ability to clap in

- the phrase *give a (warm) hand*
- *to*. Handwriting can be referred
- to simply as a hand, e.g. *written*
- *in his own hand*. Workers are
- referred to as *hands*, where the
- most pertinent part of their
- body represents the whole,
- likewise in the phrase *all hands*
- *on deck*. The multiple roles of
- a hand have led to transferred
- senses of: agency – *have a hand*
- *in*, assistance – *lend/give a*
- *hand to*, and control – *in hand*.
- Various gestures of giving are
- expressed by the phrasal verbs
- *hand over, hand out, hand on*,
- and *hand in*.

handbook NOUN = **guidebook**, guide, manual, instruction book

handcuff VERB = **shackle**, secure, restrain, fetter, manacle
▷ PLURAL NOUN = **shackles**, cuffs (*informal*), fetters, manacles

handful NOUN = **few**, sprinkling, small amount, smattering, small number ≠ a lot

handicap NOUN 1 = **disability**, defect, impairment, physical abnormality 2 = **disadvantage**, barrier, restriction, obstacle, limitation, drawback, stumbling block, impediment ≠ advantage 3 = **advantage**, head start
▷ VERB = **hinder**, limit, restrict, burden, hamstring, hamper, hold back, impede ≠ help

handle NOUN = **grip**, hilt, haft, stock
▷ VERB 1 = **manage**, deal with, tackle, cope with 2 = **deal with**,

manage 3 = **control**, manage, direct, guide, manipulate, manoeuvre 4 = **hold**, feel, touch, pick up, finger, grasp

handsome ADJECTIVE 1 = **good-looking**, attractive, gorgeous, elegant, personable, dishy (*informal, chiefly Brit.*), comely, hot (*informal*), fit (*Brit. informal*) ≠ ugly 2 = **generous**, large, princely, liberal, considerable, lavish, ample, abundant ≠ mean

handy ADJECTIVE 1 = **useful**, practical, helpful, neat, convenient, easy to use, manageable, user-friendly ≠ useless 2 = **convenient**, close, available, nearby, accessible, on hand, at hand, within reach ≠ inconvenient 3 = **skilful**, skilled, expert, adept, deft, proficient, adroit, dexterous ≠ unskilled

hang VERB 1 = **dangle**, swing, suspend 2 = **lower**, suspend, dangle 3 = **lean** 4 = **execute**, lynch, string up (*informal*)
▷ PHRASES: **get the hang of something** = **grasp**, understand, learn, master, comprehend, catch on to, acquire the technique of; **hang back** = **be reluctant**, hesitate, hold back, recoil, demur

hangover NOUN = **aftereffects**, morning after (*informal*)

hang-up NOUN (*informal*) = **preoccupation**, thing (*informal*), problem, block, difficulty, obsession, mania, inhibition

hank NOUN = **coil**, roll, length,

bunch, piece, loop, clump, skein

happen VERB **1** = **occur**, take place, come about, result, develop, transpire (*informal*), come to pass **2** = **chance**, turn out (*informal*)

happening NOUN = **event**, incident, experience, affair, proceeding, episode, occurrence

happily ADVERB **1** = **luckily**, fortunately, providentially, opportunely **2** = **joyfully**, cheerfully, gleefully, blithely, merrily, gaily, joyously **3** = **willingly**, freely, gladly, with pleasure

happiness NOUN = **pleasure**, delight, joy, satisfaction, ecstasy, bliss, contentment, elation ≠ unhappiness

happy ADJECTIVE **1** = **pleased**, delighted, content, thrilled, glad, cheerful, merry, ecstatic, stoked (*Austral. & N.Z. informal*) **2** = **contented**, joyful, blissful ≠ sad **3** = **fortunate**, lucky, timely, favourable, auspicious, propitious, advantageous ≠ unfortunate

harass VERB = **annoy**, trouble, bother, harry, plague, hound, hassle (*informal*), persecute

harassed ADJECTIVE = **hassled**, worried, troubled, strained, under pressure, tormented, distraught (*informal*), vexed

harassment NOUN = **hassle**, trouble, bother, irritation, persecution (*informal*), nuisance, annoyance, pestering

harbour NOUN = **port**, haven, dock, mooring, marina, pier, wharf, anchorage
▷ VERB **1** = **hold**, bear, maintain, nurse, retain, foster, entertain, nurture **2** = **shelter**, protect, hide, shield, provide refuge, give asylum to

hard ADJECTIVE **1** = **tough**, strong, firm, solid, stiff, rigid, resistant, compressed ≠ soft **2** = **difficult**, involved, complicated, puzzling, intricate, perplexing, impenetrable, thorny ≠ easy **3** = **exhausting**, tough, exacting, rigorous, gruelling, strenuous, arduous, laborious ≠ easy **4** = **harsh**, cold, cruel, stern, callous, unkind, unsympathetic, pitiless ≠ kind **5** = **grim**, painful, distressing, harsh, unpleasant, intolerable, grievous, disagreeable
▷ ADVERB **1** = **strenuously**, steadily, persistently, doggedly, diligently, energetically, industriously, untiringly **2** = **intently**, closely, carefully, sharply, keenly **3** = **forcefully**, strongly, heavily, sharply, severely, fiercely, vigorously, intensely ≠ softly

harden VERB **1** = **solidify**, set, freeze, cake, bake, clot, thicken, stiffen **2** = **accustom**, season, toughen, train, inure, habituate

hardened ADJECTIVE **1** = **habitual**, chronic, shameless, inveterate, incorrigible ≠ occasional **2** = **seasoned**, experienced, accustomed, toughened, inured, habituated ≠ naive

hardly ADVERB 1 = **barely**, only just, scarcely, just, with difficulty, with effort ≠ completely 2 = **only just**, just, barely, scarcely

hardship NOUN = **suffering**, need, difficulty, misfortune, adversity, tribulation, privation ≠ ease

hardy ADJECTIVE = **strong**, tough, robust, sound, rugged, sturdy, stout ≠ frail

hare NOUN ▷ RELATED WORDS: *adjective* **leporine**, *male* **buck**, *female* **doe**, *young* **leveret**, *habitation* **down, husk**

harm VERB 1 = **injure**, hurt, wound, abuse, ill-treat, maltreat ≠ heal 2 = **damage**, hurt, ruin, spoil
▷ NOUN 1 = **injury**, suffering, damage, ill, hurt, distress
2 = **damage**, loss, ill, hurt, misfortune, mischief ≠ good

harmful ADJECTIVE = **damaging**, dangerous, negative, destructive, hazardous, unhealthy, detrimental, hurtful ≠ harmless

harmless ADJECTIVE 1 = **safe**, benign, wholesome, innocuous, nontoxic ≠ dangerous
2 = **inoffensive**, innocent, innocuous, gentle, tame, unobjectionable

harmony NOUN 1 = **accord**, peace, agreement, friendship, sympathy, cooperation, rapport, compatibility ≠ conflict
2 = **tune**, melody, unison, tunefulness, euphony ≠ discord

harness VERB = **exploit**, control, channel, employ, utilize, mobilize
▷ NOUN = **equipment**, tackle, gear, tack

harrowing ADJECTIVE = **distressing**, disturbing, painful, terrifying, traumatic, tormenting, agonizing, nerve-racking

harry VERB = **pester**, bother, plague, harass, hassle (*informal*), badger, chivvy

harsh ADJECTIVE 1 = **severe**, hard, tough, stark, austere, inhospitable, bare-bones
2 = **bleak**, freezing, severe, icy 3 = **cruel**, savage, ruthless, barbarous, pitiless 4 = **hard**, severe, cruel, stern, pitiless ≠ kind 5 = **drastic**, punitive, Draconian 6 = **raucous**, rough, grating, strident, rasping, discordant, guttural, dissonant ≠ soft

harshly ADVERB = **severely**, roughly, cruelly, strictly, sternly, brutally

harvest NOUN 1 = **harvesting**, picking, gathering, collecting, reaping, harvest-time 2 = **crop**, yield, year's growth, produce
▷ VERB = **gather**, pick, collect, bring in, pluck, reap

hassle (*informal*) NOUN = **trouble**, problem, difficulty, bother, grief (*informal*), uphill (*S. African*), inconvenience
▷ VERB = **bother**, bug (*informal*), annoy, hound, harass, badger, pester

hasten VERB = **rush**, race, fly,

h

speed, dash, hurry (up), scurry, make haste ≠ dawdle

hastily ADVERB 1 = **quickly**, rapidly, promptly, speedily 2 = **hurriedly**, rashly, precipitately, impetuously

hatch VERB 1 = **incubate**, breed, sit on, brood, bring forth 2 = **devise**, design, invent, put together, conceive, brew, formulate, contrive

hate VERB 1 = **detest**, loathe, despise, dislike, abhor, recoil from, not be able to bear ≠ love 2 = **dislike**, detest, shrink from, recoil from, not be able to bear ≠ like 3 = **be unwilling**, regret, be reluctant, hesitate, be sorry, be loath, feel disinclined
▷ NOUN = **dislike**, hostility, hatred, loathing, animosity, aversion, antipathy, enmity ≠ love

hatred NOUN = **hate**, dislike, animosity, aversion, revulsion, antipathy, enmity, repugnance ≠ love

haul VERB = **drag**, draw, pull, heave
▷ NOUN = **yield**, gain, spoils, catch, harvest, loot, takings, booty

haunt VERB = **plague**, trouble, obsess, torment, possess, stay with, recur, prey on
▷ NOUN = **meeting place**, hangout (informal), rendezvous, stamping ground

haunted ADJECTIVE
1 = **possessed**, ghostly, cursed, eerie, spooky (informal), jinxed
2 = **preoccupied**, worried, troubled, plagued, obsessed, tormented

haunting ADJECTIVE = **evocative**, poignant, unforgettable

have VERB 1 = **own**, keep, possess, hold, retain, boast, be the owner of 2 = **get**, obtain, take, receive, accept, gain, secure, acquire 3 = **suffer**, experience, undergo, sustain, endure, be suffering from 4 = **give birth to**, bear, deliver, bring forth, beget 5 = **experience**, go through, undergo, meet with, come across, run into, be faced with
▷ PHRASES: **have someone on** = **tease**, kid (informal), wind up (Brit. slang), trick, deceive, take the mickey, pull someone's leg; **have something on** = **wear**, be wearing, be dressed in, be clothed in, be attired in; **have to 1** with **to** = **must**, should, be forced, ought, be obliged, be bound, have got to, be compelled 2 = **have got to**, must

haven NOUN = **sanctuary**, shelter, retreat, asylum, refuge, oasis, sanctum

havoc NOUN 1 = **devastation**, damage, destruction, ruin 2 (informal) = **disorder**, confusion, chaos, disruption, mayhem, shambles

hazard NOUN = **danger**, risk, threat, problem, menace, peril, jeopardy, pitfall
▷ VERB = **jeopardize**, risk, endanger, threaten, expose, imperil, put in jeopardy ▷ PHRASE:

hazard a guess = **guess**,
conjecture, presume, take a guess
hazardous ADJECTIVE
= **dangerous**, risky, difficult,
insecure, unsafe, precarious,
perilous, dicey (informal, chiefly
Brit.) ≠ safe
haze NOUN = **mist**, cloud, fog,
obscurity, vapour
head NOUN **1** = **skull**, crown, pate,
nut (slang), loaf (slang) **2** = **mind**,
reasoning, understanding,
thought, sense, brain, brains
(informal), intelligence **3** = **top**,
crown, summit, peak, crest,
pinnacle
4 (informal) = **head teacher**,
principal **5** = **leader**, president,
director, manager, chief, boss
(informal), captain, master,
sherang (Austral. & N.Z.)
▷ ADJECTIVE = **chief**, main,
leading, first, prime, premier,
supreme, principal
▷ VERB **1** = **lead**, precede, be
the leader of, be or go first,
be or go at the front of, lead
the way **2** = **top**, lead, crown,
cap **3** = **be in charge of**, run,
manage, lead, control, direct,
guide, command ▷ PHRASES:
go to your head 1 = **intoxicate**
2 = **make someone conceited**,
puff someone up, make someone
full of themselves; **head over
heels** = **completely**, thoroughly,
utterly, intensely, wholeheartedly,
uncontrollably
● **WORD POWER**
● The *head* is the upper or front

● part of the human body,
● containing the sensory organs
● and the brain. Many of its
● literal or figurative senses refer
● to a position at the top, at
● the front, or at the beginning
● of something. Location is
● specified in *head of the line*,
● meaning at the front; *head of
● the stairs*, meaning at the top;
● and *head of the river*, meaning
● at the source. These meanings
● have been transferred into
● other fields, with the result
● that head means leader in
● *the head of state*, and the
● forefront in *head of his field*.
● Conversely, head can also
● mean end or climax when used
● in the phrase *come/bring to a
● head*. In the human body, the
● head is regarded as the seat
● of the mind and the intellect,
● especially when contrasted
● with the heart, in the phrase
● *ruled by your heart, not your
● head*. In addition, head can
● describe an ability or a facility,
● e.g. *a head for heights* or *a head
● for figures*.
headache NOUN **1** = **migraine**,
head (informal), neuralgia
2 = **problem** (informal), worry,
trouble, bother, nuisance,
inconvenience, bane,
vexation
heading NOUN = **title**, name,
caption, headline, rubric
heady ADJECTIVE **1** = **exciting**,
thrilling, stimulating,

exhilarating, intoxicating
2 = **intoxicating**, strong, potent, inebriating

heal VERB **1** *sometimes with* **up** = **mend**, get better, get well, cure, regenerate, show improvement
2 = **cure**, restore, mend, make better, remedy, make good, make well ≠ injure

health NOUN **1** = **condition**, state, shape, constitution, fettle **2** = **wellbeing**, strength, fitness, vigour, good condition, soundness, robustness, healthiness ≠ illness **3** = **state**, condition, shape

healthy ADJECTIVE **1** = **well**, fit, strong, active, robust, in good shape (*informal*), in the pink, in fine fettle ≠ ill **2** = **wholesome**, beneficial, nourishing, nutritious, salutary, hygienic, salubrious ≠ unwholesome
3 = **invigorating**, beneficial, salutary, salubrious

heap NOUN **1** = **pile**, lot, collection, mass, stack, mound, accumulation, hoard **2** *often plural* (*informal*) = **a lot**, lots (*informal*), plenty, masses, load(s) (*informal*), great deal, tons, stack(s)
▷ VERB *sometimes with* **up** = **pile**, collect, gather, stack, accumulate, amass, hoard ▷ PHRASE: **heap something on someone** = **load with**, confer on, assign to, bestow on, shower upon

hear VERB **1** = **overhear**, catch, detect **2** = **listen to 3** (*law*) = **try**, judge, examine, investigate

4 = **learn**, discover, find out, pick up, gather, ascertain, get wind of (*informal*)

hearing NOUN = **inquiry**, trial, investigation, industrial tribunal

heart NOUN **1** = **emotions**, feelings, love, affection
2 = **nature**, character, soul, constitution, essence, temperament, disposition
3 = **root**, core, centre, nucleus, hub, gist, nitty-gritty (*informal*), nub **4** = **courage**, will, spirit, purpose, bottle (*Brit. informal*), resolution, resolve, stomach
▷ PHRASE: **by heart** = **from** or **by memory**, verbatim, word for word, pat, word-perfect, by rote, off by heart, off pat ▷ RELATED WORD: *adjective* **cardiac**

● WORD POWER
● More than any other part of the
● human body, the *heart* has been
● given special significance and
● symbolic power. It is the heart
● which expresses the essential
● character of a human being,
● in phrases such as *at heart*.
● In today's English, the heart
● represents the seat of emotions
● in contrast to the reasoning of
● the head. However, formerly,
● the heart was also considered
● to be the seat of mental
● processes, including the mind
● and memory. This is seen in
● the phrase *by heart*, meaning
● from memory. Nowadays, we
● think of the heart especially
● with reference to love and

- compassion in the phrases
- *heartbreak*, *heart-rending*, and
- *heart-warming*. Adding to the
- fervour of these emotions, we
- have *from the heart* (sincerely);
- *heart-to-heart* (candidly); and
- *heart and soul* (completely).
- When we summon emotional
- reserves of courage and will,
- they come from the heart – we
- *take heart* or *lose heart*. The
- heart's role in maintaining
- life means it is viewed as the
- centre of the body and, by
- extension, this can be the hub
- of other places, as in *the heart*
- *of the region* or *at the heart of the*
- *company*.

heat VERB *sometimes with* **up**
= **warm (up)**, cook, boil, roast,
reheat, make hot ≠ chill
▷ NOUN 1 = **warmth**, hotness,
temperature ≠ cold 2 = **hot**
weather, warmth, closeness,
high temperature, heatwave,
warm weather, hot climate,
mugginess 3 = **passion**,
excitement, intensity, fury,
fervour, vehemence ≠ calmness
▷ RELATED WORD: *adjectives*
thermal

heated ADJECTIVE
1 = **impassioned**, intense,
spirited, excited, angry, furious,
fierce, lively ≠ calm 2 = **wound**
up, worked up, keyed up, het up
(*informal*)

heaven NOUN 1 = **paradise**,
next world, hereafter, nirvana
(*Buddhism*, *hinduism*), bliss, Zion

(*christianity*), life everlasting,
Elysium *or* Elysian fields (*greek
myth*) 2 (*informal*) = **happiness**,
paradise, ecstasy, bliss, utopia,
rapture, seventh heaven
▷ PHRASE: **the heavens** (*old-
fashioned*) = **sky**, ether, firmament

heavenly ADJECTIVE 1 = **celestial**,
holy, divine, blessed, immortal,
angelic ≠ earthly 2 (*informal*)
= **wonderful**, lovely, delightful,
beautiful, divine (*informal*),
exquisite, sublime, blissful
≠ awful

heavily ADVERB 1 = **excessively**,
to excess, very much, a great
deal, considerably, copiously,
without restraint, immoderately
2 = **densely**, closely, thickly,
compactly 3 = **hard**, clumsily,
awkwardly, weightily

heavy ADJECTIVE 1 = **weighty**,
large, massive, hefty, bulky,
ponderous ≠ light 2 = **intensive**,
severe, serious, concentrated,
fierce, excessive, relentless
3 = **considerable**, large, huge,
substantial, abundant, copious,
profuse ≠ slight

- **WORD POWER**
- Many of the words which have
- come into English from Hebrew
- have their origins in the bible,
- and were part of the Jewish
- and Christian religions. A
- noticeable trend with religious
- words is that they spread
- into secular language as well.
- Two examples are *amen* and
- *hallelujah*. The literal meaning

h

- of amen is 'certainly', and it is
- used at the end of prayers as a
- concluding formula. However,
- it has also passed outside the
- religious sphere to be used as
- an expression of agreement to a
- previous utterance. It is similar
- in function to 'hear, hear'
- meaning 'I agree'. Hallelujah,
- literally 'praise the Lord', is an
- interjection used by atheists
- as well as believers as a general
- exclamation of relief. Another
- biblical word is **behemoth**, from
- the Hebrew for 'beasts', which
- was used in the Old Testament
- with specific reference
- but has now become more
- generalised. The behemoth
- was a gigantic beast, possibly
- a hippopotamus. Its modern
- figurative meaning is that of
- any huge or monstrous thing. It
- is often applied to corporations
- or industries of the modern
- world in the same way as its
- synonym 'giant', in expressions
- like the *software/corporate/*
- *steel/banking behemoth*. It
- retains the slightly negative
- connotation of its original
- meaning of 'beast'.

hectic ADJECTIVE = **frantic**,
chaotic, heated, animated,
turbulent, frenetic, feverish
≠ peaceful

hedge VERB = **prevaricate**, evade,
sidestep, duck, dodge, flannel
(*Brit. informal*), equivocate,
temporize ▷ PHRASE: hedge

against something = **protect**,
insure, guard, safeguard, shield,
cover

heed VERB = **pay attention to**,
listen to, take notice of, follow,
consider, note, observe, obey
≠ ignore
▷ NOUN = **thought**, care, mind,
attention, regard, respect, notice
≠ disregard

heel NOUN (*slang*) = **swine**, cad
(*Brit. informal*), bounder (*Brit. old-
fashioned or slang*), rotter (*slang,
chiefly Brit.*), wrong 'un (*Austral.
slang*)

hefty (*informal*) ADJECTIVE = **big**,
strong, massive, strapping,
robust, muscular, burly, hulking
≠ small

height NOUN 1 = **tallness**, stature,
highness, loftiness ≠ shortness
2 = **altitude**, measurement,
highness, elevation, tallness
≠ depth 3 = **peak**, top, crown,
summit, crest, pinnacle, apex
≠ valley 4 = **culmination**, climax,
zenith, limit, maximum, ultimate
≠ low point

heighten VERB = **intensify**,
increase, add to, improve,
strengthen, enhance, sharpen,
magnify

heir NOUN = **successor**,
beneficiary, inheritor, heiress *fem.*
next in line

hell NOUN 1 = **the underworld**, the
abyss, Hades (*greek myth*), hellfire,
the inferno, fire and brimstone,
the nether world, the bad fire
(*informal*) 2 (*informal*) = **torment**,

suffering, agony, nightmare, misery, ordeal, anguish, wretchedness

hello INTERJECTION = **hi** (*informal*), greetings, how do you do?, good morning, good evening, good afternoon, welcome, kia ora (*N.Z.*), gidday *or* g'day (*Austral. & N.Z.*)

helm NOUN (*nautical*) = **tiller**, wheel, rudder

help VERB **1** *sometimes with* **out** = **aid**, support, assist, cooperate with, abet, lend a hand, succour ≠ hinder **2** = **improve**, ease, relieve, facilitate, alleviate, mitigate, ameliorate ≠ make worse **3** = **assist**, aid, support **4** = **resist**, refrain from, avoid, prevent, keep from
▷ NOUN = **assistance**, aid, support, advice, guidance, cooperation, helping hand ≠ hindrance

helper NOUN = **assistant**, ally, supporter, mate, second, aide, attendant, collaborator

helpful ADJECTIVE
1 = **cooperative**, accommodating, kind, friendly, neighbourly, sympathetic, supportive, considerate **2** = **useful**, practical, profitable, constructive
3 = **beneficial**, advantageous

helping NOUN = **portion**, serving, ration, piece, dollop (*informal*), plateful

helpless ADJECTIVE = **powerless**, weak, disabled, incapable, challenged, paralysed, impotent, infirm ≠ powerful

hem NOUN **1** = **edge**, border, margin, trimming, fringe
▷ PHRASE: **hem something** *or* **someone in 1** = **surround**, confine, enclose, shut in
2 = **restrict**, confine, beset, circumscribe

hence ADVERB = **therefore**, thus, consequently, for this reason, in consequence, ergo, on that account

herald VERB = **indicate**, promise, usher in, presage, portend, foretoken
▷ NOUN **1** (*often literary*) = **forerunner**, sign, signal, indication, token, omen, precursor, harbinger
2 = **messenger**, courier, proclaimer, announcer, crier, town crier

herd NOUN = **flock**, crowd, collection, mass, drove, mob, swarm, horde

hereditary ADJECTIVE
1 = **genetic**, inborn, inbred, transmissible, inheritable **2** (*law*) = **inherited**, passed down, traditional, ancestral

heritage NOUN = **inheritance**, legacy, birthright, tradition, endowment, bequest

hero NOUN **1** = **protagonist**, leading man **2** = **star**, champion, victor, superstar, conqueror
3 = **idol**, favourite, pin-up (*slang*), fave (*informal*)

heroic ADJECTIVE = **courageous**, brave, daring, fearless, gallant,

intrepid, valiant, lion-hearted
≠ cowardly

heroine NOUN 1 = **protagonist**,
leading lady, diva, prima donna
2 = **idol**, favourite, pin-up (slang),
fave (informal)

● **WORD POWER**
● Note that the word heroine,
● meaning 'a female hero', has an
● e at the end. The drug heroin is
● spelled without a final e.

hesitate VERB 1 = **waver**, delay,
pause, wait, doubt, falter, dither
(chiefly Brit.), vacillate ≠ be
decisive 2 = **be reluctant**, be
unwilling, shrink from, think
twice, scruple, demur, hang back,
be disinclined ≠ be determined

hesitation NOUN = **reluctance**,
reservation(s), misgiving(s),
ambivalence, qualm(s),
unwillingness, scruple(s),
compunction

hidden ADJECTIVE 1 = **secret**,
veiled, latent 2 = **concealed**,
secret, covert, unseen,
clandestine, secreted, under
wraps

hide¹ VERB 1 = **conceal**, stash
(informal), secrete, put out of sight
≠ display 2 = **go into hiding**,
take cover, keep out of sight, hole
up, lie low, go underground, go
to ground, go to earth 3 = **keep
secret**, suppress, withhold, keep
quiet about, hush up, draw a
veil over, keep dark, keep under
your hat ≠ disclose 4 = **obscure**,
cover, mask, disguise, conceal,
veil, cloak, shroud ≠ reveal

hide² NOUN = **skin**, leather, pelt

hideous ADJECTIVE = **ugly**,
revolting, ghastly, monstrous,
grotesque, gruesome, grisly,
unsightly ≠ beautiful

hiding NOUN (informal) = **beating**,
whipping, thrashing, licking
(informal), spanking, walloping
(informal), drubbing

hierarchy NOUN = **grading**,
ranking, social order, pecking
order, class system, social stratum

high ADJECTIVE 1 = **tall**, towering,
soaring, steep, elevated, lofty
≠ short 2 = **extreme**, great,
acute, severe, extraordinary,
excessive ≠ low 3 = **strong**,
violent, extreme, blustery,
squally, sharp 4 = **important**,
chief, powerful, superior,
eminent, exalted, skookum
(Canad.) ≠ lowly 5 = **high-
pitched**, piercing, shrill,
penetrating, strident, sharp,
acute, piping ≠ deep 6 (informal)
= **intoxicated**, stoned (slang),
tripping (informal)
▷ ADVERB = **way up**, aloft, far up,
to a great height

high-flown ADJECTIVE
= **extravagant**, elaborate,
pretentious, exaggerated,
inflated, lofty, grandiose,
overblown ≠ straightforward

highlight VERB = **emphasize**,
stress, accent, show up,
underline, spotlight, accentuate,
call attention to ≠ play down
▷ NOUN = **high point**, peak,
climax, feature, focus, focal point,

high spot ≠ low point

highly ADVERB = **extremely**, very, greatly, vastly, exceptionally, immensely, tremendously

hijack or **highjack** VERB = **seize**, take over, commandeer, expropriate

hike NOUN = **walk**, march, trek, ramble, tramp, traipse
  ▷ VERB = **walk**, march, trek, ramble, tramp, back-pack

hilarious ADJECTIVE 1 = **funny**, entertaining, amusing, hysterical, humorous, comical, side-splitting 2 = **merry**, uproarious, rollicking ≠ serious

hill NOUN = **mount**, fell, height, mound, hilltop, tor, knoll, hillock, kopje or koppie (S. African)

hinder VERB = **obstruct**, stop, check, block, delay, frustrate, handicap, interrupt ≠ help

● **WORD POWER**
● Hindi is the official language
● of India, with English
● recognized as an associate
● official language. Before
● independence, India was
● part of the British Empire,
● and contact between the two
● cultures led to the borrowing
● into English of a number of loan
● words. The word *dekko*, literally
● 'look!' in Hindi, entered English
● through British army slang in
● the 19th century. It remains
● restricted to British slang,
● especially in the phrase *take/*
● *have a dekko at*, meaning 'have
● a look'. It can be contrasted
● with a couple of phrases with
● similar meaning – *have a shufti*
● *at* and *do a recce*, which also
● entered English via military
● contact with other cultures
● [See Arabic]. The word *pukka*
● derives from the Hindi word
● for 'firm' or 'mature' and is
● found particularly in Indian
● English and British English.
● It has a range of meaning in
● these two varieties; applied
● to a person it means 'genuine'
● or 'socially acceptable', and
● applied to a thing it means
● 'right' or 'real'. For example, *a*
● *pukka chap*, *a pukka way*, *a pukka*
● *job*. The meaning of *wallah* in
● British English derives from
● a misunderstanding of the
● Hindi word *-wala* which is
● equivalent to the English suffix
● -er, as in teacher, producer. It
● was thought by non-native
● speakers to mean 'man'; this
● has influenced its modern
● meaning in British English
● of a person involved with a
● specified thing, particularly in
● their employment, e.g. *a policy*
● *wallah*, *an company wallah*, *a*
● *personnel wallah*.

hint NOUN 1 = **clue**, suggestion, implication, indication, pointer, allusion, innuendo, intimation 2 = **advice**, help, tip(s), suggestion(s), pointer(s) 3 = **trace**, touch, suggestion, dash, suspicion, tinge, undertone
  ▷ VERB *sometimes with* **at**

= **suggest**, indicate, imply, intimate, insinuate

hire VERB 1 = **employ**, commission, take on, engage, appoint, sign up, enlist 2 = **rent**, charter, lease, let, engage
▷ NOUN 1 = **rental**, hiring, rent, lease 2 = **charge**, rental, price, cost, fee

hiss VERB 1 = **whistle**, wheeze, whiz, whirr, sibilate 2 = **jeer**, mock, deride
▷ NOUN = **fizz**, buzz, hissing, fizzing, sibilation

historic ADJECTIVE = **significant**, notable, momentous, famous, extraordinary, outstanding, remarkable, ground-breaking
≠ unimportant

● **WORD POWER**
● Although *historic* and
● *historical* are similarly spelt
● they are very different in
● meaning and should not
● be used interchangeably. A
● distinction is usually made
● between *historic*, which means
● 'important' or 'significant',
● and *historical*, which means
● 'pertaining to history': *a historic*
● *decision; a historical perspective.*

historical ADJECTIVE
= **factual**, real, documented, actual, authentic, attested
≠ contemporary
▷ *see* **historic**

history NOUN 1 = **the past**, antiquity, yesterday, yesteryear, olden days 2 = **chronicle**, record, story, account, narrative, recital, annals

hit VERB 1 = **strike**, beat, knock, bang, slap, smack, thump, clout (*informal*) 2 = **collide with**, run into, bump into, clash with, smash into, crash against, bang into 3 = **affect**, damage, harm, ruin, devastate, overwhelm, touch, impact on 4 = **reach**, gain, achieve, arrive at, accomplish, attain
▷ NOUN 1 = **shot**, blow 2 = **blow**, knock, stroke, belt (*informal*), rap, slap, smack, clout (*informal*) 3 = **success**, winner, triumph, smash (*informal*), sensation
▷ PHRASES: **hit it off** (*informal*) = **get on (well) with**, click (*slang*), be on good terms, get on like a house on fire (*informal*); **hit on** *or* **upon something** = **think up**, discover, arrive at, invent, stumble on, light upon, strike upon

hitch NOUN = **problem**, catch, difficulty, hold-up, obstacle, drawback, snag, uphill (*S. African*), impediment
▷ VERB 1 (*informal*) = **hitchhike**, thumb a lift 2 = **fasten**, join, attach, couple, tie, connect, harness, tether ▷ PHRASE: **hitch something up** = **pull up**, tug, jerk, yank

hitherto ADVERB (*formal*) = **previously**, so far, until now, thus far, heretofore

hobby NOUN = **pastime**, relaxation, leisure pursuit, diversion, avocation, (leisure) activity

hoist VERB = **raise**, lift, erect, elevate, heave
▷ NOUN = **lift**, crane, elevator, winch

hold VERB 1 = **embrace**, grasp, clutch, hug, squeeze, cradle, clasp, enfold 2 = **restrain** ≠ release 3 = **detain**, confine, imprison, impound ≠ release 4 = **accommodate**, take, contain, seat, have a capacity for 5 = **consider**, think, believe, judge, regard, assume, reckon, deem ≠ deny 6 = **occupy**, have, fill, maintain, retain, possess, hold down (*informal*) 7 = **conduct**, convene, call, run, preside over ≠ cancel
▷ NOUN 1 = **grip**, grasp, clasp 2 = **foothold**, footing 3 = **control**, influence, mastery, mana (*N.Z.*)

holder NOUN 1 = **owner**, bearer, possessor, keeper, proprietor 2 = **case**, cover, container

hold-up NOUN 1 = **robbery**, theft, mugging (*informal*), stick-up (*slang, chiefly U.S.*) 2 = **delay**, wait, hitch, setback, snag, traffic jam, stoppage, bottleneck

hole NOUN 1 = **cavity**, pit, hollow, chamber, cave, cavern 2 = **opening**, crack, tear, gap, breach, vent, puncture, aperture 3 = **burrow**, den, earth, shelter, lair 4 (*informal*) = **hovel**, dump (*informal*), dive (*slang*), slum 5 (*informal*) = **predicament**, spot (*informal*), fix (*informal*), mess, jam (*informal*), dilemma, scrape (*informal*), hot water (*informal*)

holiday NOUN 1 = **vacation**, leave, break, time off, recess, schoolie (*Austral.*), accumulated day off *or* ADO (*Austral.*) 2 = **festival**, fête, celebration, feast, gala

hollow ADJECTIVE 1 = **empty**, vacant, void, unfilled ≠ solid 2 = **worthless**, useless, vain, meaningless, pointless, futile, fruitless ≠ meaningful 3 = **dull**, low, deep, muted, toneless, reverberant ≠ vibrant
▷ NOUN 1 = **cavity**, hole, bowl, depression, pit, basin, crater, trough ≠ mound 2 = **valley**, dale, glen, dell, dingle ≠ hill
▷ VERB *often followed by* **out** = **scoop out**, dig out, excavate, gouge out

holocaust NOUN 1 = **devastation**, destruction, genocide, annihilation, conflagration 2 = **genocide**, massacre, annihilation

holy ADJECTIVE 1 = **sacred**, blessed, hallowed, venerable, consecrated, sacrosanct, sanctified ≠ unsanctified 2 = **devout**, godly, religious, pure, righteous, pious, virtuous, saintly ≠ sinful

homage NOUN = **respect**, honour, worship, devotion, reverence, deference, adulation, adoration ≠ contempt

home NOUN 1 = **dwelling**, house, residence, abode, habitation, pad (*slang*), domicile 2 = **birthplace**, homeland, home town, native land, Godzone (*Austral. informal*)
▷ ADJECTIVE = **domestic**, local,

internal, native ▷ **PHRASES**: **at home 1** = **in**, present, available **2** = **at ease**, relaxed, comfortable, content, at peace; **bring something home to someone** = **make clear**, emphasize, drive home, press home, impress upon

homeland NOUN = **native land**, birthplace, motherland, fatherland, country of origin, mother country, Godzone (*Austral. informal*)

homeless ADJECTIVE = **destitute**, displaced, dispossessed, down-and-out

homely ADJECTIVE
1 = **comfortable**, welcoming, friendly, cosy, homespun
2 = **plain**, simple, ordinary, modest ≠ elaborate

homicide NOUN = **murder**, killing, manslaughter, slaying, bloodshed

hone VERB **1** = **improve**, better, enhance, upgrade, refine, sharpen, help **2** = **sharpen**, point, grind, edge, file, polish, whet

● **WORD POWER**
● *Hone* is sometimes wrongly
● used where *home* is meant: *this*
● *device makes it easier to home in*
● *on* (not *hone in on*) *the target.*

honest ADJECTIVE
1 = **trustworthy**, upright, ethical, honourable, reputable, truthful, virtuous, law-abiding ≠ dishonest **2** = **open**, direct, frank, plain, sincere, candid, forthright, upfront (*informal*) ≠ secretive

honestly ADVERB **1** = **ethically**,

legally, lawfully, honourably, by fair means **2** = **frankly**, plainly, candidly, straight (out), truthfully, to your face, in all sincerity

honesty NOUN **1** = **integrity**, honour, virtue, morality, probity, rectitude, truthfulness, trustworthiness **2** = **frankness**, openness, sincerity, candour, bluntness, outspokenness, straightforwardness

honorary ADJECTIVE = **nominal**, unofficial, titular, in name or title only

honour NOUN **1** = **integrity**, morality, honesty, goodness, fairness, decency, probity, rectitude ≠ dishonour
2 = **prestige**, credit, reputation, glory, fame, distinction, dignity, renown ≠ disgrace
3 = **reputation**, standing, prestige, image, status, stature, good name, cachet
4 = **acclaim**, praise, recognition, compliments, homage, accolades, commendation ≠ contempt
5 = **privilege**, credit, pleasure, compliment
▷ VERB **1** = **acclaim**, praise, decorate, commemorate, commend **2** = **respect**, value, esteem, prize, appreciate, adore ≠ scorn **3** = **fulfil**, keep, carry out, observe, discharge, live up to, be true to **4** = **pay**, take, accept, pass, acknowledge ≠ refuse

honourable ADJECTIVE
1 = **principled**, moral, ethical, fair, upright, honest, virtuous,

trustworthy **2** = **proper**, respectable, virtuous, creditable

hook NOUN = **fastener**, catch, link, peg, clasp

▷ VERB **1** = **fasten**, fix, secure, clasp **2** = **catch**, land, trap, entrap

hooked ADJECTIVE **1** = **bent**, curved, aquiline, hook-shaped **2** (*informal*) = **obsessed**, addicted, taken, devoted, turned on (*slang*), enamoured **3** (*informal*) = **addicted**, dependent, using (*informal*), having a habit

hooligan NOUN = **delinquent**, vandal, hoon (*Austral. & N.Z.*), ruffian, lager lout, yob *or* yobbo (*Brit. slang*), cougan (*Austral. slang*), scozza (*Austral. slang*), bogan (*Austral. slang*)

hoop NOUN = **ring**, band, loop, wheel, round, girdle, circlet

hop VERB = **jump**, spring, bound, leap, skip, vault, caper

▷ NOUN = **jump**, step, spring, bound, leap, bounce, skip, vault

hope VERB = **believe**, look forward to, cross your fingers

▷ NOUN = **belief**, confidence, expectation, longing, dream, desire, ambition, assumption ≠ despair

hopeful ADJECTIVE **1** = **optimistic**, confident, looking forward to, buoyant, sanguine, expectant ≠ despairing **2** = **promising**, encouraging, bright, reassuring, rosy, heartening, auspicious ≠ unpromising

hopefully ADVERB = **optimistically**, confidently, expectantly, with anticipation

● **WORD POWER**
● Some people object to the use
● of *hopefully* as a synonym for
● the phrase 'it is hoped that' in a
● sentence such as *hopefully I'll be*
● *able to attend the meeting*. This
● use of the adverb first appeared
● in America in the 1960s, but it
● has rapidly established itself
● elsewhere. There are really no
● strong grounds for objecting
● to it, since we accept other
● sentence adverbials that fulfil
● a similar function, for example
● *unfortunately*, which means 'it is
● unfortunate that' in a sentence
● such as *unfortunately I won't be*
● *able to attend the meeting.*

hopeless ADJECTIVE = **impossible**, pointless, futile, useless, vain, no-win, unattainable

horde NOUN = **crowd**, mob, swarm, host, band, pack, drove, gang

horizon NOUN = **skyline**, view, vista

horizontal ADJECTIVE = **level**, flat, parallel

horrible ADJECTIVE **1** (*informal*) = **dreadful**, terrible, awful, nasty, cruel, mean, unpleasant, horrid ≠ wonderful **2** = **terrible**, appalling, terrifying, shocking, grim, dreadful, revolting, ghastly

horrific ADJECTIVE = **horrifying**, shocking, appalling, awful, terrifying, dreadful, horrendous, ghastly

horrify VERB **1** = **terrify**, alarm,

frighten, scare, intimidate, petrify, make your hair stand on end ≠ comfort **2** = **shock**, appal, dismay, sicken, outrage ≠ delight

horror NOUN **1** = **terror**, fear, alarm, panic, dread, fright, consternation, trepidation **2** = **hatred**, disgust, loathing, aversion, revulsion, repugnance, odium, detestation ≠ love

horse NOUN = **nag**, mount, mare, colt, filly, stallion, steed (*archaic* or *literary*), moke (*Austral. slang*), yarraman or yarramin (*Austral.*), gee-gee (*slang*) ▷ **RELATED WORDS**: *adjectives* **equestrian**, **equine**, *male* **stallion**, *female* **mare**, *young* **foal**, **colt**, **filly**

hospitality NOUN = **welcome**, warmth, kindness, friendliness, sociability, conviviality, neighbourliness, cordiality

host¹ or **hostess** NOUN
1 = **master of ceremonies**, proprietor, innkeeper, landlord or landlady **2** = **presenter**, compere (*Brit.*), anchorman or anchorwoman
▷ VERB = **present**, introduce, compere (*Brit.*), front (*informal*)

host² NOUN **1** = **multitude**, lot, load (*informal*), wealth, array, myriad, great quantity, large number **2** = **crowd**, army, pack, drove, mob, herd, legion, swarm

hostage NOUN = **captive**, prisoner, pawn

hostile ADJECTIVE
1 = **antagonistic**, opposed, contrary, ill-disposed

2 = **unfriendly**, belligerent, antagonistic, rancorous, ill-disposed ≠ friendly
3 = **inhospitable**, adverse, uncongenial, unsympathetic, unwelcoming ≠ hospitable

hostility NOUN
1 = **unfriendliness**, hatred, animosity, spite, bitterness, malice, venom, enmity ≠ friendliness **2** = **opposition**, resentment, antipathy, aversion, antagonism, ill feeling, ill-will, animus ≠ approval
▷ PLURAL NOUN = **warfare**, war, fighting, conflict, combat, armed conflict ≠ peace

hot ADJECTIVE **1** = **heated**, boiling, steaming, roasting, searing, scorching, scalding **2** = **warm**, close, stifling, humid, torrid, sultry, sweltering, balmy ≠ cold
3 = **spicy**, pungent, peppery, piquant, biting, sharp ≠ mild
4 = **intense**, passionate, heated, spirited, fierce, lively, animated, ardent **5** = **new**, latest, fresh, recent, up to date, just out, up to the minute, bang up to date (*informal*) ≠ old **6** = **popular**, hip, fashionable, cool, in demand, sought-after, must-see, in vogue ≠ unpopular **7** = **fierce**, intense, strong, keen, competitive, cut-throat **8** = **fiery**, violent, raging, passionate, stormy ≠ calm

hound VERB = **harass**, harry, bother, provoke, annoy, torment, hassle (*informal*), badger
▷ **RELATED WORD**: *collective nouns*

pack

house NOUN 1 = **home**, residence, dwelling, pad (*slang*), homestead, abode, habitation, domicile, whare (*N.Z.*) 2 = **household**, family 3 = **firm**, company, business, organization, outfit (*informal*) 4 = **assembly**, parliament, Commons, legislative body 5 = **dynasty**, tribe, clan ▷ VERB 1 = **accommodate**, quarter, take in, put up, lodge, harbour, billet 2 = **contain**, keep, hold, cover, store, protect, shelter 3 = **take**, accommodate, sleep, provide shelter for, give a bed to ▷ PHRASE: **on the house** = **free**, for free (*informal*), for nothing, free of charge, gratis

household NOUN = **family**, home, house, family circle, ainga (*N.Z.*)

housing NOUN
1 = **accommodation**, homes, houses, dwellings, domiciles
2 = **case**, casing, covering, cover, shell, jacket, holder, container

hover VERB 1 = **float**, fly, hang, drift, flutter 2 = **linger**, loiter, hang about *or* around (*informal*)
3 = **waver**, fluctuate, dither (*chiefly Brit.*), oscillate, vacillate

however ADVERB = **but**, nevertheless, still, though, yet, nonetheless, notwithstanding, anyhow

howl VERB 1 = **bay**, cry 2 = **cry**, scream, roar, weep, yell, wail, shriek, bellow
▷ NOUN 1 = **baying**, cry, bay, bark, barking, yelping 2 = **cry**, scream,

roar, bay, wail, shriek, clamour, bawl

hub NOUN = **centre**, heart, focus, core, middle, focal point, nerve centre

huddle VERB 1 = **curl up**, crouch, hunch up 2 = **crowd**, press, gather, collect, squeeze, cluster, flock, herd
▷ NOUN (*informal*) = **discussion**, conference, meeting, hui (*N.Z.*), powwow, confab (*informal*), korero (*N.Z.*)

hue NOUN = **colour**, tone, shade, dye, tint, tinge

hug VERB = **embrace**, cuddle, squeeze, clasp, enfold, hold close, take in your arms
▷ NOUN = **embrace**, squeeze, bear hug, clinch (*slang*), clasp

huge ADJECTIVE = **enormous**, large, massive, vast, tremendous, immense, gigantic, monumental ≠ tiny

hui NOUN (*N.Z.*) = **meeting**, gathering, assembly, conference, congress, rally, convention, get-together (*informal*)

hull NOUN = **framework**, casing, body, covering, frame

hum VERB 1 = **drone**, buzz, murmur, throb, vibrate, purr, thrum, whir
2 (*informal*) = **be busy**, buzz, bustle, stir, pulse, pulsate

human ADJECTIVE = **mortal**, manlike ≠ nonhuman
▷ NOUN = **human being**, person, individual, creature, mortal, man *or* woman ≠ nonhuman

h

humane ADJECTIVE = **kind**, compassionate, understanding, forgiving, tender, sympathetic, benign, merciful ≠ cruel

humanitarian ADJECTIVE
1 = **compassionate**, charitable, humane, benevolent, altruistic
2 = **charitable**, philanthropic, public-spirited
▷ NOUN = **philanthropist**, benefactor, Good Samaritan, altruist

humanity NOUN 1 = **the human race**, man, mankind, people, mortals, humankind, Homo sapiens 2 = **human nature**, mortality 3 = **kindness**, charity, compassion, sympathy, mercy, philanthropy, fellow feeling, kind-heartedness

humble ADJECTIVE 1 = **modest**, meek, unassuming, unpretentious, self-effacing, unostentatious ≠ proud
2 = **lowly**, poor, mean, simple, ordinary, modest, obscure, undistinguished ≠ distinguished
▷ VERB = **humiliate**, disgrace, crush, subdue, chasten, put (someone) in their place, take down a peg (informal) ≠ exalt

humidity NOUN = **damp**, moisture, dampness, wetness, moistness, dankness, clamminess, mugginess

humiliate VERB = **embarrass**, shame, humble, crush, put down, degrade, chasten, mortify ≠ honour

humiliating ADJECTIVE

= **embarrassing**, shaming, humbling, mortifying, crushing, degrading, ignominious, barro (Austral. slang)

humiliation NOUN
= **embarrassment**, shame, disgrace, humbling, put-down, degradation, indignity, ignominy

humorous ADJECTIVE = **funny**, comic, amusing, entertaining, witty, comical, droll, jocular ≠ serious

humour NOUN 1 = **comedy**, funniness, fun, amusement, funny side, jocularity, facetiousness, ludicrousness ≠ seriousness
2 = **mood**, spirits, temper, disposition, frame of mind
3 = **joking**, comedy, wit, farce, jesting, wisecracks (informal), witticisms
▷ VERB = **indulge**, accommodate, go along with, flatter, gratify, pander to, mollify ≠ oppose

hunch NOUN = **feeling**, idea, impression, suspicion, intuition, premonition, inkling, presentiment
▷ VERB = **crouch**, bend, curve, arch, draw in

hunger NOUN 1 = **appetite**, emptiness, hungriness, ravenousness 2 = **starvation**, famine, malnutrition, undernourishment 3 = **desire**, appetite, craving, ache, lust, yearning, itch, thirst ▷ PHRASE: **hunger for** or **after something** = **want**, desire, crave, long for, wish for, yearn for, hanker after, ache for

hungry ADJECTIVE 1 = **starving**, ravenous, famished, starved, empty, voracious, peckish (*informal, chiefly Brit.*) 2 = **eager**, keen, craving, yearning, greedy, avid, desirous, covetous

hunk NOUN = **lump**, piece, chunk, block, mass, wedge, slab, nugget

hunt VERB = **stalk**, track, chase, pursue, trail, hound
▷ NOUN = **search**, hunting, investigation, chase, pursuit, quest ▷ PHRASE: **hunt for something** *or* **someone** = **search for**, look for, seek for, forage for, scour for, fossick for (*Austral.* & *N.Z.*), ferret about for

hurdle NOUN 1 = **obstacle**, difficulty, barrier, handicap, hazard, uphill (*S. African*), obstruction, stumbling block 2 = **fence**, barrier, barricade

hurl VERB = **throw**, fling, launch, cast, pitch, toss, propel, sling

hurricane NOUN = **storm**, gale, tornado, cyclone, typhoon, tempest, twister (*U.S. informal*), willy-willy (*Austral.*)

hurried ADJECTIVE 1 = **hasty**, quick, brief, rushed, short, swift, speedy 2 = **rushed**, perfunctory, speedy, hasty, cursory

hurry VERB 1 = **rush**, fly, dash, scurry, scoot ≠ dawdle 2 = **make haste**, rush, get a move on (*informal*), step on it (*informal*), crack on (*informal*)
▷ NOUN = **rush**, haste, speed, urgency, flurry, quickness

≠ slowness

hurt VERB 1 = **injure**, damage, wound, cut, disable, bruise, scrape, impair ≠ heal 2 = **ache**, be sore, be painful, burn, smart, sting, throb, be tender 3 = **harm**, injure, ill-treat, maltreat 4 = **upset**, distress, pain, wound, annoy, grieve, sadden
▷ NOUN = **distress**, suffering, pain, grief, misery, sorrow, heartache, wretchedness
≠ happiness
▷ ADJECTIVE 1 = **injured**, wounded, damaged, harmed, cut, bruised, scarred ≠ healed 2 = **upset**, wounded, crushed, offended, aggrieved, tooshie (*Austral. slang*) ≠ calmed

hurtle VERB = **rush**, charge, race, shoot, fly, speed, tear, crash

husband NOUN = **partner**, spouse, mate, better half (*humorous*)
▷ VERB = **conserve**, budget, save, store, hoard, economize on, use economically ≠ squander

hush VERB = **quieten**, silence, mute, muzzle, shush
▷ NOUN = **quiet**, silence, calm, peace, tranquillity, stillness

hut NOUN 1 = **cabin**, shack, shanty, hovel, whare (*N.Z.*) 2 = **shed**, outhouse, lean-to, lockup

hybrid NOUN 1 = **crossbreed**, cross, mixture, compound, composite, amalgam, mongrel, half-breed 2 = **mixture**, compound, composite, amalgam

hygiene NOUN = **cleanliness**,

sanitation, disinfection, sterility

hymn NOUN 1 = **religious song**,
song of praise, carol, chant,
anthem, psalm, paean 2 = **song
of praise**, anthem, paean

hype NOUN = **publicity**,
promotion, plugging (*informal*),
razzmatazz (*slang*), brouhaha,
ballyhoo (*informal*)

hypocrisy NOUN = **insincerity**,
pretence, deception, cant,
duplicity, deceitfulness
≠ sincerity

hypothesis NOUN = **theory**,
premise, proposition,
assumption, thesis, postulate,
supposition

hysteria NOUN = **frenzy**, panic,
madness, agitation, delirium,
hysterics

hysterical ADJECTIVE 1 = **frenzied**,
frantic, raving, distracted,
distraught, crazed, overwrought,
berko (*Austral. slang*) ≠ calm
2 (*informal*) = **hilarious**,
uproarious, side-splitting,
comical ≠ serious

h

I i

icy ADJECTIVE 1 = **cold**, freezing, bitter, biting, raw, chill, chilly, frosty ≠ hot 2 = **slippery**, glassy, slippy (*informal* or *dialect*), like a sheet of glass 3 = **unfriendly**, cold, distant, aloof, frosty, frigid, unwelcoming ≠ friendly

idea NOUN 1 = **notion**, thought, view, teaching, opinion, belief, conclusion, hypothesis 2 = **understanding**, thought, view, opinion, concept, impression, perception 3 = **intention**, aim, purpose, object, plan, objective

● WORD POWER
● It is usually considered correct
● to say that someone has *the*
● *idea of doing something*, rather
● than *the idea to do something*. For
● example, you would say *he had*
● *the idea of taking a holiday*, not *he*
● *had the idea to take a holiday*.

ideal NOUN 1 = **epitome**, standard, dream, pattern, perfection, last word, paragon 2 = **model**, prototype, paradigm
▷ ADJECTIVE = **perfect**, best, model, classic, supreme, ultimate, archetypal, exemplary ≠ imperfect

ideally ADVERB = **in a perfect world**, all things being equal, if you had your way

identical ADJECTIVE = **alike**, matching, twin, duplicate, indistinguishable, interchangeable ≠ different

identification NOUN 1 = **discovery**, recognition, determining, establishment, diagnosis, confirmation, divination 2 = **recognition**, naming, distinguishing, confirmation, pinpointing 3 = **connection**, relationship, association 4 = **understanding**, relationship, involvement, unity, sympathy, empathy, rapport, fellow feeling

identify VERB 1 = **recognize**, place, name, remember, spot, diagnose, make out, pinpoint 2 = **establish**, spot, confirm, demonstrate, pick out, certify, verify, mark out, flag up
▷ PHRASES: **identify something or someone with something or someone** = **equate with**, associate with; **identify with someone** = **relate to**, respond to, feel for, empathize with

identity NOUN = **individuality**, self, character, personality, existence, originality, separateness

idiot NOUN = **fool**, moron, twit (*informal, chiefly Brit.*), chump, imbecile, cretin, simpleton, halfwit, galah (*Austral. & N.Z. informal*), dorba *or* dorb (*Austral. slang*), bogan (*Austral. slang*)

idle ADJECTIVE 1 = **unoccupied**,

unemployed, redundant, inactive ≠ occupied **2** = **unused**, inactive, out of order, out of service **3** = **lazy**, slow, slack, sluggish, lax, negligent, inactive, inert ≠ busy **4** = **useless**, vain, pointless, unsuccessful, ineffective, worthless, futile, fruitless ≠ useful
▷ VERB *often with* **away** = **fritter**, lounge, potter, loaf, dally, loiter, dawdle, laze

idol NOUN **1** = **hero**, pin-up, favourite, pet, darling, beloved (*slang*), fave (*informal*) **2** = **graven image**, god, deity

if CONJUNCTION **1** = **provided**, assuming, given that, providing, supposing, presuming, on condition that, as long as **2** = **when**, whenever, every time, any time

ignite VERB **1** = **catch fire**, burn, burst into flames, inflame, flare up, take fire **2** = **set fire to**, light, set alight, torch, kindle

ignorance NOUN **1** = **lack of education**, stupidity, foolishness ≠ knowledge **2** *with* **of** = **unawareness of**, inexperience of, unfamiliarity with, innocence of, unconsciousness of

ignorant ADJECTIVE **1** = **uneducated**, illiterate ≠ educated **2** = **insensitive**, rude, crass **3** *with* **of** = **uninformed of**, unaware of, oblivious to, innocent of, unconscious of, inexperienced of, uninitiated about, unenlightened about

≠ informed

ignore VERB **1** = **pay no attention to**, neglect, disregard, slight, overlook, scorn, spurn, rebuff ≠ pay attention to **2** = **overlook**, discount, disregard, reject, neglect, shrug off, pass over, brush aside **3** = **snub**, slight, rebuff

ill ADJECTIVE **1** = **unwell**, sick, poorly (*informal*), diseased, weak, crook (*Austral. & N.Z. slang*), ailing, frail ≠ healthy **2** = **harmful**, bad, damaging, evil, foul, unfortunate, destructive, detrimental ≠ favourable
▷ NOUN = **problem**, trouble, suffering, worry, injury, hurt, strain, harm ≠ good
▷ ADVERB **1** = **badly**, unfortunately, unfavourably, inauspiciously **2** = **hardly**, barely, scarcely, just, only just, by no means, at a push ≠ well

illegal ADJECTIVE = **unlawful**, banned, forbidden, prohibited, criminal, outlawed, illicit, unlicensed ≠ legal

illicit ADJECTIVE **1** = **illegal**, criminal, prohibited, unlawful, illegitimate, unlicensed, unauthorized, felonious ≠ legal **2** = **forbidden**, improper, immoral, guilty, clandestine, furtive

illness NOUN = **sickness**, disease, infection, disorder, bug (*informal*), ailment, affliction, malady

illuminate VERB **1** = **light up**, brighten ≠ darken **2** = **explain**, interpret, make clear, clarify, clear up, enlighten, shed light on, elucidate ≠ obscure

illuminating ADJECTIVE
= **informative**, revealing, enlightening, helpful, explanatory, instructive ≠ confusing

illusion NOUN 1 = **delusion**, misconception, misapprehension, fancy, fallacy, false impression, false belief 2 = **false impression**, appearance, impression, deception, fallacy ≠ reality 3 = **fantasy**, vision, hallucination, trick, spectre, mirage, daydream, apparition

illustrate VERB 1 = **demonstrate**, emphasize 2 = **explain**, sum up, summarize, bring home, point up, elucidate

illustrated ADJECTIVE = **pictured**, decorated, pictorial

illustration NOUN 1 = **example**, case, instance, sample, specimen, exemplar 2 = **picture**, drawing, painting, image, print, plate, figure, portrait

image NOUN 1 = **thought**, idea, vision, concept, impression, perception, mental picture, conceptualization 2 = **figure of speech** 3 = **reflection**, likeness, mirror image 4 = **figure**, idol, icon, fetish, talisman 5 = **replica**, copy, reproduction, counterpart, clone, facsimile, spitting image (*informal*), Doppelgänger 6 = **picture**, photo, photograph, representation, reproduction, snapshot

imaginary ADJECTIVE = **fictional**, made-up, invented, imagined, unreal, hypothetical, fictitious, illusory ≠ real

imagination NOUN
1 = **creativity**, vision, invention, ingenuity, enterprise, originality, inventiveness, resourcefulness 2 = **mind's eye**, fancy

imaginative ADJECTIVE
= **creative**, original, inspired, enterprising, clever, ingenious, inventive ≠ unimaginative

imagine VERB 1 = **envisage**, see, picture, plan, think of, conjure up, envision, visualize 2 = **believe**, think, suppose, assume, suspect, guess (*informal, chiefly U.S. & Canad.*), take it, reckon

imitate VERB 1 = **copy**, follow, repeat, echo, emulate, ape, simulate, mirror 2 = **do an impression of**, mimic, copy

imitation NOUN 1 = **replica**, fake, reproduction, sham, forgery, counterfeiting, likeness, duplication 2 = **copying**, resemblance, mimicry 3 = **impression**, impersonation ▷ ADJECTIVE = **artificial**, mock, reproduction, dummy, synthetic, man-made, simulated, sham ≠ real

immaculate ADJECTIVE 1 = **clean**, spotless, neat, spruce, squeaky-clean, spick-and-span ≠ dirty 2 = **pure**, perfect, impeccable, flawless, faultless, above reproach ≠ corrupt 3 = **perfect**, flawless, impeccable, faultless, unblemished, untarnished,

unexceptionable ≠ tainted
immediate ADJECTIVE
  1 = **instant**, prompt,
  instantaneous, quick, on-
  the-spot, split-second ≠ later
  2 = **nearest**, next, direct, close,
  near ≠ far
immediately ADVERB = **at once**,
  now, instantly, straight away,
  directly, promptly, right away,
  without delay
immense ADJECTIVE = **huge**,
  great, massive, vast, enormous,
  extensive, tremendous, very big,
  supersize ≠ tiny
immerse VERB 1 = **engross**,
  involve, absorb, busy, occupy,
  engage 2 = **plunge**, dip,
  submerge, sink, duck, bathe,
  douse, dunk
immigrant NOUN = **settler**,
  incomer, alien, stranger, outsider,
  newcomer, migrant, emigrant
imminent ADJECTIVE = **near**,
  coming, close, approaching,
  gathering, forthcoming, looming,
  impending ≠ remote
immoral ADJECTIVE = **wicked**, bad,
  wrong, corrupt, indecent, sinful,
  unethical, depraved ≠ moral
immortal ADJECTIVE 1 = **timeless**,
  eternal, everlasting, lasting,
  traditional, classic, enduring,
  perennial ≠ ephemeral
  2 = **undying**, eternal,
  imperishable, deathless ≠ mortal
  ▷ NOUN 1 = **hero**, genius, great
  2 = **god**, goddess, deity, divine
  being, immortal being, atua (*N.Z.*)
immune ▷ PHRASES: immune

from = **exempt from**, free from;
  immune to 1 = **resistant to**,
  free from, protected from, safe
  from, not open to, spared from,
  secure against, invulnerable to
  2 = **unaffected by**, invulnerable
  to
immunity NOUN 1 = **exemption**,
  amnesty, indemnity, release,
  freedom, invulnerability 2 *with*
  to = **resistance**, protection,
  resilience, inoculation,
  immunization ≠ susceptibility
impact NOUN 1 = **effect**,
  influence, consequences,
  impression, repercussions,
  ramifications 2 = **collision**,
  contact, crash, knock, stroke,
  smash, bump, thump
  ▷ VERB = **hit**, strike, crash, clash,
  crush, ram, smack, collide
impair VERB = **worsen**,
  reduce, damage, injure, harm,
  undermine, weaken, diminish
  ≠ improve
impaired ADJECTIVE = **damaged**,
  flawed, faulty, defective,
  imperfect, unsound
impasse NOUN = **deadlock**,
  stalemate, standstill, dead end,
  standoff
impatient ADJECTIVE 1 = **cross**,
  annoyed, irritated, prickly,
  touchy, bad-tempered, intolerant,
  ill-tempered ≠ easy-going
  2 = **eager**, longing, keen, anxious,
  hungry, enthusiastic, restless,
  avid ≠ calm
impeccable ADJECTIVE
  = **faultless**, perfect, immaculate,

flawless, squeaky-clean, unblemished, unimpeachable, irreproachable ≠ flawed

impending ADJECTIVE = **looming**, coming, approaching, near, forthcoming, imminent, upcoming, in the pipeline

imperative ADJECTIVE = **urgent**, essential, pressing, vital, crucial ≠ unnecessary

imperial ADJECTIVE = **royal**, regal, kingly, queenly, princely, sovereign, majestic, monarchial

impetus NOUN 1 = **incentive**, push, spur, motivation, impulse, stimulus, catalyst, goad 2 = **force**, power, energy, momentum

implant VERB 1 = **insert**, fix, graft 2 = **instil**, infuse, inculcate

implement VERB = **carry out**, effect, carry through, complete, apply, perform, realize, fulfil ≠ hinder
▷ NOUN = **tool**, machine, device, instrument, appliance, apparatus, gadget, utensil

implicate VERB = **incriminate**, involve, embroil, entangle, inculpate ≠ dissociate
▷ PHRASE: **implicate something** or **someone in something** = **involve in**, associate with

implication NOUN
1 = **suggestion**, hint, inference, meaning, significance, presumption, overtone, innuendo
2 = **consequence**, result, development, upshot

implicit ADJECTIVE 1 = **implied**, understood, suggested, hinted

at, taken for granted, unspoken, inferred, tacit ≠ explicit
2 = **inherent**, underlying, intrinsic, latent, ingrained, inbuilt
3 = **absolute**, full, complete, firm, fixed, constant, utter, outright

implied ADJECTIVE = **suggested**, indirect, hinted at, implicit, unspoken, tacit, undeclared, unstated

imply VERB 1 = **suggest**, hint, insinuate, indicate, intimate, signify 2 = **involve**, mean, entail, require, indicate, point to, signify, presuppose

import VERB = **bring in**, buy in, ship in, introduce
▷ NOUN 1 (*formal*) = **significance**, concern, value, weight, consequence, substance, moment, magnitude
2 = **meaning**, implication, significance, sense, intention, substance, drift, thrust

importance NOUN
1 = **significance**, interest, concern, moment, value, weight, import, consequence
2 = **prestige**, standing, status, rule, authority, influence, distinction, esteem, mana (*N.Z.*)

important ADJECTIVE
1 = **significant**, critical, substantial, urgent, serious, far-reaching, momentous, seminal ≠ unimportant 2 = **powerful**, prominent, commanding, dominant, influential, eminent, high-ranking, authoritative, skookum (*Canad.*)

impose ▷ PHRASE: **impose something on** or **upon someone** 1 = **levy**, introduce, charge, establish, fix, institute, decree, ordain 2 = **inflict**, force, enforce, visit, press, apply, thrust, saddle (someone) with

imposing ADJECTIVE = **impressive**, striking, grand, powerful, commanding, awesome, majestic, dignified ≠ unimposing

imposition NOUN 1 = **application**, introduction, levying 2 = **intrusion**, liberty, presumption

impossible ADJECTIVE 1 = **not possible**, out of the question, impracticable, unfeasible 2 = **unachievable**, out of the question, vain, unthinkable, inconceivable, far-fetched, unworkable, implausible ≠ possible 3 = **absurd**, crazy (informal), ridiculous, outrageous, ludicrous, unreasonable, preposterous, farcical

impotence NOUN = **powerlessness**, inability, helplessness, weakness, incompetence, paralysis, frailty, incapacity ≠ powerfulness

impoverish VERB 1 = **bankrupt**, ruin, beggar, break 2 = **deplete**, drain, exhaust, diminish, use up, sap, wear out, reduce

impoverished ADJECTIVE = **poor**, needy, destitute, bankrupt, poverty-stricken, impecunious, penurious ≠ rich

impress VERB = **excite**, move, strike, touch, affect, inspire, amaze, overcome ▷ PHRASE: **impress something on** or **upon someone** = **stress**, bring home to, instil in, drum into, knock into, emphasize to, fix in, inculcate in

impression NOUN 1 = **idea**, feeling, thought, sense, view, assessment, judgment, reaction 2 = **effect**, influence, impact 3 = **imitation**, parody, impersonation, send-up (Brit. informal), takeoff (informal) 4 = **mark**, imprint, stamp, outline, hollow, dent, indentation

impressive ADJECTIVE = **grand**, striking, splendid, good, great (informal), fine, powerful, exciting ≠ unimpressive

imprint NOUN = **mark**, impression, stamp, indentation ▷ VERB = **engrave**, print, stamp, impress, etch, emboss

imprison VERB = **jail**, confine, detain, lock up, put away, intern, incarcerate, send down (informal) ≠ free

imprisoned ADJECTIVE = **jailed**, confined, locked up, inside (slang), in jail, captive, behind bars, incarcerated

imprisonment NOUN = **confinement**, custody, detention, captivity, incarceration

improbable ADJECTIVE 1 = **doubtful**, unlikely, dubious, questionable, fanciful, far-fetched, implausible ≠ probable

2 = **unconvincing**, weak, unbelievable, preposterous ≠ convincing

improper ADJECTIVE
1 = **inappropriate**, unfit, unsuitable, out of place, unwarranted, uncalled-for ≠ appropriate 2 = **indecent**, vulgar, suggestive, unseemly, untoward, risqué, smutty, unbecoming ≠ decent

improve VERB 1 = **enhance**, better, add to, upgrade, touch up, ameliorate ≠ worsen 2 = **get better**, pick up, develop, advance

improvement NOUN
1 = **enhancement**, advancement, betterment 2 = **advance**, development, progress, recovery, upswing

improvise VERB 1 = **devise**, contrive, concoct, throw together 2 = **ad-lib**, invent, busk, wing it (*informal*), play it by ear (*informal*), extemporize, speak off the cuff (*informal*)

impulse NOUN = **urge**, longing, wish, notion, yearning, inclination, itch, whim

inaccurate ADJECTIVE
= **incorrect**, wrong, mistaken, faulty, unreliable, defective, erroneous, unsound ≠ accurate

inadequacy NOUN 1 = **shortage**, poverty, dearth, paucity, insufficiency, meagreness, scantiness 2 = **incompetence**, inability, deficiency, incapacity, ineffectiveness 3 = **shortcoming**, failing, weakness, defect, imperfection

inadequate ADJECTIVE
1 = **insufficient**, meagre, poor, lacking, scant, sparse, sketchy ≠ adequate 2 = **incapable**, incompetent, faulty, deficient, unqualified, not up to scratch (*informal*) ≠ capable

inadvertently ADVERB
= **unintentionally**, accidentally, by accident, mistakenly, unwittingly, by mistake, involuntarily ≠ deliberately

inaugural ADJECTIVE = **first**, opening, initial, maiden, introductory

incarnation NOUN
= **embodiment**, manifestation, epitome, type, personification

incense VERB = **anger**, infuriate, enrage, irritate, madden, inflame, rile (*informal*), make your blood boil (*informal*)

incensed ADJECTIVE = **angry**, furious, fuming, infuriated, enraged, maddened, indignant, irate, tooshie (*Austral. slang*), off the air (*Austral. slang*)

incentive NOUN = **inducement**, encouragement, spur, lure, bait, motivation, carrot (*informal*), stimulus ≠ disincentive

incident NOUN 1 = **disturbance**, scene, clash, disorder, confrontation, brawl, fracas, commotion 2 = **happening**, event, affair, business, fact, matter, occasion, episode 3 = **adventure**, drama, excitement, crisis, spectacle

incidentally ADVERB = **by the way**, in passing, en passant, parenthetically, by the bye

inclination NOUN 1 = **desire**, longing, aspiration, craving, hankering 2 = **tendency**, liking, disposition, penchant, propensity, predisposition, predilection, proclivity ≠ aversion

incline VERB = **predispose**, influence, persuade, prejudice, sway, dispose
▷ NOUN = **slope**, rise, dip, grade, descent, ascent, gradient

inclined ADJECTIVE 1 = **disposed**, given, prone, likely, liable, apt, predisposed 2 = **willing**, minded, disposed

include VERB 1 = **contain**, involve, incorporate, cover, consist of, take in, embrace, comprise ≠ exclude 2 = **count** 3 = **add**, enter, put in, insert

inclusion NOUN = **addition**, incorporation, introduction, insertion ≠ exclusion

inclusive ADJECTIVE = **comprehensive**, general, global, sweeping, blanket, umbrella, across-the-board, all-embracing ≠ limited

income NOUN = **revenue**, earnings, pay, returns, profits, wages, yield, proceeds

incoming ADJECTIVE 1 = **arriving**, landing, approaching, entering, returning, homeward ≠ departing 2 = **new**

incompatible ADJECTIVE = **inconsistent**, conflicting, contradictory, incongruous, unsuited, mismatched ≠ compatible

incompetence NOUN = **ineptitude**, inability, inadequacy, incapacity, ineffectiveness, uselessness, unfitness, incapability

incompetent ADJECTIVE = **inept**, useless, incapable, floundering, bungling, unfit, ineffectual, inexpert ≠ competent

incomplete ADJECTIVE = **unfinished**, partial, wanting, deficient, imperfect, fragmentary, half-pie (*N.Z. informal*) ≠ complete

inconsistency NOUN 1 = **unreliability**, instability, unpredictability, fickleness, unsteadiness 2 = **incompatibility**, discrepancy, disparity, disagreement, variance, divergence, incongruity

inconsistent ADJECTIVE 1 = **changeable**, variable, unpredictable, unstable, erratic, fickle, capricious, unsteady ≠ consistent 2 = **incompatible**, conflicting, at odds, contradictory, incongruous, discordant, out of step, irreconcilable ≠ compatible

inconvenience NOUN = **trouble**, difficulty, bother, fuss, disadvantage, disturbance, disruption, nuisance, uphill (*S. African*)
▷ VERB = **trouble**, bother, disturb, upset, disrupt, put out, discommode

incorporate VERB 1 = **include**, contain, take in, embrace, integrate, encompass, assimilate, comprise of 2 = **integrate**, include, absorb, merge, fuse, assimilate, subsume 3 = **blend**, combine, compound, mingle

incorrect ADJECTIVE = **false**, wrong, mistaken, flawed, faulty, inaccurate, untrue, erroneous ≠ correct

increase VERB 1 = **raise**, extend, boost, expand, develop, advance, strengthen, widen ≠ decrease 2 = **grow**, develop, spread, expand, swell, enlarge, escalate, multiply ≠ shrink ▷ NOUN = **growth**, rise, development, gain, expansion, extension, proliferation, enlargement

increasingly ADVERB = **progressively**, more and more

incredible ADJECTIVE 1 (informal) = **amazing**, wonderful, stunning, extraordinary, overwhelming, astonishing, staggering, sensational (informal) 2 = **unbelievable**, unthinkable, improbable, inconceivable, preposterous, unconvincing, unimaginable, far-fetched

incumbent NOUN = **holder**, keeper, bearer ▷ ADJECTIVE (formal) = **obligatory**, required, necessary, essential, binding, compulsory, mandatory, imperative

incur VERB = **sustain**, experience, suffer, gain, earn, collect, meet

with, provoke

indecent ADJECTIVE 1 = **obscene**, lewd, dirty, inappropriate, rude, crude, filthy, improper ≠ decent 2 = **unbecoming**, unsuitable, vulgar, unseemly, undignified, indecorous ≠ proper

indeed ADVERB 1 = **certainly**, yes, definitely, surely, truly, undoubtedly, without doubt, indisputably 2 = **really**, actually, in fact, certainly, genuinely, in truth, in actuality

indefinitely ADVERB = **endlessly**, continually, for ever, ad infinitum

independence NOUN = **freedom**, liberty, autonomy, sovereignty, self-rule, self-sufficiency, self-reliance, rangatiratanga (N.Z.) ≠ subjugation

independent ADJECTIVE 1 = **separate**, unattached, uncontrolled, unconstrained ≠ controlled 2 = **self-sufficient**, free, liberated, self-contained, self-reliant, self-supporting 3 = **self-governing**, free, autonomous, liberated, sovereign, self-determining, nonaligned ≠ subject

independently ADVERB = **separately**, alone, solo, on your own, by yourself, unaided, individually, autonomously

indicate VERB 1 = **show**, suggest, reveal, display, demonstrate, point to, imply, manifest, flag up 2 = **imply**, suggest, hint, intimate, signify, insinuate 3 = **point to**, point out, specify, gesture towards, designate 4 = **register**, show, record, read, express, display, demonstrate

indication NOUN = **sign**, mark, evidence, suggestion, symptom, hint, clue, manifestation

indicator NOUN = **sign**, mark, measure, guide, signal, symbol, meter, gauge

indict VERB = **charge**, accuse, prosecute, summon, impeach, arraign

indictment NOUN = **charge**, allegation, prosecution, accusation, impeachment, summons, arraignment

indifference NOUN = **disregard**, apathy, negligence, detachment, coolness, coldness, nonchalance, aloofness ≠ concern

indifferent ADJECTIVE
1 = **unconcerned**, detached, cold, cool, callous, aloof, unmoved, unsympathetic ≠ concerned
2 = **mediocre**, ordinary, moderate, so-so (informal), passable, undistinguished, no great shakes (informal), half-pie (N.Z. informal) ≠ excellent

indignation NOUN
= **resentment**, anger, rage, exasperation, pique, umbrage

indirect ADJECTIVE 1 = **related**, secondary, subsidiary, incidental, unintended 2 = **circuitous**, roundabout, curving, wandering, rambling, deviant, meandering, tortuous ≠ direct

indispensable ADJECTIVE
= **essential**, necessary, needed, key, vital, crucial, imperative, requisite ≠ dispensable

individual ADJECTIVE
1 = **separate**, independent, isolated, lone, solitary
≠ collective 2 = **unique**, special, fresh, novel, exclusive, singular, idiosyncratic, unorthodox
≠ conventional
▷ NOUN = **person**, being, human, unit, character, soul, creature

individually ADVERB
= **separately**, independently, singly, one by one, one at a time

induce VERB 1 = **cause**, produce, create, effect, lead to, occasion, generate, bring about ≠ prevent
2 = **persuade**, encourage, influence, convince, urge, prompt, sway, entice ≠ dissuade

indulge VERB 1 = **gratify**, satisfy, feed, give way to, yield to, pander to, gladden 2 = **spoil**, pamper, cosset, humour, give in to, coddle, mollycoddle, overindulge
▷ PHRASE: indulge yourself
= **treat yourself**, splash out, spoil yourself, luxuriate in something, overindulge yourself

indulgence NOUN 1 = **luxury**, treat, extravagance, favour, privilege 2 = **gratification**, satisfaction, fulfilment, appeasement, satiation

industrialist NOUN = **capitalist**, tycoon, magnate, manufacturer, captain of industry, big businessman

industry NOUN 1 = **business**, production, manufacturing,

trade, commerce **2** = **trade**, world, business, service, line, field, profession, occupation
3 = **diligence**, effort, labour, hard work, trouble, activity, application, endeavour

ineffective ADJECTIVE
1 = **unproductive**, useless, futile, vain, unsuccessful, pointless, fruitless, ineffectual ≠ effective
2 = **inefficient**, useless, poor, powerless, unfit, worthless, inept, impotent

inefficient ADJECTIVE
1 = **wasteful**, uneconomical, profligate **2** = **incompetent**, inept, weak, bungling, ineffectual, disorganized ≠ efficient

inequality NOUN = **disparity**, prejudice, difference, bias, diversity, irregularity, unevenness, disproportion

inevitable ADJECTIVE
= **unavoidable**, inescapable, inexorable, sure, certain, fixed, assured, fated ≠ avoidable

inevitably ADVERB
= **unavoidably**, naturally, necessarily, surely, certainly, as a result, automatically, consequently

inexpensive ADJECTIVE = **cheap**, reasonable, budget, bargain, modest, economical ≠ expensive

inexperienced ADJECTIVE = **new**, green, raw, callow, immature, untried, unpractised, unversed ≠ experienced

infamous ADJECTIVE = **notorious**, ignominious, disreputable, ill-

famed ≠ esteemed

infancy NOUN = **beginnings**, start, birth, roots, seeds, origins, dawn, outset ≠ end

infant NOUN = **baby**, child, babe, toddler, tot, bairn (*Scot.*), littlie (*Austral. informal*), ankle-biter (*Austral. slang*), tacker (*Austral. slang*)

infect VERB **1** = **contaminate**
2 = **pollute**, poison, corrupt, contaminate, taint, defile
3 = **affect**, move, upset, overcome, stir, disturb

infection NOUN = **disease**, condition, complaint, illness, virus, disorder, corruption, poison

infectious ADJECTIVE = **catching**, spreading, contagious, communicable, virulent, transmittable

inferior ADJECTIVE = **lower**, minor, secondary, subsidiary, lesser, humble, subordinate, lowly ≠ superior
▷ NOUN = **underling**, junior, subordinate, lesser, menial, minion

infertility NOUN = **sterility**, barrenness, unproductiveness, infecundity

infiltrate VERB = **penetrate**, pervade, permeate, percolate, filter through to, make inroads into, sneak into (*informal*), insinuate yourself

infinite ADJECTIVE **1** = **vast**, enormous, immense, countless, measureless **2** = **limitless**, endless, unlimited, eternal, never-ending, boundless, everlasting, inexhaustible ≠ finite

inflame VERB = **enrage**, stimulate, provoke, excite, anger, arouse, rouse, infuriate ≠ calm

inflamed ADJECTIVE = **swollen**, sore, red, hot, infected, fevered

inflate VERB 1 = **blow up**, pump up, swell, dilate, distend, bloat, puff up or out ≠ deflate 2 = **increase**, expand, enlarge ≠ diminish 3 = **exaggerate**, embroider, embellish, enlarge, amplify, overstate, overestimate, overemphasize

inflated ADJECTIVE = **exaggerated**, swollen, overblown

inflation NOUN = **increase**, expansion, extension, swelling, escalation, enlargement

inflict VERB = **impose**, administer, visit, apply, deliver, levy, wreak, mete or deal out

influence NOUN 1 = **control**, power, authority, direction, command, domination, supremacy, mastery, mana (*N.Z.*) 2 = **power**, authority, pull (*informal*), importance, prestige, clout (*informal*), leverage 3 = **spell**, hold, power, weight, magic, sway, allure, magnetism ▷ VERB 1 = **affect**, have an effect on, have an impact on, control, concern, direct, guide, bear upon 2 = **persuade**, prompt, urge, induce, entice, coax, incite, instigate

influential ADJECTIVE 1 = **important**, powerful, telling, leading, inspiring, potent, authoritative, weighty ≠ unimportant 2 = **instrumental**, important, significant, crucial

influx NOUN = **arrival**, rush, invasion, incursion, inundation, inrush

inform VERB = **tell**, advise, notify, instruct, enlighten, communicate to, tip someone off ▷ PHRASE: **inform on someone** = **betray**, denounce, shop (*slang, chiefly Brit.*), give someone away, incriminate, blow the whistle on (*informal*), grass on (*Brit. slang*), double-cross (*informal*), dob someone in (*Austral. & N.Z. slang*)

informal ADJECTIVE 1 = **natural**, relaxed, casual, familiar, unofficial, laid-back, easy-going, colloquial 2 = **relaxed**, easy, comfortable, simple, natural, casual, cosy, laid-back (*informal*) ≠ formal 3 = **casual**, comfortable, leisure, everyday, simple 4 = **unofficial**, irregular ≠ official

information NOUN = **facts**, news, report, message, notice, knowledge, data, intelligence, drum (*Austral. informal*), heads up (*U.S. & Canad.*)

informative ADJECTIVE = **instructive**, revealing, educational, forthcoming, illuminating, enlightening, chatty, communicative

informed ADJECTIVE = **knowledgeable**, up to date,

enlightened, learned, expert, familiar, versed, in the picture

infuriate VERB = **enrage**, anger, provoke, irritate, incense, madden, exasperate, rile ≠ soothe

infuriating ADJECTIVE = **annoying**, irritating, provoking, galling, maddening, exasperating, vexatious

ingenious ADJECTIVE = **creative**, original, brilliant, clever, bright, shrewd, inventive, crafty ≠ unimaginative

ingredient NOUN = **component**, part, element, feature, piece, unit, item, aspect

inhabit VERB = **live in**, occupy, populate, reside in, dwell in, abide in

inhabitant NOUN = **occupant**, resident, citizen, local, native, tenant, inmate, dweller

inhabited ADJECTIVE = **populated**, peopled, occupied, developed, settled, tenanted, colonized

inhale VERB = **breathe in**, gasp, draw in, suck in, respire ≠ exhale

inherent ADJECTIVE = **intrinsic**, natural, essential, native, fundamental, hereditary, instinctive, innate ≠ extraneous

inherit VERB = **be left**, come into, be willed, succeed to, fall heir to

inheritance NOUN = **legacy**, heritage, bequest, birthright, patrimony

inhibit VERB 1 = **hinder**, check, frustrate, curb, restrain, constrain, obstruct, impede ≠ further 2 = **prevent**, stop, frustrate ≠ allow

inhibited ADJECTIVE = **shy**, reserved, guarded, subdued, repressed, constrained, self-conscious, reticent ≠ uninhibited

initial ADJECTIVE = **opening**, first, earliest, beginning, primary, maiden, introductory, embryonic ≠ final

initially ADVERB = **at first**, first, firstly, originally, primarily, in the beginning, at or in the beginning

initiate VERB 1 = **begin**, start, open, launch, kick off (informal), embark on, originate, set about 2 = **introduce**, admit, enlist, enrol, launch, establish, invest, recruit ▷ NOUN = **novice**, member, pupil, convert, amateur, newcomer, beginner, trainee ▷ PHRASE: **initiate someone into something** = **instruct in**, train in, coach in, acquaint with, drill in, make aware of, teach about, tutor in

initiative NOUN 1 = **advantage**, start, lead, upper hand 2 = **enterprise**, drive, energy, leadership, ambition, daring, enthusiasm, dynamism

inject VERB 1 = **vaccinate**, administer, inoculate 2 = **introduce**, bring in, insert, instil, infuse, breathe

injection NOUN 1 = **vaccination**, shot (informal), jab (informal), dose, booster, immunization, inoculation 2 = **introduction**,

investment, insertion,
advancement, dose, infusion

injunction NOUN = **order**, ruling,
command, instruction, mandate,
precept, exhortation

injure VERB 1 = **hurt**, wound,
harm, damage, smash, crush,
mar, shatter, mangulate (*Austral.
slang*) 2 = **damage**, harm, ruin,
wreck, spoil, impair, crool *or* cruel
(*Austral. slang*) 3 = **undermine**,
damage

injured ADJECTIVE = **hurt**,
damaged, wounded, broken, cut,
crushed, disabled, challenged,
weakened, crook (*Austral. & N.Z.
slang*)

injury NOUN 1 = **wound**, cut,
damage, trauma (*pathology*),
gash, lesion, laceration 2 = **harm**,
suffering, damage, ill, hurt,
disability, misfortune, affliction
3 = **wrong**, offence, insult,
detriment, disservice

injustice NOUN 1 = **unfairness**,
discrimination, prejudice,
bias, inequality, oppression,
intolerance, bigotry ≠ justice
2 = **wrong**, injury, crime,
error, offence, sin, misdeed,
transgression

inland ADJECTIVE = **interior**,
internal, upcountry

inner ADJECTIVE 1 = **inside**,
internal, interior, inward ≠ outer
2 = **central**, middle, internal,
interior 3 = **hidden**, deep, secret,
underlying, obscure, repressed,
unrevealed ≠ obvious

innocence NOUN 1 = **naiveté**,

simplicity, inexperience, credulity,
gullibility, ingenuousness,
artlessness, unworldliness
≠ worldliness 2 = **blamelessness**,
clean hands, uprightness,
irreproachability, guiltlessness
≠ guilt 3 = **chastity**, virtue,
purity, modesty, celibacy,
continence, maidenhood

innocent ADJECTIVE 1 = **not
guilty**, in the clear, blameless,
clean, honest, uninvolved,
irreproachable, guiltless ≠ guilty
2 = **naive**, open, trusting,
simple, childlike, gullible,
unsophisticated, unworldly
≠ worldly 3 = **harmless**,
innocuous, inoffensive, well-
meant, unobjectionable, well-
intentioned

innovation NOUN 1 = **change**,
revolution, departure,
introduction, variation,
transformation, upheaval,
alteration 2 = **newness**,
novelty, originality, freshness,
modernization, uniqueness

inquest NOUN = **inquiry**,
investigation, probe, inquisition

inquire *or* **enquire** VERB = **ask**,
question, query, quiz ▷ PHRASE:
inquire into = **investigate**, study,
examine, research, explore, look
into, probe into, make inquiries
into

inquiry *or* **enquiry** NOUN
1 = **question**, query, investigation
2 = **investigation**, study,
review, survey, examination,
probe, inspection, exploration

3 = **research**, investigation, analysis, inspection, exploration, interrogation

insane ADJECTIVE **1** = **mad**, crazy, mentally ill, crazed, demented, deranged, out of your mind, off the air (*Austral. slang*), porangi (*N.Z.*) ≠ sane **2** = **stupid**, foolish, daft (*informal*), irresponsible, irrational, senseless, preposterous, impractical ≠ reasonable

insect NOUN = **bug**, creepy-crawly (*Brit. informal*), gogga (*S. African informal*)
  ▷ *see* **ants, bees and wasps, beetles, butterflies and moths, flies**

insecure ADJECTIVE
  1 = **unconfident**, worried, anxious, afraid, shy, uncertain, unsure, timid ≠ confident
  2 = **unsafe**, exposed, vulnerable, wide-open, unprotected, defenceless, unguarded ≠ safe

insecurity NOUN = **anxiety**, fear, worry, uncertainty ≠ confidence

insert VERB = **put**, place, position, slip, slide, slot, thrust, stick in

inside NOUN = **interior**, contents, core, nucleus
  ▷ PLURAL NOUN (*informal*)
  = **stomach**, guts, belly, bowels, innards (*informal*), entrails, viscera, vitals
  ▷ ADJECTIVE **1** = **inner**, internal, interior, inward ≠ outside
  2 = **confidential**, private, secret, internal, exclusive, restricted, privileged, classified

  ▷ ADVERB = **indoors**, in, within, under cover

insight NOUN **1** = **understanding**, perception, sense, knowledge, vision, judgment, awareness, grasp **2** *with* **into** = **understanding**, perception, awareness, experience, description, introduction, observation, judgment

insignificant ADJECTIVE = **unimportant**, minor, irrelevant, petty, trivial, meaningless, trifling, paltry ≠ important

insist VERB **1** lay down the law, put your foot down (*informal*) **2** = **demand**, order, require, command, dictate, entreat **3** = **assert**, state, maintain, claim, declare, repeat, vow, swear

insistence NOUN **1** = **demand**, command, dictate, entreaty, importunity **2** = **assertion**, claim, statement, declaration, persistence, pronouncement

inspect VERB **1** = **examine**, check, look at, view, survey, look over, scrutinize, go over *or* through **2** = **check**, examine, investigate, look at, survey, vet, look over, go over *or* through

inspection NOUN
  1 = **examination**, investigation, scrutiny, once-over (*informal*)
  2 = **check**, search, investigation, review, survey, examination, scrutiny, once-over (*informal*)

inspector NOUN = **examiner**, investigator, supervisor, monitor, superintendent, auditor, censor,

- **INSECTS**
- body louse, cootie (*U.S. & N.Z.*), *or* (*N.Z. slang*) kutu
- bookworm
- caddis worm *or* caseworm
- cankerworm
- cochineal *or* cochineal insect
- cockroach
- crab (louse)
- cricket
- earwig, *or* (*Scot. dialect*) clipshears, *or* clipshear
- flea
- grasshopper
- katydid
- locust
- louse *or* (*N.Z.*) kutu
- mantis *or* praying mantis
- measuring worm, looper, *or* inchworm
- midge
- mosquito
- nit
- phylloxera
- scale insect
- silkworm
- silverfish
- stick insect *or* (*U.S. & Canad.*) walking stick
- thrips
- treehopper
- weta (*N.Z.*)
- wireworm
- woodworm

surveyor

inspiration NOUN
1 = **imagination**, creativity, ingenuity, insight, originality, inventiveness, cleverness
2 = **motivation**, example, model, boost, spur, incentive, revelation, stimulus ≠ deterrent
3 = **influence**, spur, stimulus, muse

inspire VERB **1** = **motivate**, stimulate, encourage, influence, spur, animate, enliven, galvanize ≠ discourage **2** = **give rise to**, produce, result in, engender

inspired ADJECTIVE **1** = **brilliant**, wonderful, impressive, outstanding, thrilling, memorable, dazzling, superlative
2 = **stimulated**, uplifted, exhilarated, enthused, elated

inspiring ADJECTIVE = **uplifting**, exciting, moving, stirring, stimulating, rousing, exhilarating, heartening ≠ uninspiring

instability NOUN
1 = **uncertainty**, insecurity, vulnerability, volatility, unpredictability, fluctuation, impermanence, unsteadiness ≠ stability **2** = **imbalance**, variability, unpredictability, unsteadiness, changeableness

install VERB **1** = **set up**, put in, place, position, station, establish, lay, fix **2** = **institute**, establish, introduce, invest, ordain, inaugurate, induct **3** = **settle**, position, plant, establish, lodge, ensconce

installation NOUN **1** = **setting up**, fitting, instalment, placing, positioning, establishment
2 = **appointment**, ordination, inauguration, induction,

investiture

instalment NOUN 1 = **payment**, repayment, part payment 2 = **part**, section, chapter, episode, portion, division

instance NOUN = **example**, case, occurrence, occasion, sample, illustration
▷ VERB = **name**, mention, identify, point out, advance, quote, refer to, point to

instant NOUN 1 = **moment**, second, flash, split second, jiffy (*informal*), trice, twinkling of an eye (*informal*) 2 = **time**, point, hour, moment, stage, occasion, phase, juncture
▷ ADJECTIVE 1 = **immediate**, prompt, instantaneous, direct, quick, on-the-spot, split-second 2 = **ready-made**, fast, convenience, ready-mixed, ready-cooked, precooked

instantly ADVERB = **immediately**, at once, straight away, now, directly, right away, instantaneously, this minute

instead ADVERB = **rather**, alternatively, preferably, in preference, in lieu, on second thoughts ▷ PHRASE: **instead of** = **in place of**, rather than, in preference to, in lieu of, in contrast with

instinct NOUN 1 = **natural inclination**, talent, tendency, faculty, inclination, knack, predisposition, proclivity 2 = **talent**, skill, gift, capacity, bent, genius, faculty, knack

3 = **intuition**, impulse

instinctive ADJECTIVE = **natural**, inborn, automatic, unconscious, inherent, spontaneous, reflex, innate ≠ acquired

instinctively ADVERB = **intuitively**, naturally, automatically, without thinking, involuntarily, by instinct

institute NOUN = **establishment**, body, centre, school, university, society, association, college
▷ VERB = **establish**, start, found, launch, set up, introduce, fix, organize ≠ end

institution NOUN 1 = **establishment**, body, centre, school, university, society, association, college 2 = **custom**, practice, tradition, law, rule, procedure, convention, ritual

institutional ADJECTIVE = **conventional**, accepted, established, formal, routine, orthodox, procedural

instruct VERB 1 = **order**, tell, direct, charge, bid, command, mandate, enjoin 2 = **teach**, school, train, coach, educate, drill, tutor

instruction NOUN 1 = **order**, ruling, command, rule, demand, regulation, dictate, decree 2 = **teaching**, schooling, training, grounding, education, coaching, lesson(s), guidance
▷ PLURAL NOUN = **information**, rules, advice, directions, recommendations, guidance, specifications

instructor NOUN = **teacher**, coach, guide, adviser, trainer, demonstrator, tutor, mentor

instrument NOUN 1 = **tool**, device, implement, mechanism, appliance, apparatus, gadget, contraption (*informal*) 2 = **agent**, means, medium, agency, vehicle, mechanism, organ

instrumental ADJECTIVE = **active**, involved, influential, useful, helpful, contributory

insufficient ADJECTIVE = **inadequate**, scant, meagre, short, sparse, deficient, lacking ≠ ample

insulate VERB = **isolate**, protect, screen, defend, shelter, shield, cut off, cushion

insult VERB = **offend**, abuse, wound, slight, put down, snub, malign, affront ≠ praise
  ▷ NOUN 1 = **jibe**, slight, put-down, abuse, snub, barb, affront, abusive remark 2 = **offence**, slight, snub, slur, affront, slap in the face (*informal*), kick in the teeth (*informal*), insolence

insulting ADJECTIVE = **offensive**, rude, abusive, degrading, contemptuous, disparaging, scurrilous, insolent ≠ complimentary

insurance NOUN 1 = **assurance**, cover, security, protection, safeguard, indemnity 2 = **protection**, security, guarantee, shelter, safeguard, warranty

insure VERB 1 = **assure**, cover, protect, guarantee, warrant, underwrite, indemnify 2 = **protect**, cover, safeguard

intact ADJECTIVE = **undamaged**, whole, complete, sound, perfect, entire, unscathed, unbroken ≠ damaged

integral ADJECTIVE = **essential**, basic, fundamental, necessary, component, constituent, indispensable, intrinsic ≠ inessential

integrate VERB = **join**, unite, combine, blend, incorporate, merge, fuse, assimilate ≠ separate

integrity NOUN 1 = **honesty**, principle, honour, virtue, goodness, morality, purity, probity ≠ dishonesty 2 = **unity**, unification, cohesion, coherence, wholeness, soundness, completeness

intellect NOUN = **intelligence**, mind, reason, understanding, sense, brains (*informal*), judgment

intellectual
  ADJECTIVE = **scholarly**, learned, academic, lettered, intelligent, cerebral, erudite, scholastic ≠ stupid
  ▷ NOUN = **academic**, expert, genius, thinker, master, mastermind, maestro, highbrow, fundi (*S. African*), acca (*Austral. slang*) ≠ idiot

intelligence NOUN 1 = **intellect**, understanding, brains (*informal*), sense, knowledge, judgment, wit, perception ≠ stupidity

2 = **information**, news, facts, report, findings, knowledge, data, notification, heads up (*U.S. & Canad.*) ≠ misinformation

intelligent ADJECTIVE = **clever**, bright, smart, sharp, enlightened, knowledgeable, well-informed, brainy (*informal*) ≠ stupid

intend VERB = **plan**, mean, aim, propose, purpose, have in mind *or* view

intense ADJECTIVE **1** = **extreme**, great, severe, fierce, deep, powerful, supreme, acute ≠ mild **2** = **fierce**, tough **3** = **passionate**, emotional, fierce, heightened, ardent, fanatical, fervent, heartfelt ≠ indifferent

● **WORD POWER**
● *Intense* is sometimes wrongly
● used where *intensive* is meant:
● *the land is under intensive* (not
● *intense*) *cultivation*. *Intensely*
● is sometimes wrongly used
● where *intently* is meant: *he*
● *listened intently* (not *intensely*).

intensify VERB **1** = **increase**, raise, add to, strengthen, reinforce, widen, heighten, sharpen ≠ decrease **2** = **escalate**, increase, widen, deepen

intensity NOUN **1** = **force**, strength, fierceness **2** = **passion**, emotion, fervour, force, strength, fanaticism, ardour, vehemence

intensive ADJECTIVE = **concentrated**, thorough, exhaustive, full, demanding, detailed, complete, serious

intent ADJECTIVE = **absorbed**, intense, fascinated, preoccupied, enthralled, attentive, watchful, engrossed ≠ indifferent
▷ NOUN = **intention**, aim, purpose, meaning, end, plan, goal, design ≠ chance

intention NOUN = **aim**, plan, idea, goal, end, design, target, wish

inter VERB = **bury**, lay to rest, entomb, consign to the grave

intercept VERB = **catch**, stop, block, seize, cut off, interrupt, head off, obstruct

intercourse NOUN **1** = **sexual intercourse**, sex (*informal*), copulation, coitus, carnal knowledge **2** = **contact**, communication, commerce, dealings

interest NOUN **1** *often plural* = **hobby**, activity, pursuit, entertainment, recreation, amusement, preoccupation, diversion **2** *often plural* = **advantage**, good, benefit, profit **3** = **stake**, investment
▷ VERB = **arouse your curiosity**, fascinate, attract, grip, entertain, intrigue, divert, captivate ≠ bore

interested ADJECTIVE **1** = **curious**, attracted, excited, drawn, keen, gripped, fascinated, captivated ≠ uninterested **2** = **involved**, concerned, affected, implicated

interesting ADJECTIVE = **intriguing**, absorbing, appealing, attractive, engaging, gripping, entrancing, stimulating ≠ uninteresting

interface NOUN = **connection**,

link, boundary, border, frontier

interfere VERB = **meddle**, intervene, intrude, butt in, tamper, pry, encroach, stick your oar in (*informal*) ▷ PHRASE: **interfere with something or someone** = **conflict with**, check, clash, handicap, hamper, disrupt, inhibit, thwart

interference NOUN = **intrusion**, intervention, meddling, opposition, conflict, obstruction, prying

interim ADJECTIVE = **temporary**, provisional, makeshift, acting, caretaker, improvised, stopgap

interior NOUN = **inside**, centre, heart, middle, depths, core, nucleus ▷ ADJECTIVE 1 = **inside**, internal, inner ≠ exterior 2 = **mental**, emotional, psychological, private, personal, secret, hidden, spiritual

intermediary NOUN = **mediator**, agent, middleman, broker, go-between

intermediate ADJECTIVE = **middle**, mid, halfway, in-between (*informal*), midway, intervening, transitional, median

internal ADJECTIVE 1 = **domestic**, home, national, local, civic, in-house, intramural 2 = **inner**, inside, interior ≠ external

international ADJECTIVE = **global**, world, worldwide, universal, cosmopolitan, intercontinental

Internet NOUN ▷ PHRASE: **the Internet** = **the information superhighway**, the net (*informal*), the web (*informal*), the World Wide Web, cyberspace

interpret VERB 1 = **take**, understand, explain, construe 2 = **translate**, transliterate 3 = **explain**, make sense of, decode, decipher, elucidate 4 = **understand**, read, crack, solve, figure out (*informal*), comprehend, decode, deduce 5 = **portray**, present, perform, render, depict, enact, act out

interpretation NOUN 1 = **explanation**, analysis, exposition, elucidation 2 = **performance**, portrayal, presentation, reading, rendition 3 = **reading**, study, review, version, analysis, explanation, examination, evaluation

interpreter NOUN = **translator**

interrogation NOUN = **questioning**, inquiry, examination, grilling (*informal*), cross-examination, inquisition, third degree (*informal*)

interrupt VERB 1 = **intrude**, disturb, intervene, interfere (with), break in, heckle, butt in, barge in (*informal*) 2 = **suspend**, stop, end, delay, cease, postpone, shelve, put off

interruption NOUN 1 = **disruption**, break, disturbance, hitch, intrusion 2 = **stoppage**, pause, suspension

interval NOUN 1 = **period**, spell, space, stretch, pause, span 2 = **break**, interlude, intermission, rest, gap, pause, respite, lull

3 = **delay**, gap, hold-up, stoppage

4 = **stretch**, space

intervene VERB 1 = **step in**
(*informal*), interfere, mediate,
intrude, intercede, arbitrate, take
a hand (*informal*) 2 = **interrupt**,
involve yourself 3 = **happen**,
occur, take place, follow, arise,
ensue, befall, materialize

intervention NOUN = **mediation**,
interference, intrusion,
arbitration, conciliation, agency

interview NOUN 1 = **meeting**
2 = **audience**, talk, conference,
exchange, dialogue, consultation,
press conference
▷ VERB 1 = **examine**, talk
to 2 = **question**, interrogate,
examine, investigate, pump, grill
(*informal*), quiz, cross-examine

interviewer NOUN = **questioner**,
reporter, investigator, examiner,
interrogator

intimacy NOUN = **familiarity**,
closeness, confidentiality
≠ aloofness

intimate¹ ADJECTIVE 1 = **close**,
dear, loving, near, familiar, thick
(*informal*), devoted, confidential
≠ distant 2 = **private**, personal,
confidential, special, individual,
secret, exclusive ≠ public
3 = **detailed**, minute, full,
deep, particular, immediate,
comprehensive, profound
4 = **cosy**, relaxed, friendly,
informal, harmonious, snug,
comfy (*informal*), warm
▷ NOUN = **friend**, close friend,
crony, cobber (*Austral. & N.Z.*

old-fashioned, *informal*), confidant
or confidante, (constant)
companion, E hoa (*N.Z.*)
≠ stranger

intimate² VERB 1 = **suggest**,
indicate, hint, imply, insinuate
2 = **announce**, state, declare,
communicate, make known

intimately ADVERB 1 = **closely**,
personally, warmly, familiarly,
tenderly, affectionately,
confidentially, confidingly
2 = **fully**, very well, thoroughly, in
detail, inside out

intimidate VERB = **frighten**,
pressure, threaten, scare, bully,
plague, hound, daunt

intimidation NOUN = **bullying**,
pressure, threat(s), menaces,
coercion, arm-twisting (*informal*),
browbeating, terrorization

intricate ADJECTIVE
= **complicated**, involved, complex,
fancy, elaborate, tangled,
tortuous, convoluted ≠ simple

intrigue NOUN 1 = **plot**, scheme,
conspiracy, manoeuvre, collusion,
stratagem, chicanery, wile
2 = **affair**, romance, intimacy,
liaison, amour
▷ VERB 1 = **interest**, fascinate,
attract, rivet, titillate 2 = **plot**,
scheme, manoeuvre, conspire,
connive, machinate

intriguing ADJECTIVE
= **interesting**, fascinating,
absorbing, exciting, engaging,
gripping, stimulating, compelling

introduce VERB 1 = **bring in**,
establish, set up, start, found,

launch, institute, pioneer
2 = **present**, acquaint, make
known, familiarize **3** = **suggest**,
air, advance, submit, bring up, put
forward, broach, moot **4** = **add**,
insert, inject, throw in (*informal*),
infuse
introduction NOUN **1** = **launch**,
institution, pioneering,
inauguration ≠ elimination
2 = **opening**, prelude, preface,
lead-in, preamble, foreword,
prologue, intro (*informal*)
≠ conclusion
introductory ADJECTIVE
1 = **preliminary**, first, initial,
inaugural, preparatory
≠ concluding **2** = **starting**,
opening, initial
intruder NOUN = **trespasser**,
invader, prowler, interloper,
infiltrator, gate-crasher (*informal*)
intrusion NOUN **1** = **interruption**,
interference, infringement,
trespass, encroachment
2 = **invasion**, breach,
infringement, encroachment,
infraction, usurpation
intuition NOUN **1** = **instinct**,
perception, insight, sixth sense
2 = **feeling**, idea, impression,
suspicion, premonition, inkling,
presentiment
invade VERB **1** = **attack**, storm,
assault, capture, occupy, seize,
raid, overwhelm **2** = **infest**,
swarm, overrun, ravage, beset,
pervade, permeate
invader NOUN = **attacker**, raider,
plunderer, aggressor, trespasser

invalid[1] NOUN = **patient**, sufferer,
convalescent, valetudinarian
▷ ADJECTIVE = **disabled**,
challenged, ill, sick, ailing, frail,
infirm, bedridden
invalid[2] ADJECTIVE **1** = **null and
void**, void, worthless, inoperative
≠ valid **2** = **unfounded**, false,
illogical, irrational, unsound,
fallacious ≠ sound
invaluable ADJECTIVE = **precious**,
valuable, priceless, inestimable,
worth your *or* its weight in gold
≠ worthless
invariably ADVERB = **always**,
regularly, constantly, repeatedly,
consistently, continually,
eternally, habitually
invasion NOUN **1** = **attack**,
assault, capture, takeover, raid,
offensive, occupation, conquering
2 = **intrusion**, breach, violation,
disturbance, disruption,
infringement, encroachment,
infraction
invent VERB **1** = **create**, make,
produce, design, discover,
manufacture, devise, conceive
2 = **make up**, devise, concoct,
forge, fake, fabricate, feign, falsify
invention NOUN **1** = **creation**,
machine, device, design,
instrument, discovery,
innovation, gadget
2 = **development**, design,
production, setting up,
foundation, construction,
creation, discovery **3** = **fiction**,
fantasy, lie, yarn, fabrication,
falsehood, untruth **4** = **creativity**,

imagination, initiative, enterprise, genius, ingenuity, originality, inventiveness

inventive ADJECTIVE = **creative**, original, innovative, imaginative, inspired, fertile, ingenious, resourceful ≠ uninspired

inventor NOUN = **creator**, maker, author, designer, architect, coiner, originator

inventory NOUN = **list**, record, catalogue, listing, account, roll, file, register

invertebrate NOUN
▷ see **crustaceans, snails, slugs and other gastropods, spiders and other arachnids**

invest VERB 1 = **spend**, expend,

advance, venture, put in, devote, lay out, sink in 2 = **empower**, provide, charge, sanction, license, authorize, vest ▷ PHRASE: **invest in something** = **buy**, get, purchase, pay for, obtain, acquire, procure

investigate VERB = **examine**, study, research, go into, explore, look into, inspect, probe into

investigation NOUN = **examination**, study, inquiry, review, search, survey, probe, inspection

investigator NOUN = **examiner**, researcher, monitor, detective, analyser, explorer, scrutinizer, inquirer

● **INVERTEBRATES**

- amoeba or (U.S.) ameba
- animalcule or animalculum
- arthropod
- bardy, bardie, or bardi (Austral.)
- bivalve
- blue-ringed octopus (Austral.)
- Bluff oyster (N.Z.)
- box jellyfish or (Austral.) sea wasp
- brachiopod or lamp shell
- brandling
- bryozoan or (colloquial) sea mat
- centipede

- chiton or coat-of-mail shell
- clam
- cone (shell)
- coral
- ctenophore or comb jelly
- cunjevoi or cunje (Austral.)
- cuttlefish or cuttle
- daphnia
- earthworm
- eelworm
- gastropodart
- horseleech
- jellyfish or (Austral. slang) blubber
- kina (N.Z.)
- lancelet or amphioxus

- leech
- lugworm, lug, or lobworm
- millipede, millepede, or milleped
- mollusc
- mussel
- octopus or devilfish
- oyster
- paper nautilus, nautilus, or argonaut
- pearly nautilus, nautilus, or chambered nautilus
- piddock

- pipi or ugari
  (*Austral.*)
- Portuguese man-
  of-war or (*Austral.*)
  bluebottle
- quahog, hard-shell
  clam, hard-shell, or
  round clam
- ragworm or (*U.S.*)
  clamworm
- razor-shell or (*U.S.*)
  razor clam
- red coral or
  precious coral

- roundworm
- sandworm
  or (*Austral.*)
  pumpworm
- scallop
- sea anemone
- sea cucumber
- sea lily
- sea mouse
- sea squirt
- sea urchin
- seed oyster
- sponge
- squid

- starfish
- tapeworm
- tardigrade or water
  bear
- teredo or shipworm
- trepang or bêche-
  de-mer
- tube worm
- tubifex
- tusk shell or tooth
  shell
- worm

investment NOUN 1 = **investing**,
backing, funding, financing,
contribution, speculation,
transaction, expenditure
2 = **stake**, interest, share,
concern, portion, ante (*informal*)
3 = **buy**, asset, acquisition,
venture, risk, gamble
invisible ADJECTIVE = **unseen**,
imperceptible, indiscernible,
unseeable ≠ visible
invitation NOUN = **request**, call,
invite (*informal*), summons
invite VERB 1 = **ask** 2 = **request**,
look for, bid for, appeal for
3 = **encourage**, attract, cause,
court, ask for (*informal*), generate,
foster, tempt
inviting ADJECTIVE = **tempting**,
appealing, attractive, welcoming,
enticing, seductive, alluring,
mouthwatering ≠ uninviting
invoke VERB 1 = **apply**, use,
implement, initiate, resort to, put
into effect 2 = **call upon**, appeal

to, pray to, petition, beseech,
entreat, supplicate
involve VERB 1 = **entail**, mean,
require, occasion, imply, give rise
to, necessitate 2 = **concern**, draw
in, bear on
involved ADJECTIVE
= **complicated**, complex, intricate,
hard, confused, confusing, elaborate,
tangled ≠ straightforward
involvement NOUN
= **connection**, interest, association,
commitment, attachment
inward ADJECTIVE 1 = **incoming**,
entering, inbound, ingoing
2 = **internal**, inner, private,
personal, inside, secret, hidden,
interior ≠ outward
Ireland NOUN = **Hibernia** (*Latin*)
iron MODIFIER = **ferrous**, ferric
▷ ADJECTIVE = **inflexible**, hard,
strong, tough, rigid, adamant,
unconditional, steely ≠ weak
▷ PHRASE: **iron something out**
= **settle**, resolve, sort out, get rid

of, reconcile, clear up, put right, straighten out ▷ **RELATED WORDS**: *adjectives* **ferric, ferrous**

ironic *or* **ironical** ADJECTIVE

1 = **sarcastic**, dry, acid, bitter, mocking, wry, satirical, tongue-in-cheek **2** = **paradoxical**, contradictory, puzzling, baffling, confounding, enigmatic, incongruous

irony NOUN **1** = **sarcasm**, mockery, ridicule, satire, cynicism, derision **2** = **paradox**, incongruity

irrational ADJECTIVE = **illogical**, crazy, absurd, unreasonable, preposterous, nonsensical ≠ rational

irregular ADJECTIVE **1** = **variable**, erratic, occasional, random, casual, shaky, sporadic, haphazard ≠ steady **2** = **uneven**, rough, ragged, crooked, jagged, bumpy, contorted, lopsided ≠ even **3** = **inappropriate**, unconventional, unethical, unusual, extraordinary, exceptional, peculiar, unofficial **4** = **unofficial**, underground, guerrilla, resistance, partisan, rogue, paramilitary, mercenary

irrelevant ADJECTIVE = **unconnected**, unrelated, unimportant, inappropriate, peripheral, immaterial, extraneous, beside the point ≠ relevant

irresistible ADJECTIVE = **overwhelming**, compelling, overpowering, urgent, compulsive

irresponsible ADJECTIVE

= **thoughtless**, reckless, careless, unreliable, untrustworthy, shiftless, scatterbrained ≠ responsible

irritate VERB **1** = **annoy**, anger, bother, needle (*informal*), infuriate, exasperate, nettle, irk ≠ placate **2** = **inflame**, pain, rub, scratch, scrape, chafe

irritated ADJECTIVE = **annoyed**, cross, angry, bothered, put out, exasperated, nettled, vexed, tooshie (*Austral. slang*), hoha (*N.Z.*)

irritating ADJECTIVE = **annoying**, trying, infuriating, disturbing, nagging, troublesome, maddening, irksome ≠ pleasing

irritation NOUN **1** = **annoyance**, anger, fury, resentment, gall, indignation, displeasure, exasperation ≠ pleasure **2** = **nuisance**, irritant, drag (*informal*), pain in the neck (*informal*), thorn in your flesh

island NOUN = **isle**, atoll, islet, ait *or* eyot (*dialect*), cay *or* key ▷ **RELATED WORD**: *adjective* **insular**

isolate VERB **1** = **separate**, break up, cut off, detach, split up, insulate, segregate, disconnect **2** = **quarantine**

isolated ADJECTIVE = **remote**, far, distant, lonely, out-of-the-way, hidden, secluded, inaccessible

isolation NOUN = **separation**, segregation, detachment, solitude, seclusion, remoteness

issue NOUN **1** = **topic**, point, matter, problem, question, subject, theme **2** = **point**, question, bone of contention

3 = **edition**, printing, copy, publication, number, version

4 = **children**, offspring, babies, kids (*informal*), heirs, descendants, progeny ≠ parent

▷ **VERB** = **give out**, release, publish, announce, deliver, spread, broadcast, distribute

▷ **PHRASE**: **take issue with something** or **someone** = **disagree with**, question, challenge, oppose, dispute, object to, argue with, take exception to

● **WORD POWER**

● Italian has given English a
● great number of loan words for
● the arts, particularly musical
● terms. Some musical terms,
● which originally referred
● to quite specific parts of a
● musical composition or its
● performers, now can be applied
● more generally. For example,
● *coda* (literally 'tail') and *segue*
● (literally 'follows'), originally
● meant the concluding part of a
● piece of music, and a transition
● from one piece of music to
● another without stopping,
● respectively. Coda now has the
● broader meaning 'concluding
● statement', particularly in
● narratives of people's lives,
● e.g. He is sanguine about this
● unfortunate coda to his career.
● In the same fashion, segue is
● now applied to a link between
● two ideas or texts, especially
● in speech-making or news-
● reading, e.g. He tried to think of
● a segue from Yankee Doodle to
● the New York Yankees. Another
● group of borrowings, which
● can also now be used outside
● the field of music, relate to
● performers, including *maestro*,
● *diva*, and *prima donna*. In music,
● a maestro (literally 'master') is
● a teacher, conductor, or leading
● musician. This term now more
● broadly refers to a leader in any
● profession or art, e.g. *batting*
● *maestro*, *fashion maestro*. Diva
● (literally 'goddess') and prima
● donna (literally 'first lady')
● both describe a female lead
● singer. Both have developed
● connotations of women
● who are temperamental and
● demanding. Diva, however,
● still mainly describes women in
● musical professions, whereas
● prima donna is a term often
● used of celebrities.

itch VERB **1** = **prickle**, tickle, tingle **2** = **long**, ache, crave, pine, hunger, lust, yearn, hanker

▷ **NOUN 1** = **irritation**, tingling, prickling, itchiness **2** = **desire**, longing, craving, passion, yen (*informal*), hunger, lust, yearning

item NOUN **1** = **article**, thing, object, piece, unit, component **2** = **matter**, point, issue, case, question, concern, detail, subject **3** = **report**, story, piece, account, note, feature, notice, article

itinerary NOUN = **schedule**, programme, route, timetable

Jj

jab VERB = **poke**, dig, punch, thrust, tap, stab, nudge, prod
▷ NOUN = **poke**, dig, punch, thrust, tap, stab, nudge, prod

jacket NOUN = **covering**, casing, case, cover, skin, shell, coat, wrapping

jackpot NOUN = **prize**, winnings, award, reward, bonanza

jail NOUN = **prison**, penitentiary (*U.S.*), confinement, dungeon, nick (*Brit. slang*), slammer (*slang*), reformatory, boob (*Austral. slang*)
▷ VERB = **imprison**, confine, detain, lock up, put away, intern, incarcerate, send down

jam NOUN (*informal*)
= **predicament**, tight spot, situation, trouble, hole (*slang*), fix (*informal*), mess, pinch
▷ VERB 1 = **pack**, force, press, stuff, squeeze, ram, wedge, cram
2 = **crowd**, throng, crush, mass, surge, flock, swarm, congregate
3 = **congest**, block, clog, stick, stall, obstruct

● **WORD POWER**
● A few words of Japanese origin,
● which described concepts or
● things unique to Japanese
● culture, are now used in English
● in a novel and creative way. For
● example, in Japanese myth,
● *kamikaze* was a divine wind
● which saved the Japanese by
● sinking the Mongolian navy.
● In the Second World War, a
● kamikaze was a Japanese pilot
● who flew his plane into an
● enemy ship on a suicide mission.
● Kamikaze is now a metaphor
● for any self-destructive act, as
● in *kamikaze tactics*, *kamikaze*
● *approach*. Another Japanese
● term which has undergone a
● similar meaning development
● is *tsunami*. Literally 'harbour-
● waves', a tsunami is one or
● several large sea waves produced
● by an underwater earthquake
● or volcanic eruption. It is often
● used as a metaphor for a sudden
● increase or large volume of
● either concrete or abstract
● things, e.g. *a tsunami of aid*, *of*
● *words*, or *of support*. It can be
● compared to flood, deluge, tide,
● wave, and torrent which have
● the same metaphor. Words for
● different religions and faiths
● often develop adjectives which
● describe the particular qualities
● of their believers, e.g. That's not
● very Christian of you. Similarly,
● *Zen*, a branch of Buddhism,
● not only refers to a religion or
● philosophy, but, more loosely, a
● state of calmness or meditation.
● It is sometimes found in phrases
● like *zen-like calm*, with or
● without a capital.

jar¹ NOUN = **pot**, container, drum, vase, jug, pitcher, urn, crock

jar² VERB **1** *usually with* **on**
= **irritate**, annoy, offend, nettle,
irk, grate on, get on your nerves
(*informal*) **2** = **jolt**, rock, shake,
bump, rattle, vibrate, convulse

jargon NOUN = **parlance**, idiom,
usage, argot

jaw PLURAL NOUN = **opening**,
entrance, mouth
▷ VERB (*slang*) = **talk**, chat,
gossip, chatter, spout, natter

jealous ADJECTIVE **1** = **suspicious**,
protective, wary, doubtful,
sceptical, vigilant, watchful,
possessive ≠ trusting
2 = **envious**, grudging, resentful,
green, green with envy, desirous,
covetous ≠ satisfied

jealousy NOUN = **suspicion**,
mistrust, possessiveness, doubt,
spite, resentment, wariness, dubiety

jeer VERB = **mock**, deride, heckle,
barrack, ridicule, taunt, scoff, gibe
≠ cheer
▷ NOUN = **mockery**, abuse,
ridicule, taunt, boo, derision,
gibe, catcall ≠ applause

jeopardy NOUN = **danger**, risk,
peril, vulnerability, insecurity

jerk VERB = **jolt**, bang, bump, lurch
▷ NOUN = **lurch**, movement,
thrust, twitch, jolt

jet NOUN = **stream**, current, spring,
flow, rush, flood, burst, spray
▷ VERB = **fly**, wing, cruise, soar,
zoom

jewel NOUN **1** = **gemstone**, gem,
ornament, sparkler (*informal*),
rock (*slang*) **2** = **treasure**, wonder,
darling, pearl, gem, paragon,

pride and joy, taonga (*N.Z.*)

jewellery NOUN = **jewels**, treasure,
gems, trinkets, ornaments, finery,
regalia, bling (*slang*)

job NOUN **1** = **position**, work,
calling, business, field, career,
employment, profession **2** = **task**,
duty, work, venture, enterprise,
undertaking, assignment, chore

jobless ADJECTIVE = **unemployed**,
redundant, out of work, inactive,
unoccupied, idle

jog VERB **1** = **run**, trot, canter, lope
2 = **nudge**, push, shake, prod
3 = **stimulate**, stir, prod

join VERB **1** = **enrol in**, enter, sign
up for, enlist in **2** = **connect**,
unite, couple, link, combine,
attach, fasten, add ≠ detach

joint ADJECTIVE = **shared**, mutual,
collective, communal, united,
joined, allied, combined
▷ NOUN = **junction**, connection,
brace, bracket, hinge,
intersection, node, nexus

jointly ADVERB = **collectively**,
together, in conjunction, as
one, in common, mutually,
in partnership, in league
≠ separately

joke NOUN **1** = **jest**, gag (*informal*),
wisecrack (*informal*), witticism,
crack (*informal*), quip, pun, one-
liner (*informal*) **2** = **laugh**, jest,
jape **3** = **prank**, trick, practical
joke, lark (*informal*), escapade,
jape **4** = **laughing stock**, clown,
buffoon
▷ VERB = **jest**, kid (*informal*), mock,
tease, taunt, quip, banter, play

the fool

joker NOUN = **comedian**, comic, wit, clown, wag, jester, prankster, buffoon

jolly ADJECTIVE = **happy**, cheerful, merry, upbeat (*informal*), playful, cheery, genial, chirpy (*informal*) ≠ miserable

jolt VERB 1 = **jerk**, push, shake, knock, jar, shove, jog, jostle 2 = **surprise**, stun, disturb, stagger, startle, perturb, discompose ▷ NOUN 1 = **jerk**, start, jump, shake, bump, jar, jog, lurch 2 = **surprise**, blow, shock, setback, bombshell, bolt from the blue

journal NOUN 1 = **magazine**, publication, gazette, periodical 2 = **newspaper**, paper, daily, weekly, monthly 3 = **diary**, record, history, log, notebook, chronicle, annals, yearbook, blog (*informal*)

journalist NOUN = **reporter**, writer, correspondent, newsman or newswoman, commentator, broadcaster, hack (*derogatory*), columnist

journey NOUN 1 = **trip**, drive, tour, flight, excursion, trek, expedition, voyage 2 = **progress**, voyage, pilgrimage, odyssey ▷ VERB = **travel**, go, move, tour, progress, proceed, wander, trek, go walkabout (*Austral.*)

joy NOUN = **delight**, pleasure, satisfaction, ecstasy, enjoyment, bliss, glee, rapture ≠ sorrow

jubilee NOUN = **celebration**, holiday, festival, festivity

judge NOUN 1 = **magistrate**, justice, beak (*Brit. slang*), His, Her *or* Your Honour 2 = **referee**, expert, specialist, umpire, umpie (*Austral. slang*), mediator, examiner, connoisseur, assessor 3 = **critic**, assessor, arbiter ▷ VERB 1 = **adjudicate**, referee, umpire, mediate, officiate, arbitrate 2 = **evaluate**, rate, consider, view, value, esteem 3 = **estimate**, guess, assess, calculate, evaluate, gauge ▷ RELATED WORD: *adjective* judicial

judgment NOUN 1 = **opinion**, view, estimate, belief, assessment, diagnosis, valuation, appraisal 2 = **verdict**, finding, ruling, decision, sentence, decree, arbitration, adjudication 3 = **sense**, good sense, understanding, discrimination, perception, wisdom, wit, prudence

judicial ADJECTIVE = **legal**, official

jug NOUN = **container**, pitcher, urn, carafe, creamer (*U.S. & Canad.*), vessel, jar, crock

juggle VERB = **manipulate**, change, alter, modify, manoeuvre

juice NOUN 1 = **liquid**, extract, fluid, liquor, sap, nectar 2 = **secretion**

juicy ADJECTIVE 1 = **moist**, lush, succulent 2 = **interesting**, colourful, sensational, vivid, provocative, spicy (*informal*), suggestive, racy

jumble NOUN = **muddle**, mixture, mess, disorder, confusion, clutter, disarray, mishmash ▷ VERB = **mix**, mistake, confuse, disorder, shuffle, muddle, disorganize

jumbo ADJECTIVE = **giant**, large, huge, immense, gigantic, oversized, supersize ≠ tiny

jump VERB 1 = **leap**, spring, bound, bounce, hop, skip 2 = **vault**, hurdle, go over, sail over, hop over 3 = **spring**, bound, bounce 4 = **recoil**, start, jolt, flinch, shake, jerk, quake, shudder 5 = **increase**, rise, climb, escalate, advance, soar, surge, spiral 6 = **miss**, avoid, skip, omit, evade
▷ NOUN 1 = **leap**, spring, skip, bound, hop, vault 2 = **rise**, increase, upswing, advance, upsurge, upturn, increment

jumped-up ADJECTIVE (*informal*) = **conceited**, arrogant, pompous, overbearing, presumptuous, insolent

jumper NOUN = **sweater**, top, jersey, cardigan, woolly, pullover

junior ADJECTIVE 1 = **minor**, lower, secondary, lesser, subordinate, inferior 2 = **younger** ≠ senior

junk NOUN = **rubbish**, refuse, waste, scrap, litter, debris, garbage (*chiefly U.S.*), trash

jurisdiction NOUN 1 = **authority**, power, control, rule, influence, command, mana (*N.Z.*) 2 = **range**, area, field, bounds, province, scope, sphere, compass

just ADVERB 1 = **recently**, lately, only now 2 = **merely**, only, simply, solely 3 = **barely**, hardly, by a whisker, by the skin of your teeth 4 = **exactly**, really, quite, completely, totally, perfectly, entirely, truly
▷ ADJECTIVE 1 = **fair**, good, legitimate, upright, honest, equitable, conscientious, virtuous ≠ unfair 2 = **fitting**, due, correct, deserved, appropriate, justified, decent, merited ≠ inappropriate

● **WORD POWER**
● The expression *just exactly* is
● considered to be poor style
● because, since both words
● mean the same thing, only
● one or the other is needed. Use
● *just – it's just what they want* – or
● *exactly – it's exactly what they*
● *want*, but not both together.

justice NOUN 1 = **fairness**, equity, integrity, honesty, decency, rightfulness, right ≠ injustice 2 = **justness**, fairness, legitimacy, right, integrity, honesty, legality, rightfulness 3 = **judge**, magistrate, beak (*Brit. slang*), His, Her or Your Honour

justification NOUN = **reason**, grounds, defence, basis, excuse, warrant, rationale, vindication

justify VERB = **explain**, support, warrant, defend, excuse, uphold, vindicate, exonerate

juvenile NOUN = **child**, youth, minor, girl, boy, teenager, infant, adolescent ≠ adult
▷ ADJECTIVE 1 = **young**, junior, adolescent, youthful, immature ≠ adult 2 = **immature**, childish, infantile, puerile, young, youthful, inexperienced, callow

Kk

kai NOUN (*N.Z. informal*) = **food**, grub (*slang*), provisions, fare, tucker (*Austral. & N.Z. informal*), refreshment, foodstuffs

kak (*S. African taboo*) NOUN
1 = **faeces**, excrement, manure, dung, droppings, waste matter
2 = **rubbish**, nonsense, garbage (*informal*), rot, drivel, tripe (*informal*), bizzo (*Austral. slang*), bull's wool (*Austral. & N.Z. slang*)

keen ADJECTIVE 1 = **eager**, intense, enthusiastic, passionate, ardent, avid, fervent, impassioned ≠ unenthusiastic 2 = **earnest**, fierce, intense, vehement, passionate, heightened, ardent, fanatical 3 = **sharp**, incisive, cutting, edged, razor-like ≠ dull 4 = **perceptive**, quick, sharp, acute, smart, wise, clever, shrewd ≠ obtuse 5 = **intense**, strong, fierce, relentless, cut-throat

keep VERB 1 *usually with* **from** = **prevent**, restrain, hinder, keep back 2 = **hold on to**, maintain, retain, save, preserve, nurture, cherish, conserve ≠ lose 3 = **store**, put, place, house, hold, deposit, stack, stow 4 = **carry**, stock, sell, supply, handle 5 = **support**, maintain, sustain, provide for, mind, fund, finance, feed 6 = **raise**, own, maintain, tend, farm, breed, look after, rear 7 = **manage**, run, administer, be in charge (of), direct, handle, supervise 8 = **delay**, detain, hinder, impede, obstruct, set back ≠ release
▷ NOUN 1 = **board**, food, maintenance, living, kai (*N.Z. informal*) 2 = **tower**, castle
▷ PHRASES: **keep something up** 1 = **continue**, make, maintain, carry on, persist in, persevere with 2 = **maintain**, sustain, perpetuate, retain, preserve, prolong; **keep up** = **keep pace**

keeper NOUN = **curator**, guardian, steward, attendant, caretaker, preserver

keeping NOUN = **care**, charge, protection, possession, custody, guardianship, safekeeping
▷ PHRASE: **in keeping with** = **in agreement with**, in harmony with, in accord with, in compliance with, in conformity with, in balance with, in correspondence with, in proportion with

key NOUN 1 = **opener**, door key, latchkey 2 = **answer**
▷ MODIFIER = **essential**, leading, major, main, important, necessary, vital, crucial ≠ minor

kia ora INTERJECTION (*N.Z.*) = **hello**, hi (*informal*), greetings, gidday *or* g'day (*Austral. & N.Z.*), how do you do?, good morning, good evening, good afternoon

kick VERB 1 = **boot**, knock, punt

2 (*informal*) = **give up**, break, stop, abandon, quit, cease, eschew, leave off
▷ NOUN (*informal*) = **thrill**, buzz (*slang*), tingle, high (*slang*)
▷ PHRASES: **kick someone out** (*informal*) = **dismiss**, remove, get rid of, expel, eject, evict, sack (*informal*), kennet (*Austral. slang*), jeff (*Austral. slang*); **kick something off** (*informal*) = **begin**, start, open, commence, initiate, get on the road

kid¹ NOUN (*informal*) = **child**, baby, teenager, youngster, infant, adolescent, juvenile, toddler, littlie (*Austral. informal*), ankle-biter (*Austral. slang*), tacker (*Austral. slang*)

kid² VERB = **tease**, joke, trick, fool, pretend, wind up (*Brit. slang*), hoax, delude

kidnap VERB = **abduct**, capture, seize, snatch (*slang*), hijack, hold to ransom

kill VERB **1** = **slay**, murder, execute, slaughter, destroy, massacre, butcher, cut down **2** (*informal*) = **destroy**, crush, scotch, stop, halt, wreck, shatter, suppress

killer NOUN = **murderer**, slayer, hit man (*slang*), butcher, gunman, assassin, terminator, executioner

killing NOUN = **murder**, massacre, slaughter, dispatch, manslaughter, elimination, slaying, homicide
▷ ADJECTIVE (*informal*) = **tiring**, taxing, exhausting, punishing, fatiguing, gruelling, sapping, debilitating ▷ PHRASE: **make a killing** (*informal*) = **profit**, gain, clean up (*informal*), be lucky, be successful, make a fortune, strike it rich (*informal*), make a bomb (*slang*)

kind¹ ADJECTIVE = **considerate**, kindly, concerned, friendly, generous, obliging, charitable, benign ≠ unkind

kind² NOUN **1** = **class**, sort, type, variety, brand, category, genre
2 = **sort**, set, type, family, species, breed

● **WORD POWER**
● It is common in informal
● speech to combine singular
● and plural in sentences like
● *children enjoy those kind of*
● *stories.* However, this is not
● acceptable in careful writing,
● where the plural must be used
● consistently: *children enjoy those*
● *kinds of stories.*

kindly ADJECTIVE = **benevolent**, kind, caring, warm, helpful, pleasant, sympathetic, benign ≠ cruel
▷ ADVERB = **benevolently**, politely, generously, thoughtfully, tenderly, lovingly, cordially, affectionately ≠ unkindly

kindness NOUN = **goodwill**, understanding, charity, humanity, compassion, generosity, philanthropy, benevolence ≠ malice

king NOUN = **ruler**, monarch, sovereign, leader, lord, Crown, emperor, head of state

kingdom NOUN = **country**, state, nation, territory, realm

kiss VERB 1 = **peck** (*informal*), osculate, neck (*informal*)
2 = **brush**, touch, shave, scrape, graze, glance off, stroke
▷ NOUN = **peck** (*informal*), snog (*Brit. slang*), smacker (*slang*), French kiss, osculation

kit NOUN 1 = **equipment**, materials, tackle, tools, apparatus, paraphernalia
2 = **gear**, things, stuff, equipment, uniform ▷ PHRASE: **kit something** or **someone out** or **up** = **equip**, fit, supply, provide with, arm, stock, costume, furnish

knack NOUN = **skill**, art, ability, facility, talent, gift, capacity, trick ≠ ineptitude

kneel VERB = **genuflect**, stoop

knickers PLURAL NOUN = **underwear**, smalls, briefs, drawers, panties, bloomers

knife NOUN = **blade**, carver, cutter ▷ VERB = **cut**, wound, stab, slash, thrust, pierce, spear, jab

knit VERB 1 = **join**, unite, link, tie, bond, combine, bind, weave
2 = **heal**, unite, join, link, bind, fasten, intertwine 3 = **furrow**, tighten, knot, wrinkle, crease, screw up, pucker, scrunch up

knob NOUN = **ball**, stud, knot, lump, bump, projection, hump, protrusion

knock VERB 1 = **bang**, strike, tap, rap, thump, pummel 2 = **hit**, strike, punch, belt (*informal*), smack, thump, cuff 3 (*informal*)
= **criticize**, condemn, put down, run down, abuse, slate (*informal*), censure, denigrate, nit-pick (*informal*)
▷ NOUN 1 = **knocking**, pounding, beating, tap, bang, banging, rap, thump 2 = **bang**, blow, impact, jar, collision, jolt, smash 3 = **blow**, hit, punch, crack, clip, slap, bash, smack 4 (*informal*)
= **setback**, check, defeat, blow, reverse, disappointment, hold-up, hitch ▷ PHRASES: **knock about** or **around** = **wander**, travel, roam, rove, range, drift, stray, ramble, go walkabout (*Austral.*); **knock about** or **around with someone** = **mix with**, associate with, mingle with, consort with, hobnob with, socialize with, accompany; **knock off** (*informal*) = **stop work**, get out, call it a day (*informal*), finish work, clock off, clock out; **knock someone about** or **around** = **hit**, attack, beat, strike, abuse, injure, assault, batter; **knock someone down** = **run over**, hit, run down, knock over, mow down; **knock something down** = **demolish**, destroy, flatten, tear down, level, fell, dismantle, bulldoze, kennet (*Austral. slang*), jeff (*Austral. slang*); **knock something off** (*slang*) = **steal**, take, nick (*slang, chiefly Brit.*), thieve, rob, pinch

knockout NOUN 1 = **killer blow**, coup de grâce (*French*), KO or K.O. (*slang*) 2 (*informal*) = **success**, hit, winner, triumph, smash, sensation, smash hit ≠ failure

k

knot NOUN = **connection**, tie, bond, joint, loop, ligature
▷ VERB = **tie**, secure, bind, loop, tether

know VERB 1 = **have knowledge of**, see, understand, recognize, perceive, be aware of, be conscious of 2 = **be acquainted with**, recognize, be familiar with, be friends with, be friendly with, have knowledge of, have dealings with, socialize with ≠ be unfamiliar with 3 *sometimes with* **about** *or* **of** = **be familiar with**, understand, comprehend, have knowledge of, be acquainted with, feel certain of, have dealings in, be versed in ≠ be ignorant of

know-how NOUN (*informal*) = **expertise**, ability, skill, knowledge, facility, talent, command, capability

knowing ADJECTIVE = **meaningful**, significant, expressive, enigmatic, suggestive

knowledge NOUN
1 = **understanding**, sense, judgment, perception, awareness, insight, grasp, appreciation
2 = **learning**, education, intelligence, instruction, wisdom, scholarship, enlightenment, erudition ≠ ignorance
3 = **acquaintance**, intimacy, familiarity ≠ unfamiliarity

knowledgeable ADJECTIVE
1 = **well-informed**, conversant, au fait (*French*), experienced, aware, familiar, in the know (*informal*), cognizant 2 = **intelligent**, learned, educated, scholarly, erudite

known ADJECTIVE = **famous**, well-known, celebrated, noted, acknowledged, recognized, avowed ≠ unknown

koppie *or* **kopje** NOUN (*S. African*) = **hill**, down (*archaic*), fell, mount, hilltop, knoll, hillock, brae (*Scot.*)

k

Ll

label NOUN = **tag**, ticket, tab, marker, sticker
▷ VERB = **tag**, mark, stamp, ticket, tab

labour NOUN 1 = **workers**, employees, workforce, labourers, hands 2 = **work**, effort, employment, toil, industry 3 = **childbirth**, birth, delivery, parturition
▷ VERB 1 = **work**, toil, strive, work hard, sweat (*informal*), slave, endeavour, slog away (*informal*) ≠ rest 2 = **struggle**, work, strain, work hard, strive, grapple, toil, make an effort 3 = **overemphasize**, stress, elaborate, exaggerate, strain, dwell on, overdo, go on about 4 *usually with* **under** = **be disadvantaged by**, suffer from, be a victim of, be burdened by

Labour Party ADJECTIVE = **left-wing**, Democrat (*U.S.*)

laboured ADJECTIVE = **difficult**, forced, strained, heavy, awkward

labourer NOUN = **worker**, manual worker, hand, blue-collar worker, drudge, navvy (*Brit. informal*)

lace NOUN 1 = **netting**, net, filigree, meshwork, openwork 2 = **cord**, tie, string, lacing, shoelace, bootlace
▷ VERB 1 = **fasten**, tie, tie up, do up, secure, bind, thread 2 = **mix**, drug, doctor, add to, spike, contaminate, fortify, adulterate 3 = **intertwine**, interweave, entwine, twine, interlink

lack NOUN = **shortage**, want, absence, deficiency, need, inadequacy, scarcity, dearth ≠ abundance
▷ VERB = **miss**, want, need, require, not have, be without, be short of, be in need of ≠ have

lad NOUN = **boy**, kid (*informal*), guy (*informal*), youth, fellow, youngster, juvenile, nipper (*informal*)

laden ADJECTIVE = **loaded**, burdened, full, charged, weighed down, encumbered

lady NOUN 1 = **gentlewoman**, duchess, noble, dame, baroness, countess, aristocrat, viscountess 2 = **woman**, female, girl, damsel, charlie (*Austral. slang*), chook (*Austral. slang*), wahine (*N.Z.*)

lag VERB = **hang back**, delay, trail, linger, loiter, straggle, dawdle, tarry

laid-back ADJECTIVE = **relaxed**, calm, casual, easy-going, unflappable (*informal*), unhurried, free and easy, chilled (*informal*) ≠ tense

lake NOUN = **pond**, pool, reservoir, loch (*Scot.*), lagoon, mere, lough (*Irish*), tarn

lame ADJECTIVE 1 = **disabled**, handicapped, crippled, limping, hobbling, game

2 = **unconvincing**, poor, pathetic, inadequate, thin, weak, feeble, unsatisfactory

lament VERB = **bemoan**, grieve, mourn, weep over, complain about, regret, wail about, deplore ▷ NOUN **1** = **complaint**, moan, wailing, lamentation **2** = **dirge**, requiem, elegy, threnody

land NOUN **1** = **ground**, earth, dry land, terra firma **2** = **soil**, ground, earth, clay, dirt, sod, loam **3** = **countryside**, farmland **4** (*law*) = **property**, grounds, estate, real estate, realty, acreage, homestead (*U.S. & Canad.*) **5** = **country**, nation, region, state, district, territory, province, kingdom ▷ VERB **1** = **arrive**, dock, put down, moor, alight, touch down, disembark, come to rest **2** (*informal*) = **gain**, get, win, secure, acquire ▷ PHRASE: **land up** = **end up**, turn up, wind up, finish up, fetch up (*informal*) ▷ RELATED WORD: *adjective* terrestrial

landlord NOUN **1** = **owner**, landowner, proprietor, freeholder, lessor, landholder **2** = **innkeeper**, host, hotelier

landmark NOUN **1** = **feature**, spectacle, monument **2** = **milestone**, turning point, watershed, critical point, tipping point

landscape NOUN = **scenery**, country, view, land, scene, prospect, countryside, outlook

landslide NOUN = **landslip**, avalanche, rockfall

lane NOUN = **road**, street, track, path, way, passage, trail, pathway

language NOUN **1** = **tongue**, dialect, vernacular, patois **2** = **speech**, communication, expression, speaking, talk, talking, discourse, parlance

languish VERB **1** = **decline**, fade away, wither away, flag, weaken, wilt ≠ flourish **2** (*literary*) = **waste away**, suffer, rot, be abandoned, be neglected ≠ thrive **3** *often with* **for** = **pine**, long, desire, hunger, yearn, hanker

lap¹ NOUN = **circuit**, tour, leg, stretch, circle, orbit, loop

lap² VERB **1** = **ripple**, wash, splash, swish, gurgle, slosh, purl, plash **2** = **drink**, sip, lick, swallow, gulp, sup ▷ PHRASE: **lap something up** = **relish**, like, enjoy, delight in, savour, revel in, wallow in, accept eagerly

lapse NOUN **1** = **decline**, fall, drop, deterioration **2** = **mistake**, failing, fault, failure, error, slip, negligence, omission **3** = **interval**, break, gap, pause, interruption, lull, breathing space, intermission ▷ VERB **1** = **slip**, fall, decline, sink, drop, slide, deteriorate, degenerate **2** = **end**, stop, run out, expire, terminate

lapsed ADJECTIVE = **expired**, ended, finished, run out, invalid, out of date, discontinued

large ADJECTIVE **1** = **big**, great, huge, heavy, massive, vast, enormous, tall, supersize ≠ small

2 = **massive**, great, big, huge, vast, enormous, considerable, substantial, supersize ≠ small
▷ **PHRASES**: **at large 1** = **in general**, generally, chiefly, mainly, as a whole, in the main **2** = **free**, on the run, fugitive, at liberty, on the loose, unchained, unconfined; **by and large** = **on the whole**, generally, mostly, in general, all things considered, predominantly, in the main, all in all

largely ADVERB = **mainly**, generally, chiefly, mostly, principally, primarily, predominantly, by and large

large-scale ADJECTIVE = **wide-ranging**, global, sweeping, broad, wide, vast, extensive, wholesale

lash¹ VERB **1** = **pound**, beat, strike, hammer, drum, smack (*dialect*) **2** = **censure**, attack, blast, put down, criticize, slate (*informal*, *chiefly Brit.*), scold, tear into (*informal*) **3** = **whip**, beat, thrash, birch, flog, scourge
▷ NOUN = **blow**, hit, strike, stroke, stripe, swipe (*informal*)

lash² VERB = **fasten**, tie, secure, bind, strap, make fast

last¹ ADJECTIVE **1** = **most recent**, latest, previous **2** = **hindmost**, final, at the end, remotest, furthest behind, most distant, rearmost ≠ foremost **3** = **final**, closing, concluding, ultimate ≠ first
▷ ADVERB **1** = **in** *or* **at the end**, after, behind, in the rear, bringing

up the rear ▷ **PHRASE**: **the last word 1** = **final decision**, final say, final statement, conclusive comment **2** = **leading**, finest, cream, supreme, elite, foremost, pre-eminent, unsurpassed
● **WORD POWER**
● Since *last* can mean either *after*
● *all others* or *most recent*, it is
● better to avoid using this word
● where ambiguity might arise,
● as in *her last novel*. *Final* or *latest*
● should be used as alternatives
● in such contexts to avoid any
● possible confusion.

last² VERB = **continue**, remain, survive, carry on, endure, persist, keep on, abide ≠ end

lasting ADJECTIVE = **continuing**, long-term, permanent, enduring, remaining, abiding, long-standing, perennial ≠ passing

latch NOUN = **fastening**, catch, bar, lock, hook, bolt, hasp
▷ VERB = **fasten**, bar, secure, bolt, make fast

late ADJECTIVE **1** = **overdue**, delayed, last-minute, belated, tardy, behind time, behindhand ≠ early **2** = **dead**, deceased, departed, passed on, former, defunct ≠ alive **3** = **recent**, new, advanced, fresh ≠ old
▷ ADVERB = **behind time**, belatedly, tardily, behindhand, dilatorily ≠ early

lately ADVERB = **recently**, of late, just now, in recent times, not long ago, latterly

later ADVERB = **afterwards**, after,

eventually, in time, subsequently, later on, thereafter, in a while

▷ ADJECTIVE = **subsequent**, next, following, ensuing

latest ADJECTIVE = **up-to-date**, current, fresh, newest, modern, most recent, up-to-the-minute

- ● WORD POWER
- ● Historically, English borrowed
- ● its greatest number of words
- ● from Latin and French. Often
- ● words of the same root would
- ● come into English from both
- ● Latin and French in slightly
- ● different forms. Some of these
- ● now exist as synonyms in
- ● English with fine distinctions.
- ● This process can be seen with
- ● *gravitas* and *gravity*. Both
- ● are derived from an original
- ● Latin form meaning 'weight':
- ● gravity came into English via
- ● French in the 16th century,
- ● and gravitas was coined from
- ● Latin in the 20th century.
- ● There is a significant overlap
- ● in meaning in that both mean
- ● 'seriousness', but they are used
- ● to describe different things.
- ● Gravitas is used to describe the
- ● importance and clout attached
- ● to a person's high status
- ● or the dignity of pomp and
- ● ceremony, e.g. he lent gravitas
- ● to the proceedings. Gravity,
- ● on the other hand, has a wider
- ● meaning of seriousness,
- ● and denotes a situation or
- ● behaviour, e.g. the gravity
- ● of their crime. Numerous

- ● Latin words became legal
- ● terminology with specialized
- ● meanings in English. Many
- ● of these words are still used
- ● today by lawyers in precise
- ● technical ways, but have also
- ● developed a looser meaning
- ● in general language. For
- ● example, a *proviso* is a clause in
- ● a contract making a limitation,
- ● condition, or exception to
- ● the rest of the agreement. In
- ● general language, it also means
- ● a condition or restriction,
- ● but not one which is legally
- ● binding, in the phrase **with the**
- ● **proviso that**.

latitude NOUN = **scope**, liberty, freedom, play, space, licence, leeway, laxity

latter NOUN = **second**, last, last-mentioned, second-mentioned

▷ ADJECTIVE = **last**, ending, closing, final, concluding

≠ earlier

- ● WORD POWER
- ● *The latter* should only be used
- ● to specify the second of two
- ● items, for example in *if I had to*
- ● *choose between the hovercraft and*
- ● *the ferry, I would opt for the latter.*
- ● Where there are three or more
- ● items, the last can be referred
- ● to as *the last-named*, but not *the*
- ● *latter*.

laugh VERB = **chuckle**, giggle, snigger, cackle, chortle, guffaw, titter, be in stitches

▷ NOUN 1 = **chortle**, giggle, chuckle, snigger, guffaw, titter **2**

(*informal*) =**joke**, scream (*informal*),
hoot (*informal*), lark, prank **3**
(*informal*) =**clown**, character
(*informal*), scream (*informal*),
entertainer, card (*informal*), joker,
hoot (*informal*) ▷ **PHRASE: laugh
something off** = **disregard**,
ignore, dismiss, overlook, shrug
off, minimize, brush aside, make
light of

laughter NOUN = **amusement**,
entertainment, humour, glee, fun,
mirth, hilarity, merriment

launch VERB **1** = **propel**, fire,
dispatch, discharge, project,
send off, set in motion, send
into orbit **2** = **begin**, start,
open, initiate, introduce, found,
set up, originate ▷ **PHRASE:
launch into something** = **start
enthusiastically**, begin, initiate,
embark on, instigate, inaugurate,
embark upon

laurel NOUN ▷ **PHRASE: rest on
your laurels** = **sit back**, relax,
take it easy, relax your efforts

lavatory NOUN = **toilet**,
bathroom, loo (*Brit. informal*),
privy, cloakroom (*Brit.*), urinal,
latrine, washroom, dunny (*Austral.
& N.Z. old-fashioned, informal*),
bogger (*Austral. slang*), brasco
(*Austral. slang*)

lavish ADJECTIVE **1** = **grand**,
magnificent, splendid, abundant,
copious, profuse ≠ stingy
2 = **extravagant**, wild, excessive,
exaggerated, wasteful, prodigal,
unrestrained, immoderate
≠ thrifty **3** = **generous**, free,

liberal, bountiful, open-handed,
unstinting, munificent ≠ stingy
▷ VERB = **shower**, pour, heap,
deluge, dissipate ≠ stint

law NOUN **1** = **constitution**,
code, legislation, charter
2 = **statute**, act, bill, rule, order,
command, regulation, resolution
3 = **principle**, code, canon,
precept, axiom, kaupapa (*N.Z.*)
4 = **the legal profession**, the bar,
barristers ▷ RELATED WORDS:
adjectives **legal, judicial**

lawsuit NOUN = **case**, action,
trial, suit, proceedings, dispute,
prosecution, legal action

lawyer NOUN = **legal adviser**,
attorney, solicitor, counsel,
advocate, barrister, counsellor,
legal representative

lay¹ VERB **1** = **place**, put, set,
spread, plant, leave, deposit, put
down **2** = **devise**, plan, design,
prepare, work out, plot, hatch,
contrive **3** = **produce**, bear,
deposit **4** = **arrange**, prepare,
make, organize, position,
set out, devise, put together
5 = **attribute**, assign, allocate,
allot, ascribe, impute **6** = **put
forward**, offer, present, advance,
lodge, submit, bring forward
7 = **bet**, stake, venture, gamble,
chance, risk, hazard, wager
▷ PHRASES: **lay someone off**
= **dismiss**, fire (*informal*), release,
sack (*informal*), pay off, discharge,
let go, make redundant, kennet
(*Austral. slang*), jeff (*Austral. slang*);
lay someone out (*informal*)

= **knock out**, fell, floor, knock unconscious, knock for six; **lay something out 1** = **arrange**, order, design, display, exhibit, put out, spread out **2** (*informal*) = **spend**, pay, invest, fork out (*slang*), expend, shell out (*informal*), disburse

● **WORD POWER**
● In standard English, the verb *to*
● *lay* (meaning 'to put something
● somewhere') always needs an
● object, for example *the Queen*
● *laid a wreath*. By contrast,
● the verb *to lie* is always used
● without an object, for example
● *he was just lying there*.

lay² ADJECTIVE **1** = **nonclerical**, secular, non-ordained **2** = **nonspecialist**, amateur, unqualified, untrained, inexpert, nonprofessional

layer NOUN = **tier**, level, seam, stratum

layout NOUN = **arrangement**, design, outline, format, plan, formation

lazy ADJECTIVE **1** = **idle**, inactive, indolent, slack, negligent, inert, workshy, slothful ≠ industrious **2** = **lethargic**, languorous, slow-moving, languid, sleepy, sluggish, drowsy, somnolent ≠ quick

leach VERB = **extract**, strain, drain, filter, seep, percolate

lead VERB **1** = **go in front (of)**, head, be in front, be at the head (of), walk in front (of) **2** = **guide**, conduct, steer, escort, precede, usher, pilot, show the way

3 = **connect to**, link, open onto **4** = **be ahead (of)**, be first, exceed, be winning, excel, surpass, come first, transcend **5** = **command**, rule, govern, preside over, head, control, manage, direct **6** = **live**, have, spend, experience, pass, undergo **7** = **result in**, cause, produce, contribute, generate, bring about, bring on, give rise to **8** = **cause**, prompt, persuade, move, draw, influence, motivate, prevail

▷ NOUN **1** = **first place**, winning position, primary position, vanguard **2** = **advantage**, start, edge, margin, winning margin **3** = **example**, direction, leadership, guidance, model, pattern **4** = **clue**, suggestion, hint, indication, pointer, tip-off **5** = **leading role**, principal, protagonist, title role, principal part **6** = **leash**, line, cord, rein, tether

▷ ADJECTIVE = **main**, prime, top, leading, first, head, chief, premier

▷ PHRASES: **lead someone on** = **entice**, tempt, lure, mislead, draw on, seduce, deceive, beguile; **lead up to something** = **introduce**, prepare for, pave the way for

leader NOUN = **principal**, president, head, chief, boss (*informal*), director, manager, chairman, baas (*S. African*), sherang (*Austral. & N.Z.*) ≠ follower

leadership NOUN **1** = **authority**,

control, influence, command, premiership, captaincy, governance, headship **2** = **guidance**, government, authority, management, direction, supervision, domination, superintendency

leading ADJECTIVE = **principal**, top, major, main, first, highest, greatest, chief ≠ minor

leaf NOUN **1** = **frond**, blade, cotyledon **2** = **page**, sheet, folio ▷ PHRASE: **leaf through something** (*a book, magazine, etc*) = **skim**, glance, scan, browse, look through, dip into, flick through, flip through

leaflet NOUN = **booklet**, notice, brochure, circular, flyer, tract, pamphlet, handout

leafy ADJECTIVE = **green**, shaded, shady, verdant

league NOUN **1** = **association**, union, alliance, coalition, group, corporation, partnership, federation **2** = **class**, group, level, category

leak VERB **1** = **escape**, pass, spill, release, drip, trickle, ooze, seep **2** = **disclose**, tell, reveal, pass on, give away, make public, divulge, let slip ▷ NOUN **1** = **leakage**, discharge, drip, seepage, percolation **2** = **hole**, opening, crack, puncture, aperture, chink, crevice, fissure **3** = **disclosure**, exposé, exposure, admission, revelation, uncovering, betrayal, unearthing

lean¹ VERB **1** = **bend**, tip, slope, incline, tilt, heel, slant **2** = **rest**, prop, be supported, recline, repose **3** = **tend**, prefer, favour, incline, be prone to, be disposed to ▷ PHRASE: **lean on someone** = **depend on**, trust, rely on, cling to, count on, have faith in

lean² ADJECTIVE = **thin**, slim, slender, skinny, angular, trim, spare, gaunt ≠ fat

leaning NOUN = **tendency**, bias, inclination, bent, disposition, penchant, propensity, predilection

leap VERB = **jump**, spring, bound, bounce, hop, skip ▷ NOUN **1** = **jump**, spring, bound, vault **2** = **rise**, change, increase, soaring, surge, escalation, upsurge, upswing ▷ PHRASE: **leap at something** = **accept eagerly**, seize on, jump at

learn VERB **1** = **master**, grasp, pick up, take in, familiarize yourself with **2** = **discover**, hear, understand, find out about, become aware, discern, ascertain, come to know **3** = **memorize**, commit to memory, learn by heart, learn by rote, learn parrot-fashion, get off pat

learned ADJECTIVE = **scholarly**, academic, intellectual, versed, well-informed, erudite, highbrow, well-read ≠ uneducated

learner NOUN = **student**, novice, beginner, apprentice, neophyte, tyro ≠ expert

learning NOUN = **knowledge**, study, education, scholarship, enlightenment

lease VERB 1 = **hire**, rent, let, loan, charter, rent out, hire out

least ADJECTIVE = **smallest**, meanest, fewest, lowest, tiniest, minimum, slightest, minimal

leave¹ VERB 1 = **depart from**, withdraw from, go from, escape from, quit, flee, exit, pull out of ≠ arrive 2 = **quit**, give up, get out of, resign from, drop out of 3 = **give up**, abandon, dump (*informal*), drop, surrender, ditch (*informal*), chuck (*informal*), discard ≠ stay with 4 = **entrust**, commit, delegate, refer, hand over, assign, consign, allot 5 = **bequeath**, will, transfer, endow, confer, hand down 6 = **forget**, leave behind, mislay 7 = **cause**, produce, result in, generate, deposit ▷ PHRASE: **leave something** *or* **someone out** = **omit**, exclude, miss out, forget, reject, ignore, overlook, neglect

leave² NOUN 1 = **holiday**, break, vacation, time off, sabbatical, leave of absence, furlough, schoolie (*Austral.*), accumulated day off *or* ADO (*Austral.*) 2 = **permission**, freedom, sanction, liberty, concession, consent, allowance, warrant ≠ refusal 3 = **departure**, parting, withdrawal, goodbye, farewell, retirement, leave-taking, adieu ≠ arrival

lecture NOUN 1 = **talk**, address, speech, lesson, instruction, presentation, discourse, sermon 2 = **telling-off** (*informal*), rebuke, reprimand, talking-to (*informal*), scolding, dressing-down (*informal*), reproof ▷ VERB 1 = **talk**, speak, teach, address, discourse, spout, expound, hold forth 2 = **tell off** (*informal*), berate, scold, reprimand, censure, castigate, admonish, reprove

lees PLURAL NOUN = **sediment**, grounds, deposit, dregs

left ADJECTIVE 1 = **left-hand**, port, larboard (*nautical*) 2 (*of politics*) = **socialist**, radical, left-wing, leftist

left-wing ADJECTIVE = **socialist**, communist, red (*informal*), radical, revolutionary, militant, Bolshevik, Leninist

leg NOUN 1 = **limb**, member, shank, lower limb, pin (*informal*), stump (*informal*) 2 = **support**, prop, brace, upright 3 = **stage**, part, section, stretch, lap, segment, portion ▷ PHRASE: **pull someone's leg** (*informal*) = **tease**, trick, fool, kid (*informal*), wind up (*Brit. slang*), hoax, make fun of, lead up the garden path

● **WORD POWER**
● The core meaning of *leg* is
● either of the two lower limbs
● of the human body. Their role
● in propping up the body has
● produced the meaning of
● support in other objects like
● *the leg of a chair*. We also talk
● about giving someone *a leg up*
● when they need support and

a boost. The idea of a leg as a structural support is reiterated in the phrases *not have a leg to stand on* and *on one's last legs*. A leg can equally refer to a stage of a journey or race, historically denoting sea journeys, but now with a wider application. Another common meaning of leg is that of movement in *shake a leg* (get moving), *stretch your legs* (go for a walk), and *leg it* (run away). The expression *pull someone's leg*, meaning to tease them, may originate from a Scottish rhyme where a preacher tugged on the leg of a hung criminal to make sure they were dead. Nowadays, pulling someone's leg has a more lighthearted meaning, involving teasing and joking.

legacy NOUN = **bequest**, inheritance, gift, estate, heirloom

legal ADJECTIVE 1 = **judicial**, judiciary, forensic, juridical, jurisdictive 2 = **lawful**, allowed, sanctioned, constitutional, valid, legitimate, authorized, permissible

legend NOUN 1 = **myth**, story, tale, fiction, saga, fable, folk tale, folk story 2 = **celebrity**, star, phenomenon, genius, prodigy, luminary, megastar (*informal*) 3 = **inscription**, title, caption, device, motto, rubric

legendary ADJECTIVE 1 = **famous**, celebrated, well-known, acclaimed, renowned, famed,

immortal, illustrious ≠ unknown 2 = **mythical**, fabled, traditional, romantic, fabulous, fictitious, storybook, apocryphal ≠ factual

legion NOUN 1 = **army**, company, force, division, troop, brigade 2 = **multitude**, host, mass, drove, number, horde, myriad, throng

legislation NOUN 1 = **law**, act, ruling, rule, bill, measure, regulation, charter 2 = **lawmaking**, regulation, prescription, enactment

legislative ADJECTIVE = **lawmaking**, judicial, law-giving

legislator NOUN = **lawmaker**, lawgiver

legislature NOUN = **parliament**, congress, senate, assembly, chamber

legitimate ADJECTIVE 1 = **lawful**, legal, genuine, authentic, authorized, rightful, kosher (*informal*), dinkum (*Austral. & N.Z. informal*), licit ≠ unlawful 2 = **reasonable**, correct, sensible, valid, warranted, logical, justifiable, well-founded ≠ unreasonable
▷ VERB = **legitimize**, allow, permit, sanction, authorize, legalize, pronounce lawful

leisure NOUN = **spare**, free, rest, ease, relaxation, recreation ≠ work

lekker ADJECTIVE (*S. African slang*) = **delicious**, tasty, luscious, palatable, delectable, mouthwatering, scrumptious (*informal*), appetizing, yummo

(Austral. slang)

lemon NOUN ▷ RELATED WORDS:
adjectives **citric, citrous**
   ▷ *see* **shades of yellow**

lend VERB 1 = **loan**, advance, sub
(Brit. informal) 2 = **give**, provide,
add, supply, grant, confer, bestow,
impart ▷ PHRASE: **lend itself to
something** = **be appropriate
for**, suit, be suitable for, be
appropriate to, be serviceable for

length NOUN 1 = **distance**, reach,
measure, extent, span, longitude
2 = **duration**, term, period, space,
stretch, span, expanse 3 = **piece**,
measure, section, segment,
portion ▷ PHRASE: **at length**
1 = **at last**, finally, eventually,
in time, in the end, at long last
2 = **for a long time**, completely,
fully, thoroughly, for hours, in
detail, for ages, in depth

lengthen VERB 1 = **extend**,
continue, increase, stretch,
expand, elongate ≠ shorten
2 = **protract**, extend, prolong,
draw out, spin out, make longer
≠ cut down

lengthy ADJECTIVE 1 = **protracted**,
long, prolonged, tedious, drawn-
out, interminable, long-winded,
long-drawn-out 2 = **very
long**, rambling, interminable,
long-winded, wordy, discursive,
extended ≠ brief

lesbian ADJECTIVE = **homosexual**,
gay, les (slang), sapphic, lesbo
(slang)

less ADJECTIVE = **smaller**, shorter,
not so much

▷ PREPOSITION = **minus**, without,
lacking, excepting, subtracting
● **WORD POWER**
● Less should not be confused
● with fewer. Less refers strictly
● only to quantity and not to
● number: there is less water than
● before. Fewer means smaller in
● number: there are fewer people
● than before.

lessen VERB 1 = **reduce**, lower,
diminish, decrease, ease, narrow,
minimize ≠ increase 2 = **grow
less**, diminish, decrease, contract,
ease, shrink

lesser ADJECTIVE = **lower**,
secondary, subsidiary, inferior,
less important ≠ greater

lesson NOUN 1 = **class**, schooling,
period, teaching, coaching,
session, instruction, lecture
2 = **example**, warning, message,
moral, deterrent 3 = **Bible
reading**, reading, text, Bible
passage, Scripture passage

let VERB 1 = **allow**, permit,
authorize, give the go-ahead,
give permission 2 = **lease**,
hire, rent, rent out, hire out,
sublease ▷ PHRASES: **let on**
(informal) 1 = **reveal**, disclose, say,
tell, admit, give away, divulge,
let slip; **let someone down**
= **disappoint**, fail, abandon,
desert, disillusion, fall short,
leave stranded, leave in the
lurch; **let someone off** (informal)
= **excuse**, release, discharge,
pardon, spare, forgive, exempt,
exonerate; **let something down**

= **deflate**, empty, exhaust, flatten, puncture; **let something off 1** = **fire**, explode, set off, discharge, detonate **2** = **emit**, release, leak, exude, give off; **let something out 1** = **release**, discharge **2** = **emit**, make, produce, give vent to; **let someone in** = **admit** or **receive**, include, welcome, greet, take in, incorporate, give access to; **let up** = **stop**, diminish, decrease, subside, relax, ease (up), moderate, lessen

lethal ADJECTIVE = **deadly**, terminal, fatal, dangerous, devastating, destructive, mortal, murderous ≠ harmless

letter NOUN **1** = **message**, line, note, communication, dispatch, missive, epistle, e-mail **2** = **character**, mark, sign, symbol

level NOUN = **position**, standard, degree, grade, standing, stage, rank, status
▷ ADJECTIVE **1** = **equal**, balanced, at the same height **2** = **horizontal**, even, flat, smooth, uniform ≠ slanted **3** = **even**, tied, equal, drawn, neck and neck, all square, level pegging
▷ VERB **1** = **equalize**, balance, even up **2** = **destroy**, devastate, demolish, flatten, knock down, pull down, tear down, bulldoze, kennet (*Austral. slang*), jeff (*Austral. slang*) ≠ build **3** = **direct**, point, turn, train, aim, focus **4** = **flatten**, plane, smooth, even off or out
▷ PHRASE: **on the level** (*informal*)

= **honest**, genuine, straight, fair, square, dinkum (*Austral. & N.Z. informal*), above board

lever NOUN = **handle**, bar
▷ VERB = **prise**, force

leverage NOUN **1** = **influence**, authority, pull (*informal*), weight, clout (*informal*) **2** = **force**, hold, pull, strength, grip, grasp

levy NOUN = **tax**, fee, toll, tariff, duty, excise, exaction
▷ VERB = **impose**, charge, collect, demand, exact

liability NOUN **1** = **disadvantage**, burden, drawback, inconvenience, handicap, nuisance, hindrance, millstone **2** = **responsibility**, accountability, culpability, answerability

liable ADJECTIVE **1** = **likely**, tending, inclined, disposed, prone, apt **2** = **vulnerable**, subject, exposed, prone, susceptible, open, at risk of **3** = **responsible**, accountable, answerable, obligated
● **WORD POWER**
● In the past, it was considered
● incorrect to use *liable* to mean
● 'probable' or 'likely', as in *it's*
● *liable to happen soon*. However,
● this usage is now generally
● considered acceptable.

liaison NOUN **1** = **contact**, communication, connection, interchange **2** = **intermediary**, contact, hook-up **3** = **affair**, romance, intrigue, fling, love affair, amour, entanglement

liar NOUN = **falsifier**, perjurer,

fibber, fabricator

libel NOUN = **defamation**,
misrepresentation, denigration,
smear, calumny, aspersion
▷ VERB = **defame**, smear, slur,
blacken, malign, denigrate, revile,
vilify

liberal ADJECTIVE 1 = **tolerant**,
open-minded, permissive,
indulgent, easy-going,
broad-minded ≠ intolerant
2 = **progressive**, radical,
reformist, libertarian,
forward-looking, free-thinking
≠ conservative 3 = **abundant**,
generous, handsome, lavish,
ample, rich, plentiful, copious
≠ limited 4 = **generous**,
kind, charitable, extravagant,
open-hearted, bountiful,
magnanimous, open-handed
≠ stingy

liberate VERB = **free**, release,
rescue, save, deliver, let out, set
free, let loose ≠ imprison

liberty NOUN = **independence**,
sovereignty, liberation,
autonomy, immunity, self-
determination, emancipation,
self-government ≠ restraint
▷ PHRASES: **at liberty 1** = **free**,
escaped, unlimited, at large, not
confined, untied, on the loose,
unchained 2 = **able**, free, allowed,
permitted, entitled, authorized;
take liberties or **a liberty** = **not
show enough respect**, show
disrespect, act presumptuously,
behave too familiarly, behave
impertinently

licence NOUN 1 = **certificate**,
document, permit, charter,
warrant 2 = **permission**, the
right, authority, leave, sanction,
liberty, immunity, entitlement
≠ denial 3 = **freedom**, creativity,
latitude, independence, liberty,
deviation, leeway, free rein
≠ restraint 4 = **laxity**, excess,
indulgence, irresponsibility,
licentiousness, immoderation
≠ moderation

license VERB = **permit**, sanction,
allow, warrant, authorize,
empower, certify, accredit
≠ forbid

lick VERB 1 = **taste**, lap, tongue
2 (*informal*) = **beat**, defeat,
overcome, rout, outstrip, outdo,
trounce, vanquish 3 (*of a flame*)
= **flicker**, touch, flick, dart, ripple,
play over
▷ NOUN 1 = **dab**, bit, touch, stroke
2 (*informal*) = **pace**, rate, speed,
clip (*informal*)

lie¹ NOUN = **falsehood**, deceit,
fabrication, fib, fiction, invention,
deception, untruth
▷ VERB = **fib**, fabricate, falsify,
prevaricate, not tell the truth,
equivocate, dissimulate, tell
untruths ▷ PHRASE: **give the
lie to something** = **disprove**,
expose, discredit, contradict,
refute, negate, invalidate, rebut

lie² VERB 1 = **recline**, rest, lounge,
sprawl, stretch out, loll, repose
2 = **be placed**, be, rest, exist, be
situated 3 = **be situated**, sit, be
located, be positioned 4 = **be**

buried, remain, rest, be, be
entombed

life NOUN 1 = **being**, existence,
vitality, sentience 2 = **existence**,
being, lifetime, time, days,
span 3 = **way of life**, situation,
conduct, behaviour, life style
4 = **liveliness**, energy, spirit,
vitality, animation, vigour,
verve, zest 5 = **biography**, story,
history, profile, confessions,
autobiography, memoirs, life
story ▷ **RELATED WORDS**: *adjectives*
animate, vital

lifelong ADJECTIVE = **long-lasting**,
enduring, lasting, persistent,
long-standing, perennial

lifetime NOUN = **existence**, time,
day(s), span

lift VERB 1 = **raise**, pick up, hoist,
draw up, elevate, uplift, heave up,
upraise ≠ lower 2 = **revoke**, end,
remove, withdraw, stop, cancel,
terminate, rescind ≠ impose
3 = **disappear**, clear, vanish,
disperse, dissipate, rise, be
dispelled
▷ NOUN 1 = **boost**,
encouragement, stimulus,
pick-me-up, fillip, shot in the
arm (*informal*), gee-up ≠ blow
2 = **elevator** (*chiefly U.S.*), hoist,
paternoster 3 = **ride**, run, drive,
hitch (*informal*) ▷ PHRASE: **lift off**
= **take off**, be launched, blast off,
take to the air

light¹ NOUN 1 = **brightness**,
illumination, luminosity, shining,
glow, glare, gleam, brilliance
≠ dark 2 = **lamp**, torch, candle,

flare, beacon, lantern, taper
3 = **match**, spark, flame, lighter
4 = **aspect**, context, angle,
point of view, interpretation,
viewpoint, slant, standpoint
▷ ADJECTIVE 1 = **bright**, brilliant,
shining, illuminated, luminous,
well-lit, lustrous, well-illuminated
≠ dark 2 = **pale**, fair, faded,
blonde, blond, bleached, pastel,
light-coloured ≠ dark
▷ VERB 1 = **illuminate**, light up,
brighten ≠ darken 2 = **ignite**,
inflame, kindle, touch off, set
alight ≠ put out ▷ PHRASE:
light up 1 = **cheer**, shine, blaze,
sparkle, animate, brighten,
lighten, irradiate 2 = **shine**, flash,
beam, blaze, sparkle, flare, glare,
gleam

light² ADJECTIVE 1 = **insubstantial**,
thin, slight, portable, buoyant,
airy, flimsy, underweight ≠ heavy
2 = **weak**, soft, gentle, moderate,
slight, mild, faint, indistinct
≠ strong 3 = **digestible**,
modest, frugal ≠ substantial
4 = **insignificant**, small,
slight, petty, trivial, trifling,
inconsequential, inconsiderable
≠ serious 5 = **light-hearted**,
funny, entertaining, amusing,
witty, humorous, frivolous,
unserious ≠ serious 6 = **nimble**,
graceful, deft, agile, sprightly,
lithe, limber, lissom ≠ clumsy
▷ PHRASE: **light on** or **upon**
something 1 = **settle**, land,
perch, alight 2 = **come across**,
find, discover, encounter, stumble

on, hit upon, happen upon

lighten³ VERB = **brighten**, illuminate, light up, irradiate, become light

lighten⁴ VERB 1 = **ease**, relieve, alleviate, allay, reduce, lessen, mitigate, assuage ≠ intensify 2 = **cheer**, lift, revive, brighten, perk up, buoy up ≠ depress

lightly ADVERB 1 = **moderately**, thinly, slightly, sparsely, sparingly ≠ heavily 2 = **gently**, softly, slightly, faintly, delicately ≠ forcefully 3 = **carelessly**, breezily, thoughtlessly, flippantly, frivolously, heedlessly ≠ seriously 4 = **easily**, simply, readily, effortlessly, unthinkingly, without thought, flippantly, heedlessly ≠ with difficulty

lightweight ADJECTIVE 1 = **thin**, fine, delicate, sheer, flimsy, gossamer, diaphanous, filmy 2 = **unimportant**, shallow, trivial, insignificant, slight, petty, worthless, trifling ≠ significant

like¹ ADJECTIVE = **similar to**, same as, equivalent to, parallel to, identical to, alike, corresponding to, comparable to ≠ different

● **WORD POWER**
● The use of *like* to mean 'such
● as' was in the past considered
● undesirable in formal
● writing, but has now become
● acceptable, for example in *I*
● *enjoy team sports like football and*
● *rugby*. However, the common
● use of *look like* and *seem like*
● to mean 'look or seem as if' is
● thought by many people to be
● incorrect or nonstandard. You
● might say *it looks as if* (or *as*
● *though*) *he's coming*, but it is still
● wise to avoid *it looks like he's*
● *coming*, particularly in formal or
● written contexts.

like² VERB 1 = **enjoy**, love, delight in, go for, relish, savour, revel in, be fond of ≠ dislike 2 = **admire**, approve of, appreciate, prize, take to, esteem, cherish, hold dear ≠ dislike 3 = **wish**, want, choose, prefer, desire, fancy, care, feel inclined

likelihood NOUN = **probability**, chance, possibility, prospect

likely ADJECTIVE 1 = **inclined**, disposed, prone, liable, tending, apt 2 = **probable**, expected, anticipated, odds-on, on the cards, to be expected 3 = **plausible**, possible, reasonable, credible, feasible, believable

liken VERB = **compare**, match, relate, parallel, equate, set beside

likewise ADVERB = **similarly**, the same, in the same way, in similar fashion, in like manner

liking NOUN = **fondness**, love, taste, weakness, preference, affection, inclination, penchant ≠ dislike

limb NOUN 1 = **part**, member, arm, leg, wing, extremity, appendage 2 = **branch**, spur, projection, offshoot, bough

limelight NOUN = **publicity**, recognition, fame, the spotlight, attention, prominence, stardom, public eye

limit NOUN 1 = **end**, ultimate, deadline, breaking point, extremity 2 = **boundary**, edge, border, frontier, perimeter
▷ VERB = **restrict**, control, check, bound, confine, curb, restrain, ration

limitation NOUN 1 = **restriction**, control, check, curb, restraint, constraint 2 = **weakness**, failing, qualification, reservation, defect, flaw, shortcoming, imperfection

limited ADJECTIVE = **restricted**, controlled, checked, bounded, confined, curbed, constrained, finite ≠ unlimited

limp¹ VERB = **hobble**, stagger, stumble, shuffle, hop, falter, shamble, totter
▷ NOUN = **lameness**, hobble

limp² ADJECTIVE = **floppy**, soft, slack, drooping, flabby, pliable, flaccid ≠ stiff

line NOUN 1 = **stroke**, mark, score, band, scratch, slash, streak, stripe 2 = **wrinkle**, mark, crease, furrow, crow's foot 3 = **row**, queue, rank, file, column, convoy, procession 4 = **string**, cable, wire, rope, thread, cord 5 = **trajectory**, way, course, track, channel, direction, route, path 6 = **boundary**, limit, edge, border, frontier, partition, borderline 7 = **occupation**, work, calling, business, job, area, trade, field
▷ VERB 1 = **border**, edge, bound, fringe 2 = **mark**, crease, furrow,

rule, score ▷ PHRASE: **in line for** = **due for**, shortlisted for, in the running for

lined ADJECTIVE 1 = **wrinkled**, worn, furrowed, wizened 2 = **ruled**, feint

line-up NOUN = **arrangement**, team, row, selection, array

linger VERB = **stay**, remain, stop, wait, delay, hang around, idle, dally

link NOUN 1 = **connection**, relationship, association, tie-up, affinity 2 = **relationship**, association, bond, connection, attachment, affinity 3 = **component**, part, piece, element, constituent
▷ VERB 1 = **associate**, relate, identify, connect, bracket 2 = **connect**, join, unite, couple, tie, bind, attach, fasten ≠ separate

lip NOUN 1 = **edge**, rim, brim, margin, brink 2 (*slang*) = **impudence**, insolence, impertinence, cheek (*informal*), effrontery, backchat (*informal*), brass neck (*informal*)

● **WORD POWER**
● The *lips* are the two fleshy
● folds surrounding the mouth.
● Their physical appearance has
● prompted lip to be applied
● to other structures which
● have an edge or rim, e.g. *lip*
● *of the crater*, *cup*, and *hole*. In
● theatrical circles, the edge
● of the stage is technically
● known as the lip. The lips are

- important in the articulation
- of speech, so lip in itself can
- mean speech, specifically
- impudent backchat in *none*
- *of your lip*. The expression
- *pay lip service* means to offer
- insincere support which is not
- put into practice, stemming
- from a sense of service as duty,
- for show but not for real. Lips
- have developed connotations
- of appetite, both for food and
- love: we *smack* or *lick our lips* in
- anticipation of these things.

liquid NOUN = **fluid**, solution, juice, sap
▷ ADJECTIVE 1 = **fluid**, running, flowing, melted, molten, runny, aqueous 2 (*of an asset*) = **convertible**, disposable, negotiable, realizable

liquor NOUN 1 = **alcohol**, drink, spirits, booze (*informal*), hard stuff (*informal*), strong drink 2 = **juice**, stock, liquid, extract, broth

list¹ NOUN = **inventory**, record, series, roll, index, register, catalogue, directory
▷ VERB = **itemize**, record, enter, register, catalogue, enumerate, note down, tabulate

list² VERB = **lean**, tip, incline, tilt, heel over, careen
▷ NOUN = **tilt**, leaning, slant, cant

listen VERB 1 = **hear**, attend, pay attention, lend an ear, prick up your ears 2 = **pay attention**, observe, obey, mind, heed, take notice, take note of, take heed of

literacy NOUN = **education**, learning, knowledge

literal ADJECTIVE 1 = **exact**, close, strict, accurate, faithful, verbatim, word for word 2 = **actual**, real, true, simple, plain, genuine, bona fide, unvarnished

literally ADVERB = **exactly**, really, closely, actually, truly, precisely, strictly, faithfully

literary ADJECTIVE = **well-read**, learned, formal, intellectual, scholarly, erudite, bookish

literate ADJECTIVE = **educated**, informed, knowledgeable

literature NOUN = **writings**, letters, compositions, lore, creative writing
▷ *see* Shakespeare

litigation NOUN = **lawsuit**, case, action, prosecution

litter NOUN 1 = **rubbish**, refuse, waste, junk, debris, garbage (*chiefly U.S.*), trash, muck 2 = **brood**, young, offspring, progeny
▷ VERB 1 = **clutter**, mess up, clutter up, be scattered about, disorder, disarrange, derange, muss (*U.S. & Canad.*) 2 = **scatter**, spread, shower, strew

little ADJECTIVE 1 = **small**, minute, short, tiny, wee, compact, miniature, diminutive ≠ big 2 = **young**, small, junior, infant, immature, undeveloped, babyish
▷ ADVERB 1 = **hardly**, barely, scarcely ≠ much 2 = **rarely**, seldom, scarcely, not often, infrequently, hardly ever ≠ always
▷ NOUN = **bit**, touch, spot, trace,

hint, particle, fragment, speck ≠ lot ▷ PHRASE: **a little = to a small extent**, slightly, to some extent, to a certain extent, to a small degree

live¹ VERB 1 = **dwell**, board, settle, lodge, occupy, abide, inhabit, reside 2 = **exist**, last, prevail, be, have being, breathe, persist, be alive 3 = **survive**, get along, make a living, make ends meet, subsist, eke out a living, support yourself, maintain yourself 4 = **thrive**, flourish, prosper, have fun, enjoy yourself, live life to the full

live² ADJECTIVE 1 = **living**, alive, breathing, animate 2 = **active**, unexploded 3 = **topical**, important, pressing, current, hot, burning, controversial, prevalent

livelihood NOUN = **occupation**, work, employment, living, job, bread and butter (*informal*)

lively ADJECTIVE 1 = **animated**, spirited, quick, keen, active, alert, dynamic, vigorous ≠ dull 2 = **vivid**, strong, striking, bright, exciting, stimulating, bold, colourful ≠ dull 3 = **enthusiastic**, strong, keen, stimulating, eager, formidable, vigorous, animated

living NOUN = **lifestyle**, ways, situation, conduct, behaviour, customs, lifestyle, way of life ▷ ADJECTIVE 1 = **alive**, existing, moving, active, breathing, animate ≠ dead 2 = **current**, present, active, contemporary, in use, extant ≠ obsolete

lizard NOUN

▷ *see* **reptiles**

load VERB 1 = **fill**, stuff, pack, pile, stack, heap, cram, freight 2 = **make ready**, charge, prime ▷ NOUN 1 = **cargo**, delivery, haul, shipment, batch, freight, consignment 2 = **oppression**, charge, worry, trouble, weight, responsibility, burden, onus ▷ PHRASE: **load someone down = burden**, worry, oppress, weigh down, saddle with, encumber, snow under

loaded ADJECTIVE 1 = **tricky**, charged, sensitive, delicate, manipulative, emotive, insidious, artful 2 = **biased**, weighted, rigged, distorted 3 (*slang*) = **rich**, wealthy, affluent, well off, flush (*informal*), well-heeled (*informal*), well-to-do, moneyed, minted (*Brit. slang*)

loaf¹ NOUN 1 = **lump**, block, cake, cube, slab 2 (*slang*) = **head**, mind, sense, common sense, nous (*Brit. slang*), gumption (*Brit. informal*)

loaf² VERB = **idle**, hang around, take it easy, lie around, loiter, laze, lounge around

loan NOUN = **advance**, credit, overdraft ▷ VERB = **lend**, advance, let out

loathe VERB = **hate**, dislike, despise, detest, abhor, abominate

loathing NOUN = **hatred**, hate, disgust, aversion, revulsion, antipathy, repulsion, abhorrence

lobby VERB = **campaign**, press, pressure, push, influence, promote, urge, persuade

▷ NOUN 1 = **pressure group**, group, camp, faction, lobbyists, interest group, special-interest group, ginger group, public-interest group (*U.S. & Canad.*)
2 = **corridor**, passage, entrance, porch, hallway, foyer, entrance hall, vestibule

lobola NOUN (*S. African*) = **dowry**, portion, marriage settlement, dot (*archaic*)

local ADJECTIVE 1 = **community**, regional **2** = **confined**, limited, restricted
▷ NOUN = **resident**, native, inhabitant

locate VERB 1 = **find**, discover, detect, come across, track down, pinpoint, unearth, pin down
2 = **place**, put, set, position, seat, site, establish, settle

location NOUN = **place**, point, setting, position, situation, spot, venue, locale

lock¹ VERB 1 = **fasten**, close, secure, shut, bar, seal, bolt
2 = **unite**, join, link, engage, clench, entangle, interlock, entwine **3** = **embrace**, press, grasp, clutch, hug, enclose, clasp, encircle
▷ NOUN = **fastening**, catch, bolt, clasp, padlock ▷ PHRASE: **lock someone up** = **imprison**, jail, confine, cage, detain, shut up, incarcerate, send down (*informal*)

lock² NOUN = **strand**, curl, tuft, tress, ringlet

lodge NOUN 1 = **cabin**, shelter, cottage, hut, chalet, gatehouse

2 = **society**, group, club, section, wing, chapter, branch
▷ VERB 1 = **register**, enter, file, submit, put on record **2** = **stay**, room, board, reside **3** = **stick**, remain, implant, come to rest, imbed

lodging NOUN *often plural* = **accommodation**, rooms, apartments, quarters, digs (*Brit. informal*), shelter, residence, abode, bachelor apartment (*Canad.*)

lofty ADJECTIVE 1 = **noble**, grand, distinguished, renowned, elevated, dignified, illustrious, exalted ≠ humble **2** = **high**, raised, towering, soaring, elevated ≠ low **3** = **haughty**, proud, arrogant, patronizing, condescending, disdainful, supercilious ≠ modest

log NOUN 1 = **stump**, block, branch, chunk, trunk **2** = **record**, account, register, journal, diary, logbook, blog (*informal*)
▷ VERB = **record**, enter, note, register, chart, put down, set down

logic NOUN = **reason**, reasoning, sense, good sense

logical ADJECTIVE 1 = **rational**, clear, reasoned, sound, consistent, valid, coherent, well-organized ≠ illogical
2 = **reasonable**, sensible, natural, wise, plausible ≠ unlikely

lone ADJECTIVE = **solitary**, single, one, only, sole, unaccompanied

loneliness NOUN = **solitude**,

isolation, desolation, seclusion

lonely ADJECTIVE 1 = **solitary**, alone, isolated, abandoned, lone, withdrawn, single, forsaken, lonesome (*chiefly U.S. & Canad.*) ≠ accompanied 2 = **desolate**, deserted, remote, isolated, out-of-the-way, secluded, uninhabited, godforsaken ≠ crowded

lonesome ADJECTIVE (*chiefly U.S. & Canad.*) = **lonely**, gloomy, dreary, desolate, forlorn, friendless, companionless

long¹ ADJECTIVE 1 = **elongated**, extended, stretched, expanded, extensive, lengthy, far-reaching, spread out ≠ short 2 = **prolonged**, sustained, lengthy, lingering, protracted, interminable, spun out, long-drawn-out ≠ brief

long² VERB = **desire**, want, wish, burn, pine, lust, crave, yearn

longing NOUN = **desire**, hope, wish, burning, urge, ambition, hunger, yen (*informal*) ≠ indifference

long-standing ADJECTIVE = **established**, fixed, enduring, abiding, long-lasting, long-established, time-honoured

look VERB 1 = **see**, view, consider, watch, eye, study, survey, examine 2 = **search**, seek, hunt, forage, fossick (*Austral. & N.Z.*) 3 = **consider**, contemplate 4 = **face**, overlook 5 = **hope**, expect, await, anticipate, reckon on 6 = **seem**, appear, look like, strike you as

▷ NOUN 1 = **glimpse**, view, glance, observation, sight, examination, gaze, inspection 2 = **appearance**, bearing, air, style, aspect, manner, expression, impression

▷ PHRASES: **look after something** *or* **someone** = **take care of**, mind, protect, tend, guard, nurse, care for, supervise; **look down on** *or* **upon someone** = **disdain**, despise, scorn, sneer at, spurn, contemn (*formal*); **look forward to something** = **anticipate**, expect, look for, wait for, await, hope for, long for; **look out for something** = **be careful of**, beware, watch out for, pay attention to, be wary of, keep an eye out for; **look someone up** = **visit**, call on, drop in on (*informal*), look in on; **look something up** = **research**, find, search for, hunt for, track down, seek out; **look up** = **improve**, develop, advance, pick up, progress, get better, shape up (*informal*), perk up; **look up to someone** = **respect**, honour, admire, esteem, revere, defer to, think highly of

lookout NOUN 1 = **watchman**, guard, sentry, sentinel 2 = **watch**, guard, vigil 3 = **watchtower**, post, observatory, observation post 4 (*informal*) = **concern**, business, worry

loom VERB = **appear**, emerge, hover, take shape, threaten, bulk, menace, come into view

loop NOUN = **curve**, ring, circle, twist, curl, spiral, coil, twirl

▷ VERB = **twist**, turn, roll, knot, curl, spiral, coil, wind round

loophole NOUN = **let-out**, escape, excuse

loose ADJECTIVE 1 = **free**, detached, insecure, unfettered, unrestricted, untied, unattached, unfastened 2 = **slack**, easy, relaxed, sloppy, loose-fitting ≠ tight 3 (*old-fashioned*) = **promiscuous**, fast, abandoned, immoral, dissipated, profligate, debauched, dissolute ≠ chaste 4 = **vague**, random, inaccurate, rambling, imprecise, ill-defined, indistinct, inexact ≠ precise

▷ VERB = **free**, release, liberate, detach, unleash, disconnect, set free, untie ≠ fasten

loosen VERB = **untie**, undo, release, separate, detach, unloose

▷ PHRASE: **loosen up** = **relax**, chill (*slang*), soften, unwind, go easy (*informal*), hang loose, outspan (*S. African*), ease up or off

loot VERB = **plunder**, rob, raid, sack, rifle, ravage, ransack, pillage

▷ NOUN = **plunder**, goods, prize, haul, spoils, booty, swag (*slang*)

lord NOUN 1 = **peer**, nobleman, count, duke, gentleman, earl, noble, baron 2 = **ruler**, leader, chief, master, governor, commander, superior, liege

▷ PHRASES: **lord it over someone** = **boss around** or **about** (*informal*), order around, threaten, bully, menace, intimidate, hector, bluster; **the Lord** or **Our Lord** = **Jesus Christ**, God, Christ, Messiah, Jehovah, the Almighty

lose VERB 1 = **be defeated**, be beaten, lose out, come to grief 2 = **mislay**, drop, forget, be deprived of, lose track of, misplace 3 = **forfeit**, miss, yield, be deprived of, pass up (*informal*)

loser NOUN = **failure**, flop (*informal*), also-ran, no-hoper (*Austral. slang*), dud (*informal*), non-achiever

loss NOUN 1 = **losing**, waste, squandering, forfeiture ≠ gain 2 *sometimes plural* = **deficit**, debt, deficiency, debit, depletion ≠ gain 3 = **damage**, cost, injury, hurt, harm ≠ advantage

▷ PHRASE: **at a loss** = **confused**, puzzled, baffled, bewildered, helpless, stumped, perplexed, mystified

lost ADJECTIVE = **missing**, disappeared, vanished, wayward, misplaced, mislaid

lot NOUN 1 = **bunch** (*informal*), group, crowd, crew, set, band, quantity, assortment 2 = **destiny**, situation, circumstances, fortune, chance, accident, fate, doom

▷ PHRASE: **a lot** or **lots 1** = **plenty**, scores, masses (*informal*), load(s) (*informal*), wealth, piles (*informal*), a great deal, stack(s) 2 = **often**, regularly, a great deal, frequently, a good deal

lotion NOUN = **cream**, solution, balm, salve, liniment, embrocation

lottery NOUN 1 = **raffle**, draw, lotto (*Brit., N.Z. & S. African*),

loud ADJECTIVE 1 = **noisy**, booming, roaring, thundering, forte (*music*), resounding, deafening, thunderous ≠ quiet 2 = **garish**, bold, glaring, flamboyant, brash, flashy, lurid, gaudy ≠ sombre

loudly ADVERB = **noisily**, vigorously, vehemently, vociferously, uproariously, lustily, shrilly, fortissimo (*music*)

lounge VERB = **relax**, loaf, sprawl, lie about, take it easy, loiter, loll, laze, outspan (*S. African*)
▷ NOUN = **sitting room**, living room, parlour, drawing room, front room, reception room, television room

love VERB 1 = **adore**, care for, treasure, cherish, prize, worship, be devoted to, dote on ≠ hate 2 = **enjoy**, like, appreciate, relish, delight in, savour, take pleasure in, have a soft spot for ≠ dislike
▷ NOUN 1 = **passion**, affection, warmth, attachment, intimacy, devotion, tenderness, adoration, aroha (*N.Z.*) ≠ hatred 2 = **liking**, taste, bent for, weakness for, relish for, enjoyment, devotion to, penchant for 3 = **beloved**, dear, dearest, lover, darling, honey, sweetheart, truelove ≠ enemy 4 = **sympathy**, understanding, pity, humanity, warmth, mercy, sorrow, kindness, aroha (*N.Z.*)
▷ PHRASE: **make love** = **have sexual intercourse**, have sex, go to bed, sleep together, do it (*informal*), mate, have sexual relations, have it off (*slang*)

love affair NOUN = **romance**, relationship, affair, intrigue, liaison, amour

lovely ADJECTIVE 1 = **beautiful**, appealing, attractive, charming, pretty, handsome, good-looking, exquisite, fit (*Brit. informal*) ≠ ugly 2 = **wonderful**, pleasing, nice, pleasant, engaging, marvellous, delightful, enjoyable ≠ horrible

lover NOUN = **sweetheart**, beloved, loved one, flame (*informal*), mistress, admirer, suitor, woman friend

loving ADJECTIVE 1 = **affectionate**, dear, devoted, tender, fond, doting, amorous, warm-hearted ≠ cruel 2 = **tender**, kind, caring, warm, gentle, sympathetic, considerate

low ADJECTIVE 1 = **small**, little, short, stunted, squat ≠ tall 2 = **inferior**, bad, poor, inadequate, unsatisfactory, deficient, second-rate, shoddy, half-pie (*N.Z. informal*), bodger *or* bodgie (*Austral. slang*) 3 = **quiet**, soft, gentle, whispered, muted, subdued, hushed, muffled ≠ loud 4 = **dejected**, depressed, miserable, fed up, moody, gloomy, glum, despondent ≠ happy 5 = **coarse**, common, rough, crude, rude, vulgar, undignified, disreputable 6 = **ill**, weak, frail, stricken, debilitated ≠ strong

lower ADJECTIVE 1 = **subordinate**,

under, smaller, junior, minor, secondary, lesser, inferior **2** = **reduced**, cut, diminished, decreased, lessened, curtailed ≠ increased
▷ VERB **1** = **drop**, sink, depress, let down, submerge, take down, let fall ≠ raise **2** = **lessen**, cut, reduce, diminish, slash, decrease, prune, minimize ≠ increase

low-key ADJECTIVE = **subdued**, quiet, restrained, muted, understated, toned down

loyal ADJECTIVE = **faithful**, true, devoted, dependable, constant, staunch, trustworthy, trusty ≠ disloyal

loyalty NOUN = **faithfulness**, commitment, devotion, allegiance, fidelity, homage, obedience, constancy

luck NOUN **1** = **good fortune**, success, advantage, prosperity, blessing, windfall, godsend, serendipity **2** = **fortune**, lot, stars, chance, accident, fate, destiny, twist of fate

luckily ADVERB = **fortunately**, happily, opportunely

lucky ADJECTIVE = **fortunate**, successful, favoured, charmed, blessed, jammy (*Brit. slang*), serendipitous ≠ unlucky

lucrative ADJECTIVE = **profitable**, rewarding, productive, fruitful, well-paid, advantageous, remunerative

ludicrous ADJECTIVE = **ridiculous**, crazy, absurd, preposterous, silly, laughable, farcical, outlandish

≠ sensible

luggage NOUN = **baggage**, things, cases, bags, gear, suitcases, paraphernalia, impedimenta

lull NOUN = **respite**, pause, quiet, silence, calm, hush, let-up (*informal*)
▷ VERB = **calm**, soothe, subdue, quell, allay, pacify, tranquillize

lumber¹ VERB (*Brit. informal*) = **burden**, land, load, saddle, encumber
▷ NOUN (*Brit.*) = **junk**, refuse, rubbish, trash, clutter, jumble

lumber² VERB = **plod**, shuffle, shamble, trudge, stump, waddle, trundle

lumbering ADJECTIVE = **awkward**, heavy, hulking, ponderous, ungainly

lump NOUN **1** = **piece**, ball, block, mass, chunk, hunk, nugget **2** = **swelling**, growth, bump, tumour, bulge, hump, protrusion
▷ VERB = **group**, throw, mass, combine, collect, pool, consolidate, conglomerate

lunatic NOUN = **madman**, maniac, psychopath, nutcase (*slang*), crazy (*informal*)
▷ ADJECTIVE = **mad**, crazy, insane, irrational, daft, deranged, crackpot (*informal*), crackbrained, off the air (*Austral. slang*)

lunge VERB = **pounce**, charge, dive, leap, plunge, thrust
▷ NOUN = **thrust**, charge, pounce, spring, swing, jab

lurch VERB **1** = **tilt**, roll, pitch, list, rock, lean, heel **2** = **stagger**, reel, stumble, weave, sway, totter

lure VERB = **tempt**, draw, attract, invite, trick, seduce, entice, allure
▷ NOUN = **temptation**, attraction, incentive, bait, carrot (*informal*), inducement, enticement, allurement

lurk VERB = **hide**, sneak, prowl, lie in wait, slink, skulk, conceal yourself

lush ADJECTIVE 1 = **abundant**, green, flourishing, dense, rank, verdant 2 = **luxurious**, grand, elaborate, lavish, extravagant, sumptuous, plush (*informal*), ornate

lust NOUN 1 = **lechery**, sensuality, lewdness, lasciviousness 2 = **desire**, longing, passion, appetite, craving, greed, thirst
▷ PHRASE: **lust for** *or* **after someone** *or* **something** = **desire**, want, crave, yearn for, covet, hunger for *or* after

luxurious ADJECTIVE
= **sumptuous**, expensive, comfortable, magnificent, splendid, lavish, plush (*informal*), opulent

● **WORD POWER**
● *Luxurious* is sometimes wrongly
● used where *luxuriant* is meant:
● *he had a luxuriant (not luxurious)*
● *moustache; the walls were covered*
● *with a luxuriant growth of*
● *wisteria.*

luxury NOUN 1 = **opulence**, splendour, richness, extravagance, affluence, hedonism, a bed of roses, the life of Riley ≠ poverty 2 = **extravagance**, treat, extra, indulgence, frill ≠ necessity

lyrical ADJECTIVE = **enthusiastic**, inspired, poetic, impassioned, effusive, rhapsodic

Mm

machine NOUN 1 = **appliance**, device, apparatus, engine, tool, instrument, mechanism, gadget 2 = **system**, structure, organization, machinery, setup (*informal*)

machinery NOUN = **equipment**, gear, instruments, apparatus, technology, tackle, tools, gadgetry

macho ADJECTIVE = **manly**, masculine, chauvinist, virile

mad ADJECTIVE 1 = **insane**, crazy (*informal*), nuts (*slang*), raving, unstable, psychotic, demented, deranged, off the air (*Austral. slang*) ≠ sane 2 = **foolish**, absurd, wild, stupid, daft (*informal*), irrational, senseless, preposterous ≠ sensible 3 (*informal*) = **angry**, furious, incensed, enraged, livid (*informal*), berserk, berko (*Austral. slang*), tooshie (*Austral. slang*), off the air (*Austral. slang*) ≠ calm 4 *usually with* **about** = **enthusiastic**, wild, crazy (*informal*), ardent, fanatical, avid, impassioned, infatuated ≠ nonchalant 5 = **frenzied**, wild, excited, frenetic, uncontrolled, unrestrained

madden VERB = **infuriate**, irritate, incense, enrage, upset, annoy, inflame, drive you crazy ≠ calm

madly ADVERB 1 (*informal*) = **passionately**, wildly, desperately, intensely, to distraction, devotedly 2 = **foolishly**, wildly, absurdly, ludicrously, irrationally, senselessly 3 = **energetically**, wildly, furiously, excitedly, recklessly, speedily, like mad (*informal*) 4 = **insanely**, frantically, hysterically, crazily, deliriously, distractedly, frenziedly

madness NOUN 1 = **insanity**, mental illness, delusion, mania, dementia, distraction, aberration, psychosis 2 = **foolishness**, nonsense, folly, absurdity, idiocy, wildness, daftness (*informal*), foolhardiness

magazine NOUN = **journal**, publication, supplement, rag (*informal*), issue, glossy (*informal*), pamphlet, periodical

magic NOUN 1 = **sorcery**, wizardry, witchcraft, enchantment, black art, necromancy 2 = **conjuring**, illusion, trickery, sleight of hand, legerdemain, prestidigitation 3 = **charm**, power, glamour, fascination, magnetism, enchantment, allurement ▷ ADJECTIVE = **miraculous**, entrancing, charming, fascinating, marvellous, magical, enchanting, bewitching

magician NOUN 1 = **conjuror**, illusionist, prestidigitator 2 = **sorcerer**, witch, wizard, illusionist, warlock, necromancer, enchanter or enchantress

magistrate NOUN =**judge**, justice, justice of the peace, J.P.

magnetic ADJECTIVE =**attractive**, irresistible, seductive, captivating, charming, fascinating, charismatic, hypnotic ≠ repulsive

magnificent ADJECTIVE
1 =**splendid**, impressive, imposing, glorious, gorgeous, majestic, regal, sublime ≠ ordinary 2 =**brilliant**, fine, excellent, outstanding, superb, splendid

magnify VERB 1 =**enlarge**, increase, boost, expand, intensify, blow up (*informal*), heighten, amplify ≠ reduce 2 =**make worse**, exaggerate, intensify, worsen, exacerbate, increase, inflame 3 =**exaggerate**, overstate, inflate, overplay, overemphasize ≠ understate

magnitude NOUN
1 =**importance**, consequence, significance, moment, note, weight, greatness ≠ unimportance 2 =**immensity**, size, extent, enormity, volume, vastness ≠ smallness 3 =**intensity**, amplitude

maid NOUN 1 =**servant**, chambermaid, housemaid, menial, maidservant, female servant, domestic (*archaic*), parlourmaid 2 (*archaic or literary*) =**girl**, maiden, lass, damsel, lassie (*informal*), wench

maiden NOUN (*archaic or literary*) =**girl**, maid, lass, damsel, virgin, lassie (*informal*), wench
▷ MODIFIER 1 =**first**, initial, inaugural, introductory 2 =**unmarried**, unwed

mail NOUN =**letters**, post, correspondence
▷ VERB 1 =**post**, send, forward, dispatch 2 =**e-mail**, send, forward

main ADJECTIVE =**chief**, leading, head, central, essential, primary, principal, foremost ≠ minor
▷ PLURAL NOUN 1 =**pipeline**, channel, pipe, conduit, duct 2 =**cable**, line, electricity supply, mains supply ▷ PHRASE: **in the main** =**on the whole**, generally, mainly, mostly, in general, for the most part

mainly ADVERB =**chiefly**, mostly, largely, principally, primarily, on the whole, predominantly, in the main

mainstream ADJECTIVE =**conventional**, general, established, received, accepted, current, prevailing, orthodox ≠ unconventional

maintain VERB 1 =**continue**, retain, preserve, sustain, carry on, keep up, prolong, perpetuate ≠ end 2 =**assert**, state, claim, insist, declare, contend, profess, avow ≠ disavow 3 =**look after**, care for, take care of, conserve, keep in good condition

maintenance NOUN
1 =**upkeep**, keeping, care,

m

repairs, conservation, nurture, preservation **2 = allowance**, support, keep, alimony
3 = continuation, carrying-on, perpetuation, prolongation

majestic ADJECTIVE **= grand**, magnificent, impressive, superb, splendid, regal, stately, monumental ≠ modest

majesty NOUN **= grandeur**, glory, splendour, magnificence, nobility ≠ triviality

major ADJECTIVE **1 = important**, critical, significant, great, serious, crucial, outstanding, notable
2 = main, higher, greater, bigger, leading, chief, senior, supreme ≠ minor

majority NOUN **1 = most**, mass, bulk, best part, better part, lion's share, preponderance, greater number **2 = adulthood**, maturity, age of consent, seniority, manhood *or* womanhood

● WORD POWER
● The majority of should always
● refer to a countable number
● of things or people. If you
● are talking about an amount
● or quantity, rather than a
● countable number, use *most
● of*, as in *most of the harvest was
● saved* (not *the majority of the
● harvest was saved*).

make VERB **1 = produce**, cause, create, effect, lead to, generate, bring about, give rise to
2 = perform, do, effect, carry out, execute **3 = force**, cause, compel, drive, require, oblige, induce,

constrain **4 = create**, build, produce, manufacture, form, fashion, construct, assemble
5 = earn, get, gain, net, win, clear, obtain, bring in **6 = amount to**, total, constitute, add up to, count as, tot up to (*informal*)
▷ NOUN **1 = brand**, sort, style, model, kind, type, variety, marque ▷ PHRASES: **make for something = head for**, aim for, head towards, be bound for; **make it** (*informal*) **= succeed**, prosper, arrive (*informal*), get on, crack it (*informal*); **make off = flee**, clear out (*informal*), bolt, take to your heels, run away *or* off; **make something up = invent**, create, construct, compose, frame, coin, devise, originate; **make up = settle your differences**, bury the hatchet, call it quits, declare a truce, be friends again; **make up for something = compensate for**, make amends for, atone for, balance out, offset, make recompense for; **make up something 1 = form**, account for, constitute, compose, comprise
2 = complete, supply, fill, round off

maker NOUN **= manufacturer**, producer, builder, constructor

makeshift ADJECTIVE **= temporary**, provisional, substitute, expedient, stopgap

make-up NOUN **1 = cosmetics**, paint (*informal*), powder, face (*informal*), greasepaint (*theatre*) **2 = nature**, character, constitution, temperament, disposition **3** = **structure**, organization, arrangement, construction, assembly, constitution, format, composition

making NOUN = **creation**, production, manufacture, construction, assembly, composition, fabrication

▷ PLURAL NOUN = **beginnings**, potential, capacity, ingredients

male ADJECTIVE = **masculine**, manly, macho, virile ≠ female

malicious ADJECTIVE = **spiteful**, malevolent, resentful, vengeful, rancorous, ill-disposed, ill-natured ≠ benevolent

mammal ▷ see bats, carnivores, marsupials, monkeys, apes and other primates, rodents, sea mammals, whales and dolphins

● EXTINCT MAMMALS
● apeman
● aurochs
● australopithecine
● eohippus
● glyptodont
● mammoth
● mastodon
● megathere
● quagga
● sabre-toothed tiger *or* cat
● tarpan

mammoth ADJECTIVE = **colossal**, huge, giant, massive, enormous, immense, gigantic, monumental, supersize ≠ tiny

man NOUN **1** = **male**, guy (*informal*), fellow (*informal*), gentleman, bloke (*Brit. informal*), chap (*Brit. informal*), dude (*U.S. informal*), geezer (*informal*) **2** = **human**, human being, person, individual, soul **3** = **mankind**, humanity, people, human race, humankind, Homo sapiens

▷ VERB = **staff**, people, crew, occupy, garrison

mana NOUN (*N.Z.*) = **authority**, influence, power, might, standing, status, importance, eminence

manage VERB **1** = **be in charge of**, run, handle, direct, conduct, command, administer, supervise **2** = **organize**, use, handle, regulate **3** = **cope**, survive, succeed, carry on, make do, get by (*informal*), muddle through **4** = **perform**, do, achieve, carry out, undertake, cope with, accomplish, contrive **5** = **control**, handle, manipulate

management NOUN **1** = **administration**, control, running, operation, handling, direction, command, supervision **2** = **directors**, board, executive(s), administration, employers

manager NOUN = **supervisor**, head, director, executive, boss (*informal*), governor, administrator, organizer, baas (*S. African*), sherang (*Austral. & N.Z.*)

m

mandate NOUN = **command**, order, commission, instruction, decree, directive, edict

mandatory ADJECTIVE = **compulsory**, required, binding, obligatory, requisite ≠ optional

manhood NOUN = **manliness**, masculinity, virility

manifest ADJECTIVE = **obvious**, apparent, patent, evident, clear, glaring, noticeable, blatant ≠ concealed
▷ VERB = **display**, show, reveal, express, demonstrate, expose, exhibit ≠ conceal

manifestation NOUN 1 = **sign**, symptom, indication, mark, example, evidence, proof, testimony 2 = **display**, show, exhibition, expression, demonstration

manipulate VERB 1 = **influence**, control, direct, negotiate, exploit, manoeuvre 2 = **work**, use, operate, handle

mankind NOUN = **people**, man, humanity, human race, humankind, Homo sapiens

● WORD POWER
● Some people object to the use
● of *mankind* to refer to all human
● beings on the grounds that it
● is sexist. A preferable term is
● *humankind*, which refers to both
● men and women.

manly ADJECTIVE = **virile**, masculine, strong, brave, bold, strapping, vigorous, courageous ≠ effeminate

man-made ADJECTIVE = **artificial**, manufactured, mock, synthetic, ersatz

manner NOUN 1 = **style**, way, fashion, method, custom, mode 2 = **behaviour**, air, bearing, conduct, aspect, demeanour 3 = **type**, form, sort, kind, variety, brand, category
▷ PLURAL NOUN 1 = **conduct**, behaviour, demeanour 2 = **politeness**, courtesy, etiquette, refinement, decorum, p's and q's 3 = **protocol**, customs, social graces

mannered ADJECTIVE = **affected**, artificial, pretentious, stilted, arty-farty (*informal*) ≠ natural

manoeuvre VERB 1 = **scheme**, wangle (*informal*), machinate 2 = **manipulate**, arrange, organize, set up, engineer, fix, orchestrate, contrive
▷ NOUN 1 = **stratagem**, scheme, trick, tactic, intrigue, dodge, ploy, ruse 2 *often plural* = **movement**, operation, exercise, war game

mansion NOUN = **residence**, manor, hall, villa, seat

mantle NOUN 1 = **covering**, screen, curtain, blanket, veil, shroud, canopy, pall 2 (*archaic*) = **cloak**, wrap, cape, hood, shawl

manual ADJECTIVE 1 = **physical**, human 2 = **hand-operated**, hand, non-automatic
▷ NOUN = **handbook**, guide, instructions, bible

manufacture VERB 1 = **make**, build, produce, construct, create, turn out, assemble, put together

2 = **concoct**, make up, invent, devise, fabricate, think up, cook up (*informal*), trump up
▷ NOUN = **making**, production, construction, assembly, creation

manufacturer NOUN = **maker**, producer, builder, creator, industrialist, constructor

many ADJECTIVE = **numerous**, various, countless, abundant, myriad, innumerable, manifold, umpteen (*informal*)
▷ PRONOUN = **a lot**, lots (*informal*), plenty, scores, heaps (*informal*)

mar VERB **1** = **harm**, damage, hurt, spoil, stain, taint, tarnish **2** = **ruin**, spoil, scar, flaw, impair, detract from, deform, blemish ≠ improve

march VERB **1** = **parade**, walk, file, pace, stride, swagger **2** = **walk**, strut, storm, sweep, stride, flounce
▷ NOUN **1** = **walk**, trek, slog, yomp (*Brit. informal*), routemarch **2** = **progress**, development, advance, evolution, progression

margin NOUN = **edge**, side, border, boundary, verge, brink, rim, perimeter

marginal ADJECTIVE
1 = **insignificant**, small, minor, slight, minimal, negligible
2 = **borderline**, bordering, on the edge, peripheral

marijuana NOUN = **cannabis**, pot (*slang*), dope (*slang*), grass (*slang*), hemp, dagga (*S. African*)

marine ADJECTIVE = **nautical**, maritime, naval, seafaring, seagoing

mariner NOUN = **sailor**, seaman, sea dog, seafarer, salt

marital ADJECTIVE = **matrimonial**, nuptial, conjugal, connubial

maritime ADJECTIVE **1** = **nautical**, marine, naval, oceanic, seafaring **2** = **coastal**, seaside, littoral

mark NOUN **1** = **spot**, stain, streak, smudge, line, scratch, scar, blot **2** = **characteristic**, feature, standard, quality, measure, stamp, attribute, criterion **3** = **indication**, sign, symbol, token **4** = **brand**, impression, label, device, flag, symbol, token, emblem **5** = **target**, goal, aim, purpose, object, objective
▷ VERB **1** = **scar**, scratch, stain, streak, blot, smudge, blemish **2** = **label**, identify, brand, flag, stamp, characterize **3** = **grade**, correct, assess, evaluate, appraise **4** = **distinguish**, show, illustrate, exemplify, denote **5** = **observe**, mind, note, notice, attend to, pay attention to, pay heed to

marked ADJECTIVE = **noticeable**, clear, decided, striking, obvious, prominent, patent, distinct ≠ imperceptible

markedly ADVERB = **noticeably**, clearly, obviously, considerably, distinctly, decidedly, strikingly, conspicuously

market NOUN = **fair**, mart, bazaar, souk (*Arabic*)
▷ VERB = **sell**, promote, retail, peddle, vend

maroon VERB = **abandon**, leave,

m

desert, strand, leave high and dry (*informal*)

marriage NOUN = **wedding**, match, nuptials, wedlock, matrimony ▷ **RELATED WORDS**: *adjectives* **conjugal, marital, nuptial**

marry VERB 1 = **tie the knot** (*informal*), wed, get hitched (*slang*) 2 = **unite**, join, link, bond, ally, merge, knit, unify

marsh NOUN = **swamp**, bog, slough, fen, quagmire, morass, muskeg (*Canad.*)

marshal VERB 1 = **conduct**, take, lead, guide, steer, escort, shepherd, usher 2 = **arrange**, group, order, line up, organize, deploy, array, draw up

martial ADJECTIVE = **military**, belligerent, warlike, bellicose

marvel VERB = **be amazed**, wonder, gape, be awed ▷ NOUN 1 = **wonder**, phenomenon, miracle, portent 2 = **genius**, prodigy

marvellous ADJECTIVE = **excellent**, great (*informal*), wonderful, brilliant, amazing, extraordinary, superb, spectacular, booshit (*Austral. slang*), exo (*Austral. slang*), sik (*Austral. slang*), rad (*informal*), phat (*slang*), schmick (*Austral. informal*) ≠ terrible

masculine ADJECTIVE = **male**, manly, mannish, manlike, virile

mask NOUN = **façade**, disguise, front, cover, screen, veil, guise, camouflage

▷ VERB = **disguise**, hide, conceal, obscure, cover (up), screen, blanket, veil

mass NOUN 1 = **lot**, collection, load, pile, quantity, bunch, stack, heap 2 = **piece**, block, lump, chunk, hunk 3 = **size**, matter, weight, extent, bulk, magnitude, greatness

▷ ADJECTIVE = **large-scale**, general, widespread, extensive, universal, wholesale, indiscriminate

▷ VERB = **gather**, assemble, accumulate, collect, rally, swarm, throng, congregate

massacre NOUN = **slaughter**, murder, holocaust, carnage, extermination, annihilation, butchery, blood bath

▷ VERB = **slaughter**, kill, murder, butcher, wipe out, exterminate, mow down, cut to pieces

massage NOUN = **rub-down**, manipulation

▷ VERB 1 = **rub down**, manipulate, knead

2 = **manipulate**, alter, distort, doctor, cook (*informal*), fix (*informal*), rig, fiddle (*informal*)

massive ADJECTIVE = **huge**, big, enormous, immense, hefty, gigantic, monumental, mammoth, supersize ≠ tiny

master NOUN 1 = **lord**, ruler, commander, chief, director, manager, boss (*informal*), head, baas (*S. African*) ≠ servant

2 = **expert**, maestro, ace (*informal*), genius, wizard,

- **MARSUPIALS**
- bandicoot
- Bennett's tree kangaroo or tcharibeena
- bettong
- bilby, rabbit(-eared) bandicoot, long-eared bandicoot, dalgyte, or dalgite
- bobuck or mountain (brushtail) possum
- boodie (rat), burrowing rat-kangaroo, Lesueur's rat-kangaroo, tungoo, or tungo
- boongary or Lumholtz's tree kangaroo
- bridled nail-tail wallaby or merrin
- brush-tail(ed) possum
- burramys or (mountain) pygmy possum
- crest-tailed marsupial mouse, Cannings' little dog, or mulgara
- crescent nail-tail wallaby or wurrung
- cuscus
- dasyurid, dasyure, native cat, marsupial cat, or wild cat
- dibbler

- diprotodon
- dunnart
- fluffy glider or yellow-bellied glider
- flying phalanger, flying squirrel, glider, or pongo
- green ringtail possum or toolah
- hare-wallaby
- honey mouse, honey possum, noolbenger, or tait
- jerboa, jerboa pouched mouse, jerboa kangaroo, or kultarr
- kangaroo or (Austral. informal) roo
- koala (bear) or (Austral.) native bear
- kowari
- larapinta or Darling Downs dunnart
- marlu
- marsupial mole
- marsupial mouse
- munning
- ningaui
- northern native cat or satanellus
- numbat or banded anteater
- opossum or possum
- pademelon or paddymelon

- phalanger
- pitchi-pitchi or wuhl-wuhl
- platypus, duck-billed platypus, or duckbill
- potoroo
- pygmy glider, feather glider, or flying mouse
- quokka
- quoll
- rat kangaroo
- squirrel glider
- sugar glider
- tammar, damar, or dama
- Tasmanian devil or ursine dasyure
- thylacine, Tasmanian wolf, or Tasmanian tiger
- tiger cat or spotted native cat
- tree kangaroo
- tuan, phascogale, or wambenger
- wallaby
- wallaroo, uroo, or biggada
- warabi
- wombat or (Austral.) badger
- yapok
- yallara

m

virtuoso, doyen, past master, fundi (*S. African*) ≠ amateur
3 = **teacher**, tutor, instructor ≠ student
▷ ADJECTIVE = **main**, principal, chief, prime, foremost, predominant ≠ lesser
▷ VERB **1** = **learn**, understand, pick up, grasp, get the hang of (*informal*), know inside out, know backwards **2** = **overcome**, defeat, conquer, tame, triumph over, vanquish ≠ give in to

masterly ADJECTIVE = **skilful**, expert, crack (*informal*), supreme, world-class, consummate, first-rate, masterful

mastermind VERB = **plan**, manage, direct, organize, devise, conceive
▷ NOUN = **organizer**, director, manager, engineer, brain(s) (*informal*), architect, planner

masterpiece NOUN = **classic**, tour de force (*French*), pièce de résistance (*French*), magnum opus (*Latin*), jewel

mastery NOUN
1 = **understanding**, skill, know-how, expertise, prowess, finesse, proficiency, virtuosity
2 = **control**, command, domination, superiority, supremacy, upper hand, ascendancy, mana (*N.Z.*), whip hand

match NOUN **1** = **game**, test, competition, trial, tie, contest, fixture, bout **2** = **marriage**, pairing, alliance, partnership

3 = **equal**, rival, peer, counterpart
▷ VERB **1** = **correspond with**, go with, fit with, harmonize with **2** = **correspond**, agree, accord, square, coincide, tally, conform, match up **3** = **rival**, equal, compete with, compare with, emulate, measure up to

matching ADJECTIVE = **identical**, like, twin, equivalent, corresponding, coordinating ≠ different

mate NOUN **1** (*informal*) = **friend**, pal (*informal*), companion, buddy (*informal*), comrade, chum (*informal*), mucker (*Brit. informal*), crony, cobber (*Austral. & N.Z. old-fashioned, informal*), E hoa (*N.Z.*)
2 = **partner**, lover, companion, spouse, consort, helpmeet, husband *or* wife **3** = **assistant**, subordinate, apprentice, helper, accomplice, sidekick (*informal*)
4 = **colleague**, associate, companion
▷ VERB = **pair**, couple, breed

material NOUN **1** = **substance**, matter, stuff **2** = **cloth**, fabric, textile **3** = **information**, details, facts, notes, evidence, particulars, data, info (*informal*)
▷ ADJECTIVE **1** = **physical**, solid, substantial, concrete, bodily, tangible, palpable, corporeal
2 = **relevant**, important, significant, essential, vital, serious, meaningful, applicable

materially ADVERB
= **significantly**, much, greatly, essentially, seriously, gravely,

substantially ≠ insignificantly

maternal ADJECTIVE = **motherly**, protective, nurturing, maternalistic

maternity NOUN = **motherhood**, parenthood, motherliness

matted ADJECTIVE = **tangled**, knotted, unkempt, knotty, tousled, ratty, uncombed

matter NOUN 1 = **situation**, concern, business, question, event, subject, affair, incident
2 = **substance**, material, body, stuff
▷ VERB = **be important**, make a difference, count, be relevant, make any difference, carry weight, cut any ice (*informal*), be of account

matter-of-fact ADJECTIVE = **unsentimental**, plain, sober, down-to-earth, mundane, prosaic, deadpan, unimaginative

mature VERB = **develop**, grow up, bloom, blossom, come of age, age
▷ ADJECTIVE 1 = **matured**, seasoned, ripe, mellow
2 = **grown-up**, adult, of age, fully fledged, full-grown ≠ immature

maturity NOUN 1 = **adulthood**, puberty, coming of age, pubescence, manhood *or* womanhood ≠ immaturity
2 = **ripeness**

maul VERB 1 = **mangle**, claw, lacerate, tear, mangulate (*Austral. slang*) 2 = **ill-treat**, abuse, batter, molest, manhandle

maverick NOUN = **rebel**, radical, dissenter, individualist, protester, eccentric, heretic, nonconformist ≠ traditionalist
▷ ADJECTIVE = **rebel**, radical, dissenting, individualistic, eccentric, heretical, iconoclastic, nonconformist

maximum ADJECTIVE = **greatest**, highest, supreme, paramount, utmost, most, topmost ≠ minimal
▷ NOUN = **top**, peak, ceiling, utmost, upper limit ≠ minimum

maybe ADVERB = **perhaps**, possibly, perchance (*archaic*)

mayhem NOUN = **chaos**, trouble, violence, disorder, destruction, confusion, havoc, fracas

maze NOUN = **web**, confusion, tangle, labyrinth, imbroglio, complex network

meadow NOUN = **field**, pasture, grassland, lea (*poetic*)

mean¹ VERB 1 = **signify**, indicate, represent, express, stand for, convey, spell out, symbolize
2 = **imply**, suggest, intend, hint at, insinuate 3 = **intend**, want, plan, expect, design, aim, wish, think

● **WORD POWER**
● In standard British English,
● *mean* should not be followed by
● *for* when expressing intention.
● *I didn't mean this to happen* is
● acceptable, but not *I didn't mean*
● *for this to happen*.

mean² ADJECTIVE 1 = **miserly**, stingy, parsimonious, niggardly, mercenary, penny-pinching, ungenerous, tight-fisted, snoep

m

(*S. African informal*) ≠ generous
2 = **dishonourable**, petty,
shameful, shabby, vile, callous,
sordid, despicable, scungy
(*Austral. & N.Z.*) ≠ honourable

mean³ NOUN = **average**, middle,
balance, norm, midpoint
▷ ADJECTIVE = **average**, middle,
standard

meaning NOUN 1 = **significance**,
message, substance, drift,
connotation, gist 2 = **definition**,
sense

meaningful ADJECTIVE
= **significant**, important,
material, useful, relevant, valid,
worthwhile, purposeful ≠ trivial

meaningless ADJECTIVE
= **nonsensical**, senseless,
inconsequential, inane
≠ worthwhile

means PLURAL NOUN 1 = **method**,
way, process, medium, agency,
instrument, mode 2 = **money**,
funds, capital, income, resources,
fortune, wealth, affluence
▷ PHRASES: **by all means**
= **certainly**, surely, of course,
definitely, doubtlessly; **by no
means** = **in no way**, definitely
not, not in the least, on no
account

meantime *or* **meanwhile**
ADVERB = **at the same time**,
simultaneously, concurrently

meanwhile *or* **meantime**
ADVERB = **for now**, in the interim

measure VERB = **quantify**,
determine, assess, weigh,
calculate, evaluate, compute,
gauge
▷ NOUN 1 = **quantity**, share,
amount, allowance, portion,
quota, ration, allotment
2 = **action**, act, step, procedure,
means, control, initiative,
manoeuvre 3 = **gauge**, rule, scale,
metre, ruler, yardstick 4 = **law**,
act, bill, legislation, resolution,
statute

measured ADJECTIVE 1 = **steady**,
even, slow, regular, dignified,
stately, solemn, leisurely
2 = **considered**, reasoned,
studied, calculated, deliberate,
sober, well-thought-out

measurement NOUN
= **calculation**, assessment,
evaluation, valuation,
computation, calibration,
mensuration

meat NOUN = **food**, flesh, kai (*N.Z.
informal*)

mechanical ADJECTIVE
1 = **automatic**, automated,
mechanized, power-driven,
motor-driven ≠ manual
2 = **unthinking**, routine,
automatic, instinctive,
involuntary, impersonal, cursory,
perfunctory ≠ conscious

mechanism NOUN 1 = **process**,
way, means, system, operation,
agency, method, technique
2 = **machine**, device, tool,
instrument, appliance, apparatus,
contrivance

mediate VERB = **intervene**, step
in (*informal*), intercede, referee,
umpire, reconcile, arbitrate,

conciliate

mediation NOUN = **arbitration**, intervention, reconciliation, conciliation, intercession

mediator NOUN = **negotiator**, arbitrator, referee, umpire, intermediary, middleman, arbiter, peacemaker

medicine NOUN = **remedy**, drug, cure, prescription, medication, nostrum, medicament

mediocre ADJECTIVE = **second-rate**, average, ordinary, indifferent, middling, pedestrian, inferior, so-so (*informal*), half-pie (*N.Z. informal*) ≠ excellent

meditation NOUN = **reflection**, thought, study, musing, pondering, contemplation, rumination, cogitation

medium ADJECTIVE = **average**, mean, middle, middling, fair, intermediate, midway, mediocre ≠ extraordinary
▷ NOUN 1 = **spiritualist**, seer, clairvoyant, fortune teller, channeller 2 = **middle**, mean, centre, average, compromise, midpoint

meet VERB 1 = **encounter**, come across, run into, happen on, find, contact, confront, bump into (*informal*) ≠ avoid 2 = **gather**, collect, assemble, get together, come together, muster, convene, congregate ≠ disperse 3 = **fulfil**, match (up to), answer, satisfy, discharge, comply with, come up to, conform to ≠ fall short of 4 = **experience**, face, suffer, bear, go through, encounter, endure, undergo 5 = **converge**, join, cross, touch, connect, come together, link up, intersect ≠ diverge

meeting NOUN 1 = **conference**, gathering, assembly, congress, session, convention, get-together (*informal*), reunion, hui (*N.Z.*) 2 = **encounter**, introduction, confrontation, engagement, rendezvous, tryst, assignation

melancholy ADJECTIVE = **sad**, depressed, miserable, gloomy, glum, mournful, despondent, dispirited ≠ happy
▷ NOUN = **sadness**, depression, misery, gloom, sorrow, unhappiness, despondency, dejection ≠ happiness

mellow ADJECTIVE 1 = **full-flavoured**, rich, sweet, delicate 2 = **ripe**, mature, ripened ≠ unripe
▷ VERB 1 = **relax**, improve, settle, calm, mature, soften, sweeten 2 = **season**, develop, improve, ripen

melody NOUN 1 = **tune**, song, theme, air, music, strain 2 = **tunefulness**, harmony, musicality, euphony, melodiousness

melt VERB 1 = **dissolve**, run, soften, fuse, thaw, defrost, liquefy, unfreeze 2 *often with* **away** = **disappear**, fade, vanish, dissolve, disperse, evaporate, evanesce 3 = **soften**, relax, disarm, mollify

m

member NOUN = **representative**, associate, supporter, fellow, subscriber, comrade, disciple

membership NOUN
1 = **participation**, belonging, fellowship, enrolment
2 = **members**, body, associates, fellows

memoir NOUN = **account**, life, record, journal, essay, biography, narrative, monograph

memoirs PLURAL NOUN
= **autobiography**, diary, life story, experiences, memories, journals, recollections, reminiscences

memorable ADJECTIVE
= **noteworthy**, celebrated, historic, striking, famous, significant, remarkable, notable ≠ forgettable

memorandum NOUN
= **note**, minute, message, communication, reminder, memo, jotting, e-mail

memorial NOUN = **monument**, shrine, plaque, cenotaph
▷ ADJECTIVE = **commemorative**, remembrance, monumental

memory NOUN 1 = **recall**, mind, retention, ability to remember, powers of recall, powers of retention 2 = **recollection**, reminder, reminiscence, impression, echo, remembrance 3 = **commemoration**, respect, honour, recognition, tribute, remembrance, observance

menace NOUN 1 (*informal*) = **nuisance**, plague, pest, annoyance, troublemaker

2 = **threat**, warning, intimidation, ill-omen, ominousness
▷ VERB = **bully**, threaten, intimidate, terrorize, frighten, scare

menacing ADJECTIVE
= **threatening**, frightening, forbidding, looming, intimidating, ominous, louring *or* lowering ≠ encouraging

mend VERB 1 = **repair**, fix, restore, renew, patch up, renovate, refit, retouch 2 = **darn**, repair, patch, stitch, sew 3 = **heal**, improve, recover, get better, be all right, be cured, recuperate, pull through 4 = **improve**, reform, correct, revise, amend, rectify, ameliorate, emend ▷ PHRASE: on the mend = **convalescent**, improving, recovering, getting better, recuperating

mental ADJECTIVE 1 = **intellectual**, rational, theoretical, cognitive, brain, conceptual, cerebral 2 (*slang*) = **insane**, mad, disturbed, unstable, mentally ill, psychotic, unbalanced, deranged

mentality NOUN = **attitude**, character, personality, psychology, make-up, outlook, disposition, cast of mind

mentally ADVERB
= **psychologically**, intellectually, inwardly

mention VERB = **refer to**, point out, bring up, state, reveal, declare, disclose, intimate
▷ NOUN 1 *often with* **of**

= **reference**, observation, indication, remark, allusion
2 = **acknowledgment**, recognition, tribute, citation, honourable mention

mentor NOUN = **guide**, teacher, coach, adviser, tutor, instructor, counsellor, guru

menu NOUN = **bill of fare**, tariff (*chiefly Brit.*), set menu, table d'hôte (*French*), carte du jour (*French*)

merchandise NOUN = **goods**, produce, stock, products, commodities, wares

merchant NOUN = **tradesman**, dealer, trader, broker, retailer, supplier, seller, salesman

mercy NOUN **1** = **compassion**, pity, forgiveness, grace, kindness, clemency, leniency, forbearance ≠ cruelty **2** = **blessing**, boon, godsend

mere ADJECTIVE **1** = **simple**, nothing more than, common, plain, pure **2** = **bare**, slender, trifling, meagre, just, only, basic, no more than

merge VERB **1** = **combine**, blend, fuse, amalgamate, unite, join, mix, mingle ≠ separate **2** = **join**, unite, combine, fuse ≠ separate **3** = **melt**, blend, mingle

merger NOUN = **union**, fusion, consolidation, amalgamation, combination, coalition, incorporation

merit NOUN = **advantage**, value, quality, worth, strength, asset, virtue, strong point

▷ VERB = **deserve**, warrant, be entitled to, earn, have a right to, be worthy of

merry ADJECTIVE **1** = **cheerful**, happy, carefree, jolly, festive, joyous, convivial, blithe ≠ gloomy **2** (*Brit. informal*) = **tipsy**, happy, mellow, tiddly (*slang, chiefly Brit.*), squiffy (*Brit. informal*)

mesh NOUN = **net**, netting, network, web, tracery
▷ VERB = **engage**, combine, connect, knit, coordinate, interlock, dovetail, harmonize

mess NOUN **1** = **untidiness**, disorder, confusion, chaos, litter, clutter, disarray, jumble **2** = **shambles 3** = **difficulty**, dilemma, plight, hole (*informal*), fix (*informal*), jam (*informal*), muddle, pickle (*informal*), uphill (*S. African*) ▷ PHRASES: **mess about** *or* **around** = **potter about**, dabble, amuse yourself, fool about *or* around, muck about *or* around (*informal*), play about *or* around, trifle; **mess something up 1** = **botch**, muck something up (*Brit. slang*), muddle something up **2** = **dirty**, pollute, clutter, disarrange, dishevel; **mess with something** *or* **someone** = **interfere with**, play with, fiddle with (*informal*), tamper with, tinker with, meddle with

message NOUN
1 = **communication**, note, bulletin, word, letter, dispatch, memorandum, communiqué, e-mail, text **2** = **point**, meaning,

m

idea, moral, theme, import, purport

messenger NOUN = **courier**, runner, carrier, herald, envoy, go-between, emissary, delivery boy

messy ADJECTIVE
1 = **disorganized**, sloppy (*informal*), untidy 2 = **dirty**
3 = **untidy**, disordered, chaotic, muddled, cluttered, shambolic, disorganized, daggy (*Austral. & N.Z. informal*) ≠ tidy
4 = **dishevelled**, ruffled, untidy, rumpled, bedraggled, tousled, uncombed, daggy (*Austral. & N.Z. informal*) 5 = **confusing**, difficult, complex, confused, tangled, chaotic, tortuous

metaphor NOUN = **figure of speech**, image, symbol, analogy, conceit (*literary*), allegory, trope, figurative expression

method NOUN 1 = **manner**, process, approach, technique, way, system, style, procedure
2 = **orderliness**, planning, order, system, purpose, pattern, organization, regularity

midday NOUN = **noon**, twelve o'clock, noonday

middle NOUN = **centre**, heart, midst, halfway point, midpoint, midsection
▷ ADJECTIVE 1 = **central**, medium, mid, intervening, halfway, intermediate, median
2 = **intermediate**, intervening

middle-class ADJECTIVE
= **bourgeois**, traditional, conventional

middling ADJECTIVE 1 = **mediocre**, all right, indifferent, so-so (*informal*), unremarkable, tolerable, run-of-the-mill, passable, half-pie (*N.Z. informal*)
2 = **moderate**, medium, average, fair, ordinary, modest, adequate

midnight NOUN = **twelve o'clock**, middle of the night, dead of night, the witching hour

midst ▷ PHRASE: **in the midst of** 1 = **during**, in the middle of, amidst 2 = **among**, in the middle of, surrounded by, amidst, in the thick of

midway ADVERB = **halfway**, in the middle of, part-way, equidistant, at the midpoint, betwixt and between

might NOUN = **power**, force, energy, strength, vigour

mighty ADJECTIVE = **powerful**, strong, strapping, robust, vigorous, sturdy, forceful, lusty ≠ weak

migrant NOUN = **wanderer**, immigrant, traveller, rover, nomad, emigrant, itinerant, drifter
▷ ADJECTIVE = **itinerant**, wandering, drifting, roving, travelling, shifting, immigrant, transient

migrate VERB = **move**, travel, journey, wander, trek, voyage, roam, emigrate

migration NOUN = **wandering**, journey, voyage, travel, movement, trek, emigration, roving

mild ADJECTIVE 1 = **gentle**, calm, easy-going, meek, placid, docile, peaceable, equable, chilled (*informal*) ≠ harsh 2 = **temperate**, warm, calm, moderate, tranquil, balmy ≠ cold 3 = **bland**, thin, smooth, tasteless, insipid, flavourless

militant ADJECTIVE = **aggressive**, active, vigorous, assertive, combative ≠ peaceful

military ADJECTIVE = **warlike**, armed, soldierly, martial
▷ PHRASE: **the military** = **the armed forces**, the forces, the services, the army

milk VERB = **exploit**, pump, take advantage of ▷ RELATED WORD: *adjective* lactic

mill NOUN 1 = **grinder**, crusher, quern 2 = **factory**, works, plant, workshop, foundry
▷ VERB = **grind**, pound, crush, powder, grate ▷ PHRASE: **mill about** *or* **around** = **swarm**, crowd, stream, surge, throng

mimic VERB = **imitate**, do (*informal*), take off (*informal*), ape, parody, caricature, impersonate
▷ NOUN = **imitator**, impressionist, copycat (*informal*), impersonator, caricaturist

mince VERB 1 = **cut**, grind, crumble, dice, hash, chop up 2 = **tone down**, spare, moderate, weaken, soften

mincing ADJECTIVE = **affected**, camp (*informal*), precious, pretentious, dainty, sissy, effeminate, foppish

mind NOUN 1 = **memory**, recollection, remembrance, powers of recollection 2 = **intelligence**, reason, reasoning, understanding, sense, brain(s) (*informal*), wits, intellect 3 = **intention**, wish, desire, urge, fancy, leaning, notion, inclination 4 = **sanity**, reason, senses, judgment, wits, marbles (*informal*), rationality, mental balance
▷ VERB 1 = **take offence at**, dislike, care about, object to, resent, disapprove of, be bothered by, be affronted by 2 = **be careful**, watch, take care, be wary, be cautious, be on your guard 3 = **look after**, watch, protect, tend, guard, take care of, attend to, keep an eye on 4 = **pay attention to**, mark, note, listen to, observe, obey, heed, take heed of ▷ RELATED WORD: *adjective* mental

mine NOUN 1 = **pit**, deposit, shaft, colliery, excavation 2 = **source**, store, fund, stock, supply, reserve, treasury, wealth
▷ VERB = **dig up**, extract, quarry, unearth, excavate, hew, dig for

miner NOUN = **coalminer**, pitman (*Brit.*), collier (*Brit.*)

mingle VERB 1 = **mix**, combine, blend, merge, unite, join, interweave, intermingle ≠ separate 2 = **associate**, consort, socialize, rub shoulders (*informal*), hobnob, fraternize, hang about *or* around

m

≠ dissociate

miniature ADJECTIVE = **small**, little, minute, tiny, toy, scaled-down, diminutive, minuscule ≠ giant

minimal ADJECTIVE = **minimum**, smallest, least, slightest, token, nominal, negligible, least possible

minimize VERB 1 = **reduce**, decrease, shrink, diminish, prune, curtail, miniaturize ≠ increase 2 = **play down**, discount, belittle, disparage, decry, underrate, deprecate, make light or little of ≠ praise

minimum ADJECTIVE = **lowest**, smallest, least, slightest, minimal, least possible ≠ maximum ▷ NOUN = **lowest**, least, lowest level, nadir

minister NOUN = **clergyman**, priest, vicar, parson, preacher, pastor, cleric, rector ▷ PHRASE: **minister to** = **attend to**, serve, tend to, take care of, cater to, pander to, administer to

ministry NOUN 1 = **department**, office, bureau, government department 2 = **administration**, council 3 = **the priesthood**, the church, the cloth, holy orders

minor ADJECTIVE = **small**, lesser, slight, petty, trivial, insignificant, unimportant, inconsequential ≠ major

mint VERB = **make**, produce, strike, cast, stamp, punch, coin

minute¹ NOUN = **moment**, second, bit, flash, instant, tick (Brit. informal), sec (informal), short

time

minute² ADJECTIVE 1 = **small**, little, tiny, miniature, microscopic, diminutive, minuscule, infinitesimal ≠ huge 2 = **precise**, close, detailed, critical, exact, meticulous, exhaustive, painstaking ≠ imprecise

minutes PLURAL NOUN = **record**, notes, proceedings, transactions, transcript, memorandum

miracle NOUN = **wonder**, phenomenon, sensation, marvel, amazing achievement, astonishing feat

miraculous ADJECTIVE = **wonderful**, amazing, extraordinary, incredible, astonishing, unbelievable, phenomenal, astounding ≠ ordinary

mirror NOUN = **looking-glass**, glass (Brit.), reflector ▷ VERB = **reflect**, follow, copy, echo, emulate

miscarriage NOUN = **failure**, error, breakdown, mishap, perversion

misconduct NOUN = **immorality**, wrongdoing, mismanagement, malpractice, impropriety

miserable ADJECTIVE 1 = **sad**, depressed, gloomy, forlorn, dejected, despondent, sorrowful, wretched ≠ happy 2 = **pathetic**, sorry, shameful, despicable, deplorable, lamentable ≠ respectable

misery NOUN 1 = **unhappiness**,

distress, despair, grief, suffering, depression, gloom, torment ≠ happiness **2** (*Brit. informal*) = **moaner**, pessimist, killjoy, spoilsport, prophet of doom, wet blanket (*informal*), sourpuss (*informal*), wowser (*Austral. & N.Z. slang*)

misfortune NOUN **1** *often plural* = **bad luck**, adversity, hard luck, ill luck, infelicity, bad trot (*Austral. slang*) **2** = **mishap**, trouble, disaster, reverse, tragedy, setback, calamity, affliction ≠ good luck

misguided ADJECTIVE = **unwise**, mistaken, misplaced, deluded, ill-advised, imprudent, injudicious

mislead VERB = **deceive**, fool, delude, take someone in (*informal*), misdirect, misinform, hoodwink, misguide

misleading ADJECTIVE = **confusing**, false, ambiguous, deceptive, evasive, disingenuous ≠ straightforward

miss VERB **1** = **fail to notice**, overlook, pass over **2** = **long for**, yearn for, pine for, long to see, ache for, feel the loss of, regret the absence of **3** = **not go to**, skip, cut, omit, be absent from, fail to attend, skive off (*informal*), play truant from, bludge (*Austral. & N.Z. informal*) **4** = **avoid**, beat, escape, skirt, duck, cheat, bypass, dodge
▷ NOUN = **mistake**, failure, error, blunder, omission, oversight

missile NOUN = **projectile**, weapon, shell, rocket

missing ADJECTIVE = **lost**, misplaced, not present, astray, unaccounted for, mislaid

mission NOUN = **task**, job, commission, duty, undertaking, quest, assignment, vocation

missionary NOUN = **evangelist**, preacher, apostle

mist NOUN = **fog**, cloud, steam, spray, film, haze, vapour, smog

mistake NOUN **1** = **error**, blunder, oversight, slip, gaffe (*informal*), miscalculation, faux pas (*French*), barry *or* Barry Crocker (*Austral. slang*) **2** = **oversight**, error, slip, fault, howler (*informal*), erratum, barry *or* Barry Crocker (*Austral. slang*)
▷ VERB = **misunderstand**, misinterpret, misjudge, misread, misconstrue, misapprehend
▷ PHRASE: **mistake something** *or* **someone for something** *or* **someone** = **confuse with**, take for, mix up with

mistaken ADJECTIVE **1** = **wrong**, incorrect, misguided, wide of the mark ≠ correct **2** = **inaccurate**, false, faulty, erroneous, unsound ≠ accurate

mistress NOUN = **lover**, girlfriend, concubine, kept woman, paramour

misunderstand VERB **1** = **misinterpret**, misread, mistake, misjudge, misconstrue, misapprehend, be at cross-purposes with **2** = **miss the point**, get the wrong end of the stick

m

misunderstanding

misunderstanding
   NOUN = **mistake**, error,
   mix-up, misconception,
   misinterpretation, misjudgment
misuse NOUN 1 = **waste**,
   squandering 2 = **abuse**
   3 = **misapplication**, abuse, illegal
   use, wrong use 4 = **perversion**,
   desecration 5 = **misapplication**
   ▷ VERB 1 = **abuse**, misapply,
   prostitute 2 = **waste**, squander,
   embezzle, misappropriate
mix VERB 1 = **combine**, blend,
   merge, join, cross, fuse,
   mingle, jumble 2 = **socialize**,
   associate, hang out (*informal*),
   mingle, circulate, consort,
   hobnob, fraternize 3 *often with*
   up = **combine**, marry, blend,
   integrate, amalgamate, coalesce,
   meld
   ▷ NOUN = **mixture**, combination,
   blend, fusion, compound,
   assortment, alloy, medley
   ▷ PHRASE: **mix something up**
   1 = **confuse**, scramble, muddle,
   confound 2 = **blend**, beat, mix,
   stir, fold
mixed ADJECTIVE 1 = **varied**,
   diverse, different, differing,
   cosmopolitan, assorted, jumbled,
   disparate ≠ homogeneous
   2 = **combined**, blended, united,
   compound, composite, mingled,
   amalgamated ≠ pure
mixed-up ADJECTIVE = **confused**,
   disturbed, puzzled, bewildered, at
   sea, upset, distraught, muddled
mixture NOUN 1 = **blend**, mix,
   variety, fusion, assortment,

brew, jumble, medley
   2 = **composite**, compound
   3 = **cross**, combination, blend
   4 = **concoction**, compound,
   blend, brew, amalgam
mix-up NOUN = **confusion**,
   mistake, misunderstanding,
   mess, tangle, muddle
moan VERB 1 = **groan**, sigh,
   sob, whine, lament 2 (*informal*)
   = **grumble**, complain, groan,
   whine, carp, grouse, whinge
   (*informal*), bleat
   ▷ NOUN 1 = **groan**, sigh, sob,
   lament, wail, grunt, whine 2
   (*informal*) = **complaint**, protest,
   grumble, whine, grouse, gripe
   (*informal*), grouch (*informal*)
mob NOUN 1 = **crowd**, pack, mass,
   host, drove, flock, swarm, horde
   2 = **gang**, group, set, lot, crew
   (*informal*)
   ▷ VERB = **surround**, besiege,
   jostle, fall on, set upon, crowd
   around, swarm around
mobile ADJECTIVE = **movable**,
   moving, travelling, wandering,
   portable, itinerant, peripatetic
mobilize VERB 1 = **rally**, organize,
   stimulate, excite, prompt,
   marshal, activate, awaken
   2 = **deploy**, prepare, ready, rally,
   assemble, call up, marshal,
   muster
mock VERB = **laugh at**, tease,
   ridicule, taunt, scorn, sneer, scoff,
   deride ≠ respect
   ▷ ADJECTIVE = **imitation**,
   pretended, artificial, fake, false,
   dummy, sham, feigned ≠ genuine

mocking ADJECTIVE = **scornful**, scoffing, satirical, contemptuous, sarcastic, sardonic, disrespectful, disdainful

mode NOUN 1 = **method**, way, system, form, process, style, technique, manner 2 = **fashion**, style, trend, rage, vogue, look, craze

model NOUN 1 = **representation**, image, copy, miniature, dummy, replica, imitation, duplicate 2 = **pattern**, example, standard, original, ideal, prototype, paradigm, archetype 3 = **sitter**, subject, poser
▷ VERB 1 = **show off** (*informal*), wear, display, sport 2 = **shape**, form, design, fashion, carve, mould, sculpt

moderate ADJECTIVE 1 = **mild**, reasonable, controlled, limited, steady, modest, restrained, middle-of-the-road ≠ extreme 2 = **average**, middling, fair, ordinary, indifferent, mediocre, so-so (*informal*), passable, half-pie (*N.Z. informal*)
▷ VERB 1 = **soften**, control, temper, regulate, curb, restrain, subdue, lessen 2 = **lessen**, ease ≠ intensify

modern ADJECTIVE 1 = **current**, contemporary, recent, present-day, latter-day 2 = **up-to-date**, fresh, new, novel, newfangled ≠ old-fashioned

modest ADJECTIVE 1 = **moderate**, small, limited, fair, ordinary, middling, meagre, frugal 2 = **unpretentious**, reserved, retiring, shy, coy, reticent, self-effacing, demure

modesty NOUN = **reserve**, humility, shyness, reticence, timidity, diffidence, coyness, bashfulness ≠ conceit

modification NOUN = **change**, variation, qualification, adjustment, revision, alteration, refinement

modify VERB 1 = **change**, reform, convert, alter, adjust, adapt, revise, remodel 2 = **tone down**, lower, qualify, ease, moderate, temper, soften, restrain

mogul NOUN = **tycoon**, baron, magnate, big shot (*informal*), big noise (*informal*), big hitter (*informal*), heavy hitter (*informal*), V.I.P.

moist ADJECTIVE = **damp**, wet, soggy, humid, clammy, dewy

moisture NOUN = **damp**, water, liquid, dew, wetness

molecule NOUN = **particle**, jot, speck

mom NOUN (*U.S. & Canad.*) = **mum**, mother, ma

moment NOUN 1 = **instant**, second, flash, twinkling, split second, jiffy (*informal*), trice 2 = **time**, point, stage, juncture

momentous ADJECTIVE = **significant**, important, vital, critical, crucial, historic, pivotal, fateful ≠ unimportant

momentum NOUN = **impetus**, force, power, drive, push, energy, strength, thrust

m

monarch NOUN = **ruler**, king or queen, sovereign, tsar, potentate, emperor or empress, prince or princess

monarchy NOUN
1 = **sovereignty**, autocracy, kingship, royalism, monocracy
2 = **kingdom**, empire, realm, principality

monastery NOUN = **abbey**, convent, priory, cloister, nunnery, friary

monetary ADJECTIVE = **financial**, money, economic, capital, cash, fiscal, budgetary, pecuniary

money NOUN = **cash**, capital, currency, hard cash, readies (informal), riches, silver, coin, kembla (Austral. slang)
▷ see **currencies**

monitor VERB = **check**, follow, watch, survey, observe, keep an eye on, keep track of, keep tabs on
▷ NOUN 1 = **guide**, observer, supervisor, invigilator 2 = **prefect** (Brit.), head girl, head boy, senior boy, senior girl

monk NOUN = **friar**, brother
▷ RELATED WORD: adjective **monastic**

monkey NOUN 1 = **simian**, ape, primate 2 = **rascal**, horror, devil, rogue, imp, tyke, scallywag, scamp, nointer (Austral. slang)
▷ RELATED WORD: adjective **simian**

monster NOUN 1 = **giant**, mammoth, titan, colossus, monstrosity 2 = **brute**, devil, beast, demon, villain, fiend

monstrous ADJECTIVE
1 = **outrageous**, shocking, foul, intolerable, disgraceful, scandalous, inhuman, diabolical ≠ decent 2 = **huge**, massive, enormous, tremendous, immense, mammoth, colossal, prodigious ≠ tiny 3 = **unnatural**, horrible, hideous, grotesque, gruesome, frightful, freakish, fiendish ≠ normal

monument NOUN = **memorial**, cairn, marker, shrine, tombstone, mausoleum, commemoration, headstone

monumental ADJECTIVE
= **important**, significant, enormous, historic, memorable, awesome, majestic, unforgettable ≠ unimportant
▷ INTENSIFIER (informal)
= **immense**, great, massive, staggering, colossal ≠ tiny

mood NOUN = **state of mind**, spirit, humour, temper, disposition, frame of mind

moody ADJECTIVE 1 = **changeable**, volatile, unpredictable, erratic, fickle, temperamental, impulsive, mercurial ≠ stable 2 = **sulky**, irritable, temperamental, touchy, ill-tempered, tooshie (Austral. slang) ≠ cheerful 3 = **gloomy**, sad, sullen, glum, morose ≠ cheerful 4 = **sad**, gloomy, melancholy, sombre

moon NOUN = **satellite**
▷ VERB = **idle**, drift, loaf, languish, waste time, daydream, mope
▷ RELATED WORD: adjective **lunar**

moor[1] NOUN = **moorland**, fell

- **MONKEYS, APES AND OTHER PRIMATES**
- baboon
- Barbary ape
- bushbaby *or* galago
- capuchin
- chacma
- chimpanzee *or* chimp
- colobus
- douroucouli
- flying lemur *or* colugo
- gelada
- gibbon
- gorilla
- green monkey
- grivet
- guenon
- guereza
- howler monkey
- indris *or* indri
- langur
- lemur
- loris
- macaque
- mandrill
- mangabey
- marmoset
- mona
- monkey *or* (*archaic*) jackanapes
- orang-outang, orang-utan, *or* orang
- proboscis monkey
- rhesus monkey
- saki
- siamang
- sifaka
- spider monkey
- squirrel monkey
- tamarin
- tarsier
- vervet

m

(*Brit.*), heath

moor² VERB = **tie up**, secure, anchor, dock, lash, berth, make fast

mop NOUN 1 = **squeegee**, sponge, swab 2 = **mane**, shock, mass, tangle, mat, thatch
▷ VERB = **clean**, wash, wipe, sponge, swab

moral ADJECTIVE = **good**, just, right, principled, decent, noble, ethical, honourable ≠ immoral
▷ NOUN = **lesson**, meaning, point, message, teaching, import, significance, precept
▷ PLURAL NOUN = **morality**, standards, conduct, principles, behaviour, manners, habits, ethics

morale NOUN = **confidence**, heart, spirit, self-esteem, team spirit, esprit de corps (*French*)

morality NOUN 1 = **virtue**, justice, morals, honour, integrity, goodness, honesty, decency 2 = **ethics**, conduct, principles, morals, manners, philosophy, mores 3 = **rights and wrongs**, ethics

moratorium NOUN = **postponement**, freeze, halt, suspension, standstill

more DETERMINER = **extra**, additional, new, other,

added, further, new-found, supplementary

▷ ADVERB 1 = **to a greater extent**, longer, better, further, some more 2 = **moreover**, also, in addition, besides, furthermore, what's more, on top of that, to boot

moreover ADVERB
= **furthermore**, also, further, in addition, too, as well, besides, additionally

morning NOUN 1 = **before noon**, forenoon, morn (*poetic*), a.m. 2 = **dawn**, sunrise, first light, daybreak, break of day

mortal ADJECTIVE 1 = **human**, worldly, passing, fleshly, temporal, transient, ephemeral, perishable 2 = **fatal**, killing, terminal, deadly, destructive, lethal, murderous, death-dealing

▷ NOUN = **human being**, being, man, woman, person, human, individual, earthling

mortality NOUN 1 = **humanity**, transience, impermanence, corporeality, impermanency 2 = **death**, dying, fatality

mostly ADVERB 1 = **mainly**, largely, chiefly, principally, primarily, on the whole, predominantly 2 = **generally**, usually, on the whole, as a rule

moth NOUN ▷ RELATED WORDS: *young* **caterpillar**, *enthusiast* **lepidopterist**

▷ *see* **butterflies and moths**

mother NOUN = **female parent**, mum (*Brit. informal*), ma (*informal*), mater, dam, mummy (*Brit. informal*), foster mother, biological mother

▷ VERB = **nurture**, raise, protect, tend, nurse, rear, care for, cherish

▷ MODIFIER = **native**, natural, innate, inborn ▷ RELATED WORD: *adjective* **maternal**

motherly ADJECTIVE = **maternal**, loving, caring, comforting, sheltering, protective, affectionate

motif NOUN 1 = **design**, shape, decoration, ornament 2 = **theme**, idea, subject, concept, leitmotif

motion NOUN 1 = **movement**, mobility, travel, progress, flow, locomotion 2 = **proposal**, suggestion, recommendation, proposition, submission

▷ VERB = **gesture**, direct, wave, signal, nod, beckon, gesticulate

motivate VERB 1 = **inspire**, drive, stimulate, move, cause, prompt, stir, induce 2 = **stimulate**, drive, inspire, stir, arouse, galvanize, incentivize

motivation NOUN = **incentive**, inspiration, motive, stimulus, reason, spur, inducement, incitement

motive NOUN = **reason**, ground(s), purpose, object, incentive, inspiration, stimulus, rationale

motto NOUN = **saying**, slogan, maxim, rule, adage, proverb, dictum, precept

mould¹ NOUN 1 = **cast**, shape, pattern 2 = **design**, style, fashion, build, form, kind, shape, pattern

m

3 = **nature**, character, sort, kind, quality, type, stamp, calibre
▷ **VERB 1** = **shape**, make, work, form, create, model, fashion, construct **2** = **influence**, make, form, control, direct, affect, shape

mould² NOUN = **fungus**, blight, mildew

mound NOUN **1** = **heap**, pile, drift, stack, rick **2** = **hill**, bank, rise, dune, embankment, knoll, hillock, kopje *or* koppie (*S. African*)

mount VERB **1** = **increase**, build, grow, swell, intensify, escalate, multiply ≠ decrease **2** = **accumulate**, increase, collect, gather, build up, pile up, amass **3** = **ascend**, scale, climb (up), go up, clamber up ≠ descend **4** = **get (up) on**, jump on, straddle, climb onto, hop on to, bestride, get on the back of ≠ get off **5** = **display**, present, prepare, put on, organize, put on display
▷ NOUN **1** = **horse**, steed (*literary*) **2** = **backing**, setting, support, stand, base, frame

mountain NOUN **1** = **peak**, mount, horn, ridge, fell (*Brit.*), berg (*S. African*), alp, pinnacle **2** = **heap**, mass, masses, pile, a great deal, ton, stack, abundance

mourn VERB **1** *often with* **for** = **grieve for**, lament, weep for, wail for **2** = **bemoan**, rue, deplore, bewail

mourning NOUN **1** = **grieving**, grief, bereavement, weeping, woe, lamentation **2** = **black**, sackcloth and ashes, widow's weeds

mouth NOUN **1** = **lips**, jaws, gob (*slang, esp. Brit.*), maw, cakehole (*Brit. slang*) **2** = **entrance**, opening, gateway, door, aperture, orifice **3** = **opening 4** = **inlet**, outlet, estuary, firth, outfall, debouchure ▷ **RELATED WORD**: *adjective* **oral**

● **WORD POWER**
● The *mouth* is the opening
● through which many animals
● take in food and issue vocal
● sounds. The entrance or rim
● of other structures can also
● be referred to as a mouth, for
● example a bottle, a tunnel, or
● the point at which a river meets
● the sea. The speech of humans
● is articulated through their
● mouths, therefore mouth itself
● means talk, especially empty
● talk and boasting in *she is all*
● *mouth*. Similarly, impassioned
● talk is implicated in *mouth*
● *off*. Mouth is similar to lip and
● cheek, which all refer to the
● idea of impudence. The corners
● of the mouth turn down with
● displeasure and negative
● emotion – for this reason we
● talk about people being *down in*
● *the mouth*.

move VERB **1** = **transfer**, change, switch, shift, transpose **2** = **go**, advance, progress, shift, proceed, stir, budge, make a move **3** = **relocate**, leave, remove, quit, migrate, emigrate, decamp, up sticks (*Brit. informal*) **4** = **drive**,

cause, influence, persuade, shift, inspire, prompt, induce ≠ discourage **5** = **touch**, affect, excite, impress, stir, disquiet **6** = **propose**, suggest, urge, recommend, request, advocate, submit, put forward
▷ NOUN **1** = **action**, step, manoeuvre **2** = **ploy**, action, measure, step, initiative, stroke, tactic, manoeuvre **3** = **transfer**, posting, shift, removal, relocation **4** = **turn**, go, play, chance, shot (*informal*), opportunity

movement NOUN **1** = **group**, party, organization, grouping, front, faction **2** = **campaign**, drive, push, crusade **3** = **move**, action, motion, manoeuvre **4** = **activity**, moving, stirring, bustle **5** = **advance**, progress, flow **6** = **transfer**, transportation, displacement **7** = **development**, change, variation, fluctuation **8** = **progression**, progress **9** (*music*) = **section**, part, division, passage

movie NOUN = **film**, picture, feature, flick (*slang*)

moving ADJECTIVE **1** = **emotional**, touching, affecting, inspiring, stirring, poignant ≠ unemotional **2** = **mobile**, running, active, going, operational, in motion, driving, kinetic ≠ stationary

mow VERB = **cut**, crop, trim, shear, scythe ▷ PHRASE: mow something *or* someone down = **massacre**, butcher, slaughter, cut down, shoot down, cut to pieces

much ADVERB **1** = **greatly**, a lot, considerably, decidedly, exceedingly, appreciably ≠ hardly **2** = **often**, a lot, routinely, a great deal, many times, habitually, on many occasions, customarily
▷ ADJECTIVE = **great**, a lot of, plenty of, considerable, substantial, piles of (*informal*), ample, abundant, shedful (*slang*) ≠ little
▷ PRONOUN = **a lot**, plenty, a great deal, lots (*informal*), masses (*informal*), loads (*informal*), tons (*informal*), heaps (*informal*) ≠ little

muck NOUN **1** = **dirt**, mud, filth, ooze, sludge, mire, slime, gunge (*informal*), kak (*S. African informal*) **2** = **manure**, dung, ordure

mud NOUN = **dirt**, clay, ooze, silt, sludge, mire, slime

muddle NOUN = **confusion**, mess, disorder, chaos, tangle, mix-up, disarray, predicament
▷ VERB **1** = **jumble**, disorder, scramble, tangle, mix up **2** = **confuse**, bewilder, daze, confound, perplex, disorient, stupefy, befuddle

muddy ADJECTIVE **1** = **boggy**, swampy, marshy, quaggy **2** = **dirty**, soiled, grimy, mucky, mud-caked, bespattered

mug¹ NOUN = **cup**, pot, beaker, tankard

mug² NOUN **1** (*slang*) = **face**, features, countenance, visage **2** (*Brit.*) = **fool**, sucker (*slang*), chump (*informal*), simpleton, easy or soft touch (*slang*), dorba or dorb (*Austral. slang*), bogan (*Austral. slang*)

▷ VERB (*informal*) = **attack**, assault, beat up, rob, set about or upon ▷ PHRASE: **mug up (on) something** = **study**, cram (*informal*), bone up on (*informal*), swot up on (*Brit. informal*)

multiple ADJECTIVE = **many**, several, various, numerous, sundry, manifold, multitudinous

multiply VERB 1 = **increase**, extend, expand, spread, build up, proliferate ≠ decrease 2 = **reproduce**, breed, propagate

multitude NOUN 1 = **great number**, host, army, mass, horde, myriad 2 = **crowd**, host, mass, mob, swarm, horde, throng

mundane ADJECTIVE 1 = **ordinary**, routine, commonplace, banal, everyday, day-to-day, prosaic, humdrum ≠ extraordinary 2 = **earthly**, worldly, secular, mortal, terrestrial, temporal ≠ spiritual

municipal ADJECTIVE = **civic**, public, local, council, district, urban, metropolitan

murder NOUN = **killing**, homicide, massacre, assassination, slaying, bloodshed, carnage, butchery ▷ VERB = **kill**, massacre, slaughter, assassinate, eliminate (*slang*), butcher, slay, bump off (*slang*)

murderer NOUN = **killer**, assassin, slayer, butcher, slaughterer, cut-throat, hit man (*slang*)

murderous ADJECTIVE = **deadly**, savage, brutal, cruel, lethal, ferocious, cut-throat, bloodthirsty

murky ADJECTIVE 1 = **dark**, gloomy, grey, dull, dim, cloudy, misty, overcast ≠ bright 2 = **dark**, cloudy

murmur VERB = **mumble**, whisper, mutter ▷ NOUN = **whisper**, drone, purr

muscle NOUN 1 = **tendon**, sinew 2 = **strength**, might, power, weight, stamina, brawn ▷ PHRASE: **muscle in** (*informal*) = **impose yourself**, encroach, butt in, force your way in

muscular ADJECTIVE = **strong**, powerful, athletic, strapping, robust, vigorous, sturdy, sinewy

muse VERB = **ponder**, consider, reflect, contemplate, deliberate, brood, meditate, mull over

musical ADJECTIVE = **melodious**, lyrical, harmonious, melodic, tuneful, dulcet, sweet-sounding, euphonious ≠ discordant

muskeg NOUN (*Canad.*) = **swamp**, bog, marsh, quagmire, slough, fen, mire, morass, pakihi (*N.Z.*)

muss (*U.S. & Canad.*) VERB = **mess (up)**, disarrange, dishevel, ruffle, rumple, make untidy, tumble

must NOUN = **necessity**, essential, requirement, fundamental, imperative, requisite, prerequisite, sine qua non (*Latin*)

muster VERB 1 = **summon up**, marshal 2 = **rally**, gather, assemble, marshal, mobilize, call together 3 = **assemble**, convene ▷ NOUN = **assembly**, meeting,

m

- ● MUSIC
- ● **Instruction**   **Meaning**
- ● accelerando   with increasing speed
- ● adagio   slowly
- ● agitato   in an agitated manner
- ● allegretto   fairly quickly or briskly
- ● allegro   quickly, in a brisk, lively manner
- ● amoroso   lovingly
- ● andante   at a moderately slow tempo
- ● andantino   slightly faster than andante
- ● assai   (in combination) very
- ● cantabile   in a singing style
- ● con   (in combination) with
- ● con amore   lovingly
- ● con brio   vigorously
- ● con moto   quickly
- ● crescendo   gradual increase in loudness
- ● diminuendo   gradual decrease in loudness
- ● dolce   gently and sweetly
- ● doloroso   in a sorrowful manner
- ● espressivo   expressively
- ● forte   loud or loudly
- ● fortissimo   very loud
- ● furioso   in a frantically rushing manner
- ● giocoso   merry
- ● grave   solemn and slow
- ● grazioso   graceful
- ● largo   slowly and broadly
- ● larghetto   slowly and broadly, but less so than largo
- ● legato   smoothly and connectedly
- ● leggiero   light
- ● lento   slowly
- ● maestoso   majestically
- ● mezzo   (in combination) moderately
- ● moderato   at a moderate tempo
- ● molto   (in combination) very
- ● non troppo *or* non tanto   (in combination) not too much
- ● pianissimo   very quietly
- ● piano   softly
- ● più   (in combination) more

m

● Instruction	Meaning
● pizzicato	(in music for stringed instruments) to be plucked with the finger
● poco *or* un poco	(in combination) a little
● pomposo	in a pompous manner
● presto	very fast
● prestissimo	faster than presto
● quasi	(in combination) almost, as if
● rallentando	becoming slower
● rubato	with a flexible tempo
● scherzando	in jocular style
● semplice	simple and unforced
● sforzando	with strong initial attack
● sostenuto	in a smooth and sustained manner
● sotto voce	extremely quiet
● staccato	(of notes) short, clipped, and separate
● strepitoso	noisy
● stringendo	with increasing speed
● tanto	(in combination) too much
● troppo	(in combination) too much
● vivace	in a brisk lively manner

m

collection, gathering, rally, convention, congregation, roundup, hui (*N.Z.*), runanga (*N.Z.*)

mutation NOUN **1** = **anomaly**, variation, deviant, freak of nature **2** = **change**, variation, evolution, transformation, modification, alteration, metamorphosis, transfiguration

mute ADJECTIVE **1** = **close-mouthed**, silent **2** = **silent**, dumb, unspoken, tacit, wordless, voiceless, unvoiced **3** = **dumb**, speechless, voiceless

mutter VERB = **grumble**, complain, murmur, rumble, whine, mumble, grouse, bleat

mutual ADJECTIVE = **shared**,

common, joint, returned, reciprocal, interchangeable, requited

● **WORD POWER**
● *Mutual* is sometimes used,
● as in *a mutual friend*, to mean
● 'common to or shared by two
● or more people'. This use has
● sometimes been frowned
● on in the past because it
● does not reflect the two-way
● relationship contained in the
● origins of the word, which
● comes from Latin *mutuus*
● meaning 'reciprocal'. However,
● this usage is very common and
● is now generally regarded as
● acceptable.

myriad NOUN = **multitude**, host,
army, swarm, horde
▷ ADJECTIVE = **innumerable**,
countless, untold, incalculable,
immeasurable, multitudinous
mysterious ADJECTIVE
1 = **strange**, puzzling, secret,
weird, perplexing, uncanny,
mystifying, arcane ≠ clear
2 = **secretive**, enigmatic, evasive,
discreet, covert, reticent, furtive,
inscrutable
mystery NOUN = **puzzle**, problem,
question, secret, riddle, enigma,
conundrum, teaser
mystical or **mystic** ADJECTIVE
= **supernatural**, mysterious,
transcendental, occult,
metaphysical, paranormal,
inscrutable, otherworldly
myth NOUN 1 = **legend**, story,
fiction, saga, fable, allegory, fairy
story, folk tale 2 = **illusion**, story,
fancy, fantasy, imagination,
invention, delusion, superstition
mythology NOUN = **legend**,
folklore, tradition, lore

m

Nn

nab VERB = **catch**, arrest, apprehend, seize, grab, capture, collar (*informal*), snatch

nag¹ VERB = **scold**, harass, badger, pester, worry, plague, hassle (*informal*), upbraid
▷ NOUN = **scold**, complainer, grumbler, virago, shrew, tartar, moaner, harpy

nag² NOUN *often derog.* = **horse** (*U.S.*), hack

nagging ADJECTIVE
1 = **continuous**, persistent, continual, niggling, repeated, constant, endless, perpetual
2 = **scolding**, shrewish

nail NOUN 1 = **tack**, spike, rivet, hobnail, brad (*technical*)
2 = **fingernail**, toenail, talon, thumbnail, claw
▷ VERB 1 = **fasten**, fix, secure, attach, pin, hammer, tack 2 (*informal*) = **catch**, arrest, capture, apprehend, trap, snare, ensnare, entrap

naive *or* **naïve** *or* **naïf** ADJECTIVE = **gullible**, trusting, credulous, unsuspicious, green, simple, innocent, callow ≠ worldly

naked ADJECTIVE = **nude**, stripped, exposed, bare, undressed, starkers (*informal*), stark-naked, unclothed ≠ dressed

name NOUN = **title**, nickname, designation, term, handle (*slang*), epithet, sobriquet, moniker *or* monicker (*slang*)
▷ VERB 1 = **call**, christen, baptize, dub, term, style, label, entitle
2 = **nominate**, choose, select, appoint, specify, designate

namely ADVERB = **specifically**, to wit, viz.

nap¹ VERB = **sleep**, rest, drop off (*informal*), doze, kip (*Brit. slang*), snooze (*informal*), nod off (*informal*), catnap
▷ NOUN = **sleep**, rest, kip (*Brit. slang*), siesta, catnap, forty winks (*informal*)

nap² NOUN = **pile**, down, fibre, weave, grain

napkin NOUN = **serviette**, cloth

narcotic NOUN = **drug**, anaesthetic, painkiller, sedative, opiate, tranquillizer, anodyne, analgesic
▷ ADJECTIVE = **sedative**, calming, hypnotic, analgesic, soporific, painkilling

narrative NOUN = **story**, report, history, account, statement, tale, chronicle

narrator NOUN = **storyteller**, writer, author, reporter, commentator, chronicler

narrow ADJECTIVE 1 = **thin**, fine, slim, slender, tapering, attenuated ≠ broad 2 = **limited**, restricted, confined, tight, close, meagre, constricted ≠ wide
3 = **insular**, prejudiced, partial, dogmatic, intolerant, narrow-

minded, small-minded, illiberal
≠ broad-minded
▷ VERB 1 *often with* **down**
= **restrict**, limit, reduce, constrict
2 = **get narrower**, taper, shrink,
tighten, constrict

narrowly ADVERB = **just**, barely,
only just, scarcely, by the skin of
your teeth

nasty ADJECTIVE 1 = **unpleasant**,
ugly, disagreeable ≠ pleasant
2 = **spiteful**, mean, offensive,
vicious, unpleasant, vile,
malicious, despicable ≠ pleasant
3 = **disgusting**, unpleasant,
offensive, vile, distasteful,
obnoxious, objectionable,
disagreeable, festy (*Austral. slang*),
yucko (*Austral. slang*) 4 = **serious**,
bad, dangerous, critical, severe,
painful

nation NOUN 1 = **country**, state,
realm 2 = **public**, people, society

national ADJECTIVE = **nationwide**,
public, widespread, countrywide
▷ NOUN = **citizen**, subject,
resident, native, inhabitant

nationalism NOUN = **patriotism**,
loyalty to your country,
chauvinism, jingoism, allegiance

nationality NOUN
1 = **citizenship**, birth 2 = **race**,
nation

nationwide ADJECTIVE
= **national**, general, widespread,
countrywide

native ADJECTIVE = **mother**,
indigenous, vernacular
▷ NOUN *usually with* **of**
= **inhabitant**, national, resident,

citizen, countryman, aborigine
(*often offensive*), dweller

natural ADJECTIVE 1 = **logical**,
valid, legitimate 2 = **normal**,
common, regular, usual, ordinary,
typical, everyday ≠ abnormal
3 = **innate**, native, characteristic,
inherent, instinctive, intuitive,
inborn, essential 4 = **unaffected**,
open, genuine, spontaneous,
unpretentious, unsophisticated,
dinkum (*Austral. & N.Z. informal*),
ingenuous, real ≠ affected
5 = **pure**, plain, organic, whole,
unrefined ≠ processed

naturally ADVERB 1 = **of course**,
certainly 2 = **typically**, simply,
normally, spontaneously

nature NOUN 1 = **creation**,
world, earth, environment,
universe, cosmos, natural
world 2 = **quality**, character,
make-up, constitution, essence,
complexion 3 = **temperament**,
character, personality,
disposition, outlook, mood,
humour, temper 4 = **kind**, sort,
style, type, variety, species,
category, description

naughty ADJECTIVE
1 = **disobedient**, bad,
mischievous, badly behaved,
wayward, wicked, impish,
refractory ≠ good 2 = **obscene**,
vulgar, improper, lewd, risqué,
smutty, ribald ≠ clean

nausea NOUN = **sickness**,
vomiting, retching,
squeamishness, queasiness,
biliousness

n

naval ADJECTIVE = **nautical**, marine, maritime

navigation NOUN = **sailing**, voyaging, seamanship, helmsmanship

navy NOUN = **fleet**, flotilla, armada

near ADJECTIVE 1 = **close**, neighbouring, nearby, adjacent, adjoining ≠ far 2 = **imminent**, forthcoming, approaching, looming, impending, upcoming, nigh, in the offing ≠ far-off

nearby ADJECTIVE = **neighbouring**, adjacent, adjoining

nearly ADVERB 1 = **practically**, almost, virtually, just about, as good as, well-nigh 2 = **almost**, approaching, roughly, just about, approximately

neat ADJECTIVE 1 = **tidy**, trim, orderly, spruce, shipshape, spick-and-span ≠ untidy 2 = **methodical**, tidy, systematic, fastidious ≠ disorganized 3 = **smart**, trim, tidy, spruce, dapper, natty (*informal*), well-groomed, well-turned out 4 = **graceful**, elegant, adept, nimble, adroit, efficient ≠ clumsy 5 = **clever**, efficient, handy, apt, well-judged ≠ inefficient 6 (*chiefly U.S. & Canad. slang*) = **cool**, great (*informal*), excellent, brilliant, superb, fantastic (*informal*), tremendous, fabulous (*informal*), booshit (*Austral. slang*), exo (*Austral. slang*), sik (*Austral. slang*), rad (*informal*), phat (*slang*), schmick (*Austral. informal*)

≠ terrible 7 (*of an alcoholic drink*) = **undiluted**, straight, pure, unmixed

neatly ADVERB 1 = **tidily**, smartly, systematically, methodically, fastidiously 2 = **smartly**, elegantly, tidily, nattily 3 = **gracefully**, expertly, efficiently, adeptly, skilfully, nimbly, adroitly, dexterously 4 = **cleverly**, efficiently

necessarily ADVERB 1 = **automatically**, naturally, definitely, undoubtedly, certainly 2 = **inevitably**, of necessity, unavoidably, incontrovertibly, nolens volens (*Latin*)

necessary ADJECTIVE 1 = **needed**, required, essential, vital, compulsory, mandatory, imperative, indispensable ≠ unnecessary 2 = **inevitable**, certain, unavoidable, inescapable ≠ avoidable

necessity NOUN 1 = **essential**, need, requirement, fundamental, requisite, prerequisite, sine qua non (*Latin*), desideratum (*Latin*), must-have 2 = **inevitability**, certainty 3 = **essential**, need, requirement, fundamental

need VERB 1 = **want**, miss, require, lack, have to have, demand 2 = **require**, want, demand, call for, entail, necessitate 3 = **have to**, be obliged to ▷ NOUN 1 = **requirement**, demand, essential, necessity, requisite, desideratum (*Latin*), must-have 2 = **necessity**, call, demand, obligation

3 = **emergency**, want, necessity, urgency, exigency **4** = **poverty**, deprivation, destitution, penury

needed ADJECTIVE = **necessary**, wanted, required, lacked, called for, desired

needle VERB = **irritate**, provoke, annoy, harass, taunt, nag, goad, rile

needless ADJECTIVE
= **unnecessary**, pointless, gratuitous, useless, unwanted, redundant, superfluous, groundless ≠ essential

needy ADJECTIVE = **poor**, deprived, disadvantaged, impoverished, penniless, destitute, poverty-stricken, underprivileged
≠ wealthy

negative ADJECTIVE
1 = **pessimistic**, cynical, unwilling, gloomy, jaundiced, uncooperative ≠ optimistic
2 = **dissenting**, contradictory, refusing, denying, rejecting, opposing, resisting, contrary
≠ assenting
▷ NOUN = **denial**, no, refusal, rejection, contradiction

neglect VERB **1** = **disregard**, ignore, fail to look after ≠ look after **2** = **shirk**, forget, overlook, omit, evade, pass over, skimp, be remiss in or about **3** = **fail**, forget, omit
▷ NOUN **1** = **negligence**, inattention ≠ care **2** = **shirking**, failure, oversight, carelessness, dereliction, slackness, laxity

neglected ADJECTIVE
1 = **uncared-for**, abandoned, underestimated, disregarded, undervalued, unappreciated
2 = **run down**, derelict, overgrown, uncared-for

negligence NOUN
= **carelessness**, neglect, disregard, dereliction, slackness, inattention, laxity, thoughtlessness

negotiate VERB **1** = **bargain**, deal, discuss, debate, mediate, hold talks, cut a deal, conciliate
2 = **arrange**, work out, bring about, transact **3** = **get round**, clear, pass, cross, get over, get past, surmount

negotiation NOUN
1 = **bargaining**, debate, discussion, transaction, dialogue, mediation, arbitration, wheeling and dealing (*informal*)
2 = **arrangement**, working out, transaction, bringing about

negotiator NOUN = **mediator**, ambassador, diplomat, delegate, intermediary, moderator, honest broker

neighbourhood or (U.S.)
neighborhood NOUN
1 = **district**, community, quarter, region, locality, locale
2 = **vicinity**, environs

neighbouring or (U.S.)
neighboring ADJECTIVE
= **nearby**, next, near, bordering, surrounding, connecting, adjacent, adjoining ≠ remote

neighbourly or (U.S.)

n

neighborly ADJECTIVE
= **helpful**, kind, friendly, obliging, harmonious, considerate, sociable, hospitable

nerve NOUN 1 = **bravery**, courage, bottle (*Brit. slang*), resolution, daring, guts (*informal*), pluck, grit 2 (*informal*) = **impudence**, cheek (*informal*), audacity, boldness, temerity, insolence, impertinence, brazenness
▷ PLURAL NOUN (*informal*) = **tension**, stress, strain, anxiety, butterflies (in your stomach) (*informal*), nervousness, cold feet (*informal*), worry ▷ PHRASE: **nerve yourself** = **brace yourself**, prepare yourself, steel yourself, fortify yourself, gear yourself up, gee yourself up

● WORD POWER
● The nervous system in the
● human body is its sensory and
● control apparatus, consisting
● of a network of nerve cells.
● In the middle ages, nerve
● fibres and tendons were
● not distinguished, and so
● nerves were associated with
● strength and physical force.
● The expression *nerve yourself*
● comes from this, meaning to
● brace the body and gear up the
● mind. Nerves became symbolic
● of bravery in the expression
● *get up your nerve*, and of fear
● in *lose your nerve*. The flipside
● of courage and motivation is
● arrogance and cheek: we talk
● about people *having some* or *a*
● *nerve*. In modern times, nerves
● are particularly linked to stress,
● irritation, and excitability,
● especially in the phrases *nerve-*
● *racking*, *get on someone's nerves*,
● and *nervous breakdown*.

nervous ADJECTIVE *often with* **of**
= **apprehensive**, anxious, uneasy, edgy, worried, tense, fearful, uptight (*informal*), toey (*Austral. slang*), adrenalized ≠ calm

nest NOUN = **refuge**, retreat, haunt, den, hideaway

nestle VERB *often with* **up** *or* **down** = **snuggle**, cuddle, huddle, curl up, nuzzle

nestling NOUN = **chick**, fledgling, baby bird

net¹ NOUN = **mesh**, netting, network, web, lattice, openwork
▷ VERB = **catch**, bag, capture, trap, entangle, ensnare, enmesh

net² *or* **nett** ADJECTIVE = **after taxes**, final, clear, take-home
▷ VERB = **earn**, make, clear, gain, realize, bring in, accumulate, reap

network NOUN 1 = **web**, system, arrangement, grid, lattice
2 = **maze**, warren, labyrinth

neurotic ADJECTIVE = **unstable**, nervous, disturbed, abnormal, obsessive, compulsive, manic, unhealthy ≠ rational

neutral ADJECTIVE 1 = **unbiased**, impartial, disinterested, even-handed, uninvolved, nonpartisan, unprejudiced, nonaligned ≠ biased 2 = **expressionless**, dull 3 = **uncontroversial** *or* **noncontroversial**, inoffensive

4 = **colourless**

never ADVERB 1 = **at no time**, not once, not ever ≠ always

2 = **under no circumstances**, not at all, on no account, not ever

● **WORD POWER**
● *Never* is sometimes used in
● informal speech and writing as
● an emphatic form of *not*, with
● simple past tenses of certain
● verbs: *I never said that* – and
● in very informal speech as a
● denial in place of *did not*: *he says*
● *I hit him, but I never*. These uses
● of *never* should be avoided in
● careful writing.

nevertheless ADVERB = **even so**, still, however, yet, regardless, nonetheless, notwithstanding, in spite of that

new ADJECTIVE 1 = **modern**, recent, contemporary, up-to-date, latest, current, original, fresh ≠ old-fashioned 2 = **brand new** 3 = **extra**, more, added, new-found, supplementary

4 = **unfamiliar**, strange

5 = **renewed**, changed, improved, restored, altered, revitalized

newcomer NOUN 1 = **new arrival**, stranger 2 = **beginner**, novice, new arrival, parvenu (*French*), Johnny-come-lately (*informal*)

news NOUN = **information**, latest (*informal*), report, story, exposé, intelligence, rumour, revelation, goss (*informal*)

next ADJECTIVE 1 = **following**, later, succeeding, subsequent

2 = **adjacent**, closest, nearest, neighbouring, adjoining

▷ ADVERB = **afterwards**, then, later, following, subsequently, thereafter

nice ADJECTIVE 1 = **pleasant**, delightful, agreeable, good, attractive, charming, pleasurable, enjoyable ≠ unpleasant 2 = **kind**, helpful, obliging, considerate ≠ unkind 3 = **likable** *or* **likeable**, friendly, engaging, charming, pleasant, agreeable 4 = **polite**, courteous, well-mannered ≠ vulgar 5 = **precise**, fine, careful, strict, subtle, delicate, meticulous, fastidious ≠ vague

nicely ADVERB 1 = **pleasantly**, well, delightfully, attractively, charmingly, agreeably, acceptably, pleasurably ≠ unpleasantly

2 = **kindly**, politely, thoughtfully, amiably, courteously

niche NOUN 1 = **recess**, opening, corner, hollow, nook, alcove

2 = **position**, calling, place, slot (*informal*), vocation, pigeonhole (*informal*)

nick NOUN = **cut**, mark, scratch, chip, scar, notch, dent

▷ VERB 1 (*slang, chiefly Brit.*) = **steal**, pinch (*informal*), swipe (*slang*), pilfer 2 = **cut**, mark, score, chip, scratch, scar, notch, dent

nickname NOUN = **pet name**, label, diminutive, epithet, sobriquet, moniker *or* monicker (*slang*)

night NOUN = **darkness**, dark, night-time ▷ **RELATED WORD**:

adjective nocturnal

nightly ADJECTIVE = **nocturnal**, night-time
▷ ADVERB = **every night**, nights (*informal*), each night, night after night

nightmare NOUN 1 = **bad dream**, hallucination 2 = **ordeal**, trial, hell, horror, torture, torment, tribulation, purgatory

nil NOUN 1 = **nothing**, love, zero 2 = **zero**, nothing, none, naught

nip¹ VERB 1 *with* **along**, **up**, **out**, = **pop**, go, run, rush, dash 2 = **bite** 3 = **pinch**, squeeze, tweak
▷ PHRASE: **nip something in the bud** = **thwart**, check, frustrate

nip² NOUN = **dram**, shot (*informal*), drop, sip, draught, mouthful, snifter (*informal*)

nirvana (*Buddhism, hinduism*) NOUN = **paradise**, peace, joy, bliss, serenity, tranquillity

no SENTENCE SUBSTITUTE = **not at all**, certainly not, of course not, absolutely not, never, no way, nay ≠ yes
▷ NOUN = **refusal**, rejection, denial, negation ≠ consent

noble ADJECTIVE 1 = **worthy**, generous, upright, honourable, virtuous, magnanimous ≠ despicable 2 = **dignified**, great, imposing, impressive, distinguished, splendid, stately ≠ lowly 3 = **aristocratic**, lordly, titled, patrician, blue-blooded, highborn ≠ humble
▷ NOUN = **lord**, peer, aristocrat, nobleman ≠ commoner

nobody PRONOUN = **no-one**
▷ NOUN = **nonentity**, lightweight (*informal*), zero, cipher ≠ celebrity

nod VERB 1 = **incline**, bow 2 = **signal**, indicate, motion, gesture 3 = **salute**, acknowledge
▷ NOUN 1 = **signal**, sign, motion, gesture, indication 2 = **salute**, greeting, acknowledgment

noise NOUN = **sound**, row, racket, clamour, din, uproar, commotion, hubbub ≠ silence

noisy ADJECTIVE 1 = **rowdy**, strident, boisterous, vociferous, uproarious, clamorous ≠ quiet 2 = **loud**, piercing, deafening, tumultuous, ear-splitting, cacophonous, clamorous ≠ quiet

nominal ADJECTIVE 1 = **titular**, formal, purported, in name only, supposed, so-called, theoretical, professed 2 = **token**, small, symbolic, minimal, trivial, trifling, insignificant, inconsiderable

nominate VERB 1 = **propose**, suggest, recommend, put forward 2 = **appoint**, name, choose, select, elect, assign, designate

nomination NOUN 1 = **proposal**, suggestion, recommendation 2 = **appointment**, election, selection, designation, choice

nominee NOUN = **candidate**, applicant, entrant, contestant, aspirant, runner

none PRONOUN 1 = **not any**, nothing, zero, not one, nil 2 = **no-one**, nobody, not one

nonetheless SENTENCE CONNECTOR = **nevertheless**,

however, yet, even so, despite
that, in spite of that

nonexistent ADJECTIVE
= **imaginary**, fictional, mythical,
unreal, hypothetical, illusory
≠ real

nonsense NOUN 1 = **rubbish**, hot
air (*informal*), twaddle, drivel, tripe
(*informal*), gibberish, claptrap
(*informal*), double Dutch (*Brit.
informal*), bizzo (*Austral. slang*),
bull's wool (*Austral. & N.Z.
slang*) ≠ sense 2 = **idiocy**,
stupidity

nonstop ADJECTIVE = **continuous**,
constant, relentless,
uninterrupted, endless, unbroken,
interminable, incessant
≠ occasional
▷ ADVERB = **continuously**,
constantly, endlessly, relentlessly,
perpetually, incessantly,
ceaselessly, interminably

noon NOUN = **midday**, high noon,
noonday, twelve noon, noontide

norm NOUN = **standard**, rule,
pattern, average, par, criterion,
benchmark, yardstick

normal ADJECTIVE 1 = **usual**,
common, standard, average,
natural, regular, ordinary, typical
≠ unusual 2 = **sane**, reasonable,
rational, well-adjusted, compos
mentis (*Latin*), in your right mind,
mentally sound

normally ADVERB 1 = **usually**,
generally, commonly, regularly,
typically, ordinarily, as a rule,
habitually 2 = **as usual**, naturally,
properly, conventionally, in the

usual way

● **WORD POWER**
● English was brought into
● contact with Old Norse
● through Viking invasions
● which took place between the
● 9th century and the Norman
● Conquest. Old Norse was
● closely related to Old English,
● and extensive borrowing took
● place in all areas of language,
● including vocabulary, place
● names, and personal names.
● Unusually, part of the
● grammatical system of English
● was also affected, with the
● Old Norse personal pronouns
● 'they', 'them', and 'their' ousting
● the Old English forms. In
● contrast to loan words from
● Latin and French in English
● which tend to be of a higher
● register with several syllables,
● Norse contributed everyday,
● general words like *leg*, *sky*,
● *skirt*, and *cake*. Some of the
● most common verbs in English
● came from Old Norse, such as
● *get* and *give*. One borrowing
● which describes a unique part
● of Scandinavian culture is *saga*.
● Literally 'narrative', a saga is
● a story written in Iceland in
● the Middle Ages recounting
● the adventures of a hero or
● the history of a family. The
● term is also applied to modern
● literature which has some of
● the characteristics of a saga,
● particularly a novel or series of

- novels depicting a family over
- several generations. Those
- describing the English middle
- classes have humorously been
- tagged *Aga sagas*. Informally,
- saga can also mean any story
- stretching over a long period,
- or the recounting of a long,
- boring, involved story, e.g.
- the continuing saga of the
- leadership contest.

north ADJECTIVE = **northern**,
polar, arctic, boreal, northerly
▷ ADVERB = **northward(s)**, in a
northerly direction

nose NOUN = **snout**, bill, beak,
hooter (*slang*), proboscis
▷ VERB = **ease forward**, push,
edge, shove, nudge ▷ **RELATED
WORD**: *adjective* **nasal**
- **WORD POWER**
- The literal meaning of *nose* is
- the organ of smell in human
- beings and other animals used
- in the detection and tasting of
- food. This role, and its physical
- shape, have inspired a host
- of extended meanings and
- idioms. Humans are called
- *noses* if they are experts on
- perfume. In this case, the
- meaning is drawn from the
- most relevant body part of the
- person. A *nose* can also mean
- the characteristic fragrance
- of a wine. A human's sense of
- smell can provide clues at a
- level beyond explicit thought.
- Accordingly, nose can mean
- instinct and intuition, e.g.

- *(have) a nose for trouble*. There
- are many phrases involving
- nose, such as *nose around*,
- *nose about*, and *nose out*, all
- of which involve detection
- and investigation. However,
- too much nosing can lead to
- accusations of *nosiness* and
- *poking your nose (where it doesn't
- belong)*. The physical position
- of the nose has led to a verbal
- sense of edging forward in *nose
- your way*. A nose also means
- a winning margin, originally
- from horseracing, where a
- close win is *by a nose*.

nostalgia NOUN = **reminiscence**,
longing, pining, yearning,
remembrance, homesickness,
wistfulness

nostalgic ADJECTIVE
= **sentimental**, longing,
emotional, homesick, wistful,
maudlin, regretful

notable ADJECTIVE
1 = **remarkable**, striking, unusual,
extraordinary, outstanding,
memorable, uncommon,
conspicuous ≠ imperceptible
2 = **prominent**, famous
≠ unknown
▷ NOUN = **celebrity**, big name,
dignitary, luminary, personage,
V.I.P.

notably ADVERB = **remarkably**,
unusually, extraordinarily,
noticeably, strikingly, singularly,
outstandingly, uncommonly

notch NOUN 1 (*informal*) = **level**,
step, degree, grade 2 = **cut**, nick,

n

incision, indentation, mark, score, cleft
▷ VERB = **cut**, mark, score, nick, scratch, indent

note NOUN 1 = **message**, letter, communication, memo, memorandum, epistle, e-mail, text 2 = **record**, reminder, memo, memorandum, jotting, minute 3 = **annotation**, comment, remark 4 = **document**, form, record, certificate 5 = **symbol**, mark, sign, indication, token 6 = **tone**, touch, trace, hint, sound
▷ VERB 1 = **notice**, see, observe, perceive 2 = **bear in mind**, be aware, take into account 3 = **mention**, record, mark, indicate, register, remark 4 = **write down**, record, scribble, set down, jot down

notebook NOUN = **notepad**, exercise book, journal, diary

noted ADJECTIVE = **famous**, celebrated, distinguished, well-known, prominent, acclaimed, notable, renowned ≠ unknown

nothing PRONOUN 1 = **nought**, zero, nil, not a thing, zilch (slang) 2 = **a trifle** 3 = **void**, emptiness, nothingness, nullity
▷ NOUN (informal) = **nobody**, cipher, nonentity

notice NOUN 1 = **notification**, warning, advice, intimation, news, communication, announcement, instruction, heads up (U.S. & Canad.) 2 = **attention**, interest, note, regard, consideration, observation, scrutiny, heed ≠ oversight 3 (chiefly Brit.) = **the sack** (informal), dismissal, the boot (slang), the push (slang), marching orders (informal)
▷ VERB = **observe**, see, note, spot, distinguish, perceive, detect, discern ≠ overlook

noticeable ADJECTIVE = **obvious**, clear, striking, plain, evident, manifest, conspicuous, perceptible

notify VERB = **inform**, tell, advise, alert to, announce, warn

notion NOUN 1 = **idea**, view, opinion, belief, concept, impression, sentiment, inkling 2 = **whim**, wish, desire, fancy, impulse, inclination, caprice

notorious ADJECTIVE = **infamous**, disreputable, opprobrious

notoriously ADVERB = **infamously**, disreputably

notwithstanding PREPOSITION = **despite**, in spite of, regardless of

nought (archaic or literary) or **naught** or **ought** or **aught** NOUN = **zero**, nothing, nil

nourish VERB 1 = **feed**, supply, sustain, nurture 2 = **encourage**, support, maintain, promote, sustain, foster

nourishing ADJECTIVE = **nutritious**, beneficial, wholesome, nutritive

novel[1] NOUN = **story**, tale, fiction, romance, narrative

novel[2] ADJECTIVE = **new**, different, original, fresh, unusual, innovative, uncommon

≠ ordinary

novelty NOUN 1 = **newness**, originality, freshness, innovation, surprise, uniqueness, strangeness, unfamiliarity 2 = **curiosity**, rarity, oddity, wonder 3 = **trinket**, souvenir, memento, bauble, trifle, knick-knack

novice NOUN = **beginner**, pupil, amateur, newcomer, trainee, apprentice, learner, probationer ≠ expert

now ADVERB 1 = **nowadays**, at the moment 2 = **immediately**, promptly, instantly, at once, straightaway ▷ PHRASE: **now and then** or **again** = **occasionally**, sometimes, from time to time, on and off, intermittently, infrequently, sporadically

nowadays ADVERB = **now**, today, at the moment, in this day and age

nucleus NOUN = **centre**, heart, focus, basis, core, pivot, kernel, nub

nude ADJECTIVE = **naked**, stripped, bare, undressed, stark-naked, disrobed, unclothed, unclad ≠ dressed

nudge VERB 1 = **push**, touch, dig, jog, prod, elbow, shove, poke 2 = **prompt**, influence, persuade, spur, prod, coax ▷ NOUN 1 = **push**, touch, dig, elbow, bump, shove, poke, jog 2 = **prompting**, push, encouragement, prod

nuisance NOUN = **trouble**, problem, trial, drag (*informal*), bother, pest, irritation, hassle (*informal*) ≠ benefit

numb ADJECTIVE 1 = **unfeeling**, dead, frozen, paralysed, insensitive, deadened, immobilized, torpid ≠ sensitive 2 = **stupefied**, deadened, unfeeling ▷ VERB 1 = **stun**, knock out, paralyse, daze 2 = **deaden**, freeze, dull, paralyse, immobilize, benumb

number NOUN 1 = **numeral**, figure, character, digit, integer 2 = **amount**, quantity, collection, aggregate ≠ shortage 3 = **crowd**, horde, multitude, throng 4 = **group**, set, band, crowd, gang 5 = **issue**, copy, edition, imprint, printing ▷ VERB 1 = **amount to**, come to, total, add up to 2 = **calculate**, account, reckon, compute, enumerate ≠ guess 3 = **include**, count

numerous ADJECTIVE = **many**, several, countless, lots, abundant, plentiful, innumerable, copious ≠ few

nurse VERB 1 = **look after**, treat, tend, care for, take care of, minister to 2 = **harbour**, have, maintain, preserve, entertain, cherish 3 = **breast-feed**, feed, nurture, nourish, suckle, wet-nurse

nursery NOUN = **crèche**, kindergarten, playgroup, play-centre (*N.Z.*)

nurture NOUN = **upbringing**,
training, education, instruction,
rearing, development
▷ VERB = **bring up**, raise, look
after, rear, care for, develop
≠ neglect

nut NOUN 1 (*slang*) = **madman**,
psycho (*slang*), crank (*informal*),
lunatic, maniac, nutcase (*slang*),
crazy (*informal*) 2 (*slang*) = **head**,
skull

nutrition NOUN = **food**,
nourishment, sustenance,
nutriment

n

Oo

oath NOUN 1 = **promise**, bond, pledge, vow, word, affirmation, avowal 2 = **swear word**, curse, obscenity, blasphemy, expletive, four-letter word, profanity

obedience NOUN = **compliance**, respect, reverence, observance, subservience, submissiveness, docility ≠ disobedience

obey VERB 1 = **submit to**, surrender (to), give way to, bow to, give in to, yield to, do what you are told by ≠ disobey 2 = **carry out**, follow, implement, act upon, carry through ≠ disregard 3 = **abide by**, keep, follow, comply with, observe, heed, conform to, keep to

object¹ NOUN 1 = **thing**, article, body, item, entity 2 = **purpose**, aim, end, point, plan, idea, goal, design 3 = **target**, victim, focus, recipient

object² VERB 1 *often with* **to** = **protest against**, oppose, argue against, draw the line at, take exception to, cry out against, complain against, expostulate against ≠ accept 2 = **disagree**, demur, remonstrate, express disapproval ≠ agree

objection NOUN = **protest**, opposition, complaint, doubt, dissent, outcry, protestation, scruple ≠ agreement

objective ADJECTIVE 1 = **factual**, real 2 = **unbiased**, detached, fair, open-minded, impartial, impersonal, disinterested, even-handed ≠ subjective
▷ NOUN = **purpose**, aim, goal, end, plan, hope, idea, target

objectively ADVERB = **impartially**, neutrally, fairly, justly, without prejudice, dispassionately, with an open mind, equitably

obligation NOUN 1 = **duty**, compulsion 2 = **task**, job, duty, work, charge, role, function, mission 3 = **responsibility**, duty, liability, accountability, answerability

oblige VERB 1 = **compel**, make, force, require, bind, constrain, necessitate, impel 2 = **help**, assist, benefit, please, humour, accommodate, indulge, gratify ≠ bother

obliged ADJECTIVE 1 = **forced**, required, bound, compelled, duty-bound 2 = **grateful**, in (someone's) debt, thankful, indebted, appreciative, beholden

obliging ADJECTIVE = **accommodating**, kind, helpful, willing, polite, cooperative, agreeable, considerate ≠ unhelpful

obscene ADJECTIVE 1 = **indecent**, dirty, offensive, filthy, improper, immoral, pornographic, lewd ≠ decent 2 = **offensive**, shocking, evil, disgusting, outrageous, revolting, sickening, vile

obscure ADJECTIVE **1** = **unknown**, little-known, humble, unfamiliar, out-of-the-way, lowly, unheard-of, undistinguished ≠ famous **2** = **abstruse**, complex, confusing, mysterious, vague, unclear, ambiguous, enigmatic ≠ straightforward **3** = **unclear**, uncertain, confused, mysterious, doubtful, indeterminate ≠ well-known **4** = **indistinct**, vague, blurred, dark, faint, dim, gloomy, murky ≠ clear
▷ VERB **1** = **obstruct**, hinder **2** = **hide**, screen, mask, disguise, conceal, veil, cloak, camouflage ≠ expose

observation NOUN **1** = **watching**, study, survey, review, investigation, monitoring, examination, inspection **2** = **comment**, thought, note, statement, opinion, remark, explanation, reflection **3** = **remark**, comment, statement, reflection, utterance **4** *with* **of** = **observance of**, compliance with, honouring of, fulfilment of, carrying out of

observe VERB **1** = **watch**, study, view, look at, check, survey, monitor, keep an eye on (*informal*) **2** = **notice**, see, note, discover, spot, regard, witness, distinguish **3** = **remark**, say, comment, state, note, reflect, mention, opine **4** = **comply with**, keep, follow, respect, carry out, honour, discharge, obey ≠ disregard

observer NOUN **1** = **witness**, viewer, spectator, looker-on, watcher, onlooker, eyewitness, bystander **2** = **commentator**, reporter, special correspondent **3** = **monitor**, watchdog, supervisor, scrutineer

obsessed ADJECTIVE = **absorbed**, dominated, gripped, haunted, distracted, hung up (*slang*), preoccupied ≠ indifferent

obsession NOUN = **preoccupation**, thing (*informal*), complex, hang-up (*informal*), mania, phobia, fetish, fixation

obsessive ADJECTIVE = **compulsive**, gripping, consuming, haunting, irresistible, neurotic, besetting, uncontrollable

obsolete ADJECTIVE = **outdated**, old, passé, old-fashioned, discarded, extinct, out of date, archaic ≠ up-to-date

obstacle NOUN **1** = **obstruction**, block, barrier, hurdle, snag, impediment, blockage, hindrance **2** = **hindrance**, bar, difficulty, barrier, handicap, hurdle, hitch, drawback, uphill (*S. African*) ≠ help

obstruct VERB **1** = **block**, close, bar, plug, barricade, stop up, bung up (*informal*) **2** = **hold up**, stop, check, block, restrict, slow down, hamper, hinder **3** = **impede**, hamper, hold back, thwart, hinder ≠ help **4** = **obscure**, screen, cover

obtain VERB **1** = **get**, gain, acquire,

land, net, pick up, secure, procure ≠ lose **2** = **achieve**, get, gain, accomplish, attain **3** (*formal*) = **prevail**, hold, exist, be the case, abound, predominate, be in force, be current

obvious ADJECTIVE = **clear**, plain, apparent, evident, distinct, manifest, noticeable, conspicuous ≠ unclear

obviously ADVERB **1** = **clearly**, of course, without doubt, assuredly **2** = **plainly**, patently, undoubtedly, evidently, manifestly, markedly, without doubt, unquestionably

occasion NOUN **1** = **time**, moment, point, stage, instance, juncture **2** = **function**, event, affair, do (*informal*), happening, experience, gathering, celebration **3** = **opportunity**, chance, time, opening, window **4** = **reason**, cause, call, ground(s), excuse, incentive, motive, justification
▷ VERB (*formal*) = **cause**, produce, lead to, inspire, result in, generate, prompt, provoke

occasional ADJECTIVE = **infrequent**, odd, rare, irregular, sporadic, intermittent, few and far between, periodic ≠ constant

occasionally ADVERB = **sometimes**, at times, from time to time, now and then, irregularly, now and again, periodically, once in a while ≠ constantly

occult ADJECTIVE = **supernatural**, magical, mysterious, psychic, mystical, unearthly, esoteric, uncanny ▷ PHRASE: **the occult** = **magic**, witchcraft, sorcery, wizardry, enchantment, black art, necromancy

occupant NOUN = **occupier**, resident, tenant, inmate, inhabitant, incumbent, dweller, lessee

occupation NOUN **1** = **job**, calling, business, line (of work), trade, career, employment, profession **2** = **hobby**, pastime, diversion, relaxation, leisure pursuit, (leisure) activity **3** = **invasion**, seizure, conquest, incursion, subjugation **4** = **occupancy**, residence, holding, control, possession, tenure, tenancy

occupied ADJECTIVE **1** = **in use**, taken, full, engaged, unavailable **2** = **inhabited**, peopled, lived-in, settled, tenanted ≠ uninhabited **3** = **busy**, engaged, employed, working, active, hard at work, rushed off your feet

occupy VERB **1** = **inhabit**, own, live in, dwell in, reside in, abide in ≠ vacate **2** = **invade**, take over, capture, seize, conquer, overrun, annex, colonize ≠ withdraw **3** = **hold**, control, dominate, possess **4** = **take up**, consume, tie up, use up, monopolize **5** *often passive* = **engage**, involve, employ, divert, preoccupy, engross **6** = **fill**, take up, cover, fill up, pervade, permeate, extend over

occur VERB **1** = **happen**, take place, come about, turn up (*informal*), crop up (*informal*),

transpire (*informal*), befall
2 = **exist**, appear, be found, develop, turn up, be present, manifest itself, present itself

▷ **PHRASE: occur to someone** = **come to mind**, strike someone, dawn on someone, spring to mind, cross someone's mind, enter someone's head, suggest itself to someone

● **WORD POWER**
● It is usually regarded as
● incorrect to talk of pre-
● arranged events *occurring* or
● *happening*. For this meaning
● a synonym such as *take place*
● would be more appropriate: *the*
● *wedding took place* (not *occurred*
● or *happened*) *in the afternoon*.

occurrence NOUN **1** = **incident**, happening, event, fact, matter, affair, circumstance, episode
2 = **existence**, instance, appearance, manifestation, materialization

odd ADJECTIVE **1** = **peculiar**, strange, unusual, extraordinary, bizarre, offbeat, freakish, daggy (*Austral. & N.Z. informal*)
2 = **unusual**, strange, rare, extraordinary, remarkable, bizarre, peculiar, irregular ≠ normal **3** = **occasional**, various, random, casual, irregular, periodic, sundry, incidental ≠ regular **4** = **spare**, remaining, extra, surplus, solitary, leftover, unmatched, unpaired ≠ matched

odds PLURAL NOUN
1 = **probability**, chances,

likelihood ▷ **PHRASES**: **at odds 1** = **in conflict**, arguing, quarrelling, at loggerheads, at daggers drawn **2** = **at variance**, conflicting, contrary to, at odds, out of line, out of step, at sixes and sevens (*informal*); **odds and ends** = **scraps**, bits, remains, fragments, debris, remnants, bits and pieces, bric-a-brac

odour or (*U.S.*) **odor** NOUN = **smell**, scent, perfume, fragrance, stink, bouquet, aroma, stench

Odyssey NOUN *often not cap.* = **journey**, tour, trip, quest, trek, expedition, voyage, crusade

off ADVERB **1** = **away**, out, apart, elsewhere, aside, hence, from here
2 = **absent**, gone, unavailable
▷ ADJECTIVE **1** = **cancelled**, abandoned, postponed, shelved
2 = **bad**, rotten, rancid, mouldy, turned, spoiled, sour, decayed

offence or (*U.S.*) **offense** NOUN
1 = **crime**, sin, fault, violation, wrongdoing, trespass, felony, misdemeanour **2** = **outrage**, shock, anger, trouble, bother, resentment, irritation, hassle (*informal*) **3** = **insult**, slight, hurt, outrage, injustice, snub, affront, indignity

offend VERB **1** = **distress**, upset, outrage, wound, slight, insult, annoy, snub ≠ please **2** = **break the law**, sin, err, do wrong, fall, go astray

offended ADJECTIVE = **upset**, hurt, bothered, disturbed, distressed, outraged, stung, put out

o

(informal), tooshie (Austral. slang)

offender NOUN = **criminal**, convict, crook, villain, culprit, sinner, delinquent, felon, perp (U.S. & Canad. informal)

offensive ADJECTIVE 1 = **insulting**, rude, abusive, degrading, contemptuous, disparaging, objectionable, disrespectful ≠ respectful 2 = **disgusting**, gross, foul, unpleasant, revolting, vile, repellent, obnoxious, festy (Austral. slang), yucko (Austral. slang) ≠ pleasant 3 = **attacking**, threatening, aggressive, striking, hostile, invading, combative ≠ defensive
▷ NOUN = **attack**, charge, campaign, strike, push (informal), assault, raid, drive

offer VERB 1 = **provide**, present, furnish, afford ≠ withhold 2 = **volunteer**, come forward, offer your services 3 = **propose**, suggest, advance, submit 4 = **give**, show, bring, provide, render, impart 5 = **put up for sale**, sell 6 = **bid**, submit, propose, tender, proffer
▷ NOUN 1 = **proposal**, suggestion, proposition, submission 2 = **bid**, tender, bidding price

offering NOUN 1 = **contribution**, gift, donation, present, subscription, hand-out 2 = **sacrifice**, tribute, libation, burnt offering

office NOUN 1 = **place of work**, workplace, base, workroom, place of business 2 = **branch**, department, division, section, wing, subdivision, subsection 3 = **post**, place, role, situation, responsibility, function, occupation

officer NOUN 1 = **official**, executive, agent, representative, appointee, functionary, office-holder, office bearer 2 = **police officer**, detective, PC, police constable, police man, police woman

official ADJECTIVE 1 = **authorized**, formal, sanctioned, licensed, proper, legitimate, authentic, certified ≠ unofficial 2 = **formal**, bureaucratic, ceremonial, solemn, ritualistic
▷ NOUN = **officer**, executive, agent, representative, bureaucrat, appointee, functionary, office-holder

offset VERB = **cancel out**, balance, set off, make up for, compensate for, counteract, neutralize, counterbalance

offspring NOUN 1 = **child**, baby, kid (informal), youngster, infant, successor, babe, toddler, littlie (Austral. informal), ankle-biter (Austral. slang), tacker (Austral. slang) ≠ parent 2 = **children**, young, family, issue, stock, heirs, descendants, brood

often ADVERB = **frequently**, generally, commonly, repeatedly, time and again, habitually, not infrequently ≠ never

oil NOUN 1 = **lubricant**, grease, lubrication, fuel oil 2 = **lotion**,

o

cream, balm, salve, liniment, embrocation, solution
▷ VERB = **lubricate**, grease
oily ADJECTIVE = **greasy**, slimy, fatty, slippery, oleaginous
O.K. or **okay** SENTENCE
SUBSTITUTE = **all right**, right, yes, agreed, very good, roger, very well, ya (S. African), righto (Brit. informal), yebo (S. African informal)
▷ ADJECTIVE (informal) = **all right**, fine, fitting, in order, permitted, suitable, acceptable, allowable ≠ unacceptable **2** = **fine**, good, average, fair, all right, acceptable, adequate, satisfactory ≠ unsatisfactory **3** = **well**, all right, safe, sound, healthy, unharmed, uninjured
▷ VERB = **approve**, allow, agree to, permit, sanction, endorse, authorize, rubber-stamp (informal)
▷ NOUN = **authorization**, agreement, sanction, approval, go-ahead (informal), blessing, permission, consent
old ADJECTIVE **1** = **aged**, elderly, ancient, mature, venerable, antiquated, senile, decrepit ≠ young **2** = **former**, earlier, past, previous, prior, one-time, erstwhile **3** = **long-standing**, established, fixed, enduring, abiding, long-lasting, long-established, time-honoured **4** = **stale**, worn-out, banal, threadbare, trite, overused, timeworn
old-fashioned ADJECTIVE **1** = **out of date**, dated, outdated,

unfashionable, outmoded, passé, old hat, behind the times ≠ up-to-date **2** = **oldfangled**, square (informal), outdated, unfashionable, obsolescent
ominous ADJECTIVE = **threatening**, sinister, grim, fateful, foreboding, unpromising, portentous, inauspicious ≠ promising
omission NOUN **1** = **exclusion**, removal, elimination, deletion, excision ≠ inclusion **2** = **gap**, space, exclusion, lacuna
omit VERB **1** = **leave out**, drop, exclude, eliminate, skip ≠ include **2** = **forget**, overlook, neglect, pass over, lose sight of
once ADVERB **1** = **on one occasion**, one time, one single time **2** = **at one time**, previously, formerly, long ago, once upon a time
▷ CONJUNCTION **1** = **as soon as**, when, after, the moment, immediately, the instant ▷ PHRASE: **at once 1** = **immediately**, now, straight away, directly, promptly, instantly, right away, forthwith **2** = **simultaneously**, together, at the same time, concurrently
one-sided ADJECTIVE **1** = **unequal**, unfair, uneven, unjust, unbalanced, lopsided, ill-matched ≠ equal **2** = **biased**, prejudiced, weighted, unfair, partial, distorted, partisan, slanted ≠ unbiased
ongoing ADJECTIVE = **in progress**, developing, progressing, evolving,

unfolding, unfinished

onlooker NOUN = **spectator**, witness, observer, viewer, looker-on, watcher, eyewitness, bystander

only ADJECTIVE = **sole**, one, single, individual, exclusive, unique, lone, solitary
▷ ADVERB 1 = **just**, simply, purely, merely 2 = **hardly**, just, barely, only just, scarcely, at a push

onset NOUN = **beginning**, start, birth, outbreak, inception, commencement ≠ end

onslaught NOUN = **attack**, charge, campaign, strike, assault, raid, invasion, offensive ≠ retreat

onwards or **onward** ADVERB = **forward**, on, forwards, ahead, beyond, in front, forth

ooze¹ VERB 1 = **seep**, well, escape, leak, drain, filter, drip, trickle 2 = **emit**, release, leak, drip, dribble, give off, pour forth 3 = **exude**, emit

ooze² NOUN = **mud**, clay, dirt, silt, sludge, mire, slime, alluvium

open ADJECTIVE 1 = **unclosed**, unlocked, ajar, unfastened, yawning ≠ closed 2 = **unsealed**, unstoppered ≠ unopened 3 = **extended**, unfolded, stretched out, unfurled, straightened out, unrolled ≠ shut 4 = **frank**, direct, straightforward, sincere, transparent, honest, candid, truthful ≠ sly 5 = **receptive**, sympathetic, responsive, amenable 6 = **unresolved**, unsettled, undecided,

debatable, moot, arguable 7 = **clear**, passable, unhindered, unimpeded, navigable, unobstructed ≠ obstructed 8 = **available**, to hand, accessible, handy, at your disposal 9 = **general**, public, free, universal, blanket, across-the-board, unrestricted, overarching ≠ restricted 10 = **vacant**, free, available, empty, unoccupied, unfilled
▷ VERB 1 = **unfasten**, unlock ≠ close 2 = **unwrap**, uncover, undo, unravel, untie ≠ wrap 3 = **uncork** 4 = **unfold**, spread (out), expand, unfurl, unroll ≠ fold 5 = **clear**, unblock ≠ block 6 = **undo**, unbutton, unfasten ≠ fasten 7 = **begin business** 8 = **start**, begin, launch, trigger, kick off (informal), initiate, commence, get going ≠ end 9 = **begin**, start, commence ≠ end

open-air MODIFIER = **outdoor**, outside, out-of-door(s), alfresco

opening ADJECTIVE = **first**, earliest, beginning, premier, primary, initial, maiden, inaugural
▷ NOUN 1 = **beginning**, start, launch, dawn, outset, initiation, inception, commencement ≠ ending 2 = **hole**, space, tear, crack, gap, slot, puncture, aperture ≠ blockage 3 = **opportunity**, chance, time, moment, occasion, look-in (informal) 4 = **job**, position, post,

situation, opportunity, vacancy

openly ADVERB = **frankly**, plainly, honestly, overtly, candidly, unreservedly, unhesitatingly, forthrightly ≠ privately

open-minded ADJECTIVE = **unprejudiced**, liberal, balanced, objective, reasonable, tolerant, impartial, receptive ≠ narrow-minded

operate VERB 1 = **manage**, run, direct, handle, supervise, be in charge of 2 = **function**, work, act 3 = **run**, work, use, control, manoeuvre 4 = **work**, go, run, perform, function ≠ break down

operation NOUN = **performance**, action, movement, motion

operational ADJECTIVE = **working**, going, running, ready, functioning, operative, viable, functional ≠ inoperative

operative ADJECTIVE = **in force**, effective, functioning, active, in effect, operational, in operation ≠ inoperative
▷ NOUN 1 = **worker**, employee, labourer, workman, artisan 2 (*U.S. & Canad.*) = **spy**, undercover agent, mole, nark (*Brit., Austral. & N.Z. slang*)

operator NOUN = **worker**, driver, mechanic, operative, conductor, technician, handler

opinion NOUN 1 = **belief**, feeling, view, idea, theory, conviction, point of view, sentiment
2 = **estimation**, view, impression, assessment, judgment, appraisal, considered opinion

opponent NOUN 1 = **adversary**, rival, enemy, competitor, challenger, foe, contestant, antagonist ≠ ally 2 = **opposer**, dissident, objector ≠ supporter

opportunity NOUN = **chance**, opening, time, turn, moment, possibility, occasion, slot

oppose VERB = **be against**, fight (against), block, take on, counter, contest, resist, combat ≠ support

opposed ADJECTIVE 1 *with* **to** = **against**, hostile, adverse, in opposition, averse, antagonistic, (dead) set against 2 = **contrary**, conflicting, clashing, counter, adverse, contradictory, dissentient

opposing ADJECTIVE
1 = **conflicting**, different, contrasting, opposite, differing, contrary, contradictory, incompatible 2 = **rival**, conflicting, competing, enemy, opposite, hostile

opposite ADJECTIVE = **facing**, other, opposing 2 = **different**, conflicting, contrasted, contrasting, unlike, contrary, dissimilar, divergent ≠ alike
3 = **rival**, conflicting, opposing, competing
▷ PREPOSITION *often with* **to** = **facing**, face to face with, across from, eyeball to eyeball with (*informal*)
▷ NOUN = **reverse**, contrary, converse, antithesis, contradiction, inverse, obverse

opposition NOUN 1 = **hostility**,

resistance, resentment,
disapproval, obstruction,
animosity, antagonism, antipathy
≠ support **2** = **opponent(s)**,
competition, rival(s), enemy,
competitor(s), other side,
challenger(s), foe

oppress VERB **1** = **subjugate**,
abuse, suppress, wrong, master,
overcome, subdue, persecute
≠ liberate **2** = **depress**, burden,
discourage, torment, harass,
afflict, sadden, vex

oppression NOUN = **persecution**,
control, abuse, injury, injustice,
cruelty, domination, repression
≠ justice

oppressive ADJECTIVE
1 = **tyrannical**, severe, harsh,
cruel, brutal, authoritarian,
unjust, repressive ≠ merciful
2 = **stifling**, close, sticky, stuffy,
humid, sultry, airless, muggy

opt VERB = **choose**, decide, prefer,
select, elect ≠ reject ▷ PHRASE:
opt for something or **someone**
= **choose**, pick, select, adopt, go
for, designate, decide on, plump
for

optimistic ADJECTIVE **1** = **hopeful**,
positive, confident, encouraged,
cheerful, rosy, buoyant, sanguine
≠ pessimistic **2** = **encouraging**,
promising, bright, good,
reassuring, rosy, heartening,
auspicious ≠ discouraging

optimum ADJECTIVE = **ideal**, best,
highest, finest, perfect, supreme,
peak, outstanding ≠ worst

option NOUN = **choice**,

alternative, selection, preference,
freedom of choice, power to
choose

optional ADJECTIVE = **voluntary**,
open, discretionary, possible,
extra, elective ≠ compulsory

opus NOUN = **work**, piece,
production, creation,
composition, work of art,
brainchild, oeuvre (French)

oral ADJECTIVE = **spoken**, vocal,
verbal, unwritten

orbit NOUN **1** = **path**, course,
cycle, circle, revolution, rotation,
trajectory, sweep **2** = **sphere of
influence**, reach, range, influence,
province, scope, domain, compass
▷ VERB = **circle**, ring, go round,
revolve around, encircle,
circumscribe, circumnavigate

orchestrate VERB **1** = **organize**,
plan, run, set up, arrange, put
together, marshal, coordinate
2 = **score**, set, arrange, adapt

ordain VERB **1** = **appoint**, name,
commission, select, invest,
nominate, anoint, consecrate
2 (formal) = **order**, will, rule,
demand, require, direct,
command, dictate

ordeal NOUN = **hardship**,
trial, difficulty, test, suffering,
nightmare, torture, agony
≠ pleasure

order VERB **1** = **command**,
instruct, direct, charge, demand,
require, bid, compel ≠ forbid
2 = **decree**, rule, demand,
prescribe, pronounce, ordain
≠ ban **3** = **request**, ask (for), book,

o

seek, reserve, apply for, solicit, send away for **4** = **arrange**, group, sort, position, line up, organize, catalogue, sort out ≠ disarrange
▷ NOUN **1** = **instruction**, ruling, demand, direction, command, dictate, decree, mandate **2** = **request**, booking, demand, commission, application, reservation, requisition **3** = **sequence**, grouping, series, structure, chain, arrangement, line-up, array **4** = **organization**, system, method, pattern, symmetry, regularity, neatness, tidiness ≠ chaos **5** = **peace**, control, law, quiet, calm, discipline, law and order, tranquillity **6** = **society**, company, group, club, community, association, institute, organization **7** = **class**, set, rank, grade, caste **8** (biology) = **kind**, group, class, family, sort, type, variety, category

orderly ADJECTIVE **1** = **well-behaved**, controlled, disciplined, quiet, restrained, law-abiding, peaceable ≠ disorderly **2** = **well-organized**, regular, in order, organized, precise, neat, tidy, systematic ≠ disorganized

ordinary ADJECTIVE **1** = **usual**, standard, normal, common, regular, typical, conventional, routine **2** = **commonplace**, plain, modest, humble, mundane, banal, unremarkable, run-of-the-mill ≠ extraordinary

organ NOUN **1** = **body part**, part of the body, element, biological structure **2** = **newspaper**, medium, voice, vehicle, gazette, mouthpiece

organic ADJECTIVE **1** = **natural**, biological, living, live, animate **2** = **systematic**, ordered, structured, organized, integrated, orderly, methodical

organism NOUN = **creature**, being, thing, body, animal, structure, beast, entity

organization or **organisation** NOUN **1** = **group**, company, party, body, association, band, institution, corporation **2** = **management**, running, planning, control, operation, handling, structuring, administration **3** = **structure**, form, pattern, make-up, arrangement, construction, format, formation

organize or **organise** VERB **1** = **arrange**, run, plan, prepare, set up, devise, put together, take care of, jack up (N.Z. informal) ≠ disrupt **2** = **put in order**, arrange, group, list, file, index, classify, inventory ≠ muddle

orient or **orientate** VERB = **adjust**, adapt, alter, accustom, align, familiarize, acclimatize
▷ PHRASE: **orient yourself** = **get your bearings**, establish your location

orientation NOUN **1** = **inclination**, tendency, disposition, predisposition, predilection, proclivity, partiality

2 = **induction**, introduction, adjustment, settling in, adaptation, assimilation, familiarization, acclimatization
3 = **position**, situation, location, bearings, direction, arrangement, whereabouts

origin NOUN **1** = **beginning**, start, birth, launch, foundation, creation, emergence, onset ≠ end
2 = **root**, source, basis, base, seed, foundation, nucleus, derivation

original ADJECTIVE **1** = **first**, earliest, initial **2** = **initial**, first, starting, opening, primary, introductory ≠ final
3 = **new**, fresh, novel, unusual, unprecedented, innovative, unfamiliar, seminal ≠ unoriginal
4 = **creative**, inspired, imaginative, artistic, fertile, ingenious, visionary, inventive
▷ NOUN = **prototype**, master, pattern ≠ copy

originally ADVERB = **initially**, first, firstly, at first, primarily, to begin with, in the beginning

originate VERB **1** = **begin**, start, emerge, come, happen, rise, appear, spring ≠ end **2** = **invent**, create, design, launch, introduce, institute, generate, pioneer

ornament NOUN **1** = **decoration**, trimming, accessory, festoon, trinket, bauble, knick-knack
2 = **embellishment**, decoration, embroidery, elaboration, adornment, ornamentation
▷ VERB = **decorate**, adorn, array, do up (*informal*), embellish,

festoon, beautify, prettify

orthodox ADJECTIVE
1 = **established**, official, accepted, received, common, traditional, normal, usual ≠ unorthodox
2 = **conformist**, conservative, traditional, strict, devout, observant ≠ nonconformist

orthodoxy NOUN **1** = **doctrine**, teaching, opinion, principle, belief, convention, creed, dogma
2 = **conformity**, received wisdom, traditionalism, conventionality ≠ nonconformity

other DETERMINER **1** = **additional**, more, further, new, added, extra, fresh, spare **2** = **different**, alternative, contrasting, distinct, diverse, dissimilar, separate, alternative

otherwise SENTENCE CONNECTOR = **or else**, or, if not, or then
▷ ADVERB **1** = **apart from that**, in other ways, in (all) other respects
2 = **differently**, any other way, contrarily

ounce NOUN = **shred**, bit, drop, trace, scrap, grain, fragment, atom

oust VERB = **expel**, turn out, dismiss, exclude, exile, throw out, displace, topple

out ADJECTIVE **1** = **not in**, away, elsewhere, outside, gone, abroad, from home, absent
2 = **extinguished**, ended, finished, dead, exhausted, expired, used up, at an end
≠ alight **3** = **in bloom**, opening,

open, flowering, blooming,
in flower, in full bloom
4 = **available**, on sale, in the
shops, to be had, purchasable
5 = **revealed**, exposed, common
knowledge, public knowledge,
(out) in the open ≠ kept secret
▷ VERB = **expose**

outbreak NOUN **1** = **eruption**,
burst, explosion, epidemic,
rash, outburst, flare-up, upsurge
2 = **onset**, beginning, outset,
opening, dawn, commencement

outburst NOUN **1** = **explosion**,
surge, outbreak, eruption, flare-
up **2** = **fit**, flare-up, eruption,
spasm, outpouring

outcome NOUN = **result**, end,
consequence, conclusion, payoff
(*informal*), upshot

outcry NOUN = **protest**,
complaint, objection, dissent,
outburst, clamour, uproar,
commotion

outdated ADJECTIVE = **old-
fashioned**, dated, obsolete,
out of date, passé, archaic,
unfashionable, antiquated
≠ modern

outdoor ADJECTIVE = **open-air**,
outside, out-of-door(s), alfresco
≠ indoor

outer ADJECTIVE **1** = **external**,
outside, outward, exterior,
exposed, outermost ≠ inner
2 = **surface 3** = **outlying**, distant,
provincial, out-of-the-way,
peripheral, far-flung ≠ central

outfit NOUN **1** = **costume**,
dress, clothes, clothing, suit,

get-up (*informal*), kit, ensemble
2 (*informal*) = **group**, company,
team, party, unit, crowd, squad,
organization

outgoing ADJECTIVE **1** = **leaving**,
former, previous, retiring,
withdrawing, prior, departing,
erstwhile ≠ incoming
2 = **sociable**, open, social, warm,
friendly, expansive, affable,
extrovert ≠ reserved

outgoings PLURAL NOUN
= **expenses**, costs, payments,
expenditure, overheads, outlay

outing NOUN = **journey**, run, trip,
tour, expedition, excursion, spin
(*informal*), jaunt

outlaw NOUN = **bandit**, criminal,
thief, robber, fugitive, outcast,
felon, highwayman
▷ VERB **1** = **ban**, bar, veto, forbid,
exclude, prohibit, disallow,
proscribe ≠ legalise **2** = **banish**,
put a price on (someone's) head

outlet NOUN **1** = **shop**, store,
supermarket, market, boutique,
emporium, hypermarket
2 = **channel**, release, medium,
avenue, vent, conduit **3** = **pipe**,
opening, channel, exit, duct

outline NOUN **1** = **summary**,
review, résumé, rundown,
synopsis, précis, thumbnail
sketch, recapitulation **2** = **shape**,
lines, form, figure, profile,
silhouette, configuration,
contour(s)
▷ VERB **1** = **summarize**, draft,
plan, trace, sketch (in), sum
up, encapsulate, delineate

2 = **silhouette**, etch

outlook NOUN 1 = **attitude**, opinion, position, approach, mood, perspective, point of view, stance 2 = **prospect(s)**, future, expectations, forecast, prediction, probability, prognosis

out of date ADJECTIVE 1 = **old-fashioned**, dated, outdated, obsolete, démodé (French), antiquated, outmoded, passé ≠ modern 2 = **invalid**, expired, lapsed, void, null and void

output NOUN = **production**, manufacture, manufacturing, yield, productivity

outrage NOUN = **indignation**, shock, anger, rage, fury, hurt, resentment, scorn
▷ VERB = **offend**, shock, upset, wound, insult, infuriate, incense, madden

outrageous ADJECTIVE
1 = **atrocious**, shocking, terrible, offensive, appalling, cruel, savage, horrifying ≠ mild
2 = **unreasonable**, unfair, steep (informal), shocking, extravagant, scandalous, preposterous, unwarranted ≠ reasonable

outright ADJECTIVE 1 = **absolute**, complete, total, perfect, sheer, thorough, unconditional, unqualified 2 = **definite**, clear, certain, flat, absolute, black-and-white, straightforward, unequivocal
▷ ADVERB 1 = **openly**, frankly, plainly, overtly, candidly, unreservedly, unhesitatingly,

forthrightly 2 = **absolutely**, completely, totally, fully, entirely, thoroughly, wholly, utterly

outset NOUN = **beginning**, start, opening, onset, inauguration, inception, commencement, kickoff (informal) ≠ finish

outside ADJECTIVE = **external**, outer, exterior, outward, extraneous ≠ inner 2 = **remote**, small, unlikely, slight, slim, distant, faint, marginal
▷ ADVERB = **outdoors**, out of the house, out-of-doors
▷ NOUN = **exterior**, face, front, covering, skin, surface, shell, coating

● **WORD POWER**
● The use of *outside of* and *inside*
● *of*, although fairly common,
● is generally thought to be
● incorrect or nonstandard: *She*
● *waits outside* (not *outside of*) *the*
● *school*.

outsider NOUN = **stranger**, incomer, visitor, newcomer, intruder, interloper, odd one out

outskirts PLURAL NOUN = **edge**, boundary, suburbs, fringe, perimeter, periphery, suburbia, environs

outspan VERB (S. African) = **relax**, chill out (slang, chiefly U.S.), take it easy, loosen up, put your feet up

outspoken ADJECTIVE
= **forthright**, open, frank, straightforward, blunt, explicit, upfront (informal), unequivocal
≠ reserved

outstanding ADJECTIVE

1 = **excellent**, good, great, important, special, fine, brilliant, impressive, booshit (*Austral. slang*), exo (*Austral. slang*), sik (*Austral. slang*), rad (*informal*), phat (*slang*), schmick (*Austral. informal*) ≠ mediocre **2** = **unpaid**, remaining, due, pending, payable, unsettled, uncollected **3** = **undone**, left, omitted, unfinished, unfulfilled, unperformed

outward ADJECTIVE = **apparent**, seeming, surface, ostensible ≠ inward

outwardly ADVERB = **apparently**, externally, seemingly, it seems that, on the surface, it appears that, ostensibly, on the face of it

outweigh VERB = **override**, cancel (out), eclipse, offset, compensate for, supersede, neutralize, counterbalance

oval ADJECTIVE = **elliptical**, egg-shaped, ovoid

ovation NOUN = **applause**, hand, cheers, praise, tribute, acclaim, clapping, accolade ≠ derision

over PREPOSITION **1** = **above**, on top of **2** = **on top of**, on, across, upon **3** = **across**, (looking) onto **4** = **more than**, above, exceeding, in excess of, upwards of **5** = **about**, regarding, relating to, concerning, apropos of
▷ ADVERB **1** = **above**, overhead, in the sky, on high, aloft, up above **2** = **extra**, more, further, beyond, additional, in addition, surplus, in excess

▷ ADJECTIVE = **finished**, done (with), through, ended, closed, past, completed, complete
▷ RELATED WORDS: *prefixes* **hyper-, super-**

overall ADJECTIVE = **total**, full, whole, general, complete, entire, global, comprehensive
▷ ADVERB = **in general**, generally, mostly, all things considered, on average, on the whole, predominantly, in the main

overcome VERB **1** = **defeat**, beat, conquer, master, overwhelm, subdue, rout, overpower **2** = **conquer**, beat, master, subdue, triumph over, vanquish

overdue ADJECTIVE **1** = **delayed**, belated, late, behind schedule, tardy, unpunctual, behindhand ≠ early **2** = **unpaid**, owing

overflow VERB = **spill over**, well over, run over, pour over, bubble over, brim over
▷ NOUN **1** = **flood**, spilling over **2** = **surplus**, extra, excess, overspill, overabundance, additional people *or* things

overhaul VERB **1** = **check**, service, maintain, examine, restore, tune (up), repair, go over **2** = **overtake**, pass, leave behind, catch up with, get past, outstrip, get ahead of, outdistance
▷ NOUN = **check**, service, examination, going-over (*informal*), inspection, once-over (*informal*), checkup, reconditioning

overhead ADJECTIVE = **raised**,

suspended, elevated, aerial, overhanging
▷ ADVERB = **above**, in the sky, on high, aloft, up above ≠ underneath

overheads PLURAL NOUN = **running costs**, expenses, outgoings, operating costs

overlook VERB 1 = **look over** or **out on**, have a view of 2 = **miss**, forget, neglect, omit, disregard, pass over ≠ notice 3 = **ignore**, excuse, forgive, pardon, disregard, condone, turn a blind eye to, wink at

overpower VERB 1 = **overcome**, master, overwhelm, overthrow, subdue, quell, subjugate, prevail over 2 defeat, crush, triumph over, vanquish 3 = **overwhelm**, overcome, bowl over (*informal*), stagger

override VERB 1 = **outweigh**, eclipse, supersede, take precedence over, prevail over 2 = **overrule**, cancel, overturn, repeal, rescind, annul, nullify, countermand 3 = **ignore**, reject, discount, overlook, disregard, pass over, take no notice of

overrun VERB 1 = **overwhelm**, attack, assault, occupy, raid, invade, penetrate, rout 2 = **spread over**, overwhelm, choke, swamp, infest, inundate, permeate, swarm over 3 = **exceed**, go beyond, surpass, overshoot, run over or on

overshadow VERB 1 = **spoil**, ruin, mar, wreck, blight, crool or cruel (*Austral. slang*), mess up, put a damper on 2 = **outshine**, eclipse, surpass, dwarf, tower above, leave or put in the shade

overt ADJECTIVE = **open**, obvious, plain, public, manifest, blatant, observable, undisguised ≠ hidden

overtake VERB 1 = **pass**, leave behind, overhaul, catch up with, get past, outdistance, go by or past 2 = **outdo**, top, exceed, eclipse, surpass, outstrip, get the better of, outclass 3 = **befall**, hit, happen to, catch off guard, catch unawares 4 = **engulf**, overwhelm, hit, strike, swamp, envelop, swallow up

overthrow VERB = **defeat**, overcome, conquer, bring down, oust, topple, rout, overpower ≠ uphold
▷ NOUN = **downfall**, fall, defeat, collapse, destruction, ousting, undoing, unseating ≠ preservation

overturn VERB 1 = **tip over**, topple, upturn, capsize, upend, keel over, overbalance 2 = **knock over** or **down**, upturn, tip over, upend 3 = **reverse**, change, cancel, abolish, overthrow, set aside, repeal, quash 4 = **overthrow**, defeat, destroy, overcome, bring down, oust, topple, depose

overweight ADJECTIVE = **fat**, heavy, stout, hefty, plump, bulky, chunky, chubby ≠ underweight

overwhelm VERB 1 = **overcome**,

devastate, stagger, bowl over
(*informal*), knock (someone) for six
(*informal*), sweep (someone) off
his *or* her feet, take (someone's)
breath away **2** = **destroy**, defeat,
overcome, crush, massacre,
conquer, wipe out, overthrow

overwhelming ADJECTIVE
1 = **overpowering**, strong,
powerful, towering, stunning,
crushing, devastating,
shattering ≠ negligible **2** = **vast**,
huge, massive, enormous,
tremendous, immense, very large
≠ insignificant

owe VERB = **be in debt (to)**, be in
arrears (to), be overdrawn (by), be
obligated *or* indebted (to)

owing ▷ PHRASE: owing to
= **because of**, thanks to, as a result
of, on account of, by reason of

own DETERMINER = **personal**,
special, private, individual,
particular, exclusive
▷ VERB = **possess**, have,
keep, hold, enjoy, retain, be in
possession of, have to your name

owner NOUN = **possessor**, holder,
proprietor, titleholder, landlord *or*
landlady

ownership NOUN = **possession**,
occupation, tenure, dominion

Pp

pace NOUN 1 = **speed**, rate, tempo, velocity 2 = **step**, walk, stride, tread, gait 3 = **footstep**, step, stride
▷ VERB = **stride**, walk, pound, patrol, march up and down

pack VERB 1 = **package**, load, store, bundle, stow 2 = **cram**, crowd, press, fill, stuff, jam, ram, compress
▷ NOUN 1 = **packet**, box, package, carton 2 = **bundle**, parcel, load, burden, rucksack, knapsack, back pack, kitbag 3 = **group**, crowd, company, band, troop, gang, bunch, mob ▷ PHRASES: **pack someone off** = **send away**, dismiss, send packing (*informal*); **pack something in 1** (*Brit. & N.Z. informal*) = **resign from**, leave, give up, quit (*informal*), chuck (*informal*), jack in (*informal*) 2 = **stop**, give up, kick (*informal*), cease, chuck (*informal*)

package NOUN 1 = **parcel**, box, container, packet, carton 2 = **collection**, lot, unit, combination, compilation
▷ VERB = **pack**, box, parcel (up)

packet NOUN 1 = **container**, box, package, carton 2 = **package**, parcel 3 (*slang*) = **a fortune**, a bomb (*Brit. slang*), a pile (*informal*), a small fortune, a tidy sum (*informal*), a king's ransom (*informal*), top whack (*informal*)

pact NOUN = **agreement**, alliance, treaty, deal, understanding, bargain, covenant

pad¹ NOUN 1 = **wad**, dressing, pack, padding, compress, wadding 2 = **cushion**, filling, stuffing, pillow, bolster, upholstery 3 = **notepad**, block, notebook, jotter, writing pad 4 (*slang*) = **home**, flat, apartment, place, bachelor apartment (*Canad.*) 5 = **paw**, foot, sole
▷ VERB = **pack**, fill, protect, stuff, cushion

pad² VERB = **sneak**, creep, steal, go barefoot

padding NOUN 1 = **filling**, stuffing, packing, wadding 2 = **waffle** (*informal, chiefly Brit.*), hot air (*informal*), verbiage, wordiness, verbosity

paddle¹ NOUN = **oar**, scull
▷ VERB = **row**, pull, scull

paddle² VERB = **wade**, splash (about), slop

pagan NOUN = **heathen**, infidel, polytheist, idolater
▷ ADJECTIVE = **heathen**, infidel, polytheistic, idolatrous

page¹ NOUN = **folio**, side, leaf, sheet

page² NOUN 1 = **attendant**, pageboy 2 = **servant**, attendant, squire, pageboy
▷ VERB = **call**, summon, send for

pain NOUN 1 = **suffering**, discomfort, hurt, irritation,

P

tenderness, soreness **2** = **ache**, stinging, aching, cramp, throb, throbbing, pang, twinge
3 = **sorrow**, suffering, torture, distress, despair, misery, agony, sadness
▷ **PLURAL NOUN** = **trouble**, effort, care, bother, diligence
▷ **VERB 1** = **distress**, hurt, torture, grieve, torment, sadden, agonize, cut to the quick **2** = **hurt**
painful ADJECTIVE **1** = **sore**, smarting, aching, tender
≠ painless **2** = **distressing**, unpleasant, grievous, distasteful, agonizing, disagreeable
≠ pleasant **3** = **difficult**, arduous, trying, hard, troublesome, laborious ≠ easy
painfully ADVERB = **distressingly**, clearly, sadly, unfortunately, dreadfully
paint NOUN = **colouring**, colour, stain, dye, tint, pigment, emulsion
▷ **VERB 1** = **colour**, cover, coat, stain, whitewash, daub, distemper, apply paint to
2 = **depict**, draw, portray, picture, represent, sketch
pair NOUN **1** = **set 2** = **couple**, brace, duo
▷ **VERB** often with **off** = **team**, match (up), join, couple, twin, bracket

● **WORD POWER**
● Like other collective nouns, *pair*
● takes a singular or a plural verb
● according to whether it is seen
● as a unit or as a collection of

two things: *the pair are said to dislike each other; a pair of good shoes is essential.*
pal NOUN (*informal*) = **friend**, companion, mate (*informal*), buddy (*informal*), comrade, chum (*informal*), crony, cobber (*Austral. & N.Z. old-fashioned, informal*), E hoa (*N.Z.*)
pale ADJECTIVE **1** = **light**, soft, faded, subtle, muted, bleached, pastel, light-coloured **2** = **dim**, weak, faint, feeble, thin, wan, watery **3** = **white**, pasty, bleached, wan, colourless, pallid, ashen ≠ rosy-cheeked
▷ **VERB** = **become pale**, blanch, whiten, go white, lose colour
pamper VERB = **spoil**, indulge, pet, cosset, coddle, mollycoddle
pamphlet NOUN = **booklet**, leaflet, brochure, circular, tract
pan¹ NOUN = **pot**, container, saucepan
▷ **VERB 1** (*informal*) = **criticize**, knock, slam (*slang*), censure, tear into (*informal*) **2** = **sift out**, look for, search for
pan² VERB = **move along** or **across**, follow, track, sweep
panic NOUN = **fear**, alarm, terror, anxiety, hysteria, fright, trepidation, a flap (*informal*)
▷ **VERB 1** = **go to pieces**, become hysterical, lose your nerve
2 = **alarm**, scare, unnerve
panorama NOUN **1** = **view**, prospect, vista **2** = **survey**, perspective, overview, overall picture

pant VERB = **puff**, blow, breathe, gasp, wheeze, heave

pants PLURAL NOUN 1 (Brit.) = **underpants**, briefs, drawers, knickers, panties, boxer shorts, broekies (S. African), underdaks (Austral. slang) 2 (U.S.) = **trousers**, slacks

paper NOUN 1 = **newspaper**, daily, journal, gazette 2 = **essay**, article, treatise, dissertation 3 = **examination**, test, exam 4 = **report**
▷ PLURAL NOUN 1 = **letters**, records, documents, file, diaries, archive, paperwork, dossier 2 = **documents**, records, certificates, identification, deeds, identity papers, I.D. (informal)
▷ VERB = **wallpaper**, hang

parade NOUN 1 = **procession**, march, pageant, cavalcade 2 = **show**, display, spectacle
▷ VERB 1 = **march**, process, promenade 2 = **flaunt**, display, exhibit, show off (informal) 3 = **strut**, show off (informal), swagger, swank

paradigm NOUN = **model**, example, pattern, ideal

paradise NOUN 1 = **heaven**, Promised Land, Happy Valley, Elysian fields 2 = **bliss**, delight, heaven, felicity, utopia

paradox NOUN = **contradiction**, puzzle, anomaly, enigma, oddity

paragraph NOUN = **section**, part, item, passage, clause, subdivision

parallel NOUN 1 = **equivalent**, counterpart, match, equal, twin, analogue ≠ opposite 2 = **similarity**, comparison, analogy, resemblance, likeness ≠ difference
▷ ADJECTIVE 1 = **matching**, corresponding, like, similar, resembling, analogous ≠ different 2 = **equidistant**, alongside, side by side ≠ divergent

paralyse VERB 1 = **disable**, cripple, lame, incapacitate 2 = **freeze**, stun, numb, petrify, halt, immobilize 3 = **immobilize**, freeze, halt, disable, cripple, incapacitate, bring to a standstill

paralysis NOUN 1 = **immobility**, palsy 2 = **standstill**, breakdown, stoppage, halt

parameter NOUN (informal) usually plural = **limit**, restriction, framework, limitation, specification

paramount ADJECTIVE = **principal**, prime, first, chief, main, primary, supreme, cardinal ≠ secondary

paranoid ADJECTIVE 1 (informal) = **suspicious**, worried, nervous, fearful, antsy (informal) 2 = **obsessive**, disturbed, manic, neurotic, mentally ill, psychotic, deluded, paranoiac

parasite NOUN = **sponger** (informal), leech, hanger-on, scrounger (informal), bloodsucker (informal), quandong (Austral. slang)

parcel NOUN = **package**, case, box, pack, bundle

▷ **VERB** *often with* **up** = **wrap**, pack, package, tie up, do up, gift-wrap, box up, fasten together

pardon VERB = **acquit**, let off (*informal*), exonerate, absolve ≠ punish

▷ **NOUN 1** = **forgiveness**, absolution ≠ condemnation **2** = **acquittal**, amnesty, exoneration ≠ punishment

▷ **PHRASE**: **pardon me** = **forgive me**, excuse me

parent NOUN = **father** *or* **mother**, sire, progenitor, procreator, old (*Austral. & N.Z. informal*), oldie (*Austral. informal*), patriarch

parish NOUN **1** = **district**, community **2** = **community**, flock, church, congregation

park NOUN **1** = **recreation ground**, garden, playground, pleasure garden, playpark, domain (*N.Z.*), forest park (*N.Z.*) **2** = **parkland**, grounds, estate, lawns, woodland, grassland **3** = **field**, pitch, playing field

parliament NOUN **1** = **assembly**, council, congress, senate, convention, legislature **2** = **sitting**

parliamentary ADJECTIVE = **governmental**, legislative, law-making

parlour *or* (*U.S.*) **parlor** NOUN **1** (*old-fashioned*) = **sitting room**, lounge, living room, drawing room, front room **2** = **establishment**, shop, store, salon

parody NOUN = **takeoff** (*informal*), satire, caricature, send-up (*Brit. informal*), spoof (*informal*), skit, burlesque

▷ **VERB** = **take off** (*informal*), caricature, send up (*Brit. informal*), burlesque, satirize, do a takeoff of (*informal*)

parrot VERB = **repeat**, echo, imitate, copy, mimic

parry VERB **1** = **evade**, avoid, dodge, sidestep **2** = **ward off**, block, deflect, repel, rebuff, repulse

parson NOUN = **clergyman**, minister, priest, vicar, preacher, pastor, cleric, churchman

part NOUN **1** = **piece**, share, proportion, percentage, bit, section, scrap, portion ≠ entirety **2** *often plural* = **region**, area, district, neighbourhood, quarter, vicinity **3** = **component**, bit, unit, constituent **4** = **branch**, division, office, section, wing, subdivision, subsection **5** = **organ**, member, limb **6** (*theatre*) = **role**, representation, persona, portrayal, depiction, character part **7** (*theatre*) = **lines**, words, script, dialogue **8** = **side**, behalf

▷ **VERB 1** = **divide**, separate, break, tear, split, rend, detach, sever ≠ join **2** = **part company**, separate, split up ≠ meet

▷ **PHRASE**: **in good part** = **good-naturedly**, well, cheerfully, without offence

partial ADJECTIVE **1** = **incomplete**, unfinished, imperfect, uncompleted ≠ complete

2 = **biased**, prejudiced, discriminatory, partisan, unfair, one-sided, unjust ≠ unbiased

partially ADVERB = **partly**, somewhat, in part, not wholly, fractionally, incompletely

participant NOUN = **participator**, member, player, contributor, stakeholder

participate VERB = **take part**, be involved, perform, join, partake ≠ refrain from

participation NOUN = **taking part**, contribution, involvement, sharing in, joining in, partaking

particle NOUN = **bit**, piece, scrap, grain, shred, mite, jot, speck

particular ADJECTIVE **1** = **specific**, special, exact, precise, distinct, peculiar ≠ general **2** = **special**, exceptional, notable, uncommon, marked, unusual, remarkable, singular **3** = **fussy**, demanding, fastidious, choosy (*informal*), picky (*informal*), finicky, pernickety (*informal*), nit-picky (*informal*) ≠ indiscriminate
  ▷ NOUN *usually plural* = **detail**, fact, feature, item, circumstance, specification

particularly ADVERB
  1 = **specifically**, expressly, explicitly, especially, in particular, distinctly **2** = **especially**, notably, unusually, exceptionally, singularly, uncommonly

parting NOUN **1** = **farewell**, goodbye **2** = **division**, breaking, split, separation, rift, rupture

partisan ADJECTIVE = **prejudiced**, one-sided, biased, partial, sectarian ≠ unbiased
  ▷ NOUN **1** = **supporter**, devotee, adherent, upholder ≠ opponent
  2 = **underground fighter**, guerrilla, freedom fighter, resistance fighter

partition NOUN **1** = **screen**, wall, barrier **2** = **division**, separation, segregation
  ▷ VERB = **separate**, screen, divide

partly ADVERB = **partially**, somewhat, slightly ≠ completely
  ● WORD POWER
  ● *Partly* and *partially* are to some
  ● extent interchangeable, but
  ● *partly* should be used when
  ● referring to a part or parts of
  ● something: *the building is partly*
  ● (not *partially*) *made of stone*,
  ● while *partially* is preferred for
  ● the meaning *to some extent: his*
  ● *mother is partially* (not *partly*)
  ● *sighted*.

partner NOUN **1** = **spouse**, consort, significant other (*U.S. informal*), mate, husband or wife
  2 = **companion**, ally, colleague, associate, mate, comrade
  3 = **associate**, colleague, collaborator

partnership NOUN
  1 = **cooperation**, alliance, sharing, union, connection, participation, copartnership **2** = **company**, firm, house, interest, society, cooperative

party NOUN **1** = **faction**, set, side, league, camp, clique, coterie
  2 = **get-together** (*informal*),

celebration, do (*informal*),
gathering, function, reception,
festivity, social gathering
3 = **group**, team, band, company,
unit, squad, crew, gang
pass VERB **1** = **go by** *or* **past**,
overtake, drive past, lap, leave
behind, pull ahead of ≠ stop
2 = **go**, move, travel, progress,
flow, proceed **3** = **run**, move,
stroke **4** = **give**, hand, send,
transfer, deliver, convey **5** = **be
left**, come, be bequeathed, be
inherited by **6** = **kick**, hit, loft,
head, lob **7** = **elapse**, progress, go
by, lapse, wear on, go past, tick
by **8** = **end**, go, cease, blow over
9 = **spend**, fill, occupy, while away
10 = **exceed**, beat, overtake, go
beyond, surpass, outstrip, outdo
11 = **be successful in**, qualify (in),
succeed (in), graduate (in), get
through, do, gain a pass in ≠ fail
12 = **approve**, accept, decree,
enact, ratify, ordain, legislate (for)
≠ ban
▷ NOUN **1** = **licence**, ticket,
permit, passport, warrant,
authorization **2** = **gap**, route,
canyon, gorge, ravine ▷ PHRASES:
pass away *or* **on** (*euphemistic*)
= **die**, pass on, expire, pass over,
snuff it (*informal*), kick the bucket
(*slang*), shuffle off this mortal coil,
cark it (*Austral. & N.Z. informal*);
pass out (*informal*) = **faint**, black
out (*informal*), lose consciousness,
become unconscious; **pass
someone over**; **pass something
over** = **disregard**, ignore, not

dwell on; **pass something up**
(*informal*) = **miss**, let slip, decline,
neglect, forgo, abstain from, give
(something) a miss (*informal*)
● **WORD POWER**
● The past participle of *pass* is
● sometimes wrongly spelt *past*:
● *the time for recriminations has*
● *passed* (not *past*).
passage NOUN **1** = **corridor**, hall,
lobby, vestibule **2** = **alley**, way,
close (*Brit.*), course, road, channel,
route, path **3** = **extract**, reading,
piece, section, text, excerpt,
quotation **4** = **journey**, crossing,
trip, trek, voyage **5** = **safe-
conduct**, right to travel, freedom
to travel, permission to travel
passenger NOUN = **traveller**,
rider, fare, commuter, fare payer
passer-by NOUN = **bystander**,
witness, observer, viewer,
spectator, looker-on, watcher,
onlooker
passing ADJECTIVE
1 = **momentary**, fleeting, short-
lived, transient, ephemeral,
brief, temporary, transitory
2 = **superficial**, short, quick,
glancing, casual, summary,
cursory, perfunctory
passion NOUN **1** = **love**, desire,
lust, infatuation, ardour
2 = **emotion**, feeling, fire, heat,
excitement, intensity, warmth,
zeal ≠ indifference **3** = **mania**,
enthusiasm, obsession, bug
(*informal*), craving, fascination,
craze **4** = **rage**, fit, storm, anger,
fury, outburst, frenzy, paroxysm

passionate ADJECTIVE
1 = **emotional**, eager, strong, intense, fierce, ardent, fervent, heartfelt ≠ unemotional
2 = **loving**, erotic, hot, ardent, amorous, lustful ≠ cold

passive ADJECTIVE
1 = **submissive**, compliant, receptive, docile, quiescent ≠ spirited 2 = **inactive**, uninvolved ≠ active

past NOUN 1 = **former times**, long ago, days gone by, the olden days ≠ future 2 = **background**, life, history, past life, life story, career to date
▷ ADJECTIVE 1 = **former**, early, previous, ancient, bygone, olden ≠ future 2 = **previous**, former, one-time, ex- 3 = **last**, previous 4 = **over**, done, ended, finished, gone
▷ PREPOSITION 1 = **after**, beyond, later than 2 = **by**, across, in front of
▷ ADVERB = **on**, by, along
● **WORD POWER**
● The past participle of *pass* is
● sometimes wrongly spelt *past*:
● *the time for recrimination has*
● *passed* (not *past*).

paste NOUN 1 = **adhesive**, glue, cement, gum 2 = **purée**, pâté, spread
▷ VERB = **stick**, glue, cement, gum

pastel ADJECTIVE = **pale**, light, soft, delicate, muted ≠ bright

pastime NOUN = **activity**, game, entertainment, hobby, recreation, amusement, diversion

pastor NOUN = **clergyman**, minister, priest, vicar, parson, rector, curate, churchman

pastoral ADJECTIVE
1 = **ecclesiastical**, priestly, ministerial, clerical 2 = **rustic**, country, rural, bucolic

pasture NOUN = **grassland**, grass, meadow, grazing

pat VERB = **stroke**, touch, tap, pet, caress, fondle
▷ NOUN = **tap**, stroke, clap

patch NOUN 1 = **spot**, bit, scrap, shred, small piece 2 = **plot**, area, ground, land, tract
3 = **reinforcement**, piece of fabric, piece of cloth, piece of material, piece sewn on
▷ VERB 1 *often with* **up** = **sew (up)**, mend, repair, reinforce, stitch (up)
2 *often with* **up** = **mend**, cover, reinforce

patent NOUN = **copyright**, licence, franchise, registered trademark
▷ ADJECTIVE = **obvious**, apparent, evident, clear, glaring, manifest

path NOUN 1 = **way**, road, walk, track, trail, avenue, footpath, berm (*N.Z.*) 2 = **route**, way, course, direction 3 = **course**, way, road, route

pathetic ADJECTIVE = **sad**, moving, touching, affecting, distressing, tender, poignant, plaintive ≠ funny

patience NOUN 1 = **forbearance**, tolerance, serenity, restraint, calmness, sufferance ≠ impatience 2 = **endurance**,

P

resignation, submission, fortitude, long-suffering, perseverance, stoicism, constancy

patient NOUN = **sick person**, case, sufferer, invalid

▷ ADJECTIVE 1 = **forbearing**, understanding, forgiving, mild, tolerant, indulgent, lenient, even-tempered ≠ impatient

2 = **long-suffering**, resigned, calm, enduring, philosophical, persevering, stoical, submissive

patriot NOUN = **nationalist**, loyalist, chauvinist

patriotic ADJECTIVE = **nationalistic**, loyal, chauvinistic, jingoistic

patriotism NOUN = **nationalism**, jingoism

patrol VERB = **police**, guard, keep watch (on), inspect, safeguard, keep guard (on)

▷ NOUN = **guard**, watch, watchman, sentinel, patrolman

patron NOUN 1 = **supporter**, friend, champion, sponsor, backer, helper, benefactor, philanthropist

2 = **customer**, client, buyer, frequenter, shopper, habitué

patronage NOUN = **support**, promotion, sponsorship, backing, help, aid, assistance

pattern NOUN 1 = **order**, plan, system, method, sequence

2 = **design**, arrangement, motif, figure, device, decoration

3 = **plan**, design, original, guide, diagram, stencil, template

pause VERB = **stop briefly**, delay, break, wait, rest, halt, cease,

interrupt ≠ continue

▷ NOUN = **stop**, break, interval, rest, gap, halt, respite, lull ≠ continuance

pave VERB = **cover**, floor, surface, concrete, tile

paw (*informal*) VERB = **manhandle**, grab, maul, molest, handle roughly

pay VERB 1 = **reward**, compensate, reimburse, recompense, requite, remunerate 2 = **spend**, give, fork out (*informal*), remit, shell out (*informal*) 3 = **settle** 4 = **bring in**, earn, return, net, yield 5 = **be profitable**, make money, make a return 6 = **benefit**, repay, be worthwhile 7 = **give**, extend, present with, grant, hand out, bestow

▷ NOUN = **wages**, income, payment, earnings, fee, reward, salary, allowance ▷ PHRASES: **pay off** = **succeed**, work, be effective; **pay something off** = **settle**, clear, square, discharge, pay in full

payable ADJECTIVE = **due**, outstanding, owed, owing

payment NOUN 1 = **remittance**, advance, deposit, premium, instalment 2 = **settlement**, paying, discharge, remittance 3 = **wages**, fee, reward, hire, remuneration

peace NOUN 1 = **truce**, ceasefire, treaty, armistice ≠ war

2 = **stillness**, rest, quiet, silence, calm, hush, tranquillity, seclusion

3 = **serenity**, calm, composure, contentment, repose, equanimity,

peacefulness, harmoniousness
4 = **harmony**, accord, agreement, concord

peaceful ADJECTIVE **1** = **at peace**, friendly, harmonious, amicable, nonviolent ≠ hostile **2** = **peace-loving**, conciliatory, peaceable, unwarlike ≠ belligerent **3** = **calm**, still, quiet, tranquil, restful, chilled (*informal*) ≠ agitated **4** = **serene**, placid, undisturbed

peak NOUN **1** = **high point**, crown, climax, culmination, zenith, acme **2** = **point**, top, tip, summit, brow, crest, pinnacle, apex ▷ VERB = **culminate**, climax, come to a head

peasant NOUN = **rustic**, countryman

peck VERB **1** = **pick**, hit, strike, tap, poke, jab, prick **2** = **kiss**, plant a kiss, give someone a smacker, give someone a peck or kiss ▷ NOUN = **kiss**, smacker, osculation (*rare*)

peculiar ADJECTIVE **1** = **odd**, strange, unusual, bizarre, funny, extraordinary, curious, weird ≠ ordinary **2** = **special**, particular, unique, characteristic ≠ common

peddle VERB = **sell**, trade, push (*informal*), market, hawk, flog (*slang*)

pedestrian NOUN = **walker**, foot-traveller ≠ driver ▷ ADJECTIVE = **dull**, ordinary, boring, commonplace, mundane, mediocre, banal, prosaic, half-pie (*N.Z. informal*) ≠ exciting

pedigree MODIFIER = **purebred**, thoroughbred, full-blooded ▷ NOUN = **lineage**, family, line, race, stock, blood, breed, descent

peel NOUN = **rind**, skin, peeling ▷ VERB = **skin**, scale, strip, pare, shuck, flake off, take the skin or rind off

peep VERB = **peek**, look, eyeball (*slang*), sneak a look, steal a look ▷ NOUN = **look**, glimpse, peek, look-see (*slang*)

peer¹ NOUN **1** = **noble**, lord, aristocrat, nobleman **2** = **equal**, like, fellow, contemporary, compeer

peer² VERB = **squint**, look, spy, gaze, scan, inspect, peep, peek

peg NOUN = **pin**, spike, rivet, skewer, dowel, spigot ▷ VERB = **fasten**, join, fix, secure, attach

pen¹ VERB = **write (down)**, draft, compose, pencil, draw up, scribble, take down, inscribe

pen² NOUN = **enclosure**, pound, fold, cage, coop, hutch, sty ▷ VERB = **enclose**, confine, cage, fence in, coop up, hedge in, shut up or in

penalty NOUN = **punishment**, price, fine, handicap, forfeit

pending ADJECTIVE **1** = **undecided**, unsettled, in the balance, undetermined **2** = **forthcoming**, imminent, prospective, impending, in the wind ▷ PREPOSITION = **awaiting**, until, waiting for, till

penetrate VERB 1 = **pierce**, enter, go through, bore, stab, prick **2** = **grasp**, work out, figure out (*informal*), comprehend, fathom, decipher, suss (out) (*slang*), get to the bottom of

penetrating ADJECTIVE 1 = **sharp**, harsh, piercing, carrying, piping, loud, strident, shrill ≠ sweet **2** = **pungent** **3** = **piercing** **4** = **intelligent**, quick, sharp, keen, acute, shrewd, astute, perceptive ≠ dull **5** = **perceptive**, sharp, keen ≠ unperceptive

penetration NOUN 1 = **piercing**, entry, entrance, puncturing, incision **2** = **entry**, entrance

pension NOUN = **allowance**, benefit, welfare, annuity, superannuation

pensioner NOUN = **senior citizen**, retired person, retiree (*U.S.*), old-age pensioner, O.A.P.

people PLURAL NOUN 1 = **persons**, individuals, folk (*informal*), men and women, humanity, mankind, mortals, the human race **2** = **nation**, public, community, subjects, population, residents, citizens, folk **3** = **race**, tribe **4** = **family**, parents, relations, relatives, folk, folks (*informal*), clan, kin, rellies (*Austral. slang*) ▷ VERB = **inhabit**, occupy, settle, populate, colonize

pepper NOUN = **seasoning**, flavour, spice ▷ VERB 1 = **pelt**, hit, shower, blitz, rake, bombard, assail, strafe **2** = **sprinkle**, spot, scatter, dot,

fleck, intersperse, speck, spatter

perceive VERB 1 = **see**, notice, note, identify, discover, spot, observe, recognize **2** = **understand**, gather, see, learn, realize, grasp, comprehend, suss (out) (*slang*) **3** = **consider**, believe, judge, suppose, rate, deem, adjudge

perception NOUN 1 = **awareness**, understanding, sense, impression, feeling, idea, notion, consciousness **2** = **understanding**, intelligence, observation, discrimination, insight, sharpness, cleverness, keenness

perch VERB 1 = **sit**, rest, balance, settle **2** = **place**, put, rest, balance **3** = **land**, alight, roost ▷ NOUN = **resting place**, post, branch, pole

perennial ADJECTIVE = **continual**, lasting, constant, enduring, persistent, abiding, recurrent, incessant

perfect ADJECTIVE 1 = **faultless**, correct, pure, impeccable, exemplary, flawless, foolproof ≠ deficient **2** = **excellent**, ideal, supreme, superb, splendid, sublime, superlative **3** = **immaculate**, impeccable, flawless, spotless, unblemished ≠ flawed **4** = **complete**, absolute, sheer, utter, consummate, unmitigated ≠ partial **5** = **exact**, true, accurate, precise, correct, faithful, unerring ▷ VERB = **improve**, develop, polish, refine ≠ mar

● **WORD POWER**
● For most of its meanings, the
● adjective *perfect* describes
● an absolute state, so that
● something either is or is not
● *perfect*, and cannot be referred
● to in terms of degree – thus,
● one thing should not be
● described as *more perfect* or
● *less perfect* than another thing.
● However, when *perfect* is used
● in the sense of 'excellent in all
● respects', *more* and *most* are
● acceptable, for example *the next*
● *day the weather was even more*
● *perfect*.

perfection NOUN = **excellence**,
integrity, superiority, purity,
wholeness, sublimity,
exquisiteness, faultlessness

perfectly ADVERB 1 = **completely**,
totally, absolutely, quite, fully,
altogether, thoroughly, wholly
≠ partially 2 = **flawlessly**, ideally,
wonderfully, superbly, supremely,
impeccably, faultlessly ≠ badly

perform VERB 1 = **do**, achieve,
carry out, complete, fulfil,
accomplish, execute, pull off
2 = **fulfil**, carry out, execute,
discharge 3 = **present**, act (out),
stage, play, produce, represent,
put on, enact 4 = **appear on
stage**, act

performance NOUN
1 = **presentation**, playing, acting
(out), staging, production,
exhibition, rendering, portrayal
2 = **show**, appearance, concert,

gig (*informal*), recital 3 = **work**,
acts, conduct, exploits, feats
4 = **carrying out**, practice,
achievement, execution,
completion, accomplishment,
fulfilment

performer NOUN = **artiste**,
player, Thespian, trouper, actor *or*
actress

perfume NOUN 1 = **fragrance**,
scent 2 = **scent**, smell, fragrance,
bouquet, aroma, odour

perhaps ADVERB = **maybe**,
possibly, it may be, it is possible
(that), conceivably, perchance
(*archaic*), feasibly, happen (*N.
English dialect*)

peril NOUN 1 = **danger**, risk,
threat, hazard, menace, jeopardy,
perilousness 2 *often plural*
= **pitfall**, problem, risk, hazard
≠ safety

perimeter NOUN = **boundary**,
edge, border, bounds, limit,
margin, confines, periphery
≠ centre

period NOUN = **time**, term, season,
space, run, stretch, spell, phase

periodic ADJECTIVE = **recurrent**,
regular, repeated, occasional,
cyclical, sporadic, intermittent

peripheral ADJECTIVE
1 = **secondary**, minor, marginal,
irrelevant, unimportant,
incidental, inessential
2 = **outermost**, outside, external,
outer, exterior

perish VERB 1 = **die**, be killed,
expire, pass away, lose your life,
cark it (*Austral. & N.Z. slang*) 2 = **be**

destroyed, fall, decline, collapse, disappear, vanish **3** = **rot**, waste away, decay, disintegrate, decompose, moulder

perk NOUN (*Brit. informal*) = **bonus**, benefit, extra, plus, fringe benefit, perquisite

permanent ADJECTIVE
1 = **lasting**, constant, enduring, persistent, eternal, abiding, perpetual, everlasting
≠ temporary **2** = **long-term**, established, secure, stable, steady
≠ temporary

permission NOUN
= **authorization**, sanction, licence, approval, leave, go-ahead (*informal*), liberty, consent
≠ prohibition

permit VERB **1** = **allow**, grant, sanction, let, entitle, license, authorize, consent to ≠ forbid
2 = **enable**, let, allow, cause
▷ NOUN = **licence**, pass, document, certificate, passport, visa, warrant, authorization
≠ prohibition

perpetual ADJECTIVE
1 = **everlasting**, permanent, endless, eternal, lasting, perennial, infinite, never-ending
≠ temporary **2** = **continual**, repeated, constant, endless, continuous, persistent, recurrent, never-ending ≠ brief

perpetuate VERB = **maintain**, preserve, keep going, immortalize
≠ end

persecute VERB **1** = **victimize**, torture, torment, oppress,

pick on, ill-treat, maltreat
≠ mollycoddle **2** = **harass**, bother, annoy, tease, hassle (*informal*), badger, pester ≠ leave alone

persist VERB **1** = **continue**, last, remain, carry on, keep up, linger
2 = **persevere**, continue, go on, carry on, keep on, keep going, press on, not give up, crack on (*informal*)

persistence NOUN
= **determination**, resolution, grit, endurance, tenacity, perseverance, doggedness, pertinacity

persistent ADJECTIVE
1 = **continuous**, constant, repeated, endless, perpetual, continual, never-ending, incessant ≠ occasional
2 = **determined**, dogged, steady, stubborn, persevering, tireless, tenacious, steadfast ≠ irresolute

person NOUN **1** = **individual**, being, body, human, soul, creature, mortal, man *or* woman ▷ PHRASE: **in person**
1 = **personally**, yourself **2** = **in the flesh**, actually, physically, bodily

personal ADJECTIVE **1** = **own**, special, private, individual, particular, peculiar
2 = **individual**, special, particular, exclusive **3** = **private**
4 = **offensive**, nasty, insulting, disparaging, derogatory

personality NOUN **1** = **nature**, character, make-up, identity, temperament, disposition, individuality **2** = **character**, charm, attraction, charisma, magnetism **3** = **celebrity**, star, notable, household name, famous name, personage, megastar (*informal*)

personally ADVERB **1** = **in your opinion**, in your book, for your part, from your own viewpoint, in your own view **2** = **by yourself**, alone, independently, solely, on your own **3** = **individually**, specially, subjectively, individualistically **4** = **privately**, in private, off the record

personnel NOUN = **employees**, people, staff, workers, workforce, human resources, helpers

perspective NOUN **1** = **outlook**, attitude, context, angle, frame of reference **2** = **objectivity**, proportion, relation, relativity, relative importance

persuade VERB **1** = **talk (someone) into**, urge, influence, win (someone) over, induce, sway, entice, coax ≠ dissuade **2** = **cause**, lead, move, influence, motivate, induce, incline, dispose **3** = **convince**, satisfy, assure, cause to believe

persuasion NOUN **1** = **urging**, inducement, wheedling, enticement, cajolery **2** = **belief**, views, opinion, party, school, side, camp, faith

persuasive ADJECTIVE = **convincing**, telling, effective, sound, compelling, influential, valid, credible ≠ unconvincing

pervasive ADJECTIVE

= **widespread**, general, common, extensive, universal, prevalent, ubiquitous, rife

perverse ADJECTIVE **1** = **stubborn**, contrary, dogged, troublesome, rebellious, wayward, intractable, wilful ≠ cooperative **2** = **ill-natured**, cross, surly, fractious, churlish, ill-tempered, stroppy (*Brit. slang*), peevish ≠ good-natured **3** = **abnormal**, unhealthy, improper, deviant

pervert VERB **1** = **distort**, abuse, twist, misuse, warp, misrepresent, falsify **2** = **corrupt**, degrade, deprave, debase, debauch, lead astray
▷ NOUN = **deviant**, degenerate, sicko (*informal*), weirdo or weirdie (*informal*)

pessimistic ADJECTIVE = **gloomy**, dark, despairing, bleak, depressed, cynical, hopeless, glum ≠ optimistic

pest NOUN **1** = **infection**, bug, insect, plague, epidemic, blight, scourge, pestilence, gogga (*S. African informal*) **2** = **nuisance**, trial, pain (*informal*), drag (*informal*), bother, irritation, annoyance, bane

pet ADJECTIVE = **favourite**, favoured, dearest, cherished, fave (*informal*), dear to your heart
▷ NOUN = **favourite**, treasure, darling, jewel, idol
▷ VERB **1** = **fondle**, pat, stroke, caress **2** = **pamper**, spoil, indulge, cosset, baby, dote on, coddle, mollycoddle **3** (*informal*)

= **cuddle**, kiss, snog (*Brit. slang*),
smooch (*informal*), neck (*informal*),
canoodle (*slang*)

petition NOUN 1 = **appeal**,
round robin, list of signatures
2 = **entreaty**, appeal, suit,
application, request, prayer, plea,
solicitation
▷ VERB = **appeal**, plead, ask, pray,
beg, solicit, beseech, entreat

petty ADJECTIVE 1 = **trivial**,
insignificant, little, small, slight,
trifling, negligible, unimportant
≠ important 2 = **small-
minded**, mean, shabby, spiteful,
ungenerous, mean-minded
≠ broad-minded

phantom NOUN = **spectre**, ghost,
spirit, shade (*literary*), spook
(*informal*), apparition, wraith,
phantasm

phase NOUN = **stage**, time, point,
position, step, development,
period, chapter ▷ PHRASES: **phase
something in** = **introduce**,
incorporate, ease in, start; **phase
something out** = **eliminate**,
close, remove, withdraw, pull
out, wind up, run down,
terminate

phenomenal ADJECTIVE
= **extraordinary**, outstanding,
remarkable, fantastic, unusual,
marvellous, exceptional,
miraculous ≠ unremarkable

phenomenon NOUN
1 = **occurrence**, happening, fact,
event, incident, circumstance,
episode 2 = **wonder**, sensation,
exception, miracle, marvel,

prodigy, rarity
● **WORD POWER**
● Although *phenomena* is often
● treated as a singular, this is
● not grammatically correct.
● *Phenomenon* is the singular form
● of this word, and *phenomena* the
● plural; so *several new phenomena*
● *were recorded in his notes* is
● correct, but *that is an interesting*
● *phenomena* is not.

philosopher NOUN = **thinker**,
theorist, sage, wise man, logician,
metaphysician

philosophical *or* **philosophic**
ADJECTIVE 1 = **theoretical**,
abstract, wise, rational, logical,
thoughtful, sagacious ≠ practical
2 = **stoical**, calm, composed,
cool, collected, serene, tranquil,
unruffled ≠ emotional

philosophy NOUN 1 = **thought**,
knowledge, thinking, reasoning,
wisdom, logic, metaphysics
2 = **outlook**, values, principles,
convictions, thinking, beliefs,
doctrine, ideology

phone NOUN 1 = **telephone**,
blower (*informal*) 2 = **call**, ring
(*informal, chiefly Brit.*), tinkle (*Brit.
informal*)
▷ VERB = **call**, telephone, ring
(up) (*informal, chiefly Brit.*), give
someone a call, give someone a
ring (*informal, chiefly Brit.*), make
a call, give someone a tinkle
(*Brit. informal*), get on the blower
(*informal*)

photograph NOUN = **picture**,
photo (*informal*), shot, print, snap

(*informal*), snapshot, transparency
▷ VERB = **take a picture of**,
record, film, shoot, snap (*informal*),
take (someone's) picture
photographic ADJECTIVE
1 = **pictorial**, visual, graphic,
cinematic, filmic 2 = **accurate**,
exact, precise, faithful, retentive
phrase NOUN = **expression**,
saying, remark, construction,
quotation, maxim, idiom, adage
▷ VERB = **express**, say, word, put,
voice, communicate, convey, put
into words
physical ADJECTIVE 1 = **corporal**,
fleshly, bodily, corporeal
2 = **earthly**, fleshly, mortal,
incarnate 3 = **material**, real,
substantial, natural, solid,
tangible, palpable
physician NOUN = **doctor**, doc
(*informal*), medic (*informal*),
general practitioner, medical
practitioner, doctor of medicine,
G.P., M.D.
pick VERB 1 = **select**, choose,
identify, elect, nominate, specify,
opt for, single out, flag up
≠ reject 2 = **gather**, pull, collect,
take in, harvest, pluck, garner
3 = **provoke**, start, cause, stir up,
incite, instigate 4 = **open**, force,
crack (*informal*), break into, break
open
▷ NOUN 1 = **choice**, decision,
option, selection, preference
2 = **best**, prime, finest, elect, elite,
cream, jewel in the crown, crème
de la crème (*French*) ▷ PHRASES:
pick on someone 1 = **torment**,

bully, bait, tease, get at (*informal*),
badger, persecute, hector
2 = **choose**, select, prefer, elect,
single out, fix on, settle upon;
pick something up 1 = **learn**,
master, acquire, get the hang of
(*informal*), become proficient in
2 = **obtain**, get, find, buy, discover,
purchase, acquire, locate; **pick
something** or **someone out**
= **identify**, recognize, distinguish,
perceive, discriminate, make
someone or something out, tell
someone or something apart;
pick something or **someone
up 1** = **lift**, raise, gather, take up,
grasp, uplift 2 = **collect**, get, call
for; **pick up 1** = **improve**, recover,
rally, get better, bounce back,
make progress, perk up, turn the
corner 2 = **recover**, improve, rally,
get better, mend, turn the corner,
be on the mend, take a turn for
the better
picket VERB = **blockade**, boycott,
demonstrate outside
▷ NOUN 1 = **demonstration**,
strike, blockade 2 = **protester**,
demonstrator, picketer
3 = **lookout**, watch, guard, patrol,
sentry, sentinel 4 = **stake**, post,
pale, paling, upright, stanchion
pickle VERB = **preserve**, marinade,
steep
▷ NOUN 1 = **chutney**,
relish, piccalilli 2 (*informal*)
= **predicament**, fix (*informal*),
difficulty, bind (*informal*), jam
(*informal*), dilemma, scrape
(*informal*), hot water (*informal*),

p

uphill (*S. African*)

pick-up NOUN =**improvement**, recovery, rise, rally, strengthening, revival, upturn, change for the better

picnic NOUN =**excursion**, barbecue, barbie (*informal*), cookout (*U.S. & Canad.*), alfresco meal, clambake (*U.S. & Canad.*), outdoor meal, outing

picture NOUN 1 =**representation**, drawing, painting, portrait, image, print, illustration, sketch 2 =**photograph**, photo, still, shot, image, print, frame, slide 3 =**film**, movie (*U.S. informal*), flick (*slang*), feature film, motion picture 4 =**idea**, vision, concept, impression, notion, visualization, mental picture, mental image 5 =**description**, impression, explanation, report, account, image, sketch, depiction 6 =**personification**, embodiment, essence, epitome ▷ VERB 1 =**imagine**, see, envision, visualize, conceive of, fantasize about, conjure up an image of 2 =**represent**, show, draw, paint, illustrate, sketch, depict 3 =**show**, photograph, capture on film

picturesque ADJECTIVE 1 =**interesting**, pretty, beautiful, attractive, charming, scenic, quaint ≠ unattractive 2 =**vivid**, striking, graphic, colourful, memorable ≠ dull

piece NOUN 1 =**bit**, slice, part, block, quantity, segment, portion, fragment 2 =**component**, part, section, bit, unit, segment, constituent, module 3 =**item**, report, story, study, review, article 4 =**composition**, work, production, opus 5 =**work of art**, work, creation 6 =**share**, cut (*informal*), slice, percentage, quantity, portion, quota, fraction

pier NOUN 1 =**jetty**, wharf, quay, promenade, landing place 2 =**pillar**, support, post, column, pile, upright, buttress

pierce VERB =**penetrate**, stab, spike, enter, bore, drill, puncture, prick

piercing ADJECTIVE 1 (*of a sound*) =**penetrating**, sharp, loud, shrill, high-pitched, ear-splitting ≠ low 2 =**perceptive**, sharp, keen, alert, penetrating, shrewd, perspicacious, quick-witted ≠ unperceptive 3 =**sharp**, acute, severe, intense, painful, stabbing, excruciating, agonizing 4 (*of weather*) =**cold**, biting, freezing, bitter, arctic, wintry, nippy

pig NOUN 1 =**hog**, sow, boar, swine, porker 2 (*informal*) =**slob**, glutton 3 (*informal*) =**brute**, monster, scoundrel, rogue, swine, rotter, boor

pigment NOUN =**colour**, colouring, paint, stain, dye, tint, tincture

pile¹ NOUN 1 =**heap**, collection, mountain, mass, stack, mound, accumulation, hoard 2 (*informal*) *often plural* =**lot(s)**, mountain(s), load(s) (*informal*), oceans, wealth,

great deal, stack(s), abundance
3 = **mansion**, building, residence, manor, country house, seat, big house, stately home
▷ VERB **1** = **load**, stuff, pack, stack, charge, heap, cram, lade **2** = **crowd**, pack, rush, climb, flood, stream, crush, squeeze
▷ PHRASE: **pile up** = **accumulate**, collect, gather (up), build up, amass

pile² NOUN = **foundation**, support, post, column, beam, upright, pillar

pile³ NOUN = **nap**, fibre, down, hair, fur, plush

pile-up NOUN (*informal*)
= **collision**, crash, accident, smash, smash-up (*informal*), multiple collision

pilgrim NOUN = **traveller**, wanderer, devotee, wayfarer

pilgrimage NOUN = **journey**, tour, trip, mission, expedition, excursion

pill NOUN = **tablet**, capsule, pellet

pillar NOUN **1** = **support**, post, column, prop, shaft, upright, pier, stanchion **2** = **supporter**, leader, mainstay, leading light (*informal*), upholder

pilot NOUN **1** = **airman**, flyer, aviator, aeronaut **2** = **helmsman**, navigator, steersman
▷ VERB **1** = **fly**, operate, be at the controls of **2** = **navigate**, drive, direct, guide, handle, conduct, steer **3** = **direct**, conduct, steer
▷ MODIFIER = **trial**, test, model, sample, experimental

pin NOUN **1** = **tack**, nail, needle, safety pin **2** = **peg**, rod, brace, bolt
▷ VERB **1** = **fasten**, stick, attach, join, fix, secure, nail, clip **2** = **hold fast**, hold down, constrain, immobilize, pinion ▷ PHRASES:
pin someone down = **force**, pressure, compel, put pressure on, pressurize, nail someone down, make someone commit themselves; **pin something down** = **determine**, identify, locate, name, specify, pinpoint

pinch VERB **1** = **nip**, press, squeeze, grasp, compress **2** = **hurt**, crush, squeeze, pain, cramp **3** (*Brit. informal*) = **steal**, lift (*informal*), nick (*slang, chiefly Brit.*), swipe (*slang*), knock off (*slang*), pilfer, purloin, filch
▷ NOUN **1** = **nip**, squeeze **2** = **dash**, bit, mite, jot, speck, soupçon (*French*) **3** = **emergency**, crisis, difficulty, plight, scrape (*informal*), strait, uphill (*S. African*), predicament

pine VERB **1** = **waste**, decline, sicken, fade, languish ▷ PHRASE:
pine for something *or* **someone 1** = **long**, ache, crave, yearn, eat your heart out over **2** = **hanker after**, crave, wish for, yearn for, thirst for, hunger for

pink ADJECTIVE = **rosy**, rose, salmon, flushed, reddish, roseate
▷ *see* **shades of red**
● WORD POWER
● The colour *pink* has a number
● of associations in English.
● From the plant of this name,

p

- cultivated in gardens for its
- fragrant flowers, pink has
- come to mean 'the flower' or
- the best part of something.
- The contraction *in the pink*
- has the sense 'in good health,
- flourishing'. This phrase also
- reflects our perception that
- flushing and glowing skin is
- healthy, whereas pallor of skin
- is not. Other shades of pink are
- associated with hope, promise,
- and optimism in words such
- as *rosy*, *rose-coloured*, and
- *rose-tinted*. Pink has also
- been applied symbolically to
- different political and social
- groups. Part of the political
- spectrum is represented in
- the informal and sometimes
- derogatory epithet *pinko*
- meaning a left-winger, but
- one who is nearer to the centre
- than a red socialist. The use of
- pink to refer to male gay topics
- is now well-established in
- phrases such as *the pink pound*.

pinnacle NOUN 1 = **summit**, top, height, peak 2 = **height**, top, crown, crest, zenith, apex, vertex

pinpoint VERB 1 = **identify**, discover, define, distinguish, put your finger on 2 = **locate**, find, identify, zero in on

pioneer NOUN 1 = **founder**, leader, developer, innovator, trailblazer 2 = **settler**, explorer, colonist ▷ VERB = **develop**, create, establish, start, discover, institute, invent, initiate

pipe NOUN = **tube**, drain, canal, pipeline, line, main, passage, cylinder
▷ VERB = **convey**, channel, conduct ▷ PHRASE: **pipe down** (*informal*) = **be quiet**, shut up (*informal*), hush, stop talking, quieten down, shush, shut your mouth, hold your tongue

pipeline NOUN = **tube**, passage, pipe, conduit, duct

pirate NOUN = **buccaneer**, raider, marauder, corsair, freebooter ▷ VERB = **copy**, steal, reproduce, bootleg, appropriate, poach, crib (*informal*), plagiarize

pit NOUN 1 = **coal mine**, mine, shaft, colliery, mine shaft 2 = **hole**, depression, hollow, crater, trough, cavity, abyss, chasm
▷ VERB = **scar**, mark, dent, indent, pockmark

pitch NOUN 1 = **sports field**, ground, stadium, arena, park, field of play 2 = **tone**, sound, key, frequency, timbre, modulation 3 = **level**, point, degree, summit, extent, height, intensity, high point 4 = **talk**, patter, spiel (*informal*)
▷ VERB 1 = **throw**, cast, toss, hurl, fling, chuck (*informal*), sling, lob (*informal*) 2 = **fall**, drop, plunge, dive, tumble, topple, plummet, fall headlong 3 = **set up**, raise, settle, put up, erect 4 = **toss (about)**, roll, plunge, lurch ▷ PHRASE: **pitch in** = **help**, contribute, participate, join in,

cooperate, chip in (*informal*), get stuck in (*Brit. informal*), lend a hand

pitfall NOUN *usually plural* = **danger**, difficulty, peril, catch, trap, hazard, drawback, snag, uphill (*S. African*)

pity NOUN 1 = **compassion**, charity, sympathy, kindness, fellow feeling ≠ mercilessness 2 = **shame**, sin (*informal*), misfortune, bummer (*slang*), crying shame 3 = **mercy**, kindness, clemency, forbearance ▷ VERB = **feel sorry for**, feel for, sympathize with, grieve for, weep for, bleed for, have compassion for

pivotal ADJECTIVE = **crucial**, central, vital, critical, decisive

place NOUN 1 = **spot**, point, position, site, area, location, venue, whereabouts 2 = **region**, quarter, district, neighbourhood, vicinity, locality, locale, dorp (*S. African*) 3 = **position**, point, spot, location 4 = **space**, position, seat, chair 5 = **situation**, position, circumstances, shoes (*informal*) 6 = **job**, position, post, situation, office, employment, appointment 7 = **home**, house, room, property, accommodation, pad (*slang*), residence, dwelling, bachelor apartment (*Canad.*) 8 *used in negative constructions* = **duty**, right, job, charge, concern, role, affair, responsibility ▷ PHRASE: **know one's place** = **know one's rank**, know one's standing, know one's

position, know one's footing, know one's station, know one's status, know one's grade, know one's niche ▷ VERB 1 = **lay (down)**, put (down), set (down), stand, position, rest, station, stick (*informal*) 2 = **put**, lay, set, invest, pin 3 = **classify**, class, group, put, order, sort, rank, arrange 4 = **entrust to**, give to, assign to, appoint to, allocate to, find a home for 5 = **identify**, remember, recognize, pin someone down, put your finger on, put a name to ▷ PHRASE: **take place** = **happen**, occur, go on, go down (*U.S. & Canad.*), arise, come about, crop up, transpire (*informal*)

plague NOUN 1 = **disease**, infection, epidemic, pestilence 2 = **infestation**, invasion, epidemic, influx, host, swarm, multitude ▷ VERB 1 = **torment**, trouble, torture 2 = **pester**, trouble, bother, annoy, tease, harry, harass, hassle

plain ADJECTIVE 1 = **unadorned**, simple, basic, severe, bare, stark, austere, spartan, bare-bones ≠ ornate 2 = **clear**, obvious, patent, evident, visible, distinct, understandable, manifest ≠ hidden 3 = **straightforward**, open, direct, frank, blunt, outspoken, honest, downright ≠ roundabout 4 = **ugly**, unattractive, homely (*U.S. & Canad.*), unlovely,

p

unprepossessing, not beautiful, no oil painting (*informal*), ill-favoured ≠ attractive
5 = **ordinary**, common, simple, everyday, commonplace, unaffected, unpretentious ≠ sophisticated
▷ NOUN = **flatland**, plateau, prairie, grassland, steppe, veld

plan NOUN **1** = **scheme**, system, design, programme, proposal, strategy, method, suggestion
2 = **diagram**, map, drawing, chart, representation, sketch, blueprint, layout
▷ VERB **1** = **devise**, arrange, scheme, plot, draft, organize, outline, formulate **2** = **intend**, aim, mean, propose, purpose
3 = **design**, outline, draw up a plan of

plane NOUN **1** = **aeroplane**, aircraft, jet, airliner, jumbo jet **2** = **flat surface**, the flat, horizontal, level surface **3** = **level**, position, stage, condition, standard, degree, rung, echelon
▷ ADJECTIVE = **level**, even, flat, regular, smooth, horizontal
▷ VERB = **skim**, sail, skate, glide

plant¹ NOUN = **flower**, bush, vegetable, herb, weed, shrub
▷ VERB **1** = **sow**, scatter, transplant, implant, put in the ground **2** = **seed**, sow, implant
3 = **place**, put, set, fix **4** = **hide**, put, place, conceal **5** = **place**, put, establish, found, fix, insert

plant² NOUN **1** = **factory**, works, shop, yard, mill, foundry

2 = **machinery**, equipment, gear, apparatus

plaster NOUN **1** = **mortar**, stucco, gypsum, plaster of Paris
2 = **bandage**, dressing, sticking plaster, Elastoplast (*trademark*), adhesive plaster
▷ VERB = **cover**, spread, coat, smear, overlay, daub

plastic ADJECTIVE = **pliant**, soft, flexible, supple, pliable, ductile, mouldable ≠ rigid

plate NOUN **1** = **platter**, dish, dinner plate, salver, trencher (*archaic*) **2** = **helping**, course, serving, dish, portion, platter, plateful **3** = **layer**, panel, sheet, slab **4** = **illustration**, picture, photograph, print, engraving, lithograph
▷ VERB = **coat**, gild, laminate, cover, overlay

plateau NOUN **1** = **upland**, table, highland, tableland **2** = **levelling off**, level, stage, stability

platform NOUN **1** = **stage**, stand, podium, rostrum, dais, soapbox
2 = **policy**, programme, principle, objective(s), manifesto, party line

plausible ADJECTIVE
1 = **believable**, possible, likely, reasonable, credible, probable, persuasive, conceivable
≠ unbelievable **2** = **glib**, smooth, specious, smooth-talking, smooth-tongued

play VERB **1** = **amuse yourself**, have fun, sport, fool, romp, revel, trifle, entertain yourself **2** = **take part in**, be involved in, engage

p

in, participate in, compete in
3 = **compete against**, challenge,
take on, oppose, contend against
4 = **perform**, carry out **5** = **act**,
portray, represent, perform,
act the part of **6** = **perform on**,
strum, make music on
▷ NOUN **1** = **amusement**,
pleasure, leisure, games, sport,
fun, entertainment, relaxation,
me-time **2** = **drama**, show, piece,
comedy, tragedy, farce, soapie *or*
soapie (*Austral. slang*), pantomime
▷ PHRASES: **play on** *or* **upon**
something = **take advantage of**,
abuse, exploit, impose on, trade
on, capitalize on; **play something**
down = **minimize**, make light of,
gloss over, talk down, underrate,
underplay, pooh-pooh (*informal*),
soft-pedal (*informal*); **play**
something up = **emphasize**,
highlight, underline, stress,
accentuate; **play up 1** (*Brit.*
informal) = **hurt**, be painful, bother
you, trouble you, be sore, pain you
2 (*Brit. informal*) = **malfunction**,
not work properly, be on the
blink (*slang*) **3** (*Brit. informal*)
= **be awkward**, misbehave,
give trouble, be disobedient, be
stroppy (*Brit. slang*)
playboy NOUN = **womanizer**,
philanderer, rake, lady-killer
(*informal*), roué, ladies' man
player NOUN **1** = **sportsman**
or **sportswoman**, competitor,
participant, contestant
2 = **musician**, artist, performer,
virtuoso, instrumentalist

3 = **performer**, entertainer,
Thespian, trouper, actor *or* actress
plea NOUN **1** = **appeal**, request,
suit, prayer, petition, entreaty,
intercession, supplication
2 = **excuse**, defence, explanation,
justification
plead VERB = **appeal**, ask, request,
beg, petition, implore, beseech,
entreat
pleasant ADJECTIVE **1** = **pleasing**,
nice, fine, lovely, amusing,
delightful, enjoyable, agreeable,
lekker (*S. African slang*) ≠ horrible
2 = **friendly**, nice, agreeable,
likable *or* likeable, engaging,
charming, amiable, genial
≠ disagreeable
please VERB = **delight**, entertain,
humour, amuse, suit, satisfy,
indulge, gratify ≠ annoy
pleased ADJECTIVE = **happy**,
delighted, contented, satisfied,
thrilled, glad, gratified, over the
moon (*informal*)
pleasing ADJECTIVE **1** = **enjoyable**,
satisfying, charming, delightful,
gratifying, agreeable,
pleasurable ≠ unpleasant
2 = **likable** *or* **likeable**, engaging,
charming, delightful, agreeable
≠ disagreeable
pleasure NOUN **1** = **happiness**,
delight, satisfaction, enjoyment,
bliss, gratification, gladness,
delectation ≠ displeasure
2 = **amusement**, joy ≠ duty
pledge NOUN **1** = **promise**, vow,
assurance, word, undertaking,
warrant, oath, covenant

p

2 = **guarantee**, security, deposit, bail, collateral, pawn, surety
▷ VERB = **promise**, vow, swear, contract, engage, give your word, give your oath

plentiful ADJECTIVE = **abundant**, liberal, generous, lavish, ample, overflowing, copious, bountiful ≠ scarce

plenty NOUN **1** = **abundance**, wealth, prosperity, fertility, profusion, affluence, plenitude, fruitfulness **2** *usually with* **of** = **lots of** (*informal*), enough, a great deal of, masses of, piles of (*informal*), stacks of, heaps of (*informal*), an abundance of

plight NOUN = **difficulty**, condition, state, situation, trouble, predicament

plot¹ NOUN **1** = **plan**, scheme, intrigue, conspiracy, cabal, stratagem, machination **2** = **story**, action, subject, theme, outline, scenario, narrative, story line
▷ VERB **1** = **plan**, scheme, conspire, intrigue, manoeuvre, contrive, collude, machinate **2** = **devise**, design, lay, conceive, hatch, contrive, concoct, cook up (*informal*) **3** = **chart**, mark, map, locate, calculate, outline

plot² NOUN = **patch**, lot, area, ground, parcel, tract, allotment

plough VERB = **turn over**, dig, till, cultivate ▷ PHRASE: **plough through something** = **forge**, cut, drive, press, push, plunge, wade

ploy NOUN = **tactic**, move, trick, device, scheme, manoeuvre, dodge, ruse

pluck VERB **1** = **pull out** *or* **off**, pick, draw, collect, gather, harvest **2** = **tug**, catch, snatch, clutch, jerk, yank, tweak, pull at **3** = **strum**, pick, finger, twang
▷ NOUN = **courage**, nerve, bottle (*Brit. slang*), guts (*informal*), grit, bravery, backbone, boldness

plug NOUN **1** = **stopper**, cork, bung, spigot **2** (*informal*) = **mention**, advertisement, advert (*Brit. informal*), push, publicity, hype
▷ VERB **1** = **seal**, close, stop, fill, block, stuff, pack, cork **2** (*informal*) = **mention**, push, promote, publicize, advertise, build up, hype ▷ PHRASE: **plug away** (*informal*) = **slog away**, labour, toil away, grind away (*informal*), peg away, plod away

plum MODIFIER = **choice**, prize, first-class

plumb VERB = **delve into**, explore, probe, go into, penetrate, gauge, unravel, fathom
▷ ADVERB = **exactly**, precisely, bang, slap, spot-on (*Brit. informal*)

plummet VERB **1** = **drop**, fall, crash, nose-dive, descend rapidly **2** = **plunge**, fall, drop, crash, tumble, nose-dive, descend rapidly

plump ADJECTIVE = **chubby**, fat, stout, round, tubby, dumpy, roly-poly, rotund ≠ scrawny

plunder VERB **1** = **loot**, strip, sack, rob, raid, rifle, ransack, pillage

2 = **steal**, rob, take, nick (*informal*), pinch (*informal*), embezzle, pilfer, thieve
▷ NOUN **1** = **pillage 2** = **loot**, spoils, booty, swag (*slang*), ill-gotten gains

plunge VERB **1** = **descend**, fall, drop, crash, pitch, sink, dive, tumble **2** = **hurtle**, charge, career, jump, tear, rush, dive, dash
3 = **submerge**, dip **4** = **throw**, cast, pitch, propel **5** = **fall steeply**, drop, crash (*informal*), slump, plummet, take a nosedive (*informal*)
▷ NOUN **1** = **fall**, crash (*informal*), slump, drop, tumble **2** = **dive**, jump, duck, descent

plus PREPOSITION = **and**, with, added to, coupled with
▷ NOUN (*informal*) = **advantage**, benefit, asset, gain, extra, bonus, good point
▷ ADJECTIVE = **additional**, added, extra, supplementary, add-on

● **WORD POWER**
● When you have a sentence with
● more than one subject linked
● by *and*, this makes the subject
● plural and means it should take
● a plural verb: *the doctor and all*
● *the nurses were* (not *was*) *waiting*
● *for the patient*. However, where
● the subjects are linked by *plus*,
● *together with*, or *along with*, the
● number of the verb remains
● just as it would have been if
● the extra subjects had not
● been mentioned. Therefore you
● would say *the doctor, together*

● *with all the nurses, was* (not *were*)
● *waiting for the patient*.

plush ADJECTIVE = **luxurious**, luxury, lavish, rich, sumptuous, opulent, de luxe

ply VERB = **work at**, follow, exercise, pursue, carry on, practise

pocket NOUN = **pouch**, bag, sack, compartment, receptacle
▷ MODIFIER = **small**, compact, miniature, portable, little
▷ VERB = **steal**, take, lift (*informal*), appropriate, pilfer, purloin, filch

pod NOUN = **shell**, case, hull, husk, shuck

podium NOUN = **platform**, stand, stage, rostrum, dais

poem NOUN = **verse**, song, lyric, rhyme, sonnet, ode, verse composition

poet NOUN = **bard**, rhymer, lyricist, lyric poet, versifier, elegist
▷ see poetry

poetic ADJECTIVE **1** = **figurative**, creative, lyric, symbolic, lyrical
2 = **lyrical**, lyric, elegiac, metrical

poetry NOUN = **verse**, poems, rhyme, rhyming, verse composition

pogey NOUN (*Canad.*) = **benefits**, the dole (*Brit. & Austral.*), welfare, social security, unemployment benefit, state benefit, allowance

poignant ADJECTIVE = **moving**, touching, sad, bitter, intense, painful, distressing, pathetic

point NOUN **1** = **essence**, meaning, subject, question, heart, import, drift, thrust **2** = **purpose**,

p

aim, object, end, reason, goal, intention, objective **3** = **aspect**, detail, feature, quality, particular, respect, item, characteristic **4** = **place**, area, position, site, spot, location, locality, locale **5** = **moment**, time, stage, period, phase, instant, juncture, moment in time **6** = **stage**, level, position, condition, degree, pitch, circumstance, extent **7** = **end**, tip, sharp end, top, spur, spike, apex, prong **8** = **score**, tally, mark **9** = **pinpoint**, mark, spot, dot, fleck
▷ VERB **1** *usually followed by* **at** *or* **to** = **aim**, level, train, direct **2** = **face**, look, direct **3** = **indicate**, show, signal, point to, point out, specify, designate, gesture towards

pointed ADJECTIVE **1** = **sharp**, edged, acute, barbed **2** = **cutting**, telling, biting, sharp, keen, acute, penetrating, pertinent

pointer NOUN **1** = **hint**, tip, suggestion, recommendation, caution, piece of information, piece of advice **2** = **indicator**, hand, guide, needle, arrow

pointless ADJECTIVE = **senseless**, meaningless, futile, fruitless, stupid, silly, useless, absurd ≠ worthwhile

poised ADJECTIVE **1** = **ready**, waiting, prepared, standing by, all set **2** = **composed**, calm, together (*informal*), collected, dignified, self-confident, self-possessed ≠ agitated

poison NOUN = **toxin**, venom, bane (*archaic*)
▷ VERB **1** = **murder**, kill, give someone poison, administer poison to **2** = **contaminate**, foul, infect, spoil, pollute, blight, taint, befoul **3** = **corrupt**, colour, undermine, bias, sour, pervert, warp, taint

poisonous ADJECTIVE **1** = **toxic**, fatal, deadly, lethal, mortal, virulent, noxious, venomous **2** = **evil**, malicious, corrupting, pernicious, baleful

poke VERB **1** = **jab**, push, stick, dig, stab, thrust, shove, nudge **2** = **protrude**, stick, thrust, jut
▷ NOUN = **jab**, dig, thrust, nudge, prod

pole NOUN = **rod**, post, support, staff, bar, stick, stake, paling

police NOUN = **the law** (*informal*), police force, constabulary, fuzz (*slang*), boys in blue (*informal*), the Old Bill (*slang*), rozzers (*slang*)
▷ VERB = **control**, patrol, guard, watch, protect, regulate

policy NOUN **1** = **procedure**, plan, action, practice, scheme, code, custom **2** = **line**, rules, approach

polish NOUN **1** = **varnish**, wax, glaze, lacquer, japan **2** = **sheen**, finish, glaze, gloss, brightness, lustre **3** = **style**, class (*informal*), finish, breeding, grace, elegance, refinement, finesse
▷ VERB **1** = **shine**, wax, smooth, rub, buff, brighten, burnish **2** *often with* **up** = **perfect**, improve, enhance, refine, finish, brush up,

touch up

polished ADJECTIVE 1 = **elegant**, sophisticated, refined, polite, cultivated, suave, well-bred ≠ unsophisticated 2 = **accomplished**, professional, masterly, fine, expert, skilful, adept, superlative ≠ amateurish 3 = **shining**, bright, smooth, gleaming, glossy, burnished ≠ dull

polite ADJECTIVE 1 = **mannerly**, civil, courteous, gracious, respectful, well-behaved, complaisant, well-mannered ≠ rude 2 = **refined**, cultured, civilized, polished, sophisticated, elegant, genteel, well-bred ≠ uncultured

politic ADJECTIVE = **wise**, diplomatic, sensible, prudent, advisable, expedient, judicious

political ADJECTIVE = **governmental**, government, state, parliamentary, constitutional, administrative, legislative, ministerial

politician NOUN = **statesman** or **stateswoman**, representative, senator (U.S.), congressman (U.S.), Member of Parliament, legislator, public servant, congresswoman (U.S.)

politics NOUN 1 = **affairs of state**, government, public affairs, civics 2 = **political beliefs**, party politics, political allegiances, political leanings, political sympathies 3 = **political science**, statesmanship, civics, statecraft

poll NOUN 1 = **survey**, figures, count, sampling, returns, ballot, tally, census 2 = **election**, vote, voting, referendum, ballot, plebiscite ▷ VERB 1 = **question**, interview, survey, sample, ballot, canvass 2 = **gain**, return, record, register, tally

pollute VERB 1 = **contaminate**, dirty, poison, soil, foul, infect, spoil, stain ≠ decontaminate 2 = **defile**, corrupt, sully, deprave, debase, profane, desecrate, dishonour ≠ honour

pollution NOUN 1 = **contamination**, dirtying, corruption, taint, foulness, defilement, uncleanness 2 = **waste**, poisons, dirt, impurities

pond NOUN = **pool**, tarn, small lake, fish pond, duck pond, millpond

ponder VERB = **think about**, consider, reflect on, contemplate, deliberate about, muse on, brood on, meditate on

pool¹ NOUN 1 = **swimming pool**, lido, swimming bath(s) (Brit.), bathing pool (archaic) 2 = **pond**, lake, mere, tarn 3 = **puddle**, drop, patch

pool² NOUN 1 = **supply**, reserve, fall-back 2 = **kitty**, bank, fund, stock, store, pot, jackpot, stockpile ▷ VERB = **combine**, share, merge, put together, amalgamate, lump together, join forces on

poor ADJECTIVE 1 = **impoverished**, broke (*informal*), hard up (*informal*), short, needy, penniless, destitute, poverty-stricken ≠ rich 2 = **unfortunate**, unlucky, hapless, pitiful, luckless, wretched, ill-starred, pitiable ≠ fortunate 3 = **inferior**, unsatisfactory, mediocre, second-rate, rotten (*informal*), low-grade, below par, substandard, half-pie (*N.Z. informal*), bodger or bodgie (*Austral. slang*) ≠ excellent 4 = **meagre**, inadequate, insufficient, lacking, incomplete, scant, deficient, skimpy ≠ ample

poorly ADVERB = **badly**, incompetently, inadequately, unsuccessfully, insufficiently, unsatisfactorily, inexpertly ≠ well
▷ ADJECTIVE (*informal*) = **ill**, sick, unwell, crook (*Austral. & N.Z. informal*), seedy (*informal*), below par, off colour, under the weather (*informal*), feeling rotten (*informal*) ≠ healthy

pop NOUN = **bang**, report, crack, noise, burst, explosion
▷ VERB 1 = **burst**, crack, snap, bang, explode, go off (with a bang) 2 = **put**, insert, push, stick, slip, thrust, tuck, shove

pope NOUN = **Holy Father**, pontiff, His Holiness, Bishop of Rome, Vicar of Christ

popular ADJECTIVE 1 = **well-liked**, liked, in, accepted, favourite, approved, in favour, fashionable ≠ unpopular 2 = **common**, general, prevailing, current, conventional, universal, prevalent ≠ rare

popularity NOUN 1 = **favour**, esteem, acclaim, regard, approval, vogue 2 = **currency**, acceptance, circulation, vogue, prevalence

populate VERB 1 = **inhabit**, people, live in, occupy, reside in, dwell in (*formal*) 2 = **settle**, occupy, pioneer, colonize

population NOUN = **inhabitants**, people, community, society, residents, natives, folk, occupants

pore NOUN = **opening**, hole, outlet, orifice

pornography NOUN = **obscenity**, porn (*informal*), dirt, filth, indecency, smut

port NOUN = **harbour**, haven, anchorage, seaport

portable ADJECTIVE = **light**, compact, convenient, handy, manageable, movable, easily carried

porter¹ NOUN = **baggage attendant**, carrier, bearer, baggage-carrier

porter² NOUN (*chiefly Brit.*) = **doorman**, caretaker, janitor, concierge, gatekeeper

portion NOUN 1 = **part**, bit, piece, section, scrap, segment, fragment, chunk 2 = **helping**, serving, piece, plateful 3 = **share**, allowance, lot, measure, quantity, quota, ration, allocation

portrait NOUN 1 = **picture**, painting, image, photograph, representation, likeness 2 = **description**, profile, portrayal, depiction, characterization, thumbnail sketch

portray VERB 1 = **play**, take the role of, act the part of, represent, personate (*rare*) 2 = **describe**, present, depict, evoke, delineate, put in words 3 = **represent**, draw, paint, illustrate, sketch, figure, picture, depict 4 = **characterize**, represent, depict

portrayal NOUN
1 = **performance**, interpretation, characterization 2 = **depiction**, picture, representation, sketch, rendering 3 = **description**, account, representation
4 = **characterization**, representation, depiction

● **WORD POWER**
● Several loan words came into
● English via Portuguese but had
● a different source language.
● For example, *amok* was a
● Malay word meaning 'frenzied'
● which was, in turn, adopted
● by Portuguese explorers to
● describe a Malay in a state
● of murderous frenzy. From
● Portuguese it was borrowed
● into English, and is almost
● always found in the phrase *run*
● *amok*, though *go amok* is also
● found. Run amok means to run
● about with a desire to do harm
● or kill, e.g. hooligans ran amok
● in the streets. It is similar in
● meaning to 'on the rampage'
● and 'go berserk'. Interestingly,
● berserk, from Icelandic, also
● originally denoted a person in a
● state of murderous rage, in this
● case Norse warriors who would
● *go berserk* on the battlefield.
● Run amok can also be used
● of abstract nouns, e.g. An
● example of political correctness
● run amok – where it means
● spreading wildly or out of
● control. Another word adopted
● from Portuguese is *palaver*,
● from *palavra* meaning 'talk'.
● This origin can still be seen in
● its meaning of talk or chatter
● which is loud or confused, e.g.
● all the media palaver about
● this issue. However, the most
● common meaning of palaver
● is 'fuss' or 'effort', especially of
● a time-consuming activity,
● e.g. the palaver of changing
● your mobile phone network.
● It is close in meaning to its
● synonym 'rigmarole' in this
● sense.

pose VERB 1 = **position yourself**, sit, model, arrange yourself
2 = **put on airs**, posture, show off (*informal*)
▷ NOUN 1 = **posture**, position, bearing, attitude, stance 2 = **act**, façade, air, front, posturing, pretence, mannerism, affectation
▷ PHRASE: **pose as something** or **someone** = **impersonate**, pretend to be, profess to be, masquerade as, pass yourself off as

posh (*informal, chiefly Brit.*)
ADJECTIVE 1 = **smart**, grand, stylish, luxurious, classy (*slang*),

swish (*informal, chiefly Brit.*),
up-market, swanky (*informal*),
schmick (*Austral. informal*)
2 = **upper-class**, high-class
position NOUN **1** = **location**,
place, point, area, post, situation,
station, spot **2** = **posture**,
attitude, arrangement, pose,
stance **3** = **status**, place,
standing, footing, station,
rank, reputation, importance
4 = **job**, place, post, opening,
office, role, situation, duty
5 = **place**, standing, rank, status
6 = **attitude**, view, perspective,
point of view, opinion, belief,
stance, outlook
▷ VERB = **place**, put, set, stand,
arrange, locate, lay out
positive ADJECTIVE **1** = **beneficial**,
useful, practical, helpful,
progressive, productive,
worthwhile, constructive
≠ harmful **2** = **certain**, sure,
convinced, confident, satisfied,
assured, free from doubt
≠ uncertain **3** = **definite**, real,
clear, firm, certain, express,
absolute, decisive, nailed-on
(*slang*) ≠ inconclusive **4** (*informal*)
= **absolute**, complete, perfect,
right (*Brit. informal*), real, total,
sheer, utter
positively ADVERB **1** = **definitely**,
surely, firmly, certainly, absolutely,
emphatically, unquestionably,
categorically **2** = **really**,
completely, simply, plain
(*informal*), absolutely, thoroughly,
utterly, downright

possess VERB **1** = **own**, have, hold,
be in possession of, be the owner
of, have in your possession **2** = **be
endowed with**, have, enjoy,
benefit from, be possessed of,
be gifted with **3** = **seize**, hold,
control, dominate, occupy, take
someone over, have power over,
have mastery over
possession NOUN = **ownership**,
control, custody, hold, hands,
tenure
▷ PLURAL NOUN = **property**,
things, effects, estate, assets,
belongings, chattels
possibility NOUN **1** = **feasibility**,
likelihood, potentiality,
practicability, workableness
2 = **likelihood**, chance, risk, odds,
prospect, liability, probability **3**
often plural = **potential**, promise,
prospects, talent, capabilities,
potentiality
possible ADJECTIVE **1** = **feasible**,
viable, workable, achievable,
practicable, attainable,
doable, realizable ≠ unfeasible
2 = **likely**, potential, anticipated,
probable, odds-on, on the cards
≠ improbable **3** = **conceivable**,
likely, credible, plausible,
hypothetical, imaginable,
believable, thinkable
≠ inconceivable **4** = **aspiring**,
would-be, promising, hopeful,
prospective, wannabe (*informal*)
● **WORD POWER**
● Although it is very common to
● talk about something's being
● *very possible* or *more possible*,

- many people object to such
- uses, claiming that *possible*
- describes an absolute state,
- and therefore something can
- only be either *possible* or *not*
- *possible*. If you want to refer to
- different degrees of probability,
- a word such as *likely* or *easy*
- may be more appropriate than
- *possible*, for example *it is very*
- *likely that he will resign* (not *very*
- *possible*).

possibly ADVERB = **perhaps**, maybe, perchance (*archaic*)

post¹ NOUN = **support**, stake, pole, column, shaft, upright, pillar, picket
 ▷ VERB = **put up**, display, affix, pin something up

post² NOUN 1 = **job**, place, office, position, situation, employment, appointment, assignment 2 = **position**, place, base, beat, station
 ▷ VERB = **station**, assign, put, place, position, situate, put on duty

post³ NOUN 1 = **mail**, collection, delivery, postal service, snail mail (*informal*) 2 = **correspondence**, letters, cards, mail
 ▷ VERB = **send (off)**, forward, mail, get off, transmit, dispatch, consign ▷ PHRASE: **keep someone posted** = **notify**, brief, advise, inform, report to, keep someone informed, keep someone up to date, apprise

poster NOUN = **notice**, bill, announcement, advertisement, sticker, placard, public notice

postpone VERB = **put off**, delay, suspend, adjourn, shelve, defer, put back, put on the back burner (*informal*) ≠ go ahead with

posture NOUN = **bearing**, set, attitude, stance, carriage, disposition
 ▷ VERB = **show off** (*informal*), pose, affect, put on airs

pot NOUN = **container**, bowl, pan, vessel, basin, cauldron, skillet

potent ADJECTIVE 1 = **powerful**, commanding, dynamic, dominant, influential, authoritative 2 = **strong**, powerful, mighty, vigorous, forceful ≠ weak

potential ADJECTIVE 1 = **possible**, future, likely, promising, probable 2 = **hidden**, possible, inherent, dormant, latent
 ▷ NOUN = **ability**, possibilities, capacity, capability, aptitude, wherewithal, potentiality

potter VERB *usually with* **around** *or* **about** = **mess about**, tinker, dabble, footle (*informal*)

pottery NOUN = **ceramics**, terracotta, crockery, earthenware, stoneware

pounce VERB *often followed by* **on** *or* **upon** = **attack**, strike, jump, leap, swoop

pound¹ NOUN = **enclosure**, yard, pen, compound, kennels

pound² VERB 1 *sometimes with* **on** = **beat**, strike, hammer, batter, thrash, thump, clobber (*slang*), pummel 2 = **crush**, powder,

p

pulverize **3** = **pulsate**, beat, pulse, throb, palpitate **4** = **stomp**, tramp, march, thunder (*informal*)

pour VERB **1** = **let flow**, spill, splash, dribble, drizzle, slop (*informal*), slosh (*informal*), decant **2** = **flow**, stream, run, course, rush, emit, cascade, gush **3** = **rain**, pelt (down), teem, bucket down (*informal*) **4** = **stream**, crowd, flood, swarm, gush, throng, teem

- ● **WORD POWER**
- ● The spelling of *pour* (as
- ● in *she poured cream on her*
- ● *strudel*) should be carefully
- ● distinguished from that of *pore*
- ● *over* or *through* (as in *she pored*
- ● *over the manuscript*).

pout VERB = **sulk**, glower, look petulant, pull a long face
▷ NOUN = **sullen look**, glower, long face

poverty NOUN **1** = **pennilessness**, want, need, hardship, insolvency, privation, penury, destitution ≠ wealth **2** = **scarcity**, lack, absence, want, deficit, shortage, deficiency, inadequacy ≠ abundance

powder NOUN = **dust**, talc, fine grains, loose particles
▷ VERB = **dust**, cover, scatter, sprinkle, strew, dredge

power NOUN **1** = **control**, authority, influence, command, dominance, domination, mastery, dominion, mana (*N.Z.*) **2** = **ability**, capacity, faculty, property, potential, capability, competence, competency

≠ inability **3** = **authority**, right, licence, privilege, warrant, prerogative, authorization **4** = **strength**, might, energy, muscle, vigour, potency, brawn ≠ weakness **5** = **forcefulness**, force, strength, punch (*informal*), intensity, potency, eloquence, persuasiveness

powerful ADJECTIVE
1 = **influential**, dominant, controlling, commanding, prevailing, authoritative, skookum (*Canad.*) ≠ powerless **2** = **strong**, strapping, mighty, vigorous, potent, energetic, sturdy ≠ weak **3** = **persuasive**, convincing, telling, moving, striking, storming, dramatic, impressive

powerless ADJECTIVE
1 = **defenceless**, vulnerable, dependent, subject, tied, ineffective, unarmed **2** = **weak**, disabled, helpless, incapable, frail, feeble, debilitated, impotent ≠ strong

practical ADJECTIVE
1 = **functional**, realistic, pragmatic ≠ impractical **2** = **empirical**, real, applied, actual, hands-on, in the field, experimental, factual ≠ theoretical **3** = **sensible**, ordinary, realistic, down-to-earth, matter-of-fact, businesslike, hard-headed, grounded ≠ impractical **4** = **feasible**, possible, viable, workable, practicable, doable ≠ impractical

5 = **useful**, ordinary, appropriate, sensible, everyday, functional, utilitarian, serviceable

6 = **skilled**, experienced, efficient, accomplished, proficient ≠ inexperienced

● **WORD POWER**
● A distinction is usually
● made between *practical* and
● *practicable*. *Practical* refers to a
● person, idea, project, etc, as
● being more concerned with
● or relevant to practice than
● theory: *he is a very practical*
● *person; the idea had no practical*
● *application*. *Practicable* refers to a
● project or idea as being capable
● of being done or put into
● effect: *the plan was expensive, yet*
● *practicable*.

practically ADVERB 1 = **almost**, nearly, essentially, virtually, basically, fundamentally, all but, just about 2 = **sensibly**, reasonably, matter-of-factly, realistically, rationally, pragmatically

practice NOUN 1 = **custom**, way, system, rule, method, tradition, habit, routine, tikanga (*N.Z.*) 2 = **training**, study, exercise, preparation, drill, rehearsal, repetition 3 = **profession**, work, business, career, occupation, pursuit, vocation 4 = **business**, company, office, firm, enterprise, partnership, outfit (*informal*) 5 = **use**, experience, action, operation, application, enactment

practise VERB 1 = **rehearse**, study, prepare, perfect, repeat, go through, go over, refine 2 = **do**, train, exercise, drill 3 = **carry out**, follow, apply, perform, observe, engage in 4 = **work at**, pursue, carry on

practised ADJECTIVE = **skilled**, trained, experienced, seasoned, able, expert, accomplished, proficient ≠ inexperienced

pragmatic ADJECTIVE = **practical**, sensible, realistic, down-to-earth, utilitarian, businesslike, hard-headed ≠ idealistic

praise VERB 1 = **acclaim**, approve of, honour, cheer, admire, applaud, compliment, congratulate ≠ criticize 2 = **give thanks to**, bless, worship, adore, glorify, exalt
▷ NOUN 1 = **approval**, acclaim, tribute, compliment, congratulations, eulogy, commendation, approbation ≠ criticism 2 = **thanks**, glory, worship, homage, adoration

pray VERB 1 = **say your prayers**, offer a prayer, recite the rosary 2 = **beg**, ask, plead, petition, request, solicit, implore, beseech

prayer NOUN 1 = **supplication**, devotion 2 = **orison**, litany, invocation, intercession 3 = **plea**, appeal, request, petition, entreaty, supplication

preach VERB 1 *often with* **to** = **deliver a sermon**, address, evangelize, preach a sermon 2 = **urge**, teach, champion,

p

recommend, advise, counsel,
advocate, exhort

preacher NOUN = **clergyman**,
minister, parson, missionary,
evangelist

precarious ADJECTIVE
1 = **insecure**, dangerous, tricky,
risky, dodgy (*Brit., Austral. & N.Z.
informal*), unsure, hazardous,
shaky, shonky (*Austral. & N.Z.
informal*) ≠ secure 2 = **dangerous**,
shaky, insecure, unsafe, unreliable
≠ stable

precaution NOUN = **safeguard**,
insurance, protection, provision,
safety measure

precede VERB 1 = **go before**,
antedate 2 = **go ahead of**, lead,
head, go before 3 = **preface**,
introduce, go before

precedent NOUN = **instance**,
example, standard, model,
pattern, prototype, paradigm,
antecedent

precinct NOUN = **area**, quarter,
section, sector, district, zone

precious ADJECTIVE 1 = **valuable**,
expensive, fine, prized, dear,
costly, invaluable, priceless
≠ worthless 2 = **loved**, prized,
dear, treasured, darling, beloved,
adored, cherished 3 = **affected**,
artificial, twee (*Brit. informal*),
overrefined, overnice

precipitate VERB 1 = **quicken**,
trigger, accelerate, advance,
hurry, speed up, bring on, hasten
2 = **throw**, launch, cast, hurl, fling,
let fly

▷ ADJECTIVE 1 = **hasty**, rash,

reckless, impulsive, precipitous,
impetuous, heedless 2 = **sudden**,
quick, brief, rushing, rapid,
unexpected, swift, abrupt

precise ADJECTIVE 1 = **exact**,
specific, particular, express,
correct, absolute, accurate,
explicit ≠ vague 2 = **strict**,
particular, exact, formal, careful,
stiff, rigid, meticulous ≠ inexact

precisely ADVERB 1 = **exactly**,
squarely, correctly, absolutely,
strictly, accurately, plumb
(*informal*), square on 2 = **just so**,
yes, absolutely, exactly, quite
so, you bet (*informal*), without
a doubt, indubitably 3 = **just**,
entirely, absolutely, altogether,
exactly, in all respects 4 = **word
for word**, literally, exactly, to the
letter

precision NOUN = **exactness**,
care, accuracy, particularity,
meticulousness, preciseness

predecessor NOUN 1 = **previous
job holder**, precursor, forerunner,
antecedent 2 = **ancestor**,
forebear, antecedent, forefather,
tupuna or tipuna (*N.Z.*)

predicament NOUN = **fix**
(*informal*), situation, spot
(*informal*), hole (*slang*), mess, jam
(*informal*), dilemma, pinch

predict VERB = **foretell**, forecast,
divine, prophesy, augur, portend

predictable ADJECTIVE = **likely**,
expected, sure, certain,
anticipated, reliable, foreseeable
≠ unpredictable

prediction NOUN = **prophecy**,

p

forecast, prognosis, divination, prognostication, augury

predominantly ADVERB = **mainly**, largely, chiefly, mostly, generally, principally, primarily, for the most part

prefer VERB 1 = **like better**, favour, go for, pick, fancy, opt for, incline towards, be partial to 2 = **choose**, opt for, pick, desire, would rather, would sooner, incline towards

● **WORD POWER**
● Normally, *to* (not *than*) is used
● after *prefer* and *preferable*.
● Therefore, you would say
● *I prefer skating to skiing*, and
● *a small income is preferable*
● *to no income at all*. However,
● when expressing a preference
● between two activities stated
● as infinitive verbs, for example
● *to skate* and *to ski*, use *than*, as in
● *I prefer to skate than to ski*.

preferable ADJECTIVE = **better**, best, chosen, preferred, recommended, favoured, superior, more suitable ≠ undesirable

preferably ADVERB = **ideally**, if possible, rather, sooner, by choice, in *or* for preference

preference NOUN 1 = **liking**, wish, taste, desire, leaning, bent, bias, inclination 2 = **first choice**, choice, favourite, pick, option, selection 3 = **priority**, first place, precedence, favouritism, favoured treatment

pregnant ADJECTIVE
1 = **expectant**, expecting (*informal*), with child, in the club

(*Brit. slang*), big *or* heavy with child 2 = **meaningful**, pointed, charged, significant, telling, loaded, expressive, eloquent

prejudice NOUN
1 = **discrimination**, injustice, intolerance, bigotry, unfairness, chauvinism, narrow-mindedness 2 = **bias**, preconception, partiality, preconceived notion, prejudgment
▷ VERB 1 = **bias**, influence, colour, poison, distort, slant, predispose 2 = **harm**, damage, hurt, injure, mar, undermine, spoil, impair, crool *or* cruel (*Austral. slang*)

prejudiced ADJECTIVE = **biased**, influenced, unfair, one-sided, bigoted, intolerant, opinionated, narrow-minded ≠ unbiased

preliminary ADJECTIVE 1 = **first**, opening, trial, initial, test, pilot, prior, introductory 2 = **qualifying**, eliminating
▷ NOUN = **introduction**, opening, beginning, start, prelude, preface, overture, preamble

prelude NOUN 1 = **introduction**, beginning, start 2 = **overture**, opening, introduction, introductory movement

premature ADJECTIVE 1 = **early**, untimely, before time, unseasonable 2 = **hasty**, rash, too soon, untimely, ill-timed, overhasty

premier NOUN = **head of government**, prime minister, chancellor, chief minister, P.M.
▷ ADJECTIVE = **chief**, leading,

P

first, highest, head, main, prime, primary

premiere NOUN = **first night**, opening, debut

premise NOUN = **assumption**, proposition, argument, hypothesis, assertion, supposition, presupposition, postulation

premises PLURAL NOUN = **building(s)**, place, office, property, site, establishment

premium NOUN 1 = **fee**, charge, payment, instalment 2 = **surcharge**, extra charge, additional fee or charge 3 = **bonus**, reward, prize, perk (*Brit. informal*), bounty, perquisite ▷ PHRASE: **at a premium** = **in great demand**, rare, scarce, in short supply, hard to come by

preoccupation NOUN 1 = **obsession**, fixation, bee in your bonnet 2 = **absorption**, abstraction, daydreaming, immersion, reverie, absent-mindedness, engrossment, woolgathering

preoccupied ADJECTIVE 1 = **absorbed**, lost, wrapped up, immersed, engrossed, rapt 2 = **lost in thought**, distracted, oblivious, absent-minded

preparation NOUN 1 = **groundwork**, preparing, getting ready 2 *usually plural* = **arrangement**, plan, measure, provision 3 = **mixture**, medicine, compound, concoction

prepare VERB 1 = **make** *or* **get**

ready, arrange, jack up (*N.Z. informal*) 2 = **train**, guide, prime, direct, brief, discipline, put someone in the picture 3 = **make**, cook, put together, get, produce, assemble, muster, concoct 4 = **get ready** 5 = **practise**, get ready, train, exercise, warm up, get into shape

prepared ADJECTIVE 1 = **willing**, inclined, disposed 2 = **ready**, set 3 = **fit**, primed, in order, arranged, in readiness

prescribe VERB 1 = **specify**, order, direct, stipulate, write a prescription for 2 = **ordain**, set, order, rule, recommend, dictate, lay down, decree

prescription NOUN 1 = **instruction**, direction, formula, script (*informal*), recipe 2 = **medicine**, drug, treatment, preparation, cure, mixture, dose, remedy

presence NOUN 1 = **being**, existence, residence, attendance, showing up, occupancy, inhabitance 2 = **personality**, bearing, appearance, aspect, air, carriage, aura, poise ▷ PHRASE: **presence of mind** = **level-headedness**, assurance, composure, poise, cool (*slang*), wits, countenance, coolness

present¹ ADJECTIVE 1 = **current**, existing, immediate, contemporary, present-day, existent 2 = **here**, there, near, ready, nearby, at hand ≠ absent 3 = **in existence**, existing, existent, extant ▷ **PHRASE**: **the present** = **now**, today, the time being, here and now, the present moment

present² NOUN = **gift**, offering, grant, donation, hand-out, endowment, boon, gratuity, bonsela (*S. African*), koha (*N.Z.*) ▷ VERB 1 = **give**, award, hand over, grant, hand out, confer, bestow 2 = **put on**, stage, perform, give, show, render 3 = **launch**, display, parade, exhibit, unveil 4 = **introduce**, make known, acquaint someone with

presentation NOUN 1 = **giving**, award, offering, donation, bestowal, conferral 2 = **appearance**, look, display, packaging, arrangement, layout 3 = **performance**, production, show

presently ADVERB 1 = **at present**, currently, now, today, these days, nowadays, at the present time, in this day and age 2 = **soon**, shortly, directly, before long, momentarily (*U.S. & Canad.*), by and by, in a jiffy (*informal*)

preservation NOUN 1 = **upholding**, support, maintenance 2 = **protection**, safety, maintenance, conservation, salvation, safeguarding, safekeeping

preserve VERB 1 = **maintain**, keep, continue, sustain, keep up, prolong, uphold, conserve ≠ end 2 = **protect**, keep, save, maintain, defend, shelter, shield, care for

≠ attack ▷ NOUN = **area**, department, field, territory, province, arena, sphere

preside VERB = **officiate**, chair, moderate, be chairperson

press VERB 1 = **push (down)**, depress, lean on, press down, force down 2 = **push**, squeeze, jam, thrust, ram, wedge, shove 3 = **hug**, squeeze, embrace, clasp, crush, hold close, fold in your arms 4 = **urge**, beg, petition, exhort, implore, pressurize, entreat 5 = **plead**, present, lodge, submit, tender, advance insistently 6 = **steam**, iron, smooth, flatten 7 = **compress**, grind, reduce, mill, crush, pound, squeeze, tread 8 = **crowd**, push, gather, surge, flock, herd, swarm, seethe

pressing ADJECTIVE = **urgent**, serious, vital, crucial, imperative, important, high-priority, importunate ≠ unimportant

pressure NOUN 1 = **force**, crushing, squeezing, compressing, weight, compression 2 = **power**, influence, force, constraint, sway, compulsion, coercion 3 = **stress**, demands, strain, heat, load, burden, urgency, hassle (*informal*), uphill (*S. African*)

prestige NOUN = **status**, standing, credit, reputation, honour, importance, fame, distinction, mana (*N.Z.*)

prestigious ADJECTIVE = **celebrated**, respected, prominent, great, important, esteemed, notable, renowned ≠ unknown

presumably ADVERB = **it would seem**, probably, apparently, seemingly, on the face of it, in all probability, in all likelihood

presume VERB 1 = **believe**, think, suppose, assume, guess (*informal, chiefly U.S. & Canad.*), take for granted, infer, conjecture 2 = **dare**, venture, go so far as, take the liberty, make so bold as

pretend VERB 1 = **feign**, affect, assume, allege, fake, simulate, profess, sham 2 = **make believe**, suppose, imagine, act, make up

pretty ADJECTIVE = **attractive**, beautiful, lovely, charming, fair, good-looking, bonny, comely, fit (*Brit. informal*) ≠ plain
▷ ADVERB (*informal*) = **fairly**, rather, quite, kind of (*informal*), somewhat, moderately, reasonably

prevail VERB 1 = **win**, succeed, triumph, overcome, overrule, be victorious 2 = **be widespread**, abound, predominate, be current, be prevalent, exist generally

prevailing ADJECTIVE
1 = **widespread**, general, established, popular, common, current, usual, ordinary
2 = **predominating**, ruling, main, existing, principal

prevalent ADJECTIVE = **common**, established, popular, general, current, usual, widespread, universal ≠ rare

prevent VERB = **stop**, avoid,

frustrate, hamper, foil, inhibit, avert, thwart ≠ help

prevention NOUN = **elimination**, safeguard, precaution, thwarting, avoidance, deterrence

preview NOUN = **sample**, sneak preview, trailer, taster, foretaste, advance showing

previous ADJECTIVE 1 = **earlier**, former, past, prior, preceding, erstwhile ≠ later 2 = **preceding**, past, prior, foregoing

previously ADVERB = **before**, earlier, once, in the past, formerly, hitherto, beforehand

prey NOUN 1 = **quarry**, game, kill 2 = **victim**, target, mug (*Brit. slang*), dupe, fall guy (*informal*)

price NOUN 1 = **cost**, value, rate, charge, figure, worth, damage (*informal*), amount
2 = **consequences**, penalty, cost, result, toll, forfeit
▷ VERB = **evaluate**, value, estimate, rate, cost, assess

priceless ADJECTIVE = **valuable**, expensive, precious, invaluable, dear, costly ≠ worthless

prick VERB = **pierce**, stab, puncture, punch, lance, jab, perforate
▷ NOUN = **puncture**, hole, wound, perforation, pinhole

prickly ADJECTIVE 1 = **spiny**, barbed, thorny, bristly 2 = **itchy**, sharp, smarting, stinging, crawling, tingling, scratchy

pride NOUN 1 = **satisfaction**, achievement, fulfilment, delight, content, pleasure, joy,

- **BIRDS OF PREY**
- accipiter
- Australian goshawk *or* chicken hawk
- bald eagle
- barn owl
- buzzard
- caracara
- condor
- duck hawk
- eagle
- eagle-hawk *or* wedge-tailed eagle
- falcon *or* (*N.Z.*) bush-hawk *or* karearea
- falconet
- golden eagle
- goshawk
- gyrfalcon *or* gerfalcon
- harrier
- hawk
- hobby
- honey buzzard
- kestrel
- kite
- lammergeier, lammergeyer, bearded vulture, *or* (*archaic*) ossifrage
- lanner
- merlin
- mopoke *or* (*N.Z.*) ruru
- osprey, fish eagle, *or* (*archaic*) ossifrage
- owl
- peregrine falcon
- saker
- screech owl
- sea eagle, erne, *or* ern
- secretary bird
- snowy owl
- sparrowhawk
- tawny owl
- turkey buzzard *or* vulture
- vulture

gratification **2** = **self-respect**, honour, ego, dignity, self-esteem, self-image, self-worth **3** = **conceit**, vanity, arrogance, pretension, hubris, self-importance, egotism, self-love ≠ humility

priest NOUN = **clergyman**, minister, father, divine, vicar, pastor, cleric, curate

primarily ADVERB **1** = **chiefly**, largely, generally, mainly, essentially, mostly, principally, fundamentally **2** = **at first**, originally, initially, in the first place, in the beginning, first and foremost, at *or* from the start

primary ADJECTIVE = **chief**, main, first, highest, greatest, prime, principal, cardinal ≠ subordinate

prime ADJECTIVE = **main**, leading, chief, central, major, key, primary, supreme **2** = **best**, top, select, highest, quality, choice, excellent, first-class
▷ NOUN = **peak**, flower, bloom, height, heyday, zenith
▷ VERB **1** = **inform**, tell, train, coach, brief, fill in (*informal*), notify, clue in (*informal*)
2 = **prepare**, set up, load, equip, get ready, make ready

primitive ADJECTIVE 1 = **early**, first, earliest, original, primary, elementary, primordial, primeval ≠ modern 2 = **crude**, simple, rough, rudimentary, unrefined

prince NOUN = **ruler**, lord, monarch, sovereign, crown prince, liege, prince regent, crowned head

princely ADJECTIVE 1 = **substantial**, considerable, large, huge, massive, enormous, sizable or sizeable 2 = **regal**, royal, imperial, noble, sovereign, majestic

princess NOUN = **ruler**, lady, monarch, sovereign, liege, crowned head, crowned princess, dynast

principal ADJECTIVE = **main**, leading, chief, prime, first, key, essential, primary ≠ minor ▷ NOUN 1 = **headmaster** or **headmistress**, head (informal), dean, head teacher, rector, master or mistress 2 = **star**, lead, leader, prima ballerina, leading man or lady, coryphée 3 = **capital**, money, assets, working capital

principally ADVERB = **mainly**, largely, chiefly, especially, mostly, primarily, predominantly

principle NOUN 1 = **morals**, standards, ideals, honour, virtue, ethics, integrity, conscience, kaupapa (N.Z.) 2 = **rule**, law, truth, precept ▷ PHRASE: **in principle 1** = **in general 2** = **in theory**, ideally, on paper, theoretically, in an ideal world, en

principe (French)

● **WORD POWER**
● *Principle* and *principal* are often
● confused: *the principal* (not
● *principle*) *reason for his departure*;
● *the plan was approved in principle*
● (not *principal*).

print VERB 1 = **run off**, publish, copy, reproduce, issue, engrave 2 = **publish**, release, circulate, issue, disseminate 3 = **mark**, impress, stamp, imprint ▷ NOUN 1 = **photograph**, photo, snap 2 = **picture**, plate, etching, engraving, lithograph, woodcut, linocut 3 = **copy**, photo (informal), picture, reproduction, replica

prior ADJECTIVE = **earlier**, previous, former, preceding, foregoing, pre-existing, pre-existent ▷ PHRASE: **prior to** = **before**, preceding, earlier than, in advance of, previous to

priority NOUN 1 = **prime concern** 2 = **precedence**, preference, primacy, predominance 3 = **supremacy**, rank, precedence, seniority, right of way, pre-eminence

prison NOUN = **jail**, confinement, nick (Brit. slang), cooler (slang), jug (slang), dungeon, clink (slang), gaol, boob (Austral. slang)

prisoner NOUN 1 = **convict**, con (slang), lag (slang), jailbird 2 = **captive**, hostage, detainee, internee

privacy NOUN = **seclusion**, isolation, solitude, retirement, retreat

private ADJECTIVE 1 = **exclusive**, individual, privately owned, own, special, reserved ≠ public 2 = **secret**, confidential, covert, unofficial, clandestine, off the record, hush-hush (*informal*) ≠ public 3 = **personal**, individual, secret, intimate, undisclosed, unspoken, innermost, unvoiced 4 = **secluded**, secret, separate, isolated, sequestered ≠ busy 5 = **solitary**, reserved, retiring, withdrawn, discreet, secretive, self-contained, reclusive ≠ sociable

privilege NOUN = **right**, due, advantage, claim, freedom, liberty, concession, entitlement

privileged ADJECTIVE = **special**, advantaged, favoured, honoured, entitled, elite

prize¹ NOUN 1 = **reward**, cup, award, honour, medal, trophy, accolade 2 = **winnings**, haul, jackpot, stakes, purse ▷ MODIFIER = **champion**, best, winning, top, outstanding, award-winning, first-rate

prize² VERB = **value**, treasure, esteem, cherish, hold dear

prize³ *or* **prise** VERB 1 = **force**, pull, lever 2 = **drag**, force, draw, wring, extort

probability NOUN 1 = **likelihood**, prospect, chance, odds, expectation, liability, likeliness 2 = **chance**, odds, possibility, likelihood

probable ADJECTIVE = **likely**, possible, apparent, reasonable to think, credible, plausible, feasible, presumable ≠ unlikely

probably ADVERB = **likely**, perhaps, maybe, possibly, presumably, most likely, doubtless, perchance (*archaic*)

probation NOUN = **trial period**, trial, apprenticeship

probe VERB 1 *often with* **into** = **examine**, go into, investigate, explore, search, look into, analyze, dissect 2 = **explore**, examine, poke, prod, feel around ▷ NOUN = **investigation**, study, inquiry, analysis, examination, exploration, scrutiny, scrutinization

problem NOUN 1 = **difficulty**, trouble, dispute, plight, obstacle, dilemma, headache (*informal*), complication 2 = **puzzle**, question, riddle, enigma, conundrum, poser

problematic ADJECTIVE = **tricky**, puzzling, doubtful, dubious, debatable, problematical ≠ clear

procedure NOUN = **method**, policy, process, course, system, action, practice, strategy

proceed VERB 1 = **begin**, go ahead 2 = **continue**, go on, progress, carry on, go ahead, press on, crack on (*informal*) ≠ discontinue 3 = **go on**, continue, progress, carry on, go ahead, move on, move forward, press on, crack on (*informal*) ≠ stop 4 = **arise**, come, issue, result, spring, flow, stem, derive

proceeding NOUN = **action**,

p

process, procedure, move, act, step, measure, deed

proceeds PLURAL NOUN = **income**, profit, revenue, returns, products, gain, earnings, yield

process NOUN 1 = **procedure**, means, course, system, action, performance, operation, measure 2 = **development**, growth, progress, movement, advance, evolution, progression 3 = **method**, system, practice, technique, procedure
▷ VERB = **handle**, manage, action, deal with, fulfil

procession NOUN = **parade**, train, march, file, cavalcade, cortege

proclaim VERB 1 = **announce**, declare, advertise, publish, indicate, herald, circulate, profess ≠ keep secret 2 = **pronounce**, announce, declare

prod VERB 1 = **poke**, push, dig, shove, nudge, jab 2 = **prompt**, move, urge, motivate, spur, stimulate, rouse, incite
▷ NOUN 1 = **poke**, push, dig, shove, nudge, jab 2 = **prompt**, signal, cue, reminder, stimulus

prodigy NOUN = **genius**, talent, wizard, mastermind, whizz (informal), up-and-comer (informal)

produce VERB 1 = **cause**, effect, generate, bring about, give rise to 2 = **make**, create, develop, manufacture, construct, invent, fabricate 3 = **create**, develop, write, turn out, compose, originate, churn out (informal)

4 = **yield**, provide, grow, bear, give, supply, afford, render 5 = **bring forth**, bear, deliver, breed, give birth to, beget, bring into the world 6 = **show**, provide, present, advance, demonstrate, offer, come up with, exhibit 7 = **display**, show, present, proffer 8 = **present**, stage, direct, put on, do, show, mount, exhibit
▷ NOUN = **fruit and vegetables**, goods, food, products, crops, yield, harvest, greengrocery (Brit.)

producer NOUN 1 = **director**, promoter, impresario 2 = **maker**, manufacturer, builder, creator, fabricator 3 = **grower**, farmer

product NOUN 1 = **goods**, produce, creation, commodity, invention, merchandise, artefact 2 = **result**, consequence, effect, outcome, upshot

production NOUN 1 = **producing**, making, manufacture, manufacturing, construction, formation, fabrication 2 = **creation**, development, fashioning, composition, origination 3 = **management**, administration, direction 4 = **presentation**, staging, mounting

productive ADJECTIVE 1 = **fertile**, rich, prolific, plentiful, fruitful, fecund ≠ barren 2 = **creative**, inventive 3 = **useful**, rewarding, valuable, profitable, effective, worthwhile, beneficial, constructive ≠ useless

productivity NOUN = **output**,

production, capacity, yield, efficiency, work rate

profess VERB 1 = **claim**, allege, pretend, fake, make out, purport, feign 2 = **state**, admit, announce, declare, confess, assert, proclaim, affirm

professed ADJECTIVE
1 = **supposed**, would-be, alleged, so-called, pretended, purported, self-styled, ostensible 2 = **declared**, confirmed, confessed, proclaimed, self-confessed, avowed, self-acknowledged

profession NOUN = **occupation**, calling, business, career, employment, office, position, sphere

professional ADJECTIVE
1 = **qualified**, trained, skilled, white-collar 2 = **expert**, experienced, skilled, masterly, efficient, competent, adept, proficient ≠ amateurish
▷ NOUN = **expert**, master, pro (*informal*), specialist, guru, adept, maestro, virtuoso, fundi (*S. African*)

professor NOUN = **don** (*Brit.*), fellow (*Brit.*), prof (*informal*)

profile NOUN 1 = **outline**, lines, form, figure, silhouette, contour, side view 2 = **biography**, sketch, vignette, characterization, thumbnail sketch

profit NOUN 1 *often plural* = **earnings**, return, revenue, gain, yield, proceeds, receipts, takings ≠ loss 2 = **benefit**, good,

use, value, gain, advantage, advancement ≠ disadvantage
▷ VERB 1 = **make money**, gain, earn 2 = **benefit**, help, serve, gain, promote, be of advantage to

profitable ADJECTIVE 1 = **money-making**, lucrative, paying, commercial, worthwhile, cost-effective, fruitful, remunerative 2 = **beneficial**, useful, rewarding, valuable, productive, worthwhile, fruitful, advantageous ≠ useless

profound ADJECTIVE 1 = **sincere**, acute, intense, great, keen, extreme, heartfelt, deeply felt ≠ insincere 2 = **wise**, learned, deep, penetrating, philosophical, sage, abstruse, sagacious ≠ uninformed

programme NOUN 1 = **schedule**, plan, agenda, timetable, listing, list, line-up, calendar 2 = **course**, curriculum, syllabus 3 = **show**, performance, production, broadcast, episode, presentation, transmission, telecast, podcast

progress NOUN 1 = **development**, growth, advance, gain, improvement, breakthrough, headway ≠ regression
2 = **movement forward**, passage, advancement, course, advance, headway ≠ movement backward
▷ VERB 1 = **move on**, continue, travel, advance, proceed, go forward, make headway, crack on (*informal*) ≠ move back
2 = **develop**, improve, advance, grow, gain ≠ get behind
▷ PHRASE: in progress = **going**

on, happening, continuing, being done, occurring, taking place, proceeding, under way

progression NOUN 1 = **progress**, advance, advancement, gain, headway, furtherance, movement forward 2 = **sequence**, course, series, chain, cycle, string, succession

progressive ADJECTIVE
1 = **enlightened**, liberal, modern, advanced, radical, revolutionary, avant-garde, reformist
2 = **growing**, continuing, increasing, developing, advancing, ongoing

prohibit VERB 1 = **forbid**, ban, veto, outlaw, disallow, proscribe, debar ≠ permit 2 = **prevent**, restrict, stop, hamper, hinder, impede ≠ allow

prohibition NOUN = **ban**, boycott, embargo, bar, veto, prevention, exclusion, injunction, restraining order (U.S. law)

project NOUN 1 = **scheme**, plan, job, idea, campaign, operation, activity, venture 2 = **assignment**, task, homework, piece of research
▷ VERB 1 = **forecast**, expect, estimate, predict, reckon, calculate, gauge, extrapolate
2 = **stick out**, extend, stand out, bulge, protrude, overhang, jut

projection NOUN = **forecast**, estimate, reckoning, calculation, estimation, computation, extrapolation

proliferation NOUN
= **multiplication**, increase, spread, expansion

prolific ADJECTIVE 1 = **productive**, creative, fertile, inventive, copious 2 = **fruitful**, fertile, abundant, luxuriant, profuse, fecund ≠ unproductive

prolong VERB = **lengthen**, continue, perpetuate, draw out, extend, delay, stretch out, spin out ≠ shorten

prominence NOUN 1 = **fame**, name, reputation, importance, celebrity, distinction, prestige, eminence 2 = **conspicuousness**, markedness

prominent ADJECTIVE
1 = **famous**, leading, top, important, main, distinguished, well-known, notable ≠ unknown
2 = **noticeable**, obvious, outstanding, pronounced, conspicuous, eye-catching, obtrusive ≠ inconspicuous

promise VERB 1 = **guarantee**, pledge, vow, swear, contract, assure, undertake, warrant
2 = **seem likely**, look like, show signs of, augur, betoken
▷ NOUN 1 = **guarantee**, word, bond, vow, commitment, pledge, undertaking, assurance
2 = **potential**, ability, talent, capacity, capability, aptitude

promising ADJECTIVE
1 = **encouraging**, likely, bright, reassuring, hopeful, favourable, rosy, auspicious ≠ unpromising
2 = **talented**, able, gifted, rising

promote VERB 1 = **help**, back, support, aid, forward, encourage,

advance, boost ≠ impede
2 = **advertise**, sell, hype,
publicize, push, plug (*informal*)
3 = **raise**, upgrade, elevate, exalt
≠ demote

promotion NOUN 1 = **rise**,
upgrading, move up,
advancement, elevation,
exaltation, preferment
2 = **publicity**, advertising,
plugging (*informal*)
3 = **encouragement**, support,
boosting, advancement,
furtherance

prompt VERB 1 = **cause**, occasion,
provoke, give rise to, elicit
2 = **remind**, assist, cue, help out
▷ ADJECTIVE = **immediate**, quick,
rapid, instant, timely, early, swift,
speedy ≠ slow
▷ ADVERB (*informal*) = **exactly**,
sharp, promptly, on the dot,
punctually

promptly ADVERB
1 = **immediately**, swiftly,
directly, quickly, at once, speedily
2 = **punctually**, on time, spot on
(*informal*), bang on (*informal*), on
the dot, on the button (*U.S.*), on
the nail

prone ADJECTIVE 1 = **liable**,
given, subject, inclined, tending,
bent, disposed, susceptible
≠ disinclined 2 = **face down**, flat,
horizontal, prostrate, recumbent
≠ face up

pronounce VERB 1 = **say**, speak,
sound, articulate, enunciate
2 = **declare**, announce, deliver,
proclaim, decree, affirm

pronounced ADJECTIVE
= **noticeable**, decided, marked,
striking, obvious, evident,
distinct, definite ≠ imperceptible

proof NOUN = **evidence**,
demonstration, testimony,
confirmation, verification,
corroboration, authentication,
substantiation
▷ ADJECTIVE = **impervious**,
strong, resistant, impenetrable,
repellent

prop VERB 1 = **lean**, place, set,
stand, position, rest, lay, balance
2 *often with* **up** = **support**,
sustain, hold up, brace, uphold,
bolster, buttress
▷ NOUN 1 = **support**, stay, brace,
mainstay, buttress, stanchion
2 = **mainstay**, support, sustainer,
anchor, backbone, cornerstone,
upholder

propaganda NOUN
= **information**, advertising,
promotion, publicity, hype,
disinformation

propel VERB 1 = **drive**, launch,
force, send, shoot, push, thrust,
shove ≠ stop 2 = **impel**, drive,
push, prompt, spur, motivate
≠ hold back

proper ADJECTIVE 1 = **real**,
actual, genuine, true, bona
fide, dinkum (*Austral. & N.Z.
informal*) 2 = **correct**, accepted,
established, appropriate, right,
formal, conventional, precise
≠ improper 3 = **polite**, right,
becoming, seemly, fitting, fit,
mannerly, suitable ≠ unseemly

properly ADVERB 1 = **correctly**, rightly, fittingly, appropriately, accurately, suitably, aptly ≠ incorrectly 2 = **politely**, decently, respectably ≠ badly

property NOUN 1 = **possessions**, goods, effects, holdings, capital, riches, estate, assets 2 = **land**, holding, estate, real estate, freehold 3 = **quality**, feature, characteristic, attribute, trait, hallmark

prophecy NOUN 1 = **prediction**, forecast, prognostication, augury 2 = **second sight**, divination, augury, telling the future, soothsaying

prophet or **prophetess** NOUN = **soothsayer**, forecaster, diviner, oracle, seer, sibyl, prophesier

proportion NOUN 1 = **part**, share, amount, division, percentage, segment, quota, fraction 2 = **relative amount**, relationship, ratio 3 = **balance**, harmony, correspondence, symmetry, concord, congruity ▷ PLURAL NOUN = **dimensions**, size, volume, capacity, extent, expanse

proportional or **proportionate** ADJECTIVE = **correspondent**, corresponding, even, balanced, consistent, compatible, equitable, in proportion ≠ disproportionate

proposal NOUN = **suggestion**, plan, programme, scheme, offer, project, bid, recommendation

propose VERB 1 = **put forward**, present, suggest, advance, submit 2 = **intend**, mean, plan, aim, design, scheme, have in mind 3 = **nominate**, name, present, recommend 4 = **offer marriage**, pop the question (*informal*), ask for someone's hand (in marriage)

proposition NOUN 1 = **task**, problem, activity, job, affair, venture, undertaking 2 = **theory**, idea, argument, concept, thesis, hypothesis, theorem, premiss 3 = **proposal**, plan, suggestion, scheme, bid, recommendation 4 = **advance**, pass (*informal*), proposal, overture, improper suggestion, come-on (*informal*) ▷ VERB = **make a pass at**, solicit, accost, make an improper suggestion to

proprietor or **proprietress** NOUN = **owner**, titleholder, landlord or landlady

prosecute VERB (*law*) = **take someone to court**, try, sue, indict, arraign, put someone on trial, litigate, bring someone to trial

prospect NOUN 1 = **likelihood**, chance, possibility, hope, promise, odds, expectation, probability 2 = **idea**, outlook 3 = **view**, landscape, scene, sight, outlook, spectacle, vista ▷ PLURAL NOUN = **possibilities**, chances, future, potential, expectations, outlook, scope ▷ VERB = **look**, search, seek, dowse

prospective ADJECTIVE

1 = **potential**, possible

2 = **expected**, coming, future, likely, intended, anticipated, forthcoming, imminent

prospectus NOUN = **catalogue**, list, programme, outline, syllabus, synopsis

prosper VERB = **succeed**, advance, progress, thrive, get on, do well, flourish

prosperity NOUN = **success**, riches, plenty, fortune, wealth, luxury, good fortune, affluence ≠ poverty

prosperous ADJECTIVE

1 = **wealthy**, rich, affluent, well-off, well-heeled (*informal*), well-to-do, moneyed, minted (*Brit. slang*) ≠ poor 2 = **successful**, booming, thriving, flourishing, doing well ≠ unsuccessful

prostitute NOUN = **whore**, hooker (*U.S. slang*), pro (*slang*), tart (*informal*), call girl, harlot, streetwalker, loose woman
▷ VERB = **cheapen**, sell out, pervert, degrade, devalue, squander, demean, debase

protagonist NOUN

1 = **supporter**, champion, advocate, exponent 2 = **leading character**, principal, central character, hero *or* heroine

protect VERB = **keep someone safe**, defend, support, save, guard, preserve, look after, shelter ≠ endanger

protection NOUN 1 = **safety**, care, defence, protecting, security, custody, safeguard,

aegis 2 = **safeguard**, cover, guard, shelter, screen, barrier, shield, buffer 3 = **armour**, cover, screen, barrier, shelter, shield

protective ADJECTIVE

1 = **protecting** 2 = **caring**, defensive, motherly, fatherly, maternal, vigilant, watchful, paternal

protector NOUN 1 = **defender**, champion, guard, guardian, patron, bodyguard 2 = **guard**, screen, protection, shield, pad, cushion, buffer

protest VERB 1 = **object**, demonstrate, oppose, complain, disagree, cry out, disapprove, demur 2 = **assert**, insist, maintain, declare, affirm, profess, attest, avow
▷ NOUN 1 = **demonstration**, march, rally, sit-in, demo (*informal*), hikoi (*N.Z.*)
2 = **objection**, complaint, dissent, outcry, protestation, remonstrance

protocol NOUN = **code of behaviour**, manners, conventions, customs, etiquette, propriety, decorum

prototype NOUN = **original**, model, first, example, standard

protracted ADJECTIVE = **extended**, prolonged, drawn-out, spun out, dragged out, long-drawn-out

proud ADJECTIVE 1 = **satisfied**, pleased, content, thrilled, glad, gratified, joyful, well-pleased ≠ dissatisfied 2 = **conceited**, arrogant, lordly, imperious, overbearing, haughty, snobbish, self-satisfied ≠ humble

prove VERB 1 = **turn out**, come out, end up 2 = **verify**, establish, determine, show, confirm, demonstrate, justify, substantiate ≠ disprove

proven ADJECTIVE = **established**, proved, confirmed, tested, reliable, definite, verified, attested

provide VERB 1 = **supply**, give, distribute, outfit, equip, donate, furnish, dispense ≠ withhold 2 = **give**, bring, add, produce, present, serve, afford, yield
▷ PHRASES: **provide for someone** = **support**, care for, keep, maintain, sustain, take care of, fend for; **provide for something** *followed by* **for** *or* **against** = **take precautions against**, plan for, prepare for, anticipate, plan ahead for, forearm for

provider NOUN 1 = **supplier**, giver, source, donor 2 = **breadwinner**, supporter, earner, wage earner

providing *or* **provided**
CONJUNCTION *often with* **that** = **on condition that**, if, given that, as long as

province NOUN = **region**, section, district, zone, patch, colony, domain

provincial ADJECTIVE
1 = **regional**, state, local, county, district, territorial, parochial
2 = **rural**, country, local, rustic, homespun, hick (*informal, chiefly*

U.S. & *Canad.*), backwoods ≠ urban 3 = **parochial**, insular, narrow-minded, unsophisticated, limited, narrow, small-town (*chiefly U.S.*), inward-looking ≠ cosmopolitan

provision NOUN 1 = **supplying**, giving, providing, supply, delivery, distribution, catering, presentation 2 = **condition**, term, requirement, demand, rider, restriction, qualification, clause
▷ PLURAL NOUN = **food**, supplies, stores, fare, rations, foodstuff, kai (*N.Z. informal*), victuals, edibles

provisional ADJECTIVE
1 = **temporary**, interim ≠ permanent 2 = **conditional**, limited, qualified, contingent, tentative ≠ definite

provocation NOUN 1 = **cause**, reason, grounds, motivation, stimulus, incitement 2 = **offence**, challenge, insult, taunt, injury, dare, grievance, annoyance

provocative ADJECTIVE
= **offensive**, provoking, insulting, stimulating, annoying, galling, goading

provoke VERB 1 = **anger**, annoy, irritate, infuriate, hassle (*informal*), aggravate (*informal*), incense, enrage ≠ pacify
2 = **rouse**, cause, produce, promote, occasion, prompt, stir, induce ≠ curb

prowess NOUN 1 = **skill**, ability, talent, expertise, genius, excellence, accomplishment, mastery ≠ inability 2 = **bravery**, daring, courage, heroism, mettle, valour, fearlessness, valiance ≠ cowardice

proximity NOUN = **nearness**, closeness

proxy NOUN = **representative**, agent, deputy, substitute, factor, delegate

prudent ADJECTIVE 1 = **cautious**, careful, wary, discreet, vigilant ≠ careless 2 = **wise**, politic, sensible, shrewd, discerning, judicious ≠ unwise 3 = **thrifty**, economical, sparing, careful, canny, provident, frugal, far-sighted ≠ extravagant

prune VERB 1 = **cut**, trim, clip, dock, shape, shorten, snip 2 = **reduce**, cut, cut back, trim, cut down, pare down, make reductions in

psyche NOUN = **soul**, mind, self, spirit, personality, individuality, anima, wairua (N.Z.)

psychiatrist NOUN = **psychotherapist**, analyst, therapist, psychologist, shrink (slang), psychoanalyst, headshrinker (slang)

psychic ADJECTIVE 1 = **supernatural**, mystic, occult 2 = **mystical**, spiritual, magical, other-worldly, paranormal, preternatural 3 = **psychological**, emotional, mental, spiritual, inner, psychiatric, cognitive ▷ NOUN = **clairvoyant**, fortune teller

psychological ADJECTIVE 1 = **mental**, emotional,
intellectual, inner, cognitive, cerebral 2 = **imaginary**, psychosomatic, irrational, unreal, all in the mind

psychology NOUN 1 = **behaviourism**, study of personality, science of mind 2 (informal) = **way of thinking**, attitude, behaviour, temperament, mentality, thought processes, mental processes, what makes you tick

pub or **public house** NOUN = **tavern**, bar, inn, saloon, beer parlour (Canad.), beverage room (Canad.)

public NOUN = **people**, society, community, nation, everyone, citizens, electorate, populace ▷ ADJECTIVE 1 = **civic**, government, state, national, local, official, community, social 2 = **general**, popular, national, shared, common, widespread, universal, collective 3 = **open**, accessible, communal, unrestricted ≠ private 4 = **well-known**, leading, important, respected, famous, celebrated, recognized, distinguished 5 = **known**, open, obvious, acknowledged, plain, patent, overt ≠ secret

publication NOUN 1 = **pamphlet**, newspaper, magazine, issue, title, leaflet, brochure, periodical, blog (informal) 2 = **announcement**, publishing, broadcasting, reporting, declaration, disclosure, proclamation, notification

p

publicity NOUN 1 = **advertising**, press, promotion, hype, boost, plug (*informal*) 2 = **attention**, exposure, fame, celebrity, fuss, public interest, limelight, notoriety

publish VERB 1 = **put out**, issue, produce, print 2 = **announce**, reveal, spread, advertise, broadcast, disclose, proclaim, circulate

pudding NOUN = **dessert**, afters (*Brit. informal*), sweet, pud (*informal*)

puff VERB 1 = **smoke**, draw, drag (*slang*), suck, inhale, pull at *or* on 2 = **breathe heavily**, pant, exhale, blow, gasp, gulp, wheeze, fight for breath
▷ NOUN 1 = **drag**, pull (*slang*), moke 2 = **blast**, breath, whiff, draught, gust

pull VERB 1 = **draw**, haul, drag, trail, tow, tug, jerk, yank ≠ push 2 = **extract**, pick, remove, gather, take out, pluck, uproot, draw out ≠ insert 3 (*informal*) = **attract**, draw, bring in, tempt, lure, interest, entice, pull in ≠ repel 4 = **strain**, tear, stretch, rip, wrench, dislocate, sprain
▷ NOUN 1 = **tug**, jerk, yank, twitch, heave ≠ shove 2 = **puff**, drag (*slang*), inhalation 3 (*informal*) = **influence**, power, weight, muscle, clout (*informal*), kai (*N.Z. informal*) ▷ PHRASES: **pull out (of)** 1 = **withdraw**, quit 2 = **leave**, abandon, get out, quit, retreat from, depart, evacuate;

pull someone up = **reprimand**, rebuke, admonish, read the riot act to, tell someone off (*informal*), reprove, bawl someone out (*informal*), tear someone off a strip (*Brit. informal*); **pull something off** (*informal*) = **succeed in**, manage, carry out, accomplish; **pull something out** = **produce**, draw, bring out, draw out; **pull up** = **stop**, halt, brake

pulp NOUN 1 = **paste**, mash, mush 2 = **flesh**, meat, soft part
▷ MODIFIER = **cheap**, lurid, trashy, rubbishy
▷ VERB = **crush**, squash, mash, pulverize

pulse NOUN = **beat**, rhythm, vibration, beating, throb, throbbing, pulsation
▷ VERB = **beat**, throb, vibrate, pulsate

pump VERB 1 = **supply**, send, pour, inject 2 = **interrogate**, probe, quiz, cross-examine

punch¹ VERB = **hit**, strike, box, smash, belt (*informal*), sock (*slang*), swipe (*informal*), bop (*informal*)
▷ NOUN 1 = **blow**, hit, sock (*slang*), jab, swipe (*informal*), bop (*informal*), wallop (*informal*) 2 (*informal*) = **effectiveness**, bite, impact, drive, vigour, verve, forcefulness

punch² VERB = **pierce**, cut, bore, drill, stamp, puncture, prick, perforate

punctuate VERB = **interrupt**, break, pepper, sprinkle, intersperse

puncture NOUN 1 = **flat tyre**, flat, flattie (N.Z.) 2 = **hole**, opening, break, cut, nick, leak, slit
▷ VERB = **pierce**, cut, nick, penetrate, prick, rupture, perforate, bore a hole

punish VERB = **discipline**, correct, castigate, chastise, sentence, chasten, penalize

punishing ADJECTIVE = **hard**, taxing, wearing, tiring, exhausting, gruelling, strenuous, arduous ≠ easy

punishment NOUN
1 = **penalizing**, discipline, correction, retribution, chastening, chastisement
2 = **penalty**, penance

punitive ADJECTIVE = **retaliatory**, in reprisal, retaliative

punt VERB = **bet**, back, stake, gamble, lay, wager
▷ NOUN = **bet**, stake, gamble, wager

punter NOUN 1 = **gambler**, better, backer 2 (informal) = **person**, man in the street

pupil NOUN 1 = **student**, schoolboy or schoolgirl, schoolchild ≠ teacher
2 = **learner**, novice, beginner, disciple ≠ instructor

puppet NOUN 1 = **marionette**, doll, glove puppet, finger puppet
2 = **pawn**, tool, instrument, mouthpiece, stooge, cat's-paw

purchase VERB = **buy**, pay for, obtain, get, score (slang), gain, pick up, acquire ≠ sell
▷ NOUN 1 = **acquisition**, buy,

investment, property, gain, asset, possession 2 = **grip**, hold, support, leverage, foothold

pure ADJECTIVE 1 = **unmixed**, real, simple, natural, straight, genuine, neat, authentic ≠ adulterated 2 = **clean**, wholesome, sanitary, spotless, sterilized, squeaky-clean, untainted, uncontaminated ≠ contaminated 3 = **complete**, total, perfect, absolute, sheer, patent, utter, outright ≠ qualified
4 = **innocent**, modest, good, moral, impeccable, righteous, virtuous, squeaky-clean ≠ corrupt

purely ADVERB = **absolutely**, just, only, completely, simply, entirely, exclusively, merely

purge VERB 1 = **rid**, clear, cleanse, strip, empty, void 2 = **get rid of**, remove, expel, wipe out, eradicate, do away with, exterminate
▷ NOUN = **removal**, elimination, expulsion, eradication, ejection

purity NOUN 1 = **cleanness**, cleanliness, wholesomeness, pureness, faultlessness, immaculateness ≠ impurity
2 = **innocence**, virtue, integrity, honesty, decency, virginity, chastity, chasteness ≠ immorality

purport VERB = **claim**, allege, assert, profess

purpose NOUN 1 = **reason**, point, idea, aim, object, intention 2 = **aim**, end, plan,

p

- **SHADES OF PURPLE**
- amethyst
- aubergine
- burgundy
- claret
- heather
- indigo
- lavender
- lilac
- magenta
- mauve
- mulberry
- plum
- puce
- Tyrian purple
- violet
- wine

hope, goal, wish, desire, object
3 = **determination**, resolve, will,
resolution, ambition, persistence,
tenacity, firmness ▷ **PHRASE**:
on purpose = **deliberately**,
purposely, intentionally,
knowingly, designedly

● **WORD POWER**
● The two concepts *purposeful* and
● *on purpose* should be carefully
● distinguished. *On purpose* and
● *purposely* have roughly the same
● meaning, and imply that a
● person's action is deliberate,
● rather than accidental.
● However, *purposeful* and its
● related adverb *purposefully*
● refer to the way that someone
● acts as being full of purpose or
● determination.

purposely ADVERB
= **deliberately**, expressly,
consciously, intentionally,
knowingly, with intent, on
purpose ≠ accidentally

purse NOUN **1** = **pouch**, wallet,
money-bag **2** (*U.S.*) = **handbag**,
bag, shoulder bag, pocket book,
clutch bag **3** = **funds**, means,
money, resources, treasury, wealth,
exchequer
▷ **VERB** = **pucker**, contract,

tighten, pout, press together
pursue VERB **1** = **engage in**,
perform, conduct, carry on,
practise **2** = **try for**, seek,
desire, search for, aim for, work
towards, strive for **3** = **continue**,
maintain, carry on, keep on,
persist in, proceed in, persevere
in **4** = **follow**, track, hunt, chase,
dog, shadow, tail (*informal*), hound
≠ flee
pursuit NOUN **1** = **quest**, seeking,
search, aim of, aspiration for,
striving towards **2** = **pursuing**,
seeking, search, hunt, chase,
trailing **3** = **occupation**, activity,
interest, line, pleasure, hobby,
pastime
push VERB **1** = **shove**, force, press,
thrust, drive, knock, sweep,
plunge ≠ pull **2** = **press**, operate,
depress, squeeze, activate, hold
down **3** = **make** or **force your
way**, move, shoulder, inch,
squeeze, thrust, elbow, shove
4 = **urge**, encourage, persuade,
spur, press, incite, impel
≠ discourage
▷ **NOUN 1** = **shove**, thrust, butt,
elbow, nudge ≠ pull **2** (*informal*)
= **drive**, go (*informal*), energy,
initiative, enterprise, ambition,

vitality, vigour ▷ **PHRASE**: **the push** (*informal, chiefly Brit.*) = **dismissal**, the sack (*informal*), discharge, the boot (*slang*), your cards (*informal*)

put VERB 1 = **place**, leave, set, position, rest, park (*informal*), plant, lay 2 = **express**, state, word, phrase, utter ▷ **PHRASES**: **put someone off** 1 = **discourage**, intimidate, deter, daunt, dissuade, demoralize, scare off, dishearten 2 = **disconcert**, confuse, unsettle, throw (*informal*), dismay, perturb, faze, discomfit; **put someone up** 1 = **accommodate**, house, board, lodge, quarter, take someone in, billet 2 = **nominate**, put forward, offer, present, propose, recommend, submit; **put something across** *or* **over** = **communicate**, explain, convey, make clear, get across, make yourself understood; **put something off** = **postpone**, delay, defer, adjourn, hold over, put on the back burner (*informal*), take a rain check on (*U.S. & Canad. informal*); **put something up** 1 = **build**, raise, set up, construct, erect, fabricate 2 = **offer**, present, mount, put forward

puzzle VERB = **perplex**, confuse, baffle, stump, bewilder, confound, mystify, faze
▷ **NOUN** 1 = **problem**, riddle, question, conundrum, poser 2 = **mystery**, problem, paradox, enigma, conundrum

puzzling ADJECTIVE = **perplexing**, baffling, bewildering, involved, enigmatic, incomprehensible, mystifying, abstruse ≠ simple

P

Qq

quake VERB = **shake**, tremble, quiver, move, rock, shiver, shudder, vibrate

qualification NOUN
1 = **eligibility**, quality, ability, skill, fitness, attribute, capability, aptitude 2 = **condition**, proviso, requirement, rider, reservation, limitation, modification, caveat

qualified ADJECTIVE 1 = **capable**, trained, experienced, seasoned, able, fit, expert, chartered ≠ untrained 2 = **restricted**, limited, provisional, conditional, reserved, bounded, adjusted, moderated ≠ unconditional

qualify VERB 1 = **certify**, equip, empower, train, prepare, fit, ready, permit ≠ disqualify 2 = **restrict**, limit, reduce, ease, moderate, regulate, diminish, temper

quality NOUN 1 = **standard**, standing, class, condition, rank, grade, merit, classification 2 = **excellence**, status, merit, position, value, worth, distinction, virtue 3 = **characteristic**, feature, attribute, point, side, mark, property, aspect 4 = **nature**, character, make, sort, kind

quantity NOUN 1 = **amount**, lot, total, sum, part, number 2 = **size**, measure, mass, volume, length, capacity, extent, bulk
● **WORD POWER**
● The use of a plural noun
● after *quantity of*, as in *a large*
● *quantity of bananas*, used to
● be considered incorrect,
● the objection being that
● the word *quantity* should
● only be used to refer to an
● uncountable amount, which
● was grammatically regarded as
● a singular concept. Nowadays,
● however, most people consider
● the use of *quantity* with a plural
● noun to be acceptable.

quarrel NOUN = **disagreement**, fight, row, argument, dispute, controversy, breach, contention, biffo (*Austral. slang*) ≠ accord
▷ VERB = **disagree**, fight, argue, row, clash, dispute, differ, fall out (*informal*) ≠ get on *or* along (with)

quarry NOUN = **prey**, victim, game, goal, aim, prize, objective

quarter NOUN 1 = **district**, region, neighbourhood, place, part, side, area, zone 2 = **mercy**, pity, compassion, charity, sympathy, tolerance, kindness, forgiveness
▷ VERB = **accommodate**, house, lodge, place, board, post, station, billet

quarters PLURAL
NOUN = **lodgings**, rooms, chambers, residence, dwelling, barracks, abode, habitation

quash VERB 1 = **annul**, overturn, reverse, cancel, overthrow,

revoke, overrule, rescind
2 = **suppress**, crush, put down, beat, overthrow, squash, subdue, repress

queen NOUN **1** = **sovereign**, ruler, monarch, leader, Crown, princess, majesty, head of state **2** = **leading light**, star, favourite, celebrity, darling, mistress, big name

queer ADJECTIVE **1** = **strange**, odd, funny, unusual, extraordinary, curious, weird, peculiar ≠ normal **2** = **faint**, dizzy, giddy, queasy, light-headed

● WORD POWER
● Although the term *queer*
● meaning 'gay' is still considered
● derogatory when used by
● non-gays, it is now being used
● by gay people themselves
● as a positive term in certain
● contexts, such as *queer politics*,
● *queer cinema*. Nevertheless,
● many gay people would not
● wish to have the term applied
● to them, nor would they use it
● of themselves.

query NOUN **1** = **question**, inquiry, problem **2** = **doubt**, suspicion, objection
▷ VERB **1** = **question**, challenge, doubt, suspect, dispute, object to, distrust, mistrust **2** = **ask**, inquire or enquire, question

quest NOUN **1** = **search**, hunt, mission, enterprise, crusade **2** = **expedition**, journey, adventure

question NOUN **1** = **inquiry**, enquiry, query, investigation, examination, interrogation ≠ answer **2** = **difficulty**, problem, doubt, argument, dispute, controversy, query, contention **3** = **issue**, point, matter, subject, problem, debate, proposal, theme
▷ VERB **1** = **interrogate**, cross-examine, interview, examine, probe, quiz, ask questions **2** = **dispute**, challenge, doubt, suspect, oppose, query, mistrust, disbelieve ≠ accept
▷ PHRASE: **out of the question** = **impossible**, unthinkable, inconceivable, not on (*informal*), hopeless, unimaginable, unworkable, unattainable

questionable ADJECTIVE = **dubious**, suspect, doubtful, controversial, suspicious, dodgy (*Brit., Austral. & N.Z. informal*), debatable, moot, shonky (*Austral. & N.Z. informal*) ≠ indisputable

queue NOUN = **line**, row, file, train, series, chain, string, column

quick ADJECTIVE **1** = **fast**, swift, speedy, express, cracking (*Brit. informal*), smart, rapid, fleet ≠ slow **2** = **brief**, passing, hurried, flying, fleeting, summary, lightning, short-lived ≠ long **3** = **immediate**, instant, prompt, sudden, abrupt, instantaneous **4** = **excitable**, passionate, irritable, touchy, irascible, testy ≠ calm **5** = **intelligent**, bright (*informal*), alert, sharp, acute, smart, clever, shrewd ≠ stupid

quicken VERB **1** = **speed up**, hurry, accelerate, hasten, gee up (*informal*) **2 = stimulate**, inspire, arouse, excite, revive, incite, energize, invigorate

quickly ADVERB **1 = swiftly**, rapidly, hurriedly, fast, hastily, briskly, apace ≠ slowly
2 = soon, speedily, as soon as possible, momentarily (*U.S.*), instantaneously, pronto (*informal*), a.s.a.p. (*informal*)
3 = immediately, at once, directly, promptly, abruptly, without delay

quiet ADJECTIVE **1 = soft**, low, muted, lowered, whispered, faint, suppressed, stifled ≠ loud
2 = peaceful, silent, hushed, soundless, noiseless ≠ noisy
3 = calm, peaceful, tranquil, mild, serene, placid, restful, chilled (*informal*) ≠ exciting
4 = still, calm, peaceful, tranquil ≠ troubled **5 = undisturbed**, isolated, secluded, private, sequestered, unfrequented ≠ crowded **6 = silent**
7 = reserved, retiring, shy, gentle, mild, sedate, meek ≠ excitable
▷ NOUN **= peace**, rest, tranquillity, ease, silence, solitude, serenity, stillness ≠ noise

quietly ADVERB **1 = noiselessly**, silently **2 = softly**, inaudibly, in an undertone, under your breath
3 = calmly, serenely, placidly, patiently, mildly **4 = silently**, mutely

quilt NOUN **= bedspread**, duvet, coverlet, eiderdown, counterpane, doona (*Austral.*), continental quilt

quip NOUN **= joke**, sally, jest, riposte, wisecrack (*informal*), retort, pleasantry, gibe

quirky ADJECTIVE **= odd**, unusual, eccentric, idiosyncratic, peculiar, offbeat

quit VERB **1 = resign (from)**, leave, retire (from), pull out (of), step down (from) (*informal*), abdicate
2 = stop, give up, cease, end, drop, abandon, halt, discontinue ≠ continue **3 = leave**, depart from, go out of, go away from, pull out from

quite ADVERB **1 = somewhat**, rather, fairly, reasonably, relatively, moderately
2 = absolutely, perfectly, completely, totally, fully, entirely, wholly

quiz NOUN **= examination**, questioning, interrogation, interview, investigation, grilling (*informal*), cross-examination, cross-questioning
▷ VERB **= question**, ask, interrogate, examine, investigate

quota NOUN **= share**, allowance, ration, part, limit, slice, quantity, portion

quotation NOUN **1 = passage**, quote (*informal*), excerpt, reference, extract, citation **2** (*commerce*) **= estimate**, price, tender, rate, cost, charge, figure, quote (*informal*)

quote VERB **1 = repeat**, recite, recall **2 = refer to**, cite, give, name, detail, relate, mention, instance

Rr

race¹ NOUN 1 = **competition**, contest, chase, dash, pursuit 2 = **contest**, competition, rivalry ▷ VERB 1 = **compete against**, run against 2 = **compete**, run, contend, take part in a race 3 = **run**, fly, career, speed, tear, dash, hurry, dart

race² NOUN = **people**, nation, blood, stock, type, folk, tribe

racial ADJECTIVE = **ethnic**, ethnological, national, folk, genetic, tribal, genealogical

rack NOUN = **frame**, stand, structure, framework ▷ VERB = **torture**, torment, afflict, oppress, harrow, crucify, agonize, pain

● **WORD POWER**
● The use of the spelling *wrack*
● rather than *rack* in sentences
● such as *she was wracked by grief*
● or *the country was wracked by*
● *civil war* is very common, but is
● thought by many people to be
● incorrect.

racket NOUN 1 = **noise**, row, fuss, disturbance, outcry, clamour, din, pandemonium 2 = **fraud**, scheme

radiate VERB 1 = **emit**, spread, send out, pour, shed, scatter 2 = **shine**, be diffused 3 = **show**, display, demonstrate, exhibit, emanate, give off *or* out 4 = **spread out**, diverge, branch out

radical ADJECTIVE 1 = **extreme**, complete, entire, sweeping, severe, thorough, drastic 2 = **revolutionary**, extremist, fanatical 3 = **fundamental**, natural, basic, profound, innate, deep-seated ≠ superficial ▷ NOUN = **extremist**, revolutionary, militant, fanatic ≠ conservative

rage NOUN 1 = **fury**, temper, frenzy, rampage, tantrum, foulie (*Austral. slang*), hissy fit (*informal*), strop (*Brit. informal*) ≠ calmness 2 = **anger**, passion, madness, wrath, ire 3 = **craze**, fashion, enthusiasm, vogue, fad (*informal*), latest thing ▷ VERB = **be furious**, blow up (*informal*), fume, lose it (*informal*), seethe, lose the plot (*informal*), go ballistic (*slang, chiefly U.S.*), lose your temper ≠ stay calm

ragged ADJECTIVE 1 = **tatty**, worn, torn, rundown, shabby, seedy, scruffy, in tatters ≠ smart 2 = **rough**, rugged, unfinished, uneven, jagged, serrated

raid VERB 1 = **steal from**, plunder, pillage, sack 2 = **attack**, invade, assault 3 = **make a search of**, search, bust (*informal*), make a raid on, make a swoop on ▷ NOUN 1 = **attack**, invasion, foray, sortie, incursion, sally, inroad 2 = **bust** (*informal*), swoop

raider NOUN = **attacker**, thief,

robber, plunderer, invader,
marauder

railing NOUN = **fence**, rails, barrier,
paling, balustrade

rain NOUN = **rainfall**, fall, showers,
deluge, drizzle, downpour,
raindrops, cloudburst
▷ VERB 1 = **pour**, pelt (down),
teem, bucket down (*informal*),
drizzle, come down in buckets
(*informal*) 2 = **fall**, shower, be
dropped, sprinkle, be deposited

rainy ADJECTIVE = **wet**, damp,
drizzly, showery ≠ dry

raise VERB 1 = **lift**, elevate, uplift,
heave 2 = **set upright**, lift, elevate
3 = **increase**, intensify, heighten,
advance, boost, strengthen,
enhance, enlarge ≠ reduce
4 = **make louder**, heighten,
amplify, louden 5 = **collect**,
gather, obtain 6 = **cause**, start,
produce, create, occasion,
provoke, originate, engender
7 = **put forward**, suggest,
introduce, advance, broach,
moot 8 = **bring up**, develop, rear,
nurture 9 = **build**, construct, put
up, erect ≠ demolish

rake¹ VERB 1 = **gather**, collect,
remove 2 = **search**, comb, scour,
scrutinize, fossick (*Austral. & N.Z.*)

rake² NOUN = **libertine**, playboy,
swinger (*slang*), lecher, roué,
debauchee ≠ puritan

rally NOUN 1 = **gathering**,
convention, meeting, congress,
assembly, hui (*N.Z.*) 2 = **recovery**,
improvement, revival,
recuperation ≠ relapse
▷ VERB 1 = **gather together**,
unite, regroup, reorganize,
reassemble 2 = **recover**, improve,
revive, get better, recuperate
≠ get worse

ram VERB 1 = **hit**, force, drive into,
crash, impact, smash, dash, butt
2 = **cram**, force, stuff, jam, thrust

ramble NOUN = **walk**, tour, stroll,
hike, roaming, roving, saunter
▷ VERB 1 = **walk**, range, wander,
stroll, stray, roam, rove, saunter,
go walkabout (*Austral.*) 2 *often
with* **on** = **babble**, rabbit (on) (*Brit.
informal*), waffle (*informal, chiefly
Brit.*), witter on (*informal*)

ramp NOUN = **slope**, incline,
gradient, rise

rampage VERB = **go berserk**,
storm, rage, run riot, run amok
▷ PHRASE: **on the rampage**
= **berserk**, wild, violent, raging,
out of control, amok, riotous,
berko (*Austral. slang*)

rampant ADJECTIVE
1 = **widespread**, prevalent,
rife, uncontrolled, unchecked,
unrestrained, profuse, spreading
like wildfire 2 (*heraldry*)
= **upright**, standing, rearing, erect

random ADJECTIVE 1 = **chance**,
casual, accidental, incidental,
haphazard, fortuitous, hit or
miss, adventitious ≠ planned
2 = **casual** ▷ PHRASE: **at random**
= **haphazardly**, randomly,
arbitrarily, by chance, willy-nilly,
unsystematically

randy ADJECTIVE (*informal*)
= **lustful**, hot, turned-on (*slang*),

aroused, horny (*slang*), amorous, lascivious

range NOUN 1 = **series**, variety, selection, assortment, lot, collection, gamut 2 = **limits**, reach 3 = **scope**, area, bounds, province, orbit, radius
▷ VERB 1 = **vary**, run, reach, extend, stretch 2 = **roam**, wander, rove, ramble, traverse

rank¹ NOUN 1 = **status**, level, position, grade, order, sort, type, division 2 = **class**, caste 3 = **row**, line, file, column, group, range, series, tier
▷ VERB 1 = **order**, dispose 2 = **arrange**, sort, line up, array, align

rank² ADJECTIVE 1 = **absolute**, complete, total, gross, sheer, utter, thorough, blatant 2 = **foul**, bad, offensive, disgusting, revolting, stinking, noxious, rancid, festy (*Austral. slang*) 3 = **abundant**, lush, luxuriant, dense, profuse

ransom NOUN = **payment**, money, price, payoff

rant VERB = **shout**, roar, yell, rave, cry, declaim

rap VERB = **hit**, strike, knock, crack, tap
▷ NOUN 1 = **blow**, knock, crack, tap, clout (*informal*) 2 (*slang*) = **rebuke**, blame, responsibility, punishment

rape VERB = **sexually assault**, violate, abuse, ravish, force, outrage
▷ NOUN = **sexual assault**, violation, ravishment, outrage

rapid ADJECTIVE 1 = **sudden**, prompt, speedy, express, swift ≠ gradual 2 = **quick**, fast, hurried, swift, brisk, hasty ≠ slow

rapidly ADVERB = **quickly**, fast, swiftly, briskly, promptly, hastily, hurriedly, speedily

rare ADJECTIVE 1 = **uncommon**, unusual, few, strange, scarce, singular, sparse, infrequent ≠ common 2 = **superb**, great, fine, excellent, superlative, choice, peerless

rarely ADVERB = **seldom**, hardly, hardly ever, infrequently ≠ often
● **WORD POWER**
● Since the meaning of *rarely* is
● 'hardly ever', the combination
● *rarely ever* is repetitive and
● should be avoided in careful
● writing, even though you may
● sometimes hear this phrase
● used in informal speech.

raring ADJECTIVE ▷ PHRASE:
raring to = **eager to**, impatient to, longing to, ready to, keen to, desperate to, enthusiastic to

rarity NOUN 1 = **curio**, find, treasure, gem, collector's item 2 = **uncommonness**, scarcity, infrequency, unusualness, shortage, strangeness, sparseness

rash¹ ADJECTIVE = **reckless**, hasty, impulsive, imprudent, careless, ill-advised, foolhardy, impetuous ≠ cautious

rash² NOUN 1 = **outbreak of spots**, (skin) eruption 2 = **spate**, series, wave, flood, plague, outbreak

r

rate NOUN 1 = **speed**, pace, tempo, velocity, frequency 2 = **degree**, standard, scale, proportion, ratio 3 = **charge**, price, cost, fee, figure ▷ VERB 1 = **evaluate**, consider, rank, reckon, value, measure, estimate, count 2 = **deserve**, merit, be entitled to, be worthy of ▷ PHRASE: **at any rate** = **in any case**, anyway, anyhow, at all events

rather ADVERB 1 = **preferably**, sooner, more readily, more willingly 2 = **to some extent**, quite, a little, fairly, relatively, somewhat, moderately, to some degree

● **WORD POWER**
● It is acceptable to use either
● *would rather* or *had rather* in
● sentences such as I *would rather*
● (or *had rather*) *see a film than a*
● *play. Had rather*, however, is less
● common than *would rather*, and
● sounds a little old-fashioned
● nowadays.

ratify VERB = **approve**, establish, confirm, sanction, endorse, uphold, authorize, affirm ≠ annul

rating NOUN = **position**, placing, rate, order, class, degree, rank, status

ratio NOUN = **proportion**, rate, relation, percentage, fraction

ration NOUN = **allowance**, quota, allotment, helping, part, share, measure, portion ▷ VERB = **limit**, control, restrict, budget

rational ADJECTIVE = **sensible**, sound, wise, reasonable, intelligent, realistic, logical, sane, grounded ≠ insane

rationale NOUN = **reason**, grounds, theory, principle, philosophy, logic, motivation, raison d'être (*French*)

rattle VERB 1 = **clatter**, bang, jangle 2 = **shake**, jolt, vibrate, bounce, jar 3 (*informal*) = **fluster**, shake, upset, disturb, disconcert, perturb, faze

ravage VERB = **destroy**, ruin, devastate, spoil, demolish, ransack, lay waste, despoil ▷ NOUN *often plural* = **damage**, destruction, devastation, ruin, havoc, ruination, spoliation

rave VERB 1 = **rant**, rage, roar, go mad (*informal*), babble, be delirious 2 (*informal*) = **enthuse**, praise, gush, be mad about (*informal*), be wild about (*informal*)

raving ADJECTIVE = **mad**, wild, crazy, hysterical, insane, irrational, crazed, delirious, berko (*Austral. slang*), off the air (*Austral. slang*)

raw ADJECTIVE 1 = **unrefined**, natural, crude, unprocessed, basic, rough, coarse, unfinished ≠ refined 2 = **uncooked**, natural, fresh ≠ cooked 3 = **inexperienced**, new, green, immature, callow ≠ experienced 4 = **chilly**, biting, cold, freezing, bitter, piercing, parky (*Brit. informal*)

ray NOUN = **beam**, bar, flash, shaft, gleam

re PREPOSITION = **concerning**, about, regarding, with regard to, with reference to, apropos
● WORD POWER
● In contexts such as *re your letter*,
● *your remarks have been noted* or *he*
● *spoke to me re your complaint*, *re* is
● common in business or official
● correspondence. In spoken
● and in general written English
● *with reference to* is preferable in
● the former case and *about* or
● *concerning* in the latter. Even in
● business correspondence, the
● use of *re* is often restricted to
● the letter heading.

reach VERB 1 = **arrive at**, get to, make, attain 2 = **attain**, get to 3 = **touch**, grasp, extend to, stretch to, contact 4 = **contact**, get in touch with, get through to, communicate with, get hold of
▷ NOUN 1 = **grasp**, range, distance, stretch, capacity, extent, extension, scope 2 = **jurisdiction**, power, influence

react VERB = **respond**, act, proceed, behave

reaction NOUN 1 = **response**, answer, reply 2 = **counteraction**, backlash, recoil
3 = **conservatism**, the right
● WORD POWER
● Some people say that *reaction*
● should always refer to an
● instant response to something
● (as in *his reaction was one of*
● *amazement*), and that this word
● should not be used to refer to
● a considered response given in

● the form of a statement (as in
● *the Minister gave his reaction to*
● *the court's decision*). Use *response*
● instead.

reactionary
ADJECTIVE = **conservative**, right-wing ≠ radical
▷ NOUN = **conservative**, die-hard, right-winger ≠ radical

read VERB 1 = **scan**, study, look at, pore over, peruse 2 = **understand**, interpret, comprehend, construe, decipher, see, discover 3 = **register**, show, record, display, indicate

readily ADVERB 1 = **willingly**, freely, quickly, gladly, eagerly ≠ reluctantly 2 = **promptly**, quickly, easily, smoothly, effortlessly, speedily, unhesitatingly ≠ with difficulty

readiness NOUN 1 = **willingness**, eagerness, keenness
2 = **promptness**, facility, ease, dexterity, adroitness

reading NOUN 1 = **perusal**, study, examination, inspection, scrutiny 2 = **learning**, education, knowledge, scholarship, erudition 3 = **recital**, performance, lesson, sermon 4 = **interpretation**, version, impression, grasp

ready ADJECTIVE 1 = **prepared**, set, primed, organized ≠ unprepared 2 = **completed**, arranged 3 = **mature**, ripe, mellow, ripened, seasoned 4 = **willing**, happy, glad, disposed, keen, eager, inclined, prone ≠ reluctant 5 = **prompt**, smart, quick, bright, sharp, keen,

r

alert, clever ≠ slow **6** = **available**, handy, present, near, accessible, convenient ≠ unavailable

real ADJECTIVE **1** = **true**, genuine, sincere, factual, dinkum (*Austral. & N.Z. informal*), unfeigned **2** = **genuine**, authentic, dinkum (*Austral. & N.Z. informal*) ≠ fake **3** = **proper**, true, valid **4** = **true**, actual **5** = **typical**, true, genuine, sincere, dinkum (*Austral. & N.Z. informal*), unfeigned **6** = **complete**, total, perfect, utter, thorough

realistic ADJECTIVE **1** = **practical**, real, sensible, common-sense, down-to-earth, matter-of-fact, level-headed, grounded ≠ impractical **2** = **attainable**, sensible **3** = **lifelike**, true to life, authentic, true, natural, genuine, faithful

reality NOUN **1** = **fact**, truth, realism, validity, verity, actuality **2** = **truth**, fact, actuality

realization NOUN **1** = **awareness**, understanding, recognition, perception, grasp, conception, comprehension, cognizance **2** = **achievement**, accomplishment, fulfilment

realize VERB **1** = **become aware of**, understand, take in, grasp, comprehend, get the message **2** = **fulfil**, achieve, accomplish, make real **3** = **achieve**, do, effect, complete, perform, fulfil, accomplish, carry out *or* through

really ADVERB **1** = **certainly**, genuinely, positively, surely **2** = **truly**, actually, in fact, indeed, in actuality

realm NOUN **1** = **field**, world, area, province, sphere, department, branch, territory **2** = **kingdom**, country, empire, land, domain, dominion

reap VERB **1** = **get**, gain, obtain, acquire, derive **2** = **collect**, gather, bring in, harvest, garner, cut

rear¹ NOUN **1** = **back part**, back ≠ front **2** = **back**, end, tail, rearguard, tail end
▷ MODIFIER = **back**, hind, last, following ≠ front

rear² VERB **1** = **bring up**, raise, educate, train, foster, nurture **2** = **breed**, keep **3** *often with* **up** *or* **over** = **rise**, tower, soar, loom

reason NOUN **1** = **cause**, grounds, purpose, motive, goal, aim, object, intention **2** = **sense**, mind, understanding, judgment, logic, intellect, sanity, rationality ≠ emotion
▷ VERB = **deduce**, conclude, work out, make out, infer, think
▷ PHRASE: **reason with someone** = **persuade**, bring round, urge, win over, prevail upon (*informal*), talk into *or* out of

● **WORD POWER**
● Many people object to the
● expression *the reason is*
● *because*, on the grounds that
● it is repetitive. It is therefore
● advisable to use either *this is*
● *because* or *the reason is that*.

reasonable ADJECTIVE

1 = **sensible**, sound, practical, wise, logical, sober, plausible, sane, grounded ≠ irrational 2 = **fair**, just, right, moderate, equitable, tenable ≠ unfair 3 = **within reason**, fit, proper ≠ impossible 4 = **low**, cheap, competitive, moderate, modest, inexpensive 5 = **average**, fair, moderate, modest, O.K. or okay (*informal*)

reassure VERB = **encourage**, comfort, hearten, gee up, restore confidence to, put or set your mind at rest

rebate NOUN = **refund**, discount, reduction, bonus, allowance, deduction

rebel NOUN 1 = **revolutionary**, insurgent, secessionist, revolutionist 2 = **nonconformist**, dissenter, heretic, apostate, schismatic
  ▷ VERB 1 = **revolt**, resist, rise up, mutiny 2 = **defy**, dissent, disobey
  ▷ MODIFIER = **rebellious**, revolutionary, insurgent, insurrectionary

rebellion NOUN 1 = **resistance**, rising, revolution, revolt, uprising, mutiny 2 = **nonconformity**, defiance, heresy, schism

rebellious ADJECTIVE
  1 = **defiant**, difficult, resistant, unmanageable, refractory ≠ obedient 2 = **revolutionary**, rebel, disorderly, unruly, insurgent, disloyal, seditious, mutinous ≠ obedient

rebound VERB 1 = **bounce**, ricochet, recoil 2 = **misfire**, backfire, recoil, boomerang

rebuff VERB = **reject**, refuse, turn down, cut, slight, snub, spurn, knock back (*slang*) ≠ encourage
  ▷ NOUN = **rejection**, snub, knock-back, slight, refusal, repulse, cold shoulder, slap in the face (*informal*) ≠ encouragement

rebuke VERB = **scold**, censure, reprimand, castigate, chide, dress down (*informal*), admonish, tell off (*informal*) ≠ praise
  ▷ NOUN = **scolding**, censure, reprimand, row, dressing down (*informal*), telling-off (*informal*), admonition ≠ praise

recall VERB 1 = **recollect**, remember, evoke, call to mind 2 = **call back** 3 = **annul**, withdraw, cancel, repeal, revoke, retract, countermand
  ▷ NOUN 1 = **recollection**, memory, remembrance 2 = **annulment**, withdrawal, repeal, cancellation, retraction, rescindment

recede VERB = **fall back**, withdraw, retreat, return, retire, regress

receipt NOUN 1 = **sales slip**, proof of purchase, counterfoil 2 = **receiving**, delivery, reception, acceptance

receive VERB 1 = **get**, accept, be given, pick up, collect, obtain, acquire, take 2 = **experience**, suffer, bear, encounter, sustain, undergo 3 = **greet**, meet, admit, welcome, entertain, accommodate

recent ADJECTIVE = **new**, modern, up-to-date, late, current, fresh, novel, present-day ≠ old

recently ADVERB = **not long ago**, newly, lately, currently, freshly, of late, latterly

reception NOUN 1 = **party**, gathering, get-together, social gathering, function, celebration, festivity, soirée 2 = **response**, reaction, acknowledgment, treatment, welcome, greeting

recess NOUN 1 = **break**, rest, holiday, interval, vacation, respite, intermission, schoolie (*Austral.*) 2 = **alcove**, corner, bay, hollow, niche, nook

recession NOUN = **depression**, drop, decline, slump ≠ boom

recipe NOUN = **directions**, instructions, ingredients

recital NOUN 1 = **performance**, rendering, rehearsal, reading 2 = **account**, telling, statement, relation, narrative 3 = **recitation**

recite VERB = **perform**, deliver, repeat, declaim

reckless ADJECTIVE = **careless**, wild, rash, precipitate, hasty, mindless, headlong, thoughtless ≠ cautious

reckon VERB 1 (*informal*) = **think**, believe, suppose, imagine, assume, guess (*informal, chiefly U.S. & Canad.*) 2 = **consider**, rate, account, judge, regard, count, esteem, deem 3 = **count**, figure, total, calculate, compute, add up, tally, number

reckoning NOUN = **count**, estimate, calculation, addition

reclaim VERB 1 = **retrieve**, regain 2 = **regain**, salvage, recapture

recognition NOUN 1 = **identification**, recollection, discovery, remembrance 2 = **acceptance**, admission, allowance, confession

recognize VERB 1 = **identify**, know, place, remember, spot, notice, recall, recollect 2 = **acknowledge**, allow, accept, admit, grant, concede ≠ ignore 3 = **appreciate**, respect, notice

recollection NOUN = **memory**, recall, impression, remembrance, reminiscence

recommend VERB 1 = **advocate**, suggest, propose, approve, endorse, commend ≠ disapprove of 2 = **put forward**, approve, endorse, commend, praise 3 = **advise**, suggest, advance, propose, counsel, advocate, prescribe, put forward

recommendation NOUN 1 = **advice**, proposal, suggestion, counsel 2 = **commendation**, reference, praise, sanction, approval, endorsement, advocacy, testimonial

reconcile VERB 1 = **resolve**, settle, square, adjust, compose, rectify, put to rights 2 = **reunite**, bring back together, conciliate 3 = **make peace between**, reunite, propitiate

reconciliation NOUN = **reunion**, conciliation, pacification, reconcilement ≠ separation

reconsider VERB = **rethink**, review, revise, think again, reassess

reconstruct VERB 1 = **rebuild**, restore, recreate, remake, renovate, remodel, regenerate 2 = **build up a picture of**, build up, piece together, deduce

record NOUN 1 = **document**, file, register, log, report, account, entry, journal, blog (*informal*) 2 = **evidence**, trace, documentation, testimony, witness 3 = **disc**, single, album, LP, vinyl 4 = **background**, history, performance, career ▷ VERB 1 = **set down**, minute, note, enter, document, register, log, chronicle 2 = **make a recording of**, video, tape, video-tape, tape-record 3 = **register**, show, indicate, give evidence of

recorder NOUN = **chronicler**, archivist, historian, clerk, scribe, diarist

recording NOUN = **record**, video, tape, disc

recount VERB = **tell**, report, describe, relate, repeat, depict, recite, narrate

recover VERB 1 = **get better**, improve, get well, recuperate, heal, revive, mend, convalesce ≠ relapse 2 = **rally** 3 = **save**, rescue, retrieve, salvage, reclaim ≠ abandon 4 = **recoup**, restore, get back, regain, retrieve, reclaim, redeem, recapture ≠ lose

recovery NOUN 1 = **improvement**, healing,

revival, mending, recuperation, convalescence 2 = **retrieval**, repossession, reclamation, restoration

recreation NOUN = **leisure**, play, sport, fun, entertainment, relaxation, enjoyment, amusement, me-time

recruit VERB 1 = **gather**, obtain, engage, procure 2 = **assemble**, raise, levy, muster, mobilize 3 = **enlist**, draft, enrol ≠ dismiss ▷ NOUN = **beginner**, trainee, apprentice, novice, convert, initiate, helper, learner

recur VERB = **happen again**, return, repeat, persist, revert, reappear, come again

recycle VERB = **reprocess**, reuse, salvage, reclaim, save

red NOUN = **crimson**, scarlet, ruby, vermilion, cherry, coral, carmine ▷ ADJECTIVE 1 = **crimson**, scarlet, ruby, vermilion, cherry, coral, carmine 2 = **flushed**, embarrassed, blushing, florid, shamefaced 3 (*of hair*) = **chestnut**, reddish, flame-coloured, sandy, Titian, carroty, ginger ▷ PHRASES: **in the red** (*informal*) = **in debt**, insolvent, in arrears, overdrawn; **see red** (*informal*) = **lose your temper**, lose it (*informal*), go mad (*informal*), crack up (*informal*), lose the plot (*informal*), go ballistic (*slang, chiefly U.S.*), fly off the handle (*informal*), blow your top

● **WORD POWER**

● The symbolism of *red* can be

r

● **SHADES OF RED**

● auburn
● baby pink
● burgundy
● burnt sienna
● cardinal red
● carmine
● carnation
● carroty
● cerise
● cherry
● chestnut
● cinnabar
● copper *or* coppery
● coral
● crimson
● damask
● flame

● flesh
● foxy
● fuchsia
● ginger
● henna
● liver
● magenta
● maroon
● mulberry
● old rose
● oxblood
● oyster pink
● peach
● pink
● plum
● poppy
● puce

● raspberry
● rose
● roseate
● rosy
● ruby
● russet
● rust
● sandy
● scarlet
● strawberry
● tea rose
● terracotta
● Titian
● vermilion
● wine

seen in the many phrases involving the word. The colour of fire in nature, red has become associated with fiery emotional states in people. Passion is conceptualized in the phrase *red-hot*, meaning very hot, exciting, or passionate, as is anger in the expression *see red*, meaning lose your temper. The colour of blood and the physical effects of flushing have led to the association of red with health in *rose-red* and *ruddy*; virility in *red-blooded*; shame in *red-faced*; and soreness in *red-rimmed*. Through this combination of meanings, red symbolizes danger and risk in a *red light* in traffic, or sex in a *red light*

district in a town. The phrase *in the red*, meaning 'in debt' also has this negative connotation and stems historically from the red ink used to record debits in an account. From the colour of a communist party badge, red means left-wing politics and socialism in the phrase *red army*.

redeem VERB **1** = **reinstate**, absolve, restore to favour

2 = **make up for**, compensate for, atone for, make amends for

3 = **buy back**, recover, regain, retrieve, reclaim, repurchase

4 = **save**, free, deliver, liberate, ransom, emancipate

redemption NOUN

1 = **compensation**, amends, reparation, atonement

2 = **salvation**, release, rescue, liberation, emancipation, deliverance

redress VERB **1** = **make amends for**, make up for, compensate for **2** = **put right**, balance, correct, adjust, regulate, rectify, even up ▷ NOUN = **amends**, payment, compensation, reparation, atonement, recompense

reduce VERB **1** = **lessen**, cut, lower, moderate, weaken, diminish, decrease, cut down, kennet (*Austral. slang*), jeff (*Austral. slang*) ≠ increase **2** = **degrade**, downgrade, break, humble, bring low ≠ promote

reduced ADJECTIVE = **impoverished**, broke (*informal*), hard up (*informal*), short, needy, penniless, destitute, poverty-stricken

redundancy NOUN **1** = **layoff**, sacking, dismissal **2** = **unemployment**, the sack (*informal*), the axe (*informal*), joblessness

redundant ADJECTIVE = **superfluous**, extra, surplus, unnecessary, unwanted, inessential, supernumerary ≠ essential

reel VERB **1** = **stagger**, rock, roll, pitch, sway, lurch **2** = **whirl**, spin, revolve, swirl

refer VERB **1** = **direct**, point, send, guide ▷ PHRASE: **refer to something** *or* **someone 1** = **allude to**, mention, cite, speak of, bring up **2** = **relate to**,

concern, apply to, pertain to, be relevant to **3** = **consult**, go, apply, turn to, look up

● **WORD POWER**
● It is usually unnecessary to
● add *back* to the verb *refer*, since
● the sense of *back* is already
● contained in the *re-* part of this
● word. For example, you might
● say *This refers to* (not *refers back to*) *what has already been said*.
● *Refer back* is only considered
● acceptable when used to mean
● 'return a document or question
● to the person it came from for
● further consideration', as in *he
● referred the matter back to me.*

referee NOUN = **umpire**, umpie (*Austral. slang*), judge, ref (*informal*), arbiter, arbitrator, adjudicator ▷ VERB = **umpire**, judge, mediate, adjudicate, arbitrate

reference NOUN **1** = **allusion**, note, mention, quotation **2** = **citation 3** = **testimonial**, recommendation, credentials, endorsement, character reference

referendum NOUN = **public vote**, popular vote, plebiscite

refine VERB **1** = **purify**, process, filter, cleanse, clarify, distil **2** = **improve**, perfect, polish, hone

refined ADJECTIVE **1** = **purified**, processed, pure, filtered, clean, clarified, distilled ≠ unrefined **2** = **cultured**, polished, elegant, polite, cultivated, civilized, well-bred ≠ coarse **3** = **discerning**, fine, sensitive, delicate, precise, discriminating, fastidious

reflect VERB 1 = **show**, reveal, display, indicate, demonstrate, manifest 2 = **throw back**, return, mirror, echo, reproduce 3 *usually followed by* **on** = **consider**, think, muse, ponder, meditate, ruminate, cogitate, wonder

reflection NOUN 1 = **image**, echo, mirror image 2 = **consideration**, thinking, thought, idea, opinion, observation, musing, meditation

reflective ADJECTIVE = **thoughtful**, contemplative, meditative, pensive

reform NOUN = **improvement**, amendment, rehabilitation, betterment
  ▷ VERB 1 = **improve**, correct, restore, amend, mend, rectify 2 = **mend your ways**, go straight (*informal*), shape up (*informal*), turn over a new leaf, clean up your act (*informal*), pull your socks up (*Brit. informal*)

refrain¹ VERB = **stop**, avoid, cease, renounce, abstain, leave off, desist, forbear

refrain² NOUN = **chorus**, tune, melody

refresh VERB 1 = **revive**, freshen, revitalize, stimulate, brace, enliven, invigorate 2 = **stimulate**, prompt, renew, jog

refreshing ADJECTIVE 1 = **new**, original, novel 2 = **stimulating**, fresh, bracing, invigorating ≠ tiring

refreshment plural = **food and drink**, drinks, snacks, titbits, kai

(*N.Z. informal*)

refuge NOUN 1 = **protection**, shelter, asylum 2 = **haven**, retreat, sanctuary, hide-out

refugee NOUN = **exile**, émigré, displaced person, escapee

refund NOUN = **repayment**, reimbursement, return
  ▷ VERB = **repay**, return, restore, pay back, reimburse

refurbish VERB = **renovate**, restore, repair, clean up, overhaul, revamp, mend, do up (*informal*)

refusal NOUN = **rejection**, denial, rebuff, knock-back (*slang*)

refuse¹ VERB 1 = **decline**, reject, turn down, say no to 2 = **deny**, decline, withhold ≠ allow

refuse² NOUN = **rubbish**, waste, junk (*informal*), litter, garbage, trash

regain VERB 1 = **recover**, get back, retrieve, recapture, win back, take back, recoup 2 = **get back to**, return to, reach again

regal ADJECTIVE = **royal**, majestic, kingly or queenly, noble, princely, magnificent

regard VERB 1 = **consider**, see, rate, view, judge, think of, esteem, deem 2 = **look at**, view, eye, watch, observe, clock (*Brit. slang*), check out (*informal*), gaze at
  ▷ NOUN 1 = **respect**, esteem, thought, concern, care, consideration 2 = **look**, gaze, scrutiny, stare, glance 3 *plural* = **good wishes**, respects, greetings, compliments, best wishes ▷ PHRASE: **as regards**

= **concerning**, regarding, relating to, pertaining to

● **WORD POWER**
● The word *regard* in the
● expression *with regard to* is
● singular, and has no s at the
● end. People often make the
● mistake of saying *with regards*
● *to*, perhaps being influenced by
● the phrase *as regards*.

regarding PREPOSITION
= **concerning**, about, on the subject of, re, respecting, as regards, with reference to, in or with regard to

regardless ADVERB = **in spite of everything**, anyway, nevertheless, in any case
▷ ADJECTIVE *with* **of**
= **irrespective of**, heedless of, unmindful of

regime NOUN 1 = **government**, rule, management, leadership, reign 2 = **plan**, course, system, policy, programme, scheme, regimen

region NOUN = **area**, place, part, quarter, section, sector, district, territory

regional ADJECTIVE = **local**, district, provincial, parochial, zonal

register NOUN = **list**, record, roll, file, diary, catalogue, log, archives
▷ VERB 1 = **enrol**, enlist, list, note, enter 2 = **record**, catalogue, chronicle 3 = **indicate**, show 4 = **show**, mark, indicate, manifest 5 = **express**, show, reveal, display, exhibit

regret VERB 1 = **be** or **feel sorry about**, rue, deplore, bemoan, repent (of), bewail ≠ be satisfied with 2 = **mourn**, miss, grieve for or over
▷ NOUN 1 = **remorse**, compunction, bitterness, repentance, contrition, penitence 2 = **sorrow** ≠ satisfaction

regular ADJECTIVE 1 = **frequent** 2 = **normal**, common, usual, ordinary, typical, routine, customary, habitual ≠ infrequent 3 = **steady**, consistent 4 = **even**, level, balanced, straight, flat, fixed, smooth, uniform ≠ uneven

regulate VERB 1 = **control**, run, rule, manage, direct, guide, handle, govern 2 = **moderate**, control, modulate, fit, tune, adjust

regulation NOUN 1 = **rule**, order, law, dictate, decree, statute, edict, precept 2 = **control**, government, management, direction, supervision

rehearsal NOUN = **practice**, rehearsing, run-through, preparation, drill

rehearse VERB = **practise**, prepare, run through, go over, train, repeat, drill, recite

reign VERB 1 = **be supreme**, prevail, predominate, hold sway 2 = **rule**, govern, be in power, influence, command
▷ NOUN = **rule**, power, control, command, monarchy, dominion

● **WORD POWER**
● The words *rein* and *reign* should

- not be confused; note the
- correct spellings in *he gave full*
- *rein to his feelings* (not *reign*); and
- *it will be necessary to rein in public*
- *spending* (not *reign in*).

rein NOUN = **control**, harness, bridle, hold, check, brake, curb, restraint

reincarnation NOUN = **rebirth**

reinforce VERB 1 = **support**, strengthen, fortify, toughen, stress, prop, supplement, emphasize 2 = **increase**, extend, add to, strengthen, supplement

reinforcement NOUN
1 = **strengthening**, increase, fortification, augmentation
2 = **support**, stay, prop, brace, buttress 3 *plural* = **reserves**, support, auxiliaries, additional *or* fresh troops

reinstate VERB = **restore**, recall, re-establish, return

reiterate VERB (*formal*) = **repeat**, restate, say again, do again

reject VERB 1 = **rebuff**, jilt, turn down, spurn, refuse, say no to, repulse ≠ accept 2 = **deny**, exclude, veto, relinquish, renounce, disallow, forsake, disown ≠ approve 3 = **discard**, decline, eliminate, scrap, jettison, throw away *or* out ≠ accept
▷ NOUN 1 = **castoff**, second, discard ≠ treasure 2 = **failure**, loser, flop

rejection NOUN 1 = **denial**, veto, dismissal, exclusion, disowning, thumbs down, renunciation, repudiation ≠ approval

2 = **rebuff**, refusal, knock-back (*slang*), kick in the teeth (*slang*), brushoff (*slang*) ≠ acceptance

rejoice VERB = **be glad**, celebrate, be happy, glory, be overjoyed, exult ≠ lament

rejoin VERB = **reply**, answer, respond, retort, riposte

relate VERB 1 = **tell**, recount, report, detail, describe, recite, narrate ▷ PHRASE: **relate to something** *or* **someone**
1 = **concern**, refer to, apply to, have to do with, pertain to, be relevant to 2 = **connect with**, associate with, link with, couple with, join with, correlate to

related ADJECTIVE 1 = **associated**, linked, joint, connected, affiliated, akin, interconnected ≠ unconnected 2 = **akin**, kindred ≠ unrelated

relation NOUN 1 = **similarity**, link, bearing, bond, comparison, correlation, connection
2 = **relative**, kin, kinsman *or* kinswoman, rellie (*Austral. slang*)
▷ PLURAL NOUN 1 = **dealings**, relationship, affairs, contact, connections, interaction, intercourse 2 = **family**, relatives, tribe, clan, kin, kindred, kinsmen, kinsfolk, ainga (*N.Z.*), rellie (*Austral. slang*)

relationship NOUN
1 = **association**, bond, connection, affinity, rapport, kinship 2 = **affair**, romance, liaison, amour, intrigue
3 = **connection**, link, parallel,

similarity, tie-up, correlation

relative NOUN = **relation**, kinsman or kinswoman, member of your or the family, rellie (*Austral. slang*)

▷ ADJECTIVE 1 = **comparative** 2 = **corresponding** 3 *with* **to** = **in proportion to**, proportionate to

relatively ADVERB = **comparatively**, rather, somewhat

relax VERB 1 = **be** or **feel at ease**, chill out (*slang, chiefly U.S.*), take it easy, lighten up (*slang*), outspan (*S. African*) ≠ be alarmed 2 = **calm down**, calm, unwind 3 = **make less tense**, rest 4 = **lessen**, reduce, ease, relieve, weaken, loosen, let up, slacken ≠ tighten 5 = **moderate**, ease, relieve, weaken, slacken ≠ tighten up

relaxation NOUN = **leisure**, rest, fun, pleasure, recreation, enjoyment, me-time

relay VERB = **broadcast**, carry, spread, communicate, transmit, send out

release VERB 1 = **set free**, free, discharge, liberate, drop, loose, undo, extricate ≠ imprison 2 = **acquit**, let go, let off, exonerate, absolve 3 = **issue**, publish, make public, make known, launch, distribute, put out, circulate ≠ withhold

▷ NOUN 1 = **liberation**, freedom, liberty, discharge, emancipation, deliverance ≠ imprisonment 2 = **acquittal**, exemption, absolution, exoneration

3 = **issue**, publication, proclamation

relegate VERB = **demote**, degrade, downgrade

relentless ADJECTIVE 1 = **merciless**, fierce, cruel, ruthless, unrelenting, implacable, remorseless, pitiless ≠ merciful 2 = **unremitting**, persistent, unrelenting, incessant, nonstop, unrelieved

relevant ADJECTIVE = **significant**, appropriate, related, fitting, to the point, apt, pertinent, apposite ≠ irrelevant

reliable ADJECTIVE 1 = **dependable**, trustworthy, sure, sound, true, faithful, staunch ≠ unreliable 2 = **safe**, dependable 3 = **definitive**, sound, dependable, trustworthy

reliance NOUN 1 = **dependency**, dependence 2 = **trust**, confidence, belief, faith

relic NOUN = **remnant**, vestige, memento, trace, fragment, souvenir, keepsake

relief NOUN 1 = **ease**, release, comfort, cure, remedy, solace, deliverance, mitigation 2 = **rest**, respite, relaxation, break, breather (*informal*) 3 = **aid**, help, support, assistance, succour

relieve VERB 1 = **ease**, soothe, alleviate, relax, comfort, calm, cure, soften ≠ intensify 2 = **help**, support, aid, sustain, assist, succour

religion NOUN = **belief**, faith, theology, creed

r

religious ADJECTIVE 1 = **spiritual**, holy, sacred, devotional
2 = **conscientious**, faithful, rigid, meticulous, scrupulous, punctilious

relinquish VERB (*formal*) = **give up**, leave, drop, abandon, surrender, let go, renounce, forsake

relish VERB 1 = **enjoy**, like, savour, revel in ≠ dislike 2 = **look forward to**, fancy, delight in
▷ NOUN 1 = **enjoyment**, liking, love, taste, fancy, penchant, fondness, gusto ≠ distaste
2 = **condiment**, seasoning, sauce

reluctance NOUN
= **unwillingness**, dislike, loathing, distaste, aversion, disinclination, repugnance

reluctant ADJECTIVE = **unwilling**, hesitant, loath, disinclined, unenthusiastic ≠ willing

● **WORD POWER**
● *Reticent* is quite commonly
● used nowadays as a synonym
● of *reluctant* and followed by *to*
● and a verb. In careful writing
● it is advisable to avoid this
● use, since many people would
● regard it as mistaken.

rely on VERB 1 = **depend on**, lean on 2 = **be confident of**, bank on, trust, count on, bet on

remain VERB 1 = **stay**, continue, go on, stand, dwell 2 = **stay**

● **RELIGION**
● animism
● Babi *or* Babism
● Baha'ism
● Buddhism
● Christianity
● Confucianism
● druidism
● heliolatry
● Hinduism *or* Hindooism
● Islam
● Jainism
● Judaism

● Macumba
● Manichaeism *or* Manicheism
● Mithraism *or* Mithraicism
● Orphism
● paganism
● Rastafarianism
● Ryobu Shinto
● Santeria
● Satanism
● Scientology (*trademark*)

● shamanism
● Shango
● Shembe
● Shinto
● Sikhism
● Taoism
● voodoo *or* voodooism
● Yezidis
● Zoroastrianism *or* Zoroastrism

● **Religious festivals**
● Advent
● Al Hijrah
● Ascension Day
● Ash Wednesday

● Baisakhi
● Bodhi Day
● Candlemas
● Chanukah *or*

Hanukkah
● Ching Ming
● Christmas
● Corpus Christi

- Day of Atonement
- Dhammacakka
- Diwali
- Dragon Boat Festival
- Dussehra
- Easter
- Eid ul-Adha *or* Id-ul-Adha
- Eid ul-Fitr *or* Id-ul-Fitr
- Epiphany
- Feast of Tabernacles
- Good Friday
- Guru Nanak's Birthday
- Hirja
- Hola Mohalla
- Holi
- Janamashtami
- Lailat ul-Barah
- Lailat ul-Isra Wal Mi'raj
- Lailat ul-Qadr
- Lent
- Mahashivaratri
- Maundy Thursday
- Michaelmas
- Moon Festival
- Palm Sunday
- Passion Sunday
- Passover
- Pentecost
- Pesach
- Purim
- Quadragesima
- Quinquagesima
- Raksha Bandhan
- Ramadan
- Rama Naumi
- Rogation
- Rosh Hashanah
- Septuagesima
- Sexagesima
- Shavuot
- Shrove Tuesday
- Sukkoth *or* Succoth
- Trinity
- Wesak
- Whitsun
- Winter Festival
- Yom Kippur
- Yuan Tan

behind, wait, delay ≠ go
3 = **continue**, be left, linger
remainder NOUN = **rest**, remains, balance, excess, surplus, remnant, residue, leavings
remains PLURAL NOUN
1 = **remnants**, leftovers, rest, debris, residue, dregs, leavings
2 = **relics** **3** = **corpse**, body, carcass, cadaver
remark VERB **1** = **comment**, say, state, reflect, mention, declare, observe, pass comment
2 = **notice**, note, observe, perceive, see, mark, make out, espy
▷ NOUN = **comment**, observation, reflection, statement, utterance
remarkable ADJECTIVE
= **extraordinary**, striking, outstanding, wonderful, rare, unusual, surprising, notable

≠ ordinary
remedy NOUN = **cure**, treatment, medicine, nostrum
▷ VERB = **put right**, rectify, fix, correct, set to rights
remember VERB **1** = **recall**, think back to, recollect, reminisce about, call to mind ≠ forget
2 = **bear in mind**, keep in mind
3 = **look back (on)**, commemorate
remembrance NOUN
1 = **commemoration**, memorial
2 = **souvenir**, token, reminder, monument, memento, keepsake
3 = **memory**, recollection, thought, recall, reminiscence
remind VERB = **jog your memory**, prompt, make you remember
reminiscent ADJECTIVE
= **suggestive**, evocative, similar
remnant NOUN = **remainder**, remains, trace, fragment, end,

rest, residue, leftovers

remorse NOUN = **regret**, shame, guilt, grief, sorrow, anguish, repentance, contrition

remote ADJECTIVE 1 = **distant**, far, isolated, out-of-the-way, secluded, inaccessible, in the middle of nowhere ≠ nearby 2 = **far**, distant 3 = **slight**, small, outside, unlikely, slim, faint, doubtful, dubious ≠ strong 4 = **aloof**, cold, reserved, withdrawn, distant, abstracted, detached, uncommunicative ≠ outgoing

removal NOUN 1 = **extraction**, withdrawal, uprooting, eradication, dislodgment, taking away *or* off *or* out 2 = **dismissal**, expulsion, elimination, ejection 3 = **move**, transfer, departure, relocation, flitting (*Scot. & Northern English dialect*)

remove VERB 1 = **take out**, withdraw, extract ≠ insert 2 = **take off** ≠ put on 3 = **erase**, eliminate, take out 4 = **dismiss**, eliminate, get rid of, discharge, abolish, expel, throw out, oust ≠ appoint 5 = **get rid of**, erase, eradicate, expunge 6 = **take away**, detach, displace ≠ put back 7 = **delete**, get rid of, erase, excise 8 = **move**, depart, relocate, flit (*Scot. & Northern English dialect*)

renaissance *or* **renascence** NOUN = **rebirth**, revival, restoration, renewal, resurgence, reappearance, reawakening

rend VERB (*literary*) = **tear**, rip, separate, wrench, rupture

render VERB 1 = **make**, cause to become, leave 2 = **provide**, give, pay, present, supply, submit, tender, hand out 3 = **represent**, portray, depict, do, give, play, act, perform

renew VERB 1 = **recommence**, continue, extend, repeat, resume, reopen, recreate, reaffirm 2 = **reaffirm**, resume, recommence 3 = **replace**, refresh, replenish, restock 4 = **restore**, repair, overhaul, mend, refurbish, renovate, refit, modernize

renounce VERB 1 = **disown**, quit, forsake, recant, forswear, abjure 2 = **disclaim**, deny, give up, relinquish, waive, abjure ≠ assert

renovate VERB = **restore**, repair, refurbish, do up (*informal*), renew, overhaul, refit, modernize

renowned ADJECTIVE = **famous**, noted, celebrated, well-known, distinguished, esteemed, notable, eminent ≠ unknown

rent¹ VERB 1 = **hire**, lease 2 = **let**, lease
▷ NOUN = **hire**, rental, lease, fee, payment

rent² NOUN 1 = **tear**, split, rip, slash, slit, gash, hole 2 = **opening**, hole

repair VERB 1 = **mend**, fix, restore, heal, patch, renovate, patch up ≠ damage 2 = **put right**, make up for, compensate for, rectify, redress
▷ NOUN 1 = **mend**, restoration, overhaul 2 = **darn**, mend, patch

3 = **condition**, state, form, shape (*informal*)

repay VERB = **pay back**, refund, settle up, return, square, compensate, reimburse, recompense

repeal VERB = **abolish**, reverse, revoke, annul, recall, cancel, invalidate, nullify ≠ pass
▷ NOUN = **abolition**, cancellation, annulment, invalidation, rescindment ≠ passing

repeat VERB **1** = **reiterate**, restate **2** = **retell**, echo, replay, reproduce, rerun, reshow
▷ NOUN **1** = **repetition**, echo, reiteration **2** = **rerun**, replay, reshowing

● **WORD POWER**
● Since the sense of *again* is
● already contained within the
● re- part of the word *repeat*, it
● is unnecessary to say that
● something is *repeated again*.

repeatedly ADVERB = **over and over**, often, frequently, many times

repel VERB **1** = **drive off**, fight, resist, parry, hold off, rebuff, ward off, repulse ≠ submit to **2** = **disgust**, offend, revolt, sicken, nauseate, gross out (*U.S. slang*) ≠ delight

repertoire NOUN = **range**, list, stock, supply, store, collection, repertory

repetition NOUN **1** = **recurrence**, repeating, echo **2** = **repeating**, replication, restatement, reiteration, tautology

replace VERB **1** = **take the place of**, follow, succeed, oust, take over from, supersede, supplant **2** = **substitute**, change, exchange, switch, swap **3** = **put back**, restore

replacement NOUN
1 = **replacing 2** = **successor**, double, substitute, stand-in, proxy, surrogate, understudy

replica NOUN **1** = **reproduction**, model, copy, imitation, facsimile, carbon copy ≠ original **2** = **duplicate**, copy, carbon copy

replicate VERB = **copy**, reproduce, recreate, mimic, duplicate, reduplicate

reply VERB = **answer**, respond, retort, counter, rejoin, retaliate, reciprocate
▷ NOUN = **answer**, response, reaction, counter, retort, retaliation, counterattack, rejoinder

report VERB **1** = **inform of**, communicate, recount **2** *often with* **on** = **communicate**, tell, state, detail, describe, relate, broadcast, pass on **3** = **present yourself**, come, appear, arrive, turn up
▷ NOUN **1** = **article**, story, piece, write-up **2** = **account**, record, statement, communication, description, narrative **3** *often plural* = **news**, word **4** = **bang**, sound, crack, noise, blast, boom, explosion, discharge **5** = **rumour**, talk, buzz, gossip, goss (*informal*), hearsay

r

reporter NOUN = **journalist**,
writer, correspondent, hack
(*derogatory*), pressman, journo
(*slang*)

represent VERB 1 = **act for**,
speak for 2 = **stand for**, serve
as 3 = **express**, correspond to,
symbolize, mean 4 = **exemplify**,
embody, symbolize, typify,
personify, epitomize 5 = **depict**,
show, describe, picture, illustrate,
outline, portray, denote

representation NOUN
1 = **picture**, model, image,
portrait, illustration, likeness
2 = **portrayal**, depiction, account,
description

representative NOUN
1 = **delegate**, member, agent,
deputy, proxy, spokesman *or*
spokeswoman 2 = **agent**,
salesman, rep, commercial
traveller
▷ ADJECTIVE 1 = **typical**,
characteristic, archetypal,
exemplary ≠ uncharacteristic
2 = **symbolic**

repress VERB 1 = **control**,
suppress, hold back, bottle up,
check, curb, restrain, inhibit
≠ release 2 = **hold back**, suppress,
stifle 3 = **subdue**, abuse, wrong,
persecute, quell, subjugate,
maltreat ≠ liberate

repression NOUN
1 = **subjugation**, control,
constraint, domination, tyranny,
despotism 2 = **suppression**,
crushing, quashing
3 = **inhibition**, control, restraint,

bottling up

reprieve VERB = **grant a stay of
execution to**, pardon, let off the
hook (*slang*)
▷ NOUN = **stay of execution**,
amnesty, pardon, remission,
deferment, postponement of
punishment

reproduce VERB 1 = **copy**,
recreate, replicate, duplicate,
match, mirror, echo, imitate
2 = **print**, copy 3 (*biology*) = **breed**,
procreate, multiply, spawn,
propagate

reproduction NOUN 1 = **copy**,
picture, print, replica, imitation,
duplicate, facsimile ≠ original
2 (*biology*) = **breeding**, increase,
generation, multiplication

Republican ADJECTIVE = **right-
wing**, Conservative
▷ NOUN = **right-winger**,
Conservative

reputation NOUN = **name**,
standing, character, esteem,
stature, renown, repute

request VERB 1 = **ask for**, appeal
for, put in for, demand, desire
2 = **invite**, entreat 3 = **seek**, ask
(for), solicit
▷ NOUN 1 = **appeal**, call, demand,
plea, desire, entreaty, suit
2 = **asking**, plea

require VERB 1 = **need**, crave,
want, miss, lack, wish, desire
2 = **order**, demand, command,
compel, exact, oblige, call upon,
insist upon 3 = **ask**

● WORD POWER
● The use of *require to* as in *I require*

- **REPTILES**
- adder
- agama
- agamid
- alligator
- amphisbaena
- anaconda or (*Caribbean*) camoodi
- asp
- bandy-bandy
- black snake or red-bellied black snake
- blind snake
- blue tongue
- boa
- boa constrictor
- box turtle
- brown snake or (*Austral.*) mallee snake
- bull snake or gopher snake
- bushmaster
- carpet snake or python
- cayman or caiman
- chameleon
- chuckwalla
- cobra
- constrictor
- copperhead
- coral snake
- crocodile
- death adder or deaf adder
- diamondback, diamondback terrapin, or diamondback turtle
- diamond snake or diamond python
- elapid
- fer-de-lance
- frill-necked lizard, frilled lizard, bicycle lizard, cycling lizard, or (*Austral. informal*) frillie
- gaboon viper
- garter snake
- gecko
- giant tortoise
- Gila monster
- glass snake
- goanna, bungarra (*Austral.*), or go (*Austral. informal*)
- grass snake
- green turtle
- harlequin snake
- hawksbill or hawksbill turtle
- hognose snake or puff adder
- horned toad or lizard
- horned viper
- iguana
- jew lizard, bearded lizard, or bearded dragon
- king cobra or hamadryad
- king snake
- Komodo dragon or Komodo lizard
- krait
- leatherback or (*Brit.*) leathery turtle
- lizard
- loggerhead or loggerhead turtle
- mamba
- massasauga
- milk snake
- monitor
- mud turtle
- ngarara (*N.Z.*)
- perentie or perenty
- pit viper
- puff adder
- python
- rat snake
- rattlesnake or (*U.S. & Canad. informal*) rattler
- rock snake, rock python, amethystine python, or Schneider python
- saltwater crocodile or (*Austral. informal*) saltie
- sand lizard
- sand viper
- sea snake
- sidewinder
- skink
- slowworm or blindworm
- smooth snake
- snake
- snapping turtle

r

- soft-shelled turtle
- taipan
- terrapin
- tiger snake
- tokay
- tortoise
- tree snake
- tuatara or (*technical*) sphenodon (*N.Z.*)
- turtle
- viper
- wall lizard
- water moccasin, moccasin, or cottonmouth
- water snake
- whip snake

to see the manager or *you require to complete a special form* is thought by many people to be incorrect. Useful alternatives are: *I need to see the manager* and *you are required to complete a special form*.

requirement NOUN = **necessity**, demand, stipulation, want, need, must, essential, prerequisite

rescue VERB 1 = **save**, get out, release, deliver, recover, liberate ≠ desert 2 = **salvage**, deliver, redeem
▷ NOUN = **saving**, salvage, deliverance, release, recovery, liberation, salvation, redemption

research NOUN = **investigation**, study, analysis, examination, probe, exploration
▷ VERB = **investigate**, study, examine, explore, probe, analyse

resemblance NOUN = **similarity**, correspondence, parallel, likeness, kinship, sameness, similitude ≠ dissimilarity

resemble VERB = **be like**, look like, mirror, parallel, be similar to, bear a resemblance to

resent VERB = **be bitter about**, object to, grudge, begrudge, take exception to, take offence at ≠ be content with

resentment NOUN = **bitterness**, indignation, ill feeling, ill will, grudge, animosity, pique, rancour

reservation NOUN 1 *often plural* = **doubt**, scruples, hesitancy
2 = **reserve**, territory, preserve, sanctuary

reserve VERB 1 = **book**, prearrange, engage 2 = **put by**, secure 3 = **keep**, hold, save, store, retain, set aside, stockpile, hoard
▷ NOUN 1 = **store**, fund, savings, stock, supply, reservoir, hoard, cache 2 = **park**, reservation, preserve, sanctuary, tract, forest park (*N.Z.*) 3 = **shyness**, silence, restraint, constraint, reticence, secretiveness, taciturnity
4 = **reservation**, doubt, delay, uncertainty, indecision, hesitancy, vacillation, irresolution
5 = **substitute**, extra, spare, fallback, auxiliary

reserved ADJECTIVE
1 = **uncommunicative**, retiring, silent, shy, restrained, secretive, reticent, taciturn ≠ uninhibited
2 = **set aside**, taken, kept, held, booked, retained, engaged, restricted

reservoir NOUN 1 = **lake**, pond, basin 2 = **store**, stock, source, supply, reserves, pool

r

reside VERB (*formal*) = **live**, lodge, dwell, stay, abide ≠ visit

residence NOUN = **home**, house, dwelling, place, flat, lodging, abode, habitation

resident NOUN 1 = **inhabitant**, citizen, local ≠ nonresident
2 = **tenant**, occupant, lodger
3 = **guest**, lodger

residue NOUN = **remainder**, remains, remnant, leftovers, rest, extra, excess, surplus

resign VERB 1 = **quit**, leave, step down (*informal*), vacate, abdicate, give or hand in your notice
2 = **give up**, abandon, yield, surrender, relinquish, renounce, forsake, forgo ▷ PHRASE: resign yourself to something = **accept**, succumb to, submit to, give in to, yield to, acquiesce to

resignation NOUN 1 = **leaving**, departure, abandonment, abdication 2 = **acceptance**, patience, submission, compliance, endurance, passivity, acquiescence, sufferance
≠ resistance

resigned ADJECTIVE = **stoical**, patient, subdued, long-suffering, compliant, unresisting

resist VERB 1 = **oppose**, battle against, combat, defy, stand up to, hinder ≠ accept 2 = **refrain from**, avoid, keep from, forgo, abstain from, forbear ≠ indulge in 3 = **withstand**, be proof against

resistance NOUN 1 = **opposition**, hostility, aversion 2 = **fighting**, fight, battle, struggle, defiance, obstruction, impediment, hindrance

resistant ADJECTIVE 1 = **opposed**, hostile, unwilling, intractable, antagonistic, intransigent
2 = **impervious**, hard, strong, tough, unaffected

resolution NOUN 1 = **declaration** 2 = **decision**, resolve, intention, aim, purpose, determination, intent 3 = **determination**, purpose, resolve, tenacity, perseverance, willpower, firmness, steadfastness

resolve VERB 1 = **work out**, answer, clear up, crack, fathom
2 = **decide**, determine, agree, purpose, intend, fix, conclude
▷ NOUN 1 = **determination**, resolution, willpower, firmness, steadfastness, resoluteness
≠ indecision 2 = **decision**, resolution, objective, purpose, intention

resort NOUN 1 = **holiday centre**, spot, retreat, haunt, tourist centre
2 = **recourse to**, reference to

resound VERB 1 = **echo**, resonate, reverberate, re-echo 2 = **ring**

resounding ADJECTIVE = **echoing**, full, ringing, powerful, booming, reverberating, resonant, sonorous

resource NOUN 1 = **facility**
2 = **means**, course, resort, device, expedient
▷ PLURAL NOUN 1 = **funds**, holdings, money, capital, riches, assets, wealth 2 = **reserves**, supplies, stocks

r

respect VERB 1 = **think highly of**, value, honour, admire, esteem, look up to, defer to, have a good or high opinion of 2 = **show consideration for**, honour, observe, heed 3 = **abide by**, follow, observe, comply with, obey, heed, keep to, adhere to ≠ disregard
▷ NOUN 1 = **regard**, honour, recognition, esteem, admiration, estimation ≠ contempt
2 = **consideration**, kindness, deference, tact, thoughtfulness, considerateness 3 = **particular**, way, point, matter, sense, detail, feature, aspect

respectable ADJECTIVE
1 = **honourable**, good, decent, worthy, upright, honest, reputable, estimable ≠ disreputable 2 = **decent**, neat, spruce 3 = **reasonable**, considerable, substantial, fair, ample, appreciable, sizable or sizable ≠ small

respective ADJECTIVE = **specific**, own, individual, particular, relevant

respite NOUN = **pause**, break, rest, relief, halt, interval, recess, lull

respond VERB 1 = **answer**, return, reply, counter, retort, rejoin ≠ remain silent 2 often with **to** = **reply to**, answer 3 = **react**, retaliate, reciprocate

response NOUN = **answer**, return, reply, reaction, feedback, retort, counterattack, rejoinder

responsibility NOUN 1 = **duty**, business, job, role, task, accountability, answerability 2 = **fault**, blame, liability, guilt, culpability 3 = **obligation**, duty, liability, charge, care 4 = **authority**, power, importance, mana (N.Z.) 5 = **job**, task, function, role 6 = **level-headedness**, rationality, dependability, trustworthiness, conscientiousness, sensibleness

responsible ADJECTIVE 1 = **to blame**, guilty, at fault, culpable 2 = **in charge**, in control, in authority 3 = **accountable**, liable, answerable ≠ unaccountable 4 = **sensible**, reliable, rational, dependable, trustworthy, level-headed ≠ unreliable

responsive ADJECTIVE = **sensitive**, open, alive, susceptible, receptive, reactive, impressionable ≠ unresponsive

rest¹ VERB 1 = **relax**, take it easy, sit down, be at ease, put your feet up, outspan (S. African) ≠ work 2 = **stop**, have a break, break off, take a breather (informal), halt, cease ≠ keep going 3 = **place**, repose, sit, lean, prop 4 = **be placed**, sit, lie, be supported, recline
▷ NOUN 1 = **relaxation**, repose, leisure, me-time ≠ work 2 = **pause**, break, stop, halt, interval, respite, lull, interlude 3 = **refreshment**, release, relief, ease, comfort, cure, remedy, solace 4 = **inactivity** 5 = **support**, stand, base, holder,

prop **6** = **calm**, tranquillity, stillness

rest² NOUN = **remainder**, remains, excess, remnants, others, balance, surplus, residue

restaurant NOUN = **café**, diner (*chiefly U.S. & Canad.*), bistro, cafeteria, tearoom, eatery *or* eaterie

restless ADJECTIVE **1** = **unsettled**, nervous, edgy, fidgeting, on edge, restive, jumpy, fidgety ≠ relaxed **2** = **moving**, wandering, unsettled, unstable, roving, transient, nomadic ≠ settled

restoration NOUN
1 = **reinstatement**, return, revival, restitution, re-establishment, replacement ≠ abolition
2 = **repair**, reconstruction, renewal, renovation, revitalization ≠ demolition

restore VERB **1** = **reinstate**, re-establish, reintroduce ≠ abolish **2** = **revive**, build up, strengthen, refresh, revitalize ≠ make worse **3** = **re-establish**, replace, reinstate, give back **4** = **repair**, refurbish, renovate, reconstruct, fix (up), renew, rebuild, mend ≠ demolish **5** = **return**, replace, recover, bring back, send back, hand back

restrain VERB **1** = **hold back**, control, check, contain, restrict, curb, hamper, hinder ≠ encourage **2** = **control**, inhibit

restrained ADJECTIVE
1 = **controlled**, moderate, self-controlled, calm, mild, undemonstrative ≠ hot-headed **2** = **unobtrusive**, discreet, subdued, tasteful, quiet ≠ garish

restraint NOUN **1** = **limitation**, limit, check, ban, embargo, curb, rein, interdict, restraining order (*U.S. law*) ≠ freedom **2** = **self-control**, self-discipline, self-restraint, self-possession ≠ self-indulgence **3** = **constraint**, limitation, inhibition, control, restriction

restrict VERB **1** = **limit**, regulate, curb, ration ≠ widen **2** = **hamper**, handicap, restrain, inhibit

restriction NOUN **1** = **control**, rule, regulation, curb, restraint, confinement **2** = **limitation**, handicap, inhibition

result NOUN **1** = **consequence**, effect, outcome, end result, product, sequel, upshot ≠ cause **2** = **outcome**, end
▷ VERB *often followed by* **from** = **arise**, follow, issue, happen, appear, develop, spring, derive

resume VERB = **begin again**, continue, go on with, proceed with, carry on, reopen, restart ≠ discontinue

résumé NOUN = **summary**, synopsis, précis, rundown, recapitulation

resumption NOUN = **continuation**, carrying on, reopening, renewal, restart, resurgence, re-establishment

resurgence NOUN = **revival**, return, renaissance, resurrection,

r

resumption, rebirth, re-emergence

resurrect VERB 1 = **revive**, renew, bring back, reintroduce 2 = **restore to life**, raise from the dead

resurrection NOUN 1 = **revival**, restoration, renewal, resurgence, return, renaissance, rebirth, reappearance ≠ killing off 2 = **raising** or **rising from the dead**, return from the dead ≠ demise

retain VERB 1 = **maintain**, reserve, preserve, keep up, continue to have 2 = **keep**, save ≠ let go

retaliate VERB = **pay someone back**, hit back, strike back, reciprocate, take revenge, get even with (*informal*), get your own back (*informal*) ≠ turn the other cheek

retaliation NOUN = **revenge**, repayment, vengeance, reprisal, an eye for an eye, reciprocation, requital, counterblow

retard VERB = **slow down**, check, arrest, delay, handicap, hinder, impede, set back ≠ speed up

retire VERB 1 = **stop working**, give up work 2 = **withdraw**, leave, exit, go away, depart 3 = **go to bed**, turn in (*informal*), hit the sack (*slang*), hit the hay (*slang*)

retirement NOUN = **withdrawal**, retreat, privacy, solitude, seclusion

retiring ADJECTIVE = **shy**, reserved, quiet, timid, unassuming, self-effacing, bashful, unassertive

≠ outgoing

retort VERB = **reply**, return, answer, respond, counter, come back with, riposte ▷ NOUN = **reply**, answer, response, comeback, riposte, rejoinder

retreat VERB = **withdraw**, back off, draw back, leave, go back, depart, fall back, pull back ≠ advance ▷ NOUN 1 = **flight**, retirement, departure, withdrawal, evacuation ≠ advance 2 = **refuge**, haven, shelter, sanctuary, hideaway, seclusion

retrieve VERB 1 = **get back**, regain, recover, restore, recapture 2 = **redeem**, save, win back, recoup

retrospect NOUN = **hindsight**, review, re-examination ≠ foresight

return VERB 1 = **come back**, go back, retreat, turn back, revert, reappear ≠ depart 2 = **put back**, replace, restore, reinstate ≠ keep 3 = **give back**, repay, refund, pay back, reimburse, recompense ≠ keep 4 = **recur**, repeat, persist, revert, happen again, reappear, come again 5 = **elect**, choose, vote in ▷ NOUN 1 = **reappearance** ≠ departure 2 = **restoration**, reinstatement, re-establishment ≠ removal 3 = **recurrence**, repetition, reappearance, reversion, persistence 4 = **profit**, interest, gain, income, revenue,

yield, proceeds, takings
5 = statement, report, form, list, account, summary

revamp VERB **= renovate**, restore, overhaul, refurbish, do up (*informal*), recondition

reveal VERB **1 = make known**, disclose, give away, make public, tell, announce, proclaim, let out ≠ keep secret **2 = show**, display, exhibit, unveil, uncover, manifest, unearth, unmask ≠ hide

revel VERB **= celebrate**, carouse, live it up (*informal*), make merry
▷ NOUN *often plural*
= merrymaking, party, celebration, spree, festivity, carousal

revelation NOUN **1 = disclosure**, news, announcement, publication, leak, confession, divulgence **2 = exhibition**, publication, exposure, unveiling, uncovering, unearthing, proclamation

revenge NOUN **= retaliation**, vengeance, reprisal, retribution, an eye for an eye
▷ VERB **= avenge**, repay, take revenge for, get your own back for (*informal*)

revenue NOUN **= income**, returns, profits, gain, yield, proceeds, receipts, takings ≠ expenditure

revere VERB **= be in awe of**, respect, honour, worship, reverence, exalt, look up to, venerate ≠ despise

reverse VERB **1** (*law*) **= change**, cancel, overturn, overthrow,

undo, repeal, quash, revoke ≠ implement **2 = turn round**, turn over, turn upside down, upend **3 = transpose**, change, move, exchange, transfer, switch, shift, alter **4 = go backwards**, retreat, back up, turn back, move backwards, back ≠ go forward
▷ NOUN **1 = opposite**, contrary, converse, inverse **2 = misfortune**, blow, failure, disappointment, setback, hardship, reversal, adversity **3 = back**, rear, other side, wrong side, underside ≠ front
▷ ADJECTIVE **= opposite**, contrary, converse

revert VERB **1 = go back**, return, come back, resume **2 = return**
● WORD POWER
● Since the concept *back* is
● already contained in the
● *re-* part of the word *revert*, it
● is unnecessary to say that
● someone *reverts back* to a
● particular type of behaviour.

review NOUN **1 = survey**, study, analysis, examination, scrutiny **2 = critique**, commentary, evaluation, notice, criticism, judgment **3 = inspection**, parade, march past **4 = magazine**, journal, periodical, zine (*informal*)
▷ VERB **1 = reconsider**, revise, rethink, reassess, re-examine, re-evaluate, think over **2 = assess**, study, judge, evaluate, criticize **3 = inspect**, check, survey, examine, vet **4 = look back on**, remember, recall, reflect on,

r

recollect

reviewer NOUN = **critic**, judge, commentator

revise VERB 1 = **change**, review 2 = **edit**, correct, alter, update, amend, rework, redo, emend 3 = **study**, go over, run through, cram (*informal*), swot up on (*Brit. informal*)

revision NOUN 1 = **emendation**, updating, correction 2 = **change**, amendment 3 = **studying**, cramming (*informal*), swotting (*Brit. informal*), homework

revival NOUN 1 = **resurgence** ≠ decline 2 = **reawakening**, renaissance, renewal, resurrection, rebirth, revitalization

revive VERB 1 = **revitalize**, restore, renew, rekindle, invigorate, reanimate 2 = **bring round**, awaken 3 = **come round**, recover 4 = **refresh** ≠ exhaust

revolt NOUN = **uprising**, rising, revolution, rebellion, mutiny, insurrection, insurgency ▷ VERB 1 = **rebel**, rise up, resist, mutiny 2 = **disgust**, sicken, repel, repulse, nauseate, gross out (*U.S. slang*), turn your stomach, make your flesh creep

revolting ADJECTIVE = **disgusting**, foul, horrible, sickening, horrid, repellent, repulsive, nauseating, yucko (*Austral. slang*) ≠ delightful

revolution NOUN 1 = **revolt**, rising, coup, rebellion, uprising, mutiny, insurgency 2 = **transformation**, shift,

innovation, upheaval, reformation, sea change 3 = **rotation**, turn, cycle, circle, spin, lap, circuit, orbit

revolutionary ADJECTIVE 1 = **rebel**, radical, extremist, subversive, insurgent ≠ reactionary 2 = **innovative**, new, different, novel, radical, progressive, drastic, ground-breaking ≠ conventional ▷ NOUN = **rebel**, insurgent, revolutionist ≠ reactionary

revolve VERB 1 = **go round**, circle, orbit 2 = **rotate**, turn, wheel, spin, twist, whirl

reward NOUN 1 = **punishment**, retribution, comeuppance (*slang*), just deserts 2 = **payment**, return, prize, wages, compensation, bonus, premium, repayment ≠ penalty ▷ VERB = **compensate**, pay, repay, recompense, remunerate ≠ penalize

rewarding ADJECTIVE = **satisfying**, fulfilling, valuable, profitable, productive, worthwhile, beneficial, enriching ≠ unrewarding

rhetoric NOUN 1 = **hyperbole**, bombast, wordiness, verbosity, grandiloquence, magniloquence 2 = **oratory**, eloquence, public speaking, speech-making, elocution, declamation, grandiloquence, whaikorero (*N.Z.*)

rhetorical ADJECTIVE = **high-flown**, bombastic, verbose, oratorical, grandiloquent, declamatory, arty-farty (*informal*), magniloquent

rhyme NOUN = **poem**, song, verse, ode

rhythm NOUN 1 = **beat**, swing, accent, pulse, tempo, cadence, lilt 2 = **metre**, time

rich ADJECTIVE 1 = **wealthy**, affluent, well-off, loaded (*slang*), prosperous, well-heeled (*informal*), well-to-do, moneyed, minted (*Brit. slang*) ≠ poor 2 = **well-stocked**, full, productive, ample, abundant, plentiful, copious, well-supplied ≠ scarce 3 = **full-bodied**, sweet, fatty, tasty, creamy, luscious, succulent ≠ bland 4 = **fruitful**, productive, fertile, prolific ≠ barren 5 = **abounding**, luxurious, lush, abundant

riches PLURAL NOUN 1 = **wealth**, assets, plenty, fortune, substance, treasure, affluence, top whack (*informal*) ≠ poverty 2 = **resources**, treasures

richly ADVERB 1 = **elaborately**, lavishly, elegantly, splendidly, exquisitely, expensively, luxuriously, gorgeously 2 = **fully**, well, thoroughly, amply, appropriately, properly, suitably

rid VERB = **free**, clear, deliver, relieve, purge, unburden, make free, disencumber ▷ PHRASE: **get rid of something** *or* **someone** = **dispose of**, throw away *or* out, dump, remove, eliminate, expel, eject

riddle¹ NOUN 1 = **puzzle**, problem, conundrum, poser 2 = **enigma**, question, secret, mystery, puzzle, conundrum, teaser, problem

riddle² VERB 1 = **pierce**, pepper, puncture, perforate, honeycomb 2 = **pervade**, fill, spread through, spoil, pervade, infest, permeate

ride VERB 1 = **control**, handle, manage 2 = **travel**, be carried, go, move ▷ NOUN = **journey**, drive, trip, lift, outing, jaunt

ridicule VERB = **laugh at**, mock, make fun of, sneer at, jeer at, deride, poke fun at, chaff ▷ NOUN = **mockery**, scorn, derision, laughter, jeer, chaff, gibe, raillery

ridiculous ADJECTIVE = **laughable**, stupid, silly, absurd, ludicrous, farcical, comical, risible ≠ sensible

rife ADJECTIVE = **widespread**, rampant, general, common, universal, frequent, prevalent, ubiquitous

rifle VERB = **ransack**, rob, burgle, loot, strip, sack, plunder, pillage

rift NOUN 1 = **breach**, division, split, separation, falling out (*informal*), disagreement, quarrel 2 = **split**, opening, crack, gap, break, fault, flaw, cleft

rig VERB 1 = **fix**, engineer (*informal*), arrange, manipulate, tamper with, gerrymander 2 (*nautical*) = **equip**, fit out, kit out, outfit, supply, furnish ▷ PHRASE: **rig something up** = **set up**, build,

r

construct, put up, arrange, assemble, put together, erect

right ADJECTIVE 1 = **correct**, true, genuine, accurate, exact, precise, valid, factual, dinkum (*Austral. & N.Z. informal*) ≠ wrong 2 = **proper**, done, becoming, seemly, fitting, fit, appropriate, suitable ≠ inappropriate 3 = **just**, good, fair, moral, proper, ethical, honest, equitable ≠ unfair

▷ ADVERB 1 = **correctly**, truly, precisely, exactly, genuinely, accurately ≠ wrongly 2 = **suitably**, fittingly, appropriately, properly, aptly ≠ improperly 3 = **exactly**, squarely, precisely 4 = **directly**, straight, precisely, exactly, unswervingly, without deviation, by the shortest route, in a beeline 5 = **straight**, directly, quickly, promptly, straightaway ≠ indirectly

▷ NOUN 1 = **prerogative**, business, power, claim, authority, due, freedom, licence 2 = **justice**, truth, fairness, legality, righteousness, lawfulness ≠ injustice

▷ VERB = **rectify**, settle, fix, correct, sort out, straighten, redress, put right

right away ADVERB = **immediately**, now, directly, instantly, at once, straightaway, forthwith, pronto (*informal*)

righteous ADJECTIVE = **virtuous**, good, just, fair, moral, pure, ethical, upright ≠ wicked

rigid ADJECTIVE 1 = **strict**, fixed, exact, rigorous, stringent ≠ flexible 2 = **inflexible**, uncompromising, unbending 3 = **stiff**, inflexible, inelastic ≠ pliable

rigorous ADJECTIVE = **strict**, hard, demanding, tough, severe, exacting, harsh, stern ≠ soft

rim NOUN 1 = **edge**, lip, brim 2 = **border**, edge, trim 3 = **margin**, border, verge, brink

ring¹ VERB 1 = **phone**, call, telephone, buzz (*informal, chiefly Brit.*) 2 = **chime**, sound, toll, reverberate, clang, peal 3 = **reverberate**

▷ NOUN 1 = **call**, phone call, buzz (*informal, chiefly Brit.*) 2 = **chime**, knell, peal

● **WORD POWER**
● *Rang* is the past tense of the
● verb *ring*, as in *he rang the bell*.
● *Rung* is the past participle, as in
● *he has already rung the bell*, and
● care should be taken not to use
● it as if it were a variant form of
● the past tense.

ring² NOUN 1 = **circle**, round, band, circuit, loop, hoop, halo 2 = **arena**, enclosure, circus, rink 3 = **gang**, group, association, band, circle, mob, syndicate, cartel

▷ VERB = **encircle**, surround, enclose, girdle, gird

rinse VERB = **wash**, clean, dip, splash, cleanse, bathe

▷ NOUN = **wash**, dip, splash, bath

riot NOUN 1 = **disturbance**,

disorder, confusion, turmoil, upheaval, strife, turbulence, lawlessness **2** = **display**, show, splash, extravaganza, profusion **3** = **laugh**, joke, scream (*informal*), hoot (*informal*), lark
▷ **VERB 1** = **rampage**, run riot, go on the rampage ▷ **PHRASE: run riot 1** = **rampage**, go wild, be out of control **2** = **grow profusely**, spread like wildfire

rip **VERB 1** = **tear**, cut, split, burst, rend, slash, claw, slit **2** = **be torn**, tear, split, burst
▷ **NOUN** = **tear**, cut, hole, split, rent, slash, slit, gash ▷ **PHRASE: rip someone off** (*slang*) = **cheat**, rob, con (*informal*), skin (*slang*), fleece, defraud, swindle, scam (*slang*)

ripe **ADJECTIVE 1** = **ripened**, seasoned, ready, mature, mellow ≠ unripe **2** = **right**, suitable **3** = **mature 4** = **suitable**, timely, ideal, favourable, auspicious, opportune ≠ unsuitable

rip-off or **ripoff** **NOUN** (*slang*) = **cheat**, con (*informal*), scam (*slang*), con trick (*informal*), fraud, theft, swindle

rise **VERB 1** = **get up**, stand up, get to your feet **2** = **arise 3** = **go up**, climb, ascend ≠ descend **4** = **loom**, tower **5** = **get steeper**, ascend, go uphill, slope upwards ≠ drop **6** = **increase**, mount ≠ decrease **7** = **grow**, go up, intensify **8** = **rebel**, revolt, mutiny **9** = **advance**, progress, get on, prosper
▷ **NOUN 1** = **upward slope**,

incline, elevation, ascent, kopje or koppie (*S. African*) **2** = **increase**, upturn, upswing, upsurge ≠ decrease **3** = **pay increase**, raise (*U.S.*), increment **4** = **advancement**, progress, climb, promotion ▷ **PHRASE: give rise to something** = **cause**, produce, effect, result in, bring about

risk **NOUN 1** = **danger**, chance, possibility, hazard **2** = **gamble**, chance, speculation, leap in the dark **3** = **peril**, jeopardy
▷ **VERB 1** = **stand a chance of 2** = **dare**, endanger, jeopardize, imperil, venture, gamble, hazard

risky **ADJECTIVE** = **dangerous**, hazardous, unsafe, perilous, uncertain, dodgy (*Brit., Austral. & N.Z. informal*), dicey (*informal, chiefly Brit.*), chancy (*informal*), shonky (*Austral. & N.Z. informal*) ≠ safe

rite **NOUN** = **ceremony**, custom, ritual, practice, procedure, observance

ritual **NOUN 1** = **ceremony**, rite, observance **2** = **custom**, tradition, routine, convention, practice, procedure, habit, protocol, tikanga (*N.Z.*)
▷ **ADJECTIVE** = **ceremonial**, conventional, routine, customary, habitual

rival **NOUN** = **opponent**, competitor, contender, contestant, adversary ≠ supporter
▷ **VERB** = **compete with**, match,

r

equal, compare with, come up to, be a match for

▷ MODIFIER = **competing**, conflicting, opposing

rivalry NOUN = **competition**, opposition, conflict, contest, contention

river NOUN 1 = **stream**, brook, creek, waterway, tributary, burn (*Scot.*) 2 = **flow**, rush, flood, spate, torrent

riveting ADJECTIVE = **enthralling**, gripping, fascinating, absorbing, captivating, hypnotic, engrossing, spellbinding

road NOUN 1 = **roadway**, highway, motorway, track, route, path, lane, pathway 2 = **way**, path

roam VERB = **wander**, walk, range, travel, stray, ramble, prowl, rove

roar VERB 1 = **thunder** 2 = **guffaw**, laugh heartily, hoot, split your sides (*informal*) 3 = **cry**, shout, yell, howl, bellow, bawl, bay

▷ NOUN 1 = **guffaw**, hoot 2 = **cry**, shout, yell, howl, outcry, bellow

rob VERB 1 = **steal from**, hold up, mug (*informal*) 2 = **raid**, hold up, loot, plunder, burgle, pillage 3 = **dispossess**, con (*informal*), cheat, defraud 4 = **deprive**, do out of (*informal*)

robber NOUN = **thief**, raider, burglar, looter, fraud, cheat, bandit, plunderer, rogue trader

robbery NOUN 1 = **burglary**, raid, hold-up, rip-off (*slang*), stick-up (*slang, chiefly U.S.*), home invasion (*Austral. & N.Z.*) 2 = **theft**, stealing, mugging (*informal*),

plunder, swindle, pillage, larceny

robe NOUN = **gown**, costume, habit

robot NOUN = **machine**, automaton, android, mechanical man

robust ADJECTIVE = **strong**, tough, powerful, fit, healthy, strapping, hardy, vigorous ≠ weak

rock¹ NOUN = **stone**, boulder

rock² VERB 1 = **sway**, pitch, swing, reel, toss, lurch, roll 2 = **shock**, surprise, shake, stun, astonish, stagger, astound

rocky¹ ADJECTIVE = **rough**, rugged, stony, craggy

rocky² ADJECTIVE = **unstable**, shaky, wobbly, rickety, unsteady

rod NOUN 1 = **stick**, bar, pole, shaft, cane 2 = **staff**, baton, wand

rogue NOUN 1 = **scoundrel**, crook (*informal*), villain, fraud, blackguard, skelm (*S. African*), rorter (*Austral. slang*), wrong 'un (*Austral. slang*) 2 = **scamp**, rascal, scally (*Northwest English dialect*), nointer (*Austral. slang*)

role NOUN 1 = **job**, part, position, post, task, duty, function, capacity 2 = **part**, character, representation, portrayal

roll VERB 1 = **turn**, wheel, spin, go round, revolve, rotate, whirl, swivel 2 = **trundle**, go, move 3 = **flow**, run, course 4 *often with* **up** = **wind**, bind, wrap, swathe, envelop, furl, enfold 5 *often with* **out** = **level**, even, press, smooth, flatten 6 = **toss**, rock, lurch, reel, tumble, sway

● **RODENTS**

- agouti
- beaver
- capybara
- cavy
- chinchilla
- chipmunk
- coypu or nutria
- desert rat
- dormouse
- fieldmouse
- flying squirrel
- gerbil, gerbille, or jerbil
- gopher or pocket gopher
- gopher or ground squirrel
- grey squirrel
- groundhog or woodchuck
- guinea pig or cavy
- hamster
- harvest mouse
- hedgehog
- house mouse
- jerboa
- kangaroo rat
- kiore (N.Z.)
- lemming
- Māori rat or (N.Z.) kiore
- marmot
- mouse
- muskrat or musquash
- paca
- pack rat
- porcupine
- rat
- red squirrel or chickaree
- spinifex hopping mouse or (Austral.) dargawarra
- springhaas
- squirrel
- suslik or souslik
- viscacha or vizcacha
- vole
- water rat
- water vole or water rat

▷ NOUN 1 = **rumble**, boom, roar, thunder, reverberation
2 = **register**, record, list, index, census 3 = **turn**, spin, rotation, cycle, wheel, revolution, reel, whirl

romance NOUN 1 = **love affair**, relationship, affair, attachment, liaison, amour 2 = **excitement**, colour, charm, mystery, glamour, fascination 3 = **story**, tale, fantasy, legend, fairy tale, love story, melodrama

romantic ADJECTIVE 1 = **loving**, tender, passionate, fond, sentimental, amorous, icky (*informal*) ≠ unromantic
2 = **idealistic**, unrealistic, impractical, dreamy, starry-eyed ≠ realistic 3 = **exciting**, fascinating, mysterious, colourful, glamorous ≠ unexciting
▷ NOUN = **idealist**, dreamer, sentimentalist

romp VERB = **frolic**, sport, have fun, caper, cavort, frisk, gambol
▷ NOUN = **frolic**, lark (*informal*), caper

room NOUN 1 = **chamber**, office, apartment 2 = **space**, area, capacity, extent, expanse
3 = **opportunity**, scope, leeway, chance, range, occasion, margin

root¹ NOUN 1 = **stem**, tuber, rhizome 2 = **source**, cause, heart, bottom, base, seat, seed, foundation
▷ PLURAL NOUN = **sense of belonging**, origins, heritage,

birthplace, home, family, cradle
▷ **PHRASE**: **root something**
or **someone out** = **get rid of**,
remove, eliminate, abolish,
eradicate, do away with, weed
out, exterminate

root² VERB = **dig**, burrow, ferret

rope NOUN = **cord**, line, cable,
strand, hawser ▷ **PHRASES**: **know
the ropes** = **be experienced**,
be knowledgeable, be an old
hand; **rope someone in** or **into
something** (Brit.) = **persuade**,
involve, engage, enlist, talk into,
inveigle

rosy ADJECTIVE 1 = **glowing**,
blooming, radiant, ruddy, healthy-
looking ≠ pale 2 = **promising**,
encouraging, bright, optimistic,
hopeful, cheerful, favourable,
auspicious ≠ gloomy 3 = **pink**,
red
▷ see **shades of red**

rot VERB 1 = **decay**, spoil,
deteriorate, perish, decompose,
moulder, go bad, putrefy
2 = **crumble** 3 = **deteriorate**,
decline, waste away
▷ NOUN 1 = **decay**,
decomposition, corruption,
mould, blight, canker,
putrefaction 2 (informal)
= **nonsense**, rubbish, drivel,
twaddle, garbage (chiefly U.S.),
trash, tripe (informal), claptrap
(informal), bizzo (Austral. slang),
bull's wool (Austral. & N.Z. slang)
▷ **RELATED WORD**: adjective **putrid**

rotate VERB 1 = **revolve**, turn,
wheel, spin, reel, go round, swivel,

pivot 2 = **follow in sequence**,
switch, alternate, take turns

rotation NOUN 1 = **revolution**,
turning, turn, wheel,
spin, spinning, reel, orbit
2 = **sequence**, switching, cycle,
succession, alternation

rotten ADJECTIVE 1 = **decaying**,
bad, rank, corrupt, sour, stinking,
perished, festering, festy (Austral.
slang) ≠ fresh 2 = **crumbling**,
perished 3 (informal)
= **despicable**, mean, base, dirty,
nasty, contemptible 4 (informal)
= **inferior**, poor, inadequate, duff
(Brit. informal), unsatisfactory,
lousy (slang), substandard,
crummy (slang), bodger or bodgie
(Austral. slang) 5 = **corrupt**,
immoral, crooked (informal),
dishonest, dishonourable,
perfidious ≠ honourable

rough ADJECTIVE 1 = **uneven**,
broken, rocky, irregular, jagged,
bumpy, stony, craggy ≠ even
2 = **boisterous**, hard, tough,
arduous 3 = **ungracious**, blunt,
rude, coarse, brusque, uncouth,
impolite, uncivil ≠ refined
4 = **unpleasant**, hard, difficult,
tough, uncomfortable ≠ easy
5 = **approximate**, estimated
≠ exact 6 = **vague**, general,
sketchy, imprecise, inexact
7 = **basic**, crude, unfinished,
incomplete, imperfect,
rudimentary, sketchy, unrefined
≠ complete 8 = **stormy**, wild,
turbulent, choppy, squally ≠ calm
9 = **harsh**, tough, nasty, cruel,

unfeeling ≠ gentle
▷ NOUN = **outline**, draft, mock-up, preliminary sketch ▷ PHRASES: **rough and ready 1** = **makeshift**, crude, provisional, improvised, sketchy, stopgap **2** = **unrefined**, shabby, untidy, unkempt, unpolished, ill-groomed, daggy (*Austral. & N.Z. informal*); **rough something out** = **outline**, plan, draft, sketch

round NOUN **1** = **series**, session, cycle, sequence, succession **2** = **stage**, turn, level, period, division, session, lap **3** = **sphere**, ball, band, ring, circle, disc, globe, orb **4** = **course**, tour, circuit, beat, series, schedule, routine
▷ ADJECTIVE **1** = **spherical**, rounded, curved, circular, cylindrical, rotund, globular **2** = **plump**, full, ample, fleshy, rotund, full-fleshed
▷ VERB = **go round**, circle, skirt, flank, bypass, encircle, turn
▷ PHRASE: **round something** or **someone up** = **gather**, muster, group, drive, collect, rally, herd, marshal

roundabout ADJECTIVE
1 = **indirect**, devious, tortuous, circuitous, evasive, discursive ≠ direct **2** = **oblique**, implied, indirect, circuitous

roundup NOUN = **muster**, collection, rally, assembly, herding

rouse VERB **1** = **wake up**, call, wake, awaken **2** = **excite**, move, stir, provoke, anger, animate, agitate, inflame **3** = **stimulate**,

provoke, incite

rousing ADJECTIVE = **lively**, moving, spirited, exciting, inspiring, stirring, stimulating ≠ dull

rout VERB = **defeat**, beat, overthrow, thrash, destroy, crush, conquer, wipe the floor with (*informal*)
▷ NOUN = **defeat**, beating, overthrow, thrashing, pasting (*slang*), debacle, drubbing

route NOUN **1** = **way**, course, road, direction, path, journey, itinerary **2** = **beat**, circuit
● WORD POWER
● When adding -*ing* to the
● verb *route* to form the
● present participle, it is more
● conventional, and clearer, to
● keep the final *e* from the end
● of the verb stem: *routeing*. The
● spelling *routing* in this sense is
● also possible, but keeping the
● *e* distinguishes it from *routing*,
● which is the participle formed
● from the verb *rout* meaning 'to
● defeat'.

routine NOUN = **procedure**, programme, order, practice, method, pattern, custom
▷ ADJECTIVE **1** = **usual**, standard, normal, customary, ordinary, typical, everyday, habitual ≠ unusual **2** = **boring**, dull, predictable, tedious, tiresome, humdrum

row¹ NOUN = **line**, bank, range, series, file, string, column ▷ PHRASE: **in a row**

= **consecutively**, running, in turn, one after the other, successively, in sequence

row² NOUN 1 = **quarrel**, dispute, argument, squabble, tiff, trouble, brawl 2 = **disturbance**, noise, racket, uproar, commotion, rumpus, tumult
▷ VERB = **quarrel**, fight, argue, dispute, squabble, wrangle

royal ADJECTIVE 1 = **regal**, kingly, queenly, princely, imperial, sovereign 2 = **splendid**, grand, impressive, magnificent, majestic, stately

rub VERB 1 = **stroke**, massage, caress 2 = **polish**, clean, shine, wipe, scour 3 = **chafe**, scrape, grate, abrade
▷ NOUN 1 = **massage**, caress, kneading 2 = **polish**, stroke, shine, wipe ▷ PHRASE: **rub something out** = **erase**, remove, cancel, wipe out, delete, obliterate, efface

rubbish NOUN 1 = **waste**, refuse, scrap, junk (*informal*), litter, garbage (*chiefly U.S.*), trash, lumber 2 = **nonsense**, garbage (*chiefly U.S.*), twaddle, rot, trash, hot air (*informal*), tripe (*informal*), claptrap (*informal*), bizzo (*Austral. slang*), bull's wool (*Austral. & N.Z. slang*)

rude ADJECTIVE 1 = **impolite**, insulting, cheeky, abusive, disrespectful, impertinent, insolent, impudent ≠ polite 2 = **uncivilized**, rough, coarse, brutish, boorish, uncouth,

loutish, graceless 3 = **vulgar** ≠ refined 4 = **unpleasant**, sharp, sudden, harsh, startling, abrupt 5 = **roughly-made**, simple, rough, raw, crude, primitive, makeshift, artless ≠ well-made

rue VERB (*literary*) = **regret**, mourn, lament, repent, be sorry for, kick yourself for

ruffle VERB 1 = **disarrange**, disorder, mess up, rumple, tousle, dishevel, muss (*U.S. & Canad.*) 2 = **annoy**, upset, irritate, agitate, nettle, fluster, peeve (*informal*) ≠ calm

rugged ADJECTIVE 1 = **rocky**, broken, rough, craggy, difficult, ragged, irregular, uneven ≠ even 2 = **strong-featured**, rough-hewn, weather-beaten ≠ delicate 3 = **well-built**, strong, tough, robust, sturdy 4 (*chiefly U.S. & Canad.*) = **tough**, strong, robust, muscular, sturdy, burly, husky (*informal*), brawny ≠ delicate

ruin VERB 1 = **destroy**, devastate, wreck, defeat, smash, crush, demolish, lay waste, kennet (*Austral. slang*), jeff (*Austral. slang*) ≠ create 2 = **bankrupt**, break, impoverish, beggar, pauperize 3 = **spoil**, damage, mess up, blow (*slang*), screw up (*informal*), botch, make a mess of, crool or cruel (*Austral. slang*) ≠ improve
▷ NOUN 1 = **bankruptcy**, insolvency, destitution 2 = **disrepair**, decay, disintegration, ruination, wreckage 3 = **destruction**, fall,

breakdown, defeat, collapse, wreck, undoing, downfall ≠ preservation

rule NOUN 1 = **regulation**, law, direction, guideline, decree 2 = **precept**, principle, canon, maxim, tenet, axiom 3 = **custom**, procedure, practice, routine, tradition, habit, convention 4 = **government**, power, control, authority, command, regime, reign, jurisdiction, mana (*N.Z.*) ▷ VERB 1 = **govern**, control, direct, have power over, command over, have charge of 2 = **reign**, govern, be in power, be in authority 3 = **decree**, decide, judge, settle, pronounce 4 = **be prevalent**, prevail, predominate, be customary, preponderate ▷ PHRASES: **as a rule** = **usually**, generally, mainly, normally, on the whole, ordinarily; **rule someone out** = **exclude**, eliminate, disqualify, ban, reject, dismiss, prohibit, leave out; **rule something out** = **reject**, exclude, eliminate

ruler NOUN 1 = **governor**, leader, lord, commander, controller, monarch, sovereign, head of state 2 = **measure**, rule, yardstick

ruling ADJECTIVE 1 = **governing**, reigning, controlling, commanding 2 = **predominant**, dominant, prevailing, preponderant, chief, main, principal, pre-eminent ≠ minor ▷ NOUN = **decision**, verdict, judgment, decree, adjudication,

pronouncement

rumour NOUN = **story**, news, report, talk, word, whisper, buzz, gossip, goss (*informal*)

run VERB 1 = **race**, rush, dash, hurry, sprint, bolt, gallop, hare (*Brit. informal*) ≠ dawdle 2 = **flee**, escape, take off (*informal*), bolt, beat it (*slang*), leg it (*informal*), take flight, do a runner (*slang*) ≠ stay 3 = **take part**, compete 4 = **continue**, go, stretch, reach, extend, proceed ≠ stop 5 (*chiefly U.S. & Canad.*) = **compete**, stand, contend, be a candidate, put yourself up for, take part 6 = **manage**, lead, direct, be in charge of, head, control, operate, handle 7 = **go**, work, operate, perform, function 8 = **perform**, carry out 9 = **work**, go, operate, function 10 = **pass**, go, move, roll, glide, skim 11 = **flow**, pour, stream, go, leak, spill, discharge, gush 12 = **publish**, feature, display, print 13 = **melt**, dissolve, liquefy, go soft 14 = **smuggle**, traffic in, bootleg ▷ NOUN 1 = **race**, rush, dash, sprint, gallop, jog, spurt 2 = **ride**, drive, trip, spin (*informal*), outing, excursion, jaunt 3 = **sequence**, period, stretch, spell, course, season, series, string 4 = **enclosure**, pen, coop ▷ PHRASES: **run away** VERB = **flee**, escape, bolt, abscond, do a runner (*slang*), make a run for it, scram (*informal*), fly the coop (*U.S. & Canad. informal*), do

r

a Skase (*Austral. informal*); **run into someone** VERB = **meet**, encounter, bump into, run across, come across *or* upon; **run into something 1** = **be beset by**, encounter, come across *or* upon, face, experience **2** = **collide with**, hit, strike; **run out 1** = **be used up**, dry up, give out, fail, finish, be exhausted **2** = **expire**, end, terminate; **run over something 1** = **exceed**, overstep, go over the top of, go over the limit of **2** = **review**, check, go through, go over, run through, rehearse; **run over something** *or* **someone** = **knock down**, hit, run down, knock over; **run something** *or* **someone down 1** = **criticize**, denigrate, belittle, knock (*informal*), rubbish (*informal*), slag (off) (*slang*), disparage, decry **2** = **downsize**, cut, reduce, trim, decrease, cut back, curtail, kennet (*Austral. slang*), jeff (*Austral. slang*) **3** = **knock down**, hit, run into, run over, knock over

rundown *or* **run-down**
ADJECTIVE **1** = **exhausted**, weak, drained, weary, unhealthy, worn-out, debilitated, below par ≠ fit **2** = **dilapidated**, broken-down, shabby, worn-out, seedy, ramshackle, decrepit

runner NOUN **1** = **athlete**, sprinter, jogger **2** = **messenger**, courier, errand boy, dispatch bearer

running NOUN **1** = **management**, control, administration, direction, leadership, organization, supervision **2** = **working**, performance, operation, functioning, maintenance
▷ ADJECTIVE **1** = **continuous**, constant, perpetual, uninterrupted, incessant **2** = **in succession**, unbroken **3** = **flowing**, moving, streaming, coursing

rupture NOUN = **break**, tear, split, crack, rent, burst, breach, fissure
▷ VERB = **break**, separate, tear, split, crack, burst, sever

rural ADJECTIVE **1** = **agricultural**, country **2** = **rustic**, country, pastoral, sylvan ≠ urban

rush VERB **1** = **hurry**, run, race, shoot, fly, career, speed, tear ≠ dawdle **2** = **push**, hurry, press, hustle **3** = **attack**, storm, charge at
▷ NOUN **1** = **dash**, charge, race, scramble, stampede **2** = **hurry**, haste, hustle **3** = **surge**, flow, gush **4** = **attack**, charge, assault, onslaught
▷ ADJECTIVE = **hasty**, fast, quick, hurried, rapid, urgent, swift ≠ leisurely

● **WORD POWER**
● Most Russian words in English
● refer in a restricted way to
● specific political aspects of
● the former Soviet Union,
● e.g. *agit-prop*, *glasnost*, and
● *perestroika*. A couple of Russian
● words which have gained
● wider currency are *refusenik* and
● *intelligentsia*. The intelligentsia

were the educated class in
pre-revolutionary Russia – this
label is now applied more
generally to the intellectual or
educated section of any society.
It shares some of the meaning
of chattering classes in that
both refer to the educated
parts of a society. However,
whereas 'intelligentsia' implies
an intellectual elite who shape
their society through political
activism or the development
of culture, 'chattering
classes' is often a derogatory
description of the educated
liberal middle-class. Refusenik
is a term which originally
denoted a Jew in the Soviet
Union who was not permitted
to emigrate to Israel. It now
also refers to any protester
against a system or law, by a
change in meaning from 'one
who has been refused' to 'one
who refuses'. The **-nik** suffix is
an interesting one: by analogy
with *Sputnik*, the unmanned
satellites launched by the
Soviet Union from the 1950s,
-nik also appeared in other
English words after that time,
e.g. *beatnik*. It is the Russian
equivalent of the English suffix
-er, added to nouns to mean
'the person who performs this
action' e.g. teacher, writer.

rust NOUN 1 = **corrosion**,
oxidation 2 = **mildew**, must,
mould, rot, blight
▷ VERB = **corrode**, oxidize

rusty ADJECTIVE 1 = **corroded**,
rusted, oxidized, rust-covered
2 = **out of practice**, weak, stale,
unpractised 3 = **reddish-brown**,
chestnut, reddish, russet, coppery,
rust-coloured
▷ *see* **shades of red**

ruthless ADJECTIVE = **merciless**,
harsh, cruel, brutal, relentless,
callous, heartless, remorseless
≠ merciful

Ss

sabotage VERB = **damage**, destroy, wreck, disable, disrupt, subvert, incapacitate, vandalize
▷ NOUN = **damage**, destruction, wrecking

sack¹ NOUN = **bag**, pocket, sac, pouch, receptacle
▷ VERB (*informal*) = **dismiss**, fire (*informal*), axe (*informal*), discharge, kiss off (*slang, chiefly U.S. & Canad.*), give (someone) the push (*informal*), kennet (*Austral. slang*), jeff (*Austral. slang*)
▷ PHRASE: **the sack** (*informal*) = **dismissal**, discharge, the boot (*slang*), the axe (*informal*), the push (*slang*)

sack² VERB = **plunder**, loot, pillage, strip, rob, raid, ruin
▷ NOUN = **plundering**, looting, pillage

sacred ADJECTIVE 1 = **holy**, hallowed, blessed, divine, revered, sanctified ≠ secular
2 = **religious**, holy, ecclesiastical, hallowed ≠ unconsecrated
3 = **inviolable**, protected, sacrosanct, hallowed, inalienable, unalterable

sacrifice VERB 1 = **offer**, offer up, immolate 2 = **give up**, abandon, relinquish, lose, surrender, let go, do without, renounce
▷ NOUN 1 = **offering**, oblation
2 = **surrender**, loss, giving up, rejection, abdication, renunciation, repudiation, forswearing

sad ADJECTIVE 1 = **unhappy**, down, low, blue, depressed, melancholy, mournful, dejected ≠ happy 2 = **tragic**, moving, upsetting, depressing, dismal, pathetic, poignant, harrowing
3 = **deplorable**, bad, sorry, terrible, unfortunate, regrettable, lamentable, wretched ≠ good

sadden VERB = **upset**, depress, distress, grieve, make sad, deject

saddle VERB = **burden**, load, lumber (*Brit. informal*), encumber

sadness NOUN = **unhappiness**, sorrow, grief, depression, the blues, misery, melancholy, poignancy ≠ happiness

safe ADJECTIVE 1 = **protected**, secure, impregnable, out of danger, safe and sound, in safe hands, out of harm's way ≠ endangered 2 = **all right**, intact, unscathed, unhurt, unharmed, undamaged, O.K. or okay (*informal*) 3 = **risk-free**, sound, secure, certain, impregnable
▷ NOUN = **strongbox**, vault, coffer, repository, deposit box, safe-deposit box

safeguard VERB = **protect**, guard, defend, save, preserve, look after, keep safe
▷ NOUN = **protection**, security, defence, guard

s

safely ADVERB = **in safety**, with impunity, without risk, safe and sound

safety NOUN 1 = **security**, protection, safeguards, precautions, safety measures, impregnability ≠ risk
2 = **shelter**, haven, protection, cover, retreat, asylum, refuge, sanctuary

sag VERB 1 = **sink**, bag, droop, fall, slump, dip, give way, hang loosely
2 = **drop**, sink, slump, flop, droop, loll 3 = **decline**, tire, flag, weaken, wilt, wane, droop

saga NOUN 1 = **carry-on** (*informal*), performance (*informal*), pantomime (*informal*) 2 = **epic**, story, tale, narrative, yarn

sage NOUN = **wise man**, philosopher, guru, master, elder, tohunga (*N.Z.*)
▷ ADJECTIVE = **wise**, sensible, judicious, sagacious, sapient

sail NOUN = **sheet**, canvas
▷ VERB 1 = **go by water**, cruise, voyage, ride the waves, go by sea
2 = **set sail**, embark, get under way, put to sea, put off, leave port, hoist sail, cast *or* weigh anchor
3 = **pilot**, steer 4 = **glide**, sweep, float, fly, wing, soar, drift, skim

sailor NOUN = **mariner**, marine, seaman, sea dog, seafarer

sake NOUN = **purpose**, interest, reason, end, aim, objective, motive ▷ PHRASE: **for someone's sake** = **in someone's interests**, to someone's advantage, on someone's account, for the benefit of, for the good of, for the welfare of, out of respect for, out of consideration for

salary NOUN = **pay**, income, wage, fee, payment, wages, earnings, allowance

sale NOUN 1 = **selling**, marketing, dealing, transaction, disposal
2 = **auction**, fair, mart, bazaar

salt NOUN = **seasoning**
▷ ADJECTIVE = **salty**, saline, brackish, briny

salute VERB 1 = **greet**, welcome, acknowledge, address, hail, mihi (*N.Z.*) 2 = **honour**, acknowledge, recognize, pay tribute *or* homage to
▷ NOUN = **greeting**, recognition, salutation, address

salvage VERB = **save**, recover, rescue, get back, retrieve, redeem

salvation NOUN = **saving**, rescue, recovery, salvage, redemption, deliverance ≠ ruin

same ADJECTIVE 1 = **identical**, similar, alike, equal, twin, corresponding, duplicate
≠ different 2 = **the very same**, one and the same, selfsame
3 = **aforementioned**, aforesaid
4 = **unchanged**, consistent, constant, unaltered, invariable, unvarying, changeless ≠ altered
● **WORD POWER**
● The use of *same* as in *if you send*
● *us your order for the materials,*
● *we will deliver same tomorrow*
● is common in business and
● official English. In general
● English, however, this use of

- the word is best avoided, as it
- may sound rather stilted: *may I*
- *borrow your book? I will return it*
- (not *same*) *tomorrow.*

sample NOUN 1 = **specimen**,
example, model, pattern, instance
2 = **cross section**
▷ VERB = **test**, try, experience,
taste, inspect

sanction VERB = **permit**, allow,
approve, endorse, authorize
≠ forbid
▷ NOUN 1 *often plural* = **ban**,
boycott, embargo, exclusion,
penalty, coercive measures
≠ permission 2 = **permission**,
backing, authority, approval,
authorization, O.K. *or* okay
(*informal*), stamp *or* seal of
approval ≠ ban

sanctuary NOUN 1 = **protection**,
shelter, refuge, haven, retreat,
asylum 2 = **reserve**, park,
preserve, reservation, national
park, tract, nature reserve,
conservation area

sane ADJECTIVE 1 = **rational**, all
there (*informal*), of sound mind,
compos mentis (*Latin*), in your
right mind, mentally sound
≠ insane 2 = **sensible**, sound,
reasonable, balanced, judicious,
level-headed, grounded ≠ foolish

- **WORD POWER**
- Most of the words which
- have come into English from
- Sanskrit are connected with
- eastern religions, such as
- *mantra*, *guru*, *karma*, and
- *nirvana*. These words have

- all developed more general
- meanings alongside their
- specialised religious sense.
- For example, mantra, literally
- 'speech', in Hinduism is a
- sacred word or sound which
- aids concentration and carries
- spiritual meaning. In general
- language, mantra means a
- kind of catchphrase or slogan,
- e.g. Right now, his mantra is
- 'make love, not war'. In both
- Hinduism and Buddhism the
- concept of karma means that a
- person's past deeds will decide
- their future reincarnations.
- It has developed a looser
- meaning of 'fate' or 'destiny'
- in general language where
- bad deeds are punished and
- good deeds rewarded by the
- universe. Nirvana, literally
- 'extinction', has similarly
- generated a non-religious
- meaning. In Hinduism and
- Buddhism, nirvana is liberation
- from the cycle of reincarnation.
- In general language it means
- paradise or a state of bliss.
- Although guru refers to a Hindu
- or Sikh religious teacher, it has
- also been used of an expert or
- leader in any field, particularly
- in a mocking way, e.g. the most
- venerable management guru of
- them all.

sap^1 NOUN 1 = **juice**, essence, vital
fluid, lifeblood 2 (*slang*) = **fool**,
jerk (*slang, chiefly U.S. & Canad.*),
idiot, wally (*slang*), twit (*informal*),

simpleton, ninny, dorba or dorb
(*Austral. slang*), bogan (*Austral.
slang*)

sap² VERB = **weaken**, drain,
undermine, exhaust, deplete

satanic ADJECTIVE = **evil**, demonic,
hellish, black, wicked, devilish,
infernal, fiendish ≠ godly

satire NOUN 1 = **mockery**, irony,
ridicule **2** = **parody**, mockery,
caricature, lampoon, burlesque

satisfaction NOUN
1 = **fulfilment**, pleasure,
achievement, relish, gratification,
pride ≠ dissatisfaction
2 = **contentment**, content,
comfort, pleasure, happiness,
enjoyment, satiety, repletion
≠ discontent

satisfactory ADJECTIVE
= **adequate**, acceptable,
good enough, average, fair,
all right, sufficient, passable
≠ unsatisfactory

satisfy VERB 1 = **content**,
please, indulge, gratify, pander
to, assuage, pacify, quench
≠ dissatisfy **2** = **convince**,
persuade, assure, reassure
≠ dissuade **3** = **comply with**,
meet, fulfil, answer, serve, fill,
observe, obey ≠ fail to meet

saturate VERB 1 = **flood**,
overwhelm, swamp, overrun
2 = **soak**, steep, drench, imbue,
suffuse, wet through, waterlog,
souse

saturated ADJECTIVE = **soaked**,
soaking (wet), drenched, sodden,
dripping, waterlogged, sopping

(wet), wet through

sauce NOUN = **dressing**, dip,
relish, condiment

savage ADJECTIVE 1 = **cruel**,
brutal, vicious, fierce, harsh,
ruthless, ferocious, sadistic
≠ gentle **2** = **wild**, fierce,
ferocious, unbroken, feral,
untamed, undomesticated
≠ tame **3** = **primitive**,
undeveloped, uncultivated,
uncivilized **4** = **uncultivated**,
rugged, unspoilt, uninhabited,
rough, uncivilized ≠ cultivated
▷ **NOUN** = **lout**, yob (*Brit. slang*),
barbarian, yahoo, hoon (*Austral. &
N.Z.*), boor, cougan (*Austral. slang*),
scozza (*Austral. slang*), bogan
(*Austral. slang*)
▷ **VERB** = **maul**, tear, claw, attack,
mangle, lacerate, mangulate
(*Austral. slang*)

save VERB 1 = **rescue**, free, release,
deliver, recover, get out, liberate,
salvage ≠ endanger **2** = **keep**,
reserve, set aside, store, collect,
gather, hold, hoard ≠ spend
3 = **protect**, keep, guard, preserve,
look after, safeguard, salvage,
conserve **4** = **put aside**, keep,
reserve, collect, retain, set aside,
put by

saving NOUN = **economy**,
discount, reduction, bargain
▷ **PLURAL NOUN** = **nest egg**, fund,
store, reserves, resources

saviour NOUN = **rescuer**, deliverer,
defender, protector, liberator,
redeemer, preserver

Saviour NOUN = **Christ**, Jesus, the

Messiah, the Redeemer

savour VERB 1 = **relish**, delight in, revel in, luxuriate in 2 = **enjoy**, appreciate, relish, delight in, revel in, luxuriate in

▷ NOUN = **flavour**, taste, smell, relish, smack, tang, piquancy

say VERB 1 = **state**, declare, remark, announce, maintain, mention, assert, affirm

2 = **speak**, utter, voice, express, pronounce 3 = **suggest**, express, imply, communicate, disclose, give away, convey, divulge

4 = **suppose**, supposing, imagine, assume, presume 5 = **estimate**, suppose, guess, conjecture, surmise

▷ NOUN 1 = **influence**, power, control, authority, weight, clout (*informal*), mana (*N.Z.*) 2 = **chance to speak**, vote, voice

saying NOUN = **proverb**, maxim, adage, dictum, axiom, aphorism

scale[1] NOUN = **flake**, plate, layer, lamina

scale[2] NOUN 1 = **degree**, size, range, extent, dimensions, scope, magnitude, breadth 2 = **system of measurement**, measuring system 3 = **ranking**, ladder, hierarchy, series, sequence, progression 4 = **ratio**, proportion

▷ VERB = **climb up**, mount, ascend, surmount, clamber up, escalade

scan VERB 1 = **glance over**, skim, look over, eye, check, examine, check out (*informal*), run over, surf (*computing*) 2 = **survey**,

search, investigate, sweep, scour, scrutinize

scandal NOUN 1 = **disgrace**, crime, offence, sin, embarrassment, wrongdoing, dishonourable behaviour, discreditable behaviour

2 = **gossip**, goss (*informal*), talk, rumours, dirt, slander, tattle, aspersion 3 = **shame**, disgrace, stigma, infamy, opprobrium

4 = **outrage**, shame, insult, disgrace, injustice, crying shame

scant ADJECTIVE = **inadequate**, meagre, sparse, little, minimal, barely sufficient ≠ adequate

scapegoat NOUN = **fall guy**, whipping boy

scar NOUN 1 = **mark**, injury, wound, blemish 2 = **trauma**, suffering, pain, torture, anguish

▷ VERB = **mark**, disfigure, damage, mar, mutilate, blemish, deface

scarce ADJECTIVE 1 = **in short supply**, insufficient ≠ plentiful 2 = **rare**, few, uncommon, few and far between, infrequent ≠ common

scarcely ADVERB 1 = **hardly**, barely 2 (*often used ironically*) = **by no means**, hardly, definitely not

● WORD POWER

● Since *scarcely*, *hardly*, and *barely*

● already have negative force, it

● is unnecessary to use another

● negative word with them.

● Therefore, say *he had hardly*

● *had time to think* (not *he hadn't*

● *hardly had time to think*); and

- there was scarcely any bread left
- (not there was scarcely no bread
- left). When scarcely, hardly, and
- barely are used at the beginning
- of a sentence, as in scarcely had
- I arrived, the following clause
- should start with when: scarcely
- had I arrived when I was asked
- to chair a meeting. The word
- before can be used in place of
- when in this context, but the
- word than used in the same
- way is considered incorrect
- by many people, though this
- use is becoming increasingly
- common.

scare VERB = **frighten**, alarm,
terrify, panic, shock, startle,
intimidate, dismay
▷ NOUN 1 = **fright**, shock, start
2 = **panic**, hysteria 3 = **alert**,
warning, alarm

scared ADJECTIVE = **afraid**,
alarmed, frightened, terrified,
shaken, startled, fearful, petrified

scary ADJECTIVE (informal)
= **frightening**, alarming,
terrifying, chilling, horrifying,
spooky (informal), creepy (informal),
spine-chilling

scatter VERB 1 = **throw about**,
spread, sprinkle, strew, shower,
fling, diffuse, disseminate
≠ gather 2 = **disperse**, dispel,
disband, dissipate ≠ assemble

scenario NOUN 1 = **situation**
2 = **story line**, résumé, outline,
summary, synopsis

scene NOUN 1 = **act**, part,
division, episode 2 = **setting**,

set, background, location,
backdrop 3 = **site**, place, setting,
area, position, spot, locality 4
(informal) = **world**, business,
environment, arena 5 = **view**,
prospect, panorama, vista,
landscape, outlook 6 = **fuss**, to-
do, row, performance, exhibition,
carry-on (informal, chiefly Brit.),
tantrum, commotion, hissy fit
(informal)

scenery NOUN 1 = **landscape**,
view, surroundings, terrain,
vista 2 (theatre) = **set**, setting,
backdrop, flats, stage set

scenic ADJECTIVE = **picturesque**,
beautiful, spectacular, striking,
panoramic

scent NOUN 1 = **fragrance**, smell,
perfume, bouquet, aroma, odour
2 = **trail**, track, spoor
▷ VERB = **smell**, sense, detect,
sniff, discern, nose out

scented ADJECTIVE = **fragrant**,
perfumed, aromatic, sweet-
smelling, odoriferous

sceptic NOUN 1 = **doubter**, cynic,
disbeliever 2 = **agnostic**, doubter,
unbeliever, doubting Thomas

sceptical ADJECTIVE = **doubtful**,
cynical, dubious, unconvinced,
disbelieving, incredulous,
mistrustful ≠ convinced

scepticism NOUN = **doubt**,
suspicion, disbelief, cynicism,
incredulity

schedule NOUN = **plan**,
programme, agenda, calendar,
timetable
▷ VERB = **plan**, set up, book,

S

scheme | 500

programme, arrange, organize

scheme NOUN 1 = **plan**, programme, strategy, system, project, proposal, tactics 2 = **plot**, ploy, ruse, intrigue, conspiracy, manoeuvre, subterfuge, stratagem
▷ VERB = **plot**, plan, intrigue, manoeuvre, conspire, contrive, collude, machinate

scheming ADJECTIVE = **calculating**, cunning, sly, tricky, wily, artful, conniving, underhand ≠ straightforward

schmick ADJECTIVE 1 (*Austral. slang*) = **excellent**, outstanding, good, great, fine, cool (*informal*), brilliant, very good, superb, booshit (*Austral. slang*), exo (*Austral. slang*), sik (*Austral. slang*), rad (*informal*), phat (*slang*) ≠ terrible 2 = **stylish**, smart, chic, fashionable, trendy (*Brit. informal*), modish, dressy (*informal*), voguish ≠ scruffy

scholar NOUN 1 = **intellectual**, academic, savant, acca (*Austral. slang*) 2 = **student**, pupil, learner, schoolboy or schoolgirl

scholarly ADJECTIVE = **learned**, academic, intellectual, lettered, erudite, scholastic, bookish ≠ uneducated

scholarship NOUN 1 = **grant**, award, payment, endowment, fellowship, bursary 2 = **learning**, education, knowledge, erudition, book-learning

school NOUN 1 = **academy**, college, institution, institute, seminary 2 = **group**, set, circle, faction, followers, disciples, devotees, denomination
▷ VERB = **train**, coach, discipline, educate, drill, tutor, instruct

science NOUN = **discipline**, body of knowledge, branch of knowledge

scientific ADJECTIVE = **systematic**, accurate, exact, precise, controlled, mathematical

scientist NOUN = **researcher**, inventor, boffin (*informal*), technophile

scoff¹ VERB = **scorn**, mock, laugh at, ridicule, knock (*informal*), despise, sneer, jeer

scoff² VERB = **gobble (up)**, wolf, devour, bolt, guzzle, gulp down, gorge yourself on

scoop VERB = **win**, get, land, gain, achieve, earn, secure, obtain
▷ NOUN 1 = **ladle**, spoon, dipper 2 = **exclusive**, exposé, revelation, sensation ▷ PHRASES: **scoop something out 1** = **take out**, empty, spoon out, bail or bale out 2 = **dig**, shovel, excavate, gouge, hollow out; **scoop something or someone up** = **gather up**, lift, pick up, take up, sweep up or away

scope NOUN 1 = **opportunity**, room, freedom, space, liberty, latitude 2 = **range**, capacity, reach, area, outlook, orbit, span, sphere

scorch VERB = **burn**, sear, roast, wither, shrivel, parch, singe

scorching ADJECTIVE = **burning**, boiling, baking, flaming, roasting, searing, fiery, red-hot

score VERB 1 = **gain**, win, achieve, make, get, attain, notch up (*informal*), chalk up (*informal*) 2 (*music*) = **arrange**, set, orchestrate, adapt 3 = **cut**, scratch, mark, slash, scrape, graze, gouge, deface
▷ NOUN 1 = **rating**, mark, grade, percentage 2 = **points**, result, total, outcome 3 = **composition**, soundtrack, arrangement, orchestration 4 = **grievance**, wrong, injury, injustice, grudge ▷ PLURAL NOUN = **lots**, loads, many, millions, hundreds, masses, swarms, multitudes ▷ PHRASE: **score something out** *or* **through** = **cross out**, delete, strike out, cancel, obliterate

scorn NOUN = **contempt**, disdain, mockery, derision, sarcasm, disparagement ≠ respect
▷ VERB = **despise**, reject, disdain, slight, be above, spurn, deride, flout ≠ respect

● **WORD POWER**
● The Scots language has a
● lexicon of highly evocative and
● colourful words, some of which
● have no direct Standard English
● counterparts. Many of these
● remain restricted to Scottish
● dialects, but some have filtered
● through into Standard English,
● though sometimes only as far
● as British English. For example,
● *canny*, originally from the verb
● 'to know', means shrewd or
● knowing, and is related to

● the words cunning and ken. It
● particularly refers to financial
● astuteness in phrases like *canny*
● *with money*, *canny business*
● *sense*. It is a description very
● often applied to someone else,
● rather than oneself, with a
● mixture of awe and mistrust. It
● might be expected that *uncanny*
● would mean the opposite
● of canny, i.e. not shrewd,
● foolish, careless. However,
● in Standard English, this
● meaning has been superseded
● by the senses 'mysterious'
● and 'beyond what is normal',
● e.g. She bore an uncanny
● resemblance to her mother.
● The Scottish word *blether* has
● come into Standard English
● and sits alongside its more
● common English equivalent
● *blather*. From an Old Norse
● word meaning 'nonsense', it
● refers to foolish talk, which
● can be long-winded, gossipy,
● boasting, or inconsequential.
● A blether can be both the
● person doing the chattering
● and the conversation itself. It
● is similar in meaning to natter
● and chinwag, e.g. He always
● enjoyed a wee dram and a good
● blether.

scour¹ VERB = **scrub**, clean, polish, rub, buff, abrade

scour² VERB = **search**, hunt, comb, ransack

scout NOUN = **vanguard**, lookout, precursor, outrider, reconnoitrer,

advance guard
▷ VERB = **reconnoitre**, investigate, watch, survey, observe, spy, probe, recce (*slang*)

scramble VERB 1 = **struggle**, climb, crawl, swarm, scrabble 2 = **strive**, rush, contend, vie, run, push, jostle 3 = **jumble**, mix up, muddle, shuffle
▷ NOUN 1 = **clamber**, ascent 2 = **race**, competition, struggle, rush, confusion, commotion, melee *or* mêlée

scrap¹ NOUN = **piece**, fragment, bit, grain, particle, portion, part, crumb 2 = **waste**, junk, off cuts
▷ PLURAL NOUN = **leftovers**, remains, bits, leavings
▷ VERB = **get rid of**, drop, abandon, ditch (*slang*), discard, write off, jettison, throw away *or* out ≠ bring back

scrap² (*informal*) NOUN = **fight**, battle, row, argument, dispute, disagreement, quarrel, squabble, biffo (*Austral. slang*)
▷ VERB = **fight**, argue, row, squabble, wrangle

scrape VERB 1 = **rake**, sweep, drag, brush 2 = **grate**, grind, scratch, squeak, rasp 3 = **graze**, skin, scratch, bark, scuff, rub 4 = **clean**, remove, scour
▷ NOUN (*informal*) = **predicament**, difficulty, fix (*informal*), mess, dilemma, plight, tight spot, awkward situation

scratch VERB 1 = **rub**, scrape, claw at 2 = **mark**, cut, score, damage, grate, graze, etch, lacerate

▷ NOUN = **mark**, scrape, graze, blemish, gash, laceration, claw mark ▷ PHRASE: **not up to scratch** (*informal*) = **inadequate**, unacceptable, unsatisfactory, insufficient, not up to standard

scream VERB = **cry**, yell, shriek, screech, bawl, howl
▷ NOUN = **cry**, yell, howl, shriek, screech, yelp

screen NOUN = **cover**, guard, shade, shelter, shield, partition, cloak, canopy
▷ VERB 1 = **broadcast**, show, put on, present, air, cable, beam, transmit 2 = **cover**, hide, conceal, shade, mask, veil, cloak 3 = **investigate**, test, check, examine, scan 4 = **process**, sort, examine, filter, scan, evaluate, gauge, sift 5 = **protect**, guard, shield, defend, shelter

screw NOUN = **nail**, pin, tack, rivet, fastener, spike
▷ VERB 1 = **fasten**, fix, attach, bolt, clamp, rivet 2 = **turn**, twist, tighten 3 (*informal*) = **cheat**, do (*slang*), rip (someone) off (*slang*), skin (*slang*), trick, con, sting (*informal*), fleece 4 (*informal*) often with **out of** = **squeeze**, wring, extract, wrest ▷ PHRASE: **screw something up** 1 = **contort**, wrinkle, distort, pucker 2 (*informal*) = **bungle**, botch, mess up, spoil, mishandle, make a mess of (*slang*), make a hash of (*informal*), crool *or* cruel (*Austral. slang*)

scribble VERB = **scrawl**, write, jot,

dash off

script NOUN 1 = **text**, lines, words, book, copy, dialogue, libretto
2 = **handwriting**, writing, calligraphy, penmanship
▷ VERB = **write**, draft

scripture NOUN = **The Bible**, The Gospels, The Scriptures, The Good Book, Holy Scripture, Holy Writ, Holy Bible

scrub VERB 1 = **scour**, clean, polish, rub, wash, cleanse, buff
2 (*informal*) = **cancel**, drop, give up, abolish, forget about, call off, delete

scrutiny NOUN = **examination**, study, investigation, search, analysis, inspection, exploration, perusal

sculpture NOUN = **statue**, figure, model, bust, effigy, figurine, statuette
▷ VERB = **carve**, form, model, fashion, shape, mould, sculpt, chisel

sea NOUN 1 = **ocean**, the deep, the waves, main 2 = **mass**, army, host, crowd, mob, abundance, swarm, horde ▷ PHRASE: **at sea** = **bewildered**, lost, confused, puzzled, baffled, perplexed, mystified, flummoxed ▷ RELATED WORDS: *adjectives* **marine, maritime**

- SEA BIRDS
- albatross *or* (*informal*) gooney bird
- auk
- black-backed gull
- black shag *or* kawau (*N.Z.*)
- blue penguin, korora *or* little blue penguin (*N.Z.*)
- blue shag (*N.Z.*)
- caspian tern *or* taranui (*N.Z.*)
- coot
- cormorant
- fairy penguin, little penguin, *or* (*N.Z.*) korora
- fish hawk
- fulmar
- gannet
- guillemot
- gull *or* (*archaic or dialect*) cob(b)
- herring gull
- kittiwake

- man-of-war bird *or* frigate bird
- oystercatcher
- petrel
- razorbill *or* razor-billed auk
- scoter
- sea eagle, erne, *or* ern
- seagull
- shearwater
- short-tailed shearwater, (Tasmanian) mutton bird, *or* (*N.Z.*) titi
- skua
- storm petrel, stormy petrel, *or* Mother Carey's chicken
- wandering albatross
- white-fronted tern, black cap, kahawai bird, sea swallow *or* tara (*N.Z.*)

S

seal VERB = **settle**, clinch, conclude, consummate, finalize
▷ NOUN 1 = **sealant**, sealer, adhesive 2 = **authentication**, stamp, confirmation, ratification, insignia, imprimatur

seam NOUN 1 = **joint**, closure 2 = **layer**, vein, stratum, lode

- ● SEA MAMMALS
- ● dugong
- ● elephant seal
- ● harp seal
- ● manatee
- ● sea cow
- ● seal
- ● sea lion
- ● walrus or (*archaic*) sea horse

sear VERB = **wither**, burn, scorch, sizzle

search VERB = **examine**, investigate, explore, inspect, comb, scour, ransack, scrutinize, fossick (*Austral. & N.Z.*)
▷ NOUN = **hunt**, look, investigation, examination, pursuit, quest, inspection, exploration ▷ PHRASE: **search for something** *or* **someone** = **look for**, hunt for, pursue

searching ADJECTIVE = **keen**, sharp, probing, close, intent, piercing, penetrating, quizzical ≠ superficial

searing ADJECTIVE 1 = **acute**, intense, shooting, severe, painful, stabbing, piercing, gut-wrenching 2 = **cutting**, biting, bitter, harsh, barbed, hurtful, caustic

season NOUN = **period**, time, term, spell
▷ VERB = **flavour**, salt, spice, enliven, pep up

seasoned ADJECTIVE = **experienced**, veteran, practised, hardened, time-served ≠ inexperienced

seasoning NOUN = **flavouring**, spice, salt and pepper, condiment

seat NOUN 1 = **chair**, bench, stall, stool, pew, settle 2 = **membership**, place, constituency, chair, incumbency 3 = **centre**, place, site, heart, capital, situation, source, hub 4 = **mansion**, house, residence, abode, ancestral hall
▷ VERB 1 = **sit**, place, settle, set, fix, locate, install 2 = **hold**, take, accommodate, sit, contain, cater for

second¹ ADJECTIVE 1 = **next**, following, succeeding, subsequent 2 = **additional**, other, further, extra, alternative 3 = **inferior**, secondary, subordinate, lower, lesser
▷ NOUN = **supporter**, assistant, aide, colleague, backer, helper, right-hand man
▷ VERB = **support**, back, endorse, approve, go along with

second² NOUN = **moment**, minute, instant, flash, sec (*informal*), jiffy (*informal*), trice

secondary ADJECTIVE 1 = **subordinate**, minor, lesser,

lower, inferior, unimportant
≠ main **2** = **resultant**,
contingent, derived, indirect
≠ original

second-hand ADJECTIVE = **used**,
old, hand-me-down (*informal*),
nearly new, preloved (*Austral.
slang*)

secondly ADVERB = **next**, second,
moreover, furthermore, also, in
the second place

secrecy NOUN **1** = **mystery**,
stealth, concealment, furtiveness,
secretiveness, clandestineness,
covertness **2** = **confidentiality**,
privacy **3** = **privacy**, silence,
seclusion

secret ADJECTIVE **1** = **undisclosed**,
unknown, confidential,
underground, undercover,
unrevealed **2** = **concealed**,
hidden, disguised ≠ unconcealed
3 = **undercover**, furtive ≠ open
4 = **secretive**, reserved, close
≠ frank **5** = **mysterious**, cryptic,
abstruse, occult, clandestine,
arcane ≠ straightforward
▷ NOUN = **private affair**
▷ PHRASE: **in secret** = **secretly**,
surreptitiously, slyly

secretive ADJECTIVE = **reticent**,
reserved, close, deep,
uncommunicative, tight-lipped
≠ open

secretly ADVERB = **in secret**,
privately, surreptitiously, quietly,
covertly, furtively, stealthily,
clandestinely

sect NOUN = **group**, division,
faction, party, camp,
denomination, schism

section NOUN **1** = **part**, piece,
portion, division, slice, passage,
segment, fraction **2** = **district**,
area, region, sector, zone

sector NOUN **1** = **part**, division
2 = **area**, part, region, district,
zone, quarter

secular ADJECTIVE = **worldly**,
lay, earthly, civil, temporal,
nonspiritual ≠ religious

secure VERB **1** = **obtain**, get,
acquire, score (*slang*), gain,
procure ≠ lose **2** = **attach**, stick,
fix, bind, fasten ≠ detach
▷ ADJECTIVE **1** = **safe**, protected,
immune, unassailable
≠ unprotected **2** = **fast**, firm,
fixed, stable, steady, fastened,
immovable ≠ insecure
3 = **confident**, sure, easy, certain,
assured, reassured ≠ uneasy

security NOUN **1** = **precautions**,
defence, safeguards, protection,
safety measures **2** = **assurance**,
confidence, conviction, certainty,
reliance, sureness, positiveness
≠ insecurity **3** = **pledge**,
insurance, guarantee, hostage,
collateral, pawn, gage, surety
4 = **protection**, safety, custody,
refuge, sanctuary, safekeeping
≠ vulnerability

sediment NOUN = **dregs**,
grounds, residue, lees, deposit

seduce VERB **1** = **tempt**, lure,
entice, mislead, deceive, beguile,
lead astray, inveigle **2** = **corrupt**,
deprave, dishonour, debauch,
deflower

S

seductive ADJECTIVE = **tempting**, inviting, attractive, enticing, provocative, alluring, bewitching, hot (informal)

see VERB 1 = **perceive**, spot, notice, sight, witness, observe, distinguish, glimpse 2 = **understand**, get, follow, realize, appreciate, grasp, comprehend, fathom 3 = **find out**, learn, discover, determine, verify, ascertain 4 = **consider**, decide, reflect, deliberate, think over 5 = **make sure**, ensure, guarantee, make certain, see to it 6 = **accompany**, show, escort, lead, walk, usher 7 = **speak to**, receive, interview, consult, confer with 8 = **meet**, come across, happen on, bump into, run across, chance on 9 = **go out with**, court, date (informal, chiefly U.S.), go steady with (informal), step out with (informal) ▷ PHRASE: **seeing as** = **since**, as, in view of the fact that, inasmuch as

● **WORD POWER**
● It is common to hear seeing
● as how, as in seeing as how the
● bus is always late, I don't need to
● hurry. However, the use of how
● here is considered incorrect or
● nonstandard, and should be
● avoided.

seed NOUN 1 = **grain**, pip, germ, kernel, egg, embryo, spore, ovum 2 = **beginning**, start, germ 3 = **origin**, source, nucleus 4 (chiefly bible) = **offspring**, children, descendants, issue,

progeny ▷ PHRASE: **go** or **run to seed** = **decline**, deteriorate, degenerate, decay, go downhill (informal), let yourself go, go to pot

seek VERB 1 = **look for**, pursue, search for, be after, hunt 2 = **try**, attempt, aim, strive, endeavour, essay, aspire to

seem VERB = **appear**, give the impression of being, look

seep VERB = **ooze**, well, leak, soak, trickle, exude, permeate

seethe VERB 1 = **be furious**, rage, fume, simmer, see red (informal), be livid, go ballistic (slang, chiefly U.S.) 2 = **boil**, bubble, foam, fizz, froth

segment NOUN = **section**, part, piece, division, slice, portion, wedge

segregate VERB = **set apart**, divide, separate, isolate, discriminate against, dissociate ≠ unite

segregation NOUN = **separation**, discrimination, apartheid, isolation

seize VERB 1 = **grab**, grip, grasp, take, snatch, clutch, snap up, pluck ≠ let go 2 = **take by storm**, take over, acquire, occupy, conquer 3 = **capture**, catch, arrest, apprehend, take captive ≠ release

seizure NOUN 1 = **attack**, fit, spasm, convulsion, paroxysm 2 = **taking**, grabbing, annexation, confiscation, commandeering 3 = **capture**, arrest, apprehension

seldom ADVERB = **rarely**, not

often, infrequently, hardly ever
≠ often

select VERB = **choose**, take, pick,
opt for, decide on, single out,
adopt, settle upon ≠ reject
▷ ADJECTIVE 1 = **choice**, special,
excellent, superior, first-class,
hand-picked, top-notch (*informal*)
≠ ordinary 2 = **exclusive**,
elite, privileged, cliquish
≠ indiscriminate

selection NOUN 1 = **choice**,
choosing, pick, option, preference
2 = **anthology**, collection, medley,
choice

selective ADJECTIVE = **particular**,
discriminating, careful,
discerning, tasteful, fastidious
≠ indiscriminate

selfish ADJECTIVE = **self-
centred**, self-interested, greedy,
ungenerous, egoistic *or* egoistical,
egotistic *or* egoistical ≠ unselfish

sell VERB 1 = **trade**, exchange,
barter ≠ buy 2 = **deal in**, market,
trade in, stock, handle, retail,
peddle, traffic in ≠ buy ▷ PHRASE:
sell out of something = **run out
of**, be out of stock of

seller NOUN = **dealer**, merchant,
vendor, agent, retailer,
supplier, purveyor, salesman *or*
saleswoman

send VERB 1 = **dispatch**, forward,
direct, convey, remit 2 = **propel**,
hurl, fling, shoot, fire, cast, let
fly ▷ PHRASE: **send something**
or **someone up** (*Brit. informal*)
= **mock**, mimic, parody, spoof
(*informal*), imitate, take off

(*informal*), make fun of, lampoon

sendoff NOUN = **farewell**,
departure, leave-taking,
valediction

senior ADJECTIVE 1 = **higher
ranking**, superior ≠ subordinate
2 = **the elder**, major (*Brit.*)
≠ junior

sensation NOUN 1 = **feeling**,
sense, impression, perception,
awareness, consciousness
2 = **excitement**, thrill, stir, furore,
commotion

sensational ADJECTIVE
1 = **amazing**, dramatic, thrilling,
astounding ≠ dull 2 = **shocking**,
exciting, melodramatic, shock-
horror (*facetious*) ≠ unexciting
3 (*informal*) = **excellent**, superb,
mean (*slang*), impressive,
smashing (*informal*), fabulous
(*informal*), marvellous, out of this
world (*informal*), booshit (*Austral.
slang*), exo (*Austral. slang*), sik
(*Austral. slang*), rad (*informal*), phat
(*slang*), schmick (*Austral. informal*),
funky ≠ ordinary

sense NOUN 1 = **faculty**
2 = **feeling**, impression,
perception, awareness,
consciousness, atmosphere, aura
3 = **understanding**, awareness
4 *sometimes plural* = **intelligence**,
reason, understanding,
brains (*informal*), judgment,
wisdom, wit(s), common sense
≠ foolishness 5 = **meaning**,
significance, import, implication,
drift, gist
▷ VERB = **perceive**, feel,

S

understand, pick up, realize,
be aware of, discern, get the
impression ≠ be unaware of

sensibility NOUN *often plural*
= **feelings**, emotions, sentiments,
susceptibilities, moral sense

sensible ADJECTIVE 1 = **wise**,
practical, prudent, shrewd,
judicious ≠ foolish
2 = **intelligent**, practical, rational,
sound, realistic, sage, shrewd,
down-to-earth, grounded
≠ senseless

sensitive ADJECTIVE
1 = **thoughtful**, kindly, concerned,
patient, attentive, tactful,
unselfish 2 = **delicate**, tender
3 = **susceptible**, responsive,
easily affected 4 = **touchy**,
oversensitive, easily upset,
easily offended, easily hurt
≠ insensitive 5 = **precise**,
fine, acute, keen, responsive
≠ imprecise

sensitivity NOUN
1 = **susceptibility**,
responsiveness, receptiveness,
sensitiveness 2 = **consideration**,
patience, thoughtfulness
3 = **touchiness**, oversensitivity
4 = **responsiveness**, precision,
keenness, acuteness

sensual ADJECTIVE 1 = **sexual**,
erotic, raunchy (*slang*), lewd,
lascivious, lustful, lecherous
2 = **physical**, bodily, voluptuous,
animal, luxurious, fleshly, carnal

sentence NOUN 1 = **punishment**,
condemnation 2 = **verdict**, order,
ruling, decision, judgment, decree

▷ VERB 1 = **condemn**, doom
2 = **convict**, condemn, penalize

sentiment NOUN 1 = **feeling**,
idea, view, opinion,
attitude, belief, judgment
2 = **sentimentality**, emotion,
tenderness, romanticism,
sensibility, emotionalism,
mawkishness

sentimental ADJECTIVE
= **romantic**, touching,
emotional, nostalgic, maudlin,
weepy (*informal*), slushy
(*informal*), schmaltzy (*slang*)
≠ unsentimental

separate ADJECTIVE
1 = **unconnected**, individual,
particular, divided, divorced,
isolated, detached, disconnected
≠ connected 2 = **individual**,
independent, apart, distinct
≠ joined
▷ VERB 1 = **divide**, detach,
disconnect, disjoin ≠ combine
2 = **come apart**, split, come away
≠ connect 3 = **sever**, break apart,
split in two, divide in two ≠ join
4 = **split up**, part, divorce, break
up, part company, get divorced, be
estranged 5 = **distinguish**, mark,
single out, set apart ≠ link

separated ADJECTIVE
1 = **estranged**, parted,
separate, apart, disunited
2 = **disconnected**, parted,
divided, separate, disassociated,
disunited, sundered

separately ADVERB 1 = **alone**,
apart, not together, severally
≠ together 2 = **individually**,

singly

separation NOUN 1 = **division**, break, dissociation, disconnection, disunion 2 = **split-up**, parting, split, divorce, break-up, rift

sequel NOUN 1 = **follow-up**, continuation, development 2 = **consequence**, result, outcome, conclusion, end, upshot

sequence NOUN = **succession**, course, series, order, chain, cycle, arrangement, progression

series NOUN 1 = **sequence**, course, chain, succession, run, set, order, train 2 = **drama**, serial, soap (*informal*), sitcom (*informal*), soap opera, soapie *or* soapie (*Austral. slang*), situation comedy

serious ADJECTIVE 1 = **grave**, bad, critical, dangerous, acute, severe 2 = **important**, crucial, urgent, pressing, worrying, significant, grim, momentous ≠ unimportant 3 = **thoughtful**, detailed, careful, deep, profound, in-depth 4 = **deep**, sophisticated 5 = **solemn**, earnest, grave, sober, staid, humourless, unsmiling ≠ light-hearted 6 = **sincere**, earnest, genuine, honest, in earnest ≠ insincere

seriously ADVERB 1 = **truly**, in earnest, all joking aside 2 = **badly**, severely, gravely, critically, acutely, dangerously

seriousness NOUN 1 = **importance**, gravity, urgency, significance 2 = **solemnity**, gravity, earnestness, gravitas

sermon NOUN = **homily**, address

servant NOUN = **attendant**, domestic, slave, maid, help, retainer, skivvy (*chiefly Brit.*)

serve VERB 1 = **work for**, help, aid, assist, be in the service of 2 = **perform**, do, complete, fulfil, discharge 3 = **be adequate**, do, suffice, suit, satisfy, be acceptable, answer the purpose 4 = **present**, provide, supply, deliver, set out, dish up

service NOUN 1 = **facility**, system, resource, utility, amenity 2 = **ceremony**, worship, rite, observance 3 = **work**, labour, employment, business, office, duty 4 = **check**, maintenance check
▷ VERB = **overhaul**, check, maintain, tune (up), go over, fine tune

session NOUN = **meeting**, hearing, sitting, period, conference, congress, discussion, assembly

set¹ VERB 1 = **put**, place, lay, position, rest, plant, station, stick 2 = **arrange**, decide (upon), settle, establish, determine, fix, schedule, appoint 3 = **assign**, give, allot, prescribe 4 = **harden**, stiffen, solidify, cake, thicken, crystallize, congeal 5 = **go down**, sink, dip, decline, disappear, vanish, subside 6 = **prepare**, lay, spread, arrange, make ready
▷ ADJECTIVE 1 = **established**, planned, decided, agreed, arranged, rigid, definite,

S

inflexible **2** = **strict**, rigid,
stubborn, inflexible ≠ flexible
3 = **conventional**, traditional,
stereotyped, unspontaneous
▷ NOUN **1** = **scenery**, setting,
scene, stage set **2** = **position**,
bearing, attitude, carriage,
posture ▷ PHRASES: **set on** or
upon something = **determined
to**, intent on, bent on, resolute
about; **set something up**
1 = **arrange**, organize, prepare,
prearrange **2** = **establish**,
begin, found, institute, initiate
3 = **build**, raise, construct, put
up, assemble, put together, erect
4 = **assemble**, put up
set² NOUN **1** = **series**, collection,
assortment, batch, compendium,
ensemble **2** = **group**, company,
crowd, circle, band, gang, faction,
clique
setback NOUN = **hold-up**,
check, defeat, blow, reverse,
disappointment, hitch,
misfortune
setting NOUN = **surroundings**,
site, location, set, scene,
background, context, backdrop
settle VERB **1** = **resolve**, work
out, put an end to, straighten
out **2** = **pay**, clear, square (up),
discharge **3** = **move to**, take up
residence in, live in, dwell in,
inhabit, reside in, set up home in,
put down roots in **4** = **colonize**,
populate, people, pioneer
5 = **land**, alight, descend, light,
come to rest **6** = **calm**, quiet,
relax, relieve, reassure, soothe,

lull, quell ≠ disturb
settlement NOUN
1 = **agreement**, arrangement,
working out, conclusion,
establishment, confirmation
2 = **payment**, clearing, discharge
3 = **colony**, community, outpost,
encampment, kainga or kaika
(*N.Z.*)
settler NOUN = **colonist**,
immigrant, pioneer, frontiersman
setup NOUN (*informal*)
= **arrangement**, system,
structure, organization,
conditions, regime
sever VERB **1** = **cut**, separate,
split, part, divide, detach,
disconnect, cut in two ≠ join
2 = **discontinue**, terminate, break
off, put an end to, dissociate
≠ continue
several ADJECTIVE = **various**,
different, diverse, sundry
severe ADJECTIVE **1** = **serious**,
critical, terrible, desperate,
extreme, awful, drastic,
catastrophic **2** = **acute**, intense,
violent, piercing, harrowing,
unbearable, agonizing,
insufferable **3** = **strict**, hard,
harsh, cruel, rigid, drastic,
oppressive, austere ≠ lenient
4 = **grim**, serious, grave,
forbidding, stern, unsmiling,
tight-lipped ≠ genial **5** = **plain**,
simple, austere, classic,
restrained, Spartan, unadorned,
unfussy, bare-bones ≠ fancy
severely ADVERB **1** = **seriously**,
badly, extremely, gravely, acutely

2 = **strictly**, harshly, sternly, sharply

severity NOUN = **strictness**, harshness, toughness, hardness, sternness, severeness

sew VERB = **stitch**, tack, seam, hem

sex NOUN **1** = **gender 2** (*informal*) = **lovemaking**, sexual relations, copulation, fornication, coitus, coition

sexual ADJECTIVE **1** = **carnal**, erotic, intimate **2** = **sexy**, erotic, sensual, arousing, naughty, provocative, seductive, sensuous

sexuality NOUN = **desire**, lust, eroticism, sensuality, sexiness (*informal*), carnality

sexy ADJECTIVE = **erotic**, sensual, seductive, arousing, naughty, provocative, sensuous, suggestive, hot (*informal*)

shabby ADJECTIVE **1** = **tatty**, worn, ragged, scruffy, tattered, threadbare ≠ smart **2** = **rundown**, seedy, mean, dilapidated **3** = **mean**, low, rotten (*informal*), cheap, dirty, despicable, contemptible, scurvy ≠ fair

shack NOUN = **hut**, cabin, shanty, whare (*N.Z.*)

shade NOUN **1** = **hue**, tone, colour, tint **2** = **shadow 3** = **dash**, trace, hint, suggestion **4** = **nuance**, difference, degree **5** = **screen**, covering, cover, blind, curtain, shield, veil, canopy **6** (*literary*) = **ghost**, spirit, phantom, spectre, apparition, kehua (*N.Z.*)
▷ VERB **1** = **darken**, shadow, cloud, dim **2** = **cover**, protect, screen, hide, shield, conceal, obscure, veil

shadow NOUN **1** = **silhouette**, shape, outline, profile **2** = **shade**, dimness, darkness, gloom, cover, dusk
▷ VERB **1** = **shade**, screen, shield, darken, overhang **2** = **follow**, tail (*informal*), trail, stalk

shady ADJECTIVE **1** = **shaded**, cool, dim ≠ sunny **2** (*informal*) = **crooked**, dodgy (*Brit., Austral. & N.Z. informal*), unethical, suspect, suspicious, dubious, questionable, shifty, shonky (*Austral. & N.Z. informal*) ≠ honest

shaft NOUN **1** = **tunnel**, hole, passage, burrow, passageway, channel **2** = **handle**, staff, pole, rod, stem, baton, shank **3** = **ray**, beam, gleam

shake VERB **1** = **jiggle**, agitate **2** = **tremble**, shiver, quake, quiver **3** = **rock**, totter **4** = **wave**, wield, flourish, brandish **5** = **upset**, shock, frighten, disturb, distress, rattle (*informal*), unnerve, traumatize
▷ NOUN = **vibration**, trembling, quaking, jerk, shiver, shudder, jolt, tremor

shaky ADJECTIVE **1** = **unstable**, weak, precarious, rickety ≠ stable **2** = **unsteady**, faint, trembling, faltering, quivery **3** = **uncertain**, suspect, dubious, questionable, iffy (*informal*) ≠ reliable

shallow ADJECTIVE = **superficial**, surface, empty, slight, foolish, trivial, meaningless, frivolous

s

- **SHAKESPEARE**
- **Characters in Shakespeare**   **Play**
- Sir Andrew Aguecheek   Twelfth Night
- Antonio   The Merchant of Venice
- Antony   Antony and Cleopatra, Julius Caesar
- Ariel   The Tempest
- Aufidius   Coriolanus
- Autolycus   The Winter's Tale
- Banquo   Macbeth
- Bassanio   The Merchant of Venice
- Beatrice   Much Ado About Nothing
- Sir Toby Belch   Twelfth Night
- Benedick   Much Ado About Nothing
- Bolingbroke   Richard II
- Bottom   A Midsummer Night's Dream
- Brutus   Julius Caesar
- Caliban   The Tempest
- Casca   Julius Caesar
- Cassio   Othello
- Cassius   Julius Caesar
- Claudio   Much Ado About Nothing, Measure for Measure
- Claudius   Hamlet
- Cleopatra   Antony and Cleopatra
- Cordelia   King Lear
- Coriolanus   Coriolanus
- Cressida   Troilus and Cressida
- Demetrius   A Midsummer Night's Dream
- Desdemona   Othello
- Dogberry   Much Ado About Nothing
- Edmund   King Lear
- Enobarbus   Antony and Cleopatra
- Falstaff   Henry IV Parts I and II, The Merry Wives of Windsor
- Ferdinand   The Tempest
- Feste   Twelfth Night
- Fluellen   Henry V
- Fool   King Lear
- Gertrude   Hamlet
- Gloucester   King Lear

S

Characters in Shakespeare	Play
Goneril	King Lear
Guildenstern	Hamlet
Hamlet	Hamlet
Helena	All's Well that Ends Well, A Midsummer Night's Dream
Hermia	A Midsummer Night's Dream
Hero	Much Ado About Nothing
Hotspur	Henry IV Part I
Iago	Othello
Jaques	As You Like It
John of Gaunt	Richard II
Juliet	Romeo and Juliet
Julius Caesar	Julius Caesar
Katharina or Kate	The Taming of the Shrew
Kent	King Lear
Laertes	Hamlet
Lear	King Lear
Lysander	A Midsummer Night's Dream
Macbeth	Macbeth
Lady Macbeth	Macbeth
Macduff	Macbeth
Malcolm	Macbeth
Malvolio	Twelfth Night
Mercutio	Romeo and Juliet
Miranda	The Tempest
Oberon	A Midsummer Night's Dream
Octavius	Antony and Cleopatra
Olivia	Twelfth Night
Ophelia	Hamlet
Orlando	As You Like It
Orsino	Twelfth Night
Othello	Othello
Pandarus	Troilus and Cressida
Perdita	The Winter's Tale
Petruchio	The Taming of the Shrew
Pistol	Henry IV Part II, Henry V, The Merry Wives of Windsor
Polonius	Hamlet
Portia	The Merchant of Venice

Characters in Shakespeare

Character	Play
Prospero	The Tempest
Puck	A Midsummer Night's Dream
Mistress Quickly	The Merry Wives of Windsor
Regan	King Lear
Romeo	Romeo and Juliet
Rosalind	As You Like It
Rosencrantz	Hamlet
Sebastian	The Tempest, Twelfth Night
Shylock	The Merchant of Venice
Thersites	Troilus and Cressida
Timon	Timon of Athens
Titania	A Midsummer Night's Dream
Touchstone	As You Like It
Troilus	Troilus and Cressida
Tybalt	Romeo and Juliet
Viola	Twelfth Night

Shakespeare's Plays

- All's Well that Ends Well
- Antony and Cleopatra
- As You Like It
- The Comedy of Errors
- Coriolanus
- Cymbeline
- Hamlet
- Henry IV Part I
- Henry IV Part II
- Henry V
- Henry VI Part I
- Henry VI Part II
- Henry VI Part III
- Henry VIII
- Julius Caesar
- King John
- King Lear
- Love's Labour's Lost
- Macbeth
- Measure for Measure
- The Merchant of Venice
- The Merry Wives of Windsor
- A Midsummer Night's Dream
- Much Ado About Nothing
- Othello
- Pericles, Prince of Tyre
- Richard II
- Richard III
- Romeo and Juliet
- The Taming of the Shrew
- The Tempest
- Timon of Athens
- Titus Andronicus
- Troilus and Cressida
- Twelfth Night
- The Two Gentlemen of Verona
- The Winter's Tale

s

≠ deep

sham NOUN =**fraud**, imitation, hoax, pretence, forgery, counterfeit, humbug, impostor ≠ the real thing
▷ ADJECTIVE =**false**, artificial, bogus, pretended, mock, imitation, simulated, counterfeit ≠ real

shambles NOUN 1 =**chaos**, mess, disorder, confusion, muddle, havoc, disarray, madhouse
2 =**mess**, jumble, untidiness

shame NOUN
1 =**embarrassment**, humiliation, ignominy, mortification, abashment ≠ shamelessness
2 =**disgrace**, scandal, discredit, smear, disrepute, reproach, dishonour, infamy ≠ honour
▷ VERB 1 =**embarrass**, disgrace, humiliate, humble, mortify, abash ≠ make proud 2 =**dishonour**, degrade, stain, smear, blot, debase, defile ≠ honour

shameful ADJECTIVE
=**disgraceful**, outrageous, scandalous, mean, low, base, wicked, dishonourable ≠ admirable

shape NOUN 1 =**appearance**, form, aspect, guise, likeness, semblance 2 =**form**, profile, outline, lines, build, figure, silhouette, configuration
3 =**pattern**, model, frame, mould
4 =**condition**, state, health, trim, fettle
▷ VERB 1 =**form**, make, produce, create, model, fashion, mould
2 =**mould**, form, make, fashion, model, frame

share NOUN =**part**, portion, quota, ration, lot, due, contribution, allowance
▷ VERB 1 =**divide**, split, distribute, assign 2 =**go halves on**, go fifty-fifty on (*informal*)

sharp ADJECTIVE 1 =**keen**, jagged, serrated ≠ blunt 2 =**quick-**

S

● **SHARKS**
● angel shark, angelfish, or monkfish
● basking shark, sailfish or (*N.Z.*) reremai
● blue pointer, or (*N.Z.*) blue shark or blue whaler
● bronze whaler (*Austral.*)
● carpet shark or (*Austral.*) wobbegong
● dogfish or (*Austral.*) dog shark
● gummy (shark)
● hammerhead

● mako
● nurse shark
● porbeagle or mackerel shark
● requiem shark
● school shark (*Austral.*)
● seven-gill shark (*Austral.*)
● shovelhead
● thrasher or thresher shark
● tiger shark
● tope
● whale shark

witted, clever, astute, knowing, quick, bright, alert, penetrating ≠ dim **3** = **cutting**, biting, bitter, harsh, barbed, hurtful, caustic ≠ gentle **4** = **sudden**, marked, abrupt, extreme, distinct ≠ gradual **5** = **clear**, distinct, well-defined, crisp ≠ indistinct **6** = **sour**, tart, pungent, hot, acid, acrid, piquant ≠ bland **7** = **acute**, severe, intense, painful, shooting, stabbing, piercing, gut-wrenching

▷ ADVERB = **promptly**, precisely, exactly, on time, on the dot, punctually ≠ approximately

sharpen VERB = **make sharp**, hone, whet, grind, edge

shatter VERB **1** = **smash**, break, burst, crack, crush, pulverize **2** = **destroy**, ruin, wreck, demolish, torpedo

shattered ADJECTIVE **1** = **devastated**, crushed, gutted (slang) **2** (informal) = **exhausted**, drained, worn out, done in (informal), all in (slang), knackered (slang), tired out, ready to drop

shave VERB **1** = **trim**, crop **2** = **scrape**, trim, shear, pare

shed¹ NOUN = **hut**, shack, outhouse, whare (N.Z.)

shed² VERB **1** = **drop**, spill, scatter **2** = **cast off**, discard, moult, slough off **3** = **give out**, cast, emit, give, radiate

sheen NOUN = **shine**, gleam, gloss, polish, brightness, lustre

sheer ADJECTIVE **1** = **total**, complete, absolute, utter, pure, downright, out-and-out, unmitigated ≠ moderate **2** = **steep**, abrupt, precipitous ≠ gradual **3** = **fine**, thin, transparent, see-through, gossamer, diaphanous, gauzy ≠ thick

sheet NOUN **1** = **page**, leaf, folio, piece of paper **2** = **plate**, piece, panel, slab **3** = **coat**, film, layer, surface, stratum, veneer, overlay, lamina **4** = **expanse**, area, stretch, sweep, covering, blanket

shell NOUN **1** = **husk**, case, pod **2** = **carapace 3** = **frame**, structure, hull, framework, chassis

▷ VERB = **bomb**, bombard, attack, blitz, strafe ▷ PHRASE: **shell something out** (informal) = **pay out**, fork out (slang), give, hand over

shelter NOUN **1** = **cover**, screen **2** = **protection**, safety, refuge, cover **3** = **refuge**, haven, sanctuary, retreat, asylum

▷ VERB **1** = **take shelter**, hide, seek refuge, take cover **2** = **protect**, shield, harbour, safeguard, cover, hide, guard, defend ≠ endanger

sheltered ADJECTIVE **1** = **screened**, covered, protected, shielded, secluded ≠ exposed **2** = **protected**, screened, shielded, quiet, isolated, secluded, cloistered

shelve VERB = **postpone**, defer, freeze, suspend, put aside, put on ice, put on the back burner

(*informal*), take a rain check on
(*U.S. & Canad. informal*)

shepherd NOUN = **drover**,
stockman, herdsman, grazier
▷ VERB = **guide**, conduct, steer,
herd, usher ▷ RELATED WORD:
adjective pastoral

sherang NOUN (*Austral. & N.Z.*)
= **boss**, manager, head, leader,
director, chief, master, employer,
supervisor, baas (*S. African*)

shield NOUN = **protection**, cover,
defence, screen, guard, shelter,
safeguard
▷ VERB = **protect**, cover, screen,
guard, defend, shelter, safeguard

shift VERB 1 = **move**, move around,
budge 2 = **remove**, move,
displace, relocate, rearrange,
reposition
▷ NOUN 1 = **change**, shifting,
displacement 2 = **move**,
rearrangement

shimmer VERB = **gleam**, twinkle,
glisten, scintillate
▷ NOUN = **gleam**, iridescence

shine VERB 1 = **gleam**, flash,
beam, glow, sparkle, glitter, glare,
radiate 2 = **polish**, buff, burnish,
brush 3 = **be outstanding**, stand
out, excel, be conspicuous
▷ NOUN 1 = **polish**, gloss, sheen,
lustre 2 = **brightness**, light,
sparkle, radiance

shining ADJECTIVE = **bright**,
brilliant, gleaming, beaming,
sparkling, shimmering, radiant,
luminous

shiny ADJECTIVE = **bright**,
gleaming, glossy, glistening,

polished, lustrous

ship NOUN = **vessel**, boat, craft

shiver VERB = **shudder**, shake,
tremble, quake, quiver
▷ NOUN = **tremble**, shudder,
quiver, trembling, flutter, tremor

shock NOUN 1 = **upset**, blow,
trauma, bombshell, turn
(*informal*), distress, disturbance
2 = **impact**, blow, clash, collision
3 = **start**, scare, fright, turn, jolt
▷ VERB 1 = **shake**, stun, stagger,
jolt, stupefy 2 = **horrify**, appal,
disgust, revolt, sicken, nauseate,
scandalize

shocking ADJECTIVE 1
(*informal*) = **terrible**, appalling,
dreadful, bad, horrendous,
ghastly, deplorable, abysmal
2 = **appalling**, outrageous,
disgraceful, disgusting, dreadful,
horrifying, revolting, sickening
≠ wonderful

shoot VERB 1 = **open fire on**, blast
(*slang*), hit, kill, plug (*slang*), bring
down 2 = **fire**, launch, discharge,
project, hurl, fling, propel, emit
3 = **speed**, race, rush, charge, fly,
tear, dash, barrel (along) (*informal*,
chiefly U.S. & Canad.)
▷ NOUN = **sprout**, branch, bud,
sprig, offshoot

shop NOUN = **store**, supermarket,
boutique, emporium,
hypermarket, dairy (*N.Z.*)

shore NOUN = **beach**, coast, sands,
strand (*poetic*), seashore

short ADJECTIVE 1 = **brief**, fleeting,
momentary ≠ long 2 = **concise**,
brief, succinct, summary,

S

compressed, terse, laconic, pithy
≠ lengthy **3** = **small**, little, squat,
diminutive, petite, dumpy ≠ tall
4 = **abrupt**, sharp, terse, curt,
brusque, impolite, discourteous,
uncivil ≠ polite **5** = **scarce**,
wanting, low, limited, lacking,
scant, deficient ≠ plentiful
▷ ADVERB = **abruptly**, suddenly,
without warning ≠ gradually

shortage NOUN = **deficiency**,
want, lack, scarcity, dearth,
paucity, insufficiency
≠ abundance

shortcoming NOUN = **failing**,
fault, weakness, defect, flaw,
imperfection

shorten VERB **1** = **cut**, reduce,
decrease, diminish, lessen,
curtail, abbreviate, abridge
≠ increase **2** = **turn up**

shortly ADVERB = **soon**, presently,
before long, in a little while

shot NOUN **1** = **discharge**,
gunfire, crack, blast, explosion,
bang **2** = **ammunition**, bullet,
slug, pellet, projectile, lead,
ball **3** = **marksman**, shooter,
markswoman **4** = **strike**, throw,
lob **5** (informal) = **attempt**, go
(informal), try, turn, effort, stab
(informal), endeavour

shoulder VERB **1** = **bear**, carry,
take on, accept, assume, be
responsible for **2** = **push**, elbow,
shove, jostle, press

shout VERB = **cry (out)**, call (out),
yell, scream, roar, bellow, bawl,
holler (informal)
▷ NOUN = **cry**, call, yell, scream,

roar, bellow ▷ PHRASE: **shout
someone down** = **drown out**,
overwhelm, drown, silence

shove VERB = **push**, thrust, elbow,
drive, press, propel, jostle, impel
▷ NOUN = **push**, knock, thrust,
elbow, bump, nudge, jostle
▷ PHRASE: **shove off** (informal)
= **go away**, leave, clear off
(informal), depart, push off
(informal), scram (informal), rack off
(Austral. & N.Z. slang)

shovel VERB **1** = **move**, scoop,
dredge, load, heap **2** = **stuff**, ladle

show VERB **1** = **indicate**,
demonstrate, prove, reveal,
display, point out, manifest,
testify to, flag up ≠ disprove
2 = **display**, exhibit **3** = **guide**,
lead, conduct, accompany,
direct, escort **4** = **demonstrate**,
describe, explain, teach, illustrate,
instruct **5** = **be visible** ≠ be
invisible **6** = **express**, display,
reveal, indicate, register,
demonstrate, manifest ≠ hide
7 (informal) = **turn up**, appear,
attend **8** = **broadcast**, transmit,
air, beam, relay, televise, put on
the air, podcast
▷ NOUN **1** = **display**, sight,
spectacle, array **2** = **exhibition**,
fair, display, parade, pageant
3 = **appearance**, display,
pose, parade **4** = **pretence**,
appearance, illusion, affectation
5 = **programme**, broadcast,
presentation, production
6 = **entertainment**, production,
presentation ▷ PHRASES: **show**

off (*informal*) = **boast**, brag, blow your own trumpet, swagger; **show someone up** (*informal*) = **embarrass**, let down, mortify, put to shame; **show something off** = **exhibit**, display, parade, demonstrate, flaunt; **show something up** = **reveal**, expose, highlight, lay bare

showdown NOUN (*informal*) = **confrontation**, clash, face-off (*slang*)

shower NOUN = **deluge**
  ▷ VERB 1 = **cover**, dust, spray, sprinkle 2 = **inundate**, heap, lavish, pour, deluge

show-off NOUN (*informal*) = **exhibitionist**, boaster, poseur, braggart, figjam (*Austral. slang*)

shred NOUN 1 = **strip**, bit, piece, scrap, fragment, sliver, tatter 2 = **particle**, trace, scrap, grain, atom, jot, iota

shrewd ADJECTIVE = **astute**, clever, sharp, keen, smart, calculating, intelligent, cunning ≠ naive

shriek VERB = **scream**, cry, yell, screech, squeal
  ▷ NOUN = **scream**, cry, yell, screech, squeal

shrink VERB = **decrease**, dwindle, lessen, grow *or* get smaller, contract, narrow, diminish, shorten ≠ grow

shroud NOUN 1 = **winding sheet**, grave clothes 2 = **covering**, veil, mantle, screen, pall
  ▷ VERB = **conceal**, cover, screen, hide, blanket, veil, cloak, envelop

shudder VERB = **shiver**, shake, tremble, quake, quiver, convulse
  ▷ NOUN = **shiver**, tremor, quiver, spasm

shuffle VERB 1 = **shamble**, stagger, stumble, dodder 2 = **scuffle**, drag, scrape 3 = **rearrange**, jumble, mix, disorder, disarrange

shun VERB = **avoid**, steer clear of, keep away from

shut VERB = **close**, secure, fasten, seal, slam ≠ open
  ▷ ADJECTIVE = **closed**, fastened, sealed, locked ≠ open ▷ PHRASE: **shut down** = **stop work**, halt work, close down

shuttle VERB = **go back and forth**, commute, go to and fro, alternate

shy ADJECTIVE 1 = **timid**, self-conscious, bashful, retiring, shrinking, coy, self-effacing, diffident ≠ confident 2 = **cautious**, wary, hesitant, suspicious, distrustful, chary ≠ reckless
  ▷ VERB *sometimes with* **off** *or* **away** = **recoil**, flinch, draw back, start, balk

sick ADJECTIVE 1 = **unwell**, ill, poorly (*informal*), diseased, crook (*Austral. & N.Z. informal*), ailing, under the weather, indisposed ≠ well 2 = **nauseous**, ill, queasy, nauseated 3 (*informal*) = **tired**, bored, fed up, weary, jaded 4 (*informal*) = **morbid**, sadistic, black, macabre, ghoulish

sicken VERB 1 = **disgust**, revolt, nauseate, repel, gross out (*U.S. slang*), turn your stomach 2 = **fall**

S

ill, take sick, ail

sickening ADJECTIVE
= **disgusting**, revolting, offensive, foul, distasteful, repulsive, nauseating, loathsome, yucko (*Austral. slang*) ≠ delightful

sickness NOUN 1 = **illness**, disorder, ailment, disease, complaint, bug (*informal*), affliction, malady 2 = **nausea**, queasiness 3 = **vomiting**

side NOUN 1 = **border**, margin, boundary, verge, flank, rim, perimeter, edge ≠ middle
2 = **face**, surface, facet 3 = **party**, camp, faction, cause 4 = **point of view**, viewpoint, position, opinion, angle, slant, standpoint
5 = **team**, squad, line-up
6 = **aspect**, feature, angle, facet
▷ ADJECTIVE = **subordinate**, minor, secondary, subsidiary, lesser, marginal, incidental, ancillary ≠ main ▷ PHRASE: **side with someone** = **support**, agree with, stand up for, favour, go along with, take the part of, ally yourself with

sidewalk NOUN (*U.S. & Canad.*)
= **pavement**, footpath (*Austral. & N.Z.*)

sideways ADVERB 1 = **indirectly**, obliquely 2 = **to the side**, laterally
▷ ADJECTIVE = **sidelong**, oblique

sift VERB 1 = **part**, filter, strain, separate, sieve 2 = **examine**, investigate, go through, research, analyse, work over, scrutinize

sight NOUN 1 = **vision**, eyes, eyesight, seeing, eye

2 = **spectacle**, show, scene, display, exhibition, vista, pageant
3 = **view**, range of vision, visibility
4 (*informal*) = **eyesore**, mess, monstrosity
▷ VERB = **spot**, see, observe, distinguish, perceive, make out, discern, behold ▷ RELATED WORDS: *adjectives* optical, visual

sign NOUN 1 = **symbol**, mark, device, logo, badge, emblem
2 = **figure** 3 = **notice**, board, warning, placard 4 = **indication**, evidence, mark, signal, symptom, hint, proof, gesture 5 = **omen**, warning, portent, foreboding, augury, auspice
▷ VERB 1 = **gesture**, indicate, signal, beckon, gesticulate
2 = **autograph**, initial, inscribe

signal NOUN 1 = **flare**, beam, beacon 2 = **cue**, sign, prompting, reminder 3 = **sign**, gesture, indication, mark, note, expression, token
▷ VERB = **gesture**, sign, wave, indicate, motion, beckon, gesticulate

significance NOUN
= **importance**, consequence, moment, weight

significant ADJECTIVE
1 = **important**, serious, material, vital, critical, momentous, weighty, noteworthy
≠ insignificant 2 = **meaningful**, expressive, eloquent, indicative, suggestive ≠ meaningless

signify VERB = **indicate**, mean, suggest, imply, intimate, be a sign

S

of, denote, connote, flag up

silence NOUN 1 = **quiet**, peace, calm, hush, lull, stillness ≠ noise 2 = **reticence**, dumbness, taciturnity, muteness ≠ speech
▷ VERB = **quieten**, still, quiet, cut off, stifle, cut short, muffle, deaden ≠ make louder

silent ADJECTIVE 1 = **mute**, dumb, speechless, wordless, voiceless ≠ noisy 2 = **uncommunicative**, quiet, taciturn 3 = **quiet**, still, hushed, soundless, noiseless, muted ≠ loud

silently ADVERB 1 = **quietly**, in silence, soundlessly, noiselessly, inaudibly, without a sound 2 = **mutely**, in silence, wordlessly

silhouette NOUN = **outline**, form, shape, profile
▷ VERB = **outline**, etch

silly ADJECTIVE 1 = **stupid**, ridiculous, absurd, daft, inane, senseless, idiotic, fatuous ≠ clever 2 = **foolish**, stupid, unwise, rash, irresponsible, thoughtless, imprudent ≠ sensible

● **WORD POWER**
● Silver is a precious metal
● used in jewellery, coins, and
● cutlery. Its value is referred
● to in the expression *born with*
● *a silver spoon in one's mouth*
● which means coming from a
● wealthy family. However, when
● contrasted with gold, its worth
● is the lesser of the two, and a
● *silver medal* is given as second
● prize in a competition. Silver

● has also been opposed to the
● colour grey in various idioms.
● For example, the expression
● *every cloud has a silver lining*
● means that even dark
● situations can have comforting
● aspects. In addition, silver is
● now used instead of grey to
● refer to older people, e.g. *silver*
● *surfer*, to avoid the negative
● associations of grey. Silver
● also means articulate and
● persuasive in the expression
● *silver-tongued*.

similar ADJECTIVE 1 = **alike**, resembling, comparable ≠ different 2 *with* **to** = **like**, comparable to, analogous to, close to

● **WORD POWER**
● *As* should not be used after
● *similar* – so *Wilson held a similar*
● *position to Jones* is correct, but
● not *Wilson held a similar position*
● *as Jones*; and *the system is similar*
● *to the one in France* is correct,
● but not *the system is similar as*
● *in France*.

similarity NOUN = **resemblance**, likeness, sameness, agreement, correspondence, analogy, affinity, closeness ≠ difference

simmer VERB 1 = **bubble**, boil gently, seethe 2 = **fume**, seethe, smoulder, rage, be angry
▷ PHRASE: **simmer down** (*informal*) = **calm down**, control yourself, cool off *or* down

simple ADJECTIVE
1 = **uncomplicated**, clear,

plain, understandable, lucid, recognizable, comprehensible, intelligible ≠ complicated **2** = **easy**, straightforward, not difficult, effortless, painless, uncomplicated, undemanding **3** = **plain**, natural, classic, unfussy, unembellished, bare-bones ≠ elaborate **4** = **pure**, mere, sheer, unalloyed **5** = **artless**, innocent, naive, natural, sincere, unaffected, childlike, unsophisticated ≠ sophisticated **6** = **unpretentious**, modest, humble, homely, unfussy, unembellished ≠ fancy

simplicity NOUN
1 = **straightforwardness**, ease, clarity, clearness ≠ complexity **2** = **plainness**, restraint, purity, lack of adornment ≠ elaborateness

simplify VERB = **make simpler**, streamline, disentangle, dumb down, reduce to essentials, declutter

simply ADVERB **1** = **just**, only, merely, purely, solely **2** = **totally**, really, completely, absolutely, wholly, utterly **3** = **clearly**, straightforwardly, directly, plainly, intelligibly **4** = **plainly**, naturally, modestly, unpretentiously **5** = **without doubt**, surely, certainly, definitely, beyond question

simulate VERB = **pretend**, act, feign, affect, put on, sham

simultaneous ADJECTIVE = **coinciding**, concurrent, contemporaneous, coincident, synchronous, happening at the same time

simultaneously ADVERB = **at the same time**, together, concurrently

sin NOUN **1** = **wickedness**, evil, crime, error, transgression, iniquity **2** = **crime**, offence, error, wrongdoing, misdeed, transgression, act of evil, guilt ▷ VERB = **transgress**, offend, lapse, err, go astray, do wrong

sincere ADJECTIVE = **honest**, genuine, real, true, serious, earnest, frank, candid, dinkum (*Austral. & N.Z. informal*) ≠ false

sincerely ADVERB = **honestly**, truly, genuinely, seriously, earnestly, wholeheartedly, in earnest

sincerity NOUN = **honesty**, truth, candour, frankness, seriousness, genuineness

sing VERB **1** = **croon**, carol, chant, warble, yodel, pipe **2** = **trill**, chirp, warble

● **WORD POWER**
● *Sang* is the past tense of the
● verb *sing*, as in *she sang sweetly*.
● *Sung* is the past participle, as in
● *we have sung our song*, and care
● should be taken not to use it as
● if it were a variant form of the
● past tense.

singer NOUN = **vocalist**, crooner, minstrel, soloist, chorister, balladeer

single ADJECTIVE **1** = **one**, sole, lone, solitary, only, only one

2 = **individual**, separate, distinct
3 = **unmarried**, free, unattached, unwed 4 = **separate**, individual, exclusive, undivided, unshared
5 = **simple**, unmixed, unblended
▷ PHRASE: **single something** or **someone out** = **pick**, choose, select, separate, distinguish, fix on, set apart, pick on or out, flag up

singly ADVERB = **one by one**, individually, one at a time, separately

singular ADJECTIVE 1 = **single**, individual 2 = **remarkable**, outstanding, exceptional, notable, eminent, noteworthy ≠ ordinary 3 = **unusual**, odd, strange, extraordinary, curious, peculiar, eccentric, queer, daggy (*Austral. & N.Z. informal*) ≠ conventional

sinister ADJECTIVE = **threatening**, evil, menacing, dire, ominous, malign, disquieting ≠ reassuring

sink VERB 1 = **go down**, founder, go under, submerge, capsize 2 = **slump**, drop 3 = **fall**, drop, slip, plunge, subside, abate 4 = **drop**, fall 5 = **stoop**, be reduced to, lower yourself 6 = **decline**, fade, fail, flag, weaken, diminish, decrease, deteriorate ≠ improve 7 = **dig**, bore, drill, drive, excavate

sip VERB = **drink**, taste, sample, sup ▷ NOUN = **swallow**, drop, taste, thimbleful

sit VERB 1 = **take a seat**, perch, settle down 2 = **place**, set, put, position, rest, lay, settle,

deposit 3 = **be a member of**, serve on, have a seat on, preside on 4 = **convene**, meet, assemble, officiate

site NOUN 1 = **area**, plot 2 = **location**, place, setting, point, position, situation, spot ▷ VERB = **locate**, put, place, set, position, establish, install, situate

situation NOUN 1 = **position**, state, case, condition, circumstances, equation, plight, state of affairs 2 = **scenario**, state of affairs 3 = **location**, place, setting, position, site, spot

● WORD POWER
● It is common to hear the word
● *situation* used in sentences
● such as *the company is in a crisis*
● *situation*. This use of *situation* is
● considered bad style and the
● word should be left out, since it
● adds nothing to the sentence's
● meaning.

size NOUN = **dimensions**, extent, range, amount, mass, volume, proportions, bulk ▷ PHRASE: **size something** or **someone up** (*informal*) = **assess**, evaluate, appraise, take stock of

sizeable or **sizable** ADJECTIVE = **large**, considerable, substantial, goodly, decent, respectable, largish

sizzle VERB = **hiss**, spit, crackle, fry, frizzle

skeleton NOUN = **bones**, bare bones

sketch NOUN = **drawing**, design, draft, delineation

▷ **VERB** = **draw**, outline, represent, draft, depict, delineate, rough out

skilful ADJECTIVE = **expert**, skilled, masterly, able, professional, clever, practised, competent ≠ clumsy

skill NOUN = **expertise**, ability, proficiency, art, technique, facility, talent, craft ≠ clumsiness

skilled ADJECTIVE = **expert**, professional, able, masterly, skilful, proficient ≠ unskilled

skim VERB 1 = **remove**, separate, cream 2 = **glide**, fly, coast, sail, float 3 *usually with* **over** *or* **through** = **scan**, glance, run your eye over

skin NOUN 1 = **hide**, pelt, fell 2 = **peel**, rind, husk, casing, outside, crust 3 = **film**, coating ▷ **VERB** 1 = **peel** 2 = **scrape**, flay

skinny ADJECTIVE = **thin**, lean, scrawny, emaciated, undernourished ≠ fat

skip VERB 1 = **hop**, dance, bob, trip, bounce, caper, prance, frisk 2 = **miss out**, omit, leave out, overlook, pass over, eschew, give (something) a miss

skirt VERB 1 = **border**, edge, flank 2 *often with* **around** *or* **round** = **go round**, circumvent 3 *often with* **around** *or* **round** = **avoid**, evade, steer clear of, circumvent

skookum ADJECTIVE (*Canad.*) = **powerful**, influential, big, dominant, controlling, commanding, supreme, prevailing, authoritative

sky NOUN = **heavens**, firmament, rangi (*N.Z.*) ▷ **RELATED WORD**: *adjective* **celestial**

slab NOUN = **piece**, slice, lump, chunk, wedge, portion

slack ADJECTIVE 1 = **limp**, relaxed, loose, lax 2 = **loose**, baggy ≠ taut 3 = **slow**, quiet, inactive, dull, sluggish, slow-moving ≠ busy 4 = **negligent**, lazy, lax, idle, inactive, slapdash, neglectful, slipshod ≠ strict ▷ NOUN 1 = **surplus**, excess, glut, surfeit, superabundance, superfluity 2 = **room**, excess, leeway, give (*informal*) ▷ **VERB** = **shirk**, idle, dodge, skive (*Brit. slang*), bludge (*Austral. & N.Z. informal*)

slam VERB 1 = **bang**, crash, smash 2 = **throw**, dash, hurl, fling

slant VERB 1 = **slope**, incline, tilt, list, bend, lean, heel, cant 2 = **bias**, colour, twist, angle, distort ▷ NOUN 1 = **slope**, incline, tilt, gradient, camber 2 = **bias**, emphasis, prejudice, angle, point of view, one-sidedness

slanting ADJECTIVE = **sloping**, angled, inclined, tilted, tilting, bent, diagonal, oblique

slap VERB = **smack**, beat, clap, cuff, swipe, spank, clobber (*slang*), wallop (*informal*) ▷ NOUN = **smack**, blow, cuff, swipe, spank

slash VERB 1 = **cut**, slit, gash, lacerate, score, rend, rip, hack 2 = **reduce**, cut, decrease, drop, lower, moderate, diminish, cut down

▷ NOUN = **cut**, slit, gash, rent, rip, incision, laceration

slate VERB (*informal, chiefly Brit.*) = **criticize**, censure, rebuke, scold, tear into (*informal*)

slaughter VERB 1 = **kill**, murder, massacre, destroy, execute, assassinate 2 = **butcher**, kill, slay, massacre

▷ NOUN = **slaying**, killing, murder, massacre, bloodshed, carnage, butchery

slave NOUN 1 = **servant**, serf, vassal 2 = **drudge**, skivvy (*chiefly Brit.*)

▷ VERB = **toil**, drudge, slog

slavery NOUN = **enslavement**, servitude, subjugation, captivity, bondage ≠ freedom

slay VERB 1 (*archaic or literary*) = **kill**, slaughter, massacre, butcher 2 = **murder**, kill, massacre, slaughter, mow down

sleaze NOUN (*informal*) = **corruption**, fraud, dishonesty, bribery, extortion, venality, unscrupulousness

sleek ADJECTIVE = **glossy**, shiny, lustrous, smooth ≠ shaggy

sleep NOUN = **slumber(s)**, nap, doze, snooze (*informal*), hibernation, siesta, forty winks (*informal*), zizz (*Brit. informal*)

▷ VERB = **slumber**, doze, snooze (*informal*), hibernate, take a nap, catnap, drowse

sleepy ADJECTIVE = **drowsy**, sluggish, lethargic, heavy, dull, inactive ≠ wide-awake

slender ADJECTIVE 1 = **slim**, narrow, slight, lean, willowy ≠ chubby 2 = **faint**, slight, remote, slim, thin, tenuous ≠ strong 3 = **meagre**, little, small, scant, scanty ≠ large

slice NOUN = **piece**, segment, portion, wedge, sliver, helping, share, cut

▷ VERB = **cut**, divide, carve, sever, dissect, bisect

slick ADJECTIVE 1 = **skilful**, deft, adroit, dexterous, professional, polished ≠ clumsy 2 = **glib**, smooth, plausible, polished, specious

▷ VERB = **smooth**, sleek, plaster down

slide VERB = **slip**, slither, glide, skim, coast

slight ADJECTIVE 1 = **small**, minor, insignificant, trivial, feeble, trifling, meagre, unimportant ≠ large 2 = **slim**, small, delicate, spare, fragile, lightly-built ≠ sturdy

▷ VERB = **snub**, insult, ignore, affront, scorn, disdain ≠ compliment

▷ NOUN = **insult**, snub, affront, rebuff, slap in the face (*informal*), (the) cold shoulder ≠ compliment

slightly ADVERB = **a little**, a bit, somewhat

slim ADJECTIVE 1 = **slender**, slight, trim, thin, narrow, lean, svelte, willowy ≠ chubby 2 = **slight**, remote, faint, slender ≠ strong

▷ VERB = **lose weight**, diet ≠ put on weight

S

sling VERB 1 (*informal*) = **throw**, cast, toss, hurl, fling, chuck (*informal*), lob (*informal*), heave 2 = **hang**, suspend

slip VERB 1 = **fall**, skid 2 = **slide**, slither 3 = **sneak**, creep, steal ▷ NOUN = **mistake**, failure, error, blunder, lapse, omission, oversight, barry or Barry Crocker (*Austral. slang*) ▷ PHRASES: **give someone the slip** = **escape from**, get away from, evade, elude, lose (someone), flee, dodge; **slip up** = **make a mistake**, blunder, err, miscalculate

slippery ADJECTIVE 1 = **smooth**, icy, greasy, glassy, slippy (*informal or dialect*), unsafe 2 = **untrustworthy**, tricky, cunning, dishonest, devious, crafty, evasive, shifty

slit VERB = **cut (open)**, rip, slash, knife, pierce, lance, gash ▷ NOUN 1 = **cut**, gash, incision, tear, rent 2 = **opening**, split

slogan NOUN = **catch phrase**, motto, tag-line, catchword, catchcry (*Austral.*)

slope NOUN = **inclination**, rise, incline, tilt, slant, ramp, gradient ▷ VERB = **slant**, incline, drop away, fall, rise, lean, tilt ▷ PHRASE: **slope off** = **slink away**, slip away, creep away

sloping ADJECTIVE = **slanting**, leaning, inclined, oblique

sloppy ADJECTIVE 1 (*informal*) = **careless**, slovenly, slipshod, messy, untidy 2 (*informal*) = **sentimental**, soppy (*Brit.*

informal), slushy (*informal*), gushing, mawkish, icky (*informal*)

slot NOUN 1 = **opening**, hole, groove, vent, slit, aperture 2 (*informal*) = **place**, time, space, opening, position, vacancy ▷ VERB = **fit**, insert

slow ADJECTIVE 1 = **unhurried**, sluggish, leisurely, lazy, ponderous, dawdling, laggard, lackadaisical ≠ quick 2 = **prolonged**, protracted, long-drawn-out, lingering, gradual 3 = **late**, behind, tardy 4 = **stupid**, dim, dense, thick, retarded, dozy (*Brit. informal*), obtuse, braindead (*informal*) ≠ bright ▷ VERB 1 *often with* **down** = **decelerate**, brake 2 *often with* **down** = **delay**, hold up, handicap, retard ≠ speed up

● WORD POWER
● While not as unkind as *thick*
● and *stupid*, words like *slow*
● and *backward*, when used to
● talk about a person's mental
● abilities, are both unhelpful
● and likely to cause offence. It is
● preferable to say that a person
● has *special educational needs* or
● *learning difficulties*.

slowly ADVERB = **gradually**, unhurriedly ≠ quickly

slug NOUN ▷ *see* **snails, slugs and other gastropods**

sluggish ADJECTIVE = **inactive**, slow, lethargic, heavy, dull, inert, indolent, torpid ≠ energetic

slum NOUN = **hovel**, ghetto,

shanty

slump VERB 1 = **fall**, sink, plunge, crash, collapse, slip ≠ increase 2 = **sag**, hunch, droop, slouch, loll ▷ NOUN 1 = **fall**, drop, decline, crash, collapse, reverse, downturn, trough ≠ increase 2 = **recession**, depression, stagnation, inactivity, hard or bad times

slur NOUN = **insult**, stain, smear, affront, innuendo, calumny, insinuation, aspersion

sly ADJECTIVE 1 = **roguish**, knowing, arch, mischievous, impish 2 = **cunning**, scheming, devious, secret, clever, subtle, wily, crafty ≠ open ▷ PHRASE: **on the sly** = **secretly**, privately, covertly, surreptitiously, on the quiet

smack VERB 1 = **slap**, hit, strike, clap, cuff, swipe, spank 2 = **drive**, hit, strike ▷ NOUN = **slap**, blow, cuff, swipe, spank ▷ ADVERB (informal) = **directly**, right, straight, squarely, precisely, exactly, slap (informal)

small ADJECTIVE 1 = **little**, minute, tiny, mini, miniature, minuscule, diminutive, petite ≠ big 2 = **young**, little, junior, wee, juvenile, youthful, immature 3 = **unimportant**, minor, trivial, insignificant, little, petty, trifling, negligible ≠ important 4 = **modest**, humble, unpretentious ≠ grand

smart ADJECTIVE 1 = **chic**, trim, neat, stylish, elegant, spruce, snappy, natty (informal), schmick (Austral. informal) ≠ scruffy 2 = **clever**, bright, intelligent, quick, sharp, keen, acute, shrewd ≠ stupid 3 = **brisk**, quick, lively, vigorous ▷ VERB = **sting**, burn, hurt

smash VERB 1 = **break**, crush, shatter, crack, demolish, pulverize 2 = **shatter**, break, disintegrate, crack, splinter 3 = **collide**, crash, meet head-on, clash, come into collision 4 = **destroy**, ruin, wreck, trash (slang), lay waste ▷ NOUN = **collision**, crash, accident

smashing ADJECTIVE (informal, chiefly Brit.) = **excellent**, mean (slang), great (informal), wonderful, brilliant (informal), cracking (Brit. informal), superb, fantastic (informal), booshit (Austral. slang), exo (Austral. slang), sik (Austral. slang), rad (informal), phat (slang), schmick (Austral. informal) ≠ awful

smear VERB 1 = **spread over**, daub, rub on, cover, coat, bedaub 2 = **slander**, malign, blacken, besmirch 3 = **smudge**, soil, dirty, stain, sully ▷ NOUN 1 = **smudge**, daub, streak, blot, blotch, splotch 2 = **slander**, libel, defamation, calumny

smell NOUN 1 = **odour**, scent, fragrance, perfume, bouquet, aroma 2 = **stink**, stench, pong (Brit. informal), fetor ▷ VERB 1 = **stink**, reek, pong (Brit.

S

informal) **2** = **sniff**, scent

smile VERB = **grin**, beam, smirk, twinkle, grin from ear to ear
▷ NOUN = **grin**, beam, smirk

smooth ADJECTIVE **1** = **even**, level, flat, plane, flush, horizontal ≠ uneven **2** = **sleek**, polished, shiny, glossy, silky, velvety ≠ rough **3** = **mellow**, pleasant, mild, agreeable **4** = **flowing**, steady, regular, uniform, rhythmic **5** = **easy**, effortless, well-ordered **6** = **suave**, slick, persuasive, urbane, glib, facile, unctuous, smarmy (*Brit. informal*)
▷ VERB **1** = **flatten**, level, press, plane, iron **2** = **ease**, facilitate ≠ hinder

smother VERB **1** = **extinguish**, put out, stifle, snuff **2** = **suffocate**, choke, strangle, stifle **3** = **suppress**, stifle, repress, hide, conceal, muffle

smug ADJECTIVE = **self-satisfied**, superior, complacent, conceited

snack NOUN = **light meal**, bite, refreshment(s)

snag NOUN = **difficulty**, hitch, problem, obstacle, catch, disadvantage, complication, drawback
▷ VERB = **catch**, tear, rip

snake NOUN = **serpent** ▷ RELATED WORD: *adjective* serpentine
▷ *see* reptiles

snap VERB **1** = **break**, crack, separate **2** = **pop**, click, crackle **3** = **speak sharply**, bark, lash out at, jump down (someone's) throat (*informal*) **4** = **bite at**, bite, nip
▷ MODIFIER = **instant**, immediate, sudden, spur-of-the-moment ▷ PHRASE: snap something up = **grab**, seize, take advantage of, pounce upon

snare NOUN = **trap**, net, wire, gin, noose
▷ VERB = **trap**, catch, net, wire, seize, entrap

snatch VERB **1** = **grab**, grip, grasp, clutch **2** = **steal**, take, nick (*slang, chiefly Brit.*), pinch (*informal*), lift (*informal*), pilfer, filch, thieve **3** = **win 4** = **save**, recover, get out, salvage
▷ NOUN = **bit**, part, fragment, piece, snippet

sneak VERB **1** = **slink**, slip, steal,

S

● **SNAILS, SLUGS AND OTHER GASTROPODS**
● abalone *or* ear shell
● conch
● cowrie *or* cowry
● limpet
● murex
● nudibranch *or* sea slug
● ormer *or* sea-ear

● periwinkle *or* winkle
● slug
● snail
● triton
● wentletrap
● whelk

pad, skulk 2 = **slip**, smuggle, spirit
▷ NOUN = **informer**, betrayer, telltale, Judas, accuser, stool pigeon, nark (*Brit., Austral. & N.Z. slang*), fizgig (*Austral. slang*)

sneaking ADJECTIVE 1 = **nagging**, worrying, persistent, uncomfortable 2 = **secret**, private, hidden, unexpressed, unvoiced, undivulged

sneer VERB 1 = **scorn**, mock, ridicule, laugh, jeer, disdain, deride 2 = **say contemptuously**, snigger
▷ NOUN = **scorn**, ridicule, mockery, derision, jeer, gibe

sniff VERB 1 = **breathe in**, inhale 2 = **smell**, scent 3 = **inhale**, breathe in, suck in, draw in

snub VERB = **insult**, slight, put down, humiliate, cut (*informal*), rebuff, cold-shoulder
▷ NOUN = **insult**, put-down, affront, slap in the face

so SENTENCE CONNECTOR
= **therefore**, thus, hence, consequently, then, as a result, accordingly, thence

soak VERB 1 = **steep** 2 = **wet**, damp, saturate, drench, moisten, suffuse, wet through, waterlog 3 = **penetrate**, permeate, seep
▷ PHRASE: **soak something up**
= **absorb**, suck up, assimilate

soaking ADJECTIVE = **soaked**, dripping, saturated, drenched, sodden, streaming, sopping, wet through

soar VERB 1 = **rise**, increase, grow, mount, climb, go up, rocket,

escalate 2 = **fly**, wing, climb, ascend ≠ plunge 3 = **tower**, climb, go up

sob VERB = **cry**, weep, howl, shed tears
▷ NOUN = **cry**, whimper, howl

sober ADJECTIVE 1 = **abstinent**, temperate, abstemious, moderate ≠ drunk 2 = **serious**, cool, grave, reasonable, steady, composed, rational, solemn, grounded ≠ frivolous 3 = **plain**, dark, sombre, quiet, subdued, drab ≠ bright

so-called ADJECTIVE = **alleged**, supposed, professed, pretended, self-styled

social ADJECTIVE 1 = **communal**, community, collective, group, public, general, common
2 = **organized**, gregarious
▷ NOUN = **get-together** (*informal*), party, gathering, function, reception, social gathering

society NOUN 1 = **the community**, people, the public, humanity, civilization, mankind 2 = **culture**, community, population 3 = **organization**, group, club, union, league, association, institute, circle 4 = **upper classes**, gentry, elite, high society, beau monde 5 (*old-fashioned*) = **companionship**, company, fellowship, friendship

sofa NOUN = **couch**, settee, divan, chaise longue

soft ADJECTIVE 1 = **velvety**, smooth, silky, feathery, downy, fleecy ≠ rough 2 = **yielding**,

s

elastic ≠ hard 3 = **soggy**, swampy, marshy, boggy
4 = **squashy**, sloppy, mushy, spongy, gelatinous, pulpy
5 = **pliable**, flexible, supple, malleable, plastic, elastic, bendable, mouldable 6 = **quiet**, gentle, murmured, muted, dulcet, soft-toned ≠ loud
7 = **lenient**, easy-going, lax, indulgent, permissive, spineless, overindulgent ≠ harsh
8 = **kind**, tender, sentimental, compassionate, sensitive, gentle, tenderhearted, touchy-feely (*informal*) 9 (*informal*) = **easy**, comfortable, undemanding, cushy (*informal*) 10 = **pale**, light, subdued, pastel, bland, mellow ≠ bright 11 = **dim**, faint, dimmed ≠ bright 12 = **mild**, temperate, balmy

soften VERB 1 = **melt**, tenderize
2 = **lessen**, moderate, temper, ease, cushion, subdue, allay, mitigate

soil¹ NOUN 1 = **earth**, ground, clay, dust, dirt 2 = **territory**, country, land

soil² VERB = **dirty**, foul, stain, pollute, tarnish, sully, defile, besmirch ≠ clean

soldier NOUN = **fighter**, serviceman, trooper, warrior, man-at-arms, squaddie *or* squaddy (*Brit. slang*)

sole ADJECTIVE = **only**, one, single, individual, alone, exclusive, solitary

solely ADVERB = **only**, completely, entirely, exclusively, alone, merely

solemn ADJECTIVE 1 = **serious**, earnest, grave, sober, sedate, staid ≠ cheerful 2 = **formal**, grand, grave, dignified, ceremonial, stately, momentous ≠ informal

solid ADJECTIVE 1 = **firm**, hard, compact, dense, concrete ≠ unsubstantial 2 = **strong**, stable, sturdy, substantial, unshakable ≠ unstable
3 = **reliable**, dependable, upstanding, worthy, upright, trusty ≠ unreliable 4 = **sound**, real, reliable, good, genuine, dinkum (*Austral. & N.Z. informal*) ≠ unsound

solidarity NOUN = **unity**, unification, accord, cohesion, team spirit, unanimity, concordance, like-mindedness, kotahitanga (*N.Z.*)

solitary ADJECTIVE 1 = **unsociable**, reclusive, unsocial, isolated, lonely, cloistered, lonesome, friendless ≠ sociable 2 = **lone**, alone 3 = **isolated**, remote, out-of-the-way, hidden, unfrequented ≠ busy

solution NOUN 1 = **answer**, key, result, explanation 2 (*chemistry*) = **mixture**, mix, compound, blend, solvent

solve VERB = **answer**, work out, resolve, crack, clear up, unravel, decipher, suss (out) (*slang*)

sombre ADJECTIVE 1 = **gloomy**, sad, sober, grave, dismal, mournful, lugubrious, joyless ≠ cheerful 2 = **dark**, dull, gloomy, sober, drab ≠ bright

somebody NOUN = **celebrity**, name, star, notable, household name, dignitary, luminary, personage ≠ nobody

somehow ADVERB = **one way or another**, come what may, come hell or high water (*informal*), by fair means or foul, by hook or (by) crook, by some means or other

sometimes ADVERB = **occasionally**, at times, now and then ≠ always

song NOUN = **ballad**, air, tune, carol, chant, chorus, anthem, number, waiata (*N.Z.*)

soon ADVERB = **before long**, shortly, in the near future

soothe VERB 1 = **calm**, still, quiet, hush, appease, lull, pacify, mollify ≠ upset 2 = **relieve**, ease, alleviate, assuage ≠ irritate

soothing ADJECTIVE 1 = **calming**, relaxing, peaceful, quiet, calm, restful 2 = **emollient**, palliative

sophisticated ADJECTIVE 1 = **complex**, advanced, complicated, subtle, delicate, elaborate, refined, intricate ≠ simple 2 = **cultured**, refined, cultivated, worldly, cosmopolitan, urbane ≠ unsophisticated

sophistication NOUN = **poise**, worldliness, savoir-faire, urbanity, finesse, worldly wisdom

sore ADJECTIVE 1 = **painful**, smarting, raw, tender, burning, angry, sensitive, irritated 2 = **annoyed**, cross, angry, pained, hurt, upset, stung, irritated,

tooshie (*Austral. slang*), hoha (*N.Z.*) 3 = **annoying**, troublesome 4 = **urgent**, desperate, extreme, dire, pressing, critical, acute

sorrow NOUN 1 = **grief**, sadness, woe, regret, distress, misery, mourning, anguish ≠ joy 2 = **hardship**, trial, tribulation, affliction, trouble, woe, misfortune ≠ good fortune
▷ VERB = **grieve**, mourn, lament, be sad, bemoan, agonize, bewail ≠ rejoice

sorry ADJECTIVE 1 = **regretful**, apologetic, contrite, repentant, remorseful, penitent, shamefaced, conscience-stricken ≠ unapologetic 2 = **sympathetic**, moved, full of pity, compassionate, commiserative ≠ unsympathetic 3 = **wretched**, miserable, pathetic, mean, poor, sad, pitiful, deplorable

sort NOUN = **kind**, type, class, make, order, style, quality, nature
▷ VERB = **arrange**, group, order, rank, divide, grade, classify, categorize

● **WORD POWER**
● It is common in informal
● speech to combine singular
● and plural in sentences like
● *these sort of distinctions are*
● *becoming blurred*. This is not
● acceptable in careful writing,
● where the plural must be used
● consistently: *these sorts of*
● *distinctions are becoming blurred*.

soul NOUN 1 = **spirit**, essence, life, vital force, wairua (*N.Z.*)

2 = **embodiment**, essence, epitome, personification, quintessence, type 3 = **person**, being, individual, body, creature, man *or* woman

sound¹ NOUN 1 = **noise**, din, report, tone, reverberation 2 = **idea**, impression, drift 3 = **cry**, noise, peep, squeak 4 = **tone**, music, note
▷ VERB 1 = **toll**, set off 2 = **resound**, echo, go off, toll, set off, chime, reverberate, clang 3 = **seem**, seem to be, appear to be ▷ RELATED WORDS: *adjectives* sonic, acoustic

sound² ADJECTIVE 1 = **fit**, healthy, perfect, intact, unhurt, uninjured, unimpaired ≠ frail 2 = **sturdy**, strong, solid, stable 3 = **sensible**, wise, reasonable, right, correct, proper, valid, rational, grounded ≠ irresponsible 4 = **deep**, unbroken, undisturbed, untroubled ≠ troubled

sour ADJECTIVE 1 = **sharp**, acid, tart, bitter, pungent, acetic ≠ sweet 2 = **rancid**, turned, gone off, curdled, gone bad, off ≠ fresh 3 = **bitter**, tart, acrimonious, embittered, disagreeable, ill-tempered, waspish, ungenerous ≠ good-natured

source NOUN 1 = **cause**, origin, derivation, beginning, author 2 = **informant**, authority 3 = **origin**, fount

souvenir NOUN = **keepsake**, reminder, memento

sovereign ADJECTIVE

1 = **supreme**, ruling, absolute, royal, principal, imperial, kingly *or* queenly 2 = **excellent**, efficient, effectual
▷ NOUN = **monarch**, ruler, king *or* queen, chief, potentate, emperor *or* empress, prince *or* princess

sovereignty NOUN = **supreme power**, domination, supremacy, primacy, kingship, rangatiratanga (*N.Z.*)

sow VERB = **scatter**, plant, seed, implant

space NOUN 1 = **room**, capacity, extent, margin, scope, play, expanse, leeway 2 = **period**, interval, time, while, span, duration, time frame, timeline 3 = **outer space**, the universe, the galaxy, the solar system, the cosmos 4 = **blank**, gap, interval

spacious ADJECTIVE = **roomy**, large, huge, broad, extensive, ample, expansive, capacious ≠ limited

● **WORD POWER**
● Several Spanish words in
● English have nuances of
● meaning not shared by their
● synonyms. For example,
● *aficionado*, literally 'fond of',
● refers to a person who is
● passionate about a particular
● activity or pastime, e.g. a wine
● aficionado, an aficionado of
● classical music. Some of its
● synonyms have connotations
● of obsession, e.g. addict, buff,
● freak, fiend, and others have
● connotations of expertise, e.g.

S

- connoisseur, expert, whizz.
- Aficionado is perhaps most
- closely related in meaning to
- admirer, devotee, enthusiast,
- and fan. Another Spanish
- word which has no direct
- English equivalent is *peccadillo*.
- From 'pecado' meaning sin, a
- peccadillo is a lapse or minor
- sin. It describes a fault which
- is ethical or moral, rather than
- legal or religious, although
- there is some overlap between
- these categories. It can be
- contrasted with words relating
- to legal offences such as crime,
- offence, and violation, and
- those of religious wrongdoing
- such as sin, trespass, and
- transgression. It shares the
- meaning of misdemeanour,
- lapse, and misbehaviour, e.g.
- Speeding is indulged as the
- peccadillo of the too-busy.
- *Bonanza*, literally 'calm sea', is a
- Spanish word descended from
- Latin *bonus*, meaning 'good'.
- It signifies a source of luck
- and money, which is usually
- sudden and unexpected, e.g.
- cash bonanza, ratings bonanza.
- In comparison, bonus also has
- associations with money in
- the sense of 'dividend' in British
- English. Many of the synonyms
- of bonanza are found almost
- exclusively in the context of
- money, e.g. windfall, jackpot,
- whereas bonanza can refer to
- other types of good fortune.

span NOUN 1 = **period**, term, duration, spell 2 = **extent**, reach, spread, length, distance, stretch
▷ VERB = **extend across**, cross, bridge, cover, link, traverse

spar VERB = **argue**, row, squabble, scrap (*informal*), wrangle, bicker

spare ADJECTIVE 1 = **back-up**, reserve, second, extra, additional, auxiliary 2 = **extra**, surplus, leftover, over, free, odd, unwanted, unused ≠ necessary 3 = **free**, leisure, unoccupied 4 = **thin**, lean, meagre, gaunt, wiry ≠ plump
▷ VERB 1 = **afford**, give, grant, do without, part with, manage without, let someone have 2 = **have mercy on**, pardon, leave, let off (*informal*), go easy on (*informal*), save (from harm) ≠ show no mercy to

sparing ADJECTIVE = **economical**, frugal, thrifty, saving, careful, prudent ≠ lavish

spark NOUN 1 = **flicker**, flash, gleam, glint, flare 2 = **trace**, hint, scrap, atom, jot, vestige
▷ VERB *often with* off = **start**, stimulate, provoke, inspire, trigger (off), set off, precipitate

sparkle VERB = **glitter**, flash, shine, gleam, shimmer, twinkle, dance, glint
▷ NOUN 1 = **glitter**, flash, gleam, flicker, brilliance, twinkle, glint 2 = **vivacity**, life, spirit, dash, vitality, élan, liveliness

spate NOUN 1 = **flood**, flow, torrent, rush, deluge, outpouring

2 = **series**, sequence, course, chain, succession, run, train

speak VERB **1** = **talk**, say something **2** = **articulate**, say, pronounce, utter, tell, state, talk, express **3** = **converse**, talk, chat, discourse, confer, commune, exchange views, korero (*N.Z.*) **4** = **lecture**, address an audience

speaker NOUN = **orator**, public speaker, lecturer, spokesperson, spokesman *or* spokeswoman

spearhead VERB = **lead**, head, pioneer, launch, set off, initiate, set in motion

special ADJECTIVE **1** = **exceptional**, important, significant, particular, unique, unusual, extraordinary, memorable ≠ ordinary **2** = **specific**, particular, distinctive, individual, appropriate, precise ≠ general

specialist NOUN = **expert**, authority, professional, master, consultant, guru, buff (*informal*), connoisseur, fundi (*S. African*)

speciality NOUN = **forte**, métier, specialty, bag (*slang*), pièce de résistance (*French*)

species NOUN = **kind**, sort, type, group, class, variety, breed, category

specific ADJECTIVE **1** = **particular**, special, characteristic, distinguishing ≠ general **2** = **precise**, exact, explicit, definite, express, clear-cut, unequivocal ≠ vague **3** = **peculiar**, appropriate, individual, particular, unique

specification NOUN = **requirement**, detail, particular, stipulation, condition, qualification

specify VERB = **state**, designate, stipulate, name, detail, mention, indicate, define

specimen NOUN **1** = **sample**, example, model, type, pattern, instance, representative, exemplification **2** = **example**, model, type

spectacle NOUN **1** = **show**, display, exhibition, event, performance, extravaganza, pageant **2** = **sight**, wonder, scene, phenomenon, curiosity, marvel

spectacular ADJECTIVE = **impressive**, striking, dramatic, stunning (*informal*), grand, magnificent, splendid, dazzling ≠ unimpressive ▷ NOUN = **show**, display, spectacle

spectator NOUN = **onlooker**, observer, viewer, looker-on, watcher, bystander ≠ participant

spectre NOUN = **ghost**, spirit, phantom, vision, apparition, wraith, kehua (*N.Z.*)

speculate VERB **1** = **conjecture**, consider, wonder, guess, surmise, theorize, hypothesize **2** = **gamble**, risk, venture, hazard

speculation NOUN **1** = **theory**, opinion, hypothesis, conjecture, guess, surmise, guesswork, supposition **2** = **gamble**, risk, hazard

speculative ADJECTIVE = **hypothetical**, academic,

theoretical, notional, conjectural, suppositional

speech NOUN
1 = **communication**, talk, conversation, discussion, dialogue 2 = **diction**, pronunciation, articulation, delivery, fluency, inflection, intonation, elocution
3 = **language**, tongue, jargon, dialect, idiom, parlance, articulation, diction 4 = **talk**, address, lecture, discourse, homily, oration, spiel (*informal*), whaikorero (*N.Z.*)

speed NOUN 1 = **rate**, pace
2 = **swiftness**, rush, hurry, haste, rapidity, quickness ≠ slowness
▷ VERB 1 = **race**, rush, hurry, zoom, career, tear, barrel (along) (*informal, chiefly U.S. & Canad.*), gallop ≠ crawl 2 = **help**, advance, aid, boost, assist, facilitate, expedite ≠ hinder

● **WORD POWER**
● The past tense of *speed up* is
● *speeded up* (not *sped up*), for
● example *I speeded up to overtake*
● *the lorry*. The past participle is
● also *speeded up*, for example
● *I had already speeded up when I*
● *spotted the police car.*

speedy ADJECTIVE = **quick**, fast, rapid, swift, express, immediate, prompt, hurried ≠ slow

spell¹ VERB = **indicate**, mean, signify, point to, imply, augur, portend

spell² NOUN 1 = **incantation**, charm, makutu (*N.Z.*)

2 = **enchantment**, magic, fascination, glamour, allure, bewitchment

spell³ NOUN = **period**, time, term, stretch, course, season, interval, bout

spend VERB 1 = **pay out**, fork out (*slang*), expend, disburse ≠ save
2 = **pass**, fill, occupy, while away
3 = **use up**, waste, squander, empty, drain, exhaust, consume, run through ≠ save

sphere NOUN 1 = **ball**, globe, orb, globule, circle 2 = **field**, department, function, territory, capacity, province, patch, scope

spice NOUN 1 = **seasoning**
2 = **excitement**, zest, colour, pep, zing (*informal*), piquancy

spicy ADJECTIVE 1 = **hot**, seasoned, aromatic, savoury, piquant 2 (*informal*) = **risqué**, racy, ribald, hot (*informal*), suggestive, titillating, indelicate

spider NOUN ▷ RELATED WORD: *fear* **arachnophobia**

spike NOUN = **point**, stake, spine, barb, prong
▷ VERB = **impale**, spit, spear, stick

spill VERB 1 = **tip over**, overturn, capsize, knock over 2 = **shed**, discharge, disgorge 3 = **slop**, flow, pour, run, overflow

spin VERB 1 = **revolve**, turn, rotate, reel, whirl, twirl, gyrate, pirouette
2 = **reel**, swim, whirl
▷ NOUN 1 (*informal*) = **drive**, ride, joy ride (*informal*) 2 = **revolution**, roll, whirl, gyration ▷ PHRASE: **spin something out** = **prolong**,

- **SPIDERS AND OTHER ARACHNIDS**
- black widow
- chigger, chigoe, or (U.S. & Canad.) redbug
- chigoe, chigger, jigger, or sand flea
- harvestman or (U.S. & Canad.) daddy-longlegs
- katipo (N.Z.)
- mite
- red-back (spider) (Austral.)
- spider
- spider mite
- tarantula
- tick
- trap-door spider
- whip scorpion
- wolf spider or hunting spider

extend, lengthen, draw out, drag out, delay, amplify

spine NOUN 1 = **backbone**, vertebrae, spinal column, vertebral column 2 = **barb**, spur, needle, spike, ray, quill

- **WORD POWER**
- The *spine* or backbone of a
- human body supports the
- skeleton, and in turn the whole
- body. Various metaphors have
- developed out of this role,
- specifically the notions of
- underpinning and strength.
- The physical appearance of the
- spine as a ridge has inspired
- many analogies, from hills in
- the landscape to the backs of
- books. In sport, players can be
- described as the *spine of their*
- *team* if they are considered
- to support the rest. Although
- spine on its own means
- resolution and endurance,
- it is most commonly seen in
- the negative form *spineless*
- meaning lacking courage or
- will. Parallels for most of the
- meanings of spine are found
- in *backbone*, particularly
- the meaning 'courage', as
- in *show some backbone*. The
- perception of fear is sometimes
- experienced as *sending a chill*
- *down the spine* in *spine-chilling*
- and *spine-tingling*.

spiral ADJECTIVE = **coiled**, winding, whorled, helical
▷ NOUN = **coil**, helix, corkscrew, whorl

spirit NOUN 1 = **soul**, life 2 = **life force**, vital spark, mauri (N.Z.) 3 = **ghost**, phantom, spectre, apparition, atua (N.Z.), kehua (N.Z.) 4 = **courage**, guts (informal), grit, backbone, spunk (informal), gameness 5 = **liveliness**, energy, vigour, life, force, fire, enthusiasm, animation 6 = **attitude**, character, temper, outlook, temperament, disposition 7 = **heart**, sense, nature, soul, core, substance, essence, quintessence 8 = **intention**, meaning, purpose, purport, gist 9 = **feeling**, atmosphere, character, tone, mood, tenor, ambience 10 *plural*

S

= **mood**, feelings, morale, temper, disposition, state of mind, frame of mind

spirited ADJECTIVE = **lively**, energetic, animated, active, feisty (*informal, chiefly U.S. & Canad.*), vivacious, mettlesome, (as) game as Ned Kelly (*Austral. slang*) ≠ lifeless

spiritual ADJECTIVE
1 = **nonmaterial**, immaterial, incorporeal ≠ material
2 = **sacred**, religious, holy, divine, devotional

spit VERB 1 = **expectorate**
2 = **eject**, throw out
▷ NOUN = **saliva**, dribble, spittle, drool, slaver

spite NOUN = **malice**, malevolence, ill will, hatred, animosity, venom, spleen, spitefulness ≠ kindness
▷ VERB = **annoy**, hurt, injure, harm, vex ≠ benefit ▷ PHRASE: **in spite of** = **despite**, regardless of, notwithstanding, (even) though

splash VERB 1 = **paddle**, plunge, bathe, dabble, wade, wallow
2 = **scatter**, shower, spray, sprinkle, wet, spatter, slop
3 = **spatter**, mark, stain, speck, speckle
▷ NOUN 1 = **dash**, touch, spattering 2 = **spot**, burst, patch, spurt 3 = **blob**, spot, smudge, stain, smear, fleck, speck

splendid ADJECTIVE 1 = **excellent**, wonderful, marvellous, great (*informal*), cracking (*Brit. informal*), fantastic (*informal*), first-class, glorious, booshit (*Austral. slang*),

exo (*Austral. slang*), sik (*Austral. slang*), rad (*informal*), phat (*slang*), schmick (*Austral. informal*)
≠ poor 2 = **magnificent**, grand, impressive, rich, superb, costly, gorgeous, lavish ≠ squalid

splendour NOUN
= **magnificence**, grandeur, show, display, spectacle, richness, nobility, pomp ≠ squalor

splinter NOUN = **sliver**, fragment, chip, flake
▷ VERB = **shatter**, split, fracture, disintegrate

split VERB 1 = **break**, crack, burst, open, give way, come apart, come undone 2 = **cut**, break, crack, snap, chop 3 = **divide**, separate, disunite, disband, cleave
4 = **diverge**, separate, branch, fork, part 5 = **tear**, rend, rip
6 = **share out**, divide, distribute, halve, allocate, partition, allot, apportion
▷ NOUN 1 = **division**, breach, rift, rupture, discord, schism, estrangement, dissension
2 = **separation**, break-up, split-up 3 = **crack**, tear, rip, gap, rent, breach, slit, fissure
▷ ADJECTIVE 1 = **divided**
2 = **broken**, cracked, fractured, ruptured, cleft

spoil VERB 1 = **ruin**, destroy, wreck, damage, injure, harm, mar, trash (*slang*), crool or cruel (*Austral. slang*) ≠ improve
2 = **overindulge**, indulge, pamper, cosset, coddle, mollycoddle
≠ deprive 3 = **indulge**, pamper,

S

satisfy, gratify, pander to **4 = go bad**, turn, go off (*Brit. informal*), rot, decay, decompose, curdle, addle

spoils PLURAL NOUN **= booty**, loot, plunder, prey, swag (*slang*)

spoken ADJECTIVE **= verbal**, voiced, expressed, uttered, oral, said, told, unwritten

spokesperson NOUN **= speaker**, official, spokesman *or* spokeswoman, voice, spin doctor (*informal*), mouthpiece

sponsor VERB **= back**, fund, finance, promote, subsidize, patronize
▷ NOUN **= backer**, patron, promoter

spontaneous ADJECTIVE **= unplanned**, impromptu, unprompted, willing, natural, voluntary, instinctive, impulsive ≠ planned

sport NOUN **1 = game**, exercise, recreation, play, amusement, diversion, pastime **2 = fun**, joking, teasing, banter, jest, badinage
▷ VERB (*informal*) **= wear**, display, flaunt, exhibit, flourish, show off, vaunt

sporting ADJECTIVE **= fair**, sportsmanlike, game (*informal*) ≠ unfair

sporty ADJECTIVE **= athletic**, outdoor, energetic

spot NOUN **1 = mark**, stain, speck, scar, blot, smudge, blemish, speckle **2 = pimple**, pustule, zit (*slang*) **3 = place**, site, point,

position, scene, location **4** (*informal*) **= predicament**, trouble, difficulty, mess, plight, hot water (*informal*), quandary, tight spot
▷ VERB **1 = see**, observe, catch sight of, sight, recognize, detect, make out, discern **2 = mark**, stain, soil, dirty, fleck, spatter, speckle, splodge

spotlight NOUN **= attention**, limelight, public eye, fame
▷ VERB **= highlight**, draw attention to, accentuate

spotted ADJECTIVE **= speckled**, dotted, flecked, mottled, dappled

spouse NOUN **= partner**, mate, husband *or* wife, consort, significant other (*U.S. informal*)

sprawl VERB **= loll**, slump, lounge, flop, slouch

spray¹ NOUN **1 = droplets**, fine mist, drizzle **2 = aerosol**, sprinkler, atomizer
▷ VERB **= scatter**, shower, sprinkle, diffuse

spray² NOUN **= sprig**, floral arrangement, branch, corsage

spread VERB **1 = open (out)**, extend, stretch, unfold, sprawl, unroll **2 = extend**, open, stretch **3 = grow**, increase, expand, widen, escalate, proliferate, multiply, broaden **4 = circulate**, broadcast, propagate, disseminate, make known ≠ suppress **5 = diffuse**, cast, shed, radiate
▷ NOUN **1 = increase**, development, advance, expansion, proliferation,

dissemination, dispersal
2 = extent, span, stretch, sweep

spree NOUN **= fling**, binge
(*informal*), orgy

spring NOUN **= flexibility**, bounce,
resilience, elasticity, buoyancy
▷ VERB **1 = jump**, bound, leap,
bounce, vault **2** *usually followed by*
from **= originate**, come, derive,
start, issue, proceed, arise, stem
▷ RELATED WORD: *adjective* **vernal**

sprinkle VERB **= scatter**, dust,
strew, pepper, shower, spray,
powder, dredge

sprinkling NOUN **= scattering**,
dusting, few, dash, handful,
sprinkle

sprint VERB **= run**, race, shoot,
tear, dash, dart, hare (*Brit.
informal*)

sprout VERB **1 = germinate**, bud,
shoot, spring **2 = grow**, develop,
ripen

spur VERB **= incite**, drive, prompt,
urge, stimulate, animate, prod,
prick
▷ NOUN **= stimulus**, incentive,
impetus, motive, impulse,
inducement, incitement
▷ PHRASE: **on the spur of
the moment = on impulse**,
impulsively, on the spot,
impromptu, without planning

spurn VERB **= reject**, slight, scorn,
rebuff, snub, despise, disdain,
repulse ≠ accept

spy NOUN **= undercover agent**,
mole, nark (*Brit., Austral. & N.Z.
slang*)
▷ VERB **= catch sight of**, spot,

notice, observe, glimpse, espy

squabble VERB **= quarrel**, fight,
argue, row, dispute, wrangle,
bicker
▷ NOUN **= quarrel**, fight, row,
argument, dispute, disagreement,
tiff

squad NOUN **= team**, group, band,
company, force, troop, crew, gang

squander VERB **= waste**, spend,
fritter away, blow (*slang*), misuse,
expend, misspend ≠ save

square ADJECTIVE **= fair**, straight,
genuine, ethical, honest, on the
level (*informal*), kosher (*informal*),
dinkum (*Austral. & N.Z. informal*),
above board
▷ VERB *often followed by* **with**
= agree, match, fit, correspond,
tally, reconcile

squash VERB **1 = crush**, press,
flatten, mash, smash, distort,
pulp, compress **2 = suppress**,
quell, silence, crush, annihilate
3 = embarrass, put down, shame,
degrade, mortify

squeeze VERB **1 = press**, crush,
squash, pinch **2 = clutch**, press,
grip, crush, pinch, squash,
compress, wring **3 = cram**, press,
crowd, force, stuff, pack, jam, ram
4 = hug, embrace, cuddle, clasp,
enfold
▷ NOUN **1 = press**, grip, clasp,
crush, pinch, squash, wring
2 = crush, jam, squash, press,
crowd, congestion **3 = hug**,
embrace, clasp

stab VERB **= pierce**, stick, wound,
knife, thrust, spear, jab, transfix

S

▷ NOUN 1 (*informal*) = **attempt**, go, try, endeavour 2 = **twinge**, prick, pang, ache

stability NOUN = **firmness**, strength, soundness, solidity, steadiness ≠ instability

stable ADJECTIVE 1 = **secure**, lasting, strong, sound, fast, sure, established, permanent ≠ insecure 2 = **well-balanced**, balanced, sensible, reasonable, rational 3 = **solid**, firm, fixed, substantial, durable, well-made, well-built, immovable ≠ unstable

stack NOUN 1 = **pile**, heap, mountain, mass, load, mound 2 = **lot**, mass, load (*informal*), ton (*informal*), heap (*informal*), great amount
▷ VERB = **pile**, heap up, load, assemble, accumulate, amass

staff NOUN 1 = **workers**, employees, personnel, workforce, team 2 = **stick**, pole, rod, crook, cane, stave, wand, sceptre

stage NOUN = **step**, leg, phase, point, level, period, division, lap

stagger VERB 1 = **totter**, reel, sway, lurch, wobble 2 = **astound**, amaze, stun, shock, shake, overwhelm, astonish, confound

stain NOUN 1 = **mark**, spot, blot, blemish, discoloration, smirch 2 = **stigma**, shame, disgrace, slur, dishonour 3 = **dye**, colour, tint
▷ VERB 1 = **mark**, soil, discolour, dirty, tinge, spot, blot, blemish 2 = **dye**, colour, tint

stake¹ NOUN = **pole**, post, stick, pale, paling, picket, palisade

stake² NOUN 1 = **bet**, ante, wager 2 = **interest**, share, involvement, concern, investment
▷ VERB = **bet**, gamble, wager, chance, risk, venture, hazard

stale ADJECTIVE 1 = **old**, hard, dry, decayed ≠ fresh 2 = **musty**, fusty 3 = **tasteless**, flat, sour 4 = **unoriginal**, banal, trite, stereotyped, worn-out, threadbare, hackneyed, overused ≠ original

stalk VERB = **pursue**, follow, track, hunt, shadow, haunt

stall¹ VERB = **stop dead**, jam, seize up, catch, stick, stop short
▷ NOUN = **stand**, table, counter, booth, kiosk

stall² VERB = **play for time**, delay, hedge, temporize

stalwart ADJECTIVE 1 = **loyal**, faithful, firm, true, dependable, steadfast 2 = **strong**, strapping, sturdy, stout ≠ puny

stamina NOUN = **staying power**, endurance, resilience, force, power, energy, strength

stammer VERB = **stutter**, falter, pause, hesitate, stumble over your words

stamp NOUN = **imprint**, mark, brand, signature, earmark, hallmark
▷ VERB 1 = **print**, mark, impress 2 = **trample**, step, tread, crush 3 = **identify**, mark, brand, label, reveal, show to be, categorize
▷ PHRASE: **stamp something out** = **eliminate**, destroy, eradicate, crush, suppress, put down,

scotch, quell

stance NOUN 1 = **attitude**, stand, position, viewpoint, standpoint 2 = **posture**, carriage, bearing, deportment

stand VERB 1 = **be upright**, be erect, be vertical 2 = **get to your feet**, rise, stand up, straighten up 3 = **be located**, be, sit, be positioned, be situated or located 4 = **be valid**, continue, exist, prevail, remain valid 5 = **put**, place, position, set, mount 6 = **sit**, mellow 7 = **resist**, endure, tolerate, stand up to 8 = **tolerate**, bear, abide, stomach, endure, brook 9 = **take**, bear, handle, endure, put up with (*informal*), countenance
▷ NOUN 1 = **position**, attitude, stance, opinion, determination 2 = **stall**, booth, kiosk, table
▷ PHRASES: **stand by** = **be prepared**, wait; **stand for something** 1 = **represent**, mean, signify, denote, indicate, symbolize, betoken; **stand in for someone** = **be a substitute for**, represent, cover for, take the place of, deputize for; **stand up for something** or **someone** = **support**, champion, defend, uphold, stick up for (*informal*)

standard NOUN 1 = **level**, grade 2 = **criterion**, measure, guideline, example, model, average, norm, gauge 3 = *often plural* = **principles**, ideals, morals, ethics 4 = **flag**, banner, ensign
▷ ADJECTIVE 1 = **usual**, normal, customary, average, basic, regular, typical, orthodox ≠ unusual 2 = **accepted**, official, established, approved, recognized, definitive, authoritative ≠ unofficial

stand-in NOUN = **substitute**, deputy, replacement, reserve, surrogate, understudy, locum, stopgap

standing NOUN 1 = **status**, position, footing, rank, reputation, eminence, repute 2 = **duration**, existence, continuance
▷ ADJECTIVE 1 = **permanent**, lasting, fixed, regular 2 = **upright**, erect, vertical

staple ADJECTIVE = **principal**, chief, main, key, basic, fundamental, predominant

star NOUN 1 = **heavenly body**, celestial body 2 = **celebrity**, big name, megastar (*informal*), name, luminary, leading man or lady, hero or heroine, principal, main attraction
▷ VERB = **play the lead**, appear, feature, perform ▷ RELATED WORDS: *adjectives* **astral**, **stellar**

stare VERB = **gaze**, look, goggle, watch, gape, eyeball (*slang*), gawp (*Brit. slang*), gawk

stark ADJECTIVE 1 = **plain**, harsh, basic, grim, straightforward, blunt 2 = **sharp**, clear, striking, distinct, clear-cut 3 = **austere**, severe, plain, bare, harsh, bare-bones 4 = **bleak**, grim, barren, hard 5 = **absolute**, pure, sheer,

utter, downright, out-and-out, unmitigated
▷ ADVERB = **absolutely**, quite, completely, entirely, altogether, wholly, utterly
start VERB 1 = **set about**, begin, proceed, embark upon, take the first step, make a beginning ≠ stop 2 = **begin**, arise, originate, issue, appear, commence ≠ end 3 = **set in motion**, initiate, instigate, open, trigger, originate, get going, kick-start ≠ stop 4 = **establish**, begin, found, create, launch, set up, institute, pioneer ≠ terminate 5 = **start up**, activate, get something going ≠ turn off 6 = **jump**, shy, jerk, flinch, recoil
▷ NOUN 1 = **beginning**, outset, opening, birth, foundation, dawn, onset, initiation ≠ end 2 = **jump**, spasm, convulsion
startle VERB = **surprise**, shock, frighten, scare, make (someone) jump
starving ADJECTIVE = **hungry**, starved, ravenous, famished
state NOUN 1 = **country**, nation, land, republic, territory, federation, commonwealth, kingdom 2 = **government**, ministry, administration, executive, regime, powers-that-be 3 = **condition**, shape 4 = **frame of mind**, condition, spirits, attitude, mood, humour 5 = **ceremony**, glory, grandeur, splendour, majesty, pomp 6 = **circumstances**, situation,

position, predicament
▷ VERB = **say**, declare, present, voice, express, assert, utter
stately ADJECTIVE = **grand**, majestic, dignified, royal, august, noble, regal, lofty ≠ lowly
statement NOUN 1 = **announcement**, declaration, communication, communiqué, proclamation 2 = **account**, report
station NOUN 1 = **railway station**, stop, stage, halt, terminal, train station, terminus 2 = **headquarters**, base, depot 3 = **position**, rank, status, standing, post, situation 4 = **post**, place, location, position, situation
▷ VERB = **assign**, post, locate, set, establish, install
stature NOUN 1 = **height**, build, size 2 = **importance**, standing, prestige, rank, prominence, eminence
status NOUN 1 = **position**, rank, grade 2 = **prestige**, standing, authority, influence, weight, honour, importance, fame, mana (N.Z.) 3 = **state of play**, development, progress, condition, evolution
staunch ADJECTIVE = **loyal**, faithful, stalwart, firm, sound, true, trusty, steadfast
stay VERB 1 = **remain**, continue to be, linger, stop, wait, halt, pause, abide ≠ go 2 *often with* **at** = **lodge**, visit, sojourn, put up at, be accommodated at 3 = **continue**, remain, go on,

survive, endure
▷ NOUN 1 = **visit**, stop,
holiday, stopover, sojourn
2 = **postponement**, delay,
suspension, stopping, halt,
deferment

steady ADJECTIVE 1 = **continuous**,
regular, constant, consistent,
persistent, unbroken,
uninterrupted, incessant
≠ irregular 2 = **stable**, fixed,
secure, firm, safe ≠ unstable
3 = **regular**, established
4 = **dependable**, sensible, reliable,
secure, calm, supportive, sober,
level-headed ≠ undependable

steal VERB 1 = **take**, nick (slang,
chiefly Brit.), pinch (informal),
lift (informal), embezzle, pilfer,
misappropriate, purloin 2 = **copy**,
take, appropriate, pinch (informal)
3 = **sneak**, slip, creep, tiptoe, slink

stealth NOUN = **secrecy**,
furtiveness, slyness, sneakiness,
unobtrusiveness, stealthiness,
surreptitiousness

steep¹ ADJECTIVE 1 = **sheer**,
precipitous, abrupt, vertical
≠ gradual 2 = **sharp**, sudden,
abrupt, marked, extreme, distinct
3 (informal) = **high**, exorbitant,
extreme, unreasonable,
overpriced, extortionate
≠ reasonable

steep² VERB = **soak**, immerse,
marinate (cookery), submerge,
drench, moisten, souse

steeped ADJECTIVE = **saturated**,
pervaded, permeated, filled,
infused, imbued, suffused

steer VERB 1 = **drive**, control,
direct, handle, pilot 2 = **direct**,
lead, guide, conduct, escort

stem¹ NOUN = **stalk**, branch, trunk,
shoot, axis ▷ PHRASE: **stem from
something** = **originate from**, be
caused by, derive from, arise from

stem² VERB = **stop**, hold back,
staunch, check, dam, curb

step NOUN 1 = **pace**, stride,
footstep 2 = **footfall** 3 = **move**,
measure, action, means, act,
deed, expedient 4 = **stage**, point,
phase 5 = **level**, rank, degree
▷ VERB = **walk**, pace, tread, move
▷ PHRASES: **step in** (informal)
= **intervene**, take action, become
involved; **step something up**
= **increase**, intensify, raise

stereotype NOUN = **formula**,
pattern
▷ VERB = **categorize**, typecast,
pigeonhole, standardize

sterile ADJECTIVE 1 = **germ-free**,
sterilized, disinfected, aseptic
≠ unhygienic 2 = **barren**,
infertile, unproductive, childless
≠ fertile

sterling ADJECTIVE = **excellent**,
sound, fine, superlative

stern ADJECTIVE 1 = **strict**,
harsh, hard, grim, rigid, austere,
inflexible ≠ lenient 2 = **severe**,
serious, forbidding ≠ friendly

stick¹ NOUN 1 = **twig**, branch
2 = **cane**, staff, pole, rod, crook,
baton 3 (slang) = **abuse**,
criticism, flak (informal), fault-
finding

stick² VERB 1 (informal) = **put**,

S

place, set, lay, deposit **2** = **poke**, dig, stab, thrust, pierce, penetrate, spear, prod **3** = **fasten**, fix, bind, hold, bond, attach, glue, paste **4** = **adhere**, cling, become joined, become welded **5** = **stay**, remain, linger, persist **6** (*slang*) = **tolerate**, take, stand, stomach, abide ▷ PHRASES: **stick out** = **protrude**, stand out, jut out, show, project, bulge, obtrude; **stick up for someone** (*informal*) = **defend**, support, champion, stand up for

sticky ADJECTIVE **1** = **adhesive**, gummed, adherent **2** = **gooey**, tacky (*informal*), viscous, glutinous, gummy, icky (*informal*), gluey, clinging **3** (*informal*) = **difficult**, awkward, tricky, embarrassing, nasty, delicate, unpleasant, barro (*Austral. slang*) **4** = **humid**, close, sultry, oppressive, sweltering, clammy, muggy

stiff ADJECTIVE **1** = **inflexible**, rigid, unyielding, hard, firm, tight, solid, tense ≠ flexible **2** = **formal**, constrained, forced, unnatural, stilted, unrelaxed ≠ informal **3** = **vigorous**, great, strong **4** = **severe**, strict, harsh, hard, heavy, extreme, drastic **5** = **difficult**, hard, tough, exacting, arduous

stifle VERB **1** = **suppress**, repress, stop, check, silence, restrain, hush, smother **2** = **restrain**, suppress, repress, smother

stigma NOUN = **disgrace**, shame, dishonour, stain, slur, smirch

still ADJECTIVE **1** = **motionless**, stationary, calm, peaceful, serene, tranquil, undisturbed, restful ≠ moving **2** = **silent**, quiet, hushed ≠ noisy ▷ VERB = **quieten**, calm, settle, quiet, silence, soothe, hush, lull ≠ get louder ▷ SENTENCE CONNECTOR = **however**, but, yet, nevertheless, notwithstanding

stimulate VERB = **encourage**, inspire, prompt, fire, spur, provoke, arouse, rouse

stimulating ADJECTIVE = **exciting**, inspiring, stirring, rousing, provocative, exhilarating ≠ boring

stimulus NOUN = **incentive**, spur, encouragement, impetus, inducement, goad, incitement, fillip

sting VERB **1** = **hurt**, burn, wound **2** = **smart**, burn, pain, hurt, tingle

stink VERB = **reek**, pong (*Brit. informal*) ▷ NOUN = **stench**, pong (*Brit. informal*), foul smell, fetor

stint NOUN = **term**, time, turn, period, share, shift, stretch, spell ▷ VERB = **be mean**, hold back, be sparing, skimp on, be frugal

stipulate VERB = **specify**, agree, require, contract, settle, covenant, insist upon

stir VERB **1** = **mix**, beat, agitate **2** = **stimulate**, move, excite, spur, provoke, arouse, awaken, rouse ≠ inhibit **3** = **spur**, drive, prompt,

S

stimulate, prod, urge, animate, prick

▷ NOUN = **commotion**, excitement, activity, disorder, fuss, disturbance, bustle, flurry

stock NOUN 1 = **shares**, holdings, securities, investments, bonds, equities 2 = **property**, capital, assets, funds 3 = **goods**, merchandise, wares, range, choice, variety, selection, commodities 4 = **supply**, store, reserve, fund, stockpile, hoard 5 = **livestock**, cattle, beasts, domestic animals

▷ VERB 1 = **sell**, supply, handle, keep, trade in, deal in 2 = **fill**, supply, provide with, equip, furnish, fit out

▷ ADJECTIVE 1 = **hackneyed**, routine, banal, trite, overused 2 = **regular**, usual, ordinary, conventional, customary

stomach NOUN 1 = **belly**, gut (informal), abdomen, tummy (informal), puku (N.Z.) 2 = **tummy**, pot 3 = **inclination**, taste, desire, appetite, relish

▷ VERB = **bear**, take, tolerate, endure, swallow, abide ▷ RELATED WORD: adjective gastric

stone NOUN 1 = **masonry**, rock 2 = **rock**, pebble 3 = **pip**, seed, pit, kernel

stoop VERB 1 = **hunch** 2 = **bend**, lean, bow, duck, crouch

▷ NOUN = **slouch**, bad posture, round-shoulderedness

stop VERB 1 = **quit**, cease, refrain, put an end to, discontinue, desist

≠ start 2 = **prevent**, cut short, arrest, restrain, hold back, hinder, repress, impede ≠ facilitate 3 = **end**, conclude, finish, terminate ≠ continue 4 = **cease**, shut down, discontinue, desist ≠ continue 5 = **halt**, pause ≠ keep going 6 = **pause**, wait, rest, take a break, have a breather (informal), stop briefly 7 = **stay**, rest, lodge

▷ NOUN 1 = **halt**, standstill 2 = **station**, stage, depot, terminus 3 = **stay**, break, rest

store NOUN 1 = **shop**, outlet, market, mart 2 = **supply**, stock, reserve, fund, quantity, accumulation, stockpile, hoard 3 = **repository**, warehouse, depository, storeroom

▷ VERB 1 often with **away** or **up** = **put by**, save, hoard, keep, reserve, deposit, garner, stockpile 2 = **put away**, put in storage, put in store 3 = **keep**, hold, preserve, maintain, retain, conserve

storm NOUN 1 = **tempest**, hurricane, gale, blizzard, squall 2 = **outburst**, row, outcry, furore, outbreak, turmoil, disturbance, strife

▷ VERB 1 = **rush**, stamp, flounce, fly 2 = **rage**, rant, thunder, rave, bluster 3 = **attack**, charge, rush, assault, assail

stormy ADJECTIVE 1 = **wild**, rough, raging, turbulent, windy, blustery, inclement, squally 2 = **rough**, wild, turbulent, raging 3 = **angry**, heated, fierce, passionate, fiery,

S

impassioned

story NOUN 1 = **tale**, romance, narrative, history, legend, yarn 2 = **anecdote**, account, tale, report 3 = **report**, news, article, feature, scoop, news item

stout ADJECTIVE 1 = **fat**, big, heavy, overweight, plump, bulky, burly, fleshy ≠ slim 2 = **strong**, strapping, muscular, robust, sturdy, stalwart, brawny, able-bodied ≠ puny 3 = **brave**, bold, courageous, fearless, resolute, gallant, intrepid, valiant ≠ timid

straight ADJECTIVE 1 = **direct** ≠ indirect 2 = **level**, even, right, square, true, smooth, aligned, horizontal ≠ crooked 3 = **frank**, plain, straightforward, blunt, outright, honest, candid, forthright ≠ evasive 4 = **successive**, consecutive, continuous, running, solid, nonstop ≠ discontinuous 5 (slang) = **conventional**, conservative, bourgeois ≠ fashionable 6 = **honest**, just, fair, reliable, respectable, upright, honourable, law-abiding ≠ dishonest 7 = **undiluted**, pure, neat, unadulterated, unmixed 8 = **in order**, organized, arranged, neat, tidy, orderly, shipshape ≠ untidy
▷ ADVERB 1 = **directly**, precisely, exactly, unswervingly, by the shortest route, in a beeline 2 = **immediately**, directly, promptly, instantly, at once, straight away, without delay,

forthwith

straightaway ADVERB = **immediately**, now, at once, directly, instantly, right away

straighten VERB = **neaten**, arrange, tidy (up), order, put in order

straightforward ADJECTIVE 1 (chiefly Brit.) = **simple**, easy, uncomplicated, routine, elementary, easy-peasy (slang) ≠ complicated 2 = **honest**, open, direct, genuine, sincere, candid, truthful, forthright, dinkum (Austral. & N.Z. informal) ≠ devious

strain¹ NOUN 1 = **pressure**, stress, demands, burden 2 = **stress**, anxiety 3 = **worry**, effort, struggle ≠ ease 4 = **burden**, tension 5 = **injury**, wrench, sprain, pull
▷ VERB 1 = **stretch**, tax, overtax 2 = **strive**, struggle, endeavour, labour, go for it (informal), bend over backwards (informal), give it your best shot (informal), knock yourself out (informal) ≠ relax 3 = **sieve**, filter, sift, purify

strain² NOUN 1 = **trace**, suggestion, tendency, streak 2 = **breed**, family, race, blood, descent, extraction, ancestry, lineage

strained ADJECTIVE 1 = **tense**, difficult, awkward, embarrassed, stiff, uneasy ≠ relaxed 2 = **forced**, put on, false, artificial, unnatural ≠ natural

strait NOUN often plural = **channel**, sound, narrows
▷ PLURAL NOUN = **difficulty**,

dilemma, plight, hardship, uphill (*S. African*), predicament, extremity

strand NOUN = **filament**, fibre, thread, string

stranded ADJECTIVE 1 = **beached**, grounded, marooned, ashore, shipwrecked, aground 2 = **helpless**, abandoned, high and dry

strange ADJECTIVE 1 = **odd**, curious, weird, wonderful, extraordinary, bizarre, peculiar, abnormal, daggy (*Austral. & N.Z. informal*) ≠ ordinary 2 = **unfamiliar**, new, unknown, foreign, novel, alien, exotic, untried ≠ familiar

stranger NOUN 1 = **unknown person** 2 = **newcomer**, incomer, foreigner, guest, visitor, alien, outlander

strangle VERB 1 = **throttle**, choke, asphyxiate, strangulate 2 = **suppress**, inhibit, subdue, stifle, repress, overpower, quash, quell

strap NOUN = **tie**, thong, belt ▷ VERB = **fasten**, tie, secure, bind, lash, buckle

strapping ADJECTIVE = **well-built**, big, powerful, robust, sturdy, husky (*informal*), brawny

strategic ADJECTIVE 1 = **tactical**, calculated, deliberate, planned, politic, diplomatic 2 = **crucial**, important, key, vital, critical, decisive, cardinal

strategy NOUN 1 = **policy**, procedure, approach, scheme

2 = **plan**, approach, scheme

stray VERB 1 = **wander**, go astray, drift 2 = **drift**, wander, roam, meander, rove 3 = **digress**, diverge, deviate, get off the point ▷ MODIFIER = **lost**, abandoned, homeless, roaming, vagrant ▷ ADJECTIVE = **random**, chance, accidental

streak NOUN 1 = **band**, line, strip, stroke, layer, slash, vein, stripe 2 = **trace**, touch, element, strain, dash, vein ▷ VERB = **speed**, fly, tear, flash, sprint, dart, zoom, whizz (*informal*)

stream NOUN 1 = **river**, brook, burn (*Scot.*), beck, tributary, bayou, rivulet 2 = **flow**, current, rush, run, course, drift, surge, tide ▷ VERB 1 = **flow**, run, pour, issue, flood, spill, cascade, gush 2 = **rush**, fly, speed, tear, flood, pour

streamlined ADJECTIVE = **efficient**, organized, rationalized, slick, smooth-running

street NOUN = **road**, lane, avenue, terrace, row, roadway

strength NOUN 1 = **might**, muscle, brawn ≠ weakness 2 = **will**, resolution, courage, character, nerve, determination, pluck, stamina 3 = **health**, fitness, vigour 4 = **mainstay** 5 = **toughness**, soundness, robustness, sturdiness 6 = **force**, power, intensity ≠ weakness 7 = **potency**, effectiveness,

S

efficacy **8 = strong point**, skill, asset, advantage, talent, forte, speciality ≠ failing

strengthen VERB **1 = fortify**, harden, toughen, consolidate, stiffen, gee up, brace up ≠ weaken **2 = reinforce**, support, intensify, bolster, buttress **3 = bolster**, harden, reinforce **4 = heighten**, intensify **5 = make stronger**, build up, invigorate, restore, give strength to **6 = support**, brace, reinforce, consolidate, harden, bolster, augment, buttress **7 = become stronger**, intensify, gain strength

stress VERB **1 = emphasize**, underline, dwell on **2 = place the emphasis on**, emphasize, give emphasis to, lay emphasis upon
▷ NOUN **1 = emphasis**, significance, force, weight **2 = strain**, pressure, worry, tension, burden, anxiety, trauma **3 = accent**, beat, emphasis, accentuation

stretch VERB **1 = extend**, cover, spread, reach, put forth, unroll **2 = last**, continue, go on, carry on, reach **3 = expand 4 = pull**, distend, strain, tighten, draw out, elongate
▷ NOUN **1 = expanse**, area, tract, spread, distance, extent **2 = period**, time, spell, stint, term, space

strict ADJECTIVE **1 = severe**, harsh, stern, firm, stringent ≠ easy-going **2 = stern**, firm, severe, harsh, authoritarian **3 = exact**,

accurate, precise, close, true, faithful, meticulous, scrupulous **4 = absolute**, total, utter

strife NOUN **= conflict**, battle, clash, quarrel, friction, discord, dissension

strike NOUN **= walkout**, industrial action, mutiny, revolt
▷ VERB **1 = walk out**, down tools, revolt, mutiny **2 = hit**, smack, thump, beat, knock, punch, hammer, slap **3 = drive**, hit, smack, wallop (*informal*) **4 = collide with**, hit, run into, bump into **5 = knock**, smack, thump, beat **6 = affect**, touch, devastate, overwhelm, leave a mark on **7 = attack**, assault someone, set upon someone, lay into someone (*informal*) **8 = occur to**, hit, come to, register (*informal*), dawn on *or* upon **9 = seem to**, appear to, look to, give the impression to **10 = move**, touch, hit, affect, overcome, stir, disturb, perturb

striking ADJECTIVE **= impressive**, dramatic, outstanding, noticeable, conspicuous, jaw-dropping ≠ unimpressive

string NOUN **1 = cord**, twine, fibre **2 = series**, line, row, file, sequence, succession, procession **3 = sequence**, run, series, chain, succession

stringent ADJECTIVE **= strict**, tough, rigorous, tight, severe, rigid, inflexible ≠ lax

strip[1] VERB **1 = undress**, disrobe, unclothe **2 = plunder**, rob, loot, empty, sack, ransack, pillage, divest

strip² NOUN 1 = **piece**, shred, band, belt 2 = **stretch**, area, tract, expanse, extent

strive VERB = **try**, labour, struggle, attempt, toil, go all out (*informal*), bend over backwards (*informal*), do your best

stroke VERB = **caress**, rub, fondle, pet
▷ NOUN 1 = **apoplexy**, fit, seizure, attack, collapse 2 = **blow**, hit, knock, pat, rap, thump, swipe

stroll VERB = **walk**, ramble, amble, promenade, saunter
▷ NOUN = **walk**, promenade, constitutional, ramble, breath of air

strong ADJECTIVE 1 = **powerful**, muscular, tough, athletic, strapping, hardy, sturdy, burly ≠ weak 2 = **fit**, robust, lusty 3 = **durable**, substantial, sturdy, heavy-duty, well-built, hard-wearing ≠ flimsy 4 = **extreme**, radical, drastic, strict, harsh, rigid, forceful, uncompromising 5 = **decisive**, firm, forceful, decided, determined, resolute, incisive 6 = **persuasive**, convincing, compelling, telling, sound, effective, potent, weighty 7 = **keen**, deep, acute, fervent, zealous, vehement 8 = **intense**, deep, passionate, ardent, fierce, fervent, vehement, fervid 9 = **staunch**, firm, fierce, ardent, enthusiastic, passionate, fervent 10 = **distinct**, marked,

clear, unmistakable ≠ slight 11 = **bright**, brilliant, dazzling, bold ≠ dull

stronghold NOUN 1 = **bastion**, fortress, bulwark 2 = **refuge**, haven, retreat, sanctuary, hide-out

structure NOUN
1 = **arrangement**, form, make-up, design, organization, construction, formation, configuration 2 = **building**, construction, erection, edifice
▷ VERB = **arrange**, organize, design, shape, build up, assemble

struggle VERB 1 = **strive**, labour, toil, work, strain, go all out (*informal*), give it your best shot (*informal*), exert yourself 2 = **fight**, battle, wrestle, grapple, compete, contend
▷ NOUN 1 = **effort**, labour, toil, work, pains, scramble, exertion 2 = **fight**, battle, conflict, clash, contest, brush, combat, tussle, biffo (*Austral. slang*)

strut VERB = **swagger**, parade, peacock, prance

stubborn ADJECTIVE = **obstinate**, dogged, inflexible, persistent, intractable, tenacious, recalcitrant, unyielding ≠ compliant

stuck ADJECTIVE 1 = **fastened**, fast, fixed, joined, glued, cemented 2 (*informal*) = **baffled**, stumped, beaten

student NOUN
1 = **undergraduate**, scholar
2 = **pupil**, scholar, schoolchild,

S

schoolboy *or* schoolgirl
3 = **learner**, trainee, apprentice,
disciple

studied ADJECTIVE = **planned**,
deliberate, conscious, intentional,
premeditated ≠ unplanned

studio NOUN = **workshop**,
workroom, atelier

study VERB **1** = **learn**, cram
(*informal*), swot (up) (*Brit. informal*),
read up, mug up (*Brit. slang*)
2 = **examine**, survey, look at,
scrutinize **3** = **contemplate**, read,
examine, consider, go into, pore
over
▷ NOUN **1** = **examination**,
investigation, analysis,
consideration, inspection,
scrutiny, contemplation **2** = **piece
of research**, survey, report,
review, inquiry, investigation
3 = **learning**, lessons, school
work, reading, research, swotting
(*Brit. informal*)

stuff NOUN **1** = **things**, gear,
possessions, effects, equipment,
objects, tackle, kit **2** = **substance**,
material, essence, matter
▷ VERB **1** = **shove**, force, push,
squeeze, jam, ram **2** = **cram**, fill,
pack, crowd

stuffing NOUN = **wadding**, filling,
packing

stumble VERB **1** = **trip**, fall,
slip, reel, stagger, falter, lurch
2 = **totter**, reel, lurch, wobble
▷ PHRASE: **stumble across** *or* **on**
or **upon something** *or* **someone**
= **discover**, find, come across,
chance upon

stump NOUN = **tail end**, end,
remnant, remainder
▷ VERB = **baffle**, confuse, puzzle,
bewilder, perplex, mystify,
flummox, nonplus

stun VERB **1** = **overcome**, shock,
confuse, astonish, stagger,
bewilder, astound, overpower
2 = **daze**, knock out, stupefy,
numb, benumb

stunning ADJECTIVE (*informal*)
= **wonderful**, beautiful,
impressive, striking, lovely,
spectacular, marvellous, splendid
≠ unimpressive

stunt NOUN = **feat**, act, trick,
exploit, deed

stunted ADJECTIVE = **undersized**,
little, small, tiny, diminutive

stupid ADJECTIVE
1 = **unintelligent**, thick, simple,
slow, dim, dense, simple-minded,
moronic ≠ intelligent **2** = **silly**,
foolish, daft (*informal*), rash,
pointless, senseless, idiotic,
fatuous ≠ sensible **3** = **senseless**,
dazed, groggy, insensate,
semiconscious

sturdy ADJECTIVE **1** = **robust**,
hardy, powerful, athletic,
muscular, lusty, brawny ≠ puny
2 = **substantial**, solid, durable,
well-made, well-built ≠ flimsy

style NOUN **1** = **manner**, way,
method, approach, technique,
mode **2** = **elegance**, taste, chic,
flair, polish, sophistication,
panache, élan **3** = **design**, form,
cut **4** = **type**, sort, kind, variety,
category, genre **5** = **fashion**,

trend, mode, vogue, rage
6 = **luxury**, ease, comfort, elegance, grandeur, affluence
▷ VERB **1** = **design**, cut, tailor, fashion, shape, arrange, adapt
2 = **call**, name, term, label, entitle, dub, designate

stylish ADJECTIVE = **smart**, chic, fashionable, trendy (*Brit. informal*), modish, dressy (*informal*), voguish, schmick (*Austral. informal*), funky ≠ scruffy

subdue VERB **1** = **overcome**, defeat, master, break, control, crush, conquer, tame
2 = **moderate**, suppress, soften, mellow, tone down, quieten down ≠ arouse

subdued ADJECTIVE **1** = **quiet**, serious, sad, chastened, dejected, downcast, crestfallen, down in the mouth ≠ lively **2** = **hushed**, soft, quiet, muted ≠ loud

subject NOUN **1** = **topic**, question, issue, matter, point, business, affair, object **2** = **citizen**, resident, native, inhabitant, national
3 = **dependant**, subordinate
▷ ADJECTIVE = **subordinate**, dependent, satellite, inferior, obedient
▷ VERB = **put through**, expose, submit, lay open ▷ PHRASE:
subject to 1 = **liable to**, open to, exposed to, vulnerable to, prone to, susceptible to **2** = **bound by**
3 = **dependent on**, contingent on, controlled by, conditional on

subjective ADJECTIVE = **personal**, prejudiced, biased, nonobjective

≠ objective

sublime ADJECTIVE = **noble**, glorious, high, great, grand, elevated, lofty, exalted ≠ lowly

submerge VERB **1** = **flood**, swamp, engulf, overflow, inundate, deluge **2** = **immerse**, plunge, duck **3** = **sink**, plunge, go under water **4** = **overwhelm**, swamp, engulf, deluge

submission NOUN **1** = **surrender**, yielding, giving in, cave-in (*informal*), capitulation
2 = **presentation**, handing in, entry, tendering **3** = **compliance**, obedience, meekness, resignation, deference, passivity, docility

submit VERB **1** = **surrender**, yield, give in, agree, endure, tolerate, comply, succumb **2** = **present**, hand in, tender, put forward, table, proffer

subordinate NOUN = **inferior**, junior, assistant, aide, second, attendant ≠ superior
▷ ADJECTIVE = **inferior**, lesser, lower, junior, subject, minor, secondary, dependent ≠ superior

subscribe to VERB **1** = **support**, advocate, endorse **2** = **contribute to**, give to, donate to

subscription NOUN (*chiefly Brit.*) = **membership fee**, dues, annual payment

subsequent ADJECTIVE = **following**, later, succeeding, after, successive, ensuing ≠ previous

subsequently ADVERB = **later**,

S

afterwards

subside VERB 1 = **decrease**, diminish, lessen, ease, wane, ebb, abate, slacken ≠ increase 2 = **collapse**, sink, cave in, drop, lower, settle

subsidiary NOUN = **branch**, division, section, office, department, wing, subdivision, subsection

▷ ADJECTIVE = **secondary**, lesser, subordinate, minor, supplementary, auxiliary, ancillary ≠ main

subsidy NOUN = **aid**, help, support, grant, assistance, allowance

substance NOUN 1 = **material**, body, stuff, fabric 2 = **importance**, significance, concreteness 3 = **meaning**, main point, gist, import, significance, essence 4 = **wealth**, means, property, assets, resources, estate

substantial ADJECTIVE = **big**, significant, considerable, large, important, ample, sizable or sizeable ≠ small

substitute VERB = **replace**, exchange, swap, change, switch, interchange

▷ NOUN = **replacement**, reserve, surrogate, deputy, sub, proxy, locum

● **WORD POWER**
● Although *substitute* and *replace*
● have the same meaning, the
● structures they are used in are
● different. You replace A *with*
● B, while you substitute B *for*

A. Accordingly, *he replaced the worn tyre with a new one*, and *he substituted a new tyre for the worn one* are both correct ways of saying the same thing.

subtle ADJECTIVE 1 = **faint**, slight, implied, delicate, understated ≠ obvious 2 = **crafty**, cunning, sly, shrewd, ingenious, devious, wily, artful ≠ straightforward 3 = **muted**, soft, subdued, low-key, toned down 4 = **fine**, minute, narrow, tenuous, hair-splitting

subtlety NOUN 1 = **fine point**, refinement, sophistication, delicacy 2 = **skill**, ingenuity, cleverness, deviousness, craftiness, artfulness, slyness, wiliness

subversive
ADJECTIVE = **seditious**, riotous, treasonous
▷ NOUN = **dissident**, terrorist, saboteur, fifth columnist

succeed VERB 1 = **triumph**, win, prevail 2 = **work out**, work, be successful 3 = **make it** (*informal*), do well, be successful, triumph, thrive, flourish, make good, prosper ≠ fail 4 = **take over from**, assume the office of 5 *with* **to** = **take over**, assume, attain, come into, inherit, accede to, come into possession of 6 = **follow**, come after, follow after ≠ precede

success NOUN 1 = **victory**, triumph ≠ failure 2 = **prosperity**, fortune, luck, fame 3 = **hit** (*informal*), winner, smash (*informal*), triumph, sensation ≠ flop (*informal*) **4** = **big name**, star, hit (*informal*), celebrity, sensation, megastar (*informal*) ≠ nobody

successful ADJECTIVE
1 = **triumphant**, victorious, lucky, fortunate **2** = **thriving**, profitable, rewarding, booming, flourishing, fruitful ≠ unprofitable **3** = **top**, prosperous, wealthy

successfully ADVERB = **well**, favourably, with flying colours, victoriously

succession NOUN **1** = **series**, run, sequence, course, order, train, chain, cycle **2** = **taking over**, assumption, inheritance, accession

successive ADJECTIVE = **consecutive**, following, in succession

succumb VERB **1** *often with* **to** = **surrender (to)**, yield (to), submit (to), give in (to), cave in (to) (*informal*), capitulate (to) ≠ beat **2** *with* **to** (*an illness*) = **catch**, fall ill with

suck VERB **1** = **drink**, sip, draw **2** = **take**, draw, pull, extract

sudden ADJECTIVE = **quick**, rapid, unexpected, swift, hurried, abrupt, hasty ≠ gradual

suddenly ADVERB = **abruptly**, all of a sudden, unexpectedly

sue VERB (*law*) = **take (someone) to court**, prosecute, charge, summon, indict

suffer VERB **1** = **be in pain**, hurt, ache **2** = **be affected**, have

trouble with, be afflicted, be troubled with **3** = **undergo**, experience, sustain, bear, go through, endure **4** = **tolerate**, stand, put up with (*informal*), bear, endure

suffering NOUN = **pain**, distress, agony, misery, ordeal, discomfort, torment, hardship

suffice VERB = **be enough**, do, be sufficient, be adequate, serve, meet requirements

sufficient ADJECTIVE = **adequate**, enough, ample, satisfactory ≠ insufficient

suggest VERB **1** = **recommend**, propose, advise, advocate, prescribe **2** = **indicate 3** = **hint at**, imply, intimate **4** = **bring to mind**, evoke

suggestion NOUN
1 = **recommendation**, proposal, proposition, plan, motion
2 = **hint**, insinuation, intimation
3 = **trace**, touch, hint, breath, indication, whisper, intimation

suit NOUN **1** = **outfit**, costume, ensemble, dress, clothing, habit **2** = **lawsuit**, case, trial, proceeding, cause, action, prosecution
▷ VERB **1** = **be acceptable to**, please, satisfy, do, gratify **2** = **agree with**, become, match, go with, harmonize with

suitable ADJECTIVE
1 = **appropriate**, right, fitting, fit, becoming, satisfactory, apt, befitting ≠ inappropriate
2 = **seemly**, fitting, becoming,

S

proper, correct ≠ unseemly
3 = **suited**, appropriate,
in keeping with ≠ out of
keeping **4** = **pertinent**,
relevant, applicable, fitting,
appropriate, to the point, apt
≠ irrelevant **5** = **convenient**,
timely, appropriate, well-timed,
opportune ≠ inopportune

suite NOUN = **rooms**, apartment

sum NOUN **1** = **amount**, quantity,
volume **2** = **calculation**, figures,
arithmetic, mathematics, maths
(*Brit. informal*), tally, math (*U.S.
informal*), arithmetical problem
3 = **total**, aggregate **4** = **totality**,
whole

summarize VERB = **sum
up**, condense, encapsulate,
epitomize, abridge, précis

summary NOUN = **synopsis**,
résumé, précis, review, outline,
rundown, abridgment

summit NOUN **1** = **peak**, top,
tip, pinnacle, apex, head ≠ base
2 = **height**, pinnacle, peak, zenith,
acme ≠ depths

summon VERB **1** = **send for**,
call, bid, invite **2** *often with* **up**
= **gather**, muster, draw on

sumptuous ADJECTIVE
= **luxurious**, grand, superb,
splendid, gorgeous, lavish,
opulent ≠ plain

sunny ADJECTIVE **1** = **bright**, clear,
fine, radiant, sunlit, summery,
unclouded ≠ dull **2** = **cheerful**,
happy, cheery, buoyant, joyful,
light-hearted ≠ gloomy

sunset NOUN = **nightfall**, dusk,

eventide, close of (the) day

superb ADJECTIVE **1** = **splendid**,
excellent, magnificent, fine,
grand, superior, marvellous,
world-class, booshit (*Austral.
slang*), exo (*Austral. slang*), sik
(*Austral. slang*), rad (*informal*), phat
(*slang*), schmick (*Austral. informal*)
≠ inferior **2** = **magnificent**,
superior, marvellous, exquisite,
superlative ≠ terrible

superficial ADJECTIVE
1 = **shallow**, frivolous, empty-
headed, silly, trivial ≠ serious
2 = **hasty**, cursory, perfunctory,
hurried, casual, sketchy, desultory,
slapdash ≠ thorough **3** = **slight**,
surface, external, on the surface,
exterior ≠ profound

superintendent NOUN
= **supervisor**, director, manager,
chief, governor, inspector,
controller, overseer

superior ADJECTIVE **1** = **better**,
higher, greater, grander,
surpassing, unrivalled ≠ inferior
2 = **first-class**, excellent,
first-rate, choice, exclusive,
exceptional, de luxe, booshit
(*Austral. slang*), exo (*Austral.
slang*), sik (*Austral. slang*),
rad (*informal*), phat (*slang*),
schmick (*Austral. informal*)
≠ average **3** = **supercilious**,
patronizing, condescending,
haughty, disdainful, lordly, lofty,
pretentious
▷ NOUN = **boss**, senior, director,
manager, chief (*informal*),
principal, supervisor, baas

s

(S. African), sherang (Austral. & N.Z.) ≠ subordinate

● **WORD POWER**
● *Superior* should not be used
● with *than*: *he is a better* (not *a*
● *superior*) *poet than his brother; his*
● *poetry is superior to* (not *than*) *his*
● *brother's.*

superiority NOUN = **supremacy**, lead, advantage, excellence, ascendancy, predominance

supernatural ADJECTIVE = **paranormal**, unearthly, uncanny, ghostly, psychic, mystic, miraculous, occult

supervise VERB 1 = **observe**, guide, monitor, oversee, keep an eye on 2 = **oversee**, run, manage, control, direct, handle, look after, superintend

supervision NOUN = **superintendence**, direction, control, charge, care, management, guidance

supervisor NOUN = **boss** (*informal*), manager, chief, inspector, administrator, foreman, overseer, baas (*S. African*)

supplement VERB = **add to**, reinforce, augment, extend
▷ NOUN 1 = **pull-out**, insert 2 = **appendix**, add-on, postscript 3 = **addition**, extra

supply VERB 1 = **provide**, give, furnish, produce, stock, grant, contribute, yield 2 = **furnish**, provide, equip, endow
▷ NOUN = **store**, fund, stock, source, reserve, quantity, hoard, cache

▷ PLURAL NOUN = **provisions**, necessities, stores, food, materials, equipment, rations

support VERB 1 = **help**, back, champion, second, aid, defend, assist, side with ≠ oppose 2 = **provide for**, maintain, look after, keep, fund, finance, sustain ≠ live off 3 = **bear out**, confirm, verify, substantiate, corroborate ≠ refute 4 = **bear**, carry, sustain, prop (up), reinforce, hold, brace, buttress
▷ NOUN 1 = **furtherance**, backing, promotion, assistance, encouragement 2 = **help**, loyalty ≠ opposition 3 = **aid**, help, benefits, relief, assistance 4 = **prop**, post, foundation, brace, pillar 5 = **supporter**, prop, mainstay, tower of strength, second, backer ≠ antagonist 6 = **upkeep**, maintenance, keep, subsistence, sustenance

supporter NOUN = **follower**, fan, advocate, friend, champion, sponsor, patron, helper ≠ opponent

supportive ADJECTIVE = **helpful**, encouraging, understanding, sympathetic

suppose VERB 1 = **imagine**, consider, conjecture, postulate, hypothesize 2 = **think**, imagine, expect, assume, guess (*informal*, *chiefly U.S. & Canad.*), presume, conjecture

supposed ADJECTIVE 1 *usually with* **to** = **meant**, expected, required, obliged 2 = **presumed**, alleged,

S

professed, accepted, assumed
supposedly ADVERB
= **presumably**, allegedly,
ostensibly, theoretically,
hypothetically ≠ actually
suppress VERB 1 = **stamp out**,
stop, check, crush, conquer,
subdue, put an end to, overpower
≠ encourage 2 = **check**, inhibit,
subdue, stop, quell 3 = **restrain**,
stifle, contain, silence, conceal,
curb, repress, smother
suppression NOUN
1 = **elimination**, crushing,
check, quashing 2 = **inhibition**,
blocking, restraint, smothering
supremacy NOUN = **domination**,
sovereignty, sway, mastery,
primacy, predominance, supreme
power
supreme ADJECTIVE
1 = **paramount** ≠ least 2 = **chief**,
leading, principal, highest, head,
top, prime, foremost ≠ lowest
3 = **ultimate**, highest, greatest
supremo NOUN (Brit. informal)
= **head**, leader, boss (informal),
director, master, governor,
commander, principal, baas
(S. African)
sure ADJECTIVE 1 = **certain**,
positive, decided, convinced,
confident, assured, definite
≠ uncertain 2 = **inevitable**,
guaranteed, bound, assured,
inescapable, nailed-on (slang)
≠ unsure 3 = **reliable**, accurate,
dependable, undoubted,
undeniable, foolproof, infallible,
unerring ≠ unreliable

surely ADVERB 1 = **it must be the
case that** 2 = **undoubtedly**,
certainly, definitely, without
doubt, unquestionably,
indubitably, doubtlessly
surface NOUN 1 = **covering**,
face, exterior, side, top, veneer
2 = **façade**
▷ VERB 1 = **emerge**, come up,
come to the surface 2 = **appear**,
emerge, arise, come to light,
crop up (informal), transpire,
materialize
surge NOUN 1 = **rush**, flood
2 = **flow**, wave, rush, roller, gush,
outpouring 3 = **tide**, swell,
billowing 4 = **rush**, wave, storm,
torrent, eruption
▷ VERB 1 = **rush**, pour, rise, gush
2 = **roll**, rush, heave 3 = **sweep**,
rush, storm
surpass VERB = **outdo**, beat,
exceed, eclipse, excel, transcend,
outstrip, outshine
surpassing ADJECTIVE = **supreme**,
extraordinary, outstanding,
exceptional, unrivalled,
incomparable, matchless
surplus NOUN = **excess**, surfeit
≠ shortage
▷ ADJECTIVE = **extra**, spare,
excess, remaining, odd,
superfluous ≠ insufficient
surprise NOUN 1 = **shock**,
revelation, jolt, bombshell,
eye-opener (informal)
2 = **amazement**, astonishment,
wonder, incredulity
▷ VERB 1 = **amaze**, astonish,
stun, startle, stagger, take aback

S

2 = **catch unawares** *or* **off-guard**, spring upon

surprised ADJECTIVE = **amazed**, astonished, speechless, thunderstruck

surprising ADJECTIVE = **amazing**, remarkable, incredible, astonishing, unusual, extraordinary, unexpected, staggering

surrender VERB **1** = **give in**, yield, submit, give way, succumb, cave in (*informal*), capitulate ≠ resist
2 = **give up**, abandon, relinquish, yield, concede, part with, renounce, waive
▷ NOUN = **submission**, cave-in (*informal*), capitulation, resignation, renunciation, relinquishment

surround VERB = **enclose**, ring, encircle, encompass, envelop, hem in

surrounding ADJECTIVE = **nearby**, neighbouring

surroundings PLURAL NOUN = **environment**, setting, background, location, milieu

surveillance NOUN = **observation**, watch, scrutiny, supervision, inspection

survey NOUN **1** = **poll**, study, research, review, inquiry, investigation **2** = **examination**, inspection, scrutiny
3 = **valuation**, estimate, assessment, appraisal
▷ VERB **1** = **interview**, question, poll, research, investigate
2 = **look over**, view, examine, observe, contemplate, inspect, eyeball (*slang*), scrutinize
3 = **measure**, estimate, assess, appraise

survive VERB **1** = **remain alive**, last, live on, endure **2** = **continue**, last, live on **3** = **live longer than**, outlive, outlast

susceptible ADJECTIVE
1 = **responsive**, sensitive, receptive, impressionable, suggestible ≠ unresponsive **2** *usually with* **to** = **liable**, inclined, prone, given, subject, vulnerable, disposed ≠ resistant

suspect VERB **1** = **believe**, feel, guess, consider, suppose, speculate ≠ know **2** = **distrust**, doubt, mistrust ≠ trust
▷ ADJECTIVE = **dubious**, doubtful, questionable, iffy (*informal*), shonky (*Austral. & N.Z. informal*) ≠ innocent

suspend VERB **1** = **postpone**, put off, cease, interrupt, shelve, defer, cut short, discontinue ≠ continue **2** = **hang**, attach, dangle

suspension NOUN = **postponement**, break, breaking off, interruption, abeyance, deferment, discontinuation

suspicion NOUN **1** = **distrust**, scepticism, mistrust, doubt, misgiving, qualm, wariness, dubiety **2** = **idea**, notion, hunch, guess, impression **3** = **trace**, touch, hint, suggestion, shade, streak, tinge, soupçon (*French*)

suspicious ADJECTIVE

S

1 = **distrustful**, sceptical, doubtful, unbelieving, wary ≠ trusting **2** = **suspect**, dubious, questionable, doubtful, dodgy (*Brit., Austral. & N.Z. informal*), fishy (*informal*), shonky (*Austral. & N.Z. informal*) ≠ beyond suspicion

sustain VERB **1** = **maintain**, continue, keep up, prolong, protract **2** = **suffer**, experience, undergo, feel, bear, endure, withstand **3** = **help**, aid, assist **4** = **keep alive**, nourish, provide for **5** = **support**, bear, uphold

sustained ADJECTIVE = **continuous**, constant, steady, prolonged, perpetual, unremitting, nonstop ≠ periodic

swallow VERB **1** = **eat**, consume, devour, swig (*informal*) **2** = **gulp**, drink

swamp NOUN **1** = **bog**, marsh, quagmire, slough, fen, mire, morass, pakihi (*N.Z.*), muskeg (*Canad.*)
▷ VERB **1** = **flood**, engulf, submerge, inundate **2** = **overload**, overwhelm, inundate

swap *or* **swop** VERB = **exchange**, trade, switch, interchange, barter

swarm NOUN = **multitude**, crowd, mass, army, host, flock, herd, horde
▷ VERB **1** = **crowd**, flock, throng, mass, stream **2** = **teem**, crawl, abound, bristle

swath *or* **swathe** NOUN = **area**, section, tract

swathe VERB = **wrap**, drape, envelop, cloak, shroud, bundle up

sway VERB **1** = **move from side to side**, rock, roll, swing, bend, lean **2** = **influence**, affect, guide, persuade, induce
▷ NOUN = **power**, control, influence, authority, clout (*informal*)

swear VERB **1** = **curse**, blaspheme, be foul-mouthed **2** = **vow**, promise, testify, attest **3** = **declare**, assert, affirm

swearing NOUN = **bad language**, cursing, profanity, blasphemy, foul language

sweat NOUN **1** = **perspiration 2** (*informal*) = **panic**, anxiety, worry, distress, agitation
▷ VERB **1** = **perspire**, glow **2** (*informal*) = **worry**, fret, agonize, torture yourself

sweep VERB **1** = **brush**, clean **2** = **clear**, remove, brush, clean **3** = **sail**, pass, fly, tear, zoom, glide, skim
▷ NOUN **1** = **movement**, move, swing, stroke **2** = **extent**, range, stretch, scope

sweeping ADJECTIVE **1** = **indiscriminate**, blanket, wholesale, exaggerated, overstated, unqualified **2** = **wide-ranging**, global, comprehensive, wide, broad, extensive, all-inclusive, all-embracing ≠ limited

sweet ADJECTIVE **1** = **sugary**, cloying, saccharine, icky (*informal*) ≠ sour **2** = **fragrant**, aromatic ≠ stinking **3** = **fresh**, clean,

pure **4** = **melodious**, musical, harmonious, mellow, dulcet ≠ harsh **5** = **charming**, kind, agreeable ≠ nasty **6** = **delightful**, appealing, cute, winning, engaging, lovable, likable *or* likeable ≠ unpleasant
▷ NOUN **1** (*Brit.*) *usually plural* = **confectionery**, candy (*U.S.*), lolly (*Austral. & N.Z.*), bonbon **2** (*Brit.*) = **dessert**, pudding

sweetheart NOUN **1** = **dearest**, beloved, sweet, angel, treasure, honey, dear, sweetie (*informal*) **2** = **love**, boyfriend *or* girlfriend, beloved, lover, darling

swell VERB **1** = **increase**, rise, grow, mount, expand, accelerate, escalate, multiply ≠ decrease **2** = **expand**, increase, grow, rise, balloon, enlarge, bulge, dilate ≠ shrink
▷ NOUN = **wave**, surge, billow

swelling NOUN = **enlargement**, lump, bump, bulge, inflammation, protuberance, distension

swift ADJECTIVE **1** = **quick**, prompt, rapid **2** = **fast**, quick, rapid, hurried, speedy ≠ slow

swiftly ADVERB **1** = **quickly**, rapidly, speedily **2** = **fast**, promptly, hurriedly

swing VERB **1** = **brandish**, wave, shake, flourish, wield, dangle **2** = **sway**, rock, wave, veer, oscillate **3** *usually with* **round** = **turn**, swivel, curve, rotate, pivot **4** = **hit out**, strike, swipe, lash out at, slap **5** = **hang**, dangle, suspend

▷ NOUN **1** = **swaying**, sway **2** = **fluctuation**, change, shift, switch, variation

swirl VERB = **whirl**, churn, spin, twist, eddy

switch NOUN **1** = **control**, button, lever, on/off device **2** = **change**, shift, reversal
▷ VERB **1** = **change**, shift, divert, deviate **2** = **exchange**, swap, substitute

swollen ADJECTIVE = **enlarged**, bloated, inflamed, puffed up, distended

swoop VERB **1** = **pounce**, attack, charge, rush, descend **2** = **drop**, plunge, dive, sweep, descend, pounce, stoop

symbol NOUN **1** = **metaphor**, image, sign, representation, token **2** = **representation**, sign, figure, mark, image, token, logo, badge

symbolic ADJECTIVE **1** = **representative**, emblematic, allegorical **2** = **representative**, figurative

sympathetic ADJECTIVE **1** = **caring**, kind, understanding, concerned, interested, warm, pitying, supportive ≠ uncaring **2** = **like-minded**, compatible, agreeable, friendly, congenial, companionable ≠ uncongenial

sympathy NOUN **1** = **compassion**, understanding, pity, commiseration, aroha (*N.Z.*) ≠ indifference **2** = **affinity**, agreement, rapport, fellow feeling ≠ opposition

S

symptom NOUN 1 = **sign**,
  mark, indication, warning
  2 = **manifestation**, sign,
  indication, mark, evidence,
  expression, proof, token
synthetic ADJECTIVE = **artificial**,
  fake, man-made ≠ real
system NOUN 1 = **arrangement**,
  structure, organization, scheme,
  classification 2 = **method**,
  practice, technique, procedure,
  routine
systematic ADJECTIVE
  = **methodical**, organized,
  efficient, orderly ≠ unmethodical

Tt

table NOUN 1 = **counter**, bench, stand, board, surface, work surface 2 = **list**, chart, tabulation, record, roll, register, diagram, itemization
▷ VERB (*Brit.*) = **submit**, propose, put forward, move, suggest, enter, file, lodge

taboo *or* **tabu**
ADJECTIVE = **forbidden**, banned, prohibited, unacceptable, outlawed, anathema, proscribed, unmentionable ≠ permitted
▷ NOUN = **prohibition**, ban, restriction, anathema, interdict, proscription, tapu (*N.Z.*)

tack NOUN = **nail**, pin, drawing pin
▷ VERB 1 = **fasten**, fix, attach, pin, nail, affix 2 (*Brit.*) = **stitch**, sew, hem, bind, baste ▷ PHRASE: **tack something on to something** = **append**, add, attach, tag

tackle NOUN 1 (*sport*) = **block**, challenge 2 = **rig**, apparatus
▷ VERB 1 = **deal with**, set about, get stuck into (*informal*), come *or* get to grips with 2 = **undertake**, attempt, embark upon, get stuck into (*informal*), have a go *or* stab at (*informal*) 3 (*sport*) = **intercept**, stop, challenge

tactic NOUN = **policy**, approach, move, scheme, plans, method, manoeuvre, ploy

tactical ADJECTIVE = **strategic**, shrewd, smart, diplomatic, cunning ≠ impolitic

tactics PLURAL NOUN = **strategy**, campaigning, manoeuvres, generalship

tag NOUN = **label**, tab, note, ticket, slip, identification, marker, flap
▷ VERB = **label**, mark

tail NOUN 1 = **extremity**, appendage, brush, rear end, hindquarters, hind part 2 (*astronomy*) = **train**, end, trail, tailpiece
▷ VERB (*informal*) = **follow**, track, shadow, trail, stalk ▷ PHRASE: **turn tail** = **run away**, flee, run off, retreat, cut and run, take to your heels

tailor NOUN = **outfitter**, couturier, dressmaker, seamstress, clothier, costumier
▷ VERB = **adapt**, adjust, modify, style, fashion, shape, alter, mould

taint VERB = **spoil**, ruin, contaminate, damage, stain, corrupt, pollute, tarnish ≠ purify

take VERB 1 = **grip**, grab, seize, catch, grasp, clasp, take hold of 2 = **carry**, bring, bear, transport, ferry, haul, convey, fetch ≠ send 3 = **accompany**, lead, bring, guide, conduct, escort, convoy, usher 4 = **remove**, draw, pull, fish, withdraw, extract 5 = **steal**, appropriate, pocket, pinch (*informal*), misappropriate, purloin ≠ return 6 = **capture**, seize, take into custody, lay hold of ≠ release **7** = **tolerate**, stand, bear, stomach, endure, abide, put up with (*informal*), withstand ≠ avoid **8** = **require**, need, involve, demand, call for, entail, necessitate **9** = **understand**, follow, comprehend, get, see, grasp, apprehend **10** = **have room for**, hold, contain, accommodate, accept ▷ **PHRASES**: **take off 1** = **lift off**, take to the air **2** (*informal*) = **depart**, go, leave, disappear, abscond, decamp, slope off; **take someone for something** (*informal*) = **regard as**, believe to be, consider to be, perceive to be, presume to be; **take someone in** (*informal*) = **deceive**, fool, con (*informal*), trick, cheat, mislead, dupe, swindle, scam (*slang*); **take someone off** (*informal*) = **parody**, imitate, mimic, mock, caricature, send up (*Brit. informal*), lampoon, satirize; **take something in** = **understand**, absorb, grasp, digest, comprehend, assimilate, get the hang of (*informal*); **take something up 1** = **start**, begin, engage in, adopt, become involved in **2** = **occupy**, absorb, consume, use up, cover, fill, waste, squander

takeover NOUN = **merger**, coup, incorporation

tale NOUN = **story**, narrative, anecdote, account, legend, saga, yarn (*informal*), fable

talent NOUN = **ability**, gift, aptitude, capacity, genius, flair, knack

talented ADJECTIVE = **gifted**, able, expert, master, masterly, brilliant, ace (*informal*), consummate

talk VERB **1** = **speak**, chat, chatter, converse, communicate, natter, earbash (*Austral. & N.Z. slang*) **2** = **discuss**, confer, negotiate, parley, confabulate, korero (*N.Z.*) **3** = **inform**, grass (*Brit. slang*), tell all, give the game away, blab, let the cat out of the bag ▷ NOUN = **speech**, lecture, presentation, report, address, discourse, sermon, symposium, whaikorero (*N.Z.*)

talking-to NOUN (*informal*) = **reprimand**, lecture, rebuke, scolding, criticism, reproach, ticking-off (*informal*), dressing-down (*informal*) ≠ praise

tall ADJECTIVE **1** = **lofty**, big, giant, long-legged, lanky, leggy **2** = **high**, towering, soaring, steep, elevated, lofty ≠ short

tally VERB = **agree**, match, accord, fit, square, coincide, correspond, conform ≠ disagree ▷ NOUN = **record**, score, total, count, reckoning, running total

tame ADJECTIVE **1** = **domesticated**, docile, broken, gentle, obedient, amenable, tractable ≠ wild **2** = **submissive**, meek, compliant, subdued, manageable, obedient, docile, unresisting ≠ stubborn **3** = **unexciting**, boring, dull, bland, uninspiring, humdrum, uninteresting, insipid ≠ exciting ▷ VERB **1** = **domesticate**, train, break in, house-train ≠ make fiercer **2** = **subdue**, suppress, master, discipline, humble, conquer, subjugate ≠ arouse

tangible ADJECTIVE = **definite**, real, positive, material, actual, concrete, palpable, perceptible ≠ intangible

tangle NOUN **1** = **knot**, twist, web, jungle, coil, entanglement **2** = **mess**, jam, fix (*informal*), confusion, complication, mix-up, shambles, entanglement ▷ VERB = **twist**, knot, mat, coil, mesh, entangle, interweave, ravel ≠ disentangle ▷ PHRASE: **tangle with someone** = **come into conflict with**, come up against, cross swords with, dispute with, contend with, contest with, lock horns with

tantrum NOUN = **outburst**, temper, hysterics, fit, flare-up, foulie (*Austral. slang*), hissy fit (*informal*), strop (*Brit. informal*)

tap¹ VERB = **knock**, strike, pat, rap, beat, touch, drum ▷ NOUN = **knock**, pat, rap, touch, drumming

tap² NOUN = **valve**, faucet (*U.S. & Canad.*), stopcock ▷ VERB = **listen in on**, monitor, bug (*informal*), spy on, eavesdrop on, wiretap ▷ PHRASE: **on tap 1** (*informal*) = **available**, ready, standing by, to hand, on hand, at hand, in reserve **2** = **on draught**, cask-conditioned, from barrels, not bottled *or* canned

tape NOUN = **binding**, strip, band, string, ribbon ▷ VERB **1** = **record**, video, tape-record, make a recording of **2** *sometimes with* **up** = **bind**, secure, stick, seal, wrap

target NOUN **1** = **mark**, goal **2** = **goal**, aim, objective, end, mark, object, intention, ambition **3** = **victim**, butt, prey, scapegoat

tariff NOUN **1** = **tax**, duty, toll, levy, excise **2** = **price list**, schedule

tarnish VERB **1** = **stain**, discolour, darken, blot, blemish ≠ brighten **2** = **damage**, taint, blacken, sully, smirch ≠ enhance ▷ NOUN = **stain**, taint, discoloration, spot, blot, blemish

tart¹ NOUN = **pie**, pastry, pasty, tartlet, patty

tart² ADJECTIVE = **sharp**, acid, sour, bitter, pungent, tangy, piquant, vinegary ≠ sweet

tart³ NOUN (*informal*) = **slut**, prostitute, whore, call girl, trollop, floozy (*slang*), hornbag (*Austral. slang*)

task NOUN = **job**, duty, assignment, exercise, mission, enterprise, undertaking, chore ▷ PHRASE: **take someone to task** = **criticize**, blame, censure, rebuke, reprimand, reproach, scold, tell off (*informal*)

taste NOUN **1** = **flavour**, savour, relish, smack, tang ≠ blandness **2** = **bit**, bite, mouthful, sample, dash, spoonful, morsel, titbit **3** = **liking**, preference, penchant, fondness, partiality, fancy, appetite, inclination ≠ dislike

4 = **refinement**, style, judgment, discrimination, appreciation, elegance, sophistication, discernment ≠ lack of judgment
▷ VERB 1 *often with of* = **have a flavour of**, smack of, savour of 2 = **sample**, try, test, sip, savour 3 = **distinguish**, perceive, discern, differentiate 4 = **experience**, know, undergo, partake of, encounter, meet with ≠ miss

tasty ADJECTIVE = **delicious**, luscious, palatable, delectable, savoury, full-flavoured, scrumptious (*informal*), appetizing, lekker (*S. African slang*), yummo (*Austral. slang*) ≠ bland

tattletale NOUN (*chiefly U.S. & Canad.*) = **gossip**, busybody, chatterbox (*informal*), chatterer, bigmouth (*slang*), scandalmonger, gossipmonger

taunt VERB = **jeer**, mock, tease, ridicule, provoke, insult, torment, deride
▷ NOUN = **jeer**, dig, insult, ridicule, teasing, provocation, derision, sarcasm

tavern NOUN = **inn**, bar, pub (*informal, chiefly Brit.*), public house, beer parlour (*Canad.*), beverage room (*Canad.*), hostelry, alehouse (*archaic*)

tax NOUN = **charge**, duty, toll, levy, tariff, excise, tithe
▷ VERB 1 = **charge**, rate, assess 2 = **strain**, stretch, try, test, load, burden, exhaust, weaken

teach VERB 1 = **instruct**, train, coach, inform, educate, drill, tutor, enlighten 2 *often with* **how** = **show**, train

teacher NOUN = **instructor**, coach, tutor, guide, trainer, lecturer, mentor, educator

team NOUN 1 = **side**, squad 2 = **group**, company, set, body, band, gang, line-up, bunch
▷ PHRASE: **team up** = **join**, unite, work together, cooperate, couple, link up, get together, band together

tear VERB 1 = **rip**, split, rend, shred, rupture 2 = **run** 3 = **scratch**, cut (open), gash, lacerate, injure, mangle, cut to pieces, cut to ribbons, mangulate (*Austral. slang*) 4 = **pull apart**, claw, lacerate, mutilate, mangle, mangulate (*Austral. slang*) 5 = **rush**, run, charge, race, fly, speed, dash, hurry
▷ NOUN = **hole**, split, rip, rent, snag, rupture

tears PLURAL NOUN = **crying**, weeping, sobbing, wailing, blubbering ▷ PHRASE: **in tears** = **weeping**, crying, sobbing, blubbering

tease VERB 1 = **mock**, provoke, torment, taunt, goad, pull someone's leg (*informal*), make fun of 2 = **tantalize**, lead on, flirt with, titillate

technical ADJECTIVE = **scientific**, technological, skilled, specialist, specialized, hi-tech *or* high-tech

technique NOUN 1 = **method**, way, system, approach, means, style, manner, procedure

2 = **skill**, performance, craft, touch, execution, artistry, craftsmanship, proficiency

tedious ADJECTIVE = **boring**, dull, dreary, monotonous, drab, tiresome, laborious, humdrum ≠ exciting

teenager NOUN = **youth**, minor, adolescent, juvenile, girl, boy

telephone NOUN = **phone**, mobile (phone), handset, dog and bone (*slang*)
▷ VERB = **call**, phone, ring (*chiefly Brit.*), dial

telescope NOUN = **glass**, scope (*informal*), spyglass
▷ VERB = **shorten**, contract, compress, shrink, condense, abbreviate, abridge ≠ lengthen

television NOUN = **TV**, telly (*Brit. informal*), small screen (*informal*), the box (*Brit. informal*), the tube (*slang*)

tell VERB **1** = **inform**, notify, state to, reveal to, express to, disclose to, proclaim to, divulge, flag up **2** = **describe**, relate, recount, report, portray, depict, chronicle, narrate **3** = **instruct**, order, command, direct, bid **4** = **distinguish**, discriminate, discern, differentiate, identify **5** = **have** *or* **take effect**, register, weigh, count, take its toll, carry weight, make its presence felt ▷ PHRASE: **tell someone off** = **reprimand**, rebuke, scold, lecture, censure, reproach, berate, chide

telling ADJECTIVE = **effective**, significant, considerable, marked, striking, powerful, impressive, influential ≠ unimportant

temper NOUN **1** = **irritability**, irascibility, passion, resentment, petulance, surliness, hot-headedness ≠ good humour
2 = **frame of mind**, nature, mind, mood, constitution, humour, temperament, disposition
3 = **rage**, fury, bad mood, passion, tantrum, foulie (*Austral. slang*), hissy fit (*informal*), strop (*Brit. informal*) **4** = **self-control**, composure, cool (*slang*), calmness, equanimity ≠ anger
▷ VERB **1** = **moderate**, restrain, tone down, soften, soothe, lessen, mitigate, assuage ≠ intensify
2 = **strengthen**, harden, toughen, anneal ≠ soften

temperament NOUN = **nature**, character, personality, make-up, constitution, bent, humour, temper

temple NOUN = **shrine**, church, sanctuary, house of God

temporarily ADVERB = **briefly**, for the time being, momentarily, fleetingly, pro tem

temporary ADJECTIVE
1 = **impermanent**, transitory, brief, fleeting, interim, short-lived, momentary, ephemeral ≠ permanent **2** = **short-term**, acting, interim, supply, stand-in, fill-in, caretaker, provisional

tempt VERB **1** = **attract**, allure **2** = **entice**, lure, lead on, invite, seduce, coax ≠ discourage

temptation NOUN
　1 = **enticement**, lure, inducement, pull, seduction, allurement, tantalization 2 = **appeal**, attraction

tempting ADJECTIVE = **inviting**, enticing, seductive, alluring, attractive, mouthwatering, appetizing ≠ uninviting

tenant NOUN = **leaseholder**, resident, renter, occupant, inhabitant, occupier, lodger, boarder

tend¹ VERB = **be inclined**, be liable, have a tendency, be apt, be prone, lean, incline, gravitate

tend² VERB 1 = **take care of**, look after, keep, attend, nurture, watch over ≠ neglect 2 = **maintain**, take care of, nurture, cultivate, manage ≠ neglect

tendency NOUN = **inclination**, leaning, liability, disposition, propensity, susceptibility, proclivity, proneness

tender¹ ADJECTIVE 1 = **gentle**, loving, kind, caring, sympathetic, affectionate, compassionate, considerate ≠ harsh
　2 = **vulnerable**, young, sensitive, raw, youthful, inexperienced, immature, impressionable ≠ experienced 3 = **sensitive**, painful, sore, raw, bruised, inflamed

tender² VERB = **offer**, present, submit, give, propose, volunteer, hand in, put forward
　▷ NOUN = **offer**, bid, estimate, proposal, submission

tense ADJECTIVE 1 = **strained**, uneasy, stressful, fraught, charged, difficult, worrying, exciting 2 = **nervous**, edgy, strained, anxious, apprehensive, uptight (*informal*), on edge, jumpy, adrenalized ≠ calm 3 = **rigid**, strained, taut, stretched, tight ≠ relaxed
　▷ VERB = **tighten**, strain, brace, stretch, flex, stiffen ≠ relax

tension NOUN 1 = **strain**, stress, nervousness, pressure, anxiety, unease, apprehension, suspense ≠ calmness 2 = **friction**, hostility, unease, antagonism, antipathy, enmity 3 = **rigidity**, tightness, stiffness, pressure, stress, stretching, tautness

tentative ADJECTIVE
　1 = **unconfirmed**, provisional, indefinite, test, trial, pilot, preliminary, experimental ≠ confirmed 2 = **hesitant**, cautious, uncertain, doubtful, faltering, unsure, timid, undecided ≠ confident

term NOUN 1 = **word**, name, expression, title, label, phrase 2 = **period**, time, spell, while, season, interval, span, duration
　▷ VERB = **call**, name, label, style, entitle, tag, dub, designate

terminal ADJECTIVE 1 = **fatal**, deadly, lethal, killing, mortal, incurable, inoperable, untreatable 2 = **final**, last, closing, finishing, concluding, ultimate, terminating ≠ initial
　▷ NOUN = **terminus**, station,

depot, end of the line

terminate VERB 1 = **end**, stop, conclude, finish, complete, discontinue ≠ begin 2 = **cease**, end, close, finish 3 = **abort**, end
▷ PLURAL NOUN 1 = **conditions**, particulars, provisions, provisos, stipulations, qualifications, specifications 2 = **relationship**, standing, footing, relations, status

terrain NOUN = **ground**, country, land, landscape, topography, going

terrestrial ADJECTIVE = **earthly**, worldly, global

terrible ADJECTIVE 1 = **awful**, shocking, terrifying, horrible, dreadful, horrifying, fearful, horrendous 2 (informal) = **bad**, awful, dreadful, dire, abysmal, poor, rotten (informal) ≠ wonderful 3 = **serious**, desperate, severe, extreme, dangerous, insufferable ≠ mild

terribly ADVERB 1 = **very much**, very, dreadfully, seriously, extremely, desperately, thoroughly, decidedly 2 = **extremely**, very, dreadfully, seriously, desperately, thoroughly, decidedly, awfully (informal)

terrific ADJECTIVE 1 (informal) = **excellent**, wonderful, brilliant, amazing, outstanding, superb, fantastic (informal), magnificent, booshit (Austral. slang), exo (Austral. slang), sik (Austral. slang), ka pai (N.Z.), rad (informal), phat (slang), schmick (Austral. informal)

≠ awful 2 = **intense**, great, huge, enormous, tremendous, fearful, gigantic

terrified ADJECTIVE = **frightened**, scared, petrified, alarmed, panic-stricken, horror-struck

terrify VERB = **frighten**, scare, alarm, terrorize

territory NOUN = **district**, area, land, region, country, zone, province, patch

terror NOUN 1 = **fear**, alarm, dread, fright, panic, anxiety 2 = **nightmare**, monster, bogeyman, devil, fiend, bugbear

test VERB 1 = **check**, investigate, assess, research, analyse, experiment with, try out, put something to the test 2 = **examine**, put someone to the test
▷ NOUN 1 = **trial**, research, check, investigation, analysis, assessment, examination, evaluation 2 = **examination**, paper, assessment, evaluation

testament NOUN 1 = **proof**, evidence, testimony, witness, demonstration, tribute 2 (law) = **will**, last wishes

testify VERB = **bear witness**, state, swear, certify, assert, affirm, attest, corroborate ≠ disprove

testimony NOUN 1 (law) = **evidence**, statement, submission, affidavit, deposition 2 = **proof**, evidence, demonstration, indication, support, manifestation, verification, corroboration

testing ADJECTIVE = **difficult**, demanding, taxing, challenging, searching, tough, exacting, rigorous ≠ undemanding

text NOUN 1 = **contents**, words, content, wording, body, subject matter 2 = **words**, wording 3 = **transcript**, script

texture NOUN = **feel**, consistency, structure, surface, tissue, grain

thank VERB = **say thank you to**, show your appreciation to

thanks PLURAL NOUN = **gratitude**, appreciation, credit, recognition, acknowledgment, gratefulness
▷ PHRASE: **thanks to** = **because of**, through, due to, as a result of, owing to

thaw VERB = **melt**, dissolve, soften, defrost, warm, liquefy, unfreeze ≠ freeze

theatrical ADJECTIVE
1 = **dramatic**, stage, Thespian
2 = **exaggerated**, dramatic, melodramatic, histrionic, affected, mannered, showy, ostentatious ≠ natural

theft NOUN = **stealing**, robbery, thieving, fraud, embezzlement, pilfering, larceny, purloining

theme NOUN 1 = **motif**, leitmotif
2 = **subject**, idea, topic, essence, subject matter, keynote, gist

theological ADJECTIVE
= **religious**, ecclesiastical, doctrinal

theoretical or **theoretic**
ADJECTIVE 1 = **abstract**, speculative ≠ practical

2 = **hypothetical**, academic, notional, unproven, conjectural, postulatory

theory NOUN = **belief**, feeling, speculation, assumption, hunch, presumption, conjecture, surmise

therapeutic ADJECTIVE
= **beneficial**, healing, restorative, good, corrective, remedial, salutary, curative ≠ harmful

therapist NOUN = **psychologist**, analyst, psychiatrist, shrink (*informal*), counsellor, healer, psychotherapist, psychoanalyst

therapy NOUN = **remedy**, treatment, cure, healing, method of healing

therefore ADVERB
= **consequently**, so, thus, as a result, hence, accordingly, thence, ergo

thesis NOUN 1 = **proposition**, theory, hypothesis, idea, view, opinion, proposal, contention
2 = **dissertation**, paper, treatise, essay, monograph

thick ADJECTIVE 1 = **bulky**, broad, big, large, fat, solid, substantial, hefty ≠ thin 2 = **wide**, across, deep, broad, in extent *or* diameter
3 = **dense**, close, heavy, compact, impenetrable, lush 4 = **heavy**, heavyweight, dense, chunky, bulky, woolly 5 = **opaque**, heavy, dense, impenetrable 6 = **viscous**, concentrated, stiff, condensed, gelatinous, semi-solid, viscid
≠ runny 7 = **crowded**, full, covered, bursting, bristling, brimming ≠ empty 8 = **stupid**,

slow, dense, dopey (*informal*), moronic, obtuse, brainless, dumb-ass (*informal*) ≠ clever **9** (*informal*) = **friendly**, close, intimate, familiar, pally (*informal*), devoted, inseparable ≠ unfriendly

thicken VERB = **set**, condense, congeal, clot, jell, coagulate ≠ thin

thief NOUN = **robber**, burglar, stealer, plunderer, shoplifter, embezzler, pickpocket, pilferer

thin ADJECTIVE **1** = **narrow**, fine, attenuated ≠ thick **2** = **slim**, spare, lean, slight, slender, skinny, skeletal, bony ≠ fat **3** = **meagre**, sparse, scanty, poor, scattered, inadequate, insufficient, deficient ≠ plentiful **4** = **fine**, delicate, flimsy, sheer, skimpy, gossamer, diaphanous, filmy ≠ thick **5** = **unconvincing**, inadequate, feeble, poor, weak, superficial, lame, flimsy ≠ convincing **6** = **wispy**, thinning, sparse, scarce, scanty

thing NOUN **1** = **substance**, stuff, being, body, material, fabric, entity **2** (*informal*) = **phobia**, fear, complex, horror, terror, hang-up (*informal*), aversion, neurosis **3** (*informal*) = **obsession**, liking, preoccupation, mania, fetish, fixation, soft spot, predilection **4** *often plural* = **possessions**, stuff, gear, belongings, effects, luggage, clobber (*Brit. slang*), chattels **5** = **equipment**, gear, tool, stuff, tackle, implement, kit, apparatus **6** = **circumstances**, the situation,

the state of affairs, matters, life, affairs

think VERB **1** = **believe**, be of the opinion, be of the view **2** = **judge**, consider, estimate, reckon, deem, regard as **3** = **ponder**, reflect, contemplate, deliberate, meditate, ruminate, cogitate, be lost in thought ▷ PHRASE: **think something up** = **devise**, create, come up with, invent, contrive, visualize, concoct, dream up

thinker NOUN = **philosopher**, intellect (*informal*), wise man, sage, brain (*informal*), theorist, mastermind

thinking NOUN = **reasoning**, idea, view, position, theory, opinion, judgment, conjecture ▷ ADJECTIVE = **thoughtful**, intelligent, reasoning, rational, philosophical, reflective, contemplative, meditative

thirst NOUN **1** = **dryness**, thirstiness, drought **2** = **craving**, appetite, longing, desire, passion, yearning, hankering, keenness ≠ aversion

thorn NOUN = **prickle**, spike, spine, barb

thorough ADJECTIVE **1** = **comprehensive**, full, complete, sweeping, intensive, in-depth, exhaustive ≠ cursory **2** = **careful**, conscientious, painstaking, efficient, meticulous, exhaustive, assiduous ≠ careless **3** = **complete**, total, absolute, utter, perfect, outright,

unqualified, out-and-out
≠ partial

thoroughly ADVERB
1 = **carefully**, fully, efficiently,
meticulously, painstakingly,
scrupulously, assiduously,
intensively ≠ carelessly 2 = **fully**
3 = **completely**, quite, totally,
perfectly, absolutely, utterly,
downright, to the hilt ≠ partly

though CONJUNCTION = **although**,
while, even if, even though,
notwithstanding
▷ ADVERB = **nevertheless**, still,
however, yet, nonetheless, for all
that, notwithstanding

thought NOUN 1 = **thinking**,
consideration, reflection,
deliberation, musing,
meditation, rumination,
cogitation 2 = **opinion**, view,
idea, concept, notion, judgment
3 = **consideration**, study,
attention, care, regard, scrutiny,
heed 4 = **intention**, plan, idea,
design, aim, purpose, object,
notion 5 = **hope**, expectation,
prospect, aspiration, anticipation

thoughtful ADJECTIVE
1 = **reflective**, pensive,
contemplative, meditative,
serious, studious, deliberative,
ruminative ≠ shallow
2 = **considerate**, kind,
caring, kindly, helpful,
attentive, unselfish, solicitous
≠ inconsiderate

thrash VERB 1 = **defeat**, beat,
crush, slaughter (*informal*),
rout, trounce, run rings around

(*informal*), wipe the floor with
(*informal*) 2 = **beat**, wallop, whip,
belt (*informal*), cane, flog, scourge,
spank 3 = **thresh**, flail, jerk,
writhe, toss and turn ▷ PHRASE:
thrash something out = **settle**,
resolve, discuss, debate, solve,
argue out, have out, talk over

thrashing NOUN 1 = **defeat**,
beating, hammering (*informal*),
hiding (*informal*), rout, trouncing,
drubbing 2 = **beating**, hiding
(*informal*), belting (*informal*),
whipping, flogging

thread NOUN 1 = **strand**, fibre,
yarn, filament, line, string, twine
2 = **theme**, train of thought,
direction, plot, drift, story line
▷ VERB = **move**, pass, ease, thrust,
squeeze through, pick your way

threat NOUN 1 = **danger**,
risk, hazard, menace, peril
2 = **threatening remark**, menace
3 = **warning**, foreshadowing,
foreboding

threaten VERB 1 = **intimidate**,
bully, menace, terrorize, lean
on (*slang*), pressurize, browbeat
≠ defend 2 = **endanger**,
jeopardize, put at risk, imperil,
put in jeopardy, put on the line
≠ protect 3 = **be imminent**,
impend

threshold NOUN 1 = **entrance**,
doorway, door, doorstep
2 = **start**, beginning, opening,
dawn, verge, brink, outset,
inception ≠ end 3 = **limit**,
margin, starting point, minimum

thrift NOUN = **economy**,

prudence, frugality, saving, parsimony, carefulness, thriftiness ≠ extravagance

thrill NOUN = **pleasure**, kick (*informal*), buzz (*slang*), high, stimulation, tingle, titillation ≠ tedium
▷ VERB = **excite**, stimulate, arouse, move, stir, electrify, titillate, give someone a kick

thrilling ADJECTIVE = **exciting**, gripping, stimulating, stirring, sensational, rousing, riveting, electrifying ≠ boring

thrive VERB = **prosper**, do well, flourish, increase, grow, develop, succeed, get on ≠ decline

thriving ADJECTIVE = **successful**, flourishing, healthy, booming, blooming, prosperous, burgeoning ≠ unsuccessful

throb VERB 1 = **pulsate**, pound, beat, pulse, thump, palpitate 2 = **vibrate**, pulsate, reverberate, shake, judder (*informal*)
▷ NOUN 1 = **pulse**, pounding, beat, thump, thumping, pulsating, palpitation
2 = **vibration**, throbbing, reverberation, judder (*informal*), pulsation

throng NOUN = **crowd**, mob, horde, host, pack, mass, crush, swarm
▷ VERB 1 = **crowd**, flock, congregate, converge, mill around, swarm around ≠ disperse 2 = **pack**, crowd

throttle VERB = **strangle**, choke, garrotte, strangulate

through PREPOSITION 1 = **via**, by way of, by, between, past, from one side to the other of 2 = **because of**, by way of, by means of 3 = **using**, via, by way of, by means of, by virtue of, with the assistance of 4 = **during**, throughout, for the duration of, in
▷ ADJECTIVE = **completed**, done, finished, ended ▷ PHRASE: **through and through** = **completely**, totally, fully, thoroughly, entirely, altogether, wholly, utterly

throughout PREPOSITION 1 = **right through**, everywhere in, during the whole of, through the whole of 2 = **all over**, everywhere in, through the whole of
▷ ADVERB 1 = **from start to finish**, right through 2 = **all through**, right through

throw VERB 1 = **hurl**, toss, fling, send, launch, cast, pitch, chuck (*informal*) 2 = **toss**, fling, chuck (*informal*), cast, hurl, sling 3 (*informal*) = **confuse**, baffle, faze, astonish, confound, disconcert, dumbfound
▷ NOUN = **toss**, pitch, fling, sling, lob (*informal*), heave

thrust VERB = **push**, force, shove, drive, plunge, jam, ram, propel
▷ NOUN 1 = **stab**, pierce, lunge
2 = **push**, shove, poke, prod
3 = **momentum**, impetus, drive

thug NOUN = **ruffian**, hooligan, tough, heavy (*slang*), gangster, bully boy, bruiser (*informal*), tsotsi (*S. African*)

t

thump NOUN 1 = **blow**, knock, punch, rap, smack, clout (*informal*), whack, swipe 2 = **thud**, crash, bang, clunk, thwack
▷ VERB = **strike**, hit, punch, pound, beat, knock, smack, clout (*informal*)

thunder NOUN = **rumble**, crash, boom, explosion
▷ VERB 1 = **rumble**, crash, boom, roar, resound, reverberate, peal 2 = **shout**, roar, yell, bark, bellow

thus ADVERB 1 = **in this way**, so, like this, as follows 2 = **therefore**, so, hence, consequently, accordingly, for this reason, ergo, on that account

thwart VERB = **frustrate**, foil, prevent, snooker, hinder, obstruct, outwit, stymie ≠ assist

tick NOUN 1 = **check mark**, mark, line, stroke, dash 2 = **click**, tapping, clicking, ticktock 3 (*Brit. informal*) = **moment**, second, minute, flash, instant, twinkling, split second, trice
▷ VERB 1 = **mark**, indicate, check off 2 = **click**, tap, ticktock

ticket NOUN 1 = **voucher**, pass, coupon, card, slip, certificate, token, chit 2 = **label**, tag, marker, sticker, card, slip, tab, docket

tide NOUN 1 = **current**, flow, stream, ebb, undertow, tideway 2 = **course**, direction, trend, movement, tendency, drift

tidy ADJECTIVE 1 = **neat**, orderly, clean, spruce, well-kept, well-ordered, shipshape ≠ untidy 2 = **organized**, neat, methodical

3 (*informal*) = **considerable**, large, substantial, goodly, healthy, generous, handsome, ample ≠ small
▷ VERB = **neaten**, straighten, order, clean, groom, spruce up ≠ disorder

tie VERB 1 = **fasten**, bind, join, link, connect, attach, knot ≠ unfasten 2 = **tether**, secure 3 = **restrict**, limit, confine, bind, restrain, hamper, hinder ≠ free 4 = **draw**, be level, match, equal
▷ NOUN 1 = **fastening**, binding, link, bond, knot, cord, fetter, ligature 2 = **bond**, relationship, connection, commitment, liaison, allegiance, affiliation 3 = **draw**, dead heat, deadlock, stalemate

tier NOUN = **row**, bank, layer, line, level, rank, storey, stratum

tight ADJECTIVE 1 = **close-fitting**, narrow, cramped, snug, constricted, close ≠ loose 2 = **secure**, firm, fast, fixed 3 = **taut**, stretched, rigid ≠ slack 4 = **close**, even, well-matched, hard-fought, evenly-balanced ≠ uneven 5 (*informal*) = **miserly**, mean, stingy, grasping, parsimonious, niggardly, tightfisted ≠ generous 6 (*informal*) = **drunk**, intoxicated, plastered (*slang*), under the influence (*informal*), tipsy, paralytic (*informal*), inebriated, out to it (*Austral. & N.Z. slang*) ≠ sober

tighten VERB = **close**, narrow, strengthen, squeeze, harden, constrict ≠ slacken

till¹ VERB = **cultivate**, dig, plough, work

till² NOUN = **cash register**, cash box

tilt VERB = **slant**, tip, slope, list, lean, heel, incline
▷ NOUN 1 = **slope**, angle, inclination, list, pitch, incline, slant, camber 2 (*medieval history*) = **joust**, fight, tournament, lists, combat, duel

timber NOUN 1 = **beams**, boards, planks 2 = **wood**, logs

time NOUN 1 = **period**, term, space, stretch, spell, span, time frame, timeline 2 = **occasion**, point, moment, stage, instance, point in time, juncture 3 = **age**, duration 4 = **tempo**, beat, rhythm, measure
▷ VERB = **schedule**, set, plan, book, programme, set up, fix, arrange

timeless ADJECTIVE = **eternal**, lasting, permanent, enduring, immortal, everlasting, ageless, changeless ≠ temporary

timely ADJECTIVE = **opportune**, appropriate, well-timed, suitable, convenient, judicious, propitious, seasonable ≠ untimely

timetable NOUN 1 = **schedule**, programme, agenda, list, diary, calendar 2 = **syllabus**, course, curriculum, programme, teaching programme

tinge NOUN 1 = **tint**, colour, shade 2 = **trace**, bit, drop, touch, suggestion, dash, sprinkling, smattering
▷ VERB = **tint**, colour

tinker VERB = **meddle**, play, potter, fiddle (*informal*), dabble, mess about

tint NOUN 1 = **shade**, colour, tone, hue 2 = **dye**, wash, rinse, tinge, tincture
▷ VERB = **dye**, colour

tiny ADJECTIVE = **small**, little, minute, slight, miniature, negligible, microscopic, diminutive ≠ huge

tip¹ NOUN 1 = **end**, point, head, extremity, sharp end, nib, prong 2 = **peak**, top, summit, pinnacle, zenith, spire, acme, vertex
▷ VERB = **cap**, top, crown, surmount, finish

tip² NOUN 1 = **gratuity**, gift, reward, present, sweetener (*informal*) 2 = **hint**, suggestion, piece of advice, pointer, heads up (*U.S. & Canad.*)
▷ VERB 1 = **reward**, remunerate, give a tip to, sweeten (*informal*) 2 = **predict**, back, recommend, think of

tip³ VERB 1 = **pour**, drop, empty, dump, drain, discharge, unload, jettison 2 (*Brit.*) = **dump**, empty, unload, pour out
▷ NOUN (*Brit.*) = **dump**, midden, rubbish heap, refuse heap

tire VERB 1 = **exhaust**, drain, fatigue, weary, wear out ≠ refresh 2 = **flag**, become tired, fail

tired ADJECTIVE 1 = **exhausted**, fatigued, weary, flagging, drained, sleepy, worn out,

t

drowsy, tuckered out (*Austral. & N.Z. informal*) ≠ energetic **2** = **bored**, fed up, weary, sick, hoha (*N.Z.*) ≠ enthusiastic about **3** = **hackneyed**, stale, well-worn, old, corny (*slang*), threadbare, trite, clichéd ≠ original

tiring ADJECTIVE = **exhausting**, demanding, wearing, tough, exacting, strenuous, arduous, laborious

title NOUN **1** = **name**, designation, term, handle (*slang*), moniker *or* monicker (*slang*) **2** (*sport*) = **championship**, trophy, bays, crown, honour **3** (*law*) = **ownership**, right, claim, privilege, entitlement, tenure, prerogative, freehold

toast¹ VERB **1** = **brown**, grill, crisp, roast **2** = **warm (up)**, heat (up), thaw, bring back to life

toast² NOUN **1** = **tribute**, compliment, salute, health, pledge, salutation **2** = **favourite**, celebrity, darling, talk, pet, focus of attention, hero *or* heroine, blue-eyed boy *or* girl (*Brit. informal*)
▷ VERB = **drink to**, honour, salute, drink (to) the health of

together ADVERB **1** = **collectively**, jointly, as one, with each other, in conjunction, side by side, mutually, in partnership ≠ separately **2** = **at the same time**, simultaneously, concurrently, contemporaneously, at one fell swoop
▷ ADJECTIVE (*informal*) = **self-possessed**, composed, well-

balanced, well-adjusted, grounded

toil NOUN = **hard work**, effort, application, sweat, graft (*informal*), slog, exertion, drudgery ≠ idleness
▷ VERB **1** = **labour**, work, struggle, strive, sweat (*informal*), slave, graft (*informal*), slog **2** = **struggle**, trek, slog, trudge, fight your way, footslog

toilet NOUN **1** = **lavatory**, bathroom, loo (*Brit. informal*), privy, cloakroom (*Brit.*), urinal, latrine, washroom, dunny (*Austral. & N.Z. old-fashioned*) (*informal*), bogger (*Austral. slang*), brasco (*Austral. slang*) **2** = **bathroom**, gents *or* ladies (*Brit. informal*), privy, latrine, water closet, ladies' room, W.C.

token NOUN = **symbol**, mark, sign, note, expression, indication, representation, badge
▷ ADJECTIVE = **nominal**, symbolic, minimal, hollow, superficial, perfunctory

tolerance NOUN **1** = **broad-mindedness**, indulgence, forbearance, permissiveness, open-mindedness ≠ intolerance **2** = **endurance**, resistance, stamina, fortitude, resilience, toughness, staying power, hardiness **3** = **resistance**, immunity, resilience, non-susceptibility

tolerant ADJECTIVE = **broad-minded**, understanding, open-minded, catholic, long-suffering, permissive, forbearing, unprejudiced ≠ intolerant

tolerate VERB 1 = **endure**, stand, take, stomach, put up with (*informal*) 2 = **allow**, accept, permit, take, brook, put up with (*informal*), condone ≠ forbid

toll¹ VERB = **ring**, sound, strike, chime, knell, clang, peal
▷ NOUN = **ringing**, chime, knell, clang, peal

toll² NOUN 1 = **charge**, tax, fee, duty, payment, levy, tariff 2 = **damage**, cost, loss, roll, penalty, sum, number, roster 3 = **adverse effects**, price, cost, suffering, damage, penalty, harm

tomb NOUN = **grave**, vault, crypt, mausoleum, sarcophagus, catacomb, sepulchre

tone NOUN 1 = **pitch**, inflection, intonation, timbre, modulation 2 = **volume**, timbre 3 = **character**, style, feel, air, spirit, attitude, manner, mood 4 = **colour**, shade, tint, tinge, hue
▷ VERB = **harmonize**, match, blend, suit, go well with
▷ PHRASE: **tone something down** 1 = **moderate**, temper, soften, restrain, subdue, play down 2 = **reduce**, moderate

tongue NOUN = **language**, speech, dialect, parlance

● **WORD POWER**
● In the human body, the *tongue*
● is the muscular tissue attached
● to the floor of the mouth used
● in chewing and speaking.
● Objects or areas which
● resemble a tongue also employ
● this metaphor, for example *a*
● *tongue of land*. The function of
● the tongue as one of the organs
● creating speech in humans has
● led tongue to mean a language,
● dialect, or idiom. Examples of
● this are *foreign tongue*, *native*
● *tongue*, and *mother tongue*.
● Equally, tongue can refer
● to an individual utterance
● or a manner of speaking, in
● combination with adjectives
● like quick, sharp, sweet, and
● vulgar. A tongue also describes
● a person's ability to speak:
● you can *lose your tongue* or *be*
● *tongue-tied*. The cat can even
● get your tongue!

tonic NOUN = **stimulant**, boost, pick-me-up (*informal*), fillip, shot in the arm (*informal*), restorative

too ADVERB 1 = **also**, as well, further, in addition, moreover, besides, likewise, to boot 2 = **excessively**, very, extremely, overly, unduly, unreasonably, inordinately, immoderately

tool NOUN 1 = **implement**, device, appliance, machine, instrument, gadget, utensil, contraption 2 = **puppet**, creature, pawn, stooge (*slang*), minion, lackey, flunkey, hireling

top NOUN 1 = **peak**, summit, head, crown, height, ridge, brow, crest ≠ bottom 2 = **lid**, cover, cap, plug, stopper, bung 3 = **first place**, head, peak, lead, high point
▷ ADJECTIVE 1 = **highest**,

t

loftiest, furthest up, uppermost
2 = **leading**, best, first, highest,
head, finest, elite, foremost
≠ lowest **3** = **chief**, most
important, principal, most
powerful, highest, head, leading,
main **4** = **prime**, best, select, first-
class, quality, choice, excellent,
premier
▷ **VERB 1** = **lead**, head, be at
the top of, be first in **2** = **cover**,
garnish, finish, crown, cap
3 = **surpass**, better, beat, improve
on, cap, exceed, eclipse, excel
≠ not be as good as
topic NOUN = **subject**, point,
question, issue, matter, theme,
subject matter
topical ADJECTIVE = **current**,
popular, contemporary, up-
to-date, up-to-the-minute,
newsworthy
topple VERB **1** = **fall over**, fall,
collapse, tumble, overturn, totter,
keel over, overbalance **2** = **knock
over 3** = **overthrow**, overturn,
bring down, oust, unseat, bring
low
torment VERB **1** = **torture**,
distress, rack, crucify ≠ comfort
2 = **tease**, annoy, bother, irritate,
harass, hassle (*informal*), pester,
vex
▷ **NOUN** = **suffering**, distress,
misery, pain, hell, torture, agony,
anguish ≠ bliss
torn ADJECTIVE **1** = **cut**, split, rent,
ripped, ragged, slit, lacerated
2 = **undecided**, uncertain, unsure,
wavering, vacillating, in two

minds (*informal*), irresolute
tornado NOUN = **whirlwind**,
storm, hurricane, gale, cyclone,
typhoon, tempest, squall
torture VERB **1** = **torment**, abuse,
persecute, afflict, scourge, molest,
crucify, mistreat ≠ comfort
2 = **distress**, torment, worry,
trouble, rack, afflict, harrow,
inflict anguish on
▷ **NOUN 1** = **ill-treatment**,
abuse, torment, persecution,
maltreatment, harsh treatment
2 = **agony**, suffering, anguish,
distress, torment, heartbreak
≠ bliss
toss VERB **1** = **throw**, pitch, hurl,
fling, launch, cast, flip, sling
2 = **shake 3** = **thrash (about)**,
twitch, wriggle, squirm, writhe
▷ **NOUN** = **throw**, pitch, lob
(*informal*)
tot NOUN **1** = **infant**, child, baby,
toddler, mite, littlie (*Austral.
informal*), ankle-biter (*Austral.
slang*), tacker (*Austral. slang*)
2 = **measure**, shot (*informal*),
finger, nip, slug, dram, snifter
(*informal*) ▷ **PHRASE**: **tot
something up** (*chiefly Brit.*) = **add
up**, calculate, total, reckon,
compute, tally, enumerate, count
up
total NOUN = **sum**, entirety, grand
total, whole, aggregate, totality,
full amount, sum total ≠ part
▷ **ADJECTIVE** = **complete**,
absolute, utter, whole, entire,
undivided, overarching,
thoroughgoing ≠ partial

▷ **VERB** 1 = **amount to**, make, come to, reach, equal, run to, number, add up to 2 = **add up**, work out, compute, reckon, tot up ≠ subtract

totally ADVERB = **completely**, entirely, absolutely, fully, comprehensively, thoroughly, wholly, utterly ≠ partly

touch VERB 1 = **feel**, handle, finger, stroke, brush, make contact with, caress, fondle 2 = **come into contact**, meet, contact, border, graze, adjoin, be in contact, abut 3 = **tap** 4 = **affect**, influence, inspire, impress 5 = **consume**, take, drink, eat, partake of 6 = **move**, stir, disturb 7 = **match**, rival, equal, compare with, parallel, hold a candle to (*informal*) ▷ **NOUN** 1 = **contact**, push, stroke, brush, press, tap, poke, nudge 2 = **feeling**, handling, physical contact 3 = **bit**, spot, trace, drop, dash, small amount, jot, smattering 4 = **style**, method, technique, way, manner, trademark ▷ **PHRASES**: **touch and go** = **risky**, close, near, critical, precarious, nerve-racking; **touch on** *or* **upon something** = **refer to**, cover, raise, mention, deal with, bring in, speak of, hint at

touching ADJECTIVE = **moving**, affecting, sad, stirring, pathetic, poignant, emotive, pitiable

tough ADJECTIVE 1 = **strong** ≠ weak 2 = **hardy**, strong, seasoned, strapping, vigorous, sturdy, stout 3 = **violent**, rough,

ruthless, pugnacious, hard-bitten 4 = **strict**, severe, stern, hard, firm, resolute, merciless, unbending ≠ lenient 5 = **hard**, difficult, troublesome, uphill, strenuous, arduous, laborious 6 = **resilient**, hard, resistant, durable, strong, solid, rugged, sturdy ≠ fragile ▷ **NOUN** = **ruffian**, bully, thug, hooligan, bruiser (*informal*), roughneck (*slang*), tsotsi (*S. African*)

tour NOUN = **journey**, expedition, excursion, trip, outing, jaunt, junket ▷ **VERB** 1 = **travel round**, travel through, journey round, trek round, go on a trip through 2 = **visit**, explore, go round, inspect, walk round, drive round, sightsee

tourist NOUN = **traveller**, voyager, tripper, globetrotter, holiday-maker, sightseer, excursionist

tournament NOUN = **competition**, meeting, event, series, contest

tow VERB = **drag**, draw, pull, haul, tug, yank, lug

towards PREPOSITION 1 = **in the direction of**, to, for, on the way to, en route for 2 = **regarding**, about, concerning, respecting, in relation to, with regard to, with respect to, apropos

tower NOUN = **column**, pillar, turret, belfry, steeple, obelisk

toxic ADJECTIVE = **poisonous**, deadly, lethal, harmful, pernicious, noxious, septic, pestilential ≠ harmless

toy NOUN = **plaything**, game, doll
▷ PHRASE: **toy with something**
= **play with**, consider, trifle
with, dally with, entertain the
possibility of, amuse yourself
with, think idly of

trace NOUN 1 = **bit**, drop, touch,
shadow, suggestion, hint,
suspicion, tinge 2 = **remnant**,
sign, record, mark, evidence,
indication, vestige 3 = **track**,
trail, footstep, path, footprint,
spoor, footmark
▷ VERB 1 = **search for**, track,
unearth, hunt down 2 = **find**,
track (down), discover, detect,
unearth, hunt down, ferret out,
locate 3 = **outline**, sketch, draw
4 = **copy**, map, draft, outline,
sketch, reproduce, draw over

track NOUN 1 = **path**, way, road,
route, trail, pathway, footpath
2 = **course**, line, path, orbit,
trajectory 3 = **line**, tramline
▷ VERB = **follow**, pursue, chase,
trace, tail (informal), shadow, trail,
stalk ▷ PHRASE: **track something**
or **someone down** = **find**,
discover, trace, unearth, dig up,
hunt down, sniff out, run to earth
or ground

tract¹ NOUN = **area**, region,
district, stretch, territory, extent,
plot, expanse

tract² NOUN = **treatise**, essay,
booklet, pamphlet, dissertation,
monograph, homily

trade NOUN 1 = **commerce**,
business, transactions, dealing,
exchange, traffic, truck, barter
2 = **job**, employment, business,
craft, profession, occupation, line
of work, métier
▷ VERB 1 = **deal**, do business,
traffic, truck, bargain, peddle,
transact, cut a deal 2 = **exchange**,
switch, swap, barter 3 = **operate**,
run, deal, do business

trader NOUN = **dealer**, supplier,
merchant, seller, purveyor

tradition NOUN 1 = **customs**,
institution, ritual, folklore, lore,
tikanga (N.Z.) 2 = **established**
practice, custom, convention,
habit, ritual

traditional ADJECTIVE 1 = **old-**
fashioned, old, established,
conventional, usual, accustomed,
customary, time-honoured
≠ revolutionary 2 = **folk**, old

traffic NOUN 1 = **transport**,
vehicles, transportation, freight
2 = **trade**, commerce, business,
exchange, truck, dealings,
peddling
▷ VERB often with **in** = **trade**, deal,
exchange, bargain, do business,
peddle, cut a deal, have dealings

tragedy NOUN = **disaster**,
catastrophe, misfortune,
adversity, calamity ≠ fortune

tragic or **tragical** ADJECTIVE
1 = **distressing**, sad, appalling,
deadly, unfortunate, disastrous,
dreadful, dire ≠ fortunate
2 = **sad**, miserable, pathetic,
mournful ≠ happy

trail NOUN 1 = **path**, track, route,
way, course, road, pathway,

footpath **2 = tracks**, path, marks, wake, trace, scent, footprints, spoor **3 = wake**, stream, tail
▷ VERB **1 = follow**, track, chase, pursue, dog, hunt, shadow, trace **2 = drag**, draw, pull, sweep, haul, tow, dangle, droop **3 = lag**, follow, drift, wander, linger, trudge, plod, meander

train VERB **1 = instruct**, school, prepare, coach, teach, guide, educate, drill **2 = exercise**, prepare, work out, practise, do exercise, get into shape **3 = aim**, point, level, position, direct, focus, sight, zero in
▷ NOUN **= sequence**, series, chain, string, set, cycle, trail, succession

trainer NOUN **= coach**, manager, guide, adviser, tutor, instructor, counsellor, guru

trait NOUN **= characteristic**, feature, quality, attribute, quirk, peculiarity, mannerism, idiosyncrasy

traitor NOUN **= betrayer**, deserter, turncoat, renegade, defector, Judas, quisling, apostate, fizgig (*Austral. slang*) ≠ loyalist

tramp VERB **1 = trudge**, stump, toil, plod, traipse (*informal*) **2 = hike**, walk, trek, roam, march, ramble, slog, rove
▷ NOUN **1 = vagrant**, derelict, drifter, down-and-out, derro (*Austral. slang*) **2 = tread**, stamp, footstep, footfall **3 = hike**, march, trek, ramble, slog

trample VERB *often with* **on**, **upon**, *or* **over** **= stamp**, crush,

squash, tread, flatten, run over, walk over

trance NOUN **= daze**, dream, abstraction, rapture, reverie, stupor, unconsciousness

transaction NOUN **= deal**, negotiation, business, enterprise, bargain, undertaking

transcend VERB **= surpass**, exceed, go beyond, rise above, eclipse, excel, outstrip, outdo

transcript NOUN **= copy**, record, manuscript, reproduction, duplicate, transcription

transfer VERB **= move**, transport, shift, relocate, transpose, change
▷ NOUN **= transference**, move, handover, change, shift, transmission, translation, relocation

transform VERB **1 = change**, convert, alter, transmute **2 = make over**, remodel, revolutionize

transformation NOUN **1 = change**, conversion, alteration, metamorphosis, transmutation **2 = revolution**, sea change

transit NOUN **= movement**, transfer, transport, passage, crossing, transportation, carriage, conveyance

transition NOUN **= change**, passing, development, shift, conversion, alteration, progression, metamorphosis

transitional ADJECTIVE **1 = changing**, passing, fluid, intermediate, unsettled, developmental **2** = **temporary**, working, acting, short-term, interim, fill-in, caretaker, provisional

translate VERB = **render**, put, change, convert, interpret, decode, construe, paraphrase

translation NOUN = **interpretation**, version, rendering, rendition, decoding, paraphrase

transmission NOUN **1** = **transfer**, spread, spreading, passing on, circulation, dispatch, relaying, mediation **2** = **broadcasting**, showing, putting out, relaying, sending **3** = **programme**, broadcast, show, production, telecast, podcast

transmit VERB **1** = **broadcast**, televise, relay, air, radio, send out, disseminate, beam out, podcast **2** = **pass on**, carry, spread, send, bear, transfer, hand on, convey

transparent ADJECTIVE **1** = **clear**, sheer, see-through, lucid, translucent, crystalline, limpid, diaphanous ≠ opaque **2** = **obvious**, plain, patent, evident, explicit, manifest, recognizable, unambiguous ≠ uncertain

transplant VERB **1** (*surgery*) = **implant**, transfer, graft **2** = **transfer**, take, bring, carry, remove, transport, shift, convey

transport VERB **1** = **convey**, take, move, bring, send, carry, bear, transfer **2** = **enrapture**, move, delight, entrance, enchant, captivate, ravish **3** = **exile**, banish, deport ▷ NOUN **1** = **vehicle**, transportation, conveyance **2** = **transference**, carrying, delivery, distribution, transportation, shipment, freight, haulage **3** *often plural* = **ecstasy**, delight, heaven, bliss, euphoria, rapture, enchantment, ravishment ≠ despondency

trap NOUN **1** = **snare**, net, gin, pitfall, noose **2** = **ambush**, set-up (*informal*) **3** = **trick**, set-up (*informal*), deception, ploy, ruse, trickery, subterfuge, stratagem ▷ VERB **1** = **catch**, snare, ensnare, entrap, take, corner, bag, lay hold of **2** = **trick**, fool, cheat, lure, seduce, deceive, dupe, beguile **3** = **capture**, catch, arrest, seize, take, secure, collar (*informal*), apprehend

trash NOUN **1** = **nonsense**, rubbish, rot, drivel, twaddle, tripe (*informal*), moonshine, hogwash, kak (*S. African taboo or slang*), bizzo (*Austral. slang*), bull's wool (*Austral. & N.Z. slang*) ≠ sense **2** (*chiefly U.S. & Canad.*) = **litter**, refuse, waste, rubbish, junk (*informal*), garbage, dross

trauma NOUN **1** = **shock**, suffering, pain, torture, ordeal, anguish **2** (*pathology*) = **injury**, damage, hurt, wound, agony

traumatic ADJECTIVE = **shocking**, upsetting, alarming, awful, disturbing, devastating, painful, distressing ≠ calming

travel VERB = **go**, journey, move, tour, progress, wander, trek, voyage
▷ NOUN *usually plural* = **journey**, wandering, expedition, globetrotting, tour, trip, voyage, excursion

traveller NOUN = **voyager**, tourist, explorer, globetrotter, holiday-maker, wayfarer

tread VERB = **step**, walk, march, pace, stamp, stride, hike
▷ NOUN = **step**, walk, pace, stride, footstep, gait, footfall

treason NOUN = **disloyalty**, mutiny, treachery, duplicity, sedition, perfidy, lese-majesty, traitorousness ≠ loyalty

treasure NOUN 1 = **riches**, money, gold, fortune, wealth, valuables, jewels, cash 2 = **angel**, darling, jewel, gem, paragon, nonpareil
▷ VERB = **prize**, value, esteem, adore, cherish, revere, hold dear, love

treasury NOUN = **storehouse**, bank, store, vault, hoard, cache, repository

treat VERB 1 = **behave towards**, deal with, handle, act towards, use, consider, serve, manage 2 = **take care of**, minister to, attend to, give medical treatment to, doctor (*informal*), nurse, care for, prescribe medicine for 3 *often with* **to** = **provide**, stand (*informal*), entertain, lay on, regale
▷ NOUN 1 = **entertainment**, party, surprise, gift, celebration, feast, outing, excursion

2 = **pleasure**, delight, joy, thrill, satisfaction, enjoyment, source of pleasure, fun

treatment NOUN 1 = **care**, medical care, nursing, medicine, surgery, therapy, healing, medication 2 = **cure**, remedy, medication, medicine 3 *often with* **of** = **handling**, dealings with, behaviour towards, conduct towards, management, manipulation, action towards

treaty NOUN = **agreement**, pact, contract, alliance, convention, compact, covenant, entente

trek NOUN 1 = **slog**, tramp 2 = **journey**, hike, expedition, safari, march, odyssey
▷ VERB 1 = **journey**, march, hike, tramp, rove, go walkabout (*Austral.*) 2 = **trudge**, traipse (*informal*), footslog, slog

tremble VERB 1 = **shake**, shiver, quake, shudder, quiver, totter 2 = **vibrate**, shake, quake, wobble
▷ NOUN = **shake**, shiver, quake, shudder, wobble, tremor, quiver, vibration

tremendous ADJECTIVE 1 = **huge**, great, enormous, terrific, formidable, immense, gigantic, colossal ≠ tiny 2 (*informal*) = **excellent**, great, wonderful, brilliant, amazing, extraordinary, fantastic (*informal*), marvellous, booshit (*Austral. slang*), exo (*Austral. slang*), sik (*Austral. slang*), rad (*informal*), phat (*slang*), schmick (*Austral. informal*) ≠ terrible

trench NOUN = **ditch**, channel, drain, gutter, trough, furrow, excavation

trend NOUN 1 = **tendency**, swing, drift, inclination, current, direction, flow, leaning 2 = **fashion**, craze, fad (*informal*), mode, thing, style, rage, vogue

trendy (*Brit. informal*) ADJECTIVE = **fashionable**, with it (*informal*), stylish, in fashion, in vogue, modish, voguish, schmick (*Austral. informal*), funky

trial NOUN 1 (*law*) = **hearing**, case, court case, inquiry, tribunal, lawsuit, appeal, litigation 2 = **test**, experiment, evaluation, audition, dry run (*informal*), assessment, probation, appraisal 3 = **hardship**, suffering, trouble, distress, ordeal, adversity, affliction, tribulation

tribe NOUN = **race**, people, family, clan, hapu (*N.Z.*), iwi (*N.Z.*)

tribunal NOUN = **hearing**, court, trial

tribute NOUN = **accolade**, testimonial, eulogy, recognition, compliment, commendation, panegyric ≠ criticism

trick NOUN 1 = **joke**, stunt, spoof (*informal*), prank, practical joke, antic, jape, leg-pull (*Brit. informal*) 2 = **deception**, trap, fraud, manoeuvre, ploy, hoax, swindle, ruse, fastie (*Austral. slang*) 3 = **sleight of hand**, stunt, legerdemain 4 = **secret**, skill, knack, hang (*informal*), technique, know-

how (*informal*) 5 = **mannerism**, habit, characteristic, trait, quirk, peculiarity, foible, idiosyncrasy ▷ VERB = **deceive**, trap, take someone in (*informal*), fool, cheat, con (*informal*), kid (*informal*), mislead, scam (*slang*)

trickle VERB = **dribble**, run, drop, stream, drip, ooze, seep, exude ▷ NOUN = **dribble**, drip, seepage, thin stream

tricky ADJECTIVE 1 = **difficult**, sensitive, complicated, delicate, risky, hairy (*informal*), problematic, thorny ≠ simple 2 = **crafty**, scheming, cunning, slippery, sly, devious, wily, artful ≠ open

trifle NOUN = **knick-knack**, toy, plaything, bauble, bagatelle

trifling ADJECTIVE = **insignificant**, trivial, worthless, negligible, unimportant, paltry, measly ≠ significant

trigger VERB = **bring about**, start, cause, produce, generate, prompt, provoke, set off ≠ prevent

trim ADJECTIVE 1 = **neat**, smart, tidy, spruce, dapper, natty (*informal*), well-groomed, shipshape ≠ untidy 2 = **slender**, fit, slim, sleek, streamlined, shapely, svelte, willowy ▷ VERB 1 = **cut**, crop, clip, shave, tidy, prune, pare, even up 2 = **decorate**, dress, array, adorn, ornament, embellish, deck out, beautify ▷ NOUN 1 = **decoration**, edging, border, piping, trimming, frill, embellishment, adornment

2 = **condition**, health, shape (*informal*), fitness, wellness, fettle **3** = **cut**, crop, clipping, shave, pruning, shearing, tidying up

trimming NOUN = **decoration**, edging, border, piping, frill, embellishment, adornment, ornamentation

▷ PLURAL NOUN = **extras**, accessories, ornaments, accompaniments, frills, trappings, paraphernalia

trinity NOUN = **threesome**, trio, triad, triumvirate

trio NOUN = **threesome**, trinity, trilogy, triad, triumvirate

trip NOUN **1** = **journey**, outing, excursion, day out, run, drive, tour, spin (*informal*) **2** = **stumble**, fall, slip, misstep

▷ VERB **1** *often with* **up** = **stumble**, fall, fall over, slip, tumble, topple, stagger, misstep **2** = **skip**, dance, hop, gambol ▷ PHRASE: **trip someone up** = **catch out**, trap, wrongfoot

triple ADJECTIVE **1** = **treble**, three times **2** = **three-way**, threefold, tripartite

▷ VERB = **treble**, increase threefold

triumph NOUN **1** = **success**, victory, accomplishment, achievement, coup, feat, conquest, attainment ≠ failure **2** = **joy**, pride, happiness, rejoicing, elation, jubilation, exultation

▷ VERB **1** *often with* **over** = **succeed**, win, overcome,

prevail, prosper, vanquish ≠ fail **2** = **rejoice**, celebrate, glory, revel, gloat, exult, crow

triumphant ADJECTIVE **1** = **victorious**, winning, successful, conquering ≠ defeated **2** = **celebratory**, jubilant, proud, elated, exultant, cock-a-hoop

trivial ADJECTIVE = **unimportant**, small, minor, petty, meaningless, worthless, trifling, insignificant ≠ important

troop NOUN **1** = **group**, company, team, body, unit, band, crowd, squad **2** *plural* = **soldiers**, men, armed forces, servicemen, army, soldiery

▷ VERB = **flock**, march, stream, swarm, throng, traipse (*informal*)

trophy NOUN **1** = **prize**, cup, award, laurels **2** = **souvenir**, spoils, relic, memento, booty, keepsake

tropical ADJECTIVE = **hot**, stifling, steamy, torrid, sultry, sweltering ≠ cold

trot VERB = **run**, jog, scamper, lope, canter

▷ NOUN = **run**, jog, lope, canter

trouble NOUN **1** = **bother**, problems, concern, worry, stress, difficulty (*informal*), anxiety, distress **2** *often plural* = **distress**, problem, worry, pain, anxiety, grief, torment, sorrow ≠ pleasure **3** = **ailment**, disease, failure, complaint, illness, disorder, defect, malfunction **4** = **disorder**, fighting, conflict, bother, unrest,

disturbance, to-do (*informal*), furore, biffo (*Austral. slang*), boilover (*Austral.*) ≠ peace
5 = **effort**, work, thought, care, labour, pains, hassle (*informal*), inconvenience ≠ convenience
▷ **VERB 1** = **bother**, worry, upset, disturb, distress, plague, pain, sadden ≠ please **2** = **afflict**, hurt, bother, cause discomfort to, pain, grieve **3** = **inconvenience**, disturb, burden, put out, impose upon, incommode ≠ relieve
4 = **take pains**, take the time, make an effort, exert yourself ≠ avoid

troublesome ADJECTIVE
1 = **bothersome**, trying, taxing, demanding, difficult, worrying, annoying, tricky ≠ simple
2 = **disorderly**, violent, turbulent, rebellious, unruly, rowdy, undisciplined, uncooperative ≠ well-behaved

trough NOUN = **manger**, water trough

truce NOUN = **ceasefire**, peace, moratorium, respite, lull, cessation, let-up (*informal*), armistice

true ADJECTIVE **1** = **correct**, right, accurate, precise, factual, truthful, veracious ≠ false
2 = **actual**, real, genuine, proper, authentic, dinkum (*Austral. & N.Z. informal*) **3** = **faithful**, loyal, devoted, dedicated, steady, reliable, staunch, trustworthy ≠ unfaithful **4** = **exact**, perfect, accurate, precise, spot-on (*Brit.*

informal), on target, unerring ≠ inaccurate

truly ADVERB **1** = **genuinely**, correctly, truthfully, rightly, precisely, exactly, legitimately, authentically ≠ falsely **2** = **really**, very, greatly, indeed, extremely **3** = **faithfully**, steadily, sincerely, staunchly, dutifully, loyally, devotedly

trumpet NOUN = **horn**, clarion, bugle
▷ **VERB** = **proclaim**, advertise, tout (*informal*), announce, broadcast, shout from the rooftops ≠ keep secret

trunk NOUN **1** = **stem**, stalk, bole **2** = **chest**, case, box, crate, coffer, casket **3** = **body**, torso **4** = **snout**, nose, proboscis

trust NOUN = **confidence**, credit, belief, faith, expectation, conviction, assurance, certainty ≠ distrust
▷ **VERB 1** = **believe in**, have faith in, depend on, count on, bank on, rely upon ≠ distrust **2** = **entrust**, commit, assign, confide, consign, put into the hands of, allow to look after, hand over **3** = **expect**, hope, suppose, assume, presume, surmise

trustful *or* **trusting** ADJECTIVE = **unsuspecting**, naive, gullible, unwary, credulous, unsuspicious ≠ suspicious

truth NOUN **1** = **reality**, fact(s), real life **2** = **truthfulness**, fact, accuracy, precision, validity, legitimacy, veracity, genuineness

t

≠ inaccuracy

try VERB 1 = **attempt**, seek, aim, strive, struggle, endeavour, have a go, make an effort
2 = **experiment with**, try out, put to the test, test, taste, examine, investigate, sample
▷ NOUN = **attempt**, go (*informal*), shot (*informal*), effort, crack (*informal*), stab (*informal*), bash (*informal*), whack (*informal*)

trying ADJECTIVE = **annoying**, hard, taxing, difficult, tough, stressful, exasperating, tiresome ≠ straightforward

tuck VERB = **push**, stick, stuff, slip, ease, insert, pop (*informal*)
▷ NOUN 1 (*Brit. informal*) = **food**, grub (*slang*), kai (*N.Z. informal*), nosh (*slang*) **2** = **fold**, gather, pleat, pinch

tug VERB 1 = **pull**, pluck, jerk, yank, wrench **2** = **drag**, pull, haul, tow, lug, heave, draw
▷ NOUN = **pull**, jerk, yank

tuition NOUN = **training**, schooling, education, teaching, lessons, instruction, tutoring, tutelage

tumble VERB = **fall**, drop, topple, plummet, stumble, flop
▷ NOUN = **fall**, drop, trip, plunge, spill, stumble

tumour NOUN = **growth**, cancer, swelling, lump, carcinoma (*pathology*), sarcoma (*medical*)

tune NOUN 1 = **melody**, air, song, theme, strain(s), jingle, ditty
2 = **harmony**, pitch, euphony
▷ VERB 1 = **tune up**, adjust

2 = **regulate**, adapt, modulate, harmonize, attune, pitch

tunnel NOUN = **passage**, underpass, passageway, subway, channel, hole, shaft
▷ VERB = **dig**, burrow, mine, bore, drill, excavate

turbulent ADJECTIVE = **stormy**, rough, raging, tempestuous, furious, foaming, agitated, tumultuous ≠ calm

turf NOUN 1 = **grass**, sward **2** = **sod**
▷ PHRASE: **the turf** = **horse-racing**, the flat, racing

turmoil NOUN = **confusion**, disorder, chaos, upheaval, disarray, uproar, agitation, commotion ≠ peace

turn VERB 1 *sometimes with* **round** = **change course**, swing round, wheel round, veer, move, switch, shift, swerve **2** = **rotate**, spin, go round (and round), revolve, roll, circle, twist, spiral **3** *with* **into** = **change**, transform, shape, convert, alter, mould, remodel, mutate **4** = **shape**, form, fashion, cast, frame, mould, make **5** = **go bad**, go off (*Brit. informal*), curdle **6** = **make rancid**, spoil, sour, taint
▷ NOUN 1 = **rotation**, cycle, circle, revolution, spin, twist, whirl, swivel **2** = **change of direction**, shift, departure, deviation **3** = **direction**, course, tack, tendency, drift **4** = **opportunity**, go, time, try, chance, crack (*informal*), stint **5** = **deed**, service, act, action, favour, gesture
▷ PHRASES: **turn on someone**

t

= **attack**, assault, fall on, round on, lash out at, assail, lay into (*informal*), let fly at; **turn someone on** (*slang*) = **arouse**, attract, excite, thrill, stimulate, please, titillate; **turn something down** 1 = **refuse**, decline, reject, spurn, rebuff, repudiate 2 = **lower**, soften, mute, lessen, muffle, quieten; **turn something in** = **hand in**, return, deliver, give up, hand over, submit, surrender, tender; **turn something off** = **switch off**, turn out, put out, stop, cut out, shut down, unplug, flick off; **turn something on** = **switch on**, activate, start, start up, ignite, kick-start; **turn something up** 1 = **find**, reveal, discover, expose, disclose, unearth, dig up 2 = **increase**, raise, boost, enhance, intensify, amplify; **turn up** 1 = **arrive**, come, appear, show up (*informal*), attend, put in an appearance, show your face 2 = **come to light**, show up, pop up, materialize

turning NOUN 1 = **turn-off**, turn, junction, crossroads, side road, exit 2 = **bend**, turn, curve

turning point NOUN = **crossroads**, change, crisis, crux, moment of truth, tipping point

turnout NOUN = **attendance**, crowd, audience, gate, assembly, congregation, number, throng

turnover NOUN 1 = **output**, business, productivity 2 = **movement**, coming and going, change

turtle NOUN
▷ *see* **reptiles**

tutor NOUN = **teacher**, coach, instructor, educator, guide, guardian, lecturer, guru
▷ VERB = **teach**, educate, school, train, coach, guide, drill, instruct

twig NOUN = **branch**, stick, sprig, shoot, spray

twilight NOUN 1 = **dusk**, evening, sunset, early evening, nightfall, sundown, gloaming (*Scot. poetic*), close of day, evo (*Austral. slang*) ≠ dawn 2 = **half-light**, gloom, dimness, semi-darkness

twin NOUN = **double**, counterpart, mate, match, fellow, clone, duplicate, lookalike
▷ VERB = **pair**, match, join, couple, link, yoke

twinkle VERB = **sparkle**, flash, shine, glitter, gleam, blink, flicker, shimmer
▷ NOUN = **sparkle**, flash, spark, gleam, flicker, shimmer, glimmer

twist VERB 1 = **coil**, curl, wind, wrap, screw, twirl 2 = **intertwine** 3 = **distort**, screw up, contort, mangle, mangulate (*Austral. slang*) ≠ straighten
▷ NOUN 1 = **surprise**, change, turn, development, revelation 2 = **development**, emphasis, variation, slant 3 = **wind**, turn, spin, swivel, twirl 4 = **curve**, turn, bend, loop, arc, kink, zigzag, dog-leg

twitch VERB 1 = **jerk**, flutter, jump, squirm 2 = **pull (at)**, tug (at), pluck (at), yank (at)

▷ NOUN = **jerk**, tic, spasm, jump, flutter

tycoon NOUN = **magnate**, capitalist, baron, industrialist, financier, fat cat (*slang, chiefly U.S.*), mogul, plutocrat

type NOUN = **kind**, sort, class, variety, group, order, style, species

typical ADJECTIVE 1 = **archetypal**, standard, model, normal, stock, representative, usual, regular ≠ unusual 2 = **characteristic** 3 = **average**, normal, usual, routine, regular, orthodox, predictable, run-of-the-mill

tyranny NOUN = **oppression**, cruelty, dictatorship, authoritarianism, despotism, autocracy, absolutism, high-handedness ≠ liberality

t

Uu

ubiquitous ADJECTIVE = **ever-present**, pervasive, omnipresent, everywhere, universal

ugly ADJECTIVE 1 = **unattractive**, homely (*chiefly U.S.*), plain, unsightly, unlovely, unprepossessing, ill-favoured ≠ beautiful 2 = **unpleasant**, shocking, terrible, nasty, distasteful, horrid, objectionable, disagreeable ≠ pleasant 3 = **bad-tempered**, dangerous, menacing, sinister, baleful

ulcer NOUN = **sore**, abscess, peptic ulcer, gumboil

ultimate ADJECTIVE 1 = **final**, last, end 2 = **supreme**, highest, greatest, paramount, superlative 3 = **worst**, greatest, utmost, extreme 4 = **best**, greatest, supreme, optimum, quintessential

ultimately ADVERB 1 = **finally**, eventually, in the end, after all, at last, sooner or later, in due time 2 = **fundamentally**, essentially, basically, primarily, at heart, deep down

umpire NOUN = **referee**, judge, arbiter, arbitrator, umpie (*Austral. slang*)
▷ VERB = **referee**, judge, adjudicate, arbitrate

unable ADJECTIVE *with* **to** = **incapable**, powerless, unfit, impotent, unqualified, ineffectual ≠ able

unanimous ADJECTIVE 1 = **agreed**, united, in agreement, harmonious, like-minded, of the same mind ≠ divided 2 = **united**, common, concerted, solid, consistent, harmonious, undivided, congruent ≠ split

unarmed ADJECTIVE = **defenceless**, helpless, unprotected ≠ armed

unaware ADJECTIVE = **ignorant**, unconscious, oblivious, uninformed, unknowing, not in the loop (*informal*) ≠ aware

unbearable ADJECTIVE = **intolerable**, insufferable, too much (*informal*), unacceptable ≠ tolerable

unborn ADJECTIVE = **expected**, awaited, embryonic

uncertain ADJECTIVE = **unsure**, undecided, vague, unclear, dubious, hazy, irresolute ≠ sure

uncertainty NOUN 1 = **unpredictability**, precariousness, ambiguity, unreliability, fickleness, chanciness, changeableness ≠ predictability 2 = **doubt**, confusion ≠ confidence 3 = **hesitancy**, indecision

uncomfortable ADJECTIVE 1 = **uneasy**, troubled, disturbed, embarrassed, awkward, discomfited ≠ comfortable 2 = **painful**, awkward, rough

uncommon ADJECTIVE 1 = **rare**, unusual, odd, novel, strange, peculiar, scarce, queer ≠ common 2 = **extraordinary**, remarkable, special, outstanding, distinctive, exceptional, notable ≠ ordinary

uncompromising ADJECTIVE = **inflexible**, strict, rigid, firm, tough, inexorable, intransigent, unbending

unconditional ADJECTIVE = **absolute**, full, complete, total, positive, entire, outright, unlimited ≠ qualified

unconscious ADJECTIVE 1 = **senseless**, knocked out, out cold (*informal*), out, stunned, dazed, in a coma, stupefied ≠ awake 2 = **unaware**, ignorant, oblivious, unknowing ≠ aware 3 = **unintentional**, unwitting, inadvertent, accidental ≠ intentional

uncover VERB 1 = **reveal**, expose, disclose, divulge, make known ≠ conceal 2 = **open**, unveil, unwrap, show, strip, expose, bare, lay bare

under PREPOSITION 1 = **below**, beneath, underneath ≠ over 2 = **subordinate to**, subject to, governed by, secondary to ▷ ADVERB = **below**, down, beneath ≠ up

undercover ADJECTIVE = **secret**, covert, private, hidden, concealed ≠ open

underdog NOUN = **weaker party**, little fellow (*informal*), outsider

underestimate VERB

1 = **undervalue**, understate, diminish, play down, minimize, downgrade, miscalculate, trivialize ≠ overestimate 2 = **underrate**, undervalue, belittle ≠ overrate

● **WORD POWER**
● *Underestimate* is sometimes
● wrongly used where
● *overestimate* is meant: *the*
● *importance of his work cannot*
● *be overestimated* (not *cannot be*
● *underestimated*).

undergo VERB = **experience**, go through, stand, suffer, bear, sustain, endure

underground ADJECTIVE 1 = **subterranean**, basement, lower-level, sunken, covered, buried, subterrestrial 2 = **secret**, covert, hidden, guerrilla, revolutionary, confidential, dissident, closet ▷ PHRASE: **the underground 1** = **the tube** (*Brit.*), the subway, the metro **2** = **the Resistance**, partisans, freedom fighters

underline VERB 1 = **emphasize**, stress, highlight, accentuate ≠ minimize 2 = **underscore**, mark

underlying ADJECTIVE = **fundamental**, basic, prime, primary, elementary, intrinsic

undermine VERB = **weaken**, sabotage, subvert, compromise, disable ≠ reinforce

understand VERB

1 = **comprehend**, get, take in, perceive, grasp, see, follow, realize

u

2 = **believe**, gather, think, see, suppose, notice, assume, fancy

understandable ADJECTIVE
= **reasonable**, natural, justified, expected, inevitable, legitimate, predictable, accountable

understanding NOUN
1 = **perception**, knowledge, grasp, sense, know-how (*informal*), judgment, awareness, appreciation ≠ ignorance
2 = **agreement**, deal, promise, arrangement, accord, contract, bond, pledge ≠ disagreement
3 = **belief**, view, opinion, impression, interpretation, feeling, idea, notion
▷ ADJECTIVE = **sympathetic**, kind, compassionate, considerate, patient, sensitive, tolerant ≠ unsympathetic

undertake VERB = **agree**, promise, contract, guarantee, engage, pledge

undertaking NOUN 1 = **task**, business, operation, project, attempt, effort, affair, venture
2 = **promise**, commitment, pledge, word, vow, assurance

underwear NOUN
= **underclothes**, lingerie, undies (*informal*), undergarments, underthings, broekies (*S. African informal*), underdaks (*Austral. slang*)

underworld NOUN 1 = **criminals**, gangsters, organized crime, gangland (*informal*) 2 = **nether world**, Hades, nether regions

underwrite VERB = **finance**,

back, fund, guarantee, sponsor, insure, ratify, subsidize

undesirable ADJECTIVE
= **unwanted**, unwelcome, disagreeable, objectionable, unacceptable, unsuitable, unattractive, distasteful ≠ desirable

undo VERB 1 = **open**, unfasten, loose, untie, unbutton, disentangle 2 = **reverse**, cancel, offset, neutralize, invalidate, annul 3 = **ruin**, defeat, destroy, wreck, shatter, upset, undermine, overturn

undone ADJECTIVE = **unfinished**, left, neglected, omitted, unfulfilled, unperformed ≠ finished

undoubtedly ADVERB
= **certainly**, definitely, surely, doubtless, without doubt, assuredly

unearth VERB 1 = **discover**, find, reveal, expose, uncover 2 = **dig up**, excavate, exhume, dredge up

unearthly ADJECTIVE = **eerie**, strange, supernatural, ghostly, weird, phantom, uncanny, spooky (*informal*)

uneasy ADJECTIVE 1 = **anxious**, worried, troubled, nervous, disturbed, uncomfortable, edgy, perturbed ≠ relaxed
2 = **precarious**, strained, uncomfortable, tense, awkward, shaky, insecure

unemployed ADJECTIVE = **out of work**, redundant, laid off, jobless, idle ≠ working

unfair ADJECTIVE 1 = **biased**, prejudiced, unjust, one-sided, partial, partisan, bigoted
2 = **unscrupulous**, dishonest, unethical, wrongful, unsporting ≠ ethical

unfit ADJECTIVE 1 = **out of shape**, feeble, unhealthy, flabby, in poor condition ≠ healthy
2 = **incapable**, inadequate, incompetent, no good, useless, unqualified ≠ capable
3 = **unsuitable**, inadequate, useless, unsuited ≠ suitable

unfold VERB 1 = **reveal**, tell, present, show, disclose, uncover, divulge, make known 2 = **open**, spread out, undo, expand, unfurl, unwrap, unroll

unfortunate ADJECTIVE
1 = **disastrous**, calamitous, adverse, ill-fated ≠ opportune
2 = **regrettable**, deplorable, lamentable, unsuitable, unbecoming ≠ becoming
3 = **unlucky**, unhappy, doomed, cursed, unsuccessful, hapless, wretched ≠ fortunate

unhappy ADJECTIVE 1 = **sad**, depressed, miserable, blue, melancholy, mournful, dejected, despondent ≠ happy
2 = **unlucky**, unfortunate, hapless, cursed, wretched, ill-fated ≠ fortunate

unhealthy ADJECTIVE
1 = **harmful**, detrimental, unwholesome, insanitary, insalubrious ≠ beneficial
2 = **sick**, sickly, unwell, delicate,

crook (*Austral. & N.Z. informal*), ailing, frail, feeble, invalid ≠ well
3 = **weak**, ailing ≠ strong

unification NOUN = **union**, uniting, alliance, coalition, federation, confederation, amalgamation, coalescence

uniform NOUN 1 = **regalia**, suit, livery, colours, habit 2 = **outfit**, dress, costume, attire, gear (*informal*), get-up (*informal*), ensemble, garb
▷ ADJECTIVE 1 = **consistent**, unvarying, similar, even, same, matching, regular, constant ≠ varying 2 = **alike**, similar, like, same, equal

unify VERB = **unite**, join, combine, merge, consolidate, confederate, amalgamate ≠ divide

union NOUN 1 = **joining**, uniting, unification, combination, coalition, merger, mixture, blend
2 = **alliance**, league, association, coalition, federation, confederacy

unique ADJECTIVE 1 = **distinct**, special, exclusive, peculiar, only, single, lone, solitary
2 = **unparalleled**, unmatched, unequalled, matchless, without equal

● **WORD POWER**
● *Unique* with the meaning 'being
● the only one' or 'having no
● equal' describes an absolute
● state: *a case unique in British law.*
● In this use it cannot therefore
● be qualified; something is
● either *unique* or *not unique.*
● However, *unique* is also very

u

- commonly used in the sense
- of 'remarkable' or 'exceptional',
- particularly in the language
- of advertising, and in this
- meaning it can be used with
- qualifying words such as *rather*,
- *quite*, etc. Since many people
- object to this use, it is best
- avoided in formal and serious
- writing.

unit NOUN 1 = **entity**, whole, item, feature 2 = **section**, company, group, force, detail, division, cell, squad 3 = **measure**, quantity, measurement 4 = **part**, section, segment, class, element, component, constituent, tutorial

unite VERB 1 = **join**, link, combine, couple, blend, merge, unify, fuse ≠ separate 2 = **cooperate**, ally, join forces, band, pool, collaborate ≠ split

unity NOUN 1 = **union**, unification, coalition, federation, integration, confederation, amalgamation 2 = **wholeness**, integrity, oneness, union, entity, singleness ≠ disunity 3 = **agreement**, accord, consensus, harmony, solidarity, unison, assent, concord ≠ disagreement

universal ADJECTIVE 1 = **widespread**, general, common, whole, total, unlimited, overarching 2 = **global**, worldwide, international, pandemic

universally ADVERB = **without exception**, everywhere, always, invariably

universe NOUN = **cosmos**, space, creation, nature, heavens, macrocosm, all existence

unknown ADJECTIVE 1 = **strange**, new, undiscovered, uncharted, unexplored, virgin, remote, alien 2 = **unidentified**, mysterious, anonymous, unnamed, nameless, incognito 3 = **obscure**, humble, unfamiliar ≠ famous

unlike PREPOSITION 1 = **different from**, dissimilar to, distinct from, unequal to ≠ similar to 2 = **contrasted with**, not like, in contradiction to, in contrast with *or* to, as opposed to, differently from, opposite to

unlikely ADJECTIVE 1 = **improbable**, doubtful, remote, slight, faint ≠ probable 2 = **unbelievable**, incredible, implausible, questionable ≠ believable

unload VERB 1 = **empty**, clear, unpack, dump, discharge 2 = **unburden**

unnatural ADJECTIVE 1 = **abnormal**, odd, strange, unusual, extraordinary, perverted, queer, irregular ≠ normal 2 = **false**, forced, artificial, affected, stiff, feigned, stilted, insincere ≠ genuine

unpleasant ADJECTIVE 1 = **nasty**, bad, horrid, distasteful, displeasing, objectionable, disagreeable ≠ nice 2 = **obnoxious**, rude ≠ likable *or* likeable

unravel VERB 1 = **solve**, explain,

u

work out, resolve, figure out
(*informal*) **2** = **undo**, separate,
disentangle, free, unwind,
untangle

unrest NOUN = **discontent**,
rebellion, protest, strife,
agitation, discord, sedition,
dissension ≠ peace

unsettled ADJECTIVE
1 = **unstable**, shaky, insecure,
disorderly, unsteady **2** = **restless**,
tense, shaken, confused,
disturbed, anxious, agitated,
flustered, adrenalized
3 = **inconstant**, changing,
variable, uncertain

unstable ADJECTIVE
1 = **changeable**, volatile,
unpredictable, variable,
fluctuating, fitful, inconstant
≠ constant **2** = **insecure**,
shaky, precarious, unsettled,
wobbly, tottering, unsteady
3 = **unpredictable**, irrational,
erratic, inconsistent,
temperamental, capricious,
changeable ≠ level-headed

unthinkable ADJECTIVE
1 = **impossible**, out of the
question, inconceivable, absurd,
unreasonable **2** = **inconceivable**,
incredible, unimaginable

untold ADJECTIVE
1 = **indescribable**, unthinkable,
unimaginable, undreamed
of, unutterable, inexpressible
2 = **countless**, incalculable,
innumerable, myriad,
numberless, uncountable

untrue ADJECTIVE **1** = **false**, lying,

wrong, mistaken, incorrect,
inaccurate, dishonest, deceptive
≠ true **2** = **unfaithful**, disloyal,
deceitful, treacherous, faithless,
false, untrustworthy, inconstant
≠ faithful

unusual ADJECTIVE **1** = **rare**, odd,
strange, extraordinary, different,
curious, queer, uncommon
≠ common **2** = **extraordinary**,
unique, remarkable, exceptional,
uncommon, singular,
unconventional ≠ average

upbeat ADJECTIVE (*informal*)
= **cheerful**, positive, optimistic,
encouraging, hopeful, cheery

upbringing NOUN = **education**,
training, breeding, rearing,
raising

update VERB = **bring up to date**,
improve, correct, renew, revise,
upgrade, amend, overhaul

upgrade VERB **1** = **improve**,
better, update, reform, add to,
enhance, refurbish, renovate
2 = **promote**, raise, advance,
boost, move up, elevate, kick
upstairs (*informal*), give promotion
to ≠ demote

upheaval NOUN = **disturbance**,
revolution, disorder, turmoil,
disruption

uphill ADJECTIVE **1** = **ascending**,
rising, upward, mounting,
climbing ≠ descending
2 = **arduous**, hard, taxing,
difficult, tough, exhausting,
gruelling, strenuous

uphold VERB **1** = **support**, back,
defend, aid, champion, maintain,

u

promote, sustain 2 = **confirm**, endorse

uplift VERB = **improve**, better, raise, advance, inspire, refine, edify

▷ NOUN = **improvement**, enlightenment, advancement, refinement, enhancement, enrichment, edification

upper ADJECTIVE 1 = **topmost**, top ≠ bottom 2 = **higher**, high ≠ lower 3 = **superior**, senior, higher-level, greater, top, important, chief, most important ≠ inferior

upper class ADJECTIVE = **aristocratic**, upper-class, noble, high-class, patrician, blue-blooded, highborn

upright ADJECTIVE 1 = **vertical**, straight, standing up, erect, perpendicular, bolt upright ≠ horizontal 2 = **honest**, good, principled, just, ethical, honourable, righteous, conscientious ≠ dishonourable

uprising NOUN = **rebellion**, rising, revolution, revolt, disturbance, mutiny, insurrection, insurgence

uproar NOUN 1 = **commotion**, noise, racket, riot, turmoil, mayhem, din, pandemonium 2 = **protest**, outrage, complaint, objection, fuss, stink (informal), outcry, furore

upset ADJECTIVE 1 = **distressed**, shaken, disturbed, worried, troubled, hurt, bothered, unhappy 2 = **sick**, queasy, bad, ill

▷ VERB 1 = **distress**, trouble,

disturb, worry, alarm, bother, grieve, agitate 2 = **tip over**, overturn, capsize, knock over, spill 3 = **mess up**, spoil, disturb, change, confuse, disorder, unsettle, disorganize

▷ NOUN 1 = **distress**, worry, trouble, shock, bother, disturbance, agitation 2 = **reversal**, shake-up (informal), defeat 3 = **illness**, complaint, disorder, bug (informal), sickness, malady

upside down or **upside-down** ADVERB = **wrong side up**

▷ ADJECTIVE 1 = **inverted**, overturned, upturned 2 (informal) = **confused**, disordered, chaotic, muddled, topsy-turvy, higgledy-piggledy (informal)

up-to-date ADJECTIVE = **modern**, fashionable, trendy (Brit. informal), current, stylish, in vogue, up-to-the-minute ≠ out of date

urban ADJECTIVE = **civic**, city, town, metropolitan, municipal, dorp (S. African)

urge VERB 1 = **beg**, exhort, plead, implore, beseech, entreat 2 = **advocate**, recommend, advise, support, counsel ≠ discourage

▷ NOUN = **impulse**, longing, wish, desire, drive, yearning, itch (informal), thirst ≠ reluctance

urgency NOUN = **importance**, need, necessity, gravity, pressure, hurry, seriousness, extremity

urgent ADJECTIVE = **crucial**, desperate, pressing, great,

important, crying, critical,
immediate ≠ unimportant
usage NOUN 1 = **use**, operation,
employment, running, control,
management, handling
2 = **practice**, method, procedure,
habit, regime, custom, routine,
convention
use VERB 1 = **employ**, utilize,
work, apply, operate, exercise,
practise, resort to 2 *sometimes*
with **up** = **consume**, exhaust,
spend, run through, expend
3 = **take advantage of**, exploit,
manipulate
▷ NOUN 1 = **usage**, employment,
operation, application
2 = **purpose**, end, reason, object
3 = **good**, point, help, service,
value, benefit, profit, advantage
used ADJECTIVE = **second-hand**,
cast-off, nearly new, shopsoiled,
preloved (*Austral. slang*) ≠ new
used to ADJECTIVE = **accustomed
to**, familiar with
useful ADJECTIVE = **helpful**,
effective, valuable, practical,
profitable, worthwhile,
beneficial, fruitful ≠ useless
useless ADJECTIVE 1 = **worthless**,
valueless, impractical,
fruitless, unproductive,
ineffectual, unsuitable ≠ useful
2 = **pointless**, futile, vain
≠ worthwhile 3 (*informal*)
= **inept**, no good, hopeless,
incompetent, ineffectual
usher VERB = **escort**, lead, direct,
guide, conduct
▷ NOUN = **attendant**, guide,

doorman, escort, doorkeeper
usual ADJECTIVE = **normal**,
customary, regular, general,
common, standard, ordinary,
typical ≠ unusual
usually ADVERB = **normally**,
generally, mainly, commonly,
mostly, on the whole, as a rule,
habitually
utility NOUN = **usefulness**,
benefit, convenience, practicality,
efficacy, serviceableness
utilize VERB = **use**, employ, deploy,
take advantage of, make use of,
put to use, bring into play, avail
yourself of
utmost ADJECTIVE 1 = **greatest**,
highest, maximum, supreme,
paramount, pre-eminent
2 = **farthest**, extreme, last, final
▷ NOUN = **best**, greatest,
maximum, highest, hardest
utter¹ VERB = **say**, state, speak,
voice, express, deliver, declare,
mouth
utter² ADJECTIVE = **absolute**,
complete, total, sheer,
outright, thorough, downright,
unmitigated
utterly ADVERB = **totally**,
completely, absolutely, perfectly,
fully, entirely, extremely,
thoroughly

u

Vv

vacancy NOUN 1 = **opening**, job, post, place, position, role, situation, opportunity 2 = **room**, space, available accommodation, unoccupied room

vacant ADJECTIVE 1 = **empty**, free, available, abandoned, deserted, for sale, on the market, void ≠ occupied 2 = **unfilled**, unoccupied ≠ taken 3 = **blank**, vague, dreamy, empty, abstracted, idle, vacuous, inane ≠ thoughtful

vacuum NOUN 1 = **gap**, lack, absence, space, deficiency, void 2 = **emptiness**, space, void, gap, nothingness, vacuity

vague ADJECTIVE 1 = **unclear**, indefinite, hazy, confused, loose, uncertain, unsure, superficial ≠ clear 2 = **imprecise**, unspecified, generalized, rough, loose, ambiguous, hazy, equivocal 3 = **absent-minded**, distracted, vacant, preoccupied, oblivious, inattentive 4 = **indistinct**, unclear, faint, hazy, indeterminate, nebulous, ill-defined ≠ distinct

vain ADJECTIVE 1 = **futile**, useless, pointless, unsuccessful, idle, worthless, senseless, fruitless ≠ successful 2 = **conceited**, narcissistic, proud, arrogant, swaggering, egotistical, self-important ≠ modest ▷ PHRASE: **in vain** 1 = **useless**, to no avail, unsuccessful, fruitless, vain 2 = **uselessly**, to no avail, unsuccessfully, fruitlessly, vainly, ineffectually

valid ADJECTIVE 1 = **sound**, good, reasonable, telling, convincing, rational, logical, viable ≠ unfounded 2 = **legal**, official, legitimate, genuine, authentic, lawful, bona fide ≠ invalid

validity NOUN 1 = **soundness**, force, power, weight, strength, cogency 2 = **legality**, authority, legitimacy, right, lawfulness

valley NOUN = **hollow**, dale, glen, vale, depression, dell

valuable ADJECTIVE 1 = **useful**, important, profitable, worthwhile, beneficial, helpful ≠ useless 2 = **treasured**, prized, precious 3 = **precious**, expensive, costly, dear, high-priced, priceless, irreplaceable ≠ worthless ▷ PLURAL NOUN = **treasures**, prized possessions, precious items, heirlooms, personal effects, costly articles

value NOUN 1 = **importance**, benefit, worth, merit, point, service, sense, profit ≠ worthlessness 2 = **cost**, price, worth, rate, market price, face value, asking price, selling price ▷ PLURAL NOUN = **principles**, morals, ethics, mores, standards of behaviour, (moral) standards ▷ VERB 1 = **appreciate**, rate, prize, regard highly, respect, admire, treasure, esteem ≠ undervalue **2** with **at** = **evaluate**, price, estimate, rate, cost, assess, set at, appraise

vanish VERB **1** = **disappear**, dissolve, evaporate, fade away, melt away, evanesce ≠ appear **2** = **die out**, disappear, pass away, end, fade, dwindle, cease to exist, become extinct

vanity NOUN = **pride**, arrogance, conceit, narcissism, egotism, conceitedness ≠ modesty

variable ADJECTIVE = **changeable**, unstable, fluctuating, shifting, flexible, uneven, temperamental, unsteady ≠ constant

variant ADJECTIVE = **different**, alternative, modified, divergent ▷ NOUN = **variation**, form, version, development, alternative, adaptation, revision, modification

variation NOUN **1** = **alternative**, variety, modification, departure, innovation, variant **2** = **variety**, change, deviation, difference, diversity, diversion, novelty ≠ uniformity

varied ADJECTIVE = **different**, mixed, various, diverse, assorted, miscellaneous, sundry, motley ≠ unvarying

variety NOUN **1** = **diversity**, change, variation, difference, diversification, heterogeneity, multifariousness ≠ uniformity **2** = **range**, selection, assortment, mix, collection, line-up, mixture,

array **3** = **type**, sort, kind, class, brand, species, breed, strain

various DETERMINER = **different**, assorted, miscellaneous, varied, distinct, diverse, disparate, sundry ≠ similar ▷ ADJECTIVE = **many**, numerous, countless, several, abundant, innumerable, sundry, profuse

● **WORD POWER**
● The use of *different* after
● *various*, which seems to be
● most common in speech, is
● unnecessary and should be
● avoided in serious writing: *the*
● *disease exists in various forms* (not
● *in various different forms*).

varnish NOUN = **lacquer**, polish, glaze, gloss ▷ VERB = **lacquer**, polish, glaze, gloss

vary VERB **1** = **differ**, be different, be dissimilar, disagree, diverge **2** = **change**, shift, swing, alter, fluctuate, oscillate, see-saw **3** = **alternate**

vast ADJECTIVE = **huge**, massive, enormous, great, wide, immense, gigantic, monumental ≠ tiny

vault[1] NOUN **1** = **strongroom**, repository, depository **2** = **crypt**, tomb, catacomb, cellar, mausoleum, charnel house, undercroft

vault[2] VERB = **jump**, spring, leap, clear, bound, hurdle

veer VERB = **change direction**, turn, swerve, shift, sheer, change course

vehicle NOUN **1** = **conveyance**,

machine, motor vehicle
2 = **medium**, means, channel, mechanism, organ, apparatus

veil NOUN **1** = **mask**, cover, shroud, film, curtain, cloak **2** = **screen**, mask, disguise, blind **3** = **film**, cover, curtain, cloak, shroud
▷ VERB = **cover**, screen, hide, mask, shield, disguise, conceal, obscure ≠ reveal

veiled ADJECTIVE = **disguised**, implied, hinted at, covert, masked, concealed, suppressed

vein NOUN **1** = **blood vessel**
2 = **mood**, style, note, tone, mode, temper, tenor **3** = **seam**, layer, stratum, course, current, bed, deposit, streak

velocity NOUN = **speed**, pace, rapidity, quickness, swiftness

vengeance NOUN = **revenge**, retaliation, reprisal, retribution, requital ≠ forgiveness

vent NOUN = **outlet**, opening, aperture, duct, orifice
▷ VERB = **express**, release, voice, air, discharge, utter, emit, pour out ≠ hold back

venture VERB **1** = **go**, travel, journey, set out, wander, stray, plunge into, rove **2** = **dare**, presume, have the courage to, be brave enough, hazard, go out on a limb (*informal*), take the liberty, go so far as **3** = **put forward**, volunteer
▷ NOUN = **undertaking**, project, enterprise, campaign, risk, operation, activity, scheme

verbal ADJECTIVE = **spoken**, oral,

word-of-mouth, unwritten

verdict NOUN = **decision**, finding, judgment, opinion, sentence, conclusion, conviction, adjudication

verge NOUN **1** = **brink**, point, edge, threshold **2** (*Brit.*) = **border**, edge, margin, limit, boundary, threshold, brim ▷ PHRASE: **verge on something** = **come near to**, approach, border on, resemble, incline to, be similar to, touch on, be more or less

verify VERB **1** = **check**, make sure, examine, monitor, inspect **2** = **confirm**, prove, substantiate, support, validate, bear out, corroborate, authenticate ≠ disprove

versatile ADJECTIVE
1 = **adaptable**, flexible, all-round, resourceful, multifaceted ≠ unadaptable **2** = **all-purpose**, variable, adjustable ≠ limited

versed ADJECTIVE *with* **in** = **knowledgeable**, experienced, seasoned, familiar, practised, acquainted, well-informed, proficient ≠ ignorant

version NOUN **1** = **form**, variety, variant, sort, class, design, style, model **2** = **adaptation**, edition, interpretation, form, copy, rendering, reproduction, portrayal **3** = **account**, report, description, record, reading, story, view, understanding

vertical ADJECTIVE = **upright**, sheer, perpendicular, straight (up and down), erect, plumb, on

V

end, precipitous, vertiginous
≠ horizontal

very ADVERB = **extremely**, highly, greatly, really, deeply, unusually, profoundly, decidedly
▷ ADJECTIVE 1 = **exact**, precise, selfsame 2 = **ideal**

● **WORD POWER**
● In strict usage, adverbs of
● degree such as *very*, *too*, *quite*,
● *really*, and *extremely* are used
● only to qualify adjectives: *he*
● *is very happy*; *she is too sad*. By
● this rule, these words should
● not be used to qualify past
● participles that follow the verb
● *to be*, since they would then be
● technically qualifying verbs.
● With the exception of certain
● participles, such as *tired* or
● *disappointed*, that have come
● to be regarded as adjectives,
● all other past participles are
● qualified by adverbs such
● as *much*, *greatly*, *seriously*, or
● *excessively*: *he has been much* (not
● *very*) *inconvenienced*; *she has been*
● *excessively* (not *too*) *criticized*.

vessel NOUN 1 = **ship**, boat, craft 2 = **container**, receptacle, can, bowl, tank, pot, drum, barrel

vest VERB ▷ PHRASES: **vest in something** *or* **someone** *usually passive* = **place**, invest, entrust, settle, confer, endow, bestow, consign; **vest with something** *usually passive* = **endow with**, entrust with

vet VERB = **check**, examine, investigate, review, appraise, scrutinize

veteran NOUN = **old hand**, past master, warhorse (*informal*), old stager ≠ novice
▷ MODIFIER = **long-serving**, seasoned, experienced, old, established, qualified, mature, practised

veto NOUN = **ban**, dismissal, rejection, vetoing, boycott, embargo, prohibiting, prohibition ≠ ratification
▷ VERB = **ban**, block, reject, rule out, turn down, forbid, boycott, prohibit ≠ pass

viable ADJECTIVE = **workable**, practical, feasible, suitable, realistic, operational, applicable, usable ≠ unworkable

vibrant ADJECTIVE 1 = **energetic**, dynamic, sparkling, vivid, spirited, storming, alive, vigorous 2 = **vivid**, bright, brilliant, intense, clear, rich, glowing

vice NOUN 1 = **fault**, failing, weakness, limitation, defect, deficiency, flaw, shortcoming ≠ good point 2 = **wickedness**, evil, corruption, sin, depravity, immorality, iniquity, turpitude ≠ virtue

vice versa ADVERB = **the other way round**, conversely, in reverse, contrariwise

vicious ADJECTIVE 1 = **savage**, brutal, violent, cruel, ferocious, barbarous ≠ gentle 2 = **malicious**, vindictive, spiteful, mean, cruel, venomous

victim NOUN 1 = **casualty**,

V

sufferer, fatality ≠ survivor
2 = **scapegoat**, sacrifice, martyr
victor NOUN = **winner**, champion,
conqueror, vanquisher,
prizewinner ≠ loser
victorious ADJECTIVE = **winning**,
successful, triumphant,
first, champion, conquering,
vanquishing, prizewinning
≠ losing
victory NOUN = **win**, success,
triumph, conquest, walkover
(*informal*) ≠ defeat
vie VERB *with* **with** *or* **for**
= **compete**, struggle, contend,
strive
view NOUN **1** *sometimes plural*
= **opinion**, belief, feeling, attitude,
impression, conviction, point
of view, sentiment **2** = **scene**,
picture, sight, prospect,
perspective, landscape, outlook,
spectacle **3** = **vision**, sight,
visibility, perspective, eyeshot
▷ VERB = **regard**, see, consider,
perceive, treat, estimate, reckon,
deem
viewer NOUN = **watcher**, observer,
spectator, onlooker
vigorous ADJECTIVE
1 = **strenuous**, energetic,
arduous, hard, taxing, active,
rigorous **2** = **spirited**, lively,
energetic, active, dynamic,
animated, forceful, feisty
(*informal*) ≠ lethargic **3** = **strong**,
powerful, lively, lusty ≠ weak
vigorously ADVERB
1 = **energetically**, hard,
forcefully, strongly, strenuously,

lustily **2** = **forcefully**, strongly,
vehemently, strenuously
vigour *or* (*U.S.*) **vigor** NOUN
= **energy**, vitality, power, spirit,
strength, animation, verve, gusto
≠ weakness
vile ADJECTIVE **1** = **wicked**,
evil, corrupt, perverted,
degenerate, depraved, nefarious
≠ honourable **2** = **disgusting**,
foul, revolting, offensive, nasty,
sickening, horrid, repulsive, yucko
(*Austral. slang*) ≠ pleasant
villain NOUN **1** = **evildoer**,
criminal, rogue, scoundrel,
wretch, reprobate, miscreant,
blackguard, wrong 'un (*Austral.
slang*) **2** = **baddy** (*informal*),
antihero ≠ hero
vindicate VERB **1** = **clear**, acquit,
exonerate, absolve, let off the
hook, exculpate ≠ condemn
2 = **support**, defend, excuse,
justify
vintage NOUN (*of a wine*)
= **harvest**
▷ ADJECTIVE **1** (*of a wine*)
= **high-quality**, best, prime,
quality, choice, select, superior
2 = **classic**, old, veteran, historic,
heritage, enduring, antique,
timeless
violate VERB **1** = **break**, infringe,
disobey, transgress, ignore,
defy, disregard, flout ≠ obey
2 = **invade**, infringe on, disturb,
upset, shatter, disrupt, impinge
on, encroach on **3** = **desecrate**,
profane, defile, abuse, pollute,
deface, dishonour, vandalize

≠ honour **4** = **rape**, molest, sexually assault, ravish, abuse, assault, interfere with, sexually abuse

violation NOUN **1** = **breach**, abuse, infringement, contravention, abuse, trespass, transgression, infraction
2 = **invasion**, intrusion, trespass, breach, disturbance, disruption, interruption, encroachment
3 = **desecration**, sacrilege, defilement, profanation, spoliation **4** = **rape**, sexual assault, molesting, ravishing (*old-fashioned*), abuse, sexual abuse, indecent assault, molestation

violence NOUN **1** = **brutality**, bloodshed, savagery, fighting, terrorism **2** = **force**, power, strength, might, ferocity, forcefulness, powerfulness
3 = **intensity**, force, cruelty, severity, fervour, vehemence

violent ADJECTIVE **1** = **brutal**, aggressive, savage, wild, fierce, bullying, cruel, vicious ≠ gentle
2 = **sharp 3** = **passionate**, uncontrollable, unrestrained
4 = **fiery**, fierce, passionate

VIP NOUN = **celebrity**, big name, star, somebody, luminary, big hitter (*informal*), heavy hitter (*informal*)

virgin NOUN = **maiden**, girl (*archaic*)
▷ ADJECTIVE = **pure**, chaste, immaculate, virginal, vestal, uncorrupted, undefiled ≠ corrupted

virtual ADJECTIVE = **practical**, essential, in all but name

virtually ADVERB = **practically**, almost, nearly, in effect, in essence, as good as, in all but name

virtue NOUN **1** = **goodness**, integrity, worth, morality, righteousness, probity, rectitude, incorruptibility ≠ vice **2** = **merit**, strength, asset, plus (*informal*), attribute, good point, strong point ≠ failing **3** = **advantage**, benefit, merit, credit, usefulness, efficacy

visible ADJECTIVE = **perceptible**, observable, clear, apparent, evident, manifest, in view, discernible ≠ invisible

vision NOUN **1** = **image**, idea, dream, plans, hopes, prospect, ideal, concept **2** = **hallucination**, illusion, apparition, revelation, delusion, mirage, chimera
3 = **sight**, seeing, eyesight, view, perception **4** = **foresight**, imagination, perception, insight, awareness, inspiration, innovation, creativity

visionary ADJECTIVE
1 = **idealistic**, romantic, unrealistic, utopian, speculative, impractical, unworkable, quixotic ≠ realistic **2** = **prophetic**, mystical, predictive, oracular, sibylline
▷ NOUN **1** = **idealist**, romantic, dreamer, daydreamer ≠ realist
2 = **prophet**, diviner, mystic, seer, soothsayer, sibyl, scryer, spaewife

V

(*Scot.*)

visit VERB 1 = **call on**, drop in on (*informal*), stop by, look up, go see (*U.S.*), swing by (*informal*) 2 = **stay at**, stay with, spend time with 3 = **stay in**, stop by
▷ NOUN 1 = **call**, social call 2 = **trip**, stop, stay, break, tour, holiday, vacation (*informal*), stopover

visitor NOUN = **guest**, caller, company, manu(w)hiri (*N.Z.*)

vista NOUN = **view**, scene, prospect, landscape, panorama, perspective

visual ADJECTIVE 1 = **optical**, optic, ocular 2 = **observable**, visible, perceptible, discernible ≠ imperceptible

vital ADJECTIVE 1 = **essential**, important, necessary, key, basic, significant, critical, crucial ≠ unnecessary 2 = **lively**, vigorous, energetic, spirited, dynamic, animated, vibrant, vivacious ≠ lethargic

vitality NOUN = **energy**, vivacity, life, strength, animation, vigour, exuberance, liveliness ≠ lethargy

vivid ADJECTIVE 1 = **clear**, detailed, realistic, telling, moving, affecting, arresting, powerful ≠ vague 2 = **bright**, brilliant, intense, clear, rich, glowing, colourful ≠ dull

vocabulary NOUN 1 = **language**, words, lexicon 2 = **wordbook**, dictionary, glossary, lexicon

vocal ADJECTIVE 1 = **outspoken**, frank, forthright, strident, vociferous, articulate, expressive, eloquent ≠ quiet 2 = **spoken**, voiced, uttered, oral, said

vocation NOUN = **profession**, calling, job, trade, career, mission, pursuit

vogue NOUN = **fashion**, trend, craze, style, mode, passing fancy, dernier cri (*French*)

voice NOUN 1 = **tone**, sound, articulation 2 = **utterance** 3 = **opinion**, will, feeling, wish, desire 4 = **say**, view, vote, comment, input
▷ VERB = **express**, declare, air, raise, reveal, mention, mouth, pronounce ▷ RELATED WORD: *adjective* **vocal**

void ADJECTIVE = **invalid**, null and void, inoperative, useless, ineffective, worthless
▷ NOUN 1 = **gap**, space, lack, hole, emptiness 2 = **emptiness**, space, vacuum, oblivion, blankness, nullity, vacuity
▷ VERB = **invalidate**, nullify, cancel, withdraw, reverse, undo, repeal, quash

volatile ADJECTIVE 1 = **changeable**, shifting, variable, unsettled, unstable, explosive, unreliable, unsteady ≠ stable 2 = **temperamental**, erratic, mercurial, up and down (*informal*), fickle, over-emotional ≠ calm

volley NOUN = **barrage**, blast, burst, shower, hail, bombardment, salvo, fusillade

volume NOUN 1 = **amount**, quantity, level, body, total,

measure, degree, mass
2 = **capacity**, size, mass, extent, proportions, dimensions, bulk, measurements **3** = **book**, work, title, opus, publication, manual, tome, treatise **4** = **loudness**, sound, amplification

voluntarily ADVERB = **willingly**, freely, by choice, off your own bat, of your own accord, of your own volition

voluntary ADJECTIVE
1 = **intentional**, deliberate, planned, calculated, wilful ≠ unintentional **2** = **optional**, discretionary, up to the individual, open, unforced, at your discretion, open to choice ≠ obligatory **3** = **unpaid**, free, willing, pro bono (*law*)

volunteer VERB = **offer**, step forward ≠ refuse

vomit VERB **1** = **be sick**, throw up (*informal*), spew, chuck (*Austral. & N.Z. informal*), heave (*slang*), retch **2** *often with* **up** = **bring up**, throw up, regurgitate, emit (*informal*), disgorge, spew out *or* up

vote NOUN = **poll**, election, ballot, referendum, popular vote, plebiscite, straw poll, show of hands
▷ VERB = **cast your vote**

voucher NOUN = **ticket**, token, coupon, pass, slip, chit, chitty (*Brit. informal*), docket

vow NOUN = **promise**, commitment, pledge, oath, profession, avowal
▷ VERB = **promise**, pledge, swear, commit, engage, affirm, avow, bind yourself

voyage NOUN = **journey**, trip, passage, expedition, crossing, sail, cruise, excursion
▷ VERB = **travel**, journey, tour, cruise, steam, take a trip, go on an expedition

vulgar ADJECTIVE **1** = **tasteless**, common ≠ tasteful **2** = **crude**, rude, coarse, indecent, tasteless, risqué, ribald **3** = **uncouth**, unrefined, impolite, ill-bred ≠ refined

vulnerable ADJECTIVE
1 = **susceptible**, helpless, unprotected, defenceless, exposed, weak, sensitive, tender ≠ immune **2** (*military*) = **exposed**, open, unprotected, defenceless, accessible, wide open, assailable ≠ well-protected

V

Ww

waddle VERB = **shuffle**, totter, toddle, sway, wobble

wade VERB 1 = **paddle**, splash, splash about, slop 2 = **walk through**, cross, ford, travel across

wag VERB 1 = **wave**, shake, waggle, stir, quiver, vibrate, wiggle 2 = **waggle**, wave, shake, flourish, brandish, wobble, wiggle 3 = **shake**, bob, nod
▷ NOUN 1 = **wave**, shake, quiver, vibration, wiggle, waggle 2 = **nod**, bob, shake

wage NOUN *often plural* = **payment**, pay, remuneration, fee, reward, income, allowance, recompense
▷ VERB = **engage in**, conduct, pursue, carry on, undertake, practise, prosecute, proceed with

wail VERB = **cry**, weep, grieve, lament, howl, bawl, yowl
▷ NOUN = **cry**, moan, howl, lament, yowl

wait VERB 1 = **stay**, remain, stop, pause, rest, linger, loiter, tarry ≠ go 2 = **stand by**, hold back, hang fire 3 = **be postponed**, be suspended, be delayed, be put off, be put back, be deferred, be put on hold (*informal*), be shelved
▷ NOUN = **delay**, gap, pause, interval, stay, rest, halt, hold-up

waiter NOUN = **attendant**, server, flunkey, steward, servant

waitress NOUN = **attendant**, server, stewardess, servant

waive VERB 1 = **give up**, relinquish, renounce, forsake, drop, abandon, set aside, dispense with ≠ claim 2 = **disregard**, ignore, discount, overlook, set aside, pass over, dispense with, brush aside

wake¹ VERB 1 = **awake**, stir, awaken, come to, arise, get up, rouse, get out of bed ≠ fall asleep 2 = **awaken**, arouse, rouse, waken 3 = **evoke**, recall, renew, stimulate, revive, induce, arouse, call up
▷ NOUN = **vigil**, watch, funeral, deathwatch, tangi (*N.Z.*)

● **WORD POWER**
● Both *wake* and its synonym
● *waken* can be used either with
● or without an object: *I woke/*
● *wakened my sister*, and also
● *I woke/wakened (up) at noon.*
● *Wake, wake up*, and occasionally
● *waken*, can also be used in a
● figurative sense, for example
● *seeing him again woke painful*
● *memories*; and *it's time he woke*
● *up to his responsibilities*. The
● verbs *awake* and *awaken* are
● more commonly used in the
● figurative than the literal
● sense, for example *he awoke to*
● *the danger he was in.*

wake² NOUN = **slipstream**, wash, trail, backwash, train, track, waves, path ▷ PHRASE: **in the**

wake of = **in the aftermath of**, following, because of, as a result of, on account of, as a consequence of

walk VERB 1 = **stride**, stroll, go, move, step, march, pace, hike 2 = **travel on foot** 3 = **escort**, take, see, show, partner, guide, conduct, accompany
▷ NOUN 1 = **stroll**, hike, ramble, march, trek, trudge, promenade, saunter 2 = **gait**, step, bearing, carriage, tread 3 = **path**, footpath, track, way, road, lane, trail, avenue, berm (*N.Z.*)
▷ PHRASE: **walk of life** = **area**, calling, business, line, trade, class, field, career

walker NOUN = **hiker**, rambler, wayfarer, pedestrian

wall NOUN 1 = **partition**, screen, barrier, enclosure 2 = **barrier**, obstacle, barricade, obstruction, check, bar, fence, impediment

wallet NOUN = **purse**, pocketbook, pouch, case, holder, money-bag

wander VERB = **roam**, walk, drift, stroll, range, stray, ramble, prowl
▷ NOUN = **excursion**, walk, stroll, cruise, ramble, meander, promenade, mosey (*informal*)

wanderer NOUN = **traveller**, rover, nomad, drifter, gypsy, explorer, rambler, voyager

wane VERB 1 = **decline**, weaken, diminish, fail, fade, decrease, dwindle, lessen ≠ grow 2 = **diminish**, decrease, dwindle ≠ wax

want VERB 1 = **wish for**, desire, long for, crave, covet, hope for, yearn for, thirst for ≠ have 2 = **need**, demand, require, call for 3 = **should**, need, must, ought 4 = **desire**, long for, crave, wish for, yearn for, thirst for, hanker after, burn for 5 = **lack**, need, require, miss
▷ NOUN 1 = **lack**, need, absence, shortage, deficiency, famine, scarcity, dearth ≠ abundance 2 = **poverty**, hardship, privation, penury, destitution, neediness, pennilessness ≠ wealth 3 = **wish**, will, need, desire, requirement, longing, appetite, craving

wanting ADJECTIVE 1 = **deficient**, poor, inadequate, insufficient, faulty, defective, imperfect, unsound, bodger *or* bodgie (*Austral. slang*) ≠ adequate 2 = **lacking**, missing, absent, incomplete, short, shy ≠ complete

war NOUN 1 = **conflict**, drive, attack, fighting, fight, operation, battle, movement ≠ peace 2 = **campaign**, drive, attack, operation, movement, push, mission, offensive
▷ VERB = **fight**, battle, clash, wage war, campaign, combat, do battle, take up arms ≠ make peace

ward NOUN 1 = **room**, department, unit, quarter, division, section, apartment, cubicle 2 = **district**, constituency, area, division, zone, parish, precinct 3 = **dependant**, charge, pupil, minor, protégé
▷ PHRASES: **ward someone**

W

off = **drive off**, resist, fight off, hold off, repel, fend off; **ward something off 1** = **avert**, fend off, stave off, avoid, frustrate, deflect, repel **2** = **parry**, avert, deflect, avoid, repel, turn aside

warden NOUN **1** = **steward**, guardian, administrator, superintendent, caretaker, curator, custodian **2** (*chiefly U.S. & Canad.*) = **jailer**, prison officer, guard, screw (*slang*) **3** (*Brit.*) = **governor**, head, leader, director, manager, chief, executive, commander, baas (*S. African*) **4** = **ranger**, keeper, guardian, protector, custodian, official

wardrobe NOUN **1** = **clothes cupboard**, cupboard, closet (*U.S.*), cabinet **2** = **clothes**, apparel, attire

warehouse NOUN = **store**, depot, storehouse, repository, depository, stockroom

wares PLURAL NOUN = **goods**, produce, stock, products, stuff, commodities, merchandise

warfare NOUN = **war**, fighting, battle, conflict, combat, hostilities, enmity ≠ peace

warm ADJECTIVE **1** = **balmy**, mild, temperate, pleasant, fine, bright, sunny, agreeable ≠ cool **2** = **cosy**, snug, toasty (*informal*), comfortable, homely, comfy (*informal*) **3** = **moderately hot**, heated ≠ cool **4** = **thermal**, winter, thick, chunky, woolly ≠ cool **5** = **mellow**, relaxing, pleasant, agreeable, restful

6 = **affable**, kindly, friendly, affectionate, loving, tender, amicable, cordial ≠ unfriendly **7** = **near**, close, hot, near to the truth
▷ VERB = **warm up**, heat, thaw (out), heat up ≠ cool down
▷ PHRASE: **warm something** or **someone up** = **heat**, thaw, heat up

warmth NOUN **1** = **heat**, snugness, warmness, comfort, homeliness, hotness ≠ coolness **2** = **affection**, feeling, love, goodwill, kindness, tenderness, cordiality, kindliness ≠ hostility

warn VERB **1** = **notify**, tell, remind, inform, alert, tip off, give notice, make someone aware **2** = **advise**, urge, recommend, counsel, caution, commend, exhort, admonish

warning NOUN **1** = **caution**, information, advice, injunction, notification **2** = **notice**, notification, sign, alarm, announcement, alert, tip-off (*informal*), heads up (*U.S. & Canad.*) **3** = **omen**, sign, forecast, indication, prediction, prophecy, foreboding, portent, rahui (*N.Z.*) **4** = **reprimand**, admonition

warp VERB **1** = **distort**, bend, twist, buckle, deform, disfigure, contort, malform **2** = **become distorted**, bend, twist, contort, become deformed, become misshapen **3** = **pervert**, twist, corrupt, degrade, deprave, debase, debauch, lead astray

▷ NOUN = **twist**, bend, defect, flaw, distortion, imperfection, kink, contortion

warrant VERB = **call for**, demand, require, merit, rate, earn, deserve, permit

▷ NOUN = **authorization**, permit, licence, permission, authority, sanction

warranty NOUN = **guarantee**, promise, contract, bond, pledge, certificate, assurance, covenant

warrior NOUN = **soldier**, combatant, fighter, gladiator, trooper, man-at-arms

wary ADJECTIVE 1 = **suspicious**, sceptical, guarded, distrustful, chary 2 = **watchful**, careful, alert, cautious, vigilant, circumspect, heedful ≠ careless

wash VERB 1 = **clean**, scrub, sponge, rinse, scour, cleanse 2 = **launder**, clean, rinse, dry-clean 3 = **rinse**, clean, scrub, lather 4 = **bathe**, bath, clean yourself, soak, douse, scrub yourself down 5 = **move**, overcome, touch, upset, stir, disturb, perturb, surge through 6 (informal) used in negative constructions = **be plausible**, stand up, hold up, pass muster, hold water, stick, carry weight, be convincing

▷ NOUN 1 = **laundering**, cleaning, clean, cleansing 2 = **bathe**, dip, soak, scrub, rinse 3 = **backwash**, slipstream, path, trail, train, track, waves, aftermath 4 = **splash**, surge, swell, rise and fall, undulation 5 = **coat**, film, covering, layer, coating, overlay

▷ PHRASES: **wash something away** = **erode**, wear something away; **wash something** or **someone away** = **sweep away**, carry off, bear away

wasp NOUN

▷ see **ants, bees and wasps**

waste VERB 1 = **squander**, throw away, blow (slang), lavish, misuse, dissipate, fritter away ≠ save 2 followed by **away** = **wear out**, wither

▷ NOUN 1 = **squandering**, misuse, extravagance, frittering away, dissipation, wastefulness, prodigality ≠ saving 2 = **rubbish**, refuse, debris, scrap, litter, garbage, trash, leftovers 3 usually plural = **desert**, wilderness, wasteland

▷ ADJECTIVE 1 = **unwanted**, useless, worthless, unused, leftover, superfluous, unusable, supernumerary ≠ necessary 2 = **uncultivated**, wild, bare, barren, empty, desolate, unproductive, uninhabited ≠ cultivated ▷ PHRASE: **waste away** = **decline**, dwindle, wither, fade, crumble, decay, wane, wear out

● **WORD POWER**

● *Waste* and *wastage* are to some
● extent interchangeable, but
● many people think that *wastage*
● should not be used to refer
● to loss resulting from human
● carelessness, inefficiency, etc:

w

● *a waste* (not *a wastage*) *of time,*
● *money, effort,* etc.

watch VERB 1 = **look at**,
observe, regard, eye, see, view,
contemplate, eyeball (*slang*)
2 = **spy on**, follow, track, monitor,
keep an eye on, stake out, keep
tabs on (*informal*), keep watch on
3 = **guard**, keep, mind, protect,
tend, look after, shelter, take care
of
▷ NOUN 1 = **wristwatch**,
timepiece, chronometer
2 = **guard**, surveillance,
observation, vigil, lookout
watchdog NOUN 1 = **guardian**,
monitor, protector, custodian,
scrutineer 2 = **guard dog**
water NOUN 1 = **liquid**, H_2O, wai
(*N.Z.*) 2 *often plural* = **sea**, main,
waves, ocean, depths, briny
▷ VERB 1 = **sprinkle**, spray, soak,
irrigate, hose, dampen, drench,
douse, fertigate (*Austral.*) 2 = **get
wet**, cry, weep, become wet,
exude water ▷ PHRASE: **water
something down** = **dilute**,
weaken, water, doctor, thin
▷ RELATED WORD: *adjective*
aquatic
waterfall NOUN = **cascade**, fall,
cataract
wave VERB 1 = **signal**, sign,
gesture, gesticulate 2 = **guide**,
point, direct, indicate,
signal, motion, gesture, nod
3 = **brandish**, swing, flourish,
wag, shake 4 = **flutter**, flap, stir,
shake, swing, wag, oscillate
▷ NOUN 1 = **gesture**, sign,

signal, indication, gesticulation
2 = **ripple**, breaker, swell, ridge,
roller, billow 3 = **outbreak**, rash,
upsurge, flood, surge, ground
swell 4 = **stream**, flood, surge,
spate, current, flow, rush, tide
waver VERB 1 = **hesitate**, dither
(*chiefly Brit.*), vacillate, falter,
fluctuate, seesaw, hum and haw
≠ be decisive 2 = **flicker**, shake,
tremble, wobble, quiver, totter
wax VERB 1 = **increase**, grow,
develop, expand, swell, enlarge,
magnify ≠ wane 2 = **become
fuller**, enlarge
way NOUN 1 = **method**, means,
system, process, technique,
manner, procedure, mode
2 = **manner**, style, fashion, mode
3 *often plural* = **custom**, manner,
habit, style, practice, nature,
personality, wont, tikanga (*N.Z.*)
4 = **route**, direction, course,
road, path 5 = **access**, road,
track, channel, route, path, trail,
pathway 6 = **journey**, approach,
passage 7 = **distance**, length,
stretch
wayward ADJECTIVE = **erratic**,
unruly, unmanageable,
unpredictable, capricious,
ungovernable, inconstant
≠ obedient
weak ADJECTIVE 1 = **feeble**,
frail, debilitated, fragile, sickly,
puny, unsteady, infirm ≠ strong
2 = **slight**, faint, feeble, pathetic,
hollow 3 = **fragile**, brittle,
flimsy, fine, delicate, frail, dainty,
breakable 4 = **unsafe**, exposed,

vulnerable, helpless, unprotected, defenceless, unguarded ≠ secure **5** = **unconvincing**, unsatisfactory, lame, flimsy, pathetic ≠ convincing **6** = **tasteless**, thin, diluted, watery, runny, insipid ≠ strong

weaken VERB **1** = **reduce**, undermine, moderate, diminish, lessen, sap ≠ boost **2** = **wane**, diminish, dwindle, lower, flag, fade, lessen ≠ grow **3** = **sap the strength of** ≠ strengthen

weakness NOUN **1** = **frailty**, fatigue, exhaustion, fragility, infirmity, feebleness, decrepitude ≠ strength **2** = **liking**, appetite, penchant, soft spot, passion, inclination, fondness, partiality ≠ aversion **3** = **powerlessness**, vulnerability, meekness, spinelessness, timorousness, cravenness, cowardliness **4** = **inadequacy**, deficiency, transparency, lameness, hollowness, implausibility, flimsiness, unsoundness **5** = **failing**, fault, defect, deficiency, flaw, shortcoming, blemish, imperfection ≠ strong point

wealth NOUN **1** = **riches**, fortune, prosperity, affluence, money, opulence ≠ poverty **2** = **property**, capital, fortune **3** = **abundance**, plenty, richness, profusion, fullness, cornucopia, copiousness ≠ lack

wealthy ADJECTIVE = **rich**, prosperous, affluent, well-off,

flush (*informal*), opulent, well-heeled (*informal*), well-to-do, minted (*Brit. slang*) ≠ poor

wear VERB **1** = **be dressed in**, have on, sport (*informal*), put on **2** = **show**, present, bear, display, assume, put on, exhibit **3** = **deteriorate**, fray, wear thin ▷ NOUN **1** = **clothes**, things, dress, gear (*informal*), attire, costume, garments, apparel **2** = **damage**, wear and tear, erosion, deterioration, attrition, corrosion, abrasion ≠ repair ▷ PHRASE: **wear off** = **subside**, disappear, fade, diminish, decrease, dwindle, wane, peter out

wearing ADJECTIVE = **tiresome**, trying, fatiguing, oppressive, exasperating, irksome, wearisome ≠ refreshing

weary ADJECTIVE **1** = **tired**, exhausted, drained, worn out, done in (*informal*), flagging, fatigued, sleepy, clapped out (*Austral. & N.Z. informal*) ≠ energetic **2** = **tiring**, arduous, tiresome, laborious, wearisome ≠ refreshing ▷ VERB = **grow tired**, tire, become bored ≠ invigorate

weather NOUN = **climate**, conditions, temperature, forecast, outlook, meteorological conditions, elements ▷ VERB = **withstand**, stand, survive, overcome, resist, brave, endure, come through ≠ surrender to

weave VERB 1 = **knit**, intertwine, plait, braid, entwine, interlace
2 = **zigzag**, wind, crisscross
3 = **create**, tell, recount, narrate, build, relate, make up, spin

web NOUN 1 = **cobweb**, spider's web 2 = **mesh**, lattice 3 = **tangle**, network

wed VERB 1 = **get married to**, be united to ≠ divorce 2 = **get married**, marry, be united, tie the knot (*informal*), take the plunge (*informal*) ≠ divorce 3 = **unite**, combine, join, link, ally, blend, merge, interweave ≠ divide

wedding NOUN = **marriage**, nuptials, wedding ceremony, marriage service, wedding service

wedge VERB = **squeeze**, force, lodge, jam, crowd, stuff, pack, thrust
▷ NOUN = **block**, lump, chunk

weep VERB = **cry**, shed tears, sob, whimper, mourn, lament, blubber, snivel ≠ rejoice

weigh VERB 1 = **have a weight of**, tip the scales at (*informal*)
2 = **consider**, examine, contemplate, evaluate, ponder, think over, reflect upon, meditate upon 3 = **compare**, balance, contrast, juxtapose, place side by side 4 = **matter**, carry weight, count

weight NOUN 1 = **heaviness**, mass, poundage, load, tonnage
2 = **importance**, force, power, value, authority, influence, impact, import, mana (*N.Z.*)
▷ VERB 1 *often with* **down** = **load**

2 = **bias**, load, slant, unbalance

weird ADJECTIVE 1 = **strange**, odd, unusual, bizarre, mysterious, queer, eerie, unnatural ≠ normal
2 = **bizarre**, odd, strange, unusual, queer, unnatural, creepy (*informal*), freakish ≠ ordinary

welcome VERB 1 = **greet**, meet, receive, embrace, hail, karanga (*N.Z.*), mihi (*N.Z.*) ≠ reject
2 = **accept gladly**, appreciate, embrace, approve of, be pleased by, give the thumbs up to (*informal*), be glad about, express pleasure *or* satisfaction at
▷ NOUN = **greeting**, welcoming, reception, acceptance, hail, hospitality, salutation ≠ rejection
▷ ADJECTIVE 1 = **pleasing**, appreciated, acceptable, pleasant, desirable, refreshing, delightful, gratifying ≠ unpleasant
2 = **wanted** ≠ unwanted 3 = **free**

weld VERB 1 = **join**, link, bond, bind, connect, fuse, solder
2 = **unite**, combine, blend, unify, fuse

welfare NOUN 1 = **wellbeing**, good, interest, health, security, benefit, safety, protection
2 = **state benefit**, support, benefits, pensions, dole (*slang*), social security, unemployment benefit, state benefits, pogey (*Canad.*)

well¹ ADVERB 1 = **skilfully**, expertly, adeptly, professionally, correctly, properly, efficiently, adequately ≠ badly 2 = **satisfactorily**, nicely,

smoothly, successfully, pleasantly, splendidly, agreeably ≠ badly
3 = **thoroughly**, completely, fully, carefully, effectively, efficiently, rigorously **4** = **intimately**, deeply, fully, profoundly ≠ slightly
5 = **favourably**, highly, kindly, warmly, enthusiastically, approvingly, admiringly, with admiration ≠ unfavourably
6 = **considerably**, easily, very much, significantly, substantially, markedly **7** = **fully**, highly, greatly, amply, very much, thoroughly, considerably, substantially
8 = **possibly**, probably, certainly, reasonably, conceivably, justifiably **9** = **decently**, right, kindly, fittingly, fairly, properly, politely, suitably ≠ unfairly
10 = **prosperously**, comfortably, splendidly, in comfort, in (the lap of) luxury, without hardship
▷ **ADJECTIVE 1** = **healthy**, sound, fit, blooming, in fine fettle, in good condition ≠ ill
2 = **satisfactory**, right, fine, pleasing, proper, thriving ≠ unsatisfactory **3** = **advisable**, proper, agreeable ≠ inadvisable

well² NOUN = **hole**, bore, pit, shaft
▷ **VERB 1** = **flow**, spring, pour, jet, surge, gush, spurt, spout **2** = **rise**, increase, grow, mount, surge, intensify

wet ADJECTIVE **1** = **damp**, soaking, saturated, moist, watery, soggy, sodden, waterlogged ≠ dry
2 = **rainy**, damp, drizzly, showery, raining, pouring, drizzling,

teeming ≠ sunny **3** (*informal*) = **feeble**, soft, weak, ineffectual, weedy (*informal*), spineless, effete, timorous
▷ **VERB** = **moisten**, spray, dampen, water, soak, saturate, douse, irrigate, fertigate (*Austral.*) ≠ dry
▷ **NOUN 1** = **rain**, drizzle ≠ fine weather **2** = **moisture**, water, liquid, damp, humidity, condensation, dampness, wetness ≠ dryness

whack (*informal*) VERB = **strike**, hit, belt (*informal*), bang, smack, thrash, thump, swipe
▷ **NOUN 1** = **blow**, hit, stroke, belt (*informal*), bang, smack, thump, swipe **2** (*informal*) = **share**, part, cut (*informal*), bit, portion, quota **3** (*informal*) = **attempt**, go (*informal*), try, turn, shot (*informal*), crack (*informal*), stab (*informal*), bash (*informal*)

wharf NOUN = **dock**, pier, berth, quay, jetty, landing stage

wheel NOUN = **disc**, ring, hoop
▷ **VERB 1** = **push**, trundle, roll
2 = **turn**, swing, spin, revolve, rotate, whirl, swivel **3** = **circle**, round, twirl, gyrate

whereabouts PLURAL NOUN = **position**, situation, site, location

whiff NOUN = **smell**, hint, scent, sniff, aroma, odour

whim NOUN = **impulse**, caprice, fancy, urge, notion

whine VERB **1** = **cry**, sob, wail, whimper, sniffle, snivel, moan
2 = **complain**, grumble, gripe

- **WHALES AND DOLPHINS**
- baleen whale
- beluga
- blue whale or sulphur-bottom
- bottlenose dolphin
- bowhead
- humpback whale
- killer whale, grampus, or orca
- narwhal
- porpoise
- right whale or (Austral.) bay whale
- rorqual
- sperm whale or cachalot
- toothed whale
- whalebone whale
- white whale

(informal), whinge (informal), moan, grouse, grizzle (informal, chiefly Brit.), grouch (informal)
▷ NOUN 1 = **cry**, moan, sob, wail, whimper 2 = **drone**, note, hum 3 = **complaint**, moan, grumble, grouse, gripe (informal), whinge (informal), grouch (informal)

whip NOUN = **lash**, cane, birch, crop, scourge, cat-o'-nine-tails
▷ VERB 1 = **lash**, cane, flog, beat, strap, thrash, birch, scourge 2 (informal) = **dash**, shoot, fly, tear, rush, dive, dart, whisk 3 = **whisk**, beat, mix vigorously, stir vigorously 4 = **incite**, drive, stir, spur, work up, get going, agitate, inflame

whirl VERB 1 = **spin**, turn, twist, rotate, twirl 2 = **rotate**, roll, twist, revolve, swirl, twirl, pirouette 3 = **feel dizzy**, swim, spin, reel, go round
▷ NOUN 1 = **revolution**, turn, roll, spin, twist, swirl, rotation, twirl 2 = **bustle**, round, series, succession, flurry, merry-go-round 3 = **confusion**, daze, dither (chiefly Brit.), giddiness

4 = **tumult**, spin
whisk VERB 1 = **flick**, whip, sweep, brush 2 = **beat**, mix vigorously, whip, fluff up
▷ NOUN 1 = **flick**, sweep, brush, whip 2 = **beater**, mixer, blender
whisper VERB 1 = **murmur**, breathe ≠ shout 2 = **rustle**, sigh, hiss, swish
▷ NOUN 1 = **murmur**, mutter, mumble, undertone 2 (informal) = **rumour**, report, gossip, goss (informal), innuendo, insinuation 3 = **rustle**, sigh, hiss, swish
white ADJECTIVE = **pale**, wan, pasty, pallid, ashen
▷ see **shades from black to white**
- **WORD POWER**
- *White* is a colour which has no
- hue due to the reflection of
- all light. White has long been
- associated in Western cultures
- with cleanliness and, by
- extension, purity and virginity,
- resulting in the expression
- *whiter than white*, meaning
- extremely white, clean, or pure.
- This focus on cleanliness is
- also evident in the expression

- *white-collar*, which denotes
- workers who are in professions
- that traditionally wore a white
- button-down shirt, rather than
- in manual labour. White is
- also associated with illness or
- severe emotional states, with
- the pallor of the face seen as a
- sign of ill-health or discomfort,
- in phrases like *white with*
- *fear*, *shock* or *anger*. White is
- sometimes used as a term
- relating to ethnic origin.

white-collar ADJECTIVE
= **clerical**, professional, salaried,
nonmanual

whittle VERB = **carve**, cut, hew,
shape, trim, shave, pare ▷ PHRASE:
whittle something away
= **undermine**, reduce, consume,
erode, eat away, wear away, cut
down, cut, decrease, prune, scale
down

whole NOUN = **unit**, ensemble,
entirety, totality ≠ part
▷ ADJECTIVE 1 = **complete**,
full, total, entire, uncut,
undivided, unabridged ≠ partial
2 = **undamaged**, intact,
unscathed, unbroken, untouched,
unharmed, in one piece
≠ damaged ▷ PHRASE: **on the**
whole 1 = **all in all**, altogether, all
things considered, by and large
2 = **generally**, in general, as a rule,
chiefly, mainly, mostly, principally,
on average

wholesale
ADJECTIVE = **extensive**, total,
mass, sweeping, broad,

comprehensive, wide-ranging,
blanket ≠ limited
▷ ADVERB = **extensively**,
comprehensively, across the
board, indiscriminately

wholly ADVERB = **completely**,
totally, perfectly, fully, entirely,
altogether, thoroughly, utterly
≠ partly

whore NOUN = **prostitute**, tart
(*informal*), streetwalker, call girl

wide ADJECTIVE 1 = **spacious**,
broad, extensive, roomy,
commodious ≠ confined
2 = **baggy**, full, loose, ample,
billowing, roomy, voluminous,
capacious 3 = **expanded**,
dilated, distended ≠ shut
4 = **broad**, extensive, wide-
ranging, large, sweeping, vast,
immense, expansive ≠ restricted
5 = **extensive**, general, far-
reaching, overarching 6 = **large**,
broad, vast, immense 7 = **distant**,
remote, off course, off target
▷ ADVERB 1 = **fully**, completely
≠ partly 2 = **off target**, astray, off
course, off the mark

widen VERB 1 = **broaden**, expand,
enlarge, dilate, spread, extend,
stretch ≠ narrow 2 = **get wider**,
spread, extend, expand, broaden
≠ narrow

widespread ADJECTIVE
= **common**, general, popular,
broad, extensive, universal, far-
reaching, pervasive ≠ limited

width NOUN = **breadth**, extent,
span, scope, diameter, compass,
thickness, girth

W

wield VERB 1 = **brandish**, flourish, manipulate, swing, use, manage, handle, employ 2 = **exert**, maintain, exercise, have, possess

wife NOUN = **spouse**, partner, mate, bride, better half (*humorous*), vrou (*S. African*), wahine (*N.Z.*), wifey (*informal*)

wild ADJECTIVE 1 = **untamed**, fierce, savage, ferocious, unbroken, feral, undomesticated, free, warrigal (*Austral. literary*) ≠ tame 2 = **uncultivated**, natural ≠ cultivated 3 = **stormy**, violent, rough, raging, choppy, tempestuous, blustery 4 = **excited**, crazy (*informal*), enthusiastic, raving, hysterical ≠ unenthusiastic 5 = **uncontrolled**, disorderly, turbulent, wayward, unruly, rowdy, unfettered, riotous ≠ calm 6 = **mad** (*informal*), furious, fuming, infuriated, incensed, enraged, very angry, irate, tooshie (*Austral. slang*), off the air (*Austral. slang*) 7 = **uncivilized**, fierce, savage, primitive, ferocious, barbaric, brutish, barbarous ≠ civilized ▷ PHRASE: **the wilds** = **wilderness**, desert, wasteland, middle of nowhere (*informal*), backwoods, back of beyond (*informal*)

wilderness NOUN = **wilds**, desert, wasteland, uncultivated region

will NOUN 1 = **determination**, drive, purpose, commitment, resolution, resolve, spine, backbone 2 = **wish**, mind, desire, intention, fancy, preference, inclination 3 = **choice**, prerogative, volition 4 = **decree**, wish, desire, command, dictate, ordinance 5 = **testament**, bequest(s), last wishes, last will and testament ▷ VERB 1 = **wish**, want, prefer, desire, see fit 2 = **bequeath**, give, leave, transfer, gift, hand on, pass on, confer

willing ADJECTIVE 1 = **inclined**, prepared, consenting, agreeable, compliant, amenable ≠ unwilling 2 = **ready**, game (*informal*) ≠ reluctant

willingly ADVERB = **readily**, freely, gladly, happily, eagerly, voluntarily, cheerfully, by choice ≠ unwillingly

willingness NOUN = **inclination**, will, agreement, wish, consent, volition ≠ reluctance

wilt VERB 1 = **droop**, wither, sag, shrivel 2 = **weaken**, languish, droop 3 = **wane**, flag, fade

win VERB 1 = **be victorious in**, succeed in, prevail in, come first in, be the victor in ≠ lose 2 = **be victorious**, succeed, triumph, overcome, prevail, conquer, come first, sweep the board ≠ lose 3 = **gain**, get, land, achieve, earn, secure, obtain, acquire ≠ forfeit ▷ NOUN = **victory**, success, triumph, conquest ≠ defeat ▷ PHRASE: **win someone over** *or* **round** = **convince**, influence, persuade, convert, sway, prevail upon, bring *or* talk round

wince VERB = **flinch**, start, shrink, cringe, quail, recoil, cower, draw back
▷ NOUN = **flinch**, start, cringe

wind¹ NOUN 1 = **air**, blast, hurricane, breeze, draught, gust, zephyr 2 = **flatulence**, gas 3 = **breath**, puff, respiration 4 = **nonsense**, talk, boasting, hot air, babble, bluster, humbug, twaddle (*informal*), bizzo (*Austral. slang*), bull's wool (*Austral. & N.Z. slang*) ▷ PHRASE: **get wind of something** = **hear about**, learn of, find out about, become aware of, be told about, be informed of, be made aware of, hear tell of

wind² VERB 1 = **meander**, turn, bend, twist, curve, snake, ramble, twist and turn 2 = **wrap**, twist, reel, curl, loop, coil 3 = **coil**, curl, spiral, encircle ▷ PHRASES: **wind someone up** (*informal*) 1 = **irritate**, excite, anger, annoy, exasperate, nettle, work someone up, pique 2 = **tease**, kid (*informal*), have someone on (*informal*), annoy, rag (*informal*), rib (*informal*), josh (*informal*), vex; **wind something up** 1 = **end**, finish, settle, conclude, tie up, wrap up, finalize 2 = **close down**, close, dissolve, terminate, put something into liquidation; **wind up** = **end up**, be left, finish up, fetch up (*informal*), land up

windfall NOUN = **godsend**, find, jackpot, bonanza, manna from heaven ≠ misfortune

windy ADJECTIVE = **breezy**, wild, stormy, windswept, blustery, gusty, squally, blowy ≠ calm

wing NOUN = **faction**, group, arm, section, branch
▷ VERB 1 = **fly**, soar, glide, take wing 2 = **wound**, hit, clip

wink VERB 1 = **blink**, bat, flutter 2 = **twinkle**, flash, shine, sparkle, gleam, shimmer, glimmer
▷ NOUN = **blink**, flutter

winner NOUN = **victor**, champion, master, champ (*informal*), conqueror, prizewinner ≠ loser

winning ADJECTIVE 1 = **victorious**, first, top, successful, unbeaten, conquering, triumphant, undefeated 2 = **charming**, pleasing, attractive, engaging, cute, disarming, enchanting, endearing ≠ unpleasant
▷ PLURAL NOUN = **spoils**, profits, gains, prize, proceeds, takings

wipe VERB 1 = **clean**, polish, brush, rub, sponge, mop, swab 2 = **erase**, remove
▷ NOUN = **rub**, brush ▷ PHRASE: **wipe something** *or* **someone out** = **destroy**, massacre, erase, eradicate, obliterate, annihilate, exterminate, expunge

wisdom NOUN = **understanding**, learning, knowledge, intelligence, judgment, insight, enlightenment, erudition ≠ foolishness

wise ADJECTIVE 1 = **sage**, clever, intelligent, sensible, enlightened, discerning, perceptive, erudite, grounded ≠ foolish 2 = **sensible**, clever, intelligent, prudent,

W

judicious ≠ unwise

wish NOUN = **desire**, want, hope, urge, intention, fancy (*informal*), ambition, yen (*informal*) ≠ aversion
▷ VERB = **want**, feel, choose, please, desire, think fit ▷ PHRASE: **wish for** = **desire**, want, hope for, long for, crave, aspire to, yearn for, hanker for

wit NOUN 1 = **humour**, quips, banter, puns, repartee, wordplay, witticisms, badinage ≠ seriousness 2 = **humorist**, card (*informal*), comedian, wag, joker, dag (*N.Z. informal*) 3 = **cleverness**, sense, brains, wisdom, common sense, intellect, ingenuity, acumen ≠ stupidity

witch NOUN = **enchantress**, magician, hag, crone, sorceress, Wiccan

witchcraft NOUN = **magic**, voodoo, wizardry, black magic, enchantment, occultism, sorcery, Wicca, makutu (*N.Z.*)

withdraw VERB 1 = **remove**, take off, pull out, extract, take away, pull back, draw out, draw back 2 = **take out**, extract, draw out

withdrawal NOUN = **removal**, ending, stopping, taking away, abolition, elimination, cancellation, termination

withdrawn ADJECTIVE = **uncommunicative**, reserved, retiring, distant, shy, taciturn, introverted, unforthcoming ≠ outgoing

wither VERB 1 = **wilt**, decline, decay, disintegrate, perish, shrivel ≠ flourish 2 = **waste**, decline, shrivel 3 = **fade**, decline, perish ≠ increase

withering ADJECTIVE = **scornful**, devastating, humiliating, snubbing, hurtful, mortifying

withhold VERB 1 = **keep secret**, refuse, hide, reserve, retain, conceal, suppress, hold back ≠ reveal 2 = **hold back**, suppress, keep back ≠ release

withstand VERB = **resist**, suffer, bear, oppose, cope with, endure, tolerate, stand up to ≠ give in to

witness NOUN 1 = **observer**, viewer, spectator, looker-on, watcher, onlooker, eyewitness, bystander 2 = **testifier**
▷ VERB 1 = **see**, view, watch, note, notice, observe, perceive 2 = **countersign**, sign, endorse, validate

witty ADJECTIVE = **humorous**, funny, clever, amusing, sparkling, whimsical, droll, piquant ≠ dull

wizard NOUN = **magician**, witch, shaman, sorcerer, occultist, magus, conjuror, warlock, tohunga (*N.Z.*)

wobble VERB 1 = **shake**, rock, sway, tremble, teeter, totter 2 = **tremble**, shake
▷ NOUN 1 = **unsteadiness**, shake, tremble 2 = **unsteadiness**, shake, tremor

woe NOUN 1 = **misery**, distress, grief, agony, gloom, sadness, sorrow, anguish ≠ happiness 2 = **problem**, grief, misery, sorrow

woman NOUN = **lady**, girl, female, sheila (*Austral. & N.Z. informal*), vrou (*S. African*), adult female, charlie (*Austral. slang*), chook (*Austral. slang*), wahine (*N.Z.*) ≠ man

womanly ADJECTIVE
1 = **feminine**, motherly, female, warm, tender, matronly, ladylike 2 = **curvaceous**, ample, voluptuous, shapely, curvy (*informal*), busty (*informal*), buxom, full-figured

wonder VERB 1 = **think**, question, puzzle, speculate, query, ponder, meditate, conjecture 2 = **be amazed**, stare, marvel, be astonished, gape
▷ NOUN 1 = **amazement**, surprise, admiration, awe, fascination, astonishment, bewilderment, wonderment
2 = **phenomenon**, sight, miracle, spectacle, curiosity, marvel, prodigy, rarity

wonderful ADJECTIVE
1 = **excellent**, great (*informal*), brilliant, outstanding, superb, fantastic (*informal*), tremendous, magnificent, booshit (*Austral. slang*), exo (*Austral. slang*), sik (*Austral. slang*), rad (*informal*), phat (*slang*), schmick (*Austral. informal*) ≠ terrible 2 = **remarkable**, amazing, extraordinary, incredible, astonishing, staggering, startling, phenomenal ≠ ordinary

woo VERB 1 = **seek**, cultivate 2 = **court**, pursue

wood NOUN 1 = **timber**, planks, planking, lumber (*U.S.*)
2 = **woodland**, forest, grove, thicket, copse, coppice, bushland
3 = **firewood**, fuel, logs, kindling

wooded ADJECTIVE = **tree-covered**, forested, timbered, sylvan (*poetic*), tree-clad

wooden ADJECTIVE 1 = **made of wood**, timber, woody, ligneous
2 = **expressionless**, lifeless, deadpan, unresponsive

wool NOUN 1 = **fleece**, hair, coat
2 = **yarn**

word NOUN 1 = **term**, name, expression 2 = **chat**, tête-à-tête, talk, discussion, consultation, confab (*informal*), heart-to-heart, powwow (*informal*) 3 = **comment**, remark, utterance 4 = **message**, news, report, information, notice, intelligence, dispatch, communiqué, heads up (*U.S. & Canad.*) 5 = **promise**, guarantee, pledge, vow, assurance, oath
6 = **command**, order, decree, bidding, mandate
▷ VERB = **express**, say, state, put, phrase, utter, couch, formulate
▷ RELATED WORDS: *adjective* **lexical, verbal**

wording NOUN = **phraseology**, words, language, phrasing, terminology

work VERB 1 = **be employed**, be in work 2 = **labour**, sweat, slave, toil, slog (away), drudge, peg away, exert yourself ≠ relax
3 = **function**, go, run, operate, be in working order ≠ be out of

W

order **4** = **succeed**, work out, pay off (*informal*), be successful, be effective, do the trick (*informal*), do the business (*informal*), get results **5** = **cultivate**, farm, dig, till, plough **6** = **operate**, use, move, control, drive, manage, handle, manipulate **7** = **manipulate**, form, fashion, shape, mould, knead

▷ NOUN **1** = **employment**, business, job, trade, duty, profession, occupation, livelihood ≠ play **2** = **effort**, industry, labour, sweat, toil, exertion, drudgery, elbow grease (*facetious*) ≠ leisure **3** = **task**, jobs, projects, commissions, duties, assignments, chores, yakka (*Austral. & N.Z. informal*) **4** = **handiwork**, doing, act, feat, deed **5** = **creation**, piece, production, opus, achievement, composition, handiwork

▷ PHRASE: **work out** = **solve**, find out, calculate, figure out

worker NOUN = **employee**, hand, labourer, workman, craftsman, artisan, tradesman

workman NOUN = **labourer**, hand, worker, employee, mechanic, operative, craftsman, artisan

works PLURAL NOUN **1** = **factory**, plant, mill, workshop
2 = **writings**, output, canon, oeuvre (*French*) **3** = **mechanism**, workings, parts, action, movement, machinery

workshop NOUN **1** = **factory**, plant, mill **2** = **workroom**, studio

world NOUN **1** = **earth**, planet, globe **2** = **mankind**, man, everyone, the public, everybody, humanity, humankind
3 = **sphere**, area, field, environment, realm, domain

▷ PHRASE: **a world of** = **a huge amount of**, a mountain of, a wealth of, a great deal of, a good deal of, an abundance of, an enormous amount of, a vast amount of

worldly ADJECTIVE **1** = **earthly**, physical, secular, terrestrial, temporal, profane ≠ spiritual
2 = **materialistic**, grasping, selfish, greedy ≠ nonmaterialistic
3 = **worldly-wise**, knowing, experienced, sophisticated, cosmopolitan, urbane, blasé ≠ naive

worn ADJECTIVE = **ragged**, frayed, shabby, tattered, tatty, threadbare, the worse for wear

worried ADJECTIVE = **anxious**, concerned, troubled, afraid, frightened, nervous, tense, uneasy ≠ unworried

worry VERB **1** = **be anxious**, be concerned, be worried, obsess, brood, fret, agonize, get in a lather (*informal*) ≠ be unconcerned
2 = **trouble**, upset, bother, disturb, annoy, unsettle, pester, vex ≠ soothe

▷ NOUN **1** = **anxiety**, concern, fear, trouble, unease, apprehension, misgiving, trepidation ≠ peace of mind

2 = **problem**, care, trouble, bother, hassle (*informal*)

worsen VERB 1 = **deteriorate**, decline, sink, decay, get worse, degenerate, go downhill (*informal*) ≠ improve 2 = **aggravate**, damage, exacerbate, make worse ≠ improve

worship VERB 1 = **revere**, praise, honour, adore, glorify, exalt, pray to, venerate ≠ dishonour 2 = **love**, adore, idolize, put on a pedestal ≠ despise
▷ NOUN = **reverence**, praise, regard, respect, honour, glory, devotion, adulation

worth NOUN 1 = **value**, price, rate, cost, estimate, valuation ≠ worthlessness 2 = **merit**, value, quality, importance, excellence, goodness, worthiness ≠ unworthiness 3 = **usefulness**, value, quality, importance, excellence, goodness ≠ uselessness

worthless ADJECTIVE 1 = **valueless**, rubbishy, negligible ≠ valuable 2 = **useless**, unimportant, ineffectual, negligible ≠ useful 3 = **good-for-nothing**, vile, despicable, contemptible ≠ honourable

worthwhile ADJECTIVE = **useful**, valuable, helpful, profitable, productive, beneficial, meaningful, constructive ≠ useless

worthy ADJECTIVE = **praiseworthy**, deserving, valuable, worthwhile, admirable, virtuous, creditable, laudable ≠ disreputable

would-be ADJECTIVE = **budding**, self-styled, wannabe (*informal*), unfulfilled, self-appointed

wound NOUN 1 = **injury**, cut, hurt, trauma (*pathology*), gash, lesion, laceration 2 *often plural* = **trauma**, offence, slight, insult
▷ VERB 1 = **injure**, cut, wing, hurt, pierce, gash, lacerate 2 = **offend**, hurt, annoy, sting, mortify, cut to the quick

wrangle VERB = **argue**, fight, row, dispute, disagree, contend, quarrel, squabble
▷ NOUN = **argument**, row, dispute, quarrel, squabble, bickering, tiff, altercation

wrap VERB 1 = **cover**, enclose, shroud, swathe, encase, enfold, bundle up 2 = **pack**, package, parcel (up), tie up, gift-wrap ≠ unpack 3 = **bind**, swathe ≠ unwind
▷ NOUN 1 = **cloak**, cape, stole, mantle, shawl ▷ PHRASE: **wrap something up 1** = **giftwrap**, pack, package, bundle up **2** (*informal*) = **end**, conclude, wind up, terminate, finish off, round off, polish off

wrath NOUN = **anger**, rage, temper, fury, resentment, indignation, ire, displeasure ≠ satisfaction

wreck VERB 1 = **destroy**, break, smash, ruin, devastate, shatter, spoil, demolish, kennet (*Austral. slang*), jeff (*Austral. slang*) ≠ build

W

2 = **spoil**, ruin, devastate, shatter, crool or cruel (*Austral. slang*) ≠ save

▷ NOUN 1 = **shipwreck**, hulk 2 (*wreckage*) = **remains**, pieces, ruin, fragments, debris, rubble

wrench VERB 1 = **twist**, force, pull, tear, rip, tug, jerk, yank
2 = **sprain**, strain, rick
▷ NOUN 1 = **twist**, pull, rip, tug, jerk, yank 2 = **sprain**, strain, twist
3 = **blow**, shock, upheaval, pang
4 = **spanner**, adjustable spanner

wrestle VERB = **fight**, battle, struggle, combat, grapple, tussle, scuffle

wrinkle NOUN 1 = **line**, fold, crease, furrow, crow's-foot, corrugation 2 = **crease**, fold, crumple, furrow, crinkle, corrugation
▷ VERB = **crease**, gather, fold, crumple, furrow, rumple, pucker, corrugate ≠ smooth

writ NOUN = **summons**, document, decree, indictment, court order, subpoena, arraignment

write VERB 1 = **record**, scribble, inscribe, set down, jot down
2 = **compose**, draft, pen, draw up 3 = **correspond**, get in touch, keep in touch, write a letter, drop a line, drop a note, e-mail

writer NOUN = **author**, novelist, hack, scribbler, scribe, wordsmith, penpusher
▷ *see* **dramatists, novelists, poets**

writing NOUN = **script**, hand, printing, fist (*informal*), scribble, handwriting, scrawl, calligraphy

wrong ADJECTIVE 1 = **amiss**, faulty, unsatisfactory, not right, defective, awry
2 = **incorrect**, mistaken, false, inaccurate, untrue, erroneous, wide of the mark, fallacious
3 = **inappropriate**, incorrect, unsuitable, unacceptable, undesirable, incongruous, unseemly, unbecoming ≠ correct
4 = **bad**, criminal, illegal, evil, unlawful, immoral, unjust, dishonest ≠ moral 5 = **defective**, faulty, awry, askew
▷ ADVERB 1 = **incorrectly**, badly, wrongly, mistakenly, erroneously, inaccurately ≠ correctly
2 = **amiss**, astray, awry, askew
▷ NOUN = **offence**, injury, crime, error, sin, injustice, misdeed, transgression ≠ good deed
▷ VERB = **mistreat**, abuse, hurt, harm, cheat, take advantage of, oppress, malign ≠ treat well

w

Xx

X-ray NOUN = **radiograph**, x-ray
image

Yy

yank VERB = **pull**, tug, jerk, seize, snatch, pluck, hitch, wrench
  ▷ NOUN = **pull**, tug, jerk, snatch, hitch, wrench, tweak
yarn NOUN 1 = **thread**, fibre, cotton, wool 2 (*informal*) = **story**, tale, anecdote, account, narrative, fable, reminiscence, urban myth
yawning ADJECTIVE = **gaping**, wide, huge, vast, cavernous
yearly ADJECTIVE = **annual**, each year, every year, once a year
  ▷ ADVERB = **annually**, every year, by the year, once a year, per annum
yearn VERB *often with* **for** = **long**, desire, hunger, ache, crave, covet, itch, hanker after
yell VERB = **scream**, shout, cry out, howl, call out, wail, shriek, screech ≠ whisper
  ▷ NOUN = **scream**, cry, shout, roar, howl, shriek, whoop, screech

≠ whisper
yellow NOUN = **lemon**, gold, amber
  ▷ ADJECTIVE
  ● **WORD POWER**
  ● *Yellow* is a colour which is
  ● often associated with the
  ● sun, warmth, and positivity.
  ● Conversely, there are a number
  ● of negative connotations
  ● associated with this colour
  ● to do with ageing, sickness,
  ● jealousy, cowardice, and
  ● betrayal. Paper yellows with
  ● age and plants turn yellow
  ● when they are diseased.
  ● Some illnesses, such as
  ● jaundice, cause yellowing in
  ● the skin. Formerly, jealousy
  ● was associated with yellow,
  ● because of the meaning
  ● 'jaundiced, biased in view',
  ● though this symbolism has
  ● now transferred to the colour
  ● green. The most common
  ● modern figurative meaning is
  ● that of cowardice. The slang
  ● term *yellow-belly* was used in
  ● the U.S. from the early 20th
  ● century to mean cowardly,

SHADES OF YELLOW
- amber
- buff
- canary yellow
- champagne
- cinnamon
- daffodil
- gold *or* golden
- lemon
- maize
- mustard
- oatmeal
- ochre
- old gold
- primrose
- saffron
- straw
- tea rose
- topaz
- tortoiseshell

- thought to be derived from
- the yellow underside of some
- animals and birds. Yellow
- has also been the colour of
- betrayal in Christian religious
- symbolism, with Judas
- portrayed by painters over the
- ages wearing a yellow cloak.

yen NOUN = **longing**, desire, craving, yearning, passion, hunger, ache, itch

yet ADVERB 1 = **so far**, until now, up to now, still, as yet, even now, thus far, up till now 2 = **now**, right now, just now, so soon 3 = **still**, in addition, besides, to boot, into the bargain

▷ CONJUNCTION = **nevertheless**, still, however, for all that, notwithstanding, just the same, be that as it may

- **WORD POWER**
- Yiddish is a language spoken
- mainly by Jews in Europe and
- America, and is a mixture
- of German, Hebrew, and
- Slavic languages. Yiddish has
- contributed many distinctive
- words to English; many of
- these remain slang words used
- primarily in the U.S.. A group
- of loan words from Yiddish and
- German have a characteristic
- 'sh' sound at the beginning:
- *shemozzle*, *schmuck*, *schlep*,
- *schlock*, *schmaltz*, *schmooze*,
- *shtick*, *shlub*. *Schmooze*,
- literally 'chat', means to talk
- to someone for the purpose
- of self-promotion, e.g. This

- was his chance to schmooze
- producers, distributors, and
- agents. Its onomatopoeic
- quality and similarity to 'ooze',
- have perhaps given schmooze
- connotations of insincere
- flattery, but it can simply
- mean to hobnob or mingle.
- Another word which has
- entered English from Yiddish
- is *schmaltz*. Literally 'melted
- fat', it refers to an animal fat
- used in cookery. It also means
- excessive sentimentality,
- especially in the arts, e.g.
- Finally, a boxing movie that
- doesn't descend into schmaltz
- or heroism. The widespread use
- of this word has also spawned
- the adjective *schmaltzy*. It
- is interesting to note that
- many of the synonyms for
- sentimental also refer to fatty,
- sweet, or creamy foodstuffs,
- e.g. cheesy, gooey, syrupy,
- saccharine. This food metaphor
- is often exploited in text:
- writers talk about drowning
- in schmaltz, and generous
- helpings of schmaltz, showing
- that its double meaning is still
- known.

yield VERB 1 = **bow**, submit, give in, surrender, succumb, cave in (*informal*), capitulate 2 = **relinquish**, resign, hand over, surrender, turn over, make over, give over, bequeath ≠ retain 3 = **produce**, give, provide, return, supply, bear, net, earn ≠ use up

y

▷ NOUN 1 = **produce**, crop, harvest, output 2 = **profit**, return, income, revenue, earnings, takings ≠ loss ≠ resist

yielding ADJECTIVE 1 = **soft**, pliable, springy, elastic, supple, spongy, unresisting 2 = **submissive**, obedient, compliant, docile, flexible, accommodating, pliant, acquiescent ≠ obstinate

yob or **yobbo** NOUN = **thug**, hooligan, lout, hoon (*Austral. & N.Z. slang*), ruffian, roughneck (*slang*), tsotsi (*S. African*), cougan (*Austral. slang*), scozza (*Austral. slang*), bogan (*Austral. slang*)

young ADJECTIVE 1 = **immature**, juvenile, youthful, little, green, junior, infant, adolescent ≠ old 2 = **early**, new, undeveloped, fledgling ≠ advanced
▷ NOUN = **offspring**, baby, litter, family, issue, brood, progeny ≠ parent

youngster NOUN = **youth**, girl, boy, kid (*informal*), lad, teenager, juvenile, lass

youth NOUN 1 = **immaturity**, adolescence, boyhood or girlhood, salad days ≠ old age 2 = **boy**, lad, youngster, kid (*informal*), teenager, young man, adolescent, teen (*informal*) ≠ adult

youthful ADJECTIVE = **young**, juvenile, childish, immature, boyish, girlish ≠ elderly

Zz

zeal NOUN = **enthusiasm**, passion, zest, spirit, verve, fervour, eagerness, gusto ≠ apathy

zero NOUN 1 = **nought**, nothing, nil 2 = **rock bottom**, the bottom, an all-time low, a nadir, as low as you can get

zip VERB = **speed**, shoot, fly, flash, zoom, whizz (*informal*)
▷ NOUN (*informal*) = **energy**, drive, vigour, verve, zest, gusto, liveliness ≠ lethargy

zone NOUN = **area**, region, section, sector, district, territory, belt, sphere

zoom VERB = **speed**, shoot, fly, rush, flash, dash, whizz (*informal*), hurtle

z

WORD
POWER
Supplement

CONTENTS

WORD POWER

CONTENTS

WORD POWER

ACTORS

Male

Woody Allen (*U.S.*)
Alan Arkin (*U.S.*)
Fred Astaire (*U.S.*)
Richard Attenborough (*English*)
Christian Bale (*English*)
Eric Bana (*Australian*)
Antonio Banderas (*Spanish*)
Jean-Louis Barrault (*French*)
John Barrymore (*U.S.*)
Alan Bates (*English*)
Warren Beatty (*U.S.*)
Jean-Paul Belmondo (*French*)
Alan Bennett (*English*)
Dirk Bogarde (*English*)
Humphrey Bogart (*U.S.*)
Charles Boyer (*French*)
Kenneth Branagh (*English*)
Marlon Brando (*U.S.*)
Adrien Brody (*U.S.*)
Mel Brooks (*U.S.*)
Richard Burbage (*English*)
Richard Burton (*Welsh*)
Glen Byam Shaw (*English*)
James Cagney (*U.S.*)
Michael Caine (*English*)
Simon Callow (*English*)
Robert Carlyle (*Scottish*)
Jim Carrey (*U.S.*)
Charlie Chaplin (*English*)
Maurice Chevalier (*French*)
John Cleese (*English*)
George Clooney (*U.S.*)
Sean Connery (*Scottish*)
Peter Cook (*English*)
Chris Cooper (*U.S.*)
Gary Cooper (*U.S.*)
Kevin Costner (*U.S.*)
Noel Coward (*English*)
Michael Crawford (*English*)
Russell Crowe (*Australian*)
Tom Cruise (*U.S.*)
James Dean (*U.S.*)
Robert De Niro (*U.S.*)
Gerard Depardieu (*French*)
Vittorio de Sica (*Italian*)
John Dexter (*English*)
Leonardo DiCaprio (*U.S.*)
Kirk Douglas (*U.S.*)
Michael Douglas (*U.S.*)
Clint Eastwood (*U.S.*)
Douglas Fairbanks Jr. (*U.S.*)

Douglas Fairbanks Snr. (*U.S.*)
Will Ferrell (*U.S.*)
WC Fields (*U.S.*)
Albert Finney (*English*)
Colin Firth (*English*)
Errol Flynn (*Australian*)
Henry Fonda (*U.S.*)
Harrison Ford (*U.S.*)
Jean Gabin (*France*)
Clark Gable (*U.S.*)
James Gandolfini (*U.S.*)
David Garrick (*English*)
Mel Gibson (*Australian*)
John Gielgud (*English*)
Kelsey Grammer (*U.S.*)
Cary Grant (*English-U.S.*)
Hugh Grant (*English*)
Alec Guinness (*English*)
Gene Hackman (*U.S.*)
Tom Hanks (*U.S.*)
Oliver Hardy (*U.S.*)
Rex Harrison (*English*)
Dustin Hoffman (*U.S.*)
Bob Hope (*U.S.*)
Anthony Hopkins (*Welsh*)
Michael Hordern (*English*)
Leslie Howard (*English*)
Trevor Howard (*English*)
Rock Hudson (*U.S.*)
Barry Humphries (*Australian*)
John Hurt (*English*)
Jeremy Irons (*English*)
Henry Irving (*English*)
Derek Jacobi (*English*)
Al Jolson (*U.S.*)
Boris Karloff (*English*)
Edmund Kean (*English*)
Buster Keaton (*U.S.*)
Harvey Keitel (*U.S.*)
Gene Kelly (*U.S.*)
John Kemble (*English*)
Ben Kingsley (*English*)
Burt Lancaster (*U.S.*)
Charles Laughton (*English-U.S.*)
Stan Laurel (*English-U.S.*)
Hugh Laurie (*English*)
Heath Ledger (*U.S.*)
Bruce Lee (*U.S.*)
Christopher Lee (*English*)
Harold Lloyd (*U.S.*)

Bela Lugosi (*Hungarian*)
Ewan McGregor (*Scottish*)
Ian McKellen (*English*)
Steve McQueen (*U.S.*)
William Macready (*English*)
James Mason (*English*)
Raymond Massey (*Canadian*)
Marcello Mastroianni (*Italian*)
Bernard Miles (*English*)
John Mills (*English*)
Robert Mitchum (*U.S.*)
Dudley Moore (*English*)
Robert Morley (*English*)
Sam Neill (*N.Z.*)
Paul Newman (*U.S.*)
Jack Nicholson (*U.S.*)
Liam Neeson (*Irish*)
David Niven (*English*)
Edward Norton (*U.S.*)
Gary Oldman (*English*)
Laurence Olivier (*English*)
Peter O'Toole (*Irish-British*)
Al Pacino (*U.S.*)
Gregory Peck (*U.S.*)
Donald Pleasence (*English*)
Anthony Quayle (*English*)
Anthony Quinn (*U.S.*)
Daniel Radcliffe (*English*)
Ronald Reagan (*U.S.*)
Robert Redford (*U.S.*)
Michael Redgrave (*English*)
Fernando Rey (*Spanish*)
Ralph Richardson (*English*)
Paul Robeson (*U.S.*)
Edward G Robinson (*U.S.*)
Tim Roth (*English*)
Arnold Schwarzenegger (*Austrian-U.S.*)
Paul Scofield (*English*)
Peter Sellers (*English*)
Charlie Sheen (*U.S.*)
Martin Sheen (*U.S.*)
Sam Shepard (*U.S.*)
Sylvester Stallone (*U.S.*)
Konstantin Stanislavsky (*Russian*)
James Stewart (*U.S.*)
Donald Sutherland (*Canadian*)
Kiefer Shepard (*Canadian*)
Jacques Tati (*French*)

4

Spencer Tracy (*U.S.*)
John Travolta (*U.S.*)
Peter Ustinov (*English*)
Rudolph Valentino (*Italian-U.S.*)

Max Von Sydow (*Swedish*)
Denzel Washington (*U.S.*)
John Wayne (*U.S.*)
Johnny Weissmuller (*U.S.*)
Orson Welles (*U.S.*)

Forest Whitaker (*U.S.*)
Bruce Willis (*U.S.*)
Elijah Wood (*U.S.*)

Female

Gillian Anderson (*U.S.*)
Jennifer Aniston (*U.S.*)
Yvonne Arnaud (*French*)
Peggy Ashcroft (*English*)
Tallulah Bankhead (*U.S.*)
Brigitte Bardot (*French*)
Ingrid Bergman (*Swedish-U.S.*)
Sarah Bernhardt (*French*)
Cate Blanchett (*Australian*)
Clara Bow (*U.S.*)
Fanny Brice (*U.S.*)
Glenn Close (*U.S.*)
Claudette Colbert (*French-U.S.*)
Joan Crawford (*U.S.*)
Clare Danes (*U.S.*)
Bette Davis (*U.S.*)
Geena Davis (*U.S.*)
Judy Davis (*Australian*)
Judi Dench (*English*)
Catherine Deneuve (*French*)
Marlene Dietrich (*German*)
Faye Dunaway (*U.S.*)
Edith Evans (*English*)
America Ferrera (*U.S.*)
Sally Field (*U.S.*)
Jane Fonda (*U.S.*)
Jodie Foster (*U.S.*)
Greta Garbo (*Swedish*)
Ava Gardner (*U.S.*)
Judy Garland (*U.S.*)
Jennifer Garner (*U.S.*)
Sarah Michelle Gellar (*U.S.*)
Lillian Gish (*U.S.*)

Joyce Grenfell (*English*)
Jean Harlow (*U.S.*)
Anne Hathaway (*U.S.*)
Audrey Hepburn (*Belgian-U.S.*)
Katharine Hepburn (*U.S.*)
Wendy Hiller (*English*)
Jennifer Hudson (*U.S.*)
Holly Hunter (*U.S.*)
Isabelle Huppert (*French*)
Glenda Jackson (*English*)
Diane Keaton (*U.S.*)
Grace Kelly (*U.S.*)
Fanny Kemble (*English-U.S.*)
Nicole Kidman (*Australian*)
Jessica Lange (*U.S.*)
Angela Lansbury (*English*)
Gertrude Lawrence (*English*)
Vivien Leigh (*English*)
Lotte Lenya (*Austrian*)
Margaret Lockwood (*English*)
Jennifer Lopez (*Puerto Rican*)
Sophia Loren (*Italian*)
Siobhan McKenna (*Irish*)
Shirley MacLaine (*U.S.*)
Melina Mercouri (*Greek*)
Liza Minnelli (*U.S.*)
Helen Mirren (*English*)
Marilyn Monroe (*U.S.*)
Jeanne Moreau (*French*)
Sarah Jessica Parker (*U.S.*)
Michelle Pfeiffer (*U.S.*)
Mary Pickford (*U.S.*)

Joan Plowright (*English*)
Jian Qing (*Chinese*)
Vanessa Redgrave (*English*)
Julia Roberts (*U.S.*)
Flora Robson (*English*)
Ginger Rogers (*U.S.*)
Rebecca Romijn (*U.S.*)
Margaret Rutherford (*English*)
Susan Sarandon (*U.S.*)
Jane Seymour (*English*)
Delphine Seyrig (*French*)
Sarah Siddons (*English*)
Simone Signoret (*French*)
Maggie Smith (*English*)
Meryl Streep (*U.S.*)
Barbra Streisand (*U.S.*)
Janet Suzman (*South African*)
Elizabeth Taylor (*English-U.S.*)
Shirley Temple (*U.S.*)
Ellen Terry (*English*)
Emma Thompson (*English*)
Sybil Thorndike (*English*)
Sigourney Weaver (*U.S.*)
Raquel Welch (*U.S.*)
Mae West (*U.S.*)
Billie Whitelaw (*English*)
Kate Winslet (*English*)
Peg Woffington (*Irish*)
Renée Zellweger (*U.S.*)
Catherine Zeta-Jones (*Welsh*)

WORD POWER

French regions

Alsace	Franche-Comté	Nord-Pas-de-Calais
Aquitaine	Guadeloupe	Pays de Loire
Auvergne	Guyane	Picardie
Basse-Normandie	Haute-Normandie	Poitou-Charentes
Bourgogne	Île-de-France	Provence-Alpes-Côte
Brittany	Languedoc-Roussillon	d'Azur
Burgundy	Limousin	Reunion
Centre	Lorraine	Rhône-Alpes
Champagne-Ardenne	Martinique	
Corsica	Midi-Pyrénées	

French départements

Ain	Gironde	Morbihan
Aisne	Guadeloupe	Moselle
Allier	Haut Rhin	Niveres
Alpes de Haute Provence	Haute Corse	Nord
Alpes Maritimes	Haute Garonne	Oise
Ardèche	Haute Loire	Orne
Ardennes	Haute Marne	Paris
Ariège	Haute Saône	Pas de Calais
Aube	Haute Savoie	Puy de Dôme
Aude	Haute Vienne	Pyrénées Atlantiques
Aveyron	Hautes Alpes	Pyrénées Orientales
Bas Rhin	Hautes Pyrénées	Réunion
Bouches du Rhône	Hauts de Seine	Rhône
Calvados	Hérault	Saône
Cantal	Ille et Vilaine	Saône et Loire
Charente	Indre	Sarthe
Charente Maritime	Indre et Loire	Savoie
Cher	Isère	Seine et Marne
Corrèze	Jura	Seine Maritime
Corse-du-Sud	Landes	Seine Saint Denis
Cote d'Or	Loir et Cher	Somme
Côtes du Nord	Loire	Tarn
Creuse	Loire Atlantique	Tarn et Garonne
Deux Sèvres	Loiret	Territoire de Belfort
Dordogne	Lot	Val d'Oise
Doubs	Lot et Garonne	Val de Marne
Drôme	Lozère	Var
Essone	Maine et Loire	Vaucluse
Eure	Manche	Vendée
Eure et Loir	Marne	Vienne
Finistère	Martinique	Vosges
Gard	Mayenne	Yonne
Gayane	Meurthe et Moselle	Yvelines
Gers	Meuse	

German states

Baden-Württemberg	Hessen	Saarland
Bavaria	Lower Saxony	Saxony
Berlin	Mecklenburg-West	Saxony-Anhalt
Brandenburg	Pomerania	Schleswig-Holstein
Bremen	North Rhine-Westphalia	Thuringia
Hamburg	Rhineland-Palatinate	

ADMINISTRATIVE REGIONS

Italian regions

Abruzzo	Friuli-Venezia Giulia	Molise	Trentino-Alto Adige
Basilicata	Lazio	Piedmont	Tuscany
Calabria	Liguria	Puglia	Umbria
Campania	Lombardy	Sardinia	Valle d'Aosta
Emilia-Romagna	Marche	Sicily	Veneto

Italian provinces

Agrigento	Catania	Lecce	Pavia	Siracusa
Alessandria	Catanzaro	Lecco	Perugia	Sondrio
Ancona	Chieti	Livorno	Pesaro	Taranto
Aosta	Como	Lodi	Pescara	Teramo
Arezzo	Cosenza	Lucca	Piacenza	Terni
Ascoli Piceno	Cremona	Macerata	Pisa	Torino
Asti	Crotone	Mantova	Pistoia	Trapani
Avellino	Cuneo	Massa Carrara	Pordenone	Trento
Bari	Enna	Matera	Potenza	Treviso
Belluno	Ferrara	Medio	Prato	Trieste
Benevento	Firenze	Campidano	Ragusa	Udine
Bergamo	Florence	Messina	Ravenna	Varese
Biella	Foggia	Milano	Reggio di	Venezia
Bologna	Forlì	Modena	Calabria	Verbania
Bolzano	Frosinone	Napoli	Reggio Emilia	Vercelli
Brescia	Genova	Novara	Rieti	Verona
Brindisi	Gorizia	Nuoro	Rimini	Vibo Valentia
Cagliari	Grosseto	Ogliastra	Roma	Vicenza
Caltanissetta	Imperia	Olbia-Tempio	Rovigo	Viterbo
Campobasso	Isernia	Oristano	Salerno	Repubblica di
Carbonia-	L'Aquila	Padova	Sassari	San Marino
Iglesias	La Spezia	Palermo	Savona	
Caserta	Latina	Parma	Siena	

Spanish regions

Andalucía	Castilla-La Mancha	Murcia
Aragón	Castilla-León	Navarra
Asturias	Catalonia	Valencian Community
Balearic Islands	Extremadura	Ceuta
Basque Country	Galicia	Melilla
Canary Islands	La Rioja	
Cantabria	Madrid	

Spanish provinces

Álava	Cádiz	Huelva	Murcia	Teruel
Albacete	Cantabria	Huesca	Navarra	Toledo
Alhucemas	Castellón	Jaén	Orense	Valencia
Alicante	Chafarinas	La Coruna	Palencia	Valladolid
Almerìa	Cordoba	La Rioja	Pontevedra	Vélez de la
Asturias	Cuenca	Las Palmas	Salamanca	Gomera
Ávila	Ceuta	León	Santa Cruz de	Vizcaya
Badajoz	Ciudad Real	Lleida	Tenerife	Zamora
Balearics	Girona	Lugo	Segovia	Zaragoza
Barcelona	Granada	Madrid	Sevilla	
Burgos	Gualalajara	Málaga	Soria	
Cácares	Guipúzcoa	Melilla	Tarragona	

WORD POWER

WORD POWER

Agostino di Duccio (*Italian*)
Josef Albers (*German-U.S.*)
Leon Battista Alberti (*Italian*)
Washington Allston (*U.S.*)
Lawrence Alma-Tadema (*Dutch-English*)
Albrecht Altdorfer (*German*)
Fra Angelico (*Italian*)
Pietro Annigoni (*Italian*)
Antonello da Messina (*Italian*)
Apelles (*Greek*)
Karel Appel (*Dutch*)
Aleksandr Porfiryevich Archipenko (*Russian*)
Giuseppe Arcimboldo (*Italian*)
Jean *or* Hans Arp (*French*)
John James Audubon (*U.S.*)
Frank Auerbach (*English-German*)
Francis Bacon (*Irish*)
Leon Nikolayevich Bakst (*Russian*)
Balthus (*Polish-French*)
Frédéric August Bartholdi (*French*)
Fra Bartolommeo (*Italian*)
Max Beckmann (*German*)
Vanessa Bell (*English*)
Giovanni Bellini (*Italian*)
Thomas Hart Benton (*U.S.*)
Gian Lorenzo Bernini (*Italian*)
Joseph Beuys (*German*)
Zarina Bhimji (*Ugandan*)
Peter Blake (*English*)
William Blake (*English*)
Umberto Boccioni (*Italian*)
David Bomberg (*English*)
Rosa Bonheur (*French*)
Pierre Bonnard (*French*)
Richard Parkes Bonnington (*English*)
Gutzon Borglum (*U.S.*)
Hieronymus Bosch (*Dutch*)
Sandro Botticelli (*Italian*)
Francois Boucher (*French*)
Eugène Boudin (*French*)
Arthur Boyd (*Australian*)
Donato Bramante (*Italian*)
Constantin Brancusi (*Romanian*)
Georges Braque (*French*)
Brassaï (*French*)

Agnolo Bronzino (*Italian*)
Ford Madox Brown (*English*)
Jan Brueghel (*Flemish*)
Pieter Brueghel the Elder (*Flemish*)
Pieter Brueghel the Younger (*Flemish*)
Bernard Buffet (*French*)
Edward Burne-Jones (*English*)
Edward Burra (*English*)
Reg Butler (*English*)
Alexander Calder (*U.S.*)
Callimachus (*Greek*)
Robert Campin (*Flemish*)
Antonio Canova (*Italian*)
Michelangelo Merisi da Caravaggio (*Italian*)
Anthony Caro (*English*)
Vittore Carpaccio (*Italian*)
Agostino Carracci (*Italian*)
Annibale Carracci (*Italian*)
Ludovico Carracci (*Italian*)
Mary Cassatt (*U.S.*)
Pietro Cavallini (*Italian*)
Benvenuto Cellini (*Italian*)
Lynn Chadwick (*English*)
Marc Chagall (*Russian-French*)
Philippe de Champaigne (*French*)
Jean-Baptiste Siméon Chardin (*French*)
Giorgio de Chirico (*Italian*)
Giovanni Cimabue (*Italian*)
Claude Lorrain (*French*)
François Clouet (*French*)
Jean Clouet (*French*)
Nathan Coley (*Scottish*)
John Constable (*English*)
John Copley (*U.S.*)
Jean Baptiste Camille Corot (*French*)
Antonio Allegri da Corregio (*Italian*)
Gustave Courbet (*French*)
David Cox (*English*)
Antoine Coypel (*French*)
Lucas Cranach (*German*)
Walter Crane (*English*)
John Crome (*English*)
Aelbert Cuyp *or* Kuyp (*Dutch*)
Paul Cézanne (*French*)
Richard Dadd (*English*)
Salvador Dalí (*Spanish*)
Francis Danby (*Irish*)

Charles François Daubigny (*French*)
Honoré Daumier (*French*)
Jacques Louis David (*French*)
Peter de Wint (*English*)
Hilaire Germain Edgar Degas (*French*)
Eugène Delacroix (*French*)
Paul Delaroche (*French*)
Robert Delaunay (*French*)
Paul Delvaux (*Belgian*)
Maurice Denis (*French*)
André Derain (*French*)
William Dobell (*Australian*)
Domenichino (*Italian*)
Domenico del Barbiere (*Italian*)
Donatello (*Italian*)
Gerrit Dou (*Dutch*)
George Russell Drysdale (*Australian*)
Jean Dubuffet (*French*)
Duccio di Buoninsegna (*Italian*)
Marcel Duchamp (*French-U.S.*)
Raoul Dufy (*French*)
Albrecht Dürer (*German*)
Thomas Eakins (*U.S.*)
El Greco (*Greek-Spanish*)
James Ensor (*Belgian*)
Jacob Epstein (*British*)
Max Ernst (*German*)
Henri Fantin-Latour (*French*)
Lyonel Feininger (*U.S.*)
John Flaxman (*English*)
Jean Fouquet (*French*)
Jean Honoré Fragonard (*French*)
Lucian Freud (*English*)
Caspar David Friedrich (*German*)
Roger Fry (*English*)
Henry Fuseli (*Swiss*)
Naum Gabo (*Russian-U.S.*)
Thomas Gainsborough (*English*)
Henri Gaudier-Brzeska (*French*)
Paul Gauguin (*French*)
Gentile da Fabriano (*Italian*)
Lorenzo Ghiberti (*Italian*)
Domenico Ghirlandaio (*Italian*)
Alberto Giacometti (*Swiss*)
Giambologna (*Italian*)

Grinling Gibbons (*Dutch*)
Gilbert (Proesch) and George (Passmore) (*English*)
Eric Gill (*English*)
Giorgione da Castelfranco (*Italian*)
Giotto di Bondone (*Italian*)
Giulio Romano (*Italian*)
Hugo van der Goes (*Flemish*)
Julio González (*Spanish*)
Arshile Gorky (*U.S.*)
Francisco de Goya (*Spanish*)
Jan van Goyen (*Dutch*)
Duncan Grant (*Scottish*)
Jean Baptiste Greuze (*French*)
Juan Gris (*Spanish*)
Antoine Jean Gros (*French*)
George Grosz (*German-U.S.*)
Grünewald (*German*)
Francesco Guardi (*Italian*)
François Gérard (*French*)
Théodore Géricault (*French*)
Frans Hals (*Dutch*)
Richard Hamilton (*English*)
Ando Hiroshige (*Japanese*)
Damien Hirst (*English*)
Meindert Hobbema (*Dutch*)
David Hockney (*English*)
Hans Hofmann (*German-U.S.*)
William Hogarth (*English*)
Katsushika Hokusai (*Japanese*)
Hans Holbein (*German*)
Winslow Homer (*U.S.*)
Pieter de Hooch *or* Hoogh (*Dutch*)
Edward Hopper (*U.S.*)
Jean Antoine Houdon (*French*)
William Holman Hunt (*English*)
Jean Auguste Dominique Ingres (*French*)
Augustus John (*Welsh*)
Gwen John (*Welsh*)
Jasper Johns (*U.S.*)
Johan Barthold Jongkind (*Dutch*)
Jacob Jordaens (*Flemish*)
Wassily Kandinsky (*Russian*)
Angelica Kauffmann (*Swiss*)
Ernst Ludwig Kirchner (*German*)

Ron B. Kitaj (*U.S.*)
Paul Klee (*Swiss*)
Gustav Klimt (*Austrian*)
Franz Kline (*U.S.*)
Godfrey Kneller (*German-English*)
Laura Knight (*English*)
Oscar Kokoschka (*Austrian*)
Willem de Kooning (*Dutch-U.S.*)
Leon Kossoff (*English*)
Georges de La Tour (*French*)
Edwin Landseer (*English*)
Thomas Lawrence (*English*)
Charles Lebrun (*French*)
Fernand Léger (*French*)
Wilhelm Lehmbruck (*German*)
Frederic Leighton (*English*)
Peter Lely (*Dutch-English*)
Leonardo da Vinci (*Italian*)
Wyndham Lewis (*British*)
Roy Lichtenstein (*U.S.*)
Norman Alfred William Lindsay (*Australian*)
Jacques Lipchitz (*Lithuanian-U.S.*)
Filippino Lippi (*Italian*)
L(awrence) S(tephen) Lowry (*English*)
Lysippus (*Greek*)
Jan Mabuse (*Flemish*)
Charles Rennie Mackintosh (*Scottish*)
René Magritte (*Belgian*)
Aristide Maillol (*French*)
Kasimir Severinovich Malevich (*Russian*)
Edouard Manet (*French*)
Andrea Mantegna (*Italian*)
Franz Marc (*German*)
John Martin (*English*)
Simone Martini (*Italian*)
Masaccio (*Italian*)
Quentin Massys (*Flemish*)
Henri Matisse (*French*)
Hans Memling *or* Memlinc (*Flemish*)
Franz Xavier Messerschmidt (*Austrian*)
Ivan Mestrovic (*Yugoslav-U.S.*)
Michelangelo Buonarroti (*Italian*)
Michelozzi Michelozzo (*Italian*)
John Everett Millais (*English*)

Jean François Millet (*French*)
Joan Miró (*Spanish*)
Amedeo Modigliani (*Italian*)
László Moholy-Nagy (*Hungarian*)
Piet Mondrian (*Dutch*)
Claude Oscar Monet (*French*)
Henry Moore (*British*)
Gustave Moreau (*French*)
Berthe Morisot (*French*)
William Morris (*English*)
Samuel Finley Breese Morse (*U.S.*)
Grandma Moses (*U.S.*)
Edvard Munch (*Norwegian*)
Alfred Munnings (*English*)
Bartolomé Esteban Murillo (*Spanish*)
Myron (*Greek*)
Paul Nash (*English*)
Ernst Wilhelm Nay (*German*)
Barnett Newman (*U.S.*)
Ben Nicholson (*English*)
Sidney Nolan (*Australian*)
Emil Nolde (*German*)
Joseph Nollekens (*Dutch-English*)
Georgia O'Keefe (*U.S.*)
Claes Oldenburg (*Swedish-U.S.*)
Orcagna (*Italian*)
José Clemente Orozco (*Mexican*)
Jean Baptiste Oudry (*French*)
Palma Vecchio (*Italian*)
Samuel Palmer (*English*)
Eduardo Paolozzi (*Scottish*)
Parmigianino (*Italian*)
Victor Pasmore (*English*)
Joachim Patinir *or* Patenier (*Flemish*)
Perugino (*Italian*)
Baldassare Peruzzi (*Italian*)
Antoine Pevsner (*Russian-French*)
Phidias (*Greek*)
Francis Picabia (*French*)
Pablo Picasso (*Spanish*)
Piero della Francesca (*Italian*)
Piero di Cosimo (*Italian*)
Pietro da Cortona (*Italian*)
Jean Baptiste Pigalle (*French*)
Germain Pilon (*French*)
Pinturicchio (*Italian*)

WORD POWER

John Piper (*English*)
Pisanello (*Italian*)
Andrea Pisano (*Italian*)
Giovanni Pisano (*Italian*)
Nicola Pisano (*Italian*)
Camille Pissarro (*French*)
Antonio del Pollaiuolo
  (*Italian*)
Piero del Pollaiuolo (*Italian*)
Jackson Pollock (*U.S.*)
Polyclitus (*Greek*)
Polygnotus (*Greek*)
Pontormo (*Italian*)
Paulus Potter (*Dutch*)
Nicolas Poussin (*French*)
Praxiteles (*Greek*)
Pierre Paul Prud'hon
  (*French*)
Pierre Puget (*French*)
Pierre Puvis de Chavannes
  (*French*)
Jacopa della Quercia
  (*Italian*)
Arthur Rackham (*English*)
Henry Raeburn (*Scottish*)
Allan Ramsay (*Scottish*)
Raphael (*Italian*)
Robert Rauschenberg (*U.S.*)
Man Ray (*U.S.*)
Odilon Redon (*French*)
Rembrandt Harmensz van
  Rijn (*Dutch*)
Guido Reni (*Italian*)
Pierre Auguste Renoir
  (*French*)
Joshua Reynolds (*English*)
José de Ribera (*Spanish*)
Bridget Riley (*English*)
Diego Rivera (*Mexican*)
Andrea della Robbia
  (*Italian*)
Luca della Robbia (*Italian*)
Alexander Mikhailovich
  Rodchenko (*Russian*)
Auguste Rodin (*French*)
George Romney (*English*)
Salvator Rosa (*Italian*)
Dante Gabriel Rossetti
  (*English*)
Mark Rothko (*U.S.*)
Geroges Rouault (*French*)
Louis-François Roubiliac or
  Roubillac (*French*)
Henri Julien Rousseau
  (*French*)

Théodore Rousseau (*French*)
Peter Paul Rubens (*Flemish*)
Rublyov or Rublev Andrei
  (*Russian*)
Jacob van Ruisdael (*Dutch*)
Philipp Otto Runge
  (*German*)
Salomen van Ruysdael
  (*Dutch*)
John Singer Sargent (*U.S.*)
Egon Schiele (*Austrian*)
Martin Schongauer
  (*German*)
Kurt Schwitters (*German*)
Scopas (*Greek*)
Maurice Sendak (*U.S.*)
Sesshu (*Japanese*)
Georges Seurat (*French*)
Ben Shahn (*U.S.*)
Walter Richard Sickert
  (*British*)
Paul Signac (*French*)
Luca Signorelli (*Italian*)
David Alfaro Siqueiros
  (*Mexican*)
Alfred Sisley (*French*)
John Sloan (*U.S.*)
Claus Sluter (*Dutch*)
David Smith (*U.S.*)
Chaim Soutine (*Lithuanian-
  French*)
Stanley Spencer (*English*)
Jan Steen (*Dutch*)
Veit Stoss (*German*)
George Stubbs (*English*)
Graham Sutherland
  (*English*)
Yves Tanguy (*French*)
Vladimir Tatlin (*Russian*)
David Teniers the Elder
  (*Flemish*)
David Teniers the Younger
  (*Flemish*)
Gerard Ter Borch or
  Terborch (*Dutch*)
Hendrik Terbrugghen
  (*Dutch*)
James Thornhill (*English*)
Bertel Thorvaldsen (*Danish*)
Giambattista Tiepolo
  (*Italian*)
Jacopo Tintoretto (*Italian*)
James Jacques Joseph Tissot
  (*French*)
Titian (*Italian*)

Henri Marie Raymond de
  Toulouse-Lautrec (*French*)
J(oseph) M(allord) W(illiam)
  Turner (*English*)
Paolo Uccello (*Italian*)
Utagawa Kuniyoshi
  (*Japanese*)
Maurice Utrillo (*French*)
Adriaen van de Velde
  (*Dutch*)
Willem van de Velde the
  Elder (*Dutch*)
Willem van de Velde the
  Younger (*Dutch*)
Rogier van der Weyden
  (*Flemish*)
Anthony Van Dyck
  (*Flemish*)
Jan van Eyck (*Flemish*)
Vincent van Gogh (*Dutch*)
Victor Vasarely (*Hungarian-
  French*)
Giorgio Vasari (*Italian*)
Diego Rodríguez de Silva y
  Velázquez (*Spanish*)
Jan Vermeer (*Dutch*)
Paolo Veronese (*Italian*)
Andrea del Verrocchio
  (*Italian*)
Élisabeth Vigée-Lebrun
  (*French*)
Jacques Villon (*French*)
Maurice de Vlaminck
  (*French*)
Mark Wallinger (*English*)
Andy Warhol (*U.S.*)
Jean Antoine Watteau
  (*French*)
George Frederick Watts
  (*English*)
Benjamin West (*U.S.*)
James Abbott McNeill
  Whistler (*U.S.*)
Richard Wilson (*Welsh*)
Joseph Wright (*English*)
Xia Gui or Hsia Kuei
  (*Chinese*)
Zeuxis (*Greek*)
Johann Zoffany (*German*)
Anders Zorn (*Swedish*)
Gaetano Giulio Zumbo
  (*Italian*)
Francisco Zurbarán
  (*Spanish*)

AUSTRALIAN STATES AND TERRITORIES

Australian Capital Territory
New South Wales
Northern Territory

Queensland
South Australia
Tasmania

Victoria
Western Australia

BAYS

Aboukir *or* Abukir Bay
Bay of Acre
Algoa Bay
Ariake Bay
Baffin Bay
Bay of Bengal
Bay of Biscay
Biscayne Bay
Bombetoka Bay
Botany Bay
Buzzards Bay
Bay of Cádiz
Caernarvon Bay
Callao Bay
Bay of Campeche
Cape Cod Bay
Cardigan Bay
Carmarthen Bay
Casco Bay
Chesapeake Bay
Cienfuegos Bay
Colwyn Bay
Corpus Christi Bay
Delagoa Bay
Delaware Bay
Discovery Bay
Dublin Bay
Dundalk Bay
Dvina Bay
Encounter Bay
Bay of Espírito Santo
False Bay
Famagusta Bay

Florida Bay
Bay of Fundy
Galway Bay
Bay of Gdansk
Georgian Bay
Bay of Gibraltar
Guanabara Bay
Guantánamo Bay
Hangzhou Bay
Hawke Bay
Hudson Bay
Inhambane Bay
Ise Bay
James Bay
Jervis Bay
Jiazhou Bay
Bay of Kaválla
Korea Bay
Kuskokwim Bay
Lobito Bay
Lützow-Holm Bay
Magdalena Bay
Manila Bay
Massachusetts Bay
Milne Bay
Mobile Bay
Montego Bay
Morecambe Bay
Moreton Bay
Narragansett Bay
Newark Bay
Bay of Naples
New York Bay

Omura Bay
Osaka Bay
Passamaquoddy Bay
Bay of Pigs
Bay of Plenty
Port Phillip Bay
Poverty Bay
Quiberon Bay
San Francisco Bay
San Pedro Bay
Santiago Bay
Setúbal Bay
Sligo Bay
St Austell Bay
Bay of St Michel
Swansea Bay
Table Bay
Tampa Bay
Tasman Bay
Thunder Bay
Tokyo Bay
Toyama Bay
Tralee Bay
Bay of Trincomalee
Ungava Bay
Urado Bay
Vigo Bay
Bay of Vlorë
Vyborg Bay
Walvis *or* Walfish Bay
Whitley Bay
Wick Bay

WORD POWER

CANADIAN PROVINCES

Province	Abbreviation	Province	Abbreviation
Alberta	AB	Nunavut	NU
British Columbia	BC	Ontario	ON
Manitoba	MB	Prince Edward Island	PE
New Brunswick	NB	Quebec	PQ
Newfoundland	NF	Saskatchewan	SK
Northwest Territories	NWT	Yukon Territory	YT
Nova Scotia	NS		

CANALS

Berezina Canal
Bridgewater Canal
Caledonian Canal
Champlain Canal
Corinth Canal
Dortmund-Ems Canal
Erie Canal
Göta Canal
Grand Canal

Grand Union Canal
Houston Ship Canal
Kiel Canal
Manchester Ship Canal
Canal du Midi
Mittelland Canal
Moscow Canal
New York State Barge
  Canal

Canal do Norte
Panama Canal
Rhine-Herne Canal
Canal de São Gonçalo
Suez Canal
Twente Canal
Welland Canal

WORD POWER

City	Country
Abu Dhabi	United Arab Emirates
Abuja	Nigeria
Accra	Ghana
Addis Ababa	Ethiopia
Adamstown	Pitcairn Islands
Astana	Kazakhstan
Algiers	Algeria
Alofi	Niue
Amman	Jordan
Amsterdam	Netherlands
Andorra la Vella	Andorra
Ankara	Turkey
Antananarivo	Madagascar
Apia	Samoa
Ashkhabad	Turkmenistan
Asmara	Eritrea
Asunción	Paraguay
Athens	Greece
Avarua	Cook Islands
Baghdad	Iraq
Baku	Azerbaijan
Bamako	Mali
Bandar Seri Begawan	Brunei
Bangkok	Thailand
Bangui	Central African Republic
Banjul	Gambia
Basseterre	St. Kitts and Nevis
Beijing	People's Republic of China
Beirut or Beyrouth	Lebanon
Belfast	Northern Ireland
Belgrade	Yugoslavia (Serbia and Montenegro)
Belmopan	Belize
Berlin	Germany
Berne	Switzerland
Bishkek	Kyrgyzstan
Bissau	Guinea-Bissau
Bloemfontein	judicial capital of South Africa
Bogotá	Colombia
Brasília	Brazil
Bratislava	Slovakia
Brazzaville	Congo (Republic of)
Bridgetown	Barbados
Brussels	Belgium
Bucharest	Romania
Budapest	Hungary
Buenos Aires	Argentina
Bujumbura	Burundi
Cairo	Egypt

City	Country
Canberra	Australia
Cape Town	legislative capital of South Africa
Caracas	Venezuela
Cardiff	Wales
Castries	St. Lucia
Cayenne	French Guiana
Charlotte Amalie	United States Virgin Islands
Cockburn Town	Turks and Caicos Islands
Colombo	Sri Lanka
Conakry or Konakry	Guinea
Copenhagen	Denmark
Cotonu	Benin
Dakar	Senegal
Damascus	Syria
Delhi	India
Dhaka or Dacca	Bangladesh
Dili	East Timor
Djibouti or Jibouti	Djibouti or Jibouti
Dodoma	Tanzania
Doha	Qatar
Douglas	Isle of Man
Dublin	Republic of Ireland
Dushanbe	Tajikistan
Edinburgh	Scotland
Fort-de-France	Martinique
Freetown	Sierra Leone
Funafuti	Tuvalu
Gaborone	Botswana
George Town	Cayman Islands
Georgetown	Guyana
Gibraltar	Gibralter
Guatemala City	Guatemala
Hagätna	Guam
Hamilton	Bermuda
Hanoi	Vietnam
Harare	Zimbabwe
Havana	Cuba
Helsinki	Finland
Honiara	Solomon Islands
Islamabad	Pakistan
Jakarta or Djakarta	Indonesia
Jerusalem	Israel
Kabul	Afghanistan
Kampala	Uganda
Katmandu or Kathmandu	Nepal
Khartoum or Khartum	Sudan
Kiev	Ukraine
Kigali	Rwanda
Kingston	Jamaica

CAPITAL CITIES

City	Country	City	Country
Kingstown	St. Vincent and the Grenadines	Oslo	Norway
Kinshasa	Congo (Democratic Republic of)	Ottawa	Canada
		Ouagadougou	Burkina-Faso
		Panama City	Panama
		Paramaribo	Suriname
Kishinev	Moldova	Paris	France
Palikir	Micronesia	Phnom Penh	Cambodia
Koror	Palau	Pishpek	Kirghizia
Kuala Lumpur	Malaysia	Podgorica	Montenegro
Kuwait	Kuwait	Port-au-Prince	Haiti
La Paz	administrative capital of Bolivia	Port Louis	Mauritius
		Port Moresby	Papua New Guinea
Libreville	Gabon	Port of Spain	Trinidad and Tobago
Lilongwe	Malawi		
Lima	Peru		
Lisbon	Portugal	Porto Novo	Benin
Ljubljana	Slovenia	Port Vila	Republic of Vanuatu
Lomé	Togo		
London	United Kingdom	Prague	Czech Republic
Luanda	Angola	Praia	Cape Verde
Lusaka	Zambia	Pretoria	administrative capital of South Africa
Luxembourg	Luxembourg		
Madrid	Spain		
Majuro	Marshall Islands	Pristina	Kosovo (Federal Republic of Yugoslavia)
Malabo	Equatorial Guinea		
Malé	Maldives		
Managua	Nicaragua	Pyongyang	North Korea
Manama	Bahrain	Quito	Ecuador
Manila	Philippines	Rabat	Morocco
Maputo	Mozambique	Reykjavik	Iceland
Maseru	Lesotho	Riga	Latvia
Mbabane	Swaziland	Riyadh	Saudi Arabia
Melekeok	Palau	Rome	Italy
Mexico City	Mexico	Roseau	Dominica
Minsk	Belarus	San`a	Yemen
Mogadishu	Somalia	San José	Costa Rica
Monaco-Ville	Monaco	San Juan	Puerto Rico
Monrovia	Liberia	San Marino	San Marino
Montevideo	Uruguay	San Salvador	El Slavador
Moroni	Comoros	Santiago	Chile
Moscow	Russia	Santo Domingo	Dominican Republic
Muscat	Oman		
Nairobi	Kenya	São Tomé	São Tomé and Principe
Nassau	Bahamas		
Naypyidaw	Union of Myanmar	Sarajevo	Bosnia and Herzegovina
Ndjamena	Chad	Seoul	South Korea
Niamey	Niger	Singapore	Singapore
Nicosia	Cyprus	Skopje	The Former Yugoslav Republic of Macedonia
Nouakchott	Mauritania		
Nuku'alofa	Tonga		
Nuuk	Greenland		

14

CAPITAL CITIES

City	Country	City	Country
Sofia	Bulgaria	Tripoli	Libya
Sri Jayawardenepura	Sri Lanka	Tunis	Tunisia
St. George's	Grenada	Ulan Bator	Mongolia
St. John's	Antigua and Barbuda	Vaduz	Liechtenstein
		Valletta	Malta
Stockholm	Sweden	Vatican City	Vatican City
Sucre	legislative and judicial capital of Bolivia	Victoria	Seychelles
		Vienna	Austria
		Vientiane	Laos
Suva	Fiji	Port Vila	Vanuatu
Taipei	Taiwan	Vilnius	Lithuania
Tallinn	Estonia	Warsaw	Poland
Tarawa	Kiribati	Washington DC	United States of America
Tashkent	Uzbekistan		
Tbilisi	Georgia	Wellington	New Zealand
Tegucigalpa	Honduras	Windhoek	Namibia
Tehran	Iran	Yamoussoukro	Côte d'Ivoire
Tel Aviv	Israel	Yaoundé or Yaunde	Cameroon
Thimphu	Bhutan	Yaren	Nauru
Tirana	Albania	Yerevan	Armenia
Tokyo	Japan	Zagreb	Croatia

CASTLES

Aberystwyth	Caerphilly	Forfar	Portlick
Amboise	Cahir	Fotheringhay	Rait
Arundel	Canossa	Glamis	Restormel
Ashby de la Zouch	Carisbrooke	Harlech	Richmond
Ashford	Carmarthen	Heidelberg	Rock of Cashel
Aydon	Carrickfergus	Herstmonceux	Rithes
Ballindalloch	Château-Raoul	Inverness	St Mawes
Balmoral	Cheb	Kenilworth	Sherborne
Balvenie	Chillon	Kilkea	Scarborough
Barnard	Colditz	Kilkenny	Skipton
Beaumaris	Conwy	Killaghy	Stirling
Beeston	Crathes	Kilravock	Stuart
Belvoir	Culzean	Lancaster	Taymouth
Berkeley	Darnaway	Leamaneh	Tintagel
Berkhamstead	Dinan	Launceston	Torún
Berwick-upon-Tweed	Drum	Leeds	Trausnitz
	Dublin	Leicester	Trim
Blarney	Dunnottar	Lincoln	Urquhart
Blois	Dunsinane	Ludlow	Vaduz
Braemar	Dunstaffnage	Malahide	Vincennes
Brodie	Durham	Monmouth	Wartburg
Bunraity	Edinburgh	Otranto	Warwick
Cabra	Eilean Donan	Pembroke	
Caerlaverock	Esterháza	Pendennis	
Caernarfon	Farney	Pontefract	

Classical composers

Adolphe Adam (*French*)
John Adams (*U.S.*)
Isaac Albéniz (*Spanish*)
Tomaso Albinoni (*Italian*)
Gregorio Allegri (*Italian*)
William Alwyn (*British*)
George Antheil (*U.S.*)
Thomas Arne (*English*)
Malcolm Arnold (*British*)
Daniel François Espirit Auber (*French*)
Georges Auric (*French*)
Carl Philipp Emanuel Bach (*German*)
Johann Christian Bach (*German*)
Johann Christoph Friedrich Bach (*German*)
Johann Sebastian Bach (*German*)
Wilhelm Friedemann Bach (*German*)
Mily Alexeyevich Balakirev (*Russian*)
Granville Bantock (*British*)
Samuel Barber (*U.S.*)
Béla Bartók (*Hungarian*)
Arnold Bax (*British*)
Ludwig van Beethoven (*German*)
Vincenzo Bellini (*Italian*)
Arthur Benjamin (*Australian*)
Richard Rodney Bennett (*British*)
Alban Berg (*Austrian*)
Luciano Berio (*Italian*)
Lennox Berkeley (*British*)
Hector Berlioz (*French*)
Leonard Bernstein (*U.S.*)
Heinrich Biber (*German*)
Harrison Birtwhistle (*British*)
Georges Bizet (*French*)
Arthur Bliss (*British*)
Ernest Bloch (*U.S.*)
Luigi Bocherini (*Italian*)
Arrigo Boito (*Italian*)
Francesco Antonio Bonporti (*Italian*)
Aleksandr Porfirevich Borodin (*Russian*)
Pierre Boulez (*French*)
William Boyce (*English*)
Johannes Brahms (*German*)
Havergal Brian (*British*)
Frank Bridge (*British*)
Benjamin Britten (*British*)
Max Bruch (*German*)
Anton Bruckner (*Austrian*)
John Bull (*English*)
George Butterworth (*British*)
Dietrich Buxtehude (*Danish*)
William Byrd (*English*)
John Cage (*U.S.*)

Joseph Canteloube (*French*)
John Alden Carpenter (*U.S.*)
Eliot Carter (*U.S.*)
Robert Carver (*Scottish*)
Pablo Casals (*Spanish*)
Emmanuel Chabrier (*French*)
Gustave Charpentier (*French*)
Marc-Antoine Charpentier (*French*)
Ernest Chausson (*French*)
Luigi Cherubini (*Italian*)
Frédéric Chopin (*Polish-French*)
Domenico Cimarosa (*Italian*)
Jeremiah Clarke (*English*)
Samuel Coleridge-Taylor (*British*)
Aaron Copland (*U.S.*)
Arcangelo Corelli (*Italian*)
François Couperin (*French*)
Karl Czerny (*Austrian*)
Luigi Dallapiccola (*Italian*)
Peter Maxwell Davies (*British*)
Claude Debussy (*French*)
Léo Delibes (*French*)
Frederick Delius (*British*)
Josquin des Prés (*Flemish*)
Vincent d'Indy (*French*)
Ernst von Dohnányi (*Hungarian*)
Gaetano Donizetti (*Italian*)
Antal Doráti (*U.S.*)
John Dowland (*English*)
Paul Dukas (*French*)
John Dunstable (*English*)
Henri Duparc (*French*)
Marcel Dupré (*French*)
Maurice Duruflé (*French*)
Henri Dutilleux (*French*)
Antonín Dvořák (*Czech*)
Edward Elgar (*British*)
Georges Enesco (*Romanian*)
Manuel de Falla (*Spanish*)
John Farmer (*English*)
Gabriel Fauré (*French*)
John Field (*Irish*)
Gerald Finzi (*British*)
Friedrich von Flotow (*German*)
César Franck (*Belgian-French*)
Girolamo Frescobaldi (*Italian*)
Wilhelm Fürtwangler (*German*)
Andrea Gabrieli (*Italian*)
Giovanni Gabrieli (*Italian*)
George Gershwin (*U.S.*)
Carlo Gesualdo (*Italian*)
Orlando Gibbons (*English*)

Classical composers (continued)

Alberto Ginastera (*Argentinian*)
Philip Glass (*U.S.*)
Aleksandr Konstantinovich Glazunov (*Russian*)
Mikhail Ivanovich Glinka (*Russian*)
Christoph Willibald Gluck (*German*)
Eugene Goossens (*Belgian-British*)
Henryk Górecki (*Polish*)
Charles François Gounod (*French*)
Percy Grainger (*Australian*)
Enrique Granados (*Spanish*)
Edvard Grieg (*Norwegian*)
Ivor Gurney (*British*)
Fromental Halévy (*French*)
George Frederick Handel (*German*)
Roy Harris (*U.S.*)
Franz Joseph Haydn (*Austrian*)
Michael Haydn (*Austrian*)
Hans Werner Henze (*German*)
Hildegard of Bingen (*German*)
Paul Hindemith (*German*)
Heinz Holliger (*Swiss*)
Gustav Holst (*British*)
Arthur Honegger (*French*)
Johann Nepomuk Hummel (*German*)
Englebert Humperdinck (*German*)
Jacques Ibert (*French*)
John Ireland (*British*)
Charles Ives (*U.S.*)
Leoš Janáček (*Czech*)
Émile Jaques-Dalcroze (*Swiss*)
Joseph Joachim (*Hungarian*)
Daniel Jones (*British*)
Aram Ilich Khachaturian (*Armenian*)
Otto Klemperer (*German*)
Oliver Knussen (*British*)
Zoltán Kodály (*Hungarian*)
Erich Korngold (*Austrian*)
Franz Krommer (*Moravian*)
Raphael Kubelik (*Czech*)
Édouard Lalo (*French*)
Constant Lambert (*British*)
Roland de Lassus (*Flemish*)
Henry Lawes (*English*)
William Lawes (*English*)
Franz Lehár (*Hungarian*)
Ruggiero Leoncavallo (*Italian*)
György Ligeti (*Hungarian*)
Franz Liszt (*Hungarian*)
George Lloyd (*British*)
Matthew Locke (*English*)
Karl Loewe (*German*)

Jean Baptiste Lully (*Italian-French*)
Witold Lutosławski (*Polish*)
Elisabeth Lutyens (*British*)
Guillaume de Machaut (*French*)
James MacMillan (*British*)
Elizabeth Maconchy (*British*)
Gustav Mahler (*Austrian*)
Luca Marenzio (*Italian*)
Frank Martin (*Swiss*)
Bohuslav Martinů (*Czech*)
Steve Martland (*British*)
Pietro Mascagni (*Italian*)
Jules Émile Frédéric Massenet (*French*)
Fanny Mendelssohn (*German*)
Felix Mendelssohn (*German*)
Gian Carlo Menotti (*Italian*)
André Messager (*French*)
Olivier Messiaen (*French*)
Giacomo Meyerbeer (*German*)
Darius Milhaud (*French*)
Claudio Monteverdi (*Italian*)
Thomas Morley (*English*)
Leopold Mozart (*Austrian*)
Wolfgang Amadeus Mozart (*Austrian*)
Thea Musgrave (*British*)
Modest Petrovich Mussorgsky (*Russian*)
Carl Otto Ehrenfried Nicolai (*German*)
Carl Nielsen (*Danish*)
Luigi Nono (*Italian*)
Michael Nyman (*British*)
Johannes Ockeghem (*Flemish*)
Jacques Offenbach (*German-French*)
John Ogdon (*British*)
Carl Orff (*German*)
Johann Pachelbel (*German*)
Ignace Jan Paderewski (*Polish*)
Niccolò Paganini (*Italian*)
Giovanni Pierluigi da Palestrina (*Italian*)
Andrzej Panufnik (*Polish-British*)
Hubert Parry (*British*)
Arvo Pärt (*Estonian*)
Krzystof Penderecki (*Polish*)
Giovanni Battista Pergolesi (*Italian*)
Francis Poulenc (*French*)
Michael Praetorius (*German*)
Sergei Sergeyevich Prokofiev (*Russian*)
Giacomo Puccini (*Italian*)
Henry Purcell (*English*)
Sergei Vassilievich Rachmaninov (*Russian*)
Jean Philippe Rameau (*French*)
Maurice Ravel (*French*)
Alan Rawsthorne (*British*)

Classical composers (continued)

Max Reger (*German*)
Steve Reich (*U.S.*)
Ottorino Respighi (*Italian*)
Vittorio Rieti (*Italian*)
Nikolai Andreyevich Rimsky-Korsakov (*Russian*)
Joaquín Rodrigo (*Spanish*)
Sigmund Romberg (*U.S.*)
Gioacchino Antonio Rossini (*Italian*)
Mstislav Leopoldovich Rostropovich (*Russian*)
Claude Joseph Rouget de Lisle (*French*)
Albert Roussel (*French*)
Edmund Rubbra (*British*)
Anton Grigorevich Rubinstein (*Russian*)
Camille Saint-Saëns (*French*)
Antonio Salieri (*Italian*)
Erik Satie (*French*)
Alessandro Scarlatti (*Italian*)
Domenico Scarlatti (*Italian*)
Artur Schnabel (*Austrian-U.S.*)
Alfred Schnittke (*Russian*)
Arnold Schoenberg (*Austrian*)
Franz Schubert (*Austrian*)
William Schuman (*U.S.*)
Clara Schumann (*German*)
Robert Schumann (*German*)
Heinrich Schütz (*German*)
Aleksandr Nikolayvich Scriabin (*Russian*)
Peter Sculthorpe (*Australian*)
Roger Sessions (*U.S.*)
Dmitri Dmitriyevich Shostakovich (*Russian*)
Jean Sibelius (*Finnish*)
Robert Simpson (*English*)
Bedřich Smetana (*Czech*)
Ethel Smyth (*British*)
John Philip Sousa (*U.S.*)
John Stainer (*British*)
Charles Stanford (*Irish*)
Karlheinz Stockhausen (*German*)

Oscar Straus (*French*)
Johann Strauss, the elder (*Austrian*)
Johann Strauss, the younger (*Austrian*)
Richard Strauss (*German*)
Igor Fyodorovich Stravinsky (*Russian-U.S.*)
Jan Pieterszoon Sweelinck (*Dutch*)
Karol Szymanowski (*Polish*)
Toru Takemitsu (*Japanese*)
Thomas Tallis (*English*)
John Tavener (*British*)
John Taverner (*English*)
Pyotr Ilyich Tchaikovsky (*Russian*)
Georg Philipp Telemann (*German*)
Mikis Theodorakis (*Greek*)
Ambroise Thomas (*French*)
Virgil Thomson (*U.S.*)
Michael Tippett (*British*)
Paul Tortelier (*French*)
Edgar Varèse (*French-U.S.*)
Ralph Vaughan Williams (*British*)
Giuseppi Verdi (*Italian*)
Tomás Luis de Victoria (*Spanish*)
Heitor Villa-Lobos (*Brazilian*)
Antonio Vivaldi (*Italian*)
Richard Wagner (*German*)
William Walton (*British*)
David Ward (*British*)
Peter Warlock (*British*)
Carl Maria von Weber (*German*)
Anton Webern (*Austrian*)
Thomas Weelkes (*English*)
Judith Weir (*British*)
Egon Wellesz (*Austrian-British*)
Gillian Whitehead (*New Zealand*)
Malcolm Williamson (*Australian*)
Hugo Wolf (*Austrian*)
Ermanno Wolf-Ferrari (*Italian*)
Yannis Xenakis (*Romanian-Greek*)
Alexander Zemlinsky (*Austrian*)

Popular composers, songwriters and lyricists

Harold Arlen (*U.S.*)
Burt Bacharach (*U.S.*)
Joan Baez (*U.S.*)
John Barry (*British*)
Lionel Bart (*British*)
Irving Berlin (*Russian-U.S.*)
Leonard Bernstein (*U.S.*)
David Bowie (*English*)
Jacques Brel (*Belgian*)
Nacio Herb Brown (*U.S.*)
Sammy Cahn (*U.S.*)
Hoagy Carmichael (*U.S.*)
Johnny Cash (*U.S.*)
Eric Clapton (*British*)
George Cohan (*U.S.*)
Leonard Cohen (*Canadian*)
Noel Coward (*English*)
Willie Dixon (*U.S.*)
Lamont Dozier (*U.S.*)
Vernon Duke (*Russian-U.S.*)
Bob Dylan (*U.S.*)
Duke Ellington (*U.S.*)
Stephen Foster (*U.S.*)
George Gershwin (*U.S.*)
W(illiam) S(chwenck) Gilbert (*British*)
Gerry Goffin (*U.S.*)
Elliot Goldenthal (*U.S.*)
Jerry Goldsmith (*U.S.*)
Woody Guthrie (*U.S.*)
W(illiam) C(hristopher) Handy (*U.S.*)
Marvin Hamlisch (*U.S.*)
Oscar Hammerstein (*U.S.*)
Lorenz Hart (*U.S.*)
Jerry Herman (*U.S.*)
Brian Holland (*U.S.*)
Eddie Holland (*U.S.*)
Mick Jagger (*British*)
Maurice Jarre (*French*)
Antonio Carlos Jobim (*Brazilian*)
Elton John (*British*)
Robert Johnson (*U.S.*)
Jerome (David) Kern (*U.S.*)
Alicia Keys (*U.S.*)
Carole King (*U.S.*)
Kris Kristofferson (*U.S.*)
Huddie 'Leadbelly' Ledbetter (*U.S.*)
Tom Lehrer (*U.S.*)
John Lennon (*British*)

Alan Jay Lerner (*U.S.*)
Jerry Lieber (*U.S.*)
Jay Livingston (*U.S.*)
Andrew Lloyd-Webber (*British*)
Frank Loesser (*U.S.*)
Frederick Loewe (*Austrian-U.S.*)
Paul McCartney (*British*)
Ewan McColl (*British*)
Kirsty McColl (*British*)
Jimmy McHugh (*U.S.*)
Henry Mancini (*U.S.*)
Barry Manilow (*U.S.*)
Barry Mann (*U.S.*)
John Mayer (*U.S.*)
Joni Mitchell (*Canadian*)
Thelonious (Sphere) Monk (*U.S.*)
Van Morrison (*Irish*)
Willie Nelson (*U.S.*)
Ivor Novello (*British*)
Doc Pomus (*U.S.*)
Cole Porter (*U.S.*)
Keith Richards (*British*)
William 'Smokey' Robinson (*U.S.*)
Tim Rice (*British*)
Richard Rodgers (*U.S.*)
Sigmund Romberg (*Hungarian-U.S.*)
Howard Shore (*Canadian*)
Paul Simon (*U.S.*)
Stephen Sondheim (*U.S.*)
Bruce Springsteen (*U.S.*)
Sting (*British*)
Mike Stoller (*U.S.*)
Billy Strayhorn (*U.S.*)
Barrett Strong (*U.S.*)
Jule Styne (*U.S.*)
Arthur Sullivan (*British*)
Allen Toussaint (*U.S.*)
Johnny Van Heusen (*U.S.*)
Tom Waites (*U.S.*)
Harry Warren (*U.S.*)
Jimmy Webb (*U.S.*)
Cynthia Weil (*U.S.*)
Kurt Weill (*German-U.S.*)
Norman Whitfield (*U.S.*)
Hank Williams (*U.S.*)
John Williams (*U.S.*)
Brian Wilson (*U.S.*)
Vincent Youmans (*U.S.*)

WORD POWER

—— CONTINENTS ——

Africa
Antarctica
Asia

Australia
Europe
North America

South America

COUNTIES

English counties

Bedfordshire
Berkshire
Bristol
Buckinghamshire
Cambridgeshire
Cheshire
Cornwall
Cumbria
Derbyshire
Devon
Dorset
Durham
East Riding of Yorkshire
East Sussex
Essex
Gloucestershire

Greater London
Greater Manchester
Hampshire
Herefordshire
Hertfordshire
Isle of Wight
Kent
Lancashire
Leicestershire
Lincolnshire
Merseyside
Norfolk
Northamptonshire
Northumberland
North Yorkshire
Nottinghamshire

Oxfordshire
Rutland
Shropshire
Somerset
South Yorkshire
Staffordshire
Suffolk
Surrey
Tyne and Wear
Warwickshire
West Midlands
West Sussex
West Yorkshire
Wiltshire
Worcestershire

Scottish counties

Aberdeen City
Aberdeenshire
Angus
Argyll and Bute
City of Edinburgh
Clackmannanshire
Dumfries and Galloway
Dundee City
East Ayrshire
East Dunbartonshire
East Lothian

East Renfrewshire
Falkirk
Fife
Glasgow City
Highland
Inverclyde
Midlothian
Moray
North Ayrshire
North Lanarkshire
Orkney

Perth and Kinross
Renfrewshire
Scottish Borders
Shetland
South Ayrshire
South Lanarkshire
Stirling
West Dunbartonshire
Western Isles (Eilean Siar)
West Lothian

Welsh counties

Clwyd
Dyfed
Gwent

Gwynedd
Mid Glamorgan
Powys

South Glamorgan
West Glamorgan

Northern Irish counties

Antrim
Armagh

Down
Fermanagh

Londonderry
Tyrone

Republic of Ireland counties

Carlow
Cavan
Clare
Cork
Donegal
Dublin
Galway
Kerry
Kildare

Kilkenny
Laois
Leitrim
Limerick
Longford
Louth
Mayo
Meath
Monaghan

Offaly
Roscommon
Sligo
Tipperary
Waterford
Westmeath
Wexford
Wicklow

COUNTRIES

Afghanistan
Albania
Algeria
American Samoa
Andorra
Angola
Antigua and Barbuda
Argentina
Armenia
Australia
Austria
Azerbaijan
Bahamas
Bahrain
Bangladesh
Barbados
Belarus
Belgium
Belize
Benin
Bhutan
Bolivia
Bosnia and Herzegovina
Botswana
Brazil
Brunei
Bulgaria
Burkina-Faso
Burundi
Cambodia
Cameroon
Canada
Cape Verde
Central African Republic
Chad
Chile
Colombia
Comoros
Congo (Republic of)
Congo (Democratic
  Republic of)
Costa Rica
Côte d'Ivoire
Croatia
Cuba
Cyprus
Czech Republic
Democratic People's
  Republic of Korea
Democratic Republic of
  Timor-Leste
Denmark
Djibouti
Dominica

Dominican Republic
East Timor
Ecuador
Egypt
El Salvador
England
Equatorial Guinea
Eritrea
Estonia
Ethiopia
Fiji
Finland
France
Gabon
Gambia
Georgia
Germany
Ghana
Greece
Greenland
Grenada
Guatemala
Guinea
Guinea-Bissau
Guyana
Haiti
Honduras
Hungary
Iceland
India
Indonesia
Iran
Iraq
Israel
Italy
Jamaica
Japan
Jordan
Kazakhstan
Kenya
Kirghizia
Kiribati
Kuwait
Lao People's Democratic
  Republic
Latvia
Lebanon
Lesotho
Liberia
Libya
Liechtenstein
Lithuania
Luxembourg
The Former Yugoslav

Republic of Macedonia
Madagascar
Malawi
Malaysia
Mali
Malta
Marshall Islands
Mauritania
Mauritius
Mexico
Micronesia
Moldova
Monaco
Mongolia
Montenegro
Morocco
Mozambique
Myanmar
Namibia
Nauru
Nepal
Netherlands
New Zealand
Nicaragua
Niger
Nigeria
Northern Ireland
Norway
Oman
Pakistan
Palau
Panama
Papua New Guinea
Paraguay
People's Republic of China
Peru
Philippines
Poland
Portugal
Puerto Rico
Qatar
Republic of Ireland
Republic of Korea
Republic of Maldives
Romania
Russia
Rwanda
St Kitts and Nevis
St Lucia
St Vincent and the
  Grenadines
Samoa
San Marino
São Tomé and Principe

WORD POWER

COUNTRIES

Saudi Arabia
Scotland
Senegal
Serbia
Seychelles
Sierra Leone
Singapore
Slovakia
Slovenia
Solomon Islands
Somalia
South Africa
South Korea
Spain
Sri Lanka
Sudan

Surinam
Swaziland
Sweden
Switzerland
Syria
Taiwan
Tajikistan
Tanzania
Thailand
Togo
Tonga
Trinidad and Tobago
Tunisia
Turkey
Turkmenistan
Tuvalu

Uganda
Ukraine
United Arab Emirates
United Kingdom
United States of America
Uruguay
Uzbekistan
Vanuatu
Vatican City
Venezuela
Vietnam
Wales
Yemen
Zambia
Zimbabwe

WORD POWER

Country	Currency	Country	Currency
Afghanistan	afghani	Denmark	krone
Albania	lek	Djibouti	Djibouti franc
Algeria	Algerian dinar	Dominica	East Caribbean dollar
Andorra	euro		
Angola	New Kwanza	Dominican Republic	peso
Antigua and Barbuda	East Caribbean dollar	Ecuador	US dollar
		Egypt	pound
Argentina	Austral and Argentinian Neuvo Peso	El Salvador	cólon
		Equatorial Guinea	CFA franc
		Eritrea	nakfa
Armenia	dram	Estonia	kroon
Australia	Australian dollar	Ethiopia	birr
Austria	euro	Fiji	Fiji dollar
Azerbaijan	manat	Finland	euro
Bahamas	Bahamian dollar	France	euro
Bahrain	dinar	French Guiana	euro
Bangladesh	taka	Gabon	CFA franc
Barbados	Barbados dollar	Gambia	dalasi
Belarus	rouble	Germany	euro
Belgium	euro	Ghana	cedi
Belize	Belize dollar	Greece	euro
Benin	CFA franc	Greenland	Danish krone
Bhutan	ngultrum	Grenada	East Caribbean dollar
Bolivia	boliviano		
Bosnia-Herzegovina	convertible marka	Guatemala	quetzal
Botswana	pula	Guinea	Guinea franc
Brazil	real	Guinea-Bissau	CFA franc
Brunei	Brunei dollar	Guyana	Guyana dollar
Bulgaria	lev	Haiti	gourde
Burkina-Faso	CFA franc	Honduras	lempira
Burundi	Burundi franc	Hungary	forint
Cambodia	riel	Iceland	krona
Cameroon	CFA franc	India	rupee
Canada	Canadian dollar	Indonesia	rupiah
Cape Verde	escudo	Iran	rial
Central African Republic	CFA franc	Iraq	dinar
		Ireland (Republic of)	euro
Chad	CFA franc	Israel	shekel
Chile	peso	Italy	euro
China	yuan	Jamaica	Jamaican dollar
Colombia	peso	Japan	yen
Comoros	Comorian franc	Jordan	dinar
Congo (Republic of)	New Zaire	Kazakhstan	tenge
Congo (Democratic Republic of)	Congolese franc	Kenya	shilling
		Kirghizia	som
Costa Rica	cólon	Kiribati	Australian dollar
Côte d'Ivoire	CFA franc	Kosovo	dinar; euro
Croatia	kuna	Kuwait	dinar
Cuba	peso	Kyrgyzstan	som
Cyprus	pound	Lao People's Democratic Republic	kip
Czech Republic	koruna		
Democratic People's Republic of Korea	North Korean Won	Latvia	lat
		Lebanon	pound
Democratic Republic of Timor-Leste	US dollar	Lesotho	loti
		Liberia	Liberian dollar

23

CURRENCIES

Country	Currency	Country	Currency
Libya	dinar	St. Vincent and the Grenadines	East Caribbean dollar
Liechtenstein	Swiss franc	Samoa	tala
Lithuania	litas	San Marino	euro
Luxembourg	euro	São Tomé and Principe	dobra
The Former Yugoslav Republic of Macedonia	dinar	Saudi Arabia	riyal
		Senegal	CFA franc
Madagascar	Malagasy franc	Serbia	Dinar
Malawi	kwacha	Seychelles	rupee
Malaysia	ringgit	Sierra Leone	leone
Maldives (Republic of)	rufiyaa	Singapore	Singapore dollar
Mali	CFA franc	Slovakia	koruna
Malta	lira	Slovenia	tolar
Marshall Islands	U.S. dollar	Solomon Islands	Solomon Islands dollar
Mauritania	ouguiya		
Mauritius	rupee	Somalia	shilling
Mexico	peso	South Africa	rand
Micronesia	U.S. dollar	Spain	euro
Moldova	leu	Sri Lanka	rupee
Monaco	French franc	Sudan	Pound
Mongolia	tugrik	Surinam	guilder
Montenegro	euro	Swaziland	lilangeni
Montserrat	East Caribbean dollar	Sweden	krona
		Switzerland	Swiss franc
Morocco	dirham	Syria	pound
Mozambique	metical	Taiwan	Taiwan dollar
Myanmar	kyat	Tajikistan	Tajik Rouble
Namibia	Namibian dollar	Tanzania	shilling
Nauru	Australian dollar	Thailand	baht
Nepal	rupee	Togo	CFA franc
Netherlands	euro	Tonga	pa'anga
New Zealand	New Zealand dollar	Trinidad and Tobago	Trinidad and Tobago dollar
Nicaragua	córdoba		
Niger	CFA franc	Tunisia	dinar
Nigeria	naira	Turkey	Turkish lira
Norway	krone	Turkmenistan	manat
Oman	rial	Tuvalu	Australian dollar
Pakistan	rupee	Uganda	shilling
Palau	U.S. dollar	Ukraine	hryvna
Panama	balboa	United Arab Emirates	dirham
Papua New Guinea	kina	United Kingdom	pound sterling
Paraguay	guarani	United States of America	U.S. dollar
Peru	new sol		
Philippines	Philippine peso	Uruguay	peso
Poland	zloty	Uzbekistan	som
Portugal	euro	Vanuatu	vatu
Qatar	riyal	Vatican City	euro
Republic of Korea	won	Venezuela	bolívar
Romania	leu	Vietnam	dong
Russia	rouble	Yemen	riyal
Rwanda	Rwanda franc	Zambia	kwacha
St. Kitts and Nevis	East Caribbean dollar	Zimbabwe	Zimbabwe dollar
St. Lucia	East Caribbean dollar		

DESERTS

Arabian
Atacama
Dasht-i-Lut or Dasht-e-Lut
Death Valley
Gibson
Gobi

Great Sandy
Great Victoria
Kalahari
Kara Kum
Kyzyl Kum
Libyan

Mohave or Mojave
Nubian
Rub'al Khali
Sahara
Taklimakan Shama
Thar

DIRECTORS

Robert Aldrich (*U.S.*)
Woody Allen (*U.S.*)
Pedro Almódovar (*Spanish*)
Robert Altman (*U.S.*)
Lindsay Anderson (*British*)
Michelangelo Antonioni (*Italian*)
Gillian Armstrong (*Australian*)
Anthony Asquith (*English*)
Richard Attenborough (*British*)
John Badham (*U.S.*)
Warren Beatty (*U.S.*)
Ingmar Bergman (*Swedish*)
Bernardo Bertolucci (*Italian*)
Luc Besson *French*)
Peter Bogdanovich (*U.S.*)
John Boorman (*English*)
Robert Bresson *French*)
Peter Brook (*British*)
Mel Brooks (*U.S.*)
Luis Buñuel *Spanish*)
Tim Burton (*U.S.*)
James Cameron (*U.S.*)
Jane Campion (*New Zealander*)
Frank Capra (*U.S.*)
John Carpenter (*U.S.*)
Marcel Carné (*French*)
Claude Chabrol (*French*)
Christopher Columbus (*U.S.*)
René Clair (*French*)
Jean Cocteau (*French*)
Ethan Coen (*U.S.*)
Joel Coen (*U.S.*)
Francis Ford Coppola (*U.S.*)
Roger Corman (*U.S.*)
David Cronenberg (*Canadian*)
Alfonso Cuarón (*Mexican*)
Michael Curtiz (*American-Hungarian*)
Joe Dante (*U.S.*)
Cecil B. de Mille (*U.S.*)
Johnathan Demme (*U.S.*)

Brian de Palma (*U.S.*)
Vittoria De Sicca (*Italian*)
Richard Donner (*U.S.*)
Aleksandr Petrovitch Dovzhenko (*Russian*)
Clint Eastwood (*U.S.*)
Blake Edwards (*U.S.*)
Sergei Mikhailovich Eisenstein (*Russian*)
Rainer Werner Fassbinder (*German*)
Federico Fellini (*Italian*)
Victor Fleming (*U.S.*)
Bryan Forbes (*English*)
John Ford (*U.S.*)
Milös Forman (*Czech*)
Bill Forsyth (*Scottish*)
Stephen Frears (*English*)
William Friedkin (*U.S.*)
Abel Gance (*French*)
Terry Gilliam (*U.S.*)
Jean-Luc Godard (*French*)
Peter Greenaway (*English*)
John Grierson (*Scottish*)
D(avid) W(ark) Griffith (*U.S.*)
Sacha Guitry (*French*)
Peter Hall (*English*)
Howard Hawks (*U.S.*)
Werner Herzog (*German*)
George Roy Hill (*U.S.*)
Alfred Hitchcock (*English*)
John Huston (*U.S.*)
James Ivory (*U.S.*)
Peter Jackson (*New Zealander*)
Derek Jarman (*English*)
Neil Jordan (*Irish*)
Chen Kaige (*China*)
Lawrence Kasdan (*U.S.*)
Philip Kaufman (*U.S.*)
Elia Kazan (*U.S.*)
Krzysztof Kieslowski (*Polish*)
Stanley Kubrick (*U.S.*)
Akira Kurosawa (*Japanese*)
John Landis (*U.S.*)

Fritz Lang (*Austrian*)
David Lean (*English*)
Ang Lee (*Taiwan*)
Spike Lee (*U.S.*)
Mike Leigh (*English*)
Richard Lester (*U.S.*)
Barry Levinson (*U.S.*)
Ken Loach (*English*)
George Lucas (*U.S.*)
Sidney Lumet (*U.S.*)
David Lynch (*U.S.*)
Jim McBride (*U.S.*)
Alexander Mackendrick (*Scottish*)
Louis Malle (*French*)
Joseph Mankiewicz (*U.S.*)
Georges Méliès (*French*)
Sam Mendes (*English*)
Ismail Merchant (*Indian*)
George Miller (*Australian*)
Jonathon Wolfe Miller (*English*)
Vincente Minnelli (*U.S.*)
Kenji Mizoguchi (*Japanese*)
Mike Nichols (*American-German*)
Laurence Olivier *English*)
Max Ophüls (*German*)
G(eorge) W(ilhelm) Pabst (*German*)
Marcel Pagnol (*French*)
Alan Parker (*English*)
Pier Paolo Pasolini (*Italian*)
Sam Peckinpah (*U.S.*)
Arthur Penn (*U.S.*)
Roman Polanski (*Polish*)
Sydney Pollack (*U.S.*)
Michael Powell (*English*)
Otto Preminger (*Austrian-U.S.*)
Emeric Pressburger (*Hungarian*)
Vsevolod Pudovkin (*Russian*)
David Puttnam (*English*)
Satyajit Ray (*Indian*)
Robert Redford (*U.S.*)

Directors (continued)

Carol Reed (*English*)
Carl Reiner (*U.S.*)
Rob Reiner (*U.S.*)
Edgar Reitz (*German*)
Jean Renoir (*French*)
Alain Resnais (*French*)
Leni Riefenstahl (*German*)
Guy Ritchie (*English*)
Hal Roach (*U.S.*)
Tim Robbins (*U.S.*)
Nicholas Roeg (*English*)
Eric Rohmer (*France*)
George Romero (*U.S.*)
Roberto Rossellini (*Italian*)
Ken Russell (*English*)
John Schlesinger (*English*)
Martin Scorsese (*U.S.*)
Ridley Scott (*British*)

Don Siegal (*U.S.*)
Steven Soderbergh (*U.S.*)
Steven Spielberg (*U.S.*)
Robert Stevenson (*English*)
Oliver Stone (*U.S.*)
Preston Sturges (*U.S.*)
Quentin Tarantino (*U.S.*)
Andrei Tarkovsky (*Russian*)
Jacques Tati (*French*)
Bertrand Tavernier (*French*)
François Truffaut (*French*)
Roger Vadim (*French*)
Luchino Visconti (*Italian*)
Joseph von Sternberg (*Austrian-U.S.*)
Erich von Stroheim (*Austrian-U.S.*)
Andrei Wajda (*Polish*)

Peter Weir (*Australian*)
Orson Welles (*U.S.*)
Wim Wenders (*German*)
Billy Wilder (*Austrian-U.S.*)
Michael Winner (*English*)
Robert Wise (*U.S.*)
Zhang Yimou (*Chinese*)
Franco Zeffirelli (*Italian*)
Robert Zemeckis (*U.S.*)
Fred Zinnemann (*Austrian-British*)

DRAMA

Types of Drama

comedy
comedy of manners
commedia dell'arte
costume piece *or* costume
 drama
farce
Grand Guignol
Jacobean
kabuki
Kathakali

kitchen sink
melodrama
morality play
mystery play
No *or* Noh
Pantomime
passion play
Restoration Comedy
revenge tragedy
satyrs

shadow play
situation comedy *or* sitcom
sketch
soap opera
street theatre
theatre of cruelty
theatre of the absurd
tragedy
tragicomedy

Dramatists

Aeschylus (*Greek*)
Edward Albee (*U.S.*)
Robert Amos (*Australian*)
Jean Anouilh (*French*)
Aristophanes (*Greek*)
Alan Ayckbourn (*English*)
Pierre Augustin Caron de Beaumarchais
 (*French*)
Francis Beaumont (*English*)
Samuel Beckett (*Irish*)
Brendan Behan (*Irish*)
Richard Beynon (*Australian*)
Alan Bleasdale (*English*)
Edward Bond (*English*)
Bertolt Brecht (*German*)
Eugene Brieux (*French*)
Pedro Calderón de la Barca (*Spanish*)
George Chapman (*English*)
Anton Pavlovich Chekhov (*Russian*)
William Congreve (*English*)
Pierre Corneille (*French*)
Noël (Pierce) Coward (*English*)
Thomas Dekker (*English*)
John Dryden (*English*)
T(homas) S(tearns) Eliot (*U.S.-British*)
Louis Esson (*Australian*)
Euripides (*Greek*)
John Fletcher (*English*)
Dario Fo (*Italian*)
John Ford (*English*)
Brian Friel (*Irish*)
John Galsworthy (*English*)
Jean Genet (*French*)
W(illiam) S(chwenk) Gilbert (*English*)
(Hippolyte) Jean Giraudoux (*French*)
Johann Wolfgang von Goethe (*German*)
Nikolai Gogol (*Russian*)
Oliver Goldsmith (*Irish*)
Oriel Gray (*Australian*)
Robert Greene (*English*)

David Hare (*English*)
Gerhart Johann Robert Hauptmann
 (*German*)
Václav Havel (*Czech*)
Alfred Hayes (*U.S.*)
(Christian) Friedrich Hebbel (*German*)
Dorthy Hewett (*Australian*)
Thomas Heywood (*English*)
Jack Hibberd (*Australian*)
Sidney Howard (*U.S.*)
Henrik Ibsen (*Norwegian*)
William Motter Inge (*U.S.*)
Eugène Ionesco (*Romanian-French*)
Ben Jonson (*English*)
George Kaiser (*German*)
Tony Kushner (*U.S.*)
Thomas Kyd (*English*)
Ray Lawler (*Australian*)
Liz Lochhead (*Scottish*)
Lope de Vega (*Spanish*)
Federico Garcia Lorca (*Spanish*)
Maurice Maeterlinck (*Belgian*)
David Mamet (*U.S.*)
Christopher Marlowe (*English*)
John Marston (*English*)
Menander (*Greek*)
Arthur Miller (*U.S.*)
Molière (*French*)
Barry Oakley (*Australian*)
Sean O'Casey (*Irish*)
Eugene (Gladstone) O'Neill (*U.S.*)
Joe Orton (*English*)
John Osborne (*English*)
Thomas Otway (*English*)
John Patrick (*U.S.*)
Arthur Wing Pinero (*English*)
Harold Pinter (*English*)
Luigi Pirandello (*Italian*)
Titus Maccius Plautus (*Roman*)
Hal Porter (*Australian*)

WORD POWER

Dramatists (continued)

Aleksander Sergeyevich Pushkin (*Russian*)
Jean Baptiste Racine (*French*)
Terence Mervyn Rattigan (*English*)
John Romeril (*Australian*)
Willy Russell (*English*)
Thomas Sackville (*English*)
Jean-Paul Sartre (*French*)
Johann Christoph Friedrich von Schiller (*German*)
Lucius Annaeus Seneca (*Roman*)
Alan Seymour (*Australian*)
Peter Shaffer (*English*)
William Shakespeare (*English*)
George Bernard Shaw (*Irish*)

Sam Shepard (*U.S.*)
Richard Brinsley Sheridan (*Irish*)
Robert Sherwood (*U.S.*)
Sophocles (*Greek*)
Wole Soyinka (*Nigerian*)
Tom Stoppard (*Czech-English*)
August Strindberg (*Swedish*)
John Millington Synge (*Irish*)
John Webster (*English*)
Oscar Wilde (*Irish*)
Thornton Wilder (*U.S.*)
Tennessee Williams (*U.S.*)
David Keith Williamson (*Australian*)
William Wycherly (*English*)

EUROPEAN UNION

EU member states

1958 Belgium	1981 Greece	2004 Hungary
1958 France	1986 Portugal	2004 Latvia
1958 Germany	1986 Spain	2004 Lithuania
1958 Italy	1995 Finland	2004 Malta
1958 Luxembourg	1995 Sweden	2004 Poland
1958 The Netherlands	1995 Austria	2004 Slovakia
1973 Denmark	2004 Cyprus	2004 Slovenia
1973 Republic of Ireland	2004 Czech Republic	2007 Bulgaria
1973 United Kingdom	2004 Estonia	2007 Romania

EU applications under consideration

Croatia
Former Yugoslav Republic of Macedonia
Turkey

WORD POWER

WORD POWER

Place	Inhabitant	Place	Inhabitant
Aberdeen	Aberdonian	Bolivia	Bolivian
Afghanistan	Afghan	Bordeaux	Bordelais
Alabama	Alabaman or Alabamian	the Borders	Borderer
		Bosnia	Bosnian
Alaska	Alaskan	Boston	Bostonian or (U.S. slang) Bean-eater
Albania	Albanian		
Alberta	Albertan	Botswana	Botswanan
Algeria	Algerian	Brazil	Brazilian
Alsace	Alsatian	Bristol	Bristolian
American continent	American	Brittany	Breton
American Samoa	American Samoan	British Columbia	British Columbian
Amsterdam	Amsterdammer	Bulgaria	Bulgarian
Anatolia	Anatolian	Burgundy	Burgundian
Andorra	Andorran	Burkina-Faso	Burkinabe
Angola	Angolan	Burma	Burmese
Anjou	Angevin	Burundi	Burundian
Antigua	Antiguan	Byzantium	Byzantine
Argentina	Argentine or Argentinian	California	Californian
		Cambridge	Cantabrigian
Arizona	Arizonan	Cambodia	Cambodian
Arkansas	Arkansan or (informal) Arkie	Cameroon	Cameroonian
		Canada	Canadian or (informal) Canuck
Armenia	Armenian		
Asia	Asian	Canada, Maritime Provinces	Downeaster
Assam	Assamese		
Assyria	Assyrian	Cape Verde	Cape Verdean
Australia	Australian or (informal) Aussie	Castile	Castilian
		Catalonia	Catalan
Austria	Austrian	the Caucasus	Caucasian
Azerbaijan	Azerbaijani or Azeri	Cayman Islands	Cayman Islander
		Chad	Chadian or Chadean
Babylon	Babylonian		
Bahamas	Bahamian	Chicago	Chicagoan
Bahrain	Bahraini	Chile	Chilean
Bangladesh	Bangladeshi	China	Chinese
Bali	Balinese	Circassia	Circassian
Barbados	Barbadian, Bajan (informal), or Bim (informal)	Colombia	Colombian
		Colorado	Coloradan
		Connecticut	Nutmegger
Barbuda	Barbudan or Barbudian	Cork	Corkonian
		Comoros Islands	Comorian
Bavaria	Bavarian	Congo Republic	Congolese
Belarus or Byelorussia	Belarussian or Byelorussian	Cornwall	Cornishman, Cornishwoman
Belau	Belauan	Corsica	Corsican
Belgium	Belgian	Costa Rica	Costa Rican
Benin	Beninese or Beninois	Côte d'Ivoire	Ivorian or Ivorean
		Croatia	Croat or Croatian
Berlin	Berliner	Cuba	Cuban
Bhutan	Bhutanese	Cumbria	Cumbrian
Birmingham	Brummie	Cyprus	Cypriot
Bohemia	Bohemian	Czech Republic	Czech

Place	Inhabitant	Place	Inhabitant
Czechoslovakia	Czechoslovak or Czechoslovakian	Galilee	Galilean
		Galloway	Gallovidian
Delaware	Delawarean	Galway	Galwegian
Democratic People's Republic of Korea	Korean	Gambia	Gambian
		Gascony	Gascon
Democratic Republic of Timor-Leste	Timorese	Genoa	Genoese
		Georgia (country)	Georgian
Denmark	Dane	Georgia (U.S. state)	Georgian
Delphi	Pythian	Germany	German
Devon	Devonian	Ghana	Ghanaian or Ghanian
Djibouti	Djiboutian or Djiboutien		
		Glasgow	Glaswegian
Dominica	Dominican	Greece	Greek
Dominican Republic	Dominican	Greenland	Greenlander
Dublin	Dubliner	Grenada	Grenadian
Dundee	Dundonian	Guam	Guamanian
East Timor	East Timorese	Guatemala	Guatemalan
Ecuador	Ecuadorean or Ecuadoran	Guinea	Guinean
		Guyana	Guyanese or Guyanan
Edinburgh	Edinburgher		
Egypt	Egyptian	Haiti	Haitian
El Salvador	Salvadoran, Salvadorean, or Salvadorian	Hawaii	Hawaiian
		Havana	Habanero
		Hesse	Hessian
England	Englishman, Englishwoman	Hungary	Hungarian or Magyar
Ephesus	Ephesian	Honduras	Honduran
Estonia	Estonian	Hyderabad state	Mulki
Eritrea	Eritrean	Ibiza	Ibizan
Ethiopia	Ethiopian	Iceland	Icelander
Equatorial Guinea	Equatorian	Idaho	Idahoan
Eritrea	Eritrean	Illinois	Illinoian or Illinoisian
Estonia	Estonian		
Ethiopia	Ethiopian	India	Indian
Europe	European	Indiana	Indianan, Indianian, or (informal) Hoosier
Euzkadi	Basque		
Faeroe Islands	Faeroese		
Falkland Islands	Falkland Islanders or Falklander	Indonesia	Indonesian
		Iowa	Iowan
Fife	Fifer	Iran	Iranian
Fiji	Fijian	Iraq	Iraqi
Finland	Finn	Ireland	Irishman, Irishwoman
Flanders	Fleming		
Florence	Florentine	Israel	Israeli
Florida	Floridian	Italy	Italian
France	Frenchman, Frenchwoman	Jamaica	Jamaican
		Japan	Japanese
French Guiana	Guianese	Java	Javanese
Friesland	Frisian	Jordan	Jordanian
Friuili	Friulian	Kansas	Kansan
Gabon	Gabonese	Karelia	Karelian
Galicia	Galician	Kazakhstan	Kazakh

Place	Inhabitant	Place	Inhabitant
Kent (East)	Man, Woman of Kent	Mars	Martian
		Marseilles	Marsellais
Kent (West)	Kentish Man, Woman	Marshall Islands	Marshall Islander
		Martinique	Martiniquean
Kentucky	Kentuckian	Maryland	Marylander
Kenya	Kenyan	Massachusetts	Bay Stater
Kirghizia	Kirghiz	Mauritania	Mauritanian
Korea	Korean	Mauritius	Mauritian
Kuwait	Kuwaiti	Melanesia	Melanesian
Lancashire	Lancastrian	Melbourne	Melburnian
Lancaster	Lancastrian	Mexico	Mexican
Lao People's Democratic Republic	Laotian	Michigan	Michigander, Michiganite, or Michiganian
Latvia	Latvian or Lett	Micronesia	Micronesian
Lebanon	Lebanese	Milan	Milanese
Liberia	Liberian	Minnesota	Minnesotan
Libya	Libyan	Mississippi	Mississippian
Liechtenstein	Liechtensteiner	Missouri	Missourian
Lincolnshire	yellow belly (dialect)	Moldavia	Moldavian
		Monaco	Monegasque
Lithuania	Lithuanian	Mongolia	Mongolian
Liverpool	Liverpudlian or (informal) Scouse or Scouser	Montana	Montanan
		Montenegro	Montenegrin
Lombardy	Lombard	Montserrat	Montserratian
London	Londoner or Cockney	Moravia	Moravian
		Morocco	Moroccan
Los Angeles	Angeleno	Moscow	Muscovite
Louisiana	Louisianan or Louisianian	Mozambique	Mozambican
		Namibia	Namibian
Luxembourg	Luxembourger	Nauru	Nauruan
Lyon	Lyonnais	Naples	Neapolitan
Macao	Macaonese	Nebraska	Nebraskan
The Former Yugoslav Republic of Macedonia	Macedonian	the Netherlands	Dutchman, Dutchwoman
Madagascar	Madagascan or Malagasy	New Brunswick	New Brunswicker
		Newcastle upon Tyne	Geordie
Madrid	Madrileño, Madrileña	New England	New Englander or (informal) Yankee or Downeaster
Maine	Mainer or Downeaster	Newfoundland	Newfoundlander or (informal) Newfie
Majorca	Majorcan		
Malawi	Malawian	Newfoundland fishing village	Outporter
Malaya	Malayan	New Hampshire	New Hampshirite
Malaysia	Malaysian	New Jersey	New Jerseyan or New Jerseyite
Maldive Islands	Maldivian		
Malta	Maltese	New Mexico	New Mexican
Man, Isle of	Manxman, Manxwoman	New South Wales	New South Welshman, New South Welshwoman
Manchester	Mancunian		
Manitoba	Manitoban		
Marquesas Islands	Marquesan		

WORD POWER

INHABITANTS

Place	Inhabitant	Place	Inhabitant
New York	New Yorker *or* Knickerbocker	Prussia	Prussian
		Puerto Rico	Puerto Rican
New Zealand	New Zealander *or* (*informal*) Kiwi *or* Enzedder	Qatar	Qatari
		Quebec	Quebecer, Quebecker, *or* Quebecois
Nicaragua	Nicaraguan		
Niger	Nigerien	Queensland	Queenslander
Nigeria	Nigerian	Republic of Korea	Korean
Normandy	Norman	Rhode Island	Rhode Islander
North Carolina	North Carolinian *or* Tarheel	Rhodes	Rhodian
		Rhodesia	Rhodesian
North Dakota	North Dakotan	Rio de Janeiro	Cariocan
Northern Ireland	Northern Irishman, Northern Irishwoman	Romania	Romanian
		Rome	Roman
		Russian Federation	Russian
		Ruthenia	Ruthenian
Northern Territory	Territorian	Rwanda	Rwandan
Northern Territory, northern part of	Top Ender	Samaria	Samaritan
		San Marino	San Marinese *or* Sammarinese
North Korea	North Korean		
Northumbria	Northumbrian	Sardinia	Sardinian
Norway	Norwegian	Saskatchewan	Saskatchewanian
Nova Scotia	Nova Scotian *or* (*informal*) Bluenose	Saxony	Saxon
		Saudi Arabia	Saudi *or* Saudi Arabian
Ohio	Ohioan		
Okinawa	Okinawan	Savoy	Savoyard
Oklahoma	Oklahoman *or* (*slang*) Okie	Scandinavia	Scandinavian
		Scotland	Scot, Scotsman, Scotswoman, *or* Caledonian
Oman	Omani		
Ontario	Ontarian *or* Ontarioan		
		Scottish Highlands	Highlander *or* (*old-fashioned*) Hielanman
Oregon	Oregonian		
Orkney	Orcadian		
Oxford	Oxonian	Senegal	Senegalese
Pakistan	Pakistani	Serbia	Serb *or* Serbian
Palau	Palauan	Seychelles	Seychellois
Palestine	Palestinian	Shetland	Shetlander
Panama	Panamanian	Sierra Leone	Sierra Leonean
Papua New Guinea	Papua	Sind	Sindhi
Paraguay	Paraguayan	Singapore	Singaporean
Paris	Parisian *or* Parisienne	Slovakia	Slovak
		Slovenia	Slovene *or* Slovenian
Pennsylvania	Pennsylvanian	Solomon Islands	Solomon Islander
Persia	Persian	South Africa	South African
Perth	Perthite	South Australia	South Australian *or* (*informal*) Croweater
Peru	Peruvian		
the Philippines	Filipino	South Carolina	South Carolinian
Poland	Pole	South Dakota	South Dakota
Pomerania	Pomeranian	South Korea	South Korean
Portugal	Portuguese	Spain	Spaniard
Prince Edward Island	Prince Edward Islander	Sri Lanka	Sri Lankan
		Sudan	Sudanese
Provence	Provençal		

33

WORD POWER

Place	Inhabitant	Place	Inhabitant
Suriname	Surinamese	United States of America	American *or* (*informal*) Yank *or* Yankee
Swaziland	Swazi		
Switzerland	Swiss		
Sweden	Swede	Uruguay	Uruguayan
Sydney	Sydneysider	Utah	Utahan *or* Utahn
Sydney, Western suburbs of	Westie (*informal*)	Uzbekistan	Uzbek
		Venezuela	Venezuelan
Syria	Syrian	Venice	Venetian
Taiwan	Taiwanese	Vermont	Vermonter
Tajikistan	Tajik	Victoria	Victorian
Tanzania	Tanzanian	Vienna	Viennese
Tasmania	Tasmanian *or* (*informal*) Tassie *or* Apple Islander	Vietnam	Vietnamese
		Virginia	Virginian
		Wales	Welshman, Welshwoman
Tennessee	Tennessean		
Texas	Texan	Washington	Washingtonian
Thailand	Thai	Wearside	Mackem
Thessalonika	Thessalonian	Wessex	West Saxon
Tibet	Tibetan	Western Australia	Western Australian, Westralian, *or* (*informal*) Sandgroper
Togo	Togolese		
Tonga	Tongan		
Trinidad	Trinidadian		
Tobago	Tobagan *or* Tobagonian		
		Western Sahara	Sahwari
Troy	Trojan	West Virginia	West Virginian
Tuscany	Tuscan	Winnipeg	Winnipegger
Tunisia	Tunisian	Wisconsin	Wisconsinite
Turkey	Turk	Wyoming	Wyomingite
Turkmenistan	Turkmen	Yemen	Yemeni
Tuvalu	Tuvaluan	Yorkshire	Yorkshireman, Yorkshirewoman
Tyneside	Geordie		
Tyre	Tyrian	the Yukon	Yukoner
Uganda	Ugandan	Zaire	Zairean
Ukraine	Ukrainian	Zambia	Zambian
Ulster	Ulsterman, Ulsterwoman	Zanzibar	Zanzibari
		Zimbabwe	Zimbabwean
Umbria	Umbrian		
United Kingdom	Briton, Brit (*informal*), *or* Britisher		

Achill
Admiralty
Aegean
Aegina
Alcatraz
Aldabra
Alderney
Aleutian
Alexander
Amboina
Andaman
Andaman and Nicobar
Andreanof
Andros
Anglesey
Anguilla
Anticosti
Antigua
Antilles
Antipodes
Aran
Arran
Aru or Arru
Aruba
Ascension
Auckland
Azores
Baffin
Bahamas
Balearic
Bali
Banaba
Bangka
Banks
Baranof
Barbados
Barbuda
Bardsey
Barra
Basilan
Basse-Terre
Batan
Belau
Belle
Benbecula
Bermuda
Biak
Billiton
Bioko
Bohol
Bonaire
Bonin
Bora Bora
Borneo

Bornholm
Bougainville
British
Bute
Butung
Caicos
Caldy
Calf of Man
Campobello
Canary
Canna
Canvey
Cape Breton
Capri
Caroline
Cayman
Cebú
Ceylon
Channel
Chatham
Cheju
Chichagof
Chiloé
Chios
Choiseul
Christmas
Cocos
Coll
Colonsay
Coney
Cook
Corfu
Corregidor
Corsica
Crete
Cuba
Curaçao
Cyclades
Cyprus
Cythera
Delos
D'Entrecasteaux
Diomede
Disko
Diu
Djerba or Jerba
Dodecanese
Dominica
Dry Tortugas
Easter
Eigg
Elba
Ellesmere
Espíritu Santo

Euboea
Faeroes
Faial or Fayal
Fair
Falkland
Falster
Farquhar
Fernando de Noronha
Fiji
Flannan
Flinders
Flores
Florida Keys
Foula
Foulness
Franz Josef Land
French West Indies
Frisian
Fyn
Galápagos
Gambier
Gigha
Gilbert
Gotland, Gothland, or
  Gottland
Grand Bahama
Grand Canary
Grande-Terre
Grand Manan
Greater Antilles
Greater Sunda
Greenland
Grenada
Grenadines
Guadalcanal
Guam
Guernsey
Hainan or Hainan Tao
Handa
Hawaii
Hayling
Heard and McDonald
Hebrides
Heimaey
Heligoland
Herm
Hispaniola
Hokkaido
Holy
Hong Kong
Honshu
Hormuz or Ormuz
Howland
Ibiza

ISLANDS AND ISLAND GROUPS

Icaria
Iceland
Imbros
Iona
Ionian
Ireland
Ischia
Islay
Isle Royale
Ithaca
Iwo Jima
Jamaica
Jan Mayen
Java
Jersey
Jolo
Juan Fernández
Jura
Kangaroo
Kauai
Keos
Kerrera
Kiritimati
Kodiak
Kos or Cos
Kosrae
Krakatoa or Krakatau
Kuril or Kurile
Kyushu or Kiushu
La Palma
Labuan
Lakshadweep
Lampedusa
Lanai
Lavongai
Leeward
Lemnos
Lesbos
Lesser Antilles
Levkás, Leukas, or Leucas
Lewis with Harris or Lewis
  and Harris
Leyte
Liberty
Lindisfarne
Line
Lipari
Lismore
Lolland or Laaland
Lombok
Long
Longa
Lord Howe
Luing

Lundy
Luzon
Mackinac
Macquarie
Madagascar
Madeira
Madura
Maewo
Mahé
Mainland
Majorca
Maldives
Malé
Malta
Man
Manhattan
Manitoulin
Marajó
Margarita
Marie Galante
Marinduque
Marquesas
Marshall
Martinique
Masbate
Mascarene
Matsu or Mazu
Maui
Mauritius
May
Mayotte
Melanesia
Melos
Melville
Mersea
Micronesia
Mindanao
Mindoro
Minorca
Miquelon
Molokai
Moluccas
Montserrat
Mount Desert
Muck
Mull
Mykonos
Nantucket
Nauru
Naxos
Negros
Netherlands Antilles
Nevis
New Britain

New Caledonia
Newfoundland
New Georgia
New Guinea
New Ireland
New Providence
New Siberian
Nicobar
Niue
Norfolk
North
North Uist
Nusa Tenggara
Oahu
Oceania
Okinawa
Orkneys or Orkney
Palawan
Palmyra
Panay
Pantelleria
Páros
Patmos
Pelagian
Pemba
Penang
Pescadores
Philae
Philippines
Phoenix
Pitcairn
Polynesia
Ponape
Pribilof
Prince Edward
Prince of Wales
Principe
Qeshm or Qishm
Queen Charlotte
Queen Elizabeth
Quemoy
Raasay
Ramsey
Rarotonga
Rathlin
Réunion
Rhodes
Rhum
Rialto
Roanoke
Robben
Rockall
Rona
Ross

WORD POWER

36

Ryukyu
Saba
Safety
Saipan
Sakhalin
Salamis
Saltee
Samar
Samoa
Samos
Samothrace
San Cristóbal
San Juan
San Salvador
Santa Catalina
Sao Miguel
Sao Tomé
Sardinia
Sark
Savaii
Scalpay
Schouten
Scilly
Sea
Seil
Seram or Ceram
Seychelles
Sheppey
Shetland
Sicily
Singapore
Sjælland
Skikoku
Skokholm
Skomer
Skye
Skyros or Scyros
Society
Socotra
South
Southampton

South Georgia
South Orkney
South Shetland
South Uist
Spitsbergen
Sporades
Sri Lanka
St. Croix
St. Helena
St. John
St. Kilda
St. Kitts or St. Christopher
St. Lucia
St. Martin
St. Tudwal's
St. Vincent
Staffa
Staten
Stewart
Stroma
Stromboli
Sulawesi
Sumatra
Sumba or Soemba
Sumbawa or Soembawa
Summer
Sunda or Soenda
Tahiti
Taiwan
Tasmania
Tenedos
Tenerife
Terceira
Thanet
Thásos
Thera
Thousand
Thursday
Timor
Tiree
Tobago

Tokelau
Tombo
Tonga
Tortola
Tortuga
Trinidad
Tristan da Cunha
Trobriand
Truk
Tsushima
Tuamotu
Tubuai
Turks
Tutuila
Tuvalu
Ulva
Unimak
Upolu
Ushant
Vancouver
Vanua Levu
Vanuatu
Vestmannaeyjar
Victoria
Virgin
Visayan
Viti Levu
Volcano
Walcheren
Walney
West Indies
Western
Wight
Windward
Wrangel
Yap
Youth
Zante
Zanzibar

Allen
Annecy
Aral Sea or Lake Aral
Ard
Athabaska
Averno
Awe
Baikal
Bala
Balaton
Balkhash
Bangweulu
Bassenthwaite
Belfast
Biel
Bodensee
Buttermere
Caspian Sea
Chad
Champlain
Como
Coniston Water
Constance
Crummock Water
Dead Sea
Derwentwater
Dongting
Earn
Edward
Ennerdale Water
Erie
Erne
Eyre
Frome
Fyne
Garda
Gatún
Geneva
Grasmere
Great Bear
Great Bitter
Great Lakes
Great Salt
Great Slave
Hawes Water
Huron
Ijsselmeer or Ysselmeer
Iliamna

Ilmen
Issyk-Kul
Kariba
Katrine
Kivu
Koko Nor or Kuku Nor
Kootenay
Ladoga
Laggan
Lake of the Woods
Leven
Linnhe
Little Bitter
Lochy
Lomond
Lucerne
Lugano
Léman
Maggiore
Malawi
Managua
Manitoba
Maracaibo
Mead
Meech
Memphremagog
Menteith
Michigan
Miraflores
Mistassini
Mobutu
Morar
Mweru
Nam Co or Nam Tso
Nasser
Neagh
Ness
Neuchâtel
Nicaragua
Nipigon
Nipissing
No
Nyasa
Okanagan
Okeechobee
Onega
Oneida
Onondaga

Ontario
Patos
Peipus
Pontchartrain
Poopó
Poyang or P'o-yang
Pskov
Rannoch
Reindeer
Rudolf
Saint Clair
Saint John
Sea of Galilee
Sevan
Stanley Pool
Superior
Sween
Taal
Tahoe
Tana
Tanganyika
Taupo
Tay
Thirlmere
Thun
Tien
Titicaca
Tonle Sap
Torrens
Torridon
Trasimene
Tummel
Turkana
Ullswater
Urmia
Van
Victoria
Volta
Waikaremoana
Washington
Wast Water
Windermere
Winnebago
Winnipeg
Zug
Zürich

Aconcagua
Adams
Albert Edward
Anai Mudi
Aneto
Annapurna
Apo
Aragats
Aran Fawddwy
Ararat
Arber
Argentera
Belukha
Ben Lomond
Ben Macdhui
Ben Nevis
Blackburn
Blanca Peak
Blue Mountain Peak
Bona
Brocken
Carmarthen Van
Carmel
Cerro de Mulhacén
Citlaltépetl
Clingman's Dome
Cook
Corcovado
Corno
Croagh Patrick
Demavend
Dhaulagiri
Eiger
Elbert
Elbrus
El Capitan
Emi Koussi
Estrella
Everest
Finsteraarhorn
Fuji
Gannet Peak
Gerlachovka
Grand Teton
Gran Paradiso
Harney Peak
Helicon
Helvellyn
Hermon

Humphreys Peak
Hymettus
Ida
Illimani
Isto
Jebel Musa
Jungfrau
K2 or Godwin Austen
Kamet
Kangchenjunga
Kenya
Kilimanjaro
Kinabalu
Kings Peak
Klínovec
Kommunizma Peak
Kongur Shan
Kosciusko
Lenin Peak
Leone
Logan
Longs Peak
Mansfield
Marcy
Markham
Marmolada
Masharbrum
Matterhorn
McKinley
Mitchell
Mont Blanc
Mount of Olives
Mulhacén
Munku-Sardyk
Musala
Nanda Devi
Nanga Parbat
Narodnaya
Nebo
Negoiu
Olympus
Ossa
Palomar
Parnassus
Pelion
Pentelikon
Perdido
Petermann Peak
Pikes Peak

Pilatus
Piz Bernina
Pobeda Peak
Puy de Dôme
Rainier
Rigi
Robson
Rock Creek
Rosa
Rushmore
Scafell Pike
Schneekoppe
Scopus
Sinai
Siple
Sir Sandford
Sir Wilfrid Laurier
Skalitsy
Slide Mountain
Smólikas
Snowdon
Sorata
Stanley
Sugar Loaf Mountain
Table Mountain
Tabor
Teide
Tengri Khan
Thabana Ntlenyana
Timpanogos
Tirich Mir
Toubkal
Troglav
Ulugh Muztagh
Uncompahgre Peak
Venusberg
Victoria
Viso
Waddington
Washington
Waun Fach
Weisshorn
White Mountain
Whitney
Wrangell
Zard Kuh
Zugspitze

Cook Islands	the Ross Dependency
Niue	Tokelau *or* Union Islands

WORD POWER

NOVELISTS

Peter Abrahams (*South African*)
Chinua Achebe (*Nigerian*)
Peter Ackroyd (*English*)
Douglas Adams (*English*)
Richard Adams (*English*)
Chimamanda Ngozi Adichie (*Nigerian*)
Alain-Fournier (*French*)
Brian Aldiss (*English*)
James Aldridge (*Australian*)
Monica Ali (*Bangladeshi/British*)
Al Alvarez (*English*)
Eric Ambler (*English*)
Kingsley Amis (*English*)
Martin Amis (*English*)
Mulk Raj Anand (*Indian*)
Maya Angelou (*U.S.*)
Lucius Apuleius (*Roman*)
Jeffrey Archer (*English*)
Isaac Asimov (*U.S.*)
Margaret Atwood (*Canadian*)
Louis Auchincloss (*U.S.*)
Jane Austen (*English*)
Beryl Bainbridge (*English*)
R M Ballantyne (*Scottish*)
J G Ballard (*English*)
Honoré de Balzac (*French*)
Iain Banks (*Scottish*)
Lynne Reid Banks (*English*)
Elspeth Barker (*Scottish*)
Nicola Barker (*English*)
Pat Barker (*English*)
Julian Barnes (*English*)
Stanley Barstow (*English*)
John Barth (*U.S.*)
H E Bates (*English*)
Nina Bawden (*English*)
Simone de Beauvoir (*French*)
Sybille Bedford (*British*)
Max Beerbohm (*English*)
Aphra Behn (*English*)
Saul Bellow (*Canadian*)
Andrei Bely (*Russian*)
David Benedictus (*English*)
(Enoch) Arnold Bennett (*English*)
John Berger (*English*)
Thomas Berger (*U.S.*)
Maeve Binchy (*Irish*)
R(ichard) D(oddridge)

Blackmore (*English*)
Alan Bleasdale (*English*)
Heinrich Böll (*German*)
Elizabeth Bowen (*Irish*)
Paul Bowles (*U.S.*)
William Boyd (*Scottish*)
Malcolm Bradbury (*English*)
Barbara Taylor Bradford (*English*)
Melvin Bragg (*English*)
John Braine (*English*)
André Brink (*South African*)
Vera Brittain (*English*)
Louis Bromfield (*U.S.*)
Anne Brontë (*English*)
Charlotte Brontë (*English*)
Emily (Jane) Brontë (*English*)
Christina Brooke-Rose (*English*)
Anita Brookner (*English*)
Brigid Brophy (*English*)
George Douglas Brown (*Scottish*)
George Mackay Brown (*Scottish*)
John Buchan (*Scottish*)
Pearl Buck (*U.S.*)
Mikhail Afanaseyev Bulgakov (*Russian*)
John Bunyan (*English*)
Anthony Burgess (*British*)
Fanny Burney (*English*)
Edgar Rice Burrows (*U.S.*)
William Burroughs (*U.S.*)
Samuel Butler (*English*)
A S Byatt (*English*)
Italo Calvino (*Italian*)
Albert Camus (*French*)
Elias Canetti (*Bulgarian*)
Truman Capote (*U.S.*)
Peter Carey (*Australian*)
Angela Carter (*English*)
Barbara Cartland (*English*)
Willa Cather (*U.S.*)
Camilo José Cela (*Spanish*)
Miguel de Cervantes (*Spanish*)
Raymond Chandler (*U.S.*)
G K Chesterton (*English*)
Agatha (Mary Clarissa) Christie (*English*)
Arthur C Clarke (*English*)
James Clavell (*U.S.*)

Jon Cleary (*Australian*)
J M Coatzee (*South African*)
Colette (*French*)
(William) Wilkie Collins (*English*)
Ivy Compton-Burnett (*English*)
Richard Condon (*U.S.*)
Evan Connell (*U.S.*)
Joseph Conrad (*Polish-British*)
Catherine Cookson (*English*)
James Fenimore Cooper (*U.S.*)
Jilly Cooper (*English*)
William Cooper (*English*)
Maria Corelli (*English*)
Stephen Crane (*U.S.*)
Lionel Davidson (*English*)
(William) Robertson Davies (*Canadian*)
Daniel Defoe (*English*)
Len Deighton (*English*)
E M Delafield (*English*)
Don DeLillo (*U.S.*)
Thomas de Quincy (*English*)
Anita Desai (*Indian*)
Kiran Desai (*Indian*)
Peter De Vries (*U.S.*)
Charles (John Huffam) Dickens (*English*)
Monica Dickens (*English*)
Joan Didion (*U.S.*)
Isak Dinesen (*Danish*)
Benjamin Disraeli (*English*)
J P Donleavy (*Irish*)
John Roderigo Dos Passos (*U.S.*)
Fyodor Mikhailovich Dostoevsky (*Russian*)
Arthur Conan Doyle (*Scottish*)
Roddy Doyle (*Irish*)
Margaret Drabble (*English*)
Maureen Duffy (*English*)
Alexandre Dumas (*French*)
Daphne Du Maurier (*English*)
Nell Dunn (*English*)
Gerald Durrell (*English*)
Laurence Durrell (*English*)
Umberto Eco (*Italian*)

NOVELISTS

Maria Edgeworth (*English*)
George Eliot (*English*)
Stanley Elkin (*U.S.*)
Alice Thomas Ellis (*English*)
Ben Elton (*English*)
Zöe Fairbairns (*English*)
Philip José Farmer (*U.S.*)
Howard Fast (*U.S.*)
William Faulkner (*U.S.*)
Elaine Feinstein (*English*)
Helen Fielding (*English*)
Henry Fielding (*English*)
Eva Figes (*British*)
F(rancis) Scott (Key) Fitzgerald (*U.S.*)
Penelope Fitzgerald (*English*)
Gustave Flaubert (*French*)
Ian Fleming (*English*)
Ford Madox Ford (*English*)
Richard Ford (*U.S.*)
C S Forester (*English*)
E M Forster (*English*)
Frederick Forsyth (*English*)
John Fowles (*English*)
Janet Paterson Frame (*New Zealand*)
Dick Francis (*English*)
Antonia Fraser (*English*)
Michael Frayn (*English*)
Nicholas Freeling (*English*)
Marilyn French (*U.S.*)
Roy Fuller (*English*)
William Gaddis (*U.S.*)
Janice Galloway (*Scottish*)
John Galsworthy (*English*)
Gabriel García Márquez (*Colombian*)
Helen Garner (*Australian*)
Elizabeth Gaskell (*English*)
William Alexander Gerhardie (*English*)
Lewis Grassic Gibbon (*Scottish*)
Stella Gibbons (*English*)
André Gide (*French*)
Penelope Gilliat (*English*)
George Gissing (*English*)
Ellen Glasgow (*U.S.*)
(Margaret) Rumer Godden (*English*)
William Godwin (*English*)
Johann Wolfgang von Goethe (*German*)

Nikolai Vasilievich Gogol (*Russian*)
Herbert Gold (*U.S.*)
William (Gerald) Golding (*English*)
William Goldman (*U.S.*)
Oliver Goldsmith (*Anglo-Irish*)
Ivan Aleksandrovich Goncharov (*Russian*)
Nadine Gordimer (*South African*)
Maxim Gorky (*Russian*)
Edmund Gosse (*English*)
Winston Graham (*English*)
Günter (Wilhelm) Grass (*German*)
Robert Graves (*English*)
Alasdair Gray (*Scottish*)
Graham Greene (*English*)
Philippa Gregory (*English*)
John Grisham (*U.S.*)
George Grossmith (*English*)
Weedon Grossmith (*English*)
David Guterson (*U.S.*)
Rider Haggard (*English*)
Arthur Hailey (*Anglo-Canadian*)
Thomas Hardy (*English*)
L(eslie) P(oles) Hartley (*English*)
Nathaniel Hawthorne (*U.S.*)
Shirley Hazzard (*U.S.*)
Robert A Heinlein (*U.S.*)
Joseph Heller (*U.S.*)
Ernest Hemingway (*U.S.*)
Hermann Hesse (*German*)
Georgette Heyer (*English*)
Patricia Highsmith (*U.S.*)
Susan Hill (*English*)
James Hilton (*English*)
Barry Hines (*English*)
Russell Hoban (*U.S.*)
James Hogg (*Scottish*)
Winifred Holtby (*English*)
Anthony Hope (*English*)
Paul Horgan (*U.S.*)
Elizabeth Jane Howard (*English*)
Thomas Hughes (*English*)
Victor (Marie) Hugo (*French*)
Keri Hulme (*New Zealand*)

Evan Hunter (*U.S.*)
Zora Neale Hurston (*U.S.*)
Aldous Huxley (*English*)
Hammond Innes (*English*)
John Irving (*U.S.*)
Christopher Isherwood (*English-U.S.*)
Kazuo Ishiguro (*British*)
Henry James (*U.S.-British*)
P D James (*English*)
Ruth Prawer Jhabvala (*Anglo-Polish*)
Erica Jong (*U.S.*)
James Joyce (*Irish*)
Franz Kafka (*Czech*)
Johanna Kaplan (*U.S.*)
Nikos Kazantazakis (*Greek*)
Molly Keane (*Anglo-Irish*)
James Kelman (*Scottish*)
Thomas Keneally (*Australian*)
Margaret Kennedy (*English*)
Jack Kerouac (*U.S.*)
Ken Kesey (*U.S.*)
Francis King (*English*)
Stephen King (*U.S.*)
Charles Kingsley (*English*)
Rudyard Kipling (*English*)
Milan Kundera (*French-Czech*)
Pierre Choderlos de Laclos (*French*)
George Lamming (*Barbadian*)
Guiseppe Tomasi di Lampedusa (*Italian*)
D H Lawrence (*English*)
John Le Carré (*English*)
Harper Lee (*U.S.*)
Laurie Lee (*English*)
Sheridan Le Fanu (*Irish*)
Ursula Le Guin (*U.S.*)
Rosamond Lehmann (*English*)
Mikhail Yurievich Lermontov (*Russian*)
Doris Lessing (*Rhodesian*)
Primo Levi (*Italian*)
(Harry) Sinclair Lewis (*U.S.*)
Penelope Lively (*English*)
David Lodge (*English*)
Jack London (*U.S.*)
(Clarence) Malcolm Lowry (*English*)

42

NOVELISTS

Alison Lurie (*U.S.*)
Rose Macauley (*English*)
Geraldine McCaughrean (*English*)
Carson McCullers (*U.S.*)
George MacDonald (*Scottish*)
Ian McEwan (*English*)
William McIlvanney (*Scottish*)
Colin MacInnes (*English*)
Compton MacKenzie (*English*)
Henry MacKenzie (*Scottish*)
Bernard McLaverty (*Irish*)
Alistair MacLean (*Scottish*)
Naguib Mahfouz (*Egyptian*)
Norman Mailer (*U.S.*)
Bernard Malamud (*U.S.*)
David Malouf (*Australian*)
(Cyril) Wolf Mankowitz (*English*)
Thomas Mann (*German*)
Olivia Manning (*English*)
Kamala Markandaya (*Indian*)
Frederick Marryat (*English*)
Ngaio Marsh (*New Zealand*)
Allan Massie (*Scottish*)
Somerset Maugham (*English*)
Guy de Maupassant (*French*)
Francois Mauriac (*French*)
Herman Melville (*U.S.*)
George Meredith (*English*)
James A Michener (*U.S.*)
Henry Miller (*U.S.*)
Yukio Mishima (*Japanese*)
Julian Mitchell (*English*)
Margaret Mitchell (*U.S.*)
Naomi Mitchison (*Scottish*)
Nancy Mitford (*English*)
Timothy Mo (*British*)
Nicholas Monsarrat (*English*)
Michael Moorcock (*English*)
Brian Moore (*Irish-Canadian*)
Toni Morrison (*U.S.*)
John Mortimer (*English*)
Penelope Mortimer (*Welsh*)
Nicholas Mosley (*English*)

Iris Murdoch (*Irish*)
Vladimir Vladimirovich Nabokov (*Russian-U.S.*)
V S Naipaul (*Trinidadian*)
P H Newby (*English*)
Ngugi wa Thiong'o (*Kenyan*)
Robert Nye (*English*)
Joyce Carol Oates (*U.S.*)
Edna O'Brien (*Irish*)
Kenzaburo Oë (*Japanese*)
Liam O'Flaherty (*Irish*)
John O'Hara (*U.S.*)
Ben Okri (*Nigerian*)
Margaret Oliphant (*Scottish*)
Michael Ondaatje (*Canadian*)
Baroness Emmuska Orczy (*Hungarian-British*)
George Orwell (*English*)
Ouida (*English*)
Cynthia Ozick (*U.S.*)
Boris Leonidovich Pasternak (*Russian*)
Allan Paton (*South African*)
Thomas Love Peacock (*English*)
Mervyn Peake (*English*)
Jodi Picoult (*U.S.*)
Harold Porter (*Australian*)
Katherine Anne Porter (*U.S.*)
Anthony Powell (*English*)
John Cowper Powys (*English*)
Terry Pratchett (*English*)
J B Priestley (*English*)
V S Pritchett (*English*)
E Annie Proulx (*U.S.*)
Marcel Proust (*French*)
Mario Puzo (*U.S.*)
Thomas Pynchon (*U.S.*)
Ellery Queen (*U.S.*)
Ann Radcliffe (*English*)
Ian Rankin (*Scottish*)
Raja Rao (*Indian*)
Frederic Raphael (*U.S.*)
Piers Paul Read (*English*)
Erich Maria Remarque (*German*)
Mary Renault (*English*)
Ruth Rendell (*English*)
Jean Rhys (*British*)
Dorothy Richardson

(*English*)
Samuel Richardson (*English*)
Mordecai Richler (*Canadian*)
Harold Robbins (*U.S.*)
Frederick William Rolfe (*English*)
Henry Roth (*U.S.*)
(Ahmed) Salman Rushdie (*Indian-British*)
Vita Sackville-West (*English*)
Marquis de Sade (*French*)
Antoine de Saint-Exupéry (*French*)
Saki (*British*)
J D Salinger (*U.S.*)
George Sand (*French*)
William Saroyan (*U.S.*)
Jean-Paul Sartre (*French*)
Dorothy L Sayers (*English*)
Olive Schreiner (*South African*)
Walter Scott (*Scottish*)
Hubert Selby Jr (*U.S.*)
Tom Sharpe (*English*)
Mary Shelley (*English*)
Carol Shields (*Canadian-American*)
Mikhail Alexandrovich Sholokhov (*Russian*)
Nevil Shute (*Anglo-Austrian*)
Alan Sillitoe (*English*)
Georges Simenon (*Belgian*)
Claude Simon (*French*)
Isaac Bashevis Singer (*U.S.*)
Iain Crichton Smith (*Scottish*)
Zadie Smith (*British*)
Tobias George Smollett (*Scottish*)
C P Snow (*English*)
Alexander Isayevich Solzhenitsyn (*Russian*)
Muriel Spark (*Scottish*)
Howard Spring (*Welsh*)
C K Stead (*New Zealand*)
Gertrude Stein (*U.S.*)
John Steinbeck (*U.S.*)
Stendhal (*French*)
Laurence Sterne (*Irish-British*)
Robert Louis Stevenson (*Scottish*)
J I M Stewart (*Scottish*)

NOVELISTS

Mary Stewart (*English*)
Bram Stoker (*Irish*)
Robert Stone (*U.S.*)
David Storey (*English*)
Harriet Elizabeth Beecher
  Stowe (*U.S.*)
William Styron (*U.S.*)
Patrick Süskind (*German*)
Graham Swift (*English*)
Jonathan Swift (*Irish*)
Julian Symons (*English*)
Emma Tennant (*English*)
William Makepeace
  Thackeray (*English*)
Paul Theroux (*U.S.*)
J(ohn) R(onald) R(euel)
  Tolkien (*English*)
Leo Tolstoy (*Russian*)
John Kennedy Toole (*U.S.*)
Nigel Tranter (*Scottish*)
Rose Tremain (*English*)
William Trevor (*Irish*)
Anthony Trollope (*English*)
Joanna Trollope (*English*)
Frank Tuohy (*English*)
Ivan Sergeyevich Turgenev
  (*Russian*)
Amos Tutuola (*Nigerian*)
Mark Twain (*U.S.*)

Anne Tyler (*U.S.*)
John Updike (*U.S.*)
Edward (Falaise) Upward
  (*English*)
Leon Uris (*U.S.*)
Laurens Van der Post (*South
  African*)
Peter Vansittart (*English*)
Mario Vargos Llosa
  (*Peruvian*)
Jules Verne (*French*)
Gore Vidal (*U.S.*)
Voltaire (*French*)
Kurt Vonnegut (*U.S.*)
John Wain (*English*)
Alice Walker (*U.S.*)
Horace Walpole (*English*)
Marina Warner (*English*)
Robert Penn Warren (*U.S.*)
Keith Waterhouse
  (*English*)
Sarah Waters (*English*)
Evelyn Waugh (*English*)
Fay Weldon (*English*)
H G Wells (*English*)
Irvine Welsh (*Scottish*)
Eudora Welty (*U.S.*)
Mary Wesley (*English*)
Morris West (*Australian*)

Rebecca West (*Irish*)
Edith Wharton (*U.S.*)
Antonia White (*English*)
Patrick White
  (*Australian*)
T H White (*English*)
Oscar Wilde (*Irish*)
Thornton Wilder (*U.S.*)
Michael Wilding
  (*Australian*)
A(ndrew) N(orman) Wilson
  (*English*)
Jeanette Winterson (*English*)
P(elham) G(renville)
  Wodehouse (*English-U.S.*)
Thomas Clayton Wolfe
  (*U.S.*)
Tom Wolfe (*U.S.*)
Tobias Wolff (*U.S.*)
Virginia Woolf (*English*)
Herman Wouk (*U.S.*)
Richard Nathaniel Wright
  (*U.S.*)
Frank Yerby (*U.S.*)
Marguerite Yourcenar
  (*French*)
Evgeny Ivanovich
  Zamyatin (*Russian*)
Emile Zola (*French*)

PLACES AND THEIR NICKNAMES

Place	Nickname	Place	Nickname
Aberdeen	the Granite City	Kuala Lumpur	K.L.
Adelaide	the City of Churches	London	the Big Smoke *or* the Great Wen
Amsterdam	the Venice of the North	Los Angeles	L.A.
Birmingham	Brum *or* the Venice of the North	New Jersey	the Garden State
		New Orleans	the Crescent City *or* the Big Easy
Boston	Bean Town	New South Wales	Ma State
Bruges	the Venice of the North	New York (City)	the Big Apple
California	the Golden State	New York (State)	the Empire State
Chicago	the Windy City	New Zealand	Pig Island
Dallas	the Big D	North Carolina	the Tarheel State
Detroit	the Motor City	Nottingham	Queen of the Midlands
Dresden	Florence on the Elbe		
Dublin	the Fair City	Oklahoma	the Sooner State
Dumfries	Queen of the South	Pennsylvania	the Keystone State
Edinburgh	Auld Reekie *or* the Athens of the North	Philadelphia	Philly
		Portsmouth	Pompey
Finland	Land of the Midnight Sun	Prince Edward Island	Spud Island
Florida	the Sunshine State	Queensland	Bananaland *or* the Deep North (*both derogatory*)
Fraserburgh	the Broch		
Fremantle	Freo	Rome	the Eternal City
Glasgow	the Dear Green Place	Russia	Mother Russia
Hamburg	the Venice of the North	San Francisco	Frisco
		South Africa	The Rainbow Nation
Indiana	the Hoosier State	Southeastern U.S.A.	Dixie, Dixieland, *or* the Deep South
Iowa	the Hawkeye State		
Ireland	the Emerald Isle	Tasmania	Tassie *or* the Apple Isle
Jamaica	J.A. *or* the Yard		
Japan	Land of the Rising Sun	Texas	the Lone Star State
		Utah	the Beehive State
Jerusalem	the Holy City	Venice	La Serenissima
Kentucky	the Bluegrass State		

POETRY

Poetry and prosody terms

accentual metre
accentual-syllabic metre or stress-syllabic metre
Adonic
Alcaic
Alexandrine
alliteration
amoebaean or amoebean
amphibrach
amphimacer
anacrusis
arsis
anapaest or anapest
anapaestic or anapestic
antistrophe
assonance
bacchius
ballad stanza
blank verse
bob
cadence or cadency
caesura or cesura
canto
catalectic
choriamb or choriambus
closed couplet
common measure
common metre
consonance or consonancy
couplet
cretic or amphimacer
dactyl
dactylic
diaeresis or dieresis
dipody
distich
elision
end-stopped

enjambement
envoy or envoi
epode
eye rhyme
feminine ending
feminine rhyme
foot
free verse or vers libre
half-rhyme
hemistich
heptameter
heptastich
heroic couplet
hexameter
hypermeter
iamb or iambus
iambic
ictus
internal rhyme
ionic
jabberwocky
leonine rhyme
long metre
macaronic
masculine ending
masculine rhyme
metre
octameter
octave or octet
onomatopoeia
ottava rima
paeon
paeonic
pararhyme
pentameter
pentastich
perfect rhyme or full rhyme
Pindaric

pyhrric
quantitative metre
quatrain
quintain or quintet
refrain
rhyme
rhyme royal
rhyme scheme
rhythm
rime riche
Sapphic
scansion
septet
sestet
sestina or sextain
short metre
Spenserian stanza
spondee
spondaic
sprung rhythm
stanza
stichic
strophe
syllabic metre
tercet
terza rima
tetrabrach
tetrameter
tetrapody
tetrastich
triplet
trochaic
trochee
unstopped
verse paragraph
wheel

Poetry movements and groupings

Alexandrians
Confessionalists
Decadents
Georgian Poets
imagists

Lake Poets
Liverpool Poets
Metaphysical Poets
the Movement
Objectivists

Pastoralists
Petrarchans
Romantics
Scottish Chaucerians
symbolists

Dannie Abse (*Welsh*)
(Karen) Fleur Adcock (*New Zealander*)
Conrad (Potter) Aiken (*U.S.*)
Anna Akhamatova (*Russian*)
Maya Angelou (*U.S.*)
Guillaume Apollinaire (*French*)
Ludovico Ariosto (*Italian*)
Matthew Arnold (*English*)
W(ystan) H(ugh) Auden (*English-U.S.*)
Charles Pierre Baudelaire (*French*)
Patricia Beer (*English*)
Hilaire Belloc (*British*)
John Berryman (*U.S.*)
John Betjeman (*English*)
Elizabeth Bishop (*U.S.*)
William Blake (*English*)
Edmund Blunden (*English*)
Joseph Brodsky (*Russian-American*)
Rupert (Chawner) Brooke (*English*)
Gwendolyn Brooks (*U.S.*)
Elizabeth Barrett Browning (*English*)
Robert Browning (*English*)
Robert Burns (*Scottish*)
(George Gordon) Byron (*British*)
Callimachus (*Greek*)
Luis Vaz de Camoëns (*Portuguese*)
Thomas Campion (*English*)
Raymond Carver (*U.S.*)
Gaius Valerius Catullus (*Roman*)
Charles Causley (*English*)
Geoffrey Chaucer (*English*)
Amy Clampitt (*U.S.*)
John Clare (*English*)
Samuel Taylor Coleridge (*English*)
Wendy Cope (*English*)
William Cowper (*English*)
George Crabbe (*English*)
e(dward) e(stlin) cummings (*U.S.*)
Dante (Alighieri) (*Italian*)
Cecil Day Lewis (*Irish*)
Walter de la Mare (*English*)
Emily Dickinson (*U.S.*)
John Donne (*English*)
H D (Hilda Doolittle) (*U.S.*)
John Dryden (*English*)
Carol Ann Duffy (*Scottish*)
William Dunbar (*Scottish*)
Douglas Dunn (*Scottish*)
Geoffrey Dutton (*Australian*)
T(homas) S(tearns) Eliot (*U.S.-British*)
Ebenezer Elliot (the Corn Law Rhymer)
  (*English*)
Paul Éluard (*French*)
Ralph Waldo Emerson (*U.S.*)

William Empson (*English*)
Edward Fitzgerald (*English*)
Robert Fitzgerald (*Australian*)
Robert (Lee) Frost (*U.S.*)
Allen Ginsberg (*U.S.*)
Johann Wolfgang von Goethe (*German*)
Robert Graves (*English*)
Thomas Gray (*English*)
Thom Gunn (*English*)
Seamus Heaney (*Irish*)
Adrian Henri (*English*)
Robert Henryson (*Scottish*)
George Herbert (*English*)
Robert Herrick (*English*)
Hesiod (*Greek*)
Geoffrey Hill (*English*)
Ralph Hodgson (*English*)
Homer (*Greek*)
Thomas Hood (*English*)
Gerard Manley Hopkins (*English*)
Horace (*Roman*)
A(lfred) E(dward) Housman (*English*)
Ted Hughes (*English*)
Elizabeth Jennings (*English*)
Samuel Johnson (*English*)
Ben Jonson (*English*)
Juvenal (*Roman*)
Patrick Kavanagh (*Irish*)
John Keats (*English*)
Sidney Keyes (*English*)
(Joseph) Rudyard Kipling (*English*)
Jean de La Fontaine (*French*)
Alphonse Marie Louis de Prat de Lamartine
  (*French*)
Walter Savage Landor (*English*)
William Langland (*English*)
Philip Larkin (*English*)
Tom Leonard (*Scottish*)
Gwyneth Lewis (*Welsh*)
Henry Wadsworth Longfellow (*U.S.*)
Amy Lowell (*U.S.*)
Robert Lowell (*U.S.*)
Richard Lovelace (*English*)
Lucretius (*Roman*)
Thomas Macauley (*English*)
Norman MacCaig (*Scottish*)
Hugh MacDiarmid (*Scottish*)
Roger McGough (*English*)
Sorley MacLean (*Scottish*)
Louis MacNeice (*Irish*)
Stéphane Mallarmé (*French*)
Martial (*Roman*)
Andrew Marvell (*English*)
John Masefield (*English*)

WORD POWER

Edna St Vincent Millay (*U.S.*)
John Milton (*English*)
Marianne Moore (*U.S.*)
Edwin Morgan (*Scottish*)
Andrew Motion (*English*)
Edwin Muir (*Scottish*)
Ogden Nash (*U.S.*)
Pablo Neruda (*Chilean*)
Frank O'Hara (*U.S.*)
Omar Khayyam (*Persian*)
Ovid (*Roman*)
Wilfred Owen (*British*)
Brian Patten (*English*)
Octavio Paz (*Mexican*)
Petrarch (*Italian*)
Pindar (*Greek*)
Sylvia Plath (*U.S.*)
Alexander Pope (*English*)
Peter Porter (*Australian*)
Ezra (Loomis) Pound (*U.S.*)
Sextus Propertius (*Roman*)
Aleksander Sergeyevich Pushkin (*Russian*)
Kathleen Raine (*English*)
Adrienne Rich (*U.S.*)
Laura Riding (*U.S.*)
Rainer Maria Rilke (*Austro-German*)
Arthur Rimbaud (*French*)
Robin Robertson (*Scottish*)
(John Wilmot) Rochester (*English*)
Theodore Huebner Roethke (*U.S.*)
Isaac Rosenberg (*English*)
Christina Georgina Rossetti (*English*)
Dante Gabriel Rossetti (*English*)
Saint-John Perse (*French*)
Sappho (*Greek*)
Siegfried Sassoon (*English*)

Johann Christoph Friedrich von Schiller
  (*German*)
Delmore Schwarz (*U.S.*)
Sir Walter Scott (*Scottish*)
Jaroslav Seifert (*Czech*)
William Shakespeare (*English*)
Percy Bysshe Shelley (*English*)
Sir Philip Sidney (*English*)
Edith Sitwell (*English*)
John Skelton (*English*)
Christopher Smart (*English*)
Stevie Smith (*English*)
Robert Southey (*English*)
Stephen Spender (*English*)
Edmund Spenser (*English*)
Wallace Stevens (*U.S.*)
Algernon Charles Swinburne (*English*)
Wislawa Szymborska (*Polish*)
Torquato Tasso (*Italian*)
Alfred, Lord Tennyson (*English*)
Dylan (Marlais) Thomas (*Welsh*)
Edward Thomas (*English*)
R(onald) S(tuart) Thomas (*Welsh*)
James Thomson (*Scottish*)
Paul Verlaine (*French*)
Alfred Victor de Vigny (*French*)
François Villon (*French*)
Virgil (*Roman*)
Derek Walcott (*West Indian*)
Francis Charles Webb (*Australian*)
Walt Whitman (*U.S.*)
William Wordsworth (*English*)
Judith Wright (*Australian*)
Thomas Wyatt (*English*)
W(illiam) B(utler) Yeats (*Irish*)

WORD POWER

POLITICAL PARTIES

Australia
Australian Labor Party
Liberal Party of Australia
National Party of Australia

Austria
Freedom Party (FPÖ)
People's Party (ÖVP)
Socialist Party (SPÖ)

Belgium
Flemish Bloc (VB)
Flemish Green Party (Agalev)
French Green Party (Ecolo)
Flemish Liberal Party (PVV)
French Liberal Reform Party (PRL)
Flemish Social Christian Party (CVP)
French Social Christian Party (PSC)
Flemish Socialist Party (SP)
French Socialist Party (PS)

Canada
Bloc Quebecois
Liberal Party
New Democratic Party
Progressive Conservative
Reform Party
Social Credit Party

Denmark
Centre Democrats (CD)
Christian People's Party (KrF)
Conservative People's Party (KF)
Left Socialists
Liberals (V)
Progress Party (FP)
Radical Liberals (RV)
Social Democrats (SD)
Socialist People's Party (SF)

Finland
Centre Party (KP)
Democratic Alternative
Finnish People's Democratic League (SKDL)
Finnish Rural Party (SMP)
Green League
Left Alliance
National Coalition Party (KOK)
Social Democratic Party (SD)
Swedish People's Party (SFP)

France
Communist Party (PC)
National Front
Republican Party (PR)
Socialist Party (PS)
Union for a Popular Movement (UMP)
Union for French Democracy (UDF)

Germany
Christian-Democratic Union (CDU)
Christian-Social Union (CSU)
Free Democratic Party (FDP)
Green Party
Social Democratic Party (SPD)
The Left

Greece
Coalition of the Radical Left (SYRIZA)
Greek Communist Party
New Democracy (ND)
Pan-Hellenic Socialist Movement (PASOK)
Popular Orthodox Rally (LAOS)

India
Bahujan Samaj Party (BSP)
Bharitiya Janata Party (BJP)
Communist Party of India (CPI)
Communist Party of India (Marxist) (CPI(M))
Congress (I)
Indian National Congress (INC)
Janata Dal
National Congress Party (NCP)

Irish Republic
Democratic Left
Fianna Fáil
Fine Gael
Labour Party
Progressive Democrats

Israel
Labour Party
Likud

Italy
Christian Democrat Party
Democratic Left (SD)
Forza Italia
National Alliance
Northern League

POLITICAL PARTIES

WORD POWER

Japan
Democratic Party of Japan
Japanese Communist Party (JCP)
Liberal Democratic Party
New Komeito
Social Democratic Party

Luxembourg
Communist Party
Democratic Party (PD)
Luxembourg Socialist Workers' Party
(POSL)
Christian Social Party (PCS)

Malta
Malta Labour Party
Nationalist Party

Mexico
Institutional Revolutionary Party (PRI)
National Action Party (PAN)
Party of the Democratic Revolution (PRD)

the Netherlands
Christian Democratic Appeal (CDA)
Labour Party (PvdA)
People's Party for Freedom and Democracy
(VVD)
Socialist Party (SP)

New Zealand
Labour Party
National Party

Northern Ireland
Democratic Unionist Party
Official Ulster Unionist Party
Sinn Féin
Social Democratic and Labour Party (SDLP)

Portugal .
Communist Party
Green Party
Left Bloc
Popular Party
Social Democratic Party (PSD)
Socialist Party (PS)

South Africa
African National Congress (ANC)
Inkatha Freedom Party
Pan-Africanist Congress (PAC)

Spain
Basque Nationalist Party (PNV)
Convergencia i Uni (CiU)
People's Party (PP)
Socialist Workers' Party (PSOE)
United Left (IU)

Sweden
Centre Party
Christian Democratic Party
Green Party
Left Party
Liberal Party
Moderate Party
Social Democratic Labour Party (SAP)

Turkey
Nationalist Movement Party
Republican People's Party

United Kingdom (mainland)
Conservative and Unionist Party
Labour Party
Liberal Democrats
Plaid Cymru
Scottish National Party

United States of America
Democratic Party
Republican Party

Major world ports

Abidjan
Accra
Aden
Alexandria
Algiers
Alicante
Amsterdam
Anchorage
Antwerp
Apia
Aqaba
Archangel
Ashdod
Auckland
Baku
Baltimore
Bangkok
Barcelona
Basra
Bathurst
Batum
Beira
Beirut
Belize
Benghazi
Bergen
Bilbao
Bissau
Bombay
Bordeaux
Boston
Boulogne
Bridgetown
Brindisi
Brisbane
Bristol
Buenaventura
Buenos Aires
Cádiz
Cagliari
Calais
Calcutta
Callao
Cannes
Canton
Cape Town
Cap-Haitien
Casablanca
Catania
Cebu
Charleston
Cherbourg

Chicago
Chittagong
Colombo
Colón
Conakry
Copenhagen
Corinth
Dakar
Dar es Salaam
Darwin
Dieppe
Djibouti
Dubrovnik
Duluth
Dunedin
Dunkerque
Durban
East London
Eilat or Elat
Esbjerg
Europoort
Fray Bentos
Freetown
Fremantle
Gdańsk
Genoa
Georgetown
Gijón
Göteborg or Gothenburg
Guayaquil
Haifa
Halifax
Hamburg
Hamilton
Havana
Helsinki
Hobart
Ho Chi Minh City
Honolulu
Hook of Holland
Inchon
Istanbul
Izmir
Jacksonville
Jaffa
Jidda or Jedda
Juneau
Kaohsiung or Kao-hsiung
Karachi
Kawasaki
Keflavik
Kiel

Kingston
Kobe
Kowloon
Kuwait
La Coruña
Lagos
La Guaira
Las Palmas
Launceston
Le Havre
Limassol
Lisbon
Liverpool
Livorno
Lomé
London
Los Angeles
Luanda
Lübeck
Macao
Madras
Malmo
Manama
Manaus
Manila
Maputo
Mar del Plata
Marseille
Melbourne
Mobile
Mogadiscio or Mogadishu
Mombasa
Monrovia
Montego Bay
Montevideo
Montreal
Murmansk
Muscat
Nagasaki
Naples
Nassau
New Orleans
New York
Oakland
Odense
Odessa
Oporto
Osaka
Oslo
Ostend
Phnom Penh
Piraeus

WORD POWER

Major world ports (continued)

Port Adelaide
Port au Prince
Port Elizabeth
Portland
Port Louis
Port Moresby
Port Said
Portsmouth
Port Sudan
Punta Arenas
Pusan
Recife
Reykjavik
Riga
Rimini
Rio de Janeiro
Rostock
Rotterdam
Saint Petersburg
Salvador
San Diego
San Francisco
San Juan

San Sebastian
Santander
Santo Domingo
Santos
Savannah
Seattle
Sevastopol
Seville
Shanghai
Singapore
Southampton
Split
Stavanger
Stockholm
Suez
Suva
Sydney
Szczecin
Takoradi
Tallinn or Tallin
Tampa
Tandjungpriok
Tangier

Tokyo
Townsville
Trieste
Tripoli
Trondheim
Tunis
Turku
Tyre
Valencia
Valparaíso
Vancouver
Venice
Veracruz
Vigo
Vishakhapatnam
Vladivostok
Volgograd
Walvis Bay
Wellington
Yangon
Yokohama
Zeebrugge

Major British and Irish ports

Aberdeen
Arbroath
Ayr
Barry
Belfast
Birkenhead
Bristol
Caernarfon
Cardiff
Cóbh
Cork
Dover
Dundee
Dún Laoghaire
Ellesmere Port
Fishguard
Fleetwood
Folkestone
Galway
Glasgow
Grangemouth
Gravesend
Great Yarmouth

Greenock
Grimsby
Harwich
Holyhead
Hull
Immingham
Kirkcaldy
Larne
Leith
Lerwick
Limerick
Liverpool
London
Londonderry or Derry
Lowestoft
Milford Haven
Morecambe
Newcastle upon Tyne
Newhaven
Newport
Newry
Oban
Penzance

Plymouth
Poole
Portsmouth
Port Talbot
Ramsgate
Rosslare
Scarborough
Sheerness
Sligo
Southampton
South Shields
Stornoway
Stranraer
Sunderland
Swansea
Tynemouth
Waterford
Wexford
Weymouth
Whitby
Wicklow

PRIME MINISTERS

British Prime Ministers

Prime Minister	Party	Term of office
Robert Walpole	Whig	1721–42
Earl of Wilmington	Whig	1742–43
Henry Pelham	Whig	1743–54
Duke of Newcastle	Whig	1754–56
Duke of Devonshire	Whig	1756–57
Duke of Newcastle	Whig	1757–62
Earl of Bute	Tory	1762–63
George Grenville	Whig	1763–65
Marquess of Rockingham	Whig	1765–66
Duke of Grafton	Whig	1766–70
Lord North	Tory	1770–82
Marquess of Rockingham	Whig	1782
Earl of Shelburne	Whig	1782–83
Duke of Portland	Coalition	1783
William Pitt	Tory	1783–1801
Henry Addington	Tory	1801–04
William Pitt	Tory	1804–06
Lord Grenville	Whig	1806–07
Duke of Portland	Tory	1807–09
Spencer Perceval	Tory	1809–12
Earl of Liverpool	Tory	1812–27
George Canning	Tory	1827
Viscount Goderich	Tory	1827–28
Duke of Wellington	Tory	1828–30
Earl Grey	Whig	1830–34
Viscount Melbourne	Whig	1834
Robert Peel	Conservative	1834–35
Viscount Melbourne	Whig	1835–41
Robert Peel	Conservative	1841–46
Lord John Russell	Liberal	1846–52
Earl of Derby	Conservative	1852
Lord Aberdeen	Peelite	1852–55
Viscount Palmerston	Liberal	1855–58
Earl of Derby	Conservative	1858–59
Viscount Palmerston	Liberal	1859–65
Lord John Russell	Liberal	1865–66
Earl of Derby	Conservative	1866–68
Benjamin Disraeli	Conservative	1868
William Gladstone	Liberal	1868–74
Benjamin Disraeli	Conservative	1874–80
William Gladstone	Liberal	1880–85
Marquess of Salisbury	Conservative	1885–86
William Gladstone	Liberal	1886
Marquess of Salisbury	Conservative	1886–92
William Gladstone	Liberal	1892–94
Earl of Rosebery	Liberal	1894–95
Marquess of Salisbury	Conservative	1895–1902
Arthur James Balfour	Conservative	1902–05
Henry Campbell-Bannerman	Liberal	1905–08
Herbert Henry Asquith	Liberal	1908–15
Herbert Henry Asquith	Coalition	1915–16

WORD POWER

British Prime Ministers (continued)

Prime Minister	Party	Term of office
David Lloyd George	Coalition	1916–22
Andrew Bonar Law	Conservative	1922–23
Stanley Baldwin	Conservative	1923–24
James Ramsay MacDonald	Labour	1924
Stanley Baldwin	Conservative	1924–29
James Ramsay MacDonald	Labour	1929–31
James Ramsay MacDonald	Nationalist	1931–35
Stanley Baldwin	Nationalist	1935–37
Arthur Neville Chamberlain	Nationalist	1937–40
Winston Churchill	Coalition	1940–45
Clement Attlee	Labour	1945–51
Winston Churchill	Conservative	1951–55
Anthony Eden	Conservative	1955–57
Harold Macmillan	Conservative	1957–63
Alec Douglas-Home	Conservative	1963–64
Harold Wilson	Labour	1964–70
Edward Heath	Conservative	1970–74
Harold Wilson	Labour	1974–76
James Callaghan	Labour	1976–79
Margaret Thatcher	Conservative	1979–90
John Major	Conservative	1990–97
Tony Blair	Labour	1997–2007
Gordon Brown	Labour	2007–

Australian Prime Ministers

Prime Minister	Party	Term of office
Edmund Barton	Protectionist	1901–03
Alfred Deakin	Protectionist	1903–04
John Christian Watson	Labor	1904
George Houston Reid	Free Trade	1904–05
Alfred Deakin	Protectionist	1905–08
Andrew Fisher	Labor	1908–09
Alfred Deakin	Fusion	1909–10
Andrew Fisher	Labor	1910–13
Joseph Cook	Liberal	1913–14
Andrew Fisher	Labor	1914–15
William Morris Hughes	National Labor	1915–17
William Morris Hughes	Nationalist	1917–23
Stanley Melbourne Bruce	Nationalist	1923–29
James Henry Scullin	Labor	1929–31
Joseph Aloysius Lyons	United	1931–39
Earle Christmas Page	Country	1939
Robert Gordon Menzies	United	1939–41
Arthur William Fadden	Country	1941
John Joseph Curtin	Labor	1941–45
Joseph Benedict Chifley	Labor	1945–49
Robert Gordon Menzies	Liberal	1949–66
Harold Edward Holt	Liberal	1966–67
John McEwen	Country	1967–68

Australian Prime Ministers (continued)

Prime Minister	Party	Term of office
John Grey Gorton	Liberal	1968–71
William McMahon	Liberal	1971–72
Edward Gough Whitlam	Labor	1972–75
John Malcolm Fraser	Liberal	1975–83
Robert James Lee Hawke	Labor	1983–91
Paul Keating	Labor	1991–96
John Howard	Liberal	1996–2007
Kevin Rudd	Labor	2007–

Canadian Prime Ministers

Prime Minister	Party	Term of office
John A. MacDonald	Conservative	1867–73
Alexander Mackenzie	Liberal	1873–78
John A. MacDonald	Conservative	1878–91
John J.C. Abbot	Conservative	1891–92
John S.D. Thompson	Conservative	1892–94
Mackenzie Bowell	Conservative	1894–96
Charles Tupper	Conservative	1896
Wilfrid Laurier	Liberal	1896–1911
Robert Borden	Conservative	1911–20
Arthur Meighen	Conservative	1920–21
William Lyon Mackenzie King	Liberal	1921–1926
Arthur Meighen	Conservative	1926
William Lyon Mackenzie King	Liberal	1926–30
Richard Bedford Bennet	Conservative	1930–35
William Lyon Mackenzie King	Liberal	1935–48
Louis St. Laurent	Liberal	1948–57
John George Diefenbaker	Conservative	1957–63
Lester Bowles Pearson	Liberal	1963–68
Pierre Elliott Trudeau	Liberal	1968–79
Joseph Clark	Conservative	1979–80
Pierre Elliott Trudeau	Liberal	1968–79
Joseph Clark	Conservative	1979–80
Pierre Elliott Trudeau	Liberal	1980–84
John Turner	Liberal	1984
Brian Mulroney	Conservative	1984–93
Kim Campbell	Conservative	1993
Paul Martin	Liberal	2003–2006
Stephen Harper	Conservative	2006–

New Zealand Prime Ministers

Prime Minister	Party	Term of office
Henry Sewell	–	1856
William Fox	–	1856
Edward William Stafford	–	1856–61
William Fox	–	1861–62
Alfred Domett	–	1862–63
Frederick Whitaker	–	1863–64

New Zealand Prime Ministers (continued)

Prime Minister	Party	Term of office
Frederick Aloysius Weld	–	1864–65
Edward William Stafford	–	1865–69
William Fox	–	1869–72
Edward William Stafford	–	1872
William Fox	–	1873
Julius Vogel	–	1873–75
Daniel Pollen	–	1875–76
Julius Vogel	–	1876
Harry Albert Atkinson	–	1876–77
George Grey	–	1877–79
John Hall	–	1879–82
Frederic Whitaker	–	1882–83
Harry Albert Atkinson	–	1883–84
Robert Stout	–	1884
Harry Albert Atkinson	–	1884
Robert Stout	–	1884–87
Harry Albert Atkinson	–	1887–91
John Ballance	–	1891–93
Richard John Seddon	Liberal	1893–1906
William Hall-Jones	Liberal	1906
Joseph George Ward	Liberal/National	1906–12
Thomas Mackenzie	National	1912
William Ferguson Massey	Reform	1912–25
Francis Henry Dillon Bell	Reform	1925
Joseph Gordon Coates	Reform	1925–28
Joseph George Ward	Liberal/National	1928–30
George William Forbes	United	1930–35
Michael Joseph Savage	Labour	1935–40
Peter Fraser	Labour	1940–49
Sidney George Holland	National	1949–57
Keith Jacka Holyoake	National	1957
Walter Nash	Labour	1957–60
Keith Jacka Holyoake	National	1960–72
John Ross Marshall	National	1972
Norman Eric Kirk	Labour	1972–74
Wallace Edward Rowling	Labour	1974–75
Robert David Muldoon	National	1975–84
David Russell Lange	Labour	1984–89
Geoffrey Palmer	Labour	1989–90
Mike Moore	Labour	1990
Jim Bolger	National	1990–97
Jenny Shipley	National	1997–99
Helen Clark	Labour	1999–

RIVERS

Adige
Ain
Aire
Aisne
Alabama
Albany
Aldan
Allier
Amazon
Amu Darya
Amur
Anadyr
Anderson
Angara
Apure
Apurimac
Araguaia
Aras
Arkansas
Arno
Aruwimi
Assiniboine
Atbara
Athabaska
Aube
Avon
Back
Barrow
Beni
Benue
Berezina
Bermejo
Bío-Bío
Black Volta
Blue Nile
Bomu
Boyne
Brahmaputra
Bug
Cam
Canadian
Caquetá
Cauca
Cauvery or Kaveri
Chagres
Chao Phraya
Charente
Chari or Shari
Chenab
Cher
Chindwin
Churchill
Clutha
Clyde

Colorado
Columbia
Congo
Connecticut
Cooper's Creek
Courantyne
Cuiaba
Damodar
Danube
Darling
Dee
Delaware
Demerara
Derwent
Des Moines
Detroit
Dnieper
Dniester
Don
Donets
Dordogne
Doubs
Douro
Drava or Drave
Drin
Durance
Dvina
Ebro
Elbe
Ems
Erne
Essequibo
Euphrates
Fly
Forth
Fraser
Ganges
Garonne
Glomma
Godavari
Gogra
Göta
Granta
Green
Guadalquivir
Guadiana
Guaporé
Han
Havel
Helmand
Hooghly
Hudson
Iguaçú or Iguassú
IJssel or Yssel

Illinois
Indus
Inn
Irrawaddy
Irtysh or Irtish
Isar
Isère
Isis
Japurá
Javari
Jhelum
Jordan
Juba
Jumna
Juruá
Kabul
Kagera
Kama
Kasai
Kentucky
Kizil Irmak
Klondike
Kolyma
Komati
Kootenay or
  Kootenai
Krishna
Kuban
Kura
Kuskokwim
Lachlan
Lech
Lee
Lena
Liao
Liard
Liffey
Limpopo
Lippe
Little Bighorn
Loire
Lot
Lualaba
Mackenzie
Macquarie
Madeira
Madre de Dios
Magdalena
Mahanadi
Main
Mamoré
Marañón
Maritsa
Marne

Medway
Mekong
Menderes
Mersey
Meta
Meuse
Minnesota
Miño
Mississippi
Missouri
Mohawk
Molopo
Monongahela
Morava
Moselle
Moskva
Murray
Murrumbidgee
Narmada
Neckar
Negro
Neisse
Nelson
Neman or Nyeman
Neva
Niagara
Niger
Nile
Ob
Oder
Ogooué or Ogowe
Ohio
Oise
Okanagan
Okavango
Orange
Ord
Orinoco
Orontes
Ottawa
Ouachita or
  Washita
Ouse
Paraguay
Paraíba
Paraná
Parnaíba or
  Parnahiba
Peace
Pearl
Pechora
Pecos
Piave
Pilcomayo

RIVERS

Plate
Po
Potomac
Pripet
Prut
Purús
Putamayo
Red
Rhine *or* Rhein
Rhône
Ribble
Richelieu
Rio Branco
Rio Grande
Rubicon
Saar
Sacramento
Safid Rud
Saguenay
Saint Croix
Saint John
Saint Lawrence
Salado
Salambria
Salween
Sambre
San
Santee
Saône
Saskatchewan

Sava *or* Save
Savannah
Scheldt
Seine
Severn
Shannon
Shatt-al-Arab
Shiré
Siret
Skien
Slave
Snake
Snowy
Somme
Songhua
Spey
Struma
Susquehanna
Sutlej
Suwannee *or*
  Swanee
Swan
Swat
Syr Darya
Tagus
Tana
Tanana
Tapajós
Tarim
Tarn

Tarsus
Tay
Tees
Tennessee
Thames
Tiber
Ticino
Tigris
Tisza
Tobol
Tocantins
Trent
Tugela
Tunguska
Tweed
Tyne
Ubangi
Ucayali
Uele
Ural
Usk
Ussuri
Vaal
Var
Vardar
Vienne
Vistula
Vltava
Volga
Volta

Volturno
Waal
Wabash
Waikato
Warta
Wear
Weser
White Volta
Wisconsin
Xi, Hsi, *or* Si
Xiang, Hsiang, *or*
  Siang
Xingú
Wye
Yalu
Yangtze
Yaqui
Yarra
Yellow
Yellowstone
Yenisei
Yonne
Yser
Yüan *or* Yüen
Yukon
Zambezi *or*
  Zambese
Zhu Jiang

SEAS AND OCEANS

Seas

Adriatic
Aegean
Amundsen
Andaman
Arabian
Arafura
Aral
Azov
Baltic
Banda
Barents
Beaufort
Bellingshausen
Bering
Bismarck
Black *or* Euxine
Caribbean
Caspian
Celebes

Ceram
China
Chukchi
Coral
East China
East Siberian
Flores
Icarian
Inland
Ionian
Irish
Japan
Java
Kara
Laptev
Ligurian
Lincoln
Marmara *or* Marmora
Mediterranean

Nordenskjöld
North
Norwegian
Okhotsk
Philippine
Red
Ross
Sargasso
Scotia
Solomon
South China
Sulu
Tasman
Timor
Tyrrhenian
Weddell
White
Yellow *or* Hwang Hai

Oceans

Antarctic *or* Southern
Arctic

Atlantic
Indian

Pacific

WORD POWER

SOUTH AFRICAN PROVINCES

Province	Capital	Province	Capital
Eastern Cape	Bisho	Mpumalanga	Nelspruit
Free State	Bloemfontein	North-West	Mafikeng
Gauteng	Johannesburg	Northern Cape	Kimberley
KwaZulu-Natal	Pietermaritzburg	Western Cape	Cape Town
Limpopo	Pietersburg		

U.S. PRESIDENTS

President	Party	Term of office
1. George Washington	Federalist	1789–97
2. John Adams	Federalist	1797–1801
3. Thomas Jefferson	Democratic Republican	1801–1809
4. James Madison	Democratic Republican	1809–1817
5. James Monroe	Democratic Republican	1817–25
6. John Quincy Adams	Democratic Republican	1825–29
7. Andrew Jackson	Democrat	1829–37
8. Martin Van Buren	Democrat	1837–41
9. William Henry Harrison	Whig	1841
10. John Tyler	Whig	1841–45
11. James K. Polk	Democrat	1845–49
12. Zachary Taylor	Whig	1849–50
13. Millard Fillmore	Whig	1850–53
14. Franklin Pierce	Democrat	1853–57
15. James Buchanan	Democrat	1857–61
16. Abraham Lincoln	Republican	1861–65
17. Andrew Johnson	Republican	1865–69
18. Ulysses S. Grant	Republican	1869–77
19. Rutherford B. Hayes	Republican	1877–81
20. James A. Garfield	Republican	1881
21. Chester A. Arthur	Republican	1881–85
22. Grover Cleveland	Democrat	1885–89
23. Benjamin Harrison	Republican	1889–93
24. Grover Cleveland	Democrat	1893–97
25. William McKinley	Republican	1897–1901
26. Theodore Roosevelt	Republican	1901–1909
27. William Howard Taft	Republican	1909–13
28. Woodrow Wilson	Democrat	1913–21
29. Warren G. Harding	Republican	1921–23
30. Calvin Coolidge	Republican	1923–29
31. Herbert C. Hoover	Republican	1929–33
32. Franklin D. Roosevelt	Democrat	1933–45
33. Harry S. Truman	Democrat	1945–53
34. Dwight D. Eisenhower	Republican	1953–61
35. John F. Kennedy	Democrat	1961–63
36. Lyndon B. Johnson	Democrat	1963–69
37. Richard M. Nixon	Republican	1969–74
38. Gerald R. Ford	Republican	1974–77
39. James E. Carter, Jr	Democrat	1977–81
40. Ronald W. Reagan	Republican	1981–89
41. George H. W. Bush	Republican	1989–93
42. William J. Clinton	Democrat	1993–2001
43. George W. Bush	Republican	2001–

U.S. STATES

State	Abbreviation	Zip code
Alabama	Ala.	AL
Alaska	Alas.	AK
Arizona	Ariz.	AZ
Arkansas	Ark.	AR
California	Cal.	CA
Colorado	Colo.	CO
Connecticut	Conn.	CT
Delaware	Del.	DE
District of Columbia	D.C.	DC
Florida	Fla.	FL
Georgia	Ga.	GA
Hawaii	Haw.	HI
Idaho	Id. *or* Ida.	ID
Illinois	Ill.	IL
Indiana	Ind.	IN
Iowa	Ia. *or* Io.	IA
Kansas	Kan. *or* Kans.	KS
Kentucky	Ken.	KY
Louisiana	La.	LA
Maine	Me.	ME
Maryland	Md.	MD
Massachusetts	Mass.	MA
Michigan	Mich.	MI
Minnesota	Minn.	MN
Mississippi	Miss.	MS
Missouri	Mo.	MO
Montana	Mont.	MT
Nebraska	Neb.	NE
Nevada	Nev.	NV
New Hampshire	N.H.	NH
New Jersey	N.J.	NJ
New Mexico	N.M. *or* N.Mex.	NM
New York	N.Y.	NY
North Carolina	N.C.	NC
North Dakota	N.D. *or* N.Dak.	ND
Ohio	O.	OH
Oklahoma	Okla.	OK
Oregon	Oreg.	OR
Pennsylvania	Pa., Penn., *or* Penna.	PA
Rhode Island	R.I.	RI
South Carolina	S.C.	SC
South Dakota	S.Dak.	SD
Tennessee	Tenn.	TN
Texas	Tex.	TX
Utah	Ut.	UT
Vermont	Vt.	VT
Virginia	Va.	VA
Washington	Wash.	WA
West Virginia	W.Va.	WV
Wisconsin	Wis.	WI
Wyoming	Wyo.	WY

WORD POWER

VOLCANOES

Antisana
Apo
Askja
Cameroon
Chimborazo
Citlaltépetl
Corcovado
Cotopaxi
Egmont
Elgon
El Misti
Erciyas Dagi
Erebus
Etna
Fuji
Haleakala

Hekla
Helgafell
Huascarán *or* Huascán
Iliamna
Ixtaccihuatl *or* Iztaccihuatl
Katmai
Kazbek
Kenya
Krakatoa *or* Krakatau
Lassen Peak
Mauna Kea
Mauna Loa
Mayon
Mount St. Helens
Nevado de Colima
Nevado de Toluca

Paricutín
Pelée
Popocatépetl
Santa Maria
Semeru *or* Semeroe
Soufrière
Stromboli
Suribachi
Taal
Tambora
Teide *or* Teyde
Tolima
Tristan da Cunha
Vesuvius

WATERFALLS

Angel Falls
Churchill Falls
Cleve-Garth
Cuquenan
Iguaçú Falls
Itatinga

Kaieteur Falls
Niagara Falls
Ormeli
Pilao
Ribbon
Roraima

Sutherland Falls
Tysse
Vestre Mardola
Victoria Falls
Yellowstone Falls
Yosemite Falls

WORD POWER

WORD POWER

Children's writers

Louisa May Alcott (*U.S.*)
Hans Christian Andersen (*Danish*)
Lynn Reid Banks (*English*)
J(ames) M(atthew) Barrie (*Scottish*)
Judy Blume (*U.S.*)
Enid (Mary) Blyton (*English*)
Elinor M(ary) Brent-Dyer (*English*)
Lewis Carroll (*English*)
Babette Cole (*British*)
Eoin Colfer (*Irish*)
Susan Coolidge (*U.S.*)
Karen Cushman (*U.S.*)
Roald Dahl (*British*)
Anne Digby (*English*)
Dr Seuss (*U.S.*)
Ann Fine (*English*)
Kenneth Grahame (*Scottish*)
Laura Ingalls Wilder (*U.S.*)

Mike Inkpen (*English*)
Robin Jarvis (*English*)
Diana Wynne Jones (*Welsh*)
C(live) S(taples) Lewis (*English*)
A(lan) A(lexander) Milne (*English*)
Michael Morpurgo (*English*)
Jill Murphy (*English*)
E(dith) Nesbit (*English*)
Terry Pratchett (*English*)
Philip Pullman (*English*)
Chris Riddell (*English*)
J K Rowling (*British*)
Louis Sachar (*U.S.*)
Dick King Smith (*English*)
Paul Stewart (*English*)
Noel Streatfield (*English*)
Jacqueline Wilson (*English*)

Short story writers

Giovanni Boccaccio (*Italian*)
Jorge Luis Borges (*Argentinian*)
Stephen Crane (*U.S.*)
Arthur Conan Doyle (*British*)
Joel Chandler Harris (*U.S.*)
Nathaniel Hawthorne (*U.S.*)
Washington Irving (*U.S.*)
Carson McCullers (*U.S.*)
Katherine Mansfield (*N.Z.-British*)

Herman Melville (*U.S.*)
W(illiam) Somerset Maugham (*English*)
(Henri René Albert) Guy de Maupassant (*French*)
H(ector) H(ugh) Munro (*Scottish*)
O. Henry (*U.S.*)
Dorothy Parker (*U.S.*)
Edgar Allan Poe (*U.S.*)

Non-fiction writers

Joseph Addison (*English*)
Aesop (*Greek*)
Roger Ascham (*English*)
James Boswell (*Scottish*)
John Bunyan (*English*)
Edmund Burke (*British*)
Jane Welsh Carlyle (*Scottish*)
Thomas Carlyle (*Scottish*)
William Godwin (*English*)
Marcus Tullius Cicero (*Roman*)
William Cobbett (*English*)
Desiderius Erasmus (*Dutch*)
Edward Gibbon (*English*)
William Hazlitt (*English*)
R.H. Hutton (*English*)
Thomas Jefferson (*U.S.*)

Jerome K(lapka) Jerome (*English*)
Samuel Johnson (*English*)
Margery Kempe (*English*)
Lord Chesterfield (*English*)
John Lyly (*English*)
Thomas Malory (*English*)
Michel Eyquem de Montaigne (*French*)
Tom Paine (*English-U.S.*)
Samuel Pepys (*English*)
François Rabelais (*French*)
John Ruskin (*English*)
Richard Steele (*English*)
Leslie Stephen (*English*)
Thomas Traherne (*English*)
Izaac Walton (*English*)
Mary Wollstonecraft (*English*)